For reference
W9-CCR-931

The GALE ENCYCLOPEDIA of CHILDREN'S HEALTH

INFANCY THROUGH ADOLESCENCE

The GALE ENCYCLOPEDIA of CHILDREN'S HEALTH

INFANCY THROUGH ADOLESCENCE

VOLUME

S-Z

KRISTINE KRAPP AND JEFFREY WILSON, EDITORS

Detroit • New York • San Francisco • San Diego • New Haven, Conn. • Waterville, Maine • London • Munich

The Gale Encyclopedia of Children's Health: Infancy through Adolescence

Product Manager
Kate Millson

Project Editors
Kristine M. Krapp, Jeffrey J. Wilson

Editorial
Donna Batten, Shirelle Phelps, Erin Watts

Editorial Support Services
Luann Brennan, Andrea Lopeman, Mark Springer

Rights Acquisition Management
Margaret Abendroth, Ann Taylor

Imaging
Randy Bassett, Lezlie Light, Dan Newell, Christine O'Bryan, Robyn Young

Product Design
Michelle DiMercurio, Tracey Rowens

Composition and Electronic Prepress
Evi Seoud, Mary Beth Trimper

Manufacturing
Wendy Blurton, Dorothy Maki

Indexing
Synapse Corp. of Colorado

For more information, contact
The Gale Group, Inc.
27500 Drake Rd.
Farmington Hills, MI 48331-3535
Or you can visit our Internet site at
http://www.gale.com

LIBRARY OF CONGRESS CATALOGING-IN-PUBLICATION DATA

The Gale encyclopedia of children's health : infancy through adolescence / Kristine Krapp and Jeffrey Wilson, editors.
p. cm.
Includes bibliographical references and index.
ISBN 0-7876-9241-7 (set hardcover : alk. paper) –
ISBN 0-7876-9427-4 (v. 1) – ISBN 0-7876-9428-2 (v. 2) –
ISBN 0-7876-9429-0 (v. 3) – ISBN 0-7876-9430-4 (v. 4)
1. Children–Health and hygiene–Encyclopedias.
2. Children–Diseases–Encyclopedias. 3. Pediatrics–Encyclopedias. [DNLM: 1. Pediatrics–Encyclopedias–English. 2. Pediatrics–Popular Works. 3. Child Welfare–Encyclopedias–English. 4. Child Welfare–Popular Works. 5. Infant Welfare–Encyclopedias–English. 6. Infant Welfare–Popular Works. WS 13 G1515 2005]
I. Title: Encyclopedia of children's health. II. Krapp, Kristine M. III. Wilson, Jeffrey, 1971- IV. Gale Group.

RJ26.G35 2005
618.92'0003–dc22 2005003478

This title is also available as an e-book
ISBN 0-7876-9425-8 (set)
Contact your Gale sales representative for ordering information.
ISBN 0-7876-9241-7 (set)
0-7876-9427-4 (Vol. 1)
0-7876-9428-2 (Vol. 2)
0-7876-9429-0 (Vol. 3)
0-7876-9430-4 (Vol. 4)
Printed in Canada
10 9 8 7 6 5 4 3 2 1

CONTENTS

LIST OF ENTRIES

C

D

E

F

M

N

O

P

PLEASE READ—IMPORTANT INFORMATION

The Gale Encyclopedia of Children's Health is a medical reference product designed to inform and educate readers about a wide variety of health issues related to children, ranging from prenatal to adolescence. Thomson Gale believes the product to be comprehensive, but not necessarily definitive. It is intended to supplement, not replace, consultation with a physician or other healthcare practitioner. While Thomson Gale has made substantial efforts to provide information that is accurate, comprehensive, and up-to-date, Thomson Gale makes no representations or warranties of any kind, including without limitation, warranties of merchantability or fitness for a particular purpose, nor does it guarantee the accuracy, comprehensiveness, or timeliness of the information contained in this product. Readers should be aware that the universe of medical knowledge is constantly growing and changing, and that differences of medical opinion exist among authorities. They are also advised to seek professional diagnosis and treatment for any medical condition, and to discuss information obtained from this book with their healthcare provider.

INTRODUCTION

The Gale Encyclopedia of Children's Health: Infancy Through Adolescence (GECH) is a one-stop source for medical information that covers common and rare diseases and medical conditions, immunizations and drugs, procedures, and developmental issues. It particularly addresses parents' concerns about their children's health from before birth through age 18. The book avoids medical jargon, making it easier for the layperson to use. *The Gale Encyclopedia of Children's Health* presents authoritative, balanced information and is more comprehensive than single-volume family medical guides.

SCOPE

Approximately 600 full-length articles are included in *The Gale Encyclopedia of Children's Health.* Articles follow a standardized format that provides information at a glance. Rubrics include:

Diseases/Disorders
- Definition
- Description
- Demographics
- Causes and symptoms
- Diagnosis
- Treatment
- Prognosis
- Prevention
- Parental concerns
- Resources
- Key terms

Procedures
- Definition
- Purpose
- Description
- Risks
- Normal results
- Parental concerns
- Resources
- Key terms

Immunizations/Drugs
- Definition
- Description
- General use
- Precautions
- Side effects
- Interactions
- Parental concerns
- Resources
- Key terms

Development
- Definition
- Description
- Common problems
- Parental concerns
- Resources
- Key terms

A preliminary list of diseases, conditions, procedures, drugs, and developmental issues was compiled from a wide variety of sources, including professional medical guides and textbooks, as well as consumer guides and encyclopedias. The advisory board, composed of seven doctors with specialties in pediatric medicine, evaluated the topics and made suggestions for inclusion. Final selection of topics to include was made by the medical advisors in conjunction with Thomson Gale editors.

INCLUSION CRITERIA

A preliminary list of diseases, conditions, procedures, drugs, and developmental issues was compiled from a wide variety of sources, including professional medical guides and textbooks, as well as consumer guides and encyclopedias. The advisory board, composed of seven doctors with specialties in pediatric medicine, evaluated the topics and made suggestions for inclusion. Final selection of topics to include was made by the medical advisors in conjunction with Thomson Gale editors.

ABOUT THE CONTRIBUTORS

The essays were compiled by experienced medical writers, including healthcare practitioners and educators, pharmacists, nurses, and other healthcare professionals. *GECH* medical advisors reviewed all of the completed essays to insure that they are appropriate, up-to-date, and medically accurate.

HOW TO USE THIS BOOK

The Gale Encyclopedia of Children's Health has been designed with ready reference in mind:

- Straight **alphabetical arrangement** allows users to locate information quickly.
- Bold faced terms function as *print hyperlinks* that point the reader to related entries in the encyclopedia.
- A list of **key terms** is provided where appropriate to define unfamiliar words or concepts used within the context of the essay. Additional terms may be found in the **glossary**.
- **Cross-references** placed throughout the encyclopedia direct readers to where information on subjects without their own entries can be found. Synonyms are also cross-referenced.
- A **Resources section** directs users to sources of further medical information.
- An appendix of updated **growth charts** from the U.S. Centers for Disease Control for children from birth through age 20 is included.
- An appendix of **common childhood medications** is arranged alphabetically and includes descriptions of each drug and important information about their uses.
- A comprehensive **general index** allows users to easily target detailed aspects of any topic, including Latin names.

GRAPHICS

The Gale Encyclopedia of Children's Health is enhanced with approximately 300 full color images, including photos, tables, and customized line drawings.

ADVISORY BOARD

An advisory board made up of prominent individuals from the medical community provided invaluable assistance in the formulation of this encyclopedia. They defined the scope of coverage and reviewed individual entries for accuracy and accessibility. The editors would therefore like to express our appreciation to them.

CONTRIBUTORS

Margaret Alic, PhD
Medical Writer
Eastsound, WA

Kim Saltel Allan, R.D., BHEcol
Clinical Dietitian
Winnipeg, Manitoba, Canada

Linda K. Bennington, MSN, CNS, RNC
Lecturer, School of Nursing
Old Dominion University
Norfolk, VA

Mark A. Best, MD, MBA, MPH
Pathologist
Eastview, KY

Rosalyn Carson-Dewitt, M.D.
Medical Writer
Durham, NC

Angela Costello
Medical Editor
Cleveland, OH

L. Lee Culvert
Medical Writer
Alna, ME

Tish Davidson, MA
Medical Writer
Fremont, CA

L. Fleming Fallon, Jr., MD, DrPH
Professor of Public Health
Bowling Green University
Bowling Green, OH

Paula Ford-Martin, MA
Medical Writer
Warwick, RI

Janie Franz
Medical Writer
Grand Forks, ND

Rebecca J. Frey, PhD
Medical Writer
New Haven, CT

Clare Hanrahan
Medical Writer
Asheville, NC

Crystal H. Kaczkowski, MSc.
Medical Writer
Chicago, IL

Christine Kuehn Kelly
Medical Writer
Havertown, PA

Monique Laberge, Ph.D.
Medical Writer
Philadelphia, PA

Aliene S. Linwood, BSN, DPA, FACHE
Medical and Science Writer
Athens, Ohio

Mark Mitchell, M.D.
Medical Writer
Seattle, WA

Deborah L. Nurmi, M.S.
Medical Writer, Public Health Researcher
Atlanta, GA

Martha Reilly, OD
Clinical Optometrist
Madison, WI

Joan M. Schonbeck, RN
Medical Writer
Marlborough, MA

Stephanie Dionne Sherk
Medical Writer
Ann Arbor, MI

Judith Sims, MS
Science Writer
Logan, UT

Jennifer E. Sisk, M.A.
Medical Writer
Philadelphia, PA

Genevieve Slomski, Ph.D.
Medical Writer
New Britain, CT

Deanna M. Swartout-Corbeil, RN
Medical Writer
Thompsons Station, TN

Samuel Uretsky, PharmD
Medical Writer
Wantagh, NY

Ken R. Wells
Freelance Writer
Laguna Hills, CA

S

Safety

Definition

The safety of children is potentially at risk from accidents and injuries, as well as crime. Providing a safe environment, putting prevention measures into practice, and teaching children methods of self-protection are all ways to reduce the potential for harm to children.

Description

Accidents are the leading cause of death for children aged 14 and under in the United States, claiming more than 5600 lives each year, or an average of 15 children per day. More than 16 percent of all hospitalizations for accidental injuries among children lead to permanent disability. Although the accidental injury death rate declined among children ages 14 and under by almost 40 percent from 1987 to 2000, accidental injury remained in the early 2000s the number one killer of this age group. In 2000, the leading cause of fatal accidental injury among children was motor vehicle occupant injury (28%), followed by drowning (16%) and airway obstruction injury (14%). Falls (36%) were the leading cause of nonfatal, hospital emergency room-treated childhood injury in 2001. Other frequent causes of accidental injuries and deaths are fire and burn injury, accidental firearm injury, and **poisoning**.

Another way children may have their safety jeopardized is by becoming victims of crime. Child abductions are often publicized widely and cause parents to experience a great deal of **anxiety** and **fear** regarding this possibility. Another relatively new place children face potential dangers is on the "information highway." Though the Internet opens a world of possibilities to children, there are individuals who may attempt to exploit and harm children through this technology.

Though the idea of the number of potential risks children face may seem overwhelming to parents, there are a variety of measures parents can take to reduce those risks.

Motor vehicle occupant injury

In 2001, motor vehicle accidents resulted in 36 percent of accidental deaths in children ages one to four. In the early 2000s an estimated 14 percent of children ages 14 and under continued to ride unrestrained, however, and 55 percent of those children killed in motor vehicle accidents were not restrained. Also, at that time, nearly one-third of children rode in the wrong restraint for their zage and size, and an estimated 82 percent of child safety seats were installed or used incorrectly. The following measures will help parents keep their children safe:

- Car seats need to meet federal safety standards. A car seat with a five-point harness will provide the best protection. In addition, the car seat needs to be the correct size for the child and needs to fits properly into the vehicle.
- The Lower Anchors and Tethers for Children (LATCH) system in cars manufactured after September 1, 2002, should be used. Some car seats require that parents attach additional hardware for maximum protection.
- The child must face in the right direction. Infants should ride in a car seat that faces the rear of the car until they are one year of age and weigh approximately 20 lbs (9 kg). Infants who weigh 20 lbs (9 kg) before they are one need a restraint approved for the higher weight and should also be rear-facing.
- Car seats should be installed correctly. The car seat should be held tightly against the car's back seat. After installing the car seat, parents need to make certain they cannot move it more than one inch from side to side or front to back. Police departments and community organizations frequently hold child restraint inspections, during which parents can discover if they have installed their car seats properly.
- Rear-facing car seats should not be placed in the front seat of a car that has air bags. Children 12 and under should ride in the back seat in order to avoid being hurt by inflating airbags. Generally, the back seat of the car is the safest place in a crash.

- Children need to stay in a safety seat with a full harness for as long as possible, at least until they weigh 40 lbs (18 kg). Afterwards, they can use a belt-positioning booster seat, which provides a taller sitting height so that the adult lap and shoulder belts fit correctly.
- When older children are 57 inches (1.45 m) tall and weigh 80 lbs (36 kg), they may use adult lap belts.
- Children need to be restrained every time they ride in a car.
- Children should never be left alone in or around a vehicle. Unattended children can quickly die from heat stroke or carbon monoxide poisoning.

Drowning

Drowning remains the second leading cause of accidental injury-related deaths among children ages 14 and under, claiming 943 children in 2000. An estimated 4700 children required treatment in hospital emergency departments for drowning-related incidents in 2001. As many as 20 percent of children who survive **near-drowning** suffer severe, permanent neurological disability. Children ages one to four are at the highest risk of drowning. The following measures may significantly reduce the drowning risk for your child:

- Parents and caregivers should never, even for a moment, leave children alone or in the care of another young child while in bathtubs, pools, spas, or wading pools or near any other open standing water. Infant bath seats are not a substitute for adult supervision. Parents should remove all water from containers, such as pails and buckets, immediately after use.
- If the home has a swimming pool, it should be surrounded by a fence that prevents children from having direct access to the pool from the house. Remove **toys** from in and around the pool, as toys can attract children to the pool.
- Parents should enroll their child in swimming lessons when they are old enough (usually not before age four), but should remember that these lessons do not provide protection against drowning for children of any age.
- Children should be taught to always swim with a buddy. In addition, they should be instructed never to dive into an unknown body of water, but instead jump in feet first to avoid hitting their heads.
- When boating, every person must wear a U.S. Coast Guard approved life jacket.
- Air-filled swimming aids (such as water wings) cannot take the place of life preservers.
- Parents need to teach their children about the risks of drowning in the cold weather months. Children should not walk, skate, or ride on thawing ice on any body of water.
- Parents should learn CPR and keep a telephone close to the area where their children are swimming.

Poisoning

Poisoning is a common cause of home accidents, with toddlers being the ones most vulnerable. Children are at risk of poisoning from household and personal care products, medicines, **vitamins**, indoor plants, lead, and carbon monoxide. In 2000, 91 children ages 14 and under died as a result of accidental poisoning. Approximately 114,000 children in this age group were treated in the emergency room for accidental poisonings in 2001. People can keep children safe by being aware of the potential hazards in the home and by following these guidelines:

- Medications and cleaning solutions need to be stored in locked cabinets.
- Medication lids need to be tightly closed with child-resistant caps.
- Parents should avoid taking medicine in front of children and never refer to pills as candy, as children often mimic the behavior of adults.
- Parents should check the garage for any toxic chemicals and gasoline containers. Items such as windshield washer fluid, antifreeze, and pesticides are poisonous and should be placed where children cannot reach them. In addition, these kinds of items should never be kept in juice or milk bottles.
- Poisonous plants in the home need to be identified and either removed or placed where children cannot reach them.
- Carbon monoxide detectors/alarms should be installed in homes and recreational vehicles. These should be placed in the hallway near every separate sleeping area of the home.
- Insect sprays should not be used around food.
- All painted furniture and toys should be checked for non-toxic finishes.
- The Poison Control Center phone number should be posted in a prominent place, where **family** members and other caregivers can find it quickly. Caregivers should call the Poison Control Center (1–800–222–1222) immediately when a poisoning incident is suspected. The experts at the Poison Center provide directions on the appropriate actions to take.

Fire and burn injuries

Fire and burn injury is the fifth leading cause of child accidental injury-related death. Children make up 20 percent of all fire deaths, and over 30 percent of all fires that kill children are set by children playing with fire. Children of all ages set over 100,000 fires each year, and approximately 20,000 of these are set in homes. Children aged four and under are at the greatest risk, with a fire- and burn-related death rate nearly twice that of all children. This circumstance occurs for several reasons. Young children have a less acute perception of danger and a limited ability to properly respond to a life-threatening burn or fire situation. They are also more susceptible to fire-related asphyxiation, as well as more prone to **burns** than adults. The United States Fire Administration (USFA) encourages parents to teach children at an early age about the dangers of playing with fire in order to help prevent child injuries, fire deaths, and the number of fires set in homes. The following suggestions will aid in keeping children safe from fires:

- Young children need to be supervised closely. They should not be left alone even for short periods of time.
- Lighters and matches should be kept in a secured area and children taught to tell an adult if they find lighters or matches.
- Parents should look for indications that children may be playing with fire, for burnt matches under beds or in closets.
- Families need a home fire escape plan and to practice it with the children. A meeting place outdoors should be designated.
- Children should be taught that if a fire occurs, they should crawl low on the floor, below the smoke, and get out of the house according to the escape plan. They should not attempt to get back in the house.
- Children need to know how to stop, drop to the ground, and roll if their clothes catch on fire.
- Parents should install smoke alarms on every level in the home, and familiarize children with the sound of the smoke alarm. They should test the alarm monthly and replace the battery at least yearly. Having a working smoke alarm dramatically increases residents' chances of surviving a fire.
- The thermostat on the hot water heater should be set to 120°F (49°C) or lower. The water temperature should be checked when bathing or showering children.
- Do not drink or carry very hot beverages or soup when holding a child.
- Access to the stove should be blocked if possible. Foods should be cooked on the back burners with pot handles turned away from the front of the stove. Parents and caregivers should avoid holding a baby or small child while they are cooking.

Falls

Each year, nearly 3 million children in the United States are injured in falls. For those under five, falls cause more than half of all injuries. Even close supervision is not adequate, as falls can happen very quickly. They can occur at home as well as away from home. Although most falls result in only mild bumps and **bruises**, many cause serious injuries that require immediate medical attention. Following these guidelines may help to prevent children from becoming injured in a fall:

- Playgrounds should have soft surfaces to cushion children if they should fall. Examples of soft surfaces are those made of items like bark mulch, wood chips, sand, pea gravel, or shredded tires. Avoid concrete, asphalt, and dirt surfaces. Even sod can be too hard under certain weather conditions.
- Chairs and other pieces of furniture in the home should be kept away from windows. Windows should be closed and locked when children are around. Residential windows in tall buildings should have bars or window guards. Window screens may not prevent children from falling out a window.
- Stairways must be clear to prevent children from tripping over clutter.
- Throw rugs should be secured to the floor with a rubber pad, double-sided tape, or a piece of foam carpet backing.
- Safety gates can keep toddlers away from stairs. Gates should be attached to the wall if they are used at the top of a staircase.
- Safety belts keep children from falling from shopping carts.
- As children get older and start riding a bike, a scooter, or using skates, they should always wear a correctly fitting helmet. If a child falls from one of these while wearing a helmet, the risk of a brain injury is reduced by 88 percent. A properly fitting helmet sits evenly on top of the head (low on the forehead, no more than two finger widths above the eyebrows), should be comfortable but snug, and have straps firm enough so that the helmet will not rock forward, backward, or side to side.

Airway obstruction injury

Children, especially those under the age of three, are quite vulnerable to airway obstruction injury because they have small upper airways and have relative inexperience with chewing. They also have a tendency to place objects in their mouths. On average, infants account for approximately 64 percent of **choking** deaths among children ages 14 and under. Causes of choking or airway obstruction-injury deaths include suffocation by things such as pillows, choking on food or small objects, and strangulation from window blind and clothing strings. Anything children can place in their mouths can be dangerous. Taking the following steps will help protect children:

- Parents should avoid giving children under age four any hard, smooth foods that may block or partially block their airway. These include all nuts, sunflower seeds, watermelon with seeds, cherries with pits, popcorn, hard candy, raw carrots, raw peas, and raw celery.
- Certain soft foods, such as hot dogs, grapes, and link sausages, should be chopped into small pieces. These foods can cause choking because they are the right shape to block the windpipe.
- When babies start to eat solid food, parents need to beware of foods such as raw apples or pears. Raw fruit is difficult for babies to chew properly because their teeth are just developing.
- Children should sit still while eating and chew food thoroughly.
- Children should not run, ride in the car, or **play sports** with gum, lollipops, or candy in their mouths.
- Buttons, beads, and other small objects need to be stored safely out of children's reach.
- Drawstrings should be removed from children's coats and sweatshirts. Also window blind cords that pose a risk for strangulation should be removed.
- Parents should follow manufacturer's recommendations regarding toys and check toys frequently for loose or broken parts.
- Older children should not to leave toys with small pieces or loose game parts where younger children can reach them.
- A latex balloon should not be given to a child younger than age eight. Children can choke by inhaling the balloon or a portion of it into their windpipes.
- Parents should obtain and use a "small parts tester," an inexpensive child safety device that shows if an object is small enough to fit in a child's mouth.

Accidental firearm injury

In the year 2000, 193 children in the United States ages new infant to 19 died from accidental injuries involving firearms. A child as young as three has the finger strength to pull a trigger. Some studies show that by age eight, 90 percent of children are capable of firing a gun. Whether people are gun collectors, hunters, or fierce gun control advocates, they need to ensure their families' safety by talking with their children about the potential dangers of guns and what to do if one is found. Parents should assume that their children may come across a gun at some point in their youth and proactively teach them about gun safety. There are a number of programs available that instruct children, including the very popular "Eddie Eagle," a program of the National Rifle Association (NRA). This program offers a four-step approach to gun safety: stop, don't touch, leave the area, and tell an adult. People who own firearms should follow these guidelines to prevent accidental shootings:

- Guns need to be stored unloaded in a securely locked case and out of children's reach.
- Trigger locks and other safety features should be used.
- Ammunition should be stored in a separate place from the firearms, locked in a container that is out of children's reach.
- Gun owners should take a firearms safety course to learn the correct and safe way to use the firearm, and they should practice firearm safety. Children need to be taught that guns are not toys. They need to be taught to always tell an adult about any gun they happen to find.

Online risks

While online computer exploration opens a world of possibilities to children, it also may expose them to a variety of dangers. Teenagers are particularly at risk because they are more likely to go online unsupervised and are more likely than younger children to participate in online discussions. Risks posed by the Internet include the following:

- Exposure to inappropriate material that is sexual, violent, hateful, or that encourages activities that are dangerous or illegal.
- Exposure to information or arrangements for an encounter that could risk children's safety or the safety of other family members. In some cases child molesters have used chat rooms, email, and instant messaging to gain a child's trust and then to arrange a face-to-face meeting.

There are several signs that children may be at risk online. These include their spending large amounts of time online, especially in the evenings; the presence of pornography on their computers; their making or receiving calls from men parents do not know; their receiving mail, gifts, or packages from people parents do not know; their turning off the monitor or quickly changing the screen on the monitor when parents enter the room; their becoming withdrawn from the family; and their using an online account that belongs to someone else.

Parents should not feel powerless in the face of these online risks. There are a variety of measures they can take to minimize the chances of an online exploiter victimizing their child. These include the following:

- Children need to be warned about the potential dangers online and about sexual victimization.
- Parents should spend time online with children.
- Computer should be kept in a common room in the house, not in the child's bedroom. It is more difficult for a predator to communicate with a child when the computer screen is visible to other members of the household.
- Parental controls and/or blocking software should be used.
- Parents should maintain access to the child's online account and randomly check his or her email. They should be open with children about parental access and state the reasons for it.
- Children should be instructed never to arrange a face-to-face meeting with someone they meet online; never to upload pictures of themselves onto the Internet to people they do not know; never to give out identifying information such as their name, address, school name, or telephone number; never to download pictures from an unknown source; and never to respond to messages that are suggestive, obscene, or harassing.

Abduction

Publicized crimes involving childhood abductions, although rare occurrences, frighten many parents and make them unsure about how best to protect their children. According to one study, in 57 percent of the cases, the victims of child-abduction murder were victims of opportunity. The tips noted below will help parents lessen the opportunity for abduction and kidnapping and better safeguard their children:

- Parents should teach children to run away from danger, never towards it. Danger is defined as anything or anyone that invades their personal space. Children should be taught to yell loudly, as their safety is more important than being polite.
- Children should not be allowed to go places alone, and they should always be supervised directly by parents or by another trusted adult. Older children should always take a friend along when they go somewhere.
- Parents should know where and with whom children are at all times. They should know children's friends and be clear about the places and homes they may visit. Children should habitually contact their parents when they arrive and leave a destination and if their plans change.
- Parents should talk openly with children about safety and encourage them to report to trusted adults anything or anyone makes them feel uncomfortable or frightened. Children should know they have the right to say no to any unwelcome, confusing, or uncomfortable attention by others and that they should tell parents immediately whenever such an experience occurs.
- Babysitters and caregivers should be screened and their references checked.
- Instead of confusing children with messages about avoiding strangers, Parents should identify adults to whom children may talk. Parents should list the people by name whom they permit their children to visit.
- Parents should avoid using code words but instead use the "check first" method. Children should be taught not to talk to anyone, go with anyone, or accept gifts or candy from anyone without first checking with their parents or trusted adults in charge.

Common problems

In spite of taking precautions and putting safety measures into place, accidents, injuries, and crime may still take place. All children should be taught how to call for help in an emergency. Instruct them to dial 911 when emergency assistance is needed and to remain on the phone as long as they are directed to do so.

Parental concerns

Children can injure themselves in the blink of an eye. Parents can turn their heads away for a moment, and a child could pull down a boiling pot of food or swallow something and choke on it. It is impossible for new parents to anticipate all the potential dangers or safety problems around babies and children. The trick to keeping an environment safe for children is to stay one step ahead of them at all times. By spotting dangers before an injury happens, parents can protect their children from harm and protect themselves from stress and heartache. As children develop, some of the potential dangers may change. What does not change is the responsibility parents have to provide a safe, trusting environment in which their children can thrive.

Safety rules for parents

Know where your children are at all times.

Be sensitive to changes in your child's behavior.

Talk with your child about their schoolwork and activities regularly.

Get to know your child's teachers, friends, and friends' families.

Listen sincerely to your children.

Be alert to a teenager or adult who is paying an unusual amount of attention to your child.

Make sure your children know what to do when approached by a stranger.

Don't put your child's name on clothing in a way that is visible to others.

Be aware of your child's time and activities online.

SOURCE: MetLife, "Protecting Your Child," http://www.metlife.com, 2003-5.

(Table by GGS Information Services.)

See also Childproofing.

Resources

BOOKS

Benson, Allen C. *Connecting Kids and the Web: A Handbook for Teaching Internet Use and Safety.* New York: Neal-Schuman, 2003.

Joyce, Julie. *What Should You Do?: Safety Tips for Kids.* Calumet, IL: Dynamic Publishing, 2004.

PERIODICALS

O'Neill, Heather. "How to Protect Your Child From Falls." *Parenting* (August 1, 2003): 45+.

"Prevention of Drowning in Infants, Children, and Adolescents." *Journal of Pediatrics* (August 2003): 437–40.

ORGANIZATIONS

Consumer Product Safety Commission. Washington, DC 20207–0001. Web site: <www.cpsc.gov>.

National Center for Injury Prevention and Control. Mailstop K65, 4770 Buford Highway NE, Atlanta, GA 30341–3724. Web site: <www.cdc.gov/ncipc/ncipchm.htm>.

National Center for Missing & Exploited Children. Charles B. Wang International Children's Building, 699 Prince Street, Alexandria, VA 22314–3175. Web site: <www.missingkids.org>

National Highway Traffic Safety Administration (NHTSA). 400 7th Street, SW, Washington, DC 20590. Web site: <www.nhtsa.gov>.

KEY TERMS

Airway obstruction injury—An injury that obstructs the airway and prevents proper breathing, either through strangulation, suffocation, or choking.

National SAFE KIDS Campaign. 1301 Pennsylvania Ave., NW, Suite 1000, Washington, DC 20004. Web site: <www.safekids.org>.

WEB SITES

"Buying a Safer Car for Child Passengers 2004." *National Highway Traffic Safety Administration.* Available online at <www.nhtsa.dot.gov/CPS/BASCKids2004/index.htm> (accessed August 14, 2004).

"Report to the Nation: Trends in Unintentional Childhood Injury Mortality, 1987–2000." *National Safe Kids Campaign*, May 2003. Available online at <www.safekids.org/content_documents/nskw03_report.pdf> (accessed August 14, 2004).

Deanna M. Swartout-Corbeil, RN

Safety, infant and toddler *see* **Childproofing**

Salmonella food poisoning

Definition

Salmonella **food poisoning** is a bacterial infection that causes inflammation (swelling) of the lining of the stomach and intestines (**gastroenteritis**). The causative bacteria is called *Salmonella.* While domestic and wild animals, including poultry, pigs, cattle, and pets such as turtles, iguanas, chicks, dogs, and cats can transmit this illness, most people become infected by ingesting foods contaminated with significant amounts of the causative bacteria.

Description

Improperly handled or undercooked poultry and eggs are the foods which most frequently cause salmonella food poisoning. Chickens are a major carrier of salmonella bacteria, which accounts for its prominence in poultry products. However, identifying foods which may be contaminated with salmonella is particularly difficult because infected chickens typically show no signs or symptoms. Since infected chickens have no identifying characteristics, these chickens go on to lay eggs or to be used as meat.

At one time, it was thought that salmonella bacteria were only found in eggs which had cracked, thus allowing the bacteria to enter. Ultimately, it was learned that, because the egg shell has tiny pores, even uncracked eggs which sat for a time on a surface (nest) contaminated with salmonella could themselves become contaminated. It is known also that the bacteria can be passed from the infected female chicken directly into the substance of the egg before the shell has formed around it.

Anyone may contract salmonella food poisoning, but the disease is most serious in infants, the elderly, and individuals with weakened immune systems. In these individuals, the infection may spread from the intestines to the blood stream and then to other body sites, causing death unless the person is treated promptly with **antibiotics**. In addition, people who have had part or all of their stomach or their spleen removed or who have **sickle cell anemia**, cirrhosis of the liver, leukemia, lymphoma, malaria, louse-borne relapsing fever, or acquired **Immunodeficiency** syndrome (**AIDS**) are particularly susceptible to salmonella food poisoning.

Demographics

Although salmonella food poisoning occurs worldwide, it is most frequently reported in North America and Europe. Only a small proportion of infected people are tested and diagnosed, and as few as 1 percent of cases are actually reported. While the infection rate may seem relatively low, even an attack rate of less than 0.5 percent in such a large number of exposures results in many infected individuals. The poisoning typically occurs in small, localized outbreaks in the general population or in large outbreaks in hospitals, restaurants, or institutions for children or the elderly. In the United States, salmonella is responsible for about 15 percent of all cases of food poisoning.

Causes and symptoms

Salmonella food poisoning can occur when someone drinks unpasteurized milk or eats undercooked chicken or eggs, or salad dressings or desserts which contain raw eggs. Even if salmonella-containing foods such as chicken are thoroughly cooked, any food can become contaminated during preparation if conditions and equipment for food preparation are unsanitary.

Other foods can then be accidentally contaminated if they come into contact with infected surfaces. In addition, children have become ill after playing with turtles or iguanas and then eating without washing their hands. Because the bacteria are shed in the feces for weeks after infection with salmonella, poor hygiene can allow such a carrier to spread the infection to others.

Symptoms appear about one to two days after infection and include fever (in 50% of patients), **nausea and vomiting**, **diarrhea**, and abdominal cramps and **pain**. The diarrhea is usually very liquid and rarely contains mucus or blood. Diarrhea usually lasts for about four days. The illness usually ends in about five to seven days.

Serious complications are rare, occurring most often in individuals with other medical illnesses. Complications occur when the salmonella bacteria make their way into the bloodstream (bacteremia). Once in the bloodstream, the bacteria can enter any organ system throughout the body, causing disease. Other infections which can be caused by salmonella include:

- bone infections (osteomyelitis)
- joint infections (arthritis)
- infection of the sac containing the heart (pericarditis)
- infection of the tissues which cover the brain and spinal cord (meningitis)
- infection of the liver (hepatitis)
- lung infections (pneumonia)
- infection of aneurysms (aneurysms are abnormal outpouchings which occur in weak areas of the walls of blood vessels)
- infections in the center of already-existing tumors or cysts

Diagnosis

Under appropriate laboratory conditions, salmonella can be grown and then viewed under a microscope for identification. Early in the infection, the blood is far more likely to positively show a presence of the salmonella bacterium when a sample is grown on a nutrient substance (culture) for identification purposes. Eventually, however, positive cultures can be obtained from the stool and in some cases from a urine culture.

Treatment

Even though salmonella food poisoning is a bacterial infection, most practitioners do not treat simple cases with antibiotics. Studies have shown that using antibio-

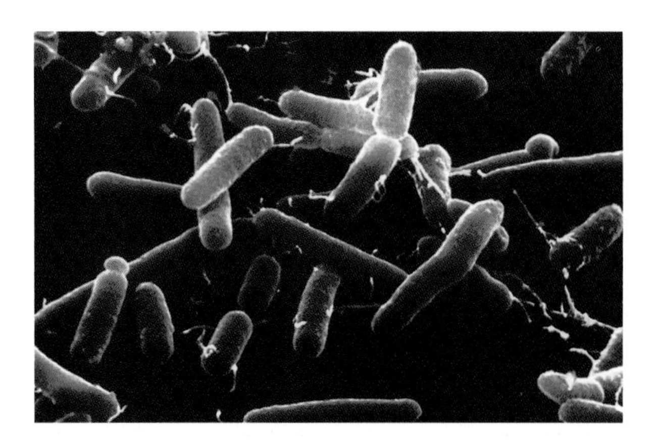

Exposure to the *Salmonella enteritidis* bacterium usually occurs by contact with contaminated food. *(Photograph by Oliver Meckes. Photo Researchers, Inc.)*

tics does not usually reduce the length of time that the patient is ill. Paradoxically, it appears that antibiotics do, however, cause the patient to shed bacteria in their feces for a longer period of time. In order to decrease the length of time that a particular individual is a carrier who can spread the disease, antibiotics are generally not given.

In situations where an individual has a more severe type of infection with salmonella bacteria, a number of antibiotics may be used. Chloramphenicol was the first antibiotic successfully used to treat salmonella food poisoning. It is still a drug of choice in developing countries because it is so inexpensive, although some resistance has developed to it. Ampicillin and trimethoprim-sulfonamide have been used successfully in the treatment of infections caused by chloramphenicol-resistant strains. Newer types of antibiotics, such as cephalosporin or quinolone, are also effective. These drugs can be given by mouth or through a needle in the vein (intravenously) for very ill patients. With effective antibiotic therapy, patients feel better in 24 to 48 hours, the temperature returns to normal in three to five days, and the patient is generally recovered by ten to 14 days.

Prognosis

The prognosis for uncomplicated cases of salmonella food poisoning is excellent. Most people recover completely within a week's time. In cases in which other medical problems complicate the illness, prognosis depends on the severity of the other medical conditions, as well as the specific organ system infected with salmonella.

KEY TERMS

Carrier—A person who possesses a gene for an abnormal trait without showing signs of the disorder. The person may pass the abnormal gene on to offspring. Also refers to a person who has a particular disease agent present within his/her body, and can pass this agent on to others, but who displays no symptoms of infection.

Gastroenteritis—Inflammation of the stomach and intestines that usually causes nausea, vomiting, diarrhea, abdominal pain, and cramps.

Prevention

Prevention of salmonella food poisoning involves the proper handling and cooking of foods likely to carry the bacteria. This means that recipes utilizing uncooked eggs (Caesar salad dressing, meringue toppings, mousses) need to be modified to eliminate the raw eggs. Not only should chicken be cooked thoroughly, until no pink juices flow, but all surfaces and utensils used on raw chicken must be carefully cleaned to prevent salmonella from contaminating other foods. Careful hand washing is a must before, during, and after all food preparation involving eggs and poultry. Hand washing is also important after handling and playing with pets such as turtles, iguanas, chicks, dogs and cats.

Parental concerns

Because children are notoriously bad at hand washing, parents want to be particularly vigilant to make sure that careful hand washing is followed, especially if someone in the home is actually ill with salmonella food poisoning. In this case, extra precautions should be taken. Children should not share foods, utensils, beverages, etc. Hand washing after toileting or diaper changes should be undertaken with extra care to avoid spreading the infection to others. The healthcare provider should give the **family** guidance regarding when a recovering child should return to school or daycare.

Resources

BOOKS

Cleary, Thomas G. "Salmonella." In *Nelson Textbook of Pediatrics*. Edited by Richard E. Behrman et al. Philadelphia: Saunders, 2004.

Eisenstein, Barry I., and Dori F. Zaleznik. "Enterobacteriaceae." In *Principles and Practice of*

Infectious Diseases. Edited by Gerald L. Mandell. London: Churchill Livingstone, Inc., 2000.

ORGANIZATIONS

Centers for Disease Control and Prevention. 1600 Clifton Rd., NE, Atlanta, GA 30333. Web site: <www.cdc.gov>.

Rosalyn Carson-DeWitt, MD

Sanfilippo's syndrome *see* **Mucopolysaccharidoses**

Sarcomas

Definition

A sarcoma is a cancerous (malignant) bone tumor.

Description

A primary bone tumor originates in or near a bone. Most primary bone tumors are benign, and the cells that compose them do not spread (metastasize) to nearby tissue or to other parts of the body.

A sarcoma is a type of malignant primary bone tumor. Malignant primary bone tumors account for less than 1 percent of all cancers diagnosed in the United States. They can infiltrate nearby tissues, enter the bloodstream, and metastasize to bones, tissues, and organs far from the original malignancy. Malignant primary bone tumors are characterized as either bone cancers which originate in the hard material of the bone or soft-tissue sarcomas which begin in blood vessels, nerves, or tissues containing muscles, fat, or fiber.

Types of bone tumors

Osteogenic sarcoma, or osteosarcoma, is the most common form of bone **cancer**, accounts for 6 percent of all instances of the disease, and for about 5 percent of all cancers that occur in children. Nine hundred new cases of osteosarcoma are diagnosed in the United States every year. The disease usually affects teenagers and is almost twice as common in boys as in girls.

Osteosarcomas, which grow very rapidly, can develop in any bone but most often occur along the edge or on the end of one of the fast-growing long bones that support the arms and legs. About 80 percent of all osteosarcomas develop in the parts of the upper and lower leg nearest the knee (the distal femur or in the proximal tibia). The next likely location for an osteosarcoma is the bone of the upper arm closest to the shoulder (the proximal humerus).

Ewing's sarcoma is the second most common form of childhood bone cancer. Accounting for fewer than 5 percent of bone tumors in children, Ewing's sarcoma usually begins in the soft tissue (the marrow) inside bones of the leg, hips, ribs, and arms. It rapidly infiltrates the lungs and may metastasize to bones in other parts of the body.

More than 80 percent of patients who have Ewing's sarcoma are white, and the disease most frequently affects children between the ages five and nine and young adults between ages 20 and 30. About 27 percent of all cases of Ewing's sarcoma occur in children under the age of ten, and 64 percent occur in adolescents between the ages of ten and 20.

Chondrosarcomas are cancerous bone tumors that most often appear in middle age. Usually originating in strong connective tissue (cartilage) in ribs or leg or hip bones, chondrosarcomas grow slowly. They rarely spread to the lungs. It takes years for a chondrosarcoma to metastasize to other parts of the body, and some of these tumors never spread.

Parosteal osteogenic sarcomas, fibrosarcomas, and chordomas are rare. Parosteal osteosarcomas generally involve both the bone and the membrane that covers it. Fibrosarcomas originate in the ends of the bones in the arm or leg and then spread to soft tissue. Chordomas develop on the skull or spinal cord.

Osteochondromas, which usually develop between the ages of ten and 20, are the most common noncancerous primary bone tumors. Giant cell tumors generally develop in a section of the thigh bone near the knee. Giant cell tumors are originally benign but sometimes become malignant.

Causes and symptoms

The cause of bone cancer is unknown, but the tendency to develop it may be inherited. Children who have bone tumors are often tall for their age, and the disease seems to be associated with growth spurts that occur during childhood and **adolescence**. Injuries can make the presence of tumors more apparent but do not cause them.

A bone that has been broken or exposed to high doses of radiation used to treat other cancers is more likely than other bones to develop osteosarcoma. A history of noncancerous bone disease also increases bone-cancer risk.

The amount of radiation in diagnostic x rays poses little or no danger of bone-cancer development, but children who have a **family** history of the most common childhood cancer of the eye (**retinoblastoma**) or who have inherited rare cancer syndromes have a greater-than-average risk of developing bone cancer. Exposure to chemicals found in some paints and dyes can slightly raise the risk.

Both benign and malignant bone tumors can distort and weaken bone and cause **pain**, but benign tumors are generally painless and asymptomatic.

It is sometimes possible to feel a lump or mass, but pain in the affected area is the most common early symptom of bone cancer. Pain is not constant in the initial stages of the disease, but it is aggravated by activity and may be worse at night. If the tumor is located on a leg bone, the patient may limp. Swelling and weakness of the limb may not be noticed until weeks after the pain begins.

Other symptoms of bone cancer include:

- a bone that breaks for no apparent reason
- difficulty moving the affected part of the body
- fatigue
- fever
- a lump on the trunk, an arm or leg, or another bone
- persistent, unexplained back pain
- weight loss

Diagnosis

Physical examination and routine x rays may yield enough evidence to diagnose benign bone tumors, but removal of tumor tissue for microscopic analysis (biopsy) is the only sure way to rule out malignancy.

A needle biopsy involves using a fine, thin needle to remove small bits of tumor, or a thick needle to extract tissue samples from the innermost part (the core) of the growth. An excisional biopsy is the surgical removal of a small, accessible tumor. An incisional biopsy is performed on tumors too large or inaccessible to be completely removed. The surgeon performing an incisional biopsy cuts into the patient's skin and removes a portion of the exposed tumor. Performed under local or general anesthetic, biopsy reveals whether a tumor is benign or malignant and identifies the type of cancer cells the malignant tumor contains.

Bone cancer is usually diagnosed about three months after symptoms first appear, and 20 percent of malignant tumors have metastasized to the lungs or other parts of the body by that time.

Imaging techniques

The following procedures are used, in conjunction with biopsy, to diagnose bone cancer:

- Bone x rays usually provide a clear image of osteosarcomas.
- Computerized axial tomography (CAT scan), a specialized x ray that uses a rotating beam to obtain detailed information about an abnormality and its physical relationship to other parts of the body, can differentiate between osteosarcomas and other types of bone tumors, illustrate how tumor cells have infiltrated other tissues, and help surgeons decide which portion of a growth would be best to biopsy. Because more than four of every five malignant bone tumors metastasize to the lungs, a CAT scan of the chest is performed to see if these organs have been affected. Chest and abdominal CAT scans are used to determine whether Ewing's sarcoma has spread to the lungs, liver, or lymph nodes.
- Magnetic resonance imaging (MRI), a specialized scan that relies on radio waves and powerful magnets to reflect energy patterns created by tissue abnormalities and specific diseases, provides more detailed information than does a CAT scan about tumors and marrow cavities of the bone and can sometimes detect clusters of cancerous cells that have separated from the original tumor. This valuable information helps surgeons select the most appropriate approach for treatment.
- Radionuclide bone scans involve injecting a small amount of radioactive material into a vein. Primary tumors or cells that have metastasized absorb the radioactive material and show up as dark spots on the scan.

Cytogenic and molecular genetic studies, which assess the structure and composition of chromosomes and genes, may also be used to diagnose osteosarcoma. These tests can sometimes indicate what form of treatment is most appropriate.

Laboratory studies

A complete blood count (CBC) reveals abnormalities in the blood and may indicate whether bone marrow has been affected. A blood test that measures levels of the enzyme lactate dehydrogenase (LDH) can help predict the likelihood of a specific patient's survival.

Immunohistochemistry involves adding special antibodies and chemicals or stains to tumor samples. This technique is effective in identifying cells that are found in Ewing's sarcoma but are not present in other malignant tumors.

Reverse transcription polymerase chain reaction (RTPCR) relies on chemical analysis of the substance in the body that transmits genetic information (RNA) to evaluate the effectiveness of cancer therapies, identify mutations consistent with the presence of Ewing's sarcoma, and reveal cancer that recurs after treatment has been completed.

Staging

Once bone cancer has been diagnosed, the tumor is staged. This process indicates how far the tumor has spread from its original location. The stage of a tumor suggests which form of treatment is most appropriate and predicts how the condition will probably respond to therapy.

An osteosarcoma may be localized or metastatic. A localized osteosarcoma has not spread beyond the bone where it arose or beyond nearby muscles, tendons, and other tissues. A metastatic osteosarcoma has spread to the lungs, to bones not directly connected to the bone in which the tumor originated, or to other tissues or organs.

Treatment

In the 1960s, amputation was the only treatment for bone cancer. Between then and the early 2000s **chemotherapy** drugs and innovative surgical techniques improved survival with intact limbs. Because osteosarcoma is so rare, patients should consider undergoing treatment at a major cancer center staffed by specialists familiar with the disease.

A treatment plan for bone cancer, developed after the tumor has been diagnosed and staged, may include the following:

- Amputation may be the only therapeutic option for large tumors involving nerves or blood vessels that have not responded to chemotherapy. MRI scans indicate how much of the diseased limb must be removed, and surgery is planned to create a cuff, formed of muscles and skin, around the amputated bone. Following surgery, an artificial (prosthetic) leg is fitted over the cuff. A patient who actively participates in the rehabilitation process may be walking independently as soon as three months after the amputation.
- Chemotherapy is usually administered in addition to surgery, to kill cancer cells that have separated from the original tumor and spread to other parts of the body. Although chemotherapy can increase the likelihood of later development of another form of cancer, the American Cancer Society maintains that the need for chemotherapeutic bone-cancer treatment is much greater than the potential risk.
- Surgery, coordinated with diagnostic biopsy, enhances the probability that limb-salvage surgery can be used to remove the cancer while preserving nearby blood vessels and bones. A metal rod or bone graft is used to replace the area of bone removed, and subsequent surgery may be needed to repair or replace rods that become loose or break. Patients who have undergone limb-salvage surgery need intensive rehabilitation. It may take as long as a year for a patient to regain full use of a leg following limb-salvage surgery, and patients who have this operation may eventually have to undergo amputation.
- Radiation therapy is used often to treat Ewing's sarcoma.
- Rotationoplasty, sometimes performed after a leg amputation, involves attaching the lower leg and foot to the thigh bone, so that the ankle replaces the knee. A prosthetic is later added to make the leg as long as it should be. Prosthetic devices are not used to lengthen limbs that remain functional after amputation to remove osteosarcomas located on the upper arm. When an osteosarcoma develops in the jawbone, the entire lower jaw is removed. Bones from other parts of the body are later grafted on remaining bone to create a new jaw.

Follow-up treatments

After a patient completes the final course of chemotherapy, CAT scans, bone scans, x rays, and other diagnostic tests may be repeated to determine if any traces of tumor remain. If none is found, treatment is discontinued, but patients are advised to see their oncologist and orthopedic surgeon every two or three months for the following year. X rays of the chest and affected bone are taken every four months. An annual echocardiogram is recommended to evaluate any adverse effect chemotherapy may have had on the heart, and CT scans are performed every six months.

Patients who have received treatment for Ewing's sarcoma are examined often—at gradually lengthening intervals—after completing therapy. Accurate growth measurements are taken during each visit and blood is drawn to be tested for side effects of treatment. X rays, CT scans, bone scans, and other imaging studies are generally performed every three months during the first year. If no evidence of tumor growth or recurrence is indicated, these tests are performed less frequently in the following years.

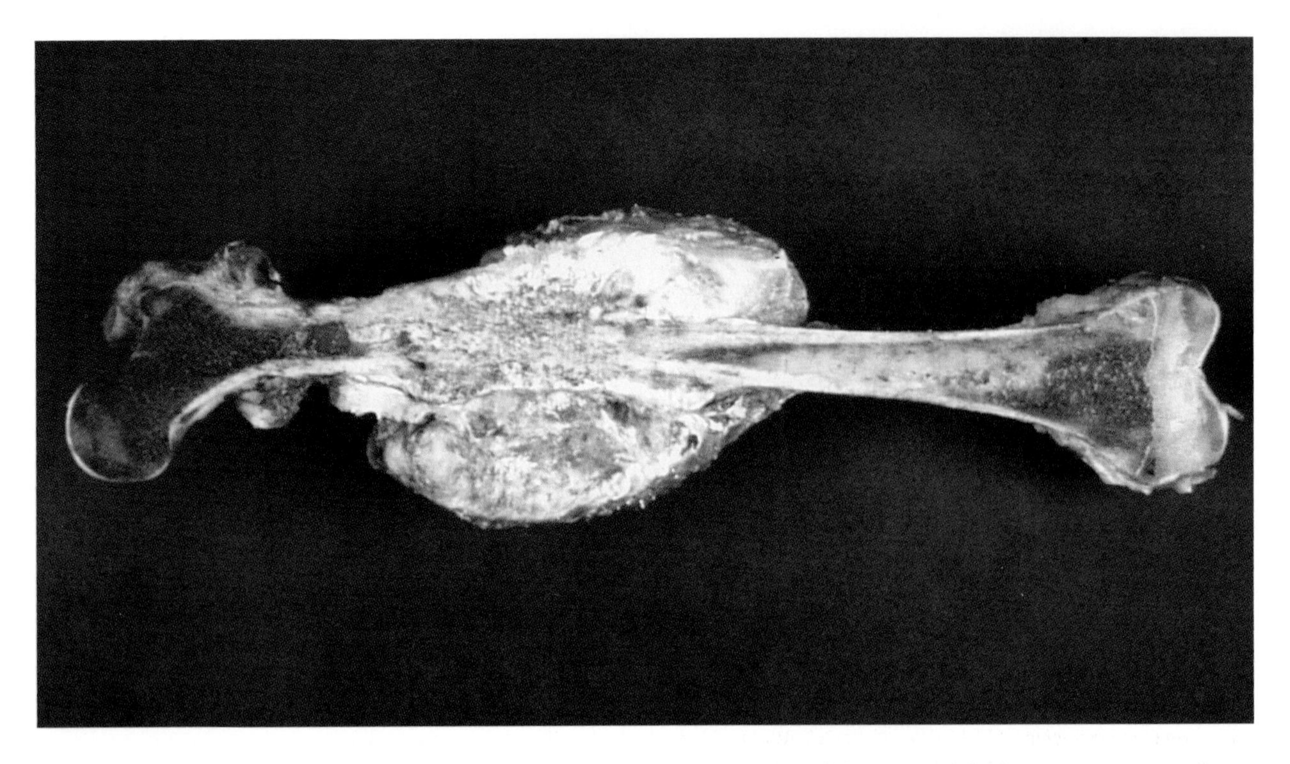

A specimen of a femur bone indicating the cancerous growth around the knee. Osteosarcoma is the most common primary cancer of the bone. *(Photo Researchers, Inc.)*

Some benign bone tumors shrink or disappear without treatment. However, regular examinations are recommended to determine whether these tumors have changed in any way.

Prognosis

Benign brain tumors rarely recur, but sarcomas can reappear after treatment was believed to have eliminated every cell.

Likelihood of long-term survival depends on the type and location of the tumor, how much the tumor has metastasized, and on what organs, bones, or tissues have been affected.

More than 85 percent of patients survive for more than five years after complete surgical removal of low-grade osteosarcomas (tumors that arise in mature tissue and contain a small number of cancerous cells). About 25 to 30 percent of patients diagnosed with high-grade osteosarcomas (tumors that develop in immature tissue and contain a large number of cancer cells) die of the disease.

Two-thirds of all children diagnosed with Ewing's sarcoma live for more than five years after the disease is detected. The outlook is most favorable for children under the age of ten, and least favorable in patients whose cancer is not diagnosed until after it has metastasized. fewer than three of every ten of these patients remain alive five years later. More than 80 percent of patients whose Ewing's sarcoma is confined to a small area and surgically removed live, for at least five years. Postsurgical radiation and chemotherapy add years to their lives. More than 70 percent of patients live five years or more with a small Ewing's sarcoma that cannot be removed, but only three out of five patients with large, unremovable tumors survive that long.

Prevention

There is no known way to prevent bone cancer.

Parental concerns

Careful attention to a child's diet can be very helpful for patients with cancer. This can be difficult when the cancer and/or the treatments are affecting the appetite, however. Whole foods, including grains, beans, fresh fruits and vegetables, and high quality fats, should be emphasized in the diet, while processed foods should be avoided. Increased consumption of fish, especially cold-water fish such as salmon, mackerel, halibut, and tuna, provides a good source of omega-3 fatty acids. Nutritional supplements can build strength and help maintain it during and following chemotherapy, radiation, or surgery.

Guided imagery and relaxation techniques can be helpful for children undergoing difficult treatments. Support groups for the child and the family can be very helpful and can give provide an important emotional outlet for the child, the parents, and the siblings.

Resources

BOOKS

Brennan, Murray F., et al. *Diagnosis and Management of Sarcoma.* Oxford, UK: Isis Medical Media Limited, 2002.

Ewing's Sarcoma: A Medical Dictionary, Bibliography, and Annotated Research Guide to Internet References. San Diego, CA: Icon Group International, 2004.

ORGANIZATIONS

American Cancer Society. 1599 Clifton Rd., NE, Atlanta, GA 30329–4251. Web site: <www.cancer.org>.

CancerCare Inc. 1180 Avenue of the Americas, New York, NY 10036. Web site: <www.cancercare.org>.

National Cancer Institute. Building 31, Room 10A31, 31 Center Drive, MSC 2580, Bethesda, MD 20892–2580. Web site: <www.nci.nih.gov>.

WEB SITES

"Ewing's Sarcoma." *Children's Cancer Web*, January 11, 2003. Available online at <www.cancerindex.org/ccw/guide2e.htm> (accessed December 30, 2004).

Maureen Haggerty
Rosalyn Carson-DeWitt, MD

Savant syndrome

Definition

Savant syndrome occurs when a person with below normal **intelligence** displays a special talent or ability in a specific area.

Description

Children who display savant syndrome have traditionally been referred to as idiot, retarded, or autistic savants. The negative connotations of the term "idiot" have led to the disuse of idiot savant. Because the syndrome is often associated with **autism**, the term autistic savant is more frequently heard. The first known description of a person displaying savant syndrome occurred in a German psychology journal in 1751. The term savant was first used in 1887 by J. Langdon Down (the doctor for whom **Down syndrome** is named).

Demographics

About half of all children with savant syndrome are autistic. Approximately 10 percent of all children with autism have savant syndrome. The rate increases to 25 percent of children with autism who have an IQ over 35. (Many autistic children have lower IQs.) About three times as many boys as girls have savant syndrome. This may be because more boys than girls are affected with autism. Less than 1 percent of the non-autistic population, including those with **mental retardation** and other developmental disorders, have savant syndrome.

Causes and symptoms

The causes of savant syndrome were as of 2004 not known. Some researchers hypothesize that it is caused by a change in a gene or genes, and others believe that it is caused by some kind of damage to the left hemisphere of the brain with compensation for this injury occurring in the right hemisphere. The reasons for the syndrome are not at all clear, however, and more research needs to be done.

Children with savant syndrome have an exceptional talent or skill in a particular area, such as the ability to process mathematical calculations at a phenomenal speed. Savant skills occur in a number of different areas, including music, visual arts, and mathematics. Experts believe that the most common skill demonstrated by savants is extraordinary memory. Children with savant syndrome may be able to memorize extensive amounts of data in such areas as **sports** statistics, population figures, and historical or biographical data. One particular skill common to those with savant syndrome is the ability to calculate what day of the week a particular date fell on or will fall on.

Diagnosis

Savant syndrome is diagnosed when a child's ability in one area is exceptionally higher than would be expected given his or her IQ or general level of functioning.

KEY TERMS

Autism—A developmental disability that appears early in life, in which normal brain development is disrupted and social and communication skills are retarded, sometimes severely.

Treatment

Savant syndrome is not known to have any drawbacks, so it does not have to be treated itself. The underlying disorders that usually accompany savant syndrome need to be treated, and it is believed that making use of the special talent of the child with savant syndrome may help treat the child's underlying developmental disorders.

Prognosis

The special skill associated with savant syndrome in a specific child is usually present for life. There has been at least one report of the skill being lost when progress was gained in other areas, but this appears to be very rare. In general, if the level of the skill changes it improves as the skill is practiced.

Prevention

There is no known way to prevent savant syndrome.

Parental concerns

Children with savant syndrome have a very special skill that can be nurtured. These children may respond better to treatments for any underlying disorder that make use in some way of the childs special underlying interest and talent.

See also Autism.

Resources

BOOKS

Hermelin, Beate. *Bright Splinters of the Mind: A Personal Story of Research with Autistics Savant.* Philadelphia: J. Kingsley, 2001.

PERIODICALS

Bolte, Sven, and Fritz Poustka. "Comparing the Intelligence Profiles of Savant and Nonsavant Individuals with Autistic Disorder." *Intelligence*– 32, no. 2 (June 2004): 121131.

WEB SITES

Edelson, Stephen M. "Autistic Savant." *Center for the Study of Autism.* Available online at <www.autism.org/savant.html> (accessed October 17, 2004).

Tish Davidson, A.M.

Scabies

Definition

Scabies is a relatively contagious infection caused by a tiny mite called *Sarcoptes scabiei.*

Description

Scabies is caused by a tiny insect about 0.3 mm long called a mite. When a human comes in contact with the female mite, the mite burrows under the skin, laying eggs along the line of its burrow. These eggs hatch, and the resulting offspring rise to the surface of the skin, mate, and repeat the cycle either within the skin of the original host or within the skin of its next victim.

The intense **itching** almost always caused by scabies is due to a reaction within the skin to the feces of the mite. The first time someone is infected with scabies, he or she may not notice any itching for a number of weeks (four to six weeks). With subsequent infections, the itchiness begins within hours of picking up the first mite.

Demographics

Prevalence rates are not clear; some studies suggest that between 6 and 27 percent of the population have scabies at any one time. Scabies is more common among schoolchildren and individuals living in crowded conditions.

Causes and symptoms

Scabies is most common among people who live in overcrowded conditions and whose ability to practice good hygiene is limited. Scabies can be passed between people by close skin contact. Although the mites can only live away from human skin for about three days, sharing clothing or bedclothes can pass scabies among **family** members or close contacts. In May 2002, the Centers for Disease Control (CDC) included scabies in its updated guidelines for the treatment of **sexually transmitted diseases**.

The itching (pruritus) from scabies is worse after a hot shower and at night. Burrows are seen as winding, slightly raised gray lines along the skin. The female mite may be seen at one end of the burrow, as a tiny pearl-like bump underneath the skin. Because of the intense itching, burrows may be obscured by scratch marks left by the patient. The most common locations for burrows are the sides of the fingers, between the fingers, the top of the wrists, around the elbows and armpits, around the nipples of the breasts in women, in the genitalia of men, around the waist (beltline), and on the lower part of the buttocks. Babies may have burrows on the soles of their feet, palms of their hands, and faces.

Scratching seems to serve some purpose in scabies, as the mites are apparently often inadvertently removed. Most infestations with scabies are caused by no more than 15 mites altogether.

Infestation with huge numbers of mites (on the order of thousands to millions) occurs when an individual does not scratch or when an individual has a weakened immune system. These patients include the elderly; those who live in institutions; the mentally retarded or physically infirm; those who have other diseases which affect the amount of sensation they have in their skin (leprosy or syringomyelia); leukemia or diabetes sufferers; those taking medications which lower their immune response (**cancer chemotherapy** or immunosuppressant drugs given after organ transplantation); or people with other diseases which lower their immune response (such as acquired **immunodeficiency** syndrome or **AIDS**). This form of scabies, with its major infestation, is referred to as crusted scabies or Norwegian scabies. Infected patients have thickened, crusty areas all over their bodies, including over the scalp. Their skin is scaly. Their fingernails may be thickened and horny.

Diagnosis

Diagnosis can be made simply by observing the characteristic burrows of the mites causing scabies. A sterilized needle can be used to explore the pearly bump at the end of a burrow, remove its contents, and place it on a slide to be examined. The mite itself may then be identified under a microscope.

Occasionally, a type of mite carried on dogs (*Sarcoptes scabiei var. canis*) may infect humans. These mites cannot survive for very long on humans, and so the infection is very light.

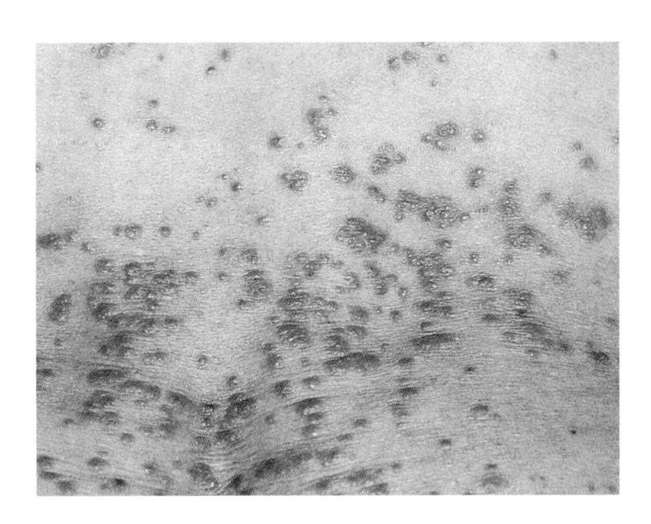

Close-up view of a scabies skin infection. *(© Dr. P Marazzi/ Photo Researchers, Inc.)*

Treatment

Several types of lotions (usually containing 5% permethrin) can be applied to the body and left on for 12 to 24 hours. One topical application is usually sufficient, although the scabicide may be reapplied after a week if mites remain. Preparations containing lindane are no longer recommended for treating scabies because of the potential for damage to the nervous system. Itching can be lessened by the use of calamine lotion or antihistamine medications.

In addition to topical medications, the doctor may prescribe oral ivermectin, a drug that was originally developed for veterinary practice as a broad-spectrum antiparasite agent. Studies done in humans, however, have found that ivermectin is as safe and effective as topical medications for treating scabies. A study published in 2003 reported that ivermectin is safe for people in high-risk categories, including those with compromised immune systems.

Prognosis

The prognosis for complete recovery from scabies infestation is excellent. In patients with weak immune systems, the biggest danger is that the areas of skin involved with scabies will become secondarily infected with bacteria.

Prevention

Good hygiene is essential in the prevention of scabies. When a member of a household is diagnosed with

KEY TERMS

Mite—An insect parasite belonging to the order Acarina. The organism that causes scabies is a mite.

Pruritus—The symptom of itching or an uncontrollable sensation leading to the urge to scratch.

Topical—Not ingested; applied to the outside of the body, for example to the skin, eye, or mouth.

scabies, all that person's recently worn clothing and bedding should be washed in very hot water.

Parental concerns

One of the biggest concerns among family members of an individual with scabies is its ready transmissibility. Care should be taken to avoid sharing bedding, towels, and clothing with an infected family member. Some healthcare providers recommend that all family members be treated with a scabicide, whether or not scabies is evident. Linens of all family members should be washed in the hottest water possible to avoid cross-contamination.

Resources

BOOKS

"Arthropod Bites and Infestations." In *Nelson Textbook of Pediatrics.* Edited by Richard E. Behrman et al. Philadelphia: Saunders, 2004.

"Infestations and Bites." In *Clinical Dermatology*, 4th ed. Edited by Thomas P. Habif et al. St. Louis, MO: Mosby, 2004.

"Scabies." In *Ferri's Clinical Advisor: Instant Diagnosis and Treatment.* Edited by Fred F. Ferri. St. Louis, MO: Mosby, 2004.

ORGANIZATIONS

American Academy of Dermatology (AAD). 930 East Woodfield Road, Schaumburg, IL 60173. Web site: <www.aad.org>.Web sites

"Facts about Scabies." Available online at <www.safe2use.com/pests/scabies/scabies.htm> (accessed December 30, 2004).

Rosalyn Carson-DeWitt, MD
Rebecca J. Frey, PhD

Scarlatina *see* **Scarlet fever**

Scarlet fever

Definition

Scarlet fever is a rash that complicates a bacterial throat infection called **strep throat**.

Description

Scarlet fever, also known as scarlatina, gets its name from the fact that the patient's skin, especially on the cheeks, is flushed. The disease primarily affects children. A **sore throat** and a raised, sandpaper-like rash over much of the body are accompanied by fever and sluggishness (lethargy). The fever usually subsides within a few days, and recovery is complete by two weeks. After the fever is gone, the skin on the face and body flakes; the skin on the palms of the hands and soles of the feet peels more dramatically. Treatment for scarlet fever is intended to offset the possibility of serious complications such as **rheumatic fever** (a heart disease) or kidney inflammation (glomerulonephritis) can develop.

Scarlet fever is highly contagious and is spread by sneezing, coughing, or direct contact. The incubation period is three to five days, with symptoms usually beginning on the second day of the disease and lasting from four to ten days.

Early in the twentieth century, severe scarlet fever epidemics were common. In the early 2000s, the disease is rare. **Antibiotics** have helped, and it is possible that the strain of bacteria that causes scarlet fever has become weaker with time.

Demographics

Scarlet fever primarily affects children between the ages of five and 15 years. Approximately 10 percent of all children who have strep throat develop the characteristic scarlet fever rash.

Causes and symptoms

Scarlet fever is caused by group A streptococcal bacteria (*S. pyogenes*), highly toxic microbes that can also cause strep throat, wound or skin infections, **pneumonia**, and serious kidney infections. The group A streptococci are hemolytic bacteria, which means that they have the ability to break red blood cells. The strain of streptococcus that causes scarlet fever, unlike the one that causes most strep throats, produces an erythrogenic toxin, which causes the skin to flush.

The main symptoms and signs of scarlet fever are fever, lethargy, sore throat, and a bumpy rash that blanches under pressure. The rash appears first on the upper chest and spreads to the neck, abdomen, legs, arms, and in folds of skin such as under the arm or groin. In scarlet fever, the skin around the mouth tends to be pale, while the cheeks are flushed. The patient usually has a "strawberry tongue," in which inflamed bumps on the tongue rise above a bright red coating. Finally, dark red lines (called Pastia's lines) may appear in the creases of skin folds.

Diagnosis

Cases of scarlet fever are usually diagnosed and treated by pediatricians or **family** medicine practitioners. The chief diagnostic signs of scarlet fever are the characteristic rash, which spares the palms and soles of the feet, and the presence of a strawberry tongue in children. Strawberry tongue is rarely seen in adults.

The doctor will take note of the signs and symptoms to eliminate the possibility of other diseases. For example, scarlet fever can be distinguished from **measles**, a viral infection that is also associated with a fever and rash, by the quality of the rash, the presence of a sore throat in scarlet fever, and the absence of the severe eye inflammation and severe runny nose that usually accompany measles.

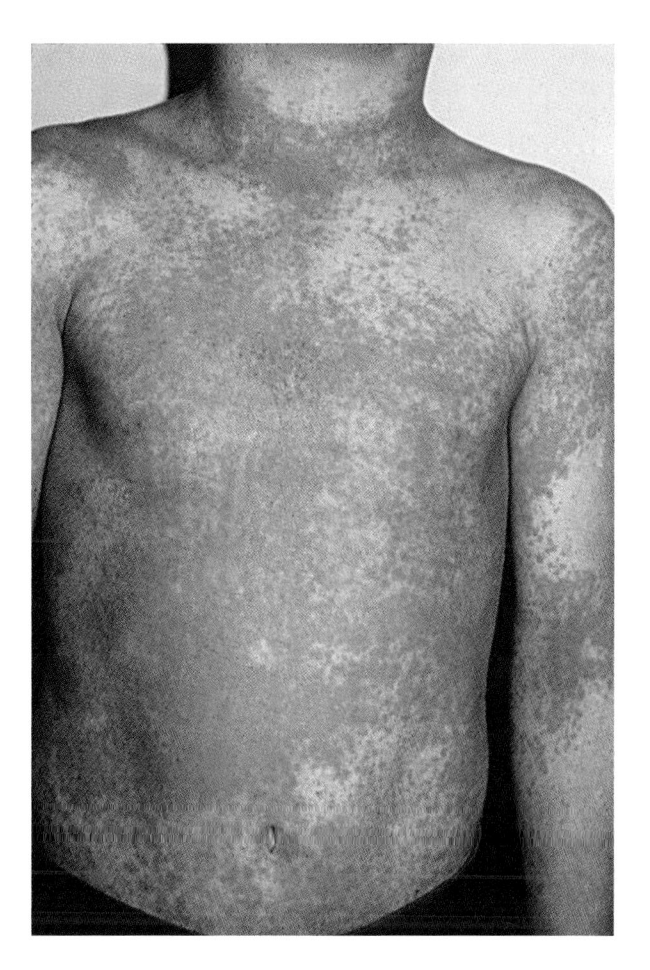

Scarlet fever is characterized by a sandpaper-like rash on reddened skin. *(© Biophoto Associates/Photo Researchers, Inc.)*

Treatment

Although scarlet fever often clears up spontaneously within a few days, antibiotic treatment with either oral or injectable penicillin is usually recommended to reduce the severity of symptoms, prevent complications, and prevent spread to others. Antibiotic treatment shortens the course of the illness in small children but may not do so in adolescents or adults. Nevertheless, treatment with antibiotics is important to prevent complications.

One benzathine penicillin injection is required for treatment. But since penicillin injections are painful, oral penicillin may be preferable. If the patient is unable to tolerate penicillin, alternative antibiotics such as erythromycin or clindamycin may be used. However, the entire course of antibiotics, usually ten days, needs to be followed for the therapy to be effective. Because symptoms subside quickly, there is a temptation to stop therapy prematurely. It is important to take all of the pills in order to kill the bacteria. Not completing the course of therapy increases the risk of developing rheumatic fever and kidney inflammation.

Bed rest is not necessary, nor is isolation of the patient. **Acetaminophen** may be given for fever or relief of **pain**.

Prognosis

If treated promptly with antibiotics, full recovery is expected. Once a patient has had scarlet fever, the person develops immunity and cannot develop it again.

Prevention

Avoiding exposure to children who have the disease helps prevent the spread of scarlet fever.

Parental concerns

The most important thing to do for children with scarlet fever is to carefully and completely follow the healthcare provider's instructions for administering a course of antibiotics.

See also Strep throat.

Resources

WEB SITES

Balentine, Jerry. "Scarlet Fever." *eMedicine*, November 2, 2004. Available online at <www.emedicine.com/emerg/topic518.htm> (accessed December 30, 2004).

Goldenring, John. "Scarlet Fever." *MedlinePlus*, November 11, 2003. Available online at <www.nlm.nih.gov/medlineplus/ency/article/000974.htm> (accessed December 30, 2004).

ORGANIZATIONS

American Academy of Pediatrics. 141 Northwest Point Blvd., Elk Grove Village, IL 60007-1098. Web site: <www.aap.org>.

Sally J. Jacobs, EdD
Rosalyn Carson-DeWitt, MD

Scheie syndrome *see* **Mucopolysaccharidoses**

Schizophrenia

Definition

Schizophrenia is a mental illness characterized by disordered thinking, delusions, hallucinations, emotional disturbance, and withdrawal from reality.

Description

Some experts view schizophrenia as a group of related illnesses with similar characteristics. Although the term, coined in 1911 by Swiss psychologist Eugene Bleuler (1857–1939), is associated with the idea of a "split" mind, the disorder is different from a "split personality" (dissociative identity disorder), with which it is frequently confused. In the United States, schizophrenics occupy more hospital beds than patients suffering from **cancer**, heart disease, or diabetes. At any given time, they account for up to half the beds in long-term care facilities and 40 percent of the treatment days.

Demographics

The incidence of childhood schizophrenia is thought to be one in 10,000 births. In comparison, the incidence among adolescents and adults is approximately one in 100. The condition occurs with equal frequency in males and females (although the onset of symptoms is usually earlier in males). At least 2.5 million Americans are thought to be afflicted with schizophrenia, with an estimated 100,000 to 200,000 new cases every year. Schizophrenia is commonly thought to disproportionately affect people in the lowest socioeconomic groups, although some people claim that socially disadvantaged persons with schizophrenia are only more visible than their more privileged counterparts, not more numerous.

Causes and symptoms

While the exact cause of schizophrenia is not known, it is believed to be caused by a combination of physiological and environmental factors. Studies have shown that there is clearly a hereditary component to the disorder. **Family** members of schizophrenics are ten times more prone to schizophrenia than the general population, and identical **twins** of schizophrenics have a 46 percent likelihood of having the illness themselves. Relatives of schizophrenics also have a higher incidence of other milder psychological disorders with some of the same symptoms as schizophrenia, such as suspicion, communication problems, and eccentric behavior.

In the years following World War II (1939–45), many doctors blamed schizophrenia on bad parenting. In the latter twentieth century, however, advanced neurological research strengthened the case for a physiological basis for the disease. It has been discovered that the brains of schizophrenics have certain features in common, including smaller volume, reduced blood flow to certain areas, and enlargement of the ventricles (cavities filled with fluid that are found at the brain's center). Much attention has focused on the connection between schizophrenia and neurotransmitters, the chemicals that transmit nerve impulses within the brain. One such chemical, dopamine, has been found to play an especially important role in the disease. Additional research has concentrated on how and when the brain abnormalities that characterize the disorder develop. Some are believed to originate prenatally for a variety of reasons, such as trauma, viral infections, **malnutrition** during pregnancy, or Rh sensitivity (a reaction caused when the mother lacks a certain blood protein called Rh that the baby has). Environmental factors associated with schizophrenia include birth complications, viral infections during infancy, and head injuries in childhood. While the notion of child-rearing practices causing schizophrenia has been largely discredited, there is evidence that certain family dynamics do contribute to the likelihood of relapse in persons who already have shown symptoms of the disease.

Researchers have found correlations between childhood behavior and the onset of schizophrenia in adulthood. A 30-year longitudinal research project studied over 4,000 people born within a single week in 1946 in order to document any unusual developmental patterns observed in those children who later became schizophrenic. It was found that a disproportionate number of them learned to sit, stand, and walk late. They were also twice as likely as their peers to have **speech disorders** at the age of six and to have played alone when they were young. Home movies have enabled other researchers to collect information about the childhood characteristics of adult schizophrenics. One study found that the routine physical movements of these children tended to be slightly abnormal in ways that most parents would not suspect were associated with a major mental illness and that the children also tended to show **fear** and anger to an unusual degree.

The initial symptoms of schizophrenia usually occur between the ages of 16 and 30, with some variation depending on the type. Disorganized schizophrenia tends to begin early, usually in **adolescence** or young adulthood, while paranoid schizophrenia tends to start later, usually after the age of 25 or 30. The onset of schizophrenia before the age of 13 is rare and is associated with more serious symptoms. The onset of acute symptoms is referred to as the first psychotic break or break from reality. In general, the earlier the onset of symptoms, the more severe the illness is. Before the disease becomes full-blown, schizophrenics may go through a period called the prodromal stage, lasting about a year, when they experience behavioral changes that precede and are less dramatic than those of the acute stage. These may include social withdrawal, trouble concentrating or sleeping, neglect of personal grooming and hygiene, and eccentric behavior.

The prodromal stage is followed by the acute phase of the disease, which usually requires medical intervention. During this stage, three-fourths of schizophrenics experience delusions, illogical and bizarre beliefs that are held despite objections. An example of a delusion is the belief that the afflicted person is under the control of a sinister force located in the sewer system that dictates his every move and thought. Hallucinations are another common symptom of acute schizophrenia. These may be auditory (hearing voices) or tactile (feeling as though worms are crawling over one's skin). The acute phase of schizophrenia is also characterized by incoherent thinking, rambling or discontinuous speech, use of nonsense words, and odd physical behavior, including grimacing, pacing, and unusual postures. Persons in the grip of acute schizophrenia may also become violent, although often this violence is directed at themselves: it is estimated that 15 to 20 percent of schizophrenics commit **suicide** out of despair over their condition or because the voices they hear "tell" them to do so, and up to 35 percent attempt to take their own lives or seriously consider doing so. In addition, about 25 to 50 percent of people with schizophrenia abuse drugs or alcohol. As the positive symptoms of the acute phase subside, they may give way to what is called residual schizophrenia. Symptoms include flat or inappropriate emotions, an inability to experience pleasure (anhedonia), lack of motivation, reduced attention span, lack of interest in one's surroundings, and social withdrawal.

When to call the doctor

Parents should contact a healthcare professional if their child begins to have auditory or visual hallucinations, has a sudden change in behavior, shows signs of suicide ideation, or exhibits other symptoms of schizophrenia

Diagnosis

Schizophrenia is generally divided into four types. The most prevalent, found in some 40 percent of affected persons, is paranoid schizophrenia, characterized by delusions and hallucinations centering on persecution, and by feelings of jealousy and grandiosity. Other possible symptoms include argumentativeness, anger, and violence. Catatonic schizophrenia is known primarily for its catatonic state, in which persons retain fixed and sometimes bizarre positions for extended periods of time without moving or speaking. Catatonic schizophrenics may also experience periods of restless movement. In disorganized (hebephrenic) schizophrenia, the patient is incoherent, with flat or inappropriate emotions, disorganized behavior, and bizarre, stereotyped movements and grimaces. Catatonic and disorganized schizophrenia affect far fewer people than paranoid schizophrenia. Most schizophrenics not diagnosed as paranoid schizophrenics fall into the large category of undifferentiated schizophrenia (the fourth type), which consists of variations of the disorder that do not correspond to the criteria of the other three types. Generally, symptoms of any type of schizophrenia must be present for six months before a diagnosis can be made.

Childhood schizophrenia has been known to appear as early as five years of age. Occurring primarily in males, it is characterized by the same symptoms as adult schizophrenia. Diagnosis of schizophrenia in children can be difficult because delusions and hallucinations may be mistaken for childhood fantasies. Other signs of schizophrenia in children include moodiness, problems relating to others, attention difficulties, and difficulty dealing with change. In many cases, children are improperly diagnosed with the disease; one study found as many as 95 percent of children initially diagnosed with childhood-onset schizophrenia did not meet the diagnostic criteria.

It is important for schizophrenia to be diagnosed as early as possible. The longer the symptoms last, the less well afflicted individuals respond to treatment.

Treatment

Even when treated, schizophrenia interferes with normal development in children and adolescents and makes new learning difficult.

Schizophrenia has historically been very difficult to treat, usually requiring **hospitalization** during its acute stage. In the late 1900s, antipsychotic drugs became the most important component of treatment. These can control delusions and hallucinations, improve thought coherence, and, if taken on a long-term maintenance basis, prevent relapses. However, antipsychotic drugs do not work for all schizophrenics, and their use has been complicated by side effects, such as akathisia (motor restlessness), dystonia (rigidity of the neck muscles), and tardive dyskinesia (uncontrollable repeated movements of the tongue and the muscles of the face and neck). In addition, many schizophrenics resist taking medication, some because of the side effects, others because they may feel better and mistakenly decide they do not need the drugs anymore, or because being dependent on medication in order to function makes them feel bad about themselves. The tendency of schizophrenics to discontinue medication is very harmful. Each time a schizophrenic goes off medication, the symptoms of the disease return with greater severity, and the effectiveness of the drugs is reduced.

Low doses of antipsychotic medication have been used successfully with children and adolescents, especially when administered shortly after the onset of symptoms. Their rate of effectiveness in children between the ages of five and 12 has been found to be as high as 80 percent. Until about 1990, the drugs most often prescribed for schizophrenia were neuroleptics such as Haldol, Prolixin, Thorazine, and Mellaril. A major breakthrough in the treatment of schizophrenia occurred in 1990 with the introduction of the drug clozapine to the U.S. market. Clozapine, which affects the neurotransmitters in the brain (specifically serotonin and dopamine), has been dramatically successful in relieving symptoms of schizophrenia, especially in patients in whom other medications have not been effective. However, even clozapine does not work for all patients. In addition, about 1 percent of those who take it develop agranulocytosis, a potentially fatal blood disease, within the first year of use, and all patients on clozapine must be monitored regularly for this side effect. (Clozapine was first developed in the mid twentieth century but could not be introduced until it became possible to screen for this disorder.) The screening itself is expensive, creating another problem for those using the drug. Risperidone, a subsequent and safer medication that offers benefits similar to those of clozapine, was introduced in 1994 and is as of the early 2000s the most frequently prescribed antipsychotic medication in the United States. Olanzapine, another in the subsequent generation of schizophrenia drugs, received FDA approval in the fall of 1996, and more medications are under development. Electroconvulsive therapy (ECT, also called electric shock treatments) has been utilized to relieve symptoms of catatonia and depression in schizophrenics, especially in cases where medication is not effective.

Although medication is an important part of treatment, psychotherapy can also play an important role in helping schizophrenics manage **anxiety** and deal with interpersonal relationships, and treatment for the disorder usually consists of a combination of medication, therapy, and various types of rehabilitation. **Family therapy** has worked well for many patients, educating both patients and their families about the nature of schizophrenia and helping them in their cooperative effort to cope with the disorder.

Alternative treatment

Some of the alternative treatments that have been used with varying success to treat children with schizophrenia include biofeedback, acupressure, chiropractic work, massage, and herbal drops.

Nutritional concerns

Some families have reported a benefit to making adjustments to or supplementing the diet of a child with schizophrenia, including reducing the amount of processed sugar consumed and supplementing with **vitamins** and **minerals** such as copper, zinc, **folic acid**, etc.

Prognosis

With the aid of antipsychotic medication to control delusions and hallucinations, about 70 percent of schizo-

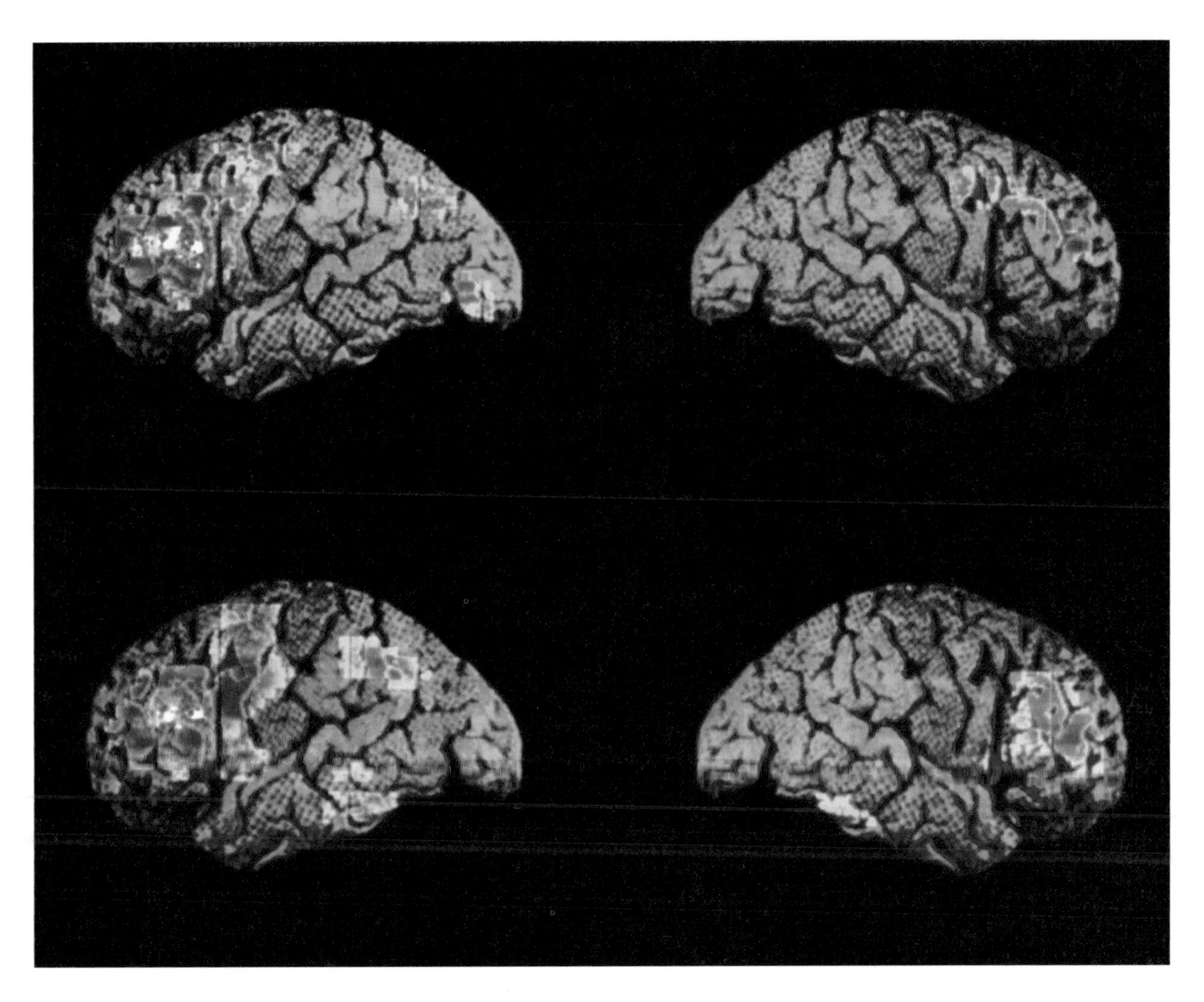

Colored positron emission tomography (PET) brain scans of a schizophrenic, bottom, and normal patient, top. *(© Wellcome Dept. of Cognitive Neurology/Science Photo Library. Photo Researchers, Inc.)*

phrenics are able to function in society. Over the long term, about one-third of patients experience recovery or remission. Children afflicted with schizophrenia have a poorer prognosis than that of adults.

Prevention

There is no proven way to prevent onset of schizophrenia. Researchers have investigated the possibility of treating schizophrenia during the prodromal stage or even before symptoms start (such as when the likelihood of hereditary transmission is high). Other areas of research include the links between schizophrenia and family stress, drug use, and exposure to certain infectious agents.

Parental concerns

Parents play a key role in the everyday treatment and management of schizophrenia. The affected child should be closely monitored to ensure he or she is taking all prescribed medications. Working with the child's school teachers to formulate a day-to-day schedule can help maintain consistency for the child and address specific developmental delays. Parents should be educated on the signs of relapse and of adverse reactions to the medication, and encourage children in remission to self-report any possible signs of relapse.

Resources

BOOKS

Dalton, Richard, Marc A. Forman, and Neil W. Boris. "Childhood Schizophrenia." In *Nelson Textbook of*

KEY TERMS

Neurotransmitters—Chemicals in the brain that transmit nerve impulses.

Ventricles—Four cavities within the brain that produce and maintain the cerebrospinal fluid that cushions and protects the brain and spinal cord.

Pediatrics, 17th ed. Edited by Richard E Behrman, Robert M. Kliegman, and Hal B. Jenson. Philadelphia: Saunders, 2004.

Moore, David P., and James W. Jefferson, eds. "Schizophrenia." In *Handbook of Medical Psychiatry*, 2nd ed. New York: Mosby, 2004.

PERIODICALS

Jarbin, Hakan, et al. "Adult Outcome of Social Function in Adolescent-Onset Schizophrenia and Affective Psychosis." *Journal of the American Academy of Child and Adolescent Psychiatry* 42, no.2 (February 2003): 176–83.

McClellan, Jon, et al. "Symptom Factors in early-Onset Psychotic Disorders." *Journal of the American Academy of Child and Adolescent Psychiatry* 41, no. 7 (July 2002): 791–8.

Schaeffer, John L., and Randal G. Ross. "Childhood-Onset Schizophrenia: Premorbid and Prodromal Diagnostic and Treatment Histories." *Journal of the American Academy of Child and Adolescent Psychiatry* 41, no. 5 (May 2002): 538–45.

ORGANIZATIONS

National Alliance for Research on Schizophrenia and Depression. 60 Cutter Mill Rd., Suite 404, Great Neck, NY 11021. Web site: <www.narsad.org>.

National Schizophrenia Foundation. 403 Seymour Ave., Suite 202, Lansing, MI 48933. Web site: <www.nsfoundation.org>.

WEB SITES

Dunn, David W. "Schizophrenia and Other Psychoses." *eMedicine*, June 17, 2004. Available online at <http://www.emedicine.com/ped/topic2057.htm> (accessed January 17, 2005).

Stephanie Dionne Sherk

School phobia/school refusal

Definition

The term school phobia was first used in 1941 to identify children who fail to attend school because attendance causes emotional distress and **anxiety**. In Great Britain and as of the early 2000s in the United States, the term school refusal is preferred.

Description

School phobia is a complex syndrome that can be influenced by the child's **temperament**, the situation at school, and the **family** situation. Current thinking defines school phobia or school refusal as an anxiety disorder related to **separation anxiety**. Children refuse to attend school because doing so causes uncomfortable feelings, stress, anxiety, or panic. Many children develop physical symptoms, such as **dizziness**, stomachache, or **headache**, when they are made to go to school. School avoidance is a milder form of refusal to attend school. With school avoidance, the child usually tries to avoid a particular situation, such as taking a test or changing clothes for physical education, rather than avoiding the school environment altogether.

School refusal usually develops after a child has been home from school for an illness or vacation. It may also follow a stressful family event, such as **divorce**, parental illness or injury, death of a relative, or a move to a new school. Usually refusal to attend school develops gradually, with children putting up increasingly intense resistance to going to school as time passes. Psychiatrists believe that in young children, the motivating factor often is a desire to stay with the parent or caregiver rather than to avoid an unpleasant situation at school. In older children, or if school refusal comes on suddenly, it may be related to avoiding a distressing situation at school such as bullying, teasing, severe teacher criticism, or it may follow a humiliating event such as throwing up in class. The longer a child stays out of school, the more difficult it is for that child to return.

School refusal is not the same as **truancy**. Children who are school refusers suffer anxiety and physical symptoms when they go to school. They may have temper **tantrums** over going to school or become depressed. They may threaten to harm themselves if made to go to school. School refusers usually work to get their parent's permission to stay home. If allowed to stay home, they usually stay in the house or near the parent or caregiver. The child is willing to do make-up school work at home, so long as he or she does not have to go to school.

Children who are truants are not anxious about school; they simply do not want to be there. They try to hide their absence from their parents and have no interest in make-up schoolwork or meeting academic expectations. Unlike school phobia, truancy often occurs with other antisocial behaviors such as shoplifting, **lying**, and drug and alcohol use.

Demographics

Boys and girls refuse to attend school at the same rates. School phobia is highest in children ages five to seven and 11 to 14. These ages correspond with starting school, and transitioning through middle school or junior high school, both unusually stressful periods. Estimates suggest that about 4.5 percent of children ages 7 to 11 and 1.3 percent of children age 14 to 16 are school refusers. School phobia is an international problem, with an estimated rate of 2.4 percent of all school-age children worldwide refusing to attend classes.

Children who are more likely to become school refusers share certain characteristics. These include:

- reluctance to stay in a room alone or **fear** of the dark
- clinging attachment to parents or caregivers
- excessive worry that something dreadful will happen at home while they are at school
- difficulties sleeping or frequent **nightmares** about separation
- homesickness when away at places other than at school, or an excessive need to stay in touch with the parent or caregiver while away

Causes and symptoms

There appears to be a genetic component to all anxiety disorders, including school phobia. Children whose parents have anxiety disorders have a higher rate of anxiety disorders than children whose parents do not have these disorders. School phobia is often associated with other anxiety disorders such as agoraphobia or other mental health disorders such as depression. Some experts theorize that another possible cause of school refusal is traumatic and prolonged separation from the primary caregiver in early childhood.

Family functioning affects school refusal. Stressful events or a dysfunctional family can cause children to feel compelled to stay home. Young children are more likely to refuse to separate from their parent or caregiver because they fear something catastrophic will happen to the adult while they are at school. Older children may refuse to leave a parent who is ill or who has a substance abuse problem, in effect trying to cope for the parent. They may also be afraid of some specific aspect of school, such as riding the bus or eating in the cafeteria.

It is not uncommon for middle and high school students to become school refusers because they are afraid of violence either at school or on the way to school, are afraid of failing academically, have been repeatedly bullied or humiliated at school, feel they have no friends at school, or are excluded.

Children who refuse to attend school usually try to win a parent's permission to stay home, although some simply refuse to leave the house. Genuine physical symptoms are common and include dizziness, headaches, **nausea**, **vomiting**, **diarrhea**, shaking or trembling, fast heart rate, chest pains, and back, joint or stomach pains. These symptoms usually improve once the child is allowed to stay home. Behavioral symptoms include temper tantrums, crying, angry outbursts, and threats to hurt themselves (**self-mutilation**).

When to call the doctor

Parents with a child who is avoiding or refusing school should call their pediatrician and arrange to have physical symptoms evaluated. If no reason for physical symptoms such as abdominal **pain** can be found, the pediatrician should make a referral to a child or adolescent psychiatrist who can evaluate the child for a range of behavioral problems including social phobia, depression, **conduct disorder**, and post-traumatic stress syndrome.

Diagnosis

The most effective form of treatment is a combination of behavioral and cognitive therapy for an average period of six months. Behavioral therapy involves teaching both parents and children strategies for overcoming certain stressful behaviors such as separation and may involve desensitization by gradual exposure to the stressful event. Cognitive therapy teaches children to redirect their thoughts and actions into a more flexible and assertive pattern. **Family therapy** may also be used to help resolve family issues that may be affecting the child.

Depending on the diagnosis, children may also be treated with drugs to help alleviate depression, panic and anxiety, or other mental health disorders. In October 2003 the United States Food and Drug Administration issued an advisory indicating that children being treated with selective serotonin re-uptake inhibitor **antidepressants** (SSRIs) for major depressive illness may be at higher risk for committing **suicide**. A similar warning was issued in the United Kingdom. Parents and physicians must weigh the benefits and risks of prescribing these medications for children on an individual basis.

Treatment

Diagnosis is made on the basis of family history, the absence of causes for physical symptoms such as heart palpitations, vomiting, or dizziness, and the results of a battery of **psychological tests**. Psychological evaluation varies with other findings and the age of the child but usually includes several assessments for anxiety and a behavioral checklist that evaluates the child's behavior at home and school.

Prognosis

The combination of cognitive and behavioral therapy appears to produce the most successful treatment results. In one study, more than 80 percent of children receiving this combination of therapies were attending school normally one year after treatment. Underlying conditions that might affect recovery from school phobia include **Tourette syndrome**, attention deficit disorder (ADD), depression, bipolar mental illness, panic disorder, or other anxiety disorders and **phobias**.

Prevention

Little can be done to prevent school refusal. However, parents can give their children appropriate opportunities to separate from them during the toddler and **preschool** years by exposing them to activities such as preschool, playgroups, **babysitters**, and daycare.

With older children, parents can step in to stop bullying behavior or remove their child from the bullying or humiliating situation as soon as it starts.

Parental concerns

Many parents recognize that their child is genuinely distressed by attending school and unwittingly encourage school refusal by allowing their child to stay home. However, the longer the child is at home, the harder it is to return to school. Parents need to make the school aware of their child's difficulties and take a firm stand in working with the school to resolve any issues of **safety** or bullying that may be preventing their child from experiencing a full education.

See also Separation anxiety.

KEY TERMS

Agoraphobia—Abnormal anxiety regarding public places or situations from which the person may wish to flee or in which he or she would be helpless in the event of a panic attack.

Selective serotonin reuptake inhibitors (SSRIs)—A class of antidepressants that work by blocking the reabsorption of serotonin in the brain, thus raising the levels of serotonin. SSRIs include fluoxetine (Prozac), sertraline (Zoloft), and paroxetine (Paxil).

Resources

BOOKS

Davidson, Tish. *School Conflict.* New York: Scholastic, 2003.

ORGANIZATIONS

*American Academy of Child and Adolescent Psychiatry.*3615 Wisconsin Avenue, NW, Washington, DC 20016 3007. Web site: <www.aacap.org>.

WEB SITES

Bernstein, Betinna E. "Anxiety Disorder: Separation Anxiety and School Refusal." *eMedicine.* Available online at <www.emedicine.com/ped/topic2657.htm> (accessed October 29, 2004).

"'Facts for Families: Children Who Wont Go to School." *American Academy of Child and Adolescent Psychiatry*, July 2004. Available online at <www.aacap.org/publications/facts fam/noschool.htm> (accessed October 29, 2004).

Fremont, Wanda P. "School Refusal in Children and Adolescents." *American Family Physician* (October 15, 2003). Available online at <www.aafp.org/2-31015/1555.html>

Tish Davidson A.M.

SCID *see* Severe combined immunodeficiency

Scoliosis

Definition

Scoliosis is a side-to-side curvature of the spine.

Description

When viewed from the rear, the spine usually appears perfectly straight. Scoliosis is a lateral (side-to-side) curve in the spine, usually combined with a rotation of the vertebrae. (The lateral curvature of scoliosis should not be confused with the normal set of front-to-back spinal curves visible from the side.) While a small degree of lateral curvature does not cause any medical problems, larger curves can cause postural imbalance and lead to muscle fatigue and **pain**. More severe scoliosis can interfere with breathing and lead to arthritis of the spine (spondylosis).

Demographics

Approximately 10 percent of all adolescents have some degree of scoliosis, although fewer than 1 percent have curves that require medical attention beyond monitoring. Scoliosis is found in both boys and girls, but a girl's spinal curve is much more likely to progress than a boy's. Girls require scoliosis treatment about five times more often than boys. The reason for these differences as of 2004 was not known.

Causes and symptoms

Four out of five cases of scoliosis are idiopathic, meaning the cause is unknown. While idiopathic scoliosis tends to run in families, no specific genes responsible for the condition have been identified. Children with idiopathic scoliosis appear to be otherwise entirely healthy and have not had any bone or joint disease early in life. Scoliosis is not caused by poor posture, diet, or carrying a heavy book bag on one shoulder.

Idiopathic scoliosis is further classified according to age of onset:

- Infantile: Curvature appears before age three. This type is quite rare in the United States but is more common in Europe.
- Juvenile: Curvature appears between ages three and ten. This type may be equivalent to the adolescent type, except for the age of onset.
- Adolescent: Curvature usually appears between ages of ten and 13, near the beginning of **puberty**. This is the most common type of idiopathic scoliosis.
- Adult: Curvature begins after physical maturation is completed.

Causes are known for three other types of scoliosis:

- Congenital scoliosis is due to abnormal formation of the bones of the spine and is often associated with other organ defects.
- Neuromuscular scoliosis is due to loss of control of the nerves or muscles that support the spine. The most common causes of this type of scoliosis are **cerebral palsy** and **muscular dystrophy**.
- Degenerative scoliosis may be caused by breaking down of the discs that separate the vertebrae or by arthritis in the joints that link them.

Scoliosis causes a noticeable asymmetry in the torso when viewed from the front or back. The first sign of scoliosis is often seen when a child is wearing a bathing suit or underwear. A child may appear to be standing with one shoulder higher than the other or to have a tilt in the waistline. One shoulder blade may appear more prominent than the other due to rotation. In girls, one breast may appear higher than the other or larger if rotation pushes one side forward.

Curve progression is greatest near the adolescent growth spurt. Scoliosis that begins early is more likely to progress significantly than scoliosis that begins later in puberty.

When to call the doctor

If the parent notices that a child's posture is abnormal, if when the child stands one hip appears to be higher than the other, if one shoulder blade appears to be sticking out, or the child appears to lean regularly to one side, the doctor should be notified. If the child is screened at school and the screener reports a suspicion of scoliosis, a doctor should be seen to follow up on this suspicion.

Diagnosis

Diagnosis for scoliosis is done by an orthopedist. A complete medical history is taken, including questions about **family** history of scoliosis. The physical examination includes determination of pubertal development in adolescents, a neurological exam (which may reveal a neuromuscular cause), and measurements of trunk asymmetry. Examination of the trunk is done while the patient is standing, bending over, and lying down and involves both visual inspection and use of a simple mechanical device called a scoliometer.

If a curve is detected, one or more x rays will usually be taken to define the curve or curves more precisely. An x ray is also used to document spinal maturity, any pelvic tilt or hip asymmetry, and the location, extent, and degree of curvature. The curve is defined in terms of where it begins and ends, in which direction it bends, and by an angle measure known as the Cobb angle. The Cobb angle is found by taking an x ray of the spine. Lines are then projected out parallel to the vertebrae at the top and bottom of the curve. Then perpendicular lines are projected from these lines and the angle at which the lines intersect is measured. These angles are referred to when the angle of the curvature is discussed. To properly track the progress of scoliosis, it is important to project from the same points of the spine each time a measurement is made; otherwise, there is a risk of getting misleading measurements.

Occasionally, **magnetic resonance imaging** (MRI) is used as a diagnostic tool, primarily to look more closely at the condition of the spinal cord and nerve roots extending from it if neurological problems are suspected.

Treatment

Treatment decisions for scoliosis are based on the degree of curvature, the likelihood of significant progression, and the presence of pain, if any.

Curves less than 20 degrees are not usually treated, except by regular follow-up for children who are still growing. Watchful waiting is usually all that is required in adolescents with curves of 20 to 30 degrees as long as there is no pain.

For children or adolescents whose curves progress to 30 degrees and who have a year or more of growth left, bracing may be required. Bracing cannot correct curvature but may be effective in halting or slowing progression.

Two styles of braces are used for daytime wear. The Milwaukee brace consists of metal uprights attached to pads at the hips, rib cage, and neck. The other kind of brace is the underarm brace, which uses rigid plastic to encircle the lower rib cage, abdomen, and hips. Both these brace types hold the spine in a vertical position. Because it can be worn out of sight beneath clothing, the underarm brace is better tolerated and often leads to better compliance. A third style, the Charleston bending brace, is used at night to bend the spine in the opposite direction. Braces are often prescribed to be worn for 22 to 23 hours per day, though some clinicians allow or encourage removal of the brace for **exercise**.

Bracing may be appropriate for scoliosis due to some types of neuromuscular disease, including **spinal muscular atrophy**, before growth is finished. Duchenne muscular dystrophy is not treated by bracing. Surgery is likely to be required.

Surgery is usually the option of last resort in cases of scoliosis. Surgery for idiopathic scoliosis is usually recommended if one of the following conditions is present:

- The curve has progressed despite bracing.
- The curve is greater than 40 to 50 degrees before growth has stopped in an adolescent.
- There is significant pain.

Orthopedic surgery for neuromuscular scoliosis is often done earlier. The goals of surgery are to correct the deformity as much as possible, to prevent further deformity, and to eliminate pain as much as possible. Surgery can usually correct 40 to 50 percent of the curve, and sometimes as much as 80 percent. Surgery cannot always completely remove pain.

The surgical procedure for scoliosis is called spinal fusion, because the goal is to straighten the spine as much as possible and then to fuse the vertebrae together to prevent further curvature. To achieve fusion, the involved vertebra are first exposed and then scraped to promote regrowth. Bone chips are usually used to splint together the vertebrae to increase the likelihood of fusion. To maintain the proper spinal posture before fusion occurs, metal rods are inserted alongside the spine and are attached to the vertebrae by hooks, screws, or wires. Fusion of the spine makes it rigid and resistant to further curvature. The metal rods are no longer needed once fusion is complete but are rarely removed unless their presence leads to complications.

Spinal fusion leaves the involved portion of the spine permanently stiff and inflexible. While this leads to some loss of normal motion, most functional activities are not strongly affected, unless the very lowest portion of the spine (the lumbar region) is fused. Normal mobility, exercise, and even contact **sports** are usually all possible after spinal fusion. Full recovery takes approximately six months. Physical therapy is part of standard treatment as well.

Alternative treatment

Numerous alternative therapies have been touted to provide relief and help for individuals with scoliosis, but none has been proven beneficial in clinical trials. These include massage and electrical stimulation. In addition, alternatives such as rolfing or chiropractic manipulation of soft tissue to improve alignment may provide improved flexibility, stronger muscles, and pain relief but cannot prevent or correct the curvature of the spine or its progression.

Although important for general health and strength, exercise has not been shown to prevent or slow the development of scoliosis. It may help relieve pain from scoliosis by helping to maintain range of motion. Aquatic exercise, in particular, can increase flexibility and improve posture, balance, coordination, and range of motion. Because it decreases joint compression, it can lessen the pain caused by scoliosis or surgery.

Good **nutrition** is also important for general health, but no specific dietary regimen has been shown to control scoliosis development. In particular, dietary calcium levels do not influence scoliosis progression.

Chiropractic treatment may relieve pain, but it cannot halt scoliosis development and should not be a substitute for conventional treatment of progressing scoliosis. Acupuncture and acupressure may also help reduce pain and discomfort, but these treatments cannot halt scoliosis development either.

Prognosis

The prognosis for a child with scoliosis depends on many factors, including the age at which scoliosis begins and the treatment received. More importantly, mostly unknown individual factors affect the likelihood of progression and the severity of the curve. Most cases of mild adolescent idiopathic scoliosis need no treatment and do not progress. Untreated severe scoliosis often leads to spondylosis and may impair breathing. Degenerative arthritis of the spine, sciatica, and severe physical deformities can also result if severe scoliosis is left untreated. Finally, scoliosis can also poorly affect the individual's **self-esteem** and cause serious emotional problems.

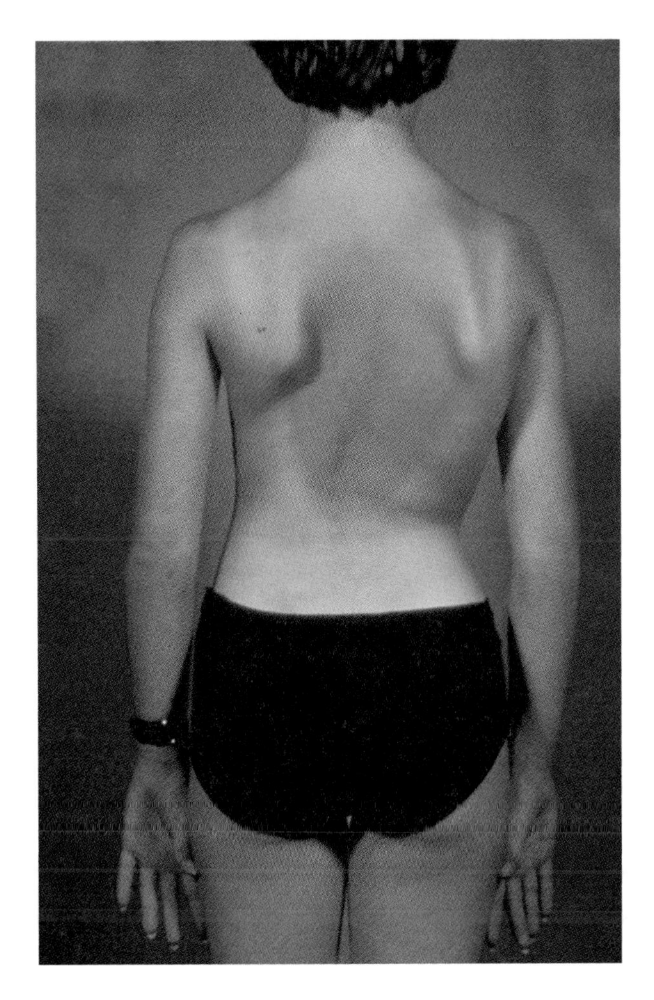

This patient suffers from scoliosis, or curvature of the spine. *(Custom Medical Stock Photo Inc.)*

Prevention

There is no known way to prevent the development of scoliosis. Progression of scoliosis may be prevented through bracing or surgery. More than 30 states have screening programs in schools for adolescent scoliosis, usually conducted by trained school nurses or physical education teachers. These programs can help to catch scoliosis early, so that treatment can begin and progression can often be halted or slowed.

Parental concerns

Children with scoliosis often have a negative self-image associated with irregular posture or having to wear a brace. This problem is being combated with new braces that can be worn under the clothing and are more discreet than traditional braces. Scoliosis can be life threatening if it is not treated and progresses to a point at which breathing is impaired. This is very rare, however. Scoliosis should be watched carefully by a physician for signs of worsening, but it usually does not progress to the point at which treatment is needed.

Resources

BOOKS

Hooper, Nancy J. *Stopping Scoliosis: The Whole Family Guide to Diagnosis and Treatment.* East Rutherford, NJ: Penguin Group, 2002.

Lenke, Lawrence, et al. *Modern Anterior Scoliosis Surgery.* St. Louis, MO: Quality Medical Publishing, 2002.

Newton, Peter O. *Adolescent Idiopathic Scoliosis.* Rosemont, IL: Academy of Orthopaedic Surgeons, 2004.

Schommer, Nancy. *Stopping Scoliosis: The Complete Guide to Diagnosis and Treatment*, 2nd ed. New York: Avery, 2002.

KEY TERMS

Cobb angle—A measure of the curvature of scoliosis, determined by measurements made on x rays.

Rolfing—A holistic system of bodywork that uses deep manipulation of the body's soft tissue to realign and rebalance the body's myofacial (connective) structure. It is used to improve posture, relieve chronic pain, and reduce stress.

Silverstein, Alvin. *Scoliosis*. Minneapolis, MN: Sagebrush Education Resources, 2003.

Spray, Michelle L., et al. *Growing Up with Scoliosis: A Young Girl's Story*. Stratford, CT: Book Shelf Inc., 2002.

PERIODICALS

Sullivan, Michele G. "Surgical Stapling Can Halt Curve of Scoliosis: Orthotics Can Be Helpful." *Family Practice News* 33 (December 15, 2003): 35.

Wachter, Kerry. "Prognosis for Scoliosis Better than Once Thought." *Family Practice News* 33 (July 1, 2003): 59.

Weomstoem. Stuart, et al. "Health and Function of Patients with Untreated Idiopathic Scoliosis: a 50-Year Natural History Study." *The Journal of the American Medical Association* 289 (February 5, 2003): 559.

ORGANIZATIONS

National Scoliosis Foundation. 5 Cabot Place, Stoughton, MA 02072. Web site: <www.scoliosis.org>.

Scoliosis Research Society. 55 East Wells St. Suite 1100. Milwaukee, WI 53202–3823. Web site: <www.srs.org>.

Tish Davidson, A.M.
Liz Meszaros

Scrapes *see* **Wounds**
Seasonal allergies *see* **Allergic rhinitis**

Seborrheic dermatitis

Definition

Seborrheic **dermatitis** is a common inflammatory disease of the scalp and skin characterized by scaly lesions usually on the scalp, hairline, face and body. In infants, it is sometimes called cradle cap.

Description

Seborrheic dermatitis appears as red, inflamed skin covered by greasy or dry scales that may be white, yellowish, or gray. It can affect the scalp, eyebrows, forehead, face, folds around the nose and ears, the chest, armpits, and groin. In infants it appears most commonly on the scalp and is called cradle cap. Dandruff is a mild form of seborrheic dermatitis and appear as fine white scales without red skin or inflammation. Dandruff can also be caused by other skin conditions, especially in children.

Seborrheic dermatitis is a common, mild disease of newborns. The red, scaly rash can spread to the forehead, behind the ears, and in the creases of the neck and armpits. The rash is not itchy and usually does not bother babies. Occasionally babies also develop this skin disease in the diaper area. When seborrheic dermatitis occurs in the diaper area, it is often accompanied by a yeast infection. When yeast is present, the rash is itchy and uncomfortable. Seborrheic dermatitis usually disappears by the end of the first year and does not reappear until **puberty**.

Transmission

Seborrheic dermatitis is not an infection and is not transmitted from individual to individual.

Demographics

Seborrheic dermatitis is a very common among newborns. It usually appears the first six weeks of life and rarely after the age of nine to 12 months. It affects babies of all races and both genders. Seborrheic dermatitis can reappear at puberty and into adulthood.

Causes and symptoms

As of 2004 the cause of seborrheic dermatitis was not clear. However, it is not an infection or an allergy, it is not contagious, and it is not caused by poor hygiene. Seborrheic refers to the sebaceous, or oil producing, glands of the skin. It appears that in pregnancy, hormone changes in the mother may cause these glands to produce too much oil. When this happens, scales develop in the area where the oil glands are most dense. Seborrheic dermatitis may also be linked to genetic factors.

Babies exhibit a characteristic non-itchy greasy red scaly rash or dry whitish or grayish scales on the scalp and possibly on other areas.

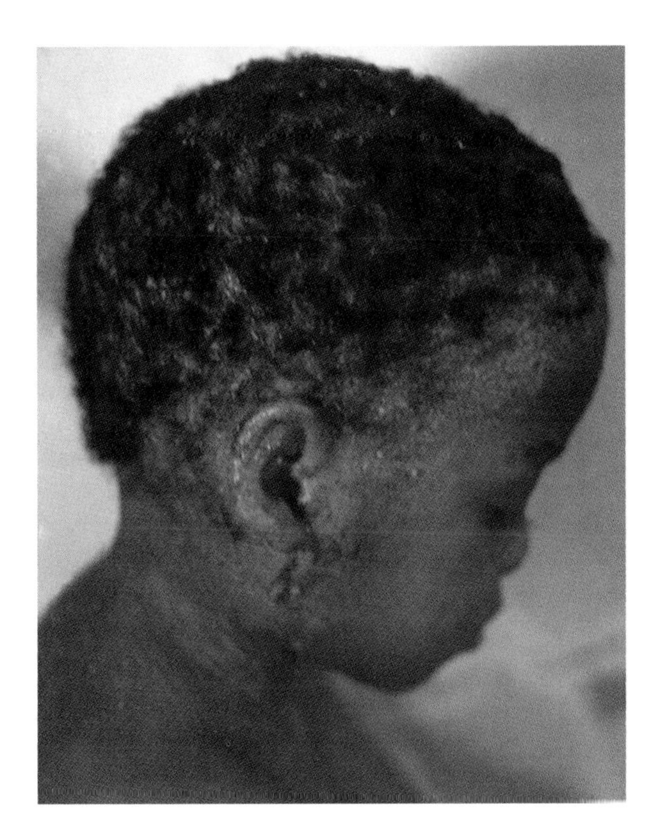

This young boy is afflicted with seborrheic dermatitis. *(Custom Medical Stock Photo Inc.)*

KEY TERMS

Cortisone—Glucocorticoid produced by the adrenal cortex in response to stress. Cortisone is a steroid with anti-inflammatory and immunosuppressive properties.

Dermatitis—Inflammation of the skin.

Salicylic acid—An agent prescribed to treat a variety of skin disorders, such as acne, dandruff, psoriasis, seborrheic dermatitis, calluses, corns, and warts.

Sebaceous—Related to the glands of the skin that produce an oily substance called sebum.

When to call the doctor

If the rash does not improve after regular washings with baby shampoo or if the rash spreads and becomes red and itchy, especially in the diaper area, the doctor should be consulted.

Diagnosis

Diagnosis is made on visual inspection of the rash.

Treatment

Frequent washing of the scalp with a mild baby shampoo followed by brushing with a soft brush to remove scales usually clears up cradle cap. In stubborn cases, a special shampoo containing sulfur and salicylic acid can be used. This treatment should be done only after consultation with a pediatrician, since this shampoo may be irritating to babies. Sometimes an ointment containing cortisone, an anti-inflammatory medication, is prescribed. If the seborrheic dermatitis is complicated by a yeast infection, an ointment containing anti-yeast medications such as nystatin is applied to the infected area three or four times daily.

Alternative treatment

Parents may rub mineral oil into their child's scalp to soften and loosen the scales, but the oil should be brushed or shampooed out and not left to accumulate.

Prognosis

Seborrheic dermatitis normally resolves without difficulty, usually by the age of six months and almost always by the end of the first year. The rash does not leave scars.

Prevention

Seborrheic dermatitis cannot be prevented from developing, although it may be controlled through frequent hair washings with a mild baby shampoo.

Parental concerns

Parents are often concerned that the rash will leave a scar on their baby's skin. However, scarring does not occur.

Resources

WEB SITES

"Cradle Cap." *Pediatric Advisor.* Available online at <www.pmhs.org/crs/pa/hhg/cradlcap.htm> (accessed November 13, 2004).

"Cradle Cap (infantile seborrhoeic dermatitis)." *DermNet NZ.* Available online at <http://dermnetnz.org/

dermatitis/cradle-cap.htlm> (assessed November 13, 2004).

Tish Davidson, A.M.
Kathleen D. Wright, RN

Security objects

Definition

Security objects are items, usually soft and easily held or carried, that offer a young child comfort. They also are referred to as transitional objects, substitute objects, cuddlies, soothers, "loveys," and security blankets.

Description

Security objects or transitional objects are items that help a young child make the emotional transition from dependence to independence. Attachment to an object often develops toward the end of the first year, although attachment to pacifiers happens earlier. Strong attachment to blankets peaks at 18 and 24 months, stays near this high level through 39 months, and then diminishes steadily. By five and a half, fewer than to 8 percent of children are attached to blankets. Other objects of attachment can be articles of clothing, cloth diapers, soft **toys**, or almost anything with a soft, pleasing texture.

In the 1940s, attachment to a special object was regarded as a childhood problem reflecting an unhealthy relationship between the mother and the child. Gradually this attitude began changing as researchers concluded that the child's attachment to a security object is normal and even desirable. Nevertheless, throughout the 1970s, but progressively less in the 1980s and 1990s, a stigma remained attached to children who, like Linus in the "Peanuts" comic strip, hugged a blanket or other security object in times of stress. The subsequently discredited stereotype was that these children were overly anxious and insecure. As a result, the security object was often taken away from the child, sometimes forcibly, just when it could have been beneficial. As of 2004 research indicated that there is no justification for such drastic actions. Evidence does not find children abnormal or overanxious just because they demonstrate an attachment to a security object. Blanket-attached children appear to be neither more nor less maladjusted or insecure than other children.

Although several theories exist about the role of security objects in development, it is not clear from any of these theories why some children engage in comfort habits with security objects while others do not. Child-rearing practices are frequently seen as contributing factors, and evidence suggests that the security of a child's attachment to its mother does predict how a security object will be used in new or stressful situations.

Despite thinking in the early 2000s that attachment to transitional objects is normal and almost universal, this attachment is actually culture-specific. For instance, in the United States, about 60 percent of children have at least a mild degree of attachment to a soft, inanimate object at some time during their life, and 32 percent exhibit strong attachment. The incidence of attachments to soft objects in the Netherlands, New Zealand, and Sweden is comparable to that in the United States. Korean children have substantially fewer attachments to blankets (18%) than do American children, but Korean-born children living in the United States display an intermediate percentage (34%). Only 5 percent of rural Italian children have transitional objects, compared to 31 percent of native Italian children living in Rome. However, only 16 percent of children living in London have a special security object. In the United States, attachments to various security objects are generally regarded as normal throughout the first five years of life.

Attachment to a security object can be beneficial to a child. The security object may serve as a substitute for the parent in his or her absence and may assist separation from the mother or father by providing the comfort of something familiar. At bedtime, it can soothe and facilitate **sleep**. Studies have also shown that during a routine third-year pediatric examination, children allowed security objects were less distressed than children undergoing the medical evaluation without their security object. The comfort provided by a blanket in new situations has even been shown to enhance children's learning.

Common problems

Parents often become frustrated with their child's need for a security object as it falls to the parent to keep track of the object and soothe the child if it is misplaced or lost. Occasionally daycare centers forbid the child to bring anything from home, including a security object, causing unnecessary stress for the child.

Parental concerns

Parents worry that as the security object becomes dirty, it will spread germs. Other concerns are related to specific objects, such as pacifiers, which may cause dental deformity or objects that, due to their size, shape, or composition, are awkward or undesirable as "loveys." In

Child using his stuffed toy as a security object. *(© Gilbert Patrick/Corbis.)*

these cases, it may be possible, with patience, to substitute one security object for another.

When to call the doctor

Attachment to a security object is normal and should be outgrown without intervention by age five, although 8 percent of children still remain attached to blankets after this age.

See also Separation anxiety.

Resources

BOOKS

O'Halloran, Barbara Collopy, et al. *Creature Comforts: People and Their Security Objects.* Boston, MA: Houghton Mifflin, 2002.

ORGANIZATIONS

American Academy of Pediatrics. 141 Northwest Point Boulevard, Elk Grove Village, IL 60007-1098. Web site: <www.aap.org>.

WEB SITES

American Academy of Pediatrics. "Transitional Objects." *Caring for Your Baby and Young Child.* Available online at <www.aap.org/pubserv/transobj.htm> (accessed November 13, 2004).

Tish Davidson, A.M.
Richard Passman, Ph.D.

Seizure disorder

Definition

A seizure is a sudden disruption of the brain's normal electrical activity accompanied by altered consciousness and/or other neurological and behavioral manifestations. Epilepsy is a disorder of the brain characterized by recurrent seizures that may include repetitive muscle jerking called convulsions.

Description

There are more than 20 different seizure disorders, although epilepsy is the most familiar. Most seizures are benign, but a seizure that lasts a long time can lead to status epilepticus, a life-threatening condition characterized by continuous seizures, sustained loss of consciousness, and respiratory distress. In addition, non-convulsive epilepsy can impair physical coordination, vision, and other senses. Undiagnosed seizures can lead to conditions that are more serious and more difficult to manage. Ten percent of Americans have a seizure at some time in their lives.

Generalized seizures

A generalized seizure occurs when electrical abnormalities exist throughout the brain. A generalized tonic-clonic (grand-mal) seizure typically begins with a loud cry before the individual having the seizure loses consciousness and falls to the ground. The muscles become rigid for about 30 seconds during the tonic phase of the seizure and alternately contract and relax during the clonic phase, which lasts 30 to 60 seconds. The skin sometimes acquires a bluish tint, and the person may bite the tongue, lose bowel or bladder control, or have trouble breathing.

A grand mal seizure lasts two to five minutes, and the person may be confused or have trouble talking after regaining consciousness (post-ictal state). The individual may complain of head or muscle aches or weakness in the arms or legs before falling into a deep **sleep**.

Primary generalized seizures

A primary generalized seizure occurs when electrical discharges begin in both halves (hemispheres) of the brain at the same time. Primary generalized seizures are more likely to be major motor attacks than to be absence seizures. Motor attacks cause parts of the body to jerk repeatedly. A motor attack usually lasts less than an hour and may last only a few minutes.

Absence seizures

Absence (petit mal) seizures generally begin at about the age of four and stop by the time the child becomes an adolescent. Absence seizures usually begin with a brief loss of consciousness and last 15 to 20 seconds. An individual having a petit mal seizure becomes very quiet and may blink, stare blankly, roll the eyes, or move the lips. When a petit mal seizure ends, individual resumes whatever he or she was doing before the seizure began and does not remember the seizure. The individual may not realize that anything unusual has happened. Untreated, petit mal seizures can recur as many as 100 times a day and may progress to grand mal seizures.

Myoclonic seizures

Myoclonic seizures are characterized by brief, involuntary spasms of the tongue or muscles of the face, arms, or legs. Myoclonic seizures are most apt to occur when waking after a night's sleep.

A Jacksonian seizure is a partial seizure characterized by tingling, stiffening, or jerking of an arm or leg. Loss of consciousness is rare. The seizure may progress in characteristic fashion along the limb.

Limp posture and a brief period of unconsciousness are features of akinetic seizures. These occur in young children. Akinetic seizures, which cause the child to fall, also are called drop attacks.

Partial seizures

Simple partial seizures do not spread from the focal area of the brain where they arise. Symptoms are determined by the part of the brain affected. The individual usually remains conscious during the seizure and can later describe it in detail. In 2003, it was reported that people who experience partial seizures are twice as likely to have sleep disturbances as people their same age and gender who do not have seizures.

Complex partial seizures

A distinctive smell, taste, or other unusual sensation (aura) may signal the start of a complex partial seizure. Complex partial seizures start as simple partial seizures but move beyond the focal area of the brain and cause loss of consciousness. Complex partial seizures can become major motor seizures. Although individuals having a complex partial seizure may not seem to be unconscious, they do not know what is happening and may behave inappropriately. They will not remember the seizure but may seem confused or intoxicated for a few minutes after it ends.

Demographics

One in ten Americans has a seizure during their lifetime, and at least 200,000 Americans have at least one seizure a month. Epilepsy affects 2.5 million Americans of all ages, and of those, 25 percent of all cases develop before the age of five. Some 181,000 new cases are diagnosed annually and 45,000 of them are children under the age of 15. Though the incidence rate for children is in the early 2000s trending down, epilepsy remains a significant problem for many children.

In all people, the risk of developing epilepsy is approximately 1 percent. However, certain groups are at higher risk. The expectations of the onset of epilepsy in these populations are as follows:

- children with **mental retardation**: 10%
- children with **cerebral palsy**: 10%
- children with both cerebral palsy and mental retardation: 50%
- children of mothers with epilepsy: 8.7%
- children of fathers with epilepsy: 2.4%

In addition, males are somewhat more likely to develop epilepsy than females, and African-Americans are more likely to develop it than Caucasians. The incidence of epilepsy is greater in those who are socioeconomically disadvantaged.

Causes and symptoms

The cause of 70 percent of new cases of epilepsy is unknown (idiopathic). Epilepsy sometimes is the result of trauma at birth. Such neonatal causes include insufficient oxygen to the brain, **head injury**, heavy bleeding, incompatibility between a woman's blood and the blood of her baby, or infection immediately before, after, or at the time of birth.

Other causes of epilepsy include the following:

- head trauma resulting from a car accident, gunshot wound, or other injury
- alcoholism
- brain abscess or inflammation of membranes covering the brain or spinal cord
- phenylketonuria (PKU) or other inherited disorders or genetic factors
- infectious diseases such as **measles**, **mumps**, and diphtheria
- degenerative disease
- lead **poisoning**, mercury poisoning, **carbon monoxide poisoning**, or ingestion of other poisonous substances

Status epilepticus, a condition in which an individual suffers from continuous seizures and may have trouble breathing, can be caused by the following factors:

- suddenly discontinuing anti-seizure medication
- hypoxic or metabolic encephalopathy (brain disease resulting from lack of oxygen or malfunctioning of other physical or chemical processes)
- acute head injury
- blood infection caused by inflammation of the brain or the membranes that cover it

Symptoms

Different types of seizures have different symptoms. Generalized epileptic seizures occur when electrical abnormalities exist throughout the brain. Partial seizures do not involve the entire brain, although a partial seizure may spread to other parts of the brain and cause a generalized seizure. Some people who have epilepsy have more than one type of seizure.

Motor attacks cause parts of the body to jerk repeatedly. Sensory seizures cause **numbness** or tingling in one area. The sensation may move along one side of the body or the back before subsiding.

Visual seizures, which affect the area of the brain that controls sight, cause people to see things that are not there. Auditory seizures affect the part of the brain that controls hearing and cause the individual to imagine voices, music, and other sounds. Other types of seizures can cause confusion, upset stomach, or emotional distress.

When to call the doctor

Parents should call the doctor or local emergency number the first time a child has a seizure. For children who have been diagnosed with epilepsy, the doctor should give guidelines about when to call. However, the following situations merit emergency attention:

- a longer seizure than the child usually has or an unusual number of seizures
- seizures that recur repeatedly in the course of a few minutes
- consciousness not regained between seizures
- occurrence of new neurological symptoms
- occurrence of side effects from medication, which could include drowsiness and rash for most anticonvulsants (Specific possible side effects should be reviewed for each medication with the physician and/or pharmacist.)

Diagnosis

Personal and **family** medical history, description of seizure activity, and physical and neurological examinations help primary care physicians, neurologists, and epileptologists diagnose this disorder. Doctors rule out conditions that cause symptoms that resemble seizure disorders, including small strokes (transient ischemic attacks, or TIAs), fainting (syncope), pseudoseizures, and sleep attacks (**narcolepsy**).

Neuropsychological testing uncovers learning or memory problems. Neuroimaging provides views of brain areas involved in seizure activity.

The **electroencephalogram** (EEG) is the main test used to diagnose epilepsy. EEGs use electrodes placed on or within the skull to record the brain's electrical activity and pinpoint the exact location of abnormal discharges.

Other tests used to diagnose seizure disorders include:

- Magnetic resonance imaging (MRI), which provides clear, detailed images of the brain. Functional MRI (fMRI), performed while the patient does various tasks, can measure shifts in electrical intensity and blood flow and indicate which brain region each activity affects.
- Positron emission tomography (PET) and single photon emission tomography (SPECT) monitor blood flow

and chemical activity in the brain area being tested. PET and SPECT are very effective in locating the brain region where metabolic changes take place between seizures.

- Urine and blood lab tests can screen for electrolyte disturbances and possible metabolic disorders.

Treatment

Seizure disorders in children are usually treated with anticonvulsant drugs. Doctors attempt to use a single drug for this purpose, but more than one may be required. Medications are prescribed based on the seizure type. Even when the drugs suppress seizures, they should not be discontinued without a doctor's advice. Most individuals require at least several years of treatment.

If medication is not successful in preventing seizures, surgery, a ketogenic diet, or vagus nerve stimulation (VNS) may be tried. Brain surgery can be useful in certain cases to remove small groups of cells causing the problem.

The ketogenic diet is a high fat, low carbohydrate, limited calorie diet that forces the child's body to burn fat instead of glucose derived from carbohydrates. Burning fat produces chemicals called ketones. One out of three children who begins the diet becomes free or almost free from seizures, while another third improve, and the final third show no improvement. This diet, which is usually begun in the hospital, is extremely rigorous and must be monitored by a doctor and dietician.

The United States Food and Drug Administration (FDA) has approved the use of vagus nerve stimulation (VNS) in patients over the age of 16 who have intractable partial seizures. This non-surgical procedure uses a pacemaker-like device implanted under the skin in the upper left chest, to provide intermittent stimulation to the vagus nerve. Stretching from the side of the neck into the brain, the vagus nerve affects swallowing, speech, breathing.

Prognosis

Prognosis depends on the type of seizures, the ability to control them with medication, the age of the individual, and the underlying cause of the seizures. Seventy percent of individuals with epilepsy can be expected to go into remission, which is defined as five or more years without seizures while on medication. Three-fourths of those who are seizure free for two to five years while on medication can have the medication reduced or eliminated. However, in 10 percent of new epilepsy cases, the seizures are not controlled by medication.

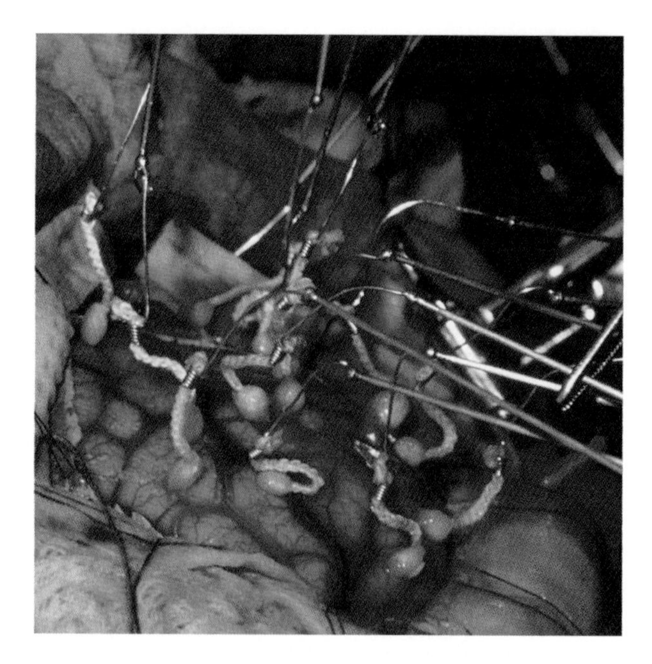

This patient's brain is exposed during surgery in order for surgeons to remove the mass responsible for epileptic seizures. *(Custom Medical Stock Photo Inc.)*

Prevention

There is no known way to prevent the onset of seizure disorders, but seizures may be controlled and sometimes prevented by the use of medication. Up to 80 percent of those with seizure disorder can have their seizures substantially or completed controlled, allowing them to live normal or close to normal lives.

Parental concerns

Seizure disorders are long-term illnesses, with the added problem of being public. Besides the difficulty of controlling medication and possibly diet, the parents of a child with a seizure disorder must sometimes deal with the public visibility of seizure episode. Parents should be supportive of the child and make sure the child does not consider himself to blame for the seizures.

Siblings are also affected by a child with a seizure disorder. Siblings may feel neglected by parents who focus on care for one child. They may also feel responsible for their brother or sister getting the disease, and they may worry about having seizures themselves. Siblings should be assured that seizure disorders are not contagious. They should be given appropriate information both for themselves and for friends who might be present during seizures.

KEY TERMS

Epileptologist—A physician who specializes in the treatment of epilepsy.

Glucose—A simple sugar that serves as the body's main source of energy.

Phenylketonuria (PKU)—A rare, inherited, metabolic disorder in which the enzyme necessary to break down and use phenylalanine, an amino acid necessary for normal growth and development, is lacking. As a result, phenylalanine builds up in the body causing mental retardation and other neurological problems.

Some parents worry that stress might bring on a seizure and are therefore unwilling to **discipline** a child with a seizure disorder and might give in to the usual childish demands. Although stress can be a factor, parents should consult with their doctor on the level of risk and methods of discipline that can be effective for their child.

Teenagers have special concerns. In many states, those who have not been seizure-free for a certain time are not allowed to drive, which affects a teen's mobility and social life. Having seizures in front of friends can be embarrassing. Parents should resist being excessively overprotective of their teenager and should consult with their physician as to which activities are safe for their child to pursue.

Some physicians recommend avoidance of swimming in children with epilepsy. Nearly all practitioners would advise against unaccompanied swimming in persons with seizure disorders. Avoidance of exposure to flashing lights or other triggers might be necessary in some persons with seizure disorders.

Resources

BOOKS

Basil, Carl W., et al. *Living Well with Epilepsy and Other Seizure Disorders: An Expert Explains What You Really Need to Know.* New York: HarperInformation, 2004.

Miles, Daniel K. *100 Questions about Your Child's Epilepsy.* Boston, MA: Jones & Bartlett Publishers, 2005.

Stafstrom, Carl E., et al. *Epilepsy and the Ketongenic Diet.* Totowa, NJ: Humana Press, 2004.

Svoboda, William B. *Childhood Epilepsy: Language, Learning, and Behavioral Complications.* Cambridge, UK: Cambridge University Press, 2004.

Wallace, Sheila J., et al. *Epilepsy in Children.* Oxford, UK: Oxford University Press, 2004.

ORGANIZATIONS

Epilepsy Foundation. 4351 Garden City Drive, Landover, MD 2078507223. Web site: <www.epilepsyfoundation.org>.

WEB SITES

Campellone, Joseph V. "Epilepsy." *MedLine Plus*, July 2, 2004. Available online at <www.nlm.nih.gov/medlineplus/ency/article/000694.htm> (accessed November 14, 2004).

"Epilepsy." *Centers for Disease Control.* Available online at <www.cdc.gov/nccdphp/epilepsy/index.htm> (accessed November 14, 2004).

Tish Davidson, A.M.
Maureen Haggerty
Teresa G. Odle

Seizure medication *see* **Antiepileptics**

Self-esteem

Definition

Considered an important component of emotional health, self-esteem encompasses both self-confidence and self-acceptance. It is the way individuals perceive themselves and their self-value.

Description

Self-esteem is the way individuals think and feel about themselves and how well they do things that are important to them. In children, self-esteem is shaped by what they think and feel about themselves. Their self-esteem is highest when they see themselves as approximating their "ideal" self, the person they would like to be. Children who have high self-esteem have an easier time handling conflicts, resisting negative pressures, and making friends. They laugh and smile more and have a generally optimistic view of the world and their life.

Children with low self-esteem have a difficult time dealing with problems, are overly self-critical, and can become passive, withdrawn, and depressed. They may hesitate to try new things, may speak negatively about themselves, are easily frustrated, and often see temporary problems as permanent conditions. They are pessimistic about themselves and their life.

Self-esteem comes from different sources for children at different stages of development. The development of self-esteem in young children is heavily influenced by parental attitudes and behavior. Supportive parental behavior, including encouragement and praise for accomplishments, as well as the child's internalization of the parents' own attitudes toward success and failure, are the most powerful factors in the development of self-esteem in early childhood. As children get older their experiences outside the home, in school, and with peers, become increasingly important in determining their self-esteem.

Schools can influence their students' self-esteem through the attitudes they foster toward competition and diversity and their recognition of achievement in academics, **sports**, and the arts. By middle childhood, friendships have assumed a pivotal role in a child's life. Studies have shown that school-age youngsters spend more time with their friends than they spend doing homework, watching television, or playing alone. In addition, the amount of time in which they interact with their parents is greatly reduced from when they were younger. At this stage, social acceptance by a child's peer group plays a major role in developing and maintaining self-esteem.

The physical and emotional changes that take place in **adolescence**, especially early adolescence, present new challenges to a child's self-esteem. Boys whose growth spurt comes late compare themselves with peers who have matured early and seem more athletic, masculine, and confident. In contrast, early physical maturation can be embarrassing for girls, who may feel gawky and self-conscious in their newly developed bodies. Both boys and girls expend inordinate amounts of time and energy on personal grooming, spending long periods of time in the bathroom trying to achieve a certain kind of look. Fitting in with their peers becomes more important than ever to their self-esteem, and, in later adolescence, relationships with the opposite sex (or sometimes the same sex) can become a major source of confidence or insecurity. Up to a certain point, adolescents need to gain a sense of competence by making and learning from their own mistakes and by being held accountable for their own actions.

Peer acceptance and relationships are important to children's social and emotional development and to their development of self-esteem. Peer acceptance, especially friendships, provides a wide range of learning and development opportunities for children. These include companionship, recreation, social skills, participating in group problem solving, and managing competition and conflict. They also allow for self-exploration, emotional growth, and moral and ethical development.

There are several factors that influence self-esteem. These include the following:

- Age: Self-esteem tends to grow steadily until middle school when the transition of moving from the familiar environment of elementary school to a new setting confronts children with new demands. Self-esteem either continues to grow after this period or begins to decrease.
- Gender: Girls tend to be more susceptible to having low self-esteem than boys, perhaps because of increased social pressure that emphasizes appearance more than **intelligence** or athletic ability.
- Socioeconomic status: Researchers have found that children from higher-income families usually have a better sense of self-esteem in the mid- to late-adolescence years.
- Body image: Especially true for teens but also important for younger children, body image is evaluated within the context of media images from television, movies, and advertising that often portray girls as thin, beautiful, and with perfect complexion. Boys are portrayed as muscular, very good looking, and tall. Girls who are overweight and boys who are thin or short often have low self-esteem because they compare themselves against these cultural and narrow standards.

Infancy

Infants start building self-esteem as soon as they are born. Their self-esteem is first built by having their basic needs met, including the need for love, comfort, and closeness. They gradually learn that they are loved as the people who care for them consistently treat them gently, kindly, comfort them when they cry, and show them attention. How their parents or primary caregivers treat them sets the stage for later development of self-esteem. Parents who give their babies love and attention teach the infants that they are important, safe, and secure.

Toddlerhood

During toddlerhood, children still have not developed a clear understanding of self-esteem or self-identity. Each time they learn a new skill they add to their sense of their ability and their comprehension of who they are. Toddlers learn about themselves by learning what they look like, what they can do, and where they belong. They find it difficult to share since they are just starting to learn who they are and what is theirs.

Toddlers see themselves through the eyes of their parents, **family**, or primary caregivers. If their parents show them love and treat them as special, toddlers will develop self-esteem. Toddlers who feel unloved find it more difficult to develop a sense of self-worth.

Preschool

By the age of three, children have a clearer understanding of who they are and how they fit into the world they know. They have begun learning about their bodies and that, within limits, they are able to think and make decisions on their own. They can handle time away from their parents or primary caregivers because they feel safe on their own or with other children and adults. They develop their self-esteem in mostly physical ways, by comparing their appearance to that of other children, such as height, size, agility, and abilities.

Preschoolers learn self-esteem in stages through developing their senses of trust, independence, and initiative. During this age, parents can help foster the child's self-esteem by teaching problem-solving skills, involving them in tasks that give them a sense of accomplishment, asking for and listening to their opinions, and introducing them to social settings, especially with their peers. Young children learn self-esteem through what they can do and what their parents think of them.

School age

A critical point in a child's development of self-esteem occurs when they start school. Many children's self-esteem falls when they have to cope with adults and peers in a new situation with rules that may be new and strange. In the early school-age years, self-esteem is about how well children manage learning tasks in school and how they perform in sports. It also depends on their physical appearance and characteristics and their ability to make friends with other children their own age.

Stresses at home, such as parents arguing a lot, and problems at school, such as difficult lessons, being bullied, or not having friends, can have a negative impact on a child's self-esteem. Children with overly developed self-esteem may tend to be **bullies**, while children with lower self-esteem may become the victims of bullies. Parents can help children develop an inner sense of self-control, which comes from having experience in making decisions.

Teenagers' self-esteem is often affected by the physical and hormonal changes they experience, especially during **puberty**. Teens undergo major changes in their lives and their self-esteem can often become fragile. They are usually extremely concerned about how they look and how they are perceived and accepted by their peers. Teens who set goals in their lives have higher self-esteem than those who do not. High self-esteem is also directly related to teens who have a very supportive family.

Body image is a major component in teenagers' self-esteem, and they are very concerned about how their peers see them. Teens who have high self-esteem like the way they look and accept themselves the way they are. Teens with low self-esteem usually have a poor body image and think they are too fat, not pretty enough, or not muscular enough. There are some physical features that teens cannot change, but accepting themselves as they are without undue self-criticism is challenging. If there are characteristics that cause low self-esteem but can be changed, teens may be able to set reasonable goals for making change. For example, if teens think they are overweight, they should first verify their perception with a healthcare provider. If they are actually overweight, they can set goals to lose weight by eating nutritiously and exercising regularly.

The "Teens Health" section of the Web site Kids Health (available online at <www.kidshealth.org>) offers the following advice for teens to improve self-esteem: "When you hear negative comments coming from within, tell yourself to stop. Your inner critic can be retrained. Try exercises like giving yourself three compliments every day. While you're at it, every evening list three things in your day that really gave you pleasure. It can be anything from the way the sun felt on your face, the sound of your favorite band, or the way someone laughed at your jokes. By focusing on the good things you do and the positive aspects of your life, you can change how you feel about yourself."

Parents can enhance teenagers' self-esteem by asking for their help or advice and listening to their opinions.

Common problems

Numerous studies have linked low self-esteem to a wide range of problems, including poor school achievement, criminal and violent behavior; being the victim of bullying; teenage pregnancy; **smoking** and the use of alcohol and other drugs; dropping out of school; depression; and thoughts of **suicide**, suicide attempts, and suicide. Also, children and teens who have low self-esteem have more physical health problems than those with higher self-esteem.

Parental concerns

Every child and teen has low self-esteem at some time in his or her life. Criticism from parents or others can make children with low self-esteem feel worse. Children can also develop low self-esteem if parents or others press them to reach unrealistic goals. Parents should be concerned when a child's low self-esteem interferes with his or her daily activities or causes depression. Some common signs of low-self esteem in children and teens are as follows:

- feeling they must always please other people
- general feelings of not liking themselves
- feelings of unhappiness most of the time
- feeling that their problems are not normal and that they to blame for their problems
- needing constant validation or approval
- not making friends easily or having no friends
- needing to prove that they are better than others

When to call the doctor

Sometimes a lack of self-esteem is too much for a child to handle alone. Parents may need to seek professional psychological help for children suffering from low self-esteem when the child is depressed or shows an inability to create friendships. Help may also be needed for adolescents whose lack of self-esteem is expressed in negative behaviors, such as criminal activities, gang affiliation, smoking, and alcohol and other drug dependency. If the child talks about or threatens suicide, professional help should be sought immediately.

Tips for raising your child's self-esteem

1. Be a role model for high self-esteem. If you have a positive attitude, chances are your children will have one too.

2. Have realistic expectations. Unreasonable goals will set your child up for feelings of failure.

3. Respect your child's individuality. Their accomplishments should be praised even if they are not in your area of interest, or if their level of academic success, for instance, is generally lower than a sibling's.

4. Praise your child's efforts, even if they are ultimately unsuccessful. Making a great effort should be rewarded, even he or she did not come in "first."

5. Be careful when correcting your child's behavior. Constructive criticism is much more useful than pinning your child with a label like "lazy" or "stupid."

SOURCE: McKesson Health Solutions, http://www.med.umich.edu/1libr/pa/pa-esteemup_pep.htm, 2004.

(Table by GGS Information Services.)

Resources

BOOKS

Koenig, Larry. *Smart Discipline: Fast, Lasting Solutions for Your Peace of Mind and Your Child's Self-Esteem.* New York: HarperResource, 2002.

Loomans, Diana, and Julia Loomans. *100 Ways to Build Self-Esteem and Teach Values.* Tiburon, CA: H. J. Kramer, 2003.

Moorman, Chick. *Parent Talk: How to Talk to Your Children in Language that Builds Self-Esteem and Encourages Responsibility.* New York: Fireside, 2003.

Owens, Karen. *Raising Your Child's Inner Self-Esteem: The Authoritative Guide from Infancy through the Teen Years.* Cambridge, MA: Da Capo Press, 2003.

PERIODICALS

Cottle, Thomas J. "Getting beyond Self-Esteem." *Childhood Education* 80 (Mid-Summer 2004): 269–271.

Dunton, Genevieve Fridlund, et al. "Physical Self-Concept in Adolescent Girls: Behavioral and Physiological Correlates." *Research Quarterly for Exercise and Sport* 74 (September 2003): 360–65.

Hoffmann, John P., et al. "Onset of Major Depressive Disorder among Adolescents." *Journal of the American Academy of Child and Adolescent Psychiatry* 42 (February 2003): 217–24.

Marmot, Michael. "Self-Esteem and Health: Autonomy, Self-Esteem, and Health are Linked Together." *British Medical Journal* 327 (September 13, 2003): 574–75.

Votta, Elizabeth, and Ian G. Manion. "Factors in the Psychological Adjustment of Homeless Adolescent Males: The Role of Coping Style." *42 (July 2003):* 778–85.

Walsh, Nancy. "Some Teens Prone to Hopelessness Depression." *Clinical Psychiatry News* 31 (June 2003): 41.

ORGANIZATIONS

National Academy of Child & Adolescent Psychiatry. 3615 Wisconsin Ave. NW, Washington, DC 20016. Web site: <www.aacap.org>.

National Association for Self-Esteem. PO Box 597, Fulton, MD 20759. Web site: <www.self-esteem-nase.org>.

WEB SITES

"How Can I Improve My Self-Esteem?" *TeensHealth*, April 2001. Available online at <www.kidshealth.org/teen/question/emotions/self_esteem.html> (accessed November 14, 2004).

KEY TERMS

Peer acceptance—The degree to which a child or adolescent is socially accepted by peers, usually of about the same age; the level of peer popularity.

Primary caregiver—A person who is responsible for the primary care and upbringing of a child.

Puberty—The point in development when the ability to reproduce begins. The gonads begin to function and secondary sexual characteristics begin to appear.

Self-identity—The awareness that an individual has of being unique.

"Self-Esteem." *ParentLink*, 2004. Available online at <www.parentlink.act.gov.au/parentguides/parentg_selfesteem.htm> (accessed November 14, 2004).

"Self-Esteem in Children." *North Carolina State University Cooperative Extension*, 2004. Available online at <www.ces.ncsu.edu/depts/fcs/human/pubs/fcsw_506.pdf> (accessed November 14, 2004).

Ken R. Wells

Self-mutilation

Definition

Self-mutilation, also called self-harm, self-injury or cutting, is the intentional destruction of tissue or alteration of the body done without the conscious wish to commit **suicide**, usually in an attempt to relieve tension.

Description

Self-mutilation has become an increasing problem among adolescents since the 1990s. Cutting one's skin with razors or knives is the most common pattern of self-mutilation. Other forms of self-harm include biting, hitting, or bruising oneself; picking or pulling at skin or hair; burning oneself with cigarettes, or amputating parts of the body. Self-mutilation can be episodic (infrequent) or repetitive. Episodic self-harm can progress to repetitive self-harm after as few as five or as many as 20 episodes.

Professional thinking about self-mutilation has evolved over the past 20 years. Before the 1990s, self-mutilation was often identified as a failed suicide attempt. This concept is no longer accepted. As of 2004 self-mutilation was not a specific diagnosis recognized by the American Psychiatric Association. Instead, it is recognized as a feature of other psychiatric disorders. Some researchers dispute this designation and feel self-mutilation should be a separate diagnosis. Self-mutilation should not be confused with current fads for **tattoos** and body **piercing**. In some cases, however, it may be difficult to distinguish between an interest in these fads and the first indications of a disorder.

Demographics

It is estimated that one in every 100 individuals in the United States, or more than 2.5 million people, are self-mutilators. Girls are four times more likely to engage in self-harm than boys, with girls between the ages of 16 and 25 at highest risk, although many girls begin cutting in middle school (ages 12 or 13). At risk individuals also include those who have underlying psychiatric disorders. Up to half of individuals who are self-mutilators were sexually abused as children.

Causes and symptoms

It is not entirely clear why some individuals mutilate themselves. However, self-injury appears to give these people an immediate release from almost unbearable tension caused by **anxiety**, anger, or sadness. Some researchers ascribe this response to the release of certain chemicals in the body in response to **pain**. Like other addictive behaviors, self-mutilation gradually takes more and more destruction to achieve release. Some researchers separate self-mutilators into several groups, based on their psychological condition, motivation for harming themselves, and degree to which they practice self-injury.

The most common form of self-mutilation, and the one usually seen in adolescents, is impulsive self-mutilation consisting of superficial skin cutting and burning. Psychiatrists generally believe that this is a maladaptive form of self-help or self-preservation and is done to achieve release from almost unbearable psychic tension and to give the individual a feeling of control. It is often a feature of psychiatric disorders including the following:

- borderline personality disorder
- antisocial personality disorder
- dissociative disorders
- anorexia or bulimia

- post traumatic stress syndrome
- substance abuse
- depression

Compulsive self-mutilation consists of repetitive hair pulling (**trichotillomania**), nail biting, and skin picking. It is often found in individuals with **obsessive-compulsive disorder** (OCD). Major self-mutilation is the least frequent form of self-harm. It involves infrequent episodes of destruction of large amounts of tissue, for example self-castration or self-amputation. Major self-mutilation occurs most often with psychotic or highly intoxicated individuals and occasionally with institutionalized mentally retarded individuals. It is also occasionally associated with **autism**, **Tourette syndrome**, and **schizophrenia**.

The symptoms of self-mutilation typically include wearing long-sleeved or baggy clothing, even in hot weather, and an unusual need for privacy. Self-mutilators are often hesitant to change their clothes or undress around others. In most cases the individual also shows signs of depression.

When to call the doctor

Parents and caregivers should consult a psychiatrist or psychotherapist with professional expertise in self-mutilation as soon as the behavior is discovered. Adolescents rarely do not outgrow this behavior. If left untreated, it can continue into adulthood.

Diagnosis

Self-mutilation is usually diagnosed by a psychiatrist or psychotherapist upon referral from a **family** member, physician, nurse, or social worker who has noticed scars, **bruises**, or other physical evidence of self-injury.

Treatment

Individuals who mutilate themselves should seek treatment from a therapist with some specialized training and experience with this behavior. Most self-mutilators are treated as outpatients, although some specialized inpatient programs for self-mutilators exist. A number of different treatment approaches are used with self-mutilators, including individual therapy, **family therapy**, and group therapy. Therapies focus on teaching self-awareness, alternate coping skills, behavior modification, and improved **communication skills**. Techniques may include journaling, music and art therapy, and role-playing.

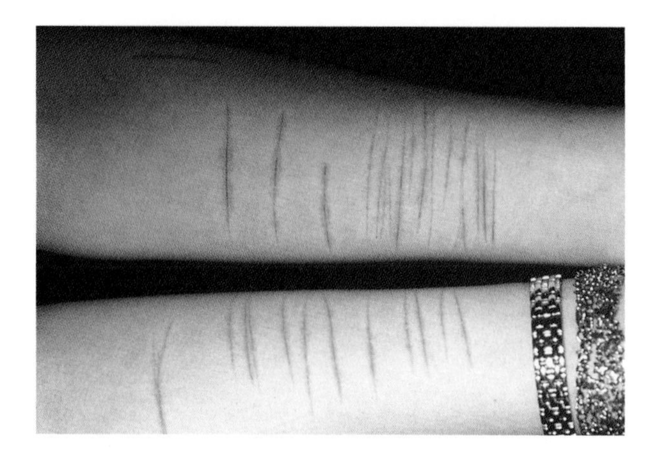

Self-inflicted lacerations on the arms of a teenage girl. *(Photo Researchers, Inc.)*

Underlying psychological disorders are also treated with medication and/or psychotherapy. Although there are no medications specifically for self-mutilation, **antidepressants** are often given, particularly if the patient meets the diagnostic criteria for a depressive disorder. However, in October 2003, the United States Food and Drug Administration issued an advisory indicating that children being treated with selective serotonin re-uptake inhibitor antidepressants (SSRIs) for major depressive illness may be at higher risk for committing suicide. A similar warning was issued in the United Kingdom. Parents and physicians must weigh the benefits and risks of prescribing these medications for children on an individual basis.

Alternative treatment

Mindfulness training, which is a form of meditation, has been used to teach self-mutilators to observe and identify their feelings in order to have some control over them.

Prognosis

The prognosis depends on the presence and severity of other emotional disorders and history of sexual abuse and/or suicide attempts. In general, teenagers without a history of abuse or other disorders have a good prognosis. Patients diagnosed with borderline personality disorder and/or a history of attempted suicide are considered to have the worst prognosis.

KEY TERMS

Borderline personality disorder (BPD)—A pattern of behavior characterized by impulsive acts, intense but chaotic relationships with others, identity problems, and emotional instability.

Dissociative disorders—A group of mental disorders in which dissociation is a prominent symptom. Patients with dissociative disorders have a high rate of self-mutilation.

Selective serotonin reuptake inhibitors (SSRIs)—A class of antidepressants that work by blocking the reabsorption of serotonin in the brain, thus raising the levels of serotonin. SSRIs include fluoxetine (Prozac), sertraline (Zoloft), and paroxetine (Paxil).

Prevention

Some society-wide factors that influence self-mutilation, such as the sexual abuse of children and media portrayals of cutting, are difficult to change. Parents should emphasize self-respect and respect for one's body. In general, young people who have learned to express themselves in words or through art and other creative activities are less likely to deal with painful feelings by injuring their bodies.

Parental concerns

Parents should be alert to Internet sites and movies that promote and/or glorify self-mutilation as a way to cope with problems. Experts feel that some children may be induced to try this behavior as a coping mechanism because of the way it is presented in these media.

See also Depressive disorders.

Resources

BOOKS

Milia, Diana. *Self-Mutilation and Art Therapy*. Herndon, VA: Kingsley Publishers, 2000.

Strong, Marilee, et al. *A Bright Red Scream: Self-Mutilation and the Language of Pain*. Collingdale, PA: DIANE Publishing Group, 2001.

Winkler, Kathleen. *Cutting and Self-Mutilation: When Teens Injure Themselves*. Berkeley Heights, NJ: Enslow Publisher, 2003.

PERIODICALS

"Self-cutting is almost epidemic in adolescents." *Pediatric News* 36 (September 2002): 29.

"Self-Injury." *Brown University Child and Adolescent Behavior Letter*– 20 (March 2004): 14.

ORGANIZATIONS

American Academy of Child and Adolescent Psychiatry.– 3615 Wisconsin Avenue, NW, Washington, DC 200163007. Web site: <www.aacap.org>.

American Psychiatric Association. 1400 K Street, NW, Washington, DC 20005. Web site: <www.psych.org>.

Focus Adolescent Services. Web site: <www.focusas.com>.

Tish Davidson, A.M.
Rebecca J. Frey, PhD

Separation anxiety

Definition

Separation **anxiety** is distress or agitation resulting from separation or **fear** of separation from a parent or caregiver to whom a child is attached.

Description

Separation anxiety is a normal part of development. It emerges during the second half year in infants. Separation anxiety reflects a stage of brain development rather than the onset of problem behaviors. On the other hand, prolonged separation anxiety that develops in school age children is considered an anxiety disorder by the American Psychiatric Association.

Normal separation anxiety

Developmentally normal separation anxiety usually begins somewhere around eight to 10 months and peaks by 18 months, after which it gradually diminishes until by age three. Only occasional bouts of separation anxiety then occur when the child is faced with new situations, such as starting **preschool** or the addition of a new baby to the **family**.

Before about six months of age, infants show little special attachment to a particular caregiver and no distress at being left alone. At about eight months, babies begin to react by crying and fussing whenever their primary caregiver leaves the room. Bedtimes may become a struggle, with the child refusing care from all but the primary caregiver and crying, fussing, and calling the caregiver when it is time to go to **sleep**. This unwillingness to be left alone can continue for many months.

When left with a babysitter, even a familiar individual that the infant formerly accepted, the child may scream and cry to exhaustion. This is likely to be due to a combination of separation anxiety and **stranger anxiety**, which arise at about the same time and has similar origins.

Separation anxiety is thought to develop because as babies mature mentally, they begin to recognize their caregivers as unique individuals. However, infants lack the mental capacity to understand that the caregiver still exists when out of sight. To the infant, once the caregiver cannot be seen, she is gone forever (lack of object permanence). This inability to project beyond what is immediately visible, coupled with the newly formed attachment to the caregiver, causes distress that is usually expressed by crying. Although this is a difficult stage for parents, the fact that a child fusses when the preferred caregiver leaves is a sign of healthy **bonding** and normal development. With experience and increased mental maturity, the child will eventually understand that he is not being abandoned permanently and that the caregiver will return.

Although separation anxiety is normal in infants and toddlers, cultural practices have an impact on the timing of its emergence and its extent. Babies who remain in constant contact with their mothers may develop separation anxiety earlier and possibly for more intense and prolonged periods than infants frequently cared for by a variety of different caregivers.

Separation anxiety disorder

Separation anxiety disorder occurs when older children refuse to leave a parent or other caregiver to whom they have become attached. Often separation anxiety disorder begins around age six or seven at a time when it can interfere with school attendance. School phobia can be a type of separation anxiety disorder.

Children with separation anxiety disorder repeatedly show at least three of the following behaviors at a developmentally inappropriate age:

- excessive distress at leaving home or leaving the primary caregiver, or even distress in anticipation of leaving
- excessive worry that something catastrophic will happen at home or to the caregiver while the child is away
- extreme fear that something will happen to them, such as getting lost or kidnapped, that will prevent their return to the caregiver
- unwillingness to be alone, even in familiar settings
- nightmares about separation from home and loved ones
- inability to stay at a friend's house overnight or go away to camp due to worry about what is happening at home
- physical complaints such as stomach pains, **dizziness**, headaches, or **vomiting** when faced with separation from home or caregiver
- refusal to attend school not related to events at school such as bullying or academic failure
- attachment to home or caregiver that interferes with social life and school attendance

Unlike developmentally normal separation anxiety, children do not outgrow separation anxiety disorder. This disorder is usually treated with a combination of behavioral and cognitive therapy. Behavioral therapy involves teaching parents and children strategies for overcoming stressful separation and may involve desensitization by gradual exposure to longer and longer periods apart. Cognitive therapy teaches children to redirect their thoughts and actions into a more flexible and assertive pattern. **Family therapy** may also be used to help resolve family issues that may be negatively affecting the child.

Separation anxiety disorder sometimes occurs in conjunction with other psychiatric disorders, such as pervasive developmental disorder, **schizophrenia**, other anxiety or panic disorders, and major depression. Depending on the diagnosis, children may also be treated with drugs to help alleviate these disorders. However, the use of **antidepressants** in minors is currently under review. In October 2003, the United States Food and Drug Administration issued an advisory indicating that children being treated with selective serotonin re-uptake inhibitor antidepressants (SSRIs) for major depressive illness may be at higher risk for committing **suicide**. A similar warning was issued in the United Kingdom. Parents and physicians must weigh the benefits and risks of prescribing these medications for children on an individual basis.

Common problems

Parents are frequently frustrated by the intensity of their child's separation anxiety while an infant and toddler and believe that something is wrong with their child rather than accepting this natural stage of development. In school-age children, refusal to attend school due to

KEY TERMS

Selective serotonin reuptake inhibitors (SSRIs)—A class of antidepressants that work by blocking the reabsorption of serotonin in the brain, thus raising the levels of serotonin. SSRIs include fluoxetine (Prozac), sertraline (Zoloft), and paroxetine (Paxil).

separation anxiety disorder is common. This can lead to academic failure and difficulty in making friends and developing relationships outside the home.

Parental concerns

Parents are distressed and concerned when their child is distressed. However, since anxiety disorders have an inherited component, in some families a parent will also have an anxiety disorder. The parent's anxieties can add to the child's concerns about separating, worsening the separation anxiety. In this case, family therapy as well as individual therapy for the parent and child may be appropriate.

When to call the doctor

Parents should call the doctor when a child in kindergarten or older shows extreme reluctance to separate from the parent to the point where it interferes with the child's normal life and social development. After a physical examination, a psychological evaluation that includes several assessments for anxiety and a behavioral checklist that evaluates the child's behavior at home and school should be done by a psychologist or psychiatrist with experience in separation anxiety.

See also Stranger anxiety; School phobia/school refusal.

Resources

BOOKS

Greenberg, Mark T., Dante Cicchetti, and E. Mark Cummings. *Attachment in the Preschool Years: Theory, Research, and Intervention.* Chicago: University of Chicago Press, 1990.

Moore, David and James Jefferson. "Separation Anxiety Disorder." *Handbook of Medical Psychiatry,*2nd ed. St Louis: Mosby, 2004 pp 52-54.

"Separation Anxiety." *The Gale Encyclopedia of Childhood and Adolescence*Detroit, MI: Gale Research, 1998.

ORGANIZATIONS

American Academy of Pediatrics T 141 Northwest Point Boulevard, Elk Grove Village, IL 60007-1098 Telephone: 847/434-4000 Fax: 847/434-8000 Web site: <http://www.aap.org>

WEB SITES

"Other Mental Disorders in Children and Adolescents: Separation Anxiety Disorder." *Mental Health: A Report Card from the Surgeon General* [accessed 6 September 2003] <http://www.surgeongeneral.gov/library/mental health/chapter3/sec6.html>.

Tish Davidson, A.M.

Serum hepatitis *see* **Hepatitis B**

Severe combined immunodeficiency

Definition

Severe combined **immunodeficiency** (SCID) is the most serious primary or congenital human immunodeficiency disorder. It is a group of congenital (present from birth) disorders in which the immune system does not work properly. Children with SCID are vulnerable to recurrent severe infections, retarded growth, and early death.

Description

The immune system is composed of elements that are needed for the body to fight infections by recognizing disease agents and attacking them. It includes many classes of T-lymphocytes (white blood cells that detect foreign proteins called antigens). It also includes B cells, which are the only cells in the body that make antibodies. Natural killer (NK) cells are cells that destroy infected cells. In children with SCID, the immune system does not function properly because T, B, and NK cells are either absent or defective. When the immune system does not function correctly, the child is left open to repeated severe diseases and infections.

Several different immune system disorders are grouped under SCID. These include the following:

- X-linked: The most common form of SCID accounts for about half of all cases. Because this is an X-linked condition, it occurs only in boys. Children with

X-linked SCID have low T-cell and natural killer (NK) cell levels but elevated B-cell levels.

- Adenosine deaminase deficiency (ADA): About 20 percent of SCID cases are of this type. ADA deficiency leads to low levels of B and T cells in the child's immune system.
- Janus Kinase 3 (Jak3) deficiency: This form of SCID accounts for about 6 percent of cases. There are very low levels of T and NK cells, or they are not present at all. There is an elevated level of B cells. In this form of SCID the lymphocyte or white blood evaluation is identical to X-linked SCID but is autosomal recessive and, therefore, occurs in girls and boys.

Demographics

The rate of SCID is not perfectly documented. It is estimated that it occurs in between one in 50,000 and one in 500,000 infants. It is about three times more common in boys than in girls.

Causes and symptoms

SCID is an inherited disorder. In all forms of SCID, B and T cells are non-functioning. They may or may not be present in various forms of SCID, but they are always non-functioning. In some forms of SCID, NK cells are also absent or non-funtioning.

For the first few months after birth, a infant with SCID is often protected by antibodies acquired before birth from the mother's blood. As early as three months of age, however, the SCID child begins to suffer from mouth infections (thrush), chronic **diarrhea**, **otitis media**, and pulmonary infections, including pneumocystis **pneumonia**. The child loses weight, becomes very weak, and if untreated eventually dies from an opportunistic infection.

When to call the doctor

If a child has unusual infections, unusually severe infections, infections with unusual organisms, or unusual complications of usual infections, a doctor should be consulted to evaluate for possible immune deficiency. This is particularly important if there is a **family** history of immune deficiency.

Diagnosis

The first screening test for SCID is a white blood cell count with a count of the lymphocytes (differential) because in most forms of SCID the lymphocyte count will be very low. Blood tests can then be done to test for the numbers of B, T, and NK type lymphocytes. If the numbers of all of these cell types are normal and SCID is still suspected, more specialized tests can be done to test the lymphocyte cell functions. Rarely there are children with SCID who have normal lymphocyte numbers and nonfunctioning cells.

Treatment

Patients with SCID should be treated aggressively with **antibiotics** for any infection, and intravenous immunoglobulin should be given to replace the antibiotics the children cannot make, but these treatments cannot cure the disorder. Bone marrow transplants are as of 2004 regarded as one of the few effective standard treatments for most types of SCID. For those children with ADA deficiency, ADA infusions are the accepted treatment of choice. Up to 95 percent of children who are treated with bone marrow transplants, especially those who are treated before three months of age, survive.

Investigational treatments

As an example of gene therapy for SCID children with ADA deficiency, the child receives periodic infusions of his or her own T cells corrected with a gene for ADA that has been implanted in an activated virus. This should allow these cells to function normally. Other types of SCID have been treated with gene therapy, but these procedures have been put on hold due to serious complications (malignancies). Researchers are as of 2004 also investigating treating SCID in the yet unborn fetus, which has been done successfully a few times.

Prognosis

There is no cure for SCID. Nearly all untreated patients die before age two, most before one year of age. Children who are treated with bone marrow transplants have a much better prognosis.

Prevention

There is no known way to prevent SCID. Genetic counseling is recommended for parents of a child with SCID who are considering having more children and for potential parents who have a family history of the disease and believe they may be carriers.

Parental concerns

Without prompt treatment SCID is nearly always fatal. Treatment can be very successful if done early, preferably within the first three months of life. Research is

KEY TERMS

Adenosine deaminase (ADA)—An enzyme that is lacking in a specific type of severe combined immunodeficiency disease (SCID). Children with an ADA deficiency have low levels of both B and T cells.

Antigen—A substance (usually a protein) identified as foreign by the body's immune system, triggering the release of antibodies as part of the body's immune response.

B cell—A type of white blood cell derived from bone marrow. B cells are sometimes called B lymphocytes. They secrete antibodies and have a number of other complex functions within the human immune system.

Congenital—Present at birth.

Gene therapy—An experimental treatment for certain genetic disorders in which a abnormal gene is replaced with the normal copy. Also called somatic-cell gene therapy.

Lymphocyte—A type of white blood cell that participates in the immune response. The two main groups are the B cells that have antibody molecules on their surface and T cells that destroy antigens.

T cell—A type of white blood cell that is produced in the bone marrow and matured in the thymus gland. It helps to regulate the immune system's response to infections or malignancy.

Thrush—An infection of the mouth, caused by the yeast *Candida albicans* and characterized by a whitish growth and ulcers.

continuing into in utero treatment options, and some in utero treatments have been successfully carried out, so fetal screening may be helpful if there is a possibility that the child has SCID.

Resources

BOOKS

Parker, James N., and Philip M. Parker. *The Official Parent's Sourcebook on Primary Immunodeficiency.* Red Hill, Australia: Icon Health, 2002.

ORGANIZATIONS

Immune Deficiency Foundation. 40 W. Chesapeake Avenue Suite 308, Towson, MD 21204. Web site: <www.primaryimmune.org>.

International Patient Organization for Patients with Primary Immunodeficiencies. Alliance House, 12 Caxton Street, London SW1H 0QS. Web site: <www.ipopi.org>

WEB SITES

Ballard, Barb. *The SCID Homepage*, September 2004. Available online at <www.scid.net/> (accessed November 14, 2004).

Tish Davidson, A.M.
Rebecca J. Frey, PhD

Sexual abuse *see* **Rape and sexual assault**

Sexually transmitted diseases

Definition

Sexually transmitted diseases (STDs) are viral and bacterial infections passed from one person to another through sexual contact.

Description

Adolescence is a time of opportunities and risk when many health behaviors are established. Although many of these behaviors are health-promoting, some are health-compromising, resulting in increasingly high rates of adolescent morbidity and mortality. For example, initiation of sexual intercourse and experimentation with alcohol and drugs are normative adolescent behaviors. However, these behaviors often result in negative health outcomes such as the acquisition of STDs. As a consequence of STDs, many adolescents experience serious health problems that often alter the course of their adult lives, including infertility, difficult pregnancy, genital and cervical **cancer**, neonatal transmission of infections, and **AIDS** (acquired **immunodeficiency** syndrome).

Examples of STDs with high prevalence among sexually-active adolescents include:

- Gonorrhea: Caused by the bacteria *Neisseria gonorrhoeae*, gonorrhea infects the reproductive tract of women, causing pelvic inflammatory disease (PID), a major cause of infertility. The bacteria are found in vaginal secretions and semen.
- Chlamydia: The bacteria that causes chlamydia, *Chlamydia trachomatis*, trigger inflammation of the reproductive tract, leading to PID in women and epididymitis (inflammation of the epididymis) in men.

- Syphilis: *Treponema pallidum* is the bacteria that causes syphilis. The course of syphilis is broken down into four distinct segments: primary syphilis, occurring within a few weeks or months of initial exposure; secondary syphilis, occurring generally between six weeks and six months of initial exposure; latent syphilis, an asymptomatic period which may stretch for years; and late syphilis, the most serious stage. If left untreated, syphilis can infect a number of organ systems and cause serious complications.
- Herpes simplex virus: Two different types of HSV (HSV-1 and HSV-2) cause lesions on the genitals, although HSV-2 is associated with the majority of cases. (HSV-1 is most commonly associated with oral lesions, or "cold sores.")
- Human papillomavirus (HPV): HPV causes condylomata acuminata, more commonly known as venereal **warts** or genital warts. The warts may affect any of the external and internal genital organs in men and women.
- Human immunodeficiency virus (HIV). HIV is the causative agent of acquired immune deficiency syndrome (AIDS), a potentially fatal condition in which the immune system fails and the individual becomes prone to frequent and unusual infections.

Transmission

The mode of transmission varies among the different sexually transmitted diseases. Some bacteria or virus are found in vaginal secretions or semen (e.g. HIV and gonorrhea), while others are shed from the skin of and around the genitals (e.g. HSV and HPV). Infection typically occurs during sexual intercourse or when the genitals come into close contact. Infection may also occur during oral sex, such as transmission of HSV from an oral lesion to the genitals or vice versa, or transmission of HIV from genital secretions through a cut in the mouth. STDs may be transmitted during nonconsensual sex acts such as **rape** or molestation.

The transmission of many STDs is more efficient from men to women than from women to men. For example, with just one unprotected sexual encounter with an infected partner, a woman is twice as likely as a man to acquire gonorrhea or chlamydia. In addition, different STDs have different rates of transmissibility. For example, with one exposure of unprotected sexual intercourse, a woman has a 1 percent chance of acquiring HIV, a 30 percent chance of acquiring herpes, and 50 percent chance of contracting gonorrhea if her partner is infected.

Demographics

STDs among sexually experienced adolescents occur at alarmingly high rates. One-fourth of the estimated 12 million new cases reported annually occur among adolescents between 15 and 19 years of age. Moreover, since many STDs are asymptomatic, they are often undiagnosed and untreated, thus increasing their potential for proliferation among adolescents.

Gonorrhea and chlamydia, the most prevalent bacterial STDs, disproportionately affect adolescents. The rates of gonorrhea in adolescents ages 15 to 19 years declined between 1990 and 2004, but in the early 2000s they continue to be higher than rates for any five-year age group between 20 and 44 years, particularly among women and African Americans.

Numerous prevalence studies for chlamydia have shown rates to be highest among adolescents and young adults under 25 years of age, many of whom are minorities. Rates of chlamydia reported by gender indicate that women, overall, have higher rates than men due in large part to increased efforts in screening women for asymptomatic chlamydial infections. The low rates of chlamydia for men suggest that the sexual partners of women diagnosed with chlamydia are not being diagnosed or treated. Chlamydia has been detected in more than 10 percent of sexually experienced women during screening.

While rates of syphilis declined between 1990 and 2004, the disease continues to be an important cause of sexually transmitted infection. The rate of syphilis infection among adolescents ages 15 to 19 is 1.3 per 100,000 population for males and 2.2 per 100,000 population for females. For comparison, the syphilis rates among males 20 to 24 is 5.5 per 100,000, and among females of the same age, 3.3 per 100,000.

HSV and HPS occur at alarming rates among sexually experienced adolescents. Studies indicate that one in six Americans is infected with HSV-2, reflecting a ninefold increase between 1975 and 2005. Prevalence of HSV-2 in adolescents and young adults varies by the demographic and behavioral characteristics of the populations studied as well as the diagnostic methods used. As of the early 2000s approximately 4 percent of Caucasians and 17 percent of African Americans are infected with HSV-2 by the end of their teenage years. One study of young pregnant women of low income status found an HSV-2 infection rate of 11 percent in women 15 to 19 years of age and 22 percent in women 25 to 29 years of age.

In 2002, there were 4,785 reported cases of AIDS among teenagers between the ages of 13 and 19, more than double the 1994 figures. Most adolescents with AIDS were infected as a result of high risk sexual and substance use behaviors. Among adolescents ages 13 to 19 years infected with HIV, 49 percent are male and 51 percent are female. Studies also indicate that African-American and Latino teens are overrepresented among persons with AIDS relative to their proportion in the population. Although these epidemiological statistics on AIDS in the United States provide a descriptive overview of the prevalence and patterns of HIV exposure in adolescents, the extent of asymptomatic **HIV infection** remains largely unknown.

Causes and symptoms

The chance for adolescents of getting and transmitting STDs is affected by complex interrelationships between key factors (sociodemographic, biologic, psychosocial, and behavioral). For example, many STD-related risk markers (e.g. age, gender, race/ethnicity) correlate with more fundamental determinants of risk status (e.g., access to health care, living in communities with high prevalence of STDs) to influence adolescents' risk for STDs.

Developmental factors such as pubertal timing, **self-esteem**, and peer affiliation may also increase their risk of exposure to STDs. An assessment of these interrelationships is critical to preventing and controlling STDs in adolescents. Moreover, since behavior is the common means by which STDs occur, an important first step in fighting STDs is to understand the prevalence and patterns of risk behaviors as well as the psychosocial context in which these behaviors occur.

Behavioral factors

Although biologic factors play an important role in the transmission of STDs, it is also the health-risking behaviors of adolescents that place them at increased risk for exposure to STDs. Behavioral risk factors include the age of sexual activity, number of sexual partners, use of contraceptives, and use of alcohol and drugs.

SEXUAL ACTIVITY Early initiation of sexual intercourse has been associated with high-risk sexual activities, including ineffective use of contraceptives, multiple sex partners over a short period of time, high-risk sex partners, and acquisition of STDs and their consequences of cervical cancer and dysplasia. The average age of first sexual intercourse is between 16 and 17 years for adolescent men and between the age of 17 and 18 years for adolescent women, and has been found to be as young as age 12 in some high-risk populations. Research on adolescents' decision to initiate sexual intercourse indicates an interaction between biological and social factors. However, much remains unknown about the interactions between hormones, behavior, and social factors.

The Youth Risk Behavior Surveillance System (YRBSS), a self-reported survey of a national representative sample of high school students in grades nine to 12, indicated that in 2003, 46.7 percent of the students reported having had sex. By grade level, the rates were 32.8 percent for ninth grade, 44.1 percent for tenth grade, 53.2 percent for eleventh grade, and 61.6 percent for twelfth grade. Approximately 7.4 percent of students reported having sex for the first time before age 13. Prevalence rates of sexual experience differed by race/ethnicity and gender. African-American students were significantly more likely (73.8% of males and 60.9% of females) than Caucasian (40.5% of males and 43.0% of females) and Hispanic (56.8% of males and 46.4% of females) students to have engaged in sexual intercourse. Moreover, data from the National Survey of Family Growth (NSFG), a large-scale national survey of women ages 15 to 44 years, reveal that family income is associated with adolescents' protection against HIV and many other STDs; adolescents from poor and low-income families are more likely to report an earlier age of sexual experience than their counterparts from higher income families.

In addition to early sexual activity, many adolescents have multiple sex partners within a short period of time in a pattern of serial monogamy which also increases their risk of acquiring STD for two important reasons: it increases the likelihood of being exposed to a sexually transmitted pathogen, and it may reflect poor choices of sexual partners. Among the sexually experienced high school students responding to the YRBSS, 14.4 percent reported having four or more sex partners. Multiple sex partners were noted more frequently among African-American students (41.7% of males and 16.3% of females), compared to Hispanic (20.5% of males and 11.2% of females) and Caucasian (11.5% of males and 10.1% of females) students.

Involuntary sexual intercourse such as rape and sexual abuse may occur more commonly among adolescents, especially younger adolescent women, and often pose a potential risk for acquisition of STDs. A study on the effects of **child abuse** (i.e., incest, extra-familial sexual abuse, and physical abuse) on adolescent males showed a strong association between abuse and a number of risk-taking behaviors, such as forcing female sexual partners into having sexual intercourse and drinking alcohol prior to sexual intercourse. Moreover, when sexual intercourse is intermittent, as it is with most sexually experienced adolescents, the adolescents are less likely to take proper measures to safeguard against STDs.

CONTRACEPTIVE USE Sexually experienced adolescents are also at risk for STDs because of their patterns of contraceptive use, especially their use of barrier-method contraceptives. Some data indicate that adolescents do not use effective methods to reduce their risk of STDs or unintended pregnancies. Sexual abstinence is the only sure method of eliminating risk for STDs. When used consistently and correctly, however, condoms offer the best protection against acquisition of STDs, including HIV. Even when condoms are used improperly they reduce the risk of acquiring infections by 50 percent.

The overall reported use of contraceptives, particularly condoms, has increased among adolescents between 1994 and 2004. Data from the 2003 YRBSS reveal that 63.0 percent of the students who reported sexual activity in the three months prior to the survey also reported using condoms during their last sexual encounter; this behavior was more common among males of virtually all ages and racial/ethnic groups. In contrast, 20.6 percent of adolescent women ages 15 to 19 years reported use of birth control pills. It appears that while the use of **oral contraceptives** provides some protection against the development of gonococcal and nongonococcal forms of PID, it may increase the risk of chlamydial endocervical infections, and provides no protection against most STDs.

Differences in the types and patterns of contraceptive use by race/ethnicity, age, and socioeconomic status have also been noted. Also, adolescent women of higher income are more likely than young women of lower income to use oral contraceptives. These factors are related to access and use of medical services for reproductive health care. Thus, providing all sexually experienced adolescents with reproductive health counseling and education about the importance of consistently and correctly using barrier-method contraceptives such as condoms may play a crucial role in reducing their risk of acquiring and transmitting STDs.

ALCOHOL AND OTHER DRUG USE Use of alcohol and other drugs is prevalent among adolescents and thus poses a significant threat to their health. About 40 percent of high school youth responding to the YRBSS have used marijuana at least once with 22.4 percent of these students reporting use of this substance within 30 days before the survey. Cocaine was used at least once by 8.7 percent of the students and by 4.1 percent within 30 days of the survey. The substance of choice, however, is alcohol: 74.9 percent of students had at least one drink at some point in time and nearly half (44.9%) consumed alcohol in the 30 days prior to the survey. Among the current alcohol users, 28.3 percent had five or more drinks on at least one occasion, suggesting that a sizeable proportion of the students are periodic heavy drinkers. Grade, age, and gender differences were noted for lifetime and current use of alcohol and other illicit substances. In general, students in higher grade levels (grades 11 and 12) and males were more likely to use all substances. Racial/ethnic differences in use of substances were also found. Heavy use of alcohol was most prevalent among Caucasian and Hispanic males and females, while marijuana use was most common among African-American and Hispanic males.

Although these data strongly suggest that adolescents are at increased risk for social and physical morbidities, and even premature mortality because of their use of alcohol and other illicit substances, they underrepresent the actual prevalence of substance use among all adolescents. Teens who have dropped out or who are repeatedly absent from school and those who are homeless or otherwise disenfranchised are not represented by the reported data; many of these teens are potentially at higher risk for STDs because of their substance use behavior.

Substance use prior to sexual intercourse is likely to be related to a number of risk-taking behaviors: sexual intercourse with a casual acquaintance, lack of communication about use of condoms or previous sexual experiences, and no use of condoms. This association remained significant regardless of demographic factors, sexual experience, and dispositional factors such as adventure and thrill seeking. It appears that early intervention to prevent the use and abuse of alcohol and other substances may significantly decrease their risk of acquiring STDs.

Psychosocial factors

One study of college students examined the relationship between sexual behavior, substance use, and specific constructs from social cognitive theory (i.e., perceptions of self-efficacy, vulnerability to HIV risk, social norms, negative outcome expectancies of condoms, and knowledge of HIV risk and prevention). The results indicate that although young men expected more negative outcomes of **condom** use and were more likely to have sexual intercourse under the influence of alcohol and other drugs, young women reported perceptions of higher self-efficacy to practice safer sex. The study further revealed that perceptions of higher self-efficacy to engage in safer sexual behaviors, perceptions of fewer negative outcomes of condom use, and less frequent alcohol and drug use with sexual intercourse were the best predictors of safer sexual behaviors.

Evaluating STD risk

The information, motivation, and behavioral skills (IMB) model is one method of evaluating risk for STDs. This model posits that information, motivation, and behavior are the primary determinants of AIDS-related preventive behavior. Specifically, the model asserts that information regarding the transmission of HIV and information concerning specific methods of preventing HIV (e.g., condom use, decreasing the number of partners) are necessary prerequisites of reducing risk behaviors.

Motivation to change risk behaviors is another determinant of prevention and affects whether a person acts on his or her knowledge of the transmission and prevention of HIV. The IMB contends that motivation to engage in prevention behaviors is a function of one's attitudes toward the behavior and of subjective norms regarding prevention behaviors. Other critical factors which are hypothesized to influence motivation to engage in prevention behaviors are perceived vulnerability to acquiring HIV, perceived costs and benefits of engaging in prevention behaviors, intention to engage in prevention behaviors regarding HIV, as well as characteristics of the sex partner and/or the sexual relationship (e.g. primary vs. secondary partner).

Behavioral skills for engaging in specific prevention behaviors are a third determinant of prevention; it affects whether a knowledgeable, highly motivated person will be able to change his or her behavior to prevent HIV. Important skills required to engage in prevention behaviors include the ability to effectively communicate with one's sex partner about safer sex, refusal to engage in unsafe sexual practices, proper use of barrier-method contraceptives, and the ability to exit a situation when prevention behaviors are not possible. In addition, individuals who are able to practice prevention skills are presumed to have a strong belief in their ability to practice these prevention behavioral skills. Overall, the IMB asserts that information and motivation trigger behavioral skills to affect the initiation and maintenance of HIV prevention behaviors.

Symptoms of common STDs

The symptoms of some STDs may seriously affect an infected individual's quality of life or eventually become fatal, while others are so mild as to go undetected. The symptoms of some of the more prevalent STDs include:

- Gonorrhea: The most common symptoms among infected adolescent girls are vaginal discharge, bleeding between menstrual cycles, and painful urination. Among adolescent boys, common symptoms are burning or painful urination and pus-like discharge from the penis. Many infections, however, remain asymptomatic in both females (32%) and males (2%). Symptoms are similar among young children who have contracted gonorrhea from a sexual abuser.
- Chlamydia: Symptoms of chlamydia are similar to those of gonorrhea and sometimes difficult to differentiate clinically. Chlamydial infections are more likely to be asymptomatic than gonorrheal infections and thus are of longer duration on average.
- Syphilis: In primarily syphilis, the characteristic symptom is the appearance of a chancre (painless ulcer) at the site of initial exposure (e.g. external genitalia, lips, tongue, nipples, or fingers). In some cases, the infected individual will experience swollen lymph glands. In secondary syphilis, the infection becomes systemic and the individual experiences symptoms such as **fever**, **headache**, **sore throat**, rash, and swollen glands. During latent syphilis, symptoms go unnoticed. During the late stage of syphilis, the infection has spread to organ systems and may cause blindness, signs of damage to the nervous system and heart, and skin lesions.
- Herpes simplex virus: The symptoms of genital herpes include burning and **itching** of the genital area, blisters or sores on the genitals, discharge from the vagina or penis, and/or flu-like symptoms such as headache and fever.
- Human papillomavirus (HPV): The warty growths of HPV can appear on the external or internal reproductive organs of males and females but are commonly found on the labia minora and the opening to the vagina in females and the penis in males. They may be small and few or combine to form larger growths.
- Human immunodeficiency virus (HIV): Some persons who are newly infected with HIV have rash, fever, enlarged lymph nodes, and a flu-like illness sometimes called HIV seroconversion syndrome. This initial syndrome passes without intervention, and later symptoms, when T-cells become depleted, include weight loss, chronic **cough**, fever, fatigue, chronic **diarrhea**, swollen glands, white spots on the tongue and inside of the mouth, and dark blotches on the skin or in the mouth.

When to call the doctor

If a child or adolescent develops any of the symptoms of STDs, he or she should be evaluated for possible infection. Routine pelvic exams are recommended for all sexually active females and all females over the age of 18.

Diagnosis

A history of sexual activity is collected from all individuals at increased risk of contracting an STD, including adolescents who admit to being sexually active or who are pregnant or have undergone therapeutic abortion, adolescents or children with symptoms indicative of infection with an STD, and adolescents or children suspected of being victims of sexual abuse or rape. The healthcare provider will take a complete medical history and perform a thorough physical examination. Depending on the STD in question, additional tests may be performed such as blood work, Papanicolaou (pap) smear, rectal swabs, or biopsy.

Treatment

The treatment of sexually transmitted diseases varies according to the diagnosed infection. Gonorrhea, chlamydia, and syphilis are curable in most cases with **antibiotics**, although antibiotic-resistant strains do exist. As viruses, HSV, HPV, and HIV are treatable but not curable. The frequency and duration of HSV lesions can be reduced with antiviral therapy, including acyclovir (Zovirax), famciclovir (Famvir), and valacyclovir (Valtrex). Common methods to reduce genital warts include application of a topical cream called imiquimod (Aldara), cryotherapy (freezing of the wart), elecrosurgery (applying an electrical current to the wart), and surgical removal. The course of HIV infection can be slowed with a number of different kinds of drugs, including reverse transcriptase inhibitors, protease inhibitors, nonnucleoside reverse transcriptase inhibitors, and fusion inhibitors.

Alternative treatment

A number of different alternative therapies may be pursued to treat STDs, such as the use of herbs, homeopathy, acupuncture, and nutritional supplements, although minimal research has been done to establish their efficacy.

Nutritional concerns

In some cases, supplementation with specific nutrients may enhance immunity and minimize outbreaks. Examples are vitamin C (to boost the immune system), zinc (to reduce the frequency of HSV outbreaks), aloe (a possible antiviral), lemon balm (to speed healing), and licorice (with anti-inflammatory and antiviral effects).

Prognosis

Most STDs have excellent prognoses and respond well to treatment. While HSV and HPS are not curable, outbreaks can be managed and infection generally has little effect on quality of life. HIV, however, is a potentially fatal disease which can be treated but not cured.

Prevention

The prevalence data on STDs, HIV, and AIDS in adolescents indicate that younger women, gay and bisexual teens, and poor, urban and racial/ethnic minority young people have higher rates of STDs and HIV relative to their peers. Primary prevention of initial STD infections through prevention and risk reduction programs are essential for stemming the tide of these sexually acquired diseases. Moreover, secondary prevention through screening at risk adolescents for asymptomatic STD infections and effectively treating the index case and his or her sexual contact(s) are the most effective means of eliminating long-term medical and psychosocial consequences from STDs.

Prevention of high risk sexual, contraceptive, and substance use behaviors through cognitive-behavioral skills training and prevention and risk reduction counseling programs is a key strategy for decreasing the high incidence of STDs in adolescents. Prevention and risk reduction strategies should be developed and implemented in settings in which most adolescents can be reached, including schools or community-based programs in which there are multiple opportunities to intervene with adolescents or clinical settings where one-to-one risk reduction counseling can occur and actual risk can be assessed.

Cognitive-behavioral skills building interventions

In order to prevent new STD infections, adolescents must not only be informed about the risk and prevention of STDs, they must also have skills to resist **peer pressure**, negotiate the use of condoms, and project the future consequences of their behaviors. In addition, prevention of STDs in adolescents requires that they have the necessary means, resources, and social support to develop self-regulative skills and self-efficacy to effectively reduce their risk of disease transmission. Such cognitive-behavioral skills building programs have been shown to be effective in developing skills, delaying the onset of sexual activity, and changing high risk behaviors associated with pregnancy, STDs, and HIV infection. Moreover, cognitive-behavioral skills building programs should be immediate, sustained, and cost-effective. Specifically, these programs should be designed to increase knowledge about the prevention and transmission of STDs and their consequences; formulate realistic attitudes and perceptions about personal susceptibility to acquiring infections; enhance self-efficacy and self-motivation; monitor and regulate STD-related risk behaviors; address the role of social peer norms; and develop appropriate decision-making, problem-solving, and **communication skills**.

Prevention and risk reduction counseling

Counseling strategies to prevent and reduce the risk of STDs should be conducted in a confidential and non-judgmental manner that is both developmental and culturally appropriate for the adolescent. Counseling should focus on a number of key elements such as maintenance and support of healthy sexual behaviors (e.g. delaying initiation of sexual intercourse, limiting the number of sexual partners), use of barrier-method contraceptives (e.g. condoms, diaphragms, spermicide), routine medical care and advice (e.g. seeking medical care if the adolescent has participated in high-risk behavior), compliance with treatment recommendations (e.g. taking all medications as directed), and encouraging sex partners to seek medical care. Adolescents should also be informed about the myths and misconceptions of acquiring STDs. Moreover, adolescents should receive anticipatory guidance to assist them in defining appropriate options and alternatives to engaging in high-risk behaviors.

Parental concerns

Parents should be encouraged to talk to their children about sexually transmitted diseases and the risks of sexual activity. By asking preteens or teenagers questions about what they knows about STDs or by using cues from television shows or newspaper articles, parents can help make their children more comfortable talking about sex and the risks of infection, thereby opening the lines of communication. It is important that adolescents be provided accurate information, even if they already have some knowledge on the topic. Research has shown teens are not more likely to have sex if they are informed about safe sex practices, but they are more likely to practice safer sex.

KEY TERMS

Opportunistic infection—An infection that is normally mild in a healthy individual, but which takes advantage of an ill person's weakened immune system to move into the body, grow, spread, and cause serious illness.

Pap test—A screening test for precancerous and cancerous cells on the cervix. This simple test is done during a routine pelvic exam and involves scraping cells from the cervix. These cells are then stained and examined under a microscope. Also known as the Papanicolaou test.

Resources

BOOKS

Hammerschlag, Margaret R., Sarah A. Rawstron, and Kenneth Bromberg. "Sexually Transmitted Diseases." In *Krugman's Infectious Diseases of Children*, 11th ed. Edited by Anne A. Gershon, Peter J. Hotez, and Samuel L. Katz. New York: Mosby, 2004.

Jenkins, Renee R. "Sexually Transmitted Diseases." In *Nelson Textbook of Pediatrics*, 17th ed. Edited by Richard E. Behrman, Robert M. Kliegman, and Hal B. Jenson. Philadelphia: Saunders, 2004.

MacDonald, Noni E., and David M. Patrick. "Sexually Transmitted Disease Syndromes." In *Principles and Practice of Pediatric Infectious Diseases*, 2nd ed. Edited by Sarah S. Long. New York: Churchill Livingstone, 2003.

PERIODICALS

Department of Health and Human Services, Centers for Disease Control and Prevention. "Youth Risk Behavior Surveillance: United States, 2003." *Morbidity and Mortality Weekly Report* 53, no. SS-2 (May 21, 2004): 12–20.

ORGANIZATIONS

Centers for Disease Control and Prevention. 1600 Clifton Rd., NE, Atlanta, GA 30333. Web site: <www.cdc.gov>.

WEB SITES

Divisions of HIV/AIDS Prevention, National Center for HIV, STD, and TB Prevention. "HIV/AIDS Surveillance in Adolescents." *Centers for Disease Control and Prevention (CDC)*, August 25, 2004. Available online at <www.cdc.gov/hiv/graphics/adolesnt.htm> (accessed January 17, 2005).

Divisions of STD Prevention, National Center for HIV, STD, and TB Prevention. "Sexually Transmitted Disease Surveillance 2002 Supplement: Syphilis Surveillance Report." *Centers for Disease Control and Prevention (CDC)*, January 2004. Available online at <www.cdc.gov/std/Syphilis2002/SyphSurvSupp2002.pdf> (accessed January 17, 2005).

Gearhart, Peter A., et al. "Human Papillomavirus." *eMedicine*, December 13,, 2004. Available online at <www.emedicine.com/med/topic1037.htm> (accessed January 17, 2005).

Lamprecht, Catherine. “Talking to Your Child about STDs.” *Nemours Foundation*, May 2001. Available online at <http://kidshealth.org/parent/positive/talk/talk_child_stds.html> (accessed January 17, 2005).

Stephanie Dionne Sherk

Shaken baby syndrome

Definition

Shaken baby syndrome (SBS) is a collective term for the internal head injuries a baby or young child sustains from being violently shaken.

Description

Shaken baby syndrome was first described in medical literature in 1972. Physicians earlier labeled these injuries as accidental, but as more about **child abuse** became known, more cases of this syndrome were properly diagnosed.

Demographics

Every year, nearly 50,000 children in the United States are forcefully shaken by their caretakers. More than 60 percent of these children are boys. Nearly 2,000 children die every year as a result of being shaken. The victims are on average six to eight months old, but may be as old as five years or as young as a few days.

Men are more likely than women to shake a child; typically, these men are in their early 20s and are the baby's father or the mother's boyfriend. Women who inflict SBS are more likely to be **babysitters** or child care providers than the baby's mother. The shaking may occur as a response of frustration to the baby's inconsolable crying or as an action of routine abuse.

Causes and symptoms

Infants and small children are especially vulnerable to SBS because their neck muscles are still too weak to adequately support their disproportionately large heads, and their young brain tissue and blood vessels are extremely fragile. When an infant is vigorously shaken by the arms, legs, shoulders, or chest, the whiplash motion repeatedly jars the baby's brain with tremendous force, causing internal damage and bleeding. While there may be no obvious external signs of injury following shaking, the child may suffer internally from brain bleeding and bruising (called subdural hemorrhage and hematoma); brain swelling and damage (called cerebral edema); **mental retardation**; blindness, hearing loss, paralysis, speech impairment, and learning disabilities; and death.

Physicians may have difficulty initially diagnosing SBS because there are usually few witnesses to give a reliable account of the events leading to the trauma, few if any external injuries, and, upon close examination, the physical findings may not agree with the account given. A shaken baby may present one or more signs, including **vomiting**; difficulty breathing, sucking, swallowing, or making sounds; seizures; and altered consciousness.

When to call the doctor

A physician should be called when a baby exhibits one or more of the following: vomiting; difficulty breathing, sucking, swallowing, or making sounds; seizures; and altered consciousness. An unresponsive child should never be put to bed, but must be taken to a hospital for immediate care.

Diagnosis

To diagnose SBS, physicians look for at least one of three classic conditions: bleeding at the back of one or both eyes (retinal hemorrhage), **subdural hematoma**, or cerebral edema. The diagnosis is confirmed by the results of either a **computed tomography** scan (CT scan) or **magnetic resonance imaging** (MRI).

Treatment

Appropriate treatment is determined by the type and severity of the trauma. Physicians may medically manage both internal and external injuries. Behavioral and educational impairments as a result of the injuries require the attention of additional specialists. Children with SBS may need physical therapy, speech therapy, vision therapy, and **special education** services.

Prognosis

Unfortunately, children who receive violent shaking have a poor prognosis for complete recovery. Those who do not die may experience permanent blindness, mental retardation, seizure disorders, or loss of motor control.

Prevention

Shaken baby syndrome is preventable with public education. Adults must be actively taught that shaking a child is never acceptable and can cause severe injury or death.

Parental concerns

When the frustration from an incessantly crying baby becomes too much, caregivers should have a strategy for coping that does not harm the baby. The first step is to place the baby in a crib or playpen and leave the room in order to calm down. Counting to 10 and taking deep breaths may help. A friend or relative may be called to come over and assist. A calm adult may then resume trying to comfort the baby. A warm bottle, a dry diaper, soft music, a bath, or a ride in a swing, stroller, or car may be offered to soothe a crying child. Crying may also indicate **pain** or illness, such as from abdominal cramps or an earache. If the crying persists, the child should be seen by a physician.

KEY TERMS

Cerebral edema—The collection of fluid in the brain, causing tissue to swell.

Hematoma—A localized collection of blood, often clotted, in body tissue or an organ, usually due to a break or tear in the wall of blood vessel.

Hemorrhage—Severe, massive bleeding that is difficult to control. The bleeding may be internal or external.

Retinal hemorrhage—Bleeding of the retina, a key structure in vision located at the back of the eye.

Subdural hematoma—A localized accumulation of blood, sometimes mixed with spinal fluid, in the space between the middle (arachnoid) and outer (dura mater) membranes covering the brain. It is caused by an injury to the head that tears blood vessels.

Resources

BOOKS

Antoon, Alia Y. and Donovan, Mary. "Brain injuries." In *Nelson Textbook of Pediatrics.* 17th ed. Ed. by Richard E. Behrman, et al., Philadelphia: Saunders, 2003, 330-7.

Augustyn, Marilyn, and Zuckerman, Barry. "Impact of viokence on children." In *Nelson Textbook of Pediatrics.* 17th ed. Ed. by Richard E. Behrman, et al., Philadelphia. Saunders, 2003, 120-1.

Lazoritz, Stephen, and Palusci, Vincent J. *Shaken Baby Syndrome: A Multidisciplinary.* Binghamton, NY: Haworth Press, Incorporated, 2002.

Minns, Robert, and Brown, Keith. *Shaken Baby Syndrome and Other Non-Accidental Head Injuries in Children.* London: MacKeith Press, 2003.

PERIODICALS

Carbaugh, S.F. "Family teaching toolbox. Preventing shaken baby syndrome." *Advances in Neonatal Care* 4, no. 2 (2004): 118-9.

Carbaugh, S.F. "Understanding shaken baby syndrome." *Advances in Neonatal Care* 4, no. 2 (2004): 105-14.

Evans, H.H. "The medical discovery of shaken baby syndrome and child physical abuse." *Pediatric Rehabilitation* 7, no. 3 (2004): 161-3.

Lin, C.L., et al. "External subdural drainage in the treatment of infantile chronic subdural hematoma." *Journal of Trauma* 57, no. 1 (2004): 104-7.

Sugarman, N. "Shaken Baby Syndrome: compensating the victims." *Pediatric Rehabilitation* 7, no. 3 (2004): 215-20.

ORGANIZATIONS

Brain Injury Association. 105 North Alfred Street, Alexandria, VA 22314. (800) 444-6443 or (703) 236-6000. Web site: <http://www.biausa.org/Sportsfs.htm>.

International Brain Injury Association. 1150 South Washington Street, Suite 210, Alexandria, VA 22314. (703) 683-8400. Web site: <www.internationalbrain.org>.

WEB SITES

"Please Don't Shake Me." *National Center on Shaken Baby Sybdrome.* Available online at <http://www.dontshake.com>.

"Shaken Baby Information Page." *National Institute of Neurological Disorders and Stroke.* Available online at <http://www.ninds.nih.gov/health_and_medical/disorders/shakenbaby.htm>.

"Shaken Baby Syndrome." *Shaken Baby Alliance.* Available online at <http://www.shakenbaby.com>.

"Shaken Baby Syndrome." *The Arc.* Available online at <http://www.thearc.org/faqs/Shaken.html.asp>.

L. Fleming Fallon, Jr., MD, DrPH

Shigellosis

Definition

Shigellosis is an infection of the intestinal tract by a group of bacteria called *Shigella.*

Description

Shigellosis is a well-known cause of traveler's **diarrhea** and illness throughout the world. The major symptoms of shigellosis are diarrhea, abdominal cramps, **fever**, and severe fluid loss (**dehydration**). The bacteria causing shigellosis is named after Shiga, a Japanese researcher, who discovered the organism in 1897. Four different groups of *Shigella* can affect humans; of these, *S. dysenteriae* generally produces the most severe attacks, and *S. sonnei* the mildest. Shigella are extremely infectious bacteria, and ingestion of just 10 organisms is enough to cause dysentery. The most serious form of the disease is called dysentery, which is characterized by severe watery (and often blood- and mucus-streaked) diarrhea, abdominal cramping, rectal **pain**, and fever. *Shigella* is only one of several organisms that can cause dysentery, but the term bacillary dysentery is usually another name for shigellosis.

Demographics

Shigella accounts for 10 to 20 percent of all cases of diarrhea worldwide, and in any given year infects over 140 million persons and kills 600,000, mostly children and the elderly.

Most deaths are in less-developed or developing countries, but even in the United States, shigellosis can be a dangerous and potentially deadly disease. Poor hygiene, overcrowding, and improper storage of food are leading causes of infection. Shigellosis is often passed within families when young children are not yet toilet-trained and hand washing is poorly done. The following statistics show the marked difference in the frequency of cases between developed and less-developed countries: in the United States, about 30,000 individuals are hit by the disease each year or about 10 cases per 100,000 population. By contrast, infection in some areas of South America is 1,000 times more frequent. Shigellosis is most common in children below the age of five years and occurs less often in adults over 20.

Causes and symptoms

Shigella share several of the characteristics of a group of bacteria that inhabit the intestinal tract. E. coli, another cause of food-borne illness, can be mistaken for *Shigella* both by physicians and the laboratory. Careful testing is needed to assure proper diagnosis and treatment.

Shigella are very resistant to the acid produced by the stomach, and this allows them to easily pass through the gastrointestinal tract and infect the colon (large intestine). The result is a colitis that produces multiple ulcers, which can bleed. *Shigella* also produce a number of toxins (Shiga toxin and others) that increase the amount of fluid secretion by the intestinal tract. This fluid secretion is a major cause of the diarrhea symptoms.

Shigella infection spreads through food or water contaminated by human waste. Sources of transmission are as follows:

- contaminated milk, ice cream, vegetables, and other foods which often cause epidemics
- household contacts (40% of adults and 20% of children develop infection from such a source)
- poor hygiene and overcrowded living conditions
- daycare centers
- sexual practices which lead to oral-anal contact, directly or indirectly

Symptoms can be limited to mild diarrhea or develop into dysentery. Dehydration results from the large fluid losses due to diarrhea, **vomiting**, and fever. Inability to eat or drink worsens the situation.

In developed countries, most infections are of the less severe type and are often due to *S. sonnei*. The period between infection and symptoms (incubation period) varies from one to seven days. Shigellosis can last from a few days to several weeks, with the average duration seven days.

Complications

Areas outside the intestine can be involved, including the following:

- nervous system (irritation of the meninges or **meningitis**, **encephalitis**, and seizures)
- kidneys (producing hemolytic uremic syndrome or HUS which leads to kidney failure)
- joints (leading to an unusual form of arthritis called Reiter's syndrome)
- skin (rash)

One of the most serious complications of this disease is HUS, which involves the kidney. The main findings are kidney failure and damage to red blood cells. As many as 15 percent of patients die from this complication, and half the survivors develop chronic kidney failure, requiring dialysis.

Another life-threatening condition is toxic megacolon. Severe inflammation causes the colon to dilate or stretch, and the thin colon wall may eventually tear. Certain medications (particularly those that diminish intestinal contractions) may increase this risk, but this interaction is unclear. Clues to this diagnosis include sudden decrease in diarrhea, swelling of the abdomen, and worsening abdominal pain.

Diagnosis

Shigellosis is one of the many causes of acute diarrhea. Culture (growing the bacteria in the laboratory) of freshly obtained diarrhea fluid is the only way to be certain of the diagnosis. But even this is not always positive, especially if the patient is already on **antibiotics**. *Shigella* are identified by their appearance under the microscope, along with various chemical tests. These studies take several days.

Treatment

The first aim of treatment is to keep up **nutrition** and avoid dehydration. Ideally, a physician should be consulted before starting any treatment. Antibiotics may not be necessary, except for the more severe infections. Many cases resolve before the diagnosis is established by culture. Medications that control diarrhea by slowing intestinal contractions can cause problems and should be avoided by patients with bloody diarrhea or fever, especially if antibiotics have not been started.

Rehydration

The World Health Organization (WHO) has developed guidelines for a standard solution taken by mouth and prepared from ingredients readily available at home. This oral rehydration solution (ORS) includes salt, baking powder, sugar, orange juice, and water. Commercial preparations, such as Pedialyte, are also available. In many patients with mild symptoms, this is the only treatment needed. Severe dehydration usually requires intravenous fluid replacement.

Antibiotics

Patients who have very mild cases of shigellosis may improve without any antibiotic therapy; therefore, these drugs are indicated only for treatment of moderate or severe disease, as found in the tropics. Choice of antibiotic is based on the type of bacteria found in the geographical area and on laboratory results. Recommended antibiotics include ampicillin, sulfa derivatives such as trimethoprim-sulfamethoxazole (TMP-SMX) sold as Bactrim, or fluoroquinolones, such as Ciprofloxacin.

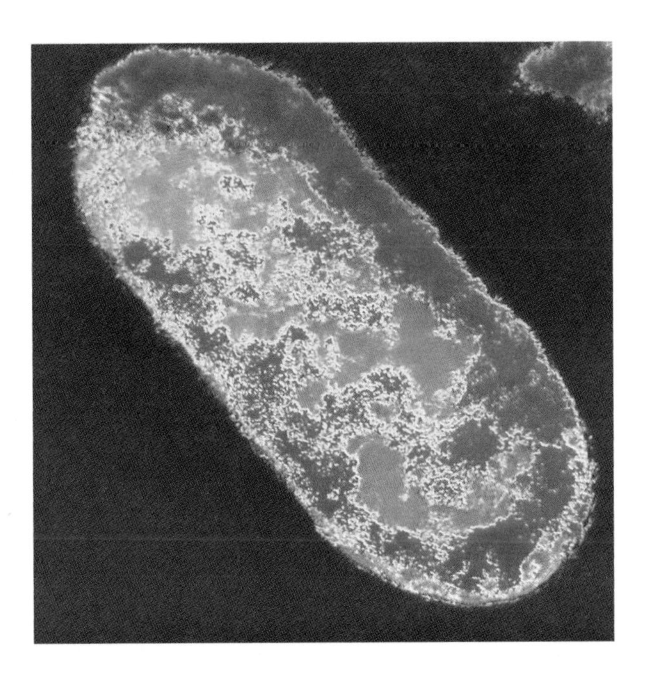

A transmission electron microscopy (TEM) scan of *Shigella*, a genus of aerobic bacteria that causes dysentery in humans and animals. *(Custom Medical Stock Photo Inc.)*

Prognosis

Many patients with mild infections need no specific treatment and recover completely. In those with severe infections, antibiotics decrease the length of symptoms and the number of days bacteria appear in the feces. In rare cases, an individual may fail to clear the bacteria from the intestinal tract; the result is a persistent carrier state. This may be more frequent in patients with acquired immune deficiency syndrome (**AIDS**). Antibiotics are about 90 percent effective in eliminating these chronic infections.

In patients who have suffered particularly severe attacks, some degree of cramping and diarrhea can last for several weeks. This is usually due to damage to the intestinal tract, which requires some time to heal. Since antibiotics can also produce a form of colitis, which may cause persistent or recurrent symptoms.

Prevention

Shigellosis is an extremely contagious disease; good hand washing techniques (especially after toileting young children or changing diapers) and proper precautions in food handling help in avoiding the spread of infection. Children in daycare centers need to be reminded about hand washing during an outbreak to minimize contagion. Shigellosis in schools or daycare

KEY TERMS

Antibiotics—Drugs that are designed to kill or inhibit the growth of the bacteria that cause infections.

Antimotility drug—A medication, such as loperamide (Imodium), dephenoxylate (Lomotil), or medications containing codeine or narcotics that decrease the ability of the intestine to contract.

Carrier state—The continued presence of an organism (bacteria, virus, or parasite) in the body that does not cause symptoms, but is able to be transmitted and infect other persons.

Colitis—Inflammation of the colon (large intestine).

Dialysis—A process of filtering and removing waste products from the bloodstream, it is used as a treatment for patients whose kidneys do not function properly. Two main types are hemodialysis and peritoneal dialysis. In hemodialysis, the blood flows out of the body into a machine that filters out the waste products and routes the cleansed blood back into the body. In peritoneal dialysis, the cleansing occurs inside the body. Dialysis fluid is injected into the peritoneal cavity and wastes are filtered through the peritoneum, the thin membrane that surrounds the abdominal organs.

Dysentery—A disease marked by frequent watery bowel movements, often with blood and mucus, and characterized by pain, urgency to have a bowel movement, fever, and dehydration.

Fluoroquinolones—A relatively new group of antibiotics used to treat infections with many gram-negative bacteria, such as *Shigella*. One drawback is that they should not be used in children under 17 years of age, because of possible effect on bone or cartilage growth.

Food-borne illness—A disease that is transmitted by eating or handling contaminated food.

Meninges—The three-layer membranous covering of the brain and spinal cord, composed of the dura mater, arachnoid, and pia mater. It provides protection for the brain and spinal cord, as well as housing many blood vessels and participating in the appropriate flow of cerebrospinal fluid.

Oral rehydration solution (ORS)—A liquid preparation of electrolytes and glucose developed by the World Health Organization that can decrease fluid loss in persons with diarrhea. Originally developed to be prepared with materials available in the home, commercial preparations have recently come into use.

Stool—The solid waste that is left after food is digested. Stool forms in the intestines and passes out of the body through the anus.

Traveler's diarrhea—An illness due to infection from a bacteria or parasite that occurs in persons traveling to areas where there is a high frequency of the illness. The disease is usually spread by contaminated food or water.

settings almost always disappears when holiday breaks occur, which severs the chain of transmission.

Traveler's diarrhea (TD)

Shigella accounts for about 10 percent of diarrhea illness in travelers to Mexico, South America, and the tropics. Most cases of TD are more of a nuisance than a life-threatening disease.

In some cases, though, aside from ruining vacation plans, these infections can interrupt business conference schedules and, in the worst instances, lead to a life-threatening illness. Therefore, researchers have tried to find a safe, yet effective, way of preventing TD. Of course the best prevention is to follow closely the rules outlined by the WHO and other groups regarding eating fresh fruits, vegetables, and other foods.

One safe and effective method of preventing TD is the use of large doses of Pepto Bismol. Tablets are easier for use during travel; usage must start a few days before departure. Patients should be aware that bismuth turns bowel movements black.

Antibiotics have also proven highly effective in preventing TD. They can also produce significant side effects. Therefore, a physician should be consulted before use. Like Pepto Bismol, antibiotics need to be started before beginning travel.

Parental concerns

Parents of children suffering from shigellosis need to follow closely their healthcare provider's directions for preventing dehydration. Excellent hand washing is crucial to prevent the spread of the infection throughout

family members. This is particularly important while helping to toilet train a child or while changing diapers.

Resources

BOOKS

Cleary, Thomas G. "Shigella." In *Nelson Textbook of Pediatrics.* Edited by Richard E. Behrman et al. Philadelphia: Saunders, 2004.

WEB SITES

Kroser, Joyann A. "Shigellosis." *eMedicine*, May 17, 2002. Available online at <www.emedicine.com/med/topic2112.htm> (accessed December 30, 2004).

"Shigellosis." *New York State Info for Consumers.* Available online at <www.health.state.ny.us/nysdoh/Communicable_diseases/en/shig.htm> (accessed December 30, 2004).

David Kaminstein, MD
Rosalyn Carson-DeWitt, MD

Shock, anaphylactic *see* **Anaphylaxis**

Shyness

Definition

Shyness is a psychological state that causes a person to feel discomfort in social situations in ways that interfere with enjoyment or that cause avoidance of social contacts altogether.

Description

Shyness can vary from mild feelings to moderately uncomfortable in social circumstances to debilitating levels of **anxiety** that interfere in children with the process of socialization (social withdrawal). Shyness is a personality trait that affects a child's **temperament**. Some infants are born shy and more sensitive. Some of them are quiet when new people enter a room. A shy baby might sink his head into his mother's shoulder, while a baby who is outgoing might smile or squeal with delight when someone new visits. Some children may feel shy in certain situations, like when meeting new people. Other children may learn to be shy because of experiences in school or at home. As of 2004, research tended to distinguish shyness from introversion. Introverts simply prefer solitary to social activities but do not **fear** social encounters as shy people do, while extroverts prefer social to solitary activities.

Evidence suggests a genetic component to shyness. Studies on the biological basis of shyness have shown that shyness in adults can often be traced as far back as the age of three. A Harvard study of two-year olds showed that, even at that age, widely different personality types can be recognized: roughly 25 percent of children are bold, sociable, and spontaneous regardless of the novelty of the situation, while 20 percent are shy and restrained in new situations. The remaining 55 percent of newborns fall between the extremes of shyness and boldness. These two basic temperaments were also recognized in studies examining infants as young as four months old. As children grow, their shy temperament tends to display itself in predictable ways: for example, in **play** groups at age seven, shy children play by themselves, while more outgoing children seek to play together in groups. Evidence of a genetic predisposition for shyness is found in parents and grandparents of shy infants who report childhood shyness more often than relatives of children who are not shy. Further evidence for a congenital link to shyness is found in studies that show that identical **twins** (who have identical genes) are more likely to be shy than fraternal twins (who are no more alike than other siblings).

Research shows, however, that 25 percent of the time genetic predisposition to shyness does not develop into shyness. Some researchers believe that a shy temperament may require environmental triggers, such as insecurity of attachment in the form of difficult relationships with parents, **family** conflict or chaos, frequent criticism, a dominating older sibling, or a stressful school environment.

Research has also identified a strong cultural link to shyness. In the United States, shyness surveys typically show that shyness is highest among Asian Americans and lowest among Jewish Americans. Using culturally sensitive adaptations of the Stanford Shyness Inventory, researchers in eight countries administered the inventory to groups of 18 to 21 year olds. Results showed that a large proportion of participants in all cultures reported experiencing shyness to a considerable degree—from 31 percent in Israel to 57 percent in Japan and 55 percent in Taiwan. In Mexico, Germany, India, and Canada, shyness levels were close to the U.S figure of 40 percent. In all countries, shyness is perceived as more negative than positive, with 60 percent or more considering shyness to be a problem. There is no gender difference in reported shyness, but males tend to conceal their shyness because it is considered a feminine trait in most countries. For example, in Mexico, males report shyness less often than females do.

Common problems

When shyness is intense, it can often lead to social anxiety disorder or to avoidant personality disorder, both characterized by the avoidance of interpersonal contacts accompanied by significant fears of embarrassment in social interaction. According to the most recent statistics, provided by the National Co-morbidity Survey—carried out in 1994—approximately 40 percent of Americans consistently report since the early 1970s that they are shy to the extent of considering it a problem in their lives. Subsequent research showed that the percentage of problem-related shyness gradually increased during the 1990s to nearly 50 percent. The National Co-morbidity Survey results were also indicative of a lifetime prevalence of social anxiety of 13.3 percent, making it the third most prevalent psychiatric disorder in the United States.

Excessive shyness usually leads to social withdrawal. If it is based on social fear and anxiety despite a desire to interact socially—such as in children who are unhappy because they are unable to make friends, it is called "conflicted shyness"; if it is based on the lack of a strong motivation to engage in social interaction, it is called "social disinterest." Both types are detected at an early age. The major behavioral components of excessive shyness in children are as follows:

- difficulty talking, stammering, **stuttering**, blushing, shaking, sweating hands when around other people
- difficulty thinking of things to say to people
- absence of outgoing mannerisms such as good eye contact or an easy smile
- reluctance to play with other kids, to go to school, to visit relatives and neighbors

Parental concerns

Parents may worry about if their shy infant, child, or teenager has a socialization problem. Parents should know that a child who seems mildly anxious or quiet at certain times may be shy. The best thing they can do is to help the child feel comfortable about being shy, by explaining that shyness can be a normal part of growing up. Teasing or being critical can make a shy child even more afraid to be around people. Sometimes, just encouraging a quiet child to play with others helps the child overcome shy feelings. Although many children who are shy remain shy all of their lives, many others overcome it in time as they develop social skills. Many children overcome shyness by themselves, some through associating with younger children, which allows them to display leadership behavior, still others through contact with other sociable children. Nothing assists in overcoming shyness more than experiencing social successes, as when a child takes the initial risk of engaging in some social activity that is rewarded, for example, in successfully developing friendships.

The use of **video games**, CD-ROM games, Web surfing, and other computer-related marvels all interfere with the time required to seek out direct contact with others for fun and friendship. Increasingly, social time is being replaced with the anonymous exchange of information within an externally imposed medium that effectively promotes shyness in young people. While some shy children may benefit from using the anonymity and structural control features of cyberspace, the danger is that for many others virtual on-line reality may become a substitute for the reality of close human relationships. Many parents are concerned because their young children prefer "chat time" on their computers more than actually talking face to face with other children, so these children may not socialize as much in the homes of neighbors and friends.

When to call the doctor

When a child is excessively shy, when shyness is persistent and results in high levels of anxiety in social settings and leads to social withdrawal and parents feel that their child is unhappy being shy, they should seek professional help. It is very important to determine if there is a social anxiety disorder, and if so, what treatment can best help the child overcome shyness. Child and adolescent psychiatrists are trained to help parents sort out whether their child's level of shyness is normal introversion or indicative of a disorder.

See also Parent-child relationships; Personality development; Personality disorders.

Resources

BOOKS

Antony, Martin M. *10 Simple Solutions to Shyness: How to Overcome Shyness, Social Anxiety, and Fear of Public Speaking*. Oakland, CA: New Harbinger Publications, 2004.

Carducci, Bernardo. *The Shyness Breakthrough: A No-Stress Plan to Help Your Shy Child Warm Up, Open Up, and Enjoy the Fun*. Emmaus, PA: Rodale Press, 2003.

Hillard, Erika B., et al. *Living Fully with Shyness and Social Anxiety: A Comprehensive Guide to Managing Social Anxiety and Gaining Social Confidence*. New York: Avalon Publishing Group, 2005.

Swallow, Ward K. *The Shy Child: Helping Children Triumph over Shyness*. New York: Warner Books, 2000.

KEY TERMS

Avoidant personality disorder—Chronic and long-standing fear of negative evaluation and tendency to avoid interpersonal situations without a guarantee of acceptance and support, accompanied by significant fears of embarrassment and shame in social interaction.

Extroversion—A personal preference for socially engaging activities and settings.

Extrovert—A person who is outgoing and performs well socially.

Introversion—A personal preference for solitary, non-social activities and settings.

Personality—The organized pattern of behaviors and attitudes that makes a human being distinctive. Personality is formed by the ongoing interaction of temperament, character, and environment.

Social anxiety disorder—Persistent avoidance and/or discomfort in social situations that significantly interferes with functioning.

Social withdrawal—Avoidance of social contacts.

Socialization—The process by which new members of a social group are integrated in the group.

Temperament—A person's natural disposition or inborn combination of mental and emotional traits.

PERIODICALS

Battaglia, M., et al. "Children's discrimination of expressions of emotions: relationship with indices of social anxiety and shyness." *Journal of the American Academy of Child & Adolescent Psychiatry* 43, no. 3 (March 2004): 358–65.

Coplan, R. J., et al. "Do you 'want' to play? Distinguishing between conflicted shyness and social disinterest in early childhood." *Developmental Psychology* 40, no. 2 (March 2004): 244–58.

Eley, T. C., et al. "A twin study of anxiety-related behaviors in pre-school children." *Journal of Child Psychology & Psychiatry* 44, no. 7 (October 2003): 945–60.

Henderson, H. A., et al. "Psychophysiological and behavioral evidence for varying forms and functions of nonsocial behavior in preschoolers." *Child Development* 75, no. 1 (January-February 2004): 251–63.

Jefferson, J. W. "Social Anxiety Disorder: More than Just a Little Shyness." *Primary Care Companion: Journal of Clinical Psychiatry* 3, no. 1 (February 2001): 4–9.

Yuen, C. N., and M. J. Lavin. "Internet dependence in the collegiate population: the role of shyness." *Cyberpsychology Behavior* 7, no. 4 (August 2004): 379–83.

Zimmermann, L. K., and K. Stansbury. "The influence of emotion regulation, level of shyness, and habituation on the neuroendocrine response of three-year-old children." *Psychoneuroendocrinology* 29, no. 8 (September 2004): 973–82.

ORGANIZATIONS

American Academy of Child & Adolescent Psychiatry (AACAP). 3615 Wisconsin Ave. NW, Washington, DC 20016–3007. Web site: <www.aacap.org>.

American Psychological Association (APA). 750 First Street, NE, Washington, DC 20002–4242. Web site: <www.apa.org>.

Anxiety Disorders Association of America (ADAA). 8730 Georgia Avenue, Suite 600, Silver Spring, MD 20910. Web site: <www.adaa.org>.

The Shyness Institute. 2000 Williams St., Palo Alto, CA 94306. Web site: <www.shyness.com>.

WEB SITES

"Shyness." *KidsHealth.* Available online at <http://kidshealth.org/kid/feeling/thought/shy.html> (accessed November 5, 2004).

The Shyness Homepage. Available online at <www.shyness.com/> (accessed November 5, 2004).

Monique Laberge, Ph.D.

Sibling rivalry

Definition

Sibling rivalry is antagonism between brothers and/or sisters that results in physical fighting, verbal hostility, teasing, or bullying.

Description

Psychologists believe that sibling rivalry comes from competition for parental attention, love, and approval. The amount of conflict depends on the perception of parents about the role of each child in the **family**, the personalities of the parents and children, the number and spacing of children in the family, outside resources available to the children, and parental beliefs about child rearing, including their attitudes toward gender, **birth order**, and competition. Sibling rivalry is also affected by the presence in the family of a special needs child, **divorce** or other family trauma, and ethnic and cultural attitudes toward family relationships.

Studies suggest that sister/sister relationships are the least competitive and hostile while brother/brother relationships, especially when brothers are close in age, are the most hostile and competitive. However, this is a generalization that does not apply in many specific instances. Some psychologists believe that moderate levels of sibling rivalry can help children learn to share, compromise, and negotiate with others.

Infancy

The birth of a new baby in the family often creates jealousy and distress for older children. Not only does a new baby increase the number children that must share parental attention, newborns are inordinately time consuming, leaving older children to feel they have been displaced and abandoned. Mothers often are exhausted and sometimes depressed after the birth of a child. While in the hospital and immediately after the birth, they may withdraw from their older children to care for the newborn, leaving day-to-day care taking of the other children to friends, relatives, or hired caregivers. Friends and other family members tend to focus on the newborn, further displacing older children. If the new baby is born with special needs, the time and energy spent focusing on the new sibling may be quite extensive.

Toddlers may react to a new baby by reverting to younger behaviors in an attempt to gain parental attention. For example, a toddler who is toilet trained may start having accidents in his or her pants. Verbal toddlers may express their disgust with the new sibling by asking, "Isn't it time to send him back?" Others may pinch and poke the new baby. Older children may become more difficult, temperamental, and uncooperative, as they see their role in the family changing. Although responses like these are, within reason, normal, they challenge parents and create conflict within the family.

Parents can help their other children prepare for the arrival of a new sibling by reading books to them about babies and involving them in preparations for their new sibling. After the child is born, in a two-parent family, the father can step in and spend extra time with older siblings, taking some of the pressure off the relationship between the mother and her older children. Many children feel more connected to their new sibling if they are given some specific age-appropriate task that helps to care for the baby.

Toddlerhood

Toddlers are active, curious people who are beginning to explore both their physical and social world. As noted above, they may respond to the birth of a new sibling by reverting to more childish behaviors. Toddlers are developing a sense of themselves as individuals and pushing the limits of their physical abilities. This testing and accompanying frustration often manifests itself in **tantrums** and other socially unacceptable behaviors such as an unwillingness to share **toys**. Since toddlers usually lack the ability to perceive the needs and desires of others and do not have the verbal capacity to express their emotions or abstract thoughts, sibling rivalry at this age usually takes the form of physical aggression.

Toddlers who are working out social boundaries may take toys from others or refuse to share or take turns. They may go through a stage of wanting whatever a sibling has, even if the moment they get it, they no longer want it. This can be a normal, if not socially desirable, stage of development. However, it creates friction with older siblings that often degenerates into kicking, hitting, punching, pinching, and even biting.

Parents need to intervene when sibling rivalry becomes physical. Younger toddlers can sometimes be distracted, but older ones need to be separated and given a break from each other. Many experts recommend punishing both children rather than becoming involved in trying to figure out who was "right" and who was "wrong."

Preschool

Preschool children are more verbal than toddlers, and much of their hostility toward siblings takes the form of name calling, verbal abuse, and teasing. Parents need to set limits on what is acceptable. Another source of sibling conflict at this age is the preschooler's desire to be part of his older siblings friendships. Although it may be easier for parents to tell their older child to include the younger one, this often intensifies the older child's hostility toward the younger one. Parents should be alert to the need to protect each child's personal possessions and friendships.

School age

Sibling rivalry can and often does continue into adulthood. By the time children reach school age, the level of sibling rivalry is affected by family attitude toward competition, ethnic and cultural attitudes, comparisons of siblings by teachers and coaches, the family's expectations for each child in the family, and their method of applying "fairness" in their relationships with their children. Hostility can take the form of physical or verbal fighting, invading each other's privacy, or destroying each other's possessions.

At this age, children often begin to carve out their own area in which to excel. One child may concentrate on soccer while another concentrates on music and a third on schoolwork. This differentiation can help reduce competition and sibling rivalry. Parents can reduce the level of sibling rivalry by supporting each child's interest with an equal investment of enthusiasm and time. At this age, the approval and support of individuals outside the family also plays a role in reducing sibling rivalry. Resentment and hostility can be increased when parents insist that all children in the family do the same activities all the time, always include each other in their **play** and friendships, and put older children in charge of younger ones for long periods on a regular basis.

Common problems

The presence of a special needs child who dominates the parents' attention can add to increased resentment and rivalry. Other common problems include assuming that the older child is always at fault in sibling fights, giving each child a label such as "the smart one" or "the wild one," that suggest one child is "good" and another is "bad," reinforcing cultural attitudes that place a higher value on sons than daughters and on first children rather than later children, and overprotecting younger children or children who are perceived as weaker than their siblings. Single parents may face an especially difficult time balancing the needs of their children in ways that reduce rivalry simply because they are the only adult in the family.

Parental concerns

Parents often worry about preferring one child over another and being fair to all their children. In reality, parents may love their children equally but find at different times in their development some of their children are more likeable and easier to get along with than others. Parents can help reduce sibling rivalry by following these steps:

- working to see each child as a unique individual with his or her own strengths and weaknesses
- spending some one-on-one time with each child every week
- encouraging children to develop their own interests and friends independent of the interests and friends of their siblings
- limiting the amount of care giving expected of older siblings for younger ones
- setting and enforcing firm rules about name calling, teasing, and physical aggression in the family
- praising cooperative behavior
- insisting that each child's personal possessions and privacy are respected by the other children in the family

When to call the doctor

Parents may wish to consult their pediatrician, a child and adolescent psychologist, or a family therapist if any of the following occurs:

- Serious attempts at reducing sibling rivalry have failed.
- Siblings physically harm each other.
- Siblings constantly tease and belittle or bully each other.
- One or more children in the family seem to have other behavioral problems at home or school.
- Siblings gang up on one child in the family.
- The level of sibling rivalry appears to be destructive to any member of the family.

Resources

BOOKS

Borden, Marian Elderman. *The Baffled Parent's Guide to Sibling Rivalry.* New York: McGraw-Hill, 2003.

Goldenthal, Peter. *Beyond Sibling Rivalry: How to Help Your Children Become Cooperative, Caring, and Compassionate.* New York: Henry Holt & Co., 2000.

Hart, Sybil. *Preventing Sibling Rivalry: Six Strategies to Build a Jealousy-Free Home.* New York: Simon & Schuster, 2001.

Sparrow, Joshua, et al. *Understanding Sibling Rivalry: The Brazelton Way.* Boulder, CO: Da Capo Press, 2005.

Thomas, Pat. *My Brother, My Sister, and Me: A First Look at Sibling Rivalry.* New York: Barrow's Educational Series, 2000.

ORGANIZATIONS

American Academy of Pediatrics. 141 Northwest Point Boulevard, Elk Grove Village, IL 60007-1098 Web site: <www.aap.org>.

WEB SITES

"Sibling Rivalry." Available online at <http://kidshealth.org/parent/emotions/feelings/sibling_rivalry.html> (accessed November 14, 2004).

Tish Davidson, A.M.

Sickle cell anemia

Definition

Sickle cell anemia, also called sickle cell disease (SS disease), is an inherited condition caused by having abnormal hemoglobin, the protein that carries oxygen in the blood. People with sickle cell anaemia have sickle hemoglobin (HbS) which is different from the normal hemoglobin (HbA).

Description

Children with sickle cell anemia produce two abnormal hemoglobin proteins (inheriting one from each parent), which makes their red blood cells easily destructible while giving them a sickle-like shape. Since the red blood cells do not have a normal shape, their circulation in the small blood vessels is impaired as well as the function of the abnormal hemoglobin (HbS) which can no longer carry oxygen with maximum efficiency.

Transmission

Sickle cell anemia is usually inherited from parents who are carriers, who have the sickle cell trait—a milder form of sickle cell anemia, or one abnormal hemoglobin.

Demographics

Sickle cell anemia and sickle cell trait are found mainly in people whose families come from Africa, the Caribbean, the Eastern Mediterranean, Middle East, and Asia. In the United States, sickle cell anemia affects some 72,000 people. The families of most of the people affected come from Africa. The disease occurs in about one in every 600 African-American births and in one in every 1,000 to 1,400 Hispanic-American births. Some 2 million Americans carry the sickle cell trait and about one in 12 African Americans have the trait.

Causes and symptoms

Sickle cell anemia is caused by an error in the gene that signals the body how to make hemoglobin. The defective gene tells the body to make the abnormal hemoglobin HbS instead of the normal HbA, and this results in deformed red blood cells. The error in the hemoglobin gene is due to a genetic mutation that occurred many thousands of years ago in people living in Africa, the Mediterranean basin, the Middle East, and India. A deadly form of malaria was very common at that time, and research has shown that in areas where malaria was endemic, children who inherited one HbS gene and who, therefore, carried the sickle cell trait, had a survival advantage because, unlike the children who had normal HbA genes, they survived malaria. They grew up, had their own children, and passed on the gene for HbS.

Symptoms or complications associated with sickle cell anemia usually start after the age of four to six months and can include all or some of the following:

- anemia, caused by low amounts of red blood cells in the bloodstream, resulting in insufficient oxygen delivery to tissues and organs
- vaso-occlusive **pain**, meaning severe episodes of pain in the arms, legs, or back, due to impaired blood circulation in the blood vessels
- chest pain and **fever** with coughing
- dactylitis, or hand-foot syndrome, with painful swelling of the bones in the hands or feet of young children
- aplastic crises, during which the body stops making new red blood cells causing severe anemia usually following an infection with the parovirus B19, which causes fifth disease
- priapism, a painful and prolonged erection
- **stroke**, usually causing sudden weakness of one side of the body
- acute splenic sequestration, with pooling of blood causing a sudden enlargement of the spleen
- jaundice, a yellowing of the skin and white of the eyes
- frequent infection with certain bacteria, particularly pneumococcus and salmonella, which are due to autoinfarction of the spleen or death of the spleen due to poor blood flow

When to call the doctor

Children suffering from sickle anemia have episodes during which they suddenly become unwell or complain of severe abdominal or chest pain, **headache**, stiffness of the neck or drowsiness. Parents should know that a child having a sickle cell crisis requires urgent hospital treatment. They should also call a doctor if the child has a temperature above 101°F (38.5°C).

Diagnosis

The diagnosis of sickle cell anemia is established during the newborn screen testing that is performed in the nursery at time of birth. For children who are not tested, an electrophoresis test of the blood can detect the abnormal hemoglobin of sickle cell anemia. This test measures the speed at which a molecule moves in a gel and can detect abnormal hemoglobin HbS.

Treatment

Treatment usually includes frequent monitoring of red blood counts, **antibiotics** for infections, transfusions for aplastic crises and splenic sequestration when required, and oxygen as well as respiratory support for chest syndrome. Some patients with severe symptoms receive regular blood transfusions to prevent crises and/or other complications such as stroke and organ damage.

Children with sickle cell disorders are at risk of developing severe infections, and penicillin is usually prescribed to prevent dangerous pneumococcal infections.

Sickle cell pain can be managed with a variety of measures including the following:

- warmth, to increase the blood flow, by massaging and rubbing and by heat from hot water bottles and deep heat creams
- bandaging to support the painful region
- rest
- getting the child to relax, by deep breathing exercises and distracting the attention, and by other psychological methods
- use of pain-killing medicines (**analgesics**)

Analgesics should only be given as recommended by the treating physician. The gentlest analgesic usually prescribed is paracetamol, given three times a day (62.5 mgm under 12 months; 125 mgm 1–4 years; 250 mgm 4–10 years; 500 mgm 10–14 years; and 1 gm 15 years upwards). The next gentlest is codeine phosphate, given four times a day, at 1–2 mgm for every kilogram of body weight.

Bone marrow transplantation has been shown to provide a cure for severely affected children with sickle cell disease, but the procedure is not entirely without risk. In addition, the marrow must come from a healthy matched sibling donor and only about 18 percent of children with sickle cell anemia are likely to have a matched sibling.

Alternative treatment

Research contributed a great deal about sickle cell anemia from 1970 to the early 2000s concerning what causes it, how it affects the patient, and how to treat it. Scientists were as of 2004 starting to be successful at developing drugs that prevent the symptoms of sickle cell anemia and procedures that they hope should eventually provide a cure. Drug research is focused on identifying drugs, such as hydroxyurea, that can increase the level of fetal hemoglobin in the blood. Fetal hemoglobin is a form of hemoglobin that all humans produce before birth, but most stop producing it after birth. It has been observed that some children with sickle cell anemia continue to produce large amounts of fetal hemoglobin after birth, and studies have shown that these children have less severe cases of the disease. Fetal hemoglobin seems to prevent "sickling" of red cells, and cells containing fetal hemoglobin tend to survive longer in the bloodstream. Butyrate, a substance widely used as a food additive, was also being investigated as of 2004 as an agent that may increase fetal hemoglobin production.

Nutritional concerns

Thirst and **dehydration** caused by not drinking enough, even if thirst is not felt, are known to trigger sickle pain. Parents should accordingly monitor fluid intake closely.

Children with sickle cell anemia are anemic to various degrees. Most of the time they feel quite well, but if the anemia gets worse, they may feel very tired. **Folic acid**, a vitamin found in fruit and vegetables, supports making blood and anemic children especially need it to prevent them from becoming run down.

Prognosis

Sickle cell anemia is an inherited disease and lasts a lifetime.

Prevention

Both sickle cell trait and sickle cell anemia are inherited. Therefore, parents can pass it to their offspring. It is important for parents to get tested. If one partner has sickle cell trait and the other does not, their children each have a 50 percent chance of having the sickle cell trait, and a 50 percent chance of having normal hemoglobin. If one parent has sickle cell trait it is extremely important that the other parent be tested. If both parents have sickle cell trait, there is a 25 percent chance that the child will have normal hemoglobin, a 50 percent chance that the child will have the sickle cell trait, and a 25 percent chance the child will have sickle cell disease. If both parents have sickle cell trait and want to know whether the unborn child has sickle cell anemia, testing can be performed as early as the tenth week of pregnancy. If the results are normal, the parents can be reassured. If the tests show that the baby will be affected, the parents can be better prepared and they can make an informed decision concerning the pregnancy.

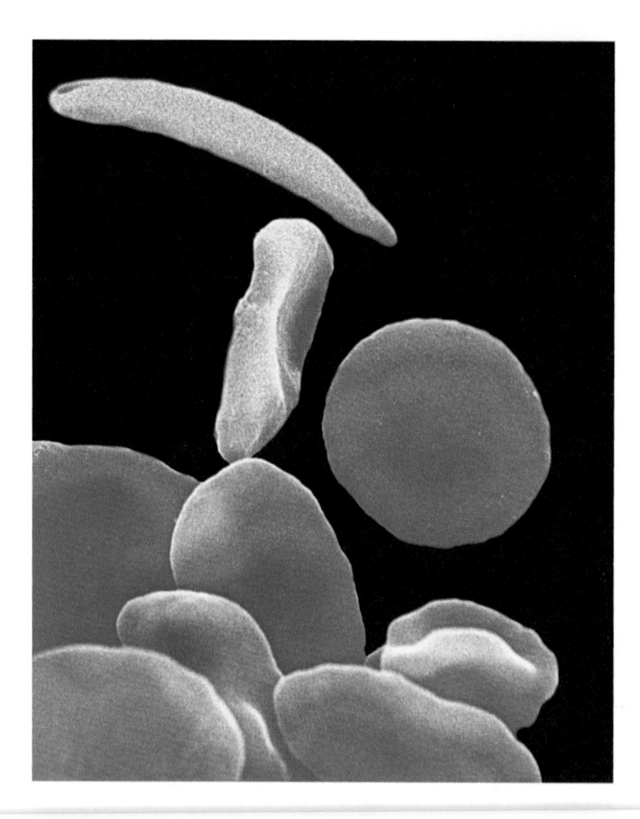

Normal red blood cells are smooth and round. In sickle cell anemia, the red blood cells become shaped like sickles or crescents. *(© Dr. Gopal Murti/Photo Researchers, Inc.)*

KEY TERMS

Acute splenic sequestration—Retention of blood in the spleen.

Anemia—A condition in which there is an abnormally low number of red blood cells in the bloodstream. It may be due to loss of blood, an increase in red blood cell destruction, or a decrease in red blood cell production. Major symptoms are paleness, shortness of breath, unusually fast or strong heart beats, and tiredness.

Aplastic anemia—A disorder in which the bone marrow greatly decreases or stops production of blood cells.

Bone marrow—The spongy tissue inside the large bones in the body that is responsible for making the red blood cells, most white blood cells, and platelets.

Dactylitis—Inflammation of the hands or feet.

Endemic—Natural to or characteristic of a particular place, population, or climate.

Hemoglobin—An iron-containing pigment of red blood cells composed of four amino acid chains (alpha, beta, gamma, delta) that delivers oxygen from the lungs to the cells of the body and carries carbon dioxide from the cells to the lungs.

Priapism—A painful, abnormally prolonged penile erection.

Sickle cell trait—Condition that occurs in people who have one of two possible genes responsible for the abnormal hemoglobin of sickle cell anemia. People with this trait may suffer milder symptoms of sickle cell anemia or may have no symptoms. Some scientists believe that the trait actually provides an advantage in tropical environments because the slightly altered shape of the blood cells cause a person to be more resistant to malaria.

Parental concerns

Parents should be aware that children with sickle cell anemia are also at increased risk of infection, especially from the *Streptococcus pneumonia* and *H. influenzae* bacteria.

Sickle cell anemia does not affect **intelligence**. Children with sickle cell disorders can almost always attend school and participate fully in normal activities. The child's teacher and the school principal should know of the diagnosis and understand the limitations sickle cell anemia can impose on a child, for instance the need for frequent drinks and easy access to the bathroom, and the triggering of pain by over-exertion or cold.

See also Anemias.

Resources

BOOKS

Gillie, Oliver. *Sickle Cell Disease (Just the Facts).* Chicago: Heineman Library, 2004.

Gordon, Melanie A. *Let's Talk about Sickle Cell Anemia.* New York: Powerkids Press, 2000.

Platt, Alan F., and A. Sacerdote. *Hope and Destiny: A Patient's and Parent's Guide to Sickle Cell Disease and Sickle Cell Trait.* Roscoe, IL: Hilton Publishing Co., 2003.

PERIODICALS

Fullerton, H. J., et al. "Declining stroke rates in Californian children with sickle cell disease." *Blood* 104, no. 2 (July 2004): 336–39.

Quinn, C. T., et al. "Survival of children with sickle cell disease." *Blood* 103, no. 11 (June 2004): 423–27.

Steinberg, M. H. "Therapies to increase fetal hemoglobin in sickle cell disease." *Current Hematology Reports* 2, no. 2 (March 2003): 95–101.

Zimmerman, S. A., et al. "Sustained long-term hematologic efficacy of hydroxyurea at maximum tolerated dose in children with sickle cell disease." *Blood* 103, no. 6 (March 2004): 239–45.

ORGANIZATIONS

American Sickle Cell Anemia Association (ASCAA). 10300 Carnegie Avenue, Cleveland Clinic EEb18, Cleveland, OH 44106. Web site: <www.ascaa.org>.

Sickle Cell Society. 54 Station Road, London, NW10 4UA, UK. Web site: <www.sicklecellsociety.org>.

WEB SITES

"Sickle Cell Anemia." *Medline Plus.* Available online at <www.nlm.nih.gov/medlineplus/sicklecellanemia.html> (accessed November 14, 2004).

Monique Laberge, Ph.D.

SIDS *see* **Sudden infant death syndrome**

Single-parent families

Definition

Single-parent families are families with children under age 18 headed by a parent who is widowed or divorced and not remarried, or by a parent who has never married.

Description

One out of every two children in the United States will live in a single-parent **family** at some time before they reach age 18. According the United States Census Bureau, in 2002 about 20 million children lived in a household with only their mother or their father. This is more than one-fourth of all children in the United States.

Since 1950, the number of one-parent families has increased substantially. In 1970, about 11 percent of children lived in single-parent families. During the 1970s, **divorce** became much more common, and the number of families headed by one parent increased rapidly. The number peaked in the 1980s and then declined slightly in the 1990s. By 1996, 31 percent of children lived in single-parent families. In 2002, the number was 28 percent. Many other children have lived in single-parent families for a time before their biological parent remarried, when they moved into a two-parent family with one biological parent and one step parent.

The reasons for single-parent families have also changed. In the mid-twentieth century, most single-parent families came about because of the death of a spouse. In the 1970s and 1980s, most single-parent families were the result of divorce. In the early 2000s, more and more single parents have never married. Many of these single parents live with an adult partner, sometimes even the unmarried father of their child. These families are counted by the Census Bureau as single-parent families, although two adults are present. Still other families are counted as single-parent families if the parents are married, but one is away for an extended period, for example, on military deployment.

The most common type of single-parent family is one that consists of a mother and her biological children. In 2002, 16.5 million or 23 percent of all children were living with their single mother. This group included 48 percent of all African-American children, 16 percent of all non-Hispanic white children, 13 percent of Asian/Pacific Islander children, and 25 percent of children of Hispanic origin. However, these numbers do not give a true picture of household organization, because 11 percent of all children were actually living in homes where their mother was sharing a home with an adult to whom she was not married. This group includes 14 percent of white children, 6 percent of African-American children, 11 percent of Asian/Pacific Islander, and 12 percent of Hispanic children.

Households headed by a single father increased substantially after the early 1980s, reflecting society's changing attitudes about the role of fathers in child rearing. In 1970, only 1 percent of children lived with a single father. In 2002, about 5 percent of children under age 18 lived with their single fathers. Single fathers, however, are much more likely to be divorced than never married and much more likely than single mothers to be sharing a home with an adult to whom they are not married. For example, 33 percent of Caucasian children lived with fathers who were unmarried but cohabiting with another adult. The rate was 29 percent for African-American children, 30 percent for Asian/Pacific Islanders, and 46 percent for children of Hispanic origin. It is clear that not all single-parent families are the same and that within different ethnic and racial groups, the number and type of single-parent families varies considerably.

Adoption by single individuals has also soared. In 1970 only 0.5 to 4 percent of adoptive parents were single. In the 1980s this rate increased from 8 to 34 percent. According the United States Department of Health and

Single parent and her children spending time together. *(© Rick Gomez/Corbis.)*

Human Services, 33 percent of children adopted from **foster care** are adopted by single parents.

Common problems

Single-parent families face special challenges. One of these is economic. In 2002, twice as many single-parent families earned less than $30,000 per year compared to families with two parents present. At the opposite end of the spectrum, 39 percent of two-parent families earned more than $75,000 compared to 6 percent of single-mother families and 11 percent of single-father families. Single-parent families are challenged in other ways. Children living with single fathers were the least likely of all children to have health insurance coverage.

Social scientists have found that children growing up in single-parent families are disadvantaged in other ways when compared to a two-biological-parent families. Many of these problems are directly related to the poor economic condition of single-parent families, not just to parenting style. These children are at risk for the following:

- lower levels of educational achievement
- twice as likely to drop out of school
- more likely to become teen parents
- more conflict with their parent(s)
- less supervised by adults
- more likely to become truants
- more frequently abuse drugs and alcohol
- more high-risk sexual behavior
- more likely to join a gang
- twice as likely to go to jail
- four times as likely to need help for emotional and behavioral problems
- more likely to participate in violent crime
- more likely to commit suicide
- twice as likely to get divorced in adulthood

Studies have also found that children who live in a two-parent family where one parent is abusive or has a high level of **antisocial behavior** do not do as well as children whose parents divorce if the child then lives in a single-parent family with the nonabusive parent.

It is important to remember that every single-parent family is different. Children who are living with a widowed mother will have a home life that is different from children with divorced parents or those whose parents were never married. Children of divorced parents will have a wide range of relationships with their parents and parents' partners depending on custody arrangements and the commitment of the non-custodial parent to maintaining a relationship with the child. Despite the fact that children from single-parent families often face a tougher time economically and emotionally than children from two-biological-parent families, children from single-parent families can grow up doing well in school and maintaining healthy behaviors and relationships.

Parental concerns

Being a single parent can be hard and lonely. There is often no other adult with whom to share decision-making, **discipline**, and financial responsibilities. The full burden of finding responsible childcare, earning a living, and parenting falls on one individual. However, the lack of a second parent often has a less negative impact on children than family instability, lack of structure, and inconsistent enforcement of parental standards. Single parents may want to follow these steps in order to create positive experiences for their children:

- Find stable, safe child care.
- Establish a home routine and stick to it.
- Apply rules and discipline clearly and consistently.
- Allow the child to be a child and not ask him or her to solve adult problems.
- Get to know the important people (teachers, coaches, friends) in the child's life.
- Answer questions about the other parent calmly and honestly.
- Avoid behavior that causes the child to feel pressed to choose between divorced parents.
- Explain financial limitations honestly.

When to get help

If parents feel their child is out of control and is not responding to their parenting, they need to get help from the child's school, social service agencies, and mental health professionals. If they feel their own life is spiraling downward and falling apart, they can seek help from many organizations that provide social, emotional, financial, and legal support for single-parent families.

Resources

BOOKS

Karst, Patricia. *The Single Mother's Survival Guide*. Freedom, CA: Crossing Press, 2000.

PERIODICALS

Fields, Jason. "Children's Living Arrangements and Characteristics: March 2002." *Current Population Reports*. United States Department of Commerce Economics and Statistics Administration, June, 2003.

Jaffee, Sara R., et al. "Life with (or without) Father: The Benefits of Living with Two Biological Parents Depend on the Father's Antisocial Behavior." *Child Development* 74 (January-February 2003): 109–27.

ORGANIZATIONS

Parents without Partners. 1650 South Dixie Highway, Suite 510, Boca Raton, Florida 33431 Web site: <www.parentswithoutpartners.org>.

Single and Custodial Fathers Network Inc. Web site: <http://scfn.org>.

WEB SITES

Single Parent Central. Available online at <www.singleparentcentral.com> (accessed November 14, 2004.).

Tish Davidson, A.M.

Sinusitis

Definition

Sinusitis is an inflammation of the sinuses, which are airspaces within the bones of the face. Sinusitis is most often due to an infection within these spaces.

Description

The sinuses are paired air pockets located within the bones of the face. There are:

- the frontal sinuses, located above the eyes, in the center region of each eyebrow
- the maxillary sinuses, located within the cheekbones, just to either side of the nose

- the ethmoid sinuses, located between the eyes, just behind the bridge of the nose
- the sphenoid sinuses, located just behind the ethmoid sinuses, and behind the eyes.

The sinuses are connected with the nose. They are lined with the same kind of skin found elsewhere within the respiratory tract. This skin has tiny little hairs projecting from it called cilia. The cilia beat constantly to help move the mucus produced in the sinuses into the respiratory tract. The beating cilia sweeping the mucus along the respiratory tract helps to clear the respiratory tract of any debris or of any organisms that may be present. When the lining of the sinuses is at all swollen, the swelling interferes with the normal flow of mucus. Trapped mucus can then fill the sinuses, causing an uncomfortable sensation of pressure and providing an excellent environment for the growth of infection-causing bacteria.

Demographics

It is estimated that about 37 million Americans are affected by sinusitis each year. Having a cold increases the chance of getting sinusitis. Immune system disorders also increase this likelihood. Children with **asthma** are also considered more likely to be affected by sinusitis.

Causes and symptoms

Sinusitis is usually due to an infection, although swelling from **allergies** can mimic the symptoms of pressure, **pain**, and congestion, and allergies can set the stage for a bacterial infection. Bacteria are the most common cause of sinus infection. *Streptococcus pneumoniae* causes about 33 percent of all cases, while *Haemophilus influenzae* causes about 25 percent of all cases. Sinusitis in children may be caused by *Moraxella catarrhalis* (20%). In people with weakened immune systems (including patients with diabetes, acquired **immunodeficiency** syndrome or **AIDS**, and patients who are taking medications that lower their immune resistance, such as **cancer** and transplant patients), sinusitis may be caused by fungi such as *Aspergillus*, *Candida*, or *Mucorales*.

Acute sinusitis usually follows some type of upper respiratory tract infection or cold. Instead of ending, the cold seems to linger on, with constant or even worsening congestion. Drainage from the nose often changes from a clear color to a thicker, yellowish-green. The individual may develop a **fever**. **Headache** and pain over the affected sinuses may occur, as well as a feeling of pressure that may worsen when the patient bends over. There may be pain in the jaw or teeth. Some children, in particular, get upset stomachs from the infected drainage going down the back of their throats and being swallowed. Some patients develop a **cough**.

Chronic sinusitis occurs when the problem has existed for at least three months. There is rarely a fever with chronic sinusitis. Sinus pain and pressure are frequent, as is nasal congestion. Because of the swelling in the sinuses, they may not be able to drain out the nose. Drainage, therefore, drips constantly down the back of the throat, resulting in a continuously **sore throat** and bad breath.

When to call the doctor

If the child is displaying the signs of sinusitis for more than a few days, the doctor should be contacted. If a cold seems to be getting better and then gets worse again, it may have developed into sinusitis. Likewise, colds that linger beyond a week may indicate sinusitis, and the doctor should be called.

Diagnosis

Diagnosis is sometimes tricky, because the symptoms so often resemble those of an uncomplicated cold. However, sinusitis should be strongly suspected when a cold lingers beyond about a week's time.

Medical practitioners have differing levels of trust in certain basic examinations commonly conducted in the office. For example, tapping over the sinuses may cause pain in patients with sinusitis, but it may not. A procedure called "sinus transillumination" may or may not also be helpful. Using a flashlight pressed up against the skin of the cheek, the practitioner will look in the patient's open mouth. When the sinuses are full of air (under normal conditions), the light will project through the sinus and will be visible on the roof of the mouth as a lit-up, reddened area. When the sinuses are full of mucus, the light will be stopped. While this simple test can be helpful, it is certainly not a perfect way to diagnose or rule out the diagnosis of sinusitis.

X-ray pictures and CT scans of the sinuses are helpful for both acute and chronic sinusitis. People with chronic sinusitis should also be checked for allergies, and they may need a procedure called nasal endoscopy where a very slender lighted fiber optic tube is placed in the nose in order for the doctor to see if any kind of anatomic obstruction is causing the illness. For example, the septum (the cartilage which separates the two nasal cavities from each other) may be slightly displaced (a deviated septum). This condition can result in chronic obstruction, setting the person up for the development of an infection.

Treatment

Antibiotic medications are used to treat acute sinusitis. Suitable **antibiotics** include sulfa drugs, amoxicillin, and a variety of cephalosporins. These medications are usually given for about two weeks but may be given for even longer periods. **Decongestants** or the short-term use of decongestant nose sprays can be useful. **Acetaminophen** (Tylenol) and ibuprofen (Motrin, Advil) can decrease the pain and headache associated with sinusitis. Also, running a humidifier can prevent mucus within the nasal passages from drying out uncomfortably and can help soothe any accompanying sore throat or cough.

Chronic sinusitis is often treated initially with antibiotics. Steroid nasal sprays may be used to decrease swelling in the nasal passages. If an anatomic reason is found for chronic sinusitis, it may need to be corrected with surgery. If a surgical procedure is necessary, samples are usually taken at the same time to allow identification of any organisms present which may be causing infection.

Fungal sinusitis requires surgery to clean out the sinuses. Then, a relatively long course of a very strong antifungal medication called amphotericin B is given through a needle in the vein (intravenously).

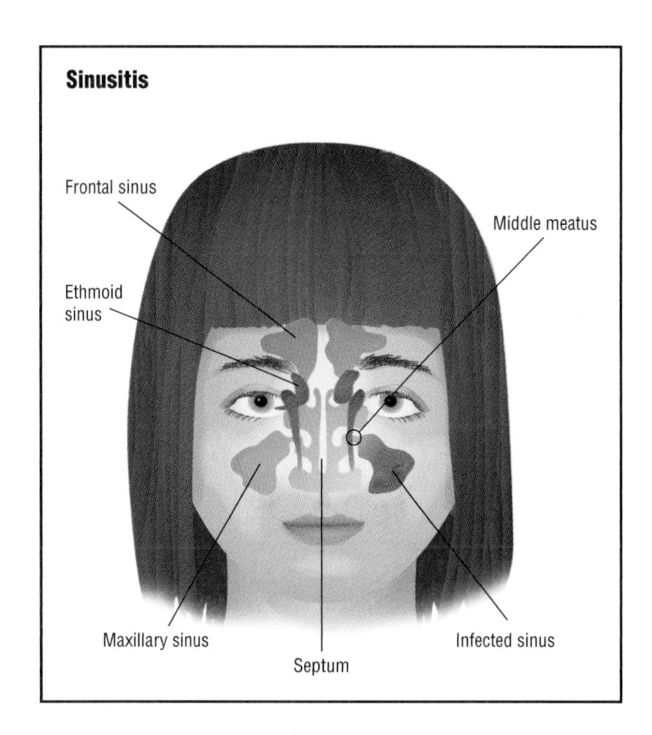

Illustration of an infected left maxillary sinus, which radiates pain and pressure to the surrounding sinus areas. *(Illustration by GGS Information Services.)*

Alternative treatment

Some practitioners believe that chronic sinusitis is associated with **food allergies**. These doctors would suggest an elimination/challenge diet to identify and eliminate allergenic foods. While linking chronic sinusitis to food is widely considered controversial, many practitioners link the problem to aero-allergies. Irrigating the sinuses with a salt-water solution is thus recommended for sinusitis and allergies, in order to clear the nasal passages of mucus. Another solution for nasal lavage (washing) uses powdered goldenseal (*Hydrastis canadensis*). Other herbal treatments, taken internally, include a mixture made of eyebright (*Euphrasia officinalis*), goldenseal, yarrow (*Achillea millefolium*), and horseradish, or, when infection is present, a mixture made of echinacea (*Echinacea* spp.), wild indigo, and poke root (*Phytolacca decandra-Americana*).

Homeopathic practitioners find a number of remedies useful for treating sinusitis. Among those they recommend are: *Arsenicum album*, *Kalium bichromium*, *Nux vomica*, *Mercurius iodatus*, and *Silica*.

Acupuncture has been used to treat sinusitis, as have a variety of dietary supplements, including **vitamins** A, C, and E, and the mineral zinc. Contrast hydrotherapy (hot and cold compresses, alternating three minutes hot, 30 seconds cold, repeated three times always ending with cold) applied directly over the sinuses can relieve pressure and enhance healing. A direct inhalation of essential oils (two drops of oil to two cups of water) using thyme, rosemary, and lavender can help open the sinuses and kill bacteria that cause infection.

Prognosis

Prognosis for sinus infections is usually excellent, although some individuals may find that they are particularly prone to contracting such infections after a cold. Fungal sinusitis, however, has a relatively high death rate.

Prevention

Prevention involves the usual standards of good hygiene to cut down on the number of colds an individual catches. Avoiding exposure to cigarette smoke, identifying and treating allergies, and avoiding deep dives in swimming pools may help prevent sinus infections. During the winter, it is a good idea to use a humidifier. Humidifiers should be adequately and frequently cleaned with bleach or comparable cleanser to avoid mold which can be aerosolized and then exacerbate existing allergies. Dry nasal passages may crack, allowing bacteria to enter. When allergies are diagnosed, a

KEY TERMS

Cilia—Tiny hairlike projections on certain cells within the body. Cilia produce lashing or whipping movements to direct or cause motion of substances or fluids within the body. Within the respiratory tract, the cilia act to move mucus along, in an effort to continually flush out and clean the respiratory tract.

Sinus—A tubular channel or cavity connecting one body part with another or with the outside. Often refers to one of the air-filled cavities surrounding the eyes and nose that are lined with mucus-producing membranes. They cleanse the nose, add resonance to the voice, and partially determine the structure of the face.

number of nasal sprays are available to assist in preventing inflammation within the nasal passageways, thus allowing the normal flow of mucus.

Parental concerns

Sinusitis can usually be treated successfully with antibiotics. It can, however, be very dangerous or even fatal if left untreated it becomes progressively worse such that the infection spreads.

See also Allergic rhinitis.

Resources

BOOKS

Bruce, Debra Fulghum, et al. *The Sinus Cure: 7 Steps to Relieve Sinusitis and Other Ear, Nose, and Throat Conditions.* Westminster, MD: Ballantine Books, 2001.

Chronic Sinusitis: A Medical Dictionary, Bibliography, and Annotated Research Guide to Internet Sources. San Diego, CA: Icon Group International, 2004.

Hirsch, Alan R. *What Your Doctor May Not Tell You about Sinusitis: Relieve Your Symptoms and Identify the Source of Your Pain.* Boston, MA: Warner Books, 2004.

Kavuru, Mani S., et al. *Diagnosis and Management of Rhinitis and Sinusitis*, 2nd ed. Cleveland, OH: Professional Communications, 2001.

Kenned, David W., et al. *Living with Chronic Sinusitis: A Patient's Guide to Sinusitis, Nasal Allergies, Polyps, and Their Treatment Options.* Long Island City, NY: Hatherleigh Co., 2004.

Plasse, Harvey, et al. *Sinusitis Relief.* New York: Henry Holt & Co., 2002.

PERIODICALS

Glaser, Gabrielle. "How to Spot a Sinus Infection." *Parents Magazine* 75 (March 2000): 89–93.

ORGANIZATIONS

American Academy of Allergy, Asthma and Immunology. 611 East Wells Street, Milwaukee, WI 53202. Web site: <www.aaaai.org>.

American Academy of Otolaryngology-Head and Neck Surgery Inc. One Prince Street, Alexandria, VA 22314–3357. Web site: <www.entnet.org>.

Joint Council of Allergy, Asthma, and Immunology. 50 N. Brockway, Suite 3.3, Palatine, IL 60067. Web site: <www.jcaai.org>.

WEB SITES

"Sinusitis." *National Institute of Allergy and Infectious Diseases*, April 2002. Available online at <www.niad.nih.gov/factsheets/sinusitis.htm> (accessed November 15, 2004).

Helen Davidson
Rosalyn Carson-DeWitt, MD

Skeletal development

Definition

Skeletal development refers to the development of the human skeletal system from the early days of pregnancy until the bones have reached full development in late **puberty**.

Description

The early development of the skeletal system begins in the third week after conception with the formation of the notochord (a rod-like structure along the back of the embryo that later becomes the spine, spinal cord, and brain), followed in the fourth week by the first signs of arms and legs. Between the fifth and eighth weeks, the limbs (first the arms, hands, and fingers, followed by the legs, feet, and toes) begin to extend and take on a definite shape.

By the end of the fifth week, the embryo has doubled in size and has grown a tail-like structure that becomes the coccyx (lowermost tip of the backbone). By the seventh week the embryo is about 2 cm (1 in) long and facial features are visible. At this stage, the 206 bones of the human body are all set down, in surprisingly adult form. However, the process of osteogenesis (development of bone) has not progressed to the point where the bones are "bony." Ossification (the process whereby tissue becomes bone) of most bony nuclei of the long bones and round bones does not complete until after birth.

The major types of human bones are:

- long (e.g. the arm and leg bones)
- short (e.g. the small bones in the wrists and ankles)
- flat (e.g. the bones of the skull or the ribs)
- irregular (e.g. vertebrae)

Long, short, and irregular bones develop by endochondral ossification, where cartilage is replaced by bone. Flat bones develop by intramembranous ossification, where bone develops within sheets of connective tissue. Compact cortical bone, representing about 80 percent of the mature skeleton, supports the body, and features extra thickness at the midpoint in long bones to prevent the bones from bending. Cancellous bone, whose porous structure with small cavities resembles sponge, predominates in the pelvis and the 33 vertebrae from the neck to the tailbone.

Bone growth is more complicated than simple elongation or simple enlargement. Most long bones add width on the outside by a process referred to as subperiosteal apposition (layers added to those already existing), while losing bone on the inside by endosteal resorption (breaking down and reabsorbing material at the center of a mass). At the same time, long bones gain in length by adding to the epiphyseal plate (the surface at the end of the bone). As they elongate, bones of this type go through a process called remodeling during which they change in outer shape as well. Conversely, the individual bones of the skull grow by circumferential apposition (adding layers at the circumference), while gaining in thickness by adding layers (apposition) at the surface with simultaneous resorption at the inner surface. By this process, the skull expands and becomes thicker while allowing for more brain space within.

Linear growth of the long bones occurs by a different process. At birth, long bones have more than one ossification center (regions from which bone growth starts). These grow during childhood until the ends of the bone (epiphyseal plates) become fused with the shaft of the bone (the diaphysis). This process is stimulated by the hormones produced by the testes and ovaries, which provide the developmental signal that the linear growth of the long bones should reach completion or full development. Both round and flat bones of the skeleton are capable of continued growth throughout life.

Ossification centers and their development

The many ossification centers of the body—hand, foot, knee, elbow, and pelvis, for example—are not visible by radiography (x rays) until they begin to mineralize or ossify, even though they are actually present long before such mineralization begins. The age at appearance of individual ossification centers then becomes a useful measure of skeletal development and especially in the form of "bone age" assessments of the hand, foot, or knee. Such assessments, made by taking a series of radiographs and comparing them against appropriate standards, are both highly reliable and useful estimates of the stage of physical development. Bone age assessments are, therefore, used in pediatric evaluation, especially when **malnutrition**, malabsorption, food intolerance, or endocrinopathies (such as hypopituitarism or **hypothyroidism**) are suspected. Bone age assessments also have forensic application, such as estimating the chronological age of a cadaver. In addition, they can provide data for making age assessments for children whose birth date in unknown or for whom a birth certificate does not exist or is suspected of being inaccurate. Families adopting infants or children from countries in which there has been socioeconomic stress may find bone age **assessment** helpful in establishing the chronological age their adopted child has attained.

The normal variability of skeletal age is about 10 percent of attained chronological age. Thus, some chronological 12-year-olds may be assessed as 14 years of age in terms of skeletal development, while others may be assessed as ten. Bone age is useful in projecting final stature; research has shown that it is more meaningful in making such projections than chronological age alone.

Factors affecting bone growth and remodeling

Girls mature earlier than boys, grow for a shorter time, and ultimately have shorter overall bone lengths by about 7 percent. Adolescent girls are, in general, shorter-legged than adolescent boys; this proportional difference is also reflected in the hand and foot skeletons as well. Thus, even at comparable stature, females are shorter-legged and shorter-handed than boys; in addition, girls' bones are more gracile (narrower) than boys and are, therefore, more affected by adult bone loss.

There are major genetically determined differences in relative growth rates of individual bones, in both length and width. Bone widths in general parallel differences in muscle mass and overall frame size. The sequence of ossification of the bones also differs significantly from child to child, and the different sequences are controlled by genetics. Differences in growth patterns even among siblings confirm this genetic component. There are also major population differences in skeletal proportions and bone sizes and ratios. Children and adults of African ancestry have relatively longer bones in their hands and feet; the same bones in children and adults of Japanese, Korean, and Chinese ancestry are relatively shorter.

Common problems

In some cases, abnormalities in skeletal development are caused by nutritional deficiencies that may or may not be reversible. Other disorders are congenital and caused by genetic abnormalities. Steroids used for chronic inflammatory illnesses can lead to thinning of bone in adults (osteoporosis) and to slower bone growth in long bones and therefore shorter status in children.

Problems relating to nutritional status

During childhood, bones are growing rapidly. Bone growth is fueled by a positive energy balance, created by a well-balanced diet and healthy living environment. Even in circumstances of severe malnutrition, there may be some formation of new bone; it will, however, occur while bone formed earlier is deteriorating. During protein malnutrition, bone growth is largely halted, and existing bone is cannibalized by the body as a source of protein. Bone growth may also be limited by **vitamin D deficiency**, resulting in a condition called rickets (osteomalacia), which leads to soft and/or deformed bones and is caused by an inability to absorb calcium due to lack of vitamin D. Treatment and prevention involves sun exposure and vitamin D supplementation.

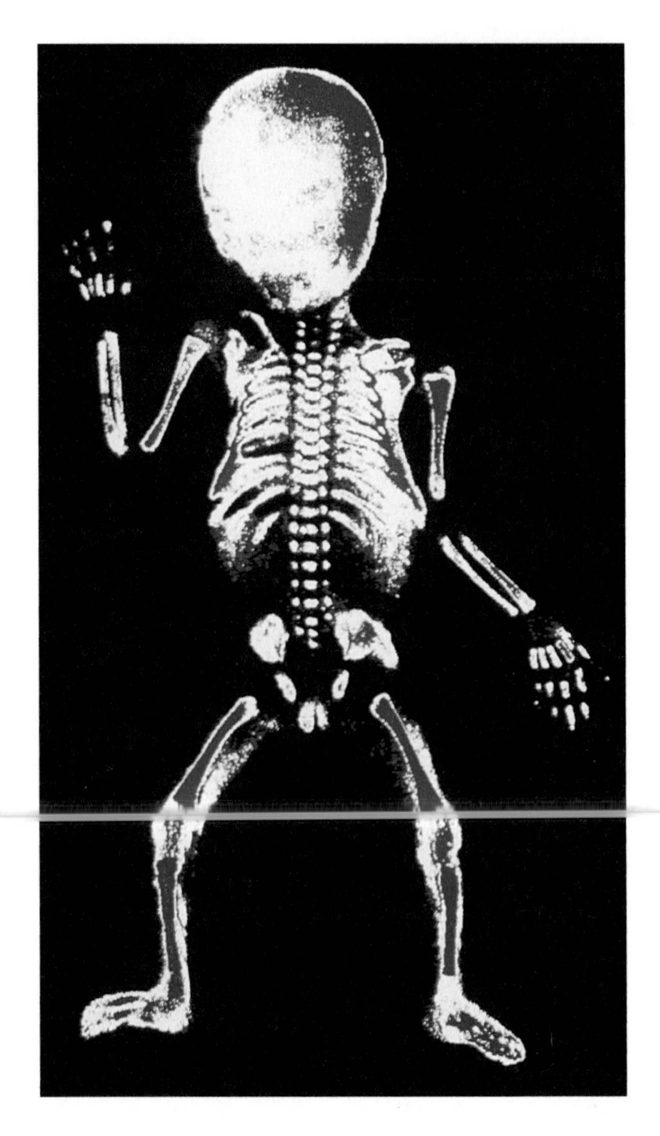

X ray showing the skeleton of a newborn. Gaps between bones indicate cartilage, which will develop into bone tissue as the child ages. *(© Howard Sochurek/Corbis.)*

With growing concern about adult osteoporosis, it is important to realize that the mass of skeleton built during childhood and into early adulthood constitutes bone banked against inevitable later withdrawals. For this reason there is much interest in the proposition that a calcium intake over 1,500 mg per day may build a greater skeletal mass. This proposition, however, in the early 2000s favored in the United States, is met with great skepticism in the United Kingdom. Moreover, calcium intakes during childhood are far greater in the United States than in most countries, but there is no particular evidence that the adult North American skeleton has a greater bone density (bone mass divided by bone volume).

Bone growth, bone remodeling, and the timing of skeletal maturation are all profoundly affected by nutritional status throughout the growing period. In bone remodeling, complex chemical signals prompt cells called osteoclasts to break down and remove (resorb) old bone, and others called osteoblasts to deposit new bone. Many elements influence bone remodeling, including whether the bone is weight-bearing, vitamin D intake, growth factors, and production of various hormones, including estrogen, thyroid, parathyroid, and calcitonin. Thus, poorly nourished boys and girls may be delayed in linear bone growth, diminished in all bone widths, later in the appearance of ossification centers, and delayed in epiphyseal union (completion of long-bone growth). Children living in poverty worldwide may exhibit evidence of smaller amounts of incremental growth of all long bones and vertebrae, and delay in epiphyseal union. By contrast, obese boys and girls evidence greater

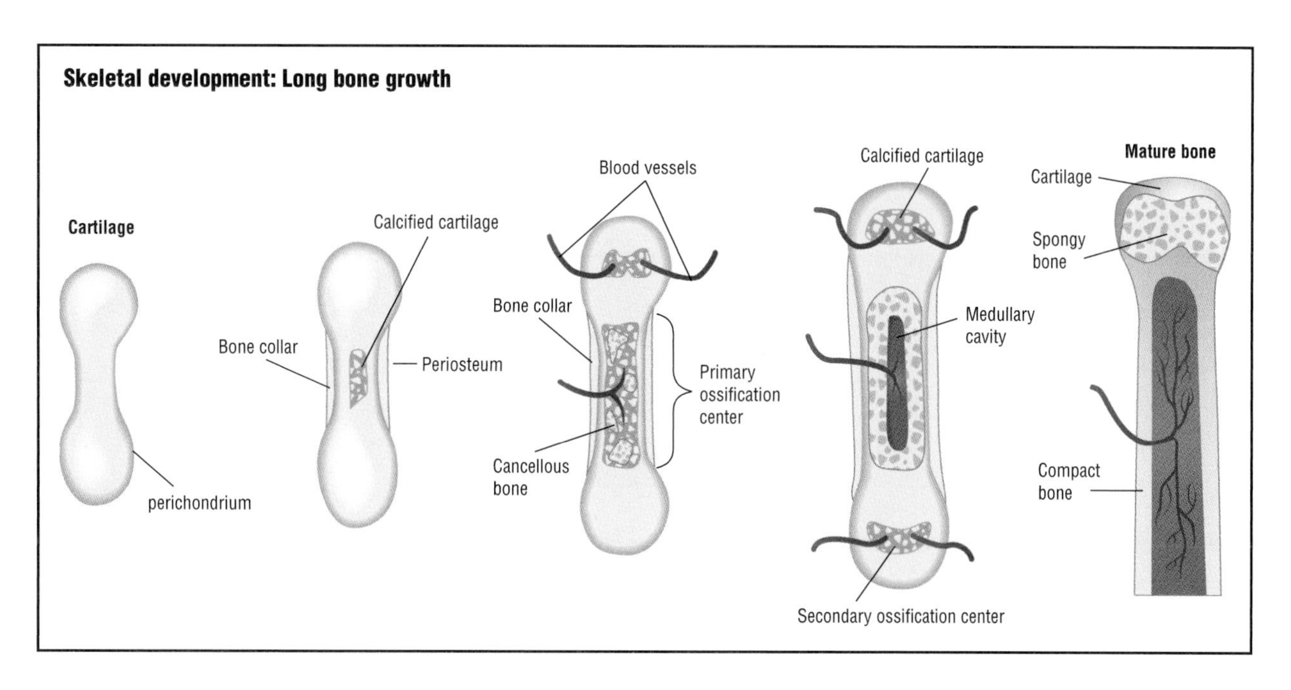

Illustration depicting the stages of long bone growth, showing the process of cartilage calcifying and becoming mature, compact bone. *(Illustration by GGS Information Services.)*

growth in bone lengths and widths, earlier appearance of ossification centers, and earlier completion of epiphyseal union. In other words, obese children grow more, though for a shorter time period, because of their elevated caloric and nutrient intake.

Bone growth is not only affected by simple caloric malnutrition due to inadequate food intake, but also if there is protein deficiency (protein-calorie malnutrition or Kwasiorkor). In protein-calorie malnutrition, lower rates of bone formation may be exceeded by higher rates of bone loss. Thus children and adolescents with protein-calorie malnutrition may show a marked thinning of the outer walls of tubular bones, and an increased incidence of bone **fractures** as a result. Excessive bone loss in protein-calorie malnutrition is also common in juvenile and adolescent cases of **anorexia nervosa**. Individuals with this condition show diminished bone density (bone mass/bone width). There is some evidence that high levels of sodium in the diet of girls ages eight to 13 can significantly increase calcium lost. This effect is particularly powerful in girls whose calcium intake is less than the recommended 1,500 mg—the amount in five glasses of milk—per day.

Congenital skeletal disorders

In some cases, skeletal abnormalities are inherited from one or both parents or occur as a result of genetic mutation. Examples of different congenital disorders of the skeletal system include:

- Achondroplasia: This form of **dwarfism** is characterized by short stature, abnormal body proportion (limbs are shorter than normal while the torso remains of average size), and facial deformities. As a genetic disease, there is no cure. Adult height is generally less than 1.2 m (4 ft).
- Giantism: This condition is characterized by excessive bone growth and is caused by too much growth hormone being produced before puberty (hyperpituitarism). Giantism is treated by inhibiting the production of pituitary hormones.
- Hypopituitarism: Caused by insufficient production of growth hormone, this condition leads to growth failure and delayed skeletal maturation. It can be treated (if diagnosed at an early enough age) with hormone replacement therapy. Hypopituitarism can also be caused by damage to the pituitary gland.
- Osteogenesis imperfecta: Also called brittle bone disease, this condition is characterized by fragile bones that are prone to fracturing. It is a genetic condition that cannot be cured; treatment may involve restricting activity to minimize stress on bones and joints.
- Osteopetrosis: The congenital form of osteopetrosis is rare and involves the formation of overly dense but fragile bones that can lead to frequent fractures, blindness, deafness, and strokes. The more severe form of congenital osteopetrosis is usually fatal within the first ten years of life unless successfully treated with a bone marrow transplant.

KEY TERMS

Cartilage—A tough, elastic connective tissue found in the joints, outer ear, nose, larynx, and other parts of the body.

Endochondral ossification—The process by which cartilage is converted into bone.

Endosteal resorption—The process by which bones are thinned from the inside.

Intramembranous ossification—The process by which bone tissue is formed within sheets of connective tissue.

Osteoporosis—Literally meaning "porous bones," this condition occurs when bones lose an excessive amount of their protein and mineral content, particularly calcium. Over time, bone mass and strength are reduced leading to increased risk of fractures.

Subperiosteal apposition—The process by which bones are made thicker from the outside.

Parental concerns

The question of long-bone growth and completion is of particular concern to parents of children whose growth falls at the outside edges of the normal range. In some cases long-bone growth may be accelerated by growth hormone administration if given by age nine, without speeding the timing of completion of long-bone growth. By encouraging the development of the three key elements of self esteem—acceptance, competence, and purpose—parents can help a child with skeletal abnormalities develop positive body image and confidence in his or her abilities.

When to call the doctor

A healthcare provider should be contacted if a child exhibits symptoms of skeletal or growth abnormalities, such as abnormally short or tall height for age, frequent bone fractures, bony growths, or bone or joint **pain**.

Resources

BOOKS

Brinker, Mark R. "Bone." In *DeLee and Drez's Orthopaedic Sports Medicine*, 2nd ed. Edited by Jesse C. DeLee and David Drez, Jr.. Philadelphia: Saunders, 2003.

Horton, William A., and Jacqueline T. Hecht. "The Skeletal Dysplasias." In *Nelson Textbook of Pediatrics*, 17th ed. Edited by Richard E. Behrman, Robert M. Kliegman, and Hal B. Jenson. Philadelphia: Saunders, 2004.

PERIODICALS

Root, Allen W. "Bone Strength and the Adolescent." *Adolescent Medicine* 13, no. 1 (February 2002): 53-72.

ORGANIZATIONS

American Academy of Orthopaedic Surgeons. 6300 North River Rd., Rosemont, IL 60018–4262. Web site: <www.aaos.org>.

WEB SITES

"Bone Development and Growth." *Surveillance, Epidemiology, and Ed Results Program, National Cancer Institute*, 2000. Available online at <http://training.seer.cancer.gov/module_anatomy/unit3_3_bone_growth.html> (accessed January 17, 2005).

Ho, Wayne, and Steven Dowshen. "Bones, Muscles, and Joints: The Musculoskeletal System." *KidsHealth*, April 2004. Available online at <http://kidshealth.org/teen/your_body/body_basics/bones_muscles_joints_p3.html> (accessed January 17, 2005).

Stephanie Dionne Sherk

Skin allergy test *see* **Allergy tests**

Skin rash *see* **Rashes**

Skin tag *see* **Polydactyly and syndactyly**

Sleep

Definition

Sleep is a biological imperative critical to the maintenance of mental and physical health. It is a state of lessened consciousness and decreased physical activity during which the organism slows down and repairs itself. The sleep cycle involves two distinct phases that alternate cyclically from light sleep to deep then deeper and deepest sleep throughout the sleep period. There are two main phases of sleep.

- rapid eye movement (REM) sleep, during which dreaming occurs
- non-rapid eye movement (NREM) or slow-wave sleep (SWS)

Description

The timing and progression of the sleep cycle and the total amount of nightly sleep required for optimal health varies from infancy to adulthood, depending on developmental stage and **temperament**. Children, particularly infants, require the most sleep during a 24-hour period. The natural sleep-wake cycle, governed by an internal "biological clock," tends toward a 25-hour day. It is affected by the relative balance of light and darkness in the environment. As darkness approaches, the hormone melatonin is secreted by the pineal gland and signals the brain that it is time to sleep.

NREM deep sleep

Sleep begins in stage one of the sleep phase known as NREM, or non-rapid eye movement, sleep. NREM sleep has four stages: light sleep, deeper sleep, and two stages of deepest sleep. Stage one is the "drifting off" period of light sleep in the transition between wakefulness and sleep and comprises about 5 percent of the entire sleep period. Stage two sleep involves a change in brain-wave patterns and increased resistance to arousal and accounts for 45–55 percent of total sleep time. Stages three and four are the deepest levels of sleep and occur only in the first third of the sleep period. NREM stage four sleep usually takes up 12 to 15 percent of total sleep time. Sleep terrors, sleep walking, and bedwetting episodes generally occur within stage four sleep or during partial arousals from this sleep stage.

It typically takes about 90 minutes to cycle through the four deepening stages of NREM sleep before onset of the second phase of sleep known as REM or dream sleep.

REM dream sleep

Rapid eye movement (REM) sleep is qualitatively different from NREM sleep. REM sleep is characterized by extensive central nervous system (CNS) activity with an increase in brain metabolism accompanied by the vivid imagery of dreams. During REM sleep the body is nearly paralyzed, a condition called "atonic," that serves to inhibit the dreamer from physical movement during active dreaming.

"Waking and dreaming are two states of consciousness, with differences that depend on chemistry," according to J. Allan Hobson, professor of psychiatry at Harvard Medical School. Physical activity and thought are suppressed in sleep, but the brain nonetheless remains active "processing information, consolidating and revising memory, and learning newly acquired skills." The brain self-activates, radically changing its chemical climate from wakefulness to sleep states.

REM sleep is also known as "paradoxical sleep" because muscle activity is suppressed even as the CNS registers intense brain activity and spontaneous rapid eye movements can be observed. Brain-wave monitoring of REM sleep with an electroencephalograph (EEG) reveals a low-voltage, fast-frequency, non-alpha wave record. Beyond infancy, REM sleep comprises 20–25 percent of the entire sleep period. This sleep phase is concerned with memory and the consolidation of new information.

Infancy

Newborn infants usually sleep for brief periods at a time around the clock, with the total of day and nighttime sleep roughly equal. A newborn's total sleep need is from 16 to 18 hours in every 24-hour period. Newborns spend approximately 50 percent of their sleep period in the REM phase. Infants are most easily awakened during this phase of sleep that is accompanied by yawning, squirming, and quiet vocalizations.

Infants move through REM and non-REM sleep stages in a 90 minute cycle, and they rise to a near-waking state every three to four hours, more often in breastfed infants. By about six months of age, babies usually will sleep through the night for 12 or more hours and will continue to nap several times throughout the day.

Researchers conducting a 2004 survey for the National Sleep Foundation discovered that children in every age group fail to meet even the low-end requirements for adequate sleep. By the third month of life, a child's sleep requirement is about 14 to 15 out of every 24 hours, a need that continues until about 11 months of age. However, research indicates that children age three months to 11 months sleep only 12.7 hours on average.

Toddlerhood

Toddlers are far more physically active than infants, and their sleeping behavior and the timing of sleep cycles reflects their maturing brains. A toddler will spend only about 30 percent of her sleep time in REM dream sleep. Toddlers on average require 12 to 14 hours of sleep and may no longer need an afternoon nap to meet this sleep requirement. But research shows that children in the one to three-year-old range may actually average only about 11.7 hours of sleep.

Preschool

Children in this age group tend to be more troubled with **nightmares** and **night terrors** than younger children. They may resist going to bed at night because of **fear** of the dark or of some monster lurking under the bed. Parental reassurance and comfort and the addition of a night light may alleviate some of these concerns.

Preschool children may also feel anxiety around the issue of **toilet training** and bedwetting.

School age

School-age children require from eight to 10 hours of sleep nightly. Adequate sleep is especially important as school children's lives become busier and stress levels rise. Sleep disruptions such as nightmares tend to increase with this age group as the child has more life experiences and anxieties to process. Parents should also monitor the child's use of caffeinated beverages which can cause sleep difficulties and add to the overall loss of adequate sleep.

Adolescents require at least 10 hours of nightly sleep. This is a busy time when many teens' lifestyles include school, work, **sports**, and other **extracurricular activities**, as well as socializing with peers. This increase in activity, together with early-morning school schedules, leaves little time for adequate sleep. Various psychological disorders also may trouble the adolescent, particularly anxiety and depression. Parents should pay attention to a young teen who shows sudden changes in eating habits, loss of interest in usual activities, and other behavioral clues that may indicate onset of depression.

Common problems

According to the "2004 Sleep in America Poll" published by the National Sleep Foundation, 69 percent of children younger than age 10 experience problems with sleep that may occur as often as several times a week. Sleep disruptions in children are usually a normal symptom of central nervous system development. In older children sleep disruptions may increase and intensify due to external stressors in the home or school environment. Sleep difficulties can also be a sign of physical or mental health problems. They are often present in children with attention-deficit/hyperactivity disorder (AD/HD) and in children who have experienced physical, psychological, or sexual abuse.

Childhood sleep problems and parasomnias include:

- Bedwetting: A common sleep problem characterized by involuntary urination during sleep. This is a routine occurrence in children up to five years of age. Bedwetting is also called "nocturnal enuresis."
- Nightmares: A common parasomnia characterized by dreams with frightening psychological content, a feeling of imminent physical danger, and a sensation of being trapped or suffocated. Nightmares occur during REM, or dream-time, sleep and trigger a partial or full awakening. The word "mare" in Old English means "demon."
- Insomnia: Difficulty falling asleep and remaining asleep, or early-morning awakenings. Insomnia may be short-term, due to stress or physical or psychological problems, or may be due to the lack of a healthy bedtime routine.
- Night terrors: A common childhood sleep disruption characterized by an abrupt arousal from stage 4 sleep within the first hour of the sleep period. The child may sit bolt upright in acute terror, screaming inconsolably. Night terrors are a confusional arousal resulting from immature sleep patterns with an intense activation of the flight or fight emotion. They occur in the deepest stage of slow-wave non-REM sleep. Night terrors are also called "pavor nocturnus."
- Sleep apnea: A serious and potentially life-threatening sleep disruption characterized by brief interruptions of airflow during sleep and frequent partial arousals throughout the night. Sleep apnea is less common than other sleep disturbances, occurring in about 2 percent of children.
- Sleep bruxism: A sleep disturbance characterized by grinding the teeth or clenching of the jaws during sleep. Sleep bruxism is common among children of all ages. This sleep problem usually subsides over time.
- Sleep rocking and head banging: A sleep disturbance characterized by rhythmical movements of the body during sleep. Rhythmical movements may be observed in children as young as six months. More dramatic movements, involving head banging and rocking, occur in as many as 60 percent of nine-month-old children. These sleep disturbances tend to decrease with age, appearing in only about 5 percent of children over two years of age.
- Sleep walking: A sleep disturbance characterized by a partial-arousal involving walking about for a few steps, or for much longer distances, with a glassy, trance-like appearance to the eyes. Sleepwalking occurs in the deepest stages of slow-wave, non-REM sleep within the first few hours of sleep onset. Researchers have found that as many as 15–30 percent of children experience at least one sleepwalking episode. Sleepwalking can be triggered by external stimuli, such as an abrupt noise, or by moving a sleeping child to a standing position. This sleep disturbance tends to run in families. Sleepwalking is also called "somnambulism."

Losing sleep

All children need regular and adequate sleep to assure optimal mental and physical health. Sleeping patterns developed in infancy usually persist into adulthood. It is important that parents help the child to establish a healthy bedtime routine that will assure adequate sleep time, minimize bedtime struggles, and help to reduce the occurrence of common childhood sleep problems.

As reported by Steven Reinberg, research by Maria M. Wong of the University of Michigan, published in 2004 in the journal *Alcoholism: Clinical and Experimental Research,* cautions parents to pay more attention to their children's sleep habits. "Sleep problems are a risk factor for alcohol and drug problems," Wong concluded from data obtained in the first study to link alcohol and drug use with **sleep disorders** in early childhood. The study obtained sleep data from 257 boys ages three to five years and followed them until they were 12–14 years old. Almost half of the children in the study who experienced childhood sleep problems began using alcohol and drugs by the time they were 14 years old.

In many households, electronic distractions interfere with the establishment of a regular bedtime routine that would help a child to settle down and prepare for restful sleep. Calming-down activities, such as being read to by a parent, have been replaced with electronic stimulation resulting in less sleep time.

As reported in *Manchester Online*, Luci Wiggs, a research fellow at Oxford University, is co-author of a 2004 poll of more than 1,000 parents with children four to 10 years of age. She found that 67 percent of these children had a television, computer, or game machine in their bedroom. These stimulating diversions, which she calls "digital distractions," resulted in a cumulative sleep deficit for at least one fifth of the children surveyed that may "compromise children's physical health, academic achievements, and mental health."

Children who consume **caffeine** throughout the day, in soda or iced tea beverages, also lose the sleep required for optimal health and cognitive functioning. A survey by the National Sleep Foundation released in 2004 found that 26 percent of children ages three and older drink at least one caffeinated beverage a day and suffer a loss of about 3.5 hours of sleep each week.

Parental concerns

Parents are on a journey of discovery with each child whose temperament, biology, and sleep habits result in a unique sleep-wake pattern. It can be frustrating when children's sleep habits do not conform to the household schedule. Helping the child develop good sleep habits in childhood takes time and parental attention, but it will have beneficial results throughout life. An understanding of the changing patterns of the typical sleep-wake cycle in children will help alleviate any unfounded concerns. Maintaining a sleep diary for each child will provide the parent with baseline information in assessing the nature and severity of childhood sleep problems. Observant parents will come to recognize unusual sleep disruptions or those that persist or intensify.

When to call the doctor

Developmental changes throughout childhood bring differences in the sleep-wake cycle and in the type and frequency of parasomnias that may interrupt sleep. Medical consultation to rule out illness, infection, or injury is prudent if the child's sleep problems prevent adequate sleep and result in an ongoing sleep deficit. As reported by *News-Medical in Child Health News*, children's sleep problems should be taken seriously as they may be a "'marker' for predicting later risk of early adolescent substance use." In the same article, University of Michigan psychiatry professor Kirk Brower, who has studied "the interplay of alcohol and sleep in adults," stressed that "The finding does not mean there's a cause-and-effect relationship."

Consultation with a child psychologist may be helpful if frightening dreams intensify and become more frequent as this may indicate a particular problem or life circumstance that needs to be changed or one that the child may need extra help working through.

Most childhood sleep disturbances will diminish over time as the brain matures and a regular sleep-wake cycle is established. Parental guidance is crucial to development of healthy sleep habits in children.

Resources

BOOKS

Hobson, J. Allan. *Dreaming: An Introduction to the Science of Sleep*. Oxford: Oxford University Press, 2002.

Moorcroft, William H. *Understanding Sleep and Dreaming*. New York: Kluwer Academic/Plenum Publishers, 2003.

Schroeder, Carolyn S., and Betty N. Gordon. *Assessment and Treatment of Childhood Problems*, 2nd ed. New York: Guildford Press, 2002.

PERIODICALS

"Kids' Sleep Problems Can Portend Alcohol and Drug Use." *Connecticut Post*, April 15, 2004. Available online at <www.lexis-nexis.com> (accessed October 6, 2004).

Moss, Lyndsay. "Computers and Games 'Keeping Children Awake.'" *Press Association News*, March 26, 2004. Available online at <lexis-nexis.com> (accessed August 3, 2004).

Wilmott, Bob. "Many Children Fall Short of the Sleep They Need." *St. Louis Post-Dispatch*, April 26, 2004. Available

KEY TERMS

Biological clock—A synonym for the body's circadian rhythm, the natural biological variations that occur over the course of a day.

Parasomnia—A type of sleep disorder characterized by abnormal changes in behavior or body functions during sleep, specific stages of sleep, or the transition from sleeping to waking.

Suprachiasmatic nuclei (SCN)—SCN is that part of the brain that functions as a person's "biological clock" to regulate many body rhythms. The SCN is located on top of the main junction of nerve fibers that connects to the eyes.

online at <www.lexis-nexis.com> (accessed August 3, 2004).

ORGANIZATIONS

American Sleep Disorders Association. 1610 14th Street, NW, Suite 300, Rochester, MN 55901–2201. Web site: <www.sleepnet.com/asda.htm>.

National Sleep Foundation. 1522 K Street, NW, Suite 500, Washington, DC, 20005. Web site: <www.livingwithillness.com/id174.htm>.

WEB SITES

"Children kept awake by computers and games." *Manchester Online*, March 26, 2004. Available online at <wwwmanchesteronline.co.uk/business/technology/s/85/85453_children_kept_awake_by_computers_and_games.html> (accessed October 7, 2004).

"Children's Bedtime Routines: Sound Sleeping Advice." *Mayo Foundation for Medical Education and Research*, September 23, 2003. Available online at <www.mayoclinic.com/invoke.cfm?id=CC00020.> (accessed July 23, 2004).

"Computers 'rob children of sleep.'" *BBC News*. Available online at <newsvote.bbc.co.uk/mpapps/pagetools/print/news.bbc.co.uk/1/hi/health/3568963.stm> (accessed August 4, 2004).

Driver, Helen. "Parasomnias." *Canadian Sleep Society*. Available online at <www.css.to/sleep/disorders/parasomnia.htm> (accessed July 29, 2004).

Reinberg, Steven. "Kids' Sleep Problems Can Portend Alcohol and Drug Use." *Healthfinder News*. Available online at <www.healthfinder.gov/news/newsstory.asp?docID=518390> (accessed October 7, 2004).

"Sleep Behavior Problems (Parasomnias)." *Kids Health for Parents*. Available online at <www.kidshealth.org/parent/general/sleep/parasomnia.html> (accessed July 26, 2004).

"Sound sleep in infants lessens likelihood of drug abuse in later years." *News-Medical in Child Health News*, April 16, 2004. Available online at <www.news-medical.net/print_article.asp?id=545> (accessed October 7, 2004).

"Tips for Healthy Sleep." *American Sleep Disorders Association*. Available online at <www.slepnet.com/> (accessed August 4, 2004).

Clare Hanrahan

Sleep apnea, infant *see* **Apnea of infancy**

Sleep disorders

Definition

Sleep disorders are a group of syndromes characterized by disturbance in the individual's amount of sleep, quality or timing of sleep, or in behaviors or physiological conditions associated with sleep.

Description

Although sleep is a basic behavior in animals as well as humans, researchers still do not completely understand all of its functions in maintaining health. Since 1975, however, laboratory studies on human volunteers have yielded information about the different types of sleep. Researchers have learned about the cyclical patterns of different types of sleep and their relationships to breathing, heart rate, brain waves, and other physical functions. These measurements are obtained by a technique called polysomnography. There are about 70 different sleep disorders. To qualify for the diagnosis of sleep disorder, the condition must be a persistent problem, cause the patient significant emotional distress, and interfere with his or her social, academic, or occupational functioning.

There are five stages of human sleep. Four stages have non-rapid eye movement (NREM) sleep, with unique brain wave patterns and physical changes occurring. Dreaming occurs in the fifth stage, during rapid eye movement (REM) sleep.

- Stage one NREM sleep. This stage occurs while a child is falling asleep. It represents about 5 percent of sleep time.

- Stage two NREM sleep. In this stage, (the beginning of "true" sleep), the child's **electroencephalogram** (EEG) will show distinctive waveforms called sleep spindles and K complexes. About 50 percent of sleep time is stage two NREM sleep.
- Stages three and four NREM sleep. Also called delta or slow wave sleep, these are the deepest levels of human sleep and represent 10 to 20 percent of sleep time. They usually occur during the first 30 to 50 percent of the sleeping period.
- REM sleep. REM sleep accounts for 20 to 25 percent of total sleep time. It usually begins about 90 minutes after the child falls asleep. It alternates with NREM sleep about every hour and a half throughout the night. REM periods increase in length over the course of the night.

Sleep cycles vary with a person's age. Children and adolescents have longer periods of stage three and stage four NREM sleep than do middle aged or elderly adults. Because of this difference, the doctor needs to consider the individual's age when evaluating a sleep disorder. Total REM sleep also declines with age.

The average length of nighttime sleep varies among individuals. Most people sleep between seven and nine hours a night. This population average appears to be constant throughout the world. In temperate climates, however, people often notice that sleep time varies with the seasons. It is not unusual for people in North America and Europe to sleep about 40 minutes longer per night during the winter. Infants can regularly sleep up to 16 hours a day. The total amount of sleep declines as the infant gets older. Teenagers may actually need more sleep than slightly younger children and often sleep nine or more hours a day.

Sleep disorders are classified based on what causes them. Primary sleep disorders are distinguished as those that are not caused by other mental disorders, prescription medications, substance abuse, or medical conditions. The two major categories of primary sleep disorders are the dyssomnias and the parasomnias.

Dyssomnias

Dyssomnias are primary sleep disorders in which the patient suffers from changes in the amount, restfulness, and timing of sleep. The most important dyssomnia is primary insomnia, which is defined as difficulty that lasts for at least one month in falling asleep or remaining asleep. Primary insomnia can be caused by many things, including a traumatic event related to sleep or bedtime, and it is often associated with increased physical or psychological arousal at night. Children who experience primary insomnia may develop **anxiety** related to not being able to sleep. The child may come to associate all sleep-related things (their bed, bedtime, etc.) with frustration, making the problem worse. The child may then becomes more stressed about not sleeping.

Hypersomnia is a condition marked by excessive sleepiness during normal waking hours. The individual has either lengthy episodes of daytime sleep or episodes of daytime sleep on a daily basis even though he or she is sleeping normally at night. In some cases, people with primary hypersomnia have difficulty waking in the morning and may appear confused or angry. This condition is sometimes called sleep drunkenness and is more common in males.

The number of people with primary hypersomnia is unknown, although 5 to 10 percent of patients in sleep disorder clinics have the disorder. Primary hypersomnia usually affects young adults between the ages of 15 and 30.

Kleine-Levin syndrome is a recurrent form of hypersomnia that usually starts in late teen years. Doctors do not know the cause of this syndrome. It is marked by excessive drowsiness and for short spells, maybe two to three days, the person sleeps 18 to 20 hours per day, overeats, and is highly irritable. Males are three or four times more likely than females to have the syndrome.

PARASOMNIAS Parasomnias are primary sleep disorders in which the individual's behavior is affected by specific sleep stages or transitions between sleeping and waking. They are sometimes described as disorders of physiological arousal during sleep.

Nightmare disorder is a parasomnia in which the child is repeatedly awakened from sleep by frightening dreams and is fully alert on awakening. The actual rate of occurrence of nightmare disorder is unknown. Approximately 10 to 50 percent of children between three and five years old have **nightmares**, as do many older children. The nightmares occur during REM sleep, usually in the second half of the night. The child is usually able to remember the content of the nightmare and may be afraid to go back to sleep. More females than males have this disorder, but it is not known whether the sex difference reflects a difference in occurrence or a difference in reporting. Nightmare disorder is most likely to occur in children under severe or traumatic stress.

Sleep terror disorder is a parasomnia in which the child awakens screaming or crying. The child also has physical signs of arousal, like sweating and shaking. Sleep terror is sometimes referred to as pavor nocturnus. Unlike nightmares, sleep terrors typically occur in stage three or stage four NREM sleep during the first third of the night. The child may be confused or disoriented for several minutes and cannot recall the content of the dream. He or she may fall asleep again and not remember the episode the next morning. Sleep terror disorder is most common in children four to 12 years old and is usually outgrown in **adolescence**. It affects about 3 percent of children. In children, more males than females have the disorder.

Sleepwalking disorder, which is sometimes called **somnambulism**, occurs when the child is capable of complex movements during sleep, including walking. Like sleep terror disorder, sleepwalking occurs during stage three and stage four NREM sleep during the first part of the night. If the child is awakened during a sleepwalking episode, he or she may be disoriented and have no memory of the behavior. In addition to walking around, individuals with sleepwalking disorder have been reported to eat, use the bathroom, unlock doors, or talk to others. It is estimated that 10 to 30 percent of children have at least one episode of sleepwalking. However, only 1 to 5 percent meet the criteria for sleepwalking disorder. The disorder is most common in children eight to 12 years old.

Demographics

In the United States, 20 to 25 percent of children have some kind of sleep problem. Nightmares are believed to occur in about 30 percent of children, usually in younger children. Sleepwalking occurs more than once in about 25 to 30 percent of children. The most common age group to experience sleepwalking is children under 10. Insomnia is reported to occur in approximately 23 percent of children. Many other sleep disorders occur less frequently but are still a problem for many children.

Causes and symptoms

The causes of sleep disorders vary depending on the disorder. Many times, stress, anxiety, or other factors are found to be the cause. Often the underlying cause of the sleep disorder is never found.

The most important symptoms of sleep disorders are insomnia and sleepiness during waking hours. Insomnia is by far the more common of the two symptoms. It covers a number of different patterns of sleep disturbance. These patterns include inability to fall asleep at bedtime, repeated awakening during the night, and/or inability to go back to sleep once awakened.

When to call the doctor

If a child does not seem to be getting enough sleep at night or the child wakes frequently or seems tired frequently during the day, it may be helpful to consult a doctor.

Diagnosis

Diagnosis of sleep disorders usually requires a psychological history as well as a medical history. Physical examinations are not usually revealing. The patient's sex and age are useful starting points in assessing the problem. The doctor may also talk to other **family** members in order to obtain information about the patient's symptoms. The family's observations are particularly important for evaluating sleepwalking, kicking in bed, snoring loudly, or other behaviors that the patient cannot remember.

Psychological testing

The doctor may use **psychological tests** or inventories to evaluate insomnia because it is frequently associated with mood or affective disorders. The **Minnesota Multiphasic Personality Inventory** (MMPI), the Millon Clinical Multiaxial Inventory (MCMI), the Beck Depression Inventory, and the Zung Depression Scale are the tests most commonly used in evaluating this symptom.

Laboratory studies

If the doctor is considering breathing-related sleep disorders, myoclonus, or **narcolepsy** as possible diagnoses, he or she may ask the patient to be tested in a sleep laboratory or at home with portable instruments.

POLYSOMNOGRAPHY Polysomnography can be used to help diagnose sleep disorders as well as conduct research into sleep. In some cases the patient is tested in a special sleep laboratory. The advantage of this testing is the availability and expertise of trained technologists, but it is expensive. Since 2001, however, portable equipment is available for home recording of certain specific physiological functions.

MULTIPLE SLEEP LATENCY TEST (MSLT) The multiple sleep latency test (MSLT) is frequently used to measure the severity of the patient's daytime sleepiness. The test measures sleep latency (the speed with which the patient falls asleep) during a series of planned naps during the day. The test also measures the amount of REM sleep that occurs. Two or more episodes of REM sleep under these conditions indicates narcolepsy. This test can also be used to help diagnose primary hypersomnia.

REPEATED TEST OF SUSTAINED WAKEFULNESS (RTSW) The repeated test of sustained wakefulness (RTSW) measures sleep latency by challenging the patient's ability to stay awake. In the RTSW, the patient is placed in a quiet room with dim lighting and is asked to stay awake. As with the MSLT, the testing pattern is repeated at intervals during the day.

Treatment

Treatment for a sleep disorder depends on what is causing the disorder. For example, if major depression is the cause of insomnia, then treatment of the depression with **antidepressants** or psychological counseling should resolve the insomnia. The use of antidepressants in minors is a matter of debate. In October 2003, the United States Food and Drug Administration issued an advisory indicating that children being treated with selective serotonin re-uptake inhibitor antidepressants (SSRIs) for major depressive illness may be at higher risk for committing **suicide**. A similar warning was issued in the United Kingdom. Parents and physicians must weigh the benefits and risks of prescribing these medications for children on an individual basis.

Medications

Medications for sleep disorders are generally not recommended for use by children. In most cases medications are the treatment of last resort. If children with sleep terror disorder or sleepwalking are treated with medication, then they may be given benzodiazepines because this type of medication suppresses stage three and stage four NREM sleep.

Psychotherapy

Psychotherapy is recommended for patients with sleep disorders associated with other mental disorders. In many cases the patient's scores on the Beck or Zung inventories will suggest the appropriate direction of treatment.

Sleep preparation

Children with sleep disorders such as insomnia may benefit from a regular pattern of pre-bedtime rituals designed to help the child relax and prepare for bed. Fluid intake should usually be limited in the hours before bed to reduce the need to get out of bed and use the toilet. Children should generally not be given **caffeine** in the evening, as it may make it harder for them to fall asleep. Children with nightmare disorder may benefit from limits on television or movies. Violent scenes or frightening science fiction stories appear to influence the frequency and intensity of children's nightmares.

Alternative treatment

Some alternative approaches may be effective in treating insomnia caused by anxiety or emotional stress. For some people, meditation practice, breathing exercises, and **yoga** can break the vicious cycle of sleeplessness, worry about inability to sleep, and further sleeplessness. Yoga can help some people to relax muscular tension in a direct fashion. The breathing exercises and meditation can keep some patients from obsessing about sleep.

Homeopathic practitioners recommend that people with chronic insomnia see a professional homeopath. They do, however, prescribe specific remedies for at-home treatment of temporary insomnia: *Nux vomica* for alcohol or substance-related insomnia, *Ignatia* for insomnia caused by grief, *Arsenicum* for insomnia caused by **fear** or anxiety, and *Passiflora* for insomnia related to mental stress.

Melatonin has also been used as an alternative treatment for sleep disorders. Melatonin is produced in the body by the pineal gland at the base of the brain. This substance is thought to be related to the body's circadian rhythms.

Practitioners of traditional Chinese medicine usually treat insomnia as a symptom of excess yang energy. Cinnabar is recommended for chronic nightmares. Either magnetic magnetite or "dragon bones" is recommended for insomnia associated with hysteria or fear. If the insomnia appears to be associated with excess yang energy arising from the liver, the practitioner will give the patient oyster shells. Acupuncture treatments can help bring about balance and facilitate sleep.

Dietary changes such as eliminating stimulant foods (coffee, cola, chocolate) and late-night meals or snacks can be effective in treating some sleep disorders. Nutritional supplementation with magnesium, as well as botanical medicines that calm the nervous system, can also be helpful. Among the botanical remedies that may be effective for sleep disorders are valerian (*Valeriana officinalis*), passionflower (*Passiflora incarnata*), and skullcap (*Scutellaria lateriflora*).

Prognosis

The prognosis depends on the specific disorder. Children usually outgrow sleep disorders. Patients with Kleine-Levin syndrome usually get better around age 40. The prognosis for sleep disorders related to many other

KEY TERMS

Apnea—The temporary absence of breathing. Sleep apnea consists of repeated episodes of temporary suspension of breathing during sleep.

Cataplexy—A symptom of narcolepsy in which there is a sudden episode of muscle weakness triggered by emotions. The muscle weakness may cause the person's knees to buckle, or the head to drop. In severe cases, the patient may become paralyzed for a few seconds to minutes.

Circadian rhythm—Any body rhythm that recurs in 24-hour cycles. The sleep-wake cycle is an example of a circadian rhythm.

Dyssomnia—A primary sleep disorder in which the patient suffers from changes in the quantity, quality, or timing of sleep.

Electroencephalogram (EEG)—A record of the tiny electrical impulses produced by the brain's activity picked up by electrodes placed on the scalp. By measuring characteristic wave patterns, the EEG can help diagnose certain conditions of the brain.

Hypersomnia—An abnormal increase of 25% or more in time spent sleeping. Individuals with hypersomnia usually have excessive daytime sleepiness.

Hypnotics—A class of drugs that are used as a sedatives and sleep aids.

Hypopnea—Shallow or excessively slow breathing usually caused by partial closure of the upper airway during sleep, leading to disruption of sleep.

Insomnia—A sleep disorder characterized by inability either to fall asleep or to stay asleep.

Jet lag—A temporary disruption of the body's sleep-wake rhythm following high-speed air travel across several time zones. Jet lag is most severe in people who have crossed eight or more time zones in 24 hours.

Kleine-Levin syndrome—A disorder that occurs primarily in young males, three or four times a year. The syndrome is marked by episodes of hypersomnia, hypersexual behavior, and excessive eating.

Narcolepsy—A life-long sleep disorder marked by four symptoms: sudden brief sleep attacks, cataplexy (a sudden loss of muscle tone usually lasting up to 30 minutes), temporary paralysis, and hallucinations. The hallucinations are associated with falling asleep or the transition from sleeping to waking.

Nocturnal myoclonus—A disorder in which the patient is awakened repeatedly during the night by cramps or twitches in the calf muscles. Also sometimes called periodic limb movement disorder.

Non-rapid eye movement (NREM) sleep—A type of sleep that differs from rapid eye movement (REM) sleep. The four stages of NREM sleep account for 75–80% of total sleeping time.

Parasomnia—A type of sleep disorder characterized by abnormal changes in behavior or body functions during sleep, specific stages of sleep, or the transition from sleeping to waking.

Pavor nocturnus—Another name for sleep terror disorder.

Polysomnography—An overnight series tests designed to evaluate a patient's basic physiological processes during sleep. Polysomnography generally includes monitoring of the patient's airflow through the nose and mouth, blood pressure, electrocardiographic activity, blood oxygen level, brain wave pattern, eye movement, and the movement of respiratory muscles and limbs

Primary sleep disorder—A sleep disorder that cannot be attributed to a medical condition, another mental disorder, or prescription medications or other substances.

Rapid eye movement (REM) latency—The amount of time it takes for the first onset of REM sleep after a person falls asleep.

Rapid eye movement (REM) sleep—A phase of sleep during which the person's eyes move rapidly beneath the lids. It accounts for 20-25% of sleep time. Dreaming occurs during REM sleep.

Restless legs syndrome (RLS)—A disorder in which the patient experiences crawling, aching, or other disagreeable sensations in the calves that can be relieved by movement. RLS is a frequent cause of difficulty falling asleep at night.

Sedative—A medication that has a calming effect and may be used to treat nervousness or restlessness. Sometimes used as a synonym for hypnotic.

Sleep latency—The amount of time that it takes to fall asleep. Sleep latency is measured in minutes and is important in diagnosing depression.

Somnambulism—Another term for sleepwalking.

conditions depends on successful treatment of the underlying problem. The prognosis for primary sleep disorders is affected by many things, including the patient's age, sex, occupation, personality characteristics, family circumstances, neighborhood environment, and similar factors.

Prevention

There is no known way to prevent sleep disorders, although having a good, regular, sleep schedule with a nighttime ritual intended to reduce stress may help.

Parental concerns

Children who do not get enough sleep, or do not get good quality sleep, may seem irritable or uncooperative during the day. Lack of sleep reduces the ability to concentrate and decreases mental functioning, so children who are not getting enough good sleep at night may have poor concentration skills and poor academic performance.

Resources

BOOKS

Kryger, Meir H., Thomas Roth, William C. Dement, eds. *Principles and Practice of Sleep Medicine*, 3rd ed. Philadelphia: Saunders, 2000.

Reite, Martin, John Ruddy, and Kim Nagel. *Concise Guide to Evaluation and Management of Sleep Disorders*, 3rd ed. Washington, DC: American Psychiatric Publishing, 2002.

ORGANIZATIONS

National Sleep Foundation. 1522 K Street, NW, Suite 500, Washington, DC 20005. Web site: <www.sleepfoundation.org>.

Tish Davidson, A.M.
Rebecca J. Frey, PhD

Small-for-gestational-age infant *see* **Intrauterine growth retardation**

Smoke inhalation

Definition

Smoke inhalation is breathing in the harmful gases, vapors, and particulate matter contained in smoke.

Description

Smoke inhalation typically occurs in victims or firefighters caught in structural fires. However, cigarette **smoking** also causes similar damage on a smaller scale over a longer period of time. People who are trapped in fires may suffer from smoke inhalation independent of receiving skin **burns**; however, the incidence of smoke inhalation increases with the percentage of total body surface area burned. Smoke inhalation contributes to the total number of fire-related deaths each year for several reasons: the damage is serious; its diagnosis is not always easy because as of 2004 there were no sensitive diagnostic tests; and people may not show symptoms until 24 to 48 hours after the event.

Demographics

According to the National Safety Council, 3,900 people died from exposure to fire, flame, and smoke in the United States in 2001, the most recent year as of 2004 for which data were available. Smoke inhalation accounts for the majority of deaths in home fires. Children under age 11 and adults over age 70 are most vulnerable to the effects of smoke inhalation.

Causes and symptoms

The harmful materials given off by combustion injure the airways and lungs in three ways: heat damage, tissue irritation, and oxygen starvation of tissues (asphyxiation). Signs of heat damage are singed nasal hairs, burns around and inside the nose and mouth, and internal swelling of the throat. Tissue irritation of the throat and lungs may appear as noisy breathing, coughing, hoarseness, black or gray spittle, and fluid in the lungs. Asphyxiation is apparent from shortness of breath and blue-gray or cherry-red skin color. In some cases, the person may not be conscious or breathing.

When to call the doctor

A doctor should be called whenever smoke is inhaled for more than a few minutes or whenever the inhaled smoke and fumes are known to contain toxic substances.

Diagnosis

In addition to looking for the signs of heat damage, tissue irritation, and asphyxiation, the physician will assess the individual's breathing by the respiratory rate (number of breaths per minute) and motion of the chest as the lungs inflate and deflate. The person's circulation is also evaluated by the pulse rate (number of heartbeats per minute) and blood pressure. Blood tests will indicate the levels of oxygen and byproducts of poisonous gases. Chest x rays are too insensitive to show damage to delicate respiratory tissues but can show fluid in the lungs (pulmonary edema).

The physician may perform a bronchoscopy, a visual examination in which the airways and lungs are seen through a fiber optic tube inserted down the person's windpipe (trachea). Other **pulmonary function tests** may be performed to measure how efficiently the lungs are working.

Treatment

Treatment varies with the severity of the damage caused. The primary focus of treatment is to maintain an open airway and provide an adequate level of oxygen. If the airway is open and stable, the individual may be given high-flow humidified 100 percent oxygen by mask. If swelling of the airway tissues is closing off the airway, the person may require the insertion of an endotracheal tube to artificially maintain an open airway.

Oxygen is often the only medication necessary. However, people who have a **cough** with wheezing (bronchospasm), indicating that the bronchial airways are narrowed or blocked, may be given a bronchodilator to relax the muscles and increase ventilation. There are also antidotes for specific poisonous gases in the blood; dosage is dependent upon the level indicated by blood tests. **Antibiotics** are not given until sputum and blood cultures confirm the presence of a bacterial infection.

In institutions where it is available, hyperbaric oxygen therapy may be used to treat smoke inhalation, resulting in severe carbon monoxide or cyanide **poisoning**. This treatment requires a special chamber in which the person receives pure oxygen at three times the normal atmospheric pressure, thus receiving more oxygen faster to overcome loss of consciousness, altered mental state, cardiovascular dysfunction, pulmonary edema, and severe neurological damage.

Botanical medicine can help to maintain open airways and heal damaged mucous membranes. It can also help support the entire respiratory system. Acupuncture and homeopathic treatment can provide support to the whole person who has suffered a traumatic injury such as smoke inhalation.

Prognosis

Although the outcome depends of the severity of the smoke inhalation and the severity of any accompanying burns or other injuries, with prompt medical treatment, the prognosis for recovery is good. However, some people may experience chronic pulmonary problems following smoke inhalation, and those with **asthma** or other chronic respiratory conditions prior to smoke inhalation may find their original conditions have been aggravated by the inhalation injury.

Prevention

Smoke inhalation is best avoided by preventing structural fires. Doing so involves inspection of wiring; safe use and storage of flammable liquids; and maintenance of clean, well-ventilated chimneys, wood stoves, and space heaters. Properly placed and working smoke detectors in combination with rapid evacuation plans minimize a person's exposure to smoke in the event of a fire. When escaping a burning building, a person should move close to the floor where there the air is cooler and clearer to breathe because hot air rises, carrying gases and particulate matter upward. Finally, firefighters should always wear proper protective gear.

Parental concerns

Parents should monitor their homes to make sure they provide a safe environment for everyone, including their children. They should also monitor **play** and recreational activities to limit exposure to smoke or toxic fumes. Parents should regularly check smoke detectors and change batteries every six months. In addition, families should have a fire escape plan, including a designated meeting area away from the house. This plan should be practiced periodically.

Resources

BOOKS

Beamis, John F., et al. *Interventional Pulmonary Medicine.* New York: Marcel Dekker, 2003.

Hanley, Michael E., and Carolyn H. Welsh. *Current Diagnosis & Treatment in Pulmonary Medicine.* New York: McGraw-Hill, 2003.

Piantadosi, Claude A. "Physical, Chemical, and Aspiration Injuries of the Lung." In *Cecil Textbook of Medicine*, 22nd ed. Edited by Lee Goldman et al. Philadelphia: Saunders, 2003, pp. 538–467.

Rodgers, George C., and Nancy J. Matyunas. "Toxic gases." In *Nelson Textbook of Pediatrics*, 17th ed. Edited by Richard E. Behrman et al. Philadelphia: Saunders, 2003, pp. 2374.

Speizer, Frank E. "Environmental Lung Diseases." In *Harrison's Principles of Internal Medicine*, 15th ed.

KEY TERMS

Asphyxiation—Oxygen starvation of tissues. Chemicals such as carbon monoxide prevent the blood from carrying sufficient oxygen to the brain and other organs. As a result, the person may lose consciousness, stop breathing, and die without artificial respiration (assisted breathing) and other means of elevating the blood oxygen level.

Hyperbaric oxygen therapy—Medical treatment in which oxygen is administered in specially designed chambers, under pressures greater than that of the atmosphere, in order to treat specific medical conditions, such as carbon monoxide poisoning, smoke inhalation, and certain bacterial infections.

Pulmonary—Referring to the lungs and respiratory system.

Pulmonary edema—An accumulation of fluid in the tissue of the lungs.

Edited by Eugene Braunwald et al. New York: McGraw-Hill, 2001, pp. 1467–74.

PERIODICALS

Stefanidou, M., and S. Athanaselis. "Toxicological aspects of fire." *Veterinary and Human Toxicology* 46, no. 4 (2004): 196–9.

ORGANIZATIONS

American Academy of Emergency Medicine. 611 East Wells St., Milwaukee, WI 53202. Web site: <www.aaem.org/>.

American College of Emergency Physicians. PO Box 619911, Dallas, TX 75261–9911. Web site: <www.acep.org/>.

American College of Occupational and Environmental Medicine. 55 West Seegers Rd., Arlington Heights, IL 60005. Web site: <www.acoem.org/>.

American College of Osteopathic Emergency Physicians. 142 E. Ontario St., Suite 550, Chicago, IL 60611. Web site: <www.acoep.org/>.

American College of Physicians. 190 N Independence Mall West, Philadelphia, PA 19106–1572. Web site: <http://www.acponline.org/>.

American Lung Association. 1740 Broadway, New York, NY 10019. Web site: <www.lungusa.org/diseases/lungtb.html>.

American Thoracic Society. 1740 Broadway, New York, NY 10019. Web site: <www.thoracic.org/>.

WEB SITES

"Burns." *Merck Manual.* Available online at <www.merck.com/mmhe/sec24/ch289/ch289a.html> (accessed December 23, 2004).

Lafferty, Keith. "Smoke Inhalation." *eMedicine*, November 2, 2004. Available online at <www.emedicine.com/EMERG/topic538.htm> (accessed December 23, 2004).

L. Fleming Fallon Jr., MD, DrPH

Smoking

Definition

Smoking is the inhalation of the smoke of burning tobacco that is used mostly in three forms: cigarettes, pipes, and cigars.

Description

Casual smoking is the act of smoking only occasionally, usually in a social situation or to relieve stress. A smoking habit is a physical **addiction** to tobacco products. Many health experts as of 2004 regarded habitual smoking as a psychological addiction, one with serious health consequences. Nicotine, the active ingredient in tobacco, is inhaled into the lungs, where most of it stays. The rest passes into the bloodstream, reaching the brain in about 10 seconds and dispersing throughout the body in about 20 seconds.

Depending on the circumstances and the amount consumed, nicotine can act as either a stimulant or tranquilizer. This dual role explains why some people report that smoking gives them energy and stimulates their mental activity, while others note that smoking relieves **anxiety** and relaxes them. The initial effect results in part from the drug's stimulation of the adrenal glands and resulting release of epinephrine into the blood. Epinephrine causes several physiological changes: it temporarily narrows the arteries, raises the blood pressure, raises the levels of fat in the blood, and increases the heart rate and flow of blood from the heart. Some researchers think epinephrine contributes to smokers' increased risk of high blood pressure.

Nicotine, by itself, increases the risk of heart disease. However, when a person smokes, he or she is ingesting a lot more than nicotine. Smoke from a cigarette, pipe, or cigar is made up of many additional toxic chemicals, including tar and carbon monoxide. Tar is a sticky substance that forms as deposits in the lungs, causing lung **cancer** and respiratory distress. Carbon monoxide limits the amount of oxygen that the red blood cells can convey throughout the body. Nicotine may also damage the inner walls of the arteries, which allows fat to build up in them.

Besides tar, nicotine, and carbon monoxide, tobacco smoke contains 4,000 different chemicals. More than 200 of these chemicals are known to be toxic. Nonsmokers who are exposed to tobacco smoke also take in these toxic chemicals. They inhale the smoke exhaled by the smoker as well as the more toxic sidestream smoke—the smoke from the end of the burning cigarette, cigar, or pipe.

The harmful effects of teenage smoking are both short-term and long-term. During **adolescence**, smoking interferes with ongoing lung growth and development, preventing the attainment of full lung function. Teenagers who smoke are less fit than their nonsmoking peers and more apt to experience shortness of breath, **dizziness**, coughing, and excess phlegm in their lungs. They are also more vulnerable to colds, flu, **pneumonia**, and other respiratory problems. Smoking for even a short time can produce a chronic smoker's **cough**. In addition to respiratory problems and a diminished level of overall well-being in adolescence, teenage smoking is also responsible for health problems in adulthood.

It is estimated that one third of the teenagers who start smoking each year eventually die of diseases related to tobacco use, diseases that will shorten their lives by an average of 12–15 years. Cigarette smoking is a major risk factor for cardiovascular disease, including coronary heart disease, atherosclerosis (hardening of the arteries), and **stroke**. Reports by the surgeon general link teenage smoking to cardiovascular disease in both adolescents and adults. The same reports cite evidence that the length of time a person has smoked has a greater impact on the risk of developing lung cancer and other smoking-related cancers than the number of cigarettes smoked; in other words, starting to smoke at an early age is an even greater health risk than being a heavy smoker.

Demographics

The National Survey on Drug Use and Health (NSDUH) is conducted annually by the Substance Abuse and Mental Health Services Administration (SAMHSA) of the U.S. Department of Health and Human Services. The study found that an estimated 70.8 million Americans reported current (past month) use of a tobacco product in 2003. This is 29.8 percent of the population aged 12 or older, similar to the rate in 2002 (30.4%). Young adults aged 18–25 reported the highest rate of past month cigarette use (40.2%), similar to the rate among young adults in 2002. An estimated 35.7 million Americans aged twelve or older in 2003 were classified as nicotine dependent in the past month because of their cigarette use (15% of the total population), about the same as for 2002.

Young adults aged 18 to 25 had the highest rate of current use of cigarettes (40.2%), similar to the rate in 2002. Past month cigarette use rates among youths in 2002 and 2003 were 13 percent and 12.2 percent, respectively, not a statistically significant change. However, there were significant declines in past year (from 20.3% to 19%) and lifetime (from 33.3% to 31%) cigarette use among youths aged 12 to 17 between 2002 and 2003. Among persons aged twelve or older, a higher proportion of males than females smoked cigarettes in the past month in 2003 (28.1% versus 23%). Among youths aged 12 to 17, however, girls (12.5%) were as likely as boys (11.9%) to smoke in the past month. There was no change in cigarette use among boys aged 12 to 17 between 2002 and 2003. However, among girls, cigarette use decreased from 13.6 percent in 2002 to 12.5 percent in 2003.

Causes and symptoms

No one starts smoking to become addicted to nicotine. It is not known how much nicotine may be consumed before the body becomes addicted. However, once smoking becomes a habit, the smoker faces a lifetime of health risks associated with one of the strongest addictions known to humans.

Smoking risks

Smoking is recognized as the leading preventable cause of death, causing or contributing to the deaths of approximately 430,700 Americans each year. Anyone with a smoking habit has an increased chance of cancer (lung, cervical, and other types); respiratory diseases (emphysema, **asthma**, and chronic **bronchitis**); and cardiovascular disease (heart attack, high blood pressure, stroke, and atherosclerosis). The risk of stroke is especially high in women who take birth control pills.

Smoking can damage fertility, making it harder to conceive, and it can interfere with the growth of the fetus during pregnancy. It accounts for an estimated 14 percent of premature births and 10 percent of infant deaths. There is some evidence that smoking may cause impotence in men. Because smoking affects so many of the body's systems, smokers often have vitamin deficiencies and suffer oxidative damage caused by free radicals.

Free radicals are molecules that steal electrons from other molecules, turning the other molecules into free radicals and destabilizing the molecules in the body's cells.

Studies reveal that the more a person smokes, the more likely he is to sustain illnesses such as cancer, chronic bronchitis, and emphysema. But even smokers who indulge in the habit only occasionally are more prone to these diseases. Some brands of cigarettes are advertised as low tar, but no cigarette is truly safe. If a smoker switches to a low-tar cigarette, he is likely to inhale longer and more deeply to get the chemicals his body craves. A smoker has to quit the habit entirely in order to improve his health and decrease the chance of disease.

Though some people believe chewing tobacco is safer, it also carries health risks. People who chew tobacco have an increased risk of heart disease and mouth and throat cancer. Pipe and cigar smokers have increased health risks as well, even though these smokers generally do not inhale as deeply as cigarette smokers do. These groups have not been studied as extensively as cigarette smokers, but there is evidence that they may be at a slightly lower risk of cardiovascular problems but a higher risk of cancer and various types of circulatory conditions. Some research reveals that passive smokers, or those who unavoidably breathe in second-hand tobacco smoke, have an increased chance of many health problems such as lung cancer, asthma, and **sudden infant death syndrome** in babies.

Smokers' symptoms

Smokers are likely to exhibit a variety of symptoms that reveal the damage caused by smoking. A nagging morning cough may be one sign of a tobacco habit. Other symptoms include shortness of breath, wheezing, and frequent occurrences of respiratory illness, such as bronchitis. Smoking also increases fatigue and decreases the smoker's sense of smell and taste. Smokers are more likely to develop poor circulation, with cold hands and feet, and premature wrinkles.

Sometimes the illnesses that result from smoking come with little warning. For instance, coronary artery disease may exhibit few or no symptoms. At other times, there will be warning signs, such as bloody discharge from a woman's vagina, a sign of cancer of the cervix. Another warning sign is a hacking cough, worse than the usual smoker's cough, that brings up phlegm or blood, a sign of lung cancer.

Withdrawal symptoms

A smoker who tries to quit may expect one or more of these withdrawal symptoms: **nausea**, **constipation** or **diarrhea**, drowsiness, loss of concentration, insomnia, **headache**, nausea, and irritability.

When to call the doctor

Smokers should seek medical help if they want to quit smoking but are unable to do so, or if they exhibit signs of any of the illnesses associated with long-term tobacco use. Persons who are frequently around smokers should seek medical advice if they show any of the symptoms associated with illnesses caused by smoking since second-hand smoke can be more damaging to health than first-hand smoke.

Diagnosis

It is not easy to quit smoking. That is why it may be wise for smokers to turn to their physician for help. For the greatest success in quitting and to help with the withdrawal symptoms, smokers should talk over a treatment plan with their doctor or alternative practitioner. They should have a general physical examination to gauge their general health and uncover any deficiencies. They should also have a thorough evaluation for some of the serious diseases that smoking can cause.

Research shows that most smokers who want to quit benefit from the support of other people. It helps to quit with a friend or to join a group such as those organized by the American Cancer Society. These groups provide support and teach behavior modification methods that can help the smoker quit. The smoker's physician can often refer him to such groups.

Other alternatives to help with the withdrawal symptoms include nicotine replacement therapy in the form of gum, patches, nasal sprays, and oral inhalers. These are available by prescription or over the counter. A physician can provide advice on how to use them. They slowly release a small amount of nicotine into the bloodstream, satisfying the smoker's physical craving. Over time, the amount of gum the smoker chews is decreased and the amount of time between applying the patches is increased. This process helps wean the smoker from nicotine slowly. However, if the smoker smokes while taking a nicotine replacement, a nicotine overdose may occur.

The drug buproprion hydrochloride has shown some success in helping smokers quit. This drug contains no nicotine and was originally developed as an antidepressant. It is not known exactly how buproprion works to suppress the desire for nicotine.

Alternative treatment

There are a wide range of alternative treatments that can help a smoker quit the habit, including hypnotherapy, herbs, acupuncture, and meditation. For example, a controlled trial demonstrated that self-massage can help smokers crave less intensely, smoke fewer cigarettes, and in some cases completely give them up.

Prognosis

Research on smoking shows that 80 percent of all smokers desire to quit. But smoking is so addictive that fewer than 20 percent of the people who try ever successfully break the habit. Still, many people attempt to quit smoking over and over again, despite the difficulties—the cravings and withdrawal symptoms, such as irritability and restlessness.

For those who do quit, it is well worth the effort. The good news is that once a smoker quits the health effects are immediate and dramatic. After the first day, oxygen and carbon monoxide levels in the blood return to normal. At two days, nerve endings begin to grow back and the senses of taste and smell revive. Within two weeks to three months, circulation and breathing improve. After one year of not smoking, the risk of heart disease is reduced by 50 percent. After 15 years of abstinence, the risks of health problems from smoking virtually vanish. A smoker who quits for good often feels a lot better too, with less fatigue and fewer respiratory illnesses.

Prevention

How do smokers give up their cigarettes for good and never go back to them again? Here are a few tips from the experts:

- People should tell their friends and neighbors that they are quitting. Doing so helps make quitting a matter of pride.
- They should chew sugarless gum or eat sugar-free hard candy to redirect the oral fixation that comes with smoking and to prevent weight gain.
- They should eat as much as they want, but only low-calorie foods and drinks. They should drink plenty of water, which may help with the feelings of tension and restlessness that quitting can bring. After eight weeks, they will lose their craving for tobacco, so it is safe then to return to their usual eating habits.
- They should stay away from situations that prompt smoking, avoiding other people who smoke and dining in the nonsmoking section of restaurants.

Parental concerns

Parents and guardians need to be aware of the power they have to influence the development of their kids throughout the pre-teen and teenage years. Adolescence brings a new and dramatic stage to **family** life. The changes that are required are not just the teen's to make; parents need to change their relationship with their teenager. It is best if parents are proactive about the challenges of this life cycle stage, particularly those that pertain to the possibility of experimenting with and using tobacco. Parents should not be afraid to talk directly to their kids about smoking, even if they have had problems with smoking themselves. Parents should give clear, no-use messages about smoking and its negative consequences on health. It is important for kids and teens to understand that the rules and expectations set by parents are based on parental love and concern for their well-being. Parents should also be actively involved and demonstrate interest in their teen's friends and social activities. Spending quality time with teens and setting good examples are essential. Even if tobacco use already exists in the teen's life, parents and families can still have a positive influence on their teen's behavior.

Resources

BOOKS

Gosselin, Kim, and Thom Buttner. *Smoking Stinks!* Plainview, NY: Jayjo Books, 2002.

Haugen, Hayley Mitchell. *Teen Smoking*. San Diego, CA: Greenhaven Press, 2004.

Shipley, Robert H. *Stop Smoking Kit: Quit Smart Stop Smoking Guide, Hypnosis Quit Smoking CD, and Cigarette Substitute*. Durham, NC: QuitSmart Stop Smoking Resources, Inc., 2004.

PERIODICALS

Brook, Judith S., et al. "Tobacco Use and Health in Young Adulthood." *Journal of Genetic Psychology* (September 2004): 310–23.

Frieden, Joyce. "Peer Pressure Likely to Prompt Tobacco Use: Behavior Predictors Studied." *Family Practice News* (June 15, 2004): 66.

McCollum, Sean. "Up in Smoke: Smoking Harms Your Health and Empties Your Wallet. How Much Does This Lethal Habit Cost? Do the Math and Find Out." *Scholastic Choices* (February-March 2004): 16–20.

KEY TERMS

Antioxidant—Any substance that reduces the damage caused by oxidation, such as the harm caused by free radicals.

Chronic bronchitis—A smoking-related respiratory illness in which the membranes that line the bronchi, or the lung's air passages, narrow over time. Symptoms include a morning cough that brings up phlegm, breathlessness, and wheezing.

Emphysema—A chronic respiratory disease that involves the destruction of air sac walls to form abnormally large air sacs that have reduced gas exchange ability and that tend to retain air within the lungs. Symptoms include labored breathing, the inability to forcefully blow air out of the lungs, and an increased susceptibility to respiratory tract infections. Emphysema is usually caused by smoking.

Epinephrine—A hormone produced by the adrenal medulla. It is important in the response to stress and partially regulates heart rate and metabolism. It is also called adrenaline.

Flavonoid—A food chemical that helps to limit oxidative damage to the body's cells, and protects against heart disease and cancer.

Free radical—An unstable molecule that causes oxidative damage by stealing electrons from surrounding molecules, thereby disrupting activity in the body's cells.

Nicotine—A colorless, oily chemical found in tobacco that makes people physically dependent on smoking. It is poisonous in large doses.

Nicotine replacement therapy—A method of weaning a smoker away from both nicotine and the oral fixation that accompanies a smoking habit by giving the smoker smaller and smaller doses of nicotine in the form of a patch or gum.

Secondhand smoke—A mixture of the smoke given off by the burning end of a cigarette, pipe, or cigar and the smoke exhaled from the lungs of smokers.

Sidestream smoke—The smoke that is emitted from the burning end of a cigarette or cigar, or that comes from the end of a pipe. Along with exhaled smoke, it is a constituent of second-hand smoke.

"Reports: Fewer U.S., Canadian Youth are Lighting Up." *Tobacco Retailer* (August 2004): 7–8.

"Tobacco Use among Middle and High School Students—United States, 2002." *Morbidity and Mortality Weekly Report* (November 14, 2003): 1096–98.

ORGANIZATIONS

Campaign for Tobacco-Free Kids. 1400 Eye Street, Suite 1200, Washington DC 20005. Web site: <www.tobaccofreekids.org>.

Youth Anti-Tobacco Collaborative. 1469 Park Ave., San Jose, CA 95128. Web site: <www.notbuyinit.org>.

WEB SITES

"Kids against Tobacco Smoke." *Roy Castle Lung Cancer Foundation.* Available online at <www.roycastle.org/kats/about.htm> (accessed November 3, 2004).

"Stand Up. Speak Out against Tobacco." Available online at <www.standonline.org> (accessed November 3, 2004).

"Tobacco vs. Kids." *Campaign for Tobacco-Free Kids.* Available online at <www.tobaccofreekids.org> (accessed November 3, 2004).

Barbara Boughton, Ph.D.
Ken R. Wells

Social competence

Definition

Social competence is the condition of possessing the social, emotional, and intellectual skills and behaviors needed to succeed as a member of society.

Description

Social competence refers to the social, emotional, and cognitive skills and behaviors that children need for successful social adaptation. Despite this simple definition, social competence is an elusive concept, because the skills and behaviors required for healthy social development vary with the age of the child and with the demands of particular situations. A socially competent **preschool** child behaves differently from a socially competent adolescent. Conversely, the same behaviors (e.g., aggression, **shyness**) have different implications for social adaptation depending on the age of the child and the particulars of the social context.

A child's social competence depends upon a number of factors including the child's social skills, social awareness, and self-confidence. The term social skills describes the child's knowledge of and ability to use a variety of social behaviors that are appropriate to a given interpersonal situation and that are pleasing to others in each situation. The capacity to inhibit egocentric, impulsive, or negative social behavior is also a reflection of a child's social skills. The term emotional **intelligence** refers to the child's ability to understand the emotions of others, perceive subtle social cues, "read" complex social situations, and demonstrate insight about others' motivations and goals. Children who have a wide repertoire of social skills and who are socially aware and perceptive are likely to be socially competent.

Social competence is the broader term used to describe a child's social effectiveness. It defines a child's ability to establish and maintain high quality and mutually satisfying relationships and to avoid negative treatment or victimization from others. In addition to social skills and emotional intelligence, factors such as the child's self-confidence or social **anxiety** can affect his or her social competence. Social competence can also be affected by the social context and the extent to which there is a good match between the child's skills, interests, and abilities and those of peers. For example, a quiet and studious boy may appear socially incompetent in a peer group full of raucous athletes but may do fine socially if a more complementary peer group can be found for him, such as children who share his interests in quiet games or computers.

Importance of social competence

Parents are the primary source of social and emotional support for children during the first years of life, but in later years peers begin to play a significant role in a child's social-emotional development. Increasingly with age, peers rather than parents become preferred companions, providing important sources of entertainment and support. In the context of peer interactions, young children engage in fantasy play that allows them to assume different roles, learn to take another person's perspective, and develop an understanding of the social rules and conventions of their culture. In addition, relationships with peers typically involve more give-and-take than relationships with adults and thus provide an opportunity for the development of social competencies such as cooperation and negotiation.

During **adolescence**, peer relations become particularly important for children. A key developmental task of adolescence is the formation of an identity or sense of the kind of person one is and the kind of person one wants to be. Adolescents try on different social roles as they interact with peers, and peers serve as a social stepping stone as adolescents move away from their emotional dependence upon their parents and toward autonomous functioning as an adult. In many ways, then, childhood peer relations serve as training grounds for future interpersonal relations, providing children with opportunities to learn about reciprocity and intimacy. These skills are associated with effective interpersonal relations in adult life, including relations with co-workers and with romantic partners.

When children experience serious difficulties in peer relations, the development of social competencies may be threatened. Rejection or victimization by peers may become a source of significant stress to children, contributing to feelings of loneliness and low **self-esteem**. In addition, peer rejection can escalate in a negative developmental spiral. That is, when children with poor social skills become rejected, they are often excluded from positive interactions with peers that are critical for learning social skills. Rejected children typically have fewer options in terms of play partners and friends than do accepted children. Observations of rejected children have revealed that they spend more time playing alone and interacting in smaller groups than their more popular peers. In addition, the companions of rejected children tend to be younger or more unpopular than the companions of accepted children. Exclusion from a normal peer group can deprive rejected children of opportunities to develop adaptive social behaviors. Hence, the social competence deficits of rejected children may increase over time, along with feelings of social anxiety and inadequacy.

Social competence deficits and peer rejection

Many children experience difficulties getting along with peers at some point during their youth. Sometimes these problems are short-lived and for some children the effects of being left out or teased by classmates are transitory. For other children, however, being ignored or rejected by peers may be a lasting problem that has lifelong consequences, such as a dislike for school, poor self-esteem, social withdrawal, and difficulties with adult relationships.

Considerable research has been undertaken to try to understand why some children experience serious and long-lasting difficulties in the area of peer relations. To explore factors leading to peer difficulties, researchers typically employ the sociometric method to identify children who are or are not successful with peers. In this method, children in a classroom or a group are asked to list the children they like most and those whom they like least. Children who receive many positive ("like most") nominations and few negative ("like least") nominations are classified as "popular." Those who receive few positive and few negative nominations are designated "neglected," and those who receive few positive and many negative nominations are classified as "rejected."

Evidence compiled from studies using child interviews, direct observations, and teacher ratings all suggest that popular children exhibit high levels of social competence. They are friendly and cooperative and engage readily in conversation. Peers describe them as helpful, nice, understanding, attractive, and good at games. Popular and socially competent children are able to consider the perspectives of others, can sustain their attention to the play task, and are able to remain self-controlled in situations involving conflict. They are agreeable and have good problem-solving skills. Socially competent children are also sensitive to the nuances of "play etiquette." They enter a group using diplomatic strategies, such as commenting upon the ongoing activity and asking permission to join in. They uphold standards of equity and show good sportsmanship, making them good companions and enjoyable play partners.

Children who have problems making friends, those who are either "neglected" or "rejected" by their peers, often show deficits in social skills. One of the most common reasons for friendship problems is behavior that annoys other children. Children, like adults, do not like behavior that is bossy, self-centered, or disruptive. It is simply not fun to play with someone who does not share or does not follow the rules. Sometimes children who have learning problems or attention problems can have trouble making friends, because they find it hard to understand and follow the rules of games. Children who get angry easily and lose their temper when things do not go their way can also have a hard time getting along with others. Children who are rejected by peers often have difficulties focusing their attention and controlling their behavior. They may show high rates of noncompliance, interference with others, or aggression (teasing or fighting). Peers often describe rejected classmates as disruptive, short-tempered, unattractive, and likely to brag, to start fights, and to get in trouble with the teacher.

Not all aggressive children are rejected by their peers. Children are particularly likely to become rejected if they show a wide range of conduct problems, including disruptive, hyperactive, and disagreeable behaviors in addition to physical aggression. Socially competent children who are aggressive tend to use aggression in a way that is accepted by peers (e.g., fighting back when provoked), whereas the aggressive acts of rejected children include **tantrums**, verbal insults, cheating, or tattling. In addition, aggressive children are more likely to be rejected if they are hyperactive, immature, and lacking in positive social skills.

Children can also have friendship problems because they are very shy and feel uncomfortable and unsure of themselves around others. Sometimes children are ignored or teased by classmates because there is something "different" about them that sets them apart from other children. When children are shy in the classroom and ignored by children, becoming classified as "neglected," it does not necessarily indicate deficits in social competence. Many neglected children have friendships outside the classroom setting, and their neglected status is simply a reflection of their quiet attitude and low profile in the classroom.

Developmentally, peer neglect is not a very stable classification, and many neglected children develop more confidence as they move into classrooms with more familiar or more compatible peers. However, some shy children are highly anxious socially and uncomfortable around peers in many situations. Shy, passive children who are actively disliked and rejected by classmates often become teased and victimized. These children often do have deficits in core areas of social competence that have a negative impact on their social development. For example, many are emotionally dependent on adults and immature in their social behavior. They may be inattentive, moody, depressed, or emotionally volatile, making it difficult for them to sustain positive play interactions with others.

The long-term consequences of sustained peer rejection can be quite serious. Often, deficits in social competence and peer rejection coincide with other emotional and behavioral problems, including attention deficits, aggression, and depression. The importance of social competence and satisfying social relations is life-long. Studies of adults have revealed that friendship is a critical source of social support that protects against the negative effects of life stress. People with few friends are at elevated risk for depression and anxiety.

Childhood peer rejection predicts a variety of difficulties in later life, including school problems, mental health disorders, and **antisocial behavior**. In fact, in one study, peer rejection proved to be a more sensitive predictor of later mental health problems than school records, achievement, intelligence quotient (IQ) scores, or teacher ratings.

It appears, then, that positive peer relations play an important role in supporting the process of healthy social and emotional development. Problematic peer relations are associated with both present and future maladjustment of children and warrant serious attention from parents and professionals working with children. When assessing the possible factors contributing to a child's social difficulties and when planning remedial interventions, it is important to understand developmental processes associated with social competence and peer relations.

Developmental changes and social competence

The key markers of social competence listed in the previous section are consistent across the developmental periods of the preschool years, middle childhood, and adolescence. Across these developmental periods, prosocial skills (friendly, cooperative, helpful behaviors) and self-control skills (anger management, negotiation skills, problem-solving skills) are key facets of social competence. In addition, however, developmental changes occur in the structure and quality of peer interactions that affect the complexity of skills contributing to social competence. That is, as children grow, their preferences for play change, and the thinking skills and language skills that provide a foundation for social competence also change. Hence, the kinds of interactions that children have with peers change qualitatively and quantitatively with development.

Preschool

During the preschool years, social competence involves the ability to separate from parents and engage with peers in shared play activities, particularly fantasy play. As preschool children are just learning to coordinate their social behavior, their interactions are often short and marked by frequent squabbles, and friendships are less stable than at later developmental stages. In addition, physical rough-and-tumble play is common, particularly among boys. During the preschool and early grade school years, children are primarily focused on group acceptance and having companions with whom they can play.

School age

By grade school, children begin to develop an interest in **sports**, structured board games, and group games with complex sets of rules. Being able to understand and follow game rules and being able to handle competition in appropriate ways (e.g., being a good sport) become important skills for social competence. Children play primarily in same-sex groups of friends and expect more stability in their friendships. Loyalty and dependability become important qualities of good friends.

During the middle to late grade school years, children begin to distinguish "regular" friends from "best" friends. The establishment of close, best friendships is an important developmental milestone. That is, in addition to gaining acceptance from a group of peers, one of the hallmarks of social competence is the ability to form and maintain satisfying close friendships.

During the preadolescent and early adolescent years, communication (including sending notes, calling on the phone, and "hanging out") becomes a major focus for peer interactions. Increasingly, social competence involves the willingness and ability to share thoughts and feelings with one another, especially for girls. When adolescent friends squabble, their conflicts typically center on issues such as gossiping, disclosing secrets, or loyalty and perceived betrayal. It is at this stage that friends and romantic partners consistently rival parents as the primary sources of intimacy and social support.

Many of the positive characteristics that promote popularity (such as cooperativeness, friendliness, and consideration for others) also assist children in developing and maintaining friendships. Friendships emerge when children share similar activities and interests and, in addition, when they develop a positive and mutual bond between them. Group acceptance and close friendships follow different timetables and serve different developmental functions, with the need for group acceptance emerging during the early grade school years and filling a need for belonging and the need for close friends emerging in preadolescence to meet newfound needs for affection, alliance, and intimacy outside the **family**. Key features of close friendships are reciprocity and similarity, mutual intimacy, and social support.

Common problems

Many children who are rejected by peers have lower self-esteem, feel lonelier, and are more dissatisfied with their social situations than are average or popular children. These feelings can cause them to give up and avoid social situations, which can in turn exacerbate their peer problems. Interestingly, not all rejected children feel badly about their social difficulties. Studies have shown that aggressive-rejected children, who tend to blame outside factors for their peer problems, are less likely to express distress than withdrawn-rejected children, who often attribute their problems to themselves.

Assessing social competence

There is an important difference between not being "popular" and having friendship problems. Some children are outgoing and have many friends. Other children are quite content with just a good friend or two. Either one of these friendship patterns is healthy. Distinguishing normal friendship problems from problem peer relations that signal serious deficits in social competence is an important goal of **assessment**. There are several key signs that a child's peer difficulties may be more serious and long-lasting rather than temporary. First, the nature of the child's social behavior is important. If children behave aggressively with peers, act bossy and domineering, or are disruptive and impulsive at school, they are more likely to have long-lasting peer difficulties than are children who are simply shy. Children who display aggressive or disruptive behavior often have many discouraging experiences at school, including **discipline** problems and learning difficulties, as well as poor peer relations. School adjustment can be a downhill slide for these children as teachers may get discouraged and peers may be angered by their behaviors. Peers may attempt to "get back" at these children by teasing, which only increases the frustrations and helplessness experienced by aggressive, disruptive children.

Second, children who are actively disliked, teased, or ostracized by peers are at more risk than children who are simply ignored. It is not necessary for a child to be popular in order for that child to gain the advantages of peer support. When children are ignored by peers and are neither disliked nor liked, teachers and parents can take steps to foster friendship development and peer support. When children are actively disliked by peers and the victims of teasing or ostracism, the task is harder for parents and teachers and the likelihood of the child reestablishing positive peer relations without help decreases.

Third, the stability and timing of peer problems should be considered. It is not unusual for children to experience short-term social difficulties when they are moving into new peer situations, such as a new school or a new classroom. Peer problems may also emerge if children are distressed about other changes in their lives, such as a reaction to parental conflict or the birth of a sibling. When peer problems emerge at a time that corresponds to other family or situational changes, they may serve as signals to let parents and teachers know that the child needs extra support at that time. When peer problems have been stable and have existed for a long time, more extensive intervention focused on improving peer relations may be needed.

A variety of methods are available for the assessment of social competence. When choosing a particular assessment strategy, it is important to consider the nature of a particular child's problem. Some children have difficulty with all types of social relationships, while others do well in their neighborhoods or in one-on-one friendships but experience problems with the peer group at school. When problems occur in the school setting, teachers and other school personnel who have opportunities to see children interacting in several peer group situations (such as the classroom, playground, and lunchroom) are often the best first step in assessment. Teachers can often provide information about how children treat and are treated by peers and can also offer opinions about how typical or unusual a child's peer problems are relative to others of the same age. Teacher assessments can include behavioral checklists and rating scales and direct observations of specific social behaviors.

Similarly, parents can provide information about children's social competence. Parents can help to identify problem behaviors such as aggression, withdrawal, and noncompliance that may interfere with social skills. In addition, parents are usually more aware than teachers of their children's social activities outside of school, such as their participation in sports, clubs, or hobbies.

Because they do not have access to the full range of situations in which children interact, however, teachers and parents may not always be the best source of information on children's peer problems. In some cases, it is most helpful to get information directly from peers themselves. One method of obtaining such information is the use of sociometric ratings and nominations. With these procedures, all of the children in a classroom are asked to rate how much they like to play with or spend time with each of their classmates. In addition, they nominate specific peers whom they particularly like or dislike, and they may be asked to identify peers who exhibit particular behavioral characteristics (e.g., nice, aggressive, shy, etc.). The sociometric method, although cumbersome to administer, identifies children who are popular, rejected, and neglected by their peers more accurately than parent or teacher reports and provides useful information about the reasons for peer dislike.

A third approach to assessment of social competence involves children's self-reports. Although input from parents, teachers, and peers can provide valuable insight into children's social behavior and their status within the peer group, information regarding children's thoughts, feelings, and perceptions of their social situations can be obtained only by asking the children themselves. Depending upon the age of the child, information about social competence can be obtained through the use of questionnaires and rating scales that measure children's self-perceptions of their peer relations, the use of stories and hypothetical social situations to elicit information about the child's social reasoning, or simply talking with children to determine their perspectives on their social situations.

Because children may have different experiences in different kinds of peer settings and because no one particular method of assessment is entirely reliable or complete, it is desirable to use a variety of sources when attempting to assess children's social competence. Teacher, parent, peer, and self-reports may yield distinct but complementary information, so by gathering multiple perspectives a more complete picture of a child's social strengths and weaknesses can be obtained.

Interventions to promote social competence

Different strategies may be needed to help children develop social competencies and establish positive peer relations depending on the age of the child and the type of peer problem being experienced. Different children have different needs when it comes to helping them get along better with others and making friends. The age of the child, the kinds of behaviors that are part of the problem, and the reasons for the friendship problem may all affect the helping strategy.

One strategy involves social skill training. Observations have revealed that children who are well liked by peers typically show helpful, courteous, and considerate behavior. The purpose of social skill training is to help unpopular children learn to treat their peers in positive ways. The specific skills taught in different programs vary depending upon the age and type of child involved. Commonly taught skills include helping, sharing, and cooperation. Often children are taught how to enter a group, how to be a good group participant, how to be a fair player (e.g., following rules, taking turns), and how to have a conversation with peers. The skills might also include anger management, negotiation, and conflict resolution skills. Problem-solving skills (e.g., identifying the problem, considering alternative solutions, choosing a solution, and making a plan) are often included in social skill training programs. Sometimes social skill training is done individually with children, but often it is done in a small group. A particular skill concept is discussed, and children may watch a short film or hear a story that illustrates the usefulness of the skill. They then have the opportunity to practice the skill during activities or role-plays with other children in the group. A trained group leader helps guide the children in their use of the skill and provides support and positive feedback to help children become more natural and spontaneous in socially skillful behavior.

Another intervention strategy focuses on helping children who are having trouble getting along with others because of angry, aggressive, or bossy behavior. It can be difficult to suppress aggressive and disruptive behaviors in peer settings for several reasons. For one thing, these behaviors often "work" in the sense that they can be instrumental in achieving desired goals. By complaining loudly, hitting, or otherwise using force or noise, children may be able to get access to a toy they want, or they may be able to get peers to stop doing something obnoxious to them. In this type of situation, an adult's expressed disapproval may suppress the behavior, but the behavior is likely to emerge again in situations where an adult supervisor is not present. Often contracts and point systems are used to suppress **aggressive behavior** and bossiness; however, positive skill training must be used in conjunction with behavior management in order to provide the child with alternative skills to use in situations requiring negotiations with peers. Often parents are included in programs to help children develop better anger management skills and to help children reduce fighting. Trained counselors, educators, or psychologists work with parents to help them find positive discipline strategies and positive **communication skills** to promote child anger management and conflict resolution skills.

A third helping strategy focuses on finding a good social "niche" for the child. Large, unstructured peer group settings (such as recess) are particularly difficult situations for many of the children who have peer problems. These children need a structured, smaller peer interaction setting in which an adult's support is available to guide positive peer interaction. Finding a good social niche for some children can be a difficult task, but an important one. Sometimes a teacher can organize cooperative learning groups that help an isolated child make friends in the classroom. Sometimes parents can help by inviting potential friends over to play or by getting their child involved in a social activity outside of school that is rewarding (such as a church group, a sports group, or a scouting club). Providing positive opportunities for friendship development is important, as it provides children with an appropriate and positive learning environment for the development of social competence.

Parental concerns

Because the family is the primary setting for social development, there are a number of ways in which family interaction patterns may help or hinder the development of children's social competence. Some researchers have speculated that the origins of social competence can be found in infancy, in the quality of the parent-child attachment relationship. Studies have shown that babies whose parents are consistent and sensitive in their responses to distress are less irritable, less anxious, and better emotionally regulated. By contrast, parents who are inconsistent and insensitive to their infants' signals are more likely to have anxious, irritable babies who are difficult to soothe. These children may learn both to model their parents' insensitivity and to rely on intrusive, demanding behavior of their own in order to get attention. If they then generalize these socially incompetent behaviors to their peer interactions, peer rejection may result.

As children get older, family interaction styles and the ways in which parents discipline may play a primary role in the development of noncompliant or aggressive behaviors in children. In families where parents are extremely demanding and use inconsistent, harsh, and punitive discipline strategies, family interaction patterns are frequently characterized by escalation and conflict, and children often exhibit behavior problems. When children generalize the aggressive and oppositional behavior that they have learned at home to their interactions with peers, other children often reject them. Indeed, research has revealed that aggressive behavior is the common link between harsh, inconsistent discipline and rejection by peers.

By contrast, parents of popular children are typically more positive and less demanding with their children than parents of unpopular children. In addition, parents of popular children set a good example by modeling appropriate social interactions and assist their children by arranging opportunities for peer interaction, carefully supervising these experiences, and providing helpful feedback about conflict resolution and making friends.

Child characteristics and social competence

In addition to family interaction patterns and various aspects of the parent-child relationship, children's own thoughts, feelings, and attitudes may influence their social behavior. Research has revealed that many rejected children make impulsive, inaccurate, and incomplete judgments about how to behave in social situations and are lacking in social problem-solving skills. They may make numerous errors in processing social information, including misinterpretation of other people's motives and behavior, setting social goals for themselves that are unrealistic or inappropriate and making poor decisions about their own conduct in social situations. For example, aggressive children are more likely to interpret an accidental push or bump from a peer as intentionally hostile and respond accordingly. Similarly, socially incompetent children are often more interested in "getting even" with peers for injustices than they are in finding positive solutions to social problems and expect that aggressive, coercive strategies will lead to desired outcomes.

When to call the doctor

If the child has significant problems with social competence, especially those which may be caused by an underlying disorder such as anxiety, a doctor or mental health professional should be consulted.

See also Peer acceptance.

Emotional and social development

Age	Activity
Two months	Smiles at person's face. Shows happiness and distress. May be soothed by rocking.
Three months	Smiles when spoken to. Coos or squeals with pleasure.
Four months	Enjoys being cuddled. Recognizes parents and distinguishes them from strangers. Recognizes patterns of feeding, bathing, and dressing. Laughs aloud.
Six months	Smiles and "talks" to mirror image. Sticks out tongue in imitation. May start to show fear of strangers and protest separation from mother or other primary care giver. Enjoys playing peek-a-boo.
Seven months	Responds to name. Tries to engage a person by coughing or making other noise.
Eight months	Responds to "no."
Ten months	May pull on clothing of caregiver to attract attention. Waves bye-bye and plays pat-a-cake. Helps with dressing by holding out arm or leg.
Twelve months	Repeats an action that evoked laughter from adults. May kiss on request, or kiss mirror image. Tends to be shy. Gives and takes objects.
Fifteen months	Asks for object by pointing. Shows affection for familiar people and objects. Shows dependency on primary caregiver. Negativism begins.
Eighteen months	Does the opposite of what is requested. May have temper tantrums.
Two years	Tends to be jealous of own toys and attention of parents. Engages in parallel play with other children. Negativism increases.
Two and a half years	Negativism peaks. Shows fear of separation. Can hit or thrash about when angry. Able to play tricks and pretend.
Three years	Has a more easy-going nature and greater sense of identity. Shows jealousy of same-sex parent and attachment for opposite-sex one. Begins to have imaginary fears of the dark or getting hurt. Engages in cooperative play.
Four years	More sure of self. Often negative and can be defiant. Tests limits. Enjoys cooperative play and group games.
Five years	More stable and secure. Likes to follow rules and enjoys some responsibility. Enjoys organized play and table games requiring taking turns and following rules.

SOURCE: *Miller-Keane Encyclopedia and Dictionary of Medicine, Nursing, and Allied Health, 5th ed.* and Child Development Institute, http://www.childdevelopmentinfo.com.

(Table by GGS Information Services.)

Resources

BOOKS

Cartledge, Gwendolyn, et al. *Teaching Social Skills to Children.* Circle Pines, MN: American Guidance Service, 2002.

Kostelnik, Marjorie, et al. *Guiding Children's Social Development: Theory to Practice*, 4th ed. Albany, NY: Delmar, 2002.

KEY TERMS

Cognitive skills—Skills required to perform higher cognitive processes, such as knowing, learning, thinking, and judging.

Emotional intelligence—The ability to perceive and interpret the emotions of others.

Social skills—The knowledge of and ability to use a variety of social behaviors that are appropriate to interact positively with other people.

Ollhoff, Jim, et al. *Getting Along: Teaching Social Skills to Children and Youth.* Eden Prairie, MN: Sparrow Media Group, 2004.

PERIODICALS

Brendgen, Mara, et al. "Is There a Dark Side of Positive Illusions? Overestimation of Social Competence and Subsequent Adjustment in Aggressive and Nonaggressive Children." *Journal of Abnormal Child Psychology* 32 (June 2004): 305–21.

Coplan, Robert J., Leanne C. Findlay, and Larry J. Nelson. "Characteristics of Preschoolers with Lower Perceived Competence." *Journal of Abnormal Child Psychology* 32 (August 2004): 399–409.

Hoglund, Wendy L., and Bonnie J. Leadbeater. "The Effects of Family, School, and Classroom Ecologies on Changes in Children's Social Competence and Emotional and Behavioral Problems in First Grade." *Developmental Psychology* 40 (July 2004): 533–45.

Tish Davidson, A.M.
Janet Welsh, Ph.D.
Karen Bierman, Ph.D.

Soft tissue cancers *see* **Sarcomas**

Somnambulism

Definition

Somnambulism is also known as sleepwalking. It is a common disorder among children that involves getting out of bed and moving about while still asleep.

Description

Somnambulism is similar to *pavor nocturnus* (**night terrors**) in that it occurs during the non-dreaming stage of **sleep**, usually within an hour or two of going to bed. The sleepwalking child feels an intense need to take action and may appear alert, purposeful, or anxious as he or she moves about. For many years, people believed that it was dangerous to awaken a sleepwalker, but there is no basis for this view. There is, however, little reason to awaken a sleepwalking child, and it may be impossible to do so. Episodes of sleepwalking may be signs of a child's heightened **anxiety** about something.

Demographics

Somnambulism, or sleepwalking, affects an estimated 15 percent of children in their early school years. It decreases in frequency with increasing age. It is very uncommon among adults.

Causes and symptoms

The root cause of sleepwalking is not known. Anxiety and stress are the most commonly given reasons for sleepwalking.

If sleepwalking is common among **family** members, it is more likely that the child may respond to even slight increases in anxiety with sleepwalking behavior.

When to call the doctor

A doctor or other health care provider should be called when episodes of sleepwalking cannot be comfortably managed in the home.

Diagnosis

A diagnosis of somnambulism is made by observation and history. There are no laboratory tests. An **electroencephalogram** may be used as a part of an analysis in a sleep laboratory, but this is the exception rather than the rule.

Treatment

Sleepwalking children should be gently guided back to bed. They will usually be cooperative in this effort.

Prognosis

The prognosis for sleepwalking is good. Most children experience a few episodes of somnambulism and then simply stop, often when a source of stress or anxiety is removed. Sleepwalking rarely affects persons outside of one's own family circle.

Prevention

There is no known way to prevent episodes of sleepwalking.

Nutritional concerns

There is no known link between sleepwalking and **nutrition**.

Parental concerns

Parents should give careful consideration to events and environmental changes that may have triggered the onset of sleepwalking. Potential hazards that may injure children should be removed from their sleeping areas.

KEY TERMS

Electroencephalogram (EEG)—A record of the tiny electrical impulses produced by the brain's activity picked up by electrodes placed on the scalp. By measuring characteristic wave patterns, the EEG can help diagnose certain conditions of the brain.

Resources

BOOKS

Carney, Paul R. et al. *Clinical Sleep Disorders*. Philadelphia: Lippincott Williams & Wilkins, 2004.

Hertz, Grett J. J. et al. *Olie's Bedtime Walk*. Long Island City, NY: Star Bright Books, 2002.

Lee-Ching, Teofilo L. et al. *Sleep Medicine*. Amsterdam: Elsevier, 2002.

Silber, Michael H. et al. *Sleep Medicine in Clinical Practice*. London: Taylor & Francis, 2004.

PERIODICALS

Cartwright, R. "Sleepwalking violence: a sleep disorder, a legal dilemma, and a psychological challenge." *American Journal of Psychiatry* 161, no. 7 (2004): 1149–58.

Guilleminault, C, et al. "Sleepwalking and sleep terrors in prepubertal children: what triggers them?" *Pediatrics* 111, no. 1 (2003): e17–25.

Kantha, S.S. "Is somnambulism a distinct disorder of humans and not seen in non-human primates?" *Medical Hypotheses* 61, no. 5–6 (2003): 517–18.

Lecendreux, M., et al. "HLA and genetic susceptibility to sleepwalking." *Molecular Psychiatry* 8, no. 1 (2003): 114–17.

Remulla, A., and C. Guilleminault. "Somnambulism (sleepwalking)." *Expert Opinion on Pharmacotherapy* 5, no. 10 (2004): 2069–74.

Zadra A, et al. "Analysis of postarousal EEG activity during somnambulistic episodes." *Journal of Sleep Research* 13, no. 3 (2004): 279–84.

ORGANIZATIONS

American Academy of Family Physicians. 11400 Tomahawk Creek Parkway, Leawood, KS 66211-2672. (913) 906-6000. fp@aafp.org. <www.aafp.org>

American Academy of Pediatrics. 141 Northwest Point Boulevard, Elk Grove Village, IL 60007-1098. (847) 434-4000, Fax: (847) 434-8000. kidsdoc@aap.org. <www.aap.org/default.htm>

American Academy of Sleep Medicine. 6301 Bandel Road NW, Suite 101, Rochester, MN 55901. (507) 287-6006. Fax: (507) 287-6008. info@aasmnet.org. <www.asda.org>

American College of Physicians, 190 N. Independence Mall West, Philadelphia, PA 19106-1572. (800) 523-1546, x2600 or (215) 351-2600. <www.acponline.org>

OTHER

"Sleep Disorders and Sleep Problems in Childhood." *American Academy of Family Physicians*. Available online at <www.aafp.org/afp/20010115/277.html>.

"Sleep Walking." *Family Practice Notebook*. Available online at <www.fpnotebook.com/PSY142.htm>.

"Sleep Walking." *National Library of Medicine*. <www.nlm.nih.gov/medlineplus/ency/article/000808.htm>

"Somnambulism (Sleep Walking)." *eMedicine*. Available online at <www.emedicine.com/neuro/topic638.htm>.

L. Fleming Fallon, Jr., M.D., Dr.PH.

Sore throat

Definition

Sore throat is a painful inflammation of the mucous membranes lining the pharynx.

Description

Sore throat is also called pharyngitis. It is a symptom of many conditions, but is most often associated with colds or **influenza**. Sore throat may be caused by either viral or bacterial infections or environmental conditions. Most sore throats heal without complications, but they should not be ignored, as some develop into serious illnesses.

Sore throats can be either acute or chronic. Acute sore throats are more common than chronic sore throats. They appear suddenly and last from three to about seven days. A chronic sore throat lasts much longer and is a symptom of an unresolved underlying condition or disease, such as a sinus infection.

Transmission

The way in which a sore throat is transmitted depends on the agent causing the sore throat. Viral and bacterial sore throats are usually passed in the same way as the **common cold**: sneezing, coughing, sharing drinking glasses or silverware, or in any other way germ particles can easily move from one person to another. Some sore throats are caused by environmental factors or **allergies**. These sore throats cannot be passed from one person to another.

Demographics

Almost everyone gets a sore throat at one time or another, although children in child care or grade school have them more often than adolescents and adults. Sore throats are most common during the winter months when upper respiratory infections (colds) are more frequent.

About 10 percent of children who go to the doctor each year have pharyngitis. Forty percent of the time that children are taken to the doctor with a sore throat, the sore throat is diagnosed as viral. An antibiotic cannot help to cure a virus; a virus has to be left to run its course.

In about 30 percent of the cases for which children are taken to the doctor, bacteria are found to be responsible for the sore throat. Many of these bacterial sore throats are cases of **strep throat**. Sore throats caused by bacteria can be successfully treated with **antibiotics**. In about 40 percent of these cases of pharyngitis, it is never clear what caused the sore throat. In these cases it is possible that the virus or bacteria was not identified, or that other factors such as environment or post-nasal drip may have been responsible.

Causes and symptoms

Sore throats have many different causes, and may or may not be accompanied by cold symptoms, **fever**, or swollen lymph glands. Proper treatment depends on understanding the cause of the sore throat.

Viral sore throat

Viruses cause most sore throats. Cold and flu viruses are the main culprits. These viruses cause an inflammation in the throat and occasionally the tonsils (**tonsillitis**). Cold symptoms usually accompany a viral sore throat. These can include a runny nose, **cough**, congestion, hoarseness, **conjunctivitis**, and fever. The level of throat **pain** varies from uncomfortable to excruciating, when it is painful for the patient to eat, breathe, swallow, or speak.

Another group of viruses that causes sore throat are the adenoviruses. These may also cause infections of the lungs and ears. In addition to a sore throat, symptoms that accompany an adenovirus infection include cough, runny nose, white bumps on the tonsils and throat, mild **diarrhea**, **vomiting**, and a rash. The sore throat lasts about one week.

A third type of virus that can cause severe sore throat is the coxsackie virus. It can cause a disease called herpangina. Although anyone can get herpangina, it is most common in children up to age 10 and is more prevalent in the summer or early autumn. Herpangina is sometimes called summer sore throat.

Three to six days after being exposed to the coxsackie virus, an infected person develops a sudden sore throat that is accompanied by a substantial fever, usually between 102–104°F (38.9–40°C). Tiny grayish-white blisters form on the throat and in the mouth. These fester and become small ulcers. Throat pain is often severe, interfering with swallowing. Children may become dehydrated if they are reluctant to eat or drink because of the pain. In addition, children with herpangina may vomit, have abdominal pain, and generally feel very ill.

One other common cause of a viral sore throat is mononucleosis. Mononucleosis occurs when the Epstein-Barr virus infects one specific type of lymphocyte. The infection spreads to the lymphatic system, respiratory system, liver, spleen, and throat. Symptoms appear 30–50 days after exposure.

Mononucleosis, sometimes called the kissing disease, is extremely common. It is estimated that by the age of 35–40, 80–95 percent of Americans will have had mononucleosis. Often, symptoms are mild, especially in young children, and are diagnosed as a cold. Since symptoms are more severe in adolescents and adults, more cases are diagnosed as mononucleosis in this age group. One of the main symptoms of mononucleosis is a severe sore throat.

Although a runny nose and cough are much more likely to accompany a sore throat caused by a virus than one caused by a bacteria, there is no absolute way to tell what is causing the sore throat without a laboratory test.

Bacterial sore throat

Fewer sore throats are caused by bacteria than are caused by viruses. The most common bacterial sore throat results from an infection by group A *Streptococcus*. This type of infection is commonly called strep throat. Anyone can get strep throat, but it is most common in school age children.

Noninfectious sore throat

Not all sore throats are caused by infection. Postnasal drip can irritate the throat and make it sore. It can be caused by hay fever and other allergies that irritate the sinuses. Environmental and other conditions, such as breathing secondhand smoke, breathing polluted air or chemical fumes, or swallowing substances that burn or scratch the throat can also cause pharyngitis. Dry air, like that in airplanes or from forced hot air furnaces, can make the throat sore. Children who breathe through their mouths at night because of nasal congestion often get sore throats that improve as the day progresses. Sore throat caused by environmental conditions is not contagious.

When to call the doctor

If the child has had a sore throat and fever for more than 24 hours, a doctor should be contacted so a strep test can be performed. Identifying and treating strep throat within about a week is vital to preventing **rheumatic fever**. If the child has had a sore throat, even without fever, for more than 48 hours, the doctor should be consulted. If the child has trouble swallowing or breathing, or is drooling excessively (in small children), emergency medical attention should be sought immediately.

Diagnosis

It is easy for people to tell if they have a sore throat, but difficult to know what has caused it without laboratory tests. Most sore throats are minor and heal without any complications. A small number of bacterial sore throats do develop into serious diseases. Because of this, it is advisable to see a doctor if a sore throat lasts more than a few days or is accompanied by fever, **nausea**, or abdominal pain.

Diagnosis of a sore throat by a doctor begins with a physical examination of the throat and chest. The doctor will also look for signs of other illness, such as a sinus infection or **bronchitis**. Since both bacterial and viral sore throat are contagious and pass easily from person to person, the doctor will seek information about whether the patient has been around other people with flu, sore throat, colds, or strep throat. If it appears that the patient may have strep throat, the doctor will do laboratory tests.

If mononucleosis is suspected, the doctor may do a mono spot test to look for antibodies indicating the presence of the Epstein-Barr virus. The strep test is inexpensive, takes only a few minutes, and can be done in a physician's office. An inexpensive blood test can also determine the presence of antibodies to the mononucleosis virus.

Treatment

Effective treatment varies depending on the cause of the sore throat. Viral sore throats are best left to run their course without drug treatment, because antibiotics have no effect on a viral sore throat. They do not shorten the length of the illness, nor do they lessen the symptoms.

Sore throat caused by streptococci or another bacteria must be treated with antibiotics. Penicillin is the preferred medication, although other antibiotics are also effective if the child is allergic to penicillin. Oral penicillin must be taken for 10 days. Patients need to take the entire amount of antibiotic prescribed, even after symptoms of the sore throat improve. If it is unlikely that the parent will be able to ensure that the child will take the full course of antibiotics, a one-time injection of antibiotics can be administered instead. Cessation of the antibiotic early can lead to a return of the sore throat.

Because a virus causes mononucleosis, there is no specific drug treatment available. Rest, a healthy diet, plenty of fluids, limiting heavy **exercise** and competitive **sports**, and treatment of aches with **acetaminophen** (Datril, Tylenol, Panadol) or ibuprofen (Advil, Nuprin, Motrin, Medipren) will help the illness pass. Nearly 90 percent of mononucleosis infections are mild. The infected person does not normally get the disease again.

In the case of chronic sore throat, it is necessary to treat the underlying disease to heal the sore throat. If a sore throat is caused by environmental factors, the aggravating stimulus should be eliminated from the sufferer's environment.

Home care for sore throat

Regardless of the cause of a sore throat, there are some home care steps that people can take to ease their discomfort. These include:

- taking acetaminophen or ibuprofen for pain (aspirin should not be given to children because of its association with increased risk for **Reye's syndrome**, a serious disease)
- gargling with warm double strength tea or warm salt water made by adding 1 tsp of salt to 8 oz (237 ml) of water
- drinking plenty of fluids, but avoiding acid juices such as orange juice, which can irritate the throat (sucking on popsicles is a good way to get fluids into children)
- eating soft, nutritious foods like noodle soup and avoiding spicy foods
- resting until the fever is gone, then resuming strenuous activities gradually
- using a room humidifier to make sore throat sufferers more comfortable
- using antiseptic lozenges and sprays with caution, as they may aggravate the sore throat rather than improve it

Alternative treatment

Alternative treatment focuses on easing the symptoms of sore throat using herbs and botanical medicines.

- Aromatherapists recommend inhaling the fragrances of the essential oils of lavender (*Lavandula officinalis*), thyme (*Thymus vulgaris*), eucalyptus (*Eucalyptus globulus*), sage (*Salvia officinalis*), and sandalwood.
- Ayurvedic practitioners suggest gargling with a mixture of water, salt, and tumeric (*Curcuma longa*) powder or astringents such as alum, sumac, sage, and bayberry (*Myrica* spp.).
- Herbalists recommend taking osha root (*Ligusticum porteri*) internally for infection or drinking ginger (*Zingiber officinale*) or slippery elm (*Ulmus fulva*) tea for pain.
- Homeopaths may treat sore throats with superdilute solutions of *Lachesis*, *Belladonna*, *Phytolacca*, or yellow jasmine (*Gelsemium*).

Nutritional concerns

Nutritional recommendations include zinc lozenges every two hours along with vitamin C with bioflavonoids, vitamin A, and beta-carotene supplements. Although it may hurt to swallow, it is very important that the child does not become dehydrated. Sucking on popsicles or drinking warm broth can help. If the child shows any signs of **dehydration** he or she should be taken to the doctor.

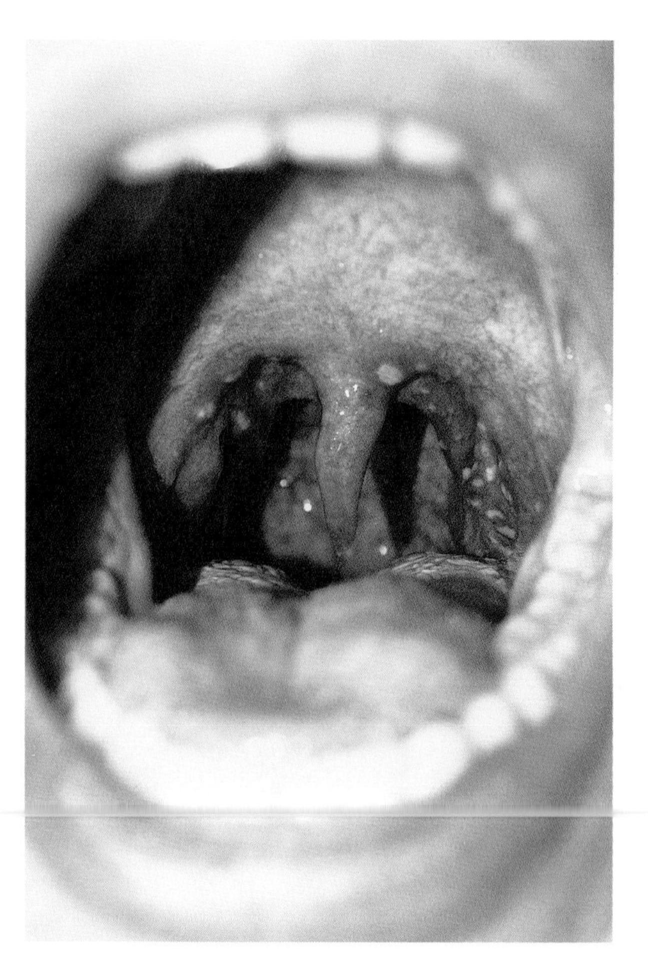

Sore throat caused by a viral infection. *(© Scott Camazine/ Photo Researchers, Inc.)*

Prognosis

Sore throat caused by a viral infection generally clears up on its own within one week with no complications. The exception is mononucleosis. Ninety percent of cases of mononucleosis clear up without medical intervention or complications, so long as dehydration does not occur. In young children, the symptoms may last only a week, but in adolescents the symptoms usually last longer. In all age groups, fatigue and weakness may continue for up to six weeks after other symptoms disappear.

In rare cases of mononucleosis, breathing may be obstructed because of swollen tonsils, adenoids, and

KEY TERMS

Antigen—A substance (usually a protein) identified as foreign by the body's immune system, triggering the release of antibodies as part of the body's immune response.

Lymphocyte—A type of white blood cell that participates in the immune response. The two main groups are the B cells that have antibody molecules on their surface and T cells that destroy antigens.

Pharynx—The throat, a tubular structure that lies between the mouth and the esophagus.

lymph glands. If this happens, the individual should seek emergency medical care immediately.

Patients with bacterial sore throat begin feeling better about 24 hours after starting antibiotics. Untreated strep throat has the potential to cause **scarlet fever**, kidney damage, or rheumatic fever. Scarlet fever causes a rash and can cause high fever and convulsions. Rheumatic fever causes inflammation of the heart and damage to the heart valves. Taking antibiotics within the first week of a strep infection will prevent these complications. People with strep throat remain contagious until they have taken antibiotics for 24 hours.

Prevention

There is no way to prevent a sore throat; however, the risk of getting one or passing one on to another person can be minimized by:

- washing hands well and frequently
- avoiding close contact with someone who has a sore throat
- not sharing food and eating utensils with anyone
- staying out of polluted air

Parental concerns

Viral sore throats usually resolve themselves fairly quickly although they may be very uncomfortable. If the child has a fever and sore throat for more than 24 hours it may be a sign of a bacterial infection and the child should be taken to the doctor. Prompt treatment with antibiotics for strep throat is important because it can prevent rheumatic fever, a serious disease that can cause damage to the heart.

See also Common cold; Mononucleosis.

Resources

PERIODICALS

"Coughs, Colds, and Sore Throat." *Practice Nurse* v.26, i.2 (July 25, 2003): 38.

Dinelli, D.L. "Sore Throat and Difficulty Breathing." *American Family Physician* 63, no. 11 (June 1, 2001): 2255.

"Sore Throat." *The Journal of the American Medical Association* 291, no. 13 (April 7, 2004): 1664.

Vincent, Miriam T., Celestin, Nadhia, Hussain, Aneela N. "Pharyngitis." *American Family Physician* 69, no. 6 (March 15, 2004): 1465.

Tish Davidson, A.M.

Spastic colon *see* **Irritable bowel syndrome**

Spasticity

Definition

Spasticity is an abnormal increase in muscle tone. It may be associated with involuntary **muscle spasms**, sustained muscle contractions (dystonia), and exaggerated deep tendon reflexes that make movement difficult or uncontrollable. Although it most commonly affects the legs and arms, spasticity can affect any part of the body including the trunk, neck, eyelids, face, or vocal cords.

Description

Spastic muscles are resistant to the normal stretching that occurs during use and may remain contracted for long periods. Spasticity may not be present all the time and varies based on initial muscle tone; length of responding muscle groups; and the person's position, posture, and state of relaxation. Spasticity may increase with **anxiety**, emotions, **pain**, or sensory stimulation. It may worsen with movement of the involved muscles. Spasticity may be aggravated by temperature extremes, humidity, skin problems such as a pressure ulcer or ingrown toenail, bladder or bowel problems, infections, and sometimes tight clothing.

The severity of spasticity ranges from slight muscle stiffness to spasms that come and go, to permanent contracture. Spasticity-induced contracture can be treated with medications. If muscle contractures are not treated, fixed contracture can occur, leaving the muscle permanently shortened.

Severe spasticity can interfere with a child's normal functioning, motor and speech development, and/or comfort. Spasticity can be painful, especially if joints are pulled into abnormal positions or if range of motion is limited.

Simple activities of daily living (such as walking, eating, dressing, and bathing) may become time-consuming and difficult for both the child and caregiver. When spasticity limits activity for long periods, it can cause additional medical problems such as **sleep** disturbances, pressure sores, and **pneumonia**.

Demographics

The exact incidence of spasticity is not known. Estimates report spasticity may affect over 500,000 Americans and over 12 million people world-wide.

Causes and symptoms

Causes

Spasticity occurs when certain nerve signals do not reach the muscles because of injury or disease that affects parts of the brain or spinal cord. With spasticity, muscles receive improper nerve signals, causing them to contract, while the brain is unable to communicate with the motor nerves to stop the muscles from contracting.

Common neurological conditions associated with spasticity include **cerebral palsy**, brain injury or trauma, severe **head injury**, **stroke**, multiple sclerosis, **spinal cord injury**, and some metabolic diseases.

Symptoms

Spasticity is characterized by increased muscle tone (hypertonicity) and by muscle stiffness.

Symptoms associated with spasticity include the following:

- increased muscle stretch reflexes
- involuntary contraction and relaxation of muscles (spasms)
- prolonged muscle contractions (dystonia)
- rapid, repetitive jerky motions (clonus)
- exaggerated deep tendon jerks or reflexes
- involuntary crossing of the legs (also called scissoring reflex)
- abnormal posture or abnormal positioning of the shoulder, arm, wrist, or finger
- increased resistance to movement of certain muscle groups

When to call the doctor

If a child has any of the following symptoms, the parent or caregiver should call the child's doctor:

- worsening spasticity
- apparent development of muscle contractures
- worsening overall health

Diagnosis

A diagnosis of spasticity is often made with the diagnosis of cerebral palsy or following a brain or spinal cord injury. A multi-disciplinary team may be consulted to provide an accurate diagnosis of spasticity so the proper treatment can be planned.

The diagnosis of spasticity includes:

- review of personal and **family** medical history
- review of current medications
- review of other health problems
- physical examination
- diagnostic tests

The medical history helps the physician evaluate the presence of other conditions or disorders that might contribute to or cause the spasticity. Records of previous diagnoses, surgeries, and treatments are reviewed. The child's family medical history is evaluated to determine if there is a history of muscular or neurological disorders.

Questions about the child's medical history may include:

- When were the symptoms first noticed?
- How long have the symptoms lasted?
- Are the symptoms always present?
- What muscles are affected?
- What makes the symptoms improve?
- What specific treatments or techniques have been tried?
- What makes the symptoms worse?
- Do certain activities, emotions, or events seem to aggravate the symptoms?
- Are other symptoms present?

- Is the spasticity preventing function or independence?

The doctor will review the presence of other health problems such as swallowing function, bowel and bladder function, and learning difficulties.

The physical exam may include an evaluation of the child's motor reflexes including muscle tone, mobility, strength, balance and endurance; heart and lung function; cranial nerve function; and an examination of the child's abdomen, spine, throat, and ears. The child's height and weight and blood pressure also are checked and recorded.

To confirm the diagnosis of spasticity, the following tests can be performed to evaluate the child's arm and leg movements, muscular activity, range of motion, and ability to perform self-care activities:

- x rays of the spine and hips
- occupational and physical therapy evaluations to determine upper and lower extremity movement patterns and passive range of motion
- diagnostic blocks with local anesthetics to provide information on the effectiveness of potential treatments
- nerve conduction studies to evaluate muscle or nerve damage
- electromyogram (EMG or myogram) to detect abnormal muscle electrical activity.

Nerve conduction studies and an electromyogram (EMG) are usually performed together to provide a comprehensive assessment of nerve and muscle function. In both tests, the examiner uses a computer, monitor, amplifier, loudspeaker, stimulator and high-tech filters to see and hear how the muscles and nerves are responding during the test.

In the nerve conduction study, small electrodes are placed on the skin over the muscles to be examined. A stimulator delivers a very small electrical current (that does not cause damage to the body) through the electrodes, causing the nerves to fire. In the electromyogram, a very thin, sterilized needle is inserted into various muscles, usually those affected most by spasticity symptoms. The needle is attached by wires to a recording machine. The patient is asked to relax and contract the muscles being examined. The electrical signals produced by the nerves and muscles during these tests are measured and recorded by a computer and displayed as electrical waves on the monitor. The test results are interpreted by a specially trained physician.

Treatment

There is no cure for spasticity, but it can be managed with the appropriate treatment. Treatment options include physical and occupational therapy, medications, surgery, or a combination of these treatments. The goals of treatment are to increase the child's comfort, decrease pain, ease mobility, help with activities of daily living including hygiene, ease rehabilitation procedures, and prevent or decrease the risk of developing a joint contracture. The type of treatment recommended will depend upon the severity of the spasticity; the patient's overall health; the potential benefits, limitations, and side effects of the treatment; and the impact of the treatment on the child's quality of life.

In some cases, treatment is not recommended or desired, because it would actually interfere with the patient's current mobility and not improve function. For example, some people with multiple sclerosis who experience significant leg weakness find that spasticity makes their legs more rigid, helping them to stand, transfer to a chair or bed, or walk.

Clinicians should work with the child and the parents or caregivers to develop an individual treatment plan. Specific treatment goals will vary from one person to the next. Treatment should be provided by a pediatric neurologist and a multi-disciplinary team of specialists that may include a physiatrist, physical therapist, occupational therapist, gait and movement specialists, social worker, and surgical specialists as applicable, such as a pediatric orthopedic surgeon or pediatric neurosurgeon.

Physical and occupational therapy

Physical therapy includes stretching exercises, muscle group strengthening exercises, and range of motion exercises to prevent muscles from shortening (contracture), preserve flexibility and range of motion, and reduce the severity of symptoms. Exercises should be practiced daily, as recommended by the physical therapist. Prolonged stretching can lengthen muscles to help decrease spasticity. Strengthening exercises can restore the proper strength to muscles affected by spasticity. Aquatic therapy also may be recommended, since in water there is less stress on the body.

A physical therapist can instruct the patient on proper posture guidelines. Proper posture is critical, especially while sitting and sleeping, to maintain proper alignment of the hips and back. Balancing rest and **exercise** is also important.

Occupational therapy may include splints, casts, or braces on the affected arm or leg to enable proper limb positioning and maintain flexibility and range of motion.

It may also include training for proper limb positioning while seated in a wheelchair or lying in bed.

Physical and occupational therapists can provide guidelines on how to adapt the child's environment to ensure **safety** and comfort.

Other treatments

Brief application (about 10 minutes) of cold packs to spastic muscles may help ease pain and improve function for a short period of time.

Electrical stimulation may be used to reduce spasticity for a short period of time or to stimulate a weak muscle to counteract the action of a stronger, spastic muscle.

Biofeedback training may be used to teach the patient how to consciously reduce muscle tension. Biofeedback uses an electrical signal that indicates when a spastic muscle relaxes. The patient may be able to use biofeedback to learn how to consciously reduce muscle tension and possibly reduce spasticity. However, little research had been conducted as of 2004 to determine the effectiveness of biofeedback on reducing spasticity.

Medications

Medications to treat spasticity are taken by mouth, injected, or received through continuous delivery systems. These medications work by preventing nerves from signaling the muscles to contract, thereby preventing muscle contractions.

If treatment with a single medicine fails to effectively treat spasticity, a different medicine may be tried or an additional medicine may be prescribed. The most important medication guidelines include making sure the child takes the medicine exactly as prescribed and not discontinuing medication without first talking to the child's doctor, even if the medication does not seem to be working or is causing unwanted side effects.

ORAL MEDICATIONS The most commonly prescribed oral medication is baclofen (Lioresal). Baclofen is a muscle relaxant that works on nerves in the spinal cord to reduce spasticity. The benefits of baclofen include decreased stretch reflexes, improved passive range of motion, and reduced muscle spasms, pain, and tightness. Side effects include drowsiness and sedation, as well as weakness, decreased muscle tone, confusion, fatigue, **nausea**, and **dizziness**. Baclofen should not be taken with central nervous system depressants or alcohol.

Benzodiazepines, such as diazepam (Valium), clonazepam (Klonopin, Rivotril), and lorazepam (Ativan) reduce spasticity by acting on the central nervous system. The benefits of benzodiazepines include improved passive range of motion, less muscle overactivity, fewer painful spasms, and overall relaxation. These medications are often taken at night because they cause drowsiness. They are also taken at night to relieve muscle spasms that interrupt sleep. Side effects include unsteadiness, loss of strength, low blood pressure, gastrointestinal symptoms, memory problems, confusion, and behavioral problems.

Datrolene sodium (Dantrium) acts on the muscles to directly interfere with the chemistry of the muscle contraction. It is generally used when other medications are not effective. Benefits may include improved passive movement, decreased muscle tone, and reduced muscle spasms, tightness, and pain. Side effects include generalized weakness, including weakness of the respiratory muscles, as well as drowsiness, fatigue, **diarrhea**, and sensitivity to the sun. Liver problems may occur with this medication, so frequent lab tests are performed to evaluate liver function.

Tizanidine (Zanaflex) reduces spasticity by acting on the central nervous system. It does not usually cause reduced muscle strength. The most common side effect is sedation, and other side effects include low blood pressure, dry mouth, dizziness, and hallucinations. Liver problems may occur with this medication, so frequent lab tests are performed to evaluate liver function.

INJECTED MEDICATIONS Botulinum toxin type A (Botox, Dysport) or type B (Myobloc) is injected locally into the affected muscle group to relax the muscles. It works by preventing nerves from sending signals to the muscles that cause them to contract. Although the treatment takes one to two weeks to reach its full effectiveness, the beneficial effects last three to four months. Botulinum-toxin allows more normal limb positioning and improved mobility. In some patients, the injections also decrease pain. Injections may be used to make casting easier, ease the adjustment of a new brace, or delay surgery.

Botulinum toxin is made by the bacteria that cause **botulism**. However, the amount of botulinum toxin injected to treat spasticity is so small that it would not cause botulism poisoning. This treatment is very safe, and the injections can be given in a doctor's office without the use of sedation or anesthesia. Injections can be repeated but should be spaced apart from three to six months to avoid exceeding the recommended dose. Botulinum-toxin injections can be used in combination with oral medications or intrathecal baclofen to treat spasticity.

Botulinum-toxin injections are typically expensive and may not be covered by insurance. A Reimbursement Hotline established by Allergan, the manufacturer of Botox, is a resource for reimbursement questions: available online at <www.botox.com>. Elan, the manufacturer of Myobloc, also has resources available to answer questions about reimbursement: available online at <www.elan.com>.

Alcohol and phenol are injected in combination but are less commonly used to treat spasticity. The medications are injected directly onto nerves that supply spastic muscles to destroy them. The injections cut off the signals to those muscles, allowing them to relax. This treatment may be used to treat spasticity in larger muscle groups closer to the trunk, such as the thigh muscles. Although this treatment is generally less expensive than botulinum-toxin injections, there are more serious side effects.

Short-term medications such as lidocaine, a local anesthetic, can be used to assess the potential benefit of botulinum toxin or alcohol and phenol injections.

CONTINUOUS DELIVERY MEDICATIONS Baclofen usually is taken as an oral medication but also can be delivered directly into the spinal fluid when the oral medication does not effectively control symptoms. An intrathecal baclofen delivery system continuously releases prescribed amounts of baclofen in small doses directly into the spinal fluid via a small catheter and pump. This type of delivery system causes fewer and less severe side effects than the oral baclofen.

To determine the potential effectiveness of the system, an initial trial of the intraspinal therapy is conducted. During this trial, the medication is delivered into the spinal fluid via a lumbar puncture procedure. The medication usually reaches its peak effectiveness within four hours. If the patient responds favorably to the trial, the intrathecal system can be considered.

The intrathecal baclofen delivery system is placed by a neurosurgeon during a surgical procedure under local or general anesthesia. First, a catheter (thin, flexible tube) is inserted through a needle and guided into the spinal canal, close to where pain pathways enter the spinal cord. The other end of the catheter is tunneled under the skin to the abdomen where a pocket is created. There, the pump is implanted under the skin (epidermal area) through an incision in the abdomen. The baclofen pump is a round, titanium disc about one inch thick and about three inches in diameter. The pump is anchored to surrounding tissue and connected to the catheter. The incision is then closed.

The pump reservoir is filled with the prescribed amount of medication. Medication can be filled and refilled in the pump by inserting a needle through the skin into a filling port (called a diaphragm) in the center of the pump.

The medication is dispensed, either continuously or at certain intervals as determined by the doctor, via a tiny motor in the pump that moves the medication from the pump reservoir through the catheter. Baclofen flows freely in the spinal canal, affecting the nerves to control hyperactive muscles. The system contains a computer chip, so adjustments to the dose, rate, and timing of the medication can be made by the physician using an external programmer. The system also has an alarm to indicate when the reservoir needs to be refilled, the battery is low, or the pump is not delivering the medication. If the system does not appear to be effective in treating spasticity, it can be turned off and eventually removed.

Pump refills and medication adjustments are generally made once every two to three months after the initial dosage is established. The pump system lasts from three to five years, at which time the system needs to be replaced.

Surgery

Surgery is only recommended when all other treatments have been tried and have not effectively controlled the child's spasticity symptoms. Surgical options for chronic spasticity include selective dorsal rhizotomy and tendon release surgery.

Selective dorsal rhizotomy surgery, also called selective posterior rhizotomy, involves a surgical resection of part of the spinal nerve. By cutting the sensory nerve rootlets that cause the spasticity, muscle stiffness is decreased while other functions are maintained. Potential benefits of this surgical procedure include pain relief, reduced spasticity to improve walking or aid sitting in a wheelchair, increased ability to bend at the waist, and improved use of the hands. Sometimes, rhizotomy results in improved breathing and better control of the arms, legs, and head.

Orthopedic surgery for spasticity may be performed to correct a contracture. During contracture release surgery, the tendon of a contractured muscle is cut, the joint is repositioned to a more normal angle, and a cast is applied. Regrowth of the tendon to this new length occurs over several weeks following surgery. After the cast is removed, physical therapy can help strengthen the muscles and improve range of motion. This procedure is most commonly performed on the Achilles tendon but may also be performed on the knees, hips, shoulders, elbows, and wrists.

Tendon transfer surgery is another technique to treat contractures. During this procedure, the tendon attached to a spastic muscle is cut and transferred to a different site, preventing the muscle from being pulled into an abnormal position.

The disadvantages of these orthopedic procedures are that they are irreversible and that they may need to be repeated.

Other orthopedic surgeries that may accompany contracture release surgery include osteotomy, in which a small wedge is removed from a bone to allow repositioning. A cast is applied while the bone heals in a more natural position. Osteotomy is more commonly performed on the bones in the hips or feet. Arthrodesis is a fusing of bones that normally move independently to limit the ability of a spastic muscle to pull the joint into an abnormal position. Arthrodesis is more commonly performed on the bones in the ankle.

Nutritional concerns

Dietary guidelines are individualized, based on the child's age, diagnosis, overall health, severity of disability, and level of functioning. Specific nutritional problems, such as swallowing or feeding difficulties, may be a concern in some patients and should be managed by a team of specialists including a speech therapist. Early identification, treatment, and correction of specific feeding problems will improve the health and nutritional status of the patient.

A well-balanced and carefully planned diet will help maintain general good health for people with spasticity. Specialists recommend that people with multiple sclerosis and other **movement disorders** adhere to the same low-fat, high-fiber diet that is recommended for the general population.

Children with spasticity may have different energy needs, depending on their condition. One study indicated that ambulatory and non-ambulatory adolescents with cerebral palsy had decreased energy needs compared with a control group of normal adolescents. Therefore, a child's specific calorie needs should be evaluated by a registered dietitian who can work with the parents to develop an individualized meal plan. The child's weight should be obtained once a week or at least once a month to determine if caloric intake is adequate.

A child's self-feeding skills can impact his or her health outcome. One study indicated that 90 percent of children with good to fair motor and feeding skills reached adulthood. In contrast, a lack of self-feeding skills was associated with a six-fold increase in mortality (rate of death).

Maintaining a healthy weight is important to prevent the development of chronic diseases such as diabetes, high blood pressure (**hypertension**), and heart disease.

Tube feedings may be required in some patients with **failure to thrive**, aspiration pneumonia, difficulty swallowing, or an inability to ingest adequate calories orally to maintain nutritional status or promote growth.

Alternative treatment

Alternative and complementary therapies include approaches that are considered to be outside the mainstream of traditional health care.

Techniques that reduce stress, such as **yoga**, Tai Chi, meditation, deep breathing exercises, guided imagery, and relaxation training, may be helpful to induce relaxation and manage spasticity. Acupuncture and biofeedback training also may help induce relaxation. Before learning or practicing any particular technique, it is important for the parent/caregiver and child to learn about the therapy, its safety and effectiveness, potential side effects, and the expertise and qualifications of the practitioner. Although some practices are beneficial, others may be harmful to certain patients.

Initial trials of cannabinoids, the active ingredient in marijuana, have shown promise in the treatment of muscle stiffness and limb straightening associated with multiple sclerosis. Further research is needed to determine the beneficial effects of marijuana-derived substances on neuromuscular symptoms associated with movement disorders. Researchers caution that **smoking** marijuana is dangerous, especially since there may be other harmful substances mixed in with the illegal drug.

Relaxation techniques and dietary supplements should not be used as a substitute for medical therapies prescribed by a doctor. Parents should discuss these alternative treatments with the child's doctor to determine the techniques and remedies that may be beneficial for the child.

Prognosis

There is no cure for spasticity, and it cannot be prevented. However, it can be well-managed with the proper combination of physical and occupational therapy, medication, and surgery. The long-term outlook for those with spasticity depends on the severity of the spasticity and the associated disorder.

KEY TERMS

Active motion (spontaneous)—Motions produced by the activity of a person. Active range of motion exercises are those that are performed by the patient without assistance.

Activities of daily living (ADL)—The activities performed during the course of a normal day, for example, eating, bathing, dressing, toileting, etc.

Anoxia—Lack of oxygen.

Central nervous system—Part of the nervous system consisting of the brain, cranial nerves, and spinal cord. The brain is the center of higher processes, such as thought and emotion and is responsible for the coordination and control of bodily activities and the interpretation of information from the senses. The cranial nerves and spinal cord link the brain to the peripheral nervous system, that is the nerves present in the rest of body.

Cerebral palsy—A nonprogressive movement disability caused by abnormal development of or damage to motor control centers of the brain.

Clonic—Referring to clonus, a series of muscle contractions and partial relaxations that alternate in some nervous diseases in the form of convulsive spasms.

Contraction—A tightening of the uterus during pregnancy. Contractions may or may not be painful and may or may not indicate labor.

Contracture—A tightening or shortening of muscles that prevents normal movement of the associated limb or other body part.

Dysphagia—Difficulty in swallowing.

Dystonia—Painful involuntary muscle cramps or spasms.

General anesthesia—Deep sleep induced by a combination of medicines that allows surgery to be performed.

Hyperactive reflexes—Reflexes that persist too long and may be too strong. For example, a hyperactive grasp reflex may cause the hand to stay clenched in a tight fist.

Hypertonia—Having excessive muscular tone or strength.

Local anesthesia—Pain-relieving medication used to numb an area while the patient remains awake. Also see general anesthesia.

Muscle spasm—Localized muscle contraction that occurs when the brain signals the muscle to contract.

Neurologist—A doctor who specializes in disorders of the nervous system, including the brain, spinal cord, and nerves.

Neurosurgeon—Physician who performs surgery on the nervous system.

Occupational therapist—A healthcare provider who specializes in adapting the physical environment to meet a patient's needs. An occupational therapist also assists patients and caregivers with activities of daily living and provide instructions on wheelchair use or other adaptive equipment.

Orthopedist—A doctor specializing in treatment of the musculoskeletal system.

Passive movement—Movement that occurs under the power of an outside source such as a clinician. There is no voluntary muscular contraction by the individual who is being passively moved.

Peripheral nerves—Nerves outside the brain and spinal cord that provide the link between the body and the central nervous system.

Physiatrist—A physician who specializes in physical medicine and rehabilitation.

Physical therapist—A healthcare provider who teaches patients how to perform therapeutic exercises to maintain maximum mobility and range of motion.

Pressure ulcer—Also known as a decubitus ulcer or bedsore, a pressure ulcer is an open wound that forms whenever prolonged pressure is applied to skin covering bony prominences of the body. Patients who are bedridden are at risk of developing pressure ulcers.

Range of motion (ROM)—The range of motion of a joint from full extension to full flexion (bending) measured in degrees like a circle.

Rigidity—A constant resistance to passive motion.

Scissoring—Involuntary crossing of the legs.

Stroke—Interruption of blood flow to a part of the brain with consequent brain damage. A stroke may be caused by a blood clot or by hemorrhage due to a burst blood vessel. Also known as a cerebrovascular accident.

Parental concerns

Parents should work closely with the child's therapists and doctors to create an effective treatment plan. It is important for parents to communicate their treatment goals with the healthcare team. Parents should take an active role in the child's exercise program and help the child practice the exercises as prescribed every day. Raising a child with a movement disorder can be challenging. There are several support groups available to provide information and assistance.

Resources

BOOKS

Barnes, Michael P., and Garth R. Johnson. *Upper Motor Neuron Syndrome & Spasticity: Clinical Management & Neurophysiology*. Cambridge, UK: Cambridge University Press, 2001.

Gelber, David A., and Douglas R. Jeffery. *Clinical Evaluation and Management of Spasticity*. Totowa, NJ: Humana Press Inc., 2001.

PERIODICALS

"Position of the American Dietetic Association: Providing Nutrition Services for Infants, Children, and Adults with Developmental Disabilities and Special Health Care Needs." *Journal of the American Dietetic Association* 104, no. 1 (2004): 97–107.

ORGANIZATIONS

Brain Injury Association of America. 8201 Greensboro Dr., Ste. 611, McLean, VA 22102. Web site: <www.biausa.org>.

National Center on Birth Defects and Developmental Disabilities, Centers for Disease Control. 4770 Buford Hwy., NE, Ste. F-35, Atlanta, GA 30341. Web site: <http://cdc.gov/ncbddd/dh>.

National Institute on Disability and Rehabilitation Research, Office of Special Education and Rehabilitative Services. U.S. Department of Education, 400 Maryland Ave., SW, Washington, DC 20202–7100. Web site: <www.ed.gov/about/offices/list/osers/nidrr/>.

National Institute of Neurological Disorders and Stroke (NINDS), National Institutes of Health. PO Box 5801, Bethesda, MD 20824. Web site: <www.ninds.nih.gov/about_ninds/>.

National Rehabilitation Information Center (NARIC). 4200 Forbes Blvd., Ste. 202, Lanham, MD 20700. Web site: <www.naric.com>.

National Spinal Cord Injury Association. 6701 Democracy Blvd., #300–9, Bethesda, MD 20817. Web site: <www.spinalcord.org>.

Worldwide Education and Awareness for Movement Disorders (WE MOVE). 204 W. 84th St. New York, NY 10024. Web site: <www.wemove.org>.

WEB SITES

"Electromyogram and Nerve Conduction Study." *North American Spine Society*. Available online at <www.spine.org/articles/emg_test.cfm> (accessed October 17, 2004).

"Severe Spasticity." *Medtronic*. Available online at <www.medtronic.com/neuro/spasticity/spasticity.html> (accessed October 17, 2004).

Spinal Cord Injury Information Network. Available online at <www.spinalcord.uab.edu> (accessed October 17, 2004).

"Task Force on Childhood Motor Disorders Consensus Report of a Meeting at the National Institutes of Health, April 22–24, 2001." Available online at <www.ninds.nih.gov/news_and_events/hypertonia_meeting_2001.htm.> (accessed October 17, 2004).

"What you need to know about Electromyograms." *The Cleveland Clinic Health Information Center*. Available online at <www.clevelandclinic.org/health/health-info/docs/0200/0225.asp?index=4825> (accessed October 17, 2004.)

Angela M. Costello

Special education

Definition

Special education refers to a range of educational and social services provided by the public school system and other educational institutions to individuals with disabilities who are between three and 21 years of age.

Purpose

Special education is designed to ensure that students with disabilities are provided with an environment that allows them to be educated effectively. Disabilities that qualify for special education include physical disabilities, such as deafness or blindness; mental disabilities, such as Down's syndrome and **autism**; medical conditions, such as oxygen dependence or traumatic brain injury; learning deficits, such as **dyslexia**; and behavioral disorders, such as attention deficit hyperactivity disorder (ADHD) and conduct disorders.

In 1975, the Education for All Handicapped Children Act (EHCA, PL 94-142) mandated that states provide a "free and appropriate public education" (FAPE) to all students, including those with physical, mental, or behavioral disabilities. This special education must include a comprehensive screening and diagnosis by a multi-disciplinary team and the development of an annual Individualized Education Plan (IEP) for each student, outlining academic and behavioral goals, services to be provided, and methods of evaluation. The student's parents must consent to initial screening and must be invited to participate in all phases of the process.

In 1997, the Individuals with Disabilities Education Act (IDEA) expanded special education services by mandating that all children with disabilities—regardless of the type or severity of their disability—between the ages of three and 21 years are entitled to FAPE in the least restrictive environment. That is, children requiring special education must by educated with nondisabled children to the maximum extent possible in an appropriate program to meet their special needs. While the majority of children with disabilities are taught at least part-time in a general classroom setting, many children are segregated, most often due to a lack of staff and resources to support special needs students in general classrooms. This stipulation that special-needs children be educated in the least restrictive environment led to the practice of mainstreaming, which is the policy of placing special education students in regular classrooms as much as possible and using separate resource rooms where the students receive special tutoring, review, and instruction.

Although gifted and talented students are not usually considered candidates for special education and there is no federal mandate to support these students, exceptionally gifted children may also be entitled to receive special education services. Gifted children who are not identified and continue to be taught in a general classroom may develop behavioral issues due to boredom. Specially designed gifted education programs are available in many school districts. In addition, bilingual children may require special education services. Children whose native language is not English may not receive appropriate education due to their language barrier. Bilingual language support services should be provided.

Description

Special education can include a range of support services, depending on the special needs of the student. Support services may involve physical assistance and therapy, counseling and psychotherapy, modified learning environments and assistive learning devices, educational and psychological assessments, and behavioral modification techniques.

According to U.S. Department of Education statistics, approximately 600,000 children aged three to five years were served by special education services in 2001. In **preschool** children, the most prevalent disability was speech or language impairment. Approximately 5.8 million students aged six to 21 years were served by special education services in 2001. Common disabilities include specific learning disabilities (e.g., dyslexia), speech or language impairment, **mental retardation**, and emotional disturbance.

In order to qualify for special education a child must be diagnosed as having a disability and the disability must be found to "adversely affect educational performance" so as to require special services. Referral and evaluation for special education varies widely. For children with severe disabilities, a physician and the parents usually identify and refer the child to special education. Other disabilities or deficits in the child's developing physical and cognitive abilities may be identified by teacher and parent observation or revealed by academic or developmental tests. Most school districts have standardized programs to screen large numbers of children between kindergarten and third grade. Other disabilities may be subtle or compensated for, such as dyslexia, and may not be discovered until demands on the student increase in college. After referral, a meeting is held to determine whether the child should be assessed or evaluated to determine the type of disability he or she may have. Tests attempt to identify the cognitive (academic), social, or physical tasks that the child has difficulty performing and why the difficulty exists, i.e., what disability or disabilities are present. Tests may include: reading, writing, spelling, and math tests; psychological or **intelligence** tests; speech and language; vision and hearing tests; or an examination by a physician. Parents must consent to all testing, evaluation, and placement and can appeal most decisions if they disagree with the conclusions.

After disabilities and special needs are identified, an IEP is developed by school staff with input from the parents. The IEP development team is interdisciplinary and usually includes the special education teacher, another regular academic teacher, the parents, a school administrator, a school psychologist, and other school staff (e.g., nurse, coach, counselor). The IEP should be comprehensive and include the following:

- current performance measures based on multiple tests and **assessment** methods
- educational goals and objectives that define how problems will be addressed in the short and long term

Special education student receiving one-on-one instruction. *(© Richard T. Nowitz/Corbis.)*

- definition of how the child's progress will be measured on an ongoing basis
- disciplinary methods (especially for children with emotional and behavioral issues)
- an individualized healthcare plan (IHP) for students also requiring special medical attention or medications

IEPs vary widely in length and complexity according to the type of disability. More effective IEPs specifically outline the child's needs; are mutually agreed upon by parents, teachers, and counselors; support activities that are typical of other students in the same age-group; promote school and community membership, and clearly facilitate the student's long-range life goals. Often IEPs do not specifically address how progress is to be measured. An effective IEP clearly defines the types of tests and assessments that are to be given to measure the child's progress. Although subjective assessment by teachers can provide valuable insight, objective tests that specifically measure academic and other skills must be included in the IEP.

After the IEP is developed, the student is placed in the appropriate educational setting. Certified special education teachers deliver programs in separate classrooms using modified educational curricula and specially designed assistive education techniques. Children with physical disabilities are provided with any assistive learning technology or equipment they need to complete educational requirements. Examples of such technology include special computers for speech/hearing/language assistance, modified desks, and writing support devices. Specially trained support staff assist students mainstreamed in general classrooms. When the public school cannot provide the appropriate environment and resources to meet the educational needs of the student, it is obligated to find and pay for an alternative educational setting, such as a day program in a mental/behavioral health facility, **home schooling** with appropriate medical/mental health support, an **alternative school** dedicated to serving disabled children, or a private school with special education support services.

Parental concerns

Children with disabilities and their parents have certain legal rights, most importantly, the right to challenge any recommendation made by a school and its staff. Parents who disagree with the school's educational program can hire legal representation, request formal and informal hearings (due process), and obtain additional evaluation from an independent consultant.

Children with emotional disturbances and related behavioral disorders have historically been unrecognized as being eligible for special education services. However, emotional problems can in fact act as a barrier to education. For children with emotional disturbances to qualify for special education, evidence from psychological testing and observation (by teachers or therapists) must demonstrate that the emotional issues significantly affect educational performance. Most public schools do not have the staff and resources to handle children with emotional disturbances, in addition to other children with disabilities. Many alternative schools exist for children with emotional disturbances and behavioral disorders who have average and above-average academic abilities. If the public school cannot adequately provide FAPE for such students, parents can seek legal representation to obtain funding from the public school for their child to attend an appropriate alternative school. Students with emotional disturbances and behavioral disorders should have mental health support services integrated with their IEP.

According to parents, 14 percent of students with disabilities in elementary and middle school had been expelled or suspended at some point in their school careers. And special needs children have a high drop-out rate—approximately 25 percent drop out of school and another 20 percent leave for other reasons. Emotionally disturbed students have the highest drop-out rate (35%), according to Department of Education statistics, while deaf-blind students have the lowest rate (4%). Graduation and employment rates for students with disabilities rose through the two decades that followed the passage of EHCA and IDEA and other disability legislation such as the Americans with Disabilities Act. Depending on the disability, as many as 45 to 70 percent of disabled adults may remain unemployed. However, some special needs students are quite successful. Students with learning disabilities and **speech disorders** have the lowest rates of unemployment, usually because they have participated in vocational education programs with a comprehensive vocational assessment, including assessment of independent living skills.

KEY TERMS

Alternative school—An educational setting designed to accommodate educational, behavioral, and/or medical needs of children and adolescents that cannot be adequately addressed in a traditional school environment.

Attention deficit hyperactivity disorder (ADHD)—A condition in which a person (usually a child) has an unusually high activity level and a short attention span. People with the disorder may act impulsively and may have learning and behavioral problems.

Dyslexia—A type of reading disorder often characterized by reversal of letters or words.

Individualized educational plan (IEP)—A detailed description of the educational goals, assessment methods, behavioral management plan, and educational performance of a student requiring special education services.

Resources

BOOKS

Gargiulo, Richard M. *Special Education in Contemporary Society*. Florence, KY: Wadsworth Publishing, 2005.

Kaufman, James, et al. *Exceptional Learners: Introduction to Special Education*. New York: Allyn & Bacon, 2005.

Kunjufu, Jawanza. *Keeping Black Boys Out of Special Education*. Chicago, IL: African American Images, 2005.

Wright, Peter W., and Pamela Darr Wright. *From Emotions to Advocacy: The Special Education Survival Guide*. Hartfield, VA: Harbor House Law Press, 2002.

PERIODICALS

Dalton, M. A. "Education Rights and the Special Needs Child." *Child and Adolescent Psychiatric Clinicals of North America* 11 (2002): 859–68.

Heller, K. W., and J. Tumlin. "Using expanded individualized health care plans to assist teachers of students with complex health care needs." *Journal of School Nursing* 20 (June 2004): 150–60.

Weist, Mark D., and Kathleen E. Albus. "Expanded School Mental Health." *Behavior Modification* 28 (July 2004): 463–71.

ORGANIZATIONS

Council for Exceptional Children. 1110 North Glebe Road, Suite 300, Arlington, VA 22201. Web site: <www.cec.sped.org/>.

MAX Foundation. PO Box 22, Rockville Center, New York, NY 11571. Web site: <http://maxfoundation.org/>.

WEB SITES

Internet Special Education Resources. Available online at <www.iser.com/index.shtml> (accessed November 4, 2004).

Special Education Resources on the Internet (SERI). Available online at <www.seriweb.com/> (accessed November 4, 2004).

Wright, Peter W., and Pamela Darr Wright. "Your Child's IEP: Practical and Legal Guidance for Parents." *Wrightslaw.* Available online at <www.wrightslaw.com/advoc/articles/iep_guidance.html> (accessed November 4, 2004).

Jennifer E. Sisk, M.A.

Specific language impairment

Definition

Specific language impairment (SLI) describes a condition of markedly delayed **language development** in the absence of any apparent handicapping conditions.

Description

Many different terms have been used to describe the childhood disorder that is characterized by markedly delayed language development in the absence of any conditions such as deafness, **autism**, or **mental retardation** that would explain the delay. SLI is also sometimes called childhood dysphasia or developmental language disorder.

Demographics

Estimates of true SLI vary according to the age of identification. Some experts argue that as many as 10 percent of two-year-olds may have a specific language impairment, but by age three or four, that percentage drops considerably, presumably because some difficulties resolve themselves. The incidence in the general population is estimated at about 1 percent. SLI is more common in boys than girls.

Causes and symptoms

Children with SLI usually begin to talk at roughly the same age as normal children but are markedly slower in the progress they make. They seem to have particular problems with inflection and word forms, such as leaving off endings when forming verb tenses (for example, the -ed ending when forming the past tense). This problem can persist much longer than early childhood, often into the grade school years and beyond, where these children encounter difficulties in reading and writing. The child with SLI also often has difficulties learning language incidentally, that is, in picking up the meaning of a new word from context or generalizing a new syntactic form. This is in decided contrast to the normal child's case, where incidental learning and generalization are the hallmarks of language acquisition. Children with SLI are not cognitively impaired and are not withdrawn or socially aloof like an autistic child.

Very little is known about the cause or origin of specific language impairment, although evidence in the early 2000s is growing that the underlying condition may be a form of brain abnormality. Any such brain abnormality, however, is not readily apparent with existing diagnostic technologies. SLI children do not have clear brain lesions or marked anatomical differences from other children in either brain hemisphere. However, there is some indication that SLI can be passed down from parents to children. Research as of 2004 suggested a possible genetic link, although there are many problems in identifying such a gene. Sometimes the siblings of an affected child show milder forms of the difficulty, complicating the picture. One of the major stumbling blocks is the definition of the disorder, because children with SLI show many different kinds of symptoms which makes it hard to determine what the genetic cause of the disorder might be.

Some investigators have attributed the difficulties that children with SLI have to problems with speech sound perception, suggesting that inflection and word forms such as endings are hard for the child to perceive because those items are fleeting and unstressed in speech. It is not that the child is deaf in general but that he or she has a specific difficulty discriminating some speech sounds.

Other researchers have argued that this difficulty is not specific to speech but reflects a general perceptual difficulty with the processing of rapidly timed events, of which speech is the most taxing example. The left hemisphere of the brain seems to be specialized for processing rapid acoustic events, so perhaps the child with SLI has a unique difficulty in that part of the brain. Some researchers investigate children with SLI who speak different languages to see if any patterns emerge in the kinds of difficulties the children experience.

When to call the doctor

If a parent notices that a child is having problems with speech or is not achieving language milestones around the usual time, a doctor should be consulted.

Diagnosis

Early identification is very important for the success of interventions for SLI. The disorder is usually diagnosed by comparing a child's linguistic abilities to those that are expected for children of the same age. If the child is significantly behind his or her age peers in terms of language development, SLI is likely. One procedure for diagnosing children aged 24 to 36 months asks parents to complete a standardized questionnaire in which they check off the vocabulary the child knows and write down examples of the child's two-word sentences. If the child's vocabulary contains fewer than 50 words and the child does not use any two-word sentences, that is an indication of SLI or another language disorder.

Treatment

SLI is generally treated by intervention that focuses on helping the child with whatever specific language problems he or she is having. The child with SLI may become increasingly aware of his or her difficulties with language and may lose spontaneity and avoid speaking as he or she gets older. Intensive language intervention can allow these children to make considerable gains, with modeling of appropriate linguistic forms that the child is having difficulty with being especially effective.

Prognosis

The prognosis for children with SLI depends very heavily on the type and severity of the language problem experienced. Many language problems can be largely overcome, although some difficulties usually persist.

Prevention

There is no known way to prevent SLI.

Parental concerns

Children with SLI are often at risk for reduced performance in other areas of their lives because of their difficulty in mastering language. SLI can lead to decreased social interaction and decreased school performance.

KEY TERMS

Inflection—Variations in the pitch or tone of a voice.

Resources

BOOKS

Leonard, Laurence B. *Children with Specific Language Impairment.* Cambridge, MA: MIT Press, 2000.

Weiss, Amy L. *Preschool Language Disorders Resource Guide: Specific Language Impairment.* San Diego, CA: Singular Thomson Learning, 2001.

PERIODICALS

Conti-Ramsden, Gina. "Processing and Linguistic Markers in Young Children with Specific Language Impairment." *Journal of Speech, Language, and Hearing Research* 46 (October 2003): 1029–38.

Fujiki, Martin, et al. "The Relationship of Language and Emotion Regulation Skills to Reticence in Children with Specific Language Impairment." *Journal of Speech, Language, and Hearing Research* 47 (June 2004): 637–47.

Nation, Kate, et al. "Hidden Language Impairments in Children: Parallels Between Poor Reading Comprehension and Specific Language Impairment?" *Journal of Speech, Language, and Hearing Research* 47 (February 2004): 199–212.

Tish Davidson, A.M.
Jill De Villers, Ph.D.

Speech disorders

Definition

Speech disorders are characterized by a difficulty in producing normal speech patterns.

Description

Children go through many stages of speech production while they are learning to communicate. What is normal in the speech of a child of one age may be a sign of a problem in an older child. Speech disorders include voice disorders (abnormalities in pitch, volume, vocal quality, resonance, or duration of sounds), articulation disorders (problems producing speech sounds), and fluency disorders (impairment in the normal rate or rhythm of speech, such as **stuttering**.

Demographics

Speech disorders are common. More than a million children in the public schools' **special education** programs have been diagnosed with a speech disorder. One in 10 people in the United States is affected by a communication disorder (speech, language, or hearing disorders).

Causes and symptoms

The causes of most speech disorders are not known. Deafness and hearing loss are significant causes of speech delays and disorders. The symptoms of a speech disorder depend heavily on the age of the child. There are no symptoms of speech disorders that apply to all ages of children. Basic guidelines about what kind of speech is normal at what age can be helpful in determining if a child is missing significant speech milestones.

- Twelve months: By this time babies should respond nonverbally, have different types of cries, and may know one or a few simple words (e.g. "mama" or "dada"). At this age babies should coo and babble.
- Eighteen months: Children of this age should be increasing their vocabularies slowly and be able to produce five to 20 common words.
- Twenty-four months: At this point vocabulary building should begin to speed up. At this age children should be able to produce simple sentences made up of two words.
- Three years: Children should begin to be able to produce speech that is understood by those outside immediate caretakers. Sentences become longer and more complex, and vocabulary increases drastically.

When to call the doctor

If a child continuously misses speech milestones, or is significantly behind what is generally considered average for his or her age, a doctor should be consulted. If hearing loss is ever suspected, such as if a child only responds when the parent speaking is in eyesight, the doctor should be consulted without delay.

Diagnosis

A doctor will do a hearing test on the child to ensure that a hearing problem is not responsible for the speech delay. The doctor may interact with the child to determine linguistic competence. In addition, he or she will interview the parents or other caregivers or have them fill out a list indicating the child's verbal skills. The doctor will typically refer the child to a speech pathologist—a professional specializing in treating speech problems. The speech pathologist will work with the child, the child's **family**, and any other caregivers to develop a plan to help the child.

Treatment

Children with isolated speech disorders are often helped by articulation therapy, in which they practice repeating specific sounds, words, phrases, and sentences. For stuttering and other fluency disorders, a popular treatment method is fluency training, which develops coordination between speech and breathing, slows down the rate of speech, and develops the ability to prolong syllables. A child may practice saying a single word fluently and then gradually add more words, slowly increasing the amount and difficulty of speech that can be mastered without stuttering. The speaking situations can gradually be made more challenging as well, beginning with speaking alone to the pathologist and ending with speaking to a group of people.

Delayed auditory feedback (DAF), in which stutterers hear an echo of their own speech sounds, has also been effective in treating stuttering. When a speech problem is caused by serious or multiple disabilities, a neurodevelopmental approach, which inhibits certain reflexes to promote normal movement, is often preferred. Other techniques used in speech therapy include the motor-kinesthetic approach and biofeedback, which helps children know whether the sounds they are producing are faulty or correct. For children with severe communication disorders, speech pathologists can assist with alternate means of communication, such as manual signing and computer-synthesized speech.

Prognosis

When speech disorders are detected and treated early, the prognosis is generally very good. Many speech disorders that are not caused by other underlying problems resolve themselves, and most others can be resolved completely or nearly completely with prompt treatment. Stuttering resolves itself without treatment in about 50–80 percent of children.

KEY TERMS

Speech pathologist—An individual certified by the American Speech-Language-Hearing Association (ASHA) to treat speech disorders.

Prevention

There is no known way to prevent most speech disorders, although making sure that children have a language-rich environment is thought to help disorders related to lack of input.

Parental concerns

Speech disorders and significant speech delays can have a lasting negative impact on children. Children who have speech disorders may not want to communicate with their peers or even adults which may adversely affect their performance in school and social development.

See also Language delay; Language disorders.

Resources

BOOKS

Bahr, Diane Chapman. *Oral Motor Assessment and Treatment: Ages and Stages.* Boston: Allyn and Bacon, 2001.

Freed, Donald B. *Motor Speech Disorders: Diagnosis & Treatment.* San Diego: Singular Pub. Group, 2000.

Merritt, Donna D. and Barbara Culatta. *Language Intervention in the Classroom.* San Diego, Calif.: Singular Pub. Group, 1998.

ORGANIZATIONS

American Speech-Language-Hearing Association. 10801 Rockville Pike, Rockville, MD 20852. (800) 638–8255. Web site: <www.asha.org>.

Tish Davidson

Spina bifida

Definition

Spina bifida is a birth abnormality in which the spine is malformed and lacks its usual protective skeletal and soft tissue coverings.

Description

Spina bifida may appear in the body midline anywhere from the neck to the buttocks. In its most severe form, termed spinal rachischisis, the entire spinal canal is open, exposing the spinal cord and nerves. More commonly, the abnormality appears as a localized mass on the back that is covered by skin or by the meninges, the three-layered membrane that envelops the spinal cord. Spina bifida is usually readily apparent at birth because of the malformation of the back and paralysis below the level of the abnormality.

Various forms of spina bifida are known as meningomyelocele, myelomeningocele, spina bifida aperta, open spina bifida, myelodysplasia, spinal dysraphism, spinal rachischisis, myelocele, and meningocele. The term meningocele is used when the spine malformation contains only the protective covering (meninges) of the spinal cord. The other terms indicate involvement of the spinal cord and nerves in the malformation. A related term, spina bifida occulta, indicates that one or more of the bony bodies in the spine are incompletely hardened, but that there is no abnormality of the spinal cord itself.

Demographics

Spina bifida occurs worldwide, but there has been a steady downward trend in occurrence rates since about 1940, particularly in regions of high prevalence. The highest prevalence rates, about one in 200 pregnancies, have been reported from certain northern provinces in China. Intermediate prevalence rates, about one in 1000 pregnancies, have been found in Central and South America. The lowest prevalence rates, less than one in 2,000 pregnancies, have been found in European countries. The highest regional prevalence in the United States of about one in 500 pregnancies has occurred in the Southeast.

Causes and symptoms

Spina bifida may occur as an isolated abnormality or in the company of other malformations. As an isolated abnormality, spina bifida is caused by the combination of genetic factors and environmental influences that bring about malformation of the spine and spinal column. The specific genes and environmental influences that contribute to the many-factored causes of spina bifida were not as of 2004 completely known. An insufficiency of **folic acid** is known to be one influential nutritional factor. Changes (mutations) in genes involving the metabolism of folic acid are believed to be significant genetic risk factors. The recurrence risk after the birth of an infant with isolated spina bifida is 3 to 5 percent.

Recurrence may be for spina bifida or another type of spinal abnormality.

Spina bifida may arise because of chromosome abnormalities, single gene mutations, or specific environmental insults such as maternal **diabetes mellitus** or prenatal exposure to certain anticonvulsant drugs. The recurrence risk varies with each of these specific causes.

In most cases, spina bifida is obvious at birth because of malformation of the spine. The spine may be completely open, exposing the spinal cord and nerves. More commonly, the spine abnormality appears as a mass on the back covered by membrane (meninges) or skin. Spina bifida may occur any where from the base of the skull to the buttocks. About 75 percent of abnormalities occur in the lower back (lumbar) region. In rare instances, the spinal cord malformation may occur internally, sometimes with a connection to the gastrointestinal tract.

In spina bifida, many complications arise, dependent in part on the level and severity of the spine malformation. As a rule, the nerves below the level of the abnormality develop in a faulty manner and fail to function, resulting in paralysis and loss of sensation below the level of the spine malformation. Since most abnormalities occur in the lumbar region, the lower limbs are paralyzed and lack sensation. Furthermore, the bowel and bladder have inadequate nerve connections, causing an inability to control bowel and bladder function. Most infants also develop hydrocephaly, an accumulation of excess fluid in the four cavities of the brain. At least one of every seven cases develops findings of Chiari II malformation, a condition in which the lower part of the brain is crowded and may be forced into the upper part of the spinal cavity.

There are a number of mild variant forms of spina bifida, including multiple vertebral abnormalities, skin dimples, tufts of hair, and localized areas of skin deficiency over the spine. Two variants, lipomeningocele and lipomyelomeningocele, typically occur in the lower back area (lumbar or sacral) of the spine. In these conditions, a tumor of fatty tissue becomes isolated among the nerves below the spinal cord, which may result in tethering of the spinal cord and complications similar to those with open spina bifida.

Diagnosis

Few disorders are to be confused with open spina bifida. The diagnosis is usually obvious based on the external findings at birth. Paralysis below the level of the abnormality and fluid on the brain (hydrocephaly) may contribute to the diagnosis. Other spine abnormalities such as congenital **scoliosis** and kyphosis, or soft tissue tumors overlying the spine, are not likely to have these accompanying findings. In cases in which there are no external findings, the diagnosis is more difficult and may not become evident until neurological abnormalities or hydrocephaly develop weeks, months, or years following birth.

Prenatal diagnosis may be made in most cases with ultrasound examination after 12 to 14 weeks of pregnancy. Many cases are also detected by the testing of the mother's blood for the level of alpha-fetoprotein at about 16 weeks of pregnancy. If the spine malformation is not skin covered, alpha-fetoprotein from the fetus's circulation may leak into the surrounding amniotic fluid, a small portion of which is absorbed into the mother's blood.

Treatment

Aggressive surgical and medical management have improved the survival and function of infants with spina bifida. Initial surgery may be carried out during the first days of life, in the hope of providing protection against injury and infection. Subsequent surgery is often necessary to protect against excessive curvature of the spine, and in the presence of hydrocephaly, to place an echanical shunt to decrease the pressure and amount of cerebrospinal fluid in the cavities of the brain. Because of weakness or paralysis below the level of the spine abnormality, most children require physical therapy, bracing, and other orthopedic assistance in order to be able to walk. A variety of approaches including periodic bladder catheterization, surgical diversion of urine, and **antibiotics** are used to protect urinary function.

Although most individuals with spina bifida have normal intellectual function, learning disabilities or **mental retardation** occur in a minority. This deficit may result, in part, from hydrocephaly and/or infections of the nervous system. Children so affected may benefit from early educational intervention, physical therapy, and occupational therapy. Counseling to improve self-image and lessen barriers to socialization becomes important in late childhood and **adolescence**.

Open fetal surgery has been performed for spina bifida during the last half of pregnancy. After direct closure of the spine malformation, the fetus is returned to the womb. By preventing chronic intrauterine exposure to mechanical and chemical trauma, **prenatal surgery** improves neurological function and leads to fewer complications after birth. Fetal surgery is considered experimental, and results have been mixed.

Prognosis

More than 80 percent of infants born with spina bifida survivc with surgical and medical management. Although complications from paralysis, hydrocephaly, Chiari II malformation, and urinary tract deterioration threaten the well-being of the survivors, the outlook for normal intellectual function is good.

Prevention

Prevention of isolated spina bifida and other spinal abnormalities became possible in the 1980s and 1990s. The major prevention is through the use of folic acid, one of the B **vitamins**, for several months prior to and following conception. The Centers for Disease Control and Prevention (CDC) recommend the intake of 400 micrograms of synthetic folic acid every day for all women of childbearing years. For women who have had a previous child with spina bifida, the CDC recommends a daily intake of 4 milligrams of synthetic folic acid to help prevent a recurrence of spina bifida in future pregnancies.

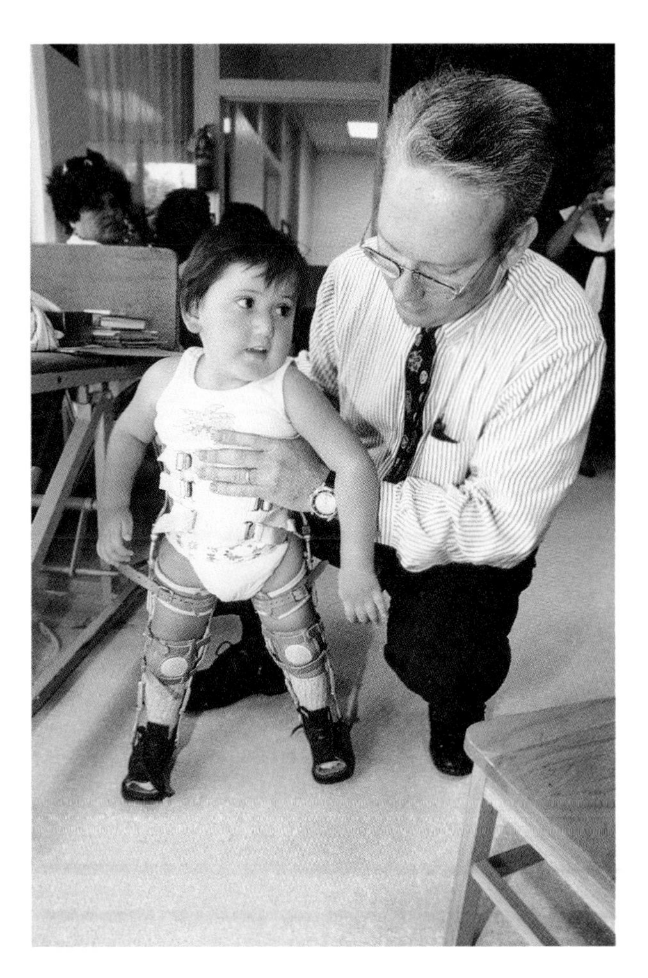

Doctor examining a child with spinal bifida. *(© Annie Griffiths Belt/Corbis.)*

Parental concerns

Caring for a child with spina bifida can be a daunting endeavor. Initially, parents may be overwhelmed with the medical decisions to be made and with the grief experienced after the birth of a special needs child. Many parents benefit from early and continuing involvement of an experienced social worker. There will be a multitude of medical decisions to be made. Children with spina bifida require a multidisciplinary team of healthcare providers, including surgeons, physicians, and therapists. Parents may find it helpful to designate a physician, usually the primary pediatrician, or an experienced rehabilitation counselor to act as an advocate for their child and to aid them in coordinating their child's treatment program.

Parental concerns may be two-fold, medical and emotional. Medical concerns include monitoring their child's condition after surgery. Children with spina bifida may have many surgical procedures throughout their lives. Post surgical complications are common but may often be avoided. Parents will be given care instructions after each surgery. Children with spina bifida face a multitude of heath issues such as monitoring bladder and bowel function, maintaining proper **nutrition**, preventing broken bones, promoting healthy growth and development, and encouraging activity and mobility. Many children with spina bifida have non-surgical treatments as well, such as positional aides to help the child sit and stand, physical therapy, and bracing and splints usually of the lower extremities.

Parents of children with spina bifida experience an array of emotions, including grief, **fear**, **anxiety**, and stress. Spina bifida impacts not only the affected child but the entire **family**. Groups and networks of other families affected by spina bifida can provide valuable support. Parents may need to be active in ensuring that their child receives the early intervention and educational services available in their community. Each state has programs to encourage healthy development in children with special needs.

Finally, parents should remember that most children with spina bifida live productive and happy lives. For the most part, children with spina bifida have average or above-average **intelligence**. Many of these children can go on to higher education, have active careers, and live self-sufficiently. It is important for parents to encourage

KEY TERMS

Bracing—Using orthopedic devices to hold joints or limbs in place.

Chiari II anomaly—A structural abnormality of the lower portion of the brain (cerebellum and brainstem) associated with spina bifida. The lower structures of the brain are crowded and may be forced into the foramen magnum, the opening through which the brain and spinal cord are connected.

Fetus—In humans, the developing organism from the end of the eighth week to the moment of birth. Until the end of the eighth week the developing organism is called an embryo.

Hydrocephalus—An abnormal accumulation of cerebrospinal fluid within the brain. This accumulation can be harmful by pressing on brain structures, and damaging them.

Splint—A thin piece of rigid or flexible material that is used to restrain, support, or immobilize a part of the body while healing takes place.

strong self esteem in their child and to foster independent living skills.

Resources

BOOKS

Behrman, Richard E., Robert M. Kliegman, and Hal B. Jenson, eds. *Nelson Textbook of Pediatrics*, 16th ed. Philadelphia: W. B. Saunders, 2000.

Sutton, Amy L. *Back and Neck Sourcebook: Basic Consumer Health Information.* Detroit, MI: Omnigraphics, 2004.

ORGANIZATIONS

March of Dimes Birth Defects Foundation. 1275 Mamaroneck Ave., White Plains, NY 10605. Web site: <www.modimes.org>.

National Birth Defects Prevention Network. Web site: <www.nbdpn.org>.

Shriners Hospitals for Children. International Shrine Headquarters, 2900 Rocky Point Dr., Tampa, FL 33607–1460. Web site: <www.shrinershq.org>.

Spina Bifida Association of America. 4590 MacArthur Blvd. NW, Suite 250, Washington, DC 20007–4226. Web site: <www.sbaa.org>.

Roger E. Stevenson
Deborah L. Nurmi, MS

Spinal cord injury

Definition

Spinal cord injury (SCI) is damage to the spinal cord that results in a loss of function such as mobility or feeling. The spinal cord does not have to be severed in order for a loss of function to occur. In most SCI cases, the spinal cord is intact, but the damage to it results in loss of function.

Description

The spinal cord and the brain are the two components of the central nervous system (CNS). The spinal cord extends from the base of the brain, down the middle of the back, to the lower back, and it coordinates movement and sensation in the body. It contains nerve cells, supporting cells, and long nerve fibers (axons) that connect to the brain and carry signals downward from the brain along descending pathways and upward to the brain along ascending pathways. Axons are covered by sheaths of an insulating whitish substance called myelin, and the region in which they lie is accordingly called white matter. The nerve cells themselves, with long branches (dendrites) that receive signals from other nerve cells, make up the gray matter that lies in a butterfly-shaped region in the center of the spinal cord. Like the brain, the spinal cord is enclosed in three membranes (meninges). The innermost layer is called the pia mater, the middle layer is the arachnoid, and the dura mater is the tougher outer layer. The spinal cord consists of several segments along its length, with higher segments controlling movement and sensation in upper parts of the body and lower segments controlling the lower parts of the body. The segments in the neck (cervical region), referred to as C1 to C8, control signals to the neck, arms, and hands. Those in the thoracic or upper back region (T1 to T12) control signals to the torso and some parts of the arms. Those in the mid-back (upper lumbar region) just below the ribs (L1 to L5) control signals to the hips and legs. Finally, the sacral segments (S1 to S5) lie just below the lumbar segments in the mid-back and control signals to the groin, toes, and some parts of the legs.

The types of disability associated with SCI thus depend directly on the type and severity of the injury, the level of the cord at which the injury occurs, and the nerve fiber pathways that are damaged. Severe injury to the spinal cord causes paralysis and complete loss of sensation to the parts of the body controlled by the spinal cord segments below the point of injury. Spinal cord injuries also can lead to many complications, including pressure sores and increased susceptibility to respiratory diseases.

Demographics

According to the National Institute of Neurological Disorders and **Stroke** (NINDS), accidents and violence cause an estimated 10,000 spinal cord injuries each year, and more than 200,000 Americans live day-to-day with the disabling effects of SCI. The incidence of spinal cord injuries peaks among people in their early 20s, with a small increase in the elderly population due to falls and degenerative diseases of the spine. SCI is an uncommon source of morbidity and mortality in children.

Causes and symptoms

According to the National Spinal Cord Injury Association (NSCIA), spinal cord injuries are caused in the United States by motor vehicle accidents (44%), acts of violence (24%), falls (22%), **sports** (8%), and other causes (2%) such as abscesses, tumors, **polio**, **spina bifida** and Friedrich's Ataxia, a rare inherited disorder. For infants, motor vehicle crash is the leading cause of SCI. Falls rank highest for ages two to nine years and sports for the 10 to 14 age group. The most common injury level for the five to 13 age group is the high cervical spine (C1-C4).

SCI symptoms usually appear immediately after the injury. However, symptoms can develop slowly, if an infection or tumor is gradually increasing pressure on the spinal cord. General symptoms are as follows:

- weakness, poor coordination or paralysis, particularly below the level of the injury
- **numbness**, tingling, or loss of sensation
- loss of bowel or bladder control
- **pain**

When to call the doctor

Immediate medical attention is required if a parent suspects a child may have injured his or her neck or back, or if a child has poor coordination or paralysis in any part of the body. Spinal cord injury is not always obvious: numbness or paralysis may result immediately after SCI or later on as swelling gradually occurs in or around the spinal cord. In either case, the time between injury and treatment is critical and can significantly influence the extent of complications and the level of recovery. Any child who has experienced significant trauma to the head, back, or neck should be medically evaluated for the possibility of SCI.

Diagnosis

The possibility of SCI is usually suspected in anyone with significant trauma to the head and/or neck. Physicians accordingly assume that such patients have a spine fracture until proven otherwise.

Diagnosis is established with the help of x-rays of the spine that allow doctors to determine the extent of the damage. The following imaging tests are also used: CT scan (**computed tomography**), MRI (**magnetic resonance imaging**), and myelogram (x ray after injection of dye into the spinal canal).

Treatment

A person suspected of having a spinal cord injury should not be moved and treatment of SCI begins with **immobilization**, commonly achieved by enclosing the cervical spine in a rigid collar and use of rigid backboards. Paramedics and other rescue workers receive extensive training in immobilizing the spine. Immobilization prevents further injuries to the cord at the scene of the injury and has helped reduce worsening of any neurological SCI injury. At the time of injury, treatment is focused on stabilizing the spine and relieving cord compression. Prompt steroid drug injections (within eight hours of the injury) are also used to minimize cell damage and improve the chance of recovery.

Surgery cannot reverse damage to the spinal cord but is often needed to stabilize the spine to prevent future pain or deformity. It may involve fusing together vertebrae or inserting metal pins; or removing bone chips, bullets, or other **foreign objects**; or draining fluid to relieve pressure. Long-term treatment of spinal cord injuries usually involves drug therapy, the use of neural prostheses, and rehabilitation. Complementary treatment includes **nutrition** management, psychological counseling, and careful monitoring by physicians.

Drug therapy

Effective drug therapy for spinal cord injury was demonstrated in 1990, when methylprednisolone, the first drug shown to improve recovery from spinal cord injury, was approved for standard use. Completely paralyzed patients given methylprednisolone recover an average of about 20 percent of their lost motor function, compared to only 8 percent recovery of function in untreated patients. Partially paralyzed patients recover an average of 75 percent of their function, compared to 59 percent in patients who do not receive the drug.

Neural prostheses

Neural prostheses are used to compensate for lost function resulting from SCI. These sophisticated electrical and mechanical devices connect with the nervous system to supplement or replace lost motor and sensory functions. Neural prostheses contain many intricate components, such as implanted stimulators, electrodes, leads and connectors, sensors, and programming systems. There are many technical considerations in selecting each component. The electronic components must be as small as possible. Biocompatibility between electrodes and body tissue is also required to prevent the patient from being harmed by contact with the device. One device, a neural prosthesis that allows rudimentary hand control, was approved by the United States Food and Drug Administration (FDA). Patients control the device using shoulder muscles. With training, most patients can open and close their hand in two different grasping movements and lock the grasp in place by moving their shoulder in different ways.

Rehabilitation

Rehabilitation techniques can greatly improve patients' health and quality of life by helping them learn to use their remaining abilities. They start by setting functional goals. Functional goals are a realistic expectation of activities that a person with SCI eventually should be able to do with a particular level of injury. These goals are set during rehabilitation with the medical team. They help the patient with SCI learn new ways to manage his/her daily activities and stay healthy. Developing independence is especially important to kids, particularly teenagers. Many hospitals have SCI units geared to help patients develop their independence, and SCI treatment centers are operational in several states with special programs for children. The SCI units include kitchens and laundry facilities and other equipment so that patients can learn independent living skills, such as cooking meals or ironing clothes. A spinal cord injury can also affect the nerves and muscles and can cause bowel and bladder problems and skin problems. Children are prepared for these changes during rehabilitation and are taught the self-care skills needed to deal with these problems. Parents of spinal cord injured children also need to learn how to take care of their spinal-cord injured child. Having a spinal cord injury does not mean that children have to stop participating in games and enjoyable activities. Most SCI units have recreational therapists on staff to show kids how to **play** wheelchair basketball, volleyball, and tennis, as well as specially adapted games.

Alternative treatment

People with spinal cord injuries caused by traumatic events have in the past been considered hopeless cases destined to a life of paralysis. But in the last decades of the twentieth century there were dramatic advances in spinal cord regeneration research. For example, Swiss scientist Martin Schwab actually managed to heal spinal cords in rats and restored their ability to walk. At the Swedish Karolinska Institute, scientists succeeded in constructing a bridge of slender nerve filaments to connect a once-severed spinal cord in rats that subsequently were able to flex their legs. These developments and others offer paralyzed people some hope. In the early 2000s envisioned treatments include an immune therapy procedure that has been tested in Israel with human subjects and possibilities for mechanical neural prostheses.

Acupuncture is a more conservative form of alternative treatment with documented evidence for the reduction of SCI-related **muscle spasms**, increased level of sensation, improved bladder and bowel function, improvement in lower limb paralysis, with younger patients reported to have better outcomes.

Nutritional concerns

Because of the changes that occur in the body after SCI, parents need to understand the role that nutrition can play in the overall health of a child following a spinal cord injury.

Special health concerns resulting from SCI are as follows:

- Bowel management. Individuals with SCI may have neurogenic bowel, with the result that the messages from the brain that control the downward muscular movements of the bowel are either absent or not working properly, making it difficult for stool to move through the intestines. SCI diets accordingly include high fiber and plenty of fluids to regulate bowel movements.
- Heart problems. SCI presents a greater risk for cardiovascular and heart problems, hence the necessity to limit salt and cholesterol intake.
- Pressure ulcers. Pressure ulcers are always a concern to individuals with SCI and a diet high in protein, **vitamins**, and **minerals** is recommended to promote skin healing.
- Kidney or bladder stones. Individuals with SCI may be prone to developing calcium stones. Certain beverages can cause crystals to form in the urine and excessive consumption of dairy products is accordingly avoided with water highly recommended as the best drink.

- Urinary tract infection. The loss of normal bladder function after SCI places an individual at risk for urinary tract infection. A high fluid intake every day has been shown to reduce the problem of infections.
- Weight control. After SCI, the metabolic rate is usually lower. Metabolic rate is how fast a body burns ingested calories. A lower muscle mass and a decrease in activities cause a lower metabolic rate, meaning that fewer calories are needed each day to maintain a desirable weight. After rehabilitation, the ideal body weight of a person with SCI is lower than for a nondisabled individual. Dieticians normally decrease the amount of calories by 5 percent for those with paraplegia and 10 to 15 percent for those with tetraplegia (quadriplegia).

Prognosis

The prognosis of SCI depends on the location and extent of injury. Once the initial injury heals, functional improvements may continue for at least six months. Any disability that remains after that point is likely to be permanent. Injuries of the neck above C4 with significant involvement of the diaphragm have worse outcomes. Although SCI often results in permanent disability, rehabilitation can maximize the level of function and help patients adapt and lead independent, productive lives.

According to the American Association of Neurological Surgeons, mortality from SCI is influenced by several factors, the most important being the severity of associated injuries. Because of the force that is required to fracture the spine, it is not uncommon for the patient to suffer significant damage to the chest and/or abdomen. Many of these associated injuries are fatal. For isolated SCIs, the mortality after one year is roughly 5 to 7 percent. If a patient survives the first 24 hours after injury, the probability of survival for ten years is approximately 75 to 80 percent. Likewise, the ten-year survival rate for patients who survived the first year after injury is 87 percent.

Prevention

The following guidelines have been shown to help prevent SCI:

- use of safe driving practices
- avoidance of situations that may become violent
- keeping firearms locked away
- taking precautions to prevent falls around the home (walkways free from obstacles, non-slip materials in bathtubs, etc)
- use of proper **safety** equipment for sports

The American Academy of Orthopedic Surgeons (AAOS) also recommends that playgrounds be made safe to prevent spinal cord injuries. It offers the following checklist to help parents assess the safety of their child's playground:

- Are any pieces of playground equipment missing supports, anchors, or footings?
- Are any supports, anchors, or footings damaged or loose?
- Has the wood started to splinter or rot?
- Are surface materials missing or damaged?
- Are there any missing, loose, or damaged nuts and bolts on the equipment?
- Are any seats broken?
- Are swing hangers and chains broken or worn?
- Are hooks, rings, or links misshapen or deformed?
- Are there any broken, missing, or loose steps?
- Are any ladder rungs missing, broken, or loose?
- Are tree roots visible or rocks sticking up that could cause a child to trip and fall?

If the answer to any of these questions is "Yes," this playground is not safe for a child. The AAOS recommends that the playground be reported to local park or school officials or to contact a local orthopedic surgeon to enquire as how to build a safe, accessible playground for the area.

Parental concerns

In most cases, SCI requires that the home be modified to be fully accessible to the injured child. Bathrooms need to be fitted with a shower chair, grab bars, a shower wand, a tub lift, or a shower bench. Grab bars should be installed on three sides of the shower, and non-skid strips should be applied to the bottom of the shower or tub. Bedrooms should be located for convenient access to the bathroom and adequate space should be provided around the bed for wheelchair access with convenient storage near the bed for braces, prostheses, and clothing. Light switches should be lowered for easy access and ramps should be built to facilitate displacements.

See also Computed tomography; Magnetic resonance imaging.

Resources

BOOKS

Nesathurai, Shanker. *The Rehabilitation of People with Spinal Cord Injury*. Oxford, UK: Blackwell Science, 2000.

KEY TERMS

Axon—A long, threadlike projection that is part of a neuron (nerve cell).

Central nervous system—Part of the nervous system consisting of the brain, cranial nerves, and spinal cord. The brain is the center of higher processes, such as thought and emotion and is responsible for the coordination and control of bodily activities and the interpretation of information from the senses. The cranial nerves and spinal cord link the brain to the peripheral nervous system, that is the nerves present in the rest of body.

Computed tomography (CT)—An imaging technique in which cross-sectional x rays of the body are compiled to create a three-dimensional image of the body's internal structures; also called computed axial tomography.

Dendrite—A threadlike extension of the cytoplasm of a neuron that conducts electrical impulses toward the cell body of the neuron. Usually it spreads out into many branches.

Gray matter—Areas of the brain and spinal cord that are comprised mostly of unmyelinated nerves.

Magnetic resonance imaging (MRI)—An imaging technique that uses a large circular magnet and radio waves to generate signals from atoms in the body. These signals are used to construct detailed images of internal body structures and organs, including the brain.

Methylpredisolone—A steroid drug. Methylpredisolone administered within eight hours of acute spinal cord trauma is the first drug shown to improve recovery from spinal cord injury.

Myelin—A fatty sheath surrounding nerves throughout the body that helps them conduct impulses more quickly.

Myelogram—An x-ray image of the spinal cord, spinal canal, and nerve roots taken with the aid of a contrast dye.

Spina bifida—A birth defect (a congenital malformation) in which part of the vertebrae fail to develop completely so that a portion of the spinal cord, which is normally protected within the vertebral column, is exposed. People with spina bifida can suffer from bladder and bowel incontinence, cognitive (learning) problems, and limited mobility.

Vertebrae—Singular, vertebra. The individual bones of the spinal column that are stacked on top of each other. There is a hole in the center of each bone, through which the spinal cord passes.

White matter—A substance, composed primarily of myelin fibers, found in the brain and nervous system that protects nerves and allows messages to be sent to and from the brain and various parts of the body. Also called white substance.

Palmer, Sara, et al. *Spinal Cord Injury: A Guide for Living.* Baltimore, MD: Johns Hopkins University Press, 2000.

Somers, Martha Freeman. *Spinal Cord Injury: Functional Rehabilitation.* New York: Pearson Education, 2001.

Vikhanski, Luba. *In Search of the Lost Cord: Solving the Mystery of Spinal Cord Regeneration.* Washington, DC: Joseph Henry Press, 2001.

PERIODICALS

Bakun, M. and K. Haddix. "Spinal cord injury prevention with children and adolescents." *SCI Nursing* 20, no. 2 (Summer, 2003): 116–118.

Beck, T. "Current spasticity management in children with spinal cord injury." *SCI Nursing* 19, no. 1 (Spring, 2002): 28–31.

Cirak, B., et al. "Spinal injuries in children." *Journal of Pediatric Surgery* 39, no. 4 (April, 2004): 607–12.

Dias, M. S. "Traumatic brain and spinal cord injury." *Pediatric Clinics of North America* 51, no. 2 (April, 2004): 271–303.

Merenda, L. A., et al. "Progressive treatment options for children with spinal cord injury." *SCI Nursing* 17, no. 3 (Fall, 2000): 102–09.

Vogel, L. C., and C. J. Anderson. "Spinal cord injuries in children and adolescents: a review." *Journal of Spinal Cord Medicine* 26, no. 3 (Fall, 2003): 193–203.

———. "Self-injurious behavior in children and adolescents with spinal cord injuries." *Spinal Cord* 40, no. 12 (December, 2002): 666–68.

Wang, M. Y., et al. "High rates of neurological improvement following severe traumatic pediatric spinal cord injury." *Spine* 29, no. 13 (July, 2004): 1493–97.

ORGANIZATIONS

American Spinal Injury Association (ASIA). 2020 Peachtree Road NW, Atlanta, GA 30309–1402. Web site: <www.asia-spinalinjury.org>.

International Spinal Cord Regeneration Center. PO Box 451, Bonita, California 91902. Web site: <www.electriciti.com/~spinal>.

National Association for Home Care (NAHC). 228 7th Street SE, Washington, DC 20003. Web site: <www.nahc.org>.

National Institute of Neurological Disorders and Stroke (NINDS). PO Box 5801, Bethesda, MD 20824. Web site: <www.ninds.nih.gov>.

National Spinal Cord Injury Association (NSCIA). 6701 Democracy Blvd, Suite 300–9, Bethesda, MD 20817. Web site: <www.spinalcord.org>.

Spinal Cord Society. 19051 County Highway 1, Fergus Falls, MN 56537–7609. Web site: <http://users.aol.com/scsweb>.

WEB SITES

"Spinal Cord Injury Rehabilitation." *Shriner's Hospitals for Children.* Available online at <http://www.shrinershq.org/hospitals/sci.html> (accessed October 13, 2004).

Monique Laberge, Ph.D.

Spinal muscular atrophy

Definition

Spinal muscular atrophy is a term that describes a number of different conditions, all of which have in common the gradual deterioration of the voluntary muscles.

Description

Several different conditions fall under the name spinal muscular atrophy (SMA). These include SMA type I, also called Werdnig-Hoffmann; SMA type II; SMA type III, also called Kugelberg-Welander disease; Kennedy syndrome, or progressive spinobulbar muscular atrophy; and congenital SMA with arthrogryposis.

Demographics

The autosomal recessive forms of spinal muscular atrophy are the most common inherited cause of infant death. Each type of spinal muscular atrophy has an incidence of about 10 to 15 cases in every 100,000 live births.

Causes and symptoms

All types of spinal muscular atrophy are genetic diseases. Most of the syndromes are autosomal recessive, meaning that they have no predilection for either sex. Parents of children with SMA usually carry the gene for the disease but have no symptoms themselves. A child who receives two genes (one from each parent) will express the symptoms of the disease.

Although the entire sequence of abnormalities that causes spinal muscular atrophy was not delineated as of 2004, there is thought to be an absence or deficiency of a specific protein necessary for the proper functioning of the nerve cells responsible for movement (motor neurons).

SMA type I (Werdnig-Hoffmann disease)

SMA type I is usually noted prior to birth, due to a decrease in the baby's movements in utero, or early in life. Babies with this type of SMA have decreased muscle and trunk tone, resulting in floppiness of the limbs and weak arm and leg movements. They have difficulty with swallowing and, therefore, with feeding, and they have breathing problems. These children are unable to learn to sit or to stand. The disease is usually fatal prior to the age of two.

SMA type II

Symptoms of SMA type II are usually noted in a child between three and 15 months of age. Symptoms include breathing problems; weak and floppy limbs; involuntary jerking and twitching of muscles in the arms, legs, and tongue; abnormal reflexes. Children with SMA type II may eventually be able to sit, but they are unable to learn to stand or to walk.

SMA type III (Kugelberg-Welander disease)

Children with SMA type III begin to experience symptoms between the ages of two and 17 years. Problems develop that hamper the child's ability to walk, run, climb stairs, and rise from a chair. Twitches and tremors may develop in the child's fingers.

Kennedy syndrome (progressive spinobulbar muscular atrophy)

This form of spinal muscular atrophy only affects men; it is an X-linked recessive disorder, meaning that the defective gene is passed from mother to son.

Individuals with Kennedy syndrome begin to develop symptoms between the ages of 15 and 60 years. Characteristic symptoms include increasing weakness of the tongue and facial muscles, problems with swallowing, impaired speech, and increased size of the male breast (gynecomastia). The severity of the symptoms of Kennedy syndrome progress gradually.

Congenital SMA with arthrogryposis

This is one of the rarest forms of spinal muscular atrophy. It is present at birth, and children exhibit severe contractures of the joints, resulting in limb deformity; spinal curvature; deformities of the chest wall; difficulties breathing; abnormally small jaw; and upper eyelid droop (ptosis).

Diagnosis

Diagnosis is by a combination of clinical observation; blood tests that reveal an increased level of creatine kinase (which appears in the blood when muscle tissue is being broken down); distinctive abnormalities on muscle biopsy; characteristic electromyographic and nerve conduction abnormalities; and genetic testing.

Treatment

There are no cures for any of the forms of spinal muscular atrophy. The treatments involve addressing the symptoms and attempting to improve quality of life. Medical treatment may be necessary for recurrent **pneumonia** and other respiratory infections. Surgery may be necessary for spinal curvature and severe contractures. Physical therapy, occupational therapy, and other types of rehabilitation programs may help individuals achieve the highest level of functioning possible.

Prognosis

The prognosis for spinal muscular atrophy is variable. Life expectancy is dependent on the degree of respiratory impairment present. Because of the slow progression of symptoms, individuals with Types III or Kennedy syndrome may have normal life spans.

Prevention

There is no way to prevent spinal muscular atrophy. However, genetic counseling is crucial so that parents can make informed decisions about having children. In general, when a **family** has already had a child with SMA, each subsequent pregnancy has a 25 percent chance of producing another child with SMA. Prenatal testing is available. Parents must then decide whether to use the information to help them prepare for the arrival of a baby with SMA or to terminate the pregnancy.

Parental concerns

Caring for a child with SMA can be very challenging and emotionally draining. Support groups, respite care, and help to support other siblings in the family can be important adjunct measures.

Resources

BOOKS

"Disorders of Neuromuscular Transmission and of Motor Neurons." In *Nelson Textbook of Pediatrics.* Edited by Richard E. Behrman et al. Philadelphia: Saunders, 2004.

Siddique, Nailah. "Degenerative Motor, Sensory, and Autonomic Disorders." In *Textbook of Clinical Neurology.* Edited by Christopher G. Goetz. Philadelphia: Saunders, 2003.

WEB SITES

Muscular Dystrophy Association—USA. 3300 E. Sunrise Drive, Tucson, AZ 85718. Web site: <www.mdausa.org>.

NIH Neurological Institute., PO Box 5801, Bethesda, MD 20824. Web site: <www.ninds.nih.gov>.

Rosalyn Carson-DeWitt, MD

Spinal tap *see* **Cerebrospinal fluid (CSF) analysis**

Spinocerebellar ataxia *see* **Friedrich's ataxia**

Spirometry *see* **Pulmonary function test**

Sports

Definition

Sports are group games and individual activities involving physical activity and skills.

Description

Sports help children develop physical skills, get **exercise**, make friends, have fun, learn to **play** as a member of a team, learn to play fair, and improve **self-esteem**.

Participation in sports is a great way of staying active and offers wonderful rewards for mental health. Being involved in sports has been proven to help children learn valuable skills for dealing with life's ups and downs. They teach youth how to interact with others and work as a team. This skill facilitates working with others in other ways such as on a class project or a school play. Sports also help students become more independent and feel better about themselves. The result is positive self-esteem and self-confidence, which are extremely important for determining later happiness and success.

Sports also offer an enjoyable, exciting environment in which to learn how to handle both failure and success. Everyone wins and loses some of the time in both sports and other endeavors. Winning feels great and empowering but can also cause a young person to feel pressure and **anxiety** in the next attempt to win. Losing usually produces feelings of sadness, depression, and disappointment. Learning how to cope with these different feelings fosters good mental health.

Another aspect of sports that contributes to a healthy mind is goal-setting. Young people who have goals are more likely to be self-motivated and are usually able to accomplish more because they know what they need to do in order to get ahead. Without goals, adolescents tend to lack direction and focus. In sports, goal setting is essential for improving individually and working as a team. This is also true in other pursuits. For example, if a student wants to get better grades, reaching specific goals, such as studying for a certain period of time each night, is the most likely way to achieve them.

SPORTSMANSHIP American sports culture has increasingly become a business. The highly stressful and competitive attitude prevalent at colleges and in professional sports affects the world of children's sports and athletics, creating an unhealthy environment. The attitudes and behavior taught to children in sports carry over into adulthood. Parents should take an active role in helping their child develop good sportsmanship, according to a 2002 health advisory issued by the journal *Clinical Reference Systems*.

To help adolescents get the most out of sports, parents need to be actively involved. Quoting from the American Academy of Child & Adolescent Psychiatry Web site, parental involvement includes the following steps:

- providing emotional support and positive feedback
- attending all or some games and talking about them afterward
- having realistic expectations for your child
- learning the sport and supporting your child's involvement
- helping your child talk with you about experiences with the coach and other team members
- helping your child handle disappointments and losing
- modeling respectful spectator behavior

EXTREME SPORTS Extreme sports in the early 2000s are becoming increasingly popular among young people. They offer the thrill of facing difficult challenges and overcoming obstacles. Extreme sports get the heart racing and put the body and mind to the test in the face of danger. However, with the many physical and mental benefits of extreme sports comes the risk of injuries. It is essential to work with a trained instructor and use the necessary **safety** equipment when doing any kind of extreme sport.

Extreme sports are not for everyone. However, those looking for bigger challenges in their quest for physical fitness have many options, including rock and ice climbing, surfing, whitewater rafting, wakeboarding, water-skiing, mountain-bike racing, bicycle stunt-riding, skydiving, skateboarding, and extreme snowboarding. There are many camps around the country that teach extreme sports to kids and teenagers. Anyone can find the nearest extreme sports camp or more general information by typing "extreme sports" on any Internet search engine. There are thousands of Web sites devoted to these activities.

Infancy

An infant is capable of participating in only a limited amount of athletic activity. Still, many parents worry about their child's motor skill development and wonder how they can help develop these skills. The American Academy of Pediatrics (AAP) advises parents that normal play with adults is more than enough physical stimulus to encourage normal development of motor skills. In years of research, no one has produced any evidence that increased stimulation of infants increases development of motor skills in later years.

Swimming is perhaps the only sport infants are really able to participate in. While infants instinctively hold their breath when immersed in water, pediatricians warn that they also swallow water, which can produce hazardous side effects. The AAP advises that infants should not participate in swimming activities until they are at least four months old.

Toddlerhood

Toddlers are naturally curious and exploratory, leading them to develop independence skills such as walking and talking. These should be encouraged by adults, as should frequent interaction with other children their own age. Athletic activity at this age should be free form and spontaneous, with adult interference or direction held to a minimum. The AAP suggests that adult intervention, such as teaching a child to throw and catch a baseball, has little effect on later motor skills development, and they warn that the repetition of such practicing often stifles the natural urge to play creatively. It has also been shown that until children reach ages of five to seven, their vision is not sufficiently developed to follow objects that are moving quickly through their line of sight, such as thrown balls.

Preschool

Children are not little adults when it comes to sports and physical activities. As reported in Heidi Splete's article on age-appropriate sports skills, Sally Harris, a pediatrician at the Palo Alto Medical Clinic in Palo Alto, California, asserts that early childhood sports should focus on skill development rather than competitiveness. Activities should allow children to learn by trial and error with minimal instruction. Competition is mostly a distraction for preschool-age children. Appropriate athletic activities for children of this age are dance, beginning gymnastics (primarily tumbling), and swimming. Free-form play with peers is probably most important, both for its socializing effect and for the creative expression it offers.

Sports activity in early childhood should have three basic components, according to Harris. They are acquisition of basic motor skills, social development by the child's interaction with coaches and teammates, and **cognitive development** in understanding and following instructions and executing strategy and tactics.

School age

By the age of five or six, children begin rapidly developing motor skills. Also, posture and balance become automatic, and reaction times become faster. However, learning complex rules is often difficult and trying to teach a child a sport requiring a great deal of instruction, such as baseball, football, or soccer, may only cause frustration and a lack of interest. A child's inability in these areas can also cause a sense of failure and provoke a life-long aversion to organized sports. One good way to get a child interested in sports during these years is to engage in physical activity the whole **family** can participate in, such as taking long walks or bicycle rides. Most pediatricians suggest that complex team sports that require coaching or memorization should be postponed until a child reaches the age of nine or ten. Between the ages of six and nine years, beginning soccer and baseball are appropriate sports, especially if the focus is on getting children interested in sports or physical activity.

By the time a child reaches **adolescence**, his or her interest in sports is most likely at its peak. Children of this age often collect sports memorabilia, wear clothes resembling the uniforms of their favorite players, and spend larger amounts of time watching, participating in, and talking about sports. At ages 10 through 12, children can improve traditional athletic skills and master complex motor skills. They are able to play sports involving strategies and teamwork, but growth spurts can bring physical and emotional changes that parents and coaches should be aware of, according to Harris.

In the last several decades of the twentieth century, there was a dramatic decrease in the number of school districts that require physical education classes for students. As a result, the U.S. Department of Health and Human Services set an objective to increase the number of children six years of age and older who exercise on a daily basis at light to moderate levels for at least 30 minutes.

A 2002 survey of student participation in extracurricular sports activities at middle schools showed a typical program was offered on average 3.6 hours per week. It also revealed that 26.7 percent of boys and 22.9 percent of girls participated in the activities. The most commonly offered activities at middle schools surveyed were basketball (31.7%), track and field (10.3%), soccer (9.4%), tennis (6.7%), and football (5.4%).

Since the middle schools offered a small number of sports activity programs, the survey recommends middle schools add a variety of noncompetitive activities, such as dance, aerobics, martial arts, jogging, walking, and **yoga**. Providing programs that appeal to a wider range of students at all grade levels of middle and high school would likely increase participation in extracurricular sports and physical activity programs.

The social benefits of athletics are especially important for young girls. In fact, it has been argued that girls are more in need of the benefits of athletics than boys. Adolescent girls tend to have lower self-esteem than boys, and many suffer from the false belief that their bodies are useful only to the extent that they are attractive to boys. Statistics compiled by the Women's Sports Foundation also demonstrate that young female athletes receive substantial benefits from participation in sports.

They found that girls who participated in school athletics are 92 percent less likely to use drugs, including tobacco and alcohol; and 80 percent less likely to get pregnant. Additionally, they are three times more likely to graduate from college.

Common problems

The most common problem in adolescent sports is sports-related injuries. An estimated 30 million children in the United States play in organized sports but about 35 percent drop out each year, usually due to physical injury or emotional stress. Each year, hospital emergency rooms see more than 2.6 million sports-related injuries in young people, according to an article in the April 8, 2002 issue of *U. S. News & World Report*.

Among children ages 5 to 14 years, the top **sports injuries** annually are: bicycling, 336,250; basketball, 193,400; football, 185,740; baseball and softball, 117,250; and soccer, 85,430. The number of other sports injuries include skateboarding, 49,930; hockey, 25,400; and gymnastics, 26,950.

Among young people ages 15 to 24 years, the top sports injuries are: basketball, 277,00; football, 171,290; bicycling, 95,720; baseball and softball, 88,340; and soccer, 68,790, according to the article. Other sports injuries included general exercising, 38,560; snowboarding, 29,700; hockey, 28,070; and skateboarding, 27,470.

Parental concerns

The National Athletic Training Association encourages parents to ask questions of coaches when their children become involved in sports. These questions include the following:

- What is the level of the coach's education? Does it include training in **cardiopulmonary resuscitation** (CPR) and first aid?
- What does the coach do when an injury happens? What is the protocol for returning to play following an injury?
- Is there an on-site athletic healthcare provider or consulting team physician? Does the coach knows about any health conditions of the child and have phone numbers where parents can be reached in an emergency?
- Are there emergency medications available for children with **asthma** or allergies?
- What are the inclement weather guidelines, especially for lightning storms and extreme heat?
- Is the athletic equipment safe, properly fitted, and in good condition?
- Are there any supervised preseason and in-season conditioning programs?

When to call the doctor

If a child receives a soft tissue injury, such as a strain or sprain, or a bone injury, the best immediate treatment is ice, compression, elevation of the injury, and rest. Get professional treatment if any injury is severe, such as a fracture, profuse bleeding, dislocated joint, prolonged swelling, or prolonged or severe **pain**. Playing rigorous sports in the heat requires close monitoring of both body and weather conditions. Heat injuries are always dangerous and can be fatal. Children perspire less than adults and require a higher core body temperature to trigger sweating. Heat-related illnesses include **dehydration**, heat exhaustion (**nausea**, **dizziness**, weakness, **headache**, pale and moist skin, heavy perspiration, normal or low body temperature, weak pulse, dilated pupils, disorientation, and fainting spells), and heat stroke (headache, dizziness, confusion, and hot dry skin, possibly leading to blood vessel collapse, coma, and death). Professional medical help should be sought for heat stroke, heat exhaustion, and any other heat-related illnesses that do not quickly clear up.

Resources

BOOKS

Erickson, Darrell. *Molding Young Athletes: How Parents and Coaches Can Positively Influence Kids in Sports.* Oregon, WI: Purington Press, 2004.

Fish, Joel. *101 Ways to Be a Terrific Sports Parent: Making Athletics a Positive Experience for Your Child.* New York: Fireside, 2003.

Malina, Robert M., and Michael A. Clark. *Youth Sports: Perspectives for a New Century.* Monterey, CA: Coaches Choice Books, 2003.

Shannon, Joyce Brennfleck. *Sports Injuries Information for Teens: Health Tips about Sports Injuries and Injury Prevention.* Detroit, MI: Omnigraphics, 2003.

PERIODICALS

Goldberg, Michael J. "Kids Dropping Out of Sports." *Pediatric News* (February 2002): 25.

Ishee, Jimmy H. "Participation in Extracurricular Physical Activity in Middle Schools." *The Journal of Physical Education, Recreation & Dance* (April 2003): 10.

Lord, Mary. "Dangerous Games: Sports Injuries among Children." *U.S. News & World Report* (April 8, 2002): 44.

Children participating in a basketball game. *(© Tom & Dee Ann McCarthy/Corbis.)*

KEY TERMS

Cardiopulmonary resuscitation (CPR)—An emergency procedure designed to stimulate breathing and blood flow through a combination of chest compressions and rescue breathing. It is used to restore circulation and prevent brain death to a person who has collapsed, is unconscious, is not breathing, and has no pulse.

Cognitive ability—Relating to the process of acquiring knowledge by using reasoning, intuition, or perception.

Dehydration—An excessive loss of water from the body. It may follow vomiting, prolonged diarrhea, or excessive sweating.

Heat exhaustion—A condition of physical weakness or collapse often accompanied by nausea, muscle cramps, and dizziness, that is caused by exposure to intense heat.

Heat stroke—A serious condition that results from exposure to extreme heat. The body loses its ability to cool itself. Severe headache, high fever, and hot, dry skin may result. In severe cases, a person with heat stroke may collapse or go into a coma.

Motor skills—Controlled movements of muscle groups. Fine motor skills involve tasks that require dexterity of small muscles, such as buttoning a shirt. Tasks such as walking or throwing a ball involve the use of gross motor skills.

Metzl, Jordan D. "Sports Should Be About Fun." *Pediatric News* (October 2002): 32.

Splete, Heidi. "Developmental Stages of Sports Readiness Can't Be Rushed: Accept Some Level of Chaos." *Family Practice News* (Sept. 1, 2002): 33.

———."Work on Age-appropriate Sports Skills: How Much, How Soon?" *Pediatric News* (October 2002): 28.

ORGANIZATIONS

American Academy of Pediatrics. 141 Northwest Point Blvd., Elk Grove Village, IL 60007. Web site: <www.aao.org>.

National Institute of Arthritis and Musculoskeletal and Skin Diseases. 1 AMS Circle, Bethesda, MD 20892. Web site: <www.nih.gov/niams>.

WEB SITES

"Children and Sports." *American Academy of Child & Adolescent Psychiatry*, January 2002. Available online at <www.aacap.org/publications/factsFam/sports.htm> (accessed October 14, 2004).

"Sports Injury Prevention: Children and Adolescents." *Safe USA*, July 14, 2002. Available online at <http://safeusa.org/sports/child.htm> (accessed October 14, 2004).

Teresa G. Odle
Ken R. Wells

Sports injuries

Definition

Sports injuries result from acute trauma or repetitive stress associated with athletic activities. Sports injuries can affect bones or soft tissue such as ligaments, muscles, and tendons.

Description

Children are more likely to suffer sports injuries than adults since a child's vulnerability is heightened by immature reflexes, an inability to recognize and evaluate risks, and underdeveloped coordination.

In 2002, about 20.3 million Americans suffered a sports injury. The highest rate is among children age 5 to 14 years (59.3 per 1000 people). As many as 20 percent of children who **play** sports get hurt, and about 25 percent of their injuries are classified as serious. Boys age 12 through 17 are the highest risk group. More than 775,000 boys and girls under age 14 are treated in hospital emergency rooms each year for sports-related injuries. Between one half and two thirds of childhood sports injuries occur during practice or in the course of unorganized athletic activity.

Types of sports injuries

About 95 percent of sports injuries are minor soft tissue traumas. The most common sports injury is a bruise (contusion). It is caused when blood collects at the site of an injury and discolors the skin.

Sprains account for one third of all sports injuries. A sprain is a partial or complete tear of a ligament, a strong band of tissue that connects bones to one another and stabilizes joints.

A strain is a partial or complete tear of a muscle (tissue composed of cells that enable the body to move) or a tendon (strong connective tissue that links muscles to bones).

Inflammation of a tendon (tendinitis) and inflammation of one of the fluid-filled sacs that allow tendons to move easily over bones (bursitis) usually result from minor stresses that repeatedly aggravate the same part of the body. These conditions often occur at the same time.

SKELETAL AND BRAIN INJURIES **Fractures** account for 5 to 6 percent of all sports injuries. The bones of the arms and legs are most apt to be broken. Sports activities rarely involve fractures of the spine or skull. The bones of the legs and feet are most susceptible to stress fractures, which occur when muscle strains or contractions make bones bend. Stress fractures are especially common in ballet dancers, long-distance runners, and in people whose bones are thin.

Shin splints are characterized by soreness and slight swelling of the front, inside, and back of the lower leg and by sharp **pain** that develops while exercising and gradually intensifies. Shin splints are caused by overuse or by stress fractures that result from the repeated foot pounding associated with activities such as aerobics, long-distance running, basketball, and volleyball.

A compartment syndrome is a potentially debilitating condition in which the muscles of the lower leg grow too large to be contained within membranes that enclose them. This condition is characterized by **numbness and tingling**. Untreated compartment syndrome can result in long-term loss of function.

Brain injury is the primary cause of fatal sports-related injuries. A **concussion** can result from even minor blows to the head. A concussion can cause loss of consciousness and may affect balance, comprehension, coordination, hearing, memory, and vision.

TREATMENT Treatment for minor soft tissue injuries generally consists of compressing the injured area with an elastic bandage, elevation, ice, and rest.

Anti-inflammatory medications, taken by mouth or injected into the swelling, may be used to treat bursitis. Anti-inflammatory medications and exercises to correct muscle imbalances are often used to treat tendinitis. If the athlete keeps stressing inflamed tendons, they may rupture, and casting or surgery is sometimes necessary to correct this condition. Orthopedic surgery may be required to repair serious **sprains and strains**.

Controlling inflammation as well as restoring normal use and mobility are the goals of treatment for overuse injuries. Athletes who have been injured are usually advised to limit their activities until their injuries are healed. The physician may suggest special exercises or behavior modifications for athletes who have had several injuries. Athletes who have been severely injured may be advised to stop playing completely.

Preschool

Appropriate athletic activities for children of this age are dance, beginning gymnastics (primarily tumbling), and swimming. The most common injuries are sprains and strains of soft tissue such as muscles and tendons.

School age

No matter what the form of specific training or sport activity, stretching and flexibility drills should be included in any pre-participation or warm-up program, even in the very young. Many studies have documented a very low incidence of injury in the total spectrum of youth sporting endeavors, according to the American Orthopaedic Society for Sports Medicine (AOSSM).

The occurrence of injury in the pre-puberty athlete has been documented as being much lower than in the post-puberty athlete, and lower in post-puberty than in the young adult. This is probably due to the fact that the younger athlete has a lower ratio of kinetic energy to body mass, which means the more immature the physical body, the lower the speed and power.

Since the magnitude of injury is almost always directly related to energy expended in a traumatic event, the younger athlete is less likely to get injured than his older counterpart. The athletic injuries that do occur are usually minor contusions and sprains. Fractures, dislocations, and major ligament injuries can happen but are more common in older age groups. Scientific studies have failed to document a significant increase in injuries to the growth areas of bones in young athletes. Only in extreme cases, such as young gymnasts in intense training for long periods of time, are some athletes at risk for growth plate injuries.

CONTACT VERSUS NON-CONTACT SPORTS The most notable examples of contact sports practiced in the United States are football, ice hockey, wrestling, and basketball. In each of these sports the athlete's body is used to physically control the opponent and, thus, to influence the play of the game. Using the body in this manner creates the opportunity for injury.

The majority of injuries in these contact sports are **bruises** and scrapes. The more significant injuries such as fractures, dislocations, or major ligament damage occur in the post-pubescent athlete. Parents should be responsive to complaints of pain and discomfort from athletes in all age groups and be aware that any athlete who is not playing up to skill level may be suffering from a significant injury.

In non-contact sports, major fractures, dislocations, or soft-tissue injuries are usually associated with accidental rather than intended collisions. Minor sprains, muscle pulls, blisters, and overuse syndrome are commonly seen injuries in non-contact sports, according to the AOSSM.

The overuse syndrome is usually related to sports requiring repetitive, high-stress motion such as tennis, swimming, track, golf, and baseball. Injury occurs as a result of constant repetition of a particular movement. Stress fractures, shin splints, and tendonitis are examples of overuse injuries.

The treatment in each case entails early recognition of the problem, followed by abstinence from competition or at least a decrease or change in training until the affected area is totally symptom free. Training intensity and duration can then increase again. Return to the previous level of training should be gradual and well planned. If the symptoms of overuse persist beyond a few days of rest or if they recur, a physician should evaluate the athlete.

Common problems

Common causes of sports injuries include athletic equipment that malfunctions or is used incorrectly, falls by athletes, forceful high-speed collisions between players, and wear and tear on areas of the body that are continually subjected to stress. Symptoms include instability or obvious dislocation of a joint, pain, swelling, and weakness.

Parental concerns

Every child who plans to participate in organized athletic activity should have an annual pre-season sports physical. This special examination is performed by a pediatrician or **family** physician who carefully evaluates the site of any previous injury, possibly recommends special stretching and strengthening exercises to help growing athletes create and preserve proper muscle and joint interaction, and pays special attention to the cardiovascular and skeletal systems.

Telling the physician which sport the athlete plays helps the physician determine which parts of the body are subjected to the most stress. The physician then is able to suggest to the athlete steps to take to minimize the chance of getting hurt.

Other injury-reducing game plans include:

- being in shape
- knowing and obeying the rules that regulate the activity
- not playing when tired, ill, or in pain
- not using steroids, which can improve athletic performance but cause life-threatening problems
- taking good care of athletic equipment and using it properly
- wearing appropriate protective equipment

When to call the doctor

A physician, pediatrician, sports medicine physician, or orthopedic surgeon should evaluate symptoms that persist, intensify, or reduce the athlete's ability to play without pain. Prompt diagnosis often can prevent

Teenage girl with a knee injury from playing soccer. *(© Tom Stewart/Corbis)*

minor injuries from becoming major problems or causing long-term damage.

A doctor should examine anyone who has the following symptoms:

- people who are prevented from playing by severe pain associated with acute injury
- people whose ability to play has declined due to chronic or long-term consequences of an injury
- people whose injury has caused visible deformities in an arm or leg.

The physician will perform a physical examination, ask how the injury occurred, and what symptoms the patient has experienced. X rays and other imaging studies of bones and soft tissues may be ordered. Anyone who has suffered a blow to the head should be examined immediately, and at five-minute intervals until normal comprehension has returned. The initial examination measures the athlete's awareness, concentration, and short-term memory. Subsequent evaluations of concussion assess **dizziness**, **headache**, **nausea**, and visual disturbances. In most cases, a physician should be consulted for athletes with head injuries.

Resources

BOOKS

Bahr, Roald, et al. *Clinical Guide to Sports Injuries.* Champaign, IL: Human Kinetics Publishers, 2003.

Griffith, H. Winter, and David A. Friscia. *Complete Guide to Sports Injuries.* Oakland, CA: Body Press, 2004.

Metzl, Jordan D., and Carol Shookhoff. *The Young Athlete.* New York: Little, Brown, 2003.

Shannon, Joyce Brennfleck. *Sports Injuries Information for Teens.* Detroit, MI: Omnigraphics, 2003.

PERIODICALS

Friedman, Manfred. "Sports Injury Prevention and Trauma." *The Exceptional Parent* 32, no. 7 (July 2002): 78–82.

Hyman, Mark. "Young Athletes, Big-League Pain: Year-Round Play and Dreams of Going Pro are Sidelining Kids with Serious Injuries." *Business Week* (July 7, 2004): 142.

KEY TERMS

Anti-inflammatory—A class of drugs, including nonsteroidal anti-inflammatory drugs (NSAIDs) and corticosteroids, used to relieve swelling, pain, and other symptoms of inflammation.

Bursitis—Inflammation of a bursa, a fluid-filled cavity or sac. In the body, bursae are located at places where friction might otherwise develop.

Cardiovascular—Relating to the heart and blood vessels.

Compartment syndrome—A condition in which the blood supply to a muscle is cut off because the muscle swells but is constricted by the connective tissue around it.

Concussion—An injury to the brain, often resulting from a blow to the head, that can cause temporary disorientation, memory loss, or unconsciousness.

Kinetic energy—The energy that the body has because of its motion.

Repetitive stress injury—An injury resulting from a repeated movement such as typing or throwing a ball.

Tendinitis—Inflammation of a tendon (a tough band of tissue that connects muscle to bone) that is often the result of overuse over a long period of time.

Lord, Mary. "Dangerous Games: Sports Injuries Among Children." *U.S. News & World Report* (April 8, 2002): 44.

Noonan, David. "When Safety is the Name of the Game: Every Year Millions of Young Athletes End Up in the Hospital. What Parents and Kids Can Do to Prevent Sports Injuries." *Newsweek* (Sept. 22, 2003): 64.

"Preventing Sports Injuries (Guide for Patients)." *Contemporary Pediatrics* 20, no. 9 (September 2003): 121.

ORGANIZATIONS

American College of Sports Medicine. 401 W. Michigan St., Indianapolis, IN 46202. Web site: <www.acsm.org>.

National Youth Sports Safety Foundation Inc. One Beacon St., Suite 3333, Boston, MA 02108. Web site: <www.nyssf.org>.

WEB SITES

"A Guide to Safety for Young Athletes." *American Academy of Orthopaedic Surgeons*, February 2002. Available online at <www.orthoinfo.aaos.org/brochure/thr_report.cfm?Thread_ID=34&topcategory=Sports%20%2F%20Exercise> (accessed October 14, 2004).

"Sports Injuries." *Medline Plus*, 2004. Available online at <www.nlm.nig.gov/medlineplus/> (accessed October 14, 2004).

Ken R. Wells

Sprains and strains

Definition

A sprain is damage to or tearing of ligaments or a joint capsule. A strain refers to damage to or tearing of a muscle.

Description

When excessive force is applied to a joint, the ligaments that hold the bones together may be torn or damaged. This action results in a sprain, and its seriousness depends on how badly the ligaments are torn. Any joint can be sprained, but the most frequently injured joints are the ankle, knee, and finger.

Strains are tears in the muscle. Sometimes called pulled muscles, they usually occur because of overexertion or improper lifting techniques. Straining the muscles of the back is common.

Demographics

Sprains and strains are common. Anyone can have them. Children under age eight are less likely to have sprains than are older people. Children's ligaments are tighter, and their bones are more apt to break before a ligament tears. People who are active in **sports** suffer more strains and sprains than less active people. However, being overweight and generally inactive also increases the chance of developing a strain or sprain. Repeated sprains in the same joint make the joint less stable and more prone to future sprains.

Causes and symptoms

Any unfamiliar activity that stresses a muscle or joint may cause a strain or sprain. Heavy lifting, falls, and playing a sport without warming up or conditioning are common causes. There are three grades of sprains.

Grade I sprains are mild injuries in which there is no tearing of the ligament and no joint function is lost, although there may be tenderness and slight swelling. Grade II sprains are caused by a partial tear in the ligament. These sprains are characterized by obvious swelling, extensive bruising, **pain**, difficulty bearing weight, and reduced function of the joint. Grade III, or third degree, sprains are caused by complete tearing of the ligament where there is severe pain, loss of joint function, widespread swelling and bruising, and the inability to bear weight. These symptoms are similar to those of bone **fractures**.

Strains can range from mild muscle stiffness to great soreness. Strains result from overuse of muscles, improper use of the muscles, or as the result of injury in another part of the body when the body compensates for pain by altering the way it moves.

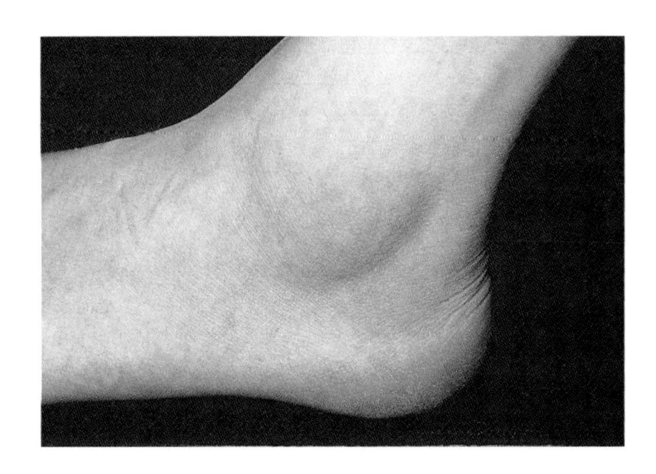

Swelling is a symptom of a sprained ankle. *(© Dr. P. Marazzi/ Photo Researchers, Inc.)*

When to call the doctor

Parents should call the doctor if their child experiences intense pain and swelling that does not improve within 24 to 48 hours; if their child cannot bear weight on the joint; if the child cannot use the muscle at all; or if there is a popping sensation in the joint when it is moved.

Diagnosis

Grade I sprains and mild strains are usually self-diagnosed. Grade II and III sprains are often seen by a physician, who x rays the area to differentiate between a sprain and a fracture. An MRI may be done to look for ruptured ligaments in a joint.

Treatment

Grade I sprains and mild strains can be treated at home. Basic first aid for sprains consists of RICE: Rest; Ice for 48 hours; Compression (wrapping in an elastic bandage); and Elevation of the sprain above the level of the heart. Over-the-counter pain medication such as **acetaminophen** (Tylenol) or ibuprofen (Motrin) can be taken for pain.

In addition to RICE, people with grade II and grade III sprains in the ankle or knee often need to use crutches until the sprains have healed enough to bear weight. Sometimes, physical therapy or home exercises are needed to restore the strength and flexibility of the joint.

Grade III sprains are usually immobilized in a cast for several weeks to see if the sprain heals. Pain medication is prescribed. Surgery may be necessary to relieve pain and restore function. Athletic people under age 40 are the most likely candidates for surgery, especially with grade III knee sprains. For complete healing, physical therapy usually follows surgery.

Alternative treatment

Alternative practitioners endorse RICE and conventional treatments. In addition, nutritional therapists recommend vitamin C and bioflavonoids to supplement a diet high in whole grains, fresh fruits, and vegetables. Anti-inflammatories such as bromelain (a proteolytic enzyme from pineapples) and tumeric (*Curcuma longa*) may also be helpful. The homeopathic remedy arnica (*Arnica montana*) may be used initially for a few days, followed by ruta (*Ruta graveolens*) for joint-related injuries or Rhus toxicodendron for muscle-related injuries. If surgery is needed, alternative practitioners can recommend pre- and post-surgical therapies that enhance healing.

Prognosis

Moderate sprains heal within two to four weeks, but it can take months to recover from severe ligament tears. Until the early 2000s, tearing the ligaments of the knee meant the end to an athlete's career. Subsequent improved surgical and rehabilitative techniques offer the possibility of complete recovery. However, once a joint has been sprained, it never is as strong as it was before.

Prevention

Sprains and strains can be prevented by warming-up before exercising, using proper lifting techniques, wearing properly fitting shoes, and taping or bracing the joint.

KEY TERMS

Ligament—A type of tough, fibrous tissue that connects bones or cartilage and provides support and strength to joints.

Parental concerns

Parents should be aware that repeated spraining of a joint weakens it. It may be necessary for the child to do exercises to strengthen the joint after a serious sprain. Parents should allow plenty of time for strains and sprains to heal before allowing their child to return to strenuous athletics.

Resources

BOOKS

DeLee, Jesse C., and David Drez. *DeLee and Drez's Orthopaedic Sports Medicine*, 2nd ed. Philadelphia: Saunders, 2003.

WEB SITES

Grayson, Charlotte. "Understanding Sprains and Strains—The Basics." *WebMD*, March 1, 2002. Available online at <http://my.webmd.com/content/article/8/1680_54419.htm> (accessed October 14, 2004).

Wedro, Benjamin C. "Sprains and Strains." *eMedicine Consumer Health*, 2003. Available online at <www.emedicinehealth.com/fulltext/5715.htm> (accessed October 14, 2004).

Tish Davidson, A.M.

Sprue *see* **Celiac disease**

SSRIs *see* **Antidepressants**

Stanford-Binet intelligence scales

Definition

The Stanford-Binet **intelligence** scale is a standardized test that assesses intelligence and cognitive abilities in children, beginning at age two, and in adults.

Purpose

The Stanford-Binet intelligence scale is used as a tool in school placement, in determining the presence of a learning disability or a **developmental delay**, and in tracking intellectual development. In addition, it is sometimes included in neuropsychological testing to assess the brain function of individuals with neurological impairments.

Description

The Stanford-Binet intelligence scale is a direct descendent of the Binet-Simon scale, the first intelligence scale created in 1905 by psychologist Alfred Binet (1857–1911) and Theophilus Simon. Lewis Terman (1877–1956) published the Stanford-Binet scale initially in 1916. As of 2004, the scale had been revised five times—in 1937, 1960 (with a scoring change of this version in 1973), 1986, and 2003.

Beginning with the fourth revision (1986), the test underwent design changes to include a larger, more diverse, representative sample in order to minimize the gender and racial inequities that had been criticized in earlier versions of the test. Originally designed for children only, with the fifth edition (2003) the Stanford-Binet can be used on anyone older than two years of age.

The Stanford-Binet scale tests intelligence across six areas: general intelligence, knowledge, fluid reasoning, quantitative reasoning, visual-spatial processing, and working memory. These areas are covered by ten subtests that include activities measuring both verbal and non-verbal intelligence. Activities include verbal absurdities, picture absurdities, verbal analogies, form patterns, procedural knowledge, sentence and word memory, position and direction, early reasoning, and quantitative reasoning.

All test subjects take two initial routing tests: a vocabulary test and a matrices test (which assesses non-verbal reasoning). The results of these tests, along with the subject's age, determines the number and level of subtests to be administered.

Total testing time is around 45 to 60 minutes, depending on the child's age and the number of subtests given. Raw scores are based on the number of items answered and are converted into a standard age score corresponding to age group, similar to an IQ measure.

Precautions

Intelligence testing requires a clinically trained examiner. The Stanford-Binet intelligence scale should

Teenage girl taking an intelligence test. *(© Lew Merrim/ Science Source/Photo Researchers, Inc.)*

be administered, scored, and interpreted by a trained professional, preferably a psychologist.

Children with physical disabilities may require certain accommodations when taking the test, such as extra time for tasks, rest breaks, or instructions received in an alternate format (e.g., signing for a deaf child). The examiner should be made aware of a child's potential limitations before the day of the test so that appropriate accommodations are available.

Normal results

Scoring for the Stanford-Binet generates a verbal IQ score (VIQ), a non-verbal IQ score (NIQ), and a full-scale IQ (FSIQ). It is a standardized test, meaning that norms are established during the design phase of the test by administering the test to a large, representative sample of the test population (in the case of the fifth edition, data from the 2000 U.S. census were used). The test has a mean, or average, standard score of 100 and a standard deviation of 15 for composite scores (subtests have a mean of 10 and a standard deviation of 3). The standard deviation indicates how far above or below the norm the subject's score is. For example, an eight-year-old is assessed with the Stanford-Binet scale and achieves a standard age score of 115. The mean score of 100 is the average level at which all eight-year-olds in the representative sample performed. This child's score would be one standard deviation above that norm.

While standard age scores provide a reference point for evaluation, they represent an average of a variety of skill areas. A trained psychologist evaluates and interprets an individual's performance on the scale's subtests to discover strengths and weaknesses and offer recommendations based upon these findings.

KEY TERMS

Norms—A fixed or ideal standard; a normative or mean score for a particular age group.

Representative sample—A random sample of people that adequately represents the test-taking population in age, gender, race, and socioeconomic standing.

Standard deviation—A measure of the distribution of scores around the average (mean). In a normal distribution, two standard deviations above and below the mean includes about 95% of all samples.

Standardization—The process of determining established norms and procedures for a test to act as a standard reference point for future test results.

Parental concerns

Test **anxiety** can have a negative impact on a child's performance, so parents should attempt to take the stress off their child by making sure they understand that it is the effort and attention they give the test, not the final score, that matters. Parents can also ensure that their children are well-rested on the testing day and have a nutritious meal beforehand.

Resources

BOOKS

Maddox, Taddy. *Tests: A Comprehensive Reference for Assessments in Psychology, Education, and Business*, 5th ed. Austin, TX: Pro-ed, 2003.

Wortham, Sue. *Assessment in Early Childhood Education*, 4th ed. Upper Saddle River, NJ: Prentice-Hall, 2004.

PERIODICALS

Becker, K. A. "History of the Stanford-Binet Intelligence Scales: Content and Psychometrics." *Stanford-Binet*

Intelligence Scales, Fifth Edition Assessment Service Bulletin, no. 1. Itasca, IL: Riverside Publishing, 2003.

Braden, Jeffery P., and Stephen N. Elliott. "Accommodations on the *Stanford-Binet Intelligence Scales*, 5th edition." In *Stanford-Binet Intelligence Scales, Fifth Edition Assessment Service Bulletin*, no. 2. Itasca, IL: Riverside Publishing, 2003.

ORGANIZATIONS

American Psychological Association (APA). 750 First St. NE, Washington, DC 20002–4242. Web site: <www.apa.org>.

WEB SITES

Riverside Publishing. *Stanford-Binet Intelligence Scales, 5th ed.* Available online at <www.riverpub.com/products/clinical/sbis5/home.html> (accessed October 30, 2004).

Paula Ford-Martin

Staphylococcal infections

Definition

Staphylococcal (staph) infections are communicable diseases caused by certain bacteria and generally characterized by the formation of abscesses. They are the leading cause of primary infections originating in hospitals in the United States.

Description

Classified since the early twentieth century as among the deadliest of all disease-causing organisms, staphylococcal bacteria exist on the skin or inside the nostrils of 20 to 30 percent of healthy people. It is sometimes found in breast tissue, the mouth, and the genital, urinary, and upper respiratory tracts.

Staph bacteria are usually harmless; however, when an injury or a break in the skin enables the organisms to invade the body and overcome the body's natural defenses, consequences can range from minor discomfort to death.

Demographics

Infection is most apt to occur in newborns; children whose immune systems have been undermined by radiation treatments, **chemotherapy**, or medication; those with surgical incisions or skin disorders; and among people with serious illnesses such as **cancer**, diabetes, and lung disease. Children are also more at risk for staph infections if they have HIV/AIDS or other diseases that compromise immune function, have a catheter or implanted prosthetics, are hospitalized, have open **wounds**, or live in close quarters with a large group of others. It is not clear exactly how many staph infections occur each year, but it is the most common infection that begins in the hospital.

Causes and symptoms

Staph infections produce pus-filled pockets (abscesses) located just beneath the surface of the skin or deep within the body. A localized staph infection is confined to a ring of dead and dying white blood cells and bacteria. The skin above it feels warm to the touch. Most of these abscesses eventually burst, and pus that leaks onto the skin can cause new infections.

A small fraction of localized staph infections enter the bloodstream and spread through the body. In children, these systemic (affecting the whole body) or disseminated infections frequently affect the ends of the long bones of the arms or legs, causing a bone infection called osteomyelitis. Other abscesses that can develop from staph infection include those of the brain, heart, kidneys, liver, lungs, or spleen.

Staphylococcus aureus

Named for the golden color of the bacteria grown under laboratory conditions, *Staphylococcus aureus* is a hardy organism that can survive in extreme temperatures or other inhospitable circumstances. About 70 to 90 percent of the population carry this type of staph in their nostrils at some time in their lives. Although present on the skin of only 5 to 20 percent of healthy people, as many as 40 percent of individuals carry it elsewhere, such as in the throat, vagina, or rectum, for varying periods of time, from hours to years, without developing symptoms or becoming ill.

S. aureus flourishes in hospitals, where it infects healthcare personnel and infects patients who have had surgery, have open wounds, have acute **dermatitis**, insulin-dependent diabetes, or dialysis-dependent kidney disease, or who receive frequent allergy-desensitization injections. Staph bacteria can also contaminate bedclothes, catheters, and other objects.

S. aureus causes a variety of infections. Boils and inflammation of the skin surrounding a hair shaft (folliculitis) are the most common. Toxic shock (TSS) and scalded skin syndrome (SSS) are among the most serious.

TOXIC SHOCK **Toxic shock syndrome** is a life-threatening infection characterized by severe **headache**, **sore throat**, **fever** as high as 105°F (40.5°C), and a sunburn-like rash that spreads from the face to the rest of the body. Symptoms appear suddenly. They also include **dehydration** and watery **diarrhea**.

Inadequate blood flow to peripheral parts of the body (shock) and loss of consciousness occur within the first 48 hours. Between the third and seventh day of illness, skin peels from the palms of the hands, soles of the feet, and other parts of the body. Kidney, liver, and muscle damage often occur.

SCALDED SKIN SYNDROME Rare in adults and most common in newborns and other children under the age of five, scalded skin syndrome originates with a localized skin infection. A mild fever and/or an increase in the number of infection-fighting white blood cells may occur.

A bright red rash spreads from the face to other parts of the body and eventually forms scales. Large, soft blisters develop at the site of infection and elsewhere. When they burst, they expose inflamed skin that looks as if it had been burned.

MISCELLANEOUS INFECTIONS *S. aureus* can also cause the following:

- arthritis
- bacteria in the bloodstream (bacteremia)
- pockets of infection and pus under the skin (carbuncles)
- tissue inflammation that spreads below the skin, causing **pain** and swelling (cellulitis)
- inflammation of the valves and walls of the heart (endocarditis)
- inflammation of tissue that encloses and protects the spinal cord and brain (meningitis)
- inflammation of bone and bone marrow (osteomyelitis)
- pneumonia

Other strains of staphylococci

S. EPIDERMIDIS Capable of clinging to tubing (such as that used for intravenous feeding), prosthetic devices, and other non-living surfaces, *S. epidermidis* is the organism that most often contaminates devices that provide direct access to the bloodstream.

The primary cause of bacterial infection in hospital patients, this strain of staph is most likely to infect cancer patients, whose immune systems have been compromised and high-risk newborns receiving intravenous supplements.

S. epidermidis also accounts for two of every five cases of prosthetic valve endocarditis. Prosthetic valve endocarditis is inflammation that occurs as a complication of the implantation of an artificial valve in the heart. Although contamination usually occurs during surgery, symptoms of infection may not become evident until a year after the operation. More than half of the patients who develop prosthetic valve endocarditis die.

Causes and symptoms

Staph bacteria can spread through the air, but infection is almost always the result of direct contact with open sores or body fluids contaminated by these organisms. Staph bacteria often enter the body through inflamed hair follicles or oil glands. Or they penetrate skin damaged by **burns**, cuts and scrapes, infection, insect **bites**, or wounds.

Multiplying beneath the skin, bacteria infect and destroy tissue in the area where they entered the body. Staph infection of the blood (staphylococcal bacteremia) develops when bacteria from a local infection infiltrate the lymph glands and bloodstream. These infections, which can usually be traced to contaminated catheters or intravenous devices, cause persistent high fever. They may cause shock. They also can cause death within a short time.

When to call the doctor

The following are common symptoms of staph infection:

- pain or swelling around a cut or an area of skin that has been scraped
- boils or other skin abscesses
- blistering, peeling, or scaling of the skin (This symptom is most common in infants and young children.)
- enlarged lymph nodes in the neck, armpits, or groin

A **family** physician should be notified whenever the following symptoms are present:

- Lymph nodes in the neck, armpits, or groin become swollen or tender.
- An area of skin that has been cut or scraped becomes painful or swollen, feels hot, or produces pus. These symptoms may mean the infection has spread to the bloodstream.

- A boil or carbuncle appears on any part of the face or spine. Staph infections affecting these areas can spread to the brain or spinal cord.
- A boil becomes very sore. Usually a sign that infection has spread, this condition may be accompanied by fever, chills, and red streaks radiating from the site of the original infection.
- Boils develop repeatedly. This type of recurrent infection could be a symptom of diabetes.

Diagnosis

Blood tests that show unusually high concentrations of white blood cells can suggest staph infection, but diagnosis is based on laboratory analysis of material removed from pus-filled sores and on analysis of normally uninfected body fluids such as blood and urine. Also, x-rays can enable doctors to locate internal abscesses and estimate the severity of infection. Needle biopsy (removing tissue with a needle, then examining it under a microscope) may be used to assess if any bones are infected.

Treatment

Superficial staph infections can generally be cured by keeping the area clean, using soaps that leave a germ-killing film on the skin, and applying warm, moist compresses to the affected area for 20 to 30 minutes three or four times a day.

Severe or recurrent infections may require a seven to 10 day course of treatment with penicillin or other oral **antibiotics**. The location of the infection and the identity of the causal bacteria determine which of several effective medications should be prescribed.

In case of a more serious infection, antibiotics may be administered intravenously for as long as six weeks. Intravenous antibiotics are also used to treat staph infections around the eyes or on other parts of the face.

Surgery may be required to drain or remove abscesses that form on internal organs or on shunts or other devices implanted inside the body.

Alternative treatment

Alternative therapies for staph infection are meant to strengthen the immune system and prevent recurrences. Among the therapies believed to be helpful for the person with a staph infection are **yoga** (to stimulate the immune system and promote relaxation), acupuncture (to draw heat away from the infection), and herbal remedies. Herbs that may help the body overcome, or withstand, staph infection include the following:

- Garlic (*Allium sativum*). This herb is believed to have antibacterial properties. Herbalists recommend consuming three garlic cloves or three garlic oil capsules a day, starting when symptoms of infection first appear.
- Cleavers (*Galium aparine*). This anti-inflammatory herb is believed to support the lymphatic system. It may be taken internally to help heal staph abscesses and reduce swelling of the lymph nodes. A cleavers compress can also be applied directly to a skin infection.
- Goldenseal (*Hydrastis canadensis*). Another herb believed to fight infection and reduce inflammation, goldenseal may be taken internally when symptoms of infection first appear. Skin infections can be treated by making a paste of water and powdered goldenseal root and applying it directly to the affected area. The preparation should be covered with a clean bandage and left in place overnight.
- Echinacea (*Echinacea* spp.). Taken internally, this herb is believed to have antibiotic properties and is also thought to strengthen the immune system.
- Thyme (*Thymus vulgaris*), lavender (*Lavandula officinalis*), or bergamot (*Citrus bergamot*) oils. These oils are believed to have antibacterial properties and may help to prevent the scarring that may result from skin infections. A few drops of these oils are added to water and then a compress soaked in the water is applied to the affected area.
- Tea tree oil (*Melaleuca* spp.). Another infection-fighting herb, this oil can be applied directly to a boil or other skin infection.

Prognosis

Most healthy people who develop staph infections recover fully within a short time. Others develop repeated infections. Some become seriously ill, requiring long-term therapy or emergency care. A small percentage die.

Doctors and researchers are becoming increasingly concerned about staph infections that are resistant to antibiotics. A bacterium that is considered resistant is one that can no longer be treated effectively using the antibiotics that are commonly prescribed for that type of infection. Resistant staph infections can usually be treated effectively with other antibiotics. Children who are most at risk for resistant staph infections are those who have been in the hospital or have serious underlying medical conditions. According to the Centers for Disease Control, although it is not clear how many cases of resistant staph infections occur each year, they are thought to be very rare. They recommend

KEY TERMS

Abscess—A localized collection of pus in the skin or other body tissue caused by infection.

Endocarditis—Inflammation of the inner membrane lining heart and/or of the heart valves caused by infection.

treating all infections promptly and only prescribing antibiotics when there is an underlying bacterial cause for the disease (antibiotics are not effective against viruses) to help reduce the occurrence of bacteria becoming resistant to antibiotics.

Prevention

Healthcare providers and patients should always wash their hands thoroughly with warm water and soap after treating a staph infection or touching an open wound or the pus it produces. Pus that oozes onto the skin from the site of an infection should be removed immediately. This affected area should then be cleansed with antiseptic or with antibacterial soap.

To prevent infection from spreading from one part of the body to another, it is important to shower rather than bathe during the healing process. Because staph infection is easily transmitted from one member of a household to others, towels, washcloths, and bed linens used by someone with a staph infection should not be used by anyone else. They should be changed daily until symptoms disappear, and laundered separately in hot water with bleach. Children should frequently be reminded not to share brushes, combs, or hair accessories.

Parental concerns

Staph infections are most likely to occur after a child has had surgery or a wound of some kind. A good way to help prevent staph infections of wounds is to keep the wound clean and dry. Children who have staph infections, especially skin infections, should be kept away from others whom they are likely to infect, and their bedding, clothes, and other things that may have touched the wound should be cleaned with hot soapy water and bleach.

Resources

BOOKS

Honeyman, Allen, Herman Friedman, and Mauro Bendinelli, eds. *Staphylococcus Aureus Infection and Disease.* New York: Kluwer Academic, 2001.

PERIODICALS

Zoler, Mitchell L. "Community-Acquired MRSA Infections Rising: Pediatric, Soft Tissue Infections." *Family Practice News* 34, no. 11 (June 2004): 7–8.

Tish Davidson, A.M.
Maureen Haggerty

STDs *see* **Sexually transmitted diseases**

Stealing

Definition

Stealing is taking another person's property without permission.

Description

Stealing is taking someone's property without permission. Very young children do not understand the concept of personal property. When they see something they want, they simply take it. Young children generally take things for immediate use only, whereas older children will take them "for keeps." Since they have no sense of personal property, young children should not be accused of stealing when they take another person's things without permission. However, the concept of stealing should be explained right from the start, even before the child can understand. If a parent, teacher, or other adult simply tells the child, "Don't take Sally's crayon," the child will believe only that taking Sally's crayon is wrong, while taking a crayon from Juan, or a cookie from Sally, is okay. A child must be told repeatedly that taking other people's things is wrong in order to develop an understanding of the broader concept of stealing.

Most children have a basic sense of "mine" and "not mine" by the age of two and can therefore begin to learn respect for other people's possessions. However, a true understanding of the harmful nature of stealing does not begin to develop until about age five to seven. At this age, children are deterred from stealing mostly by their **fear** of parental disapproval. Internal motivations of conscience and guilt do not develop until the middle childhood years. Once the recognition of property boundaries develops, stealing becomes an intentional act that must be addressed more deliberately.

Children steal for a number of reasons. Young children, or older children who have not developed sufficient self-control, may steal to achieve instant gratification when an object cannot be obtained immediately by honest means. Older children may steal to gain a sense of power, to acquire status with peers who resist authority, to get attention, to take revenge on someone who has hurt them, to alleviate boredom, or to vent unresolved feelings of anger or fear. Children who steal are often expressing displaced feelings of **anxiety**, rage, or alienation resulting from a disruption in their life, such as a parent's **divorce** or remarriage.

People who feel excluded or disconnected from society have fewer qualms about stealing, because they have less sense of respect, trust, or responsibility in relation to the community. They may even purposely steal in retaliation for the **pain** they feel society has inflicted on them. Studies have shown a direct correlation between stealing and alienation. Community-building programs in U.S. high schools have greatly reduced the incidence of theft by developing a sense of unity among the students and faculty. When a child feels integrated into a community, he or she is more likely to support all members of that community. Stealing becomes less tempting in a mutually supportive environment.

A child who is caught stealing for the first time should be treated compassionately; the focus should be on the reason(s) for the act rather than on the act itself. Parents, teachers, or other adult caregivers need to discern if the child lacks self-control, is angry (and with whom), needs attention, is bored, feels pressured by peers to cross boundaries, feels alienated from the community, has poor **self-esteem**, or needs to develop more positive moral values. A habitual stealer is expressing a serious internal problem that needs close attention. Children at risk of becoming habitual stealers often times have the following characteristics: low self-esteem; strong desires and weak self-control (impulsiveness); a lack of sensitivity to others; are angry, bored, or feel disconnected; spend a great deal of time alone; have recently experienced a significant disruption in their lives. Stealing is a behavior problem, not a character problem. The behavior can be corrected if the underlying difficulty is resolved.

Preschool

Children under the age of five generally are not sufficiently able to understand the concept of property to realize that they are stealing. Even though they might not understand, parents of children this age should make the child give back whatever was stolen and should explain why stealing is bad and how it hurts other people. The child should not be labeled bad, but the lesson should be made clear that stealing is wrong.

Elementary school

Children in elementary school generally are developed enough to understand that stealing is wrong and why it is wrong. When elementary school children steal, it is generally because they have seen something that they want, and they lack well-developed self-control. Children in this age group who are caught stealing should be made to take the item back or should be made to find ways to make enough money to pay for what they have stolen. Usually if a parent or other adult forces the child to apologize to the person from whom they stole, the embarrassment is enough to deter repeated episodes of stealing.

Middle and high school

Older children steal for different reasons than younger children. They want to feel powerful or want something expensive to try to keep up with their peers, or they may be distressed about a situation at home. Or they may want to fit in with a group. One fourth of all people caught shoplifting are between the ages of 13 and 17. In most cases children outgrow this behavior, but it still needs to be dealt with in a serious manner. Children who steal are not necessarily delinquents; however, children over the age of 15 who steal may have serious underlying troubles that need to be dealt with by a mental health professional.

Common problems

Though children who steal do so for a number of different reasons, stealing should always be treated seriously. If there is an underlying cause, such as unhappiness at home, then resolving the underlying problem usually resolves the stealing behavior, although the stealing itself should never be ignored.

Parental concerns

Just because a child has stolen does not mean he or she is going to grow up to live a life of crime. Children who steal are often helpful around the house, get good grades, and are otherwise good kids. Stealing, or a suspicion of stealing, needs to be dealt with in a serious manner, but once the matter has been dealt with, it should not be brought up again. In this way the child has a chance to start over with a clean slate.

When to call the doctor

If stealing is accompanied by other problems, such as difficulty interacting with peers or poor grades, it may be a sign of a serious underlying problem. If a child steals after the age of 15 or has gotten caught stealing more than once or there is a suspicion of underlying emotional or drug problems that might be causing the stealing, a mental health professional should be consulted.

Resources

BOOKS

Caputo, Gail. *What's in the Bag?: A Shoplifting Treatment and Education Program.* Lanham, MD: American Correctional Association, 2003.

Elquist, G. L. *Shoplifting Stories: From the Inside-Out.* Philadelphia: Xlibris Corp., 2001.

Segrave, Kerry. *Shoplifting: A Social History.* Jefferson, NC: McFarland & Co., 2001.

PERIODICALS

Nelson, Judy, Beth Nelson, and Eileen S. Nelson. "Relationship Between Parents, Peers, Morality, and Theft in an Adolescent Sample." *High School Journal* 83 (February 2000): 31.

"Toddler Steals Toys." *Contemporary Pediatrics* 17 (January 2000): 52.

ORGANIZATIONS

American Academy of Child and Adolescent Psychiatry. 3615 Wisconsin Avenue, NW, Washington, DC 20016–3007. Web site: <www.aacap.org>.

Tish Davidson, A.M.
Dianne Daeg de Mott

Steinert's disease *see* **Mytonic dystrophy**

Stepfamilies

Definition

A stepfamily is formed by the marriage or long-term cohabitation of two individuals, when one or both have at least one child from a previous relationship living part-time or full-time in the household. The individual who is not the biological parent of the child or children is referred to as the stepparent. Stepfamilies are also called blended families.

Purpose

Stepfamilies merge unrelated parents and children into a **family** unit that, with time and emotional work, can function as effectively as a traditional nuclear family. For children previously living in a single-parent family, a stepfamily can provide a more structured family environment with positive influences from two parental figures. For parents, a stepfamily can provide social support for new couples and new, emotionally rewarding relationships with biological and stepchildren.

Description

A stepfamily is a family unit in which one or both adult partners have children from a previous relationship. Stepfamilies can be formed after a **divorce** or death of a parent in a nuclear family or when a single parent chooses a long-term partner. Although in the past, marriage was usually required to define a stepfamily, marriage is not always a prerequisite for parents and children living together in the same household. Many adult partners choose to live together (cohabitation) on a long-term basis rather than marry. Children can be full-time or part-time members of a stepfamily, depending on the custody arrangement between the biological parents. Children may also be part of two stepfamilies if both parents remarry. The following terms are used to define members of a stepfamily:

- stepparent: a non-biological parent
- stepchild: a non-biological child brought into the family by marriage or cohabitation with the biological parent
- stepsiblings (stepbrother, stepsister): siblings who are not related biologically, whose parents are married to each other or cohabiting long-term
- custodial parent: the biological parent awarded primary custody by a court during divorce proceedings
- non-custodial parent: the biological parent awarded part-time custody or visitation rights by a court during divorce proceedings
- half-siblings: children who share biologically one parent
- stepgrandparents: non-biological grandparents
- mutual child: a biological child of the remarried or cohabiting couple

There are key differences between the dynamics in a stepfamily and the dynamics of a first-time nuclear family:

- Stepfamilies ultimately result from a loss, death of a parent/spouse, divorce, end of a long-term relationship, changes in lifestyle (e.g., moving, loss of job), and, therefore, involve grief on the part of both parents and children. This grief may remain unresolved and affect stepfamily relationships.
- Children in stepfamilies are members of two households and, as a result, may experience confusion, **discipline** issues, loss of stability, and conflicting feelings of loyalty.
- The role of the stepparent and status in the family is often unclear with regard to authority, level of involvement with the stepchild, and discipline. In addition, no legal relationship exists between stepparents and stepchildren.
- Stepparents must assume parental roles before there is an emotional bond with the stepchild and are often required to make instant adjustments to a parental role. In contrast, biological parents bond with their child as the child grows.
- Stepfamilies must cope with outside influences and ongoing change due to issues with the other biological parent and family members.

According to statistics from the United States Census Bureau and the Stepfamily Foundation, one in three Americans is involved in a stepfamily situation, and 1,300 new stepfamilies form each day. In addition, 50 percent of children under age 13 as of 2004 lived with one biological parent and the parent's partner. As of 2004, it is estimated that there are more stepfamilies than traditional nuclear families in the United States. The number of stepfamilies is underestimated because the U.S. Census Bureau did not as of 2004 recognize that a child can be a member of two stepfamilies; only the household where the child lives the majority of the time is counted. Because in most divorces, primary custody is awarded to the biological mother, most stepfamilies involve stepfathers who become the full-time stepparent. In rare cases, a biological father is awarded primary custody, and a stepmother can become a full-time stepparent.

Precautions

Stepfamilies are increasingly referred to as blended families, by the media and others. Stepfamily researchers, family therapists, and the Stepfamily Association of America (SAA) view this term as inaccurate because it infers that members of a stepfamily blend into an entirely new family unit, losing their individuality and attachment to other outside family members. The term stepfamily is preferred because the derivation of the prefix "step-" originates from the Old English word "steop-" which means "bereave." The term stepchild used to refer to orphans who lost their parents, and stepfather/stepmother used to refer to individuals who became parents to an orphan. Because other family types (biological, single-parent, foster, adoptive) are defined by the parent-child relationship, the SAA believes that the term stepfamily more accurately reflects that relationship and is consistent with other family definitions. Viewing the stepfamily as a blended family can lead to unrealistic expectations, confused and conflicted children, difficult adjustment, and in many cases, failure of the marriage and family.

Preparation

Divorce, remarriage, and the formation of a stepfamily are traumatic events for children. Transition can be eased by including children in discussions and preparations for the stepfamily's future. For example, for couples getting remarried, children can be included in the actual wedding ceremony (not just as ringbearers and flower girls) and given tokens, like a piece of jewelry or special gift (like the wedding rings that their parents exchange), that symbolize the joining of the new family.

Individual therapy for children whose parents are going through a divorce and remarriage can be helpful. Group **family therapy** with all members of the stepfamily can help identify issues that may undermine successful family functioning. Because grandparents can influence stepfamily dynamics, educating stepgrandparents about stepfamily issues can also help. Roles of the noncustodial parent and stepparent must be clearly defined to avoid unnecessary conflicts. Reading information on stepfamilies and joining a stepfamily support group can help ensure future success. With cooperation and understanding among stepfamily members, a stepfamily can function successfully and even heal emotional scars of past divorce.

Risks

A National Institutes of Health (NIH) study of stepfamilies found that a stepfamily has a unique natural life cycle, takes several years to develop into a family unit, and is at greatest risk for failure during its first two years. According to U.S. Census Bureau statistics, the average marriage in the United States only lasts seven years, and one of every two marriages ends in divorce. Stepfamilies are at greater risk for failure and broken marriage due to the increased stresses of stepfamily life. These stresses include the unclear role and authority of the stepparent, financial responsibility for stepchildren, conflict between custodial and noncustodial parents, and emotional tensions.

A study by British and Canadian researchers found that children in stepfamilies and **single-parent families** had more behavioral and emotional problems compared with children in intact biological families and that stresses within the family were more influential than family type in contributing to children's psychological problems. Adolescents are especially vulnerable to psychological and emotional problems resulting from a combination of **puberty** and family stresses. Medical professionals, such as pediatricians, psychologists, and therapists, can provide resources and referrals for adolescents requiring treatment and/or therapy for depression, oppositional defiance disorder, and unresolved feelings of anger, resentment, and loss.

Parental concerns

While stepmothers face some of the same issues that stepfathers face, both part-time and full-time stepmothers have a more difficult role in the stepfamily and are often expected to be more involved with their stepchild due to socialization pressures (being a mother), societal expectations, and expectations from their husband. Joining a stepmother support group can be helpful in working out frustrations and problems in the stepmother role.

Children in stepfamilies are subject to multiple parental influences and may become confused and conflicted about how they fit into each family and which parent is responsible for discipline. All parents—biological and stepparents—should strive to work out such issues for the benefit of their children. Minimizing conflicts between all parents can help children adjust to stepfamily life.

For various reasons, society does not always view stepparents as having the same responsibilities as biological parents. Employers, other family members, friends, and neighbors may have difficulty understanding and relating to stepfamily issues. One workplace psychologist estimates that businesses in the United States lose more than $10 billion annually due to problems related to stepfamily issues, working parents, and other marital stresses. Although many employers do offer employee assistance programs with substance abuse counseling, child care, and family/marriage counseling, divorced parents, working stepparents, and working live-in partners rarely seek counseling.

Parents and stepparents should be concerned during the first two years after the stepfamily is formed, since this has been identified as a crucial time period for stepfamily success. To help strengthen the stepfamily, parents can establish new and enjoyable family traditions, recognize that children need to stay in touch with noncustodial parents, and focus on being open with family communication. Organizations such as the Stepfamily Association of America offer resources and ideas for building stepfamily bonds, such as celebrating National Stepfamily Day every September and engaging in pleasurable family activities, like movie and pizza night.

KEY TERMS

Cohabitation—Sexual partners living together outside of marriage.

Nuclear family—The basic family unit, consisting of a father, a mother, and their biological children.

Resources

BOOKS

Kelley, Patricia. *Developing Healthy Stepfamilies: Twenty Families Tell Their Stories*. Binghamton, NY: Haworth Press, 2003.

Lipman-Bluementhal, Jean, et al. *Step Wars: Overcoming the Perils and Making Peace in Adult Stepfamilies*. New York: St. Martin's Press, 2004.

Lofas, Jeanette. *Stepparenting*. New York: Citadel Press Books, 2004.

PERIODICALS

Cohen, G. J. "Helping Children and Families Deal with Divorce and Separation." *Pediatrics*. 110 (November 2002):1019–1023.

Cohn, L. "Workin' Out: Feeling the Burn as Stepfamilies Help You Stretch—Emotionally." *Your Stepfamily Magazine* (March-April 2003).

O'Connor, T. G., et al. "Family Settings and Children's Adjustment: Differential Adjustment within and across Families." *British Journal of Psychiatry* 179 (2001): 110–15.

ORGANIZATIONS

Stepfamily Association of America. Web site: <www.saafamilies.org>.

Stepfamily Foundation. Web site: <www.stepfamily.org>.

WEB SITES

"Stepfamily Facts." *Stepfamily Association of America*. Available online at <www.saafamilies.org/faqs/index.htm> (accessed October 30, 2004).

"Stepfamily Law and Policy." *Stepfamily Association of America.* Available online at <www.saafamilies.org/advocacy/issues.htm> (accessed October 30, 2004).

Jennifer E. Sisk, M.A.

Steroids, anabolic *see* **Anabolic steroids**

Stimulant drugs

Definition

Stimulant drugs are drugs that excite the central nervous system.

Description

There are several drugs used as stimulants. Although in large part they share the same properties, their use is determined by how well they are absorbed from the gastrointestinal tract. These drugs are related to the body's normal stimulant hormones epinephrine and norepinephrine.

- Injectable stimulants are used to stimulate the heart or breathing. Epinephrine (adrenalin) is the most common.
- Topical stimulants are used as **decongestants**, since they cause blood vessels to contract. They are also used to stop superficial bleeding by contracting the capillaries and for relief of **conjunctivitis**. They may be applied to the skin, inhaled, or applied in the form of drops as nose drops or eye drops.
- Oral stimulants, including the two drugs in this class (**methylphenidate** [Ritalin] and amphetamine) are used to treat extreme daytime sleepiness also known as **narcolepsy** and for their calming effect in attention-deficit hyperactivity disorder (ADHD).
- Caffeine, a stimulant found in foods and drinks, is used to promote wakefulness and alertness.

The orally active stimulants were formerly used as an aid to dieting but were of little value for this purpose. They may still be used in the most extreme cases of **obesity** but are no longer routinely prescribed for this purpose. Some were widely used as decongestants for colds and **allergies**. They are subject to abuse, and amphetamines and methylphenidate are controlled substances in the United States.

Pemoline (Cylert) is also a member of this class but is rarely used because of its potential for causing severe liver problems. This drug should be reserved for treatment of children whose ADHD cannot be controlled with either first or second line drug therapy and whose condition is so severe that the potential benefits justify the risk.

Stimulant drugs, in addition to their proper medicinal use, are subject to abuse. The drugs commonly abused are methylphenidate, amphetamine, and methamphetamine. A related drug, 3,4-methylenedioxymethamphetamine (better known as ecstasy or MDMA), is also widely abused. Unlike methylphenidate and amphetamine, MDMA has no legitimate therapeutic use.

Cocaine is chemically different from the traditional stimulants but provides similar effects. It is used medicinally as a local anesthetic but is not available for self-administration. Cocaine has become a major drug abuse problem.

General use

The most common use of methylphenidate and amphetamine in children is for control of **attention-deficit/hyperactivity disorder**. This is a condition marked by general restlessness, excessive activity, and inability to concentrate on a topic. Children who have this problem are unable to concentrate on schoolwork and fall behind their classmates. They are frequently disruptive. For this condition, the stimulants have a reverse activity and have a calming, rather than a stimulating effect.

Precautions

Stimulant drugs are subject to abuse and development of tolerance. This does not appear to be a problem, however, when the drugs are appropriately used for a proper diagnosis of ADHD.

When used to treat young children, there is some evidence that stimulant drugs reduce the rate of growth. This may be made up for by a growth spurt when the drugs are discontinued.

Stimulant drugs increase blood pressure.

Side effects

The side effects for stimulant drugs are different when they are used as stimulants and when they are used for their calming effect in ADHD. The effects listed below are those seen when amphetamines and/or methylphenidate are used to treat attention-deficit hyperactivity disorder:

- reduction in rate of growth
- exacerbation of related problems such as Tourette's disorder
- appetite suppression

There are many additional side effects seen when amphetamines or methylphenidate are used or abused for their stimulant properties, but these effects are not normally seen when the stimulants are used for a proper diagnosis of ADHD and dosed appropriately.

Some of the adverse effects that may result from stimulant abuse are increased wakefulness, increased physical activity, decreased appetite, increased respiration, high **fever**, euphoria, irritability, insomnia, confusion, tremors, convulsions, **anxiety**, paranoia, and aggressiveness. The high fever and convulsions may be fatal. Long term abuse of stimulants may result in permanent brain damage that causes involuntary, Parkinson-like movements.

Methamphetamine causes increased heart rate and blood pressure and can cause irreversible damage to blood vessels in the brain, producing strokes. Other effects of methamphetamine include respiratory problems, irregular heartbeat, and extreme anorexia. Its use can result in cardiovascular collapse and death.

The reports of growth suppression associated with amphetamines and methylphenidate are not definitive but appear to be valid. This growth suppression is balanced by a growth spurt when the drugs are discontinued. For this reason, stimulants should only be administered during school hours and discontinued during summer and holiday periods.

Interactions

Stimulant drugs have no interactions with drugs that are normally prescribed for children.

Parental concerns

When used to treat ADHD, methylphenidate and amphetamines do not have the adverse effects associated with these drugs when they are abused.

ADHD is a difficult diagnosis and may be confused with normal childhood energy. A diagnosis should be made, and drug therapy initiated, only by a qualified professional experienced in this condition.

Because of the potential for abuse, methylphenidate and amphetamines must be kept out of reach of children, particularly visitors and older siblings of a child being treated for ADHD.

Because of the risk of growth suppression, stimulant drugs should only be administered during school periods. They should not be used to calm an active child for the convenience of parents or babysitters.

Children who fail a trial of one stimulant may respond to another drug in the same class. A child who does poorly on methylphenidate may respond to amphetamines and vice versa.

Approximately 15 to 30 percent of children with ADHD have underlying Tourette's disorder, a condition marked by vocal and motor **tics**. Starting treatment with methylphenidate or amphetamines may unmask the condition, and the tics will become apparent. This is not an effect of the drug, but rather a consideration of the underlying problem.

There is some dispute over the lowest age at which stimulant therapy may be appropriately started, but it seems agreed that these drugs should not be used to treat children under the age of three years.

Sometimes, drugs which are properly prescribed for ADHD are diverted and used by other children as recreational drugs. If a child who has been well stabilized on stimulants for ADHD begins to get worse, consider the possibility that the drugs are being sold to others, rather than being used therapeutically. Stimulant drugs should be administered by a parent, guardian, school nurse, or other responsible person. This will both guard against diversion and assure that children are not forgetting to take their medication.

The effects of cocaine are generally similar to those of amphetamines.

Signs of possible stimulant abuse, regarding amphetamines and cocaine, include dilated pupils, frequent lip licking and dry mouth, excessive activity, and lack of **sleep**. The drug abuser becomes talkative, but the discussion lacks continuity or coherence, and the subject changes frequently.

See also Caffeine.

Resources

BOOKS

Beers, Mark H., and Robert Berkow, eds. *The Merck Manual*, 2nd home ed. West Point, PA: Merck & Co., 2004.

Breggin, Peter. *The Ritalin Fact Book: What Your Doctor Won't Tell You.* New York: Rosen Publishing Group, 2003.

Ferreiro, Carmen. *Ritalin and Other Methylphenidate-Containing Drugs.* Langhorne, PA: Chelsea House, 2004.

Mcevoy, Gerald, et al. *AHFS Drug Information 2004.* Bethesda, MD: American Society of Healthsystems Pharmacists, 2004.

KEY TERMS

Attention deficit hyperactivity disorder (ADHD)—A condition in which a person (usually a child) has an unusually high activity level and a short attention span. People with the disorder may act impulsively and may have learning and behavioral problems.

Tic—A brief and intermittent involuntary movement or sound.

Tourette syndrome—A neurological disorder characterized by multiple involuntary movements and uncontrollable vocalizations called tics that come and go over years, usually beginning in childhood and becoming chronic. Sometimes the tics include inappropriate or obscene language (coprolalia).

Mercogliano, Chris. *Teaching the Restless: One School's No-Ritalin Approach to Helping Children Learn and Succeed.* Boston, MA: Beacon Press, 2004.

PERIODICALS

Charach, A., et al. "Stimulant treatment over five years: adherence, effectiveness, and adverse effects." *Journal of the American Academy of Child and Adolescent Psychiatry* 43 (May 2004): 559–67.

Spencer, T. J. "ADHD treatment across the life cycle." *Journal of Clinical Psychiatry* 65 Suppl. (2004): 22–6.

WEB SITES

"Amphetamines (Systemic)." *MedlinePlus.* Available online at <www.nlm.nih.gov/medlineplus/druginfo/uspdi/202031.html> (accessed January 17, 2005).

Samuel Uretsky, PharmD

Stings *see* **Bites and stings**

Stomach flu *see* **Gastroenteritis**

Stomatitis

Definition

Stomatitis is an inflammation of the mucous lining of the mouth, which may involve the cheeks, gums, tongue, lips, and roof or floor of the mouth. The word "stomatitis" literally means inflammation of the mouth.

Description

Stomatitis is an inflammation of the lining of any of the soft-tissue structures of the mouth. It is usually a painful condition, associated with redness, swelling, and occasional bleeding from the affected area. The inflammation may be caused by conditions in the mouth itself, such as poor hygiene, from **burns** from hot food or drinks, or by conditions that affect the entire body, such as medications, allergic reactions, or infections. Children may develop stomatitis at any point in their development, from infancy to **adolescence**. The two most common types seen in children are herpes stomatitis, which is caused by the **herpes simplex** virus, and aphthous stomatitis, more often referred to as **canker sores**.

Transmission

Depending upon its cause, stomatitis may or may not be contagious. Herpes stomatitis is considered contagious. Children may be exposed through kissing, sharing food, or playing in close contact with others who have an active herpes infection, such as a **cold sore**. Aphthous stomatitis is not contagious.

Demographics

Though stomatitis may occur at any time during a child's growth, different types affect children at different times. Herpes stomatitis can occur anywhere between six months and five years of age but is most common in children one to two years old who have not been exposed to the herpes virus before. Aphthous stomatitis begins in childhood or adolescence, with peak onset in those aged ten to 19 years. Aphthous ulcers may be more common in females than males. Children of higher socioeconomic status may be more affected than those who are from lower socioeconomic groups.

Causes and symptoms

Causes

A number of factors can cause stomatitis. Cheek biting, braces, or jagged teeth may persistently irritate the oral structures. Chronic mouth breathing due to plugged nasal airways may cause dryness of the mouth tissues, which in turn leads to irritation. The cause of herpes stomatitis is the herpes virus type 1 (not to be confused with genital herpes, which is caused by the herpes virus type 2 and is a sexually transmitted disease). The cause of aphthous stomatitis is unknown, although several factors are suspected. There may be an inherited tendency to develop canker sores and there may also be an immune system link. In addition, they may be triggered by emotional stress; nutritional deficiencies of iron, **folic acid**, or vitamin B12; menstrual periods; **food allergies**; or viral infections. They may occur with no identifiable cause.

Symptoms

Stomatitis is characterized by **pain** or discomfort in the mouth and the presence of open sores or ulcers in the mouth. Herpes stomatitis may cause the following symptoms:

- **fever**, sometimes as high as 101–104°F (38.3–40°C), which may precede the appearance of blisters and ulcers by one or two days
- irritability and restlessness
- blisters in the mouth, often on the tongue or cheeks or roof of the mouth, which then pop and form ulcers (These ulcers are usually small [about one to five millimeters in diameter], grayish white in the middle, and red around the edges.)
- swollen gums, which may be irritated and bleed
- pain in the mouth
- drooling
- difficulty swallowing
- foul-smelling breath

Aphthous stomatitis may cause the following symptoms:

- burning or tingling sensation in the mouth prior to the onset of other symptoms
- skin lesions on the mucous membranes of the mouth, which begin as a red spot or bump, then develop into an open ulcer, which is usually small (one to two millimeters to one centimeter in diameter) (The ulcers can be single or break out in clusters. The ulcers are painful, and the center appears white or yellow with a fibrous texture. The border of the sore may be bright red.)

When to call the doctor

Parents should call the doctor if any of the following occur:

- inability to drink or swallow
- high temperature
- fussiness and inability to settle down
- symptoms not improved after three days

If the child appears dehydrated, parents should seek immediate medical attention. Signs include dry lips, the absence of tears when crying, a sinking soft spot on an infant's head, and no urination in eight hours or very dark urine. Parents should also seek care if the child is very weak, tired, or difficult to waken.

Diagnosis

Stomatitis is diagnosed by the doctor based primarily upon the appearance of the mouth sores. Both herpes and aphthous stomatitis have lesions that are unique in appearance. Although laboratory studies are seldom performed, the physician may order further blood tests or cultures of the lesions in order to confirm the diagnosis and rule out other causes.

Treatment

The treatment of stomatitis is based upon the problem causing it. For all types, local cleansing and good **oral hygiene** is fundamental. Sharp-edged foods such as peanuts, tacos, and potato chips should be avoided. A soft-bristled toothbrush should be used, and the teeth and gums should be brushed carefully. If toothbrushing is too painful, the child should rinse out his mouth with plain water after each meal. Local factors, such as sharp teeth or braces, can be addressed by a dentist or orthodontist.

Herpes stomatitis treatment

In herpes stomatitis, the most important part of treatment is for parents to keep their child drinking as normally as possible. Bland fluids such as apple juice, liquid flavored gelatin, or lukewarm broth are easiest to drink. Sucking on a Popsicle or sherbet may be soothing. Citrus juices and spicy or salty foods should be avoided. In the event of severe disease, the doctor may use intravenous fluids to prevent **dehydration**. **Acetaminophen** may be used for temperatures over 101°F (38.3°C) and to address pain. Medicines that numb the mouth, like viscous lidocaine or topical anesthetics only last for a brief time and, by numbing the mouth, may cause your child to further injure damaged tissues without knowing it. **Antibiotics** are of no help in treating herpes stomatitis. However, if the case is particularly severe, the doctor may prescribe an antiviral medication such as acyclovir which, if given at the beginning of the outbreak, may help clear things up faster.

Aphthous stomatitis treatment

Medical treatment is usually not necessary for aphthous stomatitis, unless the ulcers are severe (larger than one centimeter or lasting longer than two weeks). In this case medical evaluation and treatment may be indicated, and topical or oral tetracycline may be given. However, tetracycline is usually not prescribed for children until after all of their permanent teeth have erupted, as it can permanently discolor teeth that are still forming. Avoid hot or spicy foods to minimize discomfort. Mild mouth washes such as salt water or over-the-counter mouthwashes may help. Over-the-counter topical medications applied to the ulcerated area may reduce discomfort and sooth the area. To prevent bacterial infections from developing, parents should encourage their child to brush and floss teeth regularly.

Alternative treatment

Placing a spent tea bag on a canker sore may provide comfort. Sodium lauryl sulfate (SLS), a component of some toothpastes, is a potential cause of canker sores. In one study, most recurrent canker sores were eliminated just by avoiding SLS-containing toothpaste for three months.

Nutritional concerns

Some physicians may recommend a variety of dietary measures to treat stomatitis. These may include eating cottage cheese, buttermilk, and yogurt, as well as foods high in B **vitamins**. Some doctors may recommend supplementation with folic acid, iron, or vitamin B12.

Prognosis

The prognosis for the resolution of stomatitis is based upon the cause of the problem. Many mouth ulcers are benign and resolve without specific treatment. In the case of herpes stomatitis, complete recovery is expected within ten days without any medical intervention. Oral acyclovir may speed up recovery. Most children are minimally inconvenienced by aphthous stomatitis, because attacks are usually infrequent and only last a few days.

Prevention

Stomatitis caused by irritants can be prevented by good oral hygiene, regular dental checkups, and good dietary habits. Because so many adults and children carry the herpes virus, and because they can pass it on even if they have no symptoms, there is no practical way to prevent herpes stomatitis. Parents can, however, discourage their child from kissing, sharing food, or playing in close contact with people who have an active herpes infection.

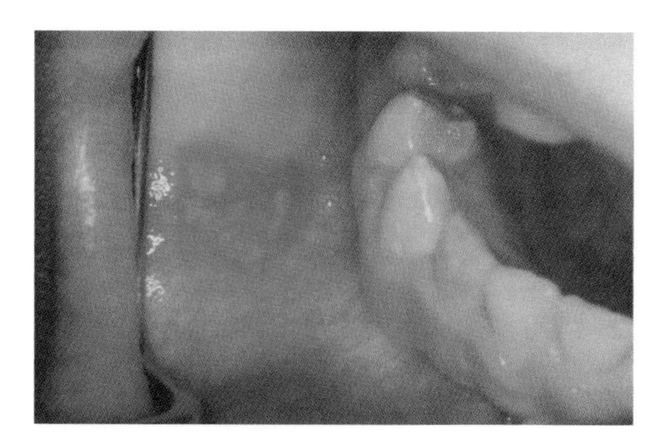

This patient is afflicted with stomatitis, a common inflammatory disease of the mouth. *(Photograph by Edward H. Gill, Custom Medical Stock Photo Inc.)*

Canker sores may be minimized by teaching children to avoid trauma, even minor trauma, to the mouth, such as hard toothbrushes and rough foods. If the doctor has determined that the child has a nutritional deficiency, parents can insure that the child is taking the appropriate supplements and eating the recommended foods. Avoiding stressful situations may also be beneficial.

Parental concerns

Most cases of stomatitis in children are benign and resolve within a relatively short period of time. Children with herpes stomatitis may return to school or **day care** when their fever is gone and the mouth sores are healed. Since aphthous stomatitis is not contagious, there is no need to curtail a child's activities unless they have developed signs of complications, such as infection.

See also Canker sores.

Resources

PERIODICALS

Vander Schaaf, Rachelle. "Cool Relief for Canker Sores." *Parenting* 17, no. 6 (August 1, 2003): 38.

ORGANIZATIONS

American Dental Association. 211 E. Chicago Ave., Chicago, IL 60612. Web site: <www.ada.org>.

WEB SITES

"Medical Encyclopedia: Herpetic Stomatitis." *Medline Plus* January 16, 2004. Available online at <www.nlm.nih.gov/medlineplus/print/ency/article/001383.htm> (accessed October 14, 2004).

KEY TERMS

Aphthous stomatitis—A specific type of stomatitis presenting with shallow, painful ulcers. Also known as canker sores.

Herpes stomatitis—A form of stomatitis caused by the herpes 1 virus, usually seen in young children.

Stomatitis—Inflammation of the mucous lining of any of the structures of the mouth, including the cheeks, gums, tongue, lips, and roof or floor of the mouth.

Stine, Annie. "Gingivostomatitis (herpes mouth sores)." *Babycenter.com* 2004. Available online at <www.babycenter.com/refcap/toddler/toddlerills/todthroatprobs/1201460.htm> (accessed October 14, 2004).

Deanna M. Swartout-Corbeil, RN
Joseph Knight, PA

Strabismus

Definition

Strabismus is a condition in which the eyes do not align in the same direction. It is also called crossed eyes or squint.

Description

With normal vision, both eyes focus on the same spot and send the brain the same message. This binocular fixation (both eyes looking directly at the same object) is necessary to see three-dimensionally and to aid in depth perception. When an eye is misaligned, the brain receives two different images. Young children learn to ignore distorted messages from a misaligned eye, but adults with strabismus often develop double vision (diplopia). A baby's eyes should be straight and parallel by three or four months of age. A child who develops strabismus after the age of eight or nine years is said to have adult-onset strabismus.

Esotropia is the most common type of strabismus. It occurs when the eyes turn inward. Infantile esotropia develops in children under the age of six months.

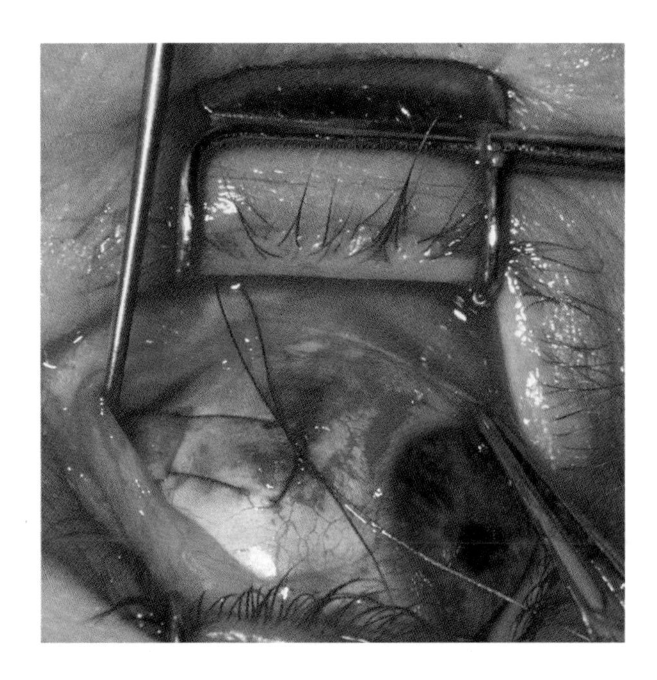

A close-up of ophthalmic surgery being performed to correct strabismus. *(Photograph by Michael English, M.D. Custom Medical Stock Photo, Inc.)*

Accommodative esotropia develops in children under age three who cross their eyes when focusing on objects nearby. This usually occurs in children who are moderately to highly farsighted (hyperopic). Congenital esotropia is a very rare form of strabismus that occurs with certain birth defects.

Another common form of strabismus is exotropia, sometimes called walleye, where the eyes turn outward. It may only be noticeable when a child looks at distant objects, daydreams, or is tired or sick. Other strabismus conditions include hypertrophia, where the eyes turn upward, and hypotropia, where the eyes turn downward.

With strabismus, in some cases the eye turn occurs always in the same eye; however, sometimes the turn alternates from one eye to the other. Most children with strabismus have comitant strabismus, which means that no matter where they look, the degree of deviation does not change. In incomitant strabismus, the amount of misalignment depends upon which direction the eyes are pointed.

False strabismus (pseudostrabismus) occurs when a child appears to have a turned eye; however, this appearance may actually be due to other factors:

- extra skin that covers the inner corner of the eye
- a broad, flat nose

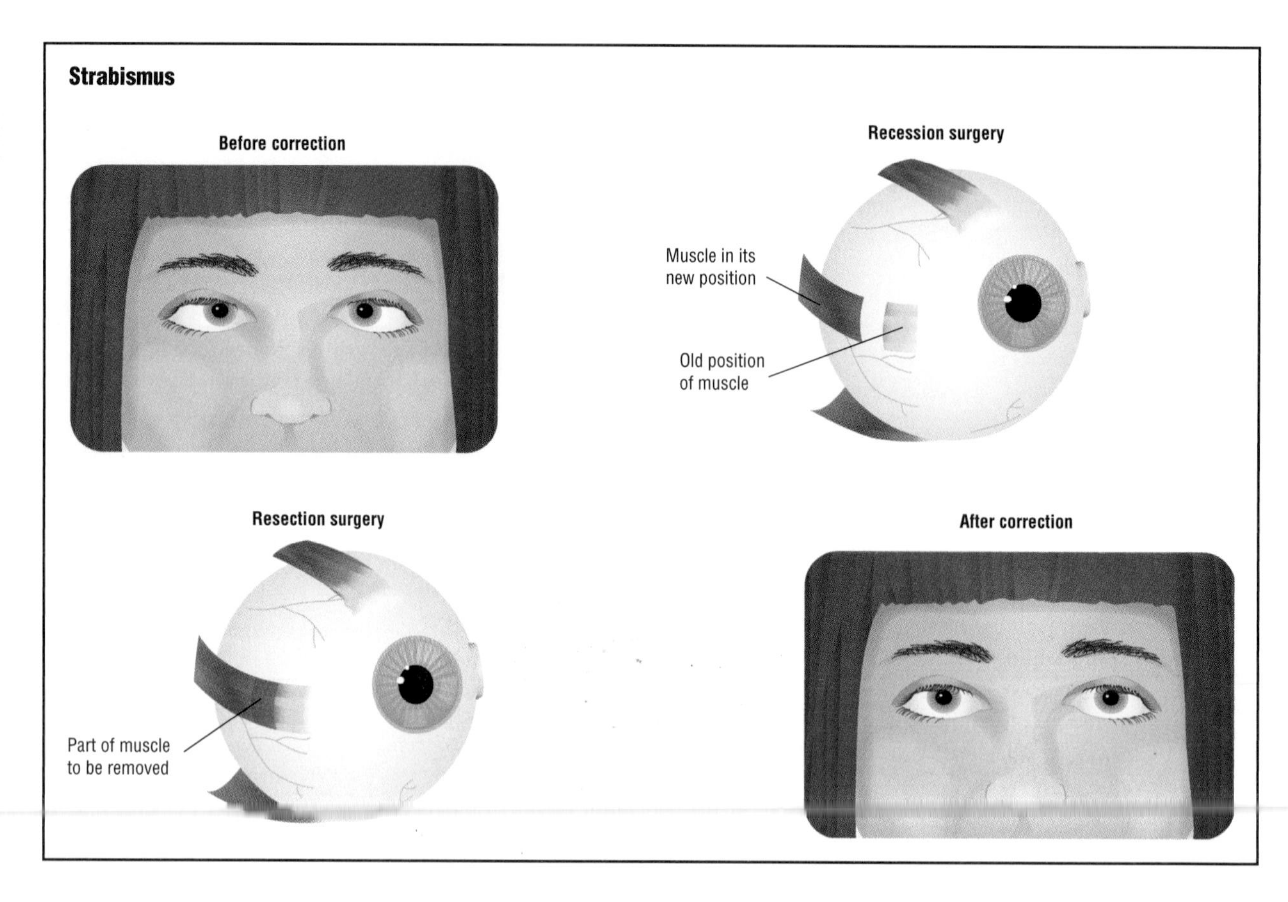

Illustration of patient with strabismus, before and after corrective surgery. During the surgery, the eye muscle may be lengthened (recession surgery) or shortened (resection surgery). *(Illustration by GGS Information Services.)*

- eyes set unusually close together or far apart

False strabismus usually disappears as the child's face grows. An eye doctor (ophthalmologist) needs to determine whether the eye turn is true strabismus or pseudostrabismus.

Demographics

Strabismus affects 5 percent of people in the United States or more than 12 million individuals, most of them children. Infantile esotropia affects about 1 percent of full term, healthy babies and a higher percentage of babies born prematurely or born with other facial defects. Congenital esotropia is rare but does not occur at a higher rate in premature babies. Strabismus occurs equally in boys and girls and shows no variation in racial or ethnic distribution. Most strabismus develops in young children, although a few diseases may cause it to develop in adults.

Causes and symptoms

Strabismus can be caused most often by a defect in the part of the brain that controls eye movement. It is caused less frequently by a defect in the muscles that control eye movement. It is especially common in children who have the following:

- brain tumors
- cerebral palsy
- Down syndrome
- hydrocephalus
- other disorders that affect the brain

Diseases that cause partial or total blindness can cause strabismus. So can extreme farsightedness, cataracts, eye injury, or having much better vision in one eye than the other.

The most obvious symptom of strabismus is an eye that is not always straight. The deviation can vary from day to day or during the day. People who have strabismus often squint in bright sunlight or tilt their heads to focus their eyes.

When to call the doctor

Parents should call their doctor whenever they notice their child's eyes appear misaligned, even if the child is very young. A baby whose eyes have not straightened by the age of four months should be examined to rule out serious disease. Strabismus is not a condition that a child will outgrow without medical intervention. Pediatricians can refer parents to an ophthalmologist (eye specialist) skilled in evaluating the vision of very young children.

Diagnosis

Every baby's eyes should be examined by the age of nine months. A pediatrician, **family** doctor, ophthalmologist, or optometrist licensed to use diagnostic drugs uses drops that dilate the pupils and temporarily paralyze eye-focusing muscles to evaluate visual status and ocular health. Early diagnosis is important. Some eye turns may result from a tumor. Untreated strabismus can damage vision and possibly result in lazy eye (**amblyopia**).

Treatment

Preserving or restoring vision and improving appearance may involve one or more of the following:

- glasses to aid in focusing and straighten the eye(s)
- patching to force infants and young children to use and straighten the weaker eye
- eye drops or ointments as a substitute for patching or glasses or to make glasses more effective
- surgery to tighten, relax, or reposition eye muscles
- medication injected into an overactive eye muscle to allow the opposite muscle to straighten the eye
- vision training (also called eye exercises)

Prognosis

Early consistent treatment usually improves vision and appearance. The most satisfactory results are achieved if the condition is corrected as early as possible and before the age of seven.

Prevention

Strabismus cannot be prevented, but it can be corrected with early intervention.

Parental concerns

Parents are often concerned that eye turn is indicative of other vision problems. Sometimes strabismus does accompany other vision defects, so a complete eye examination by a pediatric ophthalmologist is advisable. Delay only increases the difficulty in correcting strabismus, so parents should not wait to see if their child outgrows the condition.

KEY TERMS

Amblyopia—Decreased visual acuity, usually in one eye, in the absence of any structural abnormality in the eye.

Ophthalmologist—A physician who specializes in the anatomy and physiology of the eyes and in the diagnosis and treatment of eye diseases and disorders.

Resources

BOOKS

Plager, David, et al. *Strabismus Surgery: Basic and Advanced Strategies*. Oxford, UK: Oxford University Press, 2004.

ORGANIZATIONS

American Academy of Ophthalmology. PO Box 7424, 655 Beach Street, San Francisco, CA 94120–7424. Web site: <www.aao.org>.

American Academy of Optometry. 6110 Executive Boulevard, Suite 506, Rockville, MD 20852. Web site: <www.aaopt.org>.

American Academy of Pediatric Ophthalmology and Strabismus (AAPOS). PO Box 193832 San Francisco, CA 94119. Web site: <www.med-aapos.bu.edu>.

WEB SITES

Cooper, Jeffrey. "All about Strabismus." *Optometrist Network*, 2001. Available online at <www.strabismus.org> (accessed October 31, 2004).

Gerontis, Corina C. "Exotropia, Congenital." Available online at <www.emedicine.com/oph/topic330.htm> (accessed October 31, 2004).

Ocampo, Vincente V., and C. Stephen Foster. "Exotropia, Infantile." Available online at <www.emedicine.com/oph/topic328.htm> (accessed October 31, 2004).

Stidham, D. Brian, and Chris Noyes. "Exotropia, Accommodative." Available online at <www.emedicine.com/oph/topic330.htm> (accessed October 31, 2004).

Tish Davidson, A.M.
Maureen Haggerty

Stranger anxiety

Definition

Stranger anxiety is **fear** or wariness of people with whom a child is not familiar.

Description

An infant learns to recognize her parents within the first few months of birth by sight, sound, and smell. Until about six months of age, the baby will usually seem interested in other adults as well, engaging in games such as peek-a-boo. After six months, many babies undergo a period of fear and unhappiness around anyone except their parents. The child may burst into tears if an unknown person makes eye contact or shriek if left even momentarily in the care of an unfamiliar person.

This stranger anxiety is a normal part of a child's **cognitive development**. It usually begins at around eight or nine months and generally lasts into the child's second year. Normal **separation anxiety** develops during this same period. Both of these responses arise because the baby has reached a stage of mental development where she can differentiate her caretakers from other people, and she has a strong preference for familiar faces. Rather than indicating emotional difficulties, the emergence of a fear of strangers in the second half of the first year is an indicator of mental development.

Infants may react immediately and vigorously to strangers, especially if approached suddenly or picked up by someone unfamiliar. The child may be particularly upset around people who look different to her, for example, people with glasses or men with beards. The setting and way in which the stranger approaches the child can influence how the child may respond. If the stranger approaches slowly when the caregiver is nearby, smiling and speaking softly, offering a toy, the infant will sometimes show interest rather than distress. However, the degree of distress shown by an infant to a stranger varies greatly from baby to baby, a finding that many believe to be rooted in the **temperament** of the infant. A genetic basis for the development of stranger anxiety has also been shown by twin research. Identical **twins** show more similar onset of stranger distress than fraternal twins.

As infants acquire more experience in dealing with unfamiliar persons at **family** outings or in **day care**, their anxiety about strangers diminishes. Young children show a wide variety of responses depending on the situation, their past experiences, and their natural level of sociability.

Common problems

Stranger anxiety can be upsetting to friends and relatives, who may feel rebuffed by a suddenly shy child. The baby may reject a caregiver she was previously comfortable with or grow hysterical when relatives visit. It can also be a frustrating time for the child's parents, since the baby may reject the parent who is not the principal caregiver. Parents should respect the child's fear as much as possible and allow her to approach people as she is able. If the child does not want to be hugged by or sit with a relative, it is unwise to force her. Eventually children outgrow their fear and become more tolerant of strangers.

Parental concerns

All parents are concerned about teaching their children to be wary when approached by unfamiliar adults. However, parents need to find a balance between concern and encouragement of their child's natural curiosity and friendliness, while at the same time teaching them that they should always rely on parental guidance and approval in dealing with strangers.

When to call the doctor

While stranger distress and separation anxiety are normal for infants and toddlers, should a parent become concerned if they persist into the toddler or **preschool** years? The answer to this question depends in part on the nature of the child's response, its intensity, and persistence over time. For example, it is commonplace for preschoolers to show some distress on meeting new people and separating from their parents during the first week or two of daycare or in a new setting. Typically this settling in period does not last too long. If older children persists in showing excessive distress and anxiety on meeting new people, to the point where it interferes with their social development, parents should discuss this pattern with their pediatrician, who may make a referral to a child psychologist for further evaluation.

See also Separation anxiety; School phobia/school refusal.

Resources

ORGANIZATIONS

American Academy of Pediatrics. 141 Northwest Point Boulevard, Elk Grove Village, IL 60007–1098. Web site: <www.aap.org>.

WEB SITES

"Coping with Your Newborn's Stranger Anxiety." Available online at <http://va.essortment.com/newbornstranger_rzca.htm> (accessed October 31, 2004).

Honig, Alice S. "Soothing Stranger Anxiety." *Scholastic Families*. Available online at <www.scholastic.com/earlylearner/infant/childcare/baby_strangeranx.htm> (accessed October 31, 2004).

Tish Davidson, A.M.
Peter LaFrenier

Strawberry marks *see* **Birthmarks**
Strength training *see* **Exercise**
Strep culture *see* **Throat culture**

Strep throat

Definition

Streptococcal **sore throat**, or strep throat, as it is more commonly called, is a bacterial infection of the mucous membranes lining the throat or pharynx.

Description

Strep throat is caused by a type of bacteria called group A streptococci. The tonsils may also become infected (**tonsillitis**). Left untreated, strep throat may develop into **rheumatic fever** or other serious conditions.

Demographics

Strep throat accounts for between 5 and 10 percent of all sore throats. Although anyone can get strep throat, it is most common in school-age children. People who smoke, who are fatigued, run down, or who live in damp, crowded conditions are also more likely to become infected. Children under age two and adults who are not around children are less likely to get the disease.

Strep throat occurs most frequently between November to April. The disease passes directly from person to person by coughing, sneezing, and close contact. On rare occasions, the disease is passed through food, when a food handler infected with strep throat accidentally contaminates food by coughing or sneezing. Statistically, if someone in the household is infected, one out of every four other household members may get strep throat within two to seven days.

Causes and symptoms

A person with strep throat suddenly develops a painful sore throat one to five days after being exposed to the streptococcus bacteria. The **pain** is indistinguishable from sore throats caused by other diseases.

The infected person usually feels tired and has a **fever**, sometimes accompanied by chills, **headache**, muscle aches, swollen lymph glands, and **nausea**. Young children may complain of abdominal pain. The tonsils look swollen and are bright red, with white or yellow patches of pus on them. Sometimes the roof of the mouth is red or has small red spots. Often a person with strep throat has bad breath.

Despite these common symptoms, strep throat can be deceptive. It is possible to have the disease and not show any of these symptoms. Many young children complain only of a headache and stomachache, without the characteristic sore throat.

Occasionally, within a few days of developing the sore throat, an individual may develop a fine, rough, sunburn-like rash over the face and upper body and have a fever of 101–104°F (38.3–40°C). The tongue becomes bright red, with a flecked, strawberry-like appearance. When a rash develops, this form of strep throat is called **scarlet fever**. The rash is a reaction to toxins released by the streptococcus bacteria. Scarlet fever is no more dangerous than strep throat and is treated the same way. The rash disappears in about five days. One to three weeks later, patches of skin may peel off, as might occur with a **sunburn**, especially on the fingers and toes.

Untreated strep throat can cause rheumatic fever. This is a serious illness, although it occurs rarely. One outbreak appeared in the United States in the mid-1980s. Rheumatic fever occurs most often in children between the ages of five and 15 and may have a genetic component, since it seems to run in families. Although the strep throat that causes rheumatic fever is contagious, rheumatic fever itself is not.

Rheumatic fever begins one to six weeks after an untreated streptococcal infection. The joints, especially the wrists, elbows, knees, and ankles become red, sore, and swollen. The infected person develops a high fever and possibly a rapid heartbeat when lying down, paleness, shortness of breath, and fluid retention. A red rash over the trunk may come and go for weeks or months. An acute attack of rheumatic fever lasts about three months.

Rheumatic fever can cause permanent damage to the heart and heart valves. It can be prevented by promptly treating **streptococcal infections** with **antibiotics**. It does not occur if all the streptococcus bacteria are killed within the first ten to 12 days after infection.

In the 1990s, outbreaks of a virulent strain of group A streptococcus were reported to cause a toxic-shock-like illness and a severe invasive infection called necrotizing fasciitis, which destroys skin and muscle tissue. Although these diseases are caused by group A streptococci, they rarely begin with strep throat. Usually the streptococcus bacteria enters the body through a skin wound. These complications are rare. However, since the death rate in necrotizing fasciitis is 30 to 50 percent, it is wise to seek prompt treatment for any streptococcal infection.

Diagnosis

Diagnosis of a strep throat by a doctor begins with a physical examination of the throat and chest. The doctor will also look for signs of other illness, such as a sinus infection or **bronchitis**, and seek information about whether the patient has been around other people with strep throat. If it appears that the patient may have strep throat, the doctor will do laboratory tests.

There are two types of tests to determine if a person has strep throat. A rapid strep test can only determine the presence of streptococcal bacteria but will not tell if the sore throat is caused by another kind of bacteria. To perform a rapid strep test or a **throat culture**, a nurse will use a sterile swab to reach down into the throat and obtain a sample of material from the sore area. The procedure takes only a few seconds but may cause gagging. The results are available in about 20 minutes. The advantage of this test is the speed with which a diagnosis can be made.

The rapid strep test has a false negative rate of about 20 percent. In other words, in about 20 percent of cases where no strep is detected by the rapid strep test, the patient actually does have strep throat. Because of this margin of error, when a rapid strep test is negative, the doctor often does a throat culture.

For a throat culture a sample of swabbed material is cultured, or grown, in the laboratory on a medium that allows technicians to determine what kind of bacteria are present. Results take 24 to 48 hours. The test is very accurate and will show the presence of other kinds of bacteria besides streptococci. It is important not to take any leftover antibiotics before visiting the doctor and having a throat culture. Even small amounts of antibiotics can suppress the bacteria and mask its presence in the throat culture.

In the event that rheumatic fever is suspected, the doctor does a blood test. Results of this test, called an antistreptolysin-O test, tell the doctor whether the person has recently been infected with strep bacteria. This information helps the doctor distinguish between rheumatic fever and rheumatoid arthritis.

Treatment

Strep throat is treated with antibiotics. Penicillin is the preferred medication. Oral penicillin must be taken for 10 days. Patients need to take the entire amount of antibiotic prescribed and not discontinue taking the medication when they feel better. Stopping the antibiotic early can lead to a return of the strep infection. Occasionally, a single injection of long-acting penicillin (Bicillin) is given instead of ten days of oral treatment.

About 10 percent of the time, penicillin is not effective against the strep bacteria. When this happens a doctor may prescribe other antibiotics such as amoxicillin (Amoxil, Pentamox, Sumox, Trimox), clindamycin (Cleocin), or a cephalosporin (Keflex, Durocef, Ceclor). Erythromycin (Eryzole, Pediazole, Ilosone), another inexpensive antibiotic, is given to people who are allergic to penicillin. Scarlet fever is treated with the same antibiotics as strep throat.

Without treatment, the symptoms of strep throat begin subsiding in four or five days. However, because of the possibility of getting rheumatic fever, it is important to treat strep throat promptly with antibiotics. If rheumatic fever does occur, it is also treated with antibiotics. Anti-inflammatory drugs, such as steroids, are used to treat joint swelling. Diuretics are used to reduce water retention. Once the rheumatic fever becomes inactive, children may continue on low doses of antibiotics to prevent a reoccurrence. Necrotizing fasciitis is treated with intravenous antibiotics.

Prognosis

Patients with strep throat begin feeling better about 24 hours after starting antibiotics. Symptoms rarely last longer than five days.

People remain contagious until after they have been taking antibiotics for 24 hours. Children should not return to school or childcare until they are no longer contagious. Food handlers should not work for the first 24 hours after antibiotic treatment, because strep infections are occasionally passed through contaminated food. People who are not treated with antibiotics can continue to spread strep bacteria for several months.

About 10 percent of strep throat cases do not respond to penicillin. People who have even a mild sore throat after a 10-day treatment with antibiotic should return to their doctor. An explanation for this problem may be that the person is just a carrier of strep and that something else is causing the sore throat.

Taking antibiotics within the first week of a strep infection will prevent rheumatic fever and other complications. If rheumatic fever does occur, the outcomes vary considerably. Some cases may be cured. In others there may be permanent damage to the heart and heart valves. In rare cases, rheumatic fever can be fatal.

Necrotizing fasciitis has a death rate of 30 to 50 percent. Patients who survive often suffer a great deal of tissue and muscle loss. Fortunately, this complication of a streptococcus infection is very rare.

Prevention

There is no way to prevent getting a strep throat. However, the risk of getting one or passing one on to another person can be minimized by the following precautions:

- washing hands well and frequently, especially after nose blowing or sneezing and before food handling
- disposing of used tissues properly
- avoiding close contact with someone who has a strep throat
- not sharing food and eating utensils with anyone
- not smoking

Parental concerns

Children who have strep throat should be kept out of daycare, school, activities, and other public places until they have been taking their antibiotic for a full 24 hours. This will help decrease the likelihood of passing on the infection to others.

Parents who are caring for a child with strep will want to take the following steps:

- Give the child **acetaminophen** or ibuprofen for pain. Aspirin should not be given to children because of its association with **Reye's syndrome**, a serious disease.
- Encourage the child to gargle with warm double strength tea or warm salt water, made by adding one teaspoon of salt to eight ounces of water, to relieve sore throat pain.
- Make sure that the child drinks plenty of fluids but avoids acidic juices like orange juice because they irritate the throat.

KEY TERMS

Lactobacillus acidophilus—Commonly known as acidophilus, a bacteria found in yogurt that changes the balance of the bacteria in the intestine in a beneficial way.

- Offer the child soft, nutritious foods like noodle soup and avoid spicy foods.
- Help the child avoid exposure to people who are smoking.
- Encourage the child to rest until the fever is gone, then allow him or her to gradually resume activities.
- Use a room humidifier, as it may make sore throat sufferers more comfortable.
- Be aware that antiseptic lozenges and sprays may aggravate the sore throat rather than improve it.

Resources

BOOKS

Gerber, Michael A. "Group A Streptococcus." In *Nelson Textbook of Pediatrics*. Edited by Richard E. Behrman et al. Philadelphia: Saunders, 2004.

PERIODICALS

Ebell, M. H. "Strep Throat." *American Family Physician* 68 (September 1, 2000): 937–8.

Tish Davidson, A.M.
Rosalyn Carson-DeWitt, MD

Streptococcal infections

Definition

Streptococcal (strep) infections are communicable diseases that develop when bacteria of the family Streptococcus invade parts of the body and contaminate blood or tissue.

Description

Most people have some form of strep bacteria in their body at some point. A person who hosts bacteria without showing signs of infection is considered a carrier.

Types of infection

Primary strep infections invade healthy tissue and most often affect the throat. Secondary strep infections invade tissue already weakened by injury or illness. They frequently affect the bones, ears, eyes, joints, or intestines. Both primary and secondary strep infections can travel from affected tissues to lymph glands, enter the bloodstream, and spread throughout the body. Numerous strains of streptococcal bacteria have been identified. Types A, B, C, D, and G are most likely to make people sick.

GROUP A Group A strep (GAS) is the form of streptococcal bacteria most apt to be associated with serious illness. Two of the most severe invasive GAS infections are necrotizing fasciitis or flesh-eating bacteria (destruction of muscle tissue and fat) and **toxic shock syndrome** (a rapidly progressive disorder that causes shock and damages internal organs). GAS is also the type of strep responsible for **strep throat**. Strep throat is common and not usually serious. If untreated, however, strep throat can develop into rheumatic fever which can permanently damage the heart and other organs.

GROUP B Group B strep (GBS) most often affects pregnant women, infants, the elderly, and chronically ill adults. Streptococcal infection occurs when bacteria contaminate cuts or open sores or otherwise penetrate the body's natural defenses. The bacteria can be passed from pregnant women to their newborns during **childbirth**.

GROUP C Group C strep (GCS) is a common source of infection in animals. It rarely causes human illness.

GROUP D Group D strep (GDS) is a common cause of wound infections in hospital patients. GDS is also associated with the following:

- abnormal growth of tissue in the gastrointestinal tract
- urinary tract infection (UTI)
- womb infections in women who have just given birth

GROUP G Normally present on the skin, in the mouth and throat, and in the intestines and genital tract, Group G strep (GGS) is most likely to lead to infection in alcoholics and in people who have **cancer**, **diabetes mellitus**, rheumatoid arthritis, and other conditions that suppress immune-system activity.

GGS can cause a variety of infections, including the following:

- bacteria in the bloodstream (bacteremia)
- inflammation of the connective tissue structure surrounding a joint (bursitis)
- endocarditis, a condition that affects the lining of the heart chambers and the heart valves
- **meningitis**
- inflammation of bone and bone marrow (osteomyelitis)
- inflammation of the lining of the abdomen (peritonitis)

Causes and symptoms

GAS

GAS is transmitted by direct contact with saliva, nasal discharge, or open **wounds** of someone who has the infection. Chronic illness, kidney disease treated by dialysis, and steroid use increase vulnerability to infection. About one of five people with GAS infection develops a sore, inflamed throat and pus on the tonsils (strep throat). The majority of those infected by GAS either have no symptoms or develop enlarged lymph nodes, **fever**, **headache**, **nausea**, **vomiting**, weakness, and a rapid heartbeat.

Flesh-eating bacteria is characterized by fever, extreme **pain**, swelling, and redness at a site where skin is broken. Symptoms of toxic shock include abdominal pain, confusion, **dizziness**, and widespread red skin rash.

GBS

A pregnant woman who has GBS infection can develop infections of the bladder, blood, and urinary tract, and deliver a baby who is infected or stillborn. The risk of transmitting GBS infection during birth is highest in a woman whose labor begins before the thirty-seventh week of pregnancy or lasts more than 18 hours or who has the following conditions:

- has a GBS urinary-tract infection
- has already given birth to a baby infected with GBS
- develops a fever during labor

More than 13 percent of babies who develop GBS infection during birth or within the first few months of life develop neurological disorders. An equal number of them die.

Miscellaneous symptoms

Other symptoms associated with strep infections include the following:

- anemia
- elevated white blood cell counts

- inflammation of the epiglottis (epiglottitis)
- heart murmur
- high blood pressure
- infection of the heart muscle
- kidney inflammation (nephritis)
- swelling of the face and ankles

Demographics

Between 10,000 and 15,000 invasive GAS infections occur in the United States every year. In 1999, there were 300 cases of toxic shock associated with GAS infection and 600 cases of necrotizing fasciitis. There are millions of cases of strep throat every year, and similar numbers of cases of relatively mild skin infections. Strep throat is most common among school-age children and people who live in group settings (for example, dorms, boarding schools, the military).

Since first emerging in the 1970s, GBS has been the primary cause of life-threatening illness and death in newborns. GBS exists in the reproductive tract of 20 to 25 percent of all pregnant women. Although no more than 2 percent of these women develop invasive infection, if untreated 40 to 73 percent transmit bacteria to their babies during delivery. About 12,000 of the 3.5 million babies born in the United States each year develop GBS disease in infancy. About 75 percent of them develop early-onset infection. Sometimes evident within a few hours of birth and always apparent within the first week of life, this condition causes inflammation of the membranes covering the brain and spinal cord (meningitis), **pneumonia**, blood infection (sepsis), and other problems.

Late-onset GBS develops between the ages of seven days and three months. It often causes meningitis. About half of all cases of this rare condition can be traced to mothers who are GBS carriers. The cause of the others is unknown. GBS has also been linked to a history of breast cancer. Approximately 5 percent of babies who develop GBS die. However, those who survive often have debilitating problems after the disease. Infections caused by the other types of strep are rare.

When to call the doctor

If the child has a fever and **sore throat**, a wound that seems to be infected, a rash, is acting very sick, or has any other symptoms of strep infection, the doctor should be consulted.

Diagnosis

Strep bacteria can be obtained by swabbing the back of the throat, the vagina, the rectum, or the infected area with a piece of sterile cotton. A blood sample can also be taken. Microscopic examination of the smear can identify which type of bacteria has been collected. A rapid strep test may be done to test for step throat infection. This kind of test gives results within the hour. A sample may also be sent to a lab for traditional culturing, which takes from one to two days, because this form of testing is more accurate than the rapid strep test.

Treatment

Penicillin and other **antibiotics** are used to treat GAS and other types of strep infection. It usually takes less than 24 hours for antibiotics to eliminate an infected person's ability to transmit the infection, but antibiotics always need to be taken for the full course prescribed by the doctor to prevent reinfection or other complications.

Guidelines developed by the American Academy of Obstetrics and Gynecology (AAOG), the American Academy of Pediatrics (AAP), and the Centers for Disease Control and Prevention (CDC) recommend administering intravenous antibiotics during labor to a woman at high risk of passing GBS infection on to her child and offering the medication to any pregnant woman who wants it.

Initiating antibiotic therapy at least four hours before birth allows medication to become concentrated enough to protect the baby during passage through the birth canal. Babies infected with GBS during or shortly after birth need to be treated right away, but they may still die. Those who survive often require lengthy hospital stays and develop vision or hearing loss and other permanent disabilities.

Alternative treatment

Conventional medicine is very successful in treating strep infections. However, several alternative therapies, including homeopathy and botanical medicine, may help relieve symptoms or support the person with a strep infection. For example, several herbs, including garlic (*Allium sativum*), echinacea (*Echinacea* spp.), and goldenseal (*Hydrastis canadensis*), are believed to strengthen the immune system, thus helping the body fight a current infection, as well as helping prevent future infections.

Prognosis

GAS is responsible for more than 2,000 deaths a year. About one in five people infected with flesh-eating bacteria die. So do three out of every five people who develop streptococcal toxic shock syndrome. Strep throat, however, is almost never fatal, although left untreated it can result in diseases such as rheumatic fever that can affect the heart.

Early-onset GBS kills 15 percent of the infants it affects. Late-onset disease claims the lives of 10 percent of babies who develop it. GBS infections are fatal in about 20 percent of the men and non-pregnant women who develop them. About 10 to 15 percent of non-GAS strep infections are fatal. Antibiotic therapy, begun when symptoms first appear, may increase a patient's chance of survival.

Prevention

Washing the hands frequently, especially before eating and after using the bathroom, and keeping wounds clean can help prevent strep infection. Exposure to infected people should be avoided, and a family physician should be notified if the child develops an extremely sore throat or pain, redness, swelling, or drainage at the site of a wound or break in the skin.

Until vaccines to prevent strep infection become available, 12 monthly doses of oral or injected antibiotics may prevent some types of recurrent infection if necessary. Pregnant women should be screened for GBS during the last few weeks of pregnancy. About one fourth of pregnant women are thought to carry GBS in their vaginal or rectal tracts. If GBS is found to be present, antibiotics can be administered intravenously during labor. This greatly reduces the chance of GBS being transmitted from mother to baby when the baby is in the birth canal. The chances are believed to be reduced from one in 200 that the baby will develop GBS infection to one in 4000.

Parental concerns

Strep infections can develop into life-threatening or debilitating problems if not treated promptly. Ensuring the child takes the full course of antibiotics prescribed by the doctor even if the symptoms have gone away can prevent life-threatening complications such as rheumatic fever. Pregnant women should be screened for GBS during the last weeks of pregnancy to help ensure that GBS does not infect their newborns.

KEY TERMS

Bacteremia—Bacterial infection of the blood.

Bursitis—Inflammation of a bursa, a fluid-filled cavity or sac. In the body, bursae are located at places where friction might otherwise develop.

Osteomyelitis—An infection of the bone and bone marrow, usually caused by bacteria.

Resources

BOOKS

Laskey, Elizabeth. *Strep Throat.* Chicago: Heinemann Library, 2003.

Tomasz, Alexander, ed. *Streptococcus Pneumoniae: Molecular Biology & Mechanisms of Disease.* Larchmont: Mary Ann Liebert, Inc., 2000.

PERIODICALS

"Early Results Show Promise for Strep Vaccine." *Vaccine Weekly* (September 2004): 76.

Tish Davidson, A.M.
Maureen Haggerty

Stridor

Definition

Stridor is a term used to describe noisy breathing in general and to refer specifically to a high-pitched crowing sound associated with **croup**, respiratory infection, and airway obstruction.

Description

Stridor is a symptom, not a disease. It occurs when air is forced through breathing passages narrowed by the following:

- illness
- infection
- the presence of **foreign objects**
- congenital throat abnormalities

The sound is usually loud enough to be heard at a distance, although sometimes only during deep breathing and can occur on inhaling, exhaling, or both. It can be a symptom of a life-threatening respiratory emergency.

Demographics

Stridor is most common in children. Croup, an inflammation of the trachea (windpipe) and larynx (voice box), is the most common cause of stridor in children under age two. Young children also frequently develop acute stridor by inhaling a foreign object, often food such as hot dogs, popcorn, or hard candy. Stridor as a complication of bacterial infections is also common in children under age eight.

Congenital stridor is caused by abnormalities in the airways that cause them to partially collapse when the child breathes. It is present at birth and usually becomes obvious within the first six weeks of life.

Causes and symptoms

During childhood, stridor is usually caused by infection of the cartilage flap (epiglottis) that covers the opening of the trachea to prevent material from entering the lungs and **choking** a person during swallowing. It can also be caused by foreign objects, such as a food or a coin, that a child has tried to swallow.

Laryngomalacia is the most common cause of congenital stridor, accounting for 75 percent of stridor in newborns. It seems to be caused by a collapse of tissue around the larynx and usually occurs in newborns that have no other health problems. It produces a rapid, low-pitched form of stridor that may be heard when a baby inhales. This condition develops soon after birth and usually does not require medical attention. It normally disappears as the child matures and almost always by the time the child is 18 months old.

Causes of stridor in adolescents and adults include the following:

- abscess or swelling of the upper airway
- paralysis or malfunction of the vocal cords
- tumor
- enlargement of the thyroid gland goiter
- swelling of the voice box (laryngeal edema)
- narrowing of the windpipe (tracheal stenosis)

When to call the doctor

Acute stridor, especially when caused by inhaling a foreign object, can be a life-threatening emergency. Emergency medical care should be sought immediately if the individual is showing any signs of difficulty breathing or is turning blue, is unconscious, or is thought to have inhaled a foreign object. In other cases, a doctor should be consulted on a non-emergency basis whenever stridor develops in a newborn or when stridor accompanies other signs of illness such as a **fever**.

Diagnosis

When stridor is present in a newborn, pediatricians and neonatologists also look for evidence of heart defects or neurological disorders that may cause paralysis of the vocal cords. Paralysis of the vocal cords can be life threatening. If examinations do not reveal other reasons for the baby's noisy breathing, the air passages are assumed to be the cause of the problem.

Listening to an older child or adult breathe usually enables pediatricians, **family** physicians, and pulmonary specialists to estimate where an airway obstruction is located. The timing and location of the noisy breathing, whether the sound is intermittent, occurs during eating, is better or worse when lying or standing, as well as the presence or absence of fever or other signs of infection and similar information help in determining the cause of stridor. It is sometimes difficult in children for doctors to differentiate between stridor and wheezing caused by **asthma**. However, a history of the breathing problem and careful examination can usually help them make the distinction.

The extent of the obstruction can be calculated by assessing several features in the patient:

- complexion
- chest movements
- breathing rate
- level of consciousness

X rays and direct examination of the voice box (larynx) and breathing passages using a laryngoscope or bronchoscope indicate the exact location of the obstruction or inflammation. **Computed tomography** (CT) scans and **magnetic resonance imaging** (MRI) scans also may be useful, especially if surgery is needed.

Flow-volume loops and pulse oximetry are diagnostic tools used to measure how much air flows through the breathing passages and how much oxygen is available. **Pulmonary function tests** may also be performed.

Treatment

Treatment of stridor depends on the underlying cause of the breathing difficulty. Life-threatening emergencies may require the insertion of a breathing tube through the mouth and nose (tracheal intubation) or the insertion of a breathing tube directly into the windpipe (tracheotomy) and surgery to remove a foreign object.

KEY TERMS

Congenital—Present at birth.

Laryngomalacia—A birth defect that causes the tissues around the larynx to partially collapse and narrow the air passageway, causing noisy breathing.

Laryngoscope—An endoscope that is used to examine the interior of the larynx.

Bacterial infections are treated with **antibiotics**. Congenital stridor is usually left untreated and resolves on its own.

Prognosis

The outcome of stridor depends on its cause. Death by suffocation may occur when a foreign object blocks the airway. Otherwise the outcome for most cases of stridor is good to excellent, depending on the cause.

Prevention

Adults must keep small, easily swallowed objects such as coins, beads, and hard, round candies away from young children so that they do not try to swallow them. Taking precautions against colds and bronchial infections (washing hands, not sharing dishes, avoiding sick people) can cut down on stridor from infective causes. Congenital stridor is not preventable.

Parental concerns

Congenital stridor in a newborn can sound frightening to parents, but it is rarely a cause for concern or medical intervention.

See also Croup; Foreign objects; Vocal cord dysfunction.

Resources

BOOKS

Wyka, Kenneth, et al. *Foundations of Respiratory Care*. Albany, NY: Delmar Learning, 2002.

ORGANIZATIONS

American Academy of Pediatrics. 141 Northwest Point Boulevard, Elk Grove Village, IL 60007–1098. Web site: <www.aap.org>.

WEB SITES

Kumar, Murda, and Deandra Clark. "Stridor." *eMedicine Medical Library*, January 3, 2003. Available online at <www.emedicine.com/ped/topic2159.htm> (accessed November 30, 2004).

Ren, Clement L. "Congenital Stridor." *eMedicine Medical Library*, February 28, 2003. Available online at <www.emedicine.com/ped/topic2624.htm> (accessed November 30, 2004).

Tish Davidson, A.M.
Maureen Haggerty

Stroke

Definition

A stroke, also called a cerebral infarction, is a life-threatening condition marked by a sudden disruption in the blood supply to the brain.

Description

A disruption in the blood supply to the brain starves the brain of oxygen-rich blood and causes the nerve cells in that area to become damaged and die within minutes. The body parts controlled by those damaged brain cells lose their ability to function.

Depending on the area of the brain that is affected, a stroke can alter many aspects of a child's functioning such as speech, movement, behavior and learning. A stroke also may cause weakness or paralysis on one side of the body. The loss of function may be mild or severe, temporary or permanent.

If medical treatment begins within hours after symptoms are recognized, brain damage can be limited and the risk of permanent medical effects can be decreased.

Types of stroke

An ischemic stroke—the most common form of stroke in children under age 15—is caused by a blocked or narrowed artery. In children, blockages may be caused by a blood clot, injury to the artery, or rarely in children, atherosclerosis (build-up of fatty deposits on the blood vessel walls). A cerebral thrombosis is a blood clot that develops at the clogged part of the blood vessel. A cerebral embolism is a blood clot that travels to the clogged blood vessel from another location in the circulatory system.

A hemorrhagic stroke—the more common form of stroke in infants and children under age two—occurs when a weakened blood vessel leaks or bursts, causing bleeding in the brain tissue or near the surface of the brain.

Two types of weakened blood vessels usually cause hemorrhagic stroke, including:

- aneurysm: ballooning of a weakened area of a blood vessel
- arteriovenous malformations: cluster of abnormal blood vessels

A transient ischemic attack (TIA), also called a "mini stroke," is characterized by a short-term blood vessel obstruction or clot that tends to resolve itself quickly, usually within 10–20 minutes, or up to 24 hours. A TIA usually does not require intervention. However, a TIA is a strong indicator of an ischemic stroke and should be evaluated in the same way as a stroke to prevent a more serious attack.

In children, strokes can be categorized as:

- prenatal stroke: occurring before birth
- neonatal or perinatal stroke: occurring in infants less than 30 days old
- pediatric or childhood stroke: occurring in children aged 15 and under

Demographics

Childhood stroke is relatively rare, occurring in about two to three of every 100,000 children aged one to 14 per year. In comparison, stroke occurs in about 100 of every 100,000 adults per year. The rate of ischemic stroke and hemorrhagic stroke is similar among children aged one to 14.

Stroke occurs more frequently in children under age two, and peaks in the perinatal period. In the National Hospital Discharge Survey from 1980-1998, the rate of stroke for infants less than 30 days old (per 100,000 live births per year) was 26.4, with rates of 6.7 for hemorrhagic stroke and 17.8 for ischemic stroke.

More fatal strokes occur in African-American children than white children, mirroring the racial differences of stroke in adults. Compared to the stroke risk of white children, African-American children have an increased relative risk of 2.12, Hispanics a decreased relative risk of 0.76 and Asians have a similar risk. Boys have a 1.28-fold higher risk of stroke than girls and have a higher case-fatality rate for ischemic stroke than girls. The increased risk among African Americans is not explained by the presence of sickle cell disease, nor is the excess risk among boys explained by trauma.

Research conducted by the National Institute of Neurological Diseases and Stroke (NINDS) indicates a "stroke belt," or geographical area where fatal strokes are more predominant. This stroke belt includes Alabama, Arkansas, Georgia, Indiana, Kentucky, Louisiana, Mississippi, North Carolina, South Carolina, Tennessee, and Virginia. Researchers examined death certificates over a 19-year period and found a 21 percent higher risk of death from stroke in people under age 20 in the stroke belt states had compared with the same age group in other states. During the same period, people over age 25 in the stroke belt region had a 20 percent higher risk of death from stroke. Because the overall rate of stroke in children is low, researchers warn parents in these states not to be too alarmed. However, the findings indicate further investigation is needed.

Causes and symptoms

Causes

The cause of childhood stroke is unknown in one-third of cases, and an underlying medical condition or multiple conditions appear to contribute to over half of the cases. The most common causes of stroke are congenital (present at birth) and acquired heart diseases, and **sickle cell anemia**.

About 10–15 percent of children with sickle cell disease suffer a stroke, usually ischemic stroke. Sickle cell disease is a blood disorder in which the blood cells cannot carry oxygen to the brain because the blood vessels to the brain are either narrowed or closed.

One rare cause of stroke is an extreme case of the **chickenpox** virus, which causes a narrowing of blood vessels in the head for some children.

RISK FACTORS Although **obesity**, **high cholesterol**, high blood pressure, atherosclerosis, and **smoking** are common stroke risk factors in adults, they rarely contribute to stroke risk in children. Risk factors for childhood stroke include a **family** history of stroke, cardiovascular disease or diabetes, as well as the presence of the conditions listed below.

Some of the more common congenital heart diseases that increase the risk of childhood stroke include:

- aortic and mitral valve stenosis
- atrial septal defect
- patent ductus arteriosus (PDA)

- patent foramen ovale
- inherited blood clotting disorders
- ventricular septal defect
- hypercoagulable states

Some of the acquired heart conditions that increase the risk of childhood stroke include:

- bacterial meningitis
- endocarditis
- arrhythmia and atrial fibrillation
- artificial heart valve
- myocarditis
- cardiomyopathy
- rheumatic heart disease
- embolism
- anoxia
- antiphospholipid antibody syndrome
- encephalitis
- blood vessel disease
- certain blood disorders, such as **hemophilia**
- inborn errors of metabolism
- illicit drug use
- teenage pregnancy
- teen use of **oral contraceptives** (birth control pills)

Possible traumas that increase the risk of childhood stroke include birth injury or trauma, **child abuse,** or other injury or trauma.

Because of the wide range of secondary conditions that contribute to stroke, it is difficult for researchers to assess the relative contribution of each risk factor to the problem of cerebrovascular disease as a whole, according to the Child Neurology Society Ad Hoc Committee on Stroke in Children. In addition, this variability also hinders clinical research.

Symptoms

In infants and very young children, stroke symptoms are sudden and include:

- seizures
- coma
- paralysis on one side of the body
- **nausea** or vomiting

In older children, stroke symptoms are sudden and include:

- numbness or weakness of the face, arm, or leg, especially on one side of the body
- confusion or difficulty speaking or understanding speech
- vision difficulties, often in one eye
- hearing problems, often in one ear
- difficulty walking, **dizziness** or loss of balance or coordination
- severe **headache**
- difficulty swallowing
- nausea or vomiting
- painful or stiff neck

Other stroke signs and symptoms include:

- sudden severe headache with unknown cause
- sudden nausea or vomiting
- warm, flushed, clammy skin
- slow, full pulse
- appearance of unequal pupils
- facial "droop" on one side
- salivary drool
- urinary incontinence

If the child seems to recover quickly from these stroke symptoms, a TIA may have occurred. All neurological symptoms should serve as a stroke "warning sign" and could indicate a pending, more serious attack. The child should receive prompt evaluation so necessary preventive therapies can be initiated.

WHEN TO CALL THE DOCTOR If a child has any of the symptoms listed above, the parent or caregiver should immediately dial 9-1-1 to seek emergency care. It is important not to wait to see if symptoms subside; a stroke is a medical emergency. Until the paramedics arrive, the parent or caregiver should follow these first aid guidelines:

- Make sure the child is in a comfortable posture, lying on his or her side, so the airway does not become obstructed by drool or mucus.
- Talk reassuringly to the child, even if he or she is unconscious.
- Do not leave the child alone—constantly observe the child.
- Cover the child with a blanket or remove clothing as needed to maintain the child's normal body temperature.
- Do not give the child any medication, including aspirin; medication will be given later as needed.

Diagnosis

In most children, the diagnosis of stroke is delayed by more than 24 hours from the onset of symptoms. This delay is thought to occur because there is a lack of general awareness by physicians and families of cerebrovascular disorders in children. However, early recognition and treatment of a stroke could improve management, reduce the risk of brain damage and permanent disability, help prevent a recurrence, and initiate a proper treatment and rehabilitation program to maximize functional recovery.

The diagnosis of pediatric stroke generally occurs in the emergency room and includes:

- personal and family medical history
- review of current medications
- evaluation of other health problems
- physical examination
- brief neurological exam
- diagnostic tests

The medical history helps the physician evaluate the presence of other conditions or disorders that might have caused the stroke. The child's family medical history is evaluated to determine if there is a history of cardiovascular or neurological diseases that might increase the risk of blood clots.

The brief neurological exam includes a review of the patient's mental status, motor and sensory system, deep tendon reflexes, coordination, and walking pattern (gait). The cranial nerve function also will be evaluated and includes a review of the patient's visual function and eye movement, strength of facial muscles, the gag reflex, tongue and lip movements, ability to smell and taste, hearing, and sensation and movement of the face, head, and neck.

Questions about the child's condition may include:

- What symptoms occurred?
- When were the symptoms first noticed?
- How long did the symptoms last?
- What functions were affected?

During the physical exam, the child's pulse, blood pressure, and height and weight are checked and recorded.

Diagnostic tests include:

- Blood tests: Test used to detect the presence of any chemical abnormalities, infection, or blood clotting that may have caused the stroke.
- Magnetic resonance imaging (MRI) scan: An imaging technique that provides a detailed picture of the brain without the use of x rays. MRI uses a large magnet, radio waves and a computer to produce these images.
- Computed tomography (CT) scan: An imaging technique that shows the blood vessels in the brain. A CT scan is used to identify the area of the brain affected and to detect signs of swelling.
- Chest x ray: X rays are used to detect an enlarged heart, vascular abnormalities, or lung problems.
- Angiogram: An invasive imaging technique used to examine the blood vessels in the brain. An angiogram is only performed if the CT or MRI scans do not show conclusive results.
- Echocardiogram (echo): A graphic outline of the heart's movement, valves and chambers, used to determine if the stroke was caused by a blood clot traveling from the heart to the brain. Echo is often combined with Doppler ultrasound and color Doppler. During the echo, an ultrasound transducer (hand-held wand placed on the skin of the chest) emits high-frequency sound waves to produce pictures of the heart's valves and chambers.

MRI is more sensitive than CT scanning for the diagnosis of an ischemic stroke within 24 hours. However, the two tests are comparable when used to evaluate the effects of a hemorrhagic stroke.

In rare cases or when carotid artery disease is suspected, additional tests may include a carotid ultrasound or cerebral or carotid angiogram. Other tests to diagnose stroke may include a transcranial Doppler ultrasound and neurosonogram. In a transcranial Doppler ultrasound, sound waves are used to measure blood flow in the vessels of the brain. In a neurosonogram, ultra high frequency sound waves are used to analyze blood flow and possible blockages in the blood vessels in or leading to the brain.

If a pediatric stroke is diagnosed, additional tests may be performed to assess the overall function

- Electroencephalogram (EEG): Electrodes (small, sticky metal patches attached to the scalp) are connected by wires (leads) to an electroencephalograph machine to chart the brain's continuous electrical activity.
- Evoked potentials study: Wires attached to the scalp, neck, and limbs are connected to a computer to measure the electrical activity in certain areas of the brain and spinal cord when specific sensory nerve pathways are stimulated. The brain's electrical response to visual, auditory, and sensual stimulation is recorded.

Treatment

Initial treatment depends on the type of stroke. For an ischemic stroke, initial emergent treatment focuses on restoring blood flow to the brain. For a hemorrhagic stroke, the goal of initial treatment is to control the bleeding. Children with a hemorrhagic stroke may be transferred to a center with neurosurgical facilities so the proper treatment, such as decompression or **hydrocephalus** drainage, can be provided by skilled specialists.

Emergency-room treatment may include: oxygen to ensure the brain is getting the maximum amount, control of body temperature, **assessment** and treatment of breathing difficulties, intravenous fluids to prevent or treat **dehydration**, and medications to control blood pressure and prevent blood clotting. Blood transfusions may be used to treat children with sickle cell disease.

Treatment team

Treatment should be provided by a pediatric neurologist and a multi-disciplinary team of specialists that may include a physical therapist, occupational therapist, speech therapist, social worker, and other specialists as needed to meet the child's individual needs.

Medications

Adult stroke patients who receive treatment within three hours after the onset of stroke symptoms may receive a "clot busting" medication called t-PA. However, the diagnosis of stroke is rarely made within three hours, so the use of this drug in children is uncommon.

Anticoagulant medications, including heparin or warfarin and low-dose aspirin, may be used to reduce the risk of blood clot formation. Although experience with these medications in children suggests they are safe, their use in children remains controversial because of the risk of Reye's syndrome. Sometimes the potential benefits of these medications outweigh the small risk of side effects. Researchers agree that further studies are needed to determine the proper dosage and effectiveness of aspirin and other anticoagulant medications for treating stroke in children.

The most important medication guidelines are: 1) Ensure your child takes all medications exactly as prescribed; 2) Never discontinue any medication without first talking to the child's doctor, even if the medication does not seem to be working or is causing unwanted side effects; and 3) Follow-up with the child's health care provider as recommended to monitor the effects of the medication. Frequent blood tests are required for people taking anticoagulants to evaluate the dosage and effects of the medication.

Other stroke medications that are still being tested in clinical trials include:

- Citicoline as a treatment for ischemic stroke. Studies have shown both acute and long-term neuroprotective properties of citicoline in animal models of stroke and in several human clinical trials.
- Epoetin, a synthetic version of human erythropoietin, as a treatment for ischemic stroke. Epoetin aids the body in producing red blood cells and is currently used to treat anemia associated with kidney disease or caused by some drugs.
- Early administration of magnesium to serve as a potential neuroprotective agent. Studies have shown neuroprotectant properties of magnesium sulfate in animal models of stroke, and improved outcomes following magnesium sulfate treatment in humans have been observed following small pilot studies.

Rehabilitation

After the child's condition has stabilized, rehabilitation is initiated. Rehabilitation includes physical, occupational, and speech therapy. Therapy is usually initiated as soon as possible after a stroke and is often the most intense in the early stages of recovery. Clinicians should work with the child and the parents or caregivers to develop an individual treatment plan. Specific treatment goals will vary from one child to the next but will focus on restoring maximum function and independence, helping the child return to normal activities, and improving the child's quality of life. The child's progress after rehabilitation will depend upon which area of the brain was affected, the cause of stroke, the extent of injury, and the presence of other medical conditions.

Physical therapy includes stretching exercises, muscle group strengthening exercises, and range of motion exercises to preserve flexibility and range of motion. Exercises should be practiced daily, as recommended by the physical therapist. A physical therapist can instruct the patient on proper posture guidelines to maintain proper alignment of the hips and back. Balancing rest and **exercise** is also important.

Occupational therapy may include splints, casts, or braces on the affected arm or leg to enable proper limb positioning, prevent joint stiffness, and maintain flexibility and range of motion. An occupational therapist can recommend assistive equipment and devices to help the child with activities of daily living, such as bathing, dressing, and eating. If a walker or wheelchair are needed, an occupational therapist can provide specific instructions.

Physical and occupational therapists can provide guidelines on how to adapt the child's home and school environments to ensure **safety** and comfort.

Speech therapy will focus on the child's specific needs which may include any or all aspects of language use, such as speaking, reading, writing, and understanding the spoken word. Speech and language problems (aphasia) usually occur when a stroke affects the right side of the body.

Behavioral problems and learning disabilities, such as difficulties with attention or concentration, may become apparent when the child goes to school, so specific treatments and educational assistance may be needed to address these problems. A formal assessment can help parents identify potential behavioral and learning problems.

Surgery

The need for surgical treatment for pediatric stroke will depend on a number of factors, including the type of stroke, extent of damage from stroke, the child's age, and potential benefits and risks. Sometimes urgent surgery is necessary soon after the child is admitted to the emergency room to remove a blood clot and restore oxygen flow to the brain tissue.

Treatment options for hemorrhagic stroke may include surgery, sterotactic radiotherapy, or interventional neuroradiology to treat the underlying aneurysm or arteriovenous malformation.

There are several surgical procedures to repair an aneurysm that may have caused a hemorrhagic stroke. A clip may be placed across the neck of the aneurysm (like a clip at the end of a balloon) to stop the bleeding. A newer approach is to thread a long, thin tube through the artery that leads to the aneurysm. Then a tiny coil is fed through the tube into the aneurysm "balloon" to fill the space and seal off the bleeding.

An interventional procedure called carotid angioplasty may be performed to treat a blockage or blockages in the carotid arteries. During the procedure, a tiny balloon at the end of a long, thin tube (called a catheter) is pushed through the artery to the blockage. When the balloon is inflated, it opens the artery. In addition, a mesh tube (called a stent) may be placed inside the artery to help hold it open.

Carotid endarterectomy is a surgical procedure performed to remove a blockage from the carotid artery. During the operation, the surgeon scrapes away plaque from the wall of the artery so blood can flow freely through the artery to the brain.

Intracranial bypass surgery is a surgical procedure performed to restore blood flow around a blocked blood vessel in the brain. During the surgery, a healthy blood vessel, on the outside of the scalp, is re-routed to the part of the brain that is not getting enough blood flow. This new blood vessel bypasses the blocked vessel and provides an additional blood supply to areas of the brain that were deprived of blood. When blood flow is restored, the brain works normally, and the symptoms disappear. This procedure is not as common as the other surgical treatments listed above to treat pediatric stroke but it may be used to treat recurrent TIAs.

Alternative treatment

Alternative and complementary therapies include approaches that are considered to be outside the mainstream of traditional health care.

Techniques that induce relaxation and reduce stress, such as **yoga**, Tai Chi, meditation, guided imagery, and relaxation training, may be helpful in controlling blood pressure. Acupuncture and biofeedback training also may help induce relaxation. Before learning or practicing any particular technique, it is important for the parent/caregiver and child to learn about the therapy, its safety and effectiveness, potential side effects, and the expertise and qualifications of the practitioner. Although some practices are beneficial, others may be harmful to certain patients.

Alternative treatments should not be used as a substitute for medical therapies prescribed by a doctor. Parents should discuss these techniques and treatments with the child's doctor to determine the remedies that may be beneficial for the child.

Nutritional concerns

Dietary guidelines are individualized, based on the child's age, diagnosis, overall health, and level of functioning. Specific nutritional problems, such as swallowing or feeding difficulties, may be a concern in some patients and should be managed by a team of specialists including a speech therapist. Early identification, treatment, and correction of specific feeding problems will improve the health and nutritional status of the child.

A child's self-feeding skills can impact his or her health outcome. One study indicated that 90 percent of children with good to fair motor and feeding skills reached adulthood. In contrast, a lack of self-feeding skills was associated with a six-fold increase in mortality (rate of death).

Maintaining a healthy weight is important to prevent the development of chronic diseases such as diabetes, high blood pressure (**hypertension**), and heart disease.

Tube feedings may be required in some patients with **failure to thrive**, aspiration **pneumonia**, difficulty swallowing, or an inability to ingest adequate calories orally to maintain nutritional status or promote growth.

A well-balanced and carefully planned diet will help maintain general good health for children who have suffered a stroke. In general, children should follow the same low-fat, high fiber diet that is recommended for the general population.

In children older than age two, the following low-fat dietary guidelines are recommended:

- Total fat intake should comprise 30 percent or less of total calories consumed per day.
- Calories consumed as saturated fat should equal no more than 8-10 percent of total calories consumed per day.
- Total cholesterol intake should be less than 300 mg/dl per day.

If the child has high blood pressure, the DASH diet is recommended. The "Dietary Approaches to Stop Hypertension (DASH)" study, sponsored by the National Institutes of Health (NIH), showed that elevated blood pressures were reduced by an eating plan that emphasized fruits, vegetables, and low-fat dairy foods and was low in saturated fat, total fat, and cholesterol. The DASH diet includes whole grains, poultry, fish, and nuts. Fats, red meats, sodium, sweets, and sugar-sweetened beverages are limited. Sodium should also be reduced to no more than 1,500 milligrams per day.

Prognosis

Cerebrovascular disorders are among the top 10 causes of death in children, with rates highest in the first year of life. From 1979 to 1998 in the United States, childhood mortality from stroke declined sharply, by 58 percent, with reductions in all major subtypes: ischemic stroke decreased by 19 percent, subarachnoid hemorrhage by 79 percent, and intracerebral hemorrhage by 54 percent.

Some children survive a pediatric stroke with no life-long consequences. In other children, long-term complications of stroke may develop right away or within months to years after a stroke. According to a 2000 study published in the *Journal of Child Neurology*, the outcome of childhood stroke was a moderate or severe deficit in 42 percent of cases. Adverse outcomes after childhood stroke—including death in 10 percent, recurrence in 20 percent, and neurological deficits in two-thirds of survivors—can be reduced with available stroke treatments.

When a stroke affects a child whose brain is still developing, it is thought that the developing brain may be able to compensate for the functions that were lost as a result of a stroke.

Recovery from stroke is different with each child. Overall, the degree of permanent disability after a stroke is less in children than in adults. Speech and language problems usually improve rapidly in the first year after a stroke. Children may only have minor delays in the development of coordinated movement or in cognitive functioning. Almost all children recover the ability to walk independently after a stroke, unless there is another condition that causes disability. Recovery of function in the affected arm and hand is usually the most significant movement problem after a stroke. Most children who suffer from a stroke can expect to lead independent lives as adults.

Prevention

Despite current treatment, one out of 10 children with ischemic stroke will have a recurrence within five years. Although there is a high risk of repeat strokes in patients with sickle cell anemia, the risk can be reduced with regular blood transfusions. If no cause of the stroke was identified, the risk of a recurrence is low. If a cause was identified, the underlying condition should be treated, and anticoagulant or low-dose aspirin therapy may be initiated, depending on the child's diagnosis.

There is no screening for stroke, but screening exists for many of its risk factors. To prevent stroke, risk factors should be treated and managed by the child's primary care doctor or specialist. The doctor can advise if specific preventive treatment is needed.

Management of high cholesterol—especially high LDL (low-density lipoprotein) levels—high blood pressure and diabetes can help reduce the risk of a stroke.

Nutritional concerns

An adequate intake of **folic acid** (vitamin B9) has been linked to the prevention of stroke and heart disease by lowering homocysteine, an amino acid related to the early development of cardiovascular disease when high levels are present in the blood. Dietary sources of folic acid include: vegetables, especially green vegetables; potatoes; cereal and cereal products; fruits; and organ meats (liver or kidney). It is best to eat fresh fruits and vegetables whenever possible to get the most **vitamins**.

Recommended daily intake in micrograms (mcg) for folic acid supplements (oral tablets) include: 25–100 mcg in newborns to age three; 75–400 mcg in children aged four to six; 100-400 mcg in children aged seven to 10; and 150–400 mcg in children aged 11 and above.

Vitamin K is an important nutrient needed to regulate normal blood clotting. A diet deficient in vitamin K can cause prolonged blood-clotting time and easy bleeding and bruising. Vitamin K is found in: alfalfa, asparagus, broccoli, Brussels sprouts, cabbage cheddar cheese, green tea, green leafy lettuce, liver, seaweed, spinach, and turnip greens. Recommended daily intake for vitamin K supplements (for patients not on anticoagulant therapy) include: 10 mcg in newborns to age three; 20 mcg in children aged four to six; 30 mcg in children aged seven to 14; 65 mcg in boys and 55 mcg in girls aged 15–18; 70–80 mcg for males over age 18 and 60–65 mcg for females over age 18. If the patient is taking anticoagulant medications, vitamin K supplements are not recommended, and foods high in vitamin K are limited, since they counteract the action of the medication.

Vitamin E and beta carotene supplements were once thought to help decrease the risk of stroke and prevent the development of heart disease, but newer studies disprove their effectiveness. Researchers at The Cleveland Clinic Heart Center performed a meta-analysis of seven large randomized trials of vitamin E (given alone or in combination with other antioxidants) and eight of beta carotene. All trials included 1,000 or more patients and follow-up ranged from 1.4 to 12 years. The doses of vitamin E given in these trials ranged from 50–800 international units (IU) and 15–50 milligrams (mg) for beta carotene. The meta-analysis reviewed the effect of these antioxidants on death from cardiovascular disease or from any other cause ("all-cause mortality").

Their findings, published in the June, 2003 issue of *The Lancet* journal, do not support the continued use of vitamin E supplementation nor the inclusion of vitamin E in further studies. Regardless of the dosage given or the patient population, Vitamin E did not provide any benefit in lowering mortality compared to control treatments, and it did not significantly decrease the risk of cardiovascular death or stroke (cerebrovascular accident). In addition, they recommend that vitamin supplements containing beta carotene be "actively discouraged" because of the small but statistically significant increased risk of death. Researchers discourage further study of beta carotene because of the mortality risk.

Even though studies have demonstrated that vitamin E and beta carotene supplements do not reduce stroke risk, foods rich in antioxidants are still encouraged because they also contain beneficial nutrients such as flavonoids and lycopenes that are not usually included in standard oral vitamin supplements. A diet rich in antioxidant-containing foods, such as fruits, vegetables and whole grains, is linked to a reduced risk of cardiovascular disease.

Dietary supplements should not be used as a substitute for medical therapies prescribed by a doctor. Parents should discuss these **nutrition** supplements with the child's doctor to determine the remedies that may be beneficial for the child.

Parental concerns

It is common for a child to feel sad or depressed after a stroke. These emotions may be the result of not knowing what to expect or not being able to do simple tasks without becoming overly tired. Temporary feelings of sadness are normal, and should gradually go away within a few weeks, as the child starts a rehabilitation program and returns to some of his or her normal routines and activities.

When a depressed mood is severe and accompanied by other symptoms that persist every day for two or more weeks, the parent should ask for a referral to a mental health professional who can help the child cope and recover. There are many treatments for depression. A healthy lifestyle including regular exercise, proper **sleep**, a well-balanced diet, as well as relaxation and stress management techniques can help manage depression. Major depressive disorder may be treated with **antidepressants**, psychotherapy (supportive counseling or "talk therapy"), or a combination of both.

Regular follow-up visits with the child's health care provider will help identify and manage risk factors and other medical conditions. If the child has a known medical condition that increases the risk of stroke, it is important for parents and caregivers to learn the warning signs and symptoms of stroke in children and infants. If the child experiences any unexpected neurological problem, the parent should have the child evaluated by a physician. Lastly, it is important for parents to carefully follow the child's treatment plan, including following the medication schedule exactly as prescribed.

Resources

BOOKS

Burkman, Kip. *The Stroke Recovery Book: A Guide for Patients and Families.* Nebraska: Addicus Books, Inc., May, 1998.

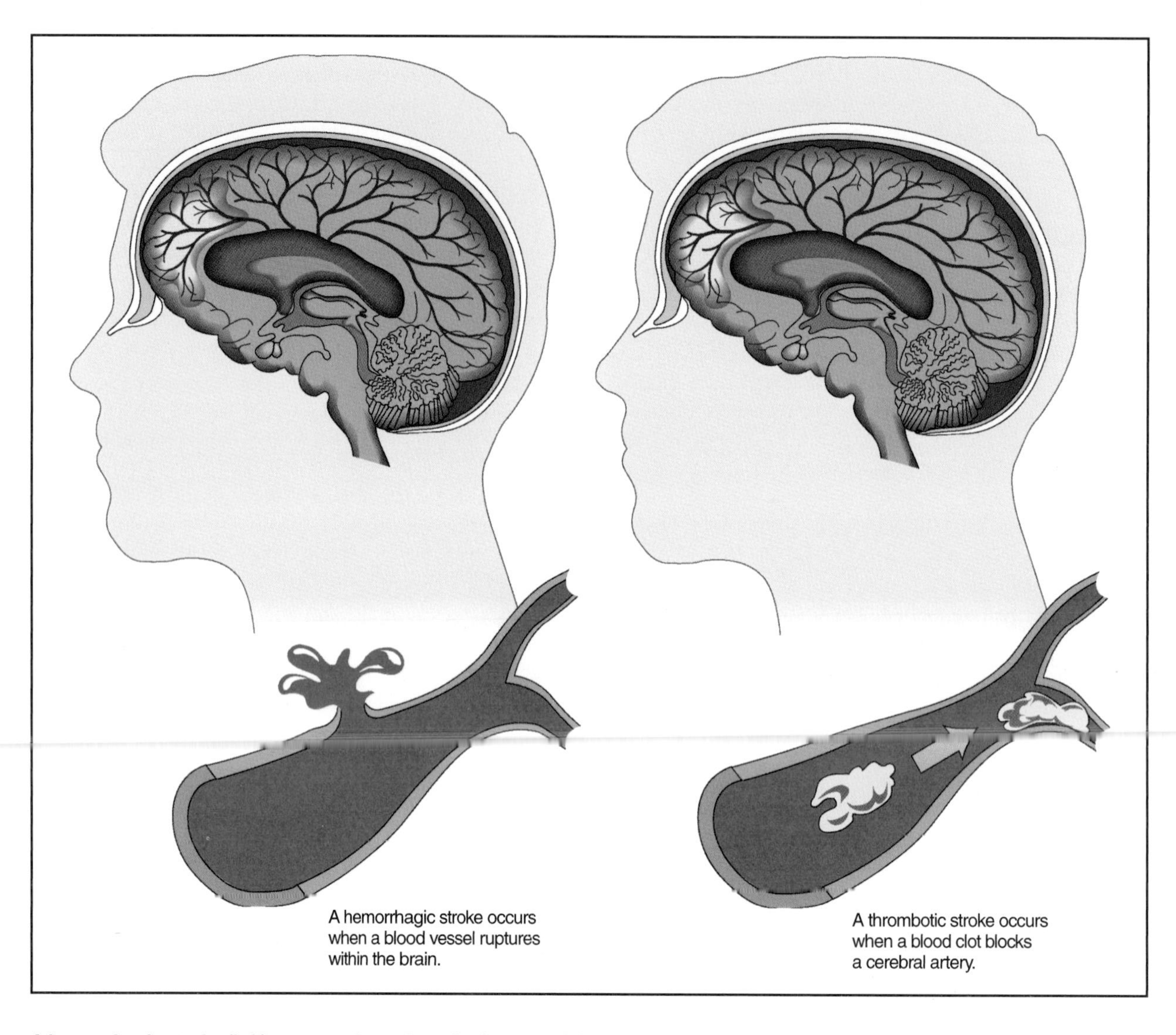

A hemorrhagic stroke (left) compared to a thrombotic stroke (right). *(Illustration by Hans & Cassidy.)*

Senelick, Richard C., Peter W. Rossi, and Karla Dougherty. *Living with Stroke: A Guide For Families: Help and New Hope for All Those Touched by Stroke*. New York: McGraw-Hill/Contemporary Books, June, 1999.

Zimmer, Judith and John P. Cooke. *The Cardiovascular Cure: How to Strengthen Your Self-Defense Against Heart Attack and Stroke*. New York: Broadway Books, August, 2002.

PERIODICALS

Abram, Harry S., MD. "Childhood Strokes: Evaluation and Treatment." Duval County Medical Society. www.dchmsonline.org/jax-medicine/1998journals/november1998/childhoodstrokes.htm.

deVeber, G., ES Roach, AR Riela, and M. Wiznitzer. "Stroke in Children: Recognition, Treatment, and Future Directions." Seminars in Pediatric Neurology. 7:4 (December, 2000): 309-317.

deVeber, G., ES Roach, AR Riela, and M. Wiznitzer. "Recognition and Treatment of Stroke in Children." Child Neurology Society Ad Hoc Committee on Stroke in Children. July, 2001.

Kirkham, FJ. "Stroke in Childhood." Archives of Disease in Childhood. 81 (July, 1999): 85-89.

Nicolaides, P. and R.E. Appleton. "Stroke in Children." Developmental Medicine and Child Neurology. 38:2 (February, 1996): 172-180.

ORGANIZATIONS

American Stroke Foundation. 11902 Lowell, Overland Park, KS 66213. (913) 649-1776. <http://www.americanstroke.org>.

KEY TERMS

Activities of daily living (ADL)—The activities performed during the course of a normal day, for example, eating, bathing, dressing, toileting, etc.

Aneurysm—A weakened area in the wall of a blood vessel which causes an outpouching or bulge. Aneurysms may be fatal if these weak areas burst, resulting in uncontrollable bleeding.

Anoxia—Lack of oxygen.

Antibody—A special protein made by the body's immune system as a defense against foreign material (bacteria, viruses, etc.) that enters the body. It is uniquely designed to attack and neutralize the specific antigen that triggered the immune response.

Antiphospholipid antibody syndrome—An immune disorder that occurs when the body recognizes phospholipids (part of a cell's membrane) as foreign and produces abnormal antibodies against them. This syndrome is associated with abnormal blood clotting, low blood platelet counts, and migraine headaches.

Aorta—The main artery located above the heart that pumps oxygenated blood out into the body. The aorta is the largest artery in the body.

Aortic valve—The valve between the heart's left ventricle and ascending aorta that prevents regurgitation of blood back into the left ventricle.

Aortic valve stenosis—Narrowing of the aortic valve.

Aphasia—The loss of the ability to speak, or to understand written or spoken language. A person who cannot speak or understand language is said to be aphasic.

Arteriosclerosis—A chronic condition characterized by thickening, loss of leasticity, and hardening of the arteries and the build-up of plaque on the arterial walls. Arteriosclerosis can slow or impair blood circulation. It includes atherosclerosis, but the two terms are often used synonymously.

Artery—A blood vessel that carries blood away from the heart to the cells, tissues, and organs of the body.

Atrial—Referring to the upper chambers of the heart.

Atrial fibrillation—A type of heart arrhythmia in which the upper chamber of the heart quivers instead of pumping in an organized way. In this condition, the upper chambers (atria) of the heart do not completely empty when the heart beats, which can allow blood clots to form.

Atrial septal defect—An opening between the right and left atria (upper chambers) of the heart.

Cardiologist—A physician who specializes in diagnosing and treating heart diseases.

Central nervous system—Part of the nervous system consisting of the brain, cranial nerves, and spinal cord. The brain is the center of higher processes, such as thought and emotion and is responsible for the coordination and control of bodily activities and the interpretation of information from the senses. The cranial nerves and spinal cord link the brain to the peripheral nervous system, that is the nerves present in the rest of body.

Cerebrospinal fluid—The clear, normally colorless fluid that fills the brain cavities (ventricles), the subarachnoid space around the brain, and the spinal cord and acts as a shock absorber.

Decompression—A decrease in pressure from the surrounding water that occurs with decreasing diving depth.

Dysphagia—Difficulty in swallowing.

Echocardiogram—A record of the internal structures of the heart obtained from beams of ultrasonic waves directed through the wall of the chest.

Electrocardiagram (ECG, EKG)—A record of the electrical activity of the heart, with each wave being labeled as P, Q, R, S, and T waves. It is often used in the diagnosis of cases of abnormal cardiac rhythm and myocardial damage.

Embolus—Plural, emboli. An embolus is something that blocks the blood flow in a blood vessel. It may be a gas bubble, a blood clot, a fat globule, a mass of bacteria, or other foreign body that forms somewhere else and travels through the circulatory system until it gets stuck.

Encephalitis—Inflammation of the brain, usually caused by a virus. The inflammation may interfere with normal brain function and may cause seizures, sleepiness, confusion, personality changes, weakness in one or more parts of the body, and even coma.

Graft—A transplanted organ or other tissue.

Heart attack—Damage that occurs to the heart when one of the coronary arteries becomes narrowed or blocked.

Hemiparesis—Weakness on one side of the body.

KEY TERMS *(contd.)*

Hemiplegia—Paralysis of one side of the body.

Hydrocephalus—An abnormal accumulation of cerebrospinal fluid within the brain. This accumulation can be harmful by pressing on brain structures, and damaging them.

Hypercoagulable states—Also called thromboembolic state or thrombophilia. A condition characterized by excess blood clotting.

Hypertension—Abnormally high arterial blood pressure, which if left untreated can lead to heart disease and stroke.

Intracerebral hemorrhage—A cause of some strokes in which vessels within the brain begin bleeding.

Ischemia—A decrease in the blood supply to an area of the body caused by obstruction or constriction of blood vessels.

Mitral valve stenosis—Narrowing of the mitral valve.

Neurologist—A doctor who specializes in disorders of the nervous system, including the brain, spinal cord, and nerves.

Neurosurgeon—Physician who performs surgery on the nervous system.

Occupational therapist—A healthcare provider who specializes in adapting the physical environment to meet a patient's needs. An occupational therapist also assists patients and caregivers with activities of daily living and provide instructions on wheelchair use or other adaptive equipment.

Patent ductus arteriosus—A congenital defect in which the temporary blood vessel connecting the left pulmonary artery to the aorta in the fetus doesn't close after birth.

Patent foramen ovale (PFO)—A congenital heart defect characterized by an open flap that remains between the two upper chambers of the heart (the left and right atria). This opening can allow a blood clot from one part of the body to travel through the flap and up to the brain, causing a stroke.

Physiatrist—A physician who specializes in physical medicine and rehabilitation.

Physical therapist—A healthcare provider who teaches patients how to perform therapeutic exercises to maintain maximum mobility and range of motion.

Reye's syndrome—A serious, life-threatening illness in children, usually developing after a bout of flu or chickenpox, and often associated with the use of aspirin. Symptoms include uncontrollable vomiting, often with lethargy, memory loss, disorientation, or delirium. Swelling of the brain may cause seizures, coma, and in severe cases, death.

Stent—A slender hollow catheter or rod placed within a vessel or duct to provide support or to keep it open.

Subarachnoid hemorrhage—A collection of blood in the subarachnoid space, the space between the arachnoid and pia mater membranes that surround the brain. This space is normally filled with cerebrospinal fluid. A subarachnoid hemorrhage can lead to stroke, seizures, permanent brain damage, and other complications.

Unilateral neglect—Also called one-sided neglect. A side effect of stroke in which the stroke survivor ignores or forgets the weaker side of the body caused by the stroke.

Vein—A blood vessel that returns blood to the heart from the body. All the veins from the body converge into two major veins that lead to the right atrium of the heart. These veins are the superior vena cava and the inferior vena cava. The pulmonary vein carries the blood from the right ventricle of the heart into the lungs.

Ventricle septal defect—A hole in the wall (septum) between the lower chambers of the heart.

Ventricles—The lower pumping chambers of the heart. The ventricles push blood to the lungs and the rest of the body.

Ventricles of the brain—The spaces within the brain where cerebrospinal fluid is made.

American Stroke Association, A Division of American Heart Association, 7272 Greenville Ave., Dallas, TX 75231. (888) 4-STROKE (787653). E-mail: strokeassociation@heart.org. <http://www.strokeassociation.org>.

Children's Hemiplegia and Stroke Association. 4101 W. Green Oaks, Ste. 305, PMB 149, Arlington, TX 76016. (817) 492-4325. E-mail: info@chasa.org. <http://www.chasa.org>.

National Heart, Lung and Blood Institute. National Institutes of Health, Building 1, 1 Center Dr., Bethesda, MD 20892. E-mail: NHLBIinfo@rover.nhlbi. <http://www.nhlbi.nih.gov>.

National Institute on Disability and Rehabilitation Research, Office of Special Education and Rehabilitative Services, U.S. Department of Education, 400 Maryland Ave. S.W., Washington, DC 20202-7100. (202) 245-7640. <http://www.ed.gov/about/offices/list/osers/nidrr/>.

National Institute of Neurological Disorders and Stroke (NINDS), National Institutes of Health. P.O. Box 5801, Bethesda, MD 20824. (800) 352-9424 or (301) 496-5751. <http://www.ninds.nih.gov/about_ninds/>.

National Rehabilitation Information Center (NARIC).4200 Forbes Blvd., Ste. 202, Lanham, MD 20700. (800) 346-2742 or (301) 459-5900. <http://www.naric.com>.

National Stroke Association. 9707 E. Easter Ln., Englewood, CO 80112-3747. (800) STROKES (787-6537) or (303) 649-9299. <http://www.stroke.org>.

Stroke Clubs International. 805 12th St. Galveston, TX 77550. (409) 762-1022 attn. Ellis Williamson. E-mail: strokeclub@aol.com.

WEB SITES

The Brain Attack Coalition. <www.stroke-site.org>

The Brain Matters, American Academy of Neurology Foundation. <www.thebrainmatters.org>

Different Strokes—A Charity for Younger Stroke Survivors. <www.differentstrokes.co.uk/>

HeartCenterOnline. <www.heartcenteronline.com>

HemiHelp—Information and Support for Children and Young People with Hemiplegia. <www.hemihelp.org.uk>

Pediatric Stroke Network. <www.pediatricstrokenetwork.com>

Angela M. Costello

Sturge-Weber syndrome

Definition

Sturge-Weber syndrome (SWS) is a rare, congenital (present at birth), noninherited disorder characterized by the vascular malformation (birthmark) called a port wine stain, usually seen on an infant's face. Sturge-Weber also is characterized by neurological abnormalities including seizures, weakness on one side of the body, **developmental delay**, and glaucoma (increased pressure within the eye). Other terms for SWS are: encephalotrigeminal angiomatosis, encephalofacial angiomatosis, or Sturge-Weber-Dimitri syndrome.

Sturge-Weber syndrome is named for the British physicians William A. Sturge (1850–1919), who first described the condition, and Frederick Parkes Weber (1863–1962) who demonstrated its intracranial calcifications.

Description

SWS is a rare congenital disorder whose most apparent indication is a port wine stain on the face that is associated with neurological abnormalities. The port wine stain is a benign tumor just under the surface of the skin, made up of overabundant blood vessels (angiomas). Port wine stain may affect either or both sides of the face and can vary in size. Other neurological abnormalities may be present, including angioma on the brain's surface.

Demographics

The incidence of SWS is estimated at one per 50,000 live births in the United States. No regional or gender differences have been noted. An estimated 13 percent of individuals with SWS will not have the port wine stain. In addition, some children with port wine stain may not have Sturge-Weber syndrome.

Causes and symptoms

The exact cause and incidence of Sturge-Weber syndrome was as of 2004 not understood. It is not thought to be genetic.

Frequency of symptoms

A child born with SWS has a higher likelihood of the following clinical signs of the disorder:

- port wine stain: 8–15 percent
- bilateral (both sides) brain involvement: 15 percent
- seizures: 72–93 percent
- hemipareis (weakness on one side of body): 25–56 percent
- hemianopsia (loss of half of the field of vision): 44 percent
- headaches: 44–62 percent
- developmental delay/mental retardation: 50–75 percent
- glaucoma (increased pressure within the eye): 30–71 percent
- choroidal hemangioma (nonmalignant blood vessel tumors in the eye): 40 percent

The following manifestations of SWS may be present:

- Port wine stain: The port wine stain is caused by excess capillaries (tiny blood vessels) just below the skin's surface. It may vary in color, shape, and location on the face. Sometimes the port wine stain covers other parts of the body as well as the face.

- Seizures: Angiomas on the surface of the brain cause seizures in nearly all children with SWS. As the child grows, the affected part of the brain can atrophy (waste away). Deposits of calcium also may occur. This can cause seizures to become more frequent and to last longer.
- Hemipareis (weakness on one side of body): In SWS, this results from frequent seizures.
- Hemianopsia (loss of half of the field of vision): Angiomas can affect the optic nerve, causing blindness in half of the eye.
- Headaches: About one-third of children aged ten years and younger with SWS suffer from migraines.
- Developmental delay/mental retardation: Seizures are responsible for learning difficulties in two out of three children with SWS.
- Glaucoma (increased pressure within the eye): Glaucoma is present in 70 percent of children with SWS whose upper eyelids have port wine stain. Fluid produced within the eye (aqueous humor) cannot exit normally. This leads to increased pressure within the eye and eventual damage to the optic nerve.
- Choroidal hemangioma (nonmalignant blood vessel tumors in the eye): Noncancerous tumors can grow within the eye on the choroid blood vessel, the vessel that nourishes the eye. If the tumor is in the central area of vision, visual function can be affected.

When to call the doctor

An infant born with a port wine stain will be immediately evaluated by healthcare staff. In some cases, infants with SWS will not have a port wine stain present at birth. In these cases, suspicion of SWS may not arise until a child has a seizure or other neurological problem.

Diagnosis

Clinical diagnosis of SWS begins with the observation of port wine stain in an infant. The port wine stain may not be obvious in children of color. Not all children with port wine stain will have SWS, however; and some children with SWS will not have port wine stain. In the absence of port wine stain, other neurological abnormalities will help determine the diagnosis. Seizures may be the first symptoms of SWS in a child, usually by the first year. The seizures are usually frequent and may be prolonged. If glaucoma is involved, there may be no symptoms in older children. Infants may avoid bright light as a result of enlarged corneas.

If neurological involvement is suspected, the following tests may be used to help make a diagnosis:

- X ray of the skull to show calcifications (calcium deposits)
- CT scan of the skull to show calcifications, abnormal veins, and brain atrophy
- MRI to show angiomas (benign tumors made up of blood vessels)
- single-photon emission **computed tomography** to measure blood flow in the brain
- EEG to evaluate seizures

Treatment

Treatment for SWS depends on the disorder involved.

- Port wine stain: Laser treatment is used to lighten or remove port wine stain. Pulsed-dye laser therapy successfully treats port wine stain without significant scarring. Treatment should start as soon as possible. Multiple treatments will be necessary.
- Seizures: Drug therapy may be used to control seizures. However, the seizures often are resistant to treatment. In some cases, early surgical removal of the part of the brain with the abnormal blood vessels may be considered.
- Vision problems: Drug therapy may be used to treat glaucoma. Photodynamic therapy also is used to treat choroidal hemangiomas that affect the eye.
- Headaches: Medications may be taken to treat migraines. Children age two and under should not take aspirin due to the risk of Reye syndrome.
- Developmental delay and learning problems: A wide range of treatment options is available to children with developmental delay and learning problems associated with SWS.
- Hemipareis (weakness on one side of body): Hemipareis can be treated with physical and occupational therapy.

Prognosis

SWS is not a fatal disease. The prognosis for SWS depends on the specific neurological abnormalities present. Some abnormalities associated with SWS may worsen with age. Successful treatment of seizures improves the outlook for children with SWS.

Prevention

There was as of 2004 no known way to prevent SWS. Nothing a parent has done or did not do causes the disorder.

Parental concerns

The seizures that are often present with SWS can place children in potentially dangerous situations.

See also Seizure disorder.

Resources

PERIODICALS

Baselga, E. "Sturge-Weber syndrome." *Seminars in Cutaneous Medicine and Surgery* 23, no. 2 (June 2004): 87–98.

Lam, Samuel, et al. "Practical Considerations in the Treatment of Capillary Vascular Malformations, or Port Wine Stains." *Facial Plastic Surgery* (2004): 71–6.

Thomas-Sohl, K. A., et al. "Sturge-Weber syndrome: a review." *Pediatric Neurology* 30 (May 2004): 303–10.

ORGANIZATIONS

American Academy of Dermatology. 930 E. Woodfield Rd., Schaumburg, IL 60168. Web site: <www.aad.org/>

Children's Hemiplegia and Stroke Association. Suite 305, PMB 149 4101 W. Green Oaks. Arlington, TX 76016. Web site: <www.hemikids.org/hemiplegia.htm>.

FACES: The National Craniofacial Association. PO Box 11082, Chattanooga, TN 37401. Web site: <www.faces-cranio.org/>.

National Association for Rare Disorders. 55 Kenosia Avenue, PO Box 1968, Danbury, CT 06813–1968. Web site: <www.rarediseases.org/info/contact.html>.

Sturge-Weber Foundation. PO Box 418, Mount Freedom, NJ 07970. Web site: <www.sturge-weber.com/>.

WEB SITES

"NINDS Sturge-Weber Syndrome Information Page." *National Institute of Neurological Disorders and Stroke*, 2001. Available online at <www.ninds.nih.gov/health_and_medical/disorders/sturge_doc.htm> (accessed November 30, 2004).

Sturge-Weber Foundation. Available online at <www.sturge-weber.com> (accessed November 30, 2004).

"Sturge-Weber Syndrome." *eMedicine*, 2001. Available online at <www.emedicine.com/neuro/topic356.htm#section~workup> (accessed November 30, 2004).

"Sturge-Weber Syndrome." *Epilepsy Action.* Available online at <www.epilepsy.org.uk/info/sturge.html> (accessed November 30, 2004).

Christine Kuehn Kelly

KEY TERMS

Angioma—A tumor (such as a hemangioma or lymphangioma) that mainly consists of blood vessels or lymphatic vessels.

Anomaly—Something that is different from what is normal or expected. Also an unusual or irregular structure.

Capillaries—The tiniest blood vessels with the smallest diameter. These vessels receive blood from the arterioles and deliver blood to the venules. In the lungs, capillaries are located next to the alveoli so that they can pick up oxygen from inhaled air.

Choroidal hemangioma—A nonmalignant blood vessel tumor in the eye.

Hemianopsia—Loss of half of the field of vision.

Hemiparesis—Weakness on one side of the body.

Stuttering

Definition

Stuttering is a speech problem characterized by repetitions; pauses; or drawn-out syllables, words, and phrases. Stutterers are different than people experiencing normal fluency problems because a stutterer's disfluency is more severe and consistent than that of people who do not stutter.

Description

Normal **language development** in a child usually includes a period of disfluency. Children might repeat syllables or words once or twice. Sometimes, children experiencing normal disfluencies hesitate during speech or use fillers, including "um," with frequency. These developmental problems usually happen between one and five years of age. Often, parents are concerned about the disfluency they hear in their children.

A child with mild stuttering, however, will repeat sounds more than twice. Parents and teachers often notice the child's facial muscles become tense and he or she might struggle to speak. The child's voice pitch might rise with repetitions, and some children experience occasional periods when airflow or voice stops for seconds at a time. Children with more severe stuttering stutter through more than 10 percent of their speech. This child exhibits considerable tension and tries to avoid stuttering by using different words. In these children, complete blocks of speech are more common than repetitions or prolongations, during which children lengthen syllables or words.

Stuttering does not affect **intelligence**. Teens often experience more noticeable problems with stuttering as they enter the dating scene and increase their social interactions. Stuttering can severely affect one's life. Often, adults who are concerned about stuttering choose their careers based on the disability.

The degree of stuttering is often inconsistent. Stutterers can be fluent in some situations. Many find that they stop stuttering when singing or doing other activities involving speech. Some have good and bad days when it comes to stuttering. On good days, a stutterer might be able to talk fluently using words that usually cause him to repeat, pause or prolong sounds, syllables, parts of words, entire words, or phrases.

Demographics

More than 3 million Americans stutter and four times more males are affected than females. Stuttering usually begins in childhood when the child is developing language skills, and it rarely develops in adulthood with only 1 percent of the population affected by the disorder. Approximately 25 percent of all children experience speech disfluencies during development that concern their parents because of their severity.

Causes and symptoms

There is no known cause of stuttering. Some believe that it has a physical cause and that it might be related to a breakdown in the neurological system. Stuttering starts early in life and often is inherited. Brain scan research has revealed that there might be abnormalities in the brains of stutterers, while they are stuttering. Myths about why stuttering occurs abound. Some cultures believe that stuttering is caused by emotional problems, tickling an infant too much, or because a mother ate improperly during breastfeeding. None has been proven to be true. It is believed that some drugs might induce stuttering-like conditions. These include **antidepressants**, **antihistamines**, tranquilizers, and selective serotonin reuptake inhibitors.

When to call the doctor

The child's doctor should be contacted if parents have concerns about the speech patterns of their child. The doctor may refer parents to a speech-language specialist for evaluation if needed.

Diagnosis

Speech and language therapists diagnose stuttering by asking stutterers to read out loud, pronounce specific words, and talk. Some also order hearing tests. The tests will determine whether a person needs speech therapy.

Treatment

As of 2004, researchers did not understand what causes stuttering. However, progress has been made regarding what contributes to the development of the disability; therefore, in some cases it can be prevented in childhood with the help of therapy early on. Therapy can help people of all ages suffering from the speech disability. While not an overnight cure, therapy can offer positive results and more fluent speech patterns. The goals of therapy are for the stutterer to reduce stuttering frequency, decrease the tension and struggle of stuttering, become educated about stuttering, and learn effective communications skills, such as making eye contact, to further enhance speech. The therapy focuses on helping stutterers to discover easier and different ways of producing sounds and expressing thoughts. The success of therapy depends largely on the stutterer's willingness to work at getting better.

The duration of stuttering therapy needed varies among stutterers. Sometimes, stutterers find intermittent therapy useful throughout their lives.

Parents, teachers and others can help ease stuttering. These include: talking slowly, but normally, clearly, and in a relaxed manner to a stutterer; answering questions after a pause to encourage a relaxed transaction; trying not to make stuttering worse by getting annoyed by a person's stuttering; giving stutterers reassurance about their stuttering; and encourage the stutterer to talk about his or her stuttering.

Electronic fluency aids help some stutterers when used as an adjunct to therapy. Medications, such as antipsychotics and neuroleptics, have been used to treat stuttering with limited success.

Some people use relaxation techniques to help their stuttering.

Prognosis

As of the early 2000s no answers had been found to explain the causes of stuttering; still, much has been learned about what contributes to stuttering's development and how to prevent it in children. People who stutter can get better through therapy. Winston Churchill, Marilyn Monroe, Carly Simon, James Earl Jones, and King George VI were childhood stutterers who went on to live successful professional lives.

Prevention

The location of some genes appears to predispose people to stuttering. While genetic factors do not explain all stuttering, genetics may help to uncover the disability's causes. Speech therapy, especially that performed at a young age, can stop the progression of stuttering.

Parental concerns

Many children experience brief episodes of stuttering. In many cases, these are transitory and disappear without treatment. Parents should be aware that some stuttering is quite normal when a child feels under pressure to talk. Thus, parents should wait to allow the child to communicate at his or her own speed, and not pressure the child to talk or make fun of the stutter.

KEY TERMS

Antipsychotic drug—A class of drugs used to control psychotic symptoms in patients with psychotic disorders such as schizophrenia and delusional disorder. Antipsychotics include risperidone (Risperdal), haloperidol (Haldol), and chlorpromazine (Thorazine).

Disfluency—An interruption in speech flow.

Neuroleptics—Antipsychotic drugs that affect psychomotor activity.

Resources

BOOKS

Boethe, Anne K. *Evidence-Based Treatment of Stuttering: Empirical Bases, Clinical Applications, and Remaining Needs.* Mahwah, NJ: Lawrence Erlbaum Associates, 2004.

Hulit, Lloyd M. *Straight Talk on Stuttering: Information, Encouragement, and Counsel for Stutterers, Caregivers, and Speech-Language Clinicians.* Springfield, IL: Charles C. Thomas, 2004.

Kent, Susan. *Let's Talk about Stuttering.* New York: Rosen Publishing Group, 2003.

Ramig, Peter R., and Darrell Dodge. *The Child and Adolescent Stuttering Treatment and Activity Resource Guide.* Albany, NY: Delmar, 2005.

PERIODICALS

Altholz, S., and M. Golensky. "Counseling, support, and advocacy for clients who stutter." *Health and Social Work* 29, no. 3 (2004): 197–205.

Maguire, G. A., et al. "Alleviating stuttering with pharmacological interventions." *Expert Opinion on Pharmacotherapy* 5, no. 7 (2004): 1565–71.

Messenger, M., et al. "Social anxiety in stuttering: measuring negative social expectancies." *Journal of Fluency Disorders* 29, no. 3 (2004): 201–12.

Michel, V., et al. "Stuttering or reflex seizure?" *Epileptic Disorders* 6, no. 3 (2004): 193–215.

Viswanath, N., et al. "Evidence for a major gene influence on persistent developmental stuttering." *Human Biology* 76, no. 3 (2004): 401–12.

ORGANIZATIONS

American Academy of Audiology. 8300 Greensboro Dr., Suite 750, McLean, VA 22102. Web site: <www.audiology.org/>.

American Speech-Language Hearing Association. 10801 Rockville Pike, Rockville, MD 20852. Web site: <www.asha.org/>.

WEB SITES

"Stuttering." *National Institute on Deafness and Other Communication Disorders*, May 2002. Available online at <www.nidcd.nih.gov/health/voice/stutter.asp> (accessed January 9, 2005).

"Stuttering." *National Library if Medicine.* Available online at <www.nlm.nih.gov/medlineplus/stuttering.html> (accessed January 9, 2005).

"Stuttering Information." *Stuttering Foundation of America.* Available online at <www.stutteringhelp.org/> (accessed January 9, 2005).

"Stuttering Support." *The National Center For Stuttering.* Available online at <www.stuttering.com/>(accessed January 9, 2005)..

"Stuttering Support." *The National Stuttering Association.* Available online at <www.nsastutter.org/> (accessed January 9, 2005).

L. Fleming Fallon, Jr., MD, DrPH

Styes and chalazia

Definition

Styes and chalazia are infections and inflammations of the tiny oil glands on the eyelids. A sty, or external hordeolum, is a common childhood infection of an oil gland on the surface of the upper or lower eyelids at the base of the eyelash. An internal hordeolum is an infection deeper inside the eyelid.

A chalazion is an inflammation or blockage of the deep oil glands within the eyelid that develops into a small hard mass.

Description

Styes and internal hordeola begin as a red, pimple-like bump on the eyelid. The eye may water and itch, and the eyelid may be swollen and painful. Styes come to a head in about three days when they open and drain. Healing is rapid. Internal hordeola are larger, last longer, and are more painful.

Chalazia develop within the Meibomian glands, or oil glands of the eyelid. There are approximately one hundred of these glands located underneath each row of eyelashes. Obstruction and infection, which often are the result of bacteria, cause the gland and the area around it to swell. Chalazia are slow growing, usually over two to three weeks, and can last several months.

A chalazion first appears as a firm lump under the skin but is usually not painful. If the oil gland is blocked and inflammation spreads beyond the eyelid, the condition can interfere with vision. Sometimes, a chalazion develops after a sty has healed.

Growths on the eyelid that are not red and painful are usually cysts and should be evaluated by a doctor. Sometimes, they are removed. In most cases, they are not.

Transmission

Staphylococcus aureus bacteria are thought to be responsible for most styes. Rubbing the eyes, especially when the sty is oozing pus, can spread the infection along the eyelid and cause other styes. There is also a chance that if transmitted to the face or other parts of the body the bacteria in the sty can cause **impetigo**, a contagious skin infection.

Demographics

Styes are more common in children than adults. Once a child has one sty, there is an increased chance of the child having another later on. They also seem to recur in children with lowered immune resistance such as children with diabetes. **Acne** also seems to trigger styes in some adolescents.

Chalazia occur more often in adults than children, and in men more than women. As is the case with styes, having acne seems to predispose some adolescents to having chalazia.

Causes and symptoms

Styes and internal hordeola in children are usually caused by *Staphylococcus aureus* bacterial infections that are transmitted from a child's eyes and nose. In most cases, the bacteria enter the eye through unwashed hands or contaminated contact lens. Bacteria may live on the eyelids or eyelash hair follicles themselves and begin to grow when the oil gland of a hair follicle becomes blocked.

Symptoms

Styes appear as red bumps on the eyelid and may cause **itching** or tearing. Sometimes children report feeling as if something is in the eye. Both styes and internal hordeola are usually painful. The eyelid may look red and be swollen. Vision is sometimes blurred, and the eyes may be sensitive to light.

Though chalazia may appear as large unsightly lumps deep within the eyelid, they are usually not painful. On rare occasions, if a chalazion becomes quite big, it can press on the cornea. If the chalazion is on the upper eye lid, it can produce various vision problems including astigmatism, a distortion of the lens that causes fuzzy vision.

When to call the doctor

It is important to call the doctor if the child has a **fever**, **pain** in the eye, swelling or redness over the entire eyelid, or a painful sty persists for one to two weeks. It may be necessary to call a doctor if the child experiences no improvement after three days of home care. In addition, if the child experiences vision problems, a doctor should be consulted.

Conjunctivitis, which appears as redness in the white of the eye, is a serious condition that must have a doctor's attention. In most cases, **antibiotics** or antibiotic ointments are prescribed.

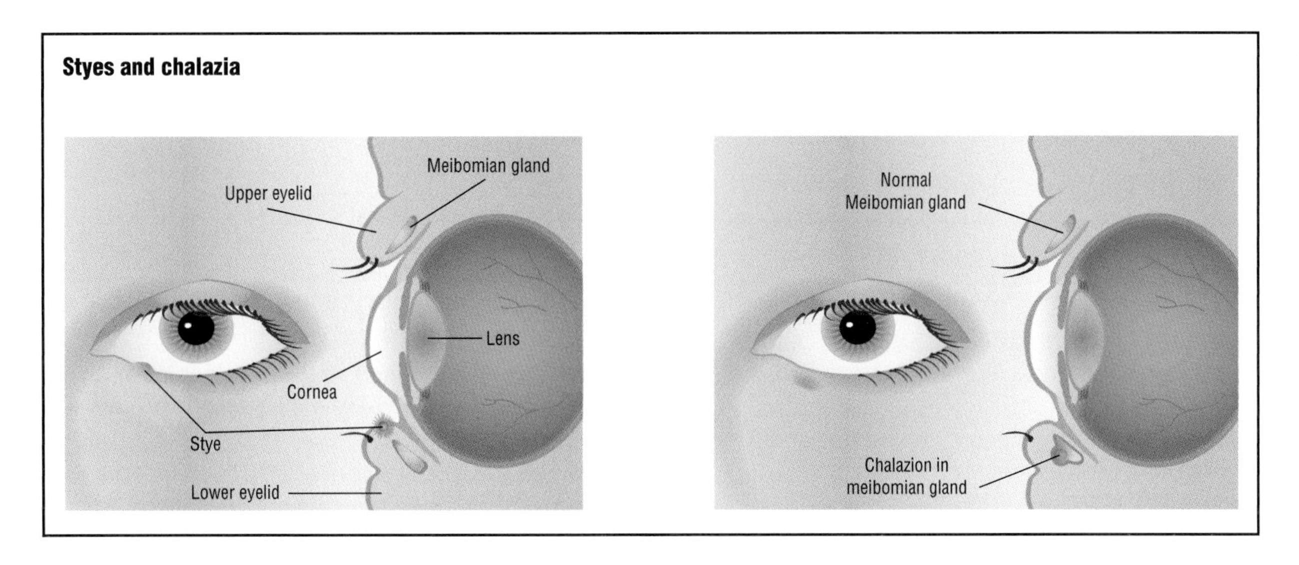

Illustration of a sty (left) and a chalazion. The sty appears on the margin of the eyelid, while the chalazion occurs deeper within the Meibomian gland of the eyelid. *(Illustration by GGS Information Services.)*

Stubborn chalazia that do not go away within six weeks or continue to enlarge require medical attention. They may need to be removed surgically, using local anesthesia.

Diagnosis

The doctor determines whether a child has a sty by visually examining the appearance of the eyelid. If the bump is hard and is located deep within the eyelid, it probably is a chalazion. For a patient whose sty has not healed with home treatment, the doctor may test the fluid in the eye to determine the type of bacteria present and prescribe treatment accordingly.

Treatment

The usual treatment for styes begins at home with the application of a warm washcloth soaked in fairly warm water. Heat is important to increase the blood supply to the eye, helping the immune system to fight off the infection. It also opens the blocked oil gland and helps remove pus. The water should be hot but not too hot. If a finger cannot remain in the water comfortably, it is too hot. Washcloths should not be heated in a microwave oven. Salt or rosewater may be added to the warm water.

The warm washcloth is applied to the eyelid of the closed eye for 10 to 15 minutes three to four times a day. Relief is usually felt within 24 hours.

The child and the parent should avoid popping the sty as one would a pimple. This can irritate the eyelid further and spread the bacteria. By allowing the style to break on its own and leak out pus, the sty can drain. Daily washing and the use of warm compresses help eliminate the bacteria released by the burst sty.

Some doctors recommend using over-the-counter eye washes, such as Bausch and Lomb Eye Wash or Collyrium Eye Wash, or medicated pads made especially for the eyes to clean around the eyelid. Others suggest washing the eyelid and the eyelash area with a mild soap wash, made from equal parts of baby shampoo and water. The soap is applied by dipping a cotton ball or clean cloth into the soap wash and washing the eye area gently. This action decreases the risk of infection, especially if the child has recurring styes. This procedure also helps prevent further styes.

Sometimes, antibiotic ointment, sulphonimide, or drops are used. Ointment is applied by putting a thin layer over the sty, usually at bedtime. To insert eye drops into the eye of an older child or adolescent, pull the lower lid down to create a pouch and then put the drops into the pouch. For a younger child, the child can lie down and then close his or her eyes. The eye drops are put into the corner of the affected eye closest to the nose. Then, the child should open his or her eyes so that the eye drops can roll into the eye. Ointment or eye drops usually are prescribed after a sty has been lanced.

The doctor may also decide to surgically drain the sty by lancing it. Usually, not all of the pus is removed if there is acute inflammation. Doing that can deform the eyelid. Sometimes, if a single eyelash is involved, it may be removed to promote healing and drainage.

If the infection does not respond to treatment or spreads to other eye areas or to the lymph nodes in front of the ear, the doctor may prescribe oral antibiotics, such as erythromycin, dicloxacillin, or cephalexin.

Internal hordeola are usually just monitored by the doctor. They may need to be opened and drained or may require antibiotics.

Chalazia are given the same treatment as styes.

Until the sty or chalazion is healed, the child should not wear **contact lenses** and the adolescent should not wear eye makeup.

Alternative treatment

Homeopathic practitioners prescribe oral homeopathic medications that reduce the bacterial growth within the sty and chalazion and thereby heal the inflammation. These medications also eliminate the itching and scaling often experienced along the eyelash line. In addition, homeopathic oral medications are aimed at boosting the immune system. Homeopathic practice usually does not use topical ointments or drops but does recommend using an antibacterial eyewash made from five drops of tincture of goldenseal in a cup of warm water. This is swabbed on the eyelid with a cotton ball. (Since goldenseal can stain, it should be used carefully.)

Prognosis

Most styes heal with minimal treatment in about a week.

Recurring styes may be an indication of a chronic eye infection called *Staphylococcus blepharitis*. In this condition, the eyelids are crusty, reddened, and swollen. The eyes may itch and burn. The base of the eyelashes may have dry scales that flake like dandruff. This condition can cause loss of eyelashes. Both *Staphylococcus blepharitis* and recurring styes can cause scarring of the eyelid.

Prevention

Cleaning the eye with a warm washcloth helps prevent the pores from clogging and a sty from forming. Using a mild, soap wash made with baby shampoo and water will also clean the area and help prevent styes from recurring.

Maintaining good hygiene is essential to preventing styes. Not touching or rubbing the eyes with the hands, especially if they are unwashed, can also prevent styes. Providing separate washcloths and towels for each child will keep bacteria from spreading. In addition, teenagers should not share makeup, especially mascara, eyeshadow, and eyeliner. Eye makeup should be replaced at least every six months because bacteria can grow in these cosmetics and cause infection.

Protecting the eyes from dust and air pollution by using safety glasses when doing dusky work outdoors, such as raking leaves, can also help prevent eye infections. These protections are also good when children are working with craft materials or other materials that may produce airborne particles.

Children's contact lens care should be monitored to maintain cleanliness. Bacteria can contaminate contact lenses or be transmitted by lenses when they are removed or inserted into the eyes. This is a common vector for bacterial transmission into the eye.

Stress has been a contributing factor to the formation of styes, especially in children with immune system disorders. Therefore, stress management techniques could help prevent styes from forming.

Parental concerns

Parents should make sure children wash their hands often and use fresh linens. Contact lenses need to be kept clean and eyes need to be protected when someone is doing dusty chores or art projects. If a child has diabetes

KEY TERMS

Autoimmune disorder—One of a group of disorders, like rheumatoid arthritis and systemic lupus erythematosus, in which the immune system is overactive and has lost the ability to distinguish between self and non-self. The body's immune cells turn on the body, attacking various tissues and organs.

Chalazion—A condition in which clogging of the Meibomiam gland causes a cyst inside the eyelid.

Conjunctivitis—Inflammation of the conjunctiva, the mucous membrane covering the white part of the eye (sclera) and lining the inside of the eyelids also called pinkeye.

Hordeolum—The medical term for sty, an infection or small abscess formation in a hair follicle of the eyelids.

Sty—An external hordeolum caused by an infection of an oil gland on the eyelid.

or an autoimmune disorder, good eye hygiene is as critical as monitoring wound healing and foot care.

See also Conjunctivitis; Eye glasses and contact lenses; Eye and vision development.

Resources

BOOKS

Neff, A. G., and C. D. Carter. "Benign eyelid lesions." In *Ophthalmology*, 2nd ed. Edited by M. Yanoof and J. S. Duker. St. Louis, MO: Mosby, 2004, pp. 698–710.

ORGANIZATIONS

National Eye Institute. 31 Center Drive, MSC 2510, Bethesda, MD, 20892–2510. Web site: <www.nei.nih.gov>.

WEB SITES

Lee, Judith, and Gretchyn Bailey. "Styes." *All About Vision*, 2003. Available online at <www.allaboutvision.com/conditions/styes.htm> (accessed November 30, 2004).

Janie Franz

Subdural hematoma

Definition

A subdural hematoma is a collection of blood in the space between the outer and middle layers of the covering of the brain. It is most often caused by torn, bleeding veins as a result of a head trauma.

Description

The covering of the brain (meninges) has three main layers. The outside is a tough, fibrous covering called the dura mater. The middle layer is the arachnoid mater, and the layer closest to the brain tissue is the pia mater. Subdural hemotamas occur when blood collects in the space between the dura mater and the arachnoid mater. Subdural hematomas usually occur because veins on the inside of the dura that connect the brain cortex and the venous sinuses (bridging veins) are ruptured as the result of a blow to the head. Symptoms can occur within minutes to hours.

Subdural hematomas in children and adolescents are usually abrupt onset or acute and are brought about by accident or injury. Another type of subdural hematoma called a chronic subdural hematoma can occur in people over age 60. However, what follows applies to acute subdural hematomas in children only.

Subdural hemotamas range from fatal or life threatening to small with only minor effects, depending on the quantity of blood released and the amount of injury to other brain tissues. With small subdural hematomas, the blood may slowly be reabsorbed over several weeks without much damage. Larger hematomas, however, can gradually get bigger even though the bleeding has stopped. This enlargement increases pressure inside the skull and can compress the brain, possibly resulting in permanent brain damage or death if the blood is not drained away and the pressure relieved through surgical intervention.

Demographics

In the United States, head injuries are the leading cause of accidental death and permanent disability in people under age 45. Not all these head injuries involve subdural hematoma, but it is the most common type of bleeding in the brain to result from trauma.

Infants are more prone to subdural hematoma than toddlers and older children, because the brain of infants has more room than the brain of older children to move around in the skull when shaken or hit. The neck muscles of infants are also less developed and unable to hold the head steady when shaken.

Children with blood clotting disorders are at an especially high risk of developing bleeding in the brain.

Causes and symptoms

In infants and children, subdural hematoma is often seen in physical **child abuse**. Its presence is one of the defining parameters (along with retinal hemorrhage) of **shaken baby syndrome**. Infants rarely fall until they start learning to walk, so falls account for only a small number of subdural hematomas in infants. However, many subdural hematomas in toddlers result from accidental falls, as they learn to walk and climb. In older children, a fall in which they hit their head is a common cause of subdural hematoma. All age groups are susceptible to developing subdural hematomas from vehicle accidents. In young children, even if the head does not contact a solid surface, the shaking, whiplash movement from some vehicle crashes causes blood vessels to burst in the brain.

Symptoms of subdural hematoma tend to fluctuate and include the following:

- **headache**
- episodes of confusion and drowsiness
- one-sided weakness or paralysis

- lethargy
- enlarged or asymmetric pupils
- convulsions
- increased intracranial pressure
- loss of consciousness after **head injury**
- coma

When to call the doctor

Individuals who show any immediate symptoms of subdural hematoma should be taken to the emergency room. Infants and children should be checked by a doctor if they have had a hard fall or accident in which they have hit their head or if child abuse or shaken baby syndrome is suspected.

Diagnosis

Diagnosis is made based on history, external signs and symptoms of head injury (although external injuries may not always be present), and confirmed through magnetic resonance imaging (MRI). X rays may be done so the doctor can look for skull fracture.

Treatment

Small hematomas that do not cause symptoms may not need to be treated. Otherwise, the hematoma should be surgically removed. Liquid blood can be drained from burr holes drilled into the skull. The surgeon may have to open a section of skull (craniotomy) to remove a large clot and/or to tie off the bleeding vein.

Corticosteroids and diuretics may be given to help control brain swelling, depending on the age of the child and the extent of the injury. After surgery, anticonvulsant drugs such as phenytoin may help control or prevent seizures, which can begin as late as two years after the head injury.

Prognosis

The outcome of subdural hematoma depends on how promptly treatment is received and how much damage the brain has received. Head injuries have a high mortality rate. The mortality rate for all patients with acute subdural hematoma is about 60 percent. Even when recovery occurs, permanent disability can occur. Headache, amnesia, attention problems, **anxiety**, and personality changes may continue for some time after surgery.

KEY TERMS

Corticosteroids—A group of hormones produced naturally by the adrenal gland or manufactured synthetically. They are often used to treat inflammation. Examples include cortisone and prednisone.

Diuretics—A group of drugs that helps remove excess water from the body by increasing the amount lost by urination.

Prevention

Preventing blunt head trauma from falls, child abuse, and assaults is the most effective way of preventing subdural hematoma.

Parental concerns

Research in the early 2000s suggests that some of the effects of brain injury do not show up in children until several years after the injury. These include the development of social and academic skills. Parents should be alert to this possibility.

See also Child abuse.

Resources

BOOKS

Beers, Mark H., and Robert Berkow, eds. *The Merck Manual*, 2nd ed., home ed. West Point, PA: Merck & Co., 2004.

ORGANIZATIONS

American Academy of Neurology. 1080 Montreal Ave., St. Paul, MN 55116. Web site: <www.aan.com>.

Brain Injury Association of America. 8201 Greensboro Dr., Suite 611, McLean, VA 22102. Web site: <www.biausa.org>.

Brain Injury Resource Center. 212 Pioneer Bldg., Seattle, WA 98104–2221. Web site: <www.headinjury.com>.

WEB SITES

Meagher, Richard J., and William F. Young. "Subdural Hematoma." *eMedicine Medical Library*, June 8, 2004. Available online at <www.emedicine.com/neuro/topic575.htm> (accessed December 1, 2004).

Moojain, Bhagwan, and Nitin Patel. "Neonatal Injuries in Child Abuse." *eMedicine Medical Library*, September 16, 2001. Available online at <www.emedicine.com/neuro/topic238.htm> (accessed December 1, 2004).

Ricci, Lawrence R., and Ann S. Botash. "Pediatrics, Child Abuse." *eMedicine Medical Library*, September 15, 2004. Available online at <www.emedicine.com/emerg/topic368.htm> (accessed December 1, 2004).

Scaletta, Tom. "Subdural Hematoma." *eMedicine Medical Library*, March 18, 2004. Available online at <www.emedicine.com/emerg/topic560.htm> (accessed December 1, 2004).

Tish Davidson, A.M.
Carol A. Turkington

Substance abuse and dependence

Definition

Substance abuse is a pattern of behavior that displays many adverse results from continual use of a substance. Substance dependence is a group of behavioral and physiological symptoms that indicate the continual, compulsive use of a substance in self-administered doses despite the problems related to the use of the substance.

Description

The characteristics of abuse are a failure to carry out obligations at home or work, continual use under circumstances that present a hazard (such as driving a car), and legal problems such as arrests. Use of the drug is persistent despite personal problems caused by the effects of the substance on the self or others. In substance dependence, as the patient's tolerance for the drug increases, increased amounts of a substance are needed to achieve the desired effect or level of intoxication. Withdrawal is a physiological and psychological change that occurs when the body's concentration of the substance declines in a person who has been a heavy user.

Substance abuse and dependence cuts across all lines of race, culture, educational, and socioeconomic status, leaving no group untouched by its devastating effects. An estimated 13 million Americans abuse or are dependent on an illegal substance. Substance abuse is an enormous public health problem, with far-ranging effects throughout society. In addition to the toll substance abuse can take on one's physical health, substance abuse is considered to be an important factor in a wide variety of social problems, affecting rates of crime, domestic violence, **sexually transmitted diseases** (including HIV/AIDS), unemployment, homelessness, teen pregnancy, and failure in school. An estimated 20 percent of the total yearly cost of health care in the United States is spent on the effects of drug and alcohol abuse.

A wide range of substances can be abused. The most common classes include the following:

- opioids, including such prescription **pain** killers as morphine and demerol, as well as illegal substances such as heroin
- benzodiazapines, including prescription drugs used for treating **anxiety**, such as valium
- sedatives or "downers," including prescription barbiturate drugs commonly referred to as tranquilizers
- stimulants or "speed," including prescription amphetamine drugs used as weight loss drugs and in the treatment of attention deficit disorder
- cannabinoid drugs obtained from the hemp plant, including marijuana and hashish
- cocaine-based drugs, including cocaine and "crack"
- hallucinogenic or psychedelic drugs, including lysergic acid diethylamide (LSD) or "acid," phencyclidine (PCP) or "angel dust," 3-4 methylenedioxymethamphetamine (MDMA) or "ecstasy," and other PCP-type drugs
- inhalants, including gaseous drugs used in the medical practice of anesthesia, as well as such common substances as paint thinner, gasoline, and glue
- alcoholic drinks
- cigarettes, cigars, and other tobacco products

Those substances of abuse that are actually prescription medications may have been obtained on the street by fraudulent means or may have been a legal, medically indicated prescription that a person begins to use without regard to the directions of his or her physician.

A number of important terms must be defined in order to have a complete discussion of substance abuse. Drug tolerance refers to a person's body being accustomed to the symptoms produced by a specific quantity of a substance. When a person first begins taking a substance, he or she will note various mental or physical reactions brought on by the drug (some of which are the very changes in consciousness that the individual is seeking through substance use). Over time with repeated use, the same dosage of the substance produces fewer of the desired feelings. In order to continue to feel the desired effect of the substance, progressively higher drug doses must be taken.

Demographics

The National Survey on Drug Use and Health (NSDUH) is conducted annually by the Substance Abuse and Mental Health Services Administration (SAMHSA) of the U.S. Department of Health and Human Services. In 2003, the study found the rate of substance dependence or abuse was 8.9 percent for youths aged 12 to 17 and 21 percent for persons aged 18 to 25. Among persons with substance dependence or abuse, illicit drugs accounted for 58.1 percent of youths and 37.2 percent of persons aged 18 to 25. In 2003, males were almost twice as likely to be classified with substance dependence or abuse as females (12.2% versus 6.2%). Among youths aged 12 to 17, however, the rate of substance dependence or abuse among females (9.1%) was similar to the rate among males (8.7%). The rate of substance dependence or abuse was highest among Native Americans and Alaska Natives (17.2%). The next highest rates were among Native Hawaiians and other Pacific Islanders (12.9%) and persons reporting mixed ethnicity (11.3%). Asian Americans had the lowest rate (6.3%). The rates among Hispanics (9.8%) and whites (9.2%) were higher than the rate among blacks (8.1%).

Rates of drug use showed substantial variation by age. For example, in 2003, 3.8 percent of youths aged 12 to 13 reported current illicit drug use compared with 10.9 percent of youths aged 14 to 15 and 19.2 percent of youths aged 16 to 17. As in other years, illicit drug use in 2003 tended to increase with age among young persons, peaking among 18 to 20-year-olds (23.3%) and declining steadily after that point with increasing age. The prevalence of current alcohol use among adolescents in 2003 increased with increasing age, from 2.9 percent at age 12 to a peak of about 70 percent for persons 21 to 22 years old. The highest prevalence of both binge and heavy drinking was for young adults aged 18 to 25, with the peak rate of both measures occurring at age 21. The rate of binge drinking was 41.6 percent for young adults aged 18 to 25 and 47.8 percent at age 21. Heavy alcohol use was reported by 15.1 percent of persons aged 18 to 25 and 18.7 percent of persons aged 21. Among youths aged 12 to 17, an estimated 17.7 percent used alcohol in the month prior to the survey interview. Of all youths, 10.6 percent were binge drinkers, and 2.6 percent were heavy drinkers, similar to the 2002 numbers.

In 2003 rates of illicit drug use varied significantly among the major racial-ethnic groups. The rate of illicit drug use was highest among Native Americans and Alaska Natives (12.1%), persons reporting two or more races (12%), and Native Hawaiians and other Pacific Islanders (11.1%). Rates were 8.7 percent for African Americans, 8.3 percent for Caucasians, and 8 percent for Hispanics. Asian Americans had the lowest rate of illicit drug use at 3.8 percent. These rates were unchanged from 2002. Native Americans and Alaska Natives were more likely than any other racial-ethnic group to report the use of tobacco products in 2003. Among persons aged 12 or older, 41.8 percent of Native Americans and Alaska Natives reported using at least one tobacco product in the past month. The lowest current tobacco use rate among racial-ethnic groups in 2003 was observed for Asian Americans (13.8%), a decrease from the 2002 rate (18.6%).

Young adults aged 18 to 25 had the highest rate of current use of cigarettes (40.2%), similar to the rate in 2002. Past month cigarette use rates among youths in 2002 and 2003 were 13 percent and 12.2 percent, respectively, not a statistically significant change. However, there were significant declines in past year (from 20.3% to 19%) and lifetime (from 33.3% to 31%) cigarette use among youths aged 12mto 17 between 2002 and 2003. Among persons aged twelve or older, a higher proportion of males than females smoked cigarettes in the past month in 2003 (28.1% versus 23%). Among youths aged 12 to 17, however, girls (12.5%) were as likely as boys (11.9%) to smoke in the past month. There was no change in cigarette use among boys aged 12 to 17 between 2002 and 2003. However, among girls, cigarette use decreased from 13.6 percent in 2002 to 12.5 percent in 2003.

Causes and symptoms

There is not thought to be a single cause of substance abuse, though scientists are as of 2004 increasingly convinced that certain people possess a genetic predisposition which can affect the development of addictive behaviors. One theory holds that a particular nerve pathway in the brain (dubbed the "mesolimbic reward pathway") holds certain chemical characteristics which can increase the likelihood that substance use will ultimately lead to substance **addiction**. Certainly, however, other social factors are involved, including **family** problems and **peer pressure**. Primary **mood disorders** (bipolar), **personality disorders**, and the role of learned behavior can influence the likelihood that a person will become substance dependent.

The symptoms of substance abuse may be related to its social effects as well as its physical effects. The social effects of substance abuse may include dropping out of school or losing a series of jobs, engaging in fighting and violence in relationships, and legal problems (ranging from driving under the influence to the commission of crimes designed to obtain the money needed to support an expensive drug habit).

When to call the doctor

The earlier one seeks help for their child or teen's substance abuse or dependence problems, the better. Regarding the matter of determining if a teen is experimenting or moving more deeply into the drug culture, parents must be careful observers, particularly of the little details that make up a teen's life. Dramatic change in appearance, friends, or physical health may be signs of trouble. If parents believe their child may be drinking or using drugs, they should seek help through a substance abuse recovery program, family physician, or mental health professional.

Diagnosis

The most difficult aspect of diagnosis involves overcoming the patient's denial. Denial is a psychological trait that prevents a person from acknowledging the reality a situation. Denial may cause a person to be completely unaware of the seriousness of the substance use or may cause the person to greatly underestimate the degree of the problem and its effects on his or her life. A physical examination may reveal signs of substance abuse in the form of needle marks, tracks, trauma to the inside of the nostrils from snorting drugs, unusually large or small pupils. With the person's permission, substance use can also be detected by examining in a laboratory an individual's blood, urine, or hair. This drug testing is limited by sensitivity, specificity, and the time elapsed since the person last used the drug.

Treatment

Treatment has several goals, which include helping a person deal with the uncomfortable and possibly life-threatening symptoms associated with withdrawal from an addictive substance (called detoxification), helping a person deal with the social effects which substance abuse has had on his or her life, and efforts to prevent relapse (resumed use of the substance). Individual or group psychotherapy is sometimes helpful.

Detoxification may take from several days to many weeks. Detoxification can be accomplished suddenly, by complete and immediate cessation of all substance use or by slowly decreasing (tapering) the dose that a person is taking, to minimize the side effects of withdrawal. Some substances absolutely must be tapered, because "cold turkey" methods of detoxification are potentially life threatening. Alternatively, a variety of medications may be used to combat the unpleasant and threatening physical symptoms of withdrawal. A substance (such as methadone in the case of heroine addiction) may be substituted for the original substance of abuse, with gradual tapering of this substituted drug. In practice, many patients may be maintained on methadone and lead a reasonably normal life style. Because of the rebound effects of wildly fluctuating blood pressure, body temperature, heart and breathing rates, as well as the potential for bizarre behavior and hallucinations, a person undergoing withdrawal must be carefully monitored.

Alternative treatment

Alternative treatments thought to improve a person's ability to stop substance use include acupuncture and hypnotherapy. Ridding the body of toxins is believed to be aided by hydrotherapy (bathing regularly in water containing baking soda, sea salt or Epsom salts). Hydrotherapy can include a constitutional effect where the body's vital force is stimulated and all organ systems are revitalized. Elimination of toxins is aided as well as by such herbs as milk thistle, burdock, and licorice. Anxiety brought on by substance withdrawal is thought to be lessened by using other herbs, for example valerian, vervain, skullcap, and kava.

Prognosis

After a person has successfully withdrawn from substance use, the even more difficult task of recovery begins. Recovery refers to the life-long efforts of a person to avoid returning to substance use. The craving can be so strong, even years and years after initial withdrawal has been accomplished, that a previously addicted person may be virtually forever in danger of slipping back into substance use. Triggers for such a relapse include any number of life stresses (problems on the job or in the marriage, loss of a relationship, death of a loved one, financial stresses), in addition to seemingly mundane exposure to a place or an acquaintance associated with previous substance use. While some people remain in counseling indefinitely as a way of maintaining contact with a professional who can help monitor behavior, others find that various support groups or twelve-step programs such as Narcotics Anonymous and Alcoholics Anonymous are the most helpful ways of monitoring the recovery process and avoiding relapse.

Prevention

Prevention is best aimed at teenagers, who are at very high risk for substance experimentation. Education regarding the risks and consequences of substance use, as well as teaching methods of resisting peer pressure, are important components of a prevention program. Furthermore, it is important to identify children at higher risk for substance abuse (including victims of physical or sexual abuse, children of parents who have a history of substance abuse, especially alcohol, and children with school failure or attention deficit disorder). These children may require a more intensive prevention program.

Parental concerns

Parents and guardians need to be aware of the power they have to influence the development of their kids throughout the teenage years. **Adolescence** brings a new and dramatic stage to family life. The changes that are required are not just the teen's to make; parents need to change their relationship with their teenager. It is best if parents are proactive about the challenges of this life cycle stage, particularly those that pertain to the possibility of experimenting with and using alcohol and drugs. Parents should not be afraid to talk directly to their kids about drug use, especially if they have had problems with drugs or alcohol themselves. Parents should give clear, no-use messages about **smoking**, drugs, and alcohol. It is important for kids and teens to understand that the rules and expectations set by parents are based on parental love and concern for their well-being. Parents should also be actively involved and demonstrate interest in their teen's friends and social activities. Spending quality time with teens and setting good examples are essential. Even if problems such as substance abuse already exist in the teen's life, parents and families can have a positive influence on their teen's behavior.

KEY TERMS

Addiction—The state of being both physically and psychologically dependent on a substance.

Dependence—A state in which a person requires a steady concentration of a particular substance to avoid experiencing withdrawal symptoms.

Detoxification—The process of physically eliminating drugs and/or alcohol from the system of a substance-dependent individual.

High—The altered state of consciousness that a person seeks when abusing a substance.

Street drug—A substance purchased from a drug dealer. It may be a legal substance, sold illicitly (without a prescription, and not for medical use), or it may be a substance which is illegal to possess.

Tolerance—A condition in which an addict needs higher doses of a substance to achieve the same effect previously achieved with a lower dose.

Withdrawal—The characteristic withdrawal syndrome for alcohol includes feelings of irritability or anxiety, elevated blood pressure and pulse, tremors, and clammy skin.

Resources

BOOKS

Haugen, Hayley Mitchell. *Teen Smoking.* Minneapolis, MN: Sagebrush Bound, 2004.

Raczek, Linda Theresa. *Teen Addiction.* San Diego, CA: Lucent Books, 2003.

Stevens, Sally J., and Andrew R. Morral. *Adolescent Substance Abuse Treatment in the United States: Exemplary Models from a National Evaluation Study.* Binghamton, NY: Haworth Press, 2002.

Townsend, John. *Drugs—Teen Issues.* Chicago, IL: Raintree, 2004.

PERIODICALS

Johnson, Kate. "Tobacco Dependence: Even Minimal Exposure Can Cause Rapid Onset; Daily Smoking Not Necessary." *Family Practice News* 34 (June 15, 2004): 66.

Kaminer, Yifah, and Chris Napolitano. "Dial for Therapy: Aftercare for Adolescent Substance Use Disorders." *Journal of the American Academy of Child and Adolescent Psychiatry* 43 (September 2004): 1171–74.

"SAMHSA Reveals State Estimates of Substance Use for the First Time: Washington, D.C. Ranks Highest in Illegal Drug Use." *Alcoholism & Drug Abuse Weekly* 16 (August 16, 2004): 1.

"Sexually Active Friends Can Signal Increase in Teen's Substance Abuse Risk." *Obesity, Fitness & Wellness Week* (September 18, 2004): 410.

Sherman, Carl. "Early Disorders Often Precede Substance Abuse." *Clinical Psychiatry News* 32 (June 2004): 34.

ORGANIZATIONS

National Council on Alcoholism and Drug Dependence Inc. 20 Exchange Place, Suite 2902, New York, NY 10005. Web site: <www.ncadd.org>.

University of Miami, Center for Treatment Research on Adolescent Drug Abuse. PO Box 019132, Miami, FL 33101. Web site: <www.miami.edu/ctrada>.

WEB SITES

"Fact Sheet: Addiction (Substance Dependence)." *New York Presbyterian Hospital.* Available online at <www.noah-health.org/english/illness/mentalhealth/cornell/conditions/substdep.html> (accessed November 4, 2004).

"Parents: The Anti-Drug." *National Youth Anti-Drug Media Campaign*. Available online at <www.theantidrug.com> (accessed November 4, 2004).

Genevieve Pham-Kanter, Ph.D.
Ken R. Wells

Sucrose intolerance *see* **Carbohydrate intolerance**

Sudden infant death syndrome

Definition

Sudden infant death syndrome (SIDS) is the sudden, unexpected death of a seemingly normal, healthy infant under one year of age that remains unexplained after a thorough postmortem investigation, including an autopsy and a review of the case history.

Description

SIDS is a defined medical disorder that is listed in the *International Classification of Diseases, 9th Revision* (ICD-9). The first published research about sudden infant death appeared in the mid-nineteenth century. Since then, researchers and healthcare providers have struggled to define the syndrome and determine its causes. The key characteristics of SIDS include:

- infant less than one year of age
- infant seemingly healthy (no preceding symptoms)
- complete investigation fails to find a cause of death
- no associated **child abuse** or illness

Demographics

In the United States, SIDS was the third leading cause of postneonatal deaths (those occurring between the ages of 28 days and one year) in 2001. According to the National Center for Health Statistics, 2,234 infants in the United States died of SIDS in 2001, or 8.1 percent of total infant deaths. (In the late 1990s, many sources placed the annual total number of deaths as high as 6,000 due to possible under-reporting.) Ninety percent of SIDS deaths occur during the first six months of life, mostly between the ages of two and four months. SIDS also occurs about 1.5 times more frequently in boys than girls. The rate of SIDS in African-American infants is twice as high as that of Caucasians, a fact often attributed to the lower quality of prenatal care received by many African-American mothers.

Causes and symptoms

Studies have identified many risk factors for SIDS, but the actual cause of the disorder remains a mystery. Although investigators are still not sure whether the immediate cause of SIDS deaths is due to respiratory failure or cardiac arrest, patterns of infant **sleep**, breathing, and arousal are a major focus of research in the early 2000s. It is known that young infants often stop breathing for short periods of time, then gasp and start again. Some researchers and physicians believe that SIDS involves a flaw in the mechanism that is responsible for resumption of breathing.

Aside from its occurrence during sleep, the other most striking feature of SIDS is its narrow age distribution, which has prompted researchers to examine the developmental changes that take place between the ages of two and four months, especially between the ages of two and four months, when most SIDS deaths occur. A growing number of experts believe that rather than a single cause, there are a number of different conditions that can cause or contribute to SIDS. This picture is complicated still further by the interaction of possible physical abnormalities with a number of environmental and developmental factors known to increase the risk of SIDS. Premature infants and low birth weight babies in general are known to be at increased risk of developing SIDS, as are infants born to teenage mothers, poor mothers, and mothers who for any reason have had inadequate prenatal care. Other risk factors include maternal **smoking** during pregnancy, exposure to smoking in the home after birth, formula feeding rather than breastfeeding, and prior death of a sibling from SIDS (although this is thought to be due to shared environmental risk factors rather than genetic predisposition). Many SIDS deaths occur in babies who have recently had colds (a possible reason that SIDS is most prevalent in winter, the time when upper respiratory infections are most frequent).

As of 2004, the most significant risk factor discovered for SIDS was placing babies to sleep in a prone position (on their stomachs). Studies have reported that anywhere from 28 percent to 52 percent of infants who die of SIDS are found lying face down. Another finding reinforcing the connection between SIDS and prone-sleeping is the fact that SIDS rates are higher in Western cultures, where women have traditionally placed children on their stomachs, than in Eastern ones, where infants usually sleep on their backs. The cause-effect relationship between prone-sleeping and SIDS is not fully understood. However, it is known that when infants sleep on their backs they are more prone to arousal, and SIDS is often thought to involve a failure to rouse from sleep. In addition, prone-sleeping raises a baby's temperature, which is another risk factor for the disorder.

When to call the doctor

Parents or caregivers should immediately call for emergency care if a child is found not breathing or without a pulse or is unable to be aroused from sleep.

Diagnosis

In most cases, three techniques are used in an attempt to determine the cause of an infant's death. These are:

- Death scene investigation. A thorough examination of the scene of death, including recording baby's position, collecting items from the surrounding area, and interviewing **family** members and/or caregivers, can sometimes point to an external cause of death.
- Autopsy. The autopsy, usually performed by a medical examiner or coroner, focuses on finding any identifiable cause of death. While parents may reject the idea of an autopsy because they feel it violates their infant's remains, it is often the only tool that can definitively rule out other potential causes of death.
- Review of family history. Healthcare providers or police interview parents and/or caregivers in order to determine the child's medical and family history, in an attempt to rule out possible illness, child abuse, or other cause of death.

Treatment

Because SIDS affects seemingly healthy infants, and death is the first symptom of the disorder, it is not possible to treat an infant who is truly affected by SIDS. If life support is implemented and the child is resuscitated, emergency care will be provided in an attempt to stabilize the child. Healthcare personnel perform a complete medical exam and record the child's medical history to exclude other potential causes.

Prognosis

By definition the prognosis for babies affected by SIDS is invariably death. In some rare cases, emergency care providers are able to resuscitate an infant who is seemingly lifeless; the prognosis remains poor in these cases.

Prevention

In the 1990s a number of countries initiated campaigns aimed at getting parents to put their infants to sleep on their backs or sides. In the United States, the American Academy of Pediatrics (AAP) in 1992 issued an official recommendation that infants be put to bed on their backs (supine position) or on their sides (lateral position). In 1994 the Public Health Service launched its "Back to Sleep" campaign, targeting parents, other care givers, and healthcare personnel with brochures advocating supine or lateral infant sleeping and also including information about other risk factors for SIDS. By the mid-1990s it was apparent that this and similar campaigns worldwide had had a significant—in many cases dramatic—impact in reducing the number of deaths from SIDS. In a number of countries the incidence of SIDS dropped by 50 percent or more. SIDS deaths in Great Britain were reduced by 91 percent between 1989 and 1992; in Denmark they declined by 72 percent between 1991 and 1993; and they were reduced by 45 percent in New Zealand between 1989 and 1992.

In the United States, the AAP recommendations reduced the incidence of front-sleeping in infants from over 70 percent in 1992 to 24 percent in 1996. A decline in SIDS rates, already observed in the 1980s, tripled its previous pace between 1990 and 1994, with SIDS deaths falling 10 to 15 percent between 1992 and 1994. Links between SIDS and other aspects of an infant's sleep environment have also emerged. The best known is the finding that soft, padded sleep surfaces can endanger infants by obstructing breathing or creating air pockets that trap their expelled carbon dioxide, which they can then inhale.

Some research also suggests that co-sleeping (having an infant sleep with the mother in her bed) can help regulate an infant's sleep pattern in ways that reduce the risk of SIDS. (Like supine infant sleeping, co-sleeping is also prevalent among Asian populations, which have a low incidence of SIDS.) Infants who share their mothers' beds become accustomed to frequent minor arousals when the mother shifts position, and their own sleep tends to be lighter and more even than that of infants who sleep alone in their cribs and are more prone to the heavier, but sporadic, breathing that stops and then starts up again with a gasp. Experts speculate that this lighter sleep not only makes it less likely for an infant to stop breathing but also that such an infant, with the "practice" gained from more frequent arousals every night, can be aroused more easily when any respiratory distress does occur. In addition, infants who co-sleep with their mothers are naturally more likely to sleep on their backs or sides, which also reduces the risk of SIDS.

In December 1996 the AAP issued the following updated recommendations regarding infant sleep:

- Infants should be put to sleep in a nonprone position. The supine position (on their backs) is safest, but sleeping on their sides can also significantly reduce the risk of SIDS. When infants sleep on their sides, the bottom arm should be extended to prevent them from rolling over on to their stomachs.
- Soft sleeping surfaces should be avoided, and a sleeping infant should not be placed on soft objects such as pillows or quilts.
- It may be better for parents, with the guidance of their pediatrician, to depart from these recommendations in the case of infants with certain health problems, such as gastroesophageal reflux (GER).
- Infants should spend some time lying on their stomachs when they are awake and supervised by an adult.

Other precautions parents can take include obtaining adequate prenatal care; avoiding exposing infants to cigarette smoke, either pre- or postnatally; breastfeeding instead of formula feeding; and not allowing an infant to become overheated while sleeping. Another measure taken by some parents is the use of a portable battery-operated monitor that sounds an alarm in response to significant deviations in infants' respiration or heart rates while they are asleep. Monitoring is based on the belief that if parents can quickly reach an infant who has stopped breathing, they can either get him breathing again themselves or call for emergency assistance. There has been no substantiated link between monitoring and the decrease in SIDS, and infants have, in fact, died while being monitored. Nevertheless, monitors provide peace of mind for many parents, especially those who have already lost an infant to SIDS or whose baby has special risk factors for the disorder. Medical opinion is generally in favor of monitoring only for newborns who have had episodes of apnea (cessation of breathing) or for any infant who has had a precipitous, life-threatening interruption of breathing or cardiovascular function.

Parental concerns

Losing a child—a traumatic experience for any parent—is especially difficult for those who lose a child to SIDS because the death is so sudden and its cause can often not be determined. Parents of a child who dies of SIDS do not gain a medical explanation of their infant's death. Although such an understanding does not lessen their loss, it can serve an important function in the healing process, one that SIDS parents do not have. In addition to the emotions that normally accompany grief, such as denial, anger, and guilt, SIDS parents may experience certain other reactions unique to their situation. They may become fearful that another unexpected disaster will strike them or members of their families. After the death of a child from SIDS, parents often become overprotective of the infant's older siblings and of any children born subsequently. Some **fear** having another child, due to misgivings that the tragedy they have experienced may repeat itself. Parents of children who die of SIDS often make major changes in their lives during the period following the death, such as relocating or changing jobs, as a way to avoid confronting painful memories or as a way to protect themselves against the SIDS death of another baby by changing the circumstances of their lives as much as possible.

SIDS deaths place a great strain on marriages. Parents' individual ways of coping with their grief may prevent them from giving each other the support they need, creating an emotional distance between them. Nevertheless, the **divorce** rate among SIDS parents appears to be no higher than that for the general population, and in one survey half the respondents reported that their marriages had ultimately been strengthened by the experience.

A SIDS death also has a significant effect on the infant's siblings. Young children often experience developmental regressions in **toilet training** or other areas. Some fear going to sleep, which they associate with the death of their baby brother or sister. As with any death in the family, children need to be reassured that they are not guilty in any way. Many pose difficult questions to their parents, wanting to know why the baby died or where he has gone, or even whether they are going to die, too. Children may also come to feel jealous of the attention paid to the infant who has died or resentful of the disruption the death has caused in their family's life. Most parents report that their way of caring for their remaining children changes after the family experiences a SIDS death. Having young children (or infants born later on) sleep with them at night makes some parents feel more confident of preventing a second tragedy from occurring. In addition to overprotecting their children and worrying about their health, SIDS parents may also spoil them and find it hard to say no to their requests. On the positive side, many parents simply value their remaining children more, spend more time with them, and become closer to them. In a minority of cases, however, the reverse happens, and parents feel emotionally distant from their surviving children. In addition, fear of being hurt sometimes makes it difficult for some parents to bond with babies born later.

Many parents of infants who die of SIDS are helped by participating in local support groups, where they can share their feelings and experiences with others who

KEY TERMS

Apnea—The temporary absence of breathing. Sleep apnea consists of repeated episodes of temporary suspension of breathing during sleep.

Co-sleeping—Having an infant sleep with the mother in her bed.

Gastroesophogeal reflux—Backward flow of stomach contents into the esophagus.

have undergone the same experience. Counseling can also be beneficial, especially with a mental health professional experienced in dealing with parental grief.

Resources

BOOKS

Byard, Roger W., et al. *Sudden Infant Death Syndrome: Problems, Progress, and Possibilities.* Oxford, UK: Oxford University Press, 2001.

Mawhiney, Robert. *S.I.D.S.: New Research into Sudden Infant Death Syndrome—Cause and Effect.* Philadelphia: Xlibris Corp., 2003.

PERIODICALS

Anderson, Robert, and Betty Smith. "Deaths: Leading Causes for 2001." *National Vital Statistics Report* 52, no. 9 (November 7, 2003): 1– 86.

ORGANIZATIONS

American Academy of Pediatrics. 141 Northwest Point Blvd., Elk Grove Village, IL 60007– 1098. Web site: <www.aap.org>.

National SIDS/Infant Death Resource Center. 2070 Chain Bridge Rd., Suite 450, Vienna, VA 22182. Web site: <www.sidscenter.org>.

SIDS Alliance. 1314 Bedord Ave., Suite 210, Baltimore, MD 21208. Web site: <www.sidsalliance.org>.

WEB SITES

National SIDS/Infant Death Resource Center. Available online at <www.sidscenter.org> (accessed November 4, 2004).

Tabib, Shahram, Thomas Tsou, and Charles Drew. "Sudden Infant Death Syndrome." *eMedicine Health*, July 22, 2004. Available online at <www.emedicinehealth.com/articles/10223-1.asp> (accessed November 4, 2004).

Stephanie Dionne Sherk

Sugar diabetes *see* **Diabetes mellitus**

Sugar intolerance *see* **Carbohydrate intolerance**

Suicide and suicidal behavior

Definition

Suicide is the act of ending one's own life. Suicidal behavior are thoughts or tendencies that put a person at risk for committing suicide.

Description

Suicide, attempted suicide, and thoughts of committing suicide are, as of the early 2000s, growing problems among adolescents in the United States and much of the world. It is the third leading cause of death among 15 to 19 year olds in the United States and the sixth leading cause of death among 10 to 14 year olds. About 2 percent of adolescent girls and 1 percent of adolescent boys attempt suicide each year in the United States. Another 5 to 10 percent of children and teens each year come up with a plan to commit suicide.

Psychologists have identified the teenage years as one of the most difficult phases of human life. Although they are often seen as a time in which to enjoy life, hang out with friends, and perform other activities that adults would not usually do, the teenage period can be difficult. Many changes in the human mind take place during **puberty**. Apart from facing the onset of sexual maturity, teenagers must also make key decisions about their future, develop their identities, change schools, and meet new friends. They may have to cope with a wide range of personal and social challenges. Many young people have difficulty dealing with stress these experiences may elicit.

The most common reasons for suicide or suicidal behavior among children and adolescents involve personal conflict or loss, most frequently with parents or romantic attachments. **Family** discord, physical or sexual abuse, and an upcoming legal or disciplinary crisis are also commonly associated with completed and attempted suicide. Adolescents who complete suicide show relatively high suicidal intent, and many are intoxicated at the time of death. The most serious suicide attempters leave suicide notes, show evidence of planning, and use an irreversible method, such as a gunshot to the head. Most adolescent suicide attempts, though, are of relatively low intent and lethality, and only a small number of these individuals actually want to die. Usually, suicide attempters want to escape psychological **pain** or unbearable circumstances, gain attention, influence others, or communicate strong feelings, such as anger or love.

Suicidal behavior is rare in children prior to puberty, probably because of their relative inability to plan and execute a suicide attempt. Psychiatric risk factors, such as depression and substance abuse, become more frequent in **adolescence**, contributing to the increase in the frequency of suicidal behavior in older children. Some view the transition from primary to middle school as particularly stressful, especially for girls. Also, parental monitoring and supervision decrease with increasing age, so that adolescents may be more likely to experience emotional difficulties without their parents' knowledge.

Repeated suicide attempts are common, but rates vary. Follow-up studies ranging from one to 12 years found a re-attempt rate among adolescents of 5 to 6 percent per year, with the greatest risk within the first three months after the initial attempt. Factors associated with a higher re-attempt rate included chronic and severe psychiatric disorders, such as depression and substance abuse; hostility and aggression; non-compliance with treatment; poor levels of social skills; family discord, neglect, or abuse; and parental psychiatric disorders.

Highest risk

Four out of five teenagers who successfully commit suicide are male, but the average female teenager is prone to attempt suicide four more times during her teen years than the average male. White teenage males are more likely to commit suicide than other ethnic groups, but as of the early 2000s teenage suicide among blacks is also increasing. Teenagers who have unsuccessfully tried to commit suicide in the past are more likely to attempt suicide in the future. The odds increase after each failed attempt. There are two groups of teens that are at a particularly high risk for committing suicide: Native Americans, and gay, lesbian, bisexual, and transgendered teens.

In Native American, including Native Alaskan, youth ages 15 to 24 years, suicide is the second leading cause of death, according to a 2001 survey by the Bureau of Indian Affairs. The survey also showed that 16 percent of Native American youth attempted suicide in the preceding year. Among Native American high school students, suicide attempts were most associated with poor school performance, poor physical health, a history of family or friends who committed or attempted suicide, family problems, and physical and sexual abuse.

Gay and bisexual male teens, which represent about 10 percent of the male teen population, are six to seven times more at risk for attempting suicide than their heterosexual peers. Several surveys show gay and lesbian youth account for 30 percent of all suicides among teens, according to the U.S. Department of Health and Human Services. Yet most studies of teen suicide have not been concerned with identifying sexual orientation.

A 1997 study by the Massachusetts Department of Education found that 46 percent of high school students who identified themselves as gay, lesbian, or bisexual, had attempted suicide in the past year compared to 8.8 percent of their heterosexual peers. Of the gay, lesbian, and bisexual teens, 23.5 percent required medical care as a result of their suicide attempt compared to 3.3 percent of heterosexual students who attempted suicide.

Common problems

The following are common risk factors for teenage suicide:

- Psychological problems: Depression, previous attempts at suicide, and having received psychiatric care in the past.
- Personal failure: Unmet high standards set by the teen or parents, including failing grades in school or poor performance in sports.
- Recent loss: Death of a close friend or family member, **divorce**, **abandonment** by a parent, pregnancy, and the breakup with a boyfriend or girlfriend.
- Substance abuse: Abuse of alcohol and other drugs as forms of self-medication for overwhelming depression. A combination of depression, substance abuse, and lowered impulse control can lead to suicide or attempted suicide. Substance abuse in other family members can also lead to suicide.
- Household guns: Easy access to a gun. Children of law enforcement officers have a much higher suicide rate because of the accessibility of guns in their houses. The most common method of suicide among teens is gunshot.
- Violence: Violence against the teen either at home or outside the home, including physical, emotional, or sexual abuse, or bullying. Violence at home or against the youth teaches teens that the way to resolve conflict is through violence, and suicide is the ultimate act of self-violence.
- Communication problems: The inability to discuss anger or other uncomfortable feelings with family members or friends. These feelings can include loneliness, rejection, and awareness of one's gay or bisexual sexual orientation.

Parental concerns

Parents who are concerned that their child is or may be suicidal should seek help immediately, such as from a psychiatrist, psychologist, or counselor. Therapists and counselors can listen to the child talk about his or her problems and may be able to suggest ways to cope which the teen will find useful.

There are a number of ways parents can help children and teens deal with loneliness, depression, and suicidal feelings. First, they can let the child do the talking, and listen carefully. They can let the child know they take his or her feelings and thoughts seriously. They can try to identify the root of the problem. Second, they can ask direct questions, such as "Are you thinking of committing suicide?" or "Are you thinking of ending your life?" Third, they can stay with the child. Parents should not leave their child alone if the child says he or she wants to commit suicide. By staying with the child, the parent may be protecting the child's life.

When to call the doctor

Many doctors recommend that teenagers be taken to a hospital immediately after they express the desire to commit suicide. At the least, immediate psychological help should be sought. There are many methods, both medical and psychological, of helping teenagers who consider committing suicide. Most teenagers who think of suicide believe their problems are too hard to solve or too embarrassing to talk about, so it is important for their helpers to show they are trustworthy and able to listen. Seeing a psychologist is widely recommended as well. A psychologist may be able to improve a teenager's vision of life by listening to the young person and conveying optimism regarding the future.

Doctors recommend that helpers not ask the teenager's reason for thinking of suicide; rather, helpers should listen and wait for the teenager to trust enough to talk openly about the problem. Helpers should, however, be understanding of the teenager's situation. Doctors also recommend that helpers not mention "reasons for living," as doing so might generate more depressing thoughts in the teenager.

There are many telephone hot lines available, on national, state, and local levels, to help teenagers who are considering suicide. Two national, 24-hour, toll-free suicide hotlines are: 800–784–2433 and 800–999–9999. Gay, lesbian, bisexual, or transgendered teens thinking of suicide can get help at 800–850–8078.

KEY TERMS

Puberty—The point in development when the ability to reproduce begins. The gonads begin to function and secondary sexual characteristics begin to appear.

Transgendered—Any person who feels their assigned gender does not completely or adequately reflect their internal gender, such as a biological male who perceives himself to be female.

Resources

BOOKS

Empfield, Maureen, and Nicholas Bakalar. *Understanding Teenage Depression: A Guide to Diagnosis, Treatment, and Management.* New York: Owl Books, 2001.

King, Robert A., et al. *Suicide in Children and Adolescents.* Cambridge, UK: Cambridge University Press, 2003.

Spirito, Anthony, and James C. Overholser. *Evaluating and Treating Adolescent Suicide Attempters: From Research to Practice.* New York: Academic Press, 2002.

Wallerstein, Claire. *Need to Know: Teenage Suicide.* Portsmouth, NH: Heinemann Educational Books, 2003.

PERIODICALS

Eckert, Tanya L., et al. "Adolescent Suicide Prevention: School Psychologists' Acceptability of School-based Programs." *School Psychology Review* (Winter 2003): 57–76.

Fritz, Gregory K. "Prevention of Child and Adolescent Suicide." *The Brown University Child and Adolescent Behavior Letter* (September 2001): 8.

Norton, Patrice G. W. "Prevention Plan Reduces Teen Suicide Attempts." *Clinical Psychiatry News* (May 2004): 44.

Perlstein, Steve. "TeenScreen Flags Adolescents at Risk of Suicide." *Clinical Psychiatry News* (April 2004): 43.

Portes, Pedro R., et al. "Understanding Adolescent Suicide: A Psycho-social Interpretation of Developmental and Contextual Factors." *Adolescence* (Winter 2002): 805–814.

ORGANIZATIONS

American Association of Suicidology. 4201 Connecticut Ave. NW, Suite 408, Washington, DC 20008. Web site: <www.suicidology.org>.

Suicide Awareness Voices of Education. 7317 Cahill Road, Suite 207, Minneapolis, MN 55424. Web site: <www.save.org>.

Yellow Ribbon International Suicide Prevention Program. PO Box 644, Westminster, CO 80036. Web site: <www.yellowribbon.org>.

WEB SITES

Columbia University. *TeenScreen*, 2003. Available online at <www.teenscreen.org> (accessed August 12, 2004).

"Depression and Suicide Page," 2004. Available online at <www.teenlineonline.org/helparchives/depression.htm> (accessed August 12, 2004).

Screening for Mental Health, Inc. "SOS High School Suicide Prevention Program", 2004. Available online at <www.mentalhealthscreening.org/sos_highschool/> (accessed August 12, 2004).

Ken R. Wells

Sulfonamides

Definition

Sulfonamides, sometimes called sulfa drugs, are medicines that prevent the growth of bacteria in the body. The sulfonamides have largely been replaced by the **antibiotics** which generally are safer and more effective.

Description

Sulfonamides are used to treat many kinds of infections caused by bacteria and certain other microorganisms. Physicians may prescribe these drugs to treat urinary tract infections, ear infections, frequent or long lasting **bronchitis**, bacterial **meningitis**, certain eye infections, *Pneumocystis carinii* **pneumonia**, traveler's **diarrhea**, and a number of other kinds of infections. These drugs will not work for colds, flu, and other infections caused by viruses.

Description

Although there were many sulfonamides, relatively few are in use as of 2004:

- Sulfisoxazole (Gantrisin) is used to treat urinary tract infections. In combination with erythromycin, sulfisoxazole may be used to treat ear infections in children.
- Trimethoprim/sulfamethoxazole (Bactrim, Septra) is a combination of two sulfonamides used together. The combination is more effective than giving either drug alone in a larger dose. The combination is commonly used to treat urinary tract infections and other infections that cannot be treated with antibiotics.
- Sulfadiazine may be used to protect people with **rheumatic fever** from infections. It is used to treat **toxoplasmosis**. An ointment containing silver sulfadiazine is widely used for treatment of burns.
- Sulfasalazine (Azulfadine) is used to treat infections of the colon and intestine.

General use

The most common use for sulfonamides in adults is treatment of urinary tract infections. In children, sulfonamides have more limited use. Sulfisoxazole may be used for prophylaxis of ear infections and prevention of meningococcal infections. Sulfasakazube is used to treat children over the age of two years with ulcerative colitis.

Precautions

Sulfonamides should never be used in infants under the age of two months. They should also be used with extreme care in patients with liver problems, kidney problems, and some types of anemia.

Side effects

Although such side effects are rare, some people have severe and life-threatening reactions to sulfonamides. These include sudden, severe liver damage; serious blood problems; breakdown of the outer layer of the skin; and a condition called Stevens-Johnson syndrome, in which people get blisters around the mouth, eyes, or anus. People should call a physician immediately if any of the following signs of a dangerous reaction occur:

- skin rash or reddish or purplish spots on the skin
- other skin problems, such as blistering or peeling
- fever
- sore throat
- cough
- shortness of breath
- joint pain
- pale skin
- yellow skin or eyes

This medicine may cause **dizziness**. Sulfonamides may also cause blood problems that can interfere with healing and lead to additional infections. This medicine may increase sensitivity to sunlight. Even brief exposure to sun can cause severe **sunburn** or rash. While being treated with this medicine, people should avoid being in direct sunlight. Very rarely, systemic sulfonamides may even cause kidney stones.

The most serious adverse effects of sulfonamides cannot be predicted. Some steps can minimize some of the less severe adverse effects. Because sulfonamides are not very soluble, they should always be taken with a full glass of water. Moreover, sulfonamides increase sensitivity to sunlight and increase the risk of sunburn. People taking sulfonamides by mouth should avoid direct sunlight and stay covered up. They should not rely on **sunscreens**. This risk does not apply, however, to people using sulfonamide eye or ear drops. Oral sulfonamides should always be taken in evenly spaced doses to maintain a steady blood level throughout the day.

Interactions

Sulfonamides may interact with a large number of other medicines. When interaction occurs, the effects of one or both of the drugs may change or the risk of side effects may be greater. People who take sulfonamides should let their physician know all other medicines they are taking. Among the drugs that may interact with sulfonamides are:

- acetaminophen (Tylenol)
- medicine for overactive thyroid
- other medicines used to treat infections
- birth control pills
- medicines for diabetes, such as glyburide (Micronase)
- anticoagulants, such as warfarin (Coumadin)
- amantadine (Symmetrel)
- water pills (diuretics) such as hydrochlorothiazide (HCTZ, HydroDIURIL)
- the anticancer drug methotrexate (Rheumatrex)
- antiseizure medicines such as valproic acid (Depakote, Depakene)

The list above does not include every drug that may interact with sulfonamides but is limited to drugs that might be used in treatment of children and adolescents. Parents should be sure to check with a physician or pharmacist before combining sulfonamides with any other prescription or nonprescription (over-the-counter) medicine.

Parental concerns

Parents giving their children eye or ear drops should be sure they know the proper way to administer these drops. Parents should review the technique with a physician or nurse to be sure the medication is given properly. If children are taking sulfonamides by mouth, parents should be sure that the children are drinking a full glass of water with each dose. Because some of the adverse effects of sulfonamides may be very serious, parents should report any suspicious symptoms to their physician promptly.

See also Cystitis; Penicillins; Tetracyclines.

Resources

BOOKS

Beers Mark H., and Robert Berkow, eds. *The Merck Manual*, 2nd ed. home edition. West Point, PA: Merck & Co., 2004.

Marx, John A. *Rosen's Emergency Medicine: Concepts and Clinical Practice*, 5th ed. St. Louis, MO: Mosby & Co, 2002.

Mcevoy, Gerald K., et al. *AHFS Drug Information 2004*. Bethesda, MD: American Society of Healthsystems Pharmacists, 2004.

Siberry, George K., and Robert Iannone, eds. *The Harriet Lane Handbook*, 15th ed. Philadelphia: Mosby Publishing, 2000.

PERIODICALS

American Academy of Pediatrics, Committee on Quality Improvement, Subcommittee on Urinary Tract Infection. "Practice parameter: the diagnosis, treatment, and evaluation of the initial urinary tract infection in febrile infants and young children." *Journal of Pediatrics* 105, no. 2 (February 2000): 463–464.

Halasa, Natasha B., et al. "Differences in antibiotic prescribing patterns for children younger than five years in the three major outpatient settings." *Journal of Pediatrics* 144, no. 2 (February 2004): 200–205.

Witman, P. M. "Pediatric oral medicine." *Dermatolgic Clinics of North America* 21, no. 1 (January 2003): 157–170.

ORGANIZATIONS

American Academy of Pediatrics. 141 Northwest Point Boulevard, Elk Grove Village, IL 60007–1098. Web site: <www.aap.org>.

WEB SITES

"Med Chem Group 7—Antibiotics." *University of Michigan, College of Pharmacy*. Available online at <http://sitemaker.umich.edu/medchemgroup7/files/sulfonamides_clinical_pharmacology.htm> (accessed September 29, 2004).

"Sulfonamides (Ophthalmic)." *MedlinePlus*. Available online at <www.nlm.nih.gov/medlineplus/druginfo/uspdi/202539.html> (accessed September 29, 2004).

Nancy Ross-Flanigan
Samuel Uretsky, PharmD

Sunburn

Definition

Sunburn is an inflammation of the skin caused by overexposure to ultraviolet radiation from the sun.

Description

Sunburn is caused by exposure to the ultraviolet (UV) rays of the sun. There are two types of ultraviolet rays, UVA and UVB. UVB radiation causes most sunburn (about 85%). However, most UVB rays are absorbed by **sunscreens**, but only about half the UVA rays are absorbed.

Although sunburn itself is not a serious health problem in the short term, skin **cancer** from sun overexposure is in the early 2000s a growing problem in the United States. Both UVA and UVB radiation play a role in the development of a form of skin cancer called malignant melanoma. According to the American Cancer Society, melanoma accounts for only 4 percent of all skin cancer, but 79 percent of skin cancer deaths, or about 7,900 deaths annually in the United States. In addition, more than 1 million Americans develop nonmelanoma skin cancer each year, although deaths from this form of cancer are much more rare (about 1,000 per year).

Skin contains a protective pigment called melanin. The darker the skin tone, the more melanin is present. Fair-skinned people are most susceptible to sunburn, because their skin produces only small amounts of the melanin. However, even the darkest-skinned people can get sunburn and skin cancer.

Infants are most susceptible to sunburn and should be kept out of the sun at all times. Children are more susceptible than adults, and because of their outdoor activities get three times more sun exposure on average than adults. It is estimated that one-half to three-quarters of an individual's total number of lifetime sunburns occur in childhood and **adolescence**.

Long-term effects of repeated sun overexposure and burning can cause premature aging and wrinkling of the skin. Overexposure can increase the risk of skin cancer, especially a serious burn in childhood. Individuals at highest risk for developing melanoma are those who have intermittent severe (blistering) sunburns in youth or adolescence.

Occasionally an allergic response to a drug will cause a skin reaction resembling sunburn in the absence of sun exposure.

KEY TERMS

Antibiotics—Drugs that are designed to kill or inhibit the growth of the bacteria that cause infections.

Prophylaxis—Protection against or prevention of a disease. Antibiotic prophylaxis is the use of antibiotics to prevent a possible infection.

Stevens-Johnson syndrome—A severe inflammatory skin eruption that occurs as a result of an allergic reaction or respiratory infection.

Toxoplasmosis—A parasitic infection caused by the intracellular protozoan *Toxoplasmosis gondii.* Humans are most commonly infected by swallowing the oocyte form of the parasite in soil (or kitty litter) contaminated by feces from an infected cat; or by swallowing the cyst form of the parasite in raw or undercooked meat.

Demographics

Infants and children are more likely to get sunburned than adults. Individuals who live in areas where the climate is mostly sunny year round (Arizona, southern California) are at higher risk both for sunburn and skin cancer. Those living at high altitudes are also at higher risk. The chance of being sunburned increases about 4 percent or every 1,000 feet (300 meters) rise in altitude. Fair-skinned, pale, freckled individuals are more likely to get sunburned than individuals with darker skin. Sunburn is extremely common. One poll found that in the summer of 1997, 13 percent of children had developed a sunburn in the preceding week.

Causes and symptoms

The ultraviolet rays in sunlight destroy cells in the outer layer of the skin, damaging tiny blood vessels underneath. When the skin is burned, the blood vessels dilate and leak fluid. Cells stop making certain proteins because their DNA is damaged by the ultraviolet rays. Repeated DNA damage can lead to cancer.

When UV rays burn the skin, immune system defenses that identify the burned skin as foreign are triggered. At the same time, the UV rays transform a substance on the skin that interferes with this immune response. While this keeps the immune system from attacking a person's own skin, it also means that any malignant (cancerous) cells in the skin will be able to grow freely.

Sunburn causes skin to turn red and blister. Symptoms appear from one to 24 hours after sun exposure and peak several days later, after which dead skin cells peel off. In severe cases, the burn may occur with sunstroke (**vomiting**, **fever**, and collapse). Severe cases of sunburn may require **hospitalization**.

When to call the doctor

The doctor should be called any time there are symptoms of heatstroke, **dehydration**, blurred vision (possible sun damage to the eyes), chills, fever, vomiting, or blistering associated with sun exposure.

Diagnosis

Sunburn is easily diagnosed by visual inspection of the skin. No laboratory tests are needed.

Treatment

In most cases, treatment involves making the sunburned person more comfortable. The individual should get out of the sun and protect tender skin against more sun exposure for at least one week. **Pain** can be treated with **acetaminophen** (Tylenol) or **nonsteroidal anti-inflammatory drugs** (NSAIDs) such as ibuprofen. Individuals with moderate sunburn over a large area should drink extra water to avoid dehydration. In addition, discomfort may be reduced by using the following:

- calamine lotion
- sunburn cream or spray
- cool tap water compress
- colloidal oatmeal baths
- moisturizer creams to reduce skin peeling

People who are severely sunburned should see a doctor who may prescribe corticosteroid cream to speed healing. Extreme sunburns that blister may require treatment in a hospital burn unit and intravenous fluids to prevent dehydration. Individuals who develop sunburn as the result of a drug reaction should see a doctor promptly.

Alternative treatment

Over-the-counter preparations containing aloe (*Aloe barbadensis*) are an effective treatment for sunburn, easing pain and inflammation while also relieving dryness of the skin. A variety of topical herbal remedies applied as lotions, poultices, or compresses may also help relieve the effects of sunburn. Calendula (*Calendula officinalis*) is one of the most frequently recommended to reduce inflammation.

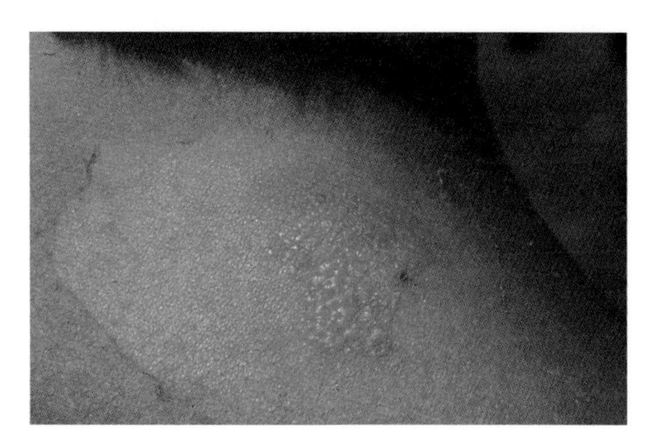

Patient with a second-degree sunburn on the back of the neck. *(Custom Medical Stock Photo Inc.)*

Prognosis

Short-term prognosis is excellent. Moderately burned skin should heal within a week. While the skin will heal after sunburn, the risk of skin cancer increases with exposure and subsequent **burns**. Even one bad burn in childhood carries an increased risk of skin cancer.

Prevention

Infants under the age of six months should be kept strictly out of the sun. Sunscreens have not been approved for use by infants. Everyone age six months and older should use a water-resistant sunscreen having a sun protective factor (SPF) of at least 15, with an SPF of 30 or more strongly recommended for children. Sunscreen should be applied 15–30 minutes before going outside, as it takes that long to bond effectively with the skin and become effective. Sunscreen should be reapplied every two hours (more often after swimming).

In addition, people should take the following steps:

- Limit sun exposure to 15 minutes the first day, even if the weather is hazy, slowly increasing exposure daily.
- Reapply waterproof sunscreen after swimming for more than 80 minutes, after toweling off, or after perspiring heavily, or every two hours if not swimming.
- Avoid the sun between 10 A.M. and 3 P.M. when the sun is strongest and most direct.
- Wear a hat or cap to protect the face.

KEY TERMS

Malignant melanoma—The most serious of the three types of skin cancer, malignant melanoma arises from the melanocytes, the skin cells that produce the pigment melanin.

Sunscreen—A product that blocks the damaging rays of the sun. Good sunscreens contain either para-aminobenzoic acid (PABA) or benzophenone, or both. Sunscreen protection factors range from two to 45.

Sunstroke—Heatstroke caused by direct exposure to the sun in which body temperature increases to dangerously high levels.

- Use sunscreen when participating in snow activities such as skiing where sunlight is reflected off the snow.
- Wear an opaque shirt on water, because reflected rays are intensified.

Parental concerns

Parents, concern about their child's sun exposure is usually influenced by their own experience with tanning and sunburn. Until the early 2000s, a tan was considered healthy rather than an increased cancer risk. Many adolescents still desire a tanned look but should be discouraged from as much sun exposure as possible. Those who insist on tanning should be encouraged to tan gradually and avoid burns.

See also Heat disorders.

Resources

BOOKS

Auerbach, Paul S. "Acute Effects of Ultraviolet Radiation on Skin: Sunburn and Tanning." *Wilderness Medicine*, 4th ed. St Louis, MO: Mosby, 2001.

Hill, David, et al. *Prevention of Skin Cancer*. London: Kluwer Law International, 2003.

McNally, Robert Aquinas. *Skin Health Information for Teens: Health Tips about Dermatological Concerns and Skin Cancer Risks*. Detroit, MI: Omnigraphics, 2003.

ORGANIZATIONS

American Cancer Society. 1599 Clifton Road, Atlanta, GA 30329. Web site: <www.cancer.org>.

WEB SITES

Guenther, Lyn, and Benjamin Barankin. "Sunburn." *eMedicine Medical Library*, October 27, 2004. Available online at <www.emedicine.com/ped/topic2561.htm> (accessed December 1, 2004).

Takayesu, James K., and Randy P. Prescilla. "Sunburn." *eMedicine Medical Library*, April 28, 2003. Available online at <www.emedicine.com/wild/topic71.htm> (accessed December 1, 2004).

Tish Davidson, A.M.
Carol A. Turkington

Sunscreens

Definition

Sunscreens are products applied to the skin to protect against the harmful effects of the sun's ultraviolet (UV) rays.

Description

Many brands of sunscreens are available, containing a variety of ingredients. The active ingredients work by absorbing, reflecting, or scattering some or all of the sun's rays. Most sunscreen products contain combinations of ingredients. Sunscreen products are sold as lotions, creams, gels, oils, sprays, sticks, and lip balms, and can be bought without a physician's prescription.

The U.S. Food and Drug Administration requires sunscreen products to carry a sun protection factor (SPF) rating on their labels. This number tells how well the sunscreen protects against burning. The higher the number, the longer a person can stay in the sun without burning.

There are three types of ultraviolet light, based on their wavelength: UVA, UVB, and UVC. UVC has the shortest wavelength and is blocked by the earth's ozone layer. Concerns about the depletion of the ozone layer focus on the serious health effects that increased exposure to UVC light would have.

UVB light is the next shortest wavelength and is called the tanning light since it is light in this range that promotes creation of the skin pigment melanin that creates a tan. UVB light only penetrates the outermost layer of the skin, but it promotes basal and squamous cell carcinoma and may worsen the effects of UVA.

Ultraviolet A is long-wave radiation generated by the sun that penetrates more deeply than UVB, causes wrinkling and leathering of the skin and damages connective tissue. UVA is the light that causes melanoma, the most serious skin **cancer**.

Several types of chemicals are used as sunscreens. They vary by the degree of protection they can provide and the types of ultraviolet light they can block:

- Cinnamates, such as octyl methoxcinnamate, give low levels of protection, and are only effective against UVB light.
- Para-amino benzoic acid (PABA) compounds, including PABA, padimate O (octyl dimethyl PABA),and glyceryl PABA, are effective only against UVB light.
- Salicylates, octylsalicylate, and homosalate offer moderate levels of protection against both UVA and UVB light, but the range of light waves against which they protect is relatively narrow.
- Benzophenones, including oxybenzone and dioxybenzone, protect against a broader range of ultraviolet light than the salicylates and are more useful for broad spectrum protection.
- Physical sunscreens are really sun blockers and include titanium dioxide, red petrolatum, and zinc oxide. Preparations containing these blockers are thick ointments and are usually reserved for skin areas at high risk of burn, such as the nose.

Other compounds, such as Parsol 1789 (avobenzone), Eusolex 8020, and menthyl anthranilate appear to be valuable broad spectrum agents. In one study, the combination of 3 percent butyl methoxydibenzoylmethane and 7 percent padimate O was the most effective of all sunscreens tested.

In addition to the chemical used as a sunscreen, the vehicle can be important in determining how well a product works. Unfortunately, thick, greasy ointments seem to work better than vanishing creams, lotions, or liquids.

General use

Users should carefully read the instructions that come with the sunscreen. Some of these products need to be applied as long as one or two hours before sun exposure. Others should be applied 30 minutes before exposure and frequently during exposure.

Users should apply sunscreen liberally to all exposed parts of the skin, including the hands, feet, nose, ears, neck, scalp (if the hair is thin or very short), and eyelids. However, they should avoid getting sunscreen in the eyes, as it can cause irritation. Use a lip balm containing sunscreen to protect the lips. Reapply sunscreen liberally every one or two hours—more frequently when perspiring heavily. People should reapply sunscreen after they go in the water.

Precautions

Sunscreen alone will not provide full protection from the sun. When possible, people should wear a hat, long pants, a long-sleeved shirt, and sunglasses. They should try to stay out of the sun between 10 A.M. and 2 P.M. (11 A.M. to 3 P.M. daylight saving time), when the sun's rays are strongest. The sun can damage the skin even on cloudy days, so people should get in the habit of using a sunscreen every day. They need to be especially careful at high elevations and in areas with surfaces that reflect the sun's rays, such as off sand, water, concrete, and snow.

Sunlamps, tanning beds, and tanning booths were once thought to be safer than the sun, because they give off mainly UVA rays. However, UVA rays are now known to cause serious skin damage and may increase the risk of melanoma. Health experts advise people not to use these tanning devices.

People with fair skin, blond, red, or light brown hair, and light colored eyes are at greatest risk for developing skin cancer. So are people with many large skin **moles**. These people should avoid exposure to the sun as much as possible. However, even dark skinned people, including African Americans and Hispanic Americans, may suffer skin damage from the sun and should be careful about exposure.

Side effects

The most common side effects are drying or tightening of the skin. This problem does not need medical attention unless it does not improve. Other side effects are rare, but possible. If any of the following symptoms occur, people should check with a physician as soon as possible:

- acne
- burning, **itching**, or stinging of the skin
- redness or swelling of the skin
- rash, with or without blisters that ooze and become crusted
- pain in hairy parts of body
- pus in hair follicles

The side effects of sunscreens cannot be prevented but can be minimized by testing a sunscreen on a small area of the body before all-over applications.

Young girl applies sunscreen to her face to protect herself from sun damage. *(© Lowell Georgia/Corbis.)*

KEY TERMS

Hair follicle—The root of a hair (that portion of a hair below the skin surface) together with its epithelial and connective tissue coverings.

Melanoma—A tumor, usually of the skin.

Ozone—A form of oxygen with three atoms in its molecule (O_3), produced by an electric spark or ultraviolet light passing through air or oxygen. A layer of ozone about 15 mi (24 km) above Earth's surface helps protect living things from the damaging effects of the sun's ultraviolet rays. Ozone is used therapeutically as a disinfectant and oxidative agent.

Pus—A thick, yellowish or greenish fluid composed of the remains of dead white blood cells, pathogens, and decomposed cellular debris. It is most often associated with bacterial infection.

Ultraviolet (UV) radiation—A portion of the light spectrum with a wavelength just below that of visible light. UV radiation is damaging to DNA and can destroy microorganisms. It may be responsible for sunburms, skins cancers, and cataracts in humans. Two bands of the UV spectrum, UVA and UVB, are used to treat psoriasis and other skin diseases.

Interactions

Anyone who is using a prescription or nonprescription (over-the-counter) drug that is applied to the skin should check with a physician before using a sunscreen.

Parental concerns

Sunscreens should not be used on children under six months of age because of the risk of side effects. Instead, children this young should be kept out of the sun. Children over six months of age should be protected with clothing and sunscreens of at least SPF 15, preferably lotions. Sunscreens containing alcohol should not be used on children because they may irritate the skin.

Before using a new sunscreen, particularly a newer formulation, it should be tested on a small area of skin. These products have some risk of causing **rashes** and other side effects.

Sunscreens should always be applied before a trip to the beach or into some other setting with intense sun exposure. Parents who start to apply sunscreen to their children upon arrival at these settings will exceed their own sun exposure limits before they begin to apply sunscreen to themselves.

Parents should consider using two to three different sunscreens at one time, to get the best results with the fewest problems. Liquids may be best for the scalp, since they can penetrate the hair. Lotions may be most appropriate for most of the body. Ointments may be the best choice for the nose and other parts of the face.

Users should always check expiration dates and not use a sunscreen past its expiration. Reapply sunscreens as directed. Children may benefit from a waterproof sunscreen. There have been claims that these sunscreens may cause eye damage, but this appears to be a hoax. There is no basis for this allegation in the medical literature.

Although sunscreen is useful, it is no replacement for subprotective clothing. While a good sunscreen has an SPF of 15 or above, denim fabric has an SPF of 1700. In contrast, a white T-shirt only has an SPF of 15, and, when wet, has an effective SPF of only 10. Sunglasses are also useful for eye protection.

Resources

PERIODICALS

Chatelain E., B. Gabard, C. Surber. "Skin penetration and sun protection factor of five UV filters: Effect of the vehicle." *Skin Pharmacology and Applied Skin Physiology* 16, no. 1 (January-February 2003): 28–35.

WEB SITES

"Child Care Health Program: Sun Protection for Child Care Providers." Available online at <www.metrokc.gov/health/childcare/sunprotection.htm> (accessed September 29, 2004).

Emery, David. "Sunscreen Warning Doesn't Hold Water." Available online at <http://urbanlegends.about.com/library/weekly/aa070898.htm> (accessed September 29, 2004).

"Sun Screen." Available online at <www.keepkidshealthy.com/medicine_cabinet/sun_screens.html> (accessed September 29, 2004).

Nancy Ross-Flanigan
Samuel Uretsky, PharmD

Sunstroke *see* **Heat disorders**

Sweat test

Definition

A sweat test, sometimes called a sweat chloride test, is a procedure used to measure the amount of sodium and/or chloride (salt) excreted by a person's sweat glands.

Purpose

The sweat test is used to diagnosis **cystic fibrosis** (CF). CF is an incurable, inherited disorder that affects glands in the lungs, intestines, bile duct, and pancreas, as well as the sweat glands. The sweat test is administered as soon as CF is suspected, either because of **family** history or symptoms, such as frequent colds, recurrent lung infections, recurrent **diarrhea**, difficulty absorbing food, and slower-than-normal growth.

Because prompt diagnosis and treatment can often ease the severity of CF, sweat tests may be administered as early as the first week of life. This timing is recommended only when a family history of CF exists or the newborn exhibits symptoms specific to the disorder. However, newborns may not make enough sweat to accurately perform the test; hence, it may be repeated when they are older. Diagnosis of CF is made based on two or more sweat tests with abnormal chloride readings. Although sweat tests are highly accurate, diagnosis may be confirmed with genetic testing.

To have CF, a child must inherit a gene for the disorder from both parents. Because siblings of CF patients have a 25 percent chance of having the disorder, they should also be tested. However, the sweat test can determine only if the child has the disorder. It cannot determine whether a child is a carrier of a single CF gene that can be passed on to the next generation.

Description

Individuals with CF produce a higher than normal level of sodium chloride (salt) in their sweat. This measurement does not normally change with diet, medication, or environmental factors, making it a good diagnostic tool. The sweat test uses a process called iontophoresis. With iontophoresis, a very small, painless electric current is used to help draw sweat to the surface of the skin, where it can be collected and analyzed. The amount of electric current is tiny, and the test is safe and painless for all ages.

For infants a sweat test is done on the right thigh; for children and adults, the right forearm is used. After the area is washed and dried, two metal electrodes are attached and fastened with straps. Two gauze pads, one soaked in salt water or bicarbonate and the other in pilocarpine, a drug that stimulates sweating, are placed under the electrodes. A tiny electric current is applied to the skin for five to ten minutes to carry the pilocarpine into the skin. This stimulates the sweat glands to begin working. The procedure is painless; the child feels only a slight tingling or tickling.

After about ten minutes, the electrodes are removed. The skin is washed with distilled water and dried again. A dry piece of filter paper is taped to the area where the pilocarpine was applied. The paper is then covered with wax or a sheet of plastic, so that evaporation does not occur. The filter paper is called a sweat patch. After 30 to 45 minutes, the plastic is removed and the paper is placed in a sealed bottle. The entire process takes between 60 and 90 minutes.

It is important that the test be performed in a certified lab because the reliability of the test is operator-dependent. In the certified lab, the sweat patch is weighed and analyzed for sodium and/or chloride content. In children, normal sodium levels are less than 70 milliequivalents per milliliter (mEq/L). A sodium level greater than 90 mEq/L is indicative of CF. Normal chloride reading is less than 40 mEq/L. A chloride reading of greater than 60 mEq/L is indicative of CF. Readings falling between these numbers are borderline and require additional testing. Results are usually available within one to two working days.

Precautions

To ensure accuracy, sweat tests should be analyzed by a laboratory certified by the Cystic Fibrosis Foundation. Some other conditions such as malfunction of the adrenal gland or kidney failure can produce abnormal chloride readings. However, these conditions have distinct symptoms that differ substantially from CF. A sweat test is never used to diagnose these conditions.

Preparation

Before the sweat test, children should not **exercise** heavily or become overheated. There are no dietary restrictions; children may eat normally before the test. The results are not affected by medication; children may take their medication on the day of the test.

Aftercare

The test area may be red and sweaty for several hours after the test.

Risks

Although there is virtually no risk of electrical shock from a sweat test, it should never be conducted on the left side of the body, nor should it be given in the chest area, because there is a very small chance that the electric current could affect the heart. The current should come from a battery-powered unit rather than from a direct current.

Parental concerns

Parents can expect to stay with their child during the test.

See also Cystic fibrosis.

KEY TERMS

Iontophoresis— Application of a small electric current to the skin.

Resources

BOOKS

Bellet, Paul S. *The Diagnostic Approach to Symptoms and Signs in Pediatrics*, 2nd ed. Philadelphia: Lippincott Williams & Wilkins, 2002.

ORGANIZATIONS

Cystic Fibrosis Foundation. 6931 Arlington Road, Bethesda, MD 20814. Web site: <www.cff.org>.

WEB SITES

Goldenring, John. "Sweat Test." *MedlinePlus Encyclopedia*, 20 January 2004. Available online at <www.nlm.nih.gov/medlineplus/ency/article/003630.htm> (accessed August 5, 2004).

"Sweat Testing." *Living with CF*. Cystic Fibrosis Foundation, April 2001. Available online at <www.cff.org/living_with_cf/sweat_testing.cfm> (accessed August 5, 2004).

Tish Davidson, A.M.

Sweating, excessive *see* **Hyperhidrosis**

Swimmer's ear *see* **Otitis externa**

Swollen glands *see* **Lyme disease**

Syndactyly *see* **Polydactyly and syndactyly**

Syphilis, nonvenereal *see* **Bejel**

Syringomyelia *see* **Chiari malformation**

Talipes *see* **Clubfoot**

Tantrums

Definition

A tantrum is an episode of extreme anger and frustration characterized by crying, screaming, and violent body motions, including throwing things, falling to the floor, and banging one's head, hands, and feet against the floor.

Description

Tantrums, also called temper tantrums, can occur by the age of 15 months, but are most frequent between the ages of two and four. All children have them at some point, and active, strong-willed youngsters may have as many as one or two a week. Generally, tantrums are an expression of frustration. Children may be frustrated by their inability to perform an activity they are attempting, such as buttoning a coat. Tantrums may also be an expression of frustration at the lack of control children have over their lives, such as at bedtime when children want to continue playing instead of going to bed. Occasionally a tantrum may also be an attempt to gain attention from a parent or other caregiver, or it may be an attempt to manipulate the situation in some way.

Aside from taking any measures needed to prevent danger to children, parents should try to ignore the tantrum and let it run its course. If the upset has occurred over something the child wants and has been denied, it is tempting to give in to the child's wishes, but doing so can be harmful because it teaches children that they can get what they want by having a tantrum. Frequently, tantrums occur in a public place, which is especially unsettling for parents. Children become over stimulated or tire more easily in busy public spaces such as supermarkets and malls and may use the tantrum as an attempt to regain parental attention that is focused elsewhere. In spite of their embarrassment, parents should treat a public tantrum in essentially the same way they treat one at home. Whenever possible, they should remove the child to the car or some other private space to avoid inconveniencing others and attracting any more unwelcome attention, after which they should ignore the tantrum and let it run its course.

While a parent cannot stop tantrums once they are in progress, it is sometimes possible to prevent them by being alert to certain danger signs, especially fatigue, hunger, and irritability. In these cases, they can change plans to give the child a needed rest, food, or change of scene. For example, a child who is getting cranky at a party or other event at which the parent is present can be taken home early. The archetypal shopping tantrum over the candy bar at the checkout counter or the elaborate toy can sometimes be countered by proposing an alternative treat or purchase instead of the flat denial that sends the child into a tantrum. Emotional upsets that occur when children are left with a babysitter or at daycare are usually a sign of **separation anxiety** and can be alleviated by preparing children in advance for the separation and giving them the opportunity to become familiar with the babysitter or daycare setting ahead of time. Keeping walking trips short can prevent tantrums over a child's demand to be carried.

Toddlerhood

Children between the ages of two and four are the most likely to have tantrums and to have them the most often. They have not acquired the verbal skills necessary to adequately express their emotions or even, in many situations, to make themselves understood. In addition, they can only use words to demand what they want, not to negotiate for it. They love to explore, but often they do not understand which places or objects are off limits and are scolded as a result. Although they are developing rapidly, they still lack the motor skills to do many things they would like to do. They want to be independent but still require continuous supervision and assistance, and their preferences are often unrecognized, ignored, or refused by their caregivers. There is also a great deal of ambivalence and indecision associated with this stage of life, meaning that there is internal conflict as well as tension between the toddler and his or her environment. The tantrum occurs because the small child, who is still learning to cope with her feelings, is simply unable to contain strong emotions of anger, frustration, or disappointment. In some cases, children are actively discouraged from showing these feelings, which creates even more tension.

School-age children

School-age children tend to have tantrums less often, but many children still have them occasionally. At this age, frustration with inability to do homework may often be the cause of tantrums. Parents should let their child calm down and then offer to help them and give encouragement. It can be helpful to remind the child that the task that causes frustration will become easier to perform with practice. If the child has tantrums at school, a doctor's advice should be sought because it could be a symptom of other another problem such as a learning disability.

Common problems

Having tantrums is a normal part of growing up; however, they are not socially acceptable behavior. Consequently, the most common problems with tantrums are problems for the parents. The tantrums often take place in public, which can be embarrassing and make them harder to deal with calmly. If the child actually hurts himself or others or has very frequent tantrums, it may be a sign of behavior problems, and the child should be assessed by a pediatrician.

Parental concerns

Most children do not actually hurt themselves or others during tantrums, although it may seem like they are going to. Holding the breath cannot actually hurt a child; the child will breathe involuntarily before harm occurs. A child's tantrums can, however, challenge parents' ability to remain calm. Tantrums may occur in busy places such as restaurants and grocery stores, and the child is more likely to be tired. It can also be very distressing for parents to see the child so upset and out of control. Parents who are concerned about their ability to calmly deal with the child's temper tantrums may talk to the child's pediatrician about ways to cope more effectively with this natural part of the child's development.

When to call the doctor

The child's doctor should be called if the child hurts herself, the parent, other people, or objects during a tantrum. If the child has more than five tantrums a day, or the tantrums reoccur in school, the doctor should also be consulted.

See also Separation anxiety.

Resources

BOOKS

Kennedy, Michelle. *Tantrums.* Hauppauge, NY: Barrons, 2003.

Levy, Ray, and Bill O'Hanlon with Tyler Norris. *Try and Make Me!: Simple Strategies that Turn Off the Tantrums and Create Cooperation.* New York, NY: Rodale/Reach, 2001.

McComas, Jennifer J. *How to Deal Effectively with Whining and Tantrum Behavior.* Austin, TX: Pro-Ed, 2003.

PERIODICALS

Chance, Paul, and Jacob Azerrad. "Tantrums: The Psychology of Violent Children." *Current* (October 2001): 29.

Mlynlec, Vicky. "Forty Ways to Prevent Tantrums." *Parents Magazine* 77 (January 2002): 84.

Potegal, Michael, and Richard J. Davidson. "Temper Tantrums in Young Children." *Journal of Developmental & Behavioral Pediatrics* 24, no. 3 (June 2003): 140.

Tish Davidson, A.M.

Tattoos *see* **Piercing and tattoos**

Tay-Sachs disease

Definition

Tay-Sachs disease is a genetic disorder caused by a missing enzyme that results in the accumulation of a fatty substance in the nervous system. This disease causes disability and death.

Description

Gangliosides are fatty substances necessary for the proper development of the brain and nerve cells (nervous system). Under normal conditions, gangliosides are continuously broken down, so that an appropriate balance is maintained. In Tay-Sachs disease, the enzyme necessary

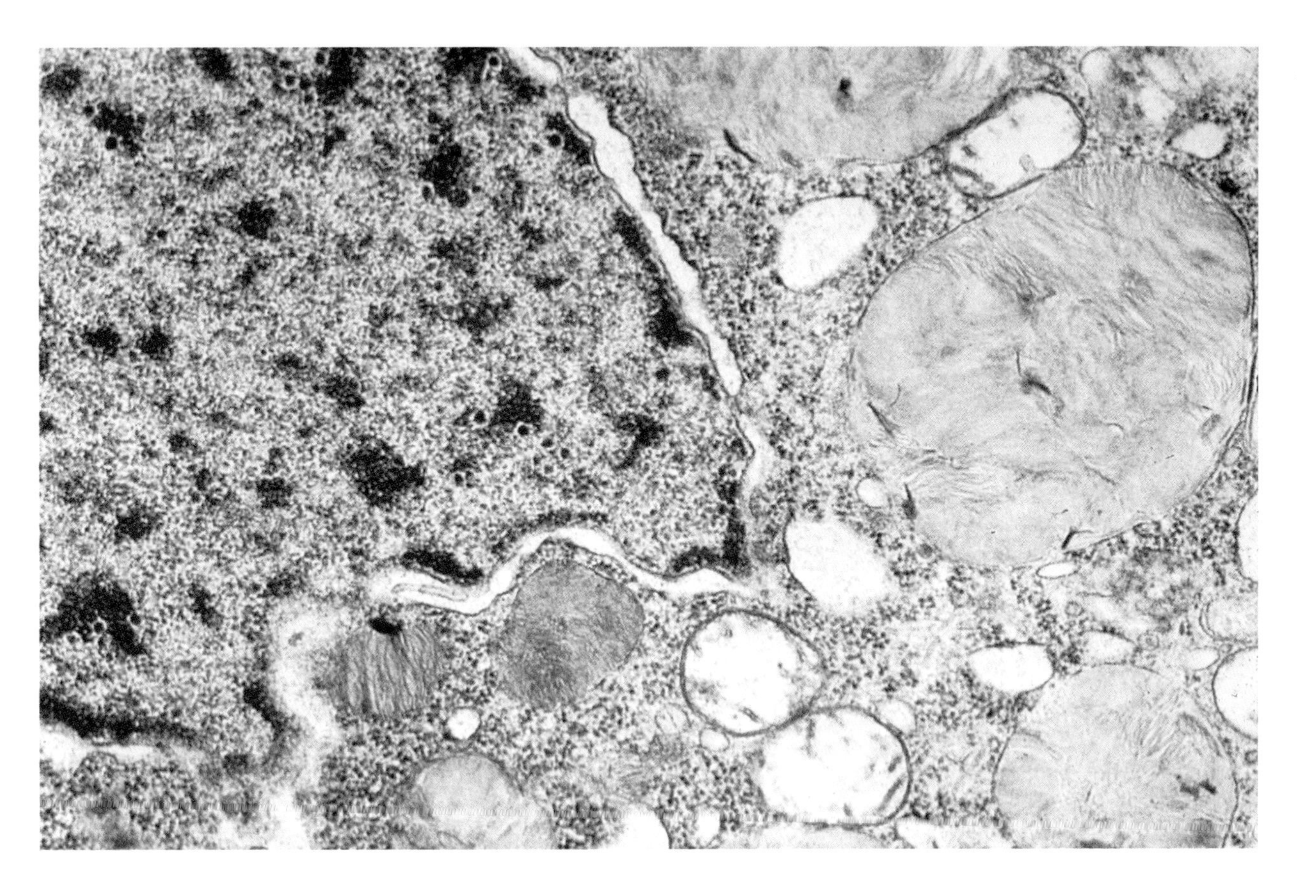

Section of brain tissue from patient with Tay-Sachs disease. *(© 1992 IMS Creative. Custom Medical Stock Photo, Inc.)*

for removing excess gangliosides is missing. This situation allows gangliosides to accumulate throughout the brain and is responsible for the disability associated with the disease.

Demographics

Tay-Sachs disease is particularly common among Jewish people of Eastern European and Russian (Ashkenazi) origin. About one out of every 2,500 to 3,600 babies born to Ashkenazi Jewish couples have the disease. In the general population about one out of every 320,000 babies born has Tay-Sachs disease. Approximately one in 30 Ashkenazi Jews is a carrier of the gene that causes the disease. Tay-Sachs is also more common among certain French-Canadian, Pennsylvania Dutch, and Cajun families.

Causes and symptoms

Tay-Sachs is caused by a defective gene. Genes are located on chromosomes and serve to direct specific developments and processes within the body. The genetic defect in Tay-Sachs disease results in the lack of an enzyme called hexosaminidase A. Without this enzyme, gangliosides cannot be broken down. They build up within the brain, interfering with nerve functioning. Because Tay-Sachs is a recessive disorder, only people who receive two defective genes (one from the mother and one from the father) will actually have the disease. People who have only one defective gene and one normal gene are called carriers. They carry the defective gene and thus the possibility of passing the gene and/or the disease onto their offspring.

When a carrier and a non-carrier have children, none of their children will actually have Tay-Sachs. The statistical probability is that 50 percent of their children will be carriers themselves. When two carriers have children, their children have a 25 percent chance of having normal genes, a 50 percent chance of being carriers of the defective gene, and a 25 percent chance of having two defective genes. Only the individual with two defective genes actually has the disease.

Classic Tay-Sachs disease strikes infants around the age of six months. Up until this age, the baby appears to develop normally. When Tay-Sachs begins to show itself, the baby stops interacting with other people and

KEY TERMS

Ganglioside—A fatty (lipid) substance found within the brain and nerve cells.

develops a staring gaze. Normal levels of noise startle the baby to an abnormal degree. By about one year of age, the baby has very weak, floppy muscles and may be completely blind. The head is quite large. Children with Tay-Sachs also have other symptoms, such as loss of peripheral (side) vision, inability to breathe and swallow, and paralysis as the disorder progresses. Seizures become a problem between ages one and two, and the baby usually dies by about age four.

A few variations from this classical progression of Tay-Sachs disease are possible:

- Juvenile hexosaminidase A deficiency: Symptoms appear between ages two and five; the disease progresses more slowly, with death by about 15 years.
- Chronic hexosaminidase A deficiency: Symptoms may begin around age five or may not occur until between 20 and 30 years of age. The disease is milder. Speech becomes slurred. The individual may have difficulty walking due to weakness, **muscle cramps**, and decreased coordination of movements. Some individuals develop mental illness. Many have changes in intellect, hearing, or vision.

When to call the doctor

If the child has any noticeable problems that might be associated with Tay-Sachs disease or appears to stop developing normally after a period of normal development, the doctor should be consulted.

Diagnosis

Examination of the eyes of a child with Tay-Sachs disease reveals a characteristic cherry-red spot at the back of the eye in an area called the retina. Tests to determine the presence and quantity of hexosaminidase A can be performed on the blood, specially treated skin cells, or white blood cells. A carrier has about half the normal level of hexosaminidase A present, while an individual with the disease has no hexosaminidase A at all.

Treatment

Providing good, supportive care and treating the symptoms as they arise is the only way to treat Tay-Sachs; there is no way to treat the disease itself.

Prognosis

The prognosis for a child with classic Tay-Sachs disease is death. Because the chronic form of Tay-Sachs was discovered near the end of the 2000s, prognosis for this type of the disease was, as of 2004, not completely known.

Prevention

There is no known way to prevent Tay-Sachs disease. It is, however, possible to identify carriers of the disease and provide them with genetic counseling and appropriate information concerning the chance of their offspring having Tay-Sachs disease. When the levels of hexosaminidase A are half the normal level, a person is a carrier of the defective gene. Blood tests of carriers reveal reduction of hexosaminidase A.

When a woman is already pregnant, tests can be performed on either the cells of the fetus (**amniocentesis**) or the placenta (chorionic villus sampling) to determine whether the baby will have Tay-Sachs disease.

Parental concerns

If parents are thinking of having a child and believe they might be carriers of Tay-Sachs, they should be screened so that they can assess their options. Children born with infantile Tay-Sachs, even with the best available care, usually die before the age of five. Children born with juvenile Tay-Sachs usually die before the age of 15.

Resources

BOOKS

Behrman, Richard E., Robert M. Kliegman, and Hal B. Jenson. *Nelson Textbook of Pediatrics*, 17th ed. Philadelphia: Saunders, 2004.

Desnick, Robert, and Michael M. Kaback, eds. *Tay-Sachs Disease*. San Diego, CA: Academic, 2001.

ORGANIZATIONS

March of Dimes Birth Defects Foundation. 1275 Mamaroneck Avenue, White Plains, NY 10605. Web site: <www.modimes.org>.

National Tay-Sachs and Allied Diseases Association. 2001 Beacon Street, Suite 204, Brighton, MA 02135. Web site: <www.ntsad.org>.

Tish Davidson, A.M.

Teething *see* **Dental development**

Television habits

Definition

Television habits consist of patterns of behavior determined by the amount of time and importance individuals give to watching television broadcasts and recorded videos and DVDs.

Description

Ever since the late 1940s when television first became available, social scientists have been interested in its effect on behavior. Originally seen as entertainment for adults and older children, television in the twenty-first century is watched by all age groups, including infants. More than 98 percent of homes in the United States have at least one television set. Many have more. One study found that 32 percent of children ages two to seven had television sets in their bedroom. This number increased to 65 percent for children ages eight to 18.

Although television can be an educational tool for children, exposing them to information and situations that they cannot experience first hand, social scientists and the American Academy of Pediatrics (AAP) have raised specific concerns about the effect of television watching on child development. Areas of concern include:

- inability of young children to distinguish between television fantasy and reality
- exposure to television violence, especially where violence is not shown to have any serious consequences
- exposure to age-inappropriate sexual situations
- effect of advertising on children
- glamorization of unrealistic body images
- promotion of alcohol use and the glamorization of cigarette and cigar smoking
- increased **obesity** when passive television watching replaces active **play**
- time taken away from school work and traditional hobby activities
- the short, segmented, hyperactive nature of children's television programming that may decrease attention span and contribute to attention deficit disorder (ADD) in children
- verifiable health risks of excessive television watching to children as concluded by the AAP

Factors that increase the likelihood of heavy television viewing by children include low socioeconomic status, living in a single parent household, and being born to a teenage mother. Viewing time is also increased by parental beliefs that television viewing does not hurt children and improves their vocabulary and imagination. Heavy parental television viewing, multiple television sets at home, television in the child's bedroom, and using television to distract young children all increase the likelihood that children will become heavy television and video watchers.

Infancy

Before the 1990s, few television programs were designed for children under the age of three. However, the success of programs such as "Teletubbies" aimed at children under age two, opened a new market to programmers. As of 2004, studies showed that by the age of 11 months, infants are watching a combined average of 75 minutes of television programming and videos daily. Between the ages of 12 and 23 months, this amount increases to almost two hours daily.

In the first two years of life the brain develops rapidly, and children learn new physical, mental, and social skills. Infants need interaction with caregivers who respond to them and interact with them. Watching television is a passive activity that does not meet these needs. The AAP recommends that television and video viewing for children under age two be discouraged and severely limited. They suggest that reading, singing, playing, and interacting with adults fosters proper, age-appropriate brain development that can be inhibited by too much television watching. They recommend that televisions be removed from childcare areas, because they are a distraction to both caregivers and children.

Toddlerhood

By the age of three, the average American child is watching more than two hours of television and videos daily. Toddlerhood is a time when motor skills develop and children begin actively moving and exploring their environment. Pediatricians are concerned that television time takes away from activities needed for physical and mental development. They recommend children of this age watch only a few selected programs or videos, after which the television should be turned off.

Preschool

Many educational programs such as "Sesame Street" are aimed at preschoolers. Properly selected and watched in moderation, these programs can increase reading readiness and number awareness and promote positive social behavior such as sharing and taking turns.

However, preschoolers are highly influenced by advertisements on commercial television. Until the age of about eight, children lack the ability to differentiate between fantasy and reality both in programming and in advertising. In addition, a three-year study of television violence found that nearly 66 percent of television programs contain violence and that children's television programs contain the most violence of all programming. **Preschool** children are often frightened by what they see on television, including the news.

School age

American school-age children watch on average 4.5 hours of television a day. Repeated studies have shown that children who watch a lot of television perform more poorly in school. In addition, there is a definite link between television watching and childhood obesity. The link is strongest among African-American and Latino children. This link is thought to result from several causes. First, television viewing is a passive activity. Children who are watching are not actively playing or exercising. Second, there is a strong tendency to eat snacks while watching television, compounding the problem. Third, advertising is often aimed at promoting high calorie, less healthful foods. The eating habits of children who watch a lot of television are influenced by this advertising.

School-age children are also influenced by the content of the programming they watch. Many studies have linked real-life violence to the repeated viewing of violence on television. Some experts theorize that children become immune to violence after seeing it repeatedly on television. For example, the average child will have seen over 8,000 television murders before finishing grade school. Other experts believe that because the hero uses violence to triumph as much as 80 percent of the time on television, children develop the idea that force is an acceptable way to solve problems. Finally, the aftermath of violence and the harm it does are rarely shown in a realistic way on television. Although television is not the only cause of social violence, most social scientists believe it is a significant contributing factor. Likewise, television's portrayal of sexual situations and the lack of on-screen consequences of sexual activity, the promotion of unrealistic body image, stereotypical gender roles, and under-representation of minorities have been found in multiple studies to promote unhealthy and unrealistic views among children and adolescents.

Common problems

The most common problems surrounding television viewing involve children being frightened by what they see, substituting television watching for health interactions with friends and **family**, and viewing material that is age-inappropriate.

Parental concerns

The most common parental concern surrounding television habits is controlling the amount and quality of television a child watches. Often parents who are heavy television viewers themselves see nothing wrong with turning on the television in the morning and letting it stay on all day. They may also be unwilling to give up watching their favorite programs, even when these programs are age-inappropriate for their children. This problem can be solved by taping programs for later viewing after children are asleep.

The new television rating system and v-chip technology required by law in all televisions with a 13-inch screen or larger manufactured after 2000 is intended to help parents control what their children watch by allowing them to lock out certain programs. However, studies have shown that very few parents understand or use the television rating system in determining what their children may see and that very few actually use the v-chip technology to lock out specific programs.

The American Academy of Pediatrics suggests the following steps to parents for controlling the television viewing habits of their children.

- Watch only specific programs; do not turn the television on and let it run.
- Remove televisions from children's bedrooms.
- Limit television viewing to two hours or less daily.
- Do not watch television during meals.
- Watch television with children and discuss what is shown.
- Substitute reading time or play time for television time.
- Teach children the difference between advertisements and program content.

When to call the doctor

Parents may want to consider seeking the advice of a pediatrician and/or child and adolescent psychiatrist if

Healthy television habits
Limit television viewing to a maximum of two hours per day.
Plan programs to watch by looking in the TV guide ahead of time.
Keep videotapes or DVDs of children's programming on hand as a backup when there is nothing appropriate for children on television.
Keep television sets out of children's rooms.
Keep the television off during meals.
Watch shows with your child, and discuss them afterward.
Criticize the negative behaviors that some TV characters exhibit, such as violence or smoking.
Explain that commercials are designed to make the viewer want something, and that not all advertised products are good or needed.
SOURCE: American Academy of Pediatrics and National Institute on Media and the Family, 2002.

(Table by GGS Information Services.)

their child appears addicted to television and videos. **Addiction** may be suggested if watching television takes priority over schoolwork and family interactions and replaces normal social activities with friends. Parents should also be concerned if they feel their child is developing unrealistic expectations about body image from television or is excessively attracted to and talks about imitating violent, gory events on television or in the movies.

Resources

PERIODICALS

American Academy of Pediatrics. "Children, Adolescents, and Television." *Journal of Pediatrics* 107, no. 2 (February 2001): 423–426.

American Academy of Pediatrics, Committee on Public Education. "Media Violence." *Journal of Pediatrics* 108, no. 5 (November 2001): 1017–1025.

Robinson, Thomas N. "Television Viewing and Childhood Obesity." *Pediatric Clinics of North America* 48, no. 4 (August 2001): 855–78.

Strasburber, Victor C. "Alcohol Advertising and Adolescents." *Pediatric Clinics of North America* 49, no. 2 (April 2002): 353–76.

Villani, Susan. "Impact of Media on Children and Adolescents: A 10-Year Review of the Research." *Journal of the American Academy of Child and Adolescent Psychiatry* 10, no.4 (April 2001): 392–401.

Yasgur, Batya S. "Parents See TV as Beneficial for Infants and Toddlers." *Family Practice News* (January 15, 2001). Available online at <www.findarticles.com/p/articles/mi_m0BJI/is_2_31/ai_70649956> (accessed September 30, 2004).

ORGANIZATIONS

American Academy of Pediatrics. 141 Northwest Point Boulevard, Elk Grove Village, IL 60007–1098. Web site: <www.aap.org>.

Tish Davidson, A.M.

Temper tantrums *see* **Tantrums**

Temperament

Definition

Individual differences in human motivation and emotion that appear early in life, usually thought to be biological in origin. Temperament is sometimes considered the biological or physiological component of personality, which refers to the sum total of the physical, emotional, mental, spiritual, and social dimensions of an individual.

Description

History

Ancient Greek and Roman physicians invoked nature, claiming that the proportions of the various humors or fluids in the bodies influenced personality. They thought that there were four basic temperaments—sanguine (cheerful), choleric (irritable), melancholic (gloomy), and phlegmatic (apathetic)—which were determined by the predominance of blood, yellow bile, black bile, and phlegm respectively in the person's physical constitution. The ancient theory survives in the form of such expressions as "being in a bad (or good) humor."

The theory of four bodily humors did not survive the rise of scientific medicine in the seventeenth century as an explanation for differences in human temperament, but it has not been replaced by any single universally accepted theory of personality either. During most of the twentieth century, political ideology, discoveries about the learning or conditioning capabilities of infants, and the emergence of psychoanalytic theory, which emphasized the importance of early experience, all combined to discredit biological explanations for human motivation and emotion. Nurture and socialization became the favored explanations of differences in temperament.

There was, however, a resurgence of interest in the contribution of temperament to children's development after the 1950s. Temperament came to be summarized as the biological dimension of personality. It was seen as a predisposition that allows two individuals to experience the same objective event very differently within the range of normal behavior and development.

Specific approaches to temperament

THE NEW YORK LONGITUDINAL STUDY Suspecting that inherent individual differences among their young patients contributed to their developmental paths, two child psychiatrists, Alexander Thomas and Stella Chess, designed a study that challenged the nature-nurture dichotomy. Beginning in 1956 and ultimately publishing their research in Temperament and Development in 1977, Thomas and Chess collected longitudinal data from over 100 children, following them from infancy through early adulthood. Using extensive clinical interviews to gather information about children's behavior as well as parents' values and expectations, they examined what they termed the goodness of fit between the individual child and his or her environment.

Thomas and Chess found that children could be rated on each of nine dimensions even in infancy:

- Activity level: The child's general level of energy and movement—whether he or she is quiet, always "on the go," or somewhere in-between.
- Rhythmicity: The child's regular biological patterns of appetite and sleep—whether the child gets hungry or tired at predictable times.
- Approach/withdrawal: The child's usual response to new people or situations—whether the child is eager for new experiences or shy and hesitant.
- Adaptability: The child's ability and pace in adjusting to changes in schedules or transitions from one activity to another.
- Threshold of responsiveness: The child's level of sensitivity to such physical stimuli as sounds, smells, and lights. For example, some children are easily startled by sudden noises while others are less sensitive to them. Some children are pickier about food than others.
- Intensity: The child's responses to people or events. Some children react strongly and loudly to even minor events while others are less demonstrative or openly emotional.
- Quality of mood: The child's overall worldview, whether positive or negative. Some children tend to focus on the negative aspects of a situation while others are more positive or hopeful. Some children tend to approach life in a serious or analytical fashion while others respond to their immediate impressions of situations.
- Distractibility: The child's ability to pay attention to tasks or instructions even when the child is not particularly interested in them. Some children have shorter attention spans than others.
- Persistence: The child's ability to continue with an activity in the face of obstacles or problems. Some children are more easily discouraged by difficulties than others.

Thomas and Chess combined the patterns of children's ratings on each of these nine dimensions to distinguish three major temperamental types:

- Easy children: About 40 percent of the NYLS sample displayed a temperamental profile marked by regularity, ease of approach to new stimuli, adaptability to change, mild to moderate mood intensity, and a generally positive mood. This profile characterizes what Thomas and Chess call the easy child.
- Difficult children: About 10 percent of children showed a very different profile and were called difficult children. They had irregular patterns of eating and sleeping, withdrew from new stimuli, did not adapt easily to change, and reacted intensely to changes. Their overall mood was often negative.
- Slow-to-adapt children: Children who were slow to warm up comprised the third temperamental group, about 15 percent of Thomas and Chess's sample. These children tended to withdraw from new stimuli and had difficulty adapting to change, but their reactions were of mild intensity and gradually became either neutral or positive with repeated exposures to the new event or person.

Some researchers prefer the terms flexible, active or feisty, and cautious instead of the somewhat judgmental terms of easy, difficult, and slow-to-adapt, respectively.

Clearly, these three temperamental types that Thomas and Chess identified did not include all of the variations seen in children across the entire sample. About one third of the children showed mixed profiles. Nonetheless, these temperamental classifications became highly influential in child development research. Perhaps the greatest contribution of the NYLS, however, was Thomas and Chess's emphasis on "goodness of fit"; that is, they maintained that the child's temperament by itself was not the most important consideration in his or her growth and development, but the extent to which that temperament agreed with the values, expectations, and style of the child's environment, whether **family**, child-care setting, school, or culture. For example, a quiet and serious child fits in well with a family of scholars or intellectuals, whereas an intense, active, and easily distracted child may not be accepted as readily in the same family context. In terms of culture, some ethnic groups place a high value on self-control and relating well to others, while other groups emphasize assertiveness and independence. A child who has a high energy level and reacts intensely to persons and events will have a better fit with the second group than with the first. The notion of goodness of fit also helps to explain why some children in a given family seem to get along better with their parents than their siblings do. Even though temperament is thought to be rooted in biology, different children in the same family may have very different temperaments.

TRAIT APPROACHES Some approaches to the study of temperament emphasize traits; that is, they assume that temperamental qualities can be rated as persisting within individuals across time in a variety of situations. In 1984, as published in their book, *Temperament: Early Developing Personality Traits*, Arnold Buss and others considered temperaments to be heritable and stable personality profiles—profiles that are genetically influenced and relatively unchanging over time. These researchers used maternal questionnaires to gather information on children's emotionality, activity, and sociability, traits they regarded as the fundamental dimensions of temperament. Interestingly, Buss and Plomin suggested that children who are rated as extreme on these dimensions may be qualitatively different from those whose scores lie closer to the middle.

Basic emotions were at the core of H. Hill Goldsmith and Joseph Campos's conception of temperament. In 1983, in an essay included in *Socio-Emotional Development,* they described temperament in terms of individual differences in experiencing and expressing such primary emotions as anger, **fear**, and pleasure. Goldsmith and Campos, however, emphasized the speed and intensity of children's responses to stimuli as well as the specific emotions involved. Their evaluations were based on three measurements: threshold (the amount of stimulation the child requires before responding); latency to respond (how rapidly the child reacts to the stimulus); and intensity of response.

In 2004, Mary Rothbart emphasized reactivity and self-regulation as core processes in organizing temperamental profiles. These processes, she believed, can be seen in six significant infant behaviors: smiling; distress when confronted by limitations; fear; activity level; soothability, and duration of orienting (how long the baby plays with or pays attention to a single object). Her Infant Behavior Questionnaire (IBQ), which was developed in the early 1980s, remained, as of 2004, one of the most widely used methods of assessing temperament in infants between the ages of three months and 12 months. In the first version of the IBQ, published in 1981, parents were asked to rate the frequency of these temperament-related behaviors in their child over a two-week period. The revised version of the IBQ, known as the IBQ-R, was developed by Rothbart and her colleague Masha Gartstein in the early 2000s. The IBQ-R expanded the original six measures of temperament to 14. The new measurements include the following:

- Approach: The infant's excitement and looking forward to a pleasurable experience or activity.
- Vocal reactivity: The baby's level of vocal responses to stimuli in its daily routine.
- Perceptual sensitivity: The infant's ability to detect low-intensity stimuli in its environment.
- Sadness.
- High-intensity pleasure: The infant's reactions to pleasurable stimuli or activities of high intensity, such as loud music or bright lights.
- Low-intensity pleasure.
- Cuddliness: The infant's physical and emotional responses to being held or cuddled by a parent or caregiver.
- Rate of recovery from distress: How long it takes the infant to return to a normal level of emotion after an exciting or upsetting experience and how readily the child falls asleep.

In contrast to Goldsmith and Campos, Rothbart emphasized cognitive processes in children as the key to understanding temperament rather than emotions by themselves. For Rothbart and her colleagues, the infant's ability to focus its attention is the basis of its later ability to regulate its reactions to people and events. In Rothbart's view, what she calls the attentional system allows the child to regulate his or her outward behavior as well as internal reactions to stimuli. As children mature, they develop the ability to turn their attention to alternative strategies when they are frustrated and to make plans in order to achieve their goals. Different patterns of self-regulation in turn help to explain differences in temperament.

Goldsmith and Rothbart collaborated to develop an **assessment** tool to gauge temperamental dimension based on systematic observations of behaviors elicited under standard laboratory conditions (for example, how a child reacts to a mechanical spider). The development of an observational protocol or test for assessing temperamental characteristics offers an advantage over reliance on questionnaires. When parents describe their children's behavior, they are influenced by their feelings about the child as well as their observations. In addition, the parents' reports include many sources of information such that reports of the child's behavior cannot be easily separated from the parents' biases, values, or expectations.

TYPE APPROACHES Another major approach to the study of temperament distinguishes among types of people characterized by different patterns of behavior. In the 1990s, in *Galen's Prophecy*, Jerome Kagan and his colleagues studied two types of children whom they defined as inhibited and uninhibited (or exuberant) respectively. Kagan's group studied the development of these two types of children through **adolescence** as well as the infant profiles that predicted the children's behavior at later ages. At early ages, inhibited children cling to their mothers and may cry and hesitate when confronted with unfamiliar persons or events. These children appear to be timid and shy and represent about 20 percent of volunteer Caucasian samples. Uninhibited or exuberant children, on the other hand, approach new events and persons without hesitation or trepidation. They appear fearless and sociable and represent about 40 percent of volunteer samples. Kagan's observations of these children over time indicated that these characteristic profiles tended to continue, although the display of temperamental tendencies varied in accordance with the child's developmental level. An older inhibited child or teenager, for example, may not cling to his or her mother or cry when coming to an unfamiliar laboratory but may hesitate to talk to the examiner and may smile infrequently.

Interestingly, Kagan found that the behavioral profiles of these children were accompanied by physiologic profiles that suggested different levels of reactivity in the children's central nervous systems, particularly in regard to fear and stress reactions. Inhibited, compared to uninhibited, children tended to have higher and more stable heart rates, higher levels of stress-related hormones like cortisol and norephinephrine, larger changes in blood pressure in response to stressors, and measurable tension in their voices when speaking under mildly stressful conditions. These differences seemed to support the contention that temperamental categories have a biological dimension.

Although young infants are not sufficiently mature to demonstrate timidity in response to new experiences, the reactivity of the structures in the human nervous system that are thought to underlie inhibited and uninhibited temperaments may appear at early ages. When infants are exposed to variations in the sights and sounds in their environment, some become aroused and demonstrate this arousal by moving their arms and legs and fretting or crying. Other infants remain calm, relatively motionless, and do not cry. Those who are highly reactive to stimulation tend to become inhibited in their reactions to novelty and uncertainty at later ages. Those whose reactivity level is low in infancy tend to grow into children who remain relaxed in novel situations so that they appear outgoing and uninhibited.

MALLEABILITY OF TEMPERAMENT Malleability refers to the extent to which temperament can be influenced or reshaped by later life events. The reader should note that the continuity of temperamental profiles from infancy through later ages is a group phenomenon; that is, individual children may change and become more or less inhibited while the groups of children remain distinct on average. Neither temperament nor biology is destiny. Temperament and environment both influence development, although relatively few researchers have studied the interaction of these two influences as of the early 2000s.

Research in early 2000s about temperament

In the early 2000s, research on temperament in children and adolescents is making use of new brain imaging technology to expand understanding of the biological processes that influence emotional self-regulation and task-related activities. This technology is known as functional **magnetic resonance imaging** (fMRI). Functional magnetic resonance imaging is based on the fact that activity in a specific part of the brain is accompanied by an increased flow of blood to that region. As the blood flow increases, the amount of deoxyhemoglobin, a form of hemoglobin that has lost its oxygen content, decreases in the affected area of the brain. Since the amount of deoxyhemoglobin in the blood affects the magnetic resonance image signal, it can be used as the source of the signal for fMRI. This discovery means that fMRI studies can be conducted without injecting radioactive materials into a subject's blood. In addition, it means that usable MRI images can be obtained in a very short period of time (1.5–2 minutes on average) rather than the longer periods of testing required when radioactive materials are used.

FMRI has many beneficial applications, ranging from more accurate planning for brain surgery to more effective **pain management**. In terms of the study of temperament, fMRI allows researchers to study such complex brain activities as problem-solving as well as visual and auditory (hearing) perception. In 2003, the National Institute of Mental Health (NIMH) began a study that uses fMRI technology on 60 children and adolescents between the ages of nine and 16. The study is designed to test the hypothesis that differences in temperament related to differences in brain functioning put some children at an increased risk of certain psychiatric disorders later in life. The type of child that Kagan's research group identified as inhibited, for example, appears to have the same pattern of disturbed nerve cell activity that has been identified in adults diagnosed with mood or **anxiety** disorders. Specifically, inhibited children seem to have a higher level of activity in a part of the brain called the amygdala, which regulates emotion, and a lower than average level of activity in the prefrontal cortex, which governs a person's ability to express emotions. Exuberant children, on the other hand, are thought to have a relatively high level of activity in the prefrontal cortex in response to certain stimuli.

In addition to its usefulness in studying the parts of the brain that are activated by sensory perception, thinking, and emotional responses to various stimuli, fMRI may also be helpful in distinguishing between problem behaviors in children that are rooted in temperament and behaviors that indicate a psychological problem. As of the early 2000s, research in the area of temperament has not been closely coordinated with research in childhood psychiatric disorders; as a result, both the causes and treatments of these disorders were, as of 2004, not well understood. Child psychiatrists have already observed that avoidant personality disorder (APD) and generalized anxiety disorder (GAD) are closely linked to the inhibited type of temperament as described in Kagan's work. To give another example, such temperamental traits as irritability and strong negative reactivity are thought to contribute to the development of **oppositional defiant disorder** in some children. Lastly, attention deficit/hyperactivity disorder is thought to be heavily influenced by genetic factors affecting the child's temperament, including the production and metabolism of certain neurotransmitters in the brain that affect the child's ability to focus his or her attention.

Common problems

The following are some of the problems that may arise in connection with differences in children's temperaments:

- Parents tend to regard certain characteristics as negative rather than as potentially positive. For example, a child's slowness to adapt may be seen as a drawback rather than as a protection against the dangers of impetuosity or being overly influenced by peer pressure.
- Behavioral problems are related to a poor fit between parent and child. Pediatricians often see families in which a vicious circle of negative interactions develops. The most common example is an angry reaction to a difficult child's aggressiveness or restlessness that takes the form of scolding or spanking. The child reacts to the parents' negative actions by increased aggressiveness, temper **tantrums**, or stubbornness. Another common pattern is the shy or inhibited child who becomes even more withdrawn when parents react to the **shyness** by lecturing or shaming the child.
- Favoritism becomes a factor when some parents find it much easier to relate to a child with a flexible temperament or one whose temperament matches their own than to a child who does not fit in as well. They may ignore the child they find less agreeable or punish him or her unfairly.

Parental concerns

Common parental concerns about evaluations of their children's temperament include the following:

- Fears about labeling or stigmatization: Some parents are concerned about the reactions of teachers or other adults if their child is identified as "difficult." This fear is one reason why some researchers prefer to describe children in this category as "active" or "feisty" rather than to use the negative term difficult.
- Concerns about fairness: Parents whose children have different temperaments are sometimes concerned that treating the children differently will be perceived as unfair or unjust.
- Concerns about the parent-child bond: Some parents worry about their ability to relate to a child with a difficult temperament or one whose temperament is different from their own. They may feel guilty about their negative emotional reactions toward such a child and doubt their ability to be good parents.

When to call the doctor

As has already been mentioned, it is not always easy for parents to distinguish between a child with a "difficult" temperament whose behaviors are still within the normal range and a child with a psychiatric disorder. Some guidelines that have been given by pediatricians include the following:

- The specific problem behavior(s) cannot be attributed to the child's developmental stage (such as "the terrible twos").
- The child's problematic behaviors occur frequently.
- The child has several problematic behaviors.
- The child's behaviors are interfering with his or her social and intellectual development.

KEY TERMS

Amygdala—An almond-shaped brain structure in the limbic system that is activated in stressful situations to trigger the emotion of fear. It is thought that the emotional overreactions in Alzheimer's patients are related to the destruction of neurons in the amygdala.

Cortisol—A steroid hormone secreted by the adrenal cortex that is important for maintenance of body fluids, electrolytes, and blood sugar levels. Also called hydrocortisone.

Goodness of fit—A term first used by Thomas and Chess to describe the importance of children's interactions with their environment as well as their basic temperament in understanding their later growth and development.

Inhibited—A type of child defined by Jerome Kagan and his colleagues as having a low level of responsiveness to strangers, a reluctance to initiate activities, and requiring a long time to relax in new situations. Children with inhibited temperaments appear to be more susceptible to anxiety disorders, depression, and certain personality disorders in their later years.

Malleability—A term that refers to the adaptability of human temperament; the extent to which it can be reshaped.

Neurotransmitter—A chemical messenger that transmits an impulse from one nerve cell to the next.

Norepinephrine—A hormone secreted by certain nerve endings of the sympathetic nervous system, and by the medulla (center) of the adrenal glands. Its primary function is to help maintain a constant blood pressure by stimulating certain blood vessels to constrict when the blood pressure falls below normal.

Personality—The organized pattern of behaviors and attitudes that makes a human being distinctive. Personality is formed by the ongoing interaction of temperament, character, and environment.

Protocol—A plan for carrying out a scientific study or a patient s course of treatment.

Reactivity—The level or intensity of a person's physical or emotional excitability.

Temperament—A person's natural disposition or inborn combination of mental and emotional traits.

Threshold—The minimum level of stimulation necessary to produce a response.

Trait—A distinguishing feature of an individual.

Type—A category used to define personality, usually based on a theory of some kind. Inhibited and uninhibited are examples of personality types.

See also Attention-deficit/hyperactivity disorder (ADHD); Magnetic resonance imaging; Personality development.

Resources

BOOKS

"Behavioral Problems." Section 19, chapter 262 in *The Merck Manual of Diagnosis and Therapy*, edited by Mark H. Beers and Robert Berkow. Whitehouse Station, NJ: Merck Research Laboratories, 2002.

Diagnostic and Statistical Manual of Mental Disorders, 4th ed., text revision. Washington, DC: American Psychiatric Association, 2000.

PERIODICALS

Austin, A. A., and B. F. Chorpita. "Temperament, Anxiety, and Depression: Comparison Across Five Ethnic Groups of Children." *Journal of Clinical Child and Adolescent Psychology* 33 (June 2004): 216–26.

Frick, P. J. "Integrating Research on Temperament and Childhood Psychopathology: Its Pitfalls and Promise." *Journal of Clinical Child and Adolescent Psychology* 33 (March 2004): 2–7.

Hyde, J. S., et al. "Children's Temperament and Behavior Problems Predict Their Employed Mothers' Work Functioning." *Child Development* 75 (March-April 2004): 580–94.

Lonigan, C. J., et al. "Temperament, Anxiety, and the Processing of Threat-Relevant Stimuli." *Journal of Clinical Child and Adolescent Psychology* 33 (March 2004): 8–20.

ORGANIZATIONS

American Academy of Child and Adolescent Psychiatry (AACAP). 3615 Wisconsin Avenue, NW, Washington, DC 20016–3007. Web site: <www.aacap.org.>.

American Psychological Association (APA). 750 First Street NE, Washington DC 20002. Web site: <www.apa.org>.

National Institute of Mental Health (NIMH), Office of Communications. 6001 Executive Boulevard, Room 8184, MSC 9663, Bethesda, MD 20892–9663. Web site: <www.nimh.nih.gov>.

WEB SITES

"The Future Role of Functional MRI in Medical Applications." *About Functional MRI (General).*

Available online at <www.fmri.org> (accessed November 5, 2004).

Larsen, Lene Holm, and Carrie Sylvester. "Anxiety Disorder: Generalized Anxiety." *eMedicine*. Available online at <www.emedicine.com/ped/topic2658.htm> (accessed November 5, 2004).

Lubit, Roy. "Posttraumatic Stress Disorder in Children." *eMedicine*. Available online at <www.emedicine.com/ped/topic3026.htm> (accessed November 5, 2004).

Montauk, Susan Louisa, and Christine Mayhall. "Attention-Deficit/Hyperactivity Disorder." *eMedicine*. Available online at <www.emedicine.com/ped/topic177.htm> (accessed November 5, 2004).

"The Psychobiology of Childhood Temperament." *National Institutes of Mental Health (NIMH) Clinical Trials*. Available online at <www.clinicaltrials.gov/ct/gui/show/NCT00060775> (accessed November 5, 2004).

Tynan, W. Douglas. "Oppositional Defiant Disorder." *eMedicine*. Available online at <www.emedicine.com/ped/topic2791.htm> (accessed November 5, 2004).

Doreen Arcus, PhD

Testicular torsion

Definition

Testicular torsion is the twisting of a testis (testicle) such that the spermatic cord becomes twisted, cutting off blood flow to the testis.

Description

The testes are suspended in the scrotum by a single bundle of tissues called the spermatic cord. Normally this bundle of tissue holds the testes in place. Each testis receives blood through the spermatic cord. When the testicle is not held firmly in place it can twist, creating a kink in the spermatic cord. When this happens blood supply to the testis is cut off. The resulting situation is an emergency, because the testis will die within hours if the blood supply is not restored.

Demographics

There is approximately one case of testicular torsion in every 4,000 men under age 25 in the United States. There are two times in life when torsion is most common, although it can occur at any age. Testicular torsion is most common in the first year of life and during **adolescence**. Torsion is more common in adolescents that it is in newborns.

Causes and symptoms

Testicular torsion is caused by the rotating of the testicle is such a way that the blood flow to it is cut off. Symptoms of testicular torsion are sudden severe **pain** in the scrotum, swelling and/or discoloration of the scrotum, **nausea**, and **vomiting**. Approximately 40 percent of patients with testicular torsion reported having a similar pain sometime before, but at that time the pain resolved without treatment.

When to call the doctor

Testicular torsion is an emergency, and the child should be taken to the doctor or emergency room immediately if he shows the signs or symptoms of testicular torsion. The chance that the testicle will be saved is directly linked to how long the testicle is without blood flow. If the torsion occurs for less than six hours, there is a high chance the testicle can be saved. If the torsion occurs for more than 24 hours, it is very unlikely that the testicle can be saved.

Diagnosis

The doctor usually first performs a visual examination of the scrotum. The affected testis may appear to be slightly higher than the unaffected one. The scrotum may be swollen or discolored. If the doctor is unsure, diagnostic tests may also be performed.

One such diagnostic test is a nuclear scan of the scrotum. In this procedure, a tiny amount of radioactive fluid is injected into the blood and detected as it flows through the scrotum and testicles. Torsion is indicated if the radioactive fluid does not flow through the sore testis. Ultrasound scan accompanied by a contrast agent can also be used to diagnose testicular torsion. Other diagnostic tests may be performed to help the doctor determine if torsion has occurred.

Treatment

Surgery performed within the first six hours has an 80 to 100 percent chance of saving the affected testis. This likelihood goes down the longer blood flow to the testis has been cut off. After 24 hours, it is very unlikely that the testicle can be saved. During the procedure, the surgeon untwists the cord and secures the testis in place

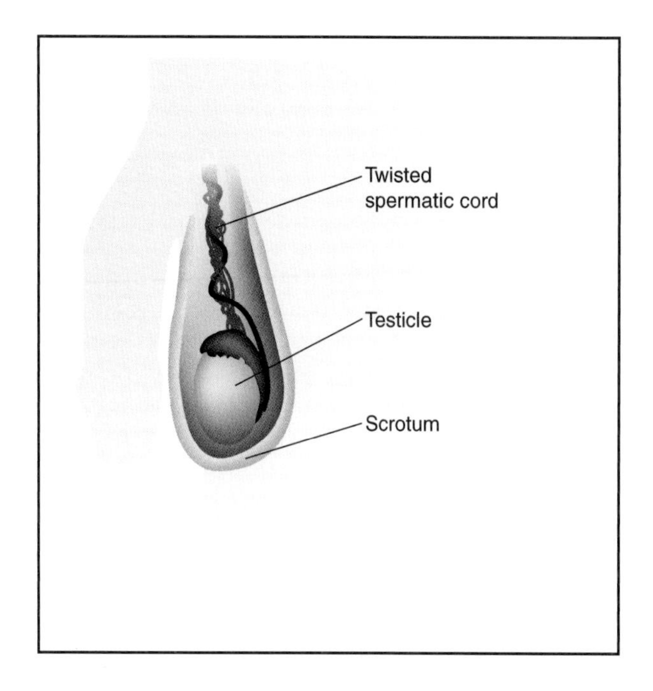

A rare condition, testicular torsion occurs when the spermatic cord is twisted and cuts off the blood supply to the testicle. *(Illustration by Argosy, Inc.)*

so that it cannot rotate again. This securing is called orchiopexy. The other testicle is also secured during the surgery to prevent future testicular torsion, because children who have had one episode of testicular torsion are likely to experience it again. If the testicle has not been untwisted in time and is dead, the surgeon will remove it.

While waiting for surgery, the doctor may try to restore blood flow to the testis by hand. This can help to save the testis if surgery is not possible right away. Surgery is still necessary, however, even if blood flow to the testis has been restored, because it is very likely that torsion will occur again.

Prognosis

If the torsion is relieved within six hours, it is very likely that the testis will recover normal blood flow and function. If the torsion continues for more than 24 hours, it is unlikely that the testis can be saved. One testis is all that is necessary for normal growth and maturation, as well as normal fertility later in life.

Prevention

The only way to prevent torsion is to surgically anchor the testes so that they cannot move. This is frequently done after an occurrence of torsion, both to the torsed testis and the unaffected testis.

KEY TERMS

Orchiopexy—A surgical procedure that places an undescended testicle in the scrotum and/or attaches a testicle to the scrotum.

Scrotum—The external pouch containing the male reproductive glands (testes) and part of the spermatic cord.

Spermatic cord—The tissue that suspends the testis inside the scrotum.

Parental concerns

Testicular torsion is usually very painful. If the torsion is not corrected quickly, the testis usually loses function. Only one healthy and functioning testis is required for normal growth and development and for normal fertility later in life.

Resources

PERIODICALS

Adelman, William P., and Alain Joffe. "The Adolescent with a Painful Scrotum." *Contemporary Pediatrics* 17 (March 2000): 111.

Kirn, Timothy, F. "Time Is Critical with Testicular Torsion." *Family Practice News* 34 (April 15, 2004): 86.

Little, Cindy. "Testicular Torsion." *Nursing* 30 (April 2000): 33.

ORGANIZATIONS

American Urological Association. 1000 Corporate Blvd., Linthicum, MD 21090. Web site: <www.auanet.org>.

WEB SITES

Paushter, David. "Testicular Torsion." *eMedicine*, July 20, 2004. Available online at <www.emedicine.com/radio/topic683.htm> (accessed December 1, 2004).

Tish Davidson, A.M.
Ricker Polsdorfer, MD

Tests for pregnant women *see* **Antenatal testing**

Tetanus

Definition

Tetanus, also called lockjaw, is a serious disease of the nervous system that can cause uncontrolled **muscle**

spasms and death. It is caused by toxins (poisons) produced by the bacterium *Clostridium tetani*.

Description

Tetanus occurs when the body is infected with spores of the bacterium *C. tetani*. This bacterium is found worldwide in soil and animal manure. The spores can remain alive in the soil for years and are resistant to heating and chemical destruction. They are more common in hot, damp environments than in cold or dry ones.

Once spores enter the body through a break in the skin, they begin producing bacteria. These bacteria multiply in areas where there is little oxygen present and produce a toxin that affects the nervous system. The toxin spreads along the nerves of the body, causing the nerves to fire (react). This results in muscle spasms and convulsions.

Transmission

The bacteria that cause tetanus enter the body through a scrape, cut, or wound, in about 70 percent of cases. The most susceptible **wounds** are those that are caused by blunt trauma such as crushing or by **bites**. The bacteria can also enter at the site of a burn, bedsore, or **frostbite**, or be introduced into the body during surgery. In developing countries, newborns often contract tetanus from contaminated instruments used to tie off the umbilical cord after birth. Often the site where the bacteria enter is insignificant, does not become swollen or red, and does not require medical attention. Any time between two and 50 days later (most commonly between days seven and 21 days), the individual begins to show the signs of tetanus.

The severity of the disease is related to several factors:

- The sooner symptoms appear, the more severe the disease.
- If the point of entry was in the head or face, symptoms are more severe.
- The very young and the very old suffer more severe symptoms and higher death rates.

Demographics

With almost universal **vaccination** starting in the 1940s, tetanus has become rare in the United States. Fewer than 50 cases have been reported annually since 1995. Worldwide, the disease is common, especially in newborns in developing parts of Asia, Africa, and South America where immunization is not universally available. The disease can affect individuals of any race, age, or gender.

Causes and symptoms

Since the incubation period can range from several days to many weeks, individuals often do not associate their initial symptoms with wound infection. The first sign of tetanus is a tightening of the jaw muscles that gives the disease its common name, lockjaw. This symptom is followed by waves of back spasms. The spasms then extend to the arms producing clenched fists and to the legs. Any stimulus, such as noise or light, can set off a round of convulsions. Other symptoms include drooling, increase in blood pressure (**hypertension**), irregular heart beat, inability to open the mouth, high **fever**, kidney failure, and respiratory failure.

When to call the doctor

Tetanus is a medical emergency, and individuals should be taken to the emergency room as soon as symptoms are noticed. About 75 percent of individuals with tetanus are first seen by a dentist or oral surgeon for **pain** and stiffness in the jaw and mouth region.

Diagnosis

Diagnosis of tetanus is based on presenting symptoms rather than laboratory tests. Less than one-third of the time can the bacteria that causes the disease be cultured from a wound.

Treatment

Treatment begins immediately in the emergency room or intensive care unit of a hospital. There are five aspects of treatment. Initially the patient is placed in a dark, quiet room and given a sedative, usually a drug in the benzodiazepine family, through direct injection into a vein (IV) in an effort to reduce muscle spasms. A tube may be inserted in to the trachea (tracheotomy) in order to keep the airways open.

The second aspect of treatment is to clean and disinfect any wounds and remove any dead flesh.

The third aspect of treatment involves killing the bacteria producing the toxin using antimicrobial drugs given as an injection. The drug of choice is metronidazole (Flagyl), with penicillin the second choice.

Fourth, the toxin already circulating in the blood must be neutralized so that it causes no further damage to the nervous system. This is done with injections of human tetanus immunoglobulin (TIG).

Finally, complications of the disease are managed. This may involve IV fluid replacement, use of a respirator, or kidney dialysis. Contracting tetanus does not provide immunity against future infections, so tetanus immunizations are also given.

Prognosis

Individuals who develop symptoms within a few days of infection have close to a 100 percent mortality rate. The mortality rate for infections originating in the head and in newborns is also very high. The sooner an individual is treated, the more likely he or she is to survive. Overall, the death rate in the United States is 10 percent. Worldwide it is 45 percent. According the United States Centers for Disease Control, the average hospital stay is 16 days. Recovery for those who survive is normally complete after about four weeks.

Prevention

Tetanus is completely preventable by immunization. The recommendation in the United States, as of 2004, is to immunize children against tetanus on the following schedule:

- initial vaccination at two months of age
- repeat at four months of age
- repeat at six months of age
- repeat at 12 to 15 months of age
- repeat at four to six years of age
- booster dose given every 10 years there after, normally at ages 15, 25, 35, etc.

Receiving the complete schedule of multiple vaccinations is necessary to ensure full protection. For children, vaccination against tetanus is normally included in a vaccine called DTaP that protects against **diphtheria**, tetanus, and **whooping cough** (acellular pertussis). Many school districts require proof of vaccination before a child may enroll.

Other prevention measures involve prompt cleaning and protection of wounds and hygiene measure such as washing well after exposure to soil containing animal manure. Sterile conditions during surgery also help prevent infection.

KEY TERMS

Intravenous—Into a vein; a needle is inserted into a vein in the back of the hand, inside the elbow, or some other location on the body. Fluids, nutrients, and drugs can be injected. Commonly called IV.

Toxin—A poisonous substance usually produced by a microorganism or plant.

Trachea—The windpipe. A tube composed of cartilage and membrane that extends from below the voice box into the chest where it splits into two branches, the bronchi, that lead to each lung.

Tracheotomy—An surgical procedure in which the surgeon cuts directly through the patient's neck into the windpipe below a blockage in order to keep the airway open.

Umbilical cord—The blood vessels that allow the developing baby to receive nutrition and oxygen from its mother; the blood vessels also eliminate the baby's waste products. One end of the umbilical cord is attached to the placenta and the other end is attached to the baby's belly button (umbilicus).

Nutritional concerns

Food is not given by mouth to individuals who are having muscle spasms for **fear** they will breathe the food into their lungs. During this time, they are fed intravenously.

Parental concerns

Some parents hesitate to vaccinate their children for religious reasons or because they fear side effects of the vaccination. The bacteria that cause tetanus are so common and the disease is so serious that protection against acquiring tetanus outweighs any risks associated with vaccination.

See also Vaccination.

Resources

BOOKS

Marx, John, et al. *Rosen's Emergency Medicine: Concepts and Clinical Practice*, 5th ed. St. Louis: Mosby, 2003.

Parker, James N., et al. *Tetanus: A Medical Dictionary, Bibliography, and Annotated Research Guide to Internet References.* Boulder, CO: netLibrary, 2004.

PERIODICALS

Roper, Martha H. "Tetanus Prophylaxis in the Emergency Department." *Annals of Emergency Medicine* 43, no. 3 (March 2004): 315–17.

WEB SITES

Sonali, Ray, and Robert W. Tolan. "Tetanus." *eMedicine Medical Library* February 24, 2004. Available online at <www.emedicine.com/ped/topic3038.htm> (accessed October 14, 2004).

Tish Davidson, A.M.

Tetracyclines

Definition

Tetracyclines are a group of **antibiotics** that are useful in treatment of many bacterial infections.

Description

Tetracyclines are called broad-spectrum antibiotics because they can be used to treat a wide variety of infections. Physicians may prescribe these drugs to treat eye infections, **pneumonia**, gonorrhea, **Rocky Mountain spotted fever**, urinary tract infections, certain bacteria that could be used in biological weapons, and other infections caused by bacteria. The medicine is also used to treat **acne**. The tetracyclines will not work for colds, flu, and other infections caused by viruses. Tetracyclines are generally a low-cost alternative among antibiotics.

There are five drugs in the tetracycline class:

- demeclocycline
- doxycycline
- minocycline
- oxytetracycline
- tetracycline

General use

All tetracyclines are used for treatment of infections in patients over the age of eight years. They may be used in several forms, including capsules, injections, ointments, eye and ear drops.

Tetracyclines are bacteriostatic. They do not kill bacteria; they prevent bacteria from growing, so that the body's natural defenses are better able to deal with an infection. For this reason, tetracyclines are not used in patients with impaired immune systems.

Although all tetracyclines are similar, and can do most of the same work, there are some differences. Doxycycline requires only one dose a day and can be used even when the patient has kidney problems. Demeclocycline and minocycline penetrate the skin better than other tetracyclines and may be preferred for treatment of acne. Demeclocycline is effective for the syndrome of inappropriate anti-diuretic hormone (SIDAH), although it is not officially approved for this purpose.

In addition to their role in treating infections, tetracyclines have a wide range of other uses. These include protection against some types of malaria and treatment of some of the infections that might be used in bioterrorism. Some tetracycline derivatives have been useful in **cancer** therapy. Tetracyclines have been useful in prevention of gum diseases of the mouth.

Precautions

Tetracyclines should normally not be used in children under the age of eight because some tetracyclines can be absorbed into the bones and teeth and give the teeth a mottled appearance. Some experts believe that tetracyclines should be avoided in children younger than ten.

Side effects

Not all tetracyclines have the same side effects, but the following list includes some of the most common problems:

- dizziness and lightheadedness
- **diarrhea**
- stomach upset
- nausea
- vomiting
- photosensitivity
- fungus infections
- tooth discoloration
- mouth irritation
- skin discoloration

On rare occasions tetracyclines may cause more severe adverse effects, including kidney damage and drug-induced lupus.

Patients taking tetracyclines should avoid prolonged sun exposure. Standard **sunscreens** are not adequate to protect against severe **sunburn** in patients taking tetracyclines.

Interactions

Tetracyclines should not be used at the same time the patient is receiving a live vaccine. The antibiotics may prevent the vaccine from growing, and this may keep the vaccine from producing immunity.

Moreover, tetracyclines may reduce the effectiveness of **oral contraceptives**.

Many antibiotics share tetracyclines' interaction with neuromuscular blocking agents. Tetracyclines should not be used at the same time as neuromuscular blocking agents since the antibiotics can increase the strength of the neuromuscular blocker, which can make breathing difficult. While this interaction is severe, it is rare, since the neuromuscular blocking agents are usually used only in surgery.

Tetracyclines should not be taken at the same time as foods containing calcium or foods containing iron, magnesium, or aluminum. The metals bind to the tetracycline, and the combination has reduced effect on bacteria.

The common interaction between tetracyclines and **minerals** can be avoided by taking tetracycline on an empty stomach, one hour before or two hours after meals, with water.

Parental concerns

Although it is recommended that tetracyclines not be given to children under the age of eight, the drug is sometimes required in severe infections. Tetracyclines may be required for children who have developed infections either in hospitals or while traveling overseas.

Parents should carefully check the expiration date of tetracycline and not use the drug past the expiration date. Expired tetracycline has been known to cause a severe kidney problem called Fanconi syndrome. Expired tetracycline should be disposed of, not saved.

Because tetracyclines can cause photosensitization, patients taking these drugs should use sunscreen and avoid direct sunlight.

Because of their interaction with metals, tetracyclines should always be taken on an empty stomach with only water. Patients should particularly avoid calcium-containing dairy products and antacids as well as multivitamin-mineral supplements.

KEY TERMS

Antibiotics—Drugs that are designed to kill or inhibit the growth of the bacteria that cause infections.

Bacteriostatic—An agent that prevents the growth of bacteria.

Fanconi's syndrome—A group of disorders involving kidney tubule malfunction and glucose, phosphate, and bicarbonate in the urine. Two forms of this syndrome have been identified: an inherited form and an acquired form caused by vitamin D deficiency or exposure to heavy metals.

Photosensitization—Development of oversensitivity to sunlight.

Tetracyclines inhibit the growth of many bacteria and other microorganisms which can lead to overgrowth of other microorganisms. Possible symptoms are discoloration of the tongue and diarrhea. Parents should report these problems to the prescriber immediately.

Parents should alert all health-care professionals about all drugs their children are taking. Both tetracycline and oral contraceptives are used to treat acne in teenage girls, but these drugs should not be used together.

See also Penicillins.

Resources

BOOKS

Beers, Mark H., and Robert Berkow, eds. *The Merck Manual*, 2nd home ed. West Point, PA: Merck & Co., 2004.

Mcevoy, Gerald K., et al. *AHFS Drug Information 2004*. Bethesda, MD: American Society of Healthsystems Pharmacists, 2004.

Siberry, George K., and Robert Iannone, eds. *The Harriet Lane Handbook*, 15th ed. Philadelphia: Mosby, 2000.

PERIODICALS

Black, Douglas J., and Allan Ellsworth. "Practical overview of antibiotics for family physicians." *Clinics in Family Practice* 6, no. 1 (March 2004): 265–89.

Cronquist, Steven D. "Tularemia: The disease and the weapon." *Dermatologic Clinics* 22, no. 3 (July 2004): 313–320.

Izzedine, Hassane, et al. "Drug-induced Fanconi's syndrome." *American Journal of Kidney Disease* 41, no. 2 (February 1, 2003): 292–309.

Sanfilippo, Angela M., et al. "Common pediatric and adolescent skin conditions." *Journal of Pediatric and Adolescent Gynecology* 16, no. 5 (October 1, 2003): 269–83.

Thompson, Matthew J., and Christopher Sanford. "Travel-related infections in primary care." *Clinics in Family Practice* 6, no. 1 (March 2004): 235–64.

ORGANIZATIONS

American Academy of Pediatrics. 141 Northwest Point Boulevard, Elk Grove Village, IL 60007–1098. Web site: <www.aap.org>.

WEB SITES

The Pediatric Infectious Disease Journal. Available online at <www.medscape.com/viewpublication/769_index> (accessed September 30, 2004).

Samuel Uretsky, PharmD

Tetralogy of Fallot

Definition

Tetralogy of Fallot is a common syndrome of congenital heart defects.

Description

The heart is two pumps in one. The ventricle on the left side pumps blood full of oxygen through the body; the ventricle on the right side pumps the same blood through the pulmonary artery to the lungs to take up oxygen. The left ventricle operates at pressures about four times as high as the right ventricle. Blood is supposed to flow through one side, then the other.

Tetralogy of Fallot is a condition that is characterized by several congenital heart defects occurring at once. They include: ventricular septal defect (abnormal passageway between the right and left ventricles), displaced aorta, narrowed pulmonary valve, thickened right ventricle wall.

Each defect acts in combination with the others to create a malfunction of the heart. The problem starts very early in the uterus with a narrowed pulmonary valve and a hole between the ventricles. This is not particularly a problem for a fetus because hardly any blood flows through the lungs until birth. It is only after birth that the defects pose a problem. The blood that is supposed to start flowing through the lungs cannot easily get there because of the narrowed valve; however, the hole between the ventricles remains open. Because of the opening between ventricles, much of the blood that comes back to the heart needing oxygen is sent out without being properly oxygenated. In addition, the right heart has to pump at the same pressure as the left side. Several changes follow. First, the baby turns blue (cyanotic) because of the deoxygenated blood that bypasses the lungs. Deoxygenated blood is darker and appears blue through the skin. Second, the right side of the heart (ventricle) hypertrophies (gets more muscular) from the extra exercise demanded of it. Next, the low oxygen causes the blood to get thicker and clot more easily. Clots in the veins can now pass through the hole in the heart and directly enter the aorta, where they can do much more damage than in the lungs such as causing infarcts in the brain. In addition, these anomalies make the lining of the heart more susceptible to infection (endocarditis), which can damage valves and lead to blood poisoning (septicemia).

Demographics

Researchers estimate that tetralogy of Fallot occurs in approximately one in every 2000 births. In the United States, almost 10 percent of **congenital heart disease** is tetralogy of Fallot. Boys are slightly more likely to have this malformation than girls.

Causes and symptoms

Tetralogy of Fallot is a congenital defect with unknown causes. Babies with tetralogy of Fallot are blue at birth or cyanotic. Sometimes the blue color appears only when they cry. They also have detectable **heart murmurs**. Infants with mild forms can have surgery postponed until they are older. Infants with more severe symptoms often have attacks of worsened cyanosis. During attacks, they turn very blue, have shortness of breath, and can faint. These symptoms usually occur during heightened activity, such as crying.

Diagnosis

A complete evaluation of the circulation is required, testing the blood for its oxygen content. Three diagnostic tests are performed: an echocardiogram, a chest x ray, and an electrocardiogram.

Treatment

Correction of the defects is done through open heart surgery. Surgery must be carefully timed with attention to the progression of the disease process, the size of the infant,

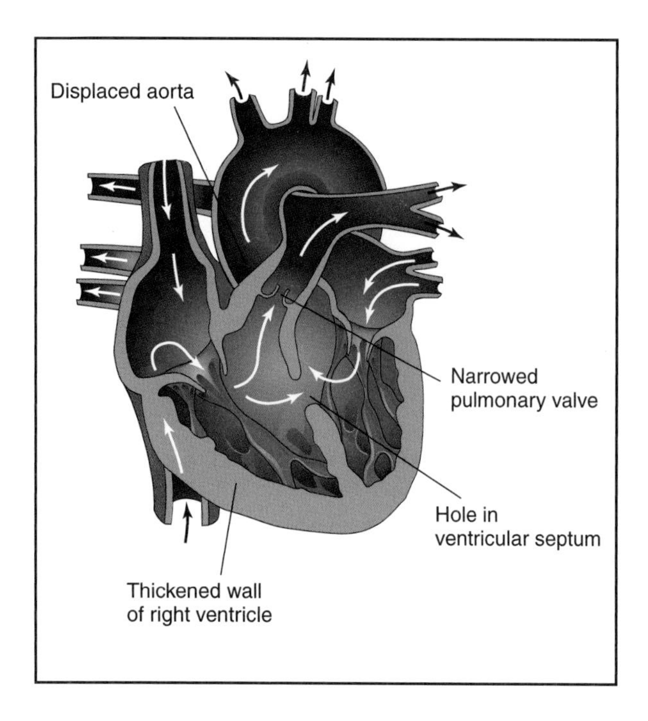

Tetralogy of Fallot is a common syndrome of congenital heart defects. This condition, present *in utero,* is caused by the narrowing of the pulmonary artery and a hole between the ventricles. When the baby is born and begins to breathe on its own, the baby turns cyanotic, or blue, due to the deoxygenated blood that bypasses the lungs because the narrowed pathway and the hole between the ventricles has remained open. *(Illustration by Electronic Illustrators Group.)*

and the size of the various defects. There are temporary surgical procedures that can prolong the time before corrective surgery, while the baby grows larger and stronger.

During surgery, the pulmonary valve is widened, the ventricular septal defect is closed, and any interim correction is removed.

Prognosis

Surgical correction has a high rate of success, returning the child to near-normal health.

Prevention

There is no known prevention for tetralogy of Fallot.

Parental concerns

Tetralogy of Fallot is a complex congenital malformation; however, open heart surgery is highly effective in correcting it. Most children have an excellent outcome and a normal healthy life. For most children, activity level, appetite, and growth eventually return to normal. Open heart surgery to repair tetralogy of Fallot is usually performed in children between the ages of six months and two years. Children with severe tetralogy of Fallot will begin the process of surgical correction in infancy. For children in whom the condition is milder, corrective surgery may be postponed until the child is older and has grown. While waiting for corrective surgery, children may experience episodes called paroxysmal hypercyanotic attacks, in which the child may cry intensely or become restless, turn blue (especially around the lips, fingernails, and toenails), and sometimes faint. These attacks can be quite serious and may require emergency medical care. For infants, holding the baby on the parent's shoulder with the infant's knees tucked underneath him may help reduce the symptoms. Older children may crouch in a squatting position.

After the child's heart surgery, parents should follow all instructions given by the healthcare team. Most children will continue to be seen by a team of doctors including the pediatrician, cardiologist, and pediatric cardiac surgeon.

KEY TERMS

Aorta—The main artery located above the heart that pumps oxygenated blood out into the body. The aorta is the largest artery in the body.

Cyanotic—Marked by a bluish tinge to the skin that occurs when the blood oxygen level drops too low. It is one of the types of congenital heart disease.

Deoxygenated blood—Blood that does not contain oxygen.

Endocarditis—Inflammation of the inner membrane lining heart and/or of the heart valves caused by infection.

Infarct—An area of dead tissue caused by inadequate blood supply.

Paroxysmal hypercyanoic attacks—Sudden episodes of cyanosis resulting from the circulation of deoxygenated blood to the body.

Septicemia—A systemic infection due to the presence of bacteria and their toxins in the bloodstream. Septicemia is sometimes called blood poisoning.

Systemic circulation—Refers to the general blood circulation of the body, not including the lungs.

Ventricles—The lower pumping chambers of the heart. The ventricles push blood to the lungs and the rest of the body.

When to call the doctor

Following open heart surgery, parents should call the doctor if any of the following occurs:

- fever of 101.5°F (38.6°C) or higher
- swelling or puffiness around the child's eyes, arms, or legs
- redness or swelling, cloudy yellow drainage, or an opening at the incision site
- rapid breathing
- increased fatigue or tiredness
- dry **cough** that was not present before surgery
- decreased appetite or refusal to eat
- increased pain

Resources

BOOKS

Behrman, Richard E., Robert M. Kliegman, and Hal B. Jenson. *Nelson Textbook of Pediatrics*, 16th ed. Philadelphia: Saunders, 2000.

Rudolph, Colin D., and Abraham M. Rudolph, eds. *Rudolph's Pediatrics*, 21st ed. New York: McGraw-Hill, 2003.

WEB SITES

C. S. Mott Children's Hospital. "Home Care after Heart Surgery." Available online at <www.med.umich.edu/1libr/chheart/care10.htm> (accessed August 11, 2004).

J. Ricker Polsdorfer, MD
Deborah L. Nurmi, MS

Thalassemia

Definition

Thalassemia describes a group of inherited disorders characterized by reduced or absent amounts of hemoglobin. Hemoglobin is the protein in red blood cells that carries oxygen throughout the body. There are two basic groups of thalassemia disorders: alpha thalassemias and beta thalassemias. These conditions cause varying degrees of anemia, which can range from insignificant to fatal.

Description

Thalassemia is a genetic disorder. It cannot be acquired from contact with other people or from the environment. In all types of thalassemia, the quantity of hemoglobin produced is reduced or absent. This circumstance affects the ability of the blood to carry oxygen to all parts of the body. Although both alpha and beta thalassemias affect hemoglobin, these diseases affect the body in distinctly different ways. Hemoglobin is made up of three components: alpha globin, beta globin, and heme. Thalassemias are classified according to the globin that is deficient.

Alpha thalassemia

Individuals inherit from each parent a gene controlling alpha globin production. Two spots (called loci) on these genes control alpha globin production. Alpha thalassemias result from changes (mutations) in these genes. There are two main types of alpha thalassemia disease: hemoglobin H disease and alpha thalassemia major. The two diseases are quite different from beta thalassemia, as well as from one another.

Individuals with hemoglobin H disease have inherited one completely defective gene and one gene that has one rather than two functional loci. This circumstance substantially reduces the amount of alpha globin that the body produces. As a result, individuals with hemoglobin H disease can experience events of hemolytic anemia—anemia caused by the rapid breakdown of the red blood cells. These events are thought to be triggered by various environmental causes, such as infection and/or exposure to certain chemicals. Hemoglobin H disease is milder than alpha thalassemia and usually milder than beta thalassemia.

Individuals with alpha thalassemia major have inherited two completely defective genes, one from each parent. Alpha thalassemia major, sometimes called hemoglobin Barts or hydrops fetalis, is a fatal disease that results in severe anemia that begins even before birth. Most affected babies do not survive to be born or die shortly after birth.

Beta thalassemia

Beta thalassemia, also called Cooley's anemia, is the most well known type of thalassemia. It is caused by a change in the gene for the beta globin component of hemoglobin. Beta thalassemia causes variable anemia that can range from moderate to severe, depending in part on the exact genetic change underlying the disease.

Beta thalassemia major causes severe anemia that usually occurs within three to six months after birth. If left untreated, severe anemia can result in stunted growth and development, as well as other characteristic physical complications that can lead to a dramatically decreased life expectancy. In developed countries, screening in the newborn period usually identifies beta thalassemia before symptoms have developed. Children who are identified early can be started on ongoing blood transfusion therapy as needed.

Beta thalassemia minor describes a disease where only one gene of the pair that control beta hemoglobin production is defective. There are few or mild events. However, the individual can pass the defective gene on to his or her offspring

Beta thalassemia intermedia is a clinical term that describes the disease in individuals who have moderate anemia that only requires blood transfusions intermittently.

Demographics

The thalassemias are among the most common genetic diseases worldwide. Both alpha and beta thalassemia have been described in individuals of almost every ancestry, but the conditions are more common among certain ethnic groups. Unaffected carriers of all types of thalassemia traits do not experience health problems.

Determining the prevalence for alpha thalassemia is difficult due to limitations in diagnostic testing. In the United States, up to 30 percent of African Americans are thought to be carriers for alpha thalassemia traits, meaning that they show no symptoms of the disorder but can pass the trait to their offspring. Despite this estimate, the number of babies born with hemoglobin H disease or alpha thalassemia major is very low. The highest frequency of alpha thalassemia diseases occurs in individuals of Southeast Asian and Chinese descent. Individuals of Greek, Middle Eastern, and North African descent also carry genes for the disease more frequently than individuals of Northern European descent. One study of 500 pregnant women in northern Thailand estimated a frequency of one in 500 pregnancies affected by alpha thalassemia major, for example. Prevalence of alpha thalassemia disease is significantly lower in the United States owing primarily to immigration patterns. However, at least one state, California, has observed growing hemoglobin H disease rates that are high enough to justify universal newborn screening for the condition.

Beta thalassemia trait is seen most commonly in people with the following ancestry: Mediterranean (including North African, and particularly Italian and Greek), Middle Eastern, Indian, African, Chinese, and Southeast Asian (including Vietnamese, Laotian, Thai, Singaporean, Filipino, Cambodian, Malaysian, Burmese, and Indonesian). It is difficult to obtain accurate prevalence figures for various types of thalassemia within different populations.

Two studies reflect prevalence figures that can be helpful counseling families and determining who to screen for beta thalassemia. Between the years of 1990 and 1996, the State of California screened over 3.1 million newborns for beta thalassemia. Approximately one in 114,000 infants had beta thalassemia major, with prevalence rates being highest among Asian Indians (about one in 4,000), Southeast Asians (about one in 10,000), and Middle Easterners (about one in 7,000). The pattern observed in California is expected to be different in other areas of the United States and the world. For example, Italians are underrepresented in this population when compared to the population of the East Coast of the United States.

Causes and symptoms

Humans normally make several types of hemoglobin. An individual's stage in development determines whether he or she makes primarily embryonic, fetal, or adult hemoglobins. All types of hemoglobin are made of three components: heme, alpha globin, and beta globin. All types of thalassemia are caused by changes in either the alpha- or beta globin gene. These changes cause little or no globin to be produced. All types of thalassemias are recessively inherited, meaning that a genetic change must be inherited from both the mother and the father to produce the disease in the child. The severity of the disease is influenced by the exact thalassemia mutations inherited, as well as other genetic and environmental factors. There are rare exceptions, notably with beta thalassemia, where globin gene mutations exhibit a dominant pattern of inheritance in which only one gene needs to be altered in order to see disease expression.

Alpha thalassemia

Most individuals have four normal copies of the alpha globin gene, two copies on each chromosome 16. These genes make the alpha globin component of normal adult hemoglobin, which is called hemoglobin A. Alpha globin is also a component of fetal hemoglobin. Since there are four genes (instead of the usual two) to consider when looking at alpha globin gene inheritance, there are several alpha globin types that are possible.

Absence of one functioning alpha globin gene leads to a condition known as silent alpha thalassemia trait. This condition causes no health problems and can be detected only by special genetic testing. Alpha thalassemia trait occurs when two alpha globin genes are missing or not functioning. There are no associated health problems, although the trait status may be detected by more routine blood screening.

Hemoglobin H disease results from the deletion of three of the four alpha globin genes. Hemoglobin H symptoms can also be a part of a unique condition called alpha thalassemia **mental retardation** syndrome. This syndrome can be caused by a deletion of a significant amount of chromosome 16, affecting the alpha globin genes. This situation is usually not inherited, but rather occurs sporadically in the affected individual. Affected individuals have mild hemoglobin H disease, mild-to-moderate mental retardation, and characteristic facial features, as well as various other developmental processes that mimic hemoglobin H disease.

Alpha thalassemia major results from the deletion of all four alpha globin genes, such that there are no functioning alpha globin genes. In this situation, there is a 25 percent chance for alpha thalassemia major in each of such a couple's children.

Beta thalassemia

Most individuals have two normal copies of the beta globin gene, which is located on chromosome 11 and makes the beta globin component of normal adult hemoglobin. There are approximately one hundred genetic mutations that have been described that cause beta thalassemia, designated as either beta0 or beta+ mutations. No beta globin is produced with a beta0 mutation, and only a small fraction of the normal amount of beta globin is produced with a beta+ mutation.

When an individual has one normal beta globin gene and one with a beta thalassemia mutation, he or she is said to carry the beta thalassemia trait. Carrying the trait is generally thought not to cause health problems, although some women with beta thalassemia trait may have an increased tendency toward anemia during pregnancy.

When both parents carry the beta thalassemia trait, there is a 25 percent chance that each of their children will inherit beta thalassemia disease by inheriting two beta thalassemia mutations, one from each parent. The clinical severity of the beta thalassemia disease depends largely on whether the mutations inherited are beta0 thalassemia or beta+ thalassemia mutations. Two beta0 mutations generally lead to beta thalassemia major, and two beta+ thalassemia mutations generally lead to beta thalassemia intermedia, a milder form of the disease. Inheritance of one beta0 and one beta+ thalassemia mutation tends to be less predictable.

Symptoms

Hemoglobin H disease

Hemoglobin H disease is a relatively mild form of thalassemia that may go unrecognized. It is not generally considered a condition that will reduce one's life expectancy. Education is an important part of managing the health of an individual with hemoglobin H disease. It is important to be able to recognize the signs of severe anemia that require medical attention. It is also important to be aware of the medications, chemicals, and other exposures to avoid due to the theoretical risk they pose of precipitating a severe anemia event. When severe anemia occurs, it is treated with blood transfusion therapy. For many individuals with hemoglobin H disease, this is rarely required. For those with a more severe form of the disease, the need for transfusions may be intermittent or ongoing, perhaps on a monthly basis, and require desferoxamine treatment. This treatment removes excess iron from the body. Individuals with this more severe form of the disease may also have an increased chance of requiring removal of an enlarged and/or overactive spleen.

Alpha thalassemia major

Because alpha globin is a necessary component of hemoglobin, absence of all functioning alpha globin genes leads to serious medical consequences that begin even before birth. Affected fetuses develop severe anemia as early as the first trimester of pregnancy. The placenta, heart, liver, spleen, and adrenal glands may all become enlarged. Fluid can begin collecting throughout the body as early as the start of the second trimester, causing damage to developing tissues and organs. Growth retardation is also common. Affected fetuses usually miscarry or die shortly after birth. In addition, women carrying affected fetuses are at increased risk of developing complications of pregnancy and delivery. Up to 80 percent of such women develop toxemia, a disturbance of metabolism that can potentially lead to convulsions and coma. Other maternal complications include premature delivery and increased rates of delivery by **cesarean section**, as well as hemorrhage after delivery.

Beta thalassemia major is characterized by severe anemia that can begin several months after birth. In the United States and other developed countries beta thalassemia is identified and treated early and effectively. Therefore, the following discussion of symptoms applies primarily to affected individuals in the past and in some underdeveloped countries as of the early 2000s. If untreated, beta thalassemia major can lead to severe lethargy, paleness, and growth and **developmental delay**. The body attempts to compensate by producing more blood, which is made inside the bones in the marrow. However, this effort is ineffective without the needed genetic instructions to make enough functioning hemoglobin. Instead, obvious bone expansion and changes occur that cause characteristic facial and other changes in appearance, as well as increased risk of **fractures**. Severe anemia taxes other organs in the body such as the heart, spleen, and liver, which must work harder than usual. This stress can lead to heart failure, as well as enlargement and other problems of the liver and spleen. When untreated, beta thalassemia major generally results in childhood death, usually due to heart failure. In developed countries, diagnosis is usually made early, often before symptoms have begun. This factor allows for treatment with blood transfusion therapy, which can prevent most of the complications of the severe anemia caused by beta thalassemia major.

Individuals with beta thalassemia intermedia have a more moderate anemia that may only require treatment with transfusion intermittently, such as when infections stress the body. As a person with beta thalassemia intermedia gets older, however, the need for blood transfusions may increase to the point that they are required on a regular basis. When this occurs the disease becomes more similar to beta thalassemia major. Other genetic and environmental factors can influence the course of the disease as well. For example, co-inheritance of one or two alpha thalassemia mutations can tend to improve some of the symptoms of beta thalassemia disease, which results in part from an imbalance in the amount of alpha- and beta-globin present in the red blood cells.

When to call the doctor

Signs of thalassemia diseases are often noted by the doctor during newborn screening. Parents should contact their doctors if they suspect any developmental delays, especially if the parents belong to one of the ethnic groups at higher risk for the disease.

Diagnosis

Diagnosis of thalassemia can occur under various circumstances and at various ages. Several states offer thalassemia screening as part of the usual battery of blood tests done on newborns. This arrangement allows for early identification and treatment. Thalassemia can be identified before birth using prenatal diagnosis. Chorionic villus sampling (CVS) can be done as early as 10 weeks of pregnancy. It involves removing a sample of the placenta and testing the cells. CVS carries a risk of causing a miscarriage that is between 0.5 percent and 1 percent. **Amniocentesis** is generally done between 15 and 22 weeks of pregnancy but can sometimes be offered earlier. Two to three tablespoons of the fluid surrounding the baby are removed. This fluid contains fetal cells that can be tested. The risk of miscarriage associated with amniocentesis ranges from 0.33 to 0.5 percent.

Pregnant women and couples may choose prenatal testing in order to prepare for the birth of a baby that may have thalassemia. Alternately, knowing the diagnosis during pregnancy allows for the option of pregnancy termination. Preimplantation genetic diagnosis (PGD) is a relatively new technique that involves in-vitro fertilization followed by genetic testing of one cell from each developing embryo. Only the embryos unaffected by the disease are transferred back into the uterus.

Thalassemia may be suspected if an individual shows signs that are suggestive of the disease. In all cases, however, laboratory tests are essential to confirm the exact diagnosis and to allow for the provision of accurate genetic counseling about recurrence risks and testing options for parents and affected individuals. Screening is likewise recommended to determine trait status for individuals of high-risk ethnic groups.

The following tests are used to screen for thalassemia disease and/or trait:

- complete blood count
- hemoglobin electrophoresis
- free erythrocyte-protoporphyrin (or ferritin or other studies of serum iron levels)

A complete blood count will identify low levels of hemoglobin, small red blood cells, and other red blood cell abnormalities that are characteristic of a thalassemia diagnosis. Since thalassemia trait can sometimes be difficult to distinguish from iron deficiency, tests to evaluate iron levels are important.

Hemoglobin electrophoresis is a test that can help identify the types and quantities of hemoglobin made by an individual. This test uses an electric field applied across a slab of gel-like material. Hemoglobins migrate through this gel at various rates and to specific locations, depending on their size, shape, and electrical charge. Isoelectric focusing and high-performance liquid chromatography (HPLC) use similar principles to separate hemoglobins. They can be used instead of or in various combinations with hemoglobin electrophoresis to determine the types and quantities of hemoglobin present. Hemoglobin electrophoresis results are usually within the normal range for all types of alpha thalassemia. Hemoglobin electrophoresis can also detect structurally abnormal hemoglobins that may be co-inherited with a thalassemia trait. Sometimes DNA testing is needed in addition to the above screening tests. This test can be performed to help confirm the diagnosis and establish the exact genetic type of thalassemia.

Treatment

Because alpha thalassemia major is most often a fatal condition in the prenatal or newborn period, treatment has previously been focused on identifying affected pregnancies in order to provide appropriate management to reduce potential maternal complications. Pregnancy termination provides one form of management. Increased prenatal surveillance and early treatment of maternal complications is an approach that is appropriate for mothers who wish to continue their pregnancy with the knowledge that the baby will most likely not survive. In the last decade of the twentieth century and early 2000s, a handful of infants with this condition have survived long-term. Most of these infants received experimental treatment including transfusions before birth, early delivery, and bone marrow transplantation before birth, although the latter procedure had, as of 2004, not yet been successful. For those infants who survive to delivery, there seems to be an increased risk of developmental problems and physical effects, particularly heart and genital malformations. Otherwise, the medical outlook is similar to a child with beta thalassemia major, with the important exception that ongoing, lifelong blood transfusions begin at birth.

Beta thalassemia

Individuals with beta thalassemia major receive regular blood transfusions, usually on a monthly basis. This helps prevent severe anemia and allow for growth and development that is more normal. Transfusion therapy does have limitations, however. Individuals can develop reactions to certain proteins in the blood, called a transfusion reaction. Such a reaction can make locating appropriately matched donor blood more difficult. Although blood supplies in the United States are very safe, there remains an increased risk of exposure to such blood-borne infections as hepatitis.

An additional side effect of repeated transfusions is that the body is unable to get rid of the excess iron that accompanies each transfusion. A medication called desferoxamine is administered, usually five nights per week over a period of several hours, using an automatic pump that can be used during **sleep** or taken anywhere the person goes. This medication is able to bind to the excess iron, which can then be eliminated through urine.

If desferoxamine is not used regularly or is unavailable, iron overload can develop and cause tissue damage and organ damage and failure. The heart, liver, and endocrine organs are particularly vulnerable. Desferoxamine itself may produce on rare occasions allergic or toxic side effects, including hearing damage. Signs of desferoxamine toxicity are screened for and generally develop in individuals who overuse the medication when body iron levels are sufficiently low. Overall, however, transfusion and desferoxamine therapy have increased the life expectancy of individuals with the most severe types of beta thalassemia major to the fourth or fifth decade.

As of 2004, new treatments including medications that target the production of red blood cells (e.g. erythropoeitin) or fetal hemoglobin (e.g. hydroxyurea and butyrate) and bone marrow transplantation may offer more effective treatment of beta thalassemia major. Other possible treatments may include gene therapy techniques aimed at increasing the amount of normal hemoglobin the body is able to make.

Prognosis

Prognosis, as noted above, depends on the type and severity of the disease. Individuals with severe disease may be stillborn or die shortly after birth. On the other hand, some individuals with mild disease have a relatively normal life expectancy.

Prevention

Thalassemias are inherited diseases that cannot be prevented. It is, however, possible to identify carriers of the disease and provide them with genetic counseling and appropriate information concerning the chance of their offspring having thalassemia disease.

Individuals with hemoglobin H disease can reduce the likelihood of symptoms by avoiding infections and certain environmental triggers.

Parental concerns

If parents are thinking of having a child and believe they might be carriers of defective hemoglobin genes, they can be screened and receive genetic counseling so that they can assess their options.

Resources

WEB SITES

Lawson, Jack P., and Leon Lenchik. "Thalassemia," June 22, 2001. Available online at <www.emedicine.com/radio/topic686.htm> (accessed October 4, 2004).

KEY TERMS

Anemia—A condition in which there is an abnormally low number of red blood cells in the bloodstream. It may be due to loss of blood, an increase in red blood cell destruction, or a decrease in red blood cell production. Major symptoms are paleness, shortness of breath, unusually fast or strong heart beats, and tiredness.

Bilirubin—A reddish yellow pigment formed from the breakdown of red blood cells, and metabolized by the liver. When levels are abnormally high, it causes the yellowish tint to eyes and skin known as jaundice. Levels of bilirubin in the blood increase in patients with liver disease, blockage of the bile ducts, and other conditions.

Bone marrow—The spongy tissue inside the large bones in the body that is responsible for making the red blood cells, most white blood cells, and platelets.

Bone marrow transplantation—A medical procedure in which a quantity of bone marrow is extracted through a needle from a donor, and then passed into a patient to replace the patient's diseased or absent bone marrow.

Desferoxamine—The primary drug used in iron chelation therapy. It aids in counteracting the life-threatening buildup of iron in the body associated with long-term blood transfusions.

Globin—One of the component protein molecules found in hemoglobin. Normal adult hemoglobin has a pair each of alpha-globin and beta-globin molecules.

Heme—The iron-containing molecule in hemoglobin that serves as the site for oxygen binding.

Hemoglobin—An iron-containing pigment of red blood cells composed of four amino acid chains (alpha, beta, gamma, delta) that delivers oxygen from the lungs to the cells of the body and carries carbon dioxide from the cells to the lungs.

Hemoglobin A—Normal adult hemoglobin that contains a heme molecule, two alpha-globin molecules, and two beta-globin molecules.

Hemoglobin electrophoresis—A laboratory test that separates molecules based on their size, shape, or electrical charge. It is used to identify abnormal hemoglobins in the blood.

Hydroxyurea—A drug that has been shown to induce production of fetal hemoglobin. Fetal hemoglobin has a pair of gamma-globin molecules in place of the typical beta-globins of adult hemoglobin. Higher-than-normal levels of fetal hemoglobin can ameliorate some of the symptoms of thalassemia.

Iron overload—A side effect of frequent blood transfusions in which the body accumulates abnormally high levels of iron. Iron deposits can form in organs, particularly the heart, and cause life-threatening damage.

Jaundice—A condition in which the skin and whites of the eyes take on a yellowish color due to an increase of bilirubin (a compound produced by the liver) in the blood. Also called icterus.

Mutation—A permanent change in the genetic material that may alter a trait or characteristic of an individual, or manifest as disease. This change can be transmitted to offspring.

Placenta—The organ that provides oxygen and nutrition from the mother to the unborn baby during pregnancy. The placenta is attached to the wall of the uterus and leads to the unborn baby via the umbilical cord.

Red blood cell—Cells that carry hemoglobin (the molecule that transports oxygen) and help remove wastes from tissues throughout the body.

Screening—A process through which carriers of a trait may be identified within a population.

"Thalassemia," April 10, 2002. Available online at <http://sicle.bwh.Harvard.edu/menu_thal.html> (accessed October 4, 2004).

ORGANIZATIONS

Children's Blood Foundation. 333 East 38th St., Room 830, New York, NY 10016–2745. Web site: <www.childrensbloodfoundation.org>.

Cooley's Anemia Foundation Inc. 129–09 26th Ave. #203, Flushing, NY 11354. Web site: <www.thalassemia.org>.

March of Dimes Birth Defects Foundation. 1275 Mamaroneck Ave., White Plains, NY 10605. Web site: <www.modimes.org>.

National Organization for Rare Disorders (NORD). PO Box 8923, New Fairfield, CT 06812–8923. Web site: <www.rarediseases.org>.

OTHER

"Alpha-thalassemia Mental Retardation Syndrome, Nondeletion Type." *Online Mendelian Inheritance of Man.* Available online at <www.ncbi.nlm.nih.gov/entrez/dispomim.cgi?id=301040> (accessed October 4, 2004).

Children's Hospital Oakland, Northern California Comprehensive Thalassemia Center Web site. Available online at <www.thalassemia.com> (accessed October 4, 2004).

Tish Davidson, A.M.

Thematic Apperception Test

Definition

The Thematic Apperception Test is a projective personality test.

Purpose

The Thematic Apperception Test (TAT) is widely used to research certain topics in psychology, such as dreams and fantasies, mate selection, the factors that motivate people's choice of occupations, and similar subjects. It is sometimes used in psychiatric evaluations to assess disordered thinking and in forensic examinations to evaluate crime suspects, even though it is not a diagnostic test. The TAT can be used to help people understand their own personality in greater depth and build on that knowledge in making important life decisions. Lastly, it is sometimes used as a screener in psychological evaluations of candidates for high-stress occupations (law enforcement, the military, religious ministry, for example).

Description

The TAT is a projective personality test that was designed at Harvard University in the 1930s by Christiana D. Morgan and Henry A. Murray. Along with the **Minnesota Multiphasic Personality Inventory** (MMPI) and the Rorschach inkblot test, the TAT is one of the most widely used **psychological tests**. A projective test is one in which a person's patterns of thought, attitudes, observational capacity, and emotional responses are evaluated on the basis of responses to ambiguous test materials. The TAT consists of 31 pictures that depict a variety of social and interpersonal situations. The subject is asked to tell a story to the examiner about each picture. Of the 31 pictures, ten are gender-specific while 21 others can be used with adults of either sex and with children.

There is no standardized procedure or set of cards for administering the TAT, except that it is a one-on-one test. It cannot be administered to groups. In one common method of administration, the examiner shows the subject only ten of the 31 cards at each of two sessions. The sessions are not timed, but average about an hour in length.

Precautions

The TAT has been criticized for its lack of a standardized method of administration as well as a lack of standard norms for interpretation. Studies of the interactions between examiners and test subjects have found that the race, sex, and social class of both participants influence both the stories that are told and the way the stories are interpreted by the examiner. Attempts have been made to design sets of TAT cards for African American and for elderly test subjects, but the results have not been encouraging. In addition, the 31 standard pictures have been criticized for being too gloomy or depressing; therefore, they may limit the range of personality characteristics that the test can assess.

Preparation

There is no specific preparation necessary before taking the TAT, although most examiners prefer to schedule sessions (if there is more than one) over two days.

Risks

The chief risks involved in taking the TAT are a bad "fit" between the examiner and the test subject and misuse of the results.

Parental concerns

The TAT does not yield a score, so its results can be difficult to interpret. It is important for parents to remember that the results of a single personality test may not accurately reflect their child's skills, talents, or problems and that there should not be too much emphasis placed upon the results of a single test.

Resources

BOOKS

Aronow, Edward, Weiss, Kim Altham, and Marvin Reznikoff. *A Practical Guide to the Thematic Apperception Test: the T.A.T. in Clinical Practice.* Philadelphia, PA: Brunner-Routledge, 2001.

KEY TERMS

Projective personality test—A personality test in which the participant interprets ambiguous images, objects, stories.

Rorschach—A projective test in which the participant is asked to interpret inkblots.

Cohen, Ronald, et al. *Psychological Testing and Assessment: An Introduction to Tests and Measurements.* New York: McGraw-Hill Companies, 2004.

Rocchio, Joseph D. *Your Child and Tests: What Every Parent Should Know about Educational and Psychological Testing.* Solon, OH: Rocklin Publications, 2002.

PERIODICALS

Karon, Bertram P. "The Clinical Interpretation of the Thematic Apperception Test, Rorschach, and Other Clinical Data: A Reexamination of Statistical versus Clinical Prediction." *Professional Psychology, Research, and Practice* 31 (April 2000): 230–34.

Lilienfeld, Scott O., James M. Wood, and Howard N. Garb. "The Scientific Status of Projective Techniques." *Psychological Science* 11 (November 2000): 27.

Tuerlinck, Francis, Paul De Boeck, and Willy Lens. "Measuring Needs with the Thematic Apperception Test: A Psychometric Study." *Journal of Personality and Social Psychology* 82 (March 2002): 448–62.

ORGANIZATIONS

American Academy of Child and Adolescent Psychiatry. 3615 Wisconsin Avenue, NW, Washington, DC 20016–3007. Web site: <www.aacap.org>.

Helen Davidson
Rebecca J. Frey, PhD

Therapeutic baths

Definition

Bathing the skin in a variety of preparations in order to remove crusts, scales, and old medications or to relieve inflammation and **itching** is called taking a therapeutic bath. The term therapeutic bath is also used to refer to various types of warm-water soaks used to speed wound healing, to apply gentle heat to sore muscles or joints, to relieve emotional stress, or to treat a variety of physical disorders ranging from **sports injuries**, rheumatoid arthritis, and chronic **sinusitis** to painful **menstruation** and vascular disorders. Therapeutic baths are one form of hydrotherapy, which is a general term for the internal or external use of water for medical treatment.

Balneotherapy is the medical term for the use of baths or soaks to treat injuries or illnesses. It comes from the Latin word *balneum*, which means bath. Balneotherapy has been used for thousands of years to treat skin disorders, arthritis, paralysis, gynecological disorders, and depression and other emotional problems. The remains of ancient baths have been found in the Indus Valley in India, and the Romans discovered mineral springs in various parts of Europe that are still used for balneotherapy.

Purpose

Baths or soaks are an easy way to treat a variety of skin disorders involving large areas of the skin, injuries to or disorders of the muscles and joints, menstrual and menopausal discomfort, fatigue, or general stress and tension. They relieve general aches and pains and can ease dry or oily, inflamed or itchy skin. Hot baths are relaxing and stimulating; cool baths can reduce inflammation.

In children as well as adults therapeutic baths are useful for itchy skin, **hives**, **sunburn**, chafing, **poison ivy** and oak, eczema, skin irritation, and dry skin. They may also help to relieve emotional tension and stress. Warm-water soaks are recommended for speeding recovery from **sprains**, muscle aches and pains, and other athletic injuries.

Many **family** care physicians recommend warm-water therapeutic baths as a way to relieve labor pains during **childbirth** without administering drugs.

Therapeutic baths are used to treat a wider variety of disorders and injuries in Europe and the French-speaking parts of Canada than in the United States. In Eastern Europe and the countries of the former Soviet Union, therapeutic baths are used to treat children suffering from the aftereffects of head trauma as well as other physical injuries. One Italian spa lists recurrent earaches, sinus infections, and **acne** among the conditions that can be treated with therapeutic baths for children and adolescents as well as adults. European doctors often use mineral water in therapeutic baths or add seaweed, dried moss, mud, or various mineral salts to the bath water.

Description

For a therapeutic bath to treat eczema, the tub should be filled half-full with water at a comfortable temperature. The water should not be allowed to cool too much.

Different types of therapeutic baths are used for different skin conditions. The following are some examples:

- Colloidal oatmeal (oatmeal that has been ground into a fine powder, e.g. Aveeno) coats, soothes, and stops itching without drying out the skin.
- Potassium permanganate—a dark purple salt—makes a good disinfectant.
- Bath oils are used as an emollient to ease itchy skin and eczema. RoBathol and cottonseed oil are recommended for younger children.
- Cornstarch is a soothing, drying bath for itchy skin.
- Sodium bicarbonate can be cooling for sunburn or other hot, dry skin conditions.
- Saline (salt) water baths can be used to treat eczema in children. The recommended amount is one cup to a tubful of warm water.
- Chlorine bleach can be added to bath water for children who develop recurrent skin infections with eczema. The recommended amount is two teaspoons per gallon of water.

Therapeutic baths to treat **sports** injuries or relieve menstrual cramps may use slightly warmer water than is used to relieve skin disorders. Adolescents using therapeutic baths to relieve emotional stress may add a few drops of essential oils of lavender or other fragrant herbs to the bath water. Some people like to add eucalyptus oil to the bath water to relieve nasal congestion when they are recovering from colds or sinusitis.

Precautions

The temperature of the water for a therapeutic bath should feel comfortable to the hand. The bath should not last longer than 20 to 30 minutes because of the tendency of these soaks to soften and wear away the skin.

A bath mat should be placed in the tub before adding water, since medications may cause the floor of the tub to be slippery.

Eczema and other skin diseases can be treated with an ointment that contains a derivative of coal tar. Parts of the coal tar are volatile, so the bathroom should be well ventilated.

Parents should not leave small children alone in the bath because of the risk of drowning.

Essential flower or herb oils used to scent therapeutic baths should always be added to the water; they should never be applied directly to the skin.

Preparation

Parents should keep the room warm to minimize temperature fluctuations. This precaution is particularly important when bathing infants or younger children.

Parents should also take appropriate **safety** precautions, including removing hair dryers, electric shavers, or other small electrical appliances from the tub area. Another important safety precaution is to check the temperature setting on the hot water heater to make sure that it does not raise the temperature of the water to the scalding point. The standard factory setting on new household water heaters is 120°F (49°C), which is the highest setting considered to be safe. It is better for large families to purchase a larger hot water heater if there is a concern about the availability of hot water than to turn the thermostat on the heater higher than 120°F (49°C).

Aftercare

After the bath, the skin should be blotted (not rubbed) carefully with a towel. The patient should wear loose, light clothing after the bath. If the child or adolescent is being treated for eczema, an emollient should be applied within three minutes. Parents may use vegetable oil, petroleum jelly, or such commercial creams as Aveeno, Curel, Purpose, Dermasil, Neutrogena, DML Forte, and Eucerin. Some doctors may recommend preparations containing urea, lactic acid, or alpha-hydroxy acid.

Teenagers using therapeutic baths as part of rehabilitation after an athletic injury should follow the recommendations of their doctor or physical therapist regarding range-of-motion exercises or other treatments following the warm-water soak.

Risks

The most common risks associated with therapeutic baths are falls caused by loss of balance on a wet or slippery surface, electrocution caused by a hair dryer or other small appliance falling into the tub, scalding accidents from overheated water, and accidental drowning.

Some older children or adolescents may experience fatigue or a drop in blood pressure from long immersion in a therapeutic bath.

KEY TERMS

Balneotherapy—The medical term for the use of baths to treat disease.

Eczema—A superficial type of inflammation of the skin that may be very itchy and weeping in the early stages; later, the affected skin becomes crusted, scaly, and thick.

Hydrotherapy—The use of water (hot, cold, steam, or ice) to relieve discomfort and promote physical well-being. Also called water therapy.

Parental concerns

Therapeutic baths are a common and inexpensive treatment for a variety of skin disorders, menstrual cramps, and minor aches and pains. The chief concern of parents should be taking appropriate safety precautions regarding the hot water supply and the bathroom or tub area.

See also Atopic dermatitis; Dysmenorrhea; Sports injuries.

Resources

BOOKS

Barron, Patrick. *Hydrotherapy: Theory and Technique.* Orlando, FL: Pine Island Publishers, 2003.

Kellogg, John Harvey. *Rational Hydrotherapy.* Brushton, NY: TEACH Services, 2001.

Pelletier, Kenneth R. *The Best Alternative Medicine, Part I: Naturopathic Medicine.* New York: Simon and Schuster, 2002.

ORGANIZATIONS

American Academy of Dermatology (AAD). PO Box 4014, Schaumburg, IL 60168–4014. Web site: <www.aad.org>.

American Association of Naturopathic Physicians. 8201 Greensboro Drive, Suite 300, McLean, Virginia 22102. Web site: <http://naturopathic.org>.

Carol A. Turkington

Therapeutic school *see* **Alternative school**

Third and fourth pharyngeal pouch syndrome *see* **DiGeorge syndrome**

Throat culture

Definition

A throat culture is a microbiological procedure for identifying disease-causing bacterial organisms in material taken from the throat. A throat swab will capture the causative organism in most cases and the culture will allow the specific organism to be grown in the microbiology laboratory under certain conditions. The bacteria can then be identified, and results from antibiotic sensitivity tests on the bacteria will determine the appropriate treatment to be prescribed.

Purpose

The primary purpose of a throat culture is to identify the specific bacterial organisms that are causing a **sore throat** or throat infection, particularly to identify or to rule out the presence of group A, beta-hemolytic streptococci, the bacterial organisms that cause **strep throat**. Hemolytic means that these streptococci are capable of destroying red blood cells.

Since most sore throats are caused by viral infections rather than by strep organisms, a correct diagnosis is important to prevent unnecessary use of **antibiotics** for viruses that do not respond to them, and to begin effective treatment of strep or other throat infections as soon as possible. Throat cultures can also be used to identify other disease organisms that are present in the patient's throat and to identify people who are carriers of organisms that cause **meningitis** and **whooping cough**, among other diseases.

Besides the use of throat cultures in diagnosis, the bacteria identified are used to determine antibiotic sensitivity, allowing physicians to select the most appropriate and effective antibiotic to treat a specific infection. It is common for physicians to order culture and sensitivity tests at the same time.

Description

A throat culture will often be performed on an individual who has a severe sore throat or known symptoms of strep throat. These symptoms include a sore throat that may be accompanied by **fever**, body aches, and loss of appetite. The tonsils and the back of the throat may appear red, swollen, and streaked with pus. Symptoms usually appear one to three days after being exposed to the group A streptococcus *S. pyogenes.* Strep throat occurs more often among children than adults, with incidence at peak in fall and winter when school is in session and contact with other children is highest. Because strep is highly contagious, **family** members and close contacts of individuals diagnosed with strep throat may also be advised to have throat cultures if they show signs of sore throat or other symptoms.

The specimen for throat culture is obtained by wiping the child's throat with a sterile cotton swab. The child is asked to tilt the head back and open the mouth wide. With the tongue depressed and the child saying "ah," the care provider wipes the back of the throat and the tonsils with the sterile swab, applying it to any area that appears either very red or is discharging pus. The swab is removed gently without touching the teeth, gums, or tongue. It is then placed in a sterile tube for immediate delivery to a laboratory. The swabbing procedure may cause gagging but is not painful. Obtaining the specimen takes less than 30 seconds. Laboratory results will be available as soon as bacteria grow in a special plate that has been streaked with the contaminated swab, usually within two to three days. Sometimes the organism cultured is not strep as suspected. The microbiology laboratory may use samples of the bacteria grown to perform other tests that will help identify the disease causing organism.

S. pyogenes is known to grow well in growth media such as rich broths or gels (agars) that are supplemented with blood. When strep is suspected, the throat material is cultured on blood agar that has been prepared as a broth and poured into petri dishes (plates) where it solidifies into a gel. Blood agar is usually made from the cell walls of red algae (also trypticase soy, heart infusion, or Todd-Hewitt agar) and sheep's blood. When the throat swab reaches the laboratory, the microbiologist uses it to make streaks directly across a blood agar plate. The covered plate is allowed to incubate at a specific temperature (35°–37°C) for 24 to 48 hours to foster the growth of bacteria. The bacteria will grow in clusters called colonies. If the organism is a group A hemolytic streptococcus, an area immediately around the bacterial colony will show hemolysis (the breaking up or lysing of red blood cells), leaving a clear zone surrounding the colony. This helps a technician identify a hemolytic strep organism visually. Other types of bacteria may grow in differently sized or shaped colonies, allowing the microbiologist to differentiate the bacteria. A sample of the bacterial colony may also be examined microscopically to evaluate bacterial type or morphology. Samples of the bacteria may be restreaked on another agar plate with small disks of specific antibiotics to see which antibiotics destroy the bacteria (sensitivity testing). The physician may then prescribe the most effective antibiotic.

When strep throat is suspected, it may be screened in a quick test in the doctor's office. These tests allow direct detection of streptococcal antigens in body fluids such as urine or blood serum or from a throat swab. The test uses a strip or disc that is chemically coated with an antibody specific for the strep antigen. If strep is present, a visible reaction occurs with the antibody on the strip when combined with material from the throat. Depending upon the manufacturer's method, results may be available in about ten to 30 minutes. These "instant" tests are not as definitive as cultures but their reliability has improved since they were first introduced. If an instant throat test is negative, however, a throat culture will still be performed to verify the negative results or to identify non-strep organisms.

Precautions

Gargling to clear the throat or treatment with antibiotics will affect culture results and may make identification of the bacteria impossible. The child should not gargle immediately before the culture.

The child's throat should be swabbed and the culture performed before any antibiotics are taken. The laboratory should be informed if the patient has recently taken antibiotics for the current infection or any other infection. After the culture, however, the physician may initiate early treatment by prescribing a broad spectrum antibiotic to be started before results of the culture are available. After the organism has been identified and sensitivity testing has indicated the most effective antibiotic, a different, more specific antibiotic can be prescribed.

The child's immunization history should be checked to evaluate the possibility that diseases other than strep are causing the sore throat. The care provider should wash his or her hands carefully after swabbing the throat and handling the specimen to prevent the spread of any infectious organisms. Hand washing should be done at home also to reduce contact with infective material. Spreading is usually from contact with droplets of material from the nose and throat of affected individuals.

Preparation

There is no special preparation involved before performing a throat culture. The individual does not need to avoid food or fluids before the test.

Aftercare

There are no special care recommendations after throat swab and culture have been performed. There are no unusual effects expected from having the throat swabbed, though the child may have a mild sensation of something present in the throat for several hours after it has been swabbed.

Risks

Healthcare professionals, parents, or other contacts are at risk of exposure to the child's illness. Strep throat is highly contagious and easily spread through contact with droplets from the nose or throat.

Normal results

Normal results would include finding organisms that grow in healthy throat tissues (normal flora). These organisms include non-hemolytic and alpha-hemolytic streptococci, some *Neisseria* species, staphylococci, **diphtheria** and hemophilus organisms, pneumococci, yeasts, and Gram-negative rods.

Abnormal results

In addition to *S. pyogenes*, other disease agents may be identified in the throat culture. Besides other varieties of strep organisms, these organisms may include *Candida albicans*, which can cause thrush; *Corynebacterium diphtheriae*, which can cause diphtheria; and *Bordetella pertussis*, which can cause whooping **cough**. In addition, the appearance of a specific normal organism in very high numbers may also be regarded as an abnormal result.

Parental concerns

Parents may be concerned that effective treatment will be delayed because of waiting for the throat culture results, which can take up to 48 hours. Physicians may prescribe a broad spectrum antibiotic as initial treatment rather than waiting for culture results. When the culture results are available and sensitivity tests indicate a more effective antibiotic, the physician will likely prescribe a new antibiotic specific for the strep or other organism identified.

See also Strep throat.

KEY TERMS

Agar—A gel made from red algae that is used to culture certain disease agents in the laboratory.

Antibiotics—Drugs that are designed to kill or inhibit the growth of the bacteria that cause infections.

Antigen—A substance (usually a protein) identified as foreign by the body's immune system, triggering the release of antibodies as part of the body's immune response.

Carrier—A person who possesses a gene for an abnormal trait without showing signs of the disorder. The person may pass the abnormal gene on to offspring. Also refers to a person who has a particular disease agent present within his/her body, and can pass this agent on to others, but who displays no symptoms of infection.

Diphtheria—A serious, frequently fatal, bacterial infection that affects the respiratory tract. Vaccinations given in childhood have made diphtheria very rare in the United States.

Hemolytic—Able to break down or dissolve red blood cells.

Morphology—Literally, the study of form. In medicine, morphology refers to size, shape, and structure rather than function.

Streptococcus—Plural, streptococci. Any of several species of spherical bacteria that form pairs or chains. They cause a wide variety of infections including scarlet fever, tonsillitis, and pneumonia.

Thrush—An infection of the mouth, caused by the yeast *Candida albicans* and characterized by a whitish growth and ulcers.

Whooping cough—An infectious disease of the respiratory tract caused by a bacterium, *Bordetella pertussis*. Also known as pertussis.

Resources

ORGANIZATIONS

American Academy of Pediatrics. 141 Northwest Point Boulevard, Elk Grove Village, IL 60007–1098. Web site: <www.aap.org>.

Centers for Disease Control. 200 Independence Avenue, SW, Washington, DC, 20201. Web site: <www.cdc.gov>.

Centers for Disease Control and Prevention. 1600 Clifton Rd., NE, Atlanta, GA 30333. Web site: <www.cdc.gov>.

WEB SITES

Rutherford, Kim. "Strep Throat." *KidsHealth*, May 2001. Available online at <http://kidshealth.org/parent/infections/lung/strep_throat.html> (accessed December 1, 2004).

Wener, Kenneth. "Throat Swab Culture." *MedlinePlus* August 11, 2003. Available online at <www.nlm.nih.gov/medlineplus/ency/article/003746.htm> (accessed December 1, 2004).

L. Lee Culvert
Cindy L. A. Jones, PhD

Thrombocyte count *see* **Platelet count**

Thrush *see* **Candidiasis**

Thumb sucking

Definition

Thumb sucking is the childhood habit of putting the thumb in the mouth for comfort or to relieve stress.

Description

About half of all children suck their thumbs during infancy, with most starting in the first weeks of life. Ultrasound pictures of intrauterine life have even shown fetuses sucking their thumbs. One way that infants explore their world is by putting objects in their mouths and sucking on them. Thumb sucking appears to be a natural habit of children in all parts of the world. Sucking the thumb is soothing for a small child, and many children continue this habit for comfort and security into the early school years. Thumb sucking is most prevalent in children under two, and most children give up the habit on their own by age four.

Thumb sucking by itself is not a cause or symptom of physical or psychological problems. It is not known why some children suck their thumbs longer than others. More girls than boys suck their thumbs beyond age two. Researchers speculate that boys receive stronger negative messages from parents and peers that thumb sucking is infantile and not acceptable. Thumb sucking offers security to a child, but this behavior does not imply that the child is insecure. Most children have some sort of self-comforting ritual that may involve sucking the thumb, fingers, or a pacifier, pulling or twisting their hair, or stroking or sucking a soft toy or blanket. These are all normal habits of infancy that are eventually outgrown.

Some nineteenth-century physicians feared a variety of consequences from thumb sucking, such as weak moral character, and earlier generations of parents were advised to break this habit forcibly. Parents were sometimes told to place mechanical constraints on their children's hands to keep their thumbs out of their mouths. Children's thumbs were sometimes coated with a bitter substance, taped, or covered with gloves. It was also considered necessary to shame and humiliate the thumb sucker.

Modern doctors find few negative health effects of thumb sucking, even if prolonged, and parents are urged to let their children outgrow the habit on their own. Thumb sucking may be more of a problem for the parent than the child, if the parent is unsettled by the behavior. Weaning a young child from the habit before he or she is ready is usually difficult and may only prolong the thumb sucking.

Infancy

Some children suck their thumbs before they are even born, and others begin sucking their thumbs soon after birth. All or nearly all infants suck on their fingers, thumbs, or a pacifier. This is completely normal and very common.

Toddlerhood

Thumb sucking is most common in children who are younger than two years old. Many children stop sucking their thumbs by age three or four without any intervention.

Preschool

Preschool children may begin to become embarrassed by their thumb sucking if the children with whom they interact do not suck their thumbs and make fun of them. Most children in this age group who still suck their thumbs will stop on their own, and intervening may stress the child and make the problem worse. Even when they have stopped thumb sucking during the day, children may continue it as part of a nighttime falling **sleep** ritual.

School age

Most children have stopped sucking their thumbs before they begin school, or else stop sucking shortly thereafter, usually in response to **peer pressure**. If a school age child seems distressed about his or her thumb sucking, the parent may want to suggest ways in which they can work together to wean the child from the thumb. If the child does not want to give up thumb sucking, the dentist should be consulted to ensure that it is not doing any damage to the alignment of the teeth.

Common problems

There are a few cases where thumb sucking may become a problem. If a school-age child sucks his or her thumb and is teased by classmates, the child may wish to quit and need help either from parents or a counselor. Some dentists warn of misalignment of permanent teeth if a child of five or six sucks the thumb with a lot of

Young boy sucking his thumb. *(© Jennie Woodcock; Reflections Photolibrary/Corbis.)*

pressure on the teeth. Not all dentists agree, however, that thumb sucking is harmful to tooth development. If a child's dentist sees evidence that thumb sucking is causing a particular problem, the child may need to be urged to quit. If the child is having trouble quitting the habit, parents may be able to help with positive reinforcement. The child can be given a sticker or small reward for a day spent without thumb sucking. Parents can also help the child find something else to do with his or her hands when the child has the urge to suck the thumb. Parents should avoid negative pressure on children to stop sucking their thumbs; this habit is eventually outgrown by all children. In extreme cases, some dentists can prescribe an oral device to alter the shape of the roof of the child's mouth, so that it is unpleasant for the child to continue sucking. If a child has recently undergone any sort of trauma such as witnessing **divorce**, a pet's death, or **family** problems, treatment for thumb sucking should not be undertaken right away.

Parental concerns

Parents tend to be more concerned with thumb sucking than is actually warranted. Until the child is five or six, or there starts to be a problem with speech formation or teeth alignment, thumb sucking is not a problem.

When to call the doctor

If the child continues to suck his or her thumb after age five or six, or sucks it frequently or very hard after age three or four, the doctor may have helpful suggestions for the concerned parent. If the child's teeth are becoming misaligned because of thumb sucking the dentist should be consulted. If the thumb sucking is combined with other problems such as **anxiety** a doctor should be consulted.

Resources

BOOKS

Dionne, Wanda. *Little Thumb.* Gretna, LA: Pelican Publishing Company, 2001.

ORGANIZATIONS

International Association of Orofacial Myology. 970 Elizabeth Street, Denver, CO 80209. Web site: <www.iaom.com>.

Tish Davidson, A.M.

Tick bite *see* **Lyme disease**

Tics

Definition

A tic is a nonvoluntary body movement or vocal sound that is made repeatedly, rapidly, and suddenly. It has a stereotyped but nonrhythmic character. The child or adolescent with a tic experiences it as irresistible but can suppress the movement or noise for a period of time. Tics are categorized as motor or vocal, and as simple or complex. The word "tic" itself is French.

Tics are a type of dyskinesia, which is the general medical term given to impairments or distortions of voluntary movements. Although tics vary considerably in severity, they are associated with several neuropsychiatric disorders in children and adolescents. The American Psychiatric Association (APA) defined four tic disorders in the fourth edition of the *Diagnostic and Statistical Manual of Mental Disorders*, or *DSM-IV*. The disorders are distinguished from one another according to three criteria: the child's age at onset; the duration of the disorder; and the number and variety of tics.

- Transient tic disorder (also known as benign tic disorder of childhood): The criteria for transient tic disorder specify that the onset must occur before the age of 18 years; the tics must occur many times a day almost every day for at least four weeks but not longer than 12 months; and the child must not meet the criteria for **Tourette syndrome** or chronic tic disorder.
- Chronic motor or vocal tic disorder: To meet the diagnosis of chronic tic disorder, the child must be younger

than 18 years of age; the tics must have occurred nearly every day or intermittently for a period longer than a year, without a tic-free interval longer than three months; the tics must be either vocal or motor but not both; and the child must not meet the criteria for Tourette disorder.

- Tourette disorder (also known as Tourette syndrome, or TS): Tourette disorder is considered the most serious of the four tic disorders. The *DSM-IV* criteria for Tourette disorder specify that the child must be younger 18 years of age at onset; the tics must include multiple vocal as well as motor tics, although not necessarily at the same time; the tics must occur many times a day, nearly every day or at intervals over a period longer than a year, without symptom-free intervals longer than six months; there must be variations in the number, location, severity, complexity, and frequency of the tics over time; and the tics cannot be attributed to the effects of a substance (such as stimulants) or a disease of the central nervous system.
- Tic disorder not otherwise specified: This category includes all cases that do not meet the full criteria for any of the other tic disorders.

Description

Tics most commonly affect the child's face, neck, voice box, and upper torso but may involve almost any body part. The experience of having a tic is difficult to describe to those who have never been troubled by them. Having tics may be compared to having the sensation of having to **cough** because something is tickling one's throat or nose. The sensation is irresistible and immediate.

Simple tics

Simple tics involve only a few muscles or sounds that are not yet words. Examples of simple motor tics include nose wrinkling, facial grimaces, eye blinking, jerking the neck, shrugging the shoulders, or tensing the muscles of the abdomen. Simple vocal tics include grunting, clucking, sniffing, chirping, or throat-clearing noises. Simple tics rarely last longer than a few hundred milliseconds.

Complex tics

Complex tics involve multiple groups or muscles or complete words or sentences. Examples of complex motor tics include such gestures as jumping, squatting, making motions with the hands, twirling around when walking, touching or smelling an object repeatedly, and holding the body in an unusual position. Complex motor tics last longer than simple motor tics, usually several seconds or longer. Two specific types of complex motor tics that often cause parents concern are *copropraxia*, in which the tic involves a vulgar or obscene gesture, and *echopraxia*, in which the tic is a spontaneous imitation of someone else's movements.

Similarly, complex vocal tics involve full speech and language, which may range from the spontaneous utterance of individual words or phrases, such as "Stop," or "Oh boy," to speech blocking or meaningless changes in the pitch, volume, or rhythm of the child's voice. Specific types of complex vocal tics include *palilalia*, which refers to the child's repetition of his or her own words; *coprolalia*, which refers to the use of obscene words or abusive terms for certain racial or religious groups; and *echolalia*, in which the child repeats someone else's last word or phrase.

Sensory tics

Sensory tics are less common than either motor or vocal tics. The term refers to repeated unwanted or uncomfortable sensations, usually in the child's throat, eyes, or shoulders. The child may feel a sensation of tickling, warmth, cold, or pressure in the affected area.

Phantom tics

Phantom tics are the least common type of tic. A phantom tic is an out-of-body variation of a sensory tic in which the person feels a sensation in other people or objects. People with phantom tics experience temporary relief from the tic by touching or scratching the object involved.

Other features of tics

Tics typically occur in bouts or episodes alternating with periods of tic-free behavior lasting from several seconds to several hours. They generally diminish in severity when the child is involved in an absorbing activity such as reading or doing homework, and increase in frequency and severity when the child is tired, ill, or stressed. Some children have tics during the lighter stages of **sleep** or wake up during the night with a tic.

Severe complex motor tics carry the risk of physical injury, as the child may damage muscles or joints, fracture bones, or fall down during an episode of these tics. Some children harm themselves deliberately by self-cutting or self-hitting, while others hurt themselves unintentionally by touching or handling lighted matches, razor blades, or other dangerous objects. Severe complex vocal tics may interfere with breathing or swallowing.

Transmission

Tics as such are symptoms and are not transmitted directly from one person to another. Tic *disorders*, however, are known to run in families. In addition, some doctors think that tic disorders are more likely to develop in children who have had certain types of infections. These theories are discussed more fully below.

Demographics

Prevalence of tic disorders

The statistics given for tics and tic disorders vary from source to source, in part because tics vary considerably in severity, and many children with mild tics may never come to a doctor's attention. Estimates for the general North American population range from 3 to 20 percent for transient tics (particularly among children below the age of ten); 2–5 percent for chronic tic disorders; and 0.1–0.8 percent for Tourette syndrome. A Swedish study done in 2003 reported that 6.6 percent of a sample of Uppsala school children between the ages of 7 and 15 met *DSM-IV* criteria for tic disorders: 4.8 percent for transient tic disorder, 0.8 percent for chronic motor tic disorder, 0.5 percent for chronic vocal tic disorder, and 0.6 percent for Tourette syndrome. One study of American volunteers for military service reported a prevalence of 0.5 cases of TS per 1000 for males and 0.3 cases per 1000 for females. Tourette syndrome is known to be more common in males than in females, although the gender ratio is variously reported as 3: 1, 5: 1, or even 10: 1.

Little is known as of 2004 about the prevalence of tic disorders across racial or ethnic groups. One small study that was done in western North Carolina reported that Caucasian children were slightly more likely to have tic disorders than either African American or Native American children (2.1 percent to 1.5 percent and 1.5 percent respectively). The authors of the study cautioned, however, against applying their findings to larger groups of children in other parts of the United States.

Tic disorders and comorbid disorders

One important characteristic of tics and tic disorders is that they rarely occur by themselves. Tic disorders—particularly TS—have a high rate of comorbidity with other childhood disorders. The term *comorbid* is used to refer to a disease or disorder that occurs at the same time as another disorder. The frequencies of the most common disorders that may be comorbid with tic disorders and Tourette syndrome are as follows:

- attention-deficit/hyperactivity disorder (ADHD): 50 percent comorbidity with tic disorders, 90 percent comorbidity with TS
- **obsessive-compulsive disorder** (OCD): 11 percent and 80 percent respectively
- major depression: 40 percent and 44 percent respectively

Other psychiatric problems that often coexist with tics and tic disorders include **learning disorders**, **impulse control disorders**, school phobia, sensory hypersensitivity, and rage attacks.

Causes and symptoms

The causes of tics and tic disorders are not fully understood as of the early 2000s, but most researchers believe that they are multifactorial, or the end result of several causes. In the early twentieth century, many doctors influenced by Freud thought that tics were caused by hysteria or other emotional problems, and treated them with psychoanalysis. Psychoanalytic treatment, however, had a very low rate of success.

Since the 1970s, researchers have been looking at genetic factors in tic disorders and Tourette syndrome. With regard to TS, genetic factors are present in about 75 percent of children diagnosed with TS, with 25 percent having inherited genetic factors from both parents. The exact pattern of genetic transmission was not known as of 2004, however; autosomal dominant, autosomal recessive, and sex-linked inheritance patterns have all been studied and rejected. Some candidate genes for TS have also been tested and excluded. What is known is that the patient's environment and heredity play a significant part in the severity and course of TS.

Tic disorders as well as OCD sometimes develop after infections (usually **scarlet fever** or **strep throat**) caused by a group of bacteria known as group A beta-hemolytic streptococci, sometimes abbreviated as GABHS. These disorders are sometimes grouped together as PANDAS disorders, which stands for Pediatric Autoimmune Neuropsychiatric Disorders Associated with Streptococci. Some researchers think that the tics develop when antibodies in the child's blood produced in response to the bacteria cross-react with proteins in the brain tissue. The connection between **streptococcal infections** and tic disorders is questioned by some researchers, however, on the grounds that most children have a GABHS infection at some point in their early years, but the vast majority (95 percent) do not develop OCD or a tic disorder. There appears to be a closer connection between Sydenham's chorea, which is a movement disorder, and GABHS infections than between tic disorders and these infections. One prospective study done at Yale reported in 2004 that new GABHS infections do *not* appear to cause a worsening of tics in children diagnosed with OCD or Tourette syndrome.

Neuroimaging studies have shown that tic disorders are related to abnormal levels of neurotransmitters known as dopamine, serotonin, and cyclic AMP in certain parts of the brain. A neurotransmitter is a chemical produced by the body that conveys nerve impulses across the gaps (synapses) between nerve cells. In addition to abnormalities in the production or absorption of these chemical messengers, imaging studies indicate that the blood flow and metabolism in a part of the brain called the basal ganglia are abnormally low. The basal ganglia are groups of nerve cells deep in the brain that control movement as well as emotion and certain aspects of thinking. In contrast to the low level of blood flow in the basal ganglia, the motor areas in the frontotemporal cortex of the brain show increased levels of activity.

The various types of tics themselves have already been described. Other symptoms that may be associated with tics and tic disorders include obsessive thoughts; difficulty concentrating or paying attention in school; forgetfulness; slowness in completing tasks; losing the thread of a conversation. These symptoms are usually regarded as side effects of interrupted thinking or behavior caused by the tics.

When to call the doctor

Most cases of mild tics do not require medical treatment and will clear up on their own over time. Doctors usually recommend that **family** members try to ignore simple tics, since teasing or other unwanted attention may make the tics worse. A visit to the doctor is recommended, however, under any of the following circumstances:

- The child is falling behind in school because of the tics.
- The child's relationships with peers and adults outside the family are affected by the tics.
- The child cannot carry out activities of daily living (self-feeding, bathing, getting dressed, etc.).
- The child has fallen, injured himself, or developed other physical problems because of the tics.
- Other family members have or have had tic disorders.
- The child has recently had an episode of strep throat or other streptococcal infection.
- The child has been diagnosed with OCD, ADHD, or depression.
- The tics have come on suddenly.

Diagnosis

Tic disorders are diagnosed by a process of excluding other possibilities; there are no definitive tests for these disorders as of the early 2000s. For this reason, the diagnosis of tic disorders is often delayed or sometimes missed altogether in milder cases. One study reported an average delay of five to 12 years between the initial symptoms and the correct diagnosis. In addition, diagnosis is complicated by the fact that children often learn to mask their tics by converting them to more socially acceptable or apparently voluntary movements or sounds.

History and physical examination

The first part of a medical workup for tics is the taking of a medical history and a general physical examination. The doctor will want to know whether there is a family history of tics or tic disorders, whether the child has been diagnosed with other childhood developmental or psychiatric disorders, and whether he or she has recently had strep throat or a similar infection.

The physical examination helps the doctor rule out such other possible diagnoses as Sydenham's chorea, a self-limited movement disorder that most commonly affects children between five and 15 years of age; other **movement disorders**; seizure disorders; **encephalitis**; neurosyphilis; Wilson's disease (a rare inherited disease that causes the body to retain copper); **schizophrenia**; **carbon monoxide poisoning**; cocaine intoxication; brain injuries caused by trauma; **cerebral palsy**; or the side effects of certain medications, particularly stimulants and antiepileptic drugs.

The doctor may not be able to observe the tic(s) during the child's first office visit, often because the child has learned to suppress or mask them. In some cases, a follow-up visit may be scheduled, or the doctor may refer the child to a child psychiatrist or neurologist for further observation. Another approach that can be used to confirm the diagnosis is to audiotape or videotape the child at home or in another less stressful setting.

Psychiatric inventories

Most child psychiatrists will administer the Yale Global Tic Severity Scale (YGTSS) during the intake interview and at follow-up visits in order to identify the particular tic disorder affecting the child, identify comorbid disorders if present, evaluate the severity of the tics, and monitor the child's response to treatment.

The YGTSS, which was first published in 1989, is a semi-structured interview that is widely used by researchers who study tic disorders. "Semi-structured" means that it is an open-ended set of questions that allow the child's parents to describe the tics and other symptoms in detail rather than just answer brief yes-or-no questions.

Laboratory tests

As mentioned earlier, there are no laboratory tests to diagnose tics as such. In some cases, however, the doctor may order a blood test to rule out Wilson's disease or other metabolic disorders, or order a **throat culture** if the child has recently had strep throat. If the doctor suspects that the child has a PANDAS disorder, he or she may order a blood test to measure the level of antibodies against group A streptococci.

Imaging studies

As of 2004, imaging studies were not routinely performed on children or adolescents with tics unless the doctor suspects a brain injury, infection, or structural abnormality. **Magnetic resonance imaging** (MRIs), PET scans, and single-photon emission **computed tomography** (SPECT) scans have been used by researchers, however, to study the brains of patients diagnosed with Tourette syndrome.

In the summer of 2004, two engineers in Taiwan reported on the development of a computerized diagnostic system that will allow radiologists to use SPECT imaging to distinguish between chronic tic disorder and Tourette syndrome with a much higher degree of accuracy. The system appears to be potentially useful in speeding up the process of diagnosis and allowing earlier treatment of TS.

Treatment

After psychoanalysis was discredited in the 1970s as a treatment for tic disorders, some doctors urged using such antipsychotic drugs as haloperidol (Haldol) to treat TS by suppressing the tics. These drugs, which are sometimes called neuroleptics, have severe side effects and are likely to interact with other medications that the child may be taking. In addition, tics are increasingly recognized as complex phenomena that have an emotional as well as a physical dimension. As a result, the treatment of tic disorders has changed in the early 2000s in the direction of minimizing the use of medications in favor of a multidisciplinary approach.

The approach to assess a child with a tic disorder is as follows:

- Administer the YGTSS in order to evaluate the areas of the child's functioning that are most severely affected by the tics.
- Identify any comorbid disorders if present. In many cases, the tics do not interfere with the child's life as much as ADHD, OCD, or depression. ADHD should be the primary target of management in children diagnosed with a tic disorder and comorbid ADHD.
- Rank the symptoms in order of importance in order to focus treatment on the ones that are most significant to the child and the family.
- Emphasize controlling the tics and learning to live with them rather than trying to eliminate them with drugs.
- Use behavioral and psychotherapeutic approaches as well as medications.
- Involve the patient's teachers and other significant adults as well as parents in order to help monitor the child's symptoms and response to treatment.

Medications

There is no medication that can cure a tic disorder; all drugs that are used to treat these disorders as of the early 2000s are used only to manage tics. In general, doctors prefer to avoid medications in treating mild tics; start the treatment of moderate or severe tics with medications that have relatively few side effects, and prescribe stronger drugs only when necessary.

Children whose throat cultures or blood tests are positive for a GABHS infection are treated aggressively with **antibiotics**, most commonly penicillin V.

Psychotherapy

Psychotherapy for tics and tic disorders typically involves education about tic disorders and therapy for the family as well as individual treatment for the child. The American Academy of Child and Adolescent Psychiatry (AACAP) urges parents to avoid blaming or punishing the child for the tics, as shaming or harsh treatment increases the child's level of emotional stress and usually makes the tics worse.

Cognitive-behavioral approaches are the most common type of individual psychotherapy used to treat tics and tic disorders. Specific behavioral approaches include the following:

- Massed negative practice: In this form of behavioral treatment, the child is asked to perform the tic intentionally for specified periods of time interspersed with rest periods.

- Competing response training: This is a form of treatment of motor tics in which the child is taught to make the opposite movement to the tic.
- Self-monitoring: In awareness training, the child keeps a diary, small notebook, or wrist counter for recording tics. It is supposed to reduce the frequency of tic bouts by increasing the child's awareness of them.
- Contingency management: This approach works best in the home and is usually carried out by the parents. The child is praised or rewarded for not performing the tics and for replacing them with acceptable alternative behaviors.

As of the early 2000s, however, no controlled studies have been done comparing the effectiveness of these various behavioral approaches. At best, they appear to produce mixed results.

Surgery

Surgery is used very rarely to treat tic disorders; it is usually tried only if the tic has not responded to any medication and interferes significantly with the patient's life. Some patients with TS, however, have been successfully treated with stereotactic surgery involving high-frequency stimulation of the thalamus. Stereotactic surgery involves an approach that calculates angles and distances from the outside of the patient's skull to locate very small lesions or structures deep inside the brain. It allows the surgeon to remove tissue or treat injured areas through much smaller incisions.

Alternative treatments

The place of alternative or complementary therapies in treating tics is debated. One group of Chinese physicians reported successfully treating patients diagnosed with TS with acupuncture. However, a group of researchers studying traditional medicine in Bali found it ineffective in treating tic disorders, and a second group at Johns Hopkins reported that relaxation therapy did not have a statistically significant effect in treating children diagnosed with TS. There is also some evidence that gingko, ginseng, and some other herbs taken for their stimulant effects may increase the severity of tics in children and adolescents.

Nutritional concerns

Although some nutritionists have suggested a possible connection between sugar or food coloring and tic severity, no studies published as of 2004 had demonstrated such a connection. One study done at the University of Kansas did find a connection between **caffeine** (which is found in cola beverages and some other soft drinks as well as tea and coffee) consumption and tic severity in children. The study sample, however, was quite small.

Prognosis

The prognosis for most tics and tic disorders is quite good. In the majority of cases, the tics diminish in severity and eventually disappear as the child grows older. Even in Tourette syndrome, about 85 percent of children find that their tics diminish or go away entirely during or after **adolescence**. Tics that persist beyond the teenage years, however, usually become permanent.

Factors associated with a poorer prognosis for all tic disorders include the following:

- history of complications during the child's birth
- chronic physical illness in childhood
- physical or emotional abuse in the family or a history of family instability
- exposure to **anabolic steroids** or cocaine
- comorbid psychiatric or developmental disorders

Prevention

There are no known ways to prevent either tics or tic disorders.

Nutritional concerns

In some cases, parents may find it helpful to monitor the child's intake of cola, iced tea, other drinks containing caffeine, and certain herbal teas.

Parental concerns

Parental concerns related to tics and tic disorders are difficult to address in general terms, because tics can range in type and severity from simple noises or movements of short duration that do not attract much attention from others to complex tics of a physically harmful or socially embarrassing nature that attract a lot of attention. In addition, tics must often be managed in the context of another disorder affecting the child. Since the treatment of tics is individualized, it is best for parents to consult with the child's doctor(s) regarding special educational programs or settings, explaining the tics or tic disorder to others, dealing with the side effects of medications, and managing rage attacks or other symptoms that may be associated with the tics.

See also Movement disorders; Tourette syndrome.

KEY TERMS

Basal ganglia—Brain structure at the base of the cerebral hemispheres involved in controlling movement.

Chorea—Involuntary movements in which the arms or legs may jerk or flail uncontrollably.

Comorbidity—A disease or condition that coexists with the disease or condition for which the patient is being primarily treated.

Compulsion—A repetitive or ritualistic behavior that a person performs to reduce anxiety. Compulsions often develop as a way of controlling or "undoing" obsessive thoughts.

Coprolalia—The involuntary use of obscene language.

Copropraxia—The involuntary display of unacceptable/obscene gestures.

Dopamine—A neurotransmitter made in the brain that is involved in many brain activities, including movement and emotion.

Dyskinesia—Impaired ability to make voluntary movements.

Echolalia—Involuntary echoing of the last word, phrase, or sentence spoken by someone else.

Echopraxia—The imitation of the movement of another individual.

Multifactorial—Describes a disease that is the product of the interaction of multiple genetic and environmental factors.

Neuroleptic—Another name for the older type of antipsychotic medications, such as haloperidol and chlorpromazine, prescribed to treat psychotic conditions.

Neurotransmitter—A chemical messenger that transmits an impulse from one nerve cell to the next.

Palilalia—A complex vocal tic in which the child repeats his or her own words, songs, or other utterances.

PANDAS disorders—A group of childhood disorders associated with such streptococcal infections as scarlet fever and strep throat. The acronym stands for Pediatric Autoimmune Neuropsychiatric Disorders Associated with Streptococci.

Semi-structured interview—A psychiatric instrument characterized by open-ended questions for discussion rather than brief questions requiring yes or no answers.

Stereotactic technique—A technique used by neurosurgeons to pinpoint locations within the brain. It employs computer imaging to guide the surgeon to the exact location for the surgical procedure.

Stereotyped—Having a persistent, repetitive, and senseless quality. Tics are stereotyped movements or sounds.

Streptococcus—Plural, streptococci. Any of several species of spherical bacteria that form pairs or chains. They cause a wide variety of infections including scarlet fever, tonsillitis, and pneumonia.

Tic—A brief and intermittent involuntary movement or sound.

Resources

BOOKS

Diagnostic and Statistical Manual of Mental Disorders, 4th ed., Text Revision. Washington, DC: American Psychiatric Association, 2000.

"Dyskinesias." Section 14, Chapter 179 in *The Merck Manual of Diagnosis and Therapy*, edited by Mark H. Beers and Robert Berkow. Whitehouse Station, NJ: Merck Research Laboratories, 2002.

PERIODICALS

Dale, R. C., et al. "Dyskinesias and Associated Psychiatric Disorders Following Streptococcal Infections." *Archives of Disease in Childhood* 89 (July 2004): 604–10.

Evidente, Virgilio G. H. "Is It a Tic or Tourette?" *Postgraduate Medicine* 108 (October 2000): 175–82.

Khalifa, N., and A. L. von Knorring. "Prevalence of Tic Disorders and Tourette Syndrome in a Swedish School Population." *Developmental Medicine and Child Neurology* 45 (May 2003): 315–19.

Lavenstein, Bennett L. "Treatment Approaches for Children with Tourette's Syndrome." *Current Neurology and Neuroscience Reports* 3 (2003): 143–48.

Lemelson, R. B. "Traditional Healing and Its Discontents: Efficacy and Traditional Therapies of Neuropsychiatric Disorders in Bali." *Medical Anthropology Quarterly* 18 (March 2004): 48–76.

Luo, F., et al. "Prospective Longitudinal Study of Children with Tic Disorders and/or Obsessive-Compulsive Disorder: Relationship of Symptom Exacerbations to Newly Acquired Streptococcal Infections." *Pediatrics* 113 (June 2004): 578–85.

McEvoy, J. P., and T. B. Allen. "The Importance of Nicotinic Acetylcholine Receptors in Schizophrenia, Bipolar Disorder, and Tourette's Syndrome." *Current Drug Targets: CNS and Neurological Disorders* 1 (August 2002): 433–42.

Yin, T. K., and N. T. Chiu. "A Computer-Aided Diagnosis for Distinguishing Tourette's Syndrome from Chronic Tic Disorder in Children by a Fuzzy System with a Two-Step Minimization Approach." *IEEE Transactions on Biomedical Engineering* 51 (July 2004): 1286–95.

ORGANIZATIONS

American Academy of Child and Adolescent Psychiatry. 3615 Wisconsin Avenue, NW, Washington, DC 20016–3007. Web site: <www.aacap.org.>.

National Institute of Neurological Disorders and Stroke (NINDS). National Institutes of Health. 9000 Rockville Pike, Bethesda, MD 20892. Web site: <www.ninds.nih.gov>.

Tourette Syndrome Association Inc. 42–40 Bell Blvd., Bayside, New York 11361–2820. Web site; <http://tsa-usa.org>.

WEB SITES

Black, Kevin J., and Heather Webb. "Tourette Syndrome and Other Tic Disorders." *eMedicine*, November 9, 2004. Available online at <www.emedicine.com/neuro/topic664.htm> (accessed December 1, 2004).

Ellis, Cynthia R., and Holly Jean Zumpfe. "Childhood Habit Behaviors and Stereotypic Movement Disorder." *eMedicine*, October 26, 2004. Available online at <www.emedicine.com/ped/topic909.htm> (accessed December 1, 2004).

OTHER

American Academy of Child and Adolescent Psychiatry (AACAP). *Tic Disorders*. AACAP Facts for Families #35. Washington, DC: AACAP, 2000.

National Institute of Neurological Disorders and Stroke (NINDS). *Tourette Syndrome Fact Sheet*. Bethesda, MD: NINDS, 2001.

Rebecca Frey, PhD

Time-out procedure

Definition

Time out is a technique in which a child is removed from activity and forced to sit alone for a few minutes in order to calm down.

Description

The time out has become an increasingly popular method of dealing with children's inappropriate behavior. If a child becomes too aggressive or angry, the parent or caregiver may remove the child from the upsetting situation. Parents may have a special place in the home for time outs: in the child's room, in a certain chair, or on a rug in an out-of-the-way place. The child may be allowed to end the time out when he or she is ready or told to stay in the time-out place for a specific length of time. The time should be very short—one guide suggests a minute for each year of the child's age—as most young children cannot easily comprehend longer time spans.

The time out is not used as a punishment so much as an opportunity for the child to try to regain control of emotions. Some children can accomplish this by themselves, and being removed from a stressful **play** situation is all that they need. Other children may not be able to recover their equilibrium without help from an adult. The parent or caregiver may ask the child to try to calm down alone in the time-out spot and then give attention only after the child has made some effort.

It should be clear to the child that the time out is not punitive, and a child should not feel humiliated for having a time out. The time-out area should not be a constraining or frightening place, such as a locked closet. The time out should serve to teach the child to manage strong feelings safely, and after he or she has done so, the child should be praised for calming down.

There may be other techniques parents or caregivers can use before a time out becomes necessary. If an activity is too stressful to one or more children, it may be better to end the activity. Changing the situation may restore tempers more readily than a spell of reflection. If children are fighting because they are hungry or tired, then that need should be addressed. Children may benefit most from a time out if the issues of aggression or out-of-control behavior have been discussed at a time when the child was not upset. Although the goal of time out may be to teach the child to take responsibility for controlling his or her own behavior, depending on the age and **temperament** of the child, this may not be possible without support and comfort from parents or other concerned adults.

Toddlerhood

Children under three may not be mature enough to comprehend a time out, although for some it may be an effective tool.

Preschool

Time outs are usually most effective with preschool-age children. If time outs are used in a **preschool** or day-care situation, parents may want to discuss this with the teachers or caregivers so that time outs can be used consistently in situations at home too. Time outs for this age group should be very brief.

School age

School age children may be more resistant to the concept of time out. It is usually possible to give these children a certain sense of autonomy by having them help choose the time out location (when they are not angry) and allowing them to take themselves there. If they do not comply, this age group often responds well to being grounded until they choose to complete the time out.

Common problems

Many times children will vocalize their distress while they are in time out. Not insisting that children maintain silence for the completion of time out can be helpful, because it allows children to vent their feelings and makes time out easier to complete successfully. Children who leave time out before time is up can be gently held in place or put in a room while the parent holds the door shut. The room should not contain anything valuable or fragile and should not contain bookshelves or other things that the child may be able to pull and injure him or her self with.

Parental concerns

Children are often very vocally adverse to time outs, but time outs have been found to be effective ways of changing behavior in many children. Helping the child understand what behavior caused the time out and what kind of behavior is considered acceptable will help the child change the behavior in the future. Children cannot change their behavior if they do not know what is expected of them. Children's angry behavior, especially during the beginning of a time out, can be embarrassing for the parent, so it may be helpful if the situation arises in a public place to have the time out in a bathroom or in the car while always keeping the child in sight.

When to call the doctor

The doctor should be consulted if the child is very violent to him or herself or others during time out, or if behavior does not improve after time outs have been regularly enforced over a few weeks.

Resources

BOOKS

Abbot, Jacob. *Gentle Measures.* Chester, NY: Anza Classics Library, 2004.

Jenson, William R., et al. *The Tough Kind Parent Book: Practical Solutions to Tough Childhood Problems.* Longmont, CO: Sopris West, 2003.

PERIODICALS

Arnoscht, Otto J. "'Time-Out' Guides Children to Productive and Positive Behaviors." *The Brown University Child and Adolescent Behavior Letter* 16 (March 2003): 1.

Tish Davidson, A.M.
A. Woodward

Toddler elbow *see* **Nursemaid's elbow**

TOF *see* **Tetralogy of Fallot**

Toilet training

Definition

Toilet training is the process of teaching a young child to control the bowel and bladder and use the bathroom for elimination. A child is considered to be toilet trained when he or she initiates going to the bathroom and can adjust clothing necessary to urinate or have a bowel movement. Toilet training is sometimes called toilet learning or potty training.

Description

The average age at which children complete toilet training in the United States is approximately three years old. In some cases children learn bladder control first; others learn bowel control before bladder control. Control is generally first achieved during the daytime, well before a child is able to stay dry at night.

Some children achieve some control over bladder and/or bowel movements as early as nine months of age and are able to cooperate in controlling themselves to some degree by the age of 12 to 15 months. Most experts agree, however, that toilet training should only be initiated when a child exhibits certain signs of readiness that usually appear between the ages of two and three years of age. Unlike infants, toddlers know when they are urinating or defecating and may assume certain postures or become quiet when they are about to move their bowels. They have also learned the vocabulary their **family** uses for elimination. Another sign is a sense of fastidiousness and desire for order that appears at this stage of development. Children are likely to ask parents to change their dirty diapers right away, and they show a general interest in orderliness that can be harnessed for purposes of toilet training. A child this age also has a pronounced desire to imitate the parent of the same sex, a trait that can be used to advantage in enticing her to use the toilet. Lastly, the child will begin to show signs of being able to delay urination or bowel movements such as waking from **sleep** still dry or refraining from urinating or defecating for longer periods of time while not wearing a diaper.

Strategies

Child care experts generally recommend a strategy that uses praise as a motivator, has little pressure from the parents, and is fun for the child. It has been found that when parents wait until their toddler has attained the greatest possible degree of readiness, the process is easier, faster, and accompanied by fewer lapses. The emphasis is on letting the child proceed at his own pace, motivated by the desire to be a "big boy" or "big girl" and imitate his parents. Measures that may cause pressure and **anxiety** need to be avoided.

The first step in toilet training is to purchase a potty. There are different versions of potties, including ones that sit on the floor and are emptied after each use, ones that have cups to protect against splatters, and ones that sit on top of an adult toilet with or without a step stool for the child to climb up to it. The floor-level model is most often recommended for the first stages of toilet training. Some recommend taking the child to the store to help pick out his or her own potty, then helping to personalize it with a name, stickers, paint, etc., with the general idea of making the potty a prized possession of the child's, not something to be feared.

The child should first spend some time sitting on the potty, first while clothed and then with clothes removed, so that he or she is comfortable sitting on it. The connection between what she is doing on her small potty and what the adults and siblings do on the big potty should be emphasized. One suggestion is to bring the child to the potty with a dirty diaper and the contents placed in it so he or she can see that this is where they belong. Parents should watch for cues from the child that he or she may be about to urinate or have a bowel movement, such as a concentrated look, yanking at his or her diaper, squatting, or grunting. Often this behavior will happen first thing in the morning, right after a nap, or approximately 20 minutes after a meal. The child should be taken to the potty, his or her diaper should be removed, and the child encouraged to sit for at least one minute. Some children may enjoy reading a book or singing a song while waiting. Special read-aloud books about toilet training are popular. Parents should never strap a child into a potty or force him or her to sit on it. If the child has not used the potty after five minutes or so, he or he should be encouraged to get dressed and try again soon.

The general consensus from experts is that much encouragement and praise should be used when a child cooperates with toilet training and when he or she begins to urinate or defecate in the potty. Rewards such as hugs and kisses, verbal praise, stickers, stars, or favorite treats can be used when the child uses the potty or tells a parent he or she has to use it. Pull-up diapers or plastic training pants can be purchased so that the child can remove them him or herself. For many children, simply progressing from diapers to training pants and then to regular underpants is an incentive in itself. When accidents occur, they should be treated casually; punishment, teasing, or chastising should be avoided.

Nighttime training usually begins when a child can stay dry all day, for at least four to six hours. Girls usually reach this point before boys, some girls begin to stay dry at naptime and even occasionally at night before the age of two. After the age of two, dry nights become more frequent: 45 percent of girls and 35 percent of boys stay dry at night at the ages of two to three. With many children, nighttime training is not done until the age of three and, in many cases, not complete until four or five. The signal from the child's bladder has to be strong enough to wake him from sleep and get him to the bathroom at least once or twice a night. As many as 25 percent of children have relapses after they have been dry at night for six months or longer, usually due to a temporary stressor. In a minority of children, nighttime bladder control does not develop until after the age of five; this situation often occurs in families where there is a history of enuresis (bedwetting).

Common problems

In some cases a child may resist all toilet training efforts from the parents, some going so far as to resist sitting on the potty or even holding back bowel movements. Toilet training resistance may be the result of a parent over-admonishing the child when accidents are made or the child does not use the potty when directed. In some cases the child is simply not ready for toilet learning. More rarely, resistance can be caused by a condition that causes the child **pain** when he or she uses the potty, such as painful urination associated with a urinary tract infection. If a child is uncooperative during the toilet training process, parents can try letting the child initiate the process when he or she is ready, using rewards and positive feedback each time the child is successful in using the potty or goes a whole day without soiling his or her pants, replacing the child's diaper or training pants with regular underwear or having the child change his or her own clothes when accidents occur.

One potential negative effect of resistance is that the child can hold back bowel movements, resulting in **constipation**. This in turn makes elimination uncomfortable and even painful, creating even greater reluctance and resistance on the part of the child. Severe cases of constipation can cause painful anal fissures, fecal soiling (**encopresis**), or rectal enlargement. Unusual delays in toilet training normal children or regressions to soiling generally indicate family stress and/or underlying emotional problems and may require counseling to be effectively resolved.

Parental concerns

Toilet training is often a dreaded and frustrating task for parents. The process can go more smoothly for parent and child if parents are educated on training techniques that emphasize waiting until a child shows signs of readiness before initiating training and taking a child-oriented approach.

When to call the doctor

Parents should contact a healthcare provider if their child exhibits any of the following behaviors:

- holding back bowel movements or constipation
- evidence of painful urination or defecation
- extended toilet training resistance (i.e. lasts several months)

Resources

BOOKS

Morgan, Richard. *Zoo Poo: A First Toilet Training Book.* New York: Barron's Educational Resources, 2004.

Warner, Penny, et al. *Toilet Training without Tears or Trauma.* Minnetonka, MN: Meadowbrook Press, 2003.

PERIODICALS

"Toilet Training." *Pediatrics for Parents* 20, no. 8 (August 2003): 2.

Schmitt, Barton D. "Toilet Training Basics." *Clinical Reference Systems* (2002): 3263–7.

———. "Toilet Training Problems: Underachievers, Refusers, and Stool Holders." *Contemporary Pediatrics* 21, no. 4 (April 2004): 71–82.

KEY TERMS

Encopresis—Fecal incontinence that can occur as a result of stress or fear.

Schonwald, Alison, et al. "Factors Associated with Difficult Toilet Training." *Pediatrics* 113, no. 6 (June 2004): 1753–7.

ORGANIZATIONS

American Academy of Pediatrics (AAP). 141 Northwest Point Boulevard, Elk Grove Village, IL 60007. Web site: <www.aap.org>.

WEB SITES

McKinney, Merritt. "Late Start May Delay Toilet Training: Study." *MedlinePlus,* August 19, 2004. <www.nlm.nih.gov/medlineplus/news/fullstory_19622.html> (accessed September 10, 2004.)

Stephanie Dionne Sherk

Tonsillitis

Definition

Tonsillitis is an infection and swelling of the tonsils, which are oval-shaped masses of lymph gland tissue located on both sides of the back of the throat.

Description

The tonsils normally help to prevent infections. They act like filters to trap bacteria and viruses entering the body through the mouth and sinuses. The tonsils also stimulate the immune system to produce antibodies that help fight infections. Anyone of any age can have tonsillitis; however, it is most common in children between the ages of five and 15 years.

Transmission

Tonsillitis is transmitted from one person to another in the same way that many common diseases are, such as by coughing and sneezing. It can also spread when a child touches his or her nose and then other children's **toys** or by children eating or drinking with the same utensils. Children with bacterial tonsillitis are usually no longer contagious 24 hours after beginning a course of **antibiotics**.

Demographics

Tonsillitis is very common among children. Nearly all children will have some form of tonsillitis at least once.

Causes and symptoms

Tonsillitis is caused by viruses or bacteria that make the tonsils swell and become inflamed. Most cases of tonsillitis are caused by viruses, which cannot be treated with antibiotics. A mild or severe **sore throat** is one of the first symptoms of tonsillitis. Symptoms can also include **fever**, chills, tiredness, muscle aches, earache, **pain** or discomfort when swallowing, and swollen glands in the neck. Very young children may be fussy and stop eating. When a doctor or nurse looks into the mouth with a flashlight, the tonsils may appear swollen and red. Sometimes, the tonsils will have white or yellow spots or flecks. Symptoms usually last four to six days.

When to call the doctor

If the child is displaying the symptoms of tonsillitis and has had a sore throat for more than 48 hours, especially when accompanied by a fever, a doctor should be called. The doctor can determine if the child has tonsillitis, if it is bacterial or viral, and treat the problem accordingly. If the child cannot breathe or cannot swallow emergency medical attention should be sought.

Diagnosis

The diagnosis of tonsillitis is made from the visible symptoms and a physical examination of the patient. The doctor examines the eyes, ears, nose, and throat, looking at the tonsils for signs of swelling, redness, or discharge. A careful examination of the throat is necessary to rule out **diphtheria** and other conditions that may cause a sore throat. Since most sore throats in children are caused by viruses rather than bacteria, the doctor may take a **throat culture** in order to test for the presence of streptococcal bacteria. A throat culture is performed by wiping a cotton swab across the tonsils and back of the throat and sending the swab to a laboratory for culturing. Streptococcus pyogenes, the bacterium that causes "strep" throat, is the most common bacterial agent responsible for tonsillitis. Depending on what type of test is used for strep, the doctor may be able to determine within a few minutes if *S. pyogenes* is present. The quick tests for strep are not as reliable as a laboratory culture, which can take 24 to 48 hours. If the results of a quick test are positive, however, the doctor can prescribe antibiotics right away. If the quick test results are negative, the doctor can do a throat culture to verify the results and wait for the laboratory report before prescribing antibiotics. A blood test may also be done to rule out a more serious infection or condition and to check the white blood cell count to see if the body is responding to the infection. In some cases, the doctor may order blood tests for mononucleosis, since about one third of patients with mononucleosis develop **streptococcal infections** of the tonsils.

Treatment

Treatment of tonsillitis usually involves keeping the patient comfortable while the illness runs its course. This supportive care includes bed rest, drinking extra fluids, gargling with warm salt water, and taking pain relievers. Children under the age of 12 should not be given aspirin as a pain reliever because of the threat of **Reye's syndrome**. Frozen juice bars and cold fruit drinks can bring some temporary relief of sore throat pain. Drinking warm tea or broth can also be soothing. If the throat culture shows that *S. pyogenes* is present, penicillin or other antibiotics will be prescribed. An injection of benzathine or procaine penicillin may be most effective in treating the infection, but it is also painful. If an oral antibiotic is prescribed, it must be taken for the full course of treatment, usually 10 to 14 days, even if the symptoms are no longer present. If the child has several episodes of severe tonsillitis, the doctor may recommend a tonsillectomy, which is the surgical removal of the tonsils.

Alternative treatment

Strengthening the immune system is important whether tonsillitis is caused by bacteria or viruses. Naturopaths often recommend dietary supplements of vitamin C, bioflavonoids, and beta-carotenes, found naturally in fruits and vegetables, to ease inflammation and fight infection. A variety of herbal remedies also may be helpful in treating tonsillitis. Calendula (*Calendula officinalis*) and cleavers (*Galium aparine*) target the lymphatic system, while echinacea (*Echinacea spp.*) and astragalus (*Astragalus membranaceus*) stimulate the immune system. Goldenseal (*Hydrastis canadensis*), myrrh (*Commiphora molmol*), and bitter orange act as antibacterials. Lomatium dissectum and ligusticum porteri have an antiviral action. Some of the homeopathic medicines that may be used to treat symptoms of tonsillitis include:

- arsenicum
- belladonna
- hepar sulphuris

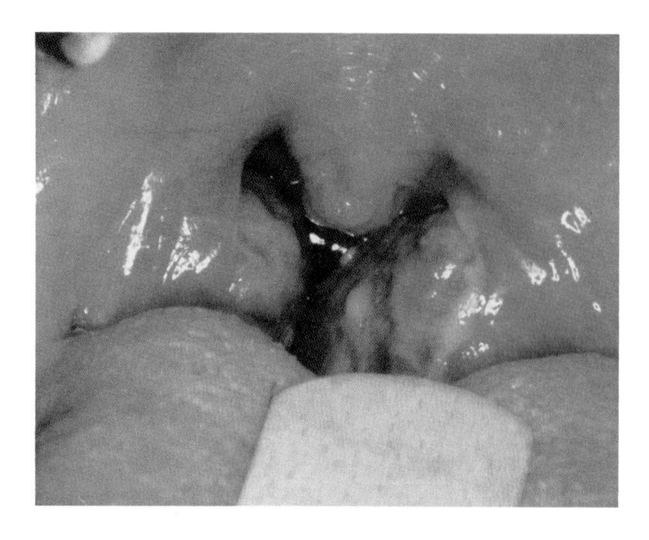

An examination of this patient's mouth reveals acute tonsillitis. *(© 1993 NMSB. Custom Medical Stock Photo, Inc.)*

KEY TERMS

Streptococcus pyogenes—A common bacterium that causes strep throat and can also cause tonsillitis.

Tonsillectomy—A surgical procedure to remove the tonsils. A tonsillectomy is performed if the patient has recurrent sore throats or throat infections, or if the tonsils have become so swollen that the patient has trouble breathing or swallowing.

Tonsils—Common name for the palatine tonsils, which are lymph masses in the back of the mouth, on either side of the tongue. Tonsils act like filters to trap bacteria and viruses.

- lachesis
- lycopodium
- mercurius
- phytolacca
- rhus toxicodendron

As with any condition, the treatment and dosage should be appropriate for the particular symptoms and age of the patient.

Prognosis

Tonsillitis usually resolves within a few days with rest and supportive care. Treating the symptoms of sore throat and fever will make the child more comfortable. If fever persists for more than 48 hours, however, or is higher than 102°F (38.9°C) the child should be seen by a doctor. If antibiotics are prescribed to treat an infection, they should be taken as directed for the complete course of treatment, even if the child starts to feel better in a few days. Prolonged symptoms may indicate that the child has other upper respiratory infections, most commonly in the ears or sinuses. An abscess behind the tonsil (a peritonsillar abscess) may also occur. In rare cases, a persistent sore throat may point to more serious conditions, such as **rheumatic fever** or **pneumonia**.

Prevention

The bacteria and viruses that cause tonsillitis are easily spread from person to person. It is not unusual for an entire **family** or several students in the same classroom to come down with similar symptoms, especially if *S. pyogenes* is the cause. The risk of transmission can be lowered by avoiding exposure to anyone who already has tonsillitis or a sore throat. Drinking glasses and eating utensils should not be shared and should be washed in hot, soapy water before reuse. Old toothbrushes should be replaced to prevent reinfection. People who are caring for someone with tonsillitis should wash their hands frequently to prevent spreading the infection to others.

Parental concerns

Tonsillitis usually has no long term effects if it is detected and treated promptly. If it is not treated it can lead to other medical conditions such as rheumatic fever, kidney inflammation, or abscesses that could block a child's breathing passage.

Resources

BOOKS

Silverstien, Alvin, Virginia Silverstein, and Laura S. Nunn. *Sore Throats and Tonsillitis*. Danbury, CT: Franklin Watts, 2000.

"Tonsillitis." In *Professional Guide to Diseases*, 7th ed. Springhouse, PA: Springhouse Corporation, 2001.

PERIODICALS

"Sore Throat." *Journal of the American Medical Association* 291, no. 13 (April 7, 2004): 1664.

Tish Davidson, A.M.

Tooth decay

Definition

Tooth decay, which is also called dental cavities or dental caries, is the destruction of the outer surface (enamel) of a tooth.

Description

Tooth decay results from the action of bacteria that live in plaque. Plaque is a sticky, whitish film formed by a protein in saliva (mucin) and sugary substances in the mouth. The plaque bacteria sticking to tooth enamel use the sugar and starch from food particles in the mouth to produce acid, which destroys the tooth's enamel.

Baby bottle tooth decay

Baby bottle tooth decay is a dental problem that develops in infants, especially infants that are put to bed with a bottle containing a sweet liquid. Baby bottle tooth decay is also called nursing-bottle caries and bottle-mouth syndrome. Bottles containing liquids such as milk, formula, fruit juices, sweetened drink mixes, and sugar water continuously bathe an infant's mouth with sugar. The bacteria in the mouth use this sugar to produce acid that destroys the child's teeth. The upper front teeth are typically the ones most severely damaged; the lower front teeth are protected to some degree by the tongue. Pacifiers dipped in sugar, honey, corn syrup, or other sweetened liquids also contribute to baby bottle tooth decay. The first signs of damage are chalky white spots or lines across the teeth. As decay progresses, the damage to the child's teeth becomes more obvious.

Demographics

Tooth decay is a common health problem, second in prevalence only to the **common cold**. It has been estimated that 90 percent of people in the United States have at least one cavity and that 75 percent of people had their first cavity by the age of five. Although anyone can have a problem with tooth decay, children are at particularly high risk. The good news is the number of children with cavities in the United States went down in the last few decades of the twentieth century. Some estimates are that as of the early 2000s cavities among adolescents have been reduced by nearly 40 percent. This rate decrease is explained in part by the fact that more areas have added fluoride to their drinking water and more children get regular, good dental care. However, children still drinking from a bottle anytime after their first birthday are more likely to have tooth decay.

Causes and symptoms

Tooth decay requires the simultaneous presence of three factors: plaque bacteria, sugar, and a vulnerable tooth surface. Although several microorganisms found in the mouth can cause tooth decay, the primary disease agent appears to be *Streptococcus mutans*. The simple sugars used by the bacteria are glucose, sucrose, and lactose. They are converted primarily into lactic acid. When this acid builds up on an unprotected tooth surface, it dissolves the **minerals** in the enamel, creating holes and weak spots (cavities). As the decay spreads inward into the middle layer (the dentin), the tooth becomes more sensitive to temperature and touch. When the decay reaches the center of the tooth (the pulp), the resulting inflammation (pulpitis) produces a **toothache**.

When to call the doctor

If a child complains of tooth or jaw **pain** and his or her cheek is swollen, and if he or she has a **fever** over 100°F (37.8°C), a dentist should be called right away. A dentist should be called during normal business hours if the child has tooth or jaw pain for more than a day, if white spots are noticed on an infant's teeth, or if there appear to be any other problems with the teeth or gums.

Diagnosis

Tooth decay develops at varying rates. It may be found during a routine six-month dental checkup before the individual is even aware of a problem. In other cases, the individual may experience common early symptoms, such as sensitivity to hot and cold liquids or localized discomfort after eating very sweet foods. The dentist or dental hygienist may suspect tooth decay if a dark spot or a pit is seen during a visual examination. Front teeth may be inspected for decay by shining a light from behind the tooth. This method is called transillumination. Areas of decay, especially between the teeth, will appear as noticeable shadows when the teeth are transilluminated. X rays may be taken to confirm the presence and extent of the decay. The dentist then makes the final clinical diagnosis by probing the enamel with a sharp instrument.

Tooth decay in pits and fissures may be differentiated from dark shadows in the crevices of the chewing surfaces by a dye that selectively stains parts of the tooth that have lost mineral content. A dentist can also use this dye to tell whether all tooth decay has been removed from a cavity before placing a filling.

Damage caused by baby bottle tooth decay is often not diagnosed until the child has a severe problem, because many parents do not schedule regular dental exams for their small children. It is recommended that a child's first trip to the dentist be before one year of age and that trips to the dentist occur regularly every six months after that.

Treatment

To treat most cases of tooth decay in older children, the dentist removes all decayed tooth structure, shapes the sides of the cavity, and fills the cavity with an appropriate material, such as silver amalgam or composite resin. The filling is put in to restore and protect the tooth. If decay has attacked the pulp, the dentist or a specialist called an endodontist may perform root canal treatment and then cover the tooth with a crown.

In cases of baby bottle tooth decay, the dentist must assess the extent of the damage before deciding on the treatment method. If the problem is caught early, the teeth involved can be treated with fluoride, followed by changes in the infant's feeding habits and better **oral hygiene**. Primary teeth with obvious decay in the enamel that has not yet progressed to the pulp need to be protected with stainless steel crowns. Fillings are not usually an option in small children because of the small size of their teeth and the concern of recurrent decay. When the decay has advanced to the pulp, pulling the tooth is often the treatment of choice. Unfortunately, loss of primary teeth at this age may hinder the young child's ability to eat and speak. It may also have negative effects on the alignment and spacing of the permanent teeth when they come in.

Prognosis

With timely diagnosis and treatment, the progression of tooth decay can be stopped relatively painlessly. If the pulp of the tooth is infected, the infection may be treated with **antibiotics** prior to root canal treatment or extraction. The longer the decay goes untreated, however, the more destructive it becomes and the longer and more intensive the necessary treatment will be. In addition, an individual with two or more areas of tooth decay is at increased risk of developing additional cavities.

Prevention

It is easier and less expensive to prevent tooth decay than to treat it. The four major prevention strategies are proper oral hygiene, fluoride, sealants, and attention to diet.

Oral hygiene

The best way to prevent tooth decay is to brush the teeth at least twice a day, preferably after every meal and snack, and floss daily. Cavities develop most easily in spaces that are hard to clean. These areas include surface grooves, spaces between teeth, and the area below the gum line. Effective brushing cleans each outer tooth surface, inner tooth surface, and the horizontal chewing surfaces of the back teeth, as well as the tongue. Flossing once a day helps prevent gum disease by removing food particles and plaque at and below the gum line, as well as between teeth. Patients should visit their dentists every six months for oral examination and professional cleaning.

Parents can easily prevent baby bottle tooth decay by not allowing a child to fall asleep with a bottle containing sweetened liquids. If a bottle is necessary when the child is falling asleep it should be filled only with plain, unsweetened water. The child should be introduced to drinking from a cup around six months of age and usually weaned from bottles by 12 months. If an infant seems to need oral comfort between feedings, a pacifier specially designed for the mouth may be used. Pacifiers, however, should never be dipped in honey, corn syrup, or other sweet liquids.

After the eruption of the first tooth, parents should begin routinely wiping the infant's teeth and gums with a moist piece of gauze or a soft cloth, especially right before bedtime. Parents may begin brushing a child's teeth with a small, soft toothbrush at about two years of age, when most of the primary teeth have come in. They should apply only a very small amount (the size of a pea) of toothpaste containing fluoride. Too much fluoride may cause spotting (fluorosis) of the tooth enamel. As the child grows, he or she will learn to handle the toothbrush, but parents should control the application of toothpaste and do the follow-up brushing until the child is about seven years old.

Fluoride application

Fluoride is a natural substance that slows the destruction of enamel and helps to repair minor tooth decay damage by remineralizing tooth structure. Toothpaste, mouthwash, fluoridated public drinking water, and vitamin supplements are all possible sources of fluoride. Children living in areas without fluoridated water should receive 0.25 mg/day of fluoride before age three, 0.5 mg/day of fluoride from three to six years of age, and 1 mg/day after age six. Sometimes children can also have their teeth treated with fluoride at the dentist's office.

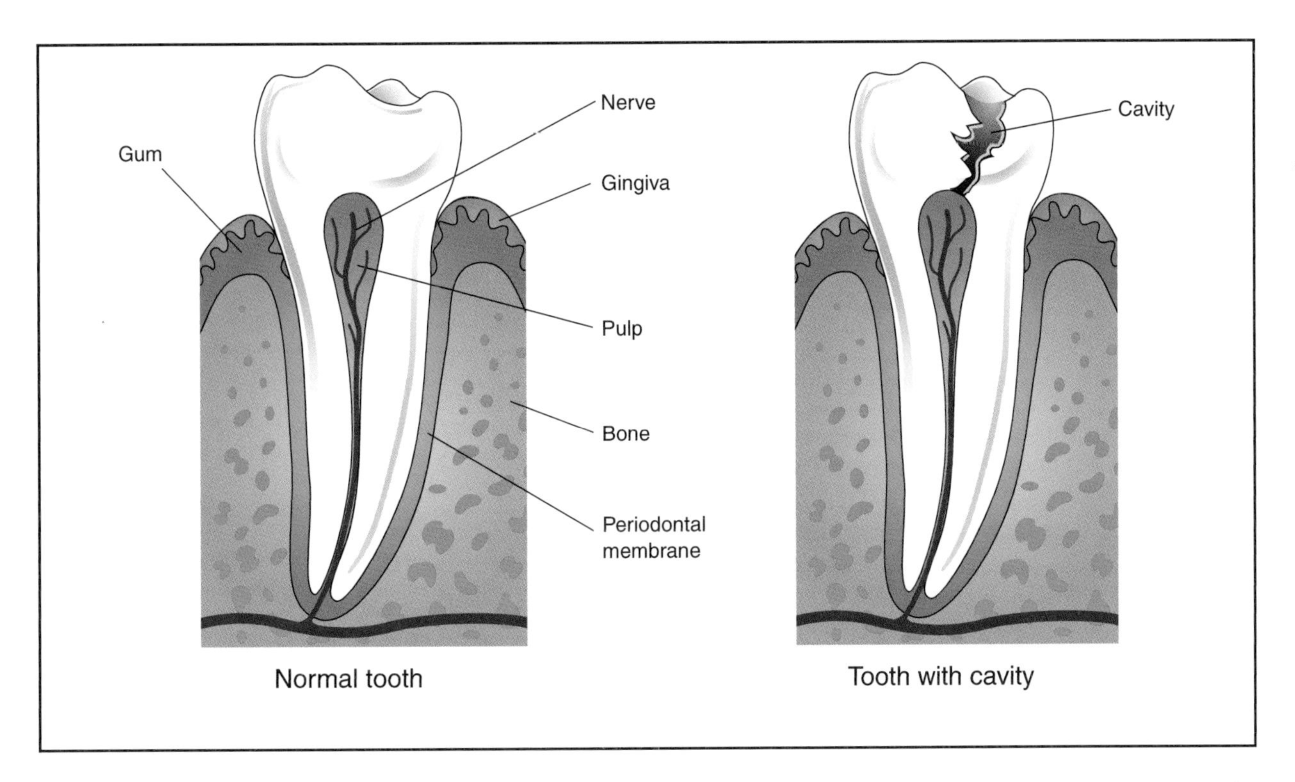

Tooth decay is the destruction of the outer surface, or enamel, of a tooth. It is caused by acid buildup from plaque bacteria, which dissolve the minerals in the enamel and create cavities. *(Illustration by Electronic Illustrators Group.)*

Sealants

Because fluoride is most beneficial on the smooth surfaces of teeth, sealants were developed to protect the irregular surfaces of teeth. A sealant is a thin plastic coating that is painted over the grooves of chewing surfaces to prevent food and plaque from being trapped there. Sealant treatment is painless, because no part of the tooth is removed, although the tooth surface is etched with acid so that the plastic will adhere to the rough surface. Sealants are usually clear or tooth-colored, making them less noticeable than silver fillings. They cost less than fillings and can last up to 10 years, although they should be checked for wear at every dental visit. Children should get sealants on their first permanent "six-year" molars, which come in between the ages of five and seven, and on the second permanent "12-year" molars, which come in between the ages of 11 and 14. Sealants should be applied to the teeth shortly after they erupt, before decay can set in. Although sealants have been used in the United States for about 25 years, one survey by the National Institute of Dental Research reported that fewer than 8 percent of American children have them.

Diet

The risk of tooth decay can be lowered by choosing foods wisely and eating less often. Foods high in sugar and starch, especially when eaten between meals, increase the risk of cavities. The bacteria in the mouth use sugar and starch to produce the acid that destroys the enamel. The damage increases with more frequent eating and longer periods of eating. For better dental health, children should eat a variety of foods, limit the number of snacks, avoid sticky and overly sweetened foods, and brush often after eating. Drinking water is also beneficial for rinsing food particles from the mouth. Children can be taught to rinse their mouth out with water after eating if they are unable to brush after lunch at school.

Parental concerns

If tooth decay is not treated, it can result in other, more serious, problems involving the gums, cheeks, or jaw. Baby bottle tooth decay that is not treated quickly can result in the affected teeth being removed. Although the child will eventually develop adult teeth to replace the baby teeth, missing baby teeth can result in overcrowding when the adult teeth come in. Missing baby teeth can also result in the adult teeth coming in crooked, the child having to chew on one side of his or her mouth, and speech delays. As of 2004, most cavities could be fixed without much discomfort by a medical professional and without any serious longterm consequences if the cavities are found and treated early.

KEY TERMS

Amalgam—A mixture (alloy) of silver and several other metals used by dentists to make fillings for cavities.

Caries—The medical term for tooth decay.

Cavity—A hole or weak spot in the tooth surface caused by decay.

Dentin—The middle layer of a tooth, which makes up most of the tooth's mass.

Enamel—The hard, outermost surface of a tooth.

Fluoride—A chemical compound containing fluorine that is used to treat water or applied directly to teeth to prevent decay.

Mucin—A protein in saliva that combines with sugars in the mouth to form plaque.

Plaque—A sticky, colorless film of bacteria, sugars, and mucin that forms on teeth and causes tooth decay.

Pulp—The soft, innermost layer of a tooth that contains its blood vessels and nerves.

Sealant—A thin plastic substance that is painted over teeth as an anti-cavity measure to seal out food particles and acids produced by bacteria.

Transillumination—A technique of checking for tooth decay by shining a light behind the patient's teeth. Decayed areas show up as spots or shadows.

Resources

BOOKS

Mittelman, Jerome, Beverly Mittelman, and Jean Barilla. *Healthy Teeth for Kids: A Preventive Program: Prebirth through the Teens*. Collingdale, PA: DIANE Publishing, 2004.

PERIODICALS

"Achievements in Public Health, 1990–1999: Fluoridation of Drinking Water to Prevent Dental Caries." *Journal of the American Medical Association* 283, no. 10 (March 8, 2000): 1283–86.

ORGANIZATIONS

American Dental Association. 211 E. Chicago Ave., Chicago, IL 60611. Web site: <www.ada.org>.

American Dental Hygienists' Association. 444 North Michigan Ave., Chicago, IL 60611. Web site: <www.adha.org>.

National Institute of Dental Research. 31 Center Drive, MSC 2190, Building 31, Room 5B49, Bethesda, MD 20892–2190. Web site: <www.nidcr.nih.gov/>.

Tish Davidson, A.M.

Toothache

Definition

A toothache is any **pain** or soreness within or around a tooth, indicating inflammation and possible infection.

Description

A toothache may feel like a sharp pain or a dull ache. The tooth may be sensitive to pressure, heat, cold, or sweets. In cases of severe pain, identifying the problem tooth is often difficult. Any patient with a toothache should see a dentist for diagnosis and treatment. Most toothaches get worse if left untreated.

Demographics

Toothaches are common. Yet people have fewer cavities on average in the early 2000s than they did in the nineteenth or twentieth century, in part because in the late 1900s many towns added fluoride to the drinking water and many dentists began prescribing fluoride tablets as a preventative measure. Fewer cavities and better tooth health have reduced the number of toothaches.

Causes and symptoms

Toothaches may result from any of a number of causes:

- **tooth decay** (dental caries)
- inflammation of the tooth pulp (pulpitis)
- abscesses
- gum disease, including periodontitis
- loose or broken filling
- cracked or impacted tooth
- exposed tooth root
- food wedged between teeth or trapped below the gum line

- tooth nerve irritated by clenching or grinding of teeth (bruxism)
- pressure from congested sinuses
- traumatic injury

When to call the doctor

If the toothache lasts for more than 24 hours an appointment with the dentist should be made. If there is **fever**, swelling, intense pain, or bleeding in addition to the toothache the dentist should be seen right away.

Diagnosis

Diagnosis includes identifying the location of the toothache, as well as the cause. The dentist begins by asking the patient specific questions about the toothache, including the types of foods that make the pain worse, whether the tooth is sensitive to temperature or biting, and whether the pain is worse at night. The dentist then examines the patient's mouth for signs of swelling, redness, and obvious tooth damage. The presence of pus indicates an abscess or gum disease. The dentist may flush the sore area with warm water to dislodge any food particles and to test for sensitivity to heat. The dentist may then dry the area with gauze to determine sensitivity to touch and pressure. The dentist may probe tooth crevices and the edges of fillings with a sharp instrument, looking for areas of tooth decay. Finally, the dentist may take x rays, looking for evidence of decay between teeth, a cracked or impacted tooth, or a disorder of the underlying bone.

Treatment

Treatment depends on the underlying cause of the toothache. If the pain is due to tooth decay, the dentist will remove the decayed area and restore the tooth with a filling of silver amalgam or composite resin. Loose or broken fillings are removed, new decay cleaned out, and a new filling is placed. If the pulp of the tooth is damaged, root canal therapy is needed. The dentist or a specialist called an endodontist removes the decayed pulp, fills the space left behind with a soothing paste, and covers the tooth with a crown to protect and seal it. If the damage cannot be treated by these methods, or if the tooth is impacted, the tooth must be extracted. If the dentist finds an infection, **antibiotics** are given to treat it.

Toothaches should always be professionally treated by a dentist. Some methods of self-treatment, however, may help manage the pain until professional care is available:

- rinsing with warm salt water
- using dental floss to remove any food particles
- taking **acetaminophen** (Tylenol) or ibuprofen (Advil) to relieve pain (Aspirin is not recommended for children because of the risk of Reye's syndrome.)
- applying a cold compress against the outside of the cheek
- using clove oil (*Syzygium aromaticum*) to numb the gums (The oil may be rubbed directly on the sore area or used to soak a small piece of cotton and applied to the sore tooth. Clove oil should not be put on the tongue because it often burns or stings.)

Alternative treatment

Toothaches caused by infection or tooth decay must be treated by a dentist. Several alternative therapies may be helpful for pain relief until dental treatment is available. Clove oil (*Syzygium aromaticum*) may be rubbed on sensitive gums to numb them or added to a small cotton pellet that is then placed into or over a hole in the tooth. The herb corydalis (*Corydalis yanhusuo*) may also help relieve toothache pain. Pain also may be reduced by using acupressure, acupuncture, or reiki.

Prognosis

Prompt dental treatment provides a positive outcome for toothache. In the absence of active infection, fillings, root canal treatments, or extractions may be performed with minimal discomfort to the patient. When a toothache is left untreated, a severe infection may develop and spread to the sinuses or jawbone, and eventually cause blood poisoning.

Prevention

Maintaining proper **oral hygiene** is the key to preventing toothaches. The best way to prevent tooth decay is to brush at least twice a day, preferably after every meal and snack. Flossing once a day also helps prevent gum disease by removing food particles and bacteria at and below the gum line, as well as between teeth. Children should visit the dentist at least every six months for oral examinations and professional cleaning. Dentists often recommend that children see the dentist for the first time before they are one year old. Parents should help young children brush their teeth. Fluoride is also very helpful in preventing tooth decay. If the town's water is not fluoridated, the parent should ask the dentist for fluoride supplements.

KEY TERMS

Abscess—A localized collection of pus in the skin or other body tissue caused by infection.

Bruxism—Habitual clenching and grinding of the teeth, especially during sleep.

Cavity—A hole or weak spot in the tooth surface caused by decay.

Dental caries—A disease of the teeth in which microorganisms convert sugar in the mouth to an acid that erodes the tooth. Commonly called a cavity.

Enamel—The hard, outermost surface of a tooth.

Endodontist—A dentist who specializes in diagnosing and treating diseases of the pulp and other inner structures of the tooth.

Impacted tooth—Any tooth that is prevented from reaching its normal position in the mouth by another tooth, bone, or soft tissue.

Periodontitis—Inflammation of the periodontium, the tissues that support and anchor the teeth. Without treatment it can destroy the structures supporting the teeth, including bone.

Pulp—The soft, innermost layer of a tooth that contains its blood vessels and nerves.

Pulpitis—Inflammation of the pulp of a tooth that involves the blood vessels and nerves.

Parental concerns

Toothaches are most often caused by cavities. If not treated promptly an infection could begin or spread. If infection spreads to the blood, serious complications can result.

Resources

BOOKS

Bagley, Katie. *Brush Well: A Look at Dental Care.* Decatur, IL: Capstone Press Inc., 2001.

Diamond, Richard. *Dental First Aid for Families.* Ravensdale, WA: Idyll Arbor Inc., 2000.

Keller, Laurie. *Open Wide: Tooth School Inside.* New York: Henry Holt & Co., 2003.

McDonald, Ralph E., et al. *Dentistry for the Child and Adolescent.* St. Louis, MO: Mosby, 2004.

PERIODICALS

Goldstein, Laura. "Two Ways to Soothe Sensitive Teeth." *Prevention* 52, i.11 (November 2000): 161.

ORGANIZATIONS

American Dental Association. 211 East Chicago Ave. Chicago, IL 60611–2678. Web site: <www.ada.org>.

WEB SITES

"Understanding a Toothache." Available online at <www.floss.com/understanding_a_toothache.htm> (accessed October 15, 2004).

Tish Davidson, A.M.
Bethany Thivierge

Topical antibiotics *see* **Antibiotics, topical**

TORCH test

Definition

The TORCH test, sometimes called the TORCH panel, belongs to a category of blood tests called infectious-disease antibody titers. A titer is the serial dilution of antibodies (protein molecules or immunoglobulins produced by the immune system in response to specific disease agents) found in blood serum that determines their level of concentration. Antibodies are proteins produced by the immune system in response to infectious agents that are foreign to the body, such as viruses, bacteria, parasites, or toxins. These infectious organisms have antigens on their surfaces that stimulate the immune system to produce corresponding antibodies. IgM antibodies are produced in response to viruses. The TORCH test screens for the presence of IgM antibodies, and the titer determines their concentration in the blood. The name of the test is an acronym derived from the initial letters of the five groups of chronic infections: **toxoplasmosis**, other viruses, **rubella**, cytomegalovirus (CMV), and **herpes simplex** virus (HSV). The "other viruses" usually include syphilis, **hepatitis B**, coxsackie virus, Epstein-Barr virus (mononucleosis), varicella-zoster virus, and human parvovirus. The test is performed by various methods in the clinical laboratory and may also be referred to as viral immunoglobulins testing. Methods used in the early 2000s are more sensitive and specific and can identify the specific virus.

Purpose

A TORCH test is performed to help screen for certain virus infections in infants who may have been exposed to a causative organism. The five groups of disease-causing organisms whose antibodies are measured by the TORCH test are grouped together because they can cause a cluster of symptomatic birth defects in newborns. This group of defects is sometimes called the TORCH syndrome. The pediatrician may order the TORCH test to be performed when a newborn has these symptoms, in order to determine if any of the five types of infection may be involved.

Symptoms of TORCH syndrome that may encourage testing include the following:

- Small size in proportion to length of the mother's pregnancy at time of delivery: Infants who are smaller than would be expected (below the tenth percentile) are referred to as small-for-gestational-age (SGA).
- Enlarged liver and spleen.
- Low level of platelets (tiny cellular elements in blood that are an important part of coagulation).
- Skin rash: The type of skin rash associated with the TORCH syndrome is usually reddish-purple or brown and is caused by the leakage of blood from broken capillaries into the baby's skin.
- Central nervous system impairment: This may include **encephalitis**, calcium deposits in brain tissue, or seizures.
- **Jaundice**: Yellow-stained skin and whites of the eyes due to elevated levels of bilirubin, a substance normally filtered out by the liver. Jaundice may indicate liver dysfunction, although it can also be a normal result of red cell turnover in the newborn.

Description

Besides general symptoms that may encourage a pediatrician to order the TORCH panel of tests, each of the TORCH infections has its own origins and may have a characteristic cluster of symptoms in newborns. These unique characteristics, the general condition and symptoms of the child, and the test results are studied in order for the physician to make a diagnosis.

Toxoplasmosis

Toxoplasmosis is caused by *Toxoplasma gondii*, a parasite that can be acquired by the mother from handling cat feces, drinking unpasteurized milk, or eating contaminated meat. The infection is carried to the infant through the mother's placenta and can cause impairment of the infant's eyes (opthalmic impairment) and central nervous system (neurological dysfunction). The organism can invade brain or muscle tissue and form cysts. Infection acquired by the mother later in pregnancy usually decreases the likelihood of infection in the infant at birth although eye problems may occur in **adolescence**. Toxoplasmosis early in pregnancy is more likely to cause miscarriage or serious birth defects. The incidence of toxoplasmosis in newborns is one in 1,000 live births.

Other viruses (syphilis)

Syphilis is caused by the spiral- or coil-shaped bacteria (spirochete), *Treponema pallidum*. It is transmitted among adults through sexual intercourse. About 2 to 5 percent of children born to mothers diagnosed with syphilis have the disease at birth. Syphilis was added to the TORCH panel because of an increase in reported cases after 1990. Syphilis can cause early delivery, miscarriage, and is a potentially life-threatening infection for an affected fetus, often resulting in stillbirth. The mortality rate in infants infected with syphilis is about 54 percent.

Rubella

Rubella is a virus that has a seasonal pattern, with epidemics most likely in the spring. Between 0.1 to 2 percent of newborns are infected with rubella. The rate of fetal infection varies according to the timing of the mother's infection during pregnancy. Birth defects, however, are most likely (85%) in infants infected during the first eight weeks of pregnancy. Infants born with rubella may already show signs of heart disease, retarded growth, hearing loss, blood disorders, vision problems, or **pneumonia**. They may also develop problems later in childhood, including **autism**, hearing loss, brain syndromes, immune system disorders, or thyroid disease.

Cytomegalovirus (CMV)

Cytomegalovirus belongs to the herpesvirus group of infections. It can be transmitted through body secretions, as well as by sexual contact; some newborns acquire CMV through the mother's breast milk. In adults, it produces symptoms resembling those of mononucleosis. About 1 to 2.2 percent of newborns in the United States are infected with CMV. Of this group, 10 percent have measurable symptoms. The mortality rate for these symptomatic newborns is 20 to 30 percent. Surviving infants with CMV may suffer from hearing problems (15%) or **mental retardation** (30%). Newborns who acquire CMV during the birth process or shortly after birth may develop pneumonia, hepatitis, or various blood disorders.

Herpes simplex virus (HSV)

Herpesvirus infections are among the most common viral infections in humans. They are spread by oral or genital contact. It is estimated that between one in 1,000 and one in 5,000 infants are born with HSV infections. About 80 percent of these infections are acquired during the birth process itself; the virus enters the infant through its eyes, skin, mouth, and upper respiratory tract. Of infants born with HSV infection, about 20 percent have localized infections of the eyes, mouth, or skin. About 50 percent of infected infants will develop the disease throughout the body (disseminated) within nine to 11 days after birth. Disseminated herpes infections attack the liver and adrenal glands, as well as other body organs. Without treatment, the mortality rate is 80 percent. Even with antiviral medication, the mortality rate is still 15 to 20 percent, with 40 to 55 percent of the survivors having long-term damage to the central nervous system. In order to begin early, effective treatment, it is critical for pediatricians to diagnose HSV infection in newborns as soon as possible.

Performing the TORCH panel requires obtaining a sample of the infant's blood. Samples from infants are usually obtained by the heelstick procedure when only a small quantity of blood is needed. The baby's foot is wrapped in a warm cloth for five minutes to bring blood to the surface and help it to flow more easily. The foot is then sterilized with an alcohol swab and a lancet is used to puncture the baby's heel on one side, avoiding the center of the heel to prevent inflammation of the bone. The blood sample is drawn in tiny capillary tubes, properly labeled, and taken to the laboratory for testing. In rare instances, a phlebotomist is not able to draw sufficient blood from a heel puncture, and a physician may draw venous blood from a femoral vein in the groin area or another vein larger than veins in an infant's arms.

Since the TORCH test is a screening or first-level test, the pediatrician may order tests of other body fluids or tissues to confirm the diagnosis of a specific infection. In suspected cases of toxoplasmosis, rubella, or syphilis, cerebrospinal fluid may be obtained from the infant by spinal tap in order to confirm the diagnosis. A diagnosis of CMV is usually confirmed by culturing the virus in a sample of the infant's urine. In HSV infections, tissue culture is the best method to confirm the diagnosis.

Precautions

Because toxoplasmosis can be transmitted by handling cat feces, pregnant women should avoid cleaning cat boxes or handling cats. Any suspected infection should be reported to the obstetrician so that testing for the causative parasite in the mother can be performed.

Medical personnel and **family** members must be aware of the possible presence of infective organisms in the infant and proper precautions taken, such as hand washing, when the infant or the infant's body fluids (blood, urine, feces) are handled.

If the infant has had blood drawn often from the same site on the heel or heels, causing scarring, inflammation, or the accumulation of tissue fluid, it may cause inaccurate test results.

False negative and false positive results can occur with the TORCH test for immunoglobulins because of cross-reacting antibodies, especially among the different types of herpes viruses.

Preparation

No special preparation, other than sterile technique by medical personnel, is required.

Aftercare

The site from which blood is withdrawn must be kept clean after the procedure and must be checked regularly for bleeding. A small adhesive patch may be used to protect the site.

Risks

The performance of the TORCH test carries no significant risk. Drawing blood for the test may involve light bleeding or bruising at the site of puncture or blood may accumulate under the puncture site (hematoma), requiring that a new location be found for subsequent tests. The infant's heel may be at risk of scarring, infection of the bone, cellulitis (inflammation of cellular tissue), small lumpy calcium deposits.

Normal results

The normal result of a TORCH panel reveals normal levels of immunoglobulin M (IgM) antibody in the infant's blood. IgM is one of five types of antibodies (protein molecules) produced by the immune system and found in blood. IgM is a specific class of antibody that seeks out virus particles. It is the most common type of immunoglobulin in newborns and, therefore, the most useful indicator of the presence of one of the TORCH virus infections.

KEY TERMS

Antibody—A special protein made by the body's immune system as a defense against foreign material (bacteria, viruses, etc.) that enters the body. It is uniquely designed to attack and neutralize the specific antigen that triggered the immune response.

Antigen—A substance (usually a protein) identified as foreign by the body's immune system, triggering the release of antibodies as part of the body's immune response.

Bacteria—Singular, bacterium; tiny, one-celled forms of life that cause many diseases and infections.

Titer—The highest dilution of a material (e.g., serum or other body fluid) that produces a reaction in an immunologic test system. Also refers to the extent to which an antibody can be diluted before it will no longer react with a specific antigen. Also spelled titre.

Virus—A small infectious agent consisting of a core of genetic material (DNA or RNA) surrounded by a shell of protein. A virus needs a living cell to reproduce.

Abnormal results

The general abnormal or "positive" result reveals high levels of IgM antibody present in the infant's blood. The test can be refined further for antibodies specific to given disease agents. The TORCH screen, however, can produce both false-positive and false-negative findings. Doctors can measure IgM levels in the infant's cerebrospinal fluid, as well as in the blood, if confirmation is needed.

Parental concerns

Parents will necessarily be concerned about the possibility of infection in the child and the amount of testing that may have to be done. Awareness of the value of the TORCH panel of tests to help confirm the presence of an infective organism and its concentration in the blood is important, especially because confirmatory tests lead to faster, more effective treatment. Medical personnel can teach parents about safe practices for handling an infant with a virus infection that can possibly spread to family members.

See also Cytomegalovirus (CMV) infection; Infectious mononucleosis; Hepatitis B.

Resources

BOOKS

Beers, Mark H., and Robert Berkow, eds. *The Merck Manual,* 2nd home ed. West Point, PA: Merck & Co., 2004.

Cohen, Margaret, et al. *Sent Before My Time: A Child Psychotherapist's View of Life on a Neonatal Intensive Care Unit.* London: Karnac Books, 2003.

Moore, Keith L., et al. *Before We Are Born: Essentials of Embryology and Birth Defects.* Kent, UK: Elsevier—Health Sciences Division, 2002.

Roberton, N. R. C., et al. *A Manual of Neonatal Intensive Care.* Oxford, UK: Oxford University Press, 2002.

ORGANIZATIONS

Centers for Disease Control and Prevention. 1600 Clifton Rd., NE, Atlanta, GA 30333. Web site: <www.cdc.gov>.

WEB SITES

"TORCH Test." *Joseph F. Smith Medical Library.* Available online at <www.chclibary.org/micromed/00068480.html> (accessed December 2, 2004).

L. Lee Culvert
Rebecca J. Frey, PhD

Torticollis *see* **Wryneck**

Tourette syndrome

Definition

Tourette syndrome (TS) is an inherited disorder of the nervous system, characterized by a variable expression of unwanted movements and noises (**tics**).

Description

Tourette syndrome is also known as Gilles de la Tourette syndrome, named after Gilles de la Tourette, a French neurologist who first described the syndrome in 1885. Children with Tourette syndrome show symptoms before the age of 18, usually around age seven, and have symptoms that usually last into adulthood. The symptoms of Tourette syndrome are usually motor and/or vocal tics, although in some children other symptoms such as socially inappropriate comments, and socially inappropriate or self-injurious behaviors sometimes occur. Children with Tourette syndrome are more likely to have **obsessive-compulsive disorder** (OCD), attention deficient disorder (ADD), and **attention deficit hyperactivity disorder** (ADHD). The symptoms of Tourette syndrome are extremely variable over time, with some symptoms beginning and some ceasing to be a problem as the child grows. Many people with Tourette syndrome experience a decrease in symptoms as they age, and some people see a complete disappearance of their symptoms.

Demographics

Tourette syndrome is found in all populations and all ethnic groups, but is three to four times more common in males than females. The exact frequency of Tourette syndrome is unknown, but estimates range from 0.05 percent to 2 percent. Estimates vary widely in part because many people with Tourette syndrome have very mild symptoms and may not seek medical attention. It is estimated that there are about 1,000 new cases of Tourette syndrome diagnosed in the United States every year.

Causes and symptoms

The causes of Tourette syndrome are not fully understood. Most studies agree that symptoms of Tourette syndrome involve the chemicals in the brain that help transmit information from one nerve cell in the brain to another. These chemicals are called neurotransmitters. Some studies suggest that the tics in Tourette syndrome are caused by an increased amount of a neurotransmitter called dopamine. Other studies suggest instead that there is a problem with a different neurotransmitter called serotonin. Still others believe the problem involves other chemicals required for normal functioning of the brain.

Most studies suggest that Tourette syndrome is an autosomal dominant disorder with decreased penetrance. An autosomal disorder is one that occurs because of an abnormal gene on a chromosome that is not a sex-linked chromosome. A dominant disorder means that it only takes one abnormal gene in a pair of genes to have the disorder. Parents each pass one copy of each gene to their child. Because in autosomal dominant disorders one gene is abnormal, people with this disorder have about a 50 percent chance of passing the abnormal gene to their offspring. Decreased penetrance means that not all people who inherit the abnormal gene develop symptoms. There is some evidence that females who inherit the Tourette syndrome gene have a lower probability of exhibiting symptoms than males who inherit the gene.

The principal symptoms of Tourette syndrome include simple and complex motor and vocal tics. Simple motor tics are characterized by brief muscle contractions of only one or a small number of muscle groups. An eye twitch is an example of a simple motor tic. Complex motor tics tend to appear more complicated and purposeful than simple tics and involve coordinated contractions of several muscle groups. Some examples of complex motor tics include the act of hitting oneself or jumping.

Vocal tics are actually manifestations of motor tics that involve the muscles required for producing sound. Simple vocal tics include **stuttering**, stammering, abnormal emphasis of part of a word or phrase, and inarticulate noises such as throat clearing, grunts, and high-pitched sounds. Complex vocal tics typically involve the involuntary expression of words. Perhaps the most striking example of this is coprolalia, the involuntary expression of obscene or socially inappropriate words or phrases, which occurs in fewer than one-third of people with Tourette syndrome. The involuntary echoing of the last word, phrase, sentence, or sound vocalized by oneself (phalilalia) or by another person or sound in the environment (echolalia) are also classified as complex tics.

The type, frequency, and severity of tics exhibited varies tremendously among individuals with Tourette syndrome. Tourette syndrome has a variable age of onset, and tics can start anytime between infancy and age 18. Initial symptoms usually occur before the early teens; the average age of onset for both males and females is approximately seven years. Most individuals with symptoms initially experience simple muscle tics involving the eyes and the head. These symptoms can progress to tics involving the upper torso, neck, arms, hands, and occasionally the legs and feet. Complex motor tics are usually the latest-onset motor tics. Vocal tics usually have a later onset than motor tics.

Not only is there extreme variability in symptoms among individuals with Tourette syndrome, but individuals commonly experience variability in type, frequency, and severity of symptoms over the course of their lifetime. Adolescents with Tourette syndrome often experience unpredictable and more severe than usual symptoms, which may be related to fluctuating hormone levels and decreased compliance in taking medications. Many people who as children have Tourette syndrome experience a decrease in symptoms or a complete end to symptoms in their adult years.

Several factors appear to affect the severity and frequency of tics. Stress appears to increase the frequency and severity of tics, while concentration on another part of the body that is not involved in a tic can result in the temporary alleviation of symptoms. Relaxation following attempts to suppress the occurrence of tics may result in an increased frequency of tics. An increased frequency and severity of tics can also result from exposure to such drugs as steroids, cocaine, amphetamines, and **caffeine**. Hormonal changes, such as those that occur prior to the menstrual cycle, can also increase the severity of symptoms.

Other associated symptoms

People with Tourette syndrome are more likely to exhibit non-obscene, socially inappropriate behaviors such as expressing insulting or socially unacceptable comments or performing socially unacceptable actions. It is not known whether these symptoms stem from more general dysfunction of impulse control that might be part of Tourette syndrome.

Tourette syndrome appears to also be associated with attention deficit disorder (ADD), a disorder characterized by a short attention span and impulsivity, and in some cases hyperactivity. Researchers have found that 21 to 90 percent of individuals with Tourette syndrome also exhibit symptoms of ADD.

People with Tourette syndrome are also at higher risk for having symptoms of obsessive-compulsive disorder (OCD), a disorder characterized by persistent, intrusive, and senseless thoughts (obsessions) or compulsions to perform repetitive behaviors that interfere with normal functioning. A person with OCD, for example, may be obsessed with germs and may counteract this obsession with continual hand washing. Symptoms of OCD are present in 1.9 to 3 percent of the general population, whereas 28 to 50 percent of people with Tourette syndrome have symptoms of OCD.

Self-injurious behavior (SIB) is also seen more frequently in those with Tourette syndrome. Approximately 34 to 53 percent of individuals with Tourette syndrome exhibit some form of self-injuring behavior. The SIB is often related to OCD but can also occur in those with Tourette syndrome who do not have OCD.

Symptoms of **anxiety** and depression are also found more commonly in people with Tourette syndrome. It is not clear, however, whether these are symptoms of Tourette syndrome or occur as a result of having to deal with the symptoms of moderate to severe Tourette syndrome.

People with Tourette syndrome may also be at increased risk for having learning disabilities and **personality disorders** and may be more predisposed to such behaviors as aggression, antisocial behaviors, severe temper outbursts, and inappropriate sexual behavior.

When to call the doctor

Parents should call the doctor if they notice the symptoms of Tourette syndrome. The initial tics usually initially involve the face or head, but the doctor should be consulted if any uncontrolled repetitive behavior is observed.

Diagnosis

Tourette syndrome cannot be diagnosed through laboratory tests. Sometimes laboratory tests can be helpful, however, in ruling out other possible conditions. The diagnosis of Tourette syndrome is made by observing and interviewing the child, looking at the family's medical history, and talking to the child's **family** and sometimes to other caregivers. The diagnosis of Tourette syndrome is complicated by a variety of factors. The extreme range of symptoms of this disorder can make it difficult to differentiate Tourette syndrome from other disorders with similar symptoms. Diagnosis is further complicated by the fact that some tics appear to be within the range of normal behavior. For example, an individual who only exhibits such tics as throat clearing and sniffing may be misdiagnosed with a medical problem such as **allergies**. In addition, such bizarre and complex tics as coprolalia may be mistaken for psychotic or so-called bad behavior. Diagnosis is also made more difficult because often individuals attempt to control tics in public, and, therefore, the healthcare professional may have difficulty observing the symptoms firsthand. Although there is some disagreement over what criteria should be used to diagnose Tourette syndrome, the most common aid in the diagnosis is the *DSM-IV*. The *DSM-IV* outlines suggested diagnostic criteria for a variety of conditions, including Tourette syndrome.

DSM-IV criteria are:

- presence of both motor and vocal tics at some time during the course of the illness
- the occurrence of multiple tics nearly every day through a period of more than one year without a remission of tics for a period of greater than three consecutive months
- distress or impairment in functioning caused by symptoms
- onset occurs prior to age 18
- symptoms not due to medications or drugs and not related to another medical condition

Some physicians criticize the *DSM-IV* criteria, arguing that they do not include the full range of behaviors and symptoms seen in Tourette syndrome. Others criticize the criteria because they limit the diagnosis to those who experience a significant impairment, which may exclude individuals who have the syndrome but exhibit milder symptoms. For these reasons many physicians use their clinical judgment as well as the *DSM-IV* criteria as a guide to diagnosing Tourette syndrome.

Treatment

There is no cure for Tourette syndrome. Treatment involves the control of symptoms through educational and psychological interventions and/or medications. The treatment and management of Tourette syndrome varies from patient to patient and should focus on the alleviation of the symptoms that are most bothersome to the individual or that cause the most interference with daily functioning.

Psychological and educational interventions

Psychological treatments such as counseling are not generally useful for the treatment of tics but can be beneficial in the treatment of associated symptoms such as obsessive-compulsive behavior and attention deficit disorder. Counseling may also help individuals to cope better with the symptoms of Tourette syndrome and to have more positive social interactions. Psychological interventions may also help people cope better with stressors that can normally trigger tics. The education of family members, teachers, and peers about Tourette syndrome can be helpful and may help to foster acceptance and prevent social isolation.

Medications

Many people with mild symptoms of Tourette syndrome never require medication. Those with more severe symptoms may require medication for all or part of their lifetime. As of 2004, the most effective treatment of tics associated with Tourette syndrome involved the use of drugs such as haloperidol, pimozide, sulpiride, and tiapride, which decrease the amount of dopamine in the body. Unfortunately, even at low dosages, these drugs bring a high incidence of side effects. The short-term side effects can include sedation, dysphoria, weight gain, movement abnormalities, depression, and poor school performance. Long-term side effects can include **phobias**, memory difficulties, and personality changes. These drugs are, therefore, better suited for short-term rather than long-term therapy.

In many cases, treatment of associated conditions such as ADD and OCD is considered more important than the tics themselves. Clonidine used in conjunction with such stimulants as Ritalin may be useful for treating people with Tourette syndrome who also have symptoms of ADD. Stimulants should be used with caution in individuals with Tourette syndrome, since they can sometimes increase the frequency and severity of tics. OCD symptoms in those with Tourette syndrome are often treated with such drugs as Prozac, Luvox, Paxil, and Zoloft.

In many cases the treatment of Tourette syndrome with medications can be discontinued after **adolescence**. Trials should be performed through the gradual tapering off of medications and should always be done under a doctor's supervision.

Prognosis

The prognosis for Tourette syndrome is fairly good. Although symptoms generally get worse during early adolescence, many people with Tourette syndrome experience a lessening of the severity of their symptoms during late adolescence and early adulthood. Approximately one third of children with Tourette syndrome will experience complete or nearly complete remission during their late adolescent and early adult years. Another third will experience a significant drop off in the severity and/or frequency of their symptoms during this time. It is difficult to tell how many children with Tourette syndrome experience complete remission over their entire adult lives, but it has been estimated to be about 8 percent. Many children who do not have complete and lasting remission will experience months or even years without significant symptoms. There does not appear to be a definite correlation between the type, frequency, and severity of symptoms and the eventual prognosis. People with Tourette syndrome who have other symptoms such as obsessive-compulsive disorder, attention deficit disorder, and self-injurious behavior usually have a poorer prognosis.

Prevention

There is no known way to prevent Tourette syndrome.

Parental concerns

Tourette syndrome does not, in itself, negatively affect **intelligence** or cognition. It is, however, often associated with other disorders such as obsessive-compulsive disorder and attention deficit disorder. It is also sometimes associated with learning and psychological disorders, many of which are often more debilitating than Tourette syndrome itself. Tourette syndrome does not reduce life expectancy. Children with Tourette syn-

KEY TERMS

Attention deficit disorder (ADD)—Disorder characterized by a short attention span, impulsivity, and in some cases hyperactivity.

Autosomal dominant—A pattern of inheritance in which only one of the two copies of an autosomal gene must be abnormal for a genetic condition or disease to occur. An autosomal gene is a gene that is located on one of the autosomes or non-sex chromosomes. A person with an autosomal dominant disorder has a 50% chance of passing it to each of their offspring.

Coprolalia—The involuntary use of obscene language.

Copropraxia—The involuntary display of unacceptable/obscene gestures.

Decreased penetrance—Individuals who inherit a changed disease gene but do not develop symptoms.

Dysphoria—Feelings of anxiety, restlessness, and dissatisfaction.

Echolalia—Involuntary echoing of the last word, phrase, or sentence spoken by someone else.

Echopraxia—The imitation of the movement of another individual.

Neurotransmitter—A chemical messenger that transmits an impulse from one nerve cell to the next.

Obsessive-compulsive disorder—An anxiety disorder marked by the recurrence of intrusive or disturbing thoughts, impulses, images, or ideas (obsessions) accompanied by repeated attempts to supress these thoughts through the performance of certain irrational and ritualistic behaviors or mental acts (compulsions).

Phalilalia—Involuntary echoing by an individual of the last word, phrase, sentence, or sound he/she vocalized.

Tic—A brief and intermittent involuntary movement or sound.

drome often have problems socializing because of embarrassment over uncontrollable tics and negative reactions from parents, teachers, and peers who do not understand the disorder. Children with Tourette syndrome may need special attention to help them cope with the social implications of their disorder.

Resources

BOOKS

Chowdhury, Uttom. *Tics and Tourette Syndrome: A Handbook for Parents and Professionals.* New York: Taylor & Francis Inc., 2004.

Cohen, Donald J., et al. *Tourette Syndrome.* London: Lippincott Williams & Wilkins, 2000.

Lechman, James F. *Tourette's Syndrome—Tics, Obsessions, Compulsions: Developmental Psychopathology and Clinical Care.* New York: John Wiley & Sons, 2001.

Waltz, Mitzi, et al. *Tourette's Syndrome: Finding Answers and Getting Help.* Cambridge, MA: O'Reilly Media, 2001.

PERIODICALS

Prestia, Kelly. "Tourette's Syndrome: Characteristics and Interventions." *Intervention in School & Clinic*, 39, no. 2 (November 2003): 67.

ORGANIZATIONS

National Tourette Syndrome Association. 42–40 Bell Blvd., Bayside, NY 11361–2820. Web site: <http://tsa-usa.org/>.

Tish Davidson, A.M.

Toxic shock syndrome

Definition

Toxic shock syndrome (TSS) is an uncommon, but potentially serious, illness that occurs when poisonous substances (toxins) produced by bacteria enter the bloodstream. The toxins cause a type of blood poisoning that results in high **fever**, symptoms of shock, and potentially organ failure.

Description

Initially toxic shock syndrome was associated with the use of ultra-absorbent tampons by menstruating girls and women. Between 1978 and 1980 thousands went to emergency rooms with high fever, **vomiting**, low blood pressure, **diarrhea**, and a rash resembling **sunburn**. Once ultra-absorbent tampons were taken off the market, the number of cases of toxic shock syndrome decreased substantially.

As of 2004, two different causes of toxic shock were recognized. Staphylococcal toxic shock syndrome (TSS) is caused by the bacteria *Staphylococcus aureus*. Streptococcal toxic shock syndrome (STSS, first described in

1987, is caused by *Streptococcus pyogenes* bacteria. Although both types of toxic shock are rare, STSS is more common and has a higher rate of serious complications and death.

Transmission

TSS is caused by a strain of *S. aureus* found in the nose, mouth, and occasionally the vagina. The bacteria produce a characteristic toxin. In large enough quantities, the toxin can enter the bloodstream, causing a potentially fatal reaction.

Although scientists still do not fully understand the link between TSS and tampons, most medical researchers suspect that tampons introduce oxygen into the vagina, which is normally an oxygen-free area of the body. Oxygen triggers bacterial growth, and the more absorbent the tampon, the longer it is left in place and the more toxin-producing bacteria it can harbor.

The streptococcal bacteria that cause STSS often enter the body through an infected wound in the skin, infection following surgery, postpartum or post abortion infection, or bone infection. STSS almost never develops following a simple **strep throat** infection.

Demographics

Although the majority of cases of TSS occur in menstruating girls and women, the disease may occur in people of any race and age, including children. STSS infection may occur in individuals who are weakened from surgery, injury, or disease that weakens the immune system. New mothers also are at higher risk for toxic shock syndrome, as are those who have recently had chicken pox. This disease is rare. Only about 100 cases of TSS and 300 cases of STSS were reported in the United States in 1996.

Causes and symptoms

Toxic shock syndrome begins suddenly about two days after infection occurs with a fever of 102°F (38.9°C) or above, vomiting and watery diarrhea, **headache**, and sunburn-like rash, together with a **sore throat** and body aches. Blood pressure may plummet a day or two after the first symptoms appear. When blood pressure drops, an individual may become disoriented or go into shock. The kidneys or liver may fail. After these developments, the skin on the hands and feet may peel. With STSS, flesh around the infected site may become damaged and die (become necrotic).

When to call the doctor

Toxic shock is a medical emergency that needs to be treated immediately in the hospital. Parents should go to the emergency room or call an ambulance if their child has a fast, weak pulse; cold hands and feet with pale moist skin; mental confusion or lethargy; abnormal breathing; a sunburn-like rash; high fever; or skin that is red, swollen, and infected.

Diagnosis

Diagnosis is made based on history, presenting symptoms, and culture of bacteria from the blood or wound. A rapid streptococcal test can be done with results available in 15 minutes. This test is positive in more than 85 percent of cases of toxic shock.

Treatment

Because toxic shock is a medical emergency, treatment is usually begun before laboratory results are available. The first line of treatment is to attempt to reverse the symptoms of shock. This process usually involves the administration of fluids intravenously. The site of infection is cleaned, and **antibiotics** are administered. If organ failure occurs, oxygen, the use of a respirator, or kidney dialysis may be necessary. It may also be necessary to surgically remove any infected and dying tissue.

Prognosis

Many otherwise healthy individuals recover from toxic shock in two to three weeks; however, the length of recovery is variable and depends on how early and how aggressively the disease is treated. About 3 percent of individuals with TSS die. The death rate with STSS can be as high as 30 to 70 percent.

Prevention

Women and girls who use tampons should always wash their hands before inserting a tampon and change the tampon every four to six hours. Skin **wounds** should be cleaned with an antiseptic and covered with a bandage.

Parental concerns

Although the risk of TSS is very low, parents may prefer that their daughters use pads rather than tampons when menstruating.

KEY TERMS

Shock—A medical emergency in which the organs and tissues of the body are not receiving an adequate flow of blood. This deprives the organs and tissues of oxygen and allows the build-up of waste products. Shock can be caused by certain diseases, serious injury, or blood loss.

Staphylococcal infection—Infection with one of several species of *Staphylococcus* bacteria. Staphylococcal infections can affect any part of the body and are characterized by the formation of abscesses. Also known popularly as a staph infection.

Streptococcus—Plural, streptococci. Any of several species of spherical bacteria that form pairs or chains. They cause a wide variety of infections including scarlet fever, tonsillitis, and pneumonia.

Toxin—A poisonous substance usually produced by a microorganism or plant.

Resources

BOOKS

Marx, John. *Rosen's Emergency Medicine: Concepts and Clinical Practice*, 5th ed. St. Louis: Mosby, 2002.

PERIODICALS

"A Quick Diagnosis of Toxic Shock Syndrome Is Critical for Avoiding Mortality." *Health & Medicine Week* (December 1, 2003): 616.

WEB SITES

Sharma, Sat, and Godfrey Harding. "Toxic Shock Syndrome." *eMedicine Medical Library*, January 22, 2003. Available online at <www.emedicine.com/med/topic2292.htm> (accessed October 4, 2004).

Tish Davidson, A.M.

Toxoplasmosis

Definition

Toxoplasmosis is an infectious disease caused by the one-celled parasitic organism *Toxoplasma gondii*. Although most individuals do not experience any symptoms, the disease can be very serious and even fatal in fetuses, newborns, and individuals with weakened immune systems.

Description

Toxoplasmosis is caused by a one-celled parasite *Toxoplasma gondii*. This parasite is found worldwide. It causes infections that can be either acute or chronic. In about 60 percent of healthy adults who become infected, the organism causes no symptoms (asymptomatic). Most of the remaining 40 percent experience mild, flu-like symptoms, low-grade **fever**, and fatigue that resolve without intervention in a few weeks. Once exposed, re-infection does not occur in healthy individuals. However, in immunocompromised individuals, such as those with HIV/AIDS, symptoms can be severe, life threatening, and recurring. *T. gondii* infection of a fetus or newborn can also cause severe neurological impairment, blindness, **mental retardation**, and death. When a fetus acquires the infection through its mother, this is called congenital toxoplasmosis.

Transmission

The organism that causes toxoplasmosis can be transmitted in four ways. The most common way is through contact with feces of an infected cat. Cats, the primary carriers of the organism, become infected by eating rodents and birds infected with *T. gondii*. Once ingested, the organism reproduces in the intestines of the cat, producing millions of eggs known as oocysts. These oocysts are excreted in cat feces daily for approximately two weeks. In the United States, approximately 50 percent of cats have been infected with *T. gondii*.

Oocysts are not capable of producing infection until approximately 24 hours after being excreted in warm climates and longer in cold climates. However, they remain infective in water or moist soil for about one year. Humans become infected when they come in contact with and accidentally ingest oocysts when changing cat litter, playing in contaminated sand, working in the garden or similar activities, or by eating unwashed vegetables and fruit irrigated with untreated water that has been contaminated with cat feces.

The second way humans become infected with *T. gondii* is through eating raw or undercooked meat. When cattle, sheep, or other livestock forage through areas contaminated with cat feces, these animals become carriers of the disease. The organism forms cysts in the muscle and brain of the livestock. When humans eat raw or undercooked infected meat, the walls of the cysts are broken down in the human digestive tract, and the individual becomes actively infected. The encysted organism can be killed by freezing or cooking the meat well.

The only form of direct person-to-person transmission occurs from mother to fetus during pregnancy. This transmission occurs only if the mother is in the acute, or active, stage of infection when the organism is circulating in the mother's blood. It is estimated that about one third of women with active infections pass the infection along to their fetus. Women who have become infected six months or more before conception do not pass the infection on to their fetus, because the organism has become dormant (inactive) and formed thick-walled cysts in muscle and other tissues of the body. Reactivation of the infection in healthy individuals is extremely rare. Women who give birth to one infected child do not pass the infection to their fetus during subsequent pregnancies unless they are immunocompromised (for example, with **AIDS**) and the infection recurs.

Finally, individuals can also become infected through blood and organ transplant from an infected person.

Demographics

Men and women of all races are equally affected by *T. gondii,* however, except for immunocompromised individuals, the implications are more serious for women, as they can pass the infection on to their offspring. The rate of infection in the United States varies considerably with location. Studies have found that the infection rate in women of childbearing age ranges from 30 percent in Los Angeles to 3.3 percent in Denver. Varying sanitary conditions and culinary habits, such as eating raw meat, account for some of this variation. The rate of infection increases with the age of the individual. About 3,500 to 4,000 children are born in the United States each year with congenital toxoplasmosis. Outside the United States, fetal infection rates tend to be higher, although the number of babies born with congenital toxoplasmosis was as of 2004 declining worldwide.

Causes and symptoms

In fetuses, the severity of infection is dependent on the time of transmission. Fetuses who acquire the infection during the first trimester of pregnancy often are stillborn or die shortly after birth. Fetuses who acquire the infection late in pregnancy often show no symptoms when born.

Severe infections lead to seizure disorders, neurological disorders, abnormal muscle tone, deafness, partial or complete blindness caused by a condition called chorioretinitis, and mental retardation. These conditions may not be present at birth, especially if the infection occurred late in pregnancy. Vision deficits, especially, tend to show up later in life.

Young children can acquire toxoplasmosis in the same ways as adults. However, symptoms and complications when the disease is acquired after birth tend to be much milder than with congenital toxoplasmosis.

Children and adults with weakened immune systems have a high risk of developing serious symptoms, including cerebral toxoplasmosis, an inflammation of the brain (**encephalitis**), one-sided weakness or **numbness**, mood and personality changes, vision disturbances, **muscle spasms**, and severe headaches. If untreated, cerebral toxoplasmosis can lead to coma and death.

When to call the doctor

Women who believe they may have become infected shortly before conception or during pregnancy should call their doctor immediately. Treatment is possible during pregnancy. Symptoms in the newborn may be obvious during the newborn examination. If they are not, parents should consult their doctor if they feel their child has any neurological or vision complications or is not meeting appropriate developmental milestones.

Diagnosis

A diagnosis of toxoplasmosis is made based on clinical signs and supporting laboratory results, including visualization of the organism in body tissue or isolation in animals. Blood tests for toxoplasmosis are designed to detect increased amounts of a protein or antibody produced in response to infection with *T. gondii.* Antibody levels can be elevated for years, however, even when the disease is in a dormant state. **Amniocentesis** (sampling amniotic fluid) between 20 and 24 weeks of gestation can detect toxoplasmosis in the fetus.

Treatment

Most healthy individuals who contract toxoplasmosis do not require treatment, because the healthy immune system is able to control the disease. Symptoms are not usually present. Mild symptoms may be relieved by taking over-the-counter medications, such as **acetaminophen** (Tylenol) and ibuprofen (Motrin, Advil). **Sore throat** lozenges and rest may also ease the symptoms.

The benefits of treating women who contract toxoplasmosis during pregnancy almost always outweigh any risks involved. Treatment is with antibiotic and antimicrobial drugs. Transmission of toxoplasmosis from the mother to the fetus may be prevented or reduced if the mother takes the antibiotic spiramycin. Later in a pregnancy, if the fetus has contracted the disease, treatment with the antibiotic pyrimethamine (Daraprim, Fansidar) and folinic acid (an active form of **folic acid**) may be effective. Babies born with toxoplasmosis who show symptoms of the disease may be treated with pyrimethamine, the sulfa drug sulfadiazine (Microsulfon), and folinic acid. Healthy children over the age of five usually do not require treatment. Infected individuals with weakened immune systems may require lifetime drug treatment to keep the infection from recurring.

Prognosis

The prognosis is poor when congenital toxoplasmosis is acquired during the first three months of pregnancy. Afflicted children die in infancy or suffer damage to their central nervous systems that can result in physical and mental retardation. Infection later in pregnancy often results in only mild symptoms, if any. The prognosis for acquired toxoplasmosis in adults with strong immune systems is excellent. The disease often disappears by itself after several weeks. However, the prognosis for immunodeficient patients is not as positive. These patients often relapse when treatment is stopped. The disease can be fatal to all immunocompromised patients, especially individuals with AIDS, and particularly if not treated.

Prevention

There are no drugs that can eliminate T. gondii cysts in animal or human tissues. Humans can reduce their risks of developing toxoplasmosis by practicing the following measures:

- freezing foods (to 10.4°F/–12°C) and cooking foods to an internal temperature of 152°F/67°C to kill the cysts
- practicing sanitary kitchen techniques, such as washing utensils and cutting boards that come into contact with raw meat
- keeping pregnant women and children away from household cats and cat litter
- disposing of cat feces daily because the oocysts do not become infective until after 24 hours
- helping cats to remain free of infection by feeding them dry, canned, or boiled food and by discouraging hunting and scavenging
- washing hands after outdoor activities involving soil contact and wearing gloves when gardening

KEY TERMS

Cyst—An abnormal sac or enclosed cavity in the body filled with liquid or partially solid material. Also refers to a protective, walled-off capsule in which an organism lies dormant.

Immunocompromised—A state in which the immune system is suppressed or not functioning properly.

Oocyst—A developmental stage of certain parasitic organisms, including those responsible for malaria and toxoplasmosis, in which the zygote of the organism is enclosed in a cyst.

Parental concerns

Fear of infection during pregnancy is the most common parental concern. When a fetus is found early in pregnancy to be infected, parents are faced with the decision of whether to continue the pregnancy given the likelihood of serious complications to the fetus.

Resources

BOOKS

Ambrose-Thomas, P., et al. *Congenital Toxoplasmosis: Scientific Background, Clinical Management, and Control.* New York: Springer, 2000.

Joynson, David H. M., et al. *Toxoplasmosis: A Comprehensive Clinical Guide.* Cambridge, UK: Cambridge University Press, 2001.

PERIODICALS

Jones, J. "Congenital Toxoplasmosis." *American Family Physician* 67 (May 15, 2003): 2131–8.

WEB SITES

Leblebicioglu, Hakan, and Murat Hökelek. "Toxoplasmosis." *eMedicine.com* August 10, 2004. Available online at <www.emedicine.com/ped/topic2271.htm> (accessed October 15, 2004).

The Merck Manual of Diagnosis and Therapy, 17th ed. Edited by Mark Beers and Robert Berkow. Available online at <www.merck.com/mrkshared/mmanual/home.jsp> (accessed October 15, 2004).

Tish Davidson, A.M.

Toys

Definition

Toys are physical items used in **play** by children.

Description

An estimated 2.6 billion toys, including electronic toys and **video games**, are sold in the United States each year, according to the Toy Industry Association, Inc. Toys can support cognitive growth, development of fine motor and **gross motor skills**, and improve problem solving and attention. Children may find extended periods of play with a toy, whether it was purchased in a store or found in the home (recycled plastic containers and empty spools of thread, for example). Most children will be happy to play with a few favorite toys—the size of the toy inventory is not critical to successful play. Parents and others who choose toys for children should take into account the following characteristics of the child for whom the toy is intended. These include the age and developmental stage, his or her interests, ease of use of the toy, the necessity for adult supervision, the presence of younger siblings for whom the toy could pose a hazard, and whether the toy is designed for independent play or group play.

While computer and video game sales have more than tripled in the past decade, to nearly $240 million last year from $65 million in 1996, toys were expected to have their third straight year of slight decline in 2004. Children are still riding bikes, sipping from play tea sets, and enjoying some of the same toys their parents did, including building blocks, erector sets, and Lincoln Logs. But the pressures bearing down on traditional toys are many. Kids are growing up faster and putting down Barbie dolls and G.I. Joe action figures at an earlier age, increasingly smitten by the grownup images of young celebrities such as high-profile athletes, movie and television stars, and recording artists. The prime audience for toys has shrunk as the children of the immense baby boom generation have grown into teenagers and beyond. And as in other industries, giant retailers have taken sales from specialized toy chains and squeezed some of the incentive to devise the next great toy.

Toy labeling

The U.S. Consumer Product Safety Commission has developed guidelines for age grading of toys and related products. Most toy manufacturers use these guidelines in labeling toys and games for age-appropriateness. Manufacturers also consider recommendations of experts in child development regarding the stages of physical, emotional, and intellectual development. Four main criteria are considered in establishing age guidelines:

- Physical skills: Can the child manipulate and play with the features of the toy as it was designed?
- Understanding: Can the child understand how to use the toy?
- Interest: Is the toy of interest to a child of a particular age?
- Safety: Is the toy safe for a child at this particular stage?

The Consumer Product Safety Commission (CPSC) has established a number of regulations related to toy safety. These are published by the American Society for Testing and Measurement (ASTM) under the safety standard known as ASTM F963. This standard is voluntary, but the majority of U.S. toy manufacturers comply with its guidelines. In fact, many incorporate a message about the toy's compliance with ASTM F963 on the toy packaging.

Infancy and toddlerhood

Toy manufacturers consider the size of toy parts—which are likely to be put into the mouth by an older infant or toddler—in designing toys. Anyone purchasing a toy for the youngest children must take the **choking** hazard seriously and make appropriate selections. When a new toy is brought into the home or child-care setting, all wrapping material should be promptly discarded. Plastic wrapping in particular may pose a suffocation hazard to the youngest children. The U.S. government maintains statistics on toy-related injuries and deaths. Many accidents involving toys are not caused by the toy itself; for example, a child may trip over a toy that was not put away after play. When an unsafe toy reaches the marketplace, U.S. government inspectors may discover it and order its recall; additionally, vigilant parents and caregivers can observations about toy safety to the CPSC. Manufacturers routinely cooperate with the CPSC in recalling products that are deemed unsafe or dangerous.

In 2002, the medical journal *Clinical Reference Systems* issued pediatric advisories on age-appropriate toys. Some of the recommendations follow. Suggested play things for infants include: interesting objects hung in view, such as brightly colored mobiles, crib decals, and colorful wall posters; sturdy rattles; large plastic rings; soft toys for throwing; colorful balls; light plastic blocks; cloth cubes; music boxes; teething toys; floating bath animals; washable squeak toys; nests of hollow blocks; and rough-smooth touching books; washable cloth picture books; and sturdy, colorful picture books.

Suggested toys for toddlers include: pyramid rings; large nesting blocks; large and small colored building blocks; cuddly stuffed animals; large, soft balls; washable, unbreakable dolls; push-pull toys with rounded handles; simple musical instruments; sand box and sand toys; water toys; transportation toys (trucks, cars, trains, and airplanes); objects to imitate adults such as plastic garden tools, toy telephones, and toy dishes or pots; and sturdy, colorful picture books.

Preschool and school age

U.S. law requires that toys and games for young children (ages three to six) carry a warning about choking hazards. If the toy or game includes small parts, marbles, or balloons, it must be marked that it is not appropriate for children under the age of three. Beyond toddlerhood, children begin to develop their own ideas about play activities and the toys that they want. They will be influenced by what they see advertised on television and by their peers. Toy fads and television show tie-ins can be powerfully persuasive to children. Parents may experience their first opportunities to teach about **peer pressure** and independent decision-making over toy requests. Toys should be selected to stimulate play and related cognitive and physical development; fad toys are less likely to sustain play activity and support development beyond the fad stage.

Toys and play items appropriate for preschool-age children include: large and small transportation toys; cuddly toy animals; simple musical instruments; farm and zoo animal sets; miniature circus; hospital, police, and fire station sets; bean bags; large balls; art materials such as paints, modeling clay, paste, and colored paper; wagons; tricycles; crawl-through play equipment; simple construction sets; nursery rhyme books; humorous and playful books; activity books; and books about familiar people and places.

For early school-age children, six to nine years old, suggested toys include: construction sets; art materials such as crayons, chalk, paint, modeling clay, and simple weaving materials; chalk, Velcro, or flannel boards; small bicycles; wagons; jump ropes; simple board games; playhouses; puzzles; kites; globes or planetarium sets; aquariums; terrariums; and books about jokes, riddles, tongue twisters, animals, insects, birds, reptiles, and children from other lands and cultures.

Appropriate toys for older school-age children, nine to 12 years, include: croquet, badminton, and shuffleboard sets; **sports** equipment (baseball, basketball, soccer, football, and tennis); skates and skateboards; aquariums and terrariums; craft sets; hobby sets; electric trains; radio-controlled vehicles; model kits; board games; microscopes; binoculars; compact disc players; camping and backpacking equipment; and books about adventure, science fiction, fantasy, science topics, simple biographies, and jokes, puzzles, riddles, and tongue twisters.

Parental concerns

Violent toys and video games

In addition to product safety, one of the biggest concerns of parents is the growing trend towards toys and video games that promote violence, crime, and war. In 2002, a national department store chain published an advertisement on its web site for a toy called "Forward Command Post" that featured an American soldier standing in a bombed-out house. It's an example of the growing collaboration, in recent years, between the toy and entertainment industry and the U.S. military, according to the activist group Worldwatch Institute. Video games with themes of terrorism and war in Middle-Eastern settings are selling well. In video games, kids can experience virtual combat, are exposed to exploding virtual body parts, and practice committing murder and theft to win games.

Traditionally, boys' and girls' toys have often been contrasted as being "rough-and-tumble" versus "nurturing." But that distinction may be disappearing, not only for healthy reasons of waning gender stereotyping, but for more questionable reasons such as the growing tolerance of—or obliviousness to—aggression and hostility in play by both sexes, according to an article in the May-June 2003 issue of *World Watch*, the institute's official publication.

Many parents are concerned about the growing number and level of acceptance of toys and video games that promote violence and war. However, not everyone agrees on what constitutes a violent toy. Most parents agree guns are symbols of violence. But at what point is the line drawn between a child perceiving a play gun as a toy or a device of violence? Many might agree a BB gun is violent since it can kill and wound small animals and birds and injure humans. But what about a squirt gun that shots water or a Nerf gun that shoots foam balls? To help answer these questions, Daphne White, founder of the Lion & Lamb Project, published a list of guidelines in the November-December 2004 issue of *Mothering* magazine. Lion & Lamb is an organization founded in 1995 to stop the marketing of violent toys and entertainment to children.

According to White's guidelines, violent toys and video games:

Age-appropriate toys

Age range	Toys
Birth to two months	Activity centers to look at and listen to; mobiles over cribs
Two to four months	Rattles, teethers, activity centers to hit or kick while on back.
Four to six months	Soft books, roly poly toys
Seven to nine months	Nesting cups, pop-up toys
Ten to twelve months	Push and pull toys, large blocks, board books, toys that require hand manipulation to "make something happen"
Thirteen to fifteen months	Toy telephone, walk-behind toys like doll stroller, soft dolls and animals, balls
Sixteen to eighteen months	Simple toy musical instruments, playing with water or sand, shape sorters
Nineteen months to two years	Rocking horse, easy puzzles, make-believe toys (plastic houses and people, toy cars and trucks, play food and dishes), crayons and paper
Two to three years	Tricycle, toy basketball hoop and balls, toy trains with tracks, dolls with bottles and other equipment, toy kitchen equipment, coloring books and crayons, books
Three to four years	Simple crafts (including scissors, glue, and paper), beginning board games, toys for imaginative play
Four to five years	Simple sports equipment, books, board and card games, computer games, collections, building blocks
Five to six years	Small blocks and building sets, art supplies, activity books, beginning reader books, games
Six years and up	Music, books, games, sports equipment. By this age, kids may get particular about their toys according to what is popular with their friends

(Table by GGS Information Services.)

- Promote violence and aggression as the best way to settle disputes.
- Depict violent actions as fun, harmless, and "cool."
- Encourage children to act out aggressive scenarios.
- Foster aggressive competition.
- Depend on "enemies" that must be "destroyed."

When to call the doctor

An inability to play with or lack of interest in toys at an early age may indicate a developmental problem in such areas as gross and **fine motor skills**. If this is suspected, a pediatrician, psychologist, or other specialist should be consulted.

See also Cognitive development; Fine motor skills; Gross motor skills.

KEY TERMS

Cognitive—The ability (or lack of) to think, learn, and memorize.

Fine motor skill—The abilities required to control the smaller muscles of the body for writing, playing an instrument, artistic expression and craft work. The muscles required to perform fine motor skills are generally found in the hands, feet and head.

Gross motor skills—The abilities required to control the large muscles of the body for walking, running, sitting, crawling, and other activities. The muscles required to perform gross motor skills are generally found in the arms, legs, back, abdomen and torso.

Resources

BOOKS

Neufeld, Les. *Making Toys That Teach: With Step-by-Step Instructions and Plans.* Newtown, CT: Taunton Press, 2003.

Oppenheim, Joanne, et al. *Oppenheim Toy Portfolio, 2005: The Best Toys, Books, Videos, Music, and Software for Kids.* New York: Oppenheim Toy Portfolio (Publishers), 2004.

Whittaker, Nicholas. *Toys Were Us: A Twentieth-Century History of Toys and Toy-Making.* Collingdale, PA: Diane Publishing Co., 2004.

PERIODICALS

(No author). "Between the Lines." *World Watch* (May-June 2003): 28–29.

Morantz, Carrie, and Brian Torrey. "Selecting Toys for Young Children." *American Family Physician* (Aug. 15, 2003): 763.

Rubin, Judith L. "No More Junk Toys: Rethinking Children's Gifts." *Mothering* (November-December 2003): 46–53.

Walker, Andrea K. "Joystick and Mouse Cut Regular Toy Sales." *The Detroit News* (Dec. 15, 2004): Business 1.

White, Daphne. "From War Chests to Toy Chests: How to Change Your Child's Worldview for the Better, One Toy at a Time." *Mothering* (November-December 2004): 40–42.

ORGANIZATIONS

Toy Industry Association, Inc. 1115 Broadway, Suite 400, New York, NY 10010. (212) 675-1141. Web site: <www.toy-tia.org>.

U.S. Consumer Product Safety Commission. Washington, DC 20207-0001. (800) 638-2772. Web site: <www.cpsc.gov>.

WEB SITES

U.S. Consumer Product Safety Commission. *Toy Safety Publications*. Dec. 13, 2004. Available online at: <www.cpsc.gov/cpscpub/pubs/toy_sfy.html> (accessed Jan. 2, 2005).

Ken R. Wells

Tracheoesophageal fistula

Definition

Tracheoesophageal fistula (TEF) is a birth defect in which the trachea is connected to the esophagus. In most cases, the esophagus is discontinuous (an **esophageal atresia**), causing immediate feeding difficulties.

Description

The trachea, or windpipe, carries air to the lungs. The esophagus carries food to the stomach. Sometimes during development these two tubes do not separate completely but remain connected by a short passage. When this happens, air enters the gastrointestinal system, causing the bowels to distend, and mucus is breathed into the lungs causing aspiration **pneumonia** and breathing problems.

There are three main types of TEF. In 85 to 90 percent of tracheoesophageal fistulas, the top part of the esophagus ends in a blind sac, and the lower part inserts into the trachea. In the second type, the upper part of the esophagus is connected directly to the trachea, while the lower part ends in a pouch. In a rare type of fistula called an H type, both the esophagus and trachea are complete, but they are connected by a small passageway. This is the most difficult type of tracheoesophageal fistula to diagnose, because both eating and breathing are possible. TEFs often occur in babies with additional birth defects.

Demographics

TEFs occur in about one of every 3,000 live births. They are slightly more common in boys than in girls. Some studies suggest that the occurrence of TEFs increases with the age of the mother.

KEY TERMS

Endoscopy—Visual examination of an organ or body cavity using an endoscope, a thin, tubular instrument containing a camera and light source. Many endoscopes also allow the retrieval of a small sample (biopsy) of the area being examined, in order to more closely view the tissue under a microscope.

Esophageal atresia—Blockage or closure of the esophagus, the tube leading from the mouth to the stomach.

Gastrostomy tube—A tube that is inserted through a small incision in the abdominal wall and that extends through the stomach wall into the stomach for the purpose of introducing parenteral feedings. Also called a gastric tube, gastrointestinal tube, or stomach tube.

Causes and symptoms

Tracheoesophageal fistulas arise as a developmental abnormality. At birth, the infant has difficulty swallowing. Eating produces severe coughing spells that interfere with breathing. Aspiration pneumonia can develop from fluid breathed into the lungs.

Small H type fistulas may go undiagnosed until later in life. Symptoms of an H type fistula include frequent pulmonary infections and bouts of abdominal bloating.

When to call the doctor

TEFs are normally diagnosed within hours of birth, because feeding and breathing problems are immediately apparent. Some H type defects are not detected until later in life.

Diagnosis

Diagnosis that the esophagus is interrupted is confirmed by the inability to insert a nasogastric suction tube into the stomach. The exact type and location of the fistula can be determined using a radiopaque catheter, which allows pictures to be taken of the esophagus. X rays may show air in the bowels. Endoscopy often fails to locate the fistula if it is small.

Treatment

Babies with all but H type fistulas are unlikely to survive without surgical separation and repair of the trachea and the esophagus. Surgery is usually done at a hospital that has special facilities for treating seriously ill newborns. However, surgery cannot always be performed immediately because of **prematurity**, the presence of other birth defects, or complications from aspiration pneumonia.

While awaiting surgery, the infant's condition is stabilized. Preoperative care concentrates on avoiding aspiration pneumonia and includes the following:

- elevating the head to avoid reflux and aspiration of the stomach contents
- using a suction catheter to continuously remove mucus and saliva that could be inhaled
- when necessary, placement of a gastrostomy tube for feeding
- withholding feeding by mouth

When surgery is performed, the esophagus is reconnected to make it continuous and separate from the trachea. If the two ends of the esophagus are too far apart to be reattached, a piece of tissue from the large intestine is used to join the parts.

Prognosis

The survival rate of infants with tracheoesophageal fistulas improved dramatically toward the end of the twentieth century. In uncomplicated cases, the survival rate is close to 100 percent. However, often babies with TEFs have other birth defects that limit their recovery.

When the esophagus is successfully separated and reattached, many infants have difficulty swallowing, because the contractility of the esophagus is impaired. Infants may also have problems with gastroesophageal reflux, in which the acidic contents of the stomach back up into the bottom of the esophagus and cause ulcers and scarring. Long-term follow-up, however, finds that 80 to 90 percent of children who have repaired TEFs as infants eat normally by the time they are in elementary school. As more individuals with corrected TEFs reach adulthood, there is some evidence that suggests they are more susceptible to esophageal cancers. However, as of 2004, there was not enough data to confirm these findings.

Prevention

Tracheoesophageal fistulas are defects in development of the fetus that cannot be prevented.

Parental concerns

Parents often worry about the effect a TEF may have on their child's later ability to eat and participate in normal activities such as **sports**. In the absence of other birth defects, almost all children have no restrictions on their eating and activities by the time they start school.

Resources

BOOKS

Moore, Keith L., et al. *Before We Are Born: Essentials of Embryology and Birth Defects.* Kent, UK: Elsevier—Health Sciences Division, 2002.

PERIODICALS

"Esophageal Atresia with or without Tracheoesophageal Fistula." *eMedicine Medical Library.* Available online at <www.emedicine.com/ped/topic2950.htm> (accessed August 18, 2004).

"Gastrointestinal Defects." *The Merck Manual of Diagnosis and Therapy*, 17th ed. Edited by Robert Berkow. Rahway, NJ: Merck Research Laboratories, 1999–2004. Available online at <www.merck.com/mrkshared/mmanual/home.jsp> (accessed October 18, 2004).

Kronemer, Keith, and Alison Snyder. "Esophageal Atresia/Tracheoesophageal Fistula." *eMedicine Medical Library.* Available online at <www.emedicine.com/radio/topic704.htm> (accessed October 18, 2004).

Minkes, Robert K., and Alison Snyder. "Congenital Anomalies of the Esophagus." *eMedicine Medical Library.* Available online at <www.emedicine.com/derm/topic396.htm> (accessed October 18, 2004).

Tish Davidson, A.M.

Trachoma

Definition

Trachoma, also called granular **conjunctivitis** or Egyptian ophthalmia, is a contagious, chronic inflammation of the mucous membranes of the eyes, caused by the bacterium *Chlamydia trachomatis.* It is characterized by swelling of the eyelids, sensitivity to light, and eventual scarring of the conjunctiva and cornea of the eye.

Description

Trachoma is a disease associated with poverty and unhygienic conditions. It is most common in hot, dry, dusty climates in the developing world where water is

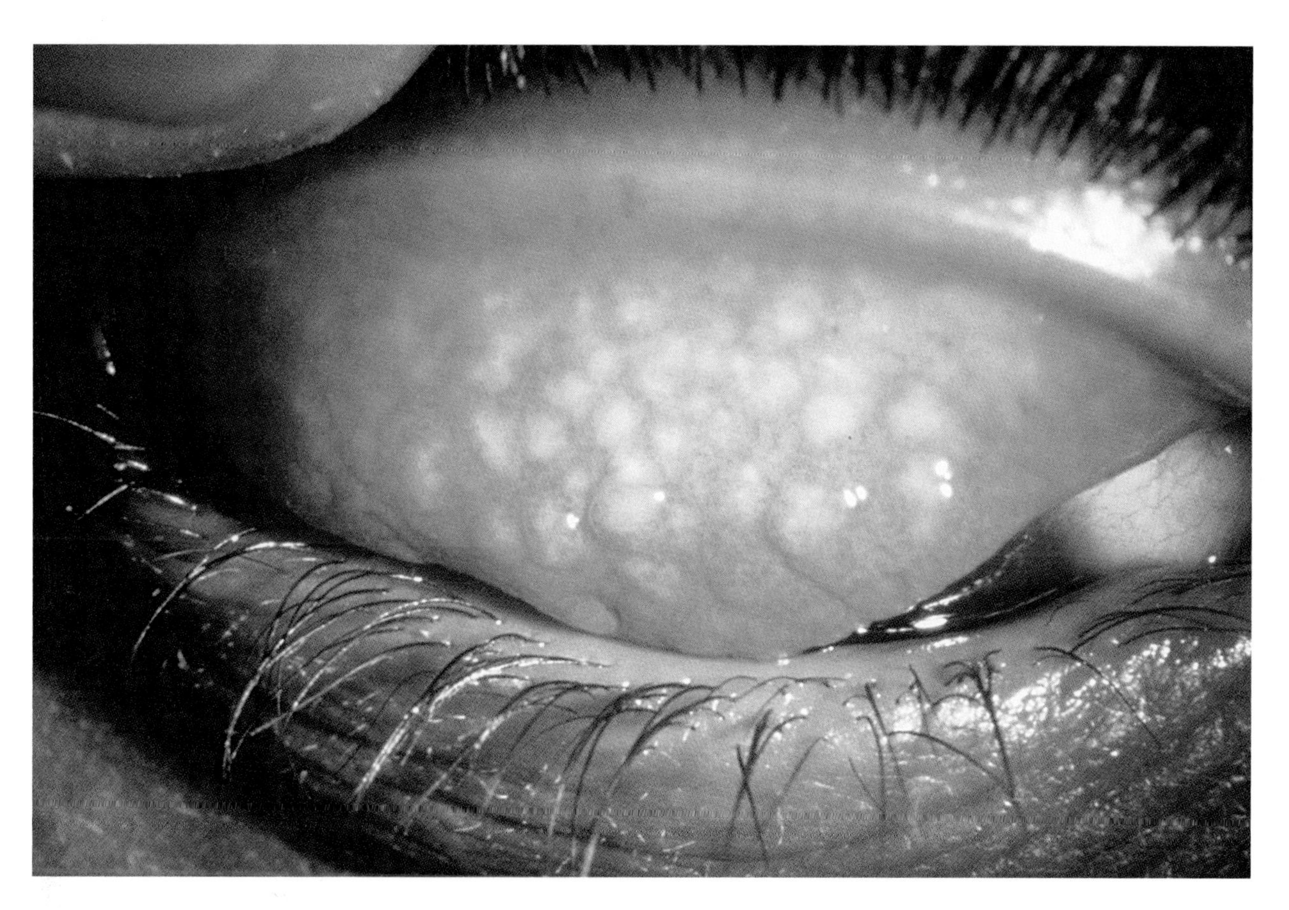

A close-up of a human eye with trachoma. Trachoma is caused by *Chlamydia trachomatis* and commonly results in blindness if left untreated. *(Custom Medical Stock Photo Inc.)*

scarce and sanitation is poor. Trachoma is the most common infectious cause of blindness in the world. It has two stages. The first stage is active infection of the conjunctiva by the bacterium *C. trachomatis*. The conjunctiva is the clear mucous membrane that lines the inside of the eyelid and covers the white part (sclera) of the eye. This stage is highly contagious.

Acquiring trachoma does not provide immunity against re-infection, so repeat infections are the norm in many communities where the disease circulates continuously among **family** members. The frequency of active infection peaks in children ages three to five. In some communities, as many as 90 percent of children under age five are actively infected.

The second stage involves damage to the cornea, the transparent covering of the front of the eye. After repeated infections, the eyelids swell and the eyelashes begin to turn inward so that they scratch the cornea every time the individual blinks. This scratching is painful, and it scars the cornea, eventually resulting in the cornea becoming opaque. Individuals are often blind by middle age. Repeated, extended, untreated periods of infection are required for blindness to occur. An occasional, treated infection does not result in blindness.

Transmission

C. trachomatis is spread through direct contact. Infected young children serve as a reservoir of infection. The bacteria are then transmitted by close physical contact with family members and other caregivers. The bacteria are also spread through shared blankets, pillows, and towels. The bazaar fly *Musca sorbens* lays its eggs in human feces that can be contaminated with trachoma bacteria. These flies pick up bacteria on their bodies and can transmit them to humans.

Certain conditions promote the spread of trachoma bacteria. These include:

- poor personal hygiene
- poor body waste and trash disposal
- insufficient water supply for washing
- shared sleeping space
- close association with domestic animals

KEY TERMS

Conjunctivitis—Inflammation of the conjunctiva, the mucous membrane covering the white part of the eye (sclera) and lining the inside of the eyelids also called pinkeye.

Cornea—The clear, dome-shaped outer covering of the eye that lies in front of the iris and pupil. The cornea lets light into the eye.

Demographics

Trachoma is widespread and present in a high percentage of the population in many parts of Africa, Iraq, Afghanistan, Burma, Thailand, and Viet Nam. Pockets of high trachoma infection also exist in southern Mexico, eastern Brazil, Ecuador, North Africa, India, China, Siberia, Indonesia, New Guinea, Borneo, and in Aboriginal communities in central Australia. Although trachoma is rare in developed countries, it is occasionally found in the United States in some Native American communities and in parts of Appalachia.

The greatest risk for contracting trachoma is having a family member with the disease. Although the disease shows no gender preference, two to three times more women eventually become blind than men, probably because they are the primary caretakers of small children who are infected. The active stage of the disease is most prevalent in children ages three to five. Blindness is most common in middle age. The World Health Organization (WHO) estimates that as of the early 2000s, between 360 and 500 million people are affected by trachoma worldwide and that six million people are blind because of the disease. In some heavily infected areas, up to 25 percent of the population becomes blind from this infection.

Causes and symptoms

The early symptoms of trachoma include the development of follicles (small sacs) on the conjunctivae of the upper eyelids; **pain**; swollen eyelids; discharge; tearing; and sensitivity to light. If the infection is not treated, the follicles develop into large yellow or gray pimples, and small blood vessels develop inside the cornea. In most cases, both eyes are infected. The incubation period is about one week.

Repeated infections eventually lead to contraction and turning-in of the eyelids. The eyelashes then scratch the corneas and conjunctivae, every time the individual blinks. This scratching leads to scarring of the cornea, eventual blockage of the tear ducts, and blindness.

When to call the doctor

U.S. parents should call the doctor if they notice any discomfort or discharge from their child's eye, especially if they have recently traveled in areas where trachoma is common.

Diagnosis

Diagnosis is based on a combination of the patient's history (especially living or traveling in areas with high rates of trachoma) and examination of the eyes. The doctor looks for the presence of follicles or scarring. In developed countries where laboratory facilities are available, the doctor takes a small sample of cells from the child's conjunctivae and examines it, following a procedure called Giemsa staining, to confirm the diagnosis. In underdeveloped countries where medical resources are scarce, diagnosis is made based on an examination only.

Treatment

The preferred treatment is the oral antibiotic azithromycin (Zithromax). This medicine has replaced treatment with other **antibiotics** (usually **tetracyclines**), because only a single dose of azithromycin is required to clear the infection. Oral single dose treatment increases compliance. Everyone in the family should be treated at the same time, whether they show clinical signs of the disease or not, because transmission among family members is so common.

Individuals with complications from untreated or repeated infections require surgery. Surgery can be used for corneal transplantation or to correct eyelid deformities. It does not, however, prevent re-infection.

Prognosis

The prognosis for full recovery is excellent if the individual is treated promptly. If the infection has progressed to the stage of follicle development, prevention of blindness depends on the size of the follicles, the presence of additional bacterial infections, and the development of scarring. The longer the period of infection, the greater the risk of corneal scarring and blindness.

Prevention

Trachoma is a preventable disease. Prevention depends upon good hygiene and public health. The

WHO has developed a program called SAFE, which aims to prevent blindness caused by trachoma. The elements of the program are surgery, antibiotic treatment, facial cleansing and improved personal hygiene, and environmental improvements. Despite this prevention program, permanent gains in controlling trachoma have been elusive.

Parental concerns

In the United States, parents should check with the Centers for Disease Control (available online at <www.cdc.gov>) for advisories about the prevalence of trachoma if they are planning to travel with their children to underdeveloped countries.

Resources

BOOKS

Bailey, Robin. "Eye Infections in the Tropics." In *Infectious Diseases*, 2nd ed. Edited by Jonathon Cohen and William Powderly. St. Louis: Mosby, 2003.

O'Brien, Terrence P. "Conjunctivitis." In *Conn's Current Therapy*, 56th ed. Edited by Robert E. Rakel. Philadelphia: W. B. Saunders Co., 2004.

WEB SITES

Mabey, Denise, and Hugh Taylor. "Trachoma." *eMedicine Medical Library*, April 17, 2001. Available online at <www.emedicine.com/0ph/topic118.htm> Accessed August 1, 2004.

"Ophthalmologic Disorders: Trachoma." In *The Merck Manual of Diagnosis and Therapy*, 17th ed. Edited by Robert Berkow. Rahway, NJ: Merck Research Laboratories, 1999–2004. Available online at <www.merck.com/mrkshared/mmanual/home.jsp> (accessed October 18, 2004).

ORGANIZATIONS

Sight Savers International. c/o Chapel & York, PMB #293, 601 Pennsylvania Avenue, NW, Suite 900, South Building, Washington, DC 20004. Web site: <www.sightsavers.org>.

Tish Davidson, A.M.

Traction *see* **Immobilization**

Transposition of the great arteries

Definition

Transposition of the great arteries (TGA) is a birth defect causing a fatal condition in which there is a reversal, or switch, in the primary connections of the two main (great) blood vessels to the heart, the aorta and pulmonary artery.

Description

There are two great arteries that transport blood away from the heart, the pulmonary artery and the aorta. Normally, the pulmonary artery carries blood from the right ventricle to the lungs. The aorta carries blood from the left ventricle to the vessels of the rest of the body.

Ordinarily, blood returning to the heart is depleted in oxygen. It goes first to the right atrium of the heart and then to the right ventricle where it is pumped to the lungs. While in the lungs, the blood picks up more oxygen. After the lungs, the blood flows to the left atrium, then the left ventricle pumps the blood out through the aorta to the rest of the body, thereby supplying the body with oxygenated blood.

In children with transposition of the great arteries, the connection of the two great arteries is reversed. This condition causes oxygen depleted blood to be circulated to the body because the aorta is connected to the right ventricle. Blood returning to the heart goes to the right atrium and ventricle, and then it goes into the aorta for distribution throughout the body instead of to the lungs to be oxygenated. At the same time, blood in the lungs goes to the left atrium, the left ventricle, but then back to the lungs rather than going to the body because the pulmonary artery is connected to the left ventricle. The result is that highly oxygenated blood keeps recycling through the lungs, while oxygen-depleted blood recycles through the body without going through the lungs to reoxygenate. The body cannot survive without oxygenated blood.

This condition occurs during the fetal development and must be treated promptly after birth if the newborn is to survive. The newborn can survive for a few days while the foramen ovale, a small hole in the septum that separates the two atria, is open, allowing some oxygenated blood to escape and mix into the blood that is being pumped throughout the body. However, within a few days after birth, the foramen ovale normally closes, and no oxygenated blood is available for the body.

Demographics

Transposition of the great arteries affects 20 to 30 of every 100,000 live births each year. It is the most common reason for cyanotic heart disease in newborns accounting for 5 to 7 percent of all infants with **congenital heart disease**. Transposition of the great arteries is most often an isolated defect and is not associated with other congenital syndromes. It affects males more than females with 60 to 70 percent of all cases occurring in males. It does not affect any race or nationality more than another.

Causes and symptoms

Transposition of the great arteries is a birth defect that occurs during fetal development. There is no identifiable disease or cause. The main symptom is a cyanotic or blue baby appearance, caused by a general lack of oxygen in the body's tissues.

Diagnosis

Diagnosis is made immediately after birth, when it is observed that the newborn has a bluish color. A definite diagnosis is made by x ray, electrocardiography (ECG), and echocardiography.

Treatment

Transposition of the great arteries may be treated by the use of medications called prostaglandins which keep the ductus arteriousus open. A procedure called a cardiac catheterization can then be performed during which a small thin tube (catheter) with a balloon tip, may be used to enlarge the opening between the two atria until surgery can be performed. However, both procedures are temporary treatments that help prolong the infant's life, in some cases allowing him or her to gain strength, until surgery can be performed. The only permanent solution for this condition is open-heart surgery. In transposition of the great arteries repair surgery, the infant's heart is stopped, and blood is circulated through the body using a mechanical heart-lung machine. The two great arteries are reconnected to their proper destination. This correction restores the normal blood flow pattern. The coronary arteries are also reconnected, so that they can supply blood to the heart itself.

Prognosis

Left untreated, this disease is fatal within the first weeks of life. After surgical repair, the survival rate is 90 percent, and most individuals grow and develop normally.

KEY TERMS

Aorta—The main artery located above the heart that pumps oxygenated blood out into the body. The aorta is the largest artery in the body.

Atrial—Referring to the upper chambers of the heart.

Cyanosis—A bluish tinge to the skin that can occur when the blood oxygen level drops too low.

Echocardiography—A non-invasive technique, using ultrasound waves, used to look at the various structures and functions of the heart.

Electrocardiagram (ECG, EKG)—A record of the electrical activity of the heart, with each wave being labeled as P, Q, R, S, and T waves. It is often used in the diagnosis of cases of abnormal cardiac rhythm and myocardial damage.

Foramen ovale—The foramen ovale is a fetal cardiac structure that allows the blood in both upper chambers (atria) of the heart to mix. After birth, the pressure rises in the left atrium pushing this opening closed, allowing the heart to function in a two-sided fashion: the right side carries the unoxygenated blood to the lungs, and the left side pumps the oxygenated blood out into the body.

Oxygenate—To supply with oxygen.

Pulmonary artery—An artery that carries blood from the heart to the lungs.

Ventricles—The lower pumping chambers of the heart. The ventricles push blood to the lungs and the rest of the body.

Prevention

Because there is no identifiable cause, there is no way to prevent this condition.

Parental concerns

Transposition of the great arteries is a complex congenital malformation; however, open heart surgery is highly effective in correcting it. Most children have an excellent outcome and a normal healthy life. For most children, activity level, appetite, and growth eventually return to normal. Open heart surgery to repair transposition of the great arteries is usually performed within the first days or weeks of life.

After the child's heart surgery parents should follow all instructions given by the healthcare team. Most children continue to be seen by a team of doctors including the pediatrician, cardiologist, and pediatric cardiac surgeon.

When to call the doctor

Following open heart surgery, parents should call the doctor if any of the following occurs:

- fever of 101.5 (38.6°C) or higher
- swelling or puffiness around the child's eyes, arms, or legs
- redness or swelling, cloudy yellow drainage, or an opening at the incision site
- rapid breathing
- increased fatigue or tiredness
- dry **cough** that was not present before surgery
- decreased appetite or refusal to eat
- increased pain

Resources

WEB SITES

Charpie, John R. "Transposition of the great arteries." *eMedicine*, October 27, 2004. Available online at <www.emedicine.com/ped/topic2548.htm> (accessed November 7, 2004).

"Transposition of the Great Arteries." *Children's Hospital Boston.* Available online at <www.childrenshospital.org/cfapps/A2ZtopicDisplay.cfm?Topic=Transposition+of+the+Great+Arteries> (accessed November 7, 2004).

John T. Lohr, PhD
Deborah L. Nurmi, MS

Traumatic amputations

Definition

Traumatic amputation is the accidental severing of some or all of a body part.

Description

Traumatic amputation most often affects limbs and appendages such as the arms, ears, feet, fingers, hands, legs, and nose. Amputations may be partial (some tissue connects the amputated part to the body) or complete (the amputated part is completely severed from the body).

Demographics

Trauma is the second leading cause of amputation in the United States. About 30,000 traumatic amputations occur in United States each year. Four of every five traumatic amputation victims are male, and most of them are between the ages of 15 and 30.

Causes and symptoms

Some of the more common causes of pediatric traumatic amputations are accidents with lawnmowers, automobiles, motorcycles, power tools, and farm equipment. Amputations may be caused by sharp objects such as knives or blades ("guillotine" amputation) or by heavy objects or mechanisms (crushing amputation). Crushing injuries are the more common cause of traumatic amputations.

Blood loss may be massive or minimal, depending on the nature of the injury and the site of the amputation. Patients who lose little blood and have less severe injuries sometimes feel more **pain** than patients who bleed heavily and whose injuries are life-threatening.

Phantom pain

About 80 percent of all amputees over the age of four experience tingling, **itching**, **numbness**, or pain in the place where the amputated part used to be. About 30 percent of amputees experience a sensation of the amputated part "telescoping" or shrinking into the viable part of the limb. Phantom sensations may begin immediately after the amputation, or they may develop months or years later. They often occur after an injury to the site of the amputation.

These intermittent feelings may have the following characteristics:

- occur frequently or only once in a while
- be mild or intense
- last for a few minutes or several hours
- help patients adjust more readily to an artificial limb (prosthesis)

When to call the doctor

A partial or complete amputation is a medical emergency and as such, the affected child (and amputated body part, if possible) should be transported to an emergency center immediately.

Diagnosis

When the patient and the amputated part(s) reach the hospital, a physician will assess the probability that the severed tissue can be successfully reattached (called replantation). The Mangled Extremity Severity Score (MESS) is a diagnostic tool used to assess the probability of successful replantation and assigns numerical values to such factors as body temperature, circulation, numbness, paralysis, tissue health, and the patient's age and general health. The total score is doubled if blood supply to the amputated part has been absent or diminished for more than six hours.

A general, emergency, or orthopedic surgeon makes the final determination about whether surgery should be performed to reattach the amputated part(s). The surgeon also considers the wishes and lifestyle of the child and parents. Additional concerns are how and to what extent the amputation will affect the child's quality of life and ability to perform everyday activities.

Treatment

First aid or emergency care given immediately after the amputation has a critical impact on both the physicians' ability to salvage and reattach the severed part(s) and the patient's ability to regain feeling and function. Muscle tissue dies quickly, but a well-preserved part can be successfully reattached as much as 24 hours after the amputation occurs. Tissue that has not been preserved will not survive for more than six hours.

Initial response

The most important steps to take when a traumatic amputation occurs are:

- Contact the nearest emergency services provider, clearly describe what has happened, and follow any instructions given.
- Make sure the victim can breathe; administer CPR if necessary.
- Control bleeding using direct pressure; minimize or avoid contact with blood and other body fluids.
- Patients should not be moved if back, head, leg, or neck injuries are suspected or if motion causes pain. If none is found by a trained professional, position the victim flat, with the feet raised 12 inches above the surface.
- Cover the victim with a coat or blanket to prevent shock.

The injured site should be cleansed with a sterile solution and wrapped in a clean towel or other thick material that will protect the wound from further injury. Tissue that is still attached to the body should not be forced back into place. If it cannot be gently replaced, it should be held in its normal position and supported until additional care is available.

Saving the patient's life is always more important than recovering the amputated part(s). Transporting the patient to a hospital or emergency center should never be delayed until missing pieces are located.

Preserving tissue

No amputated body part is too small to be salvaged. Debris or other contaminating material should be removed, but the tissue should not be allowed to get wet. An amputated body part should be wrapped in bandages, towels, or other clean, protective material and sealed in a plastic bag. Placing the sealed bag in a cooler or in a container that is inside a second container filled with cold water or ice will help prevent tissue deterioration.

Replantation

A number of factors influence whether an amputated part can be successfully reattached. These include:

- age of the patient (younger patients tend to heal better and faster)
- location of amputation (replantations of the upper extremities are more successful than those of the lower extremities)
- type of wound (sharp **wounds** are repaired more successfully than crushing injuries)
- health of the patient (e.g. if he or she is able to withstand prolonged surgery)
- amount of contamination to the wound (a grossly contaminated part has a much lower chance of successfully being reattached)
- length of time the amputated part was detached from the body (chance of successful replantation decreases after six hours)

Post-care

Techniques such as biofeedback, cognitive-behavioral **pain management**, hypnosis, acupuncture, ultra-

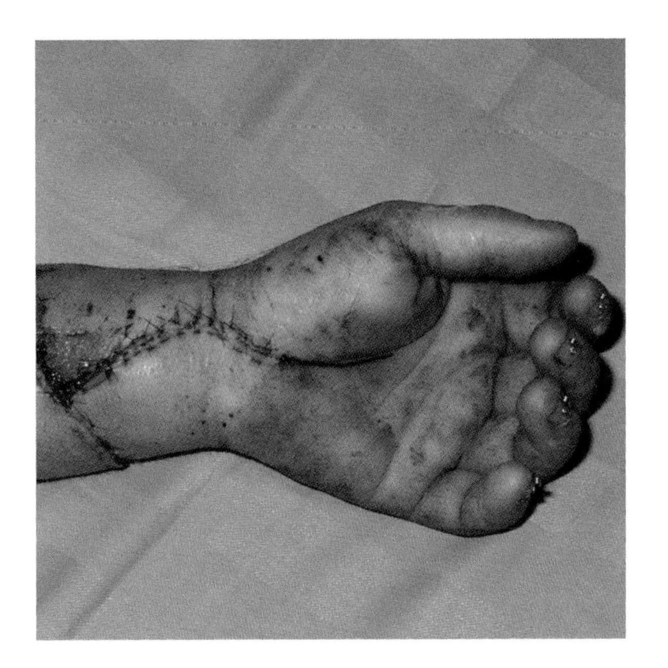

This man's hand was surgically reattached following a traumatic amputation. *(Photograph by Michael English. Custom Medical Stock Photo, Inc.)*

KEY TERMS

Phantom pain—Pain, tingling, itching, or numbness in the place where the amputated part used to be.

Pulmonary embolism—Blockage of an artery in the lungs by foreign matter such as fat, tumor tissue, or a clot originating from a vein. A pulmonary embolism can be a very serious, and in some cases fatal, condition.

Shock—A medical emergency in which the organs and tissues of the body are not receiving an adequate flow of blood. This deprives the organs and tissues of oxygen and allows the build-up of waste products. Shock can be caused by certain diseases, serious injury, or blood loss.

sound, and physical therapy have all been used to treat post-amputation and phantom pain.

Nutritional concerns

Proper **nutrition** is essential to optimize healing after an amputation or reattachment surgery. A well-balanced diet rich in **vitamins** and with adequate caloric value is recommended to promote healing.

Prognosis

Possible complications of traumatic amputation include:

- excessive bleeding and shock
- infection
- muscle shortening
- pulmonary embolism
- death

Improved medical and surgical care and rehabilitation have improved the long-term outlook for such patients. Children tend to heal faster than adults and adapt more quickly to disability.

Prevention

The best way to prevent traumatic amputation is to observe precautions such as using seat belts and obeying speed limits and other traffic regulations. It is important to take special precautions when using potentially dangerous equipment and make sure machinery is turned off and disconnected before attempting to service or repair it. Appropriate protective clothing should be worn at all times. Children should be closely monitored when in the vicinity of lawnmowers, power tools, farm equipment, or other machinery that can cause serious injury

Parental concerns

Parents of child amputees are faced with difficult decisions such as whether to get a limb prosthesis for their child and how to handle issues with negative body image. Parents will be encouraged to work with their child's rehabilitation team, which may include physicians, prosthetists, physical therapists, occupational therapists, psychologists, and/or teachers, to help the child adjust to the traumatic loss of a limb. Tools such as amputee dolls may be helpful in explaining how a prosthetic limb will be worn and to encourage positive body image.

Resources

BOOKS

Dalsey, William C., and Jeffrey Luk. "Management of Amputations." In *Clinical Procedures in Emergency Medicine*, 4th ed. Edited by James R. Roberts and Jerris R. Hedges. Philadelphia: Saunders, 2004.

PERIODICALS

Flor, Herta. "Phantom-limb Pain: Characteristics, Causes, and Treatment." *The Lancet Neurology* 1, no. 3 (July 2002): 182–9.

ORGANIZATIONS

Amputee Coalition of America. PO Box 2528, Knoxville, TN 37901–2528. Web site: <www.amputee-coalition.org>.

National Amputation Foundation. 40 Church St., Malverne, NY 11565. Web site: <www.nationalamputation.org>.

WEB SITES

Koman, L. Andrew. "Replantation." *eMedicine*, December 3, 2002. Available online at <www.emedicine.com/orthoped/topic284.htm> (accessed January 17, 2005).

Maureen Haggerty
Stephanie Dionne Sherk

Treponema infection *see* **Pinta**

Trichotillomania

Definition

Trichotillomania is a psychiatric condition in which an individual has an uncontrollable desire to pull out his own body hair. It is generally considered to be an impulse control disorder but is sometimes classified as either a subtype or variant of **obsessive-compulsive disorder** (OCD).

Description

Trichotillomania is the most common cause of hair loss in children. First described in 1889, trichotillomania is a psychiatric disorder, the result of which is **alopecia** or hair loss, caused by repeated pulling of one's hair from, most often the head, followed by the eyelashes and eye brows. But the hair of any part of the body may be pulled and multiple sites may be involved. The individual with trichotillomania will have bald spots on the head or missing eyelashes or eyebrows.

There is an immense amount of embarrassment and denial associated with trichotillomania. It is common for individuals with this disorder to deny their behavior and attempt to hide their hair loss. The hair loss may be disguised by wearing wigs, hats, scarves or hair clips, or by applying make-up or even by tattooing. The act of hair pulling is a private one. Rarely does the hair pulling occur in the presence of another, except for close **family** members. Because of this fact, social alienation is common in trichotillomania.

The hair pulling may occur either when the individual is relaxed or under stress. For some individuals with trichotillomania, certain situations, such as watching TV, lying in bed, or talking on the phone, will trigger the behavior. The individual either may focus intensely on the hair pulling or the pulling may be done unconsciously. Immediately before pulling hair, the individual with trichotillomania feels a mounting tension. This tension is relieved as a hair root is successfully pulled. Since a tingling sensation is felt upon successfully pulling a hair follicle completely from its root, a neurodermatologic connection may reinforce hair pulling as a means of tension relief. When the hair root remains intact and the hair shaft is broken, this sensation is not felt and the patient may repetitively pull hairs until successful. After pulling the hair, patient may carefully examine the hair root, and the hair bulb may be rubbed along the lips for further stimulation. The hairs may be ingested by some patients.

The amount of time each day that the patient engages in hair pulling may consist of either several brief periods, or a longer intense period. The typical trichotillomania patient will spend one to three hours daily pulling hairs. The urge to pull can be so intense that the individual with trichotillomania cannot think of anything except hair pulling. Thus, social life and work production often suffer with trichotillomania.

The act of hair pulling in trichotillomania is often ritualistic. The necessary implements, such as tweezers, are collected, the location where this is to be performed is determined, the preferred texture or color to be pulled may be planned as well as disposal of the hairs.

Rarely, the individual with trichotillomania may attempt to pull the hairs of others. The hairs of a pet or doll or the fibers of an inanimate object, such as sweater, may be pulled as well. In addition to hair pulling, the hair may be bitten off or twisted or twirled.

Co-existing psychiatric diagnoses such as **anxiety**, depression, and addictive disorders are common in trichotillomania. **Tics**, borderline **personality disorders**, and OCD are all more prevalent in trichotillomania than in the general population. The hair pulling in trichotillomania can be differentiated from that in OCD in that the hair pulling in trichotillomania is an impulse behavior where in OCD it is a repetitive act performed as part of an obsession. The individual with OCD is aware of his or her actions, while the individual with trichotillomania is not always conscious that he or she is pulling hairs.

Trichotillomania is not the underlying cause of hair pulling if there is a medical reason for the hair loss or if another co-existing psychiatric disorder such as hallucination provokes the hair pulling.

Demographics

Trichotillomania usually begins in the preteens but has been reported in children as young as one year old and has been seen first in adults over 50 years old. Patients in their seventies may suffer from trichotillomania. The mean age of onset is 12 years of age in girls and eight years of age in boys. This condition is seven times more common in children than in adults. Among young children there is no gender preference. But among adults, it is reported up to 10 times more often in females than in males. This may be skewed because females are more likely to seek attention for a medical problem, and because it is easier for males to disguise their compulsions, e.g. by shaving or because of social acceptance of male pattern hair loss.

The total number of Americans who pull their own hair at some point in their lifetime may be as high as 11 million. The prevalence of trichotillomania has been estimated to be as high as 2 percent of the general population. Among college students surveyed, more than 10 percent of college students pull their hair at some point, although only 1 percent meets the criteria for trichotillomania.

Causes and symptoms

There is no clear cause of trichotillomania, but there are psychoanalytical, behavioral, or biological theories for this disorder. Some of the more commonly accepted theories for trichotillomania are:

- childhood trauma
- stressful events
- neurochemical imbalance

The psychoanalytic model purports that trichotillomania occurs in an attempt to resolve a childhood trauma, the most common of which is sexual abuse. According to this model an unconscious unresolved past conflict triggers hair pulling.

The behavioral theory for trichotillomania states that a stressful event, such as moving or the loss of a loved one, or a family conflict precedes the onset of hair pulling and that hair pulling begins in an attempt to relieve tension caused by a stressful event. This behavior continues beyond the initial stimulus and eventually becomes habitual. Later the patient may not be aware of this initial trigger. For a child, the stressor may not be just a single event, but may occur in response to what a child may perceive as excessive demands from an authoritarian or an overbearing parent.

Biological theories for trichotillomania include a neurochemical imbalance, such as a serotonin imbalance. Drugs that correct for serotonin imbalance improve symptoms in many with this disorder. Altered dopamine levels may also play a role in trichotillomania. It is not clear if genetic factors are involved in the development of trichotillomania, although some studies report an increased percentage of relatives with various psychiatric disorders.

The most common symptom of trichotillomania is hair loss. The pattern of alopecia in trichotillomania varies among patients and the degree of hair loss will range from a barely noticeable thinning to total loss of hair. Some patients pull out hairs without regard for symmetry, while others will attempt to follow a pattern or pull out hairs in an effort to maintain symmetry of appearance. Usually, the hair loss on the head is patchy or poorly defined. There are neither scars nor any inflammation in the area of scalp hair loss. The top is the most affected region of the head. Tonsure trichotillomania is a pattern hair loss of the scalp in which hair is present only at the nape and on the outer edge of the scalp. The eyelashes and eyebrows may be plucked off, and hair loss may be noted on the arms, legs, and body. Pubic hair may be sparse.

When to call the doctor

Any continuous pulling of hair or hair loss should be reported to a medical professional, as there are medical causes for hair pulling and hair loss, and if trichotillomania is the underlying cause for this problem, then medical and psychiatric treatment needs to be initiated as soon as possible, since the earlier the intervention, the greater the likelihood that the behavior can be controlled. It is important to realize that the occasional or infrequent twisting, pulling, or chewing of hair in a child does not constitute trichotillomania and does not require medical attention.

Diagnosis

The diagnosis of trichotillomania is made by history and interview, along with histological examination of the hairs in the area of hair loss as well as skin tissue in the area. All other medical causes of hair loss must be eliminated. Since patients are adept at disguising and denying the symptoms of trichotillomania, the condition may go on for years without detection or treatment. Most patients are embarrassed to admit to hair pulling and the resultant sequelae, and elicitation of this behavior is difficult. The patient will not usually report **pain**. All of this makes the diagnosis of trichotillomania difficult. The patient must be made to feel comfortable admitting to and then discussing the behavior.

The clinician may use rating scales to assist in the diagnosis of trichotillomania and to assess the degree to which a patient has trichotillomania. These scales include the Psychiatric Institute Trichotillomania Scale, National Institutive of Mental Health-Trichotillomania Severity Scale, Yale-Brown Obsessive Scale modified for Trichotillomania, the National Institute of Mental Health-Trichotillomania Impairment Scale, and the Minnesota Trichotillomania Assessment Inventory.

According to the American Psychiatric Association there are five criteria which must be met in order for trichotillomania to be diagnosed. They are as follows:

- The hair pulling is recurrent and a noticeable pattern of hair loss is observed.
- The patient feels increased tension prior to the hair pulling.
- This tension is relieved upon pulling hairs.
- The pulling is not associated with another mental condition, and there is no medical cause for the hair pulling.
- The behavior interferes with or disrupts the patient's social and work activities.

There is a subgroup of hair-pullers who do not meet the second and third criteria listed above. These individuals are less likely to hide their behavior and do not suffer from low **self-esteem** as frequently as those who meet all of the above criteria. There is some debate about whether these people have trichotillomania and about whether these criteria for diagnosis of trichotillomania are too restrictive.

Histological examination of hair follicles and skin biopsies also help in the diagnosis of trichotillomania. In the areas of hair loss in trichotillomania there will be a mixture of short and longer hairs in the area of hair loss. Trichomalacia or distortion of the hair follicles is often present in trichotillomania.

Trichotillomania must be differentiated from medical causes of hair loss and these include: skin conditions such as **psoriasis**; trauma, such as that from radiation; endocrine disorders such as **hypothyroidism**; infectious diseases such as herpes zoster; inflammation such that of the lids margins, called blepharitis; and tinea capitis, a fungal infection of the scalp. Other psychiatric disorders, such as **schizophrenia**, must also be ruled out.

Treatment

Usually, the patient with trichotillomania does not present for treatment until, on average, two years after the hair pulling has begun. Traditional treatment for trichotillomania involves psychological or behavioral therapy, or medication. Behavior modification, especially with children, helps the child to increase his or her awareness of the hair pulling. Behavioral therapy may be as simple as acknowledging the problem and instituting a plan for desensitization of the behavior.

Habit reversal training (HRT), a cognitive behavioral therapy, has been successfully used in the treatment of trichotillomania. Under HRT treatment the patient acquires increased awareness of his or her actions and learns alternative behavior to the hair pulling. HRT has been employed in group therapy. Addressing the behavior of trichotillomania in a group setting is helpful so the patients realize that they are not the only ones with this problem. This experience also improves social interaction, as isolation is common among patients with trichotillomania.

Medication to correct biochemical imbalances in the brain is a common component of trichotillomania treatment. But since drug trials in children and adolescents have been limited, behavioral therapy is often instituted alone first, prior to using medication. But for some with trichotillomania, behavioral therapy is more successful when drug therapy helps reduce the urge to pull hair. For these individuals, relapses are more frequent when pharmacotherapy is reduced or discontinued.

There are no FDA drugs which specifically treat trichotillomania. The drugs used to treat this disorder have been developed for treatment of other psychiatric problems. The drug which has been the most successful in treatment of trichotillomania is clomipramine (Anafranil), a tricyclic antidepressant.

Since it is hypothesized that serotonin activity is abnormal in trichotillomania, selective serotonin reuptake inhibitors (SSRIs) are commonly given to improve symptoms. Prozac is a common SSRI. Drugs in this class given to treat trichotillomania in children include sertraline (Zoloft), fluvoxamine (Luvox), and clomioramine. The effectiveness of a given drug varies considerably from person to person. If one SSRI drug is not successful in controlling trichotillomania in a given individual, another drug in this class may work. Risperdone and clonazepam, which address a dopamine imbalance, can be added to SSRIs if an SSRI drug does not satisfactorily control symptoms. But these drugs, called neuroleptics, have more side effects in children than in adults.

Since those with trichotillomania do not report pain, drugs to decrease pain thresholds have been tried as well. Other drugs that are given to treat this disorder include buspirone, lithium (Lithobid), naltrexone, paroxetine (Paxil), valproate, and the antipsychotic drug, quetiapine.

Treatment of the resultant medical complications of hair pulling must be addressed. Carpal tunnel can develop from repetitive pulling. Infections at the site of the hair pulling and blepharitis at the eyelid margins can occur, both of which are treated with **topical antibiotics** and corticosteroids. If there is significant eyelash and eyebrow loss, called madarosis, blepheropigmentation or surgical tattooing can be performed. Although not done often, transplantation of hairs to these areas is possible.

Topical application of colladion can help with regrowth of hair but will not be successful long term unless the underlying behavior is controlled. If the hair pulling continues for long periods without treatment, the alopecia may be permanent.

Anemia, **malnutrition**, and digestive disorders, including bowel obstructions, can develop, if trichotillomania develops into trichotillophagia or eating of the hairs. Trichobezoars, or hairballs, can form when the hair is bitten off and ingested.

For many with trichotillomania, hair pulling is not an activity that can be stopped at will. For some, however, the suppression of hair pulling may be possible, even if the underlying urge persists. The family needs to be a part of therapy since familial stressors may have triggered trichotillomania.

Because of the shame involved with hair pulling the patient may have other medical problems which go untreated because he or she will not seek any medical care at all, for **fear** that hair pulling and its associated stigmata will be uncovered. Thus, it is important that once trichotillomania is diagnosed that the healthcare provider inquire into any other medical concerns that the patient may have.

Alternative treatment

Hypnosis has been used in treatment of childhood trichotillomania. The Erickson approach of hypnosis helps the child to substitute hair pulling for a stroking behavior. Other approaches to hypnosis in trichotillomania teach the child that he or she has control over events in his or her life, including hair pulling. There are other hypnotic techniques that employ adverse conditioning, so that the hair pulling becomes associated with pain instead of pleasure.

Other techniques, consider alternative, used to trichotillomania include biofeedback, **yoga**, and **exercise**.

Prognosis

When trichotillomania appears in early childhood, the duration of time during which the child is afflicted, is limited. The remission rate for children diagnosed before age six is high. For many children with trichotillomania, the condition resolves by adulthood.

The prognosis is much more difficult for those who develop trichotillomania after age 13. These children have a higher rate of other co-existing psychiatric disorders. Unfortunately, among those individuals who need long-term treatment for trichotillomania, as is the case when the initial presentation occurs in late childhood or as in **adolescence** or in adulthood, there is a high relapse rate in spite of intervention. A lack of definitive cause for trichotillomania makes treatment difficult, and the prognosis for a total recovery is poor, although the behavior may be satisfactorily controlled with therapy.

Prevention

Since, as of 2004, the actual cause of trichotillomania was not known, there is no known means of prevention.

Parental concerns

Parents must realize that the earlier the treatment for trichotillomania is begun, the more likely that the hair pulling can be controlled. When trichotillomania strikes the adolescent it is especially important that the behavior be addressed and treated promptly. Adolescence is a time when self-esteem and independence are developing. If the adolescent does not have a positive body image, then fear or ridicule from family and peers can affect his or her ability to interact with others. Development of normal healthy relationships as an adult may be impaired if the family and such support mechanisms as therapy are not in place.

Since often the family dynamics provoke this behavior, parental involvement in therapy is essential. If necessary, the parents must be open to establishing new boundaries within the parent-child relationship.

It is important that parents to realize that trichotillomania is a complex and not completely understood behavior. But it is increasingly believed that trichotillomania has a biological basis, and thus parents must understand that they did not cause it and that they are not the only parents with a child who has trichotillomania. Support for trichotillomania may be found through the Trichotillomania Learning Center (available online at <www.trich.org>). Many larger cities may have local support groups. Healthcare providers may help with location of such groups locally.

See also Alopecia; Obsessive-compulsive disorders.

Resources

BOOKS

Albert, Daniel M., et al. *Principles and Practice of Ophthalmology*, 2nd ed. Philadelphia: W. B. Saunders Co, 2000.

Burt, Vivien K., and Jeffery William Katzman. "Trichotillomania." In *Kaplan & Sadock's Comprehensive Textbook of Psychiatry*, vol. II. Edited by Benjamin J. Sadock and Virginia Sadock. Philadelphia: Lippinicott Williams & Wilkins, 2000.

Diagnostic and Statistical Manual of Mental Disorders, 4th ed. Washington, DC: American Psychiatric Association, 2000.

PERIODICALS

Borgfeld, Wilma, et al. "The Combined Utilization of Clinical and Histological Findings in the Diagnosis of Trichotillomania." *Journal of Cutaneous Pathology* 29 (2002): 207–14.

Diefenbach, Gretchen J., et al. "Trichotillomania: A Challenge to Research and Practice." *Clinical Psychological Review* 20, no. 3 (April 2000): 289–309.

du Troit, Pieter L., et al. "Characteristics and Phenomenology of Hair-Pulling: An Exploration of Subtypes." *Comprehensive Psychiatry* 42, no. 3 (May-June 2001): 247–56.

Enos, Stephanie, and Thomas Plante. "Trichotillomania: An Overview and Guide to Understanding." *Journal of Psychosocial Nursing and Mental Health Services* 39, no. 5 (May 2001): 10–18.

Iglesias, Alex. "Hypnosis as a Vehicle for Choice and Self-Agency in the Treatment of Children with Trichotillomania." *American Journal of Clinical Hypnosis* 46, no. 2 (October 2003): 129–37.

Jordan, D. R., and L. A. Mawn. "Trichotillomania." *Canadian Journal of Ophthalmology* 38, no. 4 (June 2003): 303–05.

Khouzam, Hani Raoul, et al. "An Overview of Trichotillomania and Its Response to Treatment with Quetiapine: A Case Report." *Psychiatry Interpersonal and Biological Processes* 65, no. 3 (Fall 2002): 262–70.

Nuss, Michelle A., et al. "Trichotillomania: A Review and Case Report." *Cutis* 72, no. 3 (September 2003): 191–96.

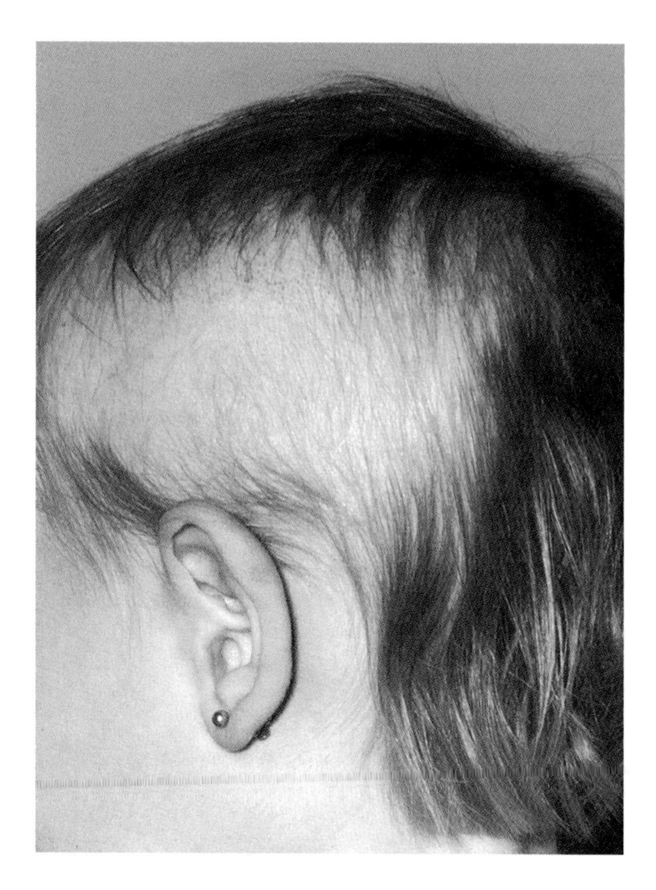

Child's scalp showing hair loss from trichotillomania. *(© NMSB/Custom Medical Stock Photo.)*

O'Sullivan, Richard L., et al. "Characterization of Trichotillomania: A Phenomenological Model with Clinical Relevance to Obsessive-Compulsive Spectrum Disorders." *The Psychiatric Clinics of North America* 23, no. 3 (September 2000): 587–604.

Springer, Karyn, et al. "Common Hair Loss Disorders." *American Family Physician* 68, no. 1 (July 1, 2004): 93–102, 107–8.

WEB SITES

"About TTM & Treatment: Alternative Therapies." *Trichotillomania Learning Center.* Available online at <www.trich.org/about-ttm/alttherapies.asp> (accessed July 24, 2004).

"About TTM & Treatment: Introduction." *Trichotillomania Learning Center.* Available online at <www.trich.org/about-ttm/intor.asp> (accessed July 24, 2004).

"About TTM & Treatment: Medications." *Trichotillomania Learning Center.* Available online at <www.trich.org/ttm/medication.asp> (accessed July 24, 2004).

KEY TERMS

Alopecia—The loss of hair, or baldness.

Dopamine—A neurotransmitter made in the brain that is involved in many brain activities, including movement and emotion.

Histology—The study of tissue structure.

Hypnosis—The technique by which a trained professional induces a trance-like state of extreme relaxation and suggestibility in a patient. Hypnosis is used to treat amnesia and identity disturbances that occur in dissociative disorders.

Obsessive-compulsive disorder—An anxiety disorder marked by the recurrence of intrusive or disturbing thoughts, impulses, images, or ideas (obsessions) accompanied by repeated attempts to supress these thoughts through the performance of certain irrational and ritualistic behaviors or mental acts (compulsions).

Remission—A disappearance of a disease and its symptoms. Complete remission means that all disease is gone. Partial remission means that the disease is significantly improved, but residual traces of the disease are still present. A remission may be due to treatment or may be spontaneous.

Serotonin—A widely distributed neurotransmitter that is found in blood platelets, the lining of the digestive tract, and the brain, and that works in combination with norepinephrine. It causes very powerful contractions of smooth muscle and is associated with mood, attention, emotions, and sleep. Low levels of serotonin are associated with depression.

"For Kids and Teens: Will it Go Away?" *Trichotillomania Learning Center*. Available online at <www.trich.org/for kidsteens/go-away.asp> (accessed July 24, 2004).

"Other Mental Illnesses: Trichotillomania." *National Mental Health Association*. Available online at <www.nmhaa.org/infoctr/factsheets/92.cfm> (accessed July 24, 2004).

Martha Reilly, OD

Triple antibiotic ointment *see* **Antiobiotics, topical**

Trisomy 13 *see* **Patau syndrome**

Trisomy 18 *see* **Edwards' syndrome**

Trisomy 21 *see* **Down syndrome**

Truancy

Definition

Truancy is unapproved absence from school, usually without a parent's knowledge.

Description

Truancy is a serious problem in many communities in the United States. All states have laws governing compulsory education. Noncompliance results in penalties for the parent(s) or guardian of the truant student. The majority of the states require that students attend school until at least age 16. Those students who do not attend school regularly are often taking the first step toward a lifetime of problems. Most experts believe that truancy is a powerful and accurate predictor of involvement in crime and violence. The United States Department of Justice reports that 80 percent of those in prison were at one time truants. The percent of juvenile offenders who started as truants is even higher, approaching 95 percent. Truancy is different from school phobia, in which a child fails to attend school because of **anxiety**.

As of 2004, no national database existed to define the number children who are truant, partly because there is no uniform definition of truancy. Some districts consider children truant only if they miss a half or full day of school, while others consider missing a single scheduled class period as truancy. The Los Angeles School District has estimated that 10 percent of its students are absent each day and that only 5 percent return with written notes from home excusing the absence. Pittsburgh, Pennsylvania, schools reported 3,500 students, or 12 percent of all students, were absent on an average school day; 70 percent of those were unexcused. Milwaukee, Wisconsin, reported 4,000 unexcused absences on an average school day. Miami, Florida, reported that over 70 percent of 13- to 16-year-olds prosecuted for crimes were truant. The No Child Left Behind Act of the early 2000s requires school districts to report truancy, so national numbers were expected to become available. Boys and girls are equally likely to be truant. The average age of truant students is 15 years, but some children begin skipping school as young as 10.

Why children are truant

According the United States Department of Education's 1996 *Manual to Combat Truancy*, skipping school is a cry for help and a signal that the child is in trouble. Psychiatrists consider truancy one of many symptoms of **oppositional defiant disorder** or the more serious diagnosis of **conduct disorder**, especially when truancy begins before age 13.

There are many reasons why children become truant. These include:

- lack of interest in education and alienation from school
- falling behind academically in school
- **fear** of violence on the way to school or at school
- alienation from authority
- lax parental supervision
- lack of parental support for education
- drug and alcohol abuse
- working long hours while attending school, resulting in chronic exhaustion
- lack of significant consequences for failure to attend school
- problems at home that require supervising younger children or helping dysfunctional adults

Truancy as a predictor of behavior

Truancy is a strong and reliable predictor of delinquent behavior, especially among males. Children who are habitual truants are more likely to engage in undesirable and antisocial behaviors such as gang membership, marijuana use, alcohol use, inhalant and hard drug use, high-risk sexual behavior, cigarette **smoking**, suicidal behaviors, theft, and vandalism. Truant girls are more likely to become pregnant and drop out of school. Most habitual truants eventually enter the juvenile court system. As adults, habitual truants have more employment and marital problems and are jailed far more often than nontruants.

Truancy is a gateway to serious violent and nonviolent crime. Law enforcement agencies have linked high rates of truancy to high rates of daytime burglary and vandalism. In addition, they have found habitual truants are more likely to belong to **gangs** and participate in violent crimes and assaults.

Combating truancy

Communities in which anti-truancy programs have been successful use a combination of incentives and sanctions to keep students in school. In the *Manual to Combat Truancy*, five key points are defined for minimizing truancy. The first step is to involve parents in all aspects of truancy prevention. To stop truants, the school must be able to provide parents with notification of their child's absence on the day the absence occurs. Schools are advised to create an efficient attendance-tracking system and to communicate students' absences to parents immediately.

Second, schools must have firm policies on the consequences for truancy, and all students should be aware of the sanctions that will be imposed if they are absent without an excuse. Some states have found that linking truancy to the ability to obtain a driver's license effectively reduces unexcused absences. Others have invoked a daytime curfew, allowing police to question any young person not in school during school hours.

Third, parents must take responsibility for keeping their children in school. Most state laws impose fines or jail terms on parents of truants. School districts vary in how aggressive they are about holding parents accountable; however, more are becoming tougher. For example, in 2003, the Upper Darby School District in suburban Philadelphia had 14,000 students. This school system sends 10 to 12 parents to jail each year for their children's failures to attend school.

Alternately, some states are investigating ways to use incentives such as linking eligibility for public assistance to truancy as an effective way to capture parents' interest in keeping their children in school. Another positive incentive provides increased eligibility for services to families whose children attend school regularly. Many communities also offer effective parenting courses, **family** counseling, and mediation for returning the student to school.

Fourth, root causes of truancy must be addressed. The root causes of truancy are complex and varied and can include drug use, membership in a peer group of truants or gangs, lack of direction in education, poor academic performance, and violence at or near school. By analyzing the reasons students are truant, the school administration may be able to correct or improve the problem and reduce truancy. For example, if students stay away from school because of inadequate academic skills, special tutoring programs may be initiated. If students have concerns about violence near the school, the administration may request increased security from the police for the surrounding neighborhood. Local businesses can be enlisted to support school-to-work programs to help students make the transition to employment.

Finally, a close link between the school, law enforcement, juvenile court, family court officials, and social service agencies may lead to solutions for truancy. Some communities have authorized the police to patrol neighborhoods where truant youth are likely to spend the school hours. Daytime curfews are also effective in some cities, where school age children can be questioned if they are on the streets during school hours.

Common problems

Truancy is not normally an isolated problem in a child's life. The following comparisons from a 2003 study published in the *Journal of the American Academy of Child and Adolescent Psychiatry* highlight the problem. The first percentage given is for truant children. The percentage of each activity in nontruant children is given in parentheses for comparison.

- all psychiatric disorders: 25.4 percent (6.8 percent)
- oppositional defiant disorder: 9.7 percent (2.3 percent)
- conduct disorder: 14.8 percent (1.6 percent)
- depression: 7.5 percent (1.6 percent)
- conflictual relationships with peers: 16.2 percent (8.7 percent)
- living in poverty: 31.3 percent (19.1 percent)
- single-parent household: 45.9 percent (21.8 percent)
- lax parental supervision: 31.5 percent (6.7 percent)
- mother currently diagnosed as depressed: 11.9 percent (5.5 percent)
- parents teenagers at time of birth: 15.3 percent (8.4 percent)

Parental concerns

Almost half of all truants live in single-parent households, usually headed by women. Parents are concerned that they have lost control of their children and fear legal sanctions if their child skips school. They also are concerned about their child dropping out of school and becoming involved in crime and the criminal justice system. Parents may also fail to understand the attendance laws or have cultural biases against the education system.

When to get help

Truancy is a symptom that things are out of control in a child's life. Parents need to seek help from the school, social service agencies, and mental health professionals at the first sign that their child is skipping school.

See also Conduct disorder.

Resources

BOOKS

Reid, Paula, and Elizabeth A. Whitmore. "Conduct Disorder." In *Psychiatric Secrets*, 2nd ed. Edited by Alan Jacobson. St. Louis: Mosby, 2001, pp. 310–13.

PERIODICALS

Baker, Myriam L., Jane Nady Sigmon, and M. Elaine Nugent. "Truancy Reduction: Keeping Students in School." *Juvenile Justice Bulletin* U.S. Department of Justice, Office of Juvenile Justice and Delinquency Prevention, September 2001.

Egger, Helen Link, E. Jane Costello, and Adrian Angold. "School Refusal and Psychiatric Disorders: A Community Study." *Journal of the American Academy of Child and Adolescent Psychiatry* (July 2003): 797–808.

ORGANIZATIONS

American Academy of Child and Adolescent Psychiatry. 3615 Wisconsin Avenue, NW, Washington, DC 20016–3007. Web site: <www.aacap.org>.

National Association of School Psychologists. 4340 East West Highway, Suite 402, Bethesda, MD 20814. Web site: <www.nasponline.org>.

Tish Davidson, A.M.

TSS *see* **Toxic shock syndrome**

Tuberculosis

Definition

Tuberculosis is a chronic, infectious disease that primarily attacks the lungs.

Description

Tuberculosis (TB) is caused by a bacteria that primarily attacks the lungs. An individual may be "TB infected," meaning the bacteria are in the body but are in an inactive state, walled off behind scab-like structures that are the body's defense mechanism, or have "TB disease," when the bacteria actively spread throughout the body and can cause damage to the lungs or other organs. The severity of the attack depends on whether the bacteria spread from the lungs to other parts of the body. TB infection in the blood, the meninges (membranes around the brain and spinal cord), or the kidneys are the most serious. Children between the ages of six and 24 months are the most susceptible to **meningitis**; it is the chief cause of tuberculin death among children.

Transmission

The bacteria that causes TB, *Mycobacterium tuberculosis*, is transmitted by droplets when an infected person coughs or sneezes. It is not spread through kissing or other physical contact. Children nearly always contract the disease from an infected adult.

Demographics

In 2003, the Centers for Disease Control and Prevention (CDC) reported 14,874 cases of tuberculosis in the United States, or 5.1 cases per 100,000 population. The actual number of TB infections, however, is estimated to be much higher, as high as ten million. In 2002, there were 802 tuberculosis-related deaths. The District of Columbia had the highest rates of TB, with 14 cases per 100,000 people in 2003; Montana and Wyoming had the lowest rate, with 0.8 cases per 100,000 population. Children less than 15 years of age represented 6 percent of reported TB cases, and 15–24-year-olds represented 11 percent of all cases. Worldwide, TB cases are the rise, with nearly 8.8 million new cases a year being estimated by the World Health Organization (WHO).

Causes and symptoms

Mycobacterium tuberculosis is a microscopic, rod-shaped bacterium. The majority of individuals who are infected with TB do not go on to have active disease. Active TB can be triggered when a person's immune system is weakened, such as from human **immunodeficiency** virus (HIV), **malnutrition**, or alcohol abuse.

Early symptoms of TB include unusual fatigue, **fever**, loss of weight, **headache**, coughing, and irritability. An infected child may have night sweats and **cough** up blood. In advanced stages, the patient will suffer persistent coughing, breathlessness, and fever. Many times TB is not diagnosed and becomes dormant; this is known as initial tuberculosis. In severe cases among young children between the ages of two and four, initial TB can be fatal. The disease can reoccur, or reactivate, during **adolescence** when resistance is low, and may disappear on its own or develop into serious lung disease.

When to call the doctor

Parents should contact their child's doctor if the child has been in contact with someone who has been diagnosed with or is suspected to have tuberculosis, or if the child exhibits the symptoms of the disease, particularly persistent fever, night sweats, and cough.

Diagnosis

Tuberculosis is nearly always diagnosed by tuberculin skin tests, although one can also be diagnosed by chest **x rays** and analysis of sputum (matter from the respiratory tract) smears and cultures. The most common tuberculin skin test is the Mantoux test, which consists of injecting a small amount of protein from the TB bacillus into the forearm. A reddening and swelling of the area after 24–72 hours signals the presence of TB. A negative result, however, may not necessarily exclude a diagnosis of TB.

Treatment

The disease is treated with a regimen of strong **antibiotics** such as Rifampin and Isoniazid for six months to two years. Because some strains of the disease are unusually drug-resistant, cultures are grown from the patient's bacteria and tested with a variety of drugs to determine the most effective treatment. In cases of strong drug-resistant strains, the child may undergo surgery to remove the infected areas.

Infants with TB are usually hospitalized but children and teenagers can generally lead active lives within two weeks of beginning medication. It is imperative that the mediation prescribed be taken faithfully.

Prognosis

With treatment, TB infection that is not drug resistant can nearly always be cured as long as patients are consistent with their medications and considerable lung damage as not already occurred. Drug-resistant TB has a lower cure rate. Without treatment, the disease will continue to progress; approximately one-half of untreated TB patients will die of the disease.

Prevention

Stopping the spread of tuberculosis is the most effective way of preventing its incidence among children. All adults who work with children should be screened regularly. In many communities, children are tested when they reach their first birthday and then at one-to-three year intervals throughout the school years. The medical profession is divided on the issue of screening; some physicians believe that the screening should be focused in areas of common occurrence or within high-risk populations such as foreign-born children. The practice of relying on parents to report results of the skin testing has also come under criticism from some members of the medical community.

While a vaccine for TB does exist (Bacille Calmette-Guerin or BCG vaccine), it is not widely available in the United States and has had conflicting reports about its efficacy. Being inoculated with BCG vaccine does not always prevent infection with the disease. The vaccine is only recommended for children in the United

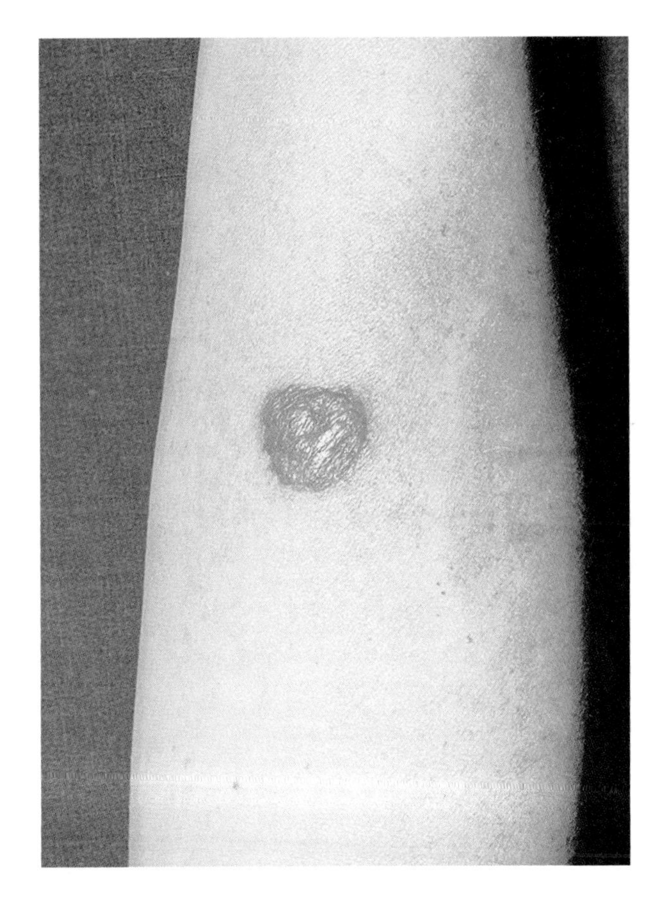

Lesion on the arm of a child infected with tuberculosis. *(© Mediscan/Visuals Unlimited.)*

States if they live with someone who has active TB that cannot be treated or is drug-resistant.

Nutritional concerns

Poor **nutrition** is closely related active tuberculosis; children with adequate nutrition are more resistant to the disease than those who suffer from malnutrition.

Parental concerns

If a child has been infected with TB and is prescribed drug therapy to treat the disease, it is imperative that parents closely monitor their child to ensure that the medication is taken as prescribed; if the medication is not taken frequently enough or until it is no longer needed, drug-resistant TB can arise.

KEY TERMS

Mantoux test—A tuberculin skin test. Also called the PPD (purified protein derivative) test.

Meningitis—An infection or inflammation of the membranes that cover the brain and spinal cord. It is usually caused by bacteria or a virus.

Sputum—The substance that is coughed up from the lungs and spit out through the mouth. It is usually a mixture of saliva and mucus, but may contain blood or pus in patients with lung abscess or other diseases of the lungs.

Resources

BOOKS

Landau, Elaine. *Tuberculosis.* New York: F. Watts, 1995.

PERIODICALS

"TB on the Rise." *Patient Care* 38, no. 6 (June 2004): 9-10.

Young, Douglas B. and Brian D. Robertson. "TB Vaccines: Global Solutions for Global Problems." *Science* 284, no. 5419 (May 28, 1999): 1479.

ORGANIZATIONS

American Lung Association. 61 Broadway, 6th Floor, New York, NY 10006. (800) 548-8252. Web site: <www.lungusa.com>.

Centers for Disease Control and Prevention. 1600 Clifton Rd., Atlanta, GA 30333. (404) 639-3311. Web site: <www,cdc.gov>.

WEB SITES

Division of Tuberculosis Elimination. "Reported Tuberculosis in the United States, 2003." *Centers for Disease Control and Prevention.* [cited September 12, 2004]. Available online at: <www.cdc.gov/nchstp/tb/surv/surv2003/default.htm>.

Sharma, Sat. "Tuberculosis." *eMedicine.* January 14, 2003 [cited September 12, 2004]. Available online at: <www.emedicine.com/aaem/topic464.htm>.

Mary McNulty
Stephanie Dionne Sherk

Tuberous sclerosis

Definition

Tuberous sclerosis is a genetic disorder in which noncancerous (benign) tumors grow on the brain, skin, kidneys, eyes, heart, and lungs.

Description

The name tuberous sclerosis refers to characteristics of the benign tumors that grow within the brain. The tumors have root-like or tuberous appendages. Over time, the tumors undergo sclerosis, meaning they calcify and grow hard.

Symptoms of tuberous sclerosis may be identifiable at birth or may develop over time.

Demographics

In the United States, as of the early 2000s, there are between 25,000 and 40,000 individuals with tuberous sclerosis. Globally, about 1 to 2 million individuals have the disease. The disease occurs in about one out of every 6,000 newborns. There is no gender, racial, or ethnic predilection.

Causes and symptoms

Tuberous sclerosis occurs when at least one of two genes (either TSC-1 on chromosome 9 or TSC-2 on chromosome 16) is defective. Normally, the two genes produce proteins called hamartin and tuberin, respectively. These proteins seem to serve as inhibitors of tumor growth. When the TS genes are defective or absent, the proteins are either absent or deficient, which allows tumor growth.

Most cases of tuberous sclerosis occur due to spontaneous mutations. This means that the disease does not occur due to the inheritance of an abnormal gene, but rather because the baby's gene is defective for some reason other than inheritance.

Symptoms

The tumors of tuberous sclerosis occur throughout the body, including the brain, heart, lungs, kidneys, eyes, and skin. Other symptoms include seizures, **developmental delay**, behavior problems, and skin problems.

KIDNEYS Cysts on the kidneys tend to appear during the second or third decade of life. In most cases, they do not interfere with kidney functioning. Rarely, there are so many cysts that the kidneys functioning is impaired, or the cysts bleed, resulting in anemia. Fatty growths within the kidneys (called angiolipomas) may grow so large that they cause **pain** and/or kidney failure. Rarely, malignant tumors of the kidney (renal cell carcinoma) occur within an existing angiolipoma.

BRAIN Several types of brain tumors can grow, resulting in blockage of the flow of cerebrospinal fluid, fluid backup, headaches, and visual disturbances.

HEART Benign tumors in the heart (rhabdomyomas) may block circulation or may exist uneventfully.

EYES White areas in the retina, called phakomas, are characteristic of the disease (and may aid in diagnosis) but do not result in visual disturbances.

SKIN A variety of skin disorders are noted in tuberous sclerosis, including areas of under-pigmented skin (hypomelanic macules); reddish bumps on the face (facial angiofibromas); raised patches on the forehead (called forehead plaques); areas of rough, thickened skin on the neck or back (shagreen patches); tiny fleshy bumps around or under the toe- or fingernails (ungula or subungual fibromas); skin tags (molluscum fibrosum); flat brown patches.

BEHAVIOR About 33 to 50 percent of all tuberous sclerosis patients have problems such as learning disabilities, severe **mental retardation**, attention deficit disorder, **obsessive-compulsive disorder**, **autism**, aggression, rage, or self-harming behavior.

Diagnosis

Tuberous sclerosis is diagnosed when the characteristic tumors are noted in the skin, heart, brain, or kidneys. Many patients come to the healthcare provider's attention after they have begun to have seizures. Further examination with CT and/or MRI scans, ultrasound, and Wood's lamps to view the eyes will reveal the presence of the characteristic tumors of tuberous sclerosis.

Treatment

As of 2004, no cure was available for tuberous sclerosis. Antiseizure medications may be prescribed, as well as medications to treat attention deficit disorder and obsessive-compulsive disorder. Skin lesions may be removed or reduced via dermabrasive or laser procedures. Surgery may be performed to remove enlarging kidney tumors, to avoid the advent of kidney failure.

Prognosis

Most individuals with tuberous sclerosis have a normal lifespan. The prognosis for their quality of life depends on the severity of their behavioral and cognitive symptoms. Individuals whose symptomatology is confined to kidneys or skin (as opposed to having multiple behavioral symptoms) may do very well.

Prevention

As of 2004, there was no way to prevent tuberous sclerosis.

Parental concerns

Parents of child with tuberous sclerosis should be prepared to answer any questions their child or the child's siblings may have about the disease. Siblings may **fear** they will catch the disease or perhaps caused it, and may need to reassured that they are not at fault.

Resources

BOOKS

Haslam, Robert H. A. "Neurocutaneous syndromes." In *Nelson Textbook of Pediatrics*. Edited by Richard E. Behrman et al. Philadelphia: Saunders, 2004.

"Neurocutaneous Disorders." In *Textbook of Clinical Neurology*. Edited by Christopher G. Goetz. Philadelphia: Saunders, 2003.

WEB SITES

"Tuberous Sclerosis Fact Sheet." *National Institute of Neurological Disorders and Stroke (NINDS)*. Available online at <www.ninds.nih.gov/disorders/tuberous_sclerosis.htm> (accessed January 9, 2005).

Rosalyn Carson-DeWitt, MD

Turner syndrome

Definition

Turner syndrome is a birth defect caused by the absence of an X chromosome in some or all cells of a female, which inhibits sexual development and usually causes infertility.

Description

Chromosomes are structures in the nucleus of every cell in the human body that contain the genetic information necessary to direct the growth and normal functioning of all cells and systems of the body. A normal individual has a total of 46 chromosomes in each cell, two of which are responsible for determining gender. Normally, females have two X chromosomes, and males have one X and one Y chromosome.

In Turner syndrome, an error occurring very early in development results in an abnormal number and arrangement of chromosomes. Most commonly, an individual with Turner syndrome will be born with 45 chromosomes in each cell rather than 46. The missing chromosome is an X chromosome. The affected person is always female.

Turner syndrome may result in a wide spectrum of symptoms, from major heart defects to minor cosmetic issues. Some individuals with Turner syndrome may only have a few symptoms while others may have many. Almost all girls with Turner syndrome have short stature and loss of ovarian function, but the severity of the symptoms varies among individuals.

Turner syndrome is also referred to as Bonnevie-Ullrich syndrome, gonadal dysgenesis, and monosomy X.

Demographics

The prevalence of Turner syndrome is widely reported as being approximately one per 2,500 live female births, although researchers have reported prevalence rates that range from one in 3,125 to one in 5,000 live female births. About 1 to 2 percent of all female conceptions have a missing X chromosome. Of these, the majority (99%) spontaneously abort, usually during the first trimester of pregnancy.

Causes and symptoms

Turner syndrome usually occurs sporadically, which means that the mutation occurs during fetal development and is not inherited from either parent. In rare cases, a parent may carry rearranged chromosomes that can result in Turner syndrome in a daughter, which is the only situation in which the Turner syndrome is inherited.

More than half of all girls with Turner syndrome are mosaics, which means that the mutation occurs in some but not all cells of their body. Therefore, Turner syndrome can vary in severity. The fewer the affected cells, the milder the disease.

Symptoms of a girl with Turner syndrome include:

- short stature
- webbed skin of the neck
- abnormal eye features (drooping eyelids)
- abnormal bone development, such as a "shield-shaped," broad flat chest
- absent or retarded development of secondary sexual characteristics that normally appear at **puberty**, including sparse pubic hair and small breasts

- coarctation (narrowing) of the aorta
- bicuspid aortic valve
- infertility
- dry eyes
- absence of **menstruation**

Growth in children with Turner syndrome is characterized by a slight **intrauterine growth retardation**, relatively normal growth rates for the first several years of life, a progressive deceleration of growth later in childhood, and the lack of a pubertal growth spurt. The average height of Turner women is 147 cm (57.8 inches), varying between 135 (53 inches) and 163 cm (64 inches). This is about 20 cm (7.8 inches) shorter than the height of women with normal chromosomes.

Normal pubertal development and spontaneous menstrual periods do not occur in the majority of children with Turner syndrome. Most girls with Turner syndrome do not have ovaries with healthy oocytes capable of fertilization and embryo formation. However, it is estimated that 3 to 8 percent of girls with a single X chromosome and 12 to 21 percent of females with sex chromosome mosaicism may have normal pubertal development and spontaneous menstrual periods. A few pregnancies have been reported in women with Turner syndrome.

Individuals with Turner syndrome report an increased incidence of **fractures** in childhood and osteoporotic fractures in adulthood. The primary cause of osteoporosis may be inadequate levels of estrogen circulating in the body; however, defects in bone structure or strength may also be related to the loss of unknown X-chromosome genes.

The incidence of type II diabetes, also known as insulin resistant diabetes (glucose intolerance), has been reported to be increased in Turner syndrome, with individuals having twice the risk of the general population for developing this disease. The muscles of many persons with Turner syndrome fail to use glucose efficiently, which may contribute to the development of high blood sugar.

Many women with Turner syndrome have high blood pressure, which may even occur during childhood. High blood pressure may be due to aortic constriction or to kidney abnormalities; however, in a majority of cases, no specific cause for high blood pressure can be identified.

Kidney problems are present in about one third of girls with Turner syndrome and may contribute to high blood pressure. Three types of kidney problems have been reported: the presence of a single horse-shoe shaped kidney (normally two distinct, bean-shaped structures are present); an abnormal urine-collecting system; or an abnormal artery supply to the kidneys.

From 5 to 10 percent of girls with Turner syndrome have a severe constriction of the major blood vessel coming from the heart (**coarctation of the aorta**). This defect is thought to be a result of an obstructed lymphatic system compressing the aorta during fetal development. Other major defects and its major vessels are reported to a lesser degree. As many as 15 percent of children with Turner syndrome have bicuspid aortic valves, where the major blood vessel from the heart has only two rather than three components to the valve regulating blood flow.

Juvenile rheumatoid arthritis, an autoimmune condition, has been associated with Turner syndrome. The prevalence seems to be at least six times greater than would be expected if the two conditions were only randomly associated. Girls with Turner syndrome have an elevated prevalence rate of dental caries and such other periodontal conditions as gum disease and plaque.

Approximately one-third of girls with Turner syndrome have a thyroid disorder, usually **hypothyroidism**. Symptoms of this condition include decreased energy, dry skin, cold-intolerance, and poor growth.

Contrary to earlier reports, most individuals with Turner syndrome are not mentally retarded. They may have some learning disabilities, particularly with regard to spatial perception, visual-motor coordination, and mathematics. This specific learning problem is referred to as Turner neurocognitive phenotype and appears to be due to loss of X chromosome genes important for selected aspects of nervous system development. The verbal skills of girls with Turner syndrome are usually normal. Some girls with Turner syndrome may also have difficulties with memory and motor coordination, which may be related to estrogen deficiency.

When to call the doctor

Parents should call their healthcare provider if their infant has symptoms of this disorder or if an adolescent girl's sexual development appears to be delayed.

Diagnosis

Turner syndrome is either diagnosed at birth because of associated anomalies or at puberty when there is absent or delayed menses and delayed development of normal secondary sexual characteristics. During a physical examination, the doctor looks for underdeveloped breasts and genitalia, webbed neck, short stature, low hairline in back, simian crease (a single crease in the palm), and abnormal development of the chest. An ultrasound may reveal small or undeveloped female reproductive organs while a gynecologic examination may reveal a dry vaginal lining. A kidney ultrasound can be used to evaluate abnormalities of the kidneys. After diagnosis, echocardiogram (heart ultrasound) and an MRI of the chest are performed to evaluate possible cardiac defects.

Hands and feet of infants with Turner syndrome may be swollen or puffy at birth; there may be swelling at the nape of the neck. These babies often have soft nails that turn upwards on the ends when they are older. These features appear to be due to obstruction of the lymphatic system during fetal development. Another characteristic cosmetic feature is the presence of multiple pigmented nevi (colored spots on the skin).

Turner syndrome is confirmed on the basis of genetic analysis of chromosomes, which can be done prior to birth. However, the predictive value of **amniocentesis** in diagnosing Turner syndrome varies from 21 to 67 percent. There is no significant relation between the mother's age and risk of Turner syndrome.

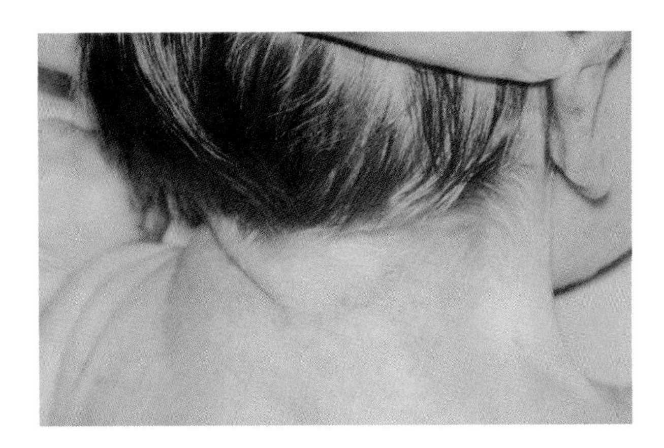

A low hairline at the back of the neck is one of several characteristics of Turner syndrome. *(NMSB/Custom Medical Stock Photo, Inc.)*

Treatment

Most individuals with Turner syndrome require female hormone therapy to promote development of secondary sexual characteristics and menstruation. The time of beginning therapy varies with individuals. Experts recommend that therapy begin when a woman expresses concern about her onset of puberty or by the age of 15. Girls and women with Turner syndrome should be treated with estrogen/progesterone to maintain their secondary sexual development and to protect their bones from osteoporosis until at the least the usual age of menopause (50 years). The use of estrogen therapy may also improve memory and motor coordination problems associated with estrogen deficiency. Assisted reproductive technology may allow for women with Turner syndrome to become pregnant with donated ooctyes.

All women receiving long-term, female hormone therapy require periodic gynecological examinations, because those with Turner syndrome have an increased risk of developing neoplasms, such as gonadoblastoma and dysgerminoma, which arise from their rudimentary streak gonads (a condition in which germ cells are absent and the ovary is replaced by a fibrous streak).

Because it is so dangerous, experts suggest early screening and surgery for aortic coarctation of the artery in girls with Turner syndrome. Bicuspid aortic valves can deteriorate or become infected, so it is advised that all girls with Turner syndrome undergo annual cardiac evaluations. Kidney problems may also be corrected surgically, but there still may be a tendency for high blood pressure and infections. Diabetes type II can be controlled through careful monitoring of blood-sugar levels, diet, **exercise**, regular health care, and medication if necessary. Hypothryoidism can be easily treated with thyroid hormone supplements.

Plastic surgery to correct webbing of the neck should be considered at an early age (before entering school) for girls with Turner syndrome.

Final adult height in individuals with Turner syndrome can be increased if growth hormone (GH) treatment is given relatively early in childhood. However, not all individuals get a good growth response to GH.

Prognosis

Most children with Turner syndrome can live relatively normal lives. The prognosis for a person with Turner syndrome is dependent on the other associated conditions that may be present. Care must be taken to regularly monitor patients for the health problems that are associated with Turner syndrome. For example, heart or kidney defects may significantly impact their quality of life. Without these types of conditions, however, their life expectancy is normal. Support will be necessary to help an adolescent girl cope with body image issues and to help some women accept the fact that they will never be able to have children.

Parental concerns

Families may wish to seek counseling regarding the effects of the syndrome on relationships within the

KEY TERMS

Bicuspid aortic valve—A condition in which the major blood vessel from the heart has only two rather than three components to the valve regulating blood flow.

Coarctation of the aorta—A congenital defect in which severe narrowing or constriction of the aorta obstructs the flow of blood.

Mosaic—A term referring to a genetic situation in which an individual's cells do not have the exact same composition of chromosomes. In Down syndrome, this may mean that some of the individual's cells have a normal 46 chromosomes, while other cells have an abnormal 47 chromosomes.

Ovary—One of the two almond-shaped glands in the female reproductive system responsible for producing eggs and the sex hormones estrogen and progesterone.

family. Many people respond with guilt, **fear**, or blame when a genetic disorder is diagnosed in the family, or they may overprotect the affected member. Support groups are often good sources of information about Turner syndrome; they can offer helpful suggestions about living with it as well as emotional support.

Resources

BOOKS

All about Me: Growing Up with Turner Syndrome and Nonverbal Learning Disabilities. Wallington, VT: Maple Leaf Center, 2004.

Roche, Alex F., and Shumei S. Sun. *Human Growth: Assessment and Interpretation.* Cambridge, UK: Cambridge University Press, 2003.

Turner Syndrome: A Medical Dictionary, Bibliography, and Annotated Research Guide to Internet References. San Diego, CA: Icon Health Publications, 2004.

ORGANIZATIONS

Human Growth Foundation. 997 Glen Cove Avenue, Glen Head, NY 11545. Web site: <www.hgfound.org>.

Turner Syndrome Society of the United States. 14450 TC Jester, Houston, TX 77014. Web site: <www.turner-syndrome-us.org>.

Turner Syndrome Support Society (UK). Hardgate, Clydebank, UK. Web site: <http://tss.org.uk>.

WEB SITES

"Turner Syndrome." *National Institute of Child Health and Human Development, National Institutes of Health.* Available online at <http://turners.nichd.nih.gov/> (accessed November 15, 2004).

Judith Sims, MS
L. Fleming Fallon, MD, PhD, DrPH

Twin pregnancy *see* **Multiple pregnancy**

Twins

Definition

Twins occur when two babies are born at the same birth.

Description

Identical, or monozygotic, twins are of the same sex and are genetically identical and physically similar, because they both come from one ovum (egg), which, after fertilization, divides in two and develops into two separate fetuses. Fraternal, or dizygotic, twins occur when the mother produces two eggs in one monthly cycle and both eggs are fertilized. The conceptions may take place on two separate occasions and could involve different fathers.

Fertilized egg division which produces twins can either happen early or late in development. In the case of early separation, the two fetuses either share an amniotic sac or each has a separate amniotic sac. If the fetuses share an amniotic sac, they also share a placenta. If the two fetuses have separate amniotic sacs, they can either share a placenta or have two separate placentas. Twins can also result from a fertilized egg that divides slightly later in development. In this case, the twins share an amniotic sac and a placenta. It is from these cases of late separation that conjoined (Siamese) twins sometimes develop.

Fraternal twins, who are no more genetically alike than ordinary siblings, may be of the same or different sex and may bear some similarity of appearance. Fraternal twinning appears to be passed on by the female members of a **family**. If the mother is a fraternal twin herself, has fraternal twin siblings, or fraternal twin relatives on her side of the family, she is more likely to give birth to fraternal twins. If she has already given birth to fraternal twins, her chances of giving birth to fraternal twins again are four times greater than those of a woman who has not had fraternal twins. In vitro fertilization increases a woman's chances for having multiple birth.

The number of twins born in the United States rose between the early 1980s and the early 2000s. In 1980, there were 69,339 sets of twins born, and in 2002 there were 125,134 sets of twins born in the United States. According to data gathered by the Centers for Disease Control (CDC), there is considerable variation among the states in number and rate of twin births. In 1994, for example, the twin birth rate ranged from 19.8 per 1,000 live births in Idaho and New Mexico to 27.7 per thousand in Connecticut and Massachusetts. One factor that may influence the distribution of multiple births is whether the state provides insurance coverage for procedures such as in vitro fertilization (IVF) and other treatments to improve fertility. These procedures increase the chance of multiple births.

Ethnicity is another factor that may correlate to the twin birth rate. For 1994, the twin birth rate among non-Hispanic white mothers was 24.3 per 1000 live births; among non-Hispanic black mothers, 28.3 per 1000; and among Hispanic mothers, 18.6 per 1000. There are also significant differences internationally in the number of twins born with the rate in Belgium almost six times the rate in China.

The CDC also studies whether maternal age has any correlation with the rate of twin births. The data seem to suggest that mothers in states with rates of twin births higher than the overall rate for the United States are older on average, and mothers in states with rates of twin births lower than the overall rate for the United States are younger. Again, as in vitro fertilization is more widely done, the incidence of multiple births will increase.

Infancy

Parents should avoid giving twins very similar names. Twins should be treated as two individuals and not as a package. They may need to be fed at different times and may develop skills at different rates. It is important to spend time with each twin separately so that they become used to being separated from each other for short times and know that they are each valued as individuals.

Toddlerhood

To help twins understand who they are as individuals, parents should avoid dressing both twins the same. It is preferable that each child receive **toys** that are geared towards their individual interests rather than each receiving the same toy.

School age

Sibling rivalry can be more intense in twins than in siblings of different ages. This is not unusual, because teachers, coaches, and even parents tend to compare twins. All children compare themselves to their siblings, and having others do this regularly can add to the pressure and stress of being a twin. Parents should consider arranging to have the twins put in different classes in school to help foster individuality. Each twin will probably have different skills, interests, and friends, and they should be encouraged to peruse activities separately if their interests diverge. Helping teachers, coaches, **babysitters**, and friends understand that it is important to treat the twins as two separate people can be very important. Friends should be encouraged to give separate gifts for birthdays and holidays, taking each child's special interests and talents into account.

Common problems

Twins often have a harder time developing their own independent identities than other children. Twins are more likely to have low birth weights or be delivered prematurely than single babies.

Parental concerns

Raising twins can be more challenging than raising two single children. The children may need to eat, **sleep**, and be changed at different times when they are infants. It can also be more expensive, because things like car seats and cribs must be purchased at the same time instead of reused for the second child. Some stores have special discounts for parents of twins.

When to call the doctor

Parents should call the doctor if one or both of their children seems ill, just as they would for any other child or children.

Resources

BOOKS

Noble, Elizabeth, with Leo Sorger. *Having Twins and More: A Parent's Guide to Multiple Pregnancy, Birth, and Early Childhood*, 3 ed. Boston, MA: Houghton Mifflin, 2003.

Pearlman, Eileen M., and Jill A. Ganon. *Raising Twins: What Parents Want to Know, and What Twins Want to Tell Them.* New York: Harper Resource, 2000.

Twin girls. Although many twins like to dress and act alike, especially at a young age, others try to differentiate themselves from each other, particularly in the teen years. *(© Dennis Degnan/Corbis.)*

KEY TERMS

Dizygotic—From two zygotes, as in non-identical, or fraternal twins. The zygote is the first cell formed by the union of sperm and egg.

Monozygotic—From one zygote, as in identical twins. The zygote is the first cell formed by the union of sperm and egg.

Placenta—The organ that provides oxygen and nutrition from the mother to the unborn baby during pregnancy. The placenta is attached to the wall of the uterus and leads to the unborn baby via the umbilical cord.

PERIODICALS

Brown, Judith E., and Marcia Carlson. "Nutrition and Multifetal Pregnancy." *Journal of the American Dietetic Association* 100 (March 2000): 343.

ORGANIZATIONS

National Organization of Mothers of Twins Clubs. PO Box 438, Thompsons Station, TN 37179–0438. Web site: <www.nomotc.org>.

Tish Davidson, A.M.

Tympanometry *see* **Audiometry**

Undescended testes

Definition

Also known as cryptorchidism, undescended testes is a congenital condition characterized by testicles that do not follow the normal developmental pattern of moving into the scrotum before birth.

Description

In the fetus, the testes are in the abdomen. As development progresses, they migrate downward through the groin and into the scrotum. This event takes place late in fetal development, during the eighth month of gestation. In some newborn boys the testes are not present in the scrotum, either because the testes did not descend or because the testes never developed in the fetus.

Demographics

Eighty percent of all undescended testes cases naturally correct themselves during the first year of life. Only 3 to 4 percent of full-term baby boys have undescended testes, and half of those complete the journey by the age of three months. Up to 30 percent of boys born prematurely have testes that have not yet made the full descent. In 5 percent of cases of undescended testes, the testis on one side is completely absent. In 10 percent of cases, both testes are completely absent.

Causes and symptoms

There are many different and complex reasons why one or both testes may not descend. Sometimes the failure is due to problems that occur during pregnancy with the tissues as they are developing or with hormone levels in the developing fetus. If the testes did not descend because they are absent, then the likely cause is different than for testes that are present but did not descend. In the case of absence, it is possible that the testes never developed at all because the blood flow was cut off to them as they were developing, preventing their formation. One or both of the testicles can be undescended; therefore, the scrotum can appear to be either missing or lopsided.

When to call the doctor

The doctor will check for the testes in the scrotum during the normal newborn examination. If the parent notices that their male infant's testes do not appear normal or do not appear to be present at all, the parent should alert the doctor. If the testes have not descended by the time the child is six months of age, the parent should call the doctor to begin discussing possible treatment options.

Diagnosis

The newborn examination always checks for testes in the scrotum. It they are not found, a search will be conducted, but not necessarily right away. If the testes are present at all, they can be anywhere within a couple inches of the appropriate spot. In most cases, the testes will drop into place later. In 5 percent of cases, one testis is completely absent. In 10 percent of cases, the condition occurs on both sides. Presence of undescended testes is differentiated from absence of testicles by measuring the amount of gonadotropin hormone in the blood.

Treatment

Once it is determined that the testes will not naturally descend, treatment options must be considered. Hormone therapy is a possible treatment but does not have a very high success rate. Another treatment option is surgery. The procedure is called an orchidopexy and is relatively simple once the testes are located. The surgery is usually performed when the boy is between one and two years old.

Prognosis

Of full-term baby boys who have undescended testes, half will descend on their own without intervention

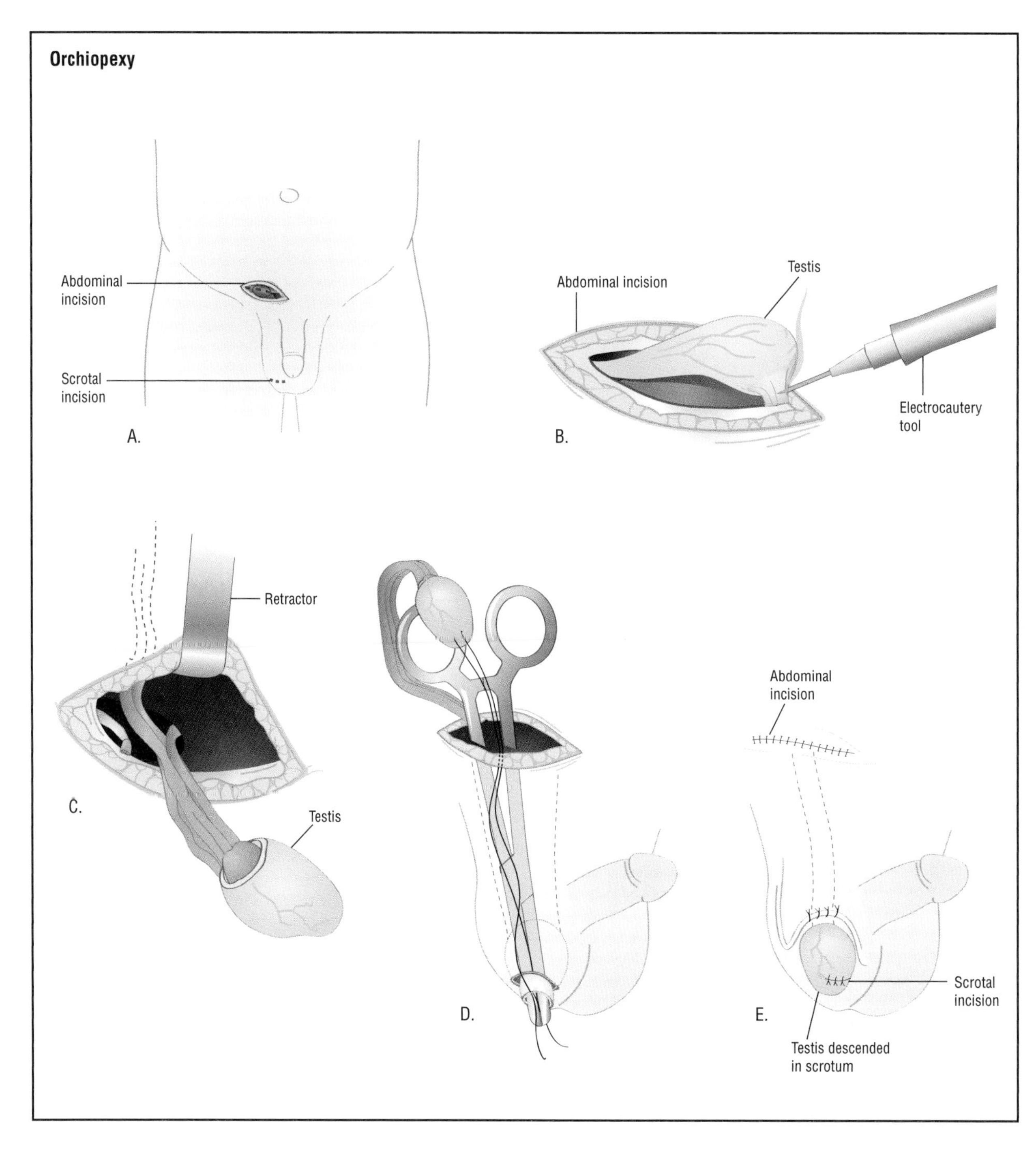

An orchiopexy is used to repair an undescended testicle in childhood. An incision is made into the abdomen, the site of the undescended testicle, and another is made in the scrotum (A). The testis is detached from surrounding tissues (B) and pulled out of the abdominal incision attached to the spermatic cord (C). The testis is then pulled down into the scrotum (D) and stitched into place (E). *(Illustration by Argosy, Inc.)*

by the age of three months. Eighty percent of all undescended testes cases naturally correct themselves during the first year of life. Of those cases that do not correct themselves naturally, intervention is very important, because undescended testes increase the likelihood of sterility and testicular **cancer**. Undescended testes are twice as likely to develop cancer as normally descended testes. Ten percent of all testicular cancers are in undescended testes. An adult man is three to 17 times more likely to develop testicular cancer if he has had a testis

KEY TERMS

Cryptorchidism—Undescended testes, a condition in which a boy is born with one or both testicles in the lower abdomen rather than the scrotum.

Embryonic—Early stages of life in the uterus.

Fetal— Refers to the fetus. In humans, the fetal period extend from the end of the eight week of pregnancy to birth.

Orchiopexy—A surgical procedure that places an undescended testicle in the scrotum and/or attaches a testicle to the scrotum.

that did not descend naturally. Surgery done to move the testis into the scrotum does not reduce the likelihood of malignancy but allows accessibility of the testes to screen for masses which will allow early treatment. The incidence of testicular cancer in men who did not have both testes descend normally is about 1 in 2000.

Many children who have undescended testes have reduced fertility as adults. It is thought that as many as 50 to 75 percent of children with undescended testes have problems with fertility as adults. Children with undescended testes are also more likely to develop hernias and have problems with their urinary tract.

Prevention

There is no known way to prevent undescended testes.

Parental concerns

Undescended testes are of concern because, although they are not known to be a threat to the child's immediate health, they are associated with an increased likelihood of negative outcomes later in life, including an increased likelihood of sterility and an increased incidence of testicular cancer.

Resources

BOOKS

Behrman, Richard E., Robert M. Kliegman, and Hal B. Jenson, eds. *Nelson Textbook of Pediatrics.* Philadelphia: Saunders, 2004.

Goldman, Lee, and J. Claude Bennett, eds. *Cecil Textbook of Medicine.* Philadelphia: Saunders, 2004.

Rajfer, Jacob. "Congenital Anomalies of the Testes and Scrotum." In *Campbell's Urology*, edited by Patrick C. Walsh, et al. Philadelphia: Saunders, 2002.

Rozauski, Thomas, et al. "Surgery of the Scrotum and Testis in Children." In *Campbell's Urology*, edited Patrick C. Walsh, et al. Philadelphia: Saunders, 2002.

PERIODICALS

Koo, Harry P. "Is It Really Cryptorchidism?" *Contemporary Urology* (January 2001): 12.

ORGANIZATIONS

American Urological Association. 1000 Corporate Blvd., Linthicum, MD 21090. Web site: <www.urologyhealth.org>.

Tish Davidson, A.M.

Ureter anomalies, congenital *see* **Congenital ureter anomalies**

Urinary reflux *see* **Vesicoureteral reflux**

Urinary tract infections *see* **Cystitis**

Urticaria *see* **Hives**

Vaccination

Definition

Vaccination introduces a vaccine into the body to produce immunity and prevent specific diseases.

Description

Many diseases that once caused widespread illness, disability, and death are now prevented by vaccines in developed countries. Vaccines are medicines that contain weakened or dead bacteria or viruses. When a child receives a vaccine, his or her immune system responds by producing antibodies, substances that weaken or destroy disease-causing organisms. When the child comes in contact with live bacteria or viruses of the same kind that are in the vaccine, the antibodies prevent those organisms from making the child sick. Vaccines also stimulate the cellular immune system. In other words, the child becomes immune to the disease the organisms normally cause. Building immunity by using a vaccine is called immunization. Childhood immunizations are safe and remain the most effective way to prevent disease.

Vaccines contain antigens (weakened or dead viruses, bacteria, and fungi that cause disease and infection). When introduced into the body, the antigens stimulate the immune system response by instructing B cells to produce antibodies, with assistance from T-cells. The antibodies are produced to fight the weakened or dead viruses in the vaccine. The antibodies "practice" on the weakened viruses, preparing the immune system to destroy real and stronger viruses in the future. When new antigens enter the body, white blood cells (called macrophages) engulf them, process the information contained in the antigens, and send it to the T-cells so that an immune system response can be mobilized.

General use

In the early 2000s, children in the United States and in other developed countries routinely have a series of vaccinations that begins at birth. Vaccinations in children began about 1900 with the smallpox vaccine. In 1960 there were only five vaccines in eight shots. The number of vaccinations children receive has steadily increased since that time. As of 2004, children receive 11 different vaccines given in up to 20 shots by age two years. Given according to a specific schedule, these vaccinations protect against **hepatitis B**; **diphtheria**, **tetanus**, pertussis (**whooping cough**) (DTP); **measles**, **mumps**, **rubella** (German measles); varicella (**chickenpox**); **polio**; pneumococcus; and *Haemophilus influenza* type B (Hib disease, a major cause of spinal **meningitis**) and, in some states, **hepatitis A**. This series of vaccinations is recommended by the American Academy of Family Physicians, the American Academy of Pediatrics, and the Centers for Disease Control and Prevention and is a requirement in all states before children can enter school. States make exceptions for children who have medical conditions such as **cancer** that prevent them from having vaccinations, and some states also make exceptions for children whose parents object for religious or other reasons.

Several vaccines are delivered in one injection, such as the measles-mumps-rubella (MMR) and diphtheria-tetanus-pertussis (DTP) combinations.

Vaccines are used in several ways. Some vaccines, such as the **rabies vaccine**, are given only when a child comes in contact with the virus that causes the disease, such as through a dog bite.

Recommendations for other vaccines and immunobiologic medicines depend on the child's health status or area of world where the family might travel. Such treatments are vaccine or immune globulin for hepatitis A, typhoid, meningitis, Japanese **encephalitis**, and **rabies**.

In addition the uses discussed above, vaccines are available for preventing anthrax, cholera, plague, **tuberculosis**, and yellow fever. Most vaccines are given as injections, but a few are taken orally.

The administration of vaccines to meet travel requirements should not interfere with or postpone any

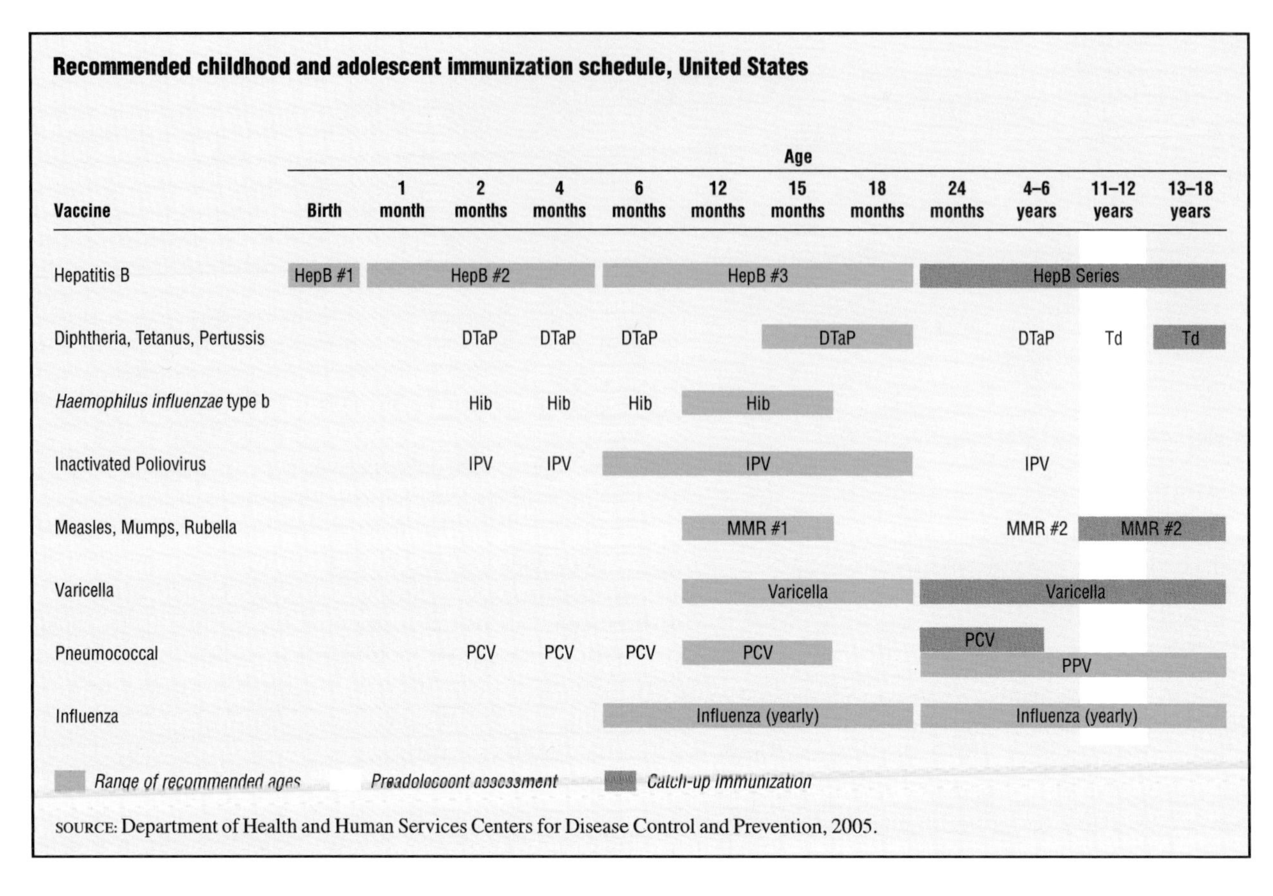

(Graph by GGS Information Services.)

of the routine childhood immunizations. If necessary, the routine immunization schedule can be accelerated to give as many vaccines as possible before departure. Decisions about vaccinations for children with chronic illnesses are made with the child's doctor.

Parents who are planning to travel with children to another country should find out what vaccinations are needed. Some vaccinations may be needed 12 weeks before the trip, so getting this information early is important. Many major hospitals and medical centers have travel clinics that provide this information. The traveler's health section of the Centers for Disease Control and Prevention also has information on vaccination requirements.

A vaccination health record helps parents and healthcare providers keep track of a child's vaccinations. The record should start when the child has his or her first vaccination and should be kept up-to-date with each added vaccination. While most doctors follow the recommended vaccination schedule, some flexibility is allowed. For example, vaccinations scheduled for age two months may be given anytime between six to ten weeks. Slight departures from the schedule do not keep the child from developing immunity, as long as all the vaccinations are received close to the right times.

Precautions

Vaccines are not always effective, and there is no way to predict whether a vaccine will "take" in any particular child. To be most effective, vaccination programs depend on the whole community participating. An increase in the number of vaccines given to children and the increased percentage of children receiving vaccines has resulted in a dramatic decrease in the number of vaccine-preventable diseases. In the United States, most young parents as of 2004 had never seen many of diseases that vaccines prevent. Even people who do not develop immunity through vaccination are safer because their friends, neighbors, children, and coworkers are immunized.

Factors influencing recommendations for childhood vaccination include age-specific risks of disease and complications, the ability of a given age group to respond to the vaccine, and the potential interference with the immune response to transferred maternal antibody. There are vaccines for the youngest age group at risk for developing the disease and known to develop a satisfactory antibody response to the vaccination.

Like most medical procedures, vaccination has risks as well as great benefits. When children receive a vaccine, parents should be told about both. Questions or concerns should be discussed with a doctor or other healthcare provider. The Centers for Disease Control and Prevention, located in Atlanta, Georgia, is also a good resource for information.

Vaccines may cause problems for children with certain **allergies**. Children who are allergic to the **antibiotics** neomycin or polymyxin B should not take rubella vaccine, measles vaccine, mumps vaccine, or the combined measles-mumps-rubella (MMR) vaccine. Children who have had a severe allergic reaction to baker's yeast should not take the **hepatitis B vaccine**. Patients who are allergic to antibiotics such as gentamicin sulfate, streptomycin sulfate, or other amino glycosides should check with their doctors before the taking influenza vaccine, as some influenza vaccines contain small amounts of these drugs. Also, some vaccines, including those for influenza, measles, and mumps, are grown in the laboratory in fluids of chick embryos, and should not be given to children who are allergic to eggs. In general, parents of children who have had an unusual reaction to a vaccine in the past should report the reaction to the doctor before taking the same vaccine again. Doctors need to know about allergies to foods, medicines, preservatives, or other substances.

Children with other medical conditions should be given vaccines with caution. Influenza vaccine may reactivate Guillain-Barre syndrome (GBS) in patients who have had it before. This vaccine also may worsen illnesses that involve the lungs, such as **bronchitis** or **pneumonia**. Vaccines that cause fever as a side effect may trigger seizures in people who have a history of seizures caused by fever.

Certain vaccines are not recommended during pregnancy. However, women who are at risk of getting specific disease such as polio may receive the vaccine to prevent medical problems in their babies. Vaccinating a pregnant woman with tetanus toxoid can prevent tetanus in the baby at birth.

Women should avoid becoming pregnant for three months after taking rubella vaccine, measles vaccine, mumps vaccine, or the combined measles-mumps-rubella (MMR) as these vaccines may cause problems in the unborn baby.

Women who are breastfeeding should check with their doctors before taking any vaccine.

Side effects

Most side effects from vaccines are minor and easily treated. The most common are **pain**, redness, and swelling at the injection site. Some children may also develop a fever or a rash. Rarely, vaccines may cause severe allergic reactions, swelling of the brain, or seizures. Unusual reaction after receiving a vaccine should be reported to the doctor right away.

Interactions

Vaccines may interact with other medicines and medical treatments. When this happens, the effects of the vaccine or the other medicine may change or the risk of side effects may be greater. Radiation therapy and cancer drugs may reduce the effectiveness of many vaccines or may increase the chance of side effects. Parents should let the doctor know of all medicines taken by the child and learn whether the possible interactions could interfere with the therapeutic effects of the vaccine or the other medicines.

Parental concerns

All vaccines used for routine child vaccinations in the United States may be given simultaneously. There is no evidence that simultaneous administration of vaccines either reduces vaccine effectiveness or increases the risk of adverse events. The only vaccines which should not be given at the same time are cholera and yellow fever vaccines.

Some vaccines are mixed in one solution, such as measles-mumps-rubella (MMR) and diphtheria-tetanus-pertussis (DTP) combination. A survey of the literature as of 2004 indicated no evidence supporting the idea that multiple vaccines in any way overwhelm or weaken the immune system. Most young infants have strong immune systems that are capable of responding to all the recommended vaccines. The protection from bacterial and viral infections provided by vaccines preserves the infant's immune systems to fight off other infections.

Most doctors follow the recommended vaccination schedule, with some flexibility. For example, vaccinations that are scheduled for age two months may be given anytime between six to 10 weeks. Slight departures from the schedule will not stop the child from developing immunity, as long as the child gets all the vaccinations close the right times.

KEY TERMS

Anthrax—A bacterial infection, primarily of livestock, that can be spread to humans. In humans it affects the skin, intestines, or lungs.

Antibody—A special protein made by the body's immune system as a defense against foreign material (bacteria, viruses, etc.) that enters the body. It is uniquely designed to attack and neutralize the specific antigen that triggered the immune response.

Bacteria—Singluar, bacterium; tiny, one-celled forms of life that cause many diseases and infections.

Cholera—An infection of the small intestine caused by a type of bacterium. The disease is spread by drinking water or eating foods that have been contaminated with the feces of infected people. It occurs in parts of Asia, Africa, Latin America, India, and the Middle East. Symptoms include watery diarrhea and exhaustion.

Encephalitis—Inflammation of the brain, usually caused by a virus. The inflammation may interfere with normal brain function and may cause seizures, sleepiness, confusion, personality changes, weakness in one or more parts of the body, and even coma.

Feces—The solid waste, also called stool, that is left after food is digested. Feces form in the intestines and pass out of the body through the anus.

Guillain-Barré syndrome—Progressive and usually reversible paralysis or weakness of multiple muscles usually starting in the lower extremities and often ascending to the muscles involved in respiration. The syndrome is due to inflammation and loss of the myelin covering of the nerve fibers, often associated with an acute infection. Also called acute idiopathic polyneuritis.

Immune system—The system of specialized organs, lymph nodes, and blood cells throughout the body that work together to defend the body against foreign invaders (bacteria, viruses, fungi, etc.).

Immunization—A process or procedure that protects the body against an infectious disease by stimulating the production of antibodies. A vaccination is a type of immunization.

Inflammation—Pain, redness, swelling, and heat that develop in response to tissue irritation or injury. It usually is caused by the immune system's response to the body's contact with a foreign substance, such as an allergen or pathogen.

Meningitis—An infection or inflammation of the membranes that cover the brain and spinal cord. It is usually caused by bacteria or a virus.

Microorganism—An organism that is too small to be seen with the naked eye, such as a bacterium, virus, or fungus.

Organism—A single, independent unit of life, such as a bacterium, a plant, or an animal.

Plague—A serious, potentially life-threatening infectious disease caused by the bacterium *Yersinia pestis*. The disease is usually transmitted to humans by the bites of infected rodent fleas. There are three major types: bubonic, pneumonic, and septicemic.

Seizure—A sudden attack, spasm, or convulsion.

Tuberculosis—Tuberculosis (TB) is a potentially fatal contagious disease that can affect almost any part of the body, but is mainly an infection of the lungs. It is caused by a bacterial microorganism, the tubercle bacillus or *Mycobacterium tuberculosis*. Symptoms include fever, weight loss, and coughing up blood.

Typhoid fever—A severe infection caused by a bacterium, *Salmonella typhi*. People with this disease have a lingering fever and feel depressed and exhausted. Diarrhea and rose-colored spots on the chest and abdomen are other symptoms. The disease is spread through poor sanitation.

Virus—A small infectious agent consisting of a core of genetic material (DNA or RNA) surrounded by a shell of protein. A virus needs a living cell to reproduce.

Yellow fever—An infectious disease caused by a virus. The disease, which is spread by mosquitoes, is most common in Central and South America and Central Africa. Symptoms include high fever, jaundice (yellow eyes and skin) and dark-colored vomit, a sign of internal bleeding. Yellow fever can be fatal.

Immunizations are not given when a child has signs of an acute illness. An interrupted primary series of immunizations need not started again but may simply continue after the child recovers. The child's doctor is the best person to decide when each vaccination should be given.

The eventual goal in child care is to reduce stress. Parents should try to increase the child's feeling of security and well-being by close involvement with the immunization process. Providing explanations of the immunization plan, special tests, and procedures suitable to the child's age is helpful. Infants and toddlers are not likely to understand verbal explanations, but they have a strong parental attachment and need affection to ease fears. Small children also have an urgent need for their mothers to defend them during medical treatments. Older children may even protest or despair in getting an injection but are usually accepting of reasonable explanations.

The health-care professional reviews the immunization record and the health status of the child at each visit. If necessary the nurse or doctor helps the parent correctly position the child and exposure of the injection site. Parents should hold a small child on their laps securely for the injection; older children may be put on the examination table in the doctor's office. After the injection, parents can give the child immediate comfort to control crying and then leave the treatment room.

Resources

BOOKS

Institute of Medicine Staff, et al. *Immunization Safety Review: Multiple Immunizations and Immune Dysfunction.* Washington, DC: National Academy Press, 2002.

Kassianos, George C., et al. *Immunization: Childhood and Travel Health.* Oxford, UK: Blackwell Publishing Inc., 2001.

Parents Guide to Childhood Immunization. Washington, DC: U.S. Government Publishing Office, 2001.

Studor, Hans-Peter, et al. *Vaccination: A Guide for Making Personal Choices.* Edinburgh, Scotland: Floris Books, 2004.

WEB SITES

Centers for Disease Control National Immunization Program. Available online at <www.cdc.gov/nip> (accessed December 3, 2004).

"Vaccination Recommendations for Infants and Children." *CDC Travelers' Health: Health Information for International Travel, 2003–2004.* Available online at <www.cdc.gov/travel/child-vax.htm> (accessed December 3, 2004).

Aliene S. Linwood, RN, DPA, FACHE

Varicella zoster *see* **Chickenpox**

Varicella zoster vaccine (VZV) *see* **Chickenpox vaccine**

Vasculitides

Definition

Vasculitides is the plural of the word vasculitis, which may be used to describe any disorder characterized by inflammation of the blood or lymph vessels. Vasculitis is not a distinctive disease in its own right, but rather a symptom or characteristic of a number of different diseases. It can affect any type or size of blood vessel—large arteries and veins as well as arterioles, venules, or capillaries. The term juvenile vasculitides is sometimes used to refer to a group of disorders that primarily affect children and adolescents. These disorders vary widely in their severity as well as the specific blood vessels and organs affected. Some are mild and may resolve even without treatment, while others are potentially life-threatening. The most common childhood vasculitides are **Kawasaki syndrome** (sometimes called Kawasaki disease) and Henoch-Schönlein purpura.

The most widely used classification scheme for the vasculitides was first proposed at an international conference in 1994. It classifies these disorders according to the size of the blood vessels involved:

- Large-sized vessel vasculitis. This category includes two disorders, only one of which—Takayasu arteritis (TA)—is found in children and adolescents.
- Medium-sized vessel vasculitis. This category includes infantile polyarteritis nodosa (IPAN) and Kawasaki disease.
- Small-sized vessel vasculitis. The disorders in this category include Henoch-Schönlein purpura (HSP) and Wegener's granulomatosis.

Description

Vasculitis may damage blood vessels in two different ways. In some cases the inflamed tissue becomes weakened and stretches, producing a bulge in the wall of the vessel known as an aneurysm. The aneurysm may eventually rupture or burst, allowing blood to escape into nearby tissues. In other cases, the inflammation causes the blood vessel to narrow, sometimes to the point that blood can no longer flow through the vessel. When enough of the larger vessels supplying a specific organan or other part of the body are closed by inflammation, the tissue that is starved for blood may die. The area of dead tissue is called an infarction or infarct.

The early symptoms of vasculitis frequently include **fever**, weakness, loss of appetite, weight loss, tiring easily, pains in the muscles or joints, and swollen joints. Some of the childhood vasculitides affect the skin, producing **rashes**, ulcers, or reddish-purple spots known as purpura. Others affect the lungs, digestive tract, kidneys, liver, nervous system, eyes, or brain, resulting in symptoms ranging from **pain** in the abdomen, **diarrhea**, coughing, or high blood pressure to shortness of breath, visual disturbances, **headache** or fainting, and **numbness** in the limbs. The specific symptoms of the more common childhood vasculitides are described in more detail below.

Transmission

Some of the childhood vasculitides may be preceded and possibly triggered by infectious diseases. In addition, Kawasaki disease sometimes occurs in epidemics, such as those reported in Japan in 1979, 1982, and 1985. No epidemics, however, have been reported since 1985.

Demographics

Most vasculitides are relatively rare disorders; one source estimates that about 100,000 persons (including adults as well as children and adolescents) are hospitalized each year in the United States for treatment of vasculitis. Although this number is small compared to the number of those treated for **cancer** or diabetes, the vasculitides can nonetheless have a significant financial and emotional impact on the families of children diagnosed with them.

The demographics of specific childhood vasculitides are as follows:

- Henoch-Schönlein purpura (HSP). HSP most commonly affects children between the ages of three and 12 years. The sex ratio is about 1.5–2 males for every one female. The disease is more common in North America between November and January; it is estimated to affect 14 or 15 children per 100,000. About 50–60 percent of children with HSP were diagnosed with **strep throat** or another upper respiratory infection two to three weeks before the onset of the vasculitis.
- Kawasaki disease. Kawasaki disease affects between one and three children per 10,000 in the United States each year. It is much more common in Japan, striking one child per thousand below the age of five. In the United States, Kawasaki disease is more common among children of Japanese descent than among children from other racial or ethnic backgrounds. It is also more likely to affect African Americans than Caucasians. The sex ratio is about 1.5 males for every one female. Kawasaki disease is primarily a disease of younger children; the average age at onset is 18 months, with 80 percent of cases found in children younger than five years.
- Infantile polyarteritis nodosa (IPAN). IPAN is a rare disease, and is sometimes described as a severe variant of Kawasaki disease. The incidence of IPAN in the United States is uncertain as of the early 2000s, primarily because of disagreements among doctors about the classification of childhood vasculitides; the most common figure given is 0.7 cases per 100,000 children. The first known case of IPAN was reported in London in 1870, although polyarteritis nodosa in adults was first described in 1852. Like Kawasaki disease, IPAN is more common in children of Asian descent. The male to female ratio is not known for certain, but is thought to be about two to one.
- Takayasu arteritis (TA). TA, which was first described by a Japanese ophthalmologist in 1908, is primarily a disease of adolescent and young adult women, although it has been diagnosed in children as young as six months. TA is relatively rare, affecting about 2.6 individuals per million. In the United States it is most common in young women of Japanese descent, with a male to female ratio of one to eight. In India, however, TA is more commonly associated with **tuberculosis**, and the sex ratio is two females for every one male.
- Wegener's granulomatosis. Wegener's granulomatosis is also a rare disease, diagnosed in one to three individuals per 100,000, with only 3 percent of these cases found in people below 20 years of age. It is, however, one of the most serious vasculitides. The male to female ratio is two to one.

Causes and symptoms

Causes

There is no single disease process that underlies all the childhood vasculitides. Various causes have been proposed for specific disorders.

- Henoch-Schönlein purpura. Although the ultimate cause of HSP was unknown as of 2004, the disease is preceded by an acute upper respiratory infection in at least half the children diagnosed with it. In other cases HSP appears to be triggered by an immune complex reaction to certain vaccines (most commonly vaccines for typhoid, **measles**, yellow fever, or cholera) or medications (most commonly penicillin, erythromycin, quinidine, or quinine). A characteristic finding in children diagnosed with HSP is higher levels of immunoglobulin A (IgA) in the blood and deposits of IgA on the walls of the child's blood vessels.

- Kawasaki disease. It is thought that an infectious organism of some kind is the cause of Kawasaki disease, although no specific virus or bacterium has been identified as of 2004. The disease has been linked to a variety of disease agents, including parvovirus B19, **HIV infection**, measles, **influenza** viruses, rotaviruses, adenoviruses, *Klebsiella pneumoniae*, and *Mycoplasma pneumoniae*. Some doctors think that genetic and immunologic factors are involved as well as an infectious organism.
- Infantile polyarteritis nodosa. As with Kawasaki disease, various infectious organisms have been proposed as the cause of IPAN, including **hepatitis B** virus, Epstein-Barr virus (EBV), various retroviruses, streptococci, and even a virus usually found in cats. None of these viruses or bacteria has been found in all patients with IPAN, however. Another theory is that IPAN is an immune complex disease, but its trigger had not been identified as of 2004.
- Takayasu arteritis. The cause of TA is unknown as of the early 2000s but may involve genetic factors, as the disease has been reported in identical twins.
- Wegener's granulomatosis. The cause of Wegener's granulomatosis was not known as of 2004. As with other childhood vasculitides, various disease organisms (including fungi as well as bacteria or viruses) have been suggested as the cause, but none have been definitely identified. A genetic cause seems unlikely, as it is unusual for two people in the same **family** to develop the disease.

Symptoms

The early symptoms of the childhood vasculitides are often difficult to distinguish from those of other illnesses. This section will focus on the symptoms specific to each disease.

- Henoch-Schönlein purpura (HSP). HSP is an acute but self-limited illness characterized by a low-grade fever (around 100.4°F [38°C]), purpura, joint pains (usually in the ankles and knees), abdominal pain, bleeding in the digestive tract, and inflammation of the kidneys. Boys with HSP often have inflammation of the testicles.
- Kawasaki disease. Kawasaki disease has three stages: an acute stage lasting about 11 days, characterized by a high fever (over 104°F [40°C]), strawberry tongue and cracked lips, **conjunctivitis**, involvement of the liver, kidneys, and digestive tract, and inflammation of the heart muscle; a subacute phase lasting about three weeks, characterized by irritability, loss of appetite, the peeling of skin from the finger tips, and the development (in about 20 percent of patients) of aneurysms in the coronary artery; and a convalescent phase marked by expansion of the aneurysms and possible heart attack. As of the early 2000s, Kawasaki disease is the leading cause of acquired heart problems for children in the developed countries.
- Infantile polyarteritis nodosa. The early symptoms of IPAN are nonspecific, usually including fever, loss of appetite, weight loss, and pain in the abdomen. The disease is most likely to affect the kidneys, heart, or liver. Depending on the organ(s) involved, the child may develop aneurysms in the arteries supplying the kidneys, kidney failure, aneurysms in the coronary artery, congestive heart failure, massive bleeding in the digestive tract, aneurysms in the arteries supplying the brain, and **stroke**. About half of patients with IPAN develop pains in the joints or skin rashes; boys frequently have pain in the testicles.
- Takayasu arteritis. Takayasu arteritis is a chronic inflammatory disorder that affects the aorta (the large artery that leaves the heart) and its major branches. Its early symptoms include fever, weight loss, and a general feeling of tiredness. The disease may not be diagnosed for months or even years, however. The inflammation of the aorta eventually leads either to the formation of aneurysms or the narrowing or complete blocking of the blood vessels. The patient may feel aching or pain in parts of the body affected by inadequate blood supply, such as aching in the legs while walking or cramping sensations in the abdomen after meals. In rare cases, the patient may suffer a heart attack or stroke. The patient may develop high blood pressure if the blood supply to the kidneys is affected. TA is sometimes called pulseless disease because the doctor may not be able to detect the pulse on one side of the patient's body. Another diagnostic clue is a significant difference (greater than 30 mm Hg) in the blood pressure on the right and left sides of the body.
- Wegener's granulomatosis. Wegener's most commonly affects the upper respiratory tract, the eyes, ears, kidneys, and skin. The disease is called a granulomatosis because it is characterized by the formation of granulomas, which are small lumps or nodules of inflammatory cells in the patient's tissues. The patient may have recurrent ear infections that are slow to heal, inflammation of the tissues inside the eye, inflamed sinuses, nosebleeds, coughing up blood, narrowing of the windpipe, and saddle nose, which is a deformity caused by the collapse of cartilage inside the nose. The

patient may also have joint pains, loss of appetite, skin lesions, and fever. Vasculitis associated with Wegener's may lead to a heart attack. If untreated, the disease eventually progresses to kidney failure and death.

When to call the doctor

Although not all children who are eventually diagnosed with vasculitis will have all of the following signs and symptoms, parents should consult the doctor if most are present:

- The child's symptoms are constitutional; that is, they affect his or her overall physical health on a basic level. Malaise (a general feeling of physical discomfort), loss of appetite, fever, and loss of energy are examples of constitutional symptoms.
- The symptoms involve more than one organ or organ system.
- The child has noticeable purpura.
- The child has **tingling** or other unusual sensations followed by numbness in certain parts of the body.

Diagnosis

The diagnosis of vasculitis is complicated by several factors. To begin with, many of the early symptoms of the childhood vasculitides are not specific to these disorders and may have a wide range of other possible causes. In many cases the doctor may not be able to make the diagnosis until specific organs or organ systems are affected. The doctor will begin by ruling out such other possible diagnoses as bacterial or viral infections, collagen vascular disease, hypersensitivity reactions, and malignant tumors.

Another factor that complicates diagnosis is that the various childhood vasculitides have overlapping symptom profiles. Although lists of diagnostic criteria have been drawn up for the various disorders in this group, some patients do not meet the full criteria of any one disorder.

The first step in diagnosis is taking a careful history. The child's doctor may be able to narrow the diagnostic possibilities on the basis of the patient's age, sex, ethnicity, and a history of recent vaccinations or upper respiratory infections. The doctor will also ask whether the child is experiencing fever, abdominal cramping, diarrhea, or pains in the muscles and joints. The second step is a general physical examination. Several of these disorders affect the circulation or eyes as well as the skin. For example, Takayasu arteritis affects the patient's pulse and blood pressure, as well as producing small hemorrhages in the retina of the eye, while Kawasaki disease is characterized by conjunctivitis (inflammation of the tissues lining the eyelids). The doctor will examine the child's skin for purpura, other skin rashes or ulcers, reddening or swelling of the skin, and will note the locations of these abnormalities. In most cases the doctor will refer the child to a specialist for further evaluation. The specialist may be a pediatric rheumatologist, cardiologist, neurologist, or specialist in infectious diseases.

Laboratory tests for vasculitis include blood and urine tests. The blood tests include a complete blood count, a blood serum chemistry panel, erythrocyte sedimentation rate (ESR), tests for rheumatoid factor and circulating immune complexes, and tests for antineutrophil cytoplasmic antibodies (c-ANCA and p-ANCA). Urinalysis is done to evaluate kidney function. The doctor may also order skin, muscle, lung, or sinus biopsies in order to distinguish among the various childhood vasculitides.

Imaging studies that are used to diagnose the various childhood vasculitides include chest **x rays** or CT scans of the sinuses (Wegener's granulomatosis); CT scan of the aorta, angiography or ultrasonography (Takayasu's arteritis); arteriography or echocardiography (IPAN); chest x ray and echocardiography (Kawasaki disease); chest x ray, abdominal ultrasound, or barium contrast study of the digestive tract (Henoch-Schönlein purpura).

Treatment

The treatment of children with one of these disorders is highly individualized; it is tailored to the specific organs affected and the child's overall condition. Henoch-Schönlein purpura usually resolves on its own without any specific therapy. The general goals of treatment for vasculitis are to reduce inflammation in the affected blood vessels; maintain an adequate blood supply to the vital organs and skin; and monitor the side effects of the medications given to treat vasculitis.

Medications

Most patients with vasculitis will be given corticosteroids (usually prednisone) to reduce joint pain if present and inflammation in the blood vessels. Other types of drugs that are commonly used are the immunosuppressants (usually cyclophosphamide, methotrexate, azathioprine, or etanercept) and anticoagulants (usually heparin). Immunosuppressants are drugs that are given to treat inflammation by lowering the intensity of the body's reaction to allergens and other triggers, while anticoagulants are given to prevent blood clots from forming and blocking blood vessels that have already been narrowed by inflammation. Children with muscle or joint pain may be given **non-steroidal anti-inflammatory drugs**, or NSAIDs, many of which are available without a prescription. An antibiotic (usually trimethoprim-sulfamethoxazole) is sometimes given to children with Wegener's granulomatosis to control flares, or recurrences of the disease.

Surgery

Patients with Takayasu arteritis often require surgical repair of damaged arteries. The most common procedures used are balloon angioplasty or stenting. Stents are small metal tubes or wires that are inserted into damaged blood vessels to hold them open. In severe cases, the damaged section of the artery may have to be removed completely and replaced with a graft made from an artificial material.

Alternative treatment

There is little information about the use of alternative treatments for vasculitides in children, most likely because the disorders in this category are relatively uncommon and vary widely with regard to the organ systems affected, symptom severity, and prognosis. One Chinese medical journal has reported on the benefits of treating children with Henoch-Schönlein purpura with a remedy made from colquhounia root, while a team of Dutch researchers has observed that acupuncture appears to be effective in reducing the inflammation associated with vasculitis. The researchers noted, however, that large randomized trials comparing acupuncture with mainstream treatments had not been undertaken as of 2004.

Some herbal preparations have been associated with harmful effects on the heart and circulatory system; however, the cases that have been reported mostly involve either contaminated or adulterated herbal products, or interactions between prescription medications and herbal preparations. The herbs most frequently mentioned in these case reports are aconite, ephedra, and licorice. The extent of the problem is not known as of the early 2000s because no large-scale analyses have been done. In any event, however, parents should *never* give a child a herbal remedy without first consulting the child's doctor, whether or not the child is taking prescription drugs.

Nutritional concerns

Children who develop high blood pressure with one of these disorders are usually placed on a low-sodium diet.

Prognosis

The prognoses for the childhood vasculitides vary widely depending on the disease and the extent of organ involvement. In general, children whose lungs or kidneys are affected have poorer outcomes.

- Henoch-Schönlein purpura. The prognosis for children with HSP is generally good, as the disease usually goes away by itself even without treatment; however, about a third of patients have recurrences.
- Kawasaki disease. Patients who are treated promptly have a good prognosis. The mortality rate in the early 2000s is estimated at 0.1–2 percent.
- Infantile polyarteritis nodosa. IPAN has a poor prognosis even when treated aggressively; the 10-year survival rate for this vasculitis is only 20 percent.
- Takayasu arteritis. TA is a chronic disorder with a high rate of relapse; the 15-year survival rate is about 95 percent.
- Wegener's granulomatosis. Untreated Wegener's is fatal, usually within five months. With treatment, about 87 percent of patients have a remission of the disease, but 53 percent have recurrences.

Prevention

Apart from minimizing a child's exposure to strep throat and similar upper respiratory infections, there is nothing that parents can do to prevent vasculitis in children, in that the cause(s) of these disorders are still unknown.

Parental concerns

The impact of childhood vasculitis on a child's family varies widely, depending on the child's age at onset, the specific symptoms of the disorder, its severity, the types of medications or other treatments that are needed, and the prognosis. Parents should work closely with the child's pediatrician and other specialists who may be involved to monitor the child's progress through regular follow-up appointments. The child's primary doctor can usually provide advice regarding such concerns as medication side effects, limitations on the child's activities if any, and explaining the disease to the child and other family members.

See also Conjunctivitis; Kawasaki syndrome.

KEY TERMS

Aneurysm—A weakened area in the wall of a blood vessel which causes an outpouching or bulge. Aneurysms may be fatal if these weak areas burst, resulting in uncontrollable bleeding.

Aorta—The main artery located above the heart that pumps oxygenated blood out into the body. The aorta is the largest artery in the body.

Conjunctivitis—Inflammation of the conjunctiva, the mucous membrane covering the white part of the eye (sclera) and lining the inside of the eyelids also called pinkeye.

Flare—A sudden worsening or recurrence of a disease.

Granuloma—An inflammatory swelling or growth composed of granulation tissue

Henoch-Schönlein purpura—A syndrome sometimes classified as a hypersensitivity vasculitis, associated with a variety of digestive symptoms, pain in the joints, and kidney involvement. Purpura comes from the Latin word for "purple" and refers to the reddish-purple spots on the skin caused by leakage of blood from inflamed capillaries.

Infarct—An area of dead tissue caused by inadequate blood supply.

Kawasaki syndrome—A syndrome of unknown origin that affects the skin, mucous membranes, and the immune system of infants and young children. It is named for the Japanese pediatrician who first identified it in 1967.

Malaise—The medical term for a general condition of unease, discomfort, or weakness.

Rheumatologist—A doctor who specializes in the diagnosis and treatment of disorders affecting the joints and connective tissues of the body.

Saddle nose—A sunken nasal bridge.

Stent—A slender hollow catheter or rod placed within a vessel or duct to provide support or to keep it open.

Strawberry tongue—A sign of scarlet fever in which the tongue appears to have a red coating with large raised bumps.

Takayasu arteritis—A disease in which the aorta and its major branches become inflamed. It is often accompanied by high blood pressure, an abnormal pulse, and visual symptoms.

Vasculopathy—Any disease or disorder that affects the blood vessels.

Resources

BOOKS

"Vasculitis." Section 5, Chapter 50 in*The Merck Manual of Diagnosis and Therapy*, edited by Mark H. Beers, MD, and Robert Berkow, MD. Whitehouse Station, NJ: Merck Research Laboratories, 2002.

"Wegener's Granulomatosis." Section 5, Chapter 50 in*The Merck Manual of Diagnosis and Therapy*, edited by Mark H. Beers, MD, and Robert Berkow, MD. Whitehouse Station, NJ: Merck Research Laboratories, 2002.

PERIODICALS

Burns, J. C., and M. P. Glode. "Kawasaki Syndrome." *Lancet* 364 (August 7, 2004): 533–544.

Ernst, E. "Cardiovascular Adverse Effects of Herbal Medicines: A Systematic Review of the Recent Literature." *Canadian Journal of Cardiology* 19 (June 2003): 818–827.

Miyata, T., O. Sato, H. Koyama, et al. "Long-Term Survival After Surgical Treatment of Patients with Takayasu's Arteritis." *Circulation* 108 (September 23, 2003): 1474–1480.

Zhou, J. H., A. X. Huang, and T. L. Liu. "Clinical Study on Treatment of Childhood Henoch-Schonlein Purpura Nephritis with Colquhounia Root Tablet." *Zhongguo Zhong Xi Yi Jie He Za Zhi* 24 (May 2004): 418–421.

Zijlstra, F. J., I. van den Berg-de Lange, F. J. Huygen, and J. Klein. "Anti-Inflammatory Actions of Acupuncture." *Mediators of Inflammation* 12 (April 2003): 59–69.

ORGANIZATIONS

American College of Rheumatology (ACR). 1800 Century Placce, Suite 250, Atlanta, GA 30345-4300. (404) 633-3777. Fax: (404) 633-1870. <http://www.rheumatology.org>.

Arthritis Foundation. P. O. Box 7669, Atlanta, GA 30357-0669. (800) 283-7800. Web site: <http://www.arthritis.org>.

National Institute of Arthritis and Musculoskeletal and Skin Diseases (NIAMS). 1 AMS Circle, Bethesda, MD 20892-3675. (301) 495-4484 or (877) 22-NIAMS. Fax: (301) 718-6366. Web site: <http://www.niams.nih.gov>.

National Institute of Neurological Disorders and Stroke (NINDS). National Institutes of Health. 9000 Rockville Pike, Bethesda, MD 20892. (301) 496-5751. Web site: <http://www.ninds.nih.gov>.

WEB SITES

Cleveland Clinic. *Vasculitis: What You Need to Know*. April 18, 2003. [cited August 17, 2004]. Available online at: <http://www.clevelandclinic.org/health/health-info/docs/0700/0746.asp?index=4969>.

Hom, Christine, MD. "Takayasu Arteritis." *eMedicine*. December 23, 2003 [cited August 18, 2004]. Available online at: <http://www.emedicine.com/ped/topic1956.htm>.

Hom, Christine, MD. "Vasculitis and Thrombophlebitis." *eMedicine*. February 14, 2003 [cited August 17, 2004]. Available online at: <http://www.emedicine.com/ped/topic2390.htm>.

Johns Hopkins Vasculitis Center. *What is Vasculitis?* 1998–2004. [cited August 18, 2004]. Available online at: <http://vasculitis.med.jhu.edu/whatis/whatis.html>.

Matteson, Eric L., MD. *A Puzzler Among Rheumatic Diseases*. American College of Rheumatology, 2004. [cited August 18, 2004]. Available online at: <http://www.rheumatology.org/public/usatoday/vasculitis.asp>.

Person, Donald A., MD. "Infantile Polyarteritis Nodosa." *eMedicine*. May 22, 2002 [cited August 18, 2004]. Available online at: <http://www.emedicine.com/ped/topic1180.htm>.

Scheinfeld, Noah S., MD, Elena L. Jones, MD, and Nanette Silverberg, MD. "Henoch-Schoenlein Purpura." *eMedicine*. May 19, 2004 [cited August 18, 2004]. Available online at: <http://www.emedicine.com/ped/topic3020.htm>.

Scheinfeld, Noah S., MD, and Nanette Silverberg, MD. "Kawasaki Disease." *eMedicine*. June 6, 2003. [cited August 23, 2004]. Available online at: <http://www.emedicine.com/ped/topic1236.htm>.

OTHER

National Institute of Arthritis and Musculoskeletal and Skin Disorders (NIAMS). *NIH Pediatric Rheumatology Clinic*. NIH Publication No. 03-5156. Bethesda, MD: NIAMS, 2003.

National Institute of Neurological Disorders and Stroke (NINDS). *NINDS Vasculitis Including Temporal Arteritis Information Page*. Bethesda, MD: NINDS, 2001.

Rebecca Frey, PhD

Vegetarianism

Definition

Vegetarianism is the voluntary abstinence from eating meat. Vegetarians refrain from eating meat for various reasons, including religious, health, and ethical ones. Lacto-ovo vegetarians supplement their diet with dairy (lactose) products and eggs (ovo). Vegans (pronounced vee-guns) do not eat any animal-derived products at all.

Description

Vegetarianism has been steadily gaining acceptance as an alternative to the meat-and-potatoes bias of the traditional American diet. Several factors contribute to the interest in vegetarianism in the United States. Outbreaks of **food poisoning** from meat products, as well as increased concern over the additives in meat such as hormones and **antibiotics**, have led some people and professionals to question meat's safety. There is also an increased awareness of the questionable treatment of farm animals in factory farming.

But the growing health consciousness of Americans is probably the major reason for the surge in interest in vegetarianism. **Nutrition** experts have built up convincing evidence that there are major problems with the conventional American diet, which is centered on meat products that are high in cholesterol and saturated fat and low in fiber. Heart disease, **cancer**, and diabetes, which cause 68 percent of all deaths in America, are all believed to be influenced by this diet.

A vegetarian diet has many well-documented health benefits. It has been shown that vegetarians have a longer life expectancy than those who eat a meat-centered diet. The U.S. Food and Drug Administration (FDA) has stated that data has shown vegetarians to have a strong or significant probability against contracting **obesity**, heart disease, lung cancer, colon cancer, **alcoholism**, **hypertension**, diabetes, gallstones, gout, kidney stones, and ulcers. However, the FDA also points out that vegetarians tend to have healthy lifestyle habits, so other factors may contribute to their increased health besides diet alone.

Vegetarians have a huge number of statistics in their favor when it comes to presenting persuasive arguments in favor of their eating habits. Vegetarians claim that a vegetarian diet is a major step in improving the health of citizens and the environment. Americans eat over 200 pounds (91 kilograms) of meat per person per year. The incidence of heart disease, cancer, diabetes, and other diseases has increased along with the dramatic increase in meat consumption during the twentieth century.

Many statistics show significantly smaller risks for vegetarians contracting certain conditions. The risks of women getting breast cancer and men contracting prostrate cancer are nearly four times as high for frequent meat eaters as for those who eat meat sparingly or not at all. For heart attacks, American men have a 50 percent risk of having one, but the risk drops to 15 percent for lacto-ovo vegetarians, and to only 4 percent for vegans. For cancer, studies of populations around the world have implied that plant-based diets have lower associated risks for certain types of cancer.

Nutritionists have repeatedly shown in studies that a healthy diet consists of plenty of fresh vegetables and fruits, complex carbohydrates such as whole grains, and foods that are high in fiber and low in cholesterol and saturated fat. Vegetarianism, a diet that fulfills all these criteria, has become part of many healthy lifestyles.

Some nutritionists have designed transition diets to help people become vegetarian in stages. Many Americans eat meat products at nearly every meal, and the first stage of a transition diet is to substitute just a few meals a week with wholly vegetarian foods. Then, particular meat products can be slowly reduced and eliminated from the diet and replaced with vegetarian foods. Red meat can be reduced and then eliminated, followed by pork, poultry, and fish. For those wishing to become pure vegetarians or vegans, the final step is to choose other nutrient-rich foods in order to eliminate eggs and dairy products. Individuals should be willing to experiment with transition diets and should have patience when learning how combine vegetarianism with social activities such as dining out.

The transition to vegetarianism can be smoother for adolescents who make informed choices with dietary practices. Sound nutritional guidelines include decreasing the intake of fat, increasing fiber, and emphasizing fresh fruits, fresh vegetables, beans and lentils, and whole grains in the diet while avoiding processed foods and sugar.

Thanks to the growing interest in vegetarianism, many meat substitutes are now readily available. Tofu and tempeh are made from soybeans that are high in protein, calcium, and other nutrients. There are "veggie-burgers" that can be grilled like hamburgers, and vegetarian substitutes for hot dogs, corn dogs, chicken, turkey, ham, bologna, pastrami, and sausage with surprisingly authentic textures and taste. Major vegetarian meat substitute brands include Morningstar Farms, Boca, Gardenburger, and Lightlife. There are many vegetarian cookbooks on the market as well as magazines such as *Vegetarian Times*, *Veggie Life*, and *Vegetarian Journal*.

Famous vegetarians, past and present, include Leonardo da Vinci, Sir Isaac Newton, Leo Tolstoy, Ralph Waldo Emerson, Gandhi, physician Albert Schweitzer, writer George Bernard Shaw, champion tri-athlete Dave Scott, and musicians Paul McCartney, George Harrison, John Lennon, Yoko Ono, Alanis Morissette, Bob Dylan, and Bruce Springsteen.

Infancy, toddlerhood, and preschool

Babies, toddlers, and preschoolers can do well on a vegetarian diet, especially one that includes eggs and dairy products. If they are not included, the young child may suffer from shortages of **vitamins** B12, B2, and D; protein; calcium; and zinc. The child may also need iron supplements because iron in plant food is not absorbed well.

Infants and toddlers require many calories in order to grow at the normal rate. At about seven to eight months of age, babies are ready to start eating protein-rich foods. Instead of pureed meats, vegetarian infants should be given protein alternatives such as pureed peas, beans, and lentils, cottage cheese, pureed tofu, and yogurt.

It is important that toddlers eat high-calorie vegetarian foods such as diced nuts, olives, dates, and avocados so they get enough calories. Most importantly, parents should make sure a vegetarian child eats a wide variety of foods, according to a 2002 advisory from the journal *Clinical Reference Systems*.

Parents must take care to insure the child gets enough food for growth, since a vegetarian diet relies heavily on bulk foods that are filling but usually short of calories. Parents who are vegetarians and want their baby to be one should discuss the topic with a pediatrician. Young children who are vegetarians should be monitored regularly to make sure their weight and height are appropriate for their age.

School age

About 2 percent of Americans age six to 17 (about 1 million) are vegetarian, the same percentage as among American adults, and 0.5 percent are vegan, according to a 2002 survey by the Vegetarian Resource Group (VRG). Six percent of six to 17 year olds do not eat meat but do eat fish and/or poultry.

Teens who follow a vegetarian diet are more likely to meet recommendations for total fat, saturated fat, and number of servings of fruits and vegetables as compared to non-vegetarians. They also have higher intakes of iron, vitamin A, fiber, and diet soda, and lower intakes of vitamin B12, cholesterol, and fast food. Most teens, whether they were vegetarian or not, do not meet recommendations for calcium, according to the VRG survey.

The survey concluded that rather than viewing adolescent vegetarianism as a phase or fad, the diet could be viewed as a healthy alternative to the traditional American meat-based diet. The survey also stated that vegetarian diets in **adolescence** could lead to lifelong health-promoting dietary practices. The survey was reported in the July-August 2002 issue of the VRG publication *Vegetarian Journal.*

Common problems

In general, a well-planned vegetarian diet is healthy and safe. However, vegetarians, and particularly vegans who eat no animal products, need to be aware of particular nutrients that may be lacking in non-animal diets. These are amino acids, vitamin B12, vitamin D, calcium, iron, zinc, and essential fatty acids. Infants and growing children have higher requirements for these nutrients.

Vegetarians should be aware of getting complete protein in their diets. A complete protein contains all of the essential amino acids, which are the building blocks for protein essential to the diet because the body cannot make them. Meat and dairy products generally contain complete proteins, but most vegetarian foods such as grains and beans contain incomplete proteins, lacking one or more of the essential amino acids. However, vegetarians can easily overcome this by combining particular foods in order to create complete proteins. For instance, beans are high in the amino acid lysine but low in tryptophan and methionine, but rice is low in lysine and high in tryptophan and methionine. Thus, combining rice and beans makes a complete protein.

Eating dairy products or nuts with grains also makes proteins complete. Oatmeal with milk on it is complete, as is peanut butter on whole wheat bread. Proteins do not necessarily need to be combined in the same meal, but generally within four hours.

Getting enough vitamin B12 may be an issue for some vegetarians, particularly vegans, because meat and dairy products are the main sources. Vitamin supplements that contain vitamin B12 are recommended. Spirulina, a nutritional supplement made from algae, is also a vegetarian source, as are fortified soy products and nutritional yeast.

Vitamin D can be obtained by vitamins, fortified foods, and sunshine. Calcium can be obtained in enriched tofu, seeds, nuts, beans, dairy products, and dark green

KEY TERMS

Amino acid—An organic compound composed of both an amino group and an acidic carboxyl group. Amino acids are the basic building blocks of proteins. There are 20 types of amino acids (eight are "essential amino acids" which the body cannot make and must therefore be obtained from food).

Cholesterol—A steroid fat found in animal foods that is also produced in the human body from saturated fat. Cholesterol is used to form cell membranes and process hormones and vitamin D. High cholesterol levels contribute to the development of atherosclerosis.

Essential fatty acid (EFA)—A fatty acid that the body requires but cannot make. It must be obtained from the diet. EFAs include omega-6 fatty acids found in primrose and safflower oils, and omega-3 fatty acids oils found in fatty fish and flaxseed, canola, soybean, and walnuts.

Gout—A metabolic disorder characterized by sudden recurring attacks of arthritis caused by deposits of crystals that build up in the joints due to abnormally high uric acid blood levels. In gout, uric acid may be overproduced, underexcreted, or both.

Hypertension—Abnormally high arterial blood pressure, which if left untreated can lead to heart disease and stroke.

Lacto-ovo vegetarian—People who do not eat meat, but do include dairy products and eggs in their diets.

Lysine—A crystalline basic amino acid essential to nutrition.

Methionine—An amino acid that, when not metabolized properly, allows homocysteine to build up in the blood. Folic acid aids methionine metabolism.

Spirulina—A genus of blue-green algae that is sometimes added to food to increase its nutrient value.

Tryptophan—An essential amino acid that has to consumed in the diet because it cannot be manufactured by the body. Tryptophan is converted by the body to niacin, one of the B vitamins, and serotonin, a neurotransmitter.

Vegan—A vegetarian who does not eat eggs or dairy products.

vegetables, including broccoli, kale, spinach, and collard greens. Iron is found in raisins, figs, beans, tofu, whole grains, potatoes, and dark green leafy vegetables. Iron is absorbed more efficiently by the body when iron-containing foods are eaten with foods that contain vitamin C, such as fruits, tomatoes, and green vegetables. Zinc is abundant in nuts, pumpkin seeds, beans, whole grains, and tofu.

For vegetarians who do not eat fish, getting enough omega-3 essential fatty acids may be an issue, and supplements such as flaxseed oil should be considered, as well as consumption of walnuts and canola oil. Another essential fatty acid, omega-6, found in fish, can be obtained from borage oil or evening primrose oil supplements.

Vegetarians do not necessarily have healthier diets. Some studies have shown that some vegetarians consume large amounts of cholesterol and saturated fat. It is quite possible to be a vegetarian yet eat an unhealthy fast-food or junk food diet. Eggs and dairy products contain cholesterol and saturated fat, while nuts, oils, and avocados are vegetable sources of saturated fat. To reap the full benefits of a vegetarian diet, vegetarians should be conscious of cholesterol and saturated fat intake.

Parental concerns

Parents should closely monitor their vegetarian child's height, weight, and general health. A child who is not getting enough vitamins, **minerals**, and other nutrients may have symptoms such as skin **rashes**, fatigue, a painful and swollen tongue, irritability, pale skin, mental slowness, or difficulty breathing. The diets of vegetarian adolescents should be monitored closely to make sure they are eating a variety of foods, including fruits, vegetables, beans, whole grains, and non-meat protein sources.

When to call the doctor

Parents should consult their child's pediatrician or physician if they are unsure the child's vegetarian diet is nutritionally adequate. A doctor should also be consulted if a child's weight or height is not appropriate for their age.

Resources

BOOKS

Poneman, Debra, and Emily Anderson Greene. *What, No Meat?! What to Do When Your Kid Becomes a Vegetarian.* Toronto, ON (Canada): ECW Press, 2003.

Schwartz, Ellen, and Farida Zaman. *I'm a Vegetarian.* New York: Tundra Books, 2002.

Stepaniak, Joanne, and Vesanto Melina. *Raising Vegetarian Children.* New York: McGraw-Hill, 2002.

PERIODICALS

Brayden, Robert. "Vegetarian Diet." *Clinical Reference Systems* (Annual 2002): 3470.

Grossman, Jeff. "Vegan with a Vengeance: Strict Form of Vegetarianism Attracts Young Adherents." *Psychology Today* 37 (March-April 2004): 16.

"How Many Teens Are Vegetarian? How Many Kids Don't Eat Meat?" *Vegetarian Journal* (January 2001): 10.

Mangels, Reed. "Good News about Vegetarian Diets for Teens." *Vegetarian Journal* 21 (July-August 2002): 20–21.

——. "Vegetarian Journal's Guide to Foods for Vegetarian Teens." *Vegetarian Journal* (September 2001): 20.

Ortinau, Rebecca. "Proud to Be a Vegetarian." *Vegetarian Baby and Child Magazine* 4 (September-October 2002): 38–40.

ORGANIZATIONS

American Vegan Society. 56 Dinshah Lane, PO Box 369, Malaga, NJ 08328. Web site: <www.americanvegan.org>.

The Vegetarian Resource Group. PO Box 1463, Baltimore, MD 21203. Web site: <www.vrg.org>.

Vegetarian Youth Network. PO Box 1141, New Paltz, NY 12561. Web site: <www.geocities.com/RainForest/Vines/4482/>.

WEB SITES

Vegetarian Baby and Child Online Magazine, 2004. Available online at <www.vegetarianbaby.com> (accessed November 14, 2004).

Vegetarianteen.com. Available online at <www.vegetarianteen.com> (accessed November 15, 2004).

Douglas Dupler
Rebecca J. Frey, PhD
Ken R. Wells

Venereal diseases *see* **Sexually transmitted diseases**

Vertigo *see* **Dizziness**

Vesicoureteral reflux

Definition

Vesicoureteral reflux (VUR) is a condition in which urine flows from the bladder, back up the ureter, and back into the kidneys.

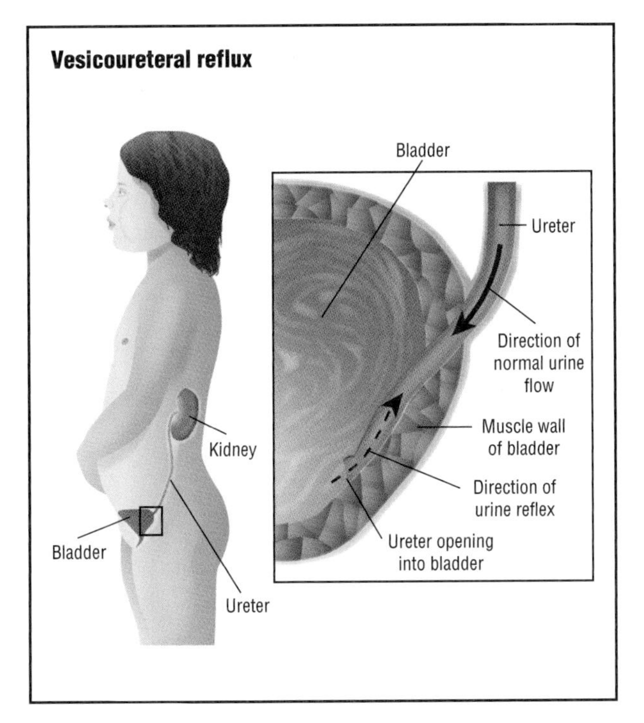

Illustration of vesicoureteral reflux in a child, a condition in which urine abnormally flows back up into the ureters, causing repeated urinary tract infections. *(Illustration by GGS Information Services.)*

Description

The normal flow of urine begins in the collecting system of each kidney. Urine then flows out of each kidney and into a tube called the ureter. Each ureter leads into the bladder, where the urine collects until it is passed out of the body. Normally, urine flows only in this direction. In vesicoureteral reflux, however, urine that has already collected in the bladder is able to flow backwards from the bladder, up the ureter, and back into the collecting system of the kidney. VUR may be present in either one or both ureters.

Vesicoureteral reflux causes damage to the kidneys in two ways. The kidney is not designed to withstand very much pressure. When VUR is present, backpressure of the urine on the kidney is significant. This can damage the kidney. Second, the kidney is usually sterile, meaning that no bacteria are normally present within it. In VUR, bacteria that enter through the urinary tract may be carried back up the ureter with the urine. These bacteria can enter the kidney, causing severe infection.

Demographics

VUR mostly occurs in the prenatal stage and may be observed at birth (congenital), although it may not be detected until an infection heralds its presence. VUR may run in families. The condition affects about 1 percent of all children. More boys than girls have VUR.

Causes and symptoms

Most cases of VUR are due to a defect in the way the ureter is implanted into the bladder. The angle may be wrong or the valve (which should allow urine only one-way entrance into the bladder) may be weak. Structural defects of the urinary system may also cause VUR. These include a situation in which two ureters leave a kidney, instead of the usual one (duplicated ureters) and in which the ureter is greatly enlarged at the end leading into the bladder (ureterocele).

VUR alone does not usually cause symptoms. Symptoms develop when an infection has set in. The usual symptoms of infection are frequent need to urinate, **pain** or burning with urination, and blood or pus in the urine. Occasionally, VUR is suspected when a child has a difficult time becoming toilet trained. In these cases, the bladder may become irritable and spastic, because it is never totally empty of urine. When the kidneys have been damaged, high blood pressure may develop. Over time, severe damage and scarring of the kidneys leads to kidney failure.

Diagnosis

Urinary tract infections are diagnosed through laboratory examination of urine samples. Kidney size and scarring can be assessed through ultrasound examination of the kidneys.

VUR itself is diagnosed by a test called a voiding cystourethrogram. This test involves inserting a small tube (catheter) into the bladder. The bladder is then filled with a dye solution, which lights up on the x-ray picture. A series of pictures are taken immediately, followed by x rays taken while the patient is urinating. This tracking allows reflux to be demonstrated and also reveals whether the level of reflux increases when pressure increases during urination. Reflux is then graded as follows based on the height and effects of the VUR:

- Grade I: VUR enters just the portion of the ureter closest to the bladder. The ureter appears normal in size.
- Grade II: VUR enters the entire ureter and goes up into the collecting system of the kidney. The ureter and the collecting system appear normal in size and structure.
- Grade III: VUR enters the entire ureter and kidney collecting system. Either the ureter or the collecting system is abnormal in size or shape.

KEY TERMS

Bladder—The muscular sac which receives urine from the kidneys, stores it, and ultimately works to remove it from the body during urination.

Reflux—The backward flow of a body fluid or secretion. Indigestion is sometimes caused by the reflux of stomach acid into the esophagus.

Ureter—The tube that carries urine from the kidney to the bladder; each kidney has one ureter.

- Grade IV: Similar to grade III, but the ureter is greatly enlarged.
- Grade V: Similar to grade IV, but the ureter is also abnormally twisted/curved, and the collecting system is greatly enlarged, with absence of the usual structural details.

Once VUR has been diagnosed, its progress may be followed with a nuclear scintigram, in which a radioactive substance is put into the bladder via catheter, and a gamma camera takes images that reveal the presence and degree of VUR. This test exposes the child to less radiation than does a standard VCUG. Doppler ultrasound techniques were as of 2004 under study as a radiation exposure-free alternative to VCUG.

Treatment

Treatment depends on the grade that is diagnosed. In grades I and II, the usual treatment involves long-term use of a small daily dose of **antibiotics** to prevent the development of infections. The urine is tested regularly to make sure that no infection occurs. The kidneys are evaluated regularly via ultrasound and VCUG (every 12 to 18 months) to make sure that they are growing normally and that no new scarring has occurred. Grades III, IV, and V VUR can be treated with antibiotics and careful monitoring. New infections, scarring, or stunting of kidney growth may result in the need for surgery. Grades IV and V are extremely likely to require surgery.

Surgery for VUR consists of reimplanting the ureters into the bladder at a more normal angle. This adjustment usually improves the functioning of the valve leading into the bladder. When structural defects of the urinary system are present, surgery will almost always be required to repair these defects.

Prognosis

Prognosis is dependent on the grade of VUR. About 80 percent of children with grades I and II VUR simply grow out of the problem. As they grow, the ureter lengthens, changing its angle of entry into the bladder and resolving the reflux. The average age of VUR resolution is about six to seven years. About 50 percent of children with grade III VUR require surgery. Nearly all children with grades IV and V VUR require surgery. In these cases, it is usually best to perform surgery when the patient is relatively young, in order to avoid damage and scarring to the kidneys.

Prevention

While as of 2004 there was no known method of preventing VUR, it is important to note that a high number of the siblings of children with VUR also have VUR. Many of these siblings (about 36%) have no symptoms but are discovered through routine examinations prompted by their brother's or sister's problems. It is important to identify these children, so that antibiotic treatment can be used to prevent the development of infection and kidney damage.

Parental concerns

It is important that parents of children with VUR understand the importance of following the instructions for antibiotic administration. Although their child may not appear at all ill, the antibiotics are crucial to protecting the health and development of their child's kidneys. Children with VUR should also be monitored for the development of **constipation**, which can complicate the VUR. Problems with bladder emptying can make toilet teaching a slower process in children with VUR.

Resources

BOOKS

Atala, Anthony, and Michael A. Keating. "Vesicoureteral reflux and megaureter." In *Campbell's Urology*, 8th ed. Edited by Meredith F. Campbell et al. St. Louis, MO: Elsevier, 2002.

"Vesicoureteral reflux." In *Nelson Textbook of Pediatrics*. Edited by Richard E. Behrman et al. Philadelphia: Saunders, 2004.

PERIODICALS

Austin, J. "Vesicoureteral reflux: Surgical approaches." In *Urology Clinics of North America* 31 (August 2004).

Cooper, C. "Vesicoureteral reflux: Who benefits from surgery?" In *Urology Clinics of North America* 31 (August 2004).

Rosalyn Carson-DeWitt, MD

Video games

Definition

Video games are electronic, interactive games known for their vibrant colors, sound effects, and complex graphics.

Description

First mass-marketed in the 1970s, video games are played by installing cartridges into a game box connected by wire to a television set. The child then manipulates a joystick or controller to control the actions of a character or series of characters as the characters face obstacles displayed on the screen. Video games, designed chiefly to appeal to children and adolescents, can also be played in arcades, on computers, and on small, hand-held screens.

As of 2004 nearly every home in the United States with children had one or more of the most popular game systems, for example, Nintendo GameCube, Sony Playstation2, or Microsoft Xbox. Few children have not been exposed to some form of video game, and access to the games is readily available to children from all walks of life.

Video games for home use proved popular from the start. Children are particularly attracted to them for a variety of reasons. Fantasy characters and situations appeal to young imaginations and provide an escape from everyday routine and the stresses presented by parents, friends, and school. In addition, the games give children a level of control that they do not experience in real life, as the characters on the screen respond to the children's commands. Players also receive immediate rewards for making the right moves. Most games can be played at a variety of skill levels so that every player can be challenged.

The popularity of video games has been matched by the controversy they have sparked among parents, psychologists, and educators. The most prevalent objection results from the violent themes and characters that dominate in most video games. A 1989 study by the National Coalition on Television Violence (NCTV) found that, of the 95 most popular home video games, 58 percent were war games and 83 percent featured violent themes. As technology has improved to allow the games to show situations and characters that are more realistic, debate has escalated about the potential effects of video games on children's behavior. One NCTV study that monitored the playground behavior of eight- to ten-year-olds immediately after playing a laser-weapon game found an 80 percent increase in fighting. There is also added concern that repeated exposure to violence desensitizes children to its effects. Other experts and video game manufacturers contend that negative effects have not been proven adequately, and, in fact, playing such games gives players an avenue for the harmless release of stress and aggression.

Public pressure prompted some video game manufacturers in the early 1990s to begin labeling games with warnings about violent or sexually explicit content. In 1994, in response to considerable political pressure and the possibility of a federal rating agency, the industry created its own rating system, overseen by the Entertainment Software Rating Board (ESRB). Ratings are assigned based on the games' suitability for various age groups. An "Early Childhood" designation on a game box indicates that the game is suitable for players ages three and older, and there is no violence, sexual content, or profanity. The designation "Everyone" indicates the game is for players ages six and older and may contain minimal violence or crude language. A "Teen" game for ages 13 and up may contain violence, profanity, and mild sexual themes. A "Mature" rating is considered suitable only for ages 17 and older and may include more intense violence, profanity, and mature sexual themes. "Adults Only" games are not intended for people under 18 and may include graphic depictions of sex and violence. The ratings system, however, is just a guide, and parents still need to oversee which video games their children buy and **play**.

In the past, the issue of gender bias in video games was another area of considerable debate. Not only were most video games male-oriented **sports** and combat games, female characters in the games were portrayed as victims to be rescued by the male hero or objects of violence or sexual desire. In the early 2000s, however, an increasing number of games had girl-oriented themes and an increasing number of gender neutral games became available.

Besides the socialization concerns presented by video games, medical concerns were also raised in the early 1990s, when video games were linked to epileptic seizures experienced by some 50 children. About one third of the children had experienced previous seizures, and there were questions about whether the seizures they experienced were related to playing or watching a video game. Two large studies later reported that the children who experienced video game-related seizures (VGRS) were particularly sensitive to light and that video games with flashing lights merely precipitated, rather than caused, the seizures. Sitting too close to the screen could exacerbate the effects of the light sensitivity, as could the increasingly complex graphic technology featured in games. Individuals with epilepsy are not thought to be particularly susceptible to VGRS, and no lasting neurological damage had as of 2004 been linked to these seizures.

Despite the controversy surrounding video games, benefits have also been noted: development of **hand-eye coordination**, increases in concentration, logical thinking skills, and healthy competition among children, as well as socialization skills gained from sharing strategies and the heightened **self-esteem** resulting from successful performances. One research study even found that doctors who had played more video games had better surgical skills.

Toddlerhood

There are a number of specialized video and computer games that are designed to be educational for toddlers. Many use familiar characters to teach basic things such as shape matching, the alphabet, and counting.

Preschool

Children in **preschool** can be exposed to video and computer games that reinforce the basic skills that they are learning, such as phonetics, shapes, colors, and basic addition.

Elementary school

School-age children can be encouraged to play educational games that reinforce what they are learning in the classroom. Parents should research the games that their children want to buy to ensure appropriate content for the child's age group. In the early 2000s marketers have developed increasing numbers of educational games that are also adventurous and exciting. Children, especially young ones, should be encouraged to play these instead of more violent games.

Middle and high school

The effect of violent games on behavior and social development is an especially important concern for older children. These children often spend much of their time playing video games when their parents are not present to supervise the content. Also, many teens buy video games with money earned from allowances or part time jobs, making it harder for parents to control which titles are purchased.

Studies have begun to find significant correlations between violence in video games and violence in real life. One study done on eighth and ninth graders compared teens who generally had personalities considered non-aggressive but who played violent games to those teens who had aggressive personalities but did not play violent games. The researchers found that the non-aggressive, video game playing teens were actually more likely to get in physical fights than the teens considered aggressive but who did not play video games.

Some states are trying to pass laws that would make it illegal to sell video games with certain ratings to people under the age for which the games are intended. Even if laws are created to try to prevent underage sale of very violent video games, parents should still be alert to what their teen is playing. Making the teen play video games in a common area and not in his or her bedroom with the door closed can be an important first step in regulating game play and facilitating discussion.

KEY TERMS

Entertainment Software Rating Board (ESRB)—The industry board that rates video games.

Video game related seizures (VGRS)—Seizures thought to be brought on by the flashing lights and complex graphics of a video game.

Common problems

Children often become very involved in video games and do not want to stop playing them. Setting concrete limits about the amount of time that can be spent playing games and then enforcing these limits is essential. Even educational games should not be played to excess, because playing video games is not a substitute for positive social interaction or traditional learning. Children can also be encouraged to play the games with other children, because discussing strategies and problem solving in a group is a positive social activity.

Parental concerns

The amount and degree of violence in video games is an important concern for parents. Monitoring the games that a child buys or rents and plays is an important way to help deal with this problem. If a child plays a violent video game at an arcade or another child's house, it can be helpful to discuss the difference between games and reality and to discuss what the real life repercussions of the actions taken in the game would be.

When to seek help

If a child has violent or **aggressive behavior** or a tendency to mimic the negative actions taken by characters in a video game it may be helpful to consult a mental health professional to discuss possible solutions.

See also Television habits.

Resources

BOOKS

Calvert, Sandra L., Amy B. Jordan, and Rodney R. Cocking, eds. *Children in the Digital Age: Influences of Electronic Media on Development.* Westport, CT: Praeger, 2002.

Gee, James Paul. *What Video Games Have to Teach Us about Learning and Literacy.* New York: Palgrave Macmillan, 2003.

PERIODICALS

Eisenman, Russell. "Video Games: Technology and Social Issues." *Journal of Evolutionary Psychology* 25 (August 2004): 170–75.

Levermore, Monique A. "Violent Media and Videogames, and Their Role in Creating Violent Youth." *The Forensic Examiner* 13 (Fall 2004): 38–42.

"Video Game Play May Increase Laparoscopic Proficiency." *AORN Journal* 80 (August 2004): 290.

Tish Davidson, A.M.
Mary Anne Klasen

Violence and violent behavior *see* **Aggressive behavior**

Vision development *see* **Eye and vision development**

Vitamin D deficiency

Definition

Vitamin D deficiency exists when the concentration of 25-hydroxy-vitamin D (25-OH-D) in the blood serum occurs at 12 nanograms/milliliter (ng/ml) or less. This is one-half to one-fourth the amount normally present. When vitamin D deficiency continues for many months in growing children, the disease commonly referred to as rickets occurs.

Description

Vitamin D is a fat-soluble vitamin, meaning it can be dissolved in fat. While some vitamin D is supplied by the diet, most of it is made in the body. To make vitamin D, cholesterol, a substance widely distributed in animal tissues, the yolk of eggs, and various oils and fats, is necessary. Once cholesterol enters the body, a slight alteration in the cholesterol molecule occurs, with one change taking place in the skin. This alteration requires ultraviolet light, a component of sunlight. Vitamin D deficiency and rickets tend to occur in children who do not get enough sunlight and who do not eat foods that are rich in vitamin D.

Once consumed or made in the body, vitamin D is further altered to produce a substance called 1,25-dihydroxy-vitamin D (1,25-diOH-D). The conversion of vitamin D to 1,25-diOH-D occurs in the liver and kidney. The role of 1,25-diOH-D in the body is to keep the concentration of calcium at a constant level in the bloodstream. Maintaining calcium at a constant level is absolutely required for human life, since dissolved calcium is required for nerves and muscles to work. One of the ways in which 1,25-diOH-D accomplishes this is by stimulating the absorption of dietary calcium by the intestines.

The sequence of events that can lead to vitamin D deficiency and later to bone disease, is as follows: a lack of vitamin D in the body creates an inability to manufacture 1,25-diOH-D. This results in decreased absorption of dietary calcium and an increased loss of calcium in the feces. When this happens, the bones are affected. Vitamin D deficiency results in a lack of bone mineralization (calcification) in growing children.

Demographics

Vitamin D deficiency is not common in the United States and other industrialized countries because of the wide availability of vitamin D fortified infant formulas and milks. It is somewhat more common in northern areas where there is not as much sunlight present during many parts of the year. Vitamin D deficiency is also slightly more common in inner city areas, because environmental factors, such as smog, can block the necessary ultraviolet (UV) component of sunlight. Children with darkly pigmented skin are more likely to be vitamin D deficient than light skinned children. Children who are exclusively breast-fed without vitamin D supplementation, particularly if they are not exposed to sunlight, are at higher risk of vitamin D deficiency.

Causes and symptoms

Vitamin D deficiency can be caused by conditions that result in little exposure to sunlight. These conditions include: living in northern regions, having dark skin, and having little chance to go outside. Children whose faces and bodies remain covered when outside can develop vitamin D deficiency even while living in a sunny climate. In-born errors of vitamin D metabolism can also cause vitamin D deficiency and rickets; these children cannot convert inactive vitamin D to active vitamin D and suffer the same symptoms as children with a nutritional deficiency.

Most foods contain little or no vitamin D. As a result, sunshine is often a deciding factor in whether vitamin D deficiency occurs. Although fortified milk and fortified infant formula contain high levels of vitamin D, human breast milk is rather low in the vitamin. (The term fortified means that **vitamins** are added to the food by the manufacturer.)

The Recommended Dietary Allowance (RDA) of vitamin D for both children and adults is 200 International Units (IU) per day. Saltwater fish such as salmon, herring, and sardines are naturally rich in vitamin D. Vitamin D fortified milk contains 400 IU per quart (liter), so half a quart (liter) of milk provides the RDA. For comparison, human breast milk contains only 4 to 60 IU per quart.

No harm is likely to result from vitamin D deficiency that occurs only a few days a year. If the deficiency occurs for a period of many months or years, however, rickets may develop. The symptoms of rickets include bowed legs and bowed arms. The bowed appearance is due to the softening of bones, and their bending if the bones are weight-bearing. Bone growth occurs through the creation of new cartilage, a soft substance at the ends of bones. When the mineral calcium phosphate is deposited onto the cartilage, a hard structure is created. In vitamin D deficiency, though, calcium is not available to create hardened bone, and the result is soft bone. Other symptoms of rickets include bony bumps on the ribs called rachitic rosary (beadlike prominences at the junction of the ribs with their cartilages) and knock-knees. Seizures may also occasionally occur in a child with rickets, because of reduced levels of dissolved calcium in the bloodstream.

When to call the doctor

The doctor should be called if the parent notices that the child has any signs of vitamin D deficiency or rickets. Such signs include skeletal **pain**, bowed limbs, and impaired growth. If there are lifestyle factors that make the child at risk for vitamin D deficiency, such as low milk or formula intake, a doctor should be consulted about the possibility of using vitamin D supplements.

Diagnosis

Vitamin D deficiency is diagnosed by measuring the level of 25-hydroxy-vitamin D in the blood serum. The normal concentration of this form of vitamin D ranges from 25 to 50 ng/ml. Deficiency occurs when this level decreases to about 12 ng/ml or less.

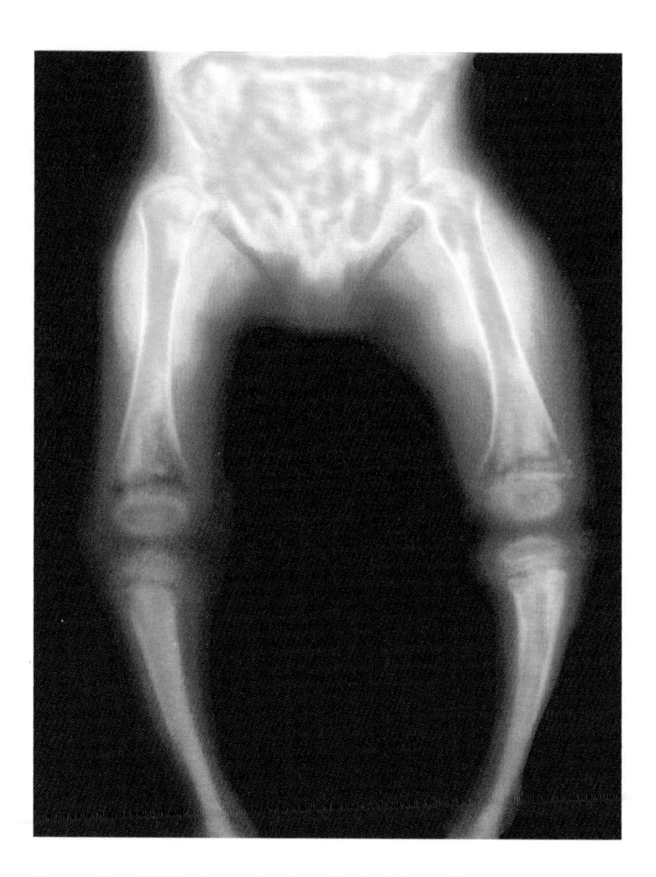

X ray of a child's lower body affected by rickets, a result of a vitamin D deficiency. *(© Dr. LR/Photo Researchers, Inc.)*

Rickets is diagnosed by x-ray examination of the leg bones. A distinct pattern of irregularities, abnormalities, and a coarse appearance can be clearly seen if a child has rickets. Measurements of blood plasma 25-OH-D, blood plasma calcium, and blood plasma parathyroid hormone must also be obtained for the diagnosis of this disease. Parathyroid hormone and 1,25-diOH-D work together in the body to regulate the levels of calcium in the blood.

Treatment

Rickets heals promptly with large doses vitamin D administered orally each day for approximately one month. During this treatment, the doctor should monitor the levels of 25-OH-D in the plasma to make sure that they are raised to a normal level. The bone abnormalities (visible by x ray) generally disappear gradually over a period of three to nine months. Parents are instructed to take their infants outdoors for approximately 20 minutes per day with their faces exposed. Children should be

KEY TERMS

25-hydroxy-vitamin D—The form of vitamin D that is measured in order to assess vitamin D deficiency.

Cholesterol—A steroid fat found in animal foods that is also produced in the human body from saturated fat. Cholesterol is used to form cell membranes and process hormones and vitamin D. High cholesterol levels contribute to the development of atherosclerosis.

Fat-soluble vitamin—A vitamin that dissolves easily in fat or oil, but not in water. The fat-soluble vitamins are vitamins D, E, A, and K.

International unit (IU)—A measurement of biological activity in which one IU is equal to one mg (milligram).

Rachitic rosary—Beadlike bumps present at the junction of the ribs with their cartilages. It is often seen in children with rickets.

Recommended Dietary Allowance (RDA)—The Recommended Dietary Allowances (RDAs) are quantities of nutrients in the diet that are required to maintain good health in people. RDAs are established by the Food and Nutrition Board of the National Academy of Sciences, and may be revised every few years. A separate RDA value exists for each nutrient. The RDA values refer to the amount of nutrient expected to maintain good health in people. The actual amounts of each nutrient required to maintain good health in specific individuals differ from person to person.

Rickets—A condition caused by the dietary deficiency of vitamin D, calcium, and usually phosphorus, seen primarily in infancy and childhood, and characterized by abnormal bone formation.

encouraged to **play** outside and to eat foods that are good sources of vitamin D. These foods include cod liver oil, egg yolks, butter, oily fish and also foods, including milk and breakfast cereals, that are fortified with synthetic vitamin D.

Care must be taken in treating vitamin D deficiency, since high doses of vitamin D are toxic (poisonous) and can result in the permanent deposit of **minerals** in the heart, lungs, and kidneys. Symptoms of toxicity are **nausea**, **vomiting**, pain in the joints, and lack of interest in eating food. In adults, vitamin D toxicity occurs with eating 50,000 IU or more per day. In infants, toxicity occurs with 1,000 IU per day. The continued intake of toxic doses results in death.

Rickets are usually treated with oral supplements of vitamin D, with the recommendation to acquire daily exposure to direct sunlight. An alternative to sunlight is the use of an ultraviolet lamp. When people use UV lamps, they need to cover their eyes to protect them against damage. Many types of sunglasses allow UV light to pass through, so only those that are opaque to UV light should be used. Attempts to acquire sunlight through glass windows fail to help the body make vitamin D because UV light does not pass through window glass.

Rickets may also occur with calcium deficiency, even when a child is regularly exposed to sunshine. This type of rickets has been found in various parts of Africa. The bone deformities are similar to, or are the same as, those that occur in typical rickets; however, calcium deficiency rickets is treated by increasing the amount of calcium in the diet. No amount of vitamin D can cure the rickets of a child with a diet that is extremely low in calcium. For this reason, it is recommended that calcium be given in conjunction with vitamin D supplementation.

Prognosis

The prognosis for correcting vitamin D deficiency and rickets is excellent. Vitamin D treatment results in the return of bone mineralization to a normal rate, the correction of low plasma calcium levels, the prevention of seizures, and a recovery from bone pain. On the other hand, already established deformities such as bowed legs and the rachitic rosary persist throughout adult life.

Prevention

Vitamin D deficiency is a very preventable. Eating foods that are high in vitamin D or foods that have been fortified with additional vitamins in combination with getting moderate amounts of exposure to direct sunlight, are usually enough to prevent vitamin D deficiency.

Some authorities still recommend exposure to sunshine as a way to prevent vitamin D deficiency, but early exposure to direct sunlight may be linked to a higher incidence of skin **cancer** later in life, so other experts recommend that infants not be taken into direct sunlight without protective coverings or sunscreen until at least six months of age. These experts recommend that supplemental drops or fortified formulas instead of direct sunlight provide infants' daily requirements of Vitamin D. Children playing in the sunlight with sunscreen on is not an effective way for them to get vitamin D because the sunscreen inhibits its production in the skin.

Nutritional concerns

Vitamin D deficiency is caused by the child not getting enough vitamin D through **nutrition** and exposure to sunshine. Even after a case of vitamin D deficiency has successfully been resolved special care should be taken with the child's diet, as vitamin D deficiency can reoccur.

Parental concerns

Vitamin D deficiency can cause rickets, which can lead to permanently stunted or irregular growth. Vitamin D deficiency can usually be easily corrected if it is noticed early, and if so the symptoms often resolve themselves. However, negative effects such as short stature and pelvic deformations can be permanent.

Resources

BOOKS

Hochber, Ze'ev, ed. *Vitamin D and Rickets.* Farmington, CT: S. Karger, 2003.

PERIODICALS

Spence, Jean, T. and Janet R. Serwint. "Secondary Prevention of Vitamin D-Deficiency Rickets" *Pediatrics* 113 (January 2004): 129.

Wharton, Brian, and Nick Bishop. "Rickets." *The Lancet* 362 (October 2003): 1389.

Tish Davidson, A.M.

Vitamins

Definition

Vitamins are organic components in food that are needed in very small amounts for growth and for maintaining good health. The vitamins include vitamins D, E, A, and K (fat-soluble vitamins), and folate (**folic acid**), vitamin B_{12}, biotin, vitamin B_6, niacin, thiamin, riboflavin, pantothenic acid, and vitamin C (ascorbic acid) (water-soluble vitamins). Vitamins are required in the diet in only tiny amounts, in contrast to the energy components of the diet. The energy components of the diet are sugars, starches, fats, and oils, and these occur in relatively large amounts in the diet.

Most of the vitamins are closely associated with a corresponding vitamin deficiency disease. **Vitamin D deficiency** causes rickets, a disease of the bones. Vitamin E deficiency occurs only very rarely and causes nerve damage. Vitamin A deficiency, common throughout the poorer parts of the world, causes night blindness. Severe vitamin A deficiency can result in xerophthalmia, a disease that, if left untreated, results in total blindness. Vitamin K deficiency results in spontaneous bleeding. Mild or moderate folate deficiency, common throughout the world, can result from the failure to eat green, leafy vegetables or fruits and fruit juices. Folate deficiency causes megaloblastic anemia, which is characterized by the presence of large abnormal cells called megaloblasts in the circulating blood. The symptoms of megaloblastic anemia are tiredness and weakness. Vitamin B_{12} deficiency occurs with the failure to consume meat, milk, or other dairy products. Vitamin B_{12} deficiency causes megaloblastic anemia and, if severe enough, can result in irreversible nerve damage. Niacin deficiency results in pellagra, which involves skin **rashes** and scabs, **diarrhea**, and mental depression. Thiamin deficiency results in beriberi, a disease resulting in atrophy, weakness of the legs, nerve damage, and heart failure. Vitamin C deficiency results in scurvy, a disease that involves bleeding. Diseases associated with deficiencies in vitamin B_6, riboflavin, or pantothenic acid have not been found in the humans, though persons who have been starving or consuming poor diets for several months, might be expected to be deficient in most of the nutrients, including vitamin B_6, riboflavin, and pantothenic acid. Rarely, deficiency in B_6 results in neurologic problems. Issues of toxicity are connected to the over consumptions of vitamins, particularly E, K, and B. Also, lack of regulation in the vitamin industry means consumers ought only to buy well-known brands.

Some of the vitamins serve only one function in the body, while other vitamins serve a variety of unrelated functions. Hence, some vitamin deficiencies tend to result in one type of defect, while other deficiencies result in a variety of problems.

Description

Vitamin treatment is usually done in three ways: by replacing a poor diet with one that supplies the recommended dietary allowance, by consuming oral supplements, or by injections. Injections are useful for persons with diseases that prevent absorption of fat-soluble vitamins. Oral vitamin supplements are especially useful for persons who otherwise cannot or will not consume food that is a good vitamin source, such as meat, milk, or other dairy products. For example, a vegetarian who will not consume meat may be encouraged to consume oral supplements of vitamin B_{12}.

Treatment of genetic diseases which impair the absorption or utilization of specific vitamins may require megadoses of the vitamin throughout one's lifetime. Megadose means a level of about 10 to 1,000 times greater than the RDA. Pernicious anemia, homocystinuria, and biotinidase deficiency are three examples of genetic diseases which are treated with megadoses of vitamins.

General use

People are treated with vitamins for three reasons. The primary reason is to relieve a vitamin deficiency, when one has been detected. Chemical tests suitable for the detection of all vitamin deficiencies are available. The diagnosis of vitamin deficiency is often aided by visual tests, such as the examination of blood cells with a microscope, the x-ray examination of bones, or a visual examination of the eyes or skin.

A second reason for vitamin treatment is to prevent the development of an expected deficiency. Here, vitamins are administered even with no test for possible deficiency. One example is vitamin K treatment of newborn infants to prevent bleeding. Food supplementation is another form of vitamin treatment. The vitamin D added to foods serves the purpose of preventing the deficiency from occurring in persons who may not be exposed much to sunlight and who fail to consume foods that are fortified with vitamin D, such as milk. Niacin supplementation prevents pellagra, a disease that occurs in people who rely heavily on corn as the main source of food and who do not eat much meat or milk. In general, the American food supply is fortified with niacin.

A third reason for vitamin treatment is to reduce the risk for diseases that may occur even when vitamin deficiency cannot be detected by chemical tests. One example is folate deficiency. The risk for cardiovascular disease can be slightly reduced for a large fraction of the population by folic acid supplements. And the risk for certain birth defects can be sharply reduced in certain women by folic acid supplements.

Vitamin treatment is important during specific diseases in which the body's normal processing of a vitamin is impaired. In these cases, high doses of the needed vitamin can force the body to process or use it in the normal manner. One example is pernicious anemia, a disease that tends to occur in middle age or old age and impairs the absorption of vitamin B_{12}. Surveys have revealed that about 0.1 percent of the general population, and 2–3 percent of the elderly, may have the disease. If left untreated, pernicious anemia leads to nervous system damage. The disease can easily be treated with large oral daily doses of vitamin B_{12} (hydroxocobalamin) or with monthly injections of the vitamin.

Vitamin supplements are widely available as over-the-counter products. But whether they work to prevent or curtail certain illnesses, particularly in people with a balanced diet, is in the early 2000s a matter of debate and ongoing research. For example, vitamin C is not proven to prevent the **common cold**. Yet millions of Americans take it for that reason. Consumers should ask a physician or pharmacist for more information on the appropriate use of multivitamin supplements.

The diagnosis of a vitamin deficiency usually involves a blood test. An overnight fast is usually recommended as preparation prior to withdrawal of the blood test so that vitamin-fortified foods do not affect the test results.

KEY TERMS

Genetic condition—A condition that is passed from one generation to the next but does not necessarily appear in each generation. Examples of genetic conditions include Down syndrome, Tay-Sach's disease, sickle cell disease, and hemophilia.

Plasma—A watery fluid containing proteins, salts, and other substances that carries red blood cells, white blood cells, and platelets throughout the body. Plasma makes up 50 percent of human blood.

Recommended dietary allowance (RDA)—The Recommended Dietary Allowances (RDAs) are quantities of nutrients in the diet that are required to maintain good health in people. RDAs are established by the Food and Nutrition Board of the National Academy of Sciences, and may be revised every few years. A separate RDA value exists for each nutrient. The RDA values refer to the amount of nutrient expected to maintain good health in people. The actual amounts of each nutrient required to maintain good health in specific individuals differ from person to person.

Serum—The fluid part of the blood that remains after blood cells, platelets, and fibrogen have been removed. Also called blood serum.

Vitamin status—The state of vitamin sufficiency or deficiency of any person. For example, a test may reveal that a patient's folate status is sufficient, borderline, or severely inadequate.

The response to vitamin treatment can be monitored by chemical tests, by an examination of red blood cells or white blood cells, or by physiological tests, depending on the exact vitamin deficiency.

Precautions

Vitamin A and vitamin D can be toxic in high doses. Side effects range from **dizziness** to kidney failure. Consumers should ask a physician or pharmacist about the correct use of a multivitamin supplement that contains these vitamins.

Side effects

Few side effects are associated with vitamin treatment if vitamins are taken within the prescribed dosages. Excessive intake of some B vitamins may impart a greenish color to urine. Any possible risks depend on the vitamin and the reason why it was prescribed. Consumers should ask a physician or pharmacist about how and when to take vitamin supplements, particularly those that have not been prescribed by a physician.

Parental concerns

The dosage of vitamin supplements should not exceed the recommended daily allowance without a recommendation by a physician. Recommended dosages vary with age, so parents should be should to give vitamins to children that are specially formulated for children. Vitamin bottles will list recommended doses for different age groups. Infants and toddlers may also benefit from vitamin supplements if they do not eat a variety of foods. Liquid vitamin supplements are available commercially for these young children.

Resources

BOOKS

Heird, William C. "Vitamin Deficiencies and Excesses." In *Nelson Textbook of Pediatrics*, 17th ed. Edited by Richard E. Behrman et al. Philadelphia: Saunders, 2003, pp. 177–90.

Litwack, Gerald. *Vitamins and Hormones.* St. Louis, MO: Elsevier, 2004.

Mason, Joel B. "Consequences of Altered Micronutrient Status." In *Cecil Textbook of Medicine*, 22nd ed. Edited by Lee Goldman et al. Philadelphia: Saunders, 2003, pp. 1326–35.

Navarra, Tova. *Encyclopedia of Vitamins, Minerals, and Supplements.* New York: Facts on File, 2004.

Russell, Robert M. "Vitamin and Trace Mineral Deficiency and Excess." In *Harrison's Principles of Internal Medicine*, 15th ed. Edited by Eugene Braunwald et al. New York: McGraw-Hill, 2001, pp. 461–9.

PERIODICALS

Bryan, J., et al. "Nutrients for cognitive development in school-aged children." *Nutrition Reviews* 62, no. 8 (2004): 295–306.

Fennell, D. "Determinants of supplement usage." *Preventive Medicine* 39, no. 5 (2004): 932–9.

Krapels, I. P., et al. "Maternal nutritional status and the risk for orofacial cleft offspring in humans." *Journal of Nutrition* 134, no. 11 (2004): 3106–13.

Mossad, S. B. "Current and future therapeutic approaches to the common cold." *Expert Review of Anti-Infective Therapy* 1, no. 4 (2004): 619–26.

ORGANIZATIONS

American Academy of Family Physicians. 11400 Tomahawk Creek Parkway, Leawood, KS 66211–2672. Web site: <www.aafp.org/>.

American Academy of Pediatrics. 141 Northwest Point Boulevard, Elk Grove Village, IL 60007–1098. Web site: <www.aap.org/default.htm>.

American Association of Naturopathic Physicians. 8201 Greensboro Drive, Suite 300, McLean, VA 22102. Web site: <http://naturopathic.org/>.

American College of Obstetricians and Gynecologists. 409 12th St., SW, PO Box 96920, Washington, DC 20090–6920. Web site: <www.acog.org/>.

WEB SITES

"Dietary Reference Intakes Tables: Vitamins Table." *Institute of Medicine of the National Academies.* Available online at <www.iom.edu/file.asp?id=7296> (accessed January 9, 2005).

"Vitamins." *Harvard School of Public Health.* Available online at <www.hsph.harvard.edu/nutritionsource/vitamins.html> (accessed January 9, 2005).

"Vitamins." *National Library of Medicine.* Available online at <www.nlm.nih.gov/medlineplus/ency/article/002399.htm> (accessed January 9, 2005).

"Vitamins and Minerals." *Food and Nutrition Information Center.* Available online at <www.nal.usda.gov/fnic/etext/000068.html> (accessed January 9, 2005).

"Vitamins and Minerals." *West Virginia Dietetic Association.* Available online at <www.wvda.org/nutrient/> (accessed January 9, 2005).

L. Fleming Fallon, Jr., MD, DrPH

Vocal cord dysfunction

Definition

Vocal cord dysfunction (VCD) is a disorder that occurs when the vocal cords move toward each other when a person breathes, narrowing the airway and causing wheezing and difficulty breathing. VCD is also called paradoxical vocal cord motion (PVCM).

Description

Normally when an individual breathes in (inhales) or out (exhales) the vocal cords are drawn apart by the muscles of the larynx (voice box) to make a wider opening for air to move into or out of the lungs. In an individual with vocal cord dysfunction, instead of being drawn apart, the vocal cords move together, narrowing and partially blocking the airway. This is called adduction of the vocal cords. Adduction of the vocal cords happens most commonly during inhalation, although it can also happen during exhalation. As a result of the narrowed airways, the individual may **cough**, wheeze, feel short of breath, or make a high-pitched, harsh sound (called **stridor**) with each breath.

VCD is often misdiagnosed as either **asthma** or exercise-induced bronchospasm. As a result, many individuals with VCD are treated with inhalers and steroids for asthma, which do not help control VCD and which have potentially harmful side effects.

Demographics

The number of people with VCD in the general U.S. population is unknown. The disorder often occurs in conjunction with asthma and is frequently a missed diagnosis. Several small studies have found that about 40 percent of individuals who have VCD also have asthma and that about 10 to 15 percent of individuals whose asthma does not respond to aggressive treatment (refractory asthma) actually have VCD.

VCD has been found in individuals as young as three and as old as 82. However, in adults it most often occurs between the ages of 20 and 40. In children it appears most often about age 14 or 15. VCD is much more common in females than in males. In children under 18, about 85 percent of individuals diagnosed with VCD are girls. In children, the disorder has a strong association with competitive **sports** and **family** orientation toward high achievement. In adults it has a strong association with **anxiety** and stress. This association with stress is present, but less frequent in children.

Causes and symptoms

VCD was first recognized in 1842, when it was thought that hysteria, a common designation at that time for several psychological conditions, brought about spasm of the muscles of the larynx. By 1900, it was generally accepted that VCD was the physical expression of stress or other psychological conditions. It was not until the 1980s that physicians began to revisit the assumptions about the disorder and examine more closely its physical causes. As of 2004, the causes of VCD was not completely clear.

In the early 2000s, it is thought that the disorder may have multiple causes and that some of the triggers may be different in children and adults. VCD appears to be associated with the following:

- injury to the brain cortex
- brainstem compression (mainly in children)
- Arnold-Chiari syndrome (mainly in children)
- gastroesophageal reflux disease (GERD; in children and adults)
- chronic sinus infection/postnasal drip
- strenuous **exercise** (often in children)
- exposure to inhaled irritants (smoke, toxic chemicals; mainly in adults)
- psychological causes (most obvious in adults)
- nerve injury during **congenital heart disease** surgery or other chest surgeries
- failure to respond to asthma treatments

VCD usually comes on suddenly. Between attacks, the individual can breathe normally. The symptoms of a VCD attack are varied, but most strongly imitate those of asthma. Its similarity to asthma, along with the fact that some people with VCD actually also have asthma, complicates diagnosis. Common signs and symptoms include the following:

- coughing (about 75% of individuals)
- wheezing
- stridor
- voice changes during an attack
- difficulty inhaling (most common)
- difficulty exhaling (less common; usually irritant-induced)
- panic, anxiety, **fear** of suffocating
- insufficient oxygen in the blood (hypoxia)
- chest tightness

- panting in short shallow breaths
- feeling like something is stuck in the throat
- skin turning blue

When to call the doctor

Immediate emergency medical assistance is essential whenever there are any signs of breathing difficulty.

Diagnosis

Diagnosis of VCD is quite difficult. VCD can mimic the symptoms of severe asthma, allergic reactions (**anaphylaxis**), spasm of the larynx (laryngospasm), or a foreign object lodged in the throat. VCD is often a diagnosis of exclusion, which means that other possibilities are considered first, and when these are eliminated, VCD is considered. This may require a lot of testing.

The best way to determine if an individual has VCD is by doing a laryngoscopy. In a laryngoscopy, a slender, flexible tube containing a fiber optic camera is inserted through the nose and down the throat to the larynx. This examination allows the doctor to see the vocal cords and watch how and when they move.

Since between attacks the vocal cords appear to move normally, it is necessary to trigger an attack. Individuals cannot voluntarily produce symptoms of VCD, so they are usually exposed to an irritant or undergo an exercise stress test in order to bring on a VCD attack. The doctor then watches the vocal cords move. A classic finding is that the vocal cords move toward each other when the individual inhales, leaving a small triangular hole or chink at the back of the larynx. Individuals with asthma do not show this triangular chink.

Most people go through a series of other tests and often get other diagnoses, most commonly refractory (unresponsive) asthma, before they have a laryngoscopy and receive a definite diagnosis of VCD. Other tests that are frequently done to pinpoint or eliminate certain respiratory disorders include arterial blood gas values (to measure oxygen in the blood), **pulmonary function tests** (to measure lung capacity), with flow-volume loops (to measure the rate of air flow at different points in the breathing process). A methacholine provocation test, which stimulates a response in asthmatics, but not in persons with VCD, also helps narrow the diagnosis.

Treatment

Treatment consists of two phases, immediate (acute) and long term. Acute care often occurs in a hospital emergency room. The most important aspect of acute care is to see that the individual is breathing and getting enough oxygen. Sometimes heliox therapy is given. Heliox is a mixture of 20 to 30 percent oxygen and 70 to 80 percent helium. Because this mixture is less dense and more oxygen-rich than regular air, it is easier to inhale. If the individual is still not getting enough oxygen, it may be necessary to perform a tracheotomy. In this operation, a tube is inserted in the larynx so that air can bypass the blockage.

Long-term therapy begins by stopping any treatments for other diagnoses such as asthma, and treating any underlying conditions, such as brainstem compression or GERD, affecting the disorder. Airborne irritants are removed from the individual's environment as much as possible. Speech therapy and teaching abdominal breathing techniques have been quite successful in preventing VCD attacks. If an individual does not respond adequately to speech therapy, psychotherapy is recommended, as in many people anxiety and stress are linked to VCD attacks. People can learn relaxation techniques and work through problems causing stress and anxiety. Occasionally anti-anxiety drugs are prescribed.

In an experimental procedure, botulinum toxin (Botox) may be injected into the larynx. The drug paralyzes the muscle, making it impossible for the vocal cords to move across the airway. This technique appears

KEY TERMS

Arnold-Chiari syndrome—A congenital malformation of the base of the brain.

Asthma—A disease in which the air passages of the lungs become inflamed and narrowed, causing wheezing, coughing, and shortness of breath.

Exercise-induced bronchospasm—A sudden contraction in the lower airway that causes breathing problems and is brought about by heavy exercise.

Gastroesophageal reflux disease (GERD)—A disorder of the lower end of the esophagus in which the lower esophageal sphincter does not open and close normally. As a result the acidic contents of the stomach can flow backward into the esophagus and irritate the tissues.

Laryngoscope—An endoscope that is used to examine the interior of the larynx.

Stridor—A term used to describe noisy breathing in general and to refer specifically to a high-pitched crowing sound associated with croup, respiratory infection, and airway obstruction.

to be successful but may require repeated injections as the toxin wears off. Another experimental device is a facemask that provides resistance when the individual inhales but not during exhalation. The resistance forces the person to breathe in more slowly and reduces stridor.

Alternative treatment

Some individuals have found biofeedback very helpful in controlling or moderating VCD attacks. Others have benefited from relaxation and mind control techniques.

Prognosis

The long-term outcome for VCD is not known and probably varies among individuals depends on the underlying cause of the disorder. Only a handful of people with VCD have been followed for 10 or more years, and all of them continued to have symptoms of the disorder. However, speech therapy and psychotherapy are often successful in reducing the number of attacks.

Prevention

Although the physical conditions that cause VCD cannot be prevented, individuals can be educated not to panic and to use certain breathing techniques when they begin to feel symptoms of VCD. In addition, airborne pollutants should be eliminated from the individual's environment. These steps can be somewhat successful in minimizing attacks.

Parental concerns

Parents have obvious reason to be concerned when their child has sudden breathing problems. Many children with VDC make multiple trips to the emergency room before the condition is correctly diagnosed. Many medical professionals are only marginally familiar with VCD, because this problem is much less common than asthma. Parents may want to suggest additional testing for VCD if their child is being treated for asthma without success.

See also Asthma; Stridor.

Resources

PERIODICALS

Leggit, Jeff. "Vocal Cord Dysfunction." *American Family Physician* 69 (March 1, 2004): 1045.

Perkins, Patrick J., and Michael J. Morris. "Vocal Cord Dysfunction Induced by Methacholine Challenge Testing." *Chest* 122 (December 2002): 1988–93.

Rundell, Kenneth W., and Barry A. Spiering. "Inspiratory Stridor in Elite Athletes." *Chest* 123 (February 2003): 468–74.

Truwit, Jonathon. "Pulmonary Disorders and Exercise." *Clinics in Sports Medicine* 22 (January 2003): 161–80.

ORGANIZATIONS

National Jewish Medical and Research Center. 1400 Jackson Street, Denver, CO 80206–2671. Web site: <www.njc.org/>.

WEB SITES

Buddiga, Praveen, and Michael O'Connell. "Vocal Cord Dysfunction." *eMedicine Medical Library*, October 27, 2003. Available online at <www.emedicine.com/med/topic3563.htm> (accessed December 3, 2004).

National Jewish Medical and Research Center. "Vocal Cord Dysfunction." *Medfacts*, July 15, 2004. Available online at <www.nationaljewish.org/medfacts/vocal.html> (accessed December 3, 2004).

Sidofsky, Carol. *Can't Breathe? Suspect Vocal Cord Dysfunction.* Available online at <www.cantbreathesuspectvcd.com> (accessed December 3, 2004).

Tish Davidson, A.M.

Volvulus *see* **Intestinal obstructions**

Vomiting *see* **Nausea and vomiting**

Von Willebrand disease

Definition

Von Willebrand disease is caused by a deficiency or an abnormality in a protein called von Willebrand factor and is characterized by prolonged bleeding.

Description

The Finnish physician Erik von Willebrand was the first to describe von Willebrand disease (VWD). In 1926, von Willebrand noticed that many male and female members of a large **family** from the Aland Islands had increased bruising (bleeding into the skin) and prolonged episodes of bleeding. The severity of the bleeding varied among family members and ranged from mild to severe and typically involved the mouth, nose, genital and urinary tracts, and occasionally the intestinal tract. Some women in the family also experienced excessive menstrual bleeding. What differentiated this bleeding disorder from classical **hemophilia** was that it appeared not to be associated with muscle and joint bleeding and affected women and men rather than just men. Dr. von Willebrand named this disorder hereditary pseudohemophilia.

Pseudohemophilia, or von Willebrand disease (VWD) as it is called in the twenty-first century, occurs when the body does not produce enough of a protein, called von Willebrand factor(vWF), or produces abnormal vWF. vWF is involved in the process of blood clotting (coagulation). Blood clotting is necessary to heal an injury to a blood vessel. When a blood vessel is injured, vWF enables blood cells called platelets to bind to the injured area and form a temporary plug to seal the hole and stop the bleeding. vWF is secreted by platelets and by the cells that line the inner wall of the blood vessels (endothelial cells). The platelets stimulate the release other chemicals, called factors, which help form a strong permanent clot. vWF binds to and stabilizes factor VIII, one of the factors involved in forming the permanent clot.

A deficiency or abnormality in vWF can interfere with the formation of the temporary platelet plug and affect the normal survival of factor VIII. This indirectly interferes with the production of the permanent clot. Individuals with VWD, therefore, have difficulty in forming blood clots, and as a result, they may bleed for a longer time. In most cases the bleeding is due to an obvious injury, although it sometimes occurs spontaneously.

VWD is classified into three basic types: type 1, 2, and 3 based on the amount and type of vWF that is produced. Type 1 is the most common and mildest form and results when the body produces slightly decreased amounts of normal vWF. Type 2 can be classified into four subtypes (A, B, M, N) and results when the body produces an abnormal type of vWF. Type 3 is the rarest and most severe form and results when the body does not produce any detectable vWF.

Demographics

Approximately one out of 100 people are affected with VWD, making it the most common inherited bleeding disorder. VWD affects people of all ethnic backgrounds. Approximately 70 to 80 percent of people with VWD have type 1, and close to 20 to 30 percent have type 2. Type 3 is very rare and occurs in less than 1 percent of people with VWD. Type 3 occurs in about one out of every million people.

Causes and symptoms

The complex genetics of VWD involve a gene found on chromosome 12. Different types of changes in the vWF gene can affect the production of vWF. Some changes cause the vWF gene to produce decreased amounts of normal vWF, while other changes cause the gene to produce abnormal vWF. Each individual inherits two copies of each gene, one from the mother and one from the father. Most of the vWF gene changes are significant enough that a change in only one vWF gene is sufficient to cause VWD. However, some types of gene changes only cause VWD if both genes are changed, which often leads to more severe symptoms.

Type 1 VWD is called an autosomal dominant condition since it is caused by a change in only one vWF gene. Since type 1 VWD results in only a slight decrease in the amount of vWF produced, the symptoms are often mild and not apparent in some individuals. Most cases of type 2 VWD are autosomal dominant since a change in only one vWF gene results in the production of an abnormal form of vWF. An autosomal dominant form of VWD can be inherited from either parent or can occur as a spontaneous gene mutation (change) in the embryo that is formed when the egg and sperm cells come together during fertilization.

Some cases of type 2 VWD and all cases of type 3 VWD are autosomal recessive, since they are caused only by changes in both vWF genes. A person with an autosomal recessive form of VWD has inherited both a changed gene from the mother and a changed gene from the father. Parents who have a child with an autosomal recessive form of VWD are called carriers, since they each possess at least one changed vWF gene. Many carriers for the autosomal recessive forms of type 2 VWD and type 3 VWD do not have any symptoms. Each child born to parents who both have one changed gene has a 25 percent chance of having VWD, a 50 percent chance of being a carrier, and a 25 percent chance of not being and not having VWD disease. A person with an autosomal dominant form of VWD has a 50 percent chance of passing the changed gene on to his or her children who may or may not have symptoms.

VWD is usually a relatively mild disorder characterized by easy bruising, recurrent nosebleeds, heavy menstrual periods, and extended bleeding after surgeries and invasive dental work. There is a great deal of variability in the severity of symptoms, which can range from clinically insignificant to life threatening. Even children within the same family who are affected with the same type of VWD may exhibit different symptoms. A child with VWD may exhibit a range of symptoms over the course of his or her lifetime and may experience an improvement in symptoms with age. The severity of the disease is partially related to the amount and type of vWF that the body produces, but it is also influenced by other genetic and non-genetic factors.

Type 1

Type 1, the mildest form of VWD, is usually associated with easy bruising, recurrent nosebleeds, heavy menstrual periods, and prolonged bleeding after surgeries and invasive work. Many people with type 1 VWD do not have any noticeable symptoms or only have prolonged bleeding after surgery or significant trauma. The amount of vWF produced by the body increases during pregnancy, so prolonged bleeding during delivery is uncommon in people with type 1 VWD.

Type 2

Children with type 2 VWD usually have symptoms from early childhood. Symptoms may even be present at birth. These children usually experience prolonged bleeding from cuts, easy bruising, nosebleeds, skin hematomas, and prolonged bleeding from the gums following tooth extraction and minor trauma. Gastrointestinal bleeding is rare but can be life-threatening. More than 50 percent of women with type 2 VWD experience heavy menstrual periods that may require a blood transfusion. Some women with type 2 VWD exhibit prolonged bleeding during delivery.

Type 3

Type 3 VWD can be quite severe and is associated with bruising and bleeding from the mouth, nose, and from the intestinal, genital, and urinary tracts. Type 3 is also associated with spontaneous bleeding into the muscles and joints, which can result in joint deformities. Some women with type 3 VWD experience prolonged bleeding during delivery.

When to call the doctor

If a child frequently experiences significant bleeding, takes longer than normal to stop bleeding, or experiences easy bruising, then the doctor should be consulted.

Diagnosis

Many children with VWD have mild symptoms or symptoms that can be confused with other bleeding disorders, making it difficult for a doctor to diagnose VWD based on clinical symptoms. VWD should be suspected in any child with a normal number of platelets in the blood and bleeding from the mucous membranes such as the nose, gums, and gastrointestinal tract. Testing for a child with suspected VWD often includes the measurement of the following:

- how long it takes for the bleeding to stop after a tiny cut is made in the skin (bleeding time)
- the amount of vWF (vWF antigen measurement)
- the activity of vWF (ristocetin co-factor activity)
- the amount of factor VIII (factor VIII antigen measurement)
- activity of factor VIII

Children with type 1 VWD usually have an increased bleeding time, but they may have an intermittently normal time. They also have a decreased amount of vWF and decreased vWF activity and usually have slightly decreased factor VIII levels and activity. Children with type 2 VWD have a prolonged bleeding time and decreased activity of vWF; they may also have decreased amounts of vWF and factor VIII and decreased factor VIII activity. Type 3 children have undetectable amounts of vWF, negligible vWF activity, factor VIII levels of less than 5 to 10 percent, and significantly reduced factor VIII activity. The activity of vWF is reduced for all types of VWD, making it the most sensitive means of identifying all three types. Individuals with borderline results should be tested two to three times over a three-month period.

Once a person is diagnosed with VWD, further testing such as vWF multimer analysis and ristocetin-induced platelet aggregation (RIPA) should be performed to determine the subtype. Multimer analysis evaluates the structure of the vWF, and RIPA measures how much ristocetin is required to cause the clumping of platelets in a blood sample. The vWF multimer analysis is able to differentiate children with a structurally normal vWF (Type 1) from children with a structurally abnormal vWF (Type 2) and is often able to identify the subtype of patients with Type 2 VWD. Children with type 1 VWD usually have normal to decreased RIPA concentrations. Depending on the subtype, patients with type 2 VWD either have increased or decreased RIPA. RIPA is usually absent and the multimer analysis shows undetectable vWF in children with type 3 VWD.

In some cases, DNA testing can be a valuable adjunct to biochemical testing. The detection of gene alteration(s) can confirm a diagnosis and can determine the type and subtype of VWD. It can also help to facilitate prenatal testing and testing of other family members. Unfortunately many people with VWD possess DNA changes that are not detectable through DNA testing. A child who has a mother, father, or sibling diagnosed with VWD should undergo biochemical testing for VWD. If the relative with VWD possesses a detectable gene change, then DNA testing should be considered.

Prenatal testing

If one parent has been diagnosed with an autosomal dominant form of VWD or both parents are carriers for an autosomal recessive form of VWD, then prenatal testing should be considered. DNA testing can be performed through **amniocentesis** or chorionic villus sampling. If the DNA change in the parent(s) is unknown, then prenatal testing can sometimes be performed through biochemical testing of blood obtained from the umbilical cord. However this procedure is less accurate and is associated with a higher risk of pregnancy loss.

Treatment

VWD is most commonly treated by replacement of vWF through the administration of blood products that contain vWF or through treatment with desmopressin (DDAVP, 1-deamino-8-D-arginine vasopressin). DDAVP functions by increasing the amount of factor VIII and vWF in the circulating blood. Treatment with blood products or DDAVP may be started in response to uncontrollable bleeding or may be administered before procedures such as surgeries or dental work. The type of treatment chosen depends on the type of VWD and a patient's response to a preliminary treatment trial.

Treatment with desmopressin (DDAVP)

DDAVP is the most common treatment for people with type 1 VWD. About 80 percent of people with type 1 VWD respond to DDAVP therapy. Treatment with DDAVP can also be used to treat some people with type 2 VWD. Patients with type 2B VWD should not be treated with this medication, since DDAVP can induce dangerous platelet clumping. Type 3 VWD should not be treated with DDAVP, since this medication does not increase the level of vWF in type 3 patients. DDAVP should only be used in people who have been shown to be responsive through a pre-treatment trial transfusion with this medication.

DDAVP can be administered intravenously or through a nasal inhaler. DDAVP has relatively few side effects although some people may experience facial flushing, tingling sensations, and headaches after treatment with this medication. Often treatment with this medication is only required prior to invasive surgeries or dental procedures.

Treatment with blood products

Patients who are unable to tolerate or are unresponsive to drug-based treatments are treated with concentrated factor VIII obtained from blood products. Not all factor VIII concentrates can be used, since some do not contain enough vWF. The concentrate is treated to kill most viruses, although caution should be used since not all types of viruses are destroyed. If the factor VIII concentrates are unable to manage a severe bleeding episode, then blood products called cryoprecipitates, which contain concentrated amounts of vWF, or platelet concentrates should be considered. Caution should be used when treating with these blood products since they are not treated to kill viruses.

Other treatments and precautions

Medications called fibrinolytic inhibitors can be helpful in controlling intestinal, mouth, and nose bleeding. Estrogens, such as are found in **oral contraceptives**, increase the synthesis of vWF and can sometimes be used in the long-term treatment of women with mild to moderate VWD. Estrogens are also sometimes used before surgery in women with type 1 VWD. Some topical agents are available to treat nose and mouth bleeds. Patients with VWD should avoid taking aspirin, which can increase their susceptibility to bleeding. Children with severe forms of VWD should avoid activities that increase their risk of injury such as contact **sports**.

Prognosis

The prognosis for VWD is generally good, and most individuals have a normal lifespan. The prognosis can depend, however, on accurate diagnosis and appropriate medical treatment.

Prevention

There is no known way to prevent VWD. If an individual planning to become a parent believes he or she may be a carrier of VWD, genetic counseling is suggested so that options may be explored.

Parental concerns

VWD is usually very mild and does not cause unusual bleeding except after trauma or surgery. Children with moderate or severe VWD may need to be discouraged from playing contact sports or participating in other activities where injury is likely. Special care should be taken before surgical or dental procedures to ensure that severe bleeding does not occur.

KEY TERMS

Amniocentesis—A procedure performed at 16–18 weeks of pregnancy in which a needle is inserted through a woman's abdomen into her uterus to draw out a small sample of the amniotic fluid from around the baby for analysis. Either the fluid itself or cells from the fluid can be used for a variety of tests to obtain information about genetic disorders and other medical conditions in the fetus.

Autosomal dominant—A pattern of inheritance in which only one of the two copies of an autosomal gene must be abnormal for a genetic condition or disease to occur. An autosomal gene is a gene that is located on one of the autosomes or non-sex chromosomes. A person with an autosomal dominant disorder has a 50% chance of passing it to each of their offspring.

Autosomal recessive—A pattern of inheritance in which both copies of an autosomal gene must be abnormal for a genetic condition or disease to occur. An autosomal gene is a gene that is located on one of the autosomes or non-sex chromosomes. When both parents have one abnormal copy of the same gene, they have a 25% chance with each pregnancy that their offspring will have the disorder.

Biochemical testing—Measuring the amount or activity of a particular enzyme or protein in a sample of blood or urine or other tissue from the body.

Carrier—A person who possesses a gene for an abnormal trait without showing signs of the disorder. The person may pass the abnormal gene on to offspring. Also refers to a person who has a particular disease agent present within his/her body, and can pass this agent on to others, but who displays no symptoms of infection.

Chorionic villus sampling—A procedure used for prenatal diagnosis at 10–12 weeks gestation. Under ultrasound guidance a needle is inserted either through the mother's vagina or abdominal wall and a sample of the chorionic membrane. These cells are then tested for chromosome abnormalities or other genetic diseases.

Chromosome—A microscopic thread-like structure found within each cell of the human body and consisting of a complex of proteins and DNA. Humans have 46 chromosomes arranged into 23 pairs. Chromosomes contain the genetic information necessary to direct the development and functioning of all cells and systems in the body. They pass on hereditary traits from parents to child (like eye color) and determine whether the child will be male or female.

Desmopressin acetate (DDAVP)—A drug used to regulate urine production.

DNA—Deoxyribonucleic acid; the genetic material in cells that holds the inherited instructions for growth, development, and cellular functioning.

DNA testing—Analysis of DNA (the genetic component of cells) in order to determine changes in genes that may indicate a specific disorder.

Endothelial cells—The cells lining the inner walls of a body cavity or the cardiovascular system. Also known as endothelium.

Factor VIII—A protein involved in blood clotting that requires von Willebrand factor for stability and long-term survival in the bloodstream.

Gene—A building block of inheritance, which contains the instructions for the production of a particular protein, and is made up of a molecular sequence found on a section of DNA. Each gene is found on a precise location on a chromosome.

Mutation—A permanent change in the genetic material that may alter a trait or characteristic of an individual, or manifest as disease. This change can be transmitted to offspring.

Platelet—A cell-like particle in the blood that plays an important role in blood clotting. Platelets are activated when an injury causes a blood vessel to break. They change shape from round to spiny, "sticking" to the broken vessel wall and to each other to begin the clotting process. In addition to physically plugging breaks in blood vessel walls, platelets also release chemicals that promote clotting.

Prenatal testing—Testing for a disease, such as a genetic condition, in an unborn baby.

Protein—An important building blocks of the body, a protein is a large, complex organic molecule composed of amino acids. It is involved in the formation of body structures and in controlling the basic functions of the human body.

Skin hematoma—Blood from a broken blood vessel that has accumulated under the skin.

von Willebrand factor (vWF)—A protein found in the blood that is involved in the process of blood clotting.

Resources

BOOKS

Berntorp, Erik, et al. *Textbook on Hemophilia.* Oxford, UK: Blackwell Publishing, 2005.

Cannon, Christopher P., et al. *Platelet Function: Assessment, Diagnosis, Treatment.* Totowa, NJ: Humana Press, 2004.

PERIODICALS

Renee Paper. "Can You Recognize and Respond to von Willebrand Disease?" *Nursing* 33 (July 2003): 54–6.

Society for the Advancement of Education. "Diagnosis Key to Treating von Willebrand Disease." *USA Today* 131 (February 2003): 546–9.

ORGANIZATIONS

National Hemophilia Foundation. 116 West 32nd Street, 11th Floor, New York, NY 10001. Web site: <www.hemophilia.org>.

Tish Davidson, A.M.
Lisa Maria Andres, MS, CGC

Walleye *see* **Strabismus**

Warts

Definition

Warts are small, benign growths caused by a viral infection of the skin or mucous membrane. The virus infects the surface layer. The viruses that cause warts are members of the human papilloma virus (HPV) family. Warts are not cancerous, but some strains of HPV, usually not associated with warts, have been linked with **cancer** formation. Warts are contagious from person to person and from one area of the body to another on the same person.

Description

There are approximately 60 types of HPV that cause warts, each preferring a specific bodily location. For instance, some types of HPV cause warts to grow on the skin, others cause them to grow inside the mouth, while still others cause them to grow on the genital and rectal areas. However, most can be active anywhere on the body. The virus enters through the skin and produces new warts after an incubation period of one to eight months. Warts are usually skin-colored and feel rough to the touch, but they also can be dark, flat, and smooth.

Warts are passed from person to person, directly and indirectly. Some people are continually susceptible to warts, while others are more resistant to HPV and seldom get them. The virus takes hold more readily when the skin has been damaged in some way, which may explain why children who bite their nails tend to have warts located on their fingers. People who take a medication to suppress their immune system or are on long-term steroid use are also prone to a wart virus infection. This tendency is seen in people with **AIDS**.

Demographics

Particularly common among children, young adults, and women, warts are a problem for 7–10 percent of the population.

Causes and symptoms

The more common types of warts include the following:

- common hand warts
- foot warts
- flat warts
- genital warts

Hand warts

Common hand warts grow around the nails, on the fingers, and on the backs of hands. They appear more frequently where skin is broken, such as in areas where fingernails are bitten or hangnails are picked.

Foot warts

Foot warts are called plantar warts because the word plantar is the medical term for the sole of the foot, the area where the wart usually appears as a single lesion or as a cluster. Plantar warts, however, do not stick up above the surface like common warts. The ball of the foot, the heel, and the plantar part of the toes are the most likely locations for the warts because the skin in those areas is subject to the most weight, pressure, and irritation, making a small break or crack more likely.

Plantar warts are familiar to all ages groups, appearing frequently in children between the ages of 12 and 16. Adolescents often come into contact with a wart virus in a locker room, swimming pool area, or by walking barefooted on dirty surfaces. The blood vessels feeding them are the black dots that are visible on the wart. If left untreated, these warts can grow to an inch or more in circumference and spread into clusters of several warts. They are known to be very painful at times, the **pain**

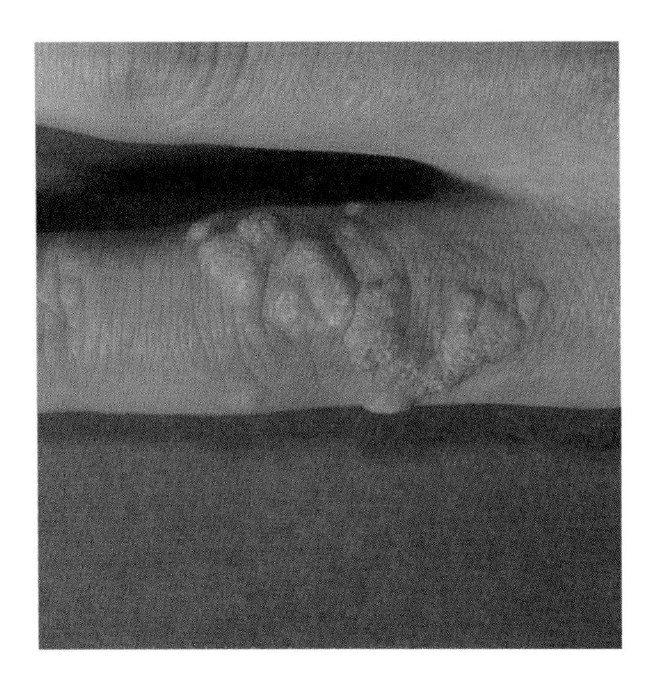

Cluster of warts on a finger. *(Custom Medical Stock Photo Inc.)*

usually compared to the feeling of a permanent stone in the shoe particularly if the wart is on a pressure point of the foot. People with **diabetes mellitus** are prone to complications from plantar warts related to the development of sores or ulceration and the poor healing potential associated with diabetes.

Flat warts

Flat warts tend to grow in great numbers and are smaller and smoother than other warts. They can erupt anywhere, appearing more frequently on the legs of women, the faces of children, and on the areas of the face that are shaved by young adult males.

Genital warts

Genital warts, also called condyloma acuminata or venereal warts, are one of the most common forms of sexually transmitted disease (STD) in this country. Most experts contend that they are contracted by sexual contact with an infected person who carries HPV and are more contagious than other warts. It is estimated that two-thirds of the people who have sexual contact with a partner with genital warts will develop the disease within three months of contact. As a result, about 1 million new cases of genital warts are diagnosed in the United States each year.

Genital warts tend to be small flat bumps but they may be thin and tall. They are usually soft and not scaly like other warts. In women, genital warts appear on the genitalia, within the vagina, on the cervix, and around the anus or within the rectum. In men, genital warts usually appear on the tip of the penis but may also be found on the scrotum or around the anus. Genital warts can also develop in the mouth of a person who has had oral sexual contact with an infected person.

When to call the doctor

Individuals who notice warts in their genital area should see a doctor. A physician should be consulted for warts that bleed, are particularly painful, or that do not disappear after six to nine months.

Diagnosis

A physician may be able to diagnose warts with a simple examination. If the warts are small, the doctor may put a vinegar-like liquid on the skin, which makes the warts turn white and easier to see, and then use a magnifying glass to look for them.

Treatment

Most people attempt to treat warts themselves. Professional treatment is usually sought after self-treatment has been unsuccessful.

Home/self treatment

Many of the nonprescription wart remedies available at drug stores will remove simple warts from hands and fingers. These medications may be lotions, ointments, or plasters and work by chemically removing the skin that was affected by the wart virus. The chemicals are strong, however, and should be used with care since they can remove healthy as well as infected skin. These solutions should be avoided by diabetics and those with cardiovascular or other circulatory disorders whose skin may be insensitive and not appreciate irritation.

Flat warts are best treated with topical retinoides (retinoic acid) or a gel containing salicylic acid. The acid does not actually kill the wart virus, but waterlogs the skin so that the surface layer, with the virus, peels off. These products can take up to three months of treatment depending on the size and depth of the wart. Patches are also good to use. Rather than applying drops, a small pad is placed on the wart and left for 48 hours and then replaced with a new one. The patch usually contains a higher concentration of salicylic acid and may irritate the surrounding skin. If this occurs, people should switch to a gel or stop medication for a period. To help the healing process for flat facial warts, men should shave with an electric shaver or temporarily grow a beard. Women with flat warts on areas that are shaved should use other methods to remove hair such as depilatory cream or wax.

Professional treatment

Physicians should be consulted if there are no signs of progress after a month of self treatment. Doctors have many ways of removing warts, including using stronger topically applied chemicals than those available in pharmacies. Some of these solutions include podofilox, topical podophyllum, and trichloracetic acid (TCA). Some burning and discomfort for one or more days following treatment can be expected. Although these chemicals are effective, they may not completely destroy all warts. A second method of removal is freezing or cryosurgery on the wart using liquid nitrogen. Cryotherapy is relatively inexpensive, does not require anesthesia, and usually does not result in scarring. Although temporarily uncomfortable, it provides an effective and safe way to deliver freezing temperatures to a particular area on the skin, and healing is usually quick. Physicians may also choose to burn the wart with liquid nitrogen or numb the skin and then scrape off the wart. Another removal process is electrocautery (electric burning), destroying the wart by burning it with an electric needle. Laser surgery is also an option for removing warts.

Genital warts are the most difficult to treat. They can be removed, but the viral infection itself cannot be cured. Often, because the warts are so small, more than one treatment may be needed. The virus continues to live in the deeper skin, which is why warts often return after they have been removed. Strong chemicals may be applied as well as surgical excision with or without electrocautery. This therapy requires a small operative procedure and a local anesthetic. Laser therapy, although more expensive, is often used for treating venereal warts that are more extensive. The use of lasers, which vaporize the lesion, can theoretically transmit the HPV. It is not at all clear, however, if this occurs.

There is no single recommended method for eliminating plantar warts. If detected early, cryotherapy is usually enough. However, they can be very resilient, requiring repeated treatment over several months. Treatment ranges from the conservative approach of applying chemical solutions to the more aggressive option of surgery. Persons with diabetes or vascular disease are usually treated with the more conservative methods.

Alternative treatment

There are a variety of alternative approaches to the treatment of warts. The following suggestions apply to common warts and plantar warts. They are not recommended for genital or cervical warts. Since genital and cervical warts are transmitted sexually, they should be treated by a physician.

For the treatment of common or plantar warts, practitioners may recommend the following remedies:

- Apply a paste made of vitamin C powder to the wart for one to two weeks.
- Place a crushed or sliced garlic clove over the wart for seven consecutive nights while sleeping.
- Soak the wart in water, put cross-hatches over it with a sterile needle, and apply drops of thuja (*Thuja occidentalis*) tincture onto the wart. Repeat the cross-hatching and tincture application until the wart is saturated with the tincture. Repeat several times each day for one to two weeks. (A tincture is an herbal extract made with alcohol.)
- Tape a piece of banana peel, smooth side down, over the wart and leave it on overnight. Repeat nightly for one to two weeks.

Prognosis

Even though genital warts may be removed, the virus itself continues to live. The HPV can cause tissue changes in the cervix of women with cervical infection. The general recommendation for women who have a history of genital warts is to see their doctors every six months for Pap smears to monitor any changes that may occur.

For plantar warts, the treatment goal is to destroy the wart and its virus without causing much damage to healthy skin. It is not unusual for treatment to cause pain until the foot heals because of the weight put on the foot.

Prevention

Plantar warts can be prevented by wearing shoes, changing shoes daily, keeping feet clean and dry, and not ignoring skin growths and changes in the skin. Genital warts can be prevented by using condoms and avoiding unprotected sex. Barrier protection will not, however, prevent the spread of wart-causing HPV to uncovered areas such as the pubis and upper thighs.

Nutritional concerns

Because warts are caused by a virus, general immune system support can be effective in helping to keep warts from coming back after treatment or to keep them from multiplying or growing. Eating a well balanced diet high in sources of **vitamins** A, C, and E can help strengthen the immune system. Avoiding stress,

KEY TERMS

Condyloma acuminata—Another term for a genital wart.

Cryotherapy—The use of a very low-temperature probe to freeze and thereby destroy tissue. Cryotherapy is used in the treatment skin lesions, Parkinson's disease, some cancers, retinal detachment, and cataracts. Also called cryosurgery.

Endometritis—Inflammation of the endometrium or mucous membrane of the uterus.

Epidermis—The outermost layer of the human skin.

Human papilloma virus (HPV)—A virus that causes common warts of the hands and feet, as well as lesions in the genital and vaginal area. More than 50 types of HPV have been identified, some of which are linked to cancerous and precancerous conditions, including cancer of the cervix.

Retinoic acid—Vitamin A_1 acid which is used topically to treat acne.

Salicylic acid—An agent prescribed to treat a variety of skin disorders, such as acne, dandruff, psoriasis, seborrheic dermatitis, calluses, corns, and warts.

which is believed to compromise the immune system, may also be helpful.

Parental concerns

Parents can help to prevent plantar warts by urging their children to wear shoes, change their shoes daily, and keep their feet clean and dry. Parents should also pay attention to growths and other changes in their child's skin. Instructing children in **condom** usage is a personal, parental decision. However, parents should tell their children that genital warts can be prevented by using condoms and avoiding unprotected sex. Barrier protection will not, however, prevent the spread of wart-causing HPV to uncovered areas such as the pubis and upper thighs.

Resources

BOOKS

Darmstadt, Gary L., and Sidbury, Robert. "Diseases of the Epidermis." In *Nelson Textbook of Pediatrics*, 17th ed. Edited by Richard E. Behrman, et al. Philadelphia: Saunders, 2003, pp. 2195-9.

Genital Warts: A Medical Dictionary, Bibliography, and Annotated Research Guide to Internet References. San Diego, CA: ICON Health Publications, 2003.

Plantar Warts: A Medical Dictionary, Bibliography, and Annotated Research Guide to Internet References. San Diego, CA: ICON Health Publications, 2003.

Royston, Angela. *Warts.* London: Heinemann, 2001.

Swerlick, Robert A., and Lawley, Thomas J. "Eczema, Psoriasis, Cutaneous Infections, Acne, and Other Common Skin Disorders." In *Harrison's Principles of Internal Medicine*, 15th ed. Edited by Eugene Braunwald, et al. New York: McGraw-Hill, 2001, pp. 309–14.

Warts: A Medical Dictionary, Bibliography, and Annotated Research Guide to Internet References. San Diego, CA: ICON Health Publications, 2003.

PERIODICALS

Bellew, S. G., et al. "Childhood warts: an update." *Cutis* 73 (2004): 379–84.

Clemons, R. J., et al. "Comparing therapy costs for physician treatment of warts." *Journal of Drugs in Dermatology* 2 (2004): 649–54.

Laube, S. "Skin infections and ageing." *Ageing Research Reviews* 3 (2004): 69–89.

Silverberg, N. B. "Human papillomavirus infections in children." *Current Opinions in Pediatrics* 16 (2004): 402–9.

Tucker, S. B., et al. "Plantar wart treatment with combination imiquimod and salicylic acid pads." *Journal of Drugs in Dermatology* 2 (2003): 124–6.

ORGANIZATIONS

American Academy of Dermatology. 930 N. Meacham Road, PO Box 4014, Schaumburg, IL 60168–4014. Web site: <www.aad.org/>.

American Academy of Family Physicians. 11400 Tomahawk Creek Parkway, Leawood, KS 66211–2672. Web site: <www.aafp.org/>.

American Academy of Pediatrics. 141 Northwest Point Boulevard, Elk Grove Village, IL 60007–1098. Web site: <www.aap.org/default.htm>.

American Association of Naturopathic Physicians. 8201 Greensboro Drive, Suite 300, McLean, VA 22102. Web site: <http://naturopathic.org/>.

American College of Physicians. 190 N Independence Mall West, Philadelphia, PA 19106–1572. Web site: <www.acponline.org/>.

American Podiatric Medical Association. 9312 Old Georgetown Road Bethesda, MD 20814–1698. Web site: <www.apma.org/>.

WEB SITES

"Human Papillomavirus and Genital Warts." *National Institute of Allergy and Infectious Disease*, July 2004. Available online at <www.niaid.nih.gov/factsheets/stdhpv.htm> (accessed December 4, 2005).

"Warts." *American Academy of Family Physicians*. Available online at <http://familydoctor.org/209.xml> (accessed December 4, 2005).

"Warts." *National Library of Medicine*. Available online at <www.nlm.nih.gov/medlineplus/warts.html> (accessed December 4, 2005).

"Warts." *University of Illinois*. Available online at <www.mckinley.uiuc.edu/health-info/dis-cond/warts/warts.html> (accessed December 4, 2005).

"What are plantar warts?" *American Podiatric Medical Association*. Available online at <www.apma.org/topics/Warts.htm> (accessed December 4, 2005).

L. Fleming Fallon, Jr., MD, DrPH

Water on the brain *see* **Hydrocephalus**

Webbed fingers and toes *see* **Polydactyly and syndactyly**

Wechsler intelligence test

Definition

The Wechsler **intelligence** tests are a widely used series of intelligence tests developed by clinical psychologist David Wechsler.

Purpose

The Wechsler Intelligence Scales for Children (regular, revised, and third edition) and Wechsler **Preschool** and Primary Scale of Intelligence are used as tools in school placement, in determining the presence of a learning disability or a **developmental delay**, in identifying giftedness, and in tracking intellectual development. They are often included in neuropsychological testing to assess the brain function of individuals with neurological impairments.

Description

The most distinctive feature of the Wechsler tests is their division into a verbal section and a nonverbal (or performance) section, with separate scores available for each subsection. All of the Wechsler scales are divided into six verbal and five performance subtests. The complete test takes 60 to 90 minutes to administer. Verbal intelligence, the component most often associated with academic success, implies the ability to think in abstract terms using either words or mathematical symbols. Performance intelligence suggests the ability to perceive relationships and fit separate parts together logically into a whole. The inclusion of the performance section in the Wechsler scales is especially helpful in assessing the cognitive ability of non-native speakers and children with speech and **language disorders**. The test can be of particular value to school psychologists screening for specific learning disabilities because of the number of specific subtests that make up each section.

The Wechsler Preschool and Primary Scales of Intelligence (WPPSI) have traditionally been geared toward children ages four to six years old, although the newest version of the test extends the age range down to three years and upward to seven years three months. The verbal section covers the following areas: general information (food, money, the body, etc.), vocabulary (definitions of increasing difficulty), comprehension (responses to questions), arithmetic (adding, subtracting, counting), sentences (repeating progressively longer sentences), and similarities (responding to questions such as "How are a pen and pencil alike?"). The performance section includes picture completion, copying geometric designs, using blocks to reproduce designs, working through a maze, and building an animal house from a model.

The Wechsler Intelligence Scale for Children (WISC) is designed for children and adolescents ages six to 16. Its makeup is similar to that of the Preschool Scale. Differences include the following: geometric designs are replaced by assembly of three-dimensional objects; children arrange groups of pictures to tell simple stories; they are asked to remember and repeat lists of digits; a coding exercise is performed in place of the animal house; mazes are a subtest. For all of the Wechsler scales (which also include the Wechsler Adult Intelligence Scale, or WAIS), separate verbal and performance scores, as well as a total score, are computed. These are then converted using a scale divided into categories (such as average and superior), and the final score is generally given as one of these categories rather than as a number or percentile ranking.

The Wechsler Intelligence Scales are standardized tests, meaning that as part of the test design, they were administered to a large representative sample of the target population, and norms were determined from the results. The scales have a mean, or average, standard score of 100 and a standard deviation of 15. The standard

KEY TERMS

Norms—A fixed or ideal standard; a normative or mean score for a particular age group.

Representative sample—A random sample of people that adequately represents the test-taking population in age, gender, race, and socioeconomic standing.

Standard deviation—A measure of the distribution of scores around the average (mean). In a normal distribution, two standard deviations above and below the mean includes about 95% of all samples.

Standardization—The process of determining established norms and procedures for a test to act as a standard reference point for future test results.

deviation indicates how far above or below the norm the subject's score is. For example, a ten-year-old is assessed with the WISC-III scale and achieves a full-scale IQ score of 85. The mean score of 100 is the average level at which all 10-year-olds in the representative sample performed. This child's score would be one standard deviation below that norm.

While the full-scale IQ score provides a reference point for evaluation, it is only an average of a variety of skill areas. A trained psychologist evaluates and interprets an child's performance on the scale's subtests to discover their strengths and weaknesses and offer recommendations based upon these findings.

Risks

The only known risk of the Wechsler intelligence tests is that the results are misused or are given undue weight.

Parental concerns

Results of intelligence tests should not be considered a complete indication of a child's future path. They are most useful in determining children who may need special attention, either because of disability or because of giftedness. Parents should consider the possible consequences carefully if they are considering telling their child the outcome of this or any other intelligence test.

Resources

BOOKS

Flanagan, Dawn P., and Alan S. Kaufman. *Essentials of WISC-IV Assessment.* Hoboken, NJ: John Wiley & Sons, 2004.

PERIODICALS

Canivez, Gary L., and Marley W. Watkins. "Long-Term Stability of the Wechsler Intelligence Scale for Children—Third Edition among Students with Disabilities." *School Psychology Review* 30 (Summer 2001): 438–54.

Caruso, John C., and Norman Cliff. "Increasing the Reliability of Wechsler Intelligence Scale for Children—Third Edition Difference Scores with Reliable Component Analysis." *Psychological Assessment* 12 (March 2000): 89–97.

Watkins, Marley W., et al. "Factor Structure of the Wechsler Intelligence Scale for Children—Third Edition among Gifted Students." *Educational and Psychological Measurement* 63 (October 2003): 164–72.

Tish Davidson, A.M.
Paula Anne Ford-Martin

Weight issues *see* **Obesity**

Well-baby examination

Definition

Well-baby examinations are scheduled regularly during the first two years of life due to the rapid growth and change that occurs during infancy. During each visit the pediatrician monitors, advises, and answers questions on a baby's growth and development.

Purpose

The American Academy of Pediatrics recommends the newborn infant see a physician for a check-up at birth, two weeks, two months, four months, six months, nine months, 12 months, 15 months, 18 months, and 24 months, and annually thereafter. Most pediatricians follow this schedule, or some variation of it, in prescribing a check-up regimen for their patients. A well-baby exam consists of questions the parents will be asked about the baby's general health and development, followed by a physical exam. The exam includes measurements of length and height, weight and head circumference (the distance around the head), vital signs, and a general physical examination. Special attention is paid to whether the baby has met normal developmental milestones. The physician will question parents or guardians about the activities of the baby to help assess developmental issues that are not observable by an office visit.

Description

A pediatrician performs a thorough physical exam at birth to determine the physical status of the newborn. This exam includes assessing size, weight, head circumference, chest circumference, genitalia, physical mobility, eyes, ears, nose, mouth, lungs, heart, elimination, presence of **neonatal reflexes**, and much more. If the hospital pediatrician is not the same as the one used for follow-up exams, it is important to obtain the birth records to bring to the first office visit. Because the majority of states have laws governing newborn testing, most hospitals do a hearing screen, metabolic screen to assess thyroid activity, and screen for **phenylketonuria** (PKU), a genetic disorder than can be easily corrected by diet.

The first well-baby visit occurs at two weeks, and a **family** medical history is usually taken at this time. The baby's height, weight, and head circumference will be measured. (Head circumference is an indirect measure of brain growth.) Abnormally slow or fast growth may indicate a problem that needs investigation. The health-care provider can show parents a graph that indicates where the baby's measurements are on a standard growth curve. The trend in growth over time is more important than what a baby's weight and height are at any particular visit. A complete head-to-toe exam will be performed, during which the parent may want to ask questions related to birth marks or anything that is perceived as unusual.

In addition to the physical exam, the physician will ask questions related to what the baby can do physically, i.e., lift the head briefly, respond to loud sounds, etc. These are developmental milestones that represent a normal progression of physical and mental maturity. Although each baby develops differently, these milestones indicate a child's progress over time. The physician may want to observe development if possible. The physician may provide guidance related to possible dangers in the home, such as the importance of installing and maintaining smoke detectors, keeping a baby away from plastic bags, and never leaving the baby unattended while on a changing table. During this visit, the parent will be asked about the stress of having a new baby and the situation at home. It is a provider's responsibility to evaluate every child for abuse, and this questioning should not be taken personally. Finally, if the **hepatitis B vaccine** was not given in the hospital, the first shot may be given at this visit. All other vaccines begin at the two-month visit.

The two-month visit will be a repeat of the two week visit with a physical exam, developmental and behavioral **assessment**, guidance for upcoming developmental changes, and immunizations. During the visit, a parent should never hesitate to ask any question that will assure them the baby is healthy and progressing normally. It is a good idea to make a list of questions before the office visit, because many parents inevitably forget what they wanted to ask. Many parents inquire about what could be given to the baby if there is a reaction to the injections. The immunizations received at this time include:

- DTP vaccine (or DtaP, **diphtheria**, **tetanus**, pertussis)—DTP (or DtaP) injections are given as a series of five injections and usually at ages two months, four months, six months, 15–18 months, and four to six years of age. At age 11 or 12, Td vaccine (tetanus and diphtheria) should be given if at least five years have elapsed since the last dose of DTaP. Td boosters are recommended every 10 years.
- Hib vaccine (*Haemophilus influenzae* type B)—Hib is given as a series of four injections at ages two months, four months, and six months, with a booster dose at 12–15 months.
- **Polio vaccine** (IPV, or inactivated poliovirus vaccine)—This is usually given in a series of five vaccines, at ages two months, four months, six to 18 months, and four to six years.
- Hep B (**hepatitis B** vaccine)—Hep B is given as a series of three injections. The first is given soon after birth and sometimes before hospital discharge. It the mother of a newborn carries the hepatitis B virus (HBV) in her blood, the baby needs to receive the first shot within 12 hours of birth. If the mother shows no evidence of HBV in her blood, the first dose may be deferred to the two-month exam. If the first shot was given in the hospital, the second shot is given at two months and the third at six months. If the first shot was given at two months, the second is given at three to four months, and the third at six to 18 months.
- PCV (Pneumococcal vaccine)—The newest addition to the immunization schedule, these vaccinations are often given as a series of four injections at two months, four months, six months, and 12–15 months of age.

The four-month exam proceeds in the same manner as the previous two—a physical exam, developmental and behavioral assessment with questions about what has been observed at home, and more immunizations. At this period, the baby should be babbling and making noises, turning over, and trying to put everything in the mouth. Parents and the physician may discuss adding solid foods to the baby's diet, usually in the form of cereal. The immunizations given will depend on how and when the series was started.

The six-month exam is again similar. Generally the baby may be able to sit alone by this stage and may be ready to add pureed food to the diet. Once more the required immunizations will depend on the baby's history and previous injections. In October 2003, the Advisory Committee on Immunization Practices (ACIP) recommended universal influenza immunization of all children six through 23 months of age. They also recommend influenza immunization of household members and out-of-home caregivers of children younger than 24 months. Children under eight years of age who are receiving the **flu vaccine** for the first time should receive two doses separated by at least six weeks. Children under five years of age should not be vaccinated with the nasal-spray flu vaccine (LAIV).

The nine-month exam represents quite a change in baby from birth. The parent usually has many questions by this time regarding the baby's **sleep** habits, feeding patterns, teething, standing up, and so on. Again, a list is helpful to remind the parent of their own questions. The physical exam is performed, plotted on the standard growth curve, and any deviations are noted. Developmental assessment is commonly done by questioning. Does he/she pay attention to small objects and try to pick them up using his/her index finger and thumb? Can he/she locate sounds? Does he/she sit by himself/herself? Does she/he transfer objects from one hand to another? Does she/he show **stranger anxiety**? Guidance of what to expect over the next three months will again be provided. For example, the baby may begin to walk alone, make sounds, say the beginnings of words, or play peek-a-boo. The physician may discuss ways to keep a baby safe, including placing gates at the top and bottom of stairs; never leaving the baby alone in the bathtub; keeping the baby rear-facing in the car seat until 20 lbs (9 kg) and one year of age; and monitoring the temperature of the hot water heater to prevent **burns**. If the hepatitis B injection was not completed at the six month visit, it will be given at this exam.

Reaching the one-year exam is a big event in itself. The baby may be walking (assisted or unassisted) and talking a bit at this stage. The pediatrician will continue in the same manner as before—doing a physical exam and noting changes, asking questions about development, and inquiring about feeding and sleeping habits. A blood test for anemia may be performed at this visit if it was not done at the nine-month exam. Formula-fed babies are more at risk for iron deficiency than breast-fed babies. If there is a risk of lead paint exposure, a test for this may be done as well. The parent may have more questions relating to physical changes or developmental changes, because the baby is now on the verge of toddlerhood. Immunizations due at this time include:

- Measles, **mumps**, and **rubella** (MMR vaccine)—These are given by injection in two doses. The first is given at 12–15 months and the second is usually given before four to six years of age.
- Varicella (**chickenpox** vaccine)—Given by injection between the ages of 12–18 months or later for children who have not had chickenpox. Susceptible teens over 13 years of age should receive two doses given at least four weeks apart.
- Flu vaccine—For influenza, if needed.

Parents who may have to move during this first year or in any subsequent years should have the child's immunization and health record with them for a new provider to review.

The 15-month visit is very comparable to the previous visits but it does mark a few milestones in the child's health. It is a time when the little boy or girl that was in the baby you have known for the last 15 months can be seen. It is usually the last time immunizations are given before the pre-kindergarten shots. The typical physical exam and developmental evaluation will be performed and guidance on future development will be given. It is important to now be certain that doors and cabinets have locks, electrical sockets are covered, and objects on which the child can choke are removed from reach. The immunizations given at this visit will depend on those given at the prior visit.

The next exam will be at 18 months and will the same as the 15-month exam. If any immunizations were missed, they can be caught-up at this time. The same is true for the two-year check-up. Many pediatricians order various tests during the first two years depending on the family's history and the child's symptoms, i.e., urinalysis, tuberculin test, and blood tests. The American Academy of Pediatrics recommends cholesterol screening of children over age two whose parents have a history of cardiovascular disease before age 55, or have blood cholesterol levels above 240mg/dl.

Precautions

There are essentially no precautions to take for a visit. However, parents who may have a history of autoimmune disorders in their family should be aware that a preservative, thimersal, which contains mercury and is used in vaccines, has a possible link to **autism** and autoimmune disorders. Many pharmaceutical companies now use a safer preservative called 2-phenoxy ethanol.

Preparation

The primary preparation for a well-baby exam involves the parent or guardian making a list of questions for the pediatrician.

Aftercare

The only aftercare necessary is when an infant has a slight reaction to the immunizations. The provider needs to inform the parent what to expect and what can be done to alleviate symptoms. **Pain** at the immunization size and a slight **fever** are often easily treated with **acetaminophen**.

Risks

There are few risks associated with well-baby visits. The risks with the preservative, thimersal, which is used in vaccines are mentioned above. Serious reactions to vaccines are extremely rare. More common problems associated with doctor visits are dealing with fears babies have of strangers touching them, and managing the child's pain from vaccinations.

Parental concerns

Concerns of many parents revolve around developmental delays and what could be done to assist advancement through these milestones. The parent needs to remember that all babies and children advance at their own pace and should never be compared to other children but only to the progress made individually. Of course, some children do have conditions that preclude normal development, and any significant lag should be monitored and investigated by the physician.

Developmental milestones that usually occur within the first year period are:

- Month one: lift head; move head from side to side; prefers the human face over shapes; turns toward familiar sounds; blinks at bright lights; focuses on items 8–12 inches (20–30 cm) away; has strong reflexes.
- Month two: smiles; tracks objects with eyes; makes noises other than crying; may make sounds that resemble vowels, as "ah" or "ooh."
- Months three and four: tracks moving objects; grasps items with hands and reaches for dangling objects; controls head; may begin trying to sit alone; recognizes people or familiar objects; develops a social smile; babbles and amuses self; responds to colors and shades; explores objects with mouth; recognizes breast or bottle; communicates pain, loneliness, or discomfort through crying; responds to rattle or bell.
- Months five and six: begins teething process; uses hands in a raking fashion to get **toys** closer; experiments with cause and effect; sits by self with minimal support; opens mouth for spoon; rolls over and back; copies facial expressions; makes two-syllable sounds.
- Months seven and eight: can self-feed some finger foods; turns in direction of voice; plays peek-a-boo; imitates many sounds; distinguishes emotions by tone of voice; responds to name; experiments with gravity by dropping things; has different reactions for different family members; gets into **crawling** position; shows some **anxiety** when removed from parent.
- Months nine and 10: picks up tiny objects; begins to identify self in mirror; drops objects and looks for them; starts to understand object permanence; goes from

KEY TERMS

Diphtheria—A serious, frequently fatal, bacterial infection that affects the respiratory tract. Vaccinations given in childhood have made diphtheria very rare in the United States.

Haemophilus influenzae—An anaerobic bacteria associated with human respiratory infections, conjunctivitis, and meningitis.

Hepatitis B—An infection of the liver that is caused by a DNA virus, is transmitted by contaminated blood or blood derivatives in transfusions, by sexual contact with an infected person, or by the use of contaminated needles and instruments.

Pertussis—Whooping cough, a highly contagious disease of the respiratory system, usually affecting children, that is caused by the bacterium Bordetella pertussis and is characterized in its advanced stage by spasms of coughing interspersed with deep, noisy inspirations.

Polio—Poliomyelitis, an acute viral disease marked by inflammation of nerve cells of the brain stem and spinal cord and can cause paralysis.

Tetanus—A potentially fatal infection caused by a toxin produced by the bacterium *Clostridium tetani*. The bacteria usually enter the body through a wound and the toxin they produce affects the central nervous system causing painful and often violent muscular contractions. Commonly called lockjaw.

tummy to sitting by self; pulls to standing; transfers object from hand to hand; gets upset if toy removed.

- Months 11 and 12: says "ma-ma" and "da-da" discrimately; understands "no" claps hands; waves bye-bye; triples birth weight and is 29–32 inches (75–81 cm) long; puts objects into containers and pulls them out; crawls well; shakes head no; afraid of strangers; interested in books; identifies self in mirror; shares toys but wants them back.

See also Cognitive development; Fine motor skills; Gross motor skills.

Resources

BOOKS

Murkhoff, H., S. Hathaway, and A. Eisenberg. *What to Expect the First Year,* 2nd ed. New York: Workman Publishing Co., 2003.

James, Walene. *Immunization: The Reality Behind the Myth.* Westport, CT: Bergin & Garvey, 1995.

PERIODICALS

Osterrieth, Paul. "Oral polio vaccine: fact vs. fiction." *Vaccine* 22 (2004): 1831–5. Available online at: <www.elsevier.com/locate/vaccine>.

ORGANIZATIONS

American Academy of Pediatrics. 141 Northwest Point Blvd., Elk Grove Village, IL, 60007. (847) 434-4000. Web site: <www.aap.org>.

WEB SITES

Center of Disease Control and Prevention. 1600 Clifton Rd., Atlanta, GA 30333. *2004 Childhood and Adolescent Immunization Schedule.* Available online at: <www.cdc.gov/nip/recs/child-schedule.htm#Printable>.

Linda K. Bennington, MSN, CNS

Wermer's syndrome *see* **Multiple endocrine neoplasia syndromes**

Werndig-Hoffman disease *see* **Spinal muscular atrophy**

Wheezing *see* **Stridor**

Whooping cough

Definition

Whooping cough, also known as pertussis, is a highly contagious disease which causes classic spasms (paroxysms) of uncontrollable coughing, followed by a sharp, high-pitched intake of air which creates the characteristic whoop that is reflected in the disease's name.

Description

Whooping cough is caused by a bacteria called *Bordetella pertussis. B. pertussis* causes its most severe symptoms by attaching itself to those cells in the respiratory tract that have cilia. Cilia are small, hair-like projections that beat continuously and serve to constantly sweep the respiratory tract clean of such debris as mucus, bacteria, viruses, and dead cells. When *B. pertussis* interferes with this normal, cleansing function, mucus and cellular debris accumulate and cause constant irritation to the respiratory tract, triggering coughing and increasing further mucus production.

Whooping cough exists throughout the world. While people of any age can contract the disease, children under the age of two are at the highest risk for both the disease and for serious complications and death. Apparently, exposure to *B. pertussis* bacteria earlier in life gives individuals some immunity against infection with it later on. Subsequent infections resemble the **common cold**.

Demographics

According to the Centers for Disease Control and Prevention, since 1990, the reported incidence of pertussis has increased in the United States. Peaks occur at three to four year intervals. Since 1990, 14 states reported the number of cases of whooping cough to be more than two per 100,000 in the population. A high proportion of those cases occurred in persons aged ten years or older.

Nearly 75 percent of pertussis cases reported worldwide are in children; half of those children affected require **hospitalization**. Prior to effective immunization programs in the United States, pertussis was the major cause of death from infectious disease among individuals under the age of 14. Because developing countries as of 2004 did not have widespread immunization available, there continue to be about 50 million cases of pertussis every year across the globe, with 300,000 leading to death. About 38 percent of all hospitalizations from pertussis are in babies under the age of six months.

Causes and symptoms

Whooping cough has four somewhat overlapping stages: incubation, catarrhal stage, paroxysmal stage, and convalescent stage.

An individual usually acquires *B. pertussis* by inhaling droplets infected with the bacteria coughed into the air by someone already suffering with the infection. Incubation is the asymptomatic period (time when no evidence of disease is present) of seven to 14 days after breathing in the *B. pertussis* bacteria, during which the bacteria multiply and penetrate the lining tissues of the entire respiratory tract.

The catarrhal stage is often mistaken for an exceedingly heavy cold. People have teary eyes, sneezing, fatigue, poor appetite, and an extremely runny nose (rhinorrhea). This stage lasts approximately ten days to two weeks.

The paroxysmal stage, lasting two to four weeks, begins with the development of the characteristic whooping cough. Spasms of uncontrollable coughing, the whooping sound of the sharp inspiration of air, and **vomiting** are all hallmarks of this stage. The whoop is believed to occur due to inflammation and increased mucus, which narrow the breathing tubes, causing people to struggle to get air into their lungs; the effort results in intense exhaustion. The paroxysms (spasms) can be induced by over activity, feeding, crying, or even overhearing someone else **cough**.

The mucus that is produced during the paroxysmal stage is thicker and more difficult to clear than the more watery mucus of the catarrhal stage. Affected persons become increasingly exhausted when attempting to clear the respiratory tract through coughing. Severely ill children may have great difficulty maintaining the normal level of oxygen in their systems and may appear somewhat blue after a paroxysm of coughing, due to the low oxygen content of their blood. Such children may also suffer from swelling and degeneration of the brain (encephalopathy), which is believed to be caused both by lack of oxygen to the brain during paroxysms and by bleeding into the brain caused by increased pressure during coughing. Seizures may result from decreased oxygen to the brain. Some children have such greatly increased abdominal pressure during coughing that hernias result. Another complicating factor during this phase is the development of **pneumonia** from infection with another agent. The second pathogen successfully invades due to the person's already-weakened condition.

If individuals survive the paroxysmal stage, recovery occurs gradually during the convalescent stage, usually taking about three to four weeks. However, spasms of coughing may continue to occur over a period of months, especially when a person contracts a cold, or other respiratory infection.

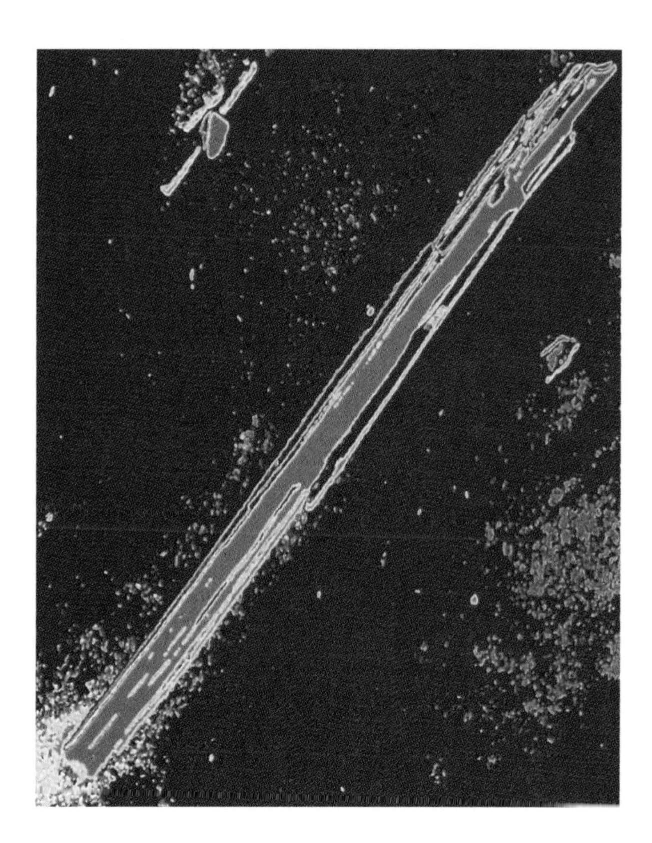

A magnified image of a pertussis toxin crystal that causes whooping cough. *(National Institutes of Health/Custom Medical Stock Photo.)*

When to call the doctor

A physician or other healthcare professional should be contacted during the first two months of life to arrange for immunization. Otherwise, a person with a cough that lasts for more than a few days should be seen by a healthcare professional.

Diagnosis

A diagnosis that is based solely on a person's symptoms is not particularly accurate, as the catarrhal stage may appear to be a heavy cold, a case of the flu, or a case of **bronchitis**. Other viruses and **tuberculosis** infections can cause symptoms similar to those found during the paroxysmal stage. The presence of a pertussis-like cough along with an increase of certain specific white blood cells (lymphocytes) is suggestive of pertussis (whooping cough). However, cough can occur from other pertussis-like viruses. The most accurate method of diagnosis is to culture (grow on a laboratory plate) the organisms obtained from swabbing mucus out of the nasopharynx (the breathing tube continuous with the nose). *B. pertussis* can then be identified by examining the culture under a microscope.

Treatment

Treatment with the antibiotic erythromycin is helpful only at very early stages of whooping cough, during incubation and early in the catarrhal stage. After the cilia and the cells bearing those cilia, are damaged, the process cannot be reversed. Such a person experiences the full progression of whooping cough symptoms; symptoms only improve when the old, damaged lining cells of the respiratory tract are replaced over time with new, healthy, cilia-bearing cells. However, treatment with erythromycin is still recommended, to decrease the likelihood of *B. pertussis* spreading. In fact, all members of the household in which an individual with whooping cough lives should be treated with erythromycin to prevent the spread of *B. pertussis* throughout the community. The only other treatment is supportive and involves careful monitoring of fluids to prevent **dehydration**, rest in a quiet, dark room to decrease paroxysms, and suctioning of mucus from the lungs.

Prognosis

Just under 1 percent of all cases of whooping cough in the United States result in death. Children who die of whooping cough usually have one or more of the following three conditions present:

- severe pneumonia, perhaps with accompanying encephalopathy
- extreme weight loss, weakness, and metabolic abnormalities due to persistent vomiting during paroxysms of coughing
- other pre-existing conditions, so that the person is already in a relatively weak, vulnerable state (such conditions may include low birth weight babies, poor **nutrition**, infection with the **measles** virus, presence of other respiratory or gastrointestinal infections or diseases)

Prevention

The mainstay of prevention lies in programs similar to the mass immunization program in the United States that begins immunization inoculations when infants are two months old. The pertussis vaccine, most often given as one immunization together with **diphtheria** and **tetanus**, has greatly reduced the incidence of whooping cough. Three injections (a primary and two booster shots) during early infancy confer complete immunity. Unfortunately, in the 1990s, there has been some concern about serious neurologic side effects from the vaccine itself. This concern led significant numbers of parents in England, Japan, and Sweden to avoid immunizing their children. Such actions led to major epidemics of the disease in those countries. However, several carefully constructed research studies disproved the idea that the pertussis vaccine is the cause of neurologic damage. Furthermore, a subsequent formulation of the pertussis vaccine became available. Unlike the former whole cell pertussis vaccine, which was composed of the entire bacterial cell that has been deactivated (and therefore unable to cause infection), the subsequent acellular pertussis vaccine does not use a whole cell of the bacteria but is comprised of between two and five chemical components of the *B. pertussis* bacteria. The acellular pertussis vaccine appears to greatly reduce the risk of unpleasant reactions to the vaccine, including high **fever** and discomfort following **vaccination**.

Nutritional concerns

Persons with whooping cough should be given adequate nutrition to assist their bodies in recovering from the infective agent.

Parental concerns

Parents should ensure that their children receive a complete series of immunizations (three injections) against whooping cough. Children who are suspected of having whooping cough should be seen by a healthcare professional. Early treatment is essential to limit the progression of the disease.

KEY TERMS

Cilia—Tiny hairlike projections on certain cells within the body. Cilia produce lashing or whipping movements to direct or cause motion of substances or fluids within the body. Within the respiratory tract, the cilia act to move mucus along, in an effort to continually flush out and clean the respiratory tract.

Encephalopathy—Any abnormality in the structure or function of brain tissues.

Hernia—A rupture in the wall of a body cavity, through which an organ may protrude.

Resources

BOOKS

Halperin, Scott A. "Pertussis and Other Bordetella Infections." In *Harrison's Principles of Internal Medicine*, 15th ed. Edited by Eugene Braunwald et al. New York: McGraw-Hill, 2001, pp. 949–52.

Johnston, Richard B. "Whooping Cough (Pertussis)." In *Cecil Textbook of Medicine*, 22nd ed. Edited by Lee Goldman et al. Philadelphia: Saunders, 2003, pp. 1829–30.

Lasky, Elizabeth. *Cecil Whooping Cough.* Portsmouth, NH: Heinemann, 2002.

Long, Sarah S. "Pertussis (Bordetella pertussis and B. parapertussis)." In *Nelson Textbook of Pediatrics*, 17th ed. Edited by Richard E. Behrman et al. Philadelphia: Saunders, 2003, pp. 908–11.

PERIODICALS

Andreae, M. C., et al. "Safety concerns regarding combination vaccines: the experience in Japan." *Vaccine* 22, no. 29–30 (2004): 3911–6.

Hviid, A., et al. "Impact of routine vaccination with a pertussis toxoid vaccine in Denmark." *Vaccine* 22, no. 27–28 (2004): 3530–4.

Steele, R. W. "Pertussis: is eradication achievable?" *Pediatric Annals* 33, no. 8 (2004): 525–34.

Zetterstrom, R. "Flawed reports of immunization complications: consequences for child health." *Acta Paediatrica* 93, no. 9 (2004): 1140–3.

WEB SITES

""Bordetella pertussis" and Whooping Cough." *University of Wisconsin-Madison.* Available online at <http://textbookofbacteriology.net/pertussis.html> (accessed January 9, 2005).

"Pertussis (Whooping Cough)." *Nemours Foundation.* Available online at <http://kidshealth.org/parent/infections/bacterial_viral/whooping_cough.html> (accessed January 9, 2005).

"Whooping Cough." *National Library of Medicine.* Available online at <www.nlm.nih.gov/medlineplus/whoopingcough.html> (accessed January 9, 2005).

"Whooping Cough, the DPT Vaccine, and Reducing Vaccine Reactions." *National Vaccine Information Center.* Available online at <www.909shot.com/Diseases/whooping.htm> (accessed January 9, 2005).

L. Fleming Fallon, Jr., MD, DrPH

Williams syndrome

Definition

A rare congenital (present from birth) genetic disorder that results in physical and developmental delays and problems.

Description

Williams syndrome (WS) is sometimes also referred to as Williams-Beuren syndrome. The disorder was first described by J. C. P. Williams of New Zealand in 1961. WS is a genetic disorder that can be inherited but often arises through spontaneous change in a chromosome (mutation). Children with WS usually have a variety of physical problems, especially problems with hearts defects. They have "elfin" faces and usually are of short stature. Children with WS are often overfriendly and have varying intellectual disabilities, with relatively good skills in music and language.

Demographics

WS is estimated to occur in about one in 20,000 births. It affects about the same number of boys and girls.

Causes and symptoms

WS is thought to be caused by a deletion of genetic information on chromosome 7. WS can be passed down from parent to child, but it often arises spontaneously. The way in which WS spontaneously arises is not clear.

Physical characteristics typical of Williams syndrome include a broad forehead, puffiness around the eyes, starburst eye pattern (usually in green or blue-eyed children), upturned nose, depressed nasal bridge, full lips, widely spaced teeth, and small chin. In addition, a child with Williams syndrome often exhibits sloping shoulders or an elongated neck. Many individuals with Williams syndrome have heart disorders, typically supravalvular aortic stenosis (SVAS), which is a narrowing of the aorta. Kidney and bladder problems are also common. Poor muscle tone and problems with the skeletal joints become evident as a child with Williams syndrome moves into **adolescence**. As the child gets older **hypertension** often becomes a problem.

Williams syndrome babies typically have a low birth weight and are often diagnosed as failing to thrive.

Elevated levels of calcium in the blood (hypercalcemia) may develop in infancy, but this usually resolves without intervention in the first two years. Digestive system symptoms such as **vomiting**, **constipation**, and feeding difficulties may occur. The infant may not be able to settle into a normal **sleep** pattern and may seem to be extremely sensitive to noise, exhibiting agitation or distress when exposed to high-pitched sounds, such as electrical appliances, motors, and loud bangs.

By the time a child with Williams syndrome is ready to enter school, mild to severe learning difficulties may appear, including impulsiveness and poor concentration. Contributing to classroom difficulties are problems with vision and spatial relations. Concepts involving numbers—especially math and time—appear to be more difficult for children with WS. In the later elementary school years, a child with Williams syndrome may be more adept at producing language than at comprehending it. Poor muscle tone and physical development continue to contribute to difficulties with gross and **fine motor skills**. The child with WS may have difficulty forming relationships with peers, preferring the company of younger children or adults. Throughout childhood, the child with Williams syndrome may exhibit deficits in the ability to reason and in self-help skills.

Children with WS are overly social and outgoing, inappropriately friendly to adults and unwary of strangers. They are usually talkative, with intense enthusiasm bordering on obsession for topics that interest them.

Special care needs to be taken when children with Williams syndrome are given anesthesia.

When to call the doctor

If a parent notices that a child has the symptoms of WS the doctor should be consulted.

Diagnosis

Williams syndrome is present from birth, although it often remains undiagnosed until a later stage of development. After a child has missed several developmental milestones, the pediatrician may refer the child to a specialist for diagnosis. Developmental delays that are typical include delay in sitting or walking. Also commonly observed are poor fine motor coordination and delayed development in language (although individuals with WS go on to develop excellent language skills). After reviewing the child's medical and **family** history, physical condition, and observing the child's behavior, a specialist in birth defects may identify Williams syndrome. In many cases, a heart murmur or suspected heart disorder may lead a cardiologist to suspect Williams syndrome, since an estimated 70 to 75 percent of people with WS have mild to severe cardiovascular problems.

Until the early 2000s, the diagnosis of WS made based on the child having a certain number of the symptoms of the disease. As of 2004, it was possible to test a child's genes for the deletion that causes WS. A test technique known as fluorescent in situ hybridization (FISH) may be used to detect this deletion. This test is only done when it is considered very likely that a child has WS because many of the clinical features are present.

Treatment

Williams syndrome cannot be cured, but the ensuing symptoms, developmental delays, learning problems, and behaviors can be treated. Many different experts work together to help develop a comprehensive treatment plan that is geared to the needs of a specific child. Children need to be monitored regularly by a doctor to ensure that problems, especially cardiac problems and hypertension, do not arise. If such problems do arise, they need to be treated promptly. Non-physical treatment often involves teaching children life skills that will eventually allow them to live on their own or with minimal care and to hold jobs. Specialists who can be helpful in treating Williams syndrome include the following:

- cardiologist, to diagnose and prescribe treatment for heart or circulatory problems
- endocrinologist, to prescribe treatment if elevated calcium levels are detected in infancy
- pediatric radiologist, to conduct diagnostic renal and bladder ultrasound tests to diagnose and prescribe treatment for any abnormalities present
- occupational therapist, to assess development delays and prescribe a plan for therapy to acquire skills necessary for daily living

Prognosis

In most cases, the child with WS will require multidisciplinary care throughout adult life, with continued medical **assessment** to diagnose and treat medical complications early. The ability to live independently and to work are usually not limited by the physical problems, which are treated successfully in the majority of cases. Rather, psychological characteristics and the inability to behave appropriately in social settings are more likely to prevent the individual from living and functioning completely on his or her own. However, each year more individuals with William syndrome are able to live independently in supervised apartment settings.

KEY TERMS

Fluorescence in situ hybridization (FISH)—A technique for diagnosing genetic disorders before birth by analyzing cells obtained by amniocentesis with DNA probes.

Hypercalcemia—A condition marked by abnormally high levels of calcium in the blood.

Supravalvular aortic stenosis (SVAS)—A narrowing of the aorta.

Prevention

There was as of 2004 no known way to prevent Williams syndrome.

Parental concerns

Children with Williams syndrome usually grow up physically healthy as long as they receive treatment for any problems, especially cardiac problems, that arise. The amount of independence that a child with Williams syndrome will eventually be able to achieve usually depends on the particular symptoms of that child.

Resources

BOOKS

Bellugi, Ursula, and Marie St. George, eds. *Journey from Cognition to Brain to Gene: Perspectives from Williams Syndrome.* Cambridge, MA: MIT Press, 2001.

Schiber, Barbara. *Fulfilling Dreams: A Handbook for Parents of Children with Williams Syndrome.* Clawson, MI: Williams Syndrome Association, 2000.

Semel, Eleanor, and Sue R. Rosner. *Understanding Williams Syndrome: Behavioral Patterns and Interventions.* Mahwah, NJ: L. Erlbaum, 2003.

PERIODICALS

Jason, Helen, et al. "Word Reading and Reading-Related Skills in Adolescents With Williams Syndrome." *Journal of Child Psychology and Psychiatry and Allied Disciplines*– 44 (May 2003): 57687.

Reis, Sally M., et al. "—Minds Music: Using a Talent Development Approach for Young Adults with Williams Syndrome." *Exceptional Children*– 69 (Spring 2003): 293314.

ORGANIZATIONS

Williams Syndrome Association. PO Box 297 Clawson, MI 480170297. Web site: <www.williams-syndrome.org>.

Williams Syndrome Foundation. Williams Syndrome Foundation, University of California, Irvine, CA 926972300. Web site: <www.wsf.org>

Tish Davidson, A.M.

Willi-Prader syndrome *see* **Prader-Willi syndrome**

Wilms' tumor

Definition

Wilms' tumor is a cancerous tumor of the kidney that usually occurs in young children.

Description

When an unborn baby is developing, the kidneys are formed from primitive cells. Over time, these cells become more specialized. The cells mature and organize into the normal kidney structure. Sometimes, clumps of these cells remain in their original, primitive form. If these more primitive cells begin to multiply after birth, they may ultimately form a large mass of abnormal cells. This is known as a Wilms' tumor. Wilms' tumor may occur in only one or in both kidneys. About 7 percent of all cases of Wilms' tumor occur bilaterally (in both kidneys simultaneously).

Wilms' tumor is a type of malignant tumor. This means that it is made up of cells that are significantly immature and abnormal. These cells are also capable of invading nearby structures within the kidney and traveling out of the kidney into other structures. Malignant cells can even travel through the body to invade other organ systems, most commonly the lungs and brain. These features of Wilms' tumor make it a type of **cancer** that, without treatment, would eventually cause death. However, advances in medicine between the 1980s and the early 2000s have made Wilms' tumor a very treatable form of cancer.

Wilms' tumor occurs almost exclusively in young children. The average patient is about three years old. Females are only slightly more likely than males to develop Wilms' tumors. In the United States, Wilms' tumor occurs in about eight children per million in white children under the age of 15 years. Wilms' tumor makes up about 6 percent of all childhood cancers and ranks as the second most frequent cancerous abdominal tumor in children. The rate is higher among African Americans and lower among Asian Americans. Wilms' tumors are found more commonly in patients with other types of birth defects. These defects include the following:

- absence of the colored part (the iris) of the eye (aniridia)
- enlargement of one arm, one leg, or half of the face (hemihypertrophy)
- certain birth defects of the urinary system or genitals
- certain genetic syndromes (WAGR syndrome, Denys-Drash syndrome, and Beckwith-Wiedemann syndrome)

Causes and symptoms

The cause of Wilms' tumor is not as of 2004 completely understood. Because 15 percent of all patients with this type of tumor have other inherited defects, it seems clear that at least some cases of Wilms' tumor may be due to an inherited alteration. It appears that the tendency to develop a Wilms' tumor can run in families. In fact, about 1.5 percent of all children with a Wilms' tumor have **family** members who have also had a Wilms' tumor. The genetic mechanisms associated with the disease are unusually complex.

Some patients with Wilms' tumor experience abdominal **pain**, **nausea**, **vomiting**, high blood pressure, or blood in the urine. However, the parents of many children with this type of tumor are the first to notice a firm, rounded mass in their child's abdomen. This discovery is often made while bathing or dressing the child and frequently occurs before any other symptoms appear. Rarely, a Wilms' tumor is diagnosed after there has been bleeding into the tumor, resulting in sudden swelling of the abdomen and a low red blood cell count (anemia).

About 5 percent of Wilms' tumor cases involve both kidneys during the initial evaluation. The tumor appears on either side equally. When pathologists look at these tumor cells under the microscope, they see great diversity in the types of cells. Some types of cells are associated with a more favorable outcome in the patient than others. In about 15 percent of cases, physicians find some degree of cancer spread (metastasis). The most common sites in the body where metastasis occurs are the liver and lungs.

Researchers have found evidence that certain types of lesions occur before the development of the Wilms' tumor. These lesions usually appear in the form of stromal, tubule, or blastemal cells.

Diagnosis

Children with Wilms' tumor generally first present to physicians with a swollen abdomen or with an obvious abdominal mass. The physician may also find that the child has **fever**, bloody urine, or abdominal pain. The physician will order a variety of tests before imaging is performed. These tests mostly involve blood analysis in the form of a white blood cell count, complete blood count, **platelet count**, and serum calcium evaluation. Liver and kidney function testing will also be performed as well as a urinalysis.

Initial diagnosis of Wilms' tumor is made by looking at the tumor using various imaging techniques. Ultrasound, **computed tomography** scans (CT scans) and **magnetic resonance imaging** (MRI scans) are helpful in diagnosing Wilms' tumor. Intravenous pyelography, in which a dye injected into a vein helps show the structures of the kidney, can also be used in diagnosing this type of tumor. Final diagnosis, however, depends on obtaining a tissue sample from the mass (biopsy) and examining it under a microscope in order to verify that it has the characteristics of a Wilms' tumor. This biopsy is usually done during surgery to remove or decrease the size of the tumor. Other studies (chest x rays, CT scan of the lungs, bone marrow biopsy) may also be done in order to see if the tumor has spread to other locations.

Treatment

Treatment for Wilms' tumor almost always begins with surgery to remove or decrease the size of the kidney tumor. Except in patients who have tumors in both kidneys, this surgery usually requires complete removal of the affected kidney. During surgery, the surrounding lymph nodes, the area around the kidneys, and the entire abdomen will also be examined. While the tumor can spread to these surrounding areas, it is less likely to do so compared to other types of cancer. In cases where the tumor affects both kidneys, surgeons will try to preserve the kidney with the smaller tumor by removing only a portion of the kidney, if possible. Additional biopsies of these areas may be done to see if the cancer has spread. The next treatment steps depend on whether the cancer has spread and if it has what other sites are involved. Samples of the tumor are also examined under a microscope to determine particular characteristics of the cells making up the tumor.

Information about the tumor cell type and the spread of the tumor is used in deciding the best kind of treatment for a particular patient. Treatment is usually a combination of surgery, medications used to kill cancer cells (**chemotherapy**), and x rays or other high-energy rays used to kill cancer cells (radiation therapy). These therapies are called adjuvant therapies, and this type of combination therapy has been shown to substantially improve outcome in patients with Wilms' tumor. It has long been known that Wilms' tumors respond to radiation therapy. Likewise, some types of chemotherapy have been found to be effective in treating Wilms' tumor. These effective drugs include dactinomycin, doxorubicin, vincristine, and cyclophosphamide. In rare cases, bone marrow transplantation may be used.

The National Wilms' Tumor Study Group developed a staging system to describe Wilms' tumors. All of the stages assume that surgical removal of the tumor has occurred. Stage I involves favorable Wilms' tumor cells and is usually treated successfully with combination chemotherapy involving dactinomycin and vincristine and without abdominal radiation therapy. Stage II tumors involving a favorable histology (cell characteristics) are usually treated with the same therapy as Stage I. Stage III tumors with favorable histology are usually treated with a combination chemotherapy with doxorubicin, dactinomycin, and vincristine along with radiation therapy to the abdomen. Stage IV disease with a favorable histology is generally treated with combination chemotherapy with dactinomycin, doxorubicin, and vincristine. These patients usually receive abdominal radiation therapy and lung radiation therapy if the tumor has spread to the lungs.

In the case of Stage II through IV tumors with unfavorable, or anaplastic, cells, then the previously-mentioned combination chemotherapy is used along with the drug cyclophosphamide. These patients also receive lung radiation therapy if the tumor has spread to the lungs. Another type of tumor cell can be present in Stages I through IV. This cell type is called clear cell sarcoma of the kidney. If this type of cell is present, then patients receive combination therapy with vincristine, doxorubicin, and dactinomycin. All of these patients receive abdominal radiation therapy and lung radiation therapy if the tumor has spread to the lungs.

Prognosis

The prognosis for patients with Wilms' tumor is quite good, compared to the prognosis for most types of cancer. The patients who have the best prognosis are usually those who have a small-sized tumor, a favorable cell type, are young (especially under two years of age), and have an early stage of cancer that has not spread. Modern treatments have been especially effective in the treatment of this cancer. Patients with the favorable type of cell have a long-term survival rate of 93 percent, whereas those with anaplasia have a long-term survival rate of 43 percent and those with the sarcoma form have a survival rate of 36 percent.

KEY TERMS

Biopsy—The surgical removal and microscopic examination of living tissue for diagnostic purposes or to follow the course of a disease. Most commonly the term refers to the collection and analysis of tissue from a suspected tumor to establish malignancy.

Blastemal—An immature material from which cells and tissues develop.

Cancer—A disease caused by uncontrolled growth of the body's cells.

Malignant—Cells that have been altered such that they have lost normal control mechanisms and are capable of local invasion and spread to other areas of the body. Often used to describe a cancer.

Sarcoma—A type of cancer that originates from connective tissue such as bone or muscle.

Stromal—Pertaining to the type of tissue that is associated with the support of an organ.

Tubule—Tissues and cells associated with the structures that connect the renal pelvis to the glomeruli.

Prevention

There are no known ways as of 2004 to prevent a Wilms' tumor, although it is important that children with birth defects associated with Wilms' tumor be carefully monitored.

Parental concerns

Clearly, a child who is undergoing the rigors of treatment for Wilms' tumor is going to have some very difficult times. Feeling ill may cause more irritability than usual. Parents will want to consult a dietician for advice on how to provide the best possible **nutrition** for their child, who may have a hard time eating due to nausea from treatment. The child's pediatrician can help provide some guidelines to help the family understand how the child's development may be affected by the illness and treatment. Support groups can be very helpful for families who are facing cancer and cancer treatment.

Resources

BOOKS

Jaffe, Norman, and Vicky Huff. "Neoplasms of the kidney." In *Nelson Textbook of Pediatrics*. Edited by Richard E. Behrman et al. Philadelphia: Saunders, 2004.

"Wilms' tumor." In *Campbell's Urology*, 8th ed. Edited by Meredith F. Campbell et al. St. Louis, MO: Elsevier, 2002.

ORGANIZATIONS

American Cancer Society. 1515 Clifton Rd. NE, Atlanta, GA 30329. Web site: <www.cancer.org>.

March of Dimes Birth Defects Foundation. 1275 Mamaroneck Ave., White Plains, NY 10605. Web site: <www.modimes.org>.

Mark A. Mitchell, M.D.
Rosalyn Carson-DeWitt, M.D.

Wiskott-Aldrich syndrome

Definition

Wiskott-Aldrich syndrome (WAS) is a rare inherited disorder marked by a low level of blood platelets, eczema, recurrent infections, and a high risk of leukemia or lymph node tumors.

Description

Wiskott-Aldrich syndrome (WAS) was named for the two physicians who reported the disorder. In 1937, A. Wiskott, a physician working in Munich, described two affected boys of German ancestry who had repeated infections, a skin rash, and poor blood-clotting ability. Nearly twenty years later, R. A. Aldrich reported similar symptoms in members of an American **family** of Dutch ancestry.

WAS is inherited as an X-linked genetic disorder and thus only affects males. The gene responsible for WAS is located on the short arm of the X chromosome. Since males have only one X chromosome they only have one copy of the gene. If that copy carries the abnormal gene, they have WAS. In contrast, females have two X chromosomes. They have a normal copy of the gene on one chromosome even if an abnormal gene is on the other because the abnormal gene is very rare. The normal copy on one X chromosome is usually sufficient to prevent females from having WAS. However, women who have one abnormal copy of the WAS gene are designated as carriers. While they will not have WAS, they have a 50 percent risk of passing the gene to each of their sons who will have WAS. Carrier females also have a 50 percent risk of passing the defective copy of the gene to their daughters who also become carriers.

Researchers identified the gene for WAS in 1994 and pinpointed its location on the short arm of the X chromosome. As of 2000, over 100 different mutations had been found in the gene among WAS patients. The fact that there are many mutations explains some of the variability of symptoms among boys with WAS. However, even within the same family, affected individuals with the identical WAS gene mutation may have different degrees of severity of the disease. The mild form, X-linked thrombocytopenia, is also caused by mutations in this same gene.

Demographics

The WAS syndrome affects one in every 250,000 male children and occurs worldwide. In the year 2000, scientists estimated that about 500 Americans had WAS.

Causes and symptoms

The syndrome is caused by a defect (mutation) in a specific gene called the WAS gene that normally codes for the protein named Wiskott-Aldrich syndrome protein (WASP). This vital protein is a component of cells that are important in the body's defense against infection (lymphocytes). The same protein also functions in the cells that help prevent bleeding (platelets). A less severe form of the disease, X-linked thrombocytopenia, affects mainly the platelets.

Increased susceptibility to infections, eczema, and excessive bleeding and bruising are the hallmarks of WAS, although the symptoms can vary significantly from one patient to another. The immune system of patients with WAS produces too few B and T cells. B cells are the cells in the body that make antibodies. There are many types of T cells. Both B and T cells are needed to defend the body against infection. Because both types of cells are affected, WAS patients are subject to repeated infections from bacteria, fungi, and viruses. Ear infections, **meningitis**, and **pneumonia** are common in boys with WAS.

WAS patients also have abnormal platelets, the specialized blood cells that help to form blood clots and control bleeding. In WAS, the platelets are often too few (called thrombocytopenia) and too small. Some of the earliest symptoms of the syndrome may be noted during early infancy, including excessive bleeding after a **cir-**

cumcision, bloody **diarrhea**, and a tendency to bruise very easily.

Some patients also have too few red blood cells (anemia) and an enlarged spleen (splenomegaly). About 10 percent of patients develop malignancies, usually leukemia or tumors in the lymph nodes (non-Hodgkin's lymphoma).

Diagnosis

The diagnosis of WAS is usually suspected in male infants who have excessive bleeding, eczema, and frequent bacterial or viral infections. Special blood tests can then be ordered to confirm WAS. The blood of Wiskott-Aldrich patients shows a low **platelet count** and a weak immune (antibody) response. Blood is analyzed to determine the quantity of immunoglobulins in the blood as well as the ability of the immune system to mount an antibody response against common pathogens. It is also possible to confirm the diagnosis by obtaining a small sample of the patient's blood and analyzing the DNA for a mutation in the WAS gene. Information about the exact mutation and the quantity of WAS protein the defective gene can produce may help predict the severity of the individual's condition.

Carrier testing

If the specific WAS gene mutation is identified in an affected child, that child's mother can then be tested to confirm that she carries the gene. Other members of the mother's family may also want to consider testing to find out if they carry the same gene mutation. The first step in studying other family members is for a geneticist or genetic counselor to obtain a detailed family history and construct a pedigree (family tree) to determine which family members should be offered testing.

Prenatal diagnosis

In families in which there one child has been born with WAS, prenatal testing should be offered in subsequent pregnancies. When the mother is a carrier, there is a 50 percent chance with each subsequent pregnancy that the new baby will receive the abnormal copy of the gene. The key is to first identify the particular WAS gene mutation in the child with WAS. Then, early in a pregnancy, cells can be obtained from the developing fetus by chorionic villus sampling or **amniocentesis** and checked for the same mutation. Women who carry the abnormal WAS gene and are considering prenatal diagnosis should discuss the risks and benefits of this type of testing with a geneticist or genetic counselor.

Treatment

Standard treatments for individuals with WAS include **antibiotics** for infections and platelet and red blood cell transfusions. Corticosteroids and immune globulin may be given in an attempt to improve thrombocytopenia. Eczema can be treated with corticosteroid creams applied directly to the skin. The spleen is sometimes removed to improve thrombocytopenia. In individuals with WAS, however, removal of the spleen also increases the risk of certain types of infections. About 50 percent of individuals with WAS are helped by treatment with transfer factor, which is a substance derived from the T cells of a healthy person. Transfer factor is given to improve both blood clotting and immune functions. Bone marrow transplantation has been successful in a number of cases. It has been most successful in boys under five years of age when the donor is a sibling whose tissue type closely matches that of the individual with WAS. As of 2000, attempts were also being made to treat individuals with WAS with umbilical cord blood from unrelated newborns in cases in which the individual diagnosed with WAS has no matched sibling donor.

Prognosis

The prognosis for males diagnosed with Wiskott-Adrich syndrome is poor. The average individual lives about eight years. Death usually occurs due to severe bleeding or overwhelming infection. Those who survive into **adolescence** often develop leukemia, lymphoma, or autoimmune diseases such as vasculitis, arthritis, inflammatory bowel disease, and kidney disease.

Prevention

Although there are no available treatments to prevent the development of WAS in an individual who receives the defective gene, prenatal genetic counseling can help couples determine their risk of having a baby with WAS.

Parental concerns

Caring for a baby or child with WAS is a highly stressful task. The child's healthcare provider should help the parents decide what steps will be necessary in order to decrease the child's risk of infection. Excellent hand washing and careful food handling should always be followed, but the healthcare provider should also provide guidance about other ways to avoid exposure to infectious disease. The parents will need to balance their child's need for a normal life with peer interaction and the desire to reduce the chance of exposure to serious

KEY TERMS

Amniocentesis—A procedure performed at 16–18 weeks of pregnancy in which a needle is inserted through a woman's abdomen into her uterus to draw out a small sample of the amniotic fluid from around the baby for analysis. Either the fluid itself or cells from the fluid can be used for a variety of tests to obtain information about genetic disorders and other medical conditions in the fetus.

Anemia—A condition in which there is an abnormally low number of red blood cells in the bloodstream. It may be due to loss of blood, an increase in red blood cell destruction, or a decrease in red blood cell production. Major symptoms are paleness, shortness of breath, unusually fast or strong heart beats, and tiredness.

Chorionic villus sampling—A procedure performed at 10 to 12 weeks of pregnancy in which a needle is inserted either through the mother's vagina or abdominal wall into the placenta to withdraw a small amount of chorionic membrane from around the early embryo. The amniotic fluid can be examined for signs of chromosome abnormalities or other genetic diseases.

Eczema—A superficial type of inflammation of the skin that may be very itchy and weeping in the early stages; later, the affected skin becomes crusted, scaly, and thick.

Immune system—The system of specialized organs, lymph nodes, and blood cells throughout the body that work together to defend the body against foreign invaders (bacteria, viruses, fungi, etc.).

Mutation—A permanent change in the genetic material that may alter a trait or characteristic of an individual, or manifest as disease. This change can be transmitted to offspring.

Platelet—A cell-like particle in the blood that plays an important role in blood clotting. Platelets are activated when an injury causes a blood vessel to break. They change shape from round to spiny, "sticking" to the broken vessel wall and to each other to begin the clotting process. In addition to physically plugging breaks in blood vessel walls, platelets also release chemicals that promote clotting.

Prenatal diagnosis—The determination of whether a fetus possesses a disease or disorder while it is still in the womb.

Syndrome—A group of signs and symptoms that collectively characterize a disease or disorder.

Thrombocytopenia—A persistent decrease in the number of blood platelets usually associated with hemorrhaging.

X-linked—A gene carried on the X chromosome, one of the two sex chromosomes.

infection. Furthermore, parents of children with WAS need to maintain a high level of suspicion; when a child with WAS begins to act ill or develop a **fever**, it may be necessary to immediately begin antibiotic treatment in order to avoid a more serious infection.

Resources

ORGANIZATIONS

Immune Deficiency Foundation. 25 W. Chesapeake Ave., Suite 206, Towson, MD 21204. Web site: <www.primaryimmune.org/inside.htm>.

WEB SITES

NORD—National Organization for Rare Disorders Inc. Available online at <www.rarediseases.org> (accessed January 9, 2005).

Sallie Boineau Freeman, PhD
Rosalyn Carson-DeWitt, MD

Working mothers

Definition

Working mothers, as a label, refers to women who are mothers and who work outside the home for income in addition to the work they perform at home in raising their children.

Demographics of working mothers

As of the early 2000s, more mothers in the United States are working than ever before. In the mid-1990s, 58 percent of mothers with children under the age of six, and nearly 75 percent of those with children between the ages of six and 18 were part of the paid labor force. The number of single mothers with full-time year-round jobs increased from 39 percent in 1996 to 49 percent in 2002. A growing percentage of married women living with their husbands work as well: 40 percent worked full time in 1992, compared with 16 percent in 1970. The rapid influx of women into the labor force that began in the 1970s was marked by the confidence of many women in their ability to successfully pursue a career while meeting the needs of their children. Throughout the 1970s and 1980s the dominant ideal of the working mother was the "Supermom"; juggling meetings, reports, and presentations with birthday parties, science projects, and soccer games. With growing numbers of women confronting the competing pressures of work and home life, observers predicted that these women's needs would be accommodated by significant changes in how things were managed on both fronts: a domestic revolution in sex roles at home and a major shift toward enlightened attitudes and policies toward women in the workplace. Although there have been some changes, they have not been substantial enough to prevent many working mothers from feeling that the price for "having it all" is too high. In the early twenty-first century, some working mothers express disenchantment with the "Supermom" ideal and look for alternatives to help them create a better balance between work and **family**.

Social and economic factors affecting working mothers

It is important to recognize that mothers in the U.S. workforce are not a homogeneous group of people; there is no typical working mother. Their attitudes toward their jobs and their decisions about child care are shaped by a range of social and economic factors:

- Marital status and family structure: Statistics indicate that working mothers who are married to the fathers of their children have more stable families. Working mothers who are single or in nontraditional relationships have a more difficult time maintaining family stability even apart from the demands of their jobs. As of 2003, only 68 percent of children in the United States under the age of 18 are living with both biological parents.
- Type of work: Working mothers in business or the professions usually earn more than women with less education and often find their work psychologically satisfying. They are also often on call outside the office and may find it difficult to leave the demands of their work behind when they go home.
- Income level: Working mothers with well-paying jobs have more choices about housing, transportation, and child care arrangements than those with limited incomes.
- Number, ages, and special needs of children: All other factors being equal, women with fewer, widely spaced, and healthy children find it easier to juggle the demands of a job with those of child care than women with several children born close together or women whose children suffer from chronic illnesses or developmental difficulties.
- Age: Working mothers over 40 are more likely to develop job-related health problems than younger women. In addition, women in this age group are often coping with the care of aging parents as well as their own offspring.

Description

There are a number of different strategies that working mothers use to balance the demands of workplace and family.

The "Mommy track"

Working mothers in many fields experience conflicts between motherhood and professional advancement. Many report that once they have children their professional aspirations are not taken as seriously by colleagues or superiors. In particular, if they quit working for a time to stay home with their children, the gap in their resumes is regarded with suspicion. One study found that the earnings of women with MBAs who took even nine months off after their children were born were still 17 percent lower 10 years later than those of employees with similar qualifications but no comparable gap in their employment record. Some women feel too threatened by the repercussions of time off the job to even take a maternity leave; others report problems on reentering the workforce after such a leave. Women in highly competitive professions are especially reluctant to lighten their work loads or schedules for **fear** that such measures will signal a lower level of commitment or ability than that of their peers, and they will be automatically assigned to the infamous "Mommy track." Many women—both with and without children—in traditionally male professions still earn lower salaries and carry greater workloads than those of male colleagues with comparable credentials and work experience because of the perception that they are not the breadwinners in their families.

Household responsibilities

On the home front, married working mothers, even those whose husbands espouse an egalitarian philosophy, still find themselves saddled with most of the housework and child care responsibilities. In effect, they often have the equivalent of two jobs, a phenomenon expressed in the title of Arlie Hochschild's highly regarded study *The Second Shift*. The book reported that the husbands of working mothers shoulder, on average, only one-third of the couple's household duties. Hochschild also noted that the tasks performed most often by men, such as repairs and home maintenance chores, can often be done at their convenience, as opposed to women's duties, such as cooking, which must be done on a daily basis and at specific times, giving women less control over their schedules. In 1990 a survey of 5,000 couples found that only 50 percent of husbands took out the garbage, 38 percent did laundry, and 14 percent ironed. Working mothers also received less help from their children, with one important exception—working single mothers, whose children helped out at home twice as much as children in other families. In addition, they often worked at tasks traditionally done by the opposite sex: boys cooked, cleaned, and babysat; girls helped with home repairs and yard work. A supplementary benefit of this development is that the daughters of single mothers have a greater than average likelihood of entering traditionally male professions offering higher pay and better opportunities for advancement.

There are signs that this "second shift" pattern may be changing. The U. S. Department of Commerce's Survey of Income and Program Participation (SIPP) reported in 1997 that one married father in four provided care for at least one child under the age of 15 while the child's mother was working. The study found that fathers who provided child care were more likely to be employed in lower-income occupations; more likely to work in service occupations (police, firefighting, maintenance, security); more likely to be military veterans; and more likely to live in the Northeast than in other parts of the United States.

Day care arrangements

More than 8 million school-age and 15 million preschool-age children in the United States are placed in the charge of substitute care givers during the hours their mothers are working. The major options for child care include staggered work hours that allow parents to meet all child care needs themselves; care by relatives or close friends; hiring a babysitter or housekeeper; and child care in a private home or at public facilities, including **day care** centers, nursery schools or preschools, and company-sponsored programs. In 1990, provisions for children under the age of five were split almost equally between in-home care by parents or other relatives and out-of-home care by nonrelatives. The percentage of child care provided by day care centers had increased from 6 percent in 1965 to 28 percent in 1990, partly because the influx of women into the workforce had narrowed the pool of female relatives and friends available to take care of other people's children. Between 1985 and 2005, employment by day care centers increased over 250 percent, representing a gain of almost 400,000 new jobs. Workplace child care facilities did not grow at the same rate: a 1995 survey found that only 10 percent of the nation's 681 major employers offered on-site care programs to their employees.

There are also a number of options for part-time child care as of the early 2000s:

- Parent babysitting cooperatives: A group of families share responsibilities for child care. Most cooperatives operate on a point basis rather than charging a monetary fee. Points are assigned to each family according to the number of its children and the number of hours of care they require.
- Sick child care: These programs send an adult caregiver to the home of a sick child on an as-needed basis. There are also day care programs run exclusively for chronically ill children.
- **Play** groups: Play groups are similar to cooperative babysitting in that several parents get together to provide opportunities for supervised play for a group of children. Most play groups meet once or twice a week for two or three hours.
- Drop-in care: Drop-in care is an option offered by some child care centers on an as-needed basis. Parents must pre-register and pay for this service, usually on an hourly basis. Drop-in care allows parents to bring their child in for three to four hours of supervised play on an occasional basis. Most child care centers that offer a drop-in option set an upper limit of 45–50 hours per child in any given month.

Alternative work arrangements

Given the failure of either home or workplace demands to ease significantly, working mothers routinely sacrifice time for themselves, and many report high levels of stress, **anxiety**, and fatigue. In addition, many still feel torn between the conflicting demands of family and career and guilt for not being able to spend more time with their children. Increasing numbers of working mothers also feel responsible for helping their own aging parents as they develop health problems and become less able to handle their own affairs. (And parents traditionally place greater demands on grown daughters than on sons.) In addition, working mothers are often expected to assume most of the responsibility in family emergencies, such as the illness of a child, which periodically disrupt their already overloaded schedules.

FLEX-TIME AND PART-TIME WORK Dissatisfied with the pressures and sacrifices of combining mothering with full-time work, many women have sought alternatives that allow them to relax the hectic pace of their lives but still maintain jobs and careers. According to one study, the number of companies offering some type of employment flexibility to their workers rose from 51 percent in 1990 to 73 percent in 1995. Fifty-five percent offered flex-time, while 51 percent offered part-time work. In 2004, *Working Mother* magazine reported that 97 percent of the companies on their list of the 100 best companies for mothers in the workforce offered compressed workweeks or job sharing opportunities. Mothers who work part-time gain more flexibility and more time with their children, as well as time to devote to their own needs. They are able to be there when their children get home from school, attend school plays and other functions, and take their children to doctor appointments without facing conflicts at work. However, part-time work also has disadvantages, aside from the cut in pay. Many part-timers carry workloads disproportionate to the number of hours they put in, sometimes being required to be available by telephone to clients or colleagues during their hours at home. In most cases they lose health insurance coverage. They may also face the resentment of coworkers who are required to keep a nine-to-five schedule. In addition, part-time work, like time taken off the job, usually places women at a disadvantage in terms of professional advancement. Promotions come later, and the "fast-track" positions are often out of reach altogether.

SHIFT WORK Another employment pattern that works well for some couples is working different job shifts, so that the father can provide child care when the mother is at work and vice versa. Many fathers in service occupations are able to share childcare responsibilities because they can work evening or night shifts. Although shift work has the advantage of allowing both parents to work full-time jobs and increase the family's total income, its disadvantage is that it decreases the time available for all family members to share meals and other activities. One study of 4,400 dual wage-earner Canadian families with children below the age of 11 found that children whose parents worked nonstandard schedules were more likely to develop difficulties than children whose parents did not do shift work. The researchers found that this correlation held whether it was the father, the mother, or both parents who worked nonstandard hours.

JOB SHARING An employment arrangement is job sharing, in which two people jointly fill one full-time position. They may alternate their hours in a variety of ways depending on what arrangement best suits the personal and professional needs of both people. For example, one pair of job sharers may work alternate days, while another arrangement may have each person working two days in a row and part of a third day. Job sharing opens up a wider arena of employment than that normally available to holders of traditional part-time jobs, and unlike most part-time employees, women who job share generally receive benefits prorated in accordance with the number of hours each works. For working mothers another advantage of job sharing is that people who job share often cover for each other when unusual family needs arise. In successful job sharing arrangements, the partners have a cooperative and supportive relationship, staying in close touch to maintain continuity on the job. Job sharing may be an option for a husband and wife in the same field as well as for two unrelated workers; some colleges and universities have allowed faculty couples to share a teaching position.

TELECOMMUTING The computer revolution makes possible yet another alternative work option for mothers seeking extra time and a more flexible schedule: telecommuting or working from home. According to reports in both the *Wall Street Journal* and the *New York Times*, telecommuting was the fastest-growing type of alternative work arrangement in the United States as of 2004. It can replace either all or part of one's hours at the workplace, and a telecommuter can work either part- or full-time. Telecommuters receive and send documents via their company's computer networks and can be available, if necessary, by e-mail, voice mail, and pager. Even when a telecommuting employee is expected to adhere to fixed work hours, the arrangement still provides a significant savings in time spent dressing for work, commuting, and socializing with other employees. Experts caution, however, that a woman who works at home should not expect to simultaneously take care of her children. Telecommuting mothers may want to arrange for child care during their working hours and may be interested in establishing boundaries between their work and their family life. Some employers may change the employment status of telecommuters to that of independent contractors, resulting in a loss of benefits for the workers.

ROLE REVERSAL A less common option is for the mother to become the sole family breadwinner while the father assumes the role of "househusband." Some men choose to become "stay-at-home dads" because their wives earn considerably higher salaries than they do; others simply want to spend more time with their children. One finding reported by the American Heart Association in April 2002, however, was that househusbands have a significantly higher risk of developing heart disease than men employed outside the home. The researchers who wrote the report theorized that the increased risk of heart disease is the result of stress caused by violating social expectations rather than the demands of child care.

SELF-EMPLOYMENT Some working mothers who want a challenging but flexible work schedule are drawn to self-employment. While the number of entrepreneurs in the United States increased 56 percent overall in the 1980s, the number of female entrepreneurs grew 82 percent. Women were expected to start 2.5 million companies in the 1990s and own half of all American businesses by 2000. In the early 1990s home-based businesses started by women were the fastest-growing type of small business. The number of women employed in these ventures tripled between 1985 and 1991. Self-employment accommodated a wide range of skills and employment backgrounds, from cooking and crafts to consulting, writing, and practicing tax law. Self-employed women working at home may put in long hours and those leaving high-powered corporate jobs usually earn less money, at least initially, but they gain flexibility and control over their schedules. Like telecommuters, self-employed women may want to daycare arrangements and find strategies for separating their business and personal lives. Fortunately, start-up costs for home-based businesses are relatively low. For women requiring assistance, low-interest loans can be obtained through the Small Business Administration, which also runs a variety of training and networking programs for female entrepreneurs. A number of states also offer programs that aid women-owned businesses.

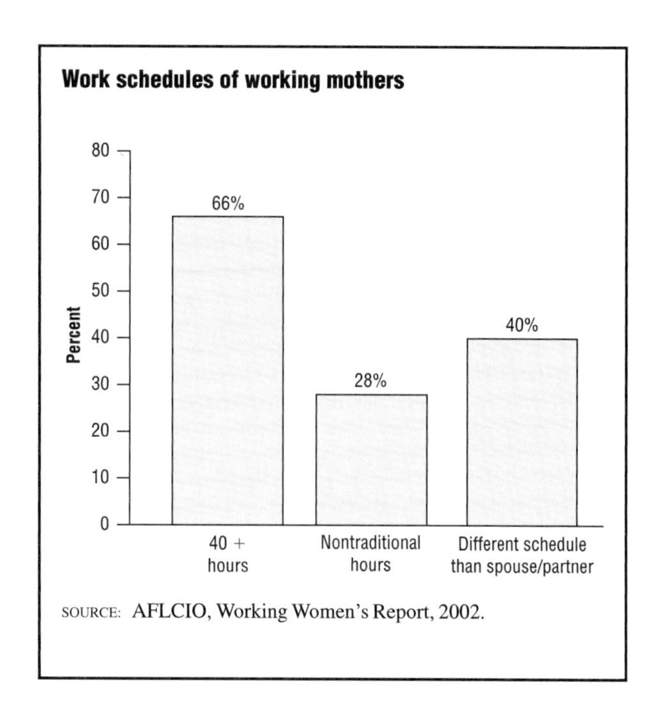

This graph of 2002 data on working mothers shows that well over half of all working mothers work over 40 hours a week. *(Graph by GGS Information Services.)*

Children of working mothers

The NICHD Study of Early Child Care, or SECC, was launched in 1991 with the enrollment of a diverse sample of 1364 children at ten different locations across the United States. Phase I of the SECC study followed these children from birth through three years of age and was completed in 1994. Phase II followed the 1226 children who remained in the study from age three through second grade between 1995 and 2000. Phase III follows the remaining 1100 participating children through 2005.

The SECC researchers reported in April 2001 that over 90 percent of the children enrolled in the study had spent some time in the care of people other than the mother, with 50 percent of the children spending 30 hours or more per week in the care of others. The report contained three major findings:

- A small minority of children (16%) who spent 30 hours or more per week in child care settings were reported to have higher levels of problem behaviors (such as fighting) than children who spent less time in care.
- The quality of nonmaternal child care makes a major difference. Children who were placed in high-quality childcare settings had better language skills and social/emotional development than those who were placed in centers with poorly trained adults or a high number of children per adult caregiver. (A good childcare center should have no more than five children per adult caregiver.) The study found that the type of care (relatives versus nonrelatives) was not significant.
- The most important single element in the children's development was their families of origin and the quality of their relationship with the mother when she was not at work.

Common problems

Common problems that working mothers confront can be summarized as follows:

- Logistical problems: These problems have to do with coordinating the details of the mother's working day, including use of the family car, arranging one's hours at work, dealing with a sick child, taking the child to the doctor for checkups, etc. Nursing mothers who return to work before an infant is weaned often have to make complicated arrangements for expressing and storing breast milk during the working day.
- Financial issues: These include the cost of child care arrangements, problems with continuity of health insurance coverage, and loss of income related to missed work. One report indicates that working mothers miss an average of 17 days of work per year due to children's healthcare needs.

- Professional development issues: Working mothers who cut back their employment to part-time work often lose opportunities for promotions as well as such benefits as health insurance. In addition, other employees often resent having to cover for working mothers who come in late, leave early, or miss work on short notice because of their child's needs.
- Health issues: Working mothers are often more vulnerable to stress-related illnesses than those who remain at home with their children. Some of the stress is related to ongoing social controversy about changing sex roles and family structures; many working mothers are made to feel guilty about their decision to continue working. In addition, working mothers often do not get enough **sleep**. Sleep deficits are known to make people more susceptible to infectious illnesses as well as automobile or workplace accidents.
- Interpersonal issues: Many working mothers, particularly those whose jobs give them little control over their work (such as food service, factory assembly-line work, retail sales work, etc.) come home at night feeling emotionally frustrated as well as physically tired. They are often concerned about the effects of job-related stress on other family members. If the family is coping with the care of elderly relatives as well as children, interpersonal stress is intensified. Parents may find themselves withdrawing emotionally from their children as well as quarreling more often with each other.

Parental concerns

Parental concerns about a mother's employment include several long-term as well as short-term issues:

- Children's future well-being: A major concern is the impact of the mother's work on her children's long-term academic success, mental health, and ability to form relationships. The SECC study appears to confirm earlier findings that the children of working mothers often benefit from her involvement in the outside world in terms of cultivating their own interests. In addition, good child care experiences often help children's social as well as emotional development.
- Stability of the marital relationship: Some couples worry about the impact of the mother's work on her relationship with her partner. In general, married couples appear to be less affected by this issue than cohabiting or lesbian couples. Many men feel less burdened by economic concerns when their wives are contributing to the family's income and report that having fewer anxieties about money actually improves their relationship with their spouse. On the other hand, some men whose wives earn higher incomes than they do may come to resent the demands of the wife's job.
- Household **safety** and security: Household safety is most likely to become an issue when the children of a working mother are too old for day care and must stay in an empty home for several hours after school before the parents return from work. Such children are sometimes called "latchkey children" because they are usually given a key to the house or apartment so that they can let themselves in when they get home. The American Academy of Adolescent and Child Psychiatry (AACAP) maintains that parents should limit as much as possible the time children must be at home alone because of the many risks involved. These risks range from physical dangers in the home (matches, knives, gas stoves, and household cleaners and other dangerous chemicals, etc.) to medical emergencies and strangers ringing the doorbell. AACAP recommends that older children should not be allowed access to "adult" channels on cable television or similar sites on the Internet. As a partial solution to parental concerns about latchkey children, some schools, churches, and synagogues offer after-school programs for children who would otherwise spend several hours at home alone.

KEY TERMS

Cohabitation—Sexual partners living together outside of marriage.

Flex-time—A system that allows employees to set their own work schedules within guidelines or limits set by the employer.

Latchkey child—A child who must spend part of the after-school day at home without supervision while the parents are at work. The name comes from the fact that such children are given a house or apartment key so that they can let themselves in when they get home from school.

Telecommuting—A form of employment in which the employee works at home on a computer linked to the company's central office.

See also Day care; Family; Parent-child relationships.

Resources

PERIODICALS

Anderson, S. G., and M. K. Eamon. "Health Coverage Instability for Mothers in Working Families." *Social Work* 49 (July 2004): 395–405.

Biagioli, Frances. "Returning to Work While Breastfeeding." *American Family Physician* 68 (December 1, 2003): 2201–17.

Draznin, J. "The 'Mommy Tenure Track.'" *Academic Medicine* 79 (April 2004): 289–90.

Harper, S. "Understanding the Implications of Population Ageing for Mid-Life Women." *Journal of the British Menopause Society* 9 (December 2003): 147–50.

Kestenbaum, C. J. "Having It All: The Professional Mother's Dilemma." *Journal of the American Academy of Psychoanalysis and Dynamic Psychiatry* 32 (Spring 2004): 117–24.

NICHD Early Child Care Research Network. "Nonmaternal Care and Family Factors in Early Development: An Overview of the NICHD Study of Early Child Care." *Journal of Applied Developmental Psychology* 22 (September-October 2001): 457–92.

Strazdins, L., et al. "Around-the-Clock: Parent Work Schedules and Children's Well-Being in a 24-H Economy." *Social Science and Medicine* 59 (October 2004): 1517–27.

Wentworth, D. K., and R. M. Chell. "The Role of Househusband and Housewife as Perceived by a College Population." *Journal of Psychology* 135 (November 2001): 639–50.

ORGANIZATIONS

American Academy of Child and Adolescent Psychiatry. 3615 Wisconsin Avenue, NW, Washington, DC 20016–3007. Web site: <www.aacap.org.>.

American Academy of Pediatrics. 141 Northwest Point Boulevard, Elk Grove Village, IL 60007. Web site: <www.aap.org>.

Families and Work Institute (FWI). 267 Fifth Avenue, Floor 2, New York, NY 10016. Web site: <www.familiesandwork.org>.

Mothers' Home Business Network. PO Box 423, East Meadow, NY 11554. Web site: <www.homeworkingmom.com>.

National Institute of Child Health and Human Development (NICHD). PO Box 3006, Rockville, MD 20847. Web site: <www.nichd.nih.gov>.

United States Small Business Administration, Online Women's Business Center. Office of Women's Business Ownership, Small Business Administration, 409 Third Street SW, Fourth Floor, Washington, DC 20416. Web site: <www.onlinewbc.gov>.

WEB SITES

"Better Benefits for Working Moms." *CNNMoney*, September 21, 2004. Available online at <http://money.cnn.com/2004/09/21/news/economy/working_mothers> (accessed December 4, 2004).

"Family Structure." *ChildTrendsDataBank*, 2004. Available online at <http://www.childtrendsdatabank.org/indicators/59FamilyStructure.cfm> (accessed December 4, 2004).

"NICHD Study of Early Child Care and Youth Development (SECC)." *National Institute of Child Health and Human Development (NICHD).* Available online at <http://secc.rti.org> (accessed December 4, 2004).

Rowland, Rhonda. "Beyond Tantrum Control: Stay-at-Home Dads Face Health Risks." *CNN.com*, April 25, 2002. Available online at <www.cnn.com/2002/HEALTH/conditions/04/24/heart.role.reversal> (accessed December 4, 2004).

"Secure Parental Employment." *Child Trends Data Bank*, 2003. Available online at <www.childtrendsdatabank.org/indicators/68ParentalEmployment.cfm> (accessed December 4, 2004).

Todd, Christine M. "The NICHD Child Care Study Results: What Do They Mean for Parents, Child-Care Professionals, Employers, and Decision Makers?" *National Network for Child Care*, 2002. Available online at <www.nncc.org/Research/NICHD.ECIresponse.html> (accessed December 4, 2004).

OTHER

American Academy of Child and Adolescent Psychiatry (AACAP). *Home Alone Children.* AACAP Facts for Families #46. Washington, DC: AACAP, 2000.

Scommegna, Paola. "Increased Cohabitation Changing Children's Family Settings." *Research on Today's Issues*, No. 13. Rockville, MD: NICHD, 2002.

Rebecca Frey, PhD

Wounds

Definition

A wound occurs when the integrity of any tissue is compromised (e.g. skin breaks, muscle tears, **burns**, or bone **fractures**). A wound may be caused by an act (such as a gunshot, a fall, or a surgical procedure), by an infectious disease, or by an underlying condition.

Description

Types and causes of wounds are wide ranging, and healthcare professionals have several different ways of classifying them. They may be chronic, such as the skin ulcers caused by **diabetes mellitus**; or acute, such as a gunshot wound or animal bite. Wounds may also be referred to as open, in which the skin has been compromised and underlying tissues are exposed, or closed, in which the skin has not been compromised, but trauma to underlying structures has occurred (e.g. a bruised rib or cerebral contusion). Emergency personnel and first-aid workers generally place acute wounds in one of eight categories:

- Abrasions. Also called scrapes, they occur when the skin is rubbed away by friction against another rough surface (e.g. rope burns and skinned knees).
- Avulsions. These occur when an entire structure or part of it is forcibly pulled away, such as the loss of a permanent tooth or an ear lobe. Explosions, gunshots, and animal **bites** may cause avulsions.
- Contusions. Also called **bruises**, these are the result of a forceful trauma that injures an internal structure without breaking the skin. Blows to the chest, abdomen, or head with a blunt instrument (e.g. a football or a fist) can cause contusions.
- Crush wounds. These occur when a heavy object falls onto a person, splitting the skin and shattering or tearing underlying structures.
- Cuts. These slicing wounds are made with a sharp instrument, leaving even edges. They may be as minimal as a paper cut or as significant as a surgical incision.
- Lacerations. Also called tears, these are separating wounds that produce ragged edges. They are produced by a tremendous force against the body, either from an internal source as in **childbirth**, or from an external source like a punch.
- Missile wounds. Also called velocity wounds, they are caused by an object entering the body at a high speed, typically a bullet.
- Punctures. These deep, narrow wounds are produced by sharp objects such as nails, knives, and broken glass.

Demographics

Wounds are very common. Nearly everyone has had a wound of one type or another. Minor wounds are especially common in childhood because children engage in so much rough-and-tumble **play**.

Causes and symptoms

Acute wounds have a wide range of causes. Often they are the unintentional results of motor vehicle accidents, falls, mishandling of sharp objects, or sports-related injury. Wounds may also be an intentional result of violence involving assault with weapons, including fists, knives, or guns.

The general symptoms of a wound are localized **pain** and bleeding. Specific symptoms include the following:

- An abrasion usually appears as lines of scraped skin with tiny spots of bleeding.
- An avulsion has heavy, rapid bleeding and a noticeable absence of tissue.
- A contusion may appear as a bruise beneath the skin or may appear only on imaging tests. An internal wound may also generate symptoms such as weakness, perspiration, and pain.
- A crush wound may have irregular margins like a laceration; however, the wound will be deeper and trauma to muscle and bone may be apparent.
- A cut may have little or profuse bleeding depending on its depth and length. Its even edges readily line up.
- A laceration too may have little or profuse bleeding, the tissue damage is generally greater, and the wound's ragged edges do not readily line up.
- A missile entry wound may be accompanied by an exit wound, and bleeding may be profuse, depending on the nature of the injury.
- A puncture wound's depth will be greater than its length; therefore, there is usually little bleeding around the outside of the wound and more bleeding inside, causing discoloration.

When to call the doctor

A child who has become impaled on a fixed object, such as a fence post or a stake in the ground, should only be moved by emergency medical personnel. **Foreign objects** embedded in the eye should only be removed by a doctor. Larger penetrating objects, such as a fishhook or an arrow, should only be removed by a doctor to prevent further damage as they exit.

Many times wounds can be treated at home; however, additional medical attention is necessary in several instances. Wounds which penetrate the muscle beneath the skin should be cleaned and treated by a doctor. Such a wound may require stitches to keep it closed during healing. Some deep wounds that do not extend to the underlying muscle may only require butterfly bandages to keep them closed during healing. Wounds to the face and neck, even small ones, should always be examined and treated by a doctor to preserve sensory function and minimize scarring. Deep wounds to the hands and wrists should be examined for nerve and tendon damage. Puncture wounds may require a **tetanus** shot to prevent serious infection. Animal bites should always be examined and the possibility of **rabies** infection determined.

Infection

Wounds that develop signs of infection should also be brought to a doctor's attention. Signs of infection are swelling, redness, tenderness, throbbing pain, localized warmth, **fever**, swollen lymph glands, the presence of pus either in the wound or draining from it, and red streaks spreading away from the wound.

Emergency treatment

Even with the loss of less than one quart of blood, a child may lose consciousness and go into traumatic shock. Because this condition is life-threatening, emergency medical assistance should be called immediately. If the child stops breathing, artificial respiration (also called mouth-to-mouth resuscitation or rescue breathing) should be administered. In the absence of a pulse, **cardiopulmonary resuscitation** (CPR) must be performed. Once the child is breathing unassisted, the bleeding may be attended to.

In cases of severe blood loss, medical treatment may include the intravenous replacement of body fluids. This treatment may be infusion with saline or plasma or a transfusion of whole blood.

Diagnosis

A diagnosis is made by visual examination and may be confirmed by a report of the causal events. Medical personnel will also assess the extent of the wound and what effect it has had on the patient's well being.

Treatment of wounds involves stopping any bleeding then cleaning and dressing the wound to prevent infection. Additional medical attention may be required if the effects of the wound have compromised the body's ability to function effectively.

Treatment

Stopping the bleeding

Most bleeding may be stopped by direct pressure. Direct pressure is applied by placing a clean cloth or dressing over the wound and pressing the palm of the hand over the entire area. This pressure limits local bleeding without disrupting a significant portion of the circulation. The cloth absorbs blood and allows clot formation. The clot should not be disturbed, so if blood soaks through the cloth, another cloth should be placed directly on top rather than replacing the original cloth.

If the wound is on an arm or leg that does not appear to have a broken bone, the wound should be elevated to a height above the child's heart while direct pressure is applied. Elevating the wound allows gravity to slow down the flow of blood to that area.

If severe bleeding cannot be stopped by direct pressure or with elevation, the next step is to apply pressure to the major artery supplying blood to the area of the wound. In the arm, pressure would be applied to the brachial artery by pressing the inside of the upper arm against the bone. In the leg, pressure would be applied to the femoral artery by pressing on the inner crease of the groin against the pelvic bone.

If the bleeding from an arm or leg is so extreme as to be life-threatening and if it cannot be stopped by any other means, a tourniquet may be required. However, in the process of limiting further blood loss, the tourniquet also drastically deprives the limb tissues of oxygen. As a result, the patient may live but the limb may die.

Dressing the wound

Once the bleeding has been stopped, cleaning and dressing the wound is important for preventing infection. Although the flowing blood flushes debris from the wound, running water should also be used to rinse away dirt. Embedded particles such as wood slivers and glass splinters, if not too deep, may be removed with a needle or pair of tweezers that has been sterilized in rubbing alcohol or in the heat of a flame. Once the wound has been cleared of foreign material and washed, it should be gently blotted dry, with care not to disturb the blood clot. An antibiotic ointment may be applied. The wound should then be covered with a clean dressing and bandaged to hold the dressing in place.

Alternative treatment

In addition to the conventional treatments described above, there are alternative therapies that may help support the injured person. Homeopathy can be very effective in acute wound situations. Ledum (*Ledum palustre*) is recommended for puncture wounds (taken internally). Calendula (*Calendula officinalis*) is the primary homeopathic remedy for wounds. An antiseptic, it is used topically as a succus (juice), tea, or salve. Another naturally occurring antiseptic is tea tree oil (*Melaleuca* spp.), which can be mixed with water for cleaning wounds. Aloe (*Aloe barbadensis*) can be applied topically to soothe skin during healing. When wounds affect the nerves, especially in the arms and legs, St. John's wort (*Hypericum perforatum*) can be helpful when taken internally or applied topically. Acupuncture can help support the healing process by restoring the energy flow in the meridians that have been affected by

KEY TERMS

Abrasion—Also called a scrape. The rubbing away of the skin surface by friction against another rough surface.

Avulsion—The forcible separation of a piece from the entire structure.

Butterfly bandage—A narrow strip of adhesive with wider flaring ends (shaped like butterfly wings) used to hold the edges of a wound together while it heals.

Cut—A slicing wound made with a sharp instrument, leaving even edges.

Laceration—A cut or separation of skin or other tissue by a tremendous force, producing irregular edges. Also called a tear.

Plasma—A watery fluid containing proteins, salts, and other substances that carries red blood cells, white blood cells, and platelets throughout the body. Plasma makes up 50% of human blood.

Puncture—An injury caused by a sharp, narrow object deeply penetrating the skin.

Tourniquet—Any device that is used to compress a blood vessel to stop bleeding or as part of collecting a blood sample. Phlebotomists usually use an elastic band as a tourniquet.

Traumatic shock—A condition of depressed body functions as a reaction to injury with loss of body fluids or lack of oxygen. Signs of traumatic shock include weak and rapid pulse, shallow and rapid breathing, and pale, cool, clammy skin.

Whole blood—Blood which contains red blood cells, white blood cells, and platelets in plasma.

the wound. In some cases, vitamin E taken orally or applied topically can speed healing and prevent scarring.

Prognosis

Without the complication of infection, most wounds heal well with time. Depending on the depth and size of the wound, it may or may not leave a visible scar. Individuals with certain underlying diseases such as diabetes mellitus may have more difficulty healing.

Prevention

Most actions that result in wounds are preventable. Injuries from motor vehicle accidents may be reduced by wearing seat belts and placing children in size-appropriate car seats in the back seat. Sharp, jagged, or pointed objects or machinery parts should be used according to the manufacturer's instructions and only for their intended purpose. Firearms and explosives should be used only by adults with explicit training; they should also be kept locked and away from children. Children engaging in **sports**, games, and recreational activities should wear proper protective equipment and follow **safety** rules.

Parental concerns

Children need to be instructed not to pick at scabs, because it slows the healing process and increases the risk of infection. Wounds tend to occur often during childhood, but most of them are minor and can successfully be treated at home.

Resources

BOOKS

Baranoski, Sharon, et al. *Wound Care Essentials: Practice Principles.* Philadelphia: Lippincott Williams & Wilkins, 2004.

Brown, Pamela A., et al. *Quick Reference to Wound Care.* Sudbury, MA: Jones & Bartlett Publishers, 2005.

ORGANIZATIONS

American Medical Association. 515 N. State Street Chicago, IL 60610. Web site: <http://www.ama-assn.org>.

Tish Davidson, A.M.
Bethany Thivierge

Wryneck

Definition

Wryneck, also called twisted neck or torticollis, is a deformity in which the neck is twisted and held at an angle to one side. A congenital (present at birth) form called congenital torticollis is the most common type of wryneck seen in children.

Description

The sternocleidomastoid (SCM) muscle runs down either side of the neck. One end is attached to the occipital bone of the skull. The other end splits, with one end attaching to the clavicle (collarbone) and the other to the top of the sternum (breastbone). This muscle is involved in the complex movements of flexing the neck bones (cervical spine) and rotating the head up and down and sideways. Wryneck affects the SCM muscle, usually on only one side of the neck, causing the neck to spasm painfully and twist.

There are several different types of wryneck. Acute wryneck is the most common type. It develops suddenly, often for no apparent reason, and causes painful spasms that make the individual tilt the neck at an angle. The condition lasts one to two weeks, then symptoms disappear on their own without medical intervention. This type of wryneck is seen most often in older children and adults.

Adults can also develop spasmodic torticollis with head tilt and jerky head movements. This condition can develop from injury to the bones of the neck or because of infection, inflammation, or tumors of the soft tissue of the head and neck. Most often adult torticollis develops between the ages of 30 and 60. Adult onset torticollis is not be discussed here.

Congenital muscular torticollis is a neck deformity that affects newborns. It limits the range of neck motion and causes infants to tilt their head. It is the most common type of wryneck seen in young children and is different from acute wryneck, because it does not cause **pain** and does not resolve on its own. It arises from different causes than adult-onset torticollis.

Infants who have congenital muscular torticollis appear normal when they are born. However, within about a month, they often develop a non-tender lump on the side of the neck. Although this lump disappears by itself after about three months, the SCM muscle becomes tight, contracted, and fibrous. It does not stretch. The child then begins to tilt his head toward the affected side and point his chin toward the opposite shoulder. About three-quarters of the time, the right side is affected, causing the head to tilt to the right.

Demographics

Congenital torticollis is a rare disorder. It affects fewer than 0.4 percent of newborns. It is more common in first children than in later children and appears to be more common in babies born with a breech presentation (feet first). For reasons that are not understood, about 20 percent of children with congenital muscular torticollis also have **congenital hip dysplasia**. Hip dysplasia is a deformity in which the ball and socket of the hip joint do not mate properly.

Causes and symptoms

Congenital torticollis is thought to be caused by trauma around the time of birth. There are two theories about how this trauma occurs. One theory suggests that damage occurs during the birth causing a blood clot to form in the SCM muscle. This blood clot eventually leads to scarring in the muscle. The scar tissue does not stretch and causes the muscle to shorten and pull the neck out of position. Support for this theory comes from the observation that children with congenital torticollis are often breech or difficult forceps deliveries.

A second theory is that the trauma occurs before birth. It is believed that either pressure on the SCM muscle due to position of the head in the uterus causes the muscle to become fibrous and shorten or that the blood supply to the muscle is disturbed and the muscle becomes scarred. In either case, the result is scarring and shortening of the SCM muscle.

In rare cases, congenital torticollis can also be a symptom of other congenital disorders including abnormalities of the neck vertebra such as **spina bifida** or Arnold-Chiari syndrome. Torticollis can also be caused at an older age by fracture or dislocation of the neck vertebra or juvenile rheumatoid arthritis.

The causes of acute wryneck in older children and adults are not usually clear but seem to be related to wrenching the neck muscles, sleeping with the neck in an odd position or similar causes. Acute wryneck is briefly uncomfortable but not serious.

Symptoms of congenital torticollis are a painless mass on the neck appearing during the first two months of life and a persistent tilt of the head to one side for no other apparent reason. The child has limited ability to turn his head or move his neck (limited range of motion).

Symptoms of acute wryneck are sudden development (often overnight) of pain and stiffness in the neck sometimes accompanied by **muscle spasms** that cause an individual to hold the neck at an angle to try to relieve the pain.

When to call the doctor

Parents of newborns should call the doctor if they notice a lump on their child's neck or any time that their child persists in holding the head at an angle.

Diagnosis

Normally x rays of the neck are done to check for **fractures**. A **computed tomography** (CT) scan and/or a **magnetic resonance imaging** (MRI) scan is done to check for abnormalities in the soft tissue, such as tumors. Electromyography (EMG) is a technique that records the electrical activity of skeletal muscles. This exam can be useful in determining the extent of muscle and nerve involvement. Electromyography is usually done before surgery.

Treatment

Treatment should begin immediately for infants with torticollis. Delayed treatment increases the chance that the head tilt will not be reversed by non-surgical means. In addition, as the child grows, the face on the tilted side may become flattened. This flattening can be reversed while the bones are young and soft but after one year of age is likely to be permanent. Another reason to begin treatment early is that children with head tilt have more difficulty learning to walk and fall more often because their balance is affected by the way their head is twisted to one side of the body.

Conservative treatment

Conservative treatment for congenital torticollis should begin as soon as the condition is diagnosed. Physical therapy is begun with turning and bending the child's head four to six times per day for 15 to 20 minutes at a time. The goal of the physical therapy is to stretch and loosen the muscle and improve the range of motion. Physical therapy is continued until the child is at least one year old before surgery is considered.

Parents can supplement physical therapy by placing **toys** in positions such that the child must turn his head to see the object. This encourages use of the affected muscle. If there is improvement in the angle of head tilt and range of motion, therapy is continued. If there is no improvement after at least one year, surgery is considered.

Another conservative treatment to supplement stretching exercises is a tubular orthosis for torticollis (TOT) collar. The TOT collar is fitted by a physical therapist on infants who are at least four months old. It is made of soft plastic tubing with hard wedges of plastic inserted on the tilt side. When the head tilts into the hard plastic, it is uncomfortable, so the child tries to straighten his neck, thus exercising and stretching the affected muscles. Children wear the collar while awake and directly supervised from the age of about four months until they begin to walk.

When congenital torticollis is caused by deformities of the neck bones (vertebrae), conservative treatment involves the use of neck braces or body jackets.

Acute wryneck is treated with heat and over-the-counter non-aspirin pain medication (**acetaminophen**, ibuprofen).

Surgical treatment

The goal of surgery in congenital muscular torticollis is to cut and then reattach the SCM muscle in a way that will remove the constricting bands of fibrous tissue, improve range of motion, and allow the head to be held vertically. Several different surgical techniques can be used. A uniploar SCM release, sometimes called an inferior open tenotomy of the SCM, cuts and then reattaches the SCM muscle where it meets both the breastbone and collarbone. This operation requires only one incision. A bipolar SCM release, also called a bipolar z-plasty, releases muscle where it is attached to the skull and at the collarbone. It requires two incisions. The SCM muscle is cut apart in a Z and then reattached. An endoscopic technique has been pioneered by plastic surgeons. This surgery involves making a small incision behind the ear and with the help of an endoscope clipping the muscle. Other surgeries are done when the cause of torticollis is a bone deformity.

After surgery children are fitted with a soft cervical collar that is worn continuously except during physical therapy and bathing or a stiff orthopedic collar that is worn during waking hours except for physical therapy. These collars are worn for about 10 weeks while the muscles heal and strengthen. Physical therapy begins about one week after surgery. The therapy involves stretching and strengthening exercises for the neck. Surgery does not instantly allow the head to be held vertically, so physical therapy and home exercises continue at least until the head tilt disappears.

Alternative treatment

Massage is said to be helpful both in stretching and releasing the muscles as a supplement, but not a replacement for, physical therapy.

Prognosis

When discovered during the first few months of life and treated promptly and consistently with stretching exercises, about 80 to 90 percent of children recover from uncomplicated congenital muscular torticollis with conservative treatment alone. Surgery is highly successful on children who do not respond to conservative treatment, so long as their torticollis is caused by restriction of the SCM muscle. In cases where torticollis is caused by or complicated by bone deformities or other congenital defects, the outcome is less likely to be successful.

KEY TERMS

Arnold-Chiari syndrome—A congenital malformation of the base of the brain.

Cervical spine—The seven bones of the neck that form the uppermost part of the spinal column.

Endoscope—A medical instrument that can be passed into an area of the body (the bladder or intestine, for example) to allow visual examination of that area. The endoscope usually has a fiberoptic camera that allows a greatly magnified image to be shown on a television screen viewed by the operator. Many endoscopes also allow the operator to retrieve a small sample (biopsy) of the area being examined, to more closely view the tissue under a microscope.

Spina bifida—A birth defect (a congenital malformation) in which part of the vertebrae fail to develop completely so that a portion of the spinal cord, which is normally protected within the vertebral column, is exposed. People with spina bifida can suffer from bladder and bowel incontinence, cognitive (learning) problems, and limited mobility.

Torticollis is unlikely to recur if stretching and flexibility exercises for the neck are continued.

Prevention

There is no sure way to prevent wryneck and congenital torticollis; however, care should be taken to avoid as much trauma to the child as possible during delivery.

Parental concerns

Parents' concerns often are focused on the psychological impact of torticollis in children who do to respond completely to treatment. Holding the head at an angle is an obvious deformity that can cause a child to retreat from social situations. The parents of a young child who has head tilt and is just learning to walk may also be concerned about the frequency with which their child loses his balance, increasing the risk of injury.

Resources

BOOKS

Rakel, Robert E. "Torticollis." In *Textbook of Family Practice*, 6th ed. Philadelphia: W. B. Saunders Company, 2002, pp. 902–03.

ORGANIZATIONS

American Academy of Orthopaedic Surgeons. 6300 North River Road Rosemont, Illinois 60018–4262. Web site: <www.aaos.org>.

WEB SITES

"Online Service Fact Sheet Congenital Torticollis (Twisted Neck)." *American Academy of Orthopaedic Surgeons*, June 2004. Available online at <www.orthoinfo.aaos.org/fact/thr_report.cfm?survey=survey> (accessed October 27, 2004).

Othee, Gurdeep S., and Carl R. Menckhoff. "Torticollis." *eMedicine Medical Library*. Available online at <www.emedicine.com/orthoped/topic452.htm> (accessed October 27, 2004).

Reynolds, Norman C., and Ma Jianxin. "Torticollis." *eMedicine Medical Library*, July 1, 2004. Available online at <www.emedicine.com/neuro/topic377.htm> (accessed October 27, 2004).

Ross, Michael, and Susan Dufel. "Torticollis." *eMedicine Medical Library*, August 17, 2004. Available online at <www.emedicine.com/emerg/topic597.htm> (accessed October 27, 2004)

Tish Davidson, A.M.

X rays

Definition

X rays are electromagnetic radiation that differentially penetrates structures within the body and creates images of these structures on photographic film or a fluorescent screen. These images are called diagnostic x rays.

Purpose

Diagnostic x rays are useful in detecting abnormalities within the body. They are a painless, non-invasive way to help diagnose problems such as broken bones, tumors, dental decay, and the presence of foreign bodies.

Description

X rays are a form of radiation similar to light rays, except that they are more energetic than light rays and are invisible to the human eye. They are created when an electric current is passed through a vacuum tube. X rays were accidentally discovered in 1895 by German physicist Wilhem Roentgen (1845-1923), who was later awarded the first Nobel Prize in physics for his discovery. Roentgen was also a photographer and almost immediately realized that the shadows created when x rays passed through the body could be permanently recorded on photographic plates. His first x-ray picture was of his wife's hand. Within a few years, x rays became a valued diagnostic tool of physicians world-wide.

How x rays work

X rays pass easily through air and soft tissue of the body. When they encounter more dense material, such as a tumor, bone, or a metal fragment, they are stopped. Diagnostic x rays are performed by positioning the part of the body to be examined between a focused beam of x rays and a plate containing film. This process is painless. The greater the density of the material that the x rays pass through, the more rays are absorbed. Thus bone absorbs more x rays than muscle or fat, and tumors may absorb more x rays than surrounding tissue. The x rays that pass through the body strike the photographic plate and interact with silver molecules on the surface of the film.

Once the film plates have been processed, dense material such as bone shows up as white, while softer tissue shows up as shades of gray, and airspaces look black. A radiologist, who is a physician trained to interpret diagnostic x rays, examines the pictures and reports to the doctor who ordered the tests. Plain film x rays normally take only a few minutes to perform and can be done in a hospital, radiological center, clinic, doctor's or dentist's office, or at bedside with a portable x-ray machine.

Special types of x-ray procedures

Mammograms are fixed plate x rays that are designed to locate tumors within the breasts. Dental x rays are designed to locate decay within the tooth. Sometimes a liquid called contrast material (for example, barium) is used to help outline internal organs such as the intestines. The contrast material absorbs x rays, helping to make soft tissue more easily visible on the x-ray films. Contrast material is commonly used in making x rays of the digestive system. The contrast liquid can be swallowed or injected, depending on the part of the body being x rayed. This may cause some minor discomfort.

Fluoroscopy is a special x-ray technique that produces real-time images on a television monitor. With fluoroscopy, contrast material is injected into a blood vessel. The physician can then watch the real-time movement of the contrast material to determine if there are blockages in circulation. Fluoroscopy is also used to help guide catheters into place in the heart during cardiac catheterization or to guide an endoscope during endoscopic surgery.

Computed tomography or CT scan works on the same principles as fixed plate x rays, only with a CT scan, an x ray tube rotates around the individual, taking hundreds of images that are then compiled by a computer to produce a two-dimensional cross section of the body. Although many images are taken to produce a CT scan, the total dose of radiation the individual is exposed to is low. Other common imaging techniques such as **magnetic resonance imaging** (MRI) and ultrasound do not use x rays.

How x rays are performed

Fixed plate x rays are extremely common diagnostic tests. A trained x-ray technologist takes the x ray. The individual is first asked to remove clothing and jewelry and to wear a hospital gown. The x ray technologist positions the patient appropriately, so that the part of the body to be x rayed will be between the x-ray beam and the film plate. Usually the individual either lies on an adjustable table or stands. Parts of the body that are especially sensitive to damage by x rays (for example, the reproductive organs, the thyroid) are shielded with a lead apron. Lead is very dense and effectively protects the body by stopping all x rays.

It is essential to remain motionless during the x ray, since movement causes the resulting picture to be blurry. Sometimes patients are asked to hold their breath briefly during the procedure. Children who are not old enough follow directions or who cannot stay still may need to be restrained or given medication to sedate them in order to keep them still enough to obtain useful results. Sometimes parents can stay with children during an x ray, unless the mother is pregnant, in which case she must protect the fetus from x-ray exposure.

If a contrast material is to be used, the individual will be given special instructions to prepare for the procedure and may be asked to remain afterwards until recovery is complete. (See Preparation and Aftercare below.)

Precautions

Although unnecessary exposure to radiation should be avoided, the low levels of radiation one is exposed to during an x ray does not cause harm with a few exceptions. Pregnant women should not have x rays unless in emergencies the benefits highly outweigh the risks. Exposure of the fetus to x rays, especially during early pregnancy can increase the risk of the child later developing leukemia. Body parts not being x rayed should be shielded with a lead apron, especially the testes, ovaries, and thyroid.

KEY TERMS

Contrast agent—Also called a contrast medium, this is usually a barium or iodine dye that is injected into the area under investigation. The dye makes the interior body parts more visible on an x-ray film.

Electromagnetic radiation—Packets of energy that develop when an electric current passes through a vacuum tube.

Endoscope—A medical instrument that can be passed into an area of the body (the bladder or intestine, for example) to allow visual examination of that area. The endoscope usually has a fiberoptic camera that allows a greatly magnified image to be shown on a television screen viewed by the operator. Many endoscopes also allow the operator to retrieve a small sample (biopsy) of the area being examined, to more closely view the tissue under a microscope.

Preparation

No special preparation is needed for fixed plate x rays unless contrast material is used. When x rays are scheduled that involve the use of contrast material, the physician will give specific instructions for preparation. For example, in a lower GI series, the individual may have to fast and use special **laxatives** to cleanse the bowel before swallowing the contrast material. Parents can prepare children for x rays be explaining what will happen and that these tests are short and painless.

Aftercare

Little aftercare is needed following an x ray. In complicated x rays where contrast material is injected into a blood vessel, the individual may need to remain under medical care for a short while to assure that there is no allergic reaction to the contrast material and recovery is complete.

Risks

Low dose exposure to x rays creates minimal cell damage and minimal risk when x rays are performed in an accredited facility. There is an increased risk that a developing fetus will develop leukemia during childhood if exposed to x-ray radiation; pregnant or potentially pregnant women should avoid x rays. There is also a slight risk of an allergic reaction to the contrast material or dye used in certain x rays.

Parental concerns

Some parents are concerned about health consequences of their child's exposure to x-ray radiation. However, doses of radiation received in most x rays are quite similar to the environmental (background) radiation one is exposed to simply by living on Earth. Although unnecessary x rays should be avoided, in most cases, the benefits greatly outweigh the potentially small increased risk of exposure.

See also Computed tomography.

Resources

BOOKS

Faculty Members at the Yale University School of Medicine and G.S. Sharpe Communications, Inc. "Chapter 3 Diagnostic Imaging." *The Patient's Guide to Medical Tests, 2nd ed. New York: Houghton Mifflin, 2002.*

PERIODICALS

Cooper, Phyllis G. "X-Rays During Pregnancy." *Clinical Reference Systems* Annual, 2002 p3574.

ORGANIZATIONS

American College of radiology 1891 Preston White Drive, Reston, Virginia 20191-4397. Telephone (800) 227-5463. <www/acr.org/flash.html>

Radiological Society of North America. 820 Jorie Boulevard, Oak Brook, Illinois 60523-2251. Telephone: (800) 381-6660. <www.rsna.org>

WEB SITES

Cameron, John R. "Understanding X-rays." *eMedicine.com Consumer Health* 2003 [cited 22 September 2004]. <www.emedicinehealth.com/fulltext/12071.htm>

Children's Virtual Hospital. "X-Rays." *Children's Hospital of Iowa/University of Iowa.* 2004 [cited 18 September 2004]. <www.vh.org/pediatric/patient/pediatrics/cqqa/xrays.html>

Harvard Medical Schools Consumer Health Education. "X-Rays." *InteliHealth Procedures and Treatments* 3 June 2003 (cited 22 September 2004) <www.intelihealth.com>

Tish Davidson, A.M.

XLA *see* **Bruton's agammaglobulinemia**

X-linked agammaglobulinemia *see* **Bruton's agammaglobulinemia**

XXY syndrome *see* **Klinefelter syndrome**

Yoga

Definition

The term "yoga" comes from a Sanskrit word meaning "union." Yoga combines physical exercises, mental meditation, and breathing techniques to strengthen the muscles and relieve stress.

Purpose

Yoga has been practiced for thousands of years as a life philosophy to join the individual self with what practitioners call the Divine, Universal Spirit, or Cosmic Consciousness. However, very few individuals in the United States as of 2004 practiced yoga in this way; rather, yoga is performed as part of an **exercise** program to increase general health, reduce stress, improve flexibility and muscle strength, and alleviate certain physical symptoms, such as chronic **pain**. Because yoga is a low-impact activity and can include gentle movements, it is commonly used as part of physical therapy and rehabilitation of injuries.

Clinical and psychological studies have demonstrated that performing yoga has the following benefits:

- Physical postures strengthen and tone muscles, and when performed in rapid succession, can provide cardiovascular conditioning.
- Meditation and deep breathing can reduce stress, thereby lowering blood pressure and inducing relaxation.
- Mind/body awareness can influence mood and **self-esteem** to improve quality of life.

In addition to exercise and stress reduction, yoga is also used therapeutically to help children and adolescents with medical conditions. Yoga instructors experienced in adapting yoga postures for individuals with special needs teach yoga to children and adolescents with **Down syndrome**, **cerebral palsy**, seizure disorders, **spinal cord injury**, multiple sclerosis, **cancer**, **autism**, Asperger's syndrome, attention deficit hyperactivity disorder (ADHD), psychiatric disorders, learning disabilities, and other disabilities to help improve physical and mental functioning. Many physicians may recommend yoga for patients with **hypertension**, **asthma**, stress-related disorders, and depression. Growing interest in alternative and complementary medicine has increased the popularity of yoga in the United States and spurred research into its medical benefits. Many hospitals offer alternative or integrative medicine centers that include yoga classes.

Some yoga instructors have even pioneered yoga for infants and toddlers, practiced with one or both parents. Yoga for infants and toddlers can improve **sleep**, ease digestive problems, facilitate neuromuscular development, strengthen the immune system, deepen parent-child bonds, serve as an outlet for creative **play** and self-expression, and reduce stress and **anxiety** for both parents and children.

Description

Yoga originated in ancient India and is considered one of the longest surviving philosophical systems in the world. Some scholars have estimated that yoga is as old as 5,000 years; artifacts detailing yoga postures have been found in India from over 3000 B.C. A recent poll conducted by *Yoga Journal* found that 11 million Americans do yoga at least occasionally and 6 million perform it regularly.

Hatha yoga is the most commonly practiced branch of yoga in the United States, and it is a highly developed system of nearly 200 physical postures, movements, and breathing techniques. The yoga philosophy maintains that the breath is the most important facet of health, as the breath is the largest source of "prana," or life force, and hatha yoga uses "pranayama," which literally means the science or control of breathing.

A typical hatha yoga routine consists of a sequence of physical poses, called asanas, and the sequence is designed to work all parts of the body, with particular emphasis on making the spine supple and increasing circulation. Each asana is named for a common thing it resembles, like the sun salutation, cobra, locust, plough, bow, eagle, tree, and the head to knee pose, to name a few. Poses named after animals are especially appealing to children, and children's yoga programs focus on those poses that mimic animals and trees. Each pose has steps for entering and exiting it, and each posture requires proper form and alignment. A pose is held for some time, depending on its level of difficulty and one's strength and stamina, and the instructor cues participants when to inhale and exhale at certain points in each posture, as breathing properly is a fundamental aspect of yoga postures. Breathing should be deep and through the nose. Mental concentration in each position is also very important, which improves awareness, poise, and posture. During a yoga routine there is often a position in which to perform meditation, called dyana, if deep relaxation is one of the goals of the sequence.

Yoga routines can take anywhere from 20 minutes to two or more hours, with one hour being a good time investment to perform a sequence of postures and a meditation. For children, 30 minutes may be the maximum span of attention for practicing yoga. Some yoga routines, depending on the teacher and school, can be as strenuous as the most difficult workout, especially those called ashtanga, or power, yoga. Other routines merely stretch and align the body while the breath and heart rate are kept slow and steady. Power yoga is only appropriate for children and adolescents who have practiced yoga for some time, or who are engaged in advanced athletic activities. Yoga achieves its best results when it is practiced as a daily discipline, and yoga can be a life-long exercise routine, offering deeper and more challenging positions as a practitioner becomes more adept. The basic positions can increase a person's strength, flexibility, and sense of well-being almost immediately, but it can take years to perfect and deepen them, which is an appealing and stimulating aspect of yoga for many.

Precautions

Children and adolescents with injuries, medical conditions, or spinal problems should consult a physician before beginning yoga. For children with special needs, parents should find a yoga teacher who is properly trained and experienced and can give children individual attention. Certain yoga positions should not be performed by a person who has a **fever** or is menstruating.

Children and adolescents who are beginners at yoga should always be properly supervised, since injuries are possible, and some advanced yoga postures, like the headstand and full lotus position, can be difficult and require strength, flexibility, and gradual preparation. Proper form and alignment should always be maintained during a stretch or posture, and the stretch or posture should be stopped if pain, **dizziness**, or excessive fatigue occurs.

While yoga can be used therapeutically to help alleviate certain symptoms in children with various medical conditions, it is not a cure. A physician should be consulted for standard medical treatment.

Risks

Injuries have been reported when yoga postures were performed without proper form or concentration, or by attempting difficult positions without working up to them gradually or having appropriate supervision. Beginners sometimes report muscle soreness and fatigue after performing yoga, but these side effects diminish with practice.

Parental concerns

Parents should make sure that the yoga instructor is qualified to teach yoga to children. Yoga instructors experienced in teaching adults may not understand that teaching children requires different skills and methods. Yoga certifications and/or training in teaching children are available.

Yoga classes for children, adolescents, and teens are held at local schools, community centers, fitness clubs, and YMCAs. In addition, yoga videos for children are available online at <www.collagevideo.com>. For children

KEY TERMS

Asana—A position or stance in yoga.

Dyana—The yoga term for meditation.

Hatha yoga—A form of yoga using postures, breathing methods, and meditation.

Meditation—A practice of concentrated focus upon a sound, object, visualization, the breath, movement, or attention itself in order to increase awareness of the present moment, reduce stress, promote relaxation, and enhance personal and spiritual growth.

Pranayama—The yoga practice of breathing cirrectly and deeply.

Yogi (female, yogini)— A trained yoga expert.

who want to perform yoga at home, parental supervision is necessary.

Resources

BOOKS

Caldwell, Micheala, et al. *The Girls' Yoga Book: Stretch Your Body, Open Your Mind, and Have Fun.* Berkeley, CA: Maple Tree Press, 2005.

Hall, Doriel. *Yoga for New Mothers: Getting Your Body and Mind Back in Shape the Natural Way after Birth.* New York: Anness, 2005.

Iyengar, B. K. S. *Yoga: The Path to Holistic Health.* London: Korling Kindersley Limited, 2001.

PERIODICALS

Cohen, L., et al. "Psychological Adjustment and Sleep Quality in a Randomized Trial of the Effects of a Tibetan Yoga Intervention in Patients with Lymphoma." *Cancer* 100 (May 15, 2004): 2253–2260.

Cooper, S., et al. "Effect of Two Breathing Exercises (Buteyko and Pranayama) on Asthma: A Randomized Controlled Trial." *Thorax* 58 (August 2003): 674–79.

Leschin-Hoar, C. "Seeking Yoga's Soothing Touch: Many Say Children with Medical Issues Benefit from its Use." *Boston Globe* November 20, 2003.

Oken, B. S., et al. "Randomized Controlled Trial of Yoga and Exercise in Multiple Sclerosis." *Neurology* 62 (June 8, 2004): 2058–2064.

Raub, J. A. "Psychophysiologic Effects of Hatha Yoga on Musculoskeletal and Cardiopulmonary Function: A Literature Review." *Journal of Alternative and Complementary Medicine* 8 (December 2002): 797–812.

ORGANIZATIONS

American Yoga Association. Web site: <www.americanyogaassociation.org>.

International Association of Yoga Therapists (IAYT). Web site: <www.iayt.org>.

WEB SITES

Itsy Bitsy Yoga. *Benefits of Yoga for Babies and Toddlers.* Available online at <www.itsybitsyyoga.com/babyandtoddleryogabenefits.htm> (accessed November 15, 2004).

Lipson, E. "Yoga Works! Medical Science Is Finally Validating What Yogis Have Known for Thousands of Years." *Yoga Journal*, Winter 1999–2000. Available online at <www.yogajournal.com/health/115.cfm> (accessed November 15, 2004).

Orkin, Lisa. "Yoga Helps Kids Find Balance in Their Lives." *The Yoga Site: The Online Yoga Resource Center*, August 2004. Available online at <www.yogasite.com/yoga%20kids.htm> (accessed November 15, 2004).

Sumar, Sonia. "Yoga for the Special Child," August 2004. Available online at <www.specialyoga.com/> (accessed November 15, 2004).

"Yoga." *Nemours Foundation: TeensHealth*, August 2001. Available online at <www.kidshealth.org/teen/food_fitness/exercise/yoga.html> (accessed November 15, 2004).

Jennifer E. Sisk, MA

GLOSSARY

A

ABANDONMENT. Legally, the refusal to provide adequate financial support for one's dependent child; the failure to maintain a parental relationship with one's dependent child.

ABDUCTION. Turning away from the body.

ABLATION. To remove or destroy tissue or a body part, such as by burning or cutting.

ABO INCOMPATABILITY. The reaction that occurs with blood groups that are of a different type.

ABRASION. Also called a scrape. The rubbing away of the skin surface by friction against another rough surface.

ABRUPTIO PLACENTAE. Premature separation of the placenta from the uterine wall. It occurs late in pregnancy and results in bleeding that may or may not establish an obstetrical emergency.

ABSCESS. A localized collection of pus in the skin or other body tissue caused by infection.

ABSENCE SEIZURE. A brief seizure with an accompanying loss of awareness or alertness. Also known as a petit mal seizure.

ACCOMMODATION. The ability of the lens to change its focus from distant to near objects and vice versa. It is achieved through the action of the ciliary muscles that change the shape of the lens.

ACELLUAR. Without whole cells. An acelluar vaccine contains on parts of the cells which can produce immunity in a person receiving the vaccine.

ACETABULUM. The large cup-shaped cavity at the junction of pelvis and femur (thigh bone).

ACETAMINOPHEN. A drug used for pain relief as well as to decrease fever. A common trade name for the drug is Tylenol.

ACETYLCHOLINE. A chemical called a neurotransmitter that functions primarily to mediate activity of the nervous system and skeletal muscles.

ACETYLSALICYLIC ACID. Aspirin; an analgesic, antipyretic, and antirheumatic drug prescribed to reduce fever and to relieve pain and inflammation.

ACHONDROPLASIA. A congenital disturbance of growth plate development in long bones that results in a person having shortened limbs and a normal trunk.

ACIDOSIS. A disturbance of the balance of acid to base in the body causing an accumulation of acid or loss of alkali (base). Blood plasma normally has a pH of 7.35-7.45. Alkaline blood has a pH value greater than pH 7.45. When the blood pH value is less than 7.35, the patient is in acidosis.

ACNE. A chronic inflammation of the sebaceous glands that manifests as blackheads, whiteheads, and/or pustules on the face or trunk.

ACOUSTIC NEUROMA. A benign tumor that grows on the nerve leading from the inner ear to the brain. As the tumor grows, it exerts pressure on the inner ear and causes severe vertigo.

ACQUIRED IMMUNODEFICIENCY SYNDROME (AIDS). An infectious disease caused by the human immunodeficiency virus (HIV). A person infected with HIV gradually loses immune function, becoming less able to resist other infections and certain cancers.

ACROCYANOSIS. A condition characterized by blueness, coldness, and sweating of the extremities. A slight cyanosis, or blueness, of the hands and feet of the newborn is considered normal.

ACROMEGALY. A rare disease resulting from excessive growth hormone caused by a benign tumor. If such a tumor develops within the first ten years of life, the result is gigantism (in which growth is accelerated) and not acromegaly. Symptoms include coarsening of the facial features, enlargement of the hands, feet, ears, and nose, jutting of the jaw, and a long face.

ACTIVE IMMUNITY. Produced by the body when the immune system is triggered to produce antibodies, either by immunization or a disease.

ACTIVE IMMUNIZATION. Treatment that provides immunity by challenging an individual's own immune system to produce antibody against a particular organism.

ACTIVE MOTION. Spontaneous; produced by active efforts. Active range of motion exercises are those that are performed by the patient without assistance.

ACTIVITIES OF DAILY LIVING (ADL). The activities performed during the course of a normal day, for example, eating, bathing, dressing, toileting, etc.

ACUPRESSURE. A traditional Chinese medical technique based on theory of *qi* (life energy) flowing in energy meridians or channels in the body. Applying pressure with the thumb and fingers to acupressure points can relieve specific conditions and promote overall balance and health.

ACUPUNCTURE. Based on the same traditional Chinese medical foundation as acupressure, acupuncture uses sterile needles inserted at specific points to treat certain conditions or relieve pain.

ACUTE. Refers to a disease or symptom that has a sudden onset and lasts a relatively short period of time.

ACUTE OTITIS MEDIA. Inflammation of the middle ear with signs of infection lasting less than three months.

ACUTE PAIN. Pain in response to injury or another stimulus that resolves when the injury heals or the stimulus is removed.

ACUTE PHASE REACTANTS. Blood proteins whose concentrations increase or decrease in reaction to the inflammation process.

ACUTE SPLENIC SEQUESTRATION. Retention of blood in the spleen.

ACYCLOVIR. An antiviral drug, available under the trade name Zovirax, used for combating chickenpox and other herpes viruses.

ADAPTIVE BEHAVIOR. The ability to do things on one's own without getting into trouble and to adapt to and manage one's surroundings.

ADDICTION. The state of being both physically and psychologically dependent on a substance or activity.

ADDUCTION. Movement toward the body.

ADENOIDS. Common name for the pharyngeal tonsils, which are lymph masses in the wall of the air passageway (pharynx) just behind the nose.

ADENOMA. A type of noncancerous (benign) tumor that often involves the overgrowth of certain cells found in glands. These tumors can secrete hormones or cause changes in hormone production in nearby glands.

ADENOMYOSIS. Uterine thickening caused when endometrial tissue, which normally lines the uterus, extends outward into the fibrous and muscular tissue of the uterus.

ADENOSINE DEAMINASE (ADA). An enzyme that is lacking in a specific type of severe combined immunodeficiency disease (SCID). Children with an ADA deficiency have low levels of both B and T cells.

ADENOVIRUS. A type of virus that can cause upper respiratory tract infections.

ADIPOSE TISSUE. Fat tissue.

ADJUVANT THERAPY. A treatment that is intended to aid primary treatment.

ADOLESCENCE. A period of life in which the biological and psychosocial transition from childhood to adulthood occurs.

ADOPTEE. A person who has been adopted.

ADOPTION. The legal process that creates a parent and child relationship between two individuals who are not biologically related at birth.

ADOPTION SUBSIDY. A short-term or long-term financial payment, either in the form of cash or services, to help an adoptive family provide for the on-going care of an adopted child. A subsidy can be medical insurance for the child, counseling services for the family, respite care for the adoptive parents; or a monthly cash allowance to help cover other extraordinary expenses and services associated with the adoption.

ADRENAL GLAND. A small gland located above the kidney (one on each side) that secretes various hormones.

ADRENALINE. Another name for epinephrine, the hormone released by the adrenal glands in response to stress. It is the principal blood-pressure raising hormone and a bronchial and intestinal smooth muscles relaxant.

ADRENOCORTICOTROPIC HORMONE (ACTH). Also called adrenocorticotropin or corticotropin, this hormone is produced by the pituitary gland to stimulate the adrenal cortex to release various corticosteroid hormones.

ADVERSE EFFECT. A negative side effect of a vaccine, drug, or other treatment.

AEROBIC. An organism that grows and thrives only in environments containing oxygen.

AFFECTIVE DISORDER. An emotional disorder involving abnormal highs and/or lows in mood. Now termed mood disorder.

AGAMMAGLOBULINEMIA. The lack of gamma globulins in the blood associated with an increased susceptibility to infection.

AGAR. A gel made from red algae that is used to culture certain disease agents in the laboratory.

AGE OUT. Becoming a legal adult at age 18 and moving out of foster care.

AGGRAVATED SEXUAL ABUSE. When an individual is forced to submit to sexual acts by use of physical force; threats of death, injury, or kidnapping; or substances that render that individual unconscious or impaired.

AGORAPHOBIA. Abnormal anxiety regarding public places or situations from which the person may wish to flee or in which he or she would be helpless in the event of a panic attack.

AILUROPHOBIA. Fear of cats.

AIRWAY OBSTRUCTION INJURY. An injury that obstructs the airway and prevents proper breathing, either through strangulation, suffocation, or choking.

ALACTASIA. A rare inherited condition causing the lack of the enzyme needed to digest milk sugar.

ALBINISM. An inherited condition that causes a lack of pigment. People with albinism typically have light skin, white or pale yellow hair, and light blue or gray eyes.

ALBUMIN. A blood protein that is made in the liver and helps to regulate water movement in the body.

ALCOHOL USE DISORDER (AUD). The repetitive, long-term ingestion of alcohol in ways that impair psychosocial functioning and health, leading to problems with personal relationships, school, or work. Alcohol use disorders include alcohol dependence, alcohol abuse, alcohol intoxication, and alcohol withdrawal.

ALCOHOL USE DISORDERS INVENTORY TEST (AUDIT). A test for alcohol use developed by the World Health Organization (WHO). Its ten questions address three specific areas of drinking over a 12-month period: the amount and frequency of drinking, dependence upon alcohol, and problems that have been encountered due to drinking alcohol.

ALDOLASE B. Also called fructose 1-phosphate aldolase, this chemical is produced in the liver, kidneys, and brain. It is needed for the breakdown of fructose, a sugar found in fruits, vegetables, honey, and other sweeteners.

ALDOSTERONE. A hormone secreted by the adrenal glands that is important for maintaining salt and water balance in the body.

ALEXANDER'S DISEASE. A progressive, degenerative disorder of the central nervous system.

ALKALOID. A type of chemical commonly found in plants and often having medicinal properties.

ALKYLATING AGENT. A chemical that alters the composition of the genetic material of rapidly dividing cells, such as cancer cells, causing selective cell death; used as a chemotherapeutic agent.

ALLELE. One of two or more alternate forms of a gene.

ALLERGEN. A foreign substance that provokes an immune reaction or allergic response in some sensitive people but not in most others.

ALLERGIC CONJUNCTIVITIS. Inflammation of the membrane lining the eyelid and covering the eyeball; congestion of the conjunctiva, with mucus secretion.

ALLERGIC REACTION. An immune system reaction to a substance in the environment; symptoms include rash, inflammation, sneezing, itchy watery eyes, and runny nose.

ALLERGIC RHINITIS. Swelling and inflammation of the nasal membranes caused by sensitivity to airborne matter like pollen or cat hair.

ALLERGISTS. Doctors who specialize in treating allergies.

ALLERGY. A hypersensitivity reaction in response to exposure to a specific substance.

ALLERGY SHOTS. Injections given by an allergy specialist to desensitize an allergic person. Also known as immunotherapy treatment.

ALOPECIA. The loss of hair, or baldness.

ALPHA FETOPROTEIN (AFP). A substance produced by a fetus's liver that can be found in the amniotic fluid and in the mother's blood.

ALPHA FETOPROTEIN TEST. A screening blood test that can be done after the sixteenth week of pregnancy to evaluate the possibility of spina bifida and other neural tube defects in the fetus.

ALTERNATIVE SCHOOL. An educational setting designed to accommodate educational, behavioral, and/or medical needs of children and adolescents that cannot be adequately addressed in a traditional school environment.

ALTRUISTIC. Thinking of others' welfare.

ALVEOLAR BONE. A set of ridges from the jawbones.

ALVEOLI. The tiny air sacs clustered at the ends of the bronchioles in the lungs in which oxygen-carbon dioxide exchange takes place.

AMALGAM. A mixture (alloy) of silver and several other metals used by dentists to make fillings for cavities.

AMBIDEXTROUS. Equally competent with either hand.

AMBIENT. Surrounding.

AMBLYOPIA. Decreased visual acuity, usually in one eye, in the absence of any structural abnormality in the eye.

AMENORRHEA. The absence or abnormal stoppage of menstrual periods.

AMINO ACID. An organic compound composed of both an amino group and an acidic carboxyl group. Amino acids are the basic building blocks of proteins. There are 20 types of amino acids (eight are "essential amino acids" which the body cannot make and must therefore be obtained from food).

AMNESIA. A general medical term for loss of memory that is not due to ordinary forgetfulness. Amnesia can be caused by head injuries, brain disease, or epilepsy, as well as by dissociation.

AMNIOCENTESIS. A procedure performed at 16-18 weeks of pregnancy in which a needle is inserted through a woman's abdomen into her uterus to draw out a small sample of the amniotic fluid from around the baby for analysis.

AMNIOINFUSION. A procedure whereby a physiologic solution such as normal saline or lactated ringer's solution is infused through a lumen in an intrauterine pressure catheter into the uterus to alleviate cord compression and to help dilute meconium staining.

AMNION. Thin, tough, innermost layer of the amniotic sac.

AMNIOTIC FLUID. The liquid in the amniotic sac that cushions the fetus and regulates temperature in the placental environment. Amniotic fluid also contains fetal cells.

AMNIOTIC MEMBRANE. The thin tissue that creates the walls of the amniotic sac.

AMNIOTIC SAC. The membranous sac that contains the fetus and the amniotic fluid during pregnancy.

AMNIOTOMY. Rupturing or breaking the amniotic sac (bag of waters) to permit the release of fluid.

AMOK. A culture-specific psychiatric syndrome first described among the Malays, in which adolescent or adult males are overcome by a sudden fit of murderous fury provoked by a perceived insult or slight. Some researchers consider amok to be a variant of intermittent explosive disorder.

AMPLIFICATION. A process by which something is made larger. In clotting, only a very few chemicals are released by the initial injury; they trigger a cascade of chemical reactions which produces increasingly larger quantities of different chemicals, resulting in an appropriately sized, strong fibrin clot.

AMPUTATION. Surgical removal of any portion of the body.

AMYGDALA. An almond-shaped brain structure in the limbic system that is activated in stressful situations to trigger the emotion of fear. It is thought that the emotional overreactions in Alzheimer's patients are related to the destruction of neurons in the amygdala.

AMYLOID. A waxy, translucent, starch-like protein that is deposited in tissues during the course of certain chronic diseases such as rheumatoid arthritis and Alzheimer's disease.

AMYLOIDOSIS. The accumulation of amyloid deposits in various organs and tissues in the body so that normal functioning is compromised. Primary amyloidosis usually occurs as a complication of multiple myeloma. Secondary amyloidosis occurs in patients suffering from chronic infections or inflammatory diseases such as tuberculosis, rheumatoid arthritis, and Crohn's disease.

AMYLOPHAGIA. The compulsive eating of purified starch, typically cornstarch or laundry starch.

ANABOLIC. Refers to metabolic processes characterized by the conversion of simple substances into more complex compounds.

ANAEROBIC. An organism that grows and thrives in an oxygen-free environment.

ANALGESICS. A class of pain-relieving medicines, including aspirin and acetaminophen (Tylenol).

ANAPHYLACTOID. A non-allergic sensitivity response resembling anaphylaxis.

ANAPHYLAXIS. Also called anaphylactic shock; a severe allergic reaction characterized by airway constriction, tissue swelling, and lowered blood pressure.

ANASTOMOSIS. Surgical reconnection of two ducts, blood vessels, or bowel segments to allow flow between the two.

ANDROGENS. Hormones (specifically testosterone) responsible for male sex characteristics.

ANEMIA. A condition in which there is an abnormally low number of red blood cells in the bloodstream. It may be due to loss of blood, an increase in red blood cell destruction, or a decrease in red blood cell production. Major symptoms are paleness, shortness of breath, unusually fast or strong heart beats, and tiredness.

ANENCEPHALY. A genetic defect resulting in the partial to complete absence of the brain and malformation of the brainstem.

ANESTHESIA. Treatment with medicine that causes a loss of feeling, especially pain. Local anesthesia numbs only part of the body; general anesthesia causes loss of consciousness.

ANESTHESIOLOGIST. A medical specialist who has special training and expertise in the delivery of anesthetics.

ANEURYSM. A weakened area in the wall of a blood vessel which causes an outpouching or bulge. Aneurysms may be fatal if these weak areas burst, resulting in uncontrollable bleeding.

ANGIOEDEMA. Patches of circumscribed swelling involving the skin and its subcutaneous layers, the mucous membranes, and sometimes the organs frequently caused by an allergic reaction to drugs or food. Also called angioneurotic edema, giant urticaria, Quincke's disease, or Quincke's edema.

ANGIOGRAPHY. Radiographic examination of blood vessels after injection with a radiopaque contrast substance or dye.

ANGIOMA. A tumor (such as a hemangioma or lymphangioma) that mainly consists of blood vessels or lymphatic vessels.

ANGIOPLASTY. A medical procedure in which a catheter, or thin tube, is threaded through blood vessels. The catheter is used to place a balloon or stent (a small metal rod) at a narrowed or blocked area and expand it mechanically.

ANISOMETROPIA. An eye condition in which there is an inequality of vision between the two eyes. There may be unequal amounts of nearsightedness, farsightedness, or astigmatism, so that one eye will be in focus while the other will not.

ANODYNE. A medicinal herb or other drug that relieves or soothes pain.

ANOMALY. Something that is different from what is normal or expected. Also an unusual or irregular structure.

ANOREXIA NERVOSA. An eating disorder marked by an unrealistic fear of weight gain, self-starvation, and distortion of body image. It most commonly occurs in adolescent females.

ANOXIA. Lack of oxygen.

ANTEPARTUM. The time period of the woman's pregnancy from conception and onset of labor.

ANTHRAX. A bacterial infection, primarily of livestock, that can be spread to humans. In humans it affects the skin, intestines, or lungs.

ANTHROPOMORPHIC. Taking on human characteristics or looking like humans.

ANTIANDROGEN. A substance that blocks the action of androgens, the hormones responsible for male characteristics.

ANTIBIOTICS. Drugs that are designed to kill or inhibit the growth of the bacteria that cause infections.

ANTIBODY. A special protein made by the body's immune system as a defense against foreign material (bacteria, viruses, etc.) that enters the body. It is uniquely designed to attack and neutralize the specific antigen that triggered the immune response.

ANTICHOLINERGIC DRUG. Drugs that block the action of the neurotransmitter acetylcholine. They are used to lessen muscle spasms in the intestines, lungs, bladder, and eye muscles.

ANTICOAGULANT DRUG. A drug used to prevent clot formation or to prevent a clot that has formed from enlarging. Anticoagulant drugs inhibit clot formation by blocking the action of clotting factors or platelets. They fall into three groups: inhibitors of clotting factor synthesis, inhibitors of thrombin, and antiplatelet drugs.

ANTICONVULSANT. Drugs used to prevent convulsions or seizures. They often are prescribed in the treatment of epilepsy.

ANTIDEPRESSANT DRUG. A medication prescribed to relieve major depression. Classes of antidepressants include selective serotonin reuptake inhibitors (fluoxetine/Prozac, sertraline/Zoloft), tricyclics (amitriptyline/Elavil), MAOIs (phenelzine/Nardil), and heterocyclics (bupropion/Wellbutrin, trazodone/Desyrel).

ANTIDIURETIC HORMONE (ADH). Also called vasopressin, a hormone that acts on the kidneys to regulate water balance.

ANTIDOTE. A remedy to counteract a poison or injury. Also refers to a substance which cancels the effect of homeopathic remedies

ANTIEMETIC DRUG. A medication that helps control nausea; also called an antinausea drug.

ANTIGEN. A substance (usually a protein) identified as foreign by the body's immune system, triggering the release of antibodies as part of the body's immune response.

ANTIHISTAMINE. A drug used to treat allergic conditions that blocks the effects of histamine, a substance in the body that causes itching, vascular changes, and mucus secretion when released by cells.

ANTI-INFLAMMATORY DRUGS. A class of drugs, including nonsteroidal anti-inflammatory drugs (NSAIDs) and corticosteroids, used to relieve swelling, pain, and other symptoms of inflammation.

ANTIMETABOLITE. A drug or other substance that interferes with a cell's growth or ability to multiply.

ANTIMOTILITY DRUG. A medication, such as loperamide (Imodium), dephenoxylate (Lomotil), or medications containing codeine or narcotics that decrease the ability of the intestine to contract.

ANTIOXIDANT. Any substance that reduces the damage caused by oxidation, such as the harm caused by free radicals.

ANTIPHOSPHOLIPID ANTIBODY SYNDROME. An immune disorder that occurs when the body recognizes phospholipids (part of a cell's membrane) as foreign and produces abnormal antibodies against them. This syndrome is associated with abnormal blood clotting, low blood platelet counts, and migraine headaches.

ANTIPLATELET DRUG. Drugs that inhibit platelets from aggregating to form a plug. They are used to prevent clotting and alter the natural course of atherosclerosis.

ANTIPSYCHOTIC DRUG. A class of drugs used to control psychotic symptoms in patients with psychotic disorders such as schizophrenia and delusional disorder. Antipsychotics include risperidone (Risperdal), haloperidol (Haldol), and chlorpromazine (Thorazine).

ANTIPYRETIC DRUG. Medications, like aspirin or acetaminophen, that lower fever.

ANTIRETROVIRAL DRUGS. Several classes of drugs that are used to treat HIV.

ANTISERUM. Human or animal blood serum containing specific antibodies.

ANTISOCIAL. Actions described as impulsively aggressive, sometimes violent, that do not comply with established social and ethical codes.

ANTISOCIAL BEHAVIOR. Behavior characterized by high levels of anger, aggression, manipulation, or violence.

ANTISOCIAL PERSONALITY DISORDER. A disorder characterized by a behavior pattern that disregards for the rights of others. People with this disorder often deceive and manipulate, or their behavior might include aggression to people or animals or property destruction, for example. This disorder has also been called sociopathy or psychopathy.

ANTITOXIN. An antibody against an exotoxin, usually derived from horse serum.

ANTITUSSIVE DRUG. A drug used to suppress coughing.

ANTIVIRAL DRUG. A medication that can destroy viruses and help treat illnesses caused by them.

ANUS. The opening at the end of the intestine through which solid waste (stool) passes as it leaves the body.

ANXIETY. Worry or tension in response to real or imagined stress, danger, or dreaded situations. Physical reactions, such as fast pulse, sweating, trembling, fatigue, and weakness, may accompany anxiety.

ANXIETY DISORDER. A mental disorder characterized by prolonged, excessive worry about circumstances in one's life. Anxiety disorders include agoraphobia and other phobias, obsessive-compulsive disorder, post-traumatic stress disorder, and panic disorder.

AORTA. The main artery located above the heart that pumps oxygenated blood out into the body. The aorta is the largest artery in the body.

AORTIC VALVE. The valve between the heart's left ventricle and ascending aorta that prevents regurgitation of blood back into the left ventricle.

AORTIC VALVE STENOSIS. Narrowing of the aortic valve.

APERT SYNDROME. A craniofacial abnormality characterized by abnormal head shape, small upper jaw, and fusion of fingers and toes.

APGAR SCORE. The results of an evaluation of a newborn's physical status, including heart rate, respiratory effort, muscle tone, response to stimulation, and color of skin.

APHASIA. The loss of the ability to speak, or to understand written or spoken language. A person who cannot speak or understand language is said to be aphasic.

APHTHOUS STOMATITIS. A specific type of stomatitis presenting with shallow, painful ulcers. Also known as canker sores.

APLASTIC ANEMIA. A disorder in which the bone marrow greatly decreases or stops production of blood cells.

APNEA. The temporary absence of breathing. Sleep apnea consists of repeated episodes of temporary suspension of breathing during sleep.

APPENDECTOMY. Surgical removal of the appendix.

APPENDIX. The worm-shaped pouch attached to the cecum, the beginning of the large intestine.

APPERCEPTION. The process of understanding through linkage with previous experience.

APPETITE SUPPRESSANT. Drug that decreases feelings of hunger. Most work by increasing levels of serotonin or catecholamine, chemicals in the brain that control appetite.

APRAXIA. Impairment of the ability to make purposeful movements, but not paralysis or loss of sensation.

ARACHNID. A large class of arthropods that includes spiders, scorpions, mites, and ticks.

ARACHNIDISM. Poisoning resulting from the bite or sting of an arachnid.

ARACHNODACTYLY. A condition characterized by abnormally long and slender fingers and toes.

ARNOLD-CHIARI SYNDROME. A congenital malformation of the base of the brain.

ARRHYTHMIA. Any deviation from a normal heart beat.

ARTERIOLE. The smallest type of artery.

ARTERIOSCLEROSIS. A chronic condition characterized by thickening, loss of elasticity, and hardening of the arteries and the build-up of plaque on the arterial walls. Arteriosclerosis can slow or impair blood circulation. It includes atherosclerosis, but the two terms are often used synonymously.

ARTERITIS. Inflammation of an artery.

ARTERY. A blood vessel that carries blood away from the heart to the cells, tissues, and organs of the body.

ARTHRITIS. A painful condition that involves inflammation of one or more joints.

ARTHROCHALASIA. Excessive looseness of the joints.

ARTICULAR BONES. Two or more bones that are connected to each other via a joint.

ASANA. A position or stance in yoga.

ASCITES. An abnormal accumulation of fluid within the abdominal cavity.

ASEPTIC. Sterile; containing no microorganisms, especially no bacteria.

ASPERGER SYNDROME. A developmental disorder of childhood characterized by autistic behavior but without the same difficulties acquiring language that children with autism have.

ASPHYXIA. Lack of oxygen.

ASPHYXIA NEONATORUM. Respiratory failure in a newborn.

ASPHYXIATION. Oxygen starvation of tissues. Chemicals such as carbon monoxide prevent the blood from carrying sufficient oxygen to the brain and other organs. As a result, the person may lose consciousness, stop breathing, and die without artificial respiration (assisted breathing) and other means of elevating the blood oxygen level.

ASPIRATION. The process of removing fluids or gases from the body by suction. Also refers to the inhalation of food or liquids into the lungs.

ASSESSMENT. In the context of psychological assessment (a structured interview), assessment is information-gathering to diagnose a mental disorder.

ASSIMILATION. The process of taking in new information by incorporating it into an existing schema.

ASSOCIATIVE PLAY. A type of play in which preschoolers engage. They participate in a similar activity but with little organization or responsibility.

ASTHMA. A disease in which the air passages of the lungs become inflamed and narrowed, causing wheezing, coughing, and shortness of breath.

ASTIGMATISM. An eye condition in which the cornea doesn't focus light properly on the retina, resulting in a blurred image.

ASYMMETRIC. Not occurring equally on both sides of the body.

ASYMPTOMATIC. Persons who carry a disease and are usually capable of transmitting the disease but who do not exhibit symptoms of the disease are said to be asymptomatic.

ATAXIA. A condition marked by impaired muscular coordination, most frequently resulting from disorders in the brain or spinal cord.

ATHEROSCLEROSIS. A disease process whereby plaques of fatty substances are deposited inside arteries, reducing the inside diameter of the vessels and eventually causing damage to the tissues located beyond the site of the blockage.

ATHETOSIS. A condition marked by slow, writhing, involuntary muscle movements.

ATOPIC DERMATITIS. An intensely itchy inflammation often found on the face, in the bend of the elbow, and behind the knees of people prone to allergies. In infants and young children, this condition is called infantile eczema.

ATOPY. A state that makes persons more likely to develop allergic reactions of any type, including the inflammation and airway narrowing typical of asthma.

ATRESIA. The congenital absence of a normal body opening or duct.

ATRIAL. Referring to the upper chambers of the heart.

ATRIAL FIBRILLATION. A type of heart arrhythmia in which the upper chamber of the heart quivers instead of pumping in an organized way. In this condition, the upper chambers (atria) of the heart do not completely empty when the heart beats, which can allow blood clots to form.

ATRIAL SEPTAL DEFECT. An opening between the right and left atria (upper chambers) of the heart.

ATROPHY. The progressive wasting and loss of function of any part of the body.

ATTACHMENT. A bond between an infant and a caregiver, usually its mother. Attachment is generally formed within the context of a family, providing the child with the necessary feelings of safety and nurturing at a time when the infant is growing and developing. This relationship between the infant and his caregiver serves as a model for all future relationships.

ATTACHMENT BEHAVIOR. Any behavior that an infant uses to seek and maintain contact with and elicit a response from the caregiver. These behaviors include crying, searching, grasping, following, smiling, reaching, and vocalizing.

ATTENDING PHYSICIAN. The doctor who is in charge of the patient's overall care and treatment in the hospital. This doctor may or may not be the child's primary physician.

ATTENTION DEFICIT HYPERACTIVITY DISORDER (ADHD). A condition in which a person (usually a child) has an unusually high activity level and a short attention span. People with the disorder may act impulsively and may have learning and behavioral problems. Sometimes called attention deficit disorder (ADD).

ATTENUATED. A live but weakened microorganism that can no longer produce disease.

AUDIOGRAM. A chart or graph of the results of a hearing test conducted with audiographic equipment. The chart reflects the softest (lowest volume) sounds that can be heard at various frequencies or pitches.

AUDIOLOGIST. A person with a degree and/or certification in the areas of identification and measurement of hearing impairments and rehabilitation of those with hearing problems.

AUDIOMETRY. The measurement of hearing ability, usually with the an audiometer.

AUDITORY BRAINSTEM RESPONSE (ABR). Brainstem auditory evoked response (BAER), brainstem evoked response (BSER), auditory evoked response (AER); a hearing test that records electrical activity in the brain in response to sound via electrodes on the scalp; used for newborns, infants, and young children.

AUDITORY DISCRIMINATION. The ability to detect small similarities and differences between sounds.

AUDITORY EVOKED POTENTIAL (AEP). A change in the neural-electrical activity in the brain in response to auditory signals.

AUDITORY PERCEPTION. The ability to comprehend and interpret auditory signals.

AURA. A subjective sensation or motor phenomenon that precedes and indicates the onset of a neurological episode, such as a migraine or an epileptic seizure. This term also is used to refer to the emanation of light from living things (plants and animals) that can be recorded by Kirlian photography.

AUTHENTIC TASK ASSESSMENT. Evaluation of a task performed by a student that is similar to tasks performed in the outside world.

AUTISM. A developmental disability that appears early in life, in which normal brain development is disrupted and social and communication skills are retarded, sometimes severely.

AUTOGENIC TRAINING. A form of self-hypnosis developed in Germany that appears to be beneficial to migraine sufferers.

AUTOIMMUNE. Pertaining to an immune response by the body against its own tissues or types of cells.

AUTONOMIC NERVOUS SYSTEM. The part of the nervous system that controls so-called involuntary functions, such as heart rate, salivary gland secretion, respiratory function, and pupil dilation.

AUTOSOMAL. Relating to any chromosome besides the X and Y sex chromosomes. Human cells contain 22 pairs of autosomes and one pair of sex chromosomes.

AUTOSOMAL DOMINANT. A pattern of inheritance in which only one of the two copies of an autosomal gene must be abnormal for a genetic condition or disease to occur. An autosomal gene is a gene that is located on one of the autosomes or non-sex chromosomes. A person with an autosomal dominant disorder has a 50% chance of passing it to each of their offspring.

AUTOSOMAL INHERITANCE. Inheritance involving any of the autosomes (22 pairs) and not involving sex-linked chromosomes X and Y.

AUTOSOMAL RECESSIVE. A pattern of inheritance in which both copies of an autosomal gene must be abnormal for a genetic condition or disease to occur. An autosomal gene is a gene that is located on one of the autosomes or non-sex chromosomes. When both parents have one abnormal copy of the same gene, they have a 25% chance with each pregnancy that their offspring will have the disorder.

AUTOSOME. A chromosome not involved in sex determination.

AVOIDANT PERSONALITY DISORDER. Chronic and longstanding fear of negative evaluation and tendency to avoid interpersonal situations without a guarantee of acceptance and support, accompanied by significant fears of embarrassment and shame in social interaction.

AVULSION. The forcible separation of a piece from the entire structure.

AVULSION FRACTURE. A fracture caused by the tearing away of a fragment of bone where a strong ligament or tendon attachment forcibly pulls the fragment away from the bone tissue.

AXILLARY. Located in or near the armpit.

AXIS. A line that passes through the center of the body or body part.

AXON. A long, threadlike projection that is part of a neuron (nerve cell).

B

BABESIOSIS. A infection transmitted by the bite of a tick and characterized by fever, headache, nausea, and muscle pain.

BABINSKI SIGN. Downward bending of the big toe on stimulating the sole of the foot.

BACILLUS. A rod-shaped bacterium, such as the diphtheria bacterium.

BACTEREMIA. Bacterial infection of the blood.

BACTERIA. Singular, bacterium; tiny, one-celled forms of life that cause many diseases and infections.

BACTERIAL ENDOCARDITIS. An infection caused by bacteria that enter the bloodstream and settle in the heart lining, a heart valve, or a blood vessel. People with congenital cardiovascular defects have an increased risk of developing bacterial endocarditis, so preventive antibiotics are prescribed before surgery, invasive tests or procedures, and dental work to reduce this risk.

BACTERIAL MENINGITIS. Meningitis caused by bacteria. Depending on the type of bacteria responsible for the infection, bacterial meningitis is either classified as monococcal or pneumococcal.

BACTERIAL SPECTRUM. The number of bacteria an antibiotic is effective against. Broad-spectrum antibiotics treat many different kinds of bacteria. Narrow-spectrum antibiotics treat fewer kinds.

BACTERIOSTATIC. An agent that prevents the growth of bacteria.

BACTERIURIA. The presence of bacteria in the urine.

BALNEOTHERAPY. The medical term for the use of baths to treat disease.

BARIATRICS. The branch of medicine that deals with the prevention and treatment of obesity and related disorders.

BARIUM ENEMA. An x ray of the bowel using a liquid called barium to enhance the image of the bowel. This test is also called a lower GI (gastrointestinal) series.

BASAL GANGLIA. Brain structure at the base of the cerebral hemispheres involved in controlling movement.

BATIK. A method of hand-printing a fabric by covering with removable wax the parts that will not be dyed.

B-CELL (B LYMPHOCYTE). A small white blood cell from bone marrow responsible for producing antibody and serving as a precursor for plasma cells.

B-CELL LYMPHOMAS. Non-Hodgkin's lymphomas that arise from B cells.

BECKER MUSCULAR DYSTROPHY (BMD). A type of muscular dystrophy that affects older boys and men and usually follows a milder course than Duchenne muscular dystrophy.

BEERY-BUKTENICA TEST. A test that identifies problems with visual perception, fine motor skills (especially hand control), and hand-eye coordination.

BEHAVIOR. A stereotyped motor response to an internal or external stimulus.

BEHAVIOR MODIFICATION. A form of therapy that uses rewards to reinforce desired behavior. An example would be to give a child a piece of chocolate for grooming appropriately.

BELL'S PALSY. Facial paralysis or weakness with a sudden onset, caused by swelling or inflammation of the seventh cranial nerve, which controls the facial muscles. Disseminated Lyme disease sometimes causes Bell's palsy.

BENIGN. In medical usage, benign is the opposite of malignant. It describes an abnormal growth that is stable, treatable, and generally not life-threatening.

BENIGN TUMOR. An abnormal proliferation of cells that does not spread to other parts of the body.

BENZODIAZEPINE. One of a class of drugs that have a hypnotic and sedative action, used mainly as tranquilizers to control symptoms of anxiety. Diazepam (Valium), alprazolam (Xanax), and chlordiazepoxide (Librium) are all benzodiazepines.

BEREAVEMENT. The emotional experience of loss after the death of a friend or relative.

BETA BLOCKERS. The popular name for a group of drugs that are usually prescribed to treat heart conditions, but that also are used to reduce the physical symptoms of anxiety and phobias, such as sweating and palpitations. These drugs, including nadolol (Corgard) and digoxin (Lanoxin), block the action of beta receptors that control the speed and strength of hear muscle contractions and blood vessel dilation. Beta blockers are also called beta-adrenergic blocking agents and antiadrenergics.

BETA-LACTAMASE. An enzyme produced by some bacteria that destroys penicillins.

BICEPS. The muscle in the front of the upper arm.

BICUSPID. Premolar; the two-cupped tooth between the first molar and the cuspid.

BICUSPID AORTIC VALVE. A condition in which the major blood vessel from the heart has only two rather than three components to the valve regulating blood flow.

BILATERAL. Occurring on two sides. For example, a patient with bilateral retinoblastoma has this retinal tumor in both eyes.

BILATERAL CLEFT LIP. A cleft that occurs on both sides of the lip.

BILE. A bitter yellow-green substance produced by the liver. Bile breaks down fats in the small intestine so that they can be used by the body. It is stored in the gallbladder and passes from the gallbladder through the common bile duct to the top of the small intestine (duodenum) as needed to digest fat.

BILE DUCTS. Tubes that carry bile, a thick yellow-green fluid that is made by the liver, stored in the gallbladder, and helps the body digest fats.

BILIARY ATRESIA. An obstruction or inflammation of a bile duct that causes bilirubin to back up into the liver.

BILIRUBIN. A reddish yellow pigment formed from the breakdown of red blood cells, and metabolized by the liver. When levels are abnormally high, it causes the yellowish tint to eyes and skin known as jaundice. Levels of bilirubin in the blood increase in patients with liver disease, blockage of the bile ducts, and other conditions.

BINGE DRINKING. Consumption of five or more alcoholic drinks in a row on a single occasion.

BINGE EATING. A pattern of eating marked by episodes of rapid consumption of large amounts of food; usually food that is high in calories.

BINOCULAR. Affecting or having to do with both eyes.

BINOCULAR VISION. Using both eyes at the same time to see an image.

BIOCHEMICAL TESTING. Measuring the amount or activity of a particular enzyme or protein in a sample of blood or urine or other tissue from the body.

BIOFEEDBACK. A training technique that enables an individual to gain some element of control over involuntary or automatic body functions.

BIOLOGICAL CLOCK. A synonym for the body's circadian rhythm, the natural biological variations that occur over the course of a day.

BIOPSY. The surgical removal and microscopic examination of living tissue for diagnostic purposes or to follow the course of a disease. Most commonly the term refers to the collection and analysis of tissue from a suspected tumor to establish malignancy.

BIOSYNTHESIS. The manufacture of materials in a biological system.

CHIROPRACTIC. A method of treatment based on the interactions of the spine and the nervous system. Chiropractors adjust or manipulate segments of the patient's spinal column in order to relieve pain.

CHLAMYDIA. The most common bacterial sexually transmitted disease in the United States. It often accompanies gonorrhea and is known for its lack of evident symptoms in the majority of women.

CHOLANGIOPANCREATOGRAPHY. An examination of the bile ducts and pancreas.

CHOLERA. An infection of the small intestine caused by a type of bacterium. The disease is spread by drinking water or eating foods that have been contaminated with the feces of infected people. It occurs in parts of Asia, Africa, Latin America, India, and the Middle East. Symptoms include watery diarrhea and exhaustion.

CHOLESTEROL. A steroid fat found in animal foods that is also produced in the human body from saturated fat. Cholesterol is used to form cell membranes and process hormones and vitamin D. High cholesterol levels contribute to the development of atherosclerosis.

CHORDEE. An abnormal curvature of the penis.

CHOREOATHETOSIS. Involuntary rapid, irregular, jerky movements or slow, writhing movements that flow into one another.

CHORES. A small or minor job; a routine duty of a household or farm.

CHORION. The outer membrane of the amniotic sac. Chorionic villi develop from its outer surface early in pregnancy. The villi establish a physical connection with the wall of the uterus and eventually develop into the placenta.

CHORIONIC VILLUS SAMPLING. A procedure used for prenatal diagnosis at 10–12 weeks gestation. Under ultrasound guidance a needle is inserted either through the mother's vagina or abdominal wall and a sample of the chorionic membrane. These cells are then tested for chromosome abnormalities or other genetic diseases.

CHOROID PLEXUS. Specialized cells located in the ventricles of the brain that produce cerebrospinal fluid.

CHOROIDAL HEMANGIOMA. A nonmalignant blood vessel tumor in the eye.

CHROMOSOME. A microscopic thread-like structure found within each cell of the human body and consisting of a complex of proteins and DNA. Humans have 46 chromosomes arranged into 23 pairs. Chromosomes contain the genetic information necessary to direct the development and functioning of all cells and systems in the body. They pass on hereditary traits from parents to child (like eye color) and determine whether the child will be male or female.

CHRONIC. Refers to a disease or condition that progresses slowly but persists or recurs over time.

CHRONIC BRONCHITIS. A smoking-related respiratory illness in which the membranes that line the bronchi, or the lung's air passages, narrow over time. Symptoms include a morning cough that brings up phlegm, breathlessness, and wheezing.

CHRONIC OTITIS MEDIA. Inflammation of the middle ear with signs of infection lasting three months or longer.

CHRONIC PAIN. Pain that lasts over a prolonged period and threatens to disrupt daily life.

CILIA. Tiny hairlike projections on certain cells within the body. Cilia produce lashing or whipping movements to direct or cause motion of substances or fluids within the body. Within the respiratory tract, the cilia act to move mucus along, in an effort to continually flush out and clean the respiratory tract.

CIRCADIAN RHYTHM. Any body rhythm that recurs in 24-hour cycles. The sleep-wake cycle is an example of a circadian rhythm.

CIRCUMCISION. A surgical procedure, usually with religious or cultural significance, where the prepuce or skin covering the tip of the penis on a boy, or the clitoris on a girl, is cut away.

CIRCUMVALLATE PLACENTA. The existence of a thick, round, white, opaque ring around the periphery of the placenta that limits the expansion of the fetal vessels.

CIRRHOSIS. A chronic degenerative disease of the liver, in which normal cells are replaced by fibrous tissue and normal liver function is disrupted. The most common symptoms are mild jaundice, fluid collection in the tissues, mental confusion, and vomiting of blood.

CLAUDICATION. Cramping or pain in a leg caused by poor blood circulation. This condition is frequently caused by hardening of the arteries (atherosclerosis). Intermittent claudication occurs only at certain times, usually after exercise, and is relieved by rest.

CLAUSTROPHOBIA. Fear of small, enclosed spaces.

CLEFT. An elongated opening or slit in an organ.

CLEFT PALATE. A congenital malformation in which there is an abnormal opening in the roof of the mouth that allows the nasal passages and the mouth to be improperly connected.

CLINICAL NURSE SPECIALIST. A nurse with advanced training as well as a master's degree.

CLIQUE. A close group of friends having similar interests and goals and whom outsiders regard as excluding them.

CLITORIS. The most sensitive area of the external female genitals. Stimulation of the clitoris causes most women to reach orgasm.

CLONIC. Referring to clonus, a series of muscle contractions and partial relaxations that alternate in some nervous diseases in the form of convulsive spasms.

CLOSED-FIST INJURY. A hand wound caused when the skin of the fist is torn open by contact with teeth.

CLOT. A soft, semi-solid mass that forms when blood coagulates.

CLOT BUSTERS. Also called thrombolytics. Medications used to break up a blood clot.

CLOTTING FACTORS. Substances in the blood, also known as coagulation factors, that act in sequence to stop bleeding by triggering the formation of a clot. Each clotting factor is designated with a Roman numeral I through XIII.

COAGULATE. To clot or cause hemostasis; in electrosurgery, to cause tissue dehydration without cutting.

COAGULOPATHY. A disorder in which blood is either too slow or too quick to coagulate (clot).

COARCTATION OF THE AORTA. A congenital defect in which severe narrowing or constriction of the aorta obstructs the flow of blood.

COBB ANGLE. A measure of the curvature of scoliosis, determined by measurements made on x rays.

COCHLEA. The hearing part of the inner ear. This snail-shaped structure contains fluid and thousands of microscopic hair cells tuned to various frequencies, in addition to the organ of Corti (the receptor for hearing).

COCHLEAR IMPLANTATION. A surgical procedure in which a small electronic device is placed under the skin behind the ear and is attached to a wire that stimulates the inner ear, allowing people who have hearing loss to hear useful sounds.

COERCIVE BEHAVIOR. Maladaptive behaviors engaged in as a means of avoiding or escaping aversive events. Coercive behavior may include whining, noncompliance, and lying.

COGNITION. The act or process of knowing or perceiving.

COGNITIVE. The ability (or lack of) to think, learn, and memorize.

COGNITIVE ABILITY. Relating to the process of acquiring knowledge by using reasoning, intuition, or perception.

COGNITIVE PROCESSES. Thought processes (i.e., reasoning, perception, judgment, memory).

COGNITIVE SKILLS. Skills required to perform higher cognitive processes, such as knowing, learning, thinking, and judging.

COGNITIVE THERAPY. Psychological treatment aimed at changing a person's way of thinking in order to change his or her behavior and emotional state.

COGNITIVE-BEHAVIORAL THERAPY. A type of psychotherapy in which people learn to recognize and change negative and self-defeating patterns of thinking and behavior.

COHABITATION. Sexual partners living together outside of marriage.

CO-INFECTION. Concurrent infection of a cell or organism with two microorganisms (pneumonia caused by coinfection with a cytomegalovirus and streptococcus).

COLCHICINE. A drug used to treat painful flare-ups of gout. It is also effective in reducing the frequency and severity of attacks in familial Mediterranean fever.

COLITIS. Inflammation of the colon (large intestine).

COLLAGEN. The main supportive protein of cartilage, connective tissue, tendon, skin, and bone.

COLOBOMA. A birth defect in which part of the eye does not form completely.

COLON. The part of the large intestine that extends from the cecum to the rectum. The sigmoid colon is the area of the intestine just above the rectum; linking the descending colon with the rectum. It is shaped like the letter S.

COLONIZATION. The presence of bacteria on a body surface (like on the skin, mouth, intestines or airway) without causing disease in the person.

COLONOSCOPY. An examination of the lining of the colon performed with a colonoscope.

COLOSTOMY. A surgical procedure in which an opening is made in the wall of the abdomen to allow a part of the large intestine (the colon) to empty outside the body. Colostomies are usually required because portions of the intestine have been removed or an intestinal obstruction exists.

COLOSTRUM. Milk secreted for a few days after birth and characterized by high protein and antibody content.

COMA. A condition of deep unconsciousness from which the person cannot be aroused

COMEDO. A hard plug composed of sebum and dead skin cells, also called a blackhead. The mildest type of acne.

COMEDOLYTIC DRUGS. Medications that break up comedones and open clogged pores.

COMING OUT. The process by which gays and bisexuals become public or tell others about their sexual orientation.

COMMINUTED FRACTURE. A fracture where there are several breaks in a bone creating numerous fragments.

COMMON COLD. A mild illness caused by upper respiratory viruses. Usual symptoms include nasal congestion, coughing, sneezing, throat irritation, and a low-grade fever.

COMMUNICATION. The act of transmitting and receiving information.

COMORBIDITY. A disease or condition that coexists with the disease or condition for which the patient is being primarily treated.

COMPARTMENT SYNDROME. A condition in which the blood supply to a muscle is cut off because the muscle swells but is constricted by the connective tissue around it.

COMPLEMENT. One of several proteins in the blood that acts with other proteins to assist in killing bacteria.

COMPLETE BLOOD COUNT (CBC). A routine analysis performed on a sample of blood taken from the patient's vein with a needle and vacuum tube. The measurements taken in a CBC include a white blood cell count, a red blood cell count, the red cell distribution width, the hematocrit (ratio of the volume of the red blood cells to the blood volume), and the amount of hemoglobin (the blood protein that carries oxygen).

COMPLETE BREECH. A breech position in which the baby is "sitting" bottom first on the cervix with legs crossed.

COMPLETE CLEFT. A cleft that extends through the entire affected mouth structure.

COMPULSION. A repetitive or ritualistic behavior that a person performs to reduce anxiety. Compulsions often develop as a way of controlling or "undoing" obsessive thoughts.

COMPUTED TOMOGRAPHY (CT). An imaging technique in which cross-sectional x rays of the body are compiled to create a three-dimensional image of the body's internal structures; also called computed axial tomography.

COMVAX. Hib-HepB, a combination vaccine that protects against the *Haemophilus influenzae* type B bacterium and the hepatitis B virus.

CONCEPTION. The union of egg and sperm to eventually form a fetus.

CONCUSSION. An injury to the brain, often resulting from a blow to the head, that can cause temporary disorientation, memory loss, or unconsciousness.

CONDUCT DISORDER. A behavioral and emotional disorder of childhood and adolescence. Children with a conduct disorder act inappropriately, infringe on the rights of others, and violate societal norms.

CONDUCTING MATERIALS. Materials that conduct electricity, materials through which electric current travels easily. Examples are metals and water.

CONDUCTIVE HEARING IMPAIRMENT. Hearing impairment associated with the outer or middle ear, often caused by infection.

CONDYLOMA ACUMINATA. Another term for a genital wart.

CONES. Receptor cells, located in the retina of the eye, that allow the perception of colors.

CONFUSIONAL AROUSAL. A partial arousal state occurring during the fourth stage of deepest sleep. Childhood night terrors are a form of confusional arousal.

CONGENITAL. Present at birth.

CONGENITAL CYSTIC ADENOMATOID MALFORMATION (CCAM). A condition in which one or more lobes of the fetal lungs develop into fluid-filled sacs called cysts.

CONGENITAL DIAPHRAGMATIC HERNIA (CDH). A condition in which the fetal diaphragm (the muscle dividing the chest and abdominal cavity) does not close completely.

CONGENITAL MALFORMATION. A deformity present at birth.

CONGENITAL RUBELLA SYNDROME (CRS). Viral illness caused by a togavirus of the genus *Rubivirus*. When rubella infection occurs during pregnancy, fetal infection is likely and often causes congenital rubella syndrome (CRS), resulting in miscarriages, stillbirths, and severe birth defects.

CONJUNCTIVA. Plural, conjunctivae. The mucous membrane that covers the white part of the eyes (sclera) and lines the eyelids.

CONJUNCTIVITIS. Inflammation of the conjunctiva, the mucous membrane covering the white part of the eye (sclera) and lining the inside of the eyelids also called pinkeye.

CONNECTIVE TISSUE. A group of tissues responsible for support throughout the body; includes cartilage, bone, fat, tissue underlying skin, and tissues that support organs, blood vessels, and nerves throughout the body.

CONSOLIDATION. A condition in which lung tissue becomes firm and solid rather than elastic and air-filled, arising because of accumulated fluids and tissue debris.

CONSTIPATION. Difficult bowel movements caused by the infrequent production of hard stools.

CONSTRICTED. Made smaller or narrower.

CONTACT DERMATITIS. Skin inflammation as a result of contact with a foreign substance.

CONTAGIOUS. The movement of disease between people. All contagious disease is infectious, but not all infections are contagious.

CONTINGENCIES. Naturally occurring or artificially designated reinforcers or punishers that follow a behavior.

CONTRACEPTIVE. A device or medication designed to prevent pregnancy by either suppressing ovulation, preventing sperm from passing through the cervix to fertilize an egg, or preventing implantation of a fertilized egg.

CONTRACTION. A tightening of the uterus during pregnancy. Contractions may or may not be painful and may or may not indicate labor.

CONTRACTURE. A tightening or shortening of muscles that prevents normal movement of the associated limb or other body part.

CONTRAST AGENT. Also called a contrast medium, this is usually a barium or iodine dye that is injected into the area under investigation. The dye makes the interior body parts more visible on an x-ray film.

CONTRAST HYDROTHERAPY. A series of hot and cold water applications. A hot compress (as hot as an individual can tolerate) is applied for three minutes followed by an ice-cold compress for 30 seconds. These applications are repeated three times each and ending with the cold compress.

CONVERGENCE. The natural movement of the eyes inward to view objects close-up.

CONVERGENT THINKING. The ability to come up with a single correct answer.

CONVULSIONS. Also termed seizures; a sudden violent contraction of a group of muscles.

COOPERATIVE PLAY. A type of play in which school-age children participate in activities with an organized structure or compete for goal or outcome.

COORDINATION. The ability to perform activities with precision and proficiency.

COPING. In psychology, a term that refers to a person's patterns of response to stress.

COPROLALIA. The involuntary use of obscene language.

COPROPRAXIA. The involuntary display of unacceptable/obscene gestures.

CORD BLOOD. The blood that remains in the umbilical cord and placenta after birth. Stem cells from cord blood can be used in place of bone marrow for treating primary immunodeficiency disorders.

CORE GENDER IDENTITY. The deep inner feeling a child has about whether he or she is a male or female.

CORNEA. The clear, dome-shaped outer covering of the eye that lies in front of the iris and pupil. The cornea lets light into the eye.

CORNEAL ABRASION. A scratch on the surface of the cornea.

CORONAL SUTURE. Skull suture that lies behind the forehead area, across the head from left side to the right side.

CORONAVIRUS. A genus of viruses that cause respiratory diseases and gastroenteritis.

CORTICOSPINAL TRACT. A tract of nerve cells that carries motor commands from the brain to the spinal cord.

CORTICOSTEROIDS. A group of hormones produced naturally by the adrenal gland or manufactured synthetically. They are often used to treat inflammation. Examples include cortisone and prednisone.

CORTISOL. A steroid hormone secreted by the adrenal cortex that is important for maintenance of body fluids, electrolytes, and blood sugar levels. Also called hydrocortisone.

CORTISONE. Glucocorticoid produced by the adrenal cortex in response to stress. Cortisone is a steroid with anti-inflammatory and immunosuppressive properties.

CO-SLEEPING. Having an infant sleep with the mother in her bed.

COUGH SUPPRESSANT. A medication that stops or prevents coughing.

COXSACKIE VIRUS. A type of enterovirus that may produce a variety of illnesses, including upper respiratory infections, myocarditis, and pericarditis. Coxsackie viruses resemble the virus that causes polio.

CRABS. An informal or slang term for pubic lice.

CRANIAL NERVES. The set of 12 nerves found on each side of the head and neck that control the sensory and muscle functions of the eyes, nose, tongue, face, and throat.

CRANIOPHARYNGIOMA. A tumor near the pituitary gland in the craniopharyngeal canal that often results in intracranial pressure.

CRANIOSYNOSTOSIS. A premature closure of one or more of the joints (fissures) between the bones of the skull, which causes an abnormally shaped skull.

CREEPING. A form of locomotion in infants, in which the baby pulls the body forward with the arms while the belly and legs drag behind.

CREEPING ERUPTION. Itchy, irregular, wandering red lines on the foot made by burrowing larvae of the hookworm family and some roundworms.

CREPITUS. A crackling sound.

CRETINISM. Severe hypothyroidism that is present at birth and characterized by severe mental retardation.

CRITERION-REFERENCED TEST. An assessment that measures the achievement of specific information or skills against a standard as opposed to being measured against how others perform.

CROHN'S DISEASE. A chronic, inflammatory disease, primarily involving the small and large intestine, but which can affect other parts of the digestive system as well.

CROSSBITE. The condition in which the upper teeth bite inside the lower teeth.

CROSS-REACTION. A reaction that occurs in blood testing when a disease agent reacts to the specific antibody for another disease agent.

CROUZON SYNDROME. A disorder characterized by malformations of the skull and face.

CROWN. The natural part of the tooth covered by enamel. A restorative crown is a protective shell that fits over a tooth.

CRYOTHERAPY. The use of a very low-temperature probe to freeze and thereby destroy tissue. Cryotherapy is used in the treatment skin lesions, Parkinson's disease, some cancers, retinal detachment, and cataracts. Also called cryosurgery.

CRYPTORCHIDISM. Undescended testes, a condition in which a boy is born with one or both testicles in the lower abdomen rather than the scrotum.

CULTURE. A test in which a sample of body fluid is placed on materials specially formulated to grow microorganisms. A culture is used to learn what type of bacterium is causing infection.

CURETTE. Also spelled curet; a small loop or scoop-shaped surgical instrument with sharpened edges that can be used to remove tissue, growths, or debris.

CUSTODIAL PARENT. A parent who has legal custody of their child or children.

CUSTODY. The care, control, and maintenance of a child, which in abuse and neglect cases can be awarded by the court to an agency or in divorce to parents. Foster parents do not have legal custody of the children who are in their care.

CUT. A slicing wound made with a sharp instrument, leaving even edges.

CUTANEOUS. Pertaining to the skin

CUTANEOUS ANGIOLIPOMAS. Benign growths consisting of fat cells and blood vessels just underneath the skin.

CYANOSIS. A bluish tinge to the skin that can occur when the blood oxygen level drops too low.

CYANOTIC. Marked by a bluish tinge to the skin that occurs when the blood oxygen level drops too low. It is one of the types of congenital heart disease.

CYCLIC VOMITING. Uncontrolled vomiting that occurs repeatedly over a certain period of time.

CYCLOOXYGENASE 2 (COX 2). The cyclooxygenase that helps mediate inflammation and that helps the brain feel pain and regulate fever.

CYST. An abnormal sac or enclosed cavity in the body filled with liquid or partially solid material. Also refers to a protective, walled-off capsule in which an organism lies dormant.

CYSTIC FIBROSIS TRANSMEMBRANE CONDUCTANCE REGULATOR (CFTR). The protein responsible for regulating chloride movement across cells in some tissues. Cystic fibrosis results when a person has two defective copies of the CFTR gene.

CYSTOSCOPY. A diagnostic procedure in which a hollow lighted tube (cystoscope) is used to look inside the bladder and the urethra.

CYTOKINES. Chemicals made by the cells that act on other cells to stimulate or inhibit their function. They are important controllers of immune functions.

CYTOMEGALOVIRUS (CMV). A common human virus causing mild or no symptoms in healthy people, but permanent damage or death to an infected fetus, a transplant patient, or a person with HIV.

CYTOTOXIC. The characteristic of being destructive to cells.

D

DACRON. A synthetic polyester fiber used to surgically repair damaged sections of heart muscle and blood vessel walls.

DACTYLITIS. Inflammation of the hands or feet.

DANDER. Loose scales shed from the fur or feathers of household pets and other animals. Dander can cause allergic reactions in susceptible people.

DARWINIAN REFLEX. An unconscious action in infants in which if a palm is touched, the infant makes a very tight fist. This instinct disappears within two to three months.

DEADBEAT PARENT. A mother or father who has abandoned his or her child or children and does not pay child custody as required by a court.

DEBRIDEMENT. The surgical removal of dead tissue and/or foreign bodies from a wound or cut.

DECELERATION. A decrease in the fetal heart rate that can indicate inadequate blood flow through the placenta.

DECIBEL. A unit of the intensity of sound or a measure of loudness. Normal speech is typically spoken in the range of about 20-50 decibels.

DECOMPRESSION. A decrease in pressure from the surrounding water that occurs with decreasing diving depth.

DECONGESTANTS. A group of medications, such as pseudoephedrine, phenylephrine, and phenylpropanolamine, that shrink blood vessels and consequently mucus membranes.

DECREASED PENETRANCE. Individuals who inherit a changed disease gene but do not develop symptoms.

DECUBITUS ULCER. A pressure sore resulting from ulceration of the skin occurring in persons confined to bed for long periods of time

DEEP BITE. A closed bite; a deep or excessive overbite in which the lower incisors bite too closely to or into the gum tissue or palate behind the upper teeth.

DEEP BREATHING. Deep breathing helps expand the lungs and forces better distribution of the air into all sections of the lung. The patient either sits in a chair or sits upright in bed and inhales, pushing the abdomen out to force maximum amounts of air into the lung. The abdomen is then contracted, and the patient exhales.

DEFECATION. The act of having a bowel movement, or the passage of feces through the anus.

DEFENSE MECHANISMS. Indirect strategies used to reduce anxiety rather than directly facing the issues causing the anxiety.

DEFIBRILLATION. A procedure to stop the type of irregular heart beat called ventricular fibrillation, usually by using electric shock.

DEFICIT. A shortfall or slowdown in development, possibly related to a disorder that slows or interrupts normal childhood development.

DEFORMATIONAL PLAGIOCEPHALY (POSITIONAL MOLDING). A form of craniosynostosis in which the head is misshapen, the result of constant pressure to the same area of the head.

DEHYDRATION. An excessive loss of water from the body. It may follow vomiting, prolonged diarrhea, or excessive sweating.

DELETION. The absence of genetic material that is normally found in a chromosome. Often, the genetic material is missing due to an error in replication of an egg or sperm cell.

DELINQUENT. A term applied to young people who behave in a manner in defiance of established social and ethical codes.

DELIRIUM. Sudden confusion with a decreased or fluctuating level of consciousness.

DELIRIUM TREMENS. A complication that may accompany alcohol withdrawal. The symptoms include body shaking (tremulousness), insomnia, agitation, confusion, hearing voices or seeing images that are not really there (hallucinations), seizures, rapid heart beat, profuse sweating, high blood pressure, and fever.

DELUSION. A belief that is resistant to reason or contrary to actual fact. Common delusions include delusions of persecution, delusions about one's importance (sometimes called delusions of grandeur), or delusions of being controlled by others.

DEMYELINATION. Disruption or destruction of the myelin sheath, leaving a bare nerve. It results in a slowing or stopping of the impulses that travel along that nerve.

DENDRITE. A threadlike extension of the cytoplasm of a neuron that conducts electrical impulses toward the cell body of the neuron. Usually it spreads out into many branches.

DENDRITIC. Branched like a tree.

DENTAL CARIES. A disease of the teeth in which microorganisms convert sugar in the mouth to an acid that erodes the tooth. Commonly called a cavity.

DENTIN. The middle layer of a tooth, which makes up most of the tooth's mass.

DEOXYGENATED BLOOD. Blood that does not contain oxygen.

DEPENDENCE. A state in which a person requires a steady concentration of a particular substance to avoid experiencing withdrawal symptoms.

DEPIGMENTED. Characterized by a loss of normal color; discolored.

DEPRESSION. A mental condition in which a person feels extremely sad and loses interest in life. A person with depression may also have sleep problems and loss of appetite and may have trouble concentrating and carrying out everyday activities.

DEPRIVATIONAL DWARFISM. A condition where emotional disturbances are associated with growth failure and abnormalities of pituitary function.

DERMATITIS. Inflammation of the skin.

DERMATITIS HERPETIFORMIS. A chronic, very itchy skin disease with groups of red lesions that leave spots behind when they heal.

DERMATOLOGIST. A physician that specializes in diseases and disorders of the skin.

DERMATOLOGY. The branch of medicine that studies and treats disorders of the skin.

DERMATOPHYTE. A type of fungus that causes diseases of the skin, including tinea or ringworm.

DERMATOSPARAXIS. Skin fragility caused by abnormal collagen.

DERMIS. The basal layer of skin; it contains blood and lymphatic vessels, nerves, glands, and hair follicles.

DESENSITIZATION. A treatment for phobias which involves exposing the phobic person to the feared situation. It is often used in conjunction with relaxation techniques. Also used to describe a technique of pain reduction in which the painful area is stimulated with whatever is causing the pain.

DESFEROXAMINE. The primary drug used in iron chelation therapy. It aids in counteracting the life-threatening buildup of iron in the body associated with long-term blood transfusions.

DESMOPRESSIN ACETATE (DDAVP). A drug used to regulate urine production.

DETOXIFICATION. The process of physically eliminating drugs and/or alcohol from the system of a substance-dependent individual.

DEVELOPMENT, EMBRYONIC. The process whereby undifferentiated embryotic cells replicate and differentiate into limbs, organ systems, and other body components of the fetus.

DEVELOPMENTAL. Referring to the growth process, particularly the growth patterns and associated skills acquired in childhood.

DEVELOPMENTAL ASSESSMENT. The ongoing process of testing, observing, and analyzing a child's skills.

DEVELOPMENTAL COORDINATION DISORDER. A disorder of motor skills.

DEVELOPMENTAL DELAY. The failure of a child to meet certain developmental milestones, such as sitting, walking, and talking, at the average age. Developmental delay may indicate a problem in development of the central nervous system.

DEVELOPMENTAL DOMAINS. Areas of a child's development.

DEVELOPMENTAL MILESTONE. The age at which an infant or toddler normally develops a particular skill. For example, by nine months, a child should be able to grasp and toss a bottle.

DEVIATED SEPTUM. A shift in the position of the nasal septum, the partition that divides the two nasal cavities.

DEXTROSE. A sugar solution used in intravenous drips.

DIABETES MELLITUS. The clinical name for common diabetes. It is a chronic disease characterized by the inability of the body to produce or respond properly to insulin, a hormone required by the body to convert glucose to energy.

DIABETIC COMA. A life-threatening, reduced level of consciousness that occurs in persons with uncontrolled diabetes mellitus.

DIABETIC RETINOPATHY. A condition seen most frequently in individuals with poorly controlled diabetes mellitus where the tiny blood vessels to the retina, the tissues that sense light at the back of the eye, are damaged. This damage causes blurred vision, sudden blindness, or black spots, lines, or flashing light in the field of vision.

DIAGNOSIS. The art or act of identifying a disease from its signs and symptoms.

DIAGNOSTIC AND STATISTICAL MANUAL OF MENTAL DISORDERS, FOURTH EDITION (DSM-IV). This reference book, published by the American Psychiatric Association, is the diagnostic standard for most mental health professionals in the United States.

DIAGNOSTIC TESTING. Testing performed to determine if a person has a particular disease.

DIALYSIS. A process of filtering and removing waste products from the bloodstream, it is used as a treatment for patients whose kidneys do not function properly. Two main types are hemodialysis and peritoneal dialysis.

DIAPER DERMATITIS (DIAPER RASH). An inflammatory reaction to irritants in the diaper area.

DIAPHRAGM. The thin layer of muscle that separates the chest cavity containing the lungs and heart from the abdominal cavity containing the intestines and digestive organs. This term is also used for a dome-shaped device used to cover the back of a woman's vagina during intercourse in order to prevent pregnancy.

DIARRHEA. A loose, watery stool.

DIASTOLIC BLOOD PRESSURE. Diastole is the period in which the left ventricle relaxes so it can refill with blood; diastolic pressure is therefore measured during diastole.

DIDASKALEINOPHOBIA. Fear of going to school.

DIETARY FIBER. Mostly indigestible material in food that stimulates the intestine to peristalsis.

DIFFERENTIATION. The ability to retain one's identity within a family system while maintaining emotional connections with the other members.

DIGESTION. The mechanical, chemical, and enzymatic process in which food is converted into the substances suitable for use by the body.

DILATE. To expand in diameter and size.

DIMERCAPROL. A chemical agent used to remove excess lead from the body.

DIOPTER (D). A unit of measure for describing the refractive power of a lens.

DIPHTHERIA. A serious, frequently fatal, bacterial infection that affects the respiratory tract. Vaccinations given in childhood have made diphtheria very rare in the United States.

DIPHTHERIA-TETANUS-PERTUSSIS (DTP) VACCINE. The standard vaccine used to immunize children against diphtheria, tetanus, and whooping cough. A so-called "acellular pertussis" vaccine (aP) is usually used since its release in the mid-1990s.

DIPLEGIA. Paralysis affecting like parts on both sides the body, such as both arms or both legs.

DISABILITY. An inability to do something others can do; sometimes referred to as handicap or impairment.

DISCHARGE PLANNER. A health care professional who helps parents arrange for health and home care needs after their child goes home from the hospital.

DISCIPLINE. In health care, a specific area of preparation or training, i.e., social work, nursing, or nutrition.

DISCLOSURE. Release of information.

DISEASE-MODIFYING ANTI-RHEUMATIC DRUGS (DMARDS). A group of medications given to treat severe cases of arthritis, JDMS, and other diseases that affect the joints. All DMARDs work by modifying the immune system.

DISFLUENCY. An interruption in speech flow.

DISLOCATION. The displacement of bones at a joint or the displacement of any part of the body from its normal position.

DISSEMINATED. Spread to other tissues.

DISSOCIATIVE DISORDERS. A group of mental disorders in which dissociation is a prominent symptom. Patients with dissociative disorders have a high rate of self-mutilation.

DISTAL MUSCULAR DYSTROPHY (DD). A form of muscular dystrophy that usually begins in middle age or later, causing weakness in the muscles of the feet and hands.

DIURETICS. A group of drugs that helps remove excess water from the body by increasing the amount lost by urination.

DIVERGENT THINKING. The ability to come up with new and unusual answers.

DIVERTICULITIS. Inflammation of the diverticula (small outpouchings) along the wall of the colon, the large intestine.

DIVERTICULUM. Plural, diverticula; an outpouching in a tubular organ caused when the inner, lining layer bulges out (herniates) through the outer, muscular layer. Diverticula are present most often in the colon (large intestine), but are also found in the stomach and the small intestine.

DIZYGOTIC. From two zygotes, as in non-identical, or fraternal twins. The zygote is the first cell formed by the union of sperm and egg.

DNA. Deoxyribonucleic acid; the genetic material in cells that holds the inherited instructions for growth, development, and cellular functioning.

DNA TESTING. Analysis of DNA (the genetic component of cells) in order to determine changes in genes that may indicate a specific disorder.

DOPA. The common name for a natural chemical (3,4-dihydroxyphenylalanine) made by the body during the process of making melanin.

DOPAMINE. A neurotransmitter made in the brain that is involved in many brain activities, including movement and emotion.

DORMANT. The biological state of being relatively inactive or in a resting state in which certain processes are slowed down or suspended.

DORSAL RHIZOTOMY. A surgical procedure that cuts nerve roots to reduce spasticity in affected muscles.

DORSUM. The medical term for the bridge of the nose.

DOULA. A doula is someone who undergoes special training to enable them to support women during childbirth and into the postpartum period.

DOWN SYNDROME. A chromosomal disorder caused by an extra copy or a rearrangement of chromosome 21. Children with Down syndrome have varying degrees of mental retardation and may have heart defects.

DUBOWITZ EXAM. Standardized test that scores responses to 33 specific neurological stimuli to estimate an infant's neural development and, hence, gestational age.

DUCHENNE MUSCULAR DYSTROPHY (DMD). The most severe form of muscular dystrophy, DMD usually affects young boys and causes progressive muscle weakness, usually beginning in the legs.

DUCTUS ARTERIOSUS. The blood vessel that joins the pulmonary artery and the aorta. When the ductus does not close at birth, it causes a type of congenital heart disease called patent ductus arteriosus.

DUODENUM. The first of the three segments of the small intestine. The duodenum is about 10 in (25 cm) long and connects the stomach and the jejunum.

DURA MATER. The strongest and outermost of three membranes that protect the brain, spinal cord, and nerves of the cauda equina.

DUST MITES. Tiny insects, unable to be seen without a microscope, that are present in carpet, stuffed animals, upholstered furniture, and bedding, including pillows, mattresses, quilts, and other bed covers. Dust mites are one of the most common asthma triggers. They grow best in areas with high humidity.

DWARFISM, PITUITARY. Short stature. When caused by hGH deficiency, as opposed to late growth spurt or genetics, abnormally slow growth and short stature with normal proportions may be seen.

DYANA. The yoga term for meditation.

DYSENTERY. A disease marked by frequent watery bowel movements, often with blood and mucus, and characterized by pain, urgency to have a bowel movement, fever, and dehydration.

DYSKINESIA. Impaired ability to make voluntary movements.

DYSLEXIA. A type of reading disorder often characterized by reversal of letters or words.

DYSMENORRHEA. Painful menstruation.

DYSMOTILITY. Abnormally slow or fast rhythmic movement of the stomach or intestine.

DYSPHAGIA. Difficulty in swallowing.

DYSPHORIA. Feelings of anxiety, restlessness, and dissatisfaction.

DYSPLASIA. Abnormal changes in cells.

DYSPNEA. Difficulty in breathing, usually associated with heart or lung diseases.

DYSSOMNIA. A primary sleep disorder in which the patient suffers from changes in the quantity, quality, or timing of sleep.

DYSTOCIA. Failure to progress in labor, either because the cervix will not dilate (expand) further or because the head does not descend through the mother's pelvis after full dilation of the cervix.

DYSTONIA. Painful involuntary muscle cramps or spasms.

DYSTROPHIN. A protein that helps muscle tissue repair itself. Both Duchenne muscular dystrophy and Becker muscular dystrophy are caused by flaws in the gene that tells the body how to make this protein.

DYSURIA. Painful or difficult urination.

E

EAR CANDLING. An alternative method for removing impacted cerumen with a lighted hollow cone of paraffin or beeswax. It does not work and is not considered an acceptable treatment for any ear problem or disorder.

EAR SPECULUM. A cone- or funnel-shaped attachment for an otoscope that is inserted into the ear canal to examine the eardrum.

EARDRUM. A paper-thin covering stretching across the ear canal that separates the middle and outer ears.

ECCENTRIC. Deviating from the center; conduct and behavior departing from accepted norms and conventions.

ECCHYMOSIS. The medical term for a bruise, or skin discoloration caused by blood seeping from broken capillaries under the skin.

ECHOCARDIOGRAM. A record of the internal structures of the heart obtained from beams of ultrasonic waves directed through the wall of the chest.

ECHOCARDIOGRAPHY. A non-invasive technique, using ultrasound waves, used to look at the various structures and functions of the heart.

ECHOLALIA. Involuntary echoing of the last word, phrase, or sentence spoken by someone else.

ECHOPRAXIA. The imitation of the movement of another individual.

ECLAMPSIA. Coma and convulsions during or immediately after pregnancy, characterized by edema, hypertension, and proteinuria.

ECTOPIA LENTIS. Dislocation of the lens of the eye. It is one of the most important single indicators in diagnosing Marfan syndrome.

ECTOPIC. Out of place or located away from the normal position.

ECTOPIC PREGNANCY. A pregnancy that develops outside of the mother's uterus, such as in the fallopian tube. Ectopic pregnancies often cause severe pain in the lower abdomen and are potentially life-threatening because of the massive blood loss that may occur as the developing embryo/fetus ruptures and damages the tissues in which it has implanted.

ECZEMA. A superficial type of inflammation of the skin that may be very itchy and weeping in the early stages; later, the affected skin becomes crusted, scaly, and thick.

EDEMA. The presence of abnormally large amounts of fluid in the intercellular tissue spaces of the body.

EDETATE CALCIUM DISODIUM. A chemical chelating agent used to remove excess lead from the body.

EDTA. A colorless compound used to keep blood samples from clotting before tests are run.

EFFERENT NERVES. Peripheral nerves that carry signals away from the brain and spinal cord.

EFFICACY. The effectiveness of a drug in treating a disease or condition.

EFFUSION. The escape of fluid from blood vessels or the lymphatic system and its collection in a cavity.

EGOCENTRIC. Limited in outlook to things mainly relating to oneself or confined to one's own affairs or activities.

EISENMENGER'S SYNDROME. A condition in which high pressures in the pulmonary arteries cause them to thicken. To compensate, the right side of the heart works harder, causing it to stretch and weaken. Eisenmenger's syndrome is a serious condition that leads to heart failure and can result in death by age 40 if left untreated.

EJACULATION. The process by which semen (made up in part of prostatic fluid) is ejected by the erect penis.

ELBOW. Hinged joint between the forearm and upper arm.

ELECTRIC CURRENT. The rate of flow of electric charge, measured in amperes. Electric current can also be described as the flow of microscopic particles called electrons flowing through wires and electronic components and appliances.

ELECTRICAL RESISTANCE. Resistance to the flow of electrical current.

ELECTROCARDIAGRAM (ECG, EKG). A record of the electrical activity of the heart, with each wave being labeled as P, Q, R, S, and T waves. It is often used in the diagnosis of cases of abnormal cardiac rhythm and myocardial damage.

ELECTROCONVULSIVE THERAPY (ECT). A psychological treatment in which a series of controlled electrical impulses are delivered to the brain in order to induce a seizure within the brain. This type of therapy is used to treat major depression and severe mental illness that does not respond to medications.

ELECTRODE. A medium for conducting an electrical current.

ELECTROENCEPHALOGRAM (EEG). A record of the tiny electrical impulses produced by the brain's activity picked up by electrodes placed on the scalp. By measuring characteristic wave patterns, the EEG can help diagnose certain conditions of the brain.

ELECTROENCEPHALOGRAPHY. The recording of electrical impulses produced by the brain's activity via electrodes attached to a patient's scalp.

ELECTROLYTES. Salts and minerals that produce electrically charged particles (ions) in body fluids. Common human electrolytes are sodium chloride, potassium, calcium, and sodium bicarbonate. Electrolytes control the fluid balance of the body and are important in muscle contraction, energy generation, and almost all major biochemical reactions in the body.

ELECTROMAGNETIC RADIATION. Packets of energy that develop when an electric current passes through a vacuum tube,

ELECTROMYOGRAPHY (EMG). A diagnostic test that records the electrical activity of muscles. In the test, small electrodes are placed on or in the skin; the patterns of electrical activity are projected on a screen or over a loudspeaker. This procedure is used to test for muscle disorders, including muscular dystrophy.

ELECTRONYSTAGMOGRAPHY. A method for measuring the electricity generated by eye movements. Electrodes are placed on the skin around the eye and the individual is subjected to a variety of stimuli so that the quality of eye movements can be assessed.

ELECTROOCULOGRAPHY (EOG). A diagnostic test that records the electrical activity of the muscles that control eye movement.

EMBOLISM. A blood clot, air bubble, or mass of foreign material that travels and blocks the flow of blood in an artery. When blood supply to a tissue or organ is blocked by an embolism, infarction, or death of the tissue the artery feeds, occurs. Without immediate and appropriate treatment, an embolism can be fatal.

EMBOLUS. Plural, emboli. An embolus is something that blocks the blood flow in a blood vessel. It may be a gas bubble, a blood clot, a fat globule, a mass of bacteria, or other foreign body that forms somewhere else and travels through the circulatory system until it gets stuck.

EMBRYO. In humans, the developing individual from the time of implantation to about the end of the second month after conception. From the third month to the point of delivery, the individual is called a fetus.

EMESIS. An act or episode of vomiting.

EMETIC. A medication intended to cause vomiting. Emetics are sometimes used in aversion therapy in place of electric shock. Their most common use in mainstream medicine is in treating accidental poisoning.

EMMENAGOGUE. A type of medication that brings on or increases a woman's menstrual flow.

EMMETROPIA. Normal vision.

EMOTIONAL INTELLIGENCE. The ability to perceive and interpret the emotions of others.

EMPATHY. A quality of the client-centered therapist, characterized by the therapist's conveying appreciation and understanding of the client's point of view.

EMPHYSEMA. A chronic respiratory disease that involves the destruction of air sac walls to form abnormally large air sacs that have reduced gas exchange ability and that tend to retain air within the lungs. Symptoms include labored breathing, the inability to forcefully blow air out of the lungs, and an increased susceptibility to respiratory tract infections. Emphysema is usually caused by smoking.

EMPIRICAL TREATMENT. Medical treatment that is given on the basis of the doctor's observations and experience.

ENAMEL. The hard, outermost surface of a tooth.

ENCEPHALITIS. Inflammation of the brain, usually caused by a virus. The inflammation may interfere with normal brain function and may cause seizures, sleepiness, confusion, personality changes, weakness in one or more parts of the body, and even coma.

ENCEPHALOMYELITIS. Encephalitis or another acute inflammation of the brain and spinal cord that can be caused by the rabies virus.

ENCEPHALOPATHY. Any abnormality in the structure or function of brain tissues.

ENCOPRESIS. Fecal incontinence that can occur as a result of stress or fear.

ENDEMIC. Natural to or characteristic of a particular place, population, or climate.

ENDEMIC DISEASE. An infectious disease that occurs frequently in a specific geographical locale. The disease often occurs in cycles.

ENDOCARDITIS. Inflammation of the inner membrane lining heart and/or of the heart valves caused by infection.

ENDOCHONDRAL OSSIFICATION. The process by which cartilage is converted into bone.

ENDOCRINE SYSTEM. A group of ductless glands and parts of glands that secrete hormones directly into the bloodstream or lymphatic system to control metabolic activity. Pituitary, thyroid, adrenals, ovaries, and testes are all part of the endocrine system.

ENDOCRINOLOGIST. A physician who specializes in treating patients who have diseases of the thyroid, parathyroid, adrenal glands, and/or the pancreas.

ENDODONTIST. A dentist who specializes in diagnosing and treating diseases of the pulp and other inner structures of the tooth.

ENDOMETRIOSIS. A condition in which the tissue that normally lines the uterus (endometrium) grows in other areas of the body, causing pain, irregular bleeding, and frequently, infertility.

ENDOMETRITIS. Inflammation of the endometrium or mucous membrane of the uterus.

ENDOMETRIUM. The mucosal layer lining the inner cavity of the uterus. The endometrium's structure changes with age and with the menstrual cycle.

ENDOSCOPE. A medical instrument that can be passed into an area of the body (the bladder or intestine, for example) to allow visual examination of that area. The endoscope usually has a fiber-optic camera that allows a greatly magnified image to be shown on a television screen viewed by the operator. Many endoscopes also allow the operator to retrieve a small sample (biopsy) of the area being examined, to more closely view the tissue under a microscope.

ENDOSCOPY. Visual examination of an organ or body cavity using an endoscope, a thin, tubular instrument containing a camera and light source. Many endoscopes also allow the retrieval of a small sample (biopsy) of the area being examined, in order to more closely view the tissue under a microscope.

ENDOSTEAL RESORPTION. The process by which bones are thinned from the inside.

ENDOTHELIAL CELLS. The cells lining the inner walls of a body cavity or the cardiovascular system. Also known as endothelium.

ENDOTRACHEAL TUBE. A hollow tube that is inserted into the trachea (windpipe) through the nose or mouth. It is used to administer anesthesia, to deliver oxygen under pressure, or to deliver medications (e.g. surfactants).

ENGLISH AS A SECOND LANGUAGE (ESL). English language instruction for English language learners (ELLs) that includes little or no use of a child's native language; a component of all bilingual education programs.

ENGLISH LANGUAGE LEARNER (ELL). A student who is learning English as a second language; also called limited English proficient (LEP).

ENTERAL NUTRITION. Liquid nutrition provided through tubes that enter the gastrointestinal tract, usually through the mouth or nose.

ENTERIC COATING. A coating or shell placed on a tablet that breaks up and releases the medicine into the intestine rather than the stomach.

ENTEROCOLITIS. Severe inflammation of the intestines that affects the intestinal lining, muscle, nerves and blood vessels.

ENTEROPATHY. A disease of the intestinal tract.

ENTEROVIRUS. Any of a group of viruses that primarily affect the gastrointestinal tract. The coxsackievirus and the poliovirus are both enteroviruses.

ENTERTAINMENT SOFTWARE RATING BOARD (ESRB). The industry board that rates video games.

ENTOMOPHOBIA. Fear of insects.

ENUCLEATION. Surgical removal of the eyeball.

ENZYME. A protein that catalyzes a biochemical reaction without changing its own structure or function.

EOSINOPHIL. A type of white blood cell containing granules that can be stained by eosin (a chemical that produces a red stain). Eosinophils increase in response to parasitic infections and allergic reactions.

EOSINOPHILIA. An abnormal increase in the number of eosinophils, a type of white blood cell.

EPIDEMIC. Refers to a situation in which a particular disease rapidly spreads among many people in the same geographical region in a relatively short period of time.

EPIDEMIC PAROTITIS. The medical name for mumps.

EPIDERMIS. The outermost layer of the human skin.

EPIGLOTTIS. A leaf-like piece of cartilage extending upwards from the larynx, which can close like a lid over the trachea to prevent the airway from receiving any food or liquid being swallowed.

EPIGLOTTITIS. Inflammation of the epiglottis, most often caused by a bacterial infection. The epiglottis is a piece of cartilage behind the tongue that closes the opening to the windpipe when a person swallows. An inflamed epiglottis can swell and close off the windpipe, thus causing the patient to suffocate. Also called supraglottitis.

EPILEPSY. A neurological disorder characterized by recurrent seizures with or without a loss of consciousness.

EPILEPTOLOGIST. A physician who specializes in the treatment of epilepsy.

EPINEPHRINE. A hormone produced by the adrenal medulla. It is important in the response to stress and partially regulates heart rate and metabolism. It is also called adrenaline.

EPISIOTOMY. An incision made in the perineum (the area between the vulva and the anus) during labor to assist in delivery and to avoid abnormal tearing of the perineum.

EPISODIC. Occurring once in a while, without a regular pattern.

EPISTAXIS. The medical term used to describe a bleeding from the nose.

EPITHELIUM. The layer of cells that covers body surfaces, lines body cavities, and forms glands.

EQUATOR. Imaginary line encircling the eyeball and dividing the eye into a front and back half.

ERB'S PALSY OR PARALYSIS. A condition caused by an injury to the upper brachial plexus, involving the cervical nerves C5, C6, and sometimes C7, affecting the upper arm and the rotation of the lower arm.

ERGOTAMINE. A drug used to prevent or treat migraine headaches. It can cause vomiting, diarrhea, and convulsions in infants and should not be taken by women who are nursing.

ERRATIC. Having no fixed course; behavior that deviates from common and accepted opinions.

ERUPTION. The process of a tooth breaking through the gum tissue to grow into place in the mouth.

ERYTHEMA. A diffuse red and inflamed area of the skin.

ERYTHEMA MIGRANS. A red skin rash that is one of the first signs of Lyme disease in about 75% of patients.

ERYTHROPOIESIS. The process through which new red blood cells are created; it begins in the bone marrow.

ERYTHROPOIETIC. Referring to the creation of new red blood cells.

ESCHERICHIA COLI. A type of enterobacterium that is responsible for most cases of severe bacterial diarrhea in the United States.

ESOPHAGEAL ATRESIA. Blockage or closure of the esophagus, the tube leading from the mouth to the stomach.

ESOPHAGOGASTRODUODENOSCOPY (EGD). An imaging test that involves visually examining the lining of the esophagus, stomach, and upper duodenum with a flexible fiberoptic endoscope.

ESOPHAGUS. The muscular tube that leads from the back of the throat to the entrance of the stomach. It is coated with mucus and surrounded by muscles, and pushes food to the stomach by sequential waves of contraction. It functions to transport food from the throat to the stomach and to keep the contents of the stomach in the stomach.

ESSENTIAL FATTY ACID (EFA). A fatty acid that the body requires but cannot make. It must be obtained from the diet. EFAs include omega-6 fatty acids found in primrose and safflower oils, and omega-3 fatty acids oils found in fatty fish and flaxseed, canola, soybean, and walnuts.

ESSENTIAL TREMOR. An uncontrollable (involuntary) shaking of the hands, head, and face. Also called familial tremor because it is sometimes inherited, it can begin in the teens or in middle age. The exact cause is not known.

ESTROGEN. Female hormone produced mainly by the ovaries and released by the follicles as they mature. Responsible for female sexual characteristics, estrogen stimulates and triggers a response from at least 300 tissues. After menopause, the production of the hormone gradually stops.

ESTRUS. A regular period of sexual excitement in females.

EUPHORIA. A feeling or state of well-being or elation.

EUROCENTRIC. Centered or focused on Europe or European peoples, especially in relation to historical or cultural influence.

EUSTACHIAN TUBE. A thin tube between the middle ear and the pharnyx. Its purpose is to equalize pressure on either side of the ear drum.

EX UTERO INTRAPARTUM TREATMENT (EXIT). A cesarean section in which the infant is removed from the uterus but the umbilical cord is not cut until after surgery for a congenital defect that blocks the air passage.

EXANTHEM. A skin eruption regarded as a characteristic sign of such diseases as measles, German measles, and scarlet fever.

EXERCISE-INDUCED BRONCHOSPASM. A sudden contraction in the lower airway that causes breathing problems and is brought about by heavy exercise.

EXFOLIATE. To shed skin. In skin care, the term exfoliate describes the process of removing dead skin cells.

EXOTOXIN. A poisonous secretion produced by bacilli that is carried in the bloodstream to other parts of the body.

EXPECTORANT. A drug that promotes the discharge of mucus from respiratory system.

EXPERIMENTAL PLAY THERAPY. Play therapy based on the belief that a child has the ability to solve his or her own problems within the context of a warm and caring therapeutic environment.

EXPRESSIVE APHASIA. A developmental disorder in which a child has lower-than-normal proficiency in vocabulary, production of complex sentences, and word recall, although language comprehension is normal.

EXPRESSIVE LANGUAGE. Communicating with language.

EXPRESSIVE LANGUAGE DEVELOPMENT. A style of language development in which a child's babble mimics the cadence and rhythm of adult speech.

EXSTROPHY. A congenital condition in which a hollow organ, such as the bladder, is turned inside out, establishing contact between the organ and the outside of the body.

EXTENDED FAMILY. Traditionally defined as the biological relatives of a nuclear family (the parents, sisters, and brothers of both members of a married couple); sometimes used to refer to the people living in the household as partners and parents with children.

EXTENDED FAMILY FIELD. A person's family of origin plus grandparents, in-laws, and other relatives.

EXTERNAL CEPHALIC VERSION. Manual manipulation of the abdomen in order to turn a breech baby; also known as version.

EXTRACTION. The removal of a tooth from its socket in the bone.

EXTRAOCULAR RETINOBLASTOMA. Cancer that has spread from the eye to other parts of the body.

EXTRAUTERINE. Occurring outside the uterus.

EXTRAVASATION. To pass from a blood vessel into the surrounding tissue.

EXTROVERSION. A personal preference for socially engaging activities and settings.

EXTROVERT. A person who is outgoing and performs well socially.

EXTUBATION. The removal of a breathing tube.

EXUDATE. Cells, protein, fluid, or other materials that pass through cell or blood vessel walls. Exudates may accumulate in the surrounding tissue or may be discharged outside the body.

EXUDATION. Leakage of cells, proteins, and fluids through the blood vessel wall into the surrounding tissue.

F

FACIOSCAPULOHUMERAL MUSCULAR DYSTROPHY (FSH). This form of muscular dystrophy, also known as Landouzy-Dejerine disease, begins in late childhood to early adulthood and affects both men and women, causing weakness in the muscles of the face, shoulders, and upper arms.

FACTITIOUS DISORDER. A mental condition in which symptoms are deliberately manufactured by patients in order to gain attention and sympathy. Patients with factitious diseases do not fake symptoms for obvious financial gain or to evade the legal system.

FACTOR VIII. A protein involved in blood clotting that requires von Willebrand factor for stability and long-term survival in the bloodstream.

FALLOPIAN TUBES. The pair of narrow tubes leading from a woman's ovaries to the uterus. After an egg is released from the ovary during ovulation, fertilization (the union of sperm and egg) normally occurs in the fallopian tubes.

FAMILY. Two or more emotionally involved people living in close proximity and having reciprocal obligations with a sense of commonness, caring, and commitment.

FAMILY SYSTEMS THEORY. An approach to treatment that emphasizes the interdependency of family members rather than focusing on individuals in isolation from the family. This theory underlies the most influential forms of contemporary family therapy.

FAMILY THERAPY. A type of therapy in which the entire immediate family participates.

FANCONI'S SYNDROME. A group of disorders involving kidney tubule malfunction and glucose, phosphate, and bicarbonate in the urine. Two forms of this syndrome have been identified: an inherited form and an acquired form caused by vitamin D deficiency or exposure to heavy metals.

FANTASY PLAY. Play activities in which children act out their fantasies.

FASCICULATIONS. Small involuntary muscle contractions visible under the skin.

FASCIITIS. Inflammation of the fascia (plural, fasciae), which refers to bands or sheaths of connective tissue that cover, support, or connect the muscles and internal organs. Human bites can lead to infection of the fasciae in the hand.

FAST-ACTING CARBOHYDRATE. A carbohydrate that causes blood sugar levels to rise quickly rather than slowly and steadily. Also called simple sugars. Examples include glucose tablets, honey, fructose, hard candy, and cake frosting.

FAT-SOLUBLE VITAMIN. A vitamin that dissolves easily in fat or oil, but not in water. The fat-soluble vitamins are vitamins D, E, A, and K.

FATTY ACID. The primary component of lipids (fats) in the body. The body requires some, called essential fatty acids, to form membranes and synthesize important compounds.

FEBRILE SEIZURE. Convulsions brought on by fever.

FECES. The solid waste, also called stool, that is left after food is digested. Feces form in the intestines and pass out of the body through the anus.

FEMALE ATHLETE TRIAD. A combination of disorders frequently found in female athletes that includes disordered eating, osteoporosis, and oligo- or amenorrhea. The triad was first officially named in 1993.

FEMUR. The thigh bone.

FERTILIZATION. The joining of the sperm and the egg; conception.

FETAL PROTEINS. Proteins that are usually produced during fetal development but may persist at high blood levels in some conditions after birth.

FETAL TISSUE TRANSPLANTATION. A method of treating Parkinson's and other neurological diseases by grafting brain cells from human fetuses onto the basal ganglia.

FETOSCOPE. A fiber optic instrument for viewing the fetus inside the uterus.

FETUS. In humans, the developing organism from the end of the eighth week to the moment of birth. Until the end of the eighth week the developing organism is called an embryo.

FIBER. Carbohydrate material in food that cannot be digested.

FIBRILLIN. A protein that is an important part of the structure of the body's connective tissue. In Marfan's syndrome, the gene responsible for fibrillin has mutated, causing the body to produce a defective protein.

FIBRIN. The last step in the blood coagulation process. Fibrin forms strands that add bulk to a forming blood clot to hold it in place and help "plug" an injured blood vessel wall.

FIBROID TUMOR. A non-cancerous tumor of connective tissue made of elongated, threadlike structures, or fibers, which usually grow slowly and are contained within an irregular shape. Fibroids are firm in consistency but may become painful if they start to break down or apply pressure to areas within the body.

FIGHT BITE. Another name for closed-fist injury.

FINANCIAL COUNSELOR. Professional who can provide assistance with financial matters associated with the patient's hospital stay. The financial counselor can help families evaluate their insurance plan's hospitalization coverage, determine a payment plan for medical expenses that are not covered, and discuss possible sources of financial aid.

FINE MOTOR SKILL. The abilities required to control the smaller muscles of the body for writing, playing an instrument, artistic expression, and craft work. The muscles required to perform fine motor skills are generally found in the hands, feet, and head.

FISTULA. An abnormal channel that connects two organs or connects an organ to the skin.

FLACCID. Flabby, limp, weak, or floppy.

FLACCID PARALYSIS. Paralysis characterized by limp, unresponsive muscles.

FLARE. A sudden worsening or recurrence of a disease.

FLAT AFFECT. Showing no emotion.

FLAVONOID. A food chemical that helps to limit oxidative damage to the body's cells, and protects against heart disease and cancer.

FLEXION. The act of bending or condition of being bent.

FLEXOR MUSCLE. A muscle that serves to flex or bend a part of the body.

FLEX-TIME. A system that allows employees to set their own work schedules within guidelines or limits set by the employer.

FLUORAPATITE. Fluoride-substituted hydroxyapatite.

FLUORESCENCE IN SITU HYBRIDIZATION (FISH). A technique for diagnosing genetic disorders before birth by analyzing cells obtained by amniocentesis with DNA probes.

FLUORESCENT ANTIBODY TEST. A test in which a fluorescent dye is linked to an antibody for diagnostic purposes.

FLUORIDE. A chemical compound containing fluorine that is used to treat water or applied directly to teeth to prevent decay.

FLUOROQUINOLONES. A relatively new group of antibiotics used to treat infections with many gram-negative bacteria, such as *Shigella*. One drawback is that they should not be used in children under 17 years of age, because of possible effect on bone or cartilage growth.

FLUOROSIS. Mottled discoloration of tooth enamel due to excessive systemic ingestion of fluoride during tooth development.

FMR-1 GENE. A gene found on the X chromosome. Its exact purpose is unknown, but it is suspected that the gene plays a role in brain development.

FOLLICLE-STIMULATING HORMONE (FSH). A pituitary hormone that in females stimulates the ovary to mature egg capsules (follicles) and in males stimulates sperm production.

FONTANELLE. One of several "soft spots" on the skull where the developing bones of the skull have yet to fuse.

FOOD-BORNE ILLNESS. A disease that is transmitted by eating or handling contaminated food.

FORAMEN MAGNUM. The opening at the base of the skull, through which the spinal cord and the brainstem pass.

FORAMEN OVALE. A fetal cardiac structure that allows the blood in both upper chambers (atria) of the heart to mix. After birth, the pressure rises in the left atrium pushing this opening closed, allowing the heart to function in a two-sided fashion: the right side carries the unoxygenated blood to the lungs, and the left side pumps the oxygenated blood out into the body.

FORCED EXHALATION. Blowing as much air out of the lungs as possible.

FORCIBLE SODOMY. Forced oral or anal intercourse.

FORENSIC. Pertaining to courtroom procedure or evidence used in courts of law.

FORESKIN. A covering fold of skin over the tip of the penis.

FRAGILE X SYNDROME. A genetic condition related to the X chromosome that affects mental, physical, and sensory development. It is the most common form of inherited mental retardation.

FRANK BREECH. A breech position where the baby is bottom first and his legs are extended upward so that his feet are near his head.

FREE RADICAL. An unstable molecule that causes oxidative damage by stealing electrons from surrounding molecules, thereby disrupting activity in the body's cells.

FREQUENCY. Sound, whether traveling through air or the human body, produces vibrations—molecules bouncing into each other—as the sound wave travels along. The frequency of a sound is the number of vibrations per second. Within the audible range, frequency means pitch—the higher the frequency, the higher a sound's pitch.

FUNDAL HEIGHT. Measured by a tape measure from the top of the symphysis pubis, over the arch of the growing uterus, to the top of the fundus.

FUNDOPLICATION. A surgical procedure that increases pressure on the lower esophageal sphincter by stretching and wrapping the upper part of the stomach around the sphincter.

FUNDUS. The inside of an organ. In the eye, fundus refers to the back area that can be seen with the ophthalmoscope.

FUNGAL. Caused by a fungus.

G

GAIT. Walking motions.

GALACTOSE. One of the two simple sugars (glucose is the other one) that makes up the protein, lactose, found in milk. Galactose can be toxic in high levels.

GANGLION. Plural, ganglia. A mass of nerve tissue or a group of neurons.

GANGLIOSIDE. A fatty (lipid) substance found within the brain and nerve cells.

GANGRENE. Decay or death of body tissue because the blood supply is cut off. Tissues that have died in this way must be surgically removed.

GASTRIC LAVAGE. Also called a stomach pump. For this procedure, a flexible tube is inserted through the nose, down the throat, and into the stomach. The contents of the stomach are then suctioned out. The inside of the stomach is rinsed with a saline (saltwater) solution.

GASTROENTERITIS. Inflammation of the stomach and intestines that usually causes nausea, vomiting, diarrhea, abdominal pain, and cramps.

GASTROENTEROLOGIST. A physician who specializes in diseases of the digestive system.

GASTROESOPHAGEAL REFLUX. The backflow of stomach contents into the esophagus.

GASTROESOPHAGEAL REFLUX DISEASE (GERD). A disorder of the lower end of the esophagus in which the lower esophageal sphincter does not open and close normally. As a result the acidic contents of the stomach can flow backward into the esophagus and irritate the tissues.

GASTROINTESTINAL. Pertaining to the digestive organs and structures, including the stomach and intestines.

GASTROINTESTINAL (GI) SYSTEM. The body system involved in digestion, the breaking down and use of food. It includes the stomach, small intestine, and large intestine. Also known as the gastrointestinal tract.

GASTROSTOMY TUBE. A tube that is inserted through a small incision in the abdominal wall and that extends through the stomach wall into the stomach for the purpose of introducing parenteral feedings. Also called a gastric tube, gastrointestinal tube, or stomach tube.

GAY BASHING. Physical or verbal violence directed against homosexuals.

GENDER IDENTITY DISORDER (GID). A strong and lasting cross-gender identification and persistent discomfort with one's biological gender (sex) role. This discomfort must cause a significant amount of distress or impairment in the functioning of the individual.

GENE. A building block of inheritance, which contains the instructions for the production of a particular protein, and is made up of a molecular sequence found on a section of DNA. Each gene is found on a precise location on a chromosome.

GENE THERAPY. An experimental treatment for certain genetic disorders in which a abnormal gene is replaced with the normal copy. Also called somatic-cell gene therapy.

GENERAL ANESTHESIA. Deep sleep induced by a combination of medicines that allows surgery to be performed.

GENETIC. Refers to genes, the basic units of biological heredity, which are contained on the chromosomes.

GENETIC DISEASE. A disease that is (partly or completely) the result of the abnormal function or expression of a gene; a disease caused by the inheritance and expression of a genetic mutation.

GENITAL. Refers to the sexual or reproductive organs that are visible outside the body.

GENITAL HERPES. A life-long, recurrent sexually transmitted infection caused by the herpes simplex virus (HSV).

GENOGRAM. A family tree diagram that represents the names, birth order, sex, and relationships of the members of a family. Therapists use genograms to detect recurrent patterns in the family history and to help the family members understand their problem(s).

GENU RECURVATUM. Hyperextension of the knee.

GEOPHAGIA. The compulsive eating of earth substances, including sand, soil, and clay.

GESTATION. The period from conception to birth, during which the developing fetus is carried in the uterus.

GESTATIONAL DIABETES. Diabetes of pregnancy leading to increased levels of blood sugar. Unlike diabetes mellitus, gestational diabetes is caused by pregnancy and goes away when pregnancy ends.

GHRELIN. A peptide hormone secreted by cells in the lining of the stomach. Ghrelin is important in appetite regulation and maintaining the body's energy balance.

GIGANTISM. Excessive growth, especially in height, resulting from overproduction of growth hormone during childhood or adolescence by a pituitary tumor. Untreated, the tumor eventually destroys the pituitary gland, resulting in death during early adulthood.

GINGIVA. The gum tissue surrounding the teeth.

GINGIVAL SULCUS. The space between the tooth and the gum that often traps food and bacteria, leading to periodontal disease.

GINGIVITIS. Inflammation of the gums in which the margins of the gums near the teeth are red, puffy, and bleeding. It is most often due to poor dental hygiene.

GLAND. A collection of cells whose function is to release certain chemicals (hormones) that are important to the functioning of other, sometimes distantly located, organs or body systems.

GLANS PENIS. The cone-shaped tip of the penis.

GLAUCOMA. A common eye disease characterized by increased fluid pressure in the eye that damages the optic nerve, which carries visual impulses to the brain. Glaucoma can be caused by another eye disorder, such as a tumor or congenital malformation, or can appear without obvious cause, but if untreated it generally leads to blindness.

GLOBIN. One of the component protein molecules found in hemoglobin. Normal adult hemoglobin has a pair each of alpha-globin and beta-globin molecules.

GLOMERULUS. Plural, glomeruli; a network of capillaries located in the nephron of the kidney where wastes are filtered from the blood.

GLOSSOPHOBIA. Fear of speaking.

GLOTTIS. The opening between the vocal cords at the upper part of the larynx.

GLUCAGON. A hormone produced in the pancreas that changes glycogen, a carbohydrate stored in muscles and the liver, into glucose. It can be used to relax muscles for a procedure such as duodenography. An injectable form of glucagon is sometimes used to treat insulin shock.

GLUCOCORTICOIDS. A general class of adrenal cortical hormones that are mainly active in protecting against stress and in protein and carbohydrate metabolism. They are widely used in medicine anti-inflammatories and immunosuppresives.

GLUCOSE. A simple sugar that serves as the body's main source of energy.

GLUCOSE-6-PHOSPHATE DEHYDROGENASE (G6PD) DEFICIENCY. A sex-linked hereditary disorder in which the body lacks an enzyme that normally protects red blood cells from toxic chemicals. When people with this condition take certain drugs, their red blood cells break down, causing anemia.

GLUTEN. A protein found in wheat, rye, barley, and oats.

GLYCATED HEMOGLOBIN. A test that measures the amount of hemoglobin bound to glucose. It is a measure of how much glucose has been in the blood during a two to three month period beginning approximately one month prior to sample collection.

GLYCEMIC. The presence of glucose in the blood.

GOITER. Chronic enlargement of the thyroid gland.

GONADOTROPHIN. Hormones that stimulate the ovary and testicles.

GONADS. Organs that produce gametes (eggs or sperm), i.e. the ovaries and testes.

GONOCOCCAL. Refers to the bacterium *Neisseria gonorrheae*. This bacterium causes gonorrhea, a sexually transmitted infection of the genitals and urinary tract. The gonococcal organism may occasionally affect the eye, causing blindness if not treated.

GONORRHEA. A sexually transmitted disease that causes infection in the genital organs and may cause disease in other parts of the body.

GOODNESS OF FIT. A term first used by Thomas and Chess to describe the importance of children's interactions with their environment as well as their basic temperament in understanding their later growth and development.

GOUT. A metabolic disorder characterized by sudden recurring attacks of arthritis caused by deposits of crystals that build up in the joints due to abnormally high uric acid blood levels.

GRAFT. A transplanted organ or other tissue.

GRAM STAIN. A staining procedure used to visualize and classify bacteria. The Gram stain procedure allows the identification of purple (gram positive) organisms and red (gram negative) organisms. This identification aids in determining treatment.

GRAM-NEGATIVE. Refers to bacteria that have a cell wall composed of a thin layer of peptidoglycan surrounded by an outer membrane made of polysaccharides and proteins. They take on the red color of the counterstain used in the Gram stain procedure.

GRANULES. Small packets of reactive chemicals stored within cells.

GRANULOCYTOPENIA. A condition characterized by a deficiency of white blood cells.

GRANULOMA. An inflammatory swelling or growth composed of granulation tissue

GRAY MATTER. Areas of the brain and spinal cord that are comprised mostly of unmyelinated nerves.

GRIEF REACTION. The normal depression felt after a traumatic major life occurrence such as the loss of a loved one.

GROSS MOTOR SKILLS. The abilities required to control the large muscles of the body for walking, running, sitting, crawling, and other activities. The muscles required to perform gross motor skills are generally found in the arms, legs, back, abdomen and torso.

GROUP B STREPTOCOCCUS. A serotype of streptococcus, *Streptococcus agalactiae*, which is beta hemolytic and can cause neonatal sepsis, pneumonia, or meningitis if present in the birth canal at the time of delivery especially when the delivery is difficult.

GROWTH HORMONE. A hormone that eventually stimulates growth. Also called somatotropin.

GUILLAIN-BARRÉ SYNDROME. Progressive and usually reversible paralysis or weakness of multiple muscles usually starting in the lower extremities and often ascending to the muscles involved in respiration. The syndrome is due to inflammation and loss of the myelin covering of the nerve fibers, often associated with an acute infection. Also called acute idiopathic polyneuritis.

H

H2RAS. Medications used to treat some gastroesophageal reflux disease symptoms, for example, Tagamet, Pepcid, Axid.

HAEMOPHILUS INFLUENZAE **TYPE B.** An anaerobic bacteria associated with human respiratory infections, conjunctivitis, and meningitis.

HAIR CELLS. Sensory receptors in the inner ear that transform sound vibrations into messages that travel to the brain.

HAIR FOLLICLE. The root of a hair (that portion of a hair below the skin surface) together with its epithelial and connective tissue coverings.

HAIRBULB. The root of a strand of hair from which growth and coloration of the hair develops.

HALO EFFECT. An observer bias in which the observer interprets a child's actions in a way that confirm the observer's preconceived ideas about the child.

HAND-EYE COORDINATION. The ability to grasp or touch an object while looking at it.

HATHA YOGA. A form of yoga using postures, breathing methods, and meditation.

HEAD START. A federal program started in 1965 that provides free education for young children in many low-income families across the United States.

HEART ATTACK. Damage that occurs to the heart when one of the coronary arteries becomes narrowed or blocked.

HEART FAILURE. A condition in which the heart is unable to pump enough blood to supply the needs of the body

HEARTBURN. A burning sensation in the chest that can extend to the neck, throat, and face. It is the primary symptom of gastroesophageal reflux (the movement of stomach acid into the esophagus).

HEAT EXHAUSTION. A condition of physical weakness or collapse often accompanied by nausea, muscle cramps, and dizziness, that is caused by exposure to intense heat.

HEAT STROKE. A serious condition that results from exposure to extreme heat. The body loses its ability to cool itself. Severe headache, high fever, and hot, dry skin may result. In severe cases, a person with heat stroke may collapse or go into a coma.

HEAVY METAL. One of 23 chemical elements that has a specific gravity (a measure of density) at least five times that of water.

HEIMLICH MANEUVER. An emergency procedure for removing a foreign object lodged in the airway that is preventing the person from breathing. To perform the Heimlich maneuver on a conscious adult, the rescuer stands behind the victim and encircles his waist. The rescuer makes a fist with one hand and places the other hand on top, positioned below the rib cage and above the waist. The rescuer then applies pressure by a series of upward and inward thrusts to force the foreign object back up the victim's trachea.

HEMANGIOMA. A benign skin tumor composed of abnormal blood vessels.

HEMATIN. A drug administered intravenously to halt an acute porphyria attack. It causes heme biosynthesis to decrease, preventing the further accumulation of heme precursors.

HEMATOCRIT. A measure of the percentage of red blood cells in the total volume of blood in the human body.

HEMATOMA. A localized collection of blood, often clotted, in body tissue or an organ, usually due to a break or tear in the wall of blood vessel.

HEMATURIA. The presence of blood in the urine.

HEME. The iron-containing molecule in hemoglobin that serves as the site for oxygen binding.

HEMIANOPSIA. Loss of half of the field of vision.

HEMIPLEGIA. Paralysis of one side of the body.

HEMOCHROMATOSIS. An inherited blood disorder that causes the body to retain excessive amounts of iron. This iron overload can lead to serious health consequences, including painful joints, diabetes, and liver damage, if the iron concentration is not lowered.

HEMOCYTOMETER. An instrument used to count platelets or other blood cells.

HEMOGLOBIN. An iron-containing pigment of red blood cells composed of four amino acid chains (alpha, beta, gamma, delta) that delivers oxygen from the lungs to the cells of the body and carries carbon dioxide from the cells to the lungs.

HEMOGLOBIN A. Normal adult hemoglobin that contains a heme molecule, two alpha-globin molecules, and two beta-globin molecules.

HEMOGLOBIN ELECTROPHORESIS. A laboratory test that separates molecules based on their size, shape, or electrical charge. It is used to identify abnormal hemoglobins in the blood.

HEMOGLOBINOPATHY. A disorder of hemoglobin, which can be either the presence of abnormal types of hemoglobin or abnormal levels of specific types of hemoglobin, i.e., sickle cell disease and thalessemia.

HEMOLYSIS. The process of breaking down of red blood cells. As the cells are destroyed, hemoglobin, the component of red blood cells which carries the oxygen, is liberated.

HEMOLYTIC. Able to break down or dissolve red blood cells.

HEMOLYTIC ANEMIA. A form of anemia characterized by chronic premature destruction of red cells in the bloodstream. Hemolytic anemias are classified as either inherited or acquired.

HEMOLYTIC-UREMIC SYNDROME (HUS). A potentially fatal complication of *E. coli* infection characterized by kidney failure and destruction of red blood cells.

HEMOPHILIA. Any of several hereditary blood coagulation disorders occurring almost exclusively in males. Because blood does not clot properly, even minor injuries can cause significant blood loss that may require a blood transfusion, with its associated minor risk of infection.

HEMORRHAGE. Severe, massive bleeding that is difficult to control. The bleeding may be internal or external.

HENOCH-SCHÖNLEIN PURPURA. A syndrome sometimes classified as a hypersensitivity vasculitis, associated with a variety of digestive symptoms, pain in the joints, and kidney involvement. Purpura comes from the Latin word for "purple" and refers to the reddish-purple spots on the skin caused by leakage of blood from inflamed capillaries.

HEPARIN. An organic acid that occurs naturally in the body and prevents blood clots. Heparin is also made synthetically and can be given as an anticoagulant treatment.

HEPATIC. Refers to the liver.

HEPATITIS. An inflammation of the liver, with accompanying liver cell damage or cell death, caused most frequently by viral infection, but also by certain drugs, chemicals, or poisons. May be either acute (of limited duration) or chronic (continuing).

HEPATITIS A. Commonly called infectious hepatitis, caused by the hepatitis A virus (HAV). Most often spread by food and water contamination.

HEPATITIS B. An infection of the liver that is caused by a DNA virus, is transmitted by contaminated blood or blood derivatives in transfusions, by sexual contact with an infected person, or by the use of contaminated needles and instruments.

HEPATITIS B IMMUNE GLOBULIN. HBIG, a blood serum preparation containing anti-hepatitis-B antibodies (anti-HBs) that is administered along with HBV to children born to hepatitis-B-infected mothers.

HEPATITIS B VIRUS (HBV). Also called Hepadna virus, the pathogen responsible for hepatitis B infection.

HEREDITARY. Something which is inherited, that is passed down from parents to offspring. In biology and medicine, the word pertains to inherited genetic characteristics.

HEREDITARY ATAXIA. One of a group of hereditary degenerative diseases of the spinal cord or cerebellum. These diseases cause tremor, spasm, and wasting of muscle.

HERMANSKY-PUDLAK SYNDROME. A rare type of albinism, most common in the Puerto Rican community, which can cause pigment changes, lung disease, intestinal disorders, and blood disorders.

HERNIA. A rupture in the wall of a body cavity, through which an organ may protrude.

HERNIATION. Bulging of tissue through opening in a membrane, muscle, or bone.

HERNIORRHAPHY. Surgical repair of a hernia.

HERPES SIMPLEX VIRUS. A virus that can cause fever and blistering on the skin and mucous membranes. Herpes simplex 1 infections usually occur on the face (cold sores) and herpes simplex 2 infections usually occur in the genital region.

HERPES STOMATITIS. A form of stomatitis caused by the herpes 1 virus, usually seen in young children.

HERPES ZOSTER VIRUS. Acute inflammatory virus that attacks the nerve cells on the root of each spinal nerve with skin eruptions along a sensory nerve ending. It causes chickenpox and shingles. Also called varicella zoster virus.

HERPES VIRUS. A family of viruses including herpes simplex types 1 and 2, and herpes zoster (also called varicella zoster). Herpes viruses cause several infections, all characterized by blisters and ulcers, including chickenpox, shingles, genital herpes, and cold sores or fever blisters.

HERPETIC GINGIVOSTOMATITIS. A severe oral infection that affects children under five years of age; vesicles and ulcerations, edematous throat, enlarged painful cervical lymph nodes occur; chills, fever, malaise, bed breath, and drooling.

HETEROZYGOTE/HETEROZYGOUS. Having two different versions of the same gene.

HIATAL HERNIA. A condition in which part of the stomach protrudes through the diaphragm into the chest cavity.

HIB DISEASE. An infection caused by *Haemophilus influenza* type b (Hib). This disease mainly affects children under the age of five. In that age group, it is the leading cause of bacterial meningitis, pneumonia, joint and bone infections, and throat inflammations.

HIGH. The altered state of consciousness that a person seeks when abusing a substance.

HISTAMINE. A substance released by immune system cells in response to the presence of an allergen. It stimulates widening of blood vessels and increased porousness of blood vessel walls so that fluid and protein leak out from the blood into the surrounding tissue, causing localized inflammation of the tissue.

HISTOLOGY. The study of tissue structure.

HISTRIONIC PERSONALITY DISORDER. A mental disorder characterized by inappropriate attention-seeking behavior, rapid emotional shifts, and exaggerated expression of emotion.

HODGKIN'S DISEASE. One of two general types of lymphoma (cancers that arise in the the lymphatic system and can invade other organs), Hodgkin's disease is characterized by lymph node enlargement and the presence of a large polyploid cells called Reed-Sternberg cells.

HOME CARE. Health care services provided in the patient's home. If home health services will be needed after the patient is discharged, they can be arranged by the social worker or nursing staff.

HOMEOPATHY. A holistic system of treatment developed in the eighteenth century. It is based on the idea that substances that produce symptoms of sickness in healthy people will have a curative effect when given in very dilute quantities to sick people who exhibit those same symptoms. Homeopathic remedies are believed to stimulate the body's own healing processes.

HOMEOSTASIS. The balanced internal environment of the body and the automatic tendency of the body to maintain this internal "steady state." Also refers to the tendency of a family system to maintain internal stability and to resist change.

HOMOCYSTEINE. An sulfur-containing amino acid.

HOMOPHOBIA. An irrational hatred, disapproval, or fear of homosexuality and homosexuals.

HOMOZYGOTE/HOMOZYGOUS. Having two identical copies of a gene.

HONEYMOON PHASE. A period of time shortly following diagnosis of type 1 diabetes during which a child's need for insulin may decrease or disappear altogether. The honeymoon phase is transitional, and insulin requirements eventually increases again.

HORDEOLUM. The medical term for stye, an infection or small abscess formation in a hair follicle of the eyelids.

HORMONE. A chemical messenger secreted by a gland or organ and released into the bloodstream. It travels via the bloodstream to distant cells where it exerts an effect.

HORMONE THERAPY. Treating cancers by changing the hormone balance of the body, instead of by using cell-killing drugs.

HUMAN DIPLOID CELL VACCINE (HDCV). A rabies vaccine in which the virus is grown in cultures of human cells, concentrated, and inactivated for IM or ID injection.

HUMAN IMMUNODEFICIENCY VIRUS (HIV). A transmissible retrovirus that causes AIDS in humans. Two forms of HIV are now recognized: HIV-1, which causes most cases of AIDS in Europe, North and South America, and most parts of Africa; and HIV-2, which is chiefly found in West African patients. HIV-2, discovered in 1986, appears to be less virulent than HIV-1 and may also have a longer latency period.

HUMAN LEUCKOCYTE ANTIGEN (HLA). A group of protein molecules located on bone marrow cells that can provoke an immune response. A donor's and a recipient's HLA types should match as closely as possible to prevent the recipient's immune system from attacking the donor's marrow as a foreign material that does not belong in the body.

HUMAN PAPILLOMA VIRUS (HPV). A virus that causes common warts of the hands and feet, as well as lesions in the genital and vaginal area. More than 50 types of HPV have been identified, some of which are linked to cancerous and precancerous conditions, including cancer of the cervix.

HUNTINGTON'S DISEASE. A rare hereditary disease that causes progressive chorea (jerky muscle movements) and mental deterioration that ends in dementia. Huntington's symptoms usually appear in patients in their 40s. Also called Huntington's chorea.

HYALINE MEMBRANE. A fibrous layer that settles in the alveoli in respiratory distress syndrome and prevents oxygen from escaping from inhaled air to the bloodstream.

HYDROCELE. A collection of fluid between two layers of tissue surrounding the testicle; the most common cause of painless scrotal swelling.

HYDROCEPHALUS. An abnormal accumulation of cerebrospinal fluid within the brain. This accumulation can be harmful by pressing on brain structures, and damaging them.

HYDROGEN BREATH TEST. A test used to determine if a person is lactose intolerant or if abnormal bacteria are present in the colon.

HYDROPS FETALIS. A condition in which a fetus or newborn baby accumulates fluids, causing swollen arms and legs and impaired breathing.

HYDROTHERAPY. The use of water (hot, cold, steam, or ice) to relieve discomfort and promote physical well-being. Also called water therapy.

HYDROXYUREA. A drug that has been shown to induce production of fetal hemoglobin. Fetal hemoglobin has a pair of gamma-globin molecules in place of the typical beta-globins of adult hemoglobin. Higher-than-normal levels of fetal hemoglobin can ameliorate some of the symptoms of thalassemia.

HYPERACTIVE REFLEXES. Reflexes that persist too long and may be too strong. For example, a hyperactive grasp reflex may cause the hand to stay clenched in a tight fist.

HYPERALIMENTATION. A method of refeeding anorexics by infusing liquid nutrients and electrolytes directly into central veins through a catheter.

HYPERANDROGENISM. The excessive secretion of androgens.

HYPERBARIC OXYGEN THERAPY. Medical treatment in which oxygen is administered in specially designed chambers, under pressures greater than that of the atmosphere, in order to treat specific medical conditions, such as carbon monoxide poisoning, smoke inhalation, and certain bacterial infections.

HYPERBILIRUBINEMIA. A condition characterized by a high level of bilirubin in the blood. Bilirubin is a natural byproduct of the breakdown of red blood cells, however, a high level of bilirubin may indicate a problem with the liver.

HYPERCALCEMIA. A condition marked by abnormally high levels of calcium in the blood.

HYPERCOAGULABLE STATE. (Also called thromboembolic state or thrombophilia.) A condition characterized by excess blood clotting.

HYPEREXTENSIBILITY. The ability to extend a joint beyond the normal range.

HYPERGLYCEMIA. A condition characterized by excessively high levels of glucose in the blood. It occurs when the body does not have enough insulin or cannot use the insulin it does have to turn glucose into energy.

HYPERKALEMIA. An abnormally high level of potassium in the blood.

HYPERLIPIDEMIA. A condition characterized by abnormally high levels of lipids in blood plasma.

HYPERMOBILITY. Unusual flexibility of the joints, allowing them to be bent or moved beyond their normal range of motion.

HYPERNATREMIA. An abnormally high level of sodium in the blood.

HYPEROSMOTIC. Hypertonic, containing a higher concentration of salts or other dissolved materials than normal tissues.

HYPERPHAGIA. Over-eating.

HYPERPLASIA. A condition where cells, such as those making up the prostate gland, rapidly divide abnormally and cause the organ to become enlarged.

HYPERPLASTIC. Refers to an increase in the size of an organ or tissue due to an increase in the number of cells.

HYPERPLASTIC OBESITY. Excessive weight gain in childhood, characterized by an increase in the number of new fat cells.

HYPERPYREXIA. Fever greater than 105.8°F (41°C).

HYPERSENSITIVITY. A condition characterized by an excessive response by the body to a foreign substance. In hypersensitive individuals even a tiny amount of allergen can cause a severe allergic reaction.

HYPERSOMNIA. An abnormal increase of 25% or more in time spent sleeping. Individuals with hypersomnia usually have excessive daytime sleepiness.

HYPERTENSION. Abnormally high arterial blood pressure, which if left untreated can lead to heart disease and stroke.

HYPERTHERMIA. Body temperature that is much higher than normal (i.e. higher than 98.6°F [37°C]).

HYPERTHYROIDISM. A condition characterized by abnormal over-functioning of the thyroid glands. Patients are hypermetabolic, lose weight, are nervous, have muscular weakness and fatigue, sweat more, and have increased urination and bowel movements. Also called thyrotoxicosis.

HYPERTONIA. Having excessive muscular tone or strength.

HYPERTONIC SALINE SOLUTION. Fluid that contains salt in a concentration higher than that of healthy blood.

HYPERTROPHIC OBESITY. Excessive weight gain in adulthood, characterized by expansion of already existing fat cells.

HYPERTROPHY. An increase in the size of a tissue or organ brought about by the enlargement of its cells rather than cell multiplication.

HYPERVENTILATION. Rapid, deep breathing, possibly exceeding 40 breaths/minute. The most common cause is anxiety, although fever, aspirin overdose, serious infections, stroke, or other diseases of the brain or nervous system. Also refers to a respiratory therapy involving deeper and/or faster breathing to keep the carbon dioxide pressure in the blood below normal.

HYPNOGOGIC HALLUCINATION. A vivid, dreamlike hallucination, such as the sensation of falling, that occurs at the onset of sleep.

HYPNOSIS. The technique by which a trained professional induces a trance-like state of extreme relaxation and suggestibility in a patient. Hypnosis is used to treat amnesia and identity disturbances that occur in dissociative disorders.

HYPNOTICS. A class of drugs that are used as a sedatives and sleep aids.

HYPOCALCEMIA. A condition characterized by an abnormally low level of calcium in the blood.

HYPOCHROMIC. A descriptive term applied to a red blood cell with a decreased concentration of hemoglobin.

HYPOCRETINS. Chemicals secreted in the hypothalamus that regulate the sleep/wake cycle.

HYPOGLYCEMIA. A condition characterized by abnormally low levels of glucose in the blood.

HYPOGLYCEMIC UNAWARENESS. A condition in which normal warning signals of a blood sugar low, such as shakiness, sweating, or rapid heartbeat, are no longer felt.

HYPOKALEMIA. A condition characterized by a deficiency of potassium in the blood.

HYPOMANIA. A milder form of mania that is characteristic of bipolar II disorder.

HYPOPLASIA. An underdeveloped or incomplete tissue or organ usually due to a decrease in the number of cells.

HYPOPLASTIC. Refers to incomplete or underdeveloped tissues or organs. Hypoplastic left heart syndrome is the most serious type of congenital heart disease.

HYPOPNEA. Shallow or excessively slow breathing usually caused by partial closure of the upper airway during sleep, leading to disruption of sleep.

HYPOSPADIAS. A congenital abnormality of the penis in which the urethral opening is located on the underside of the penis rather than at its tip.

HYPOTENSION. Low blood pressure.

HYPOTHALAMUS. A part of the forebrain that controls heartbeat, body temperature, thirst, hunger, body temperature and pressure, blood sugar levels, and other functions.

HYPOTHERMIA. A serious condition in which body temperature falls below 95°F (35 °C). It is usually caused by prolonged exposure to the cold.

HYPOTHYROIDISM. A disorder in which the thyroid gland produces too little thyroid hormone causing a decrease in the rate of metabolism with associated effects on the reproductive system. Symptoms include fatigue, difficulty swallowing, mood swings, hoarse voice, sensitivity to cold, forgetfulness, and dry/coarse skin and hair.

HYPOTONIA. Having reduced or diminished muscle tone or strength.

HYPOXEMIA. A condition characterized by an abnormally low amount of oxygen in the arterial blood. It is the major consequence of respiratory failure, when the lungs no longer are able to perform their chief function of gas exchange.

I

IATROGENIC. A condition that is caused by the diagnostic procedures or treatments administered by medical professionals. Iatrogenic conditions may be caused by any number of things including contaminated medical instruments or devices, contaminated blood or implants, or contaminated air within the medical facility.

ICHTHYOSIS. A group of congenital skin disorders of keratinization characterized by dryness and scaling of the skin.

IDEAL WEIGHT. Weight corresponding to the lowest death rate for individuals of a specific height, gender, and age.

IDENTIFIED PATIENT (IP). The family member in whom the family's symptom has emerged or is most obvious.

IDENTITY. The condition of being the same with, or possessing, a character that is well described, asserted, or defined.

IDIOPATHIC. Refers to a disease or condition of unknown origin.

ILEUS. An obstruction of the intestines usually caused by the absence of peristalsis.

IMMERSION. A language education approach in which English is the only language used.

IMMUNE GLOBULIN. Preparation of antibodies that can be given before exposure for short-term protection against hepatitis A and for persons who have already been exposed to hepatitis A virus. Immune globulin must be given within two weeks after exposure to hepatitis A virus for maximum protection.

IMMUNE HYPERSENSITIVITY REACTION. An allergic reaction that is mediated by mast cells and occurs within minutes of allergen contact.

IMMUNE RESPONSE. A physiological response of the body controlled by the immune system that involves the production of antibodies to fight off specific foreign substances or agents (antigens).

IMMUNE SYSTEM. The system of specialized organs, lymph nodes, and blood cells throughout the body that work together to defend the body against foreign invaders (bacteria, viruses, fungi, etc.).

IMMUNITY. Ability to resist the effects of agents, such as bacteria and viruses, that cause disease.

IMMUNIZATION. A process or procedure that protects the body against an infectious disease by stimulating the production of antibodies. A vaccination is a type of immunization.

IMMUNOCOMPROMISED. A state in which the immune system is suppressed or not functioning properly.

IMMUNODEFICIENCY. A condition in which the body's immune response is damaged, weakened, or is not functioning properly.

IMMUNODEFICIENCY DISEASE. A disease characterized chiefly by an increased susceptibility to infection. It is caused by very low levels of immunoglobulins that result in an impaired immune system. Affected people develop repeated infections.

IMMUNOGLOBIN A. A sugar protein with a high molecular weight that acts like an antibody and is produced by white blood cells during an immune response.

IMMUNOGLOBULIN E (IGE). A type of protein in blood plasma that acts as an antibody to activate allergic reactions. About 50% of patients with allergic disorders have increased IgE levels in their blood serum.

IMMUNOGLOBULIN G (IGG). Immunoglobulin type gamma, the most common type found in the blood and tissue fluids.

IMMUNOSUPPRESSED. A state in which the immune system is suppressed by medications during the treatment of other disorders, like cancer, or following an organ transplantation.

IMMUNOTHERAPY. A mode of cancer treatment in which the immune system is stimulated to fight the cancer.

IMPACTED TOOTH. Any tooth that is prevented from reaching its normal position in the mouth by another tooth, bone, or soft tissue.

IMPACTION. A condition in which earwax has become tightly packed in the outer ear to the point that the external ear canal is blocked.

IMPETIGO. A bacterial infection of the skin characterized by skin blistering.

IMPLANTATION. The process in which the fertilized egg embeds itself in the wall of the uterus.

IMPRESSION. In dentistry, an imprint of the upper or lower teeth made in a pliable material that sets. When this material has hardened, it may be filled with plaster, plastic, or artificial stone to make an exact model of the teeth.

IMPRINTING. A process that silences a gene or group of genes. The genes are silenced depending on whether they are inherited through the egg or the sperm.

INBORN ERROR OF METABOLISM. One of a group of rare conditions characterized by an inherited defect in an enzyme or other protein. Inborn errors of metabolism can cause brain damage and mental retardation if left untreated. Phenylketonuria, Tay-Sachs disease, and galactosemia are inborn errors of metabolism.

INCARCERATED HERNIA. A hernia of the bowel that can not return to its normal place without manipulation or surgery.

INCEST. Unlawful sexual contact between persons who are biologically related. Many therapists, however, use the term to refer to inappropriate sexual contact between any members of a family, including stepparents and stepsiblings.

INCIDENCE. The rate of development of a disease in a given population over time.

INCISOR. One of the eight front teeth.

INCOMPLETE BREECH. Also called a footling breech, in this position the baby has one or both feet down towards the pelvis so that his leg(s) are poised to deliver first.

INCONTINENCE. A condition characterized by the inability to control urination or bowel functions.

INCUBATION PERIOD. The time period between exposure to an infectious agent, such as a virus or bacteria, and the appearance of symptoms of illness. Also called the latent period.

INDEX OF REFRACTION. A constant number for any material and any given color of light that is an indicator of the degree of bending of the light caused by that material.

INDIVIDUALIZED EDUCATIONAL PLAN (IEP). A detailed description of the educational goals, assessment methods, behavioral management plan, and educational performance of a student requiring special education services.

INFANTILE MASTURBATION. The masturbation by infants, also called gratification disorder.

INFARCT. An area of dead tissue caused by inadequate blood supply.

INFECTIOUS DISEASE. A disease caused by a virus or a bacterium. Examples of viruses causing an infectious disease are: HIV-1 virus, herpes simplex, cytomegalovirus, Epstein-Barr virus, leukemia virus. Examples of bacterial infectious diseases are: syphilis and tuberculosis.

INFLAMMATION. Pain, redness, swelling, and heat that develop in response to tissue irritation or injury. It usually is caused by the immune system's response to the body's contact with a foreign substance, such as an allergen or pathogen.

INFLAMMATORY. Pertaining to inflammation.

INFLECTION. Variations in the pitch or tone of a voice.

INFLUENZA. An infectious disease caused by a virus that affects the respiratory system, causing fever, congestion, muscle aches, and headaches.

INFLUENZA VIRUS TYPE. The nature of the proteins in the outer coat of an influenza virus. Depending on the proteins, influenza viruses may be classified as A, B, or C.

INFUSION. Introduction of a substance directly into a vein or tissue by gravity flow.

INHALANT. Medication that is breathed into the lungs.

INHIBITED. A type of child defined by Jerome Kagan and his colleagues as having a low level of responsiveness to strangers, a reluctance to initiate activities, and requiring a long time to relax in new situations. Children with inhibited temperaments appear to be more susceptible to anxiety disorders, depression, and certain personality disorders in their later years.

INNER EAR. The interior section of the ear, where sound vibrations and information about balance are translated into nerve impulses.

INORGANIC. Pertaining to chemical compounds that are not hydrocarbons or their derivatives.

INORGANIC CAUSES. Cases of failure to thrive brought on by a caregiver's actions.

INPATIENT SURGERY. Surgery that requires an overnight stay of one or more days in the hospital. The number of days spent in the hospital after surgery depends on the type of procedure performed.

INSECTICIDE. Any substance used to kill insects.

INSECURE ATTACHMENT. Develops when a primary caregiver does not consistently respond in ways that are warm, affectionate, and sensitive to a baby's needs.

INSOMNIA. A sleep disorder characterized by inability either to fall asleep or to stay asleep.

INSULIN. A hormone or chemical produced by the pancreas that is needed by cells of the body in order to use glucose (sugar), a major source of energy for the human body.

INTELLIGENCE QUOTIENT (IQ). A measure of somebody's intelligence, obtained through a series of aptitude tests concentrating on different aspects of intellectual functioning.

INTELLIGENCE TEST. A questionnaire or series of exercises designed to attempt to measure intelligence.

INTERCEPTIVE ORTHODONTICS. Preventative orthodontics; early, simpler orthodontic treatment.

INTERFERON. A potent immune-defense protein produced by virus-infected cells; used as an anti-cancer and anti-viral drug.

INTERNATIONAL UNIT (IU). A measurement of biological activity in which one IU is equal to one mg (milligram).

INTRACEREBRAL HEMORRHAGE. A cause of some strokes in which vessels within the brain begin bleeding.

INTRACUTANEOUS. Into the skin, in this case directly under the top layer of skin.

INTRADERMAL. An injection into a deep layer of skin.

INTRAMEMBRANOUS OSSIFICATION. The process by which bone tissue is formed within sheets of connective tissue.

INTRAMUSCULAR (IM) INJECTION. An injection into a muscle.

INTRAOCULAR RETINOBLASTOMA. Cancer of the retina that is limited to the eye and has not spread to other parts of the body.

INTRAPARTUM. Refers to the period of time that includes labor and delivery of a baby.

INTRAUTERINE. Situated or occurring in the uterus.

INTRAVENOUS. Into a vein; a needle is inserted into a vein in the back of the hand, inside the elbow, or some other location on the body. Fluids, nutrients, and drugs can be injected. Commonly called IV.

INTRAVENTRICULAR HEMORRHAGE (IVH). A condition in which fragile blood vessels within the brain burst and bleed into the hollow chambers (ventricles) of the brain and into the tissue surrounding them.

INTRINSIC BIAS. An assumed bias that favors one group over another; as in systems and hand implements that assume that all people are right-handed.

INTROVERSION. A personal preference for solitary, non-social activities and settings

INTUBATION. A procedure in which a tube is inserted through the mouth and into the trachea to keep the airway open and to help a patient breathe.

INTUSSUSCEPTION. The slipping or telescoping of one part of the intestine into the section next to it.

INVOLUTION. The return of a large organ to normal size.

IONIZING RADIATION. Radiation that can damage living tissue by disrupting and destroying individual cells at the molecular level. All types of nuclear radiation—x rays, gamma rays, and beta rays—are potentially ionizing. Sound waves physically vibrate the material through which they pass, but do not ionize it.

IONTOPHORESIS. Application of a small electric current to the skin.

IQ. Intelligence quotient, a measure of intellectual functioning determined by performance on standardized intelligence tests. It is usually calculated by dividing an individual's mental age (determined by testing) by his/her chronological age and multiplying that result by 100.

IRON OVERLOAD. A side effect of frequent blood transfusions in which the body accumulates abnormally high levels of iron. Iron deposits can form in organs, particularly the heart, and cause life-threatening damage.

IRRIGATION. Cleansing a wound with large amounts of water and/or an antiseptic solution. Also refers to the technique of removing wax (cerumen) from the ear canal by flushing it with water.

ISCHEMIA. A decrease in the blood supply to an area of the body caused by obstruction or constriction of blood vessels.

ISOIMMUNIZATION. The development of antibodies in a species in response to antigens from the same species.

ISOTRETINOIN. A powerful vitamin A derivative used in the treatment of acne.

J

JAUNDICE. A condition in which the skin and whites of the eyes take on a yellowish color due to an increase of bilirubin (a compound produced by the liver) in the blood. Also called icterus.

JET LAG. A temporary disruption of the body's sleep-wake rhythm following high-speed air travel across several time zones. Jet lag is most severe in people who have crossed eight or more time zones in 24 hours.

JOINT. The connection point where two bones meet.

JOINT CONTRACTURES. Stiffness of the joints that prevents full extension.

JOINT DISLOCATION. The displacement of a bone from its socket or normal position.

JUVENILE ARTHRITIS. A chronic inflammatory disease characterized predominantly by arthritis with onset before the sixteenth birthday.

K

KALLMAN'S SYNDROME. A disorder of hypogonadotropic hypogonadism, delayed puberty, and anosmia. Kallman's syndrome is a birth defect in the brain that prevents release of hormones and appears as failure of male puberty.

KAPOSI'S SARCOMA. A cancer characterized by bluish-red nodules on the skin, usually on the lower extremities, that often occurs in people with AIDS.

KARYOTYPE. A standard arrangement of photographic or computer-generated images of chromosome pairs from a cell in ascending numerical order, from largest to smallest.

KARYOTYPING. A laboratory test used to study an individual's chromosome make-up. Chromosomes are separated from cells, stained, and arranged in order from largest to smallest so that their number and structure can be studied under a microscope.

KASABACH-MERRIT SYNDROME. A combination of rapidly enlarging hemangioma and thrombocytopenia; it is usually clinically evident during early infancy, but occasionally the onset is later. The hemangiomas are large and may increase in size rapidly and may cause severe anemia in infants.

KAUFMAN ASSESSMENT BATTERY FOR CHILDREN. An intelligence and achievement test for children ages 2.5 to 12.5 years.

KAWASAKI SYNDROME. A syndrome of unknown origin that affects the skin, mucous membranes, and the immune system of infants and young children. It is named for the Japanese pediatrician who first identified it in 1967.

KERATIN. A tough, nonwater-soluble protein found in the nails, hair, and the outermost layer of skin. Human hair is made up largely of keratin.

KERATOCONUS. An eye condition in which the central part of the cornea bulges outward, interfering with normal vision. Usually both eyes are affected.

KERNICTERUS. A potentially lethal disease of newborns caused by excessive accumulation of the bile pigment bilirubin in tissues of the central nervous system.

KETOACIDOSIS. Usually caused by uncontrolled type I diabetes, when the body isn't able to use glucose for energy. As an alternate source of energy, fat cells are broken down, producing ketones, toxic compounds that make the blood acidic. Symptoms of ketoacidosis include excessive thirst and urination, abdominal pain, vomiting, rapid breathing, extreme tiredness, and drowsiness.

KETONES. Poisonous acidic chemicals produced by the body when fat instead of glucose is burned for energy. Breakdown of fat occurs when not enough insulin is present to channel glucose into body cells.

KIESSELBACH'S PLEXUS. The mass of blood vessels on either side of the septum.

KILLER BEES. Hybrids of African bees accidentally introduced into the wild in South and North America in 1956 and first reported in Texas in 1990. They were first imported by Brazilian scientists attempting to create a new hybrid bee to improve honey production.

KINETIC ENERGY. The energy that the body has because of its motion.

KLEINE-LEVIN SYNDROME. A disorder that occurs primarily in young males, three or four times a year. The syndrome is marked by episodes of hypersomnia, hypersexual behavior, and excessive eating.

KLEPTOMANIA. An impulse control disorder in which one steals objects that are of little or no value.

KLUMPKE'S PALSY OR PARALYSIS. A condition caused by an injury to the lower brachial plexus, involving the cervical nerves C7 and C8, and sometimes the thoracic nerve T1, causing weakness or paralysis in the hands and fingers.

KOPLIK'S SPOTS. Tiny spots occurring inside the mouth, especially on the inside of the cheek. These spots consist of minuscule white dots (like grains of salt or sand) set onto a reddened bump and are characteristic of measles.

KYPHOSCOLIOSIS. Abnormal front-to-back and side-to-side curvature of the spine.

KYPHOSIS. An extreme, abnormal outward curvature of the spine, with a hump at the upper back.

L

LABYRINTH. The bony cavity of the inner ear.

LACERATION. A cut or separation of skin or other tissue by a tremendous force, producing irregular edges. Also called a tear.

LACTASE. The enzyme produced by cells that line the small intestine that allows the body to break down lactose.

LACTOBACILLUS ACIDOPHILUS. Commonly known as acidophilus, a bacteria found in yogurt that changes the balance of the bacteria in the intestine in a beneficial way.

LACTOBACILLUS BIFIDUS. A beneficial bacteria in breast milk that interferes with the growth of pathogenic bacteria in the gastrointestinal tracts of babies, reducing the incidence of diarrhea. *Lactobacillus bifidus* can be added to infant formulas to help control diarrhea.

LACTOGENESIS. The initiation of milk secretion.

LACTO-OVO VEGETARIAN. People who do not eat meat, but do include dairy products and eggs in their diets.

LACTOSE. A sugar found in milk and milk products.

LACTOSE INTOLERANCE. An inability to properly digest the lactose found in milk and dairy products.

LAMBDOIDAL SUTURE. The suture between the two parietal bones and the occipital bone in the skull.

LANUGO. A soft, downy body hair that covers a normal fetus beginning in the fifth month and usually shed by the ninth month. Also refers to the fine, soft hair that develops on the chest and arms of anorexic women. Also called vellus hair.

LAPAROSCOPIC SURGERY. Minimally invasive surgery in which a camera and surgical instruments are inserted through a small incision.

LAPAROSCOPY. A surgical procedure in which a small incision is made, usually in the navel, through which a viewing tube (laparoscope) is inserted. This allows the doctor to examine abdominal and pelvic organs. Other small incisions can be mad to insert instruments to perform procedures. Laparoscopy is done to diagnose conditions or to perform certain types of surgeries.

LARYNGOMALACIA. A birth defect that causes the tissues around the larynx to partially collapse and narrow the air passageway, causing noisy breathing.

LARYNGOSCOPE. An endoscope that is used to examine the interior of the larynx.

LARYNGOSPASM. Spasmodic closure of the larynx.

LARYNX. Also known as the voice box, the larynx is the part of the airway that lies between the pharynx and the trachea. It is composed of cartilage that contains the apparatus for voice production–the vocal cords and the muscles and ligaments that move the cords.

LATCHKEY CHILD. A child who must spend part of the after-school day at home without supervision while the parents are at work. The name comes from the fact that such children are given a house or apartment key so that they can let themselves in when they get home from school.

LATENT VIRUS. A nonactive virus that is in a dormant state within a cell. The herpes virus is latent in the nervous system.

LEARNING DISABILITIES. An impairment of the cognitive processes of understanding and using spoken and written language that results in difficulties with one or more academic skill sets (e.g., reading, writing, mathematics).

LEARNING DISORDERS. Academic difficulties experienced by children and adults of average to above-average intelligence that involve reading, writing, and/or mathematics, and which significantly interfere with academic achievement or daily living.

LEGUMES. A family of plants, including beans, peas, and lentils, that bear edible seeds in pods. These seeds are high in protein, fiber, and other nutrients.

LENNOX-GASTAUT SYNDROME. A severe form of epilepsy that is characterized by the onset in early childhood of frequent seizures of multiple types and by developmental delay.

LENS. The transparent, elastic, curved structure behind the iris (colored part of the eye) that helps focus light on the retina. Also refers to any device that bends light waves.

LEPTIN. A protein hormone that affects feeding behavior and hunger in humans. As of 2004 it was thought that obesity in humans may result in part from insensitivity to leptin.

LESION. A disruption of the normal structure and function of a tissue by an injury or disease process. Wounds, sores, rashes, and boils are all lesions.

LEUKEMIA. A cancer of the blood-forming organs (bone marrow and lymph system) characterized by an abnormal increase in the number of white blood cells in the tissues. There are many types of leukemias and they are classified according to the type of white blood cell involved.

LEUKOCYTE. A white blood cell that defends the body against invading viruses, bacteria, and cancer cells. There are five types of leukocytes—neutrophils, basophils, eosinophils, lymphocytes, and monocytes.

LEUKOCYTOSIS. An increased level of white cells in the blood. Leukocytosis is a common reaction to infections.

LEUKOTRIENE ANTAGONIST. An agent or class of drugs which exerts an action opposite to that of leukotrienes.

LEUKOTRIENES. Substances that are produced by white blood cells in response to antigens and contribute to inflammatory and asthmatic reactions.

LEVODOPA (L-DOPA). A substance used in the treatment of Parkinson's disease. Levodopa can cross the blood-brain barrier that protects the brain. Once in the brain, it is converted to dopamine and thus can replace the dopamine lost in Parkinson's disease.

LICHEN PLANUS. A noncancerous, chronic itchy skin disease that causes small, flat purple plaques on wrists, forearm, ankles.

LICHENIFICATION. Thickening of the outer layer of skin cells caused by prolonged scratching or rubbing and resulting in a leathery or bark-like appearance of the skin.

LIGAMENT. A type of tough, fibrous tissue that connects bones or cartilage and provides support and strength to joints.

LIGAND. Any type of small molecule that binds to a larger molecule. Hyper-IgM syndrome is caused by a lack of a ligand known as CD40 on the surfaces of the T cells in the child's blood.

LIMB-GIRDLE MUSCULAR DYSTROPHY (LGMD). A form of muscular dystrophy that begins in late childhood to early adulthood and affects both men and women. It causes weakness in the muscles around the hips and shoulders.

LIMBIC SYSTEM. A group of structures in the brain that includes the hypothalamus, amygdala, olfactory bulbs, and hippocampus. The limbic system plays an important part in regulation of human moods and emotions. Many psychiatric disorders are related to malfunctioning of the limbic system.

LIMITED ENGLISH PROFICIENT (LEP). Used to identify children who have insufficient English to succeed in English-only classrooms; also called English language learner (ELL).

LINCOLN-OSERETSKY MOTOR DEVELOPMENT SCALE. A test that assesses the development of motor skills.

LINDANE. A benzene compound that is used to kill body and pubic lice. Lindane is absorbed into the louse's central nervous system, causing seizures and death.

LIPIDS. Organic compounds not soluble in water, but soluble in fat solvents such as alcohol. Lipids are stored in the body as energy reserves and are also important components of cell membranes. Commonly known as fats.

LIPOSUCTION. A surgical technique for removing fat from under the skin by vacuum suctioning.

LISTERIA. An uncommon food-borne, life-threatening pathogen that can cause perinatal infection, which is associated with a high rate of fetal loss (including full-term stillbirths) and serious neonatal disease.

LITHIUM. A medication prescribed to treat the manic (excited) phases of bipolar disorder.

LIVER BIOPSY. A surgical procedure where a small piece of the liver is removed for examination. A needle or narrow tube may be inserted either directly through the skin and muscle or through a small incision and passed into the liver for collection of a sample of liver tissue.

LOCAL ANESTHESIA. Pain-relieving medication used to numb an area while the patient remains awake. Also see general anesthesia.

LOCOMOTION. The ability to move from one place to another.

LOEFFLER'S MEDIUM. A special substance used to grow diphtheria bacilli to confirm the diagnosis.

LOWER ESOPHAGEAL SPHINCTER (LES). A muscle located at the base of the esophagus which keeps the stomach contents from coming back into the esophagus.

LUMBAR PUNCTURE. A procedure in which the doctor inserts a small needle into the spinal cavity in the lower back to withdraw spinal fluid for testing. Also known as a spinal tap.

LUMEN. The inner cavity or canal of a tube-shaped organ, such as the bowel.

LUTEINIZING HORMONE. A hormone secreted by the pituitary gland that regulates the menstrual cycle and triggers ovulation in females. In males it stimulates the testes to produce testosterone.

LYME BORRELIOSIS. Another name for Lyme disease.

LYME DISEASE. An acute, recurrent, inflammatory disease involving one or a few joints, and transmitted by the bite of ticks carrying the spiral-shaped bacterium *Borrelia burgdorferi*. The condition was originally described in the community of Lyme, Connecticut, but has also been reported in other parts of the United States and other countries. Knees and other large joints are most commonly involved with local inflammation and swelling.

LYMPH FLUID. Clear, colorless fluid found in lymph vessels and nodes. The lymph nodes contain organisms that destroy bacteria and other disease causing organisms (also called pathogens).

LYMPH NODES. Small, bean-shaped collections of tissue located throughout the lymphatic system. They produce cells and proteins that fight infection and filter lymph. Nodes are sometimes called lymph glands.

LYMPHADENOPATHY. A disorder characterized by local or generalized enlargement of the lymph nodes or lymphatic vessels.

LYMPHANGIOMA. A benign skin tumor composed of abnormal lymph vessels.

LYMPHANGITIS. Inflammation of the lymphatic vessels. It often occurs together with lymphadenitis (inflammation of the lymph nodes).

LYMPHATIC VESSELS. Part of the lymphatic system, these vessels connect lymph capillaries with the lymph nodes. They carry lymph, a thin, watery fluid resembling blood plasma and containing white blood cells. Also called lymphatic channels.

LYMPHOCYTE. A type of white blood cell that participates in the immune response. The two main groups are the B cells that have antibody molecules on their surface and T cells that destroy antigens.

LYMPHOCYTIC LEUKEMIA. An acute form of childhood leukemia characterized by the development of abnormal cells in the bone marrow.

LYMPHOMA. A diverse group of cancers of the lymphatic system characterized by abnormal growth of lymphatic cells. Two general types are commonly recognized—Hodgkin's disease and non-Hodgkin's lymphoma.

LYSINE. A crystalline basic amino acid essential to nutrition.

LYSOSOME. A membrane-enclosed compartment in cells, containing many hydrolytic enzymes, where large molecules and cellular components are broken down.

M

MACROCYTIC. A descriptive term applied to a larger than normal red blood cell.

MACROPHAGE. A large white blood cell that engulfs and digests foreign invaders, such as bacteria and viruses, in an attempt to stop them from causing disease within the body.

MACULE. A flat, discolored area on the skin.

MAGNETIC RESONANCE IMAGING (MRI). An imaging technique that uses a large circular magnet and radio waves to generate signals from atoms in the body. These signals are used to construct detailed images of internal body structures and organs, including the brain.

MAJOR DEPRESSIVE DISORDER. A mood disorder characterized by profound feelings of sadness or despair.

MALABSORPTION. The inability of the digestive tract to absorb all the nutrients from food due to some malfunction or disability.

MALADAPTIVE BEHAVIOR. Undesirable and socially unacceptable behavior that interferes with the acquisition of desired skills or knowledge and with the performance of everyday activities.

MALAISE. The medical term for a general condition of unease, discomfort, or weakness.

MALATHION. An insecticide that can be used in 1% powdered form to disinfect the clothes of patients with body lice.

MALFORMATION. An irregular or abnormal formation or structure.

MALIGNANT. Cells that have been altered such that they have lost normal control mechanisms and are capable of local invasion and spread to other areas of the body. Often used to describe a cancer.

MALIGNANT HYPERTHERMIA. A type of reaction (probably with a genetic origin) that can occur during general anesthesia and in which the patient experiences a high fever, muscle rigidity, and irregular heart rate and blood pressure.

MALIGNANT MELANOMA. The most serious of the three types of skin cancer, malignant melanoma arises from the melanocytes, the skin cells that produce the pigment melanin.

MALIGNANT TUMOR. An abnormal proliferation of cells that can spread to other sites.

MALINGERING. Pretending to be sick in order to be relieved of an unwanted duty or obtain some other obvious benefit.

MALLEABILITY. A term that refers to the adaptability of human temperament; the extent to which it can be reshaped.

MALOCCLUSION. The misalignment of opposing teeth in the upper and lower jaws.

MAMMARY. Relating to the breast.

MANDIBLE. The lower jaw, a U-shaped bone attached to the skull at the temporomandibular joints.

MANIA. An elevated or euphoric mood or irritable state that is characteristic of bipolar I disorder. This state is characterized by mental and physical hyperactivity, disorganization of behavior, and inappropriate elevation of mood.

MANIC DEPRESSION. A psychiatric disorder characterized by extreme mood swings, ranging between episodes of acute euphoria (mania) and severe depression; also called bipolar depression.

MANIC EPISODE. A distinct period of abnormally and persistently elevated, expansive, or irritable mood, lasting at least one week, characterized by inflated sense of self-importance, decreased need for sleep, extreme talkativeness, racing thoughts, and excessive participation in pleasure-seeking activities.

MANIPULATION. Moving muscles or connective tissue to enhance function, ease tension, and reduce pain in those tissues as well as other beneficial effects.

MANOMETRY. A technique for measuring changes in pressure.

MANTOUX TEST. A tuberculin skin test. Also called the PPD (purified protein derivative) test.

MASK. An expressionless look, caused by reduced movements of the face.

MAST CELLS. A type of immune system cell that is found in the lining of the nasal passages and eyelids. It displays a type of antibody called immunoglobulin type E (IgE) on its cell surface and participates in the allergic response by releasing histamine from intracellular granules.

MASTOID BONE. The prominent bone behind the ear that projects from the temporal bone of the skull.

MASTOIDITIS. An inflammation of the bone behind the ear (the mastoid bone) caused by an infection spreading from the middle ear to the cavity in the mastoid bone.

MATERNAL SERUM ANALYTE SCREENING. A medical procedure in which a pregnant woman's blood is drawn and analyzed for the levels of certain hormones and proteins. These levels can indicate whether there may be an abnormality in the unborn child. This test is not a definitive indicator of a problem and is followed by more specific testing such as amniocentesis or chorionic villus sampling.

MATERNAL UNIPARENTAL DISOMY. A chromosome abnormality in which both chromosomes in a pair are inherited from one's mother.

MATURATION. The process by which stem cells transform from immature cells without a specific function into a particular type of blood cell with defined functions.

MATURATION DELAY. Developmental language delay; a language delay caused by the slow maturation of speech centers in the brain; often causes late talking.

MATURITY. A state of full development or completed growth.

MAXILLA. The bone of the upper jaw which serves as a foundation of the face and supports the orbits.

MEAN CORPUSCULAR HEMOGLOBIN CONCENTRATION (MCHC). A measurement of the average concentration of hemoglobin in a red blood cell.

MEAN CORPUSCULAR VOLUME (MCV). A measurement of the average volume of a red blood cell.

MECKEL'S DIVERTICULUM. A congenital abnormality of the digestive tract consisting of a small pouch off the wall of the small bowel that was not reabsorbed before birth. A Meckel's diverticulum increases the risk that a foreign object in the digestive tract will get trapped or stuck in the small intestine and cause problems.

MECONIUM. A greenish fecal material that forms the first bowel movement of an infant.

MECONIUM ASPIRATION SYNDROME. Breathing in of meconium (a newborn's first stool) by a fetus or newborn, which can block air passages and interfere with lung expansion.

MEDICAID. A program jointly funded by state and federal governments that reimburses hospitals and physicians for the care of individuals who cannot pay for their own medical expenses. These individuals may be in low-income households or may have chronic disabilities.

MEDITATION. A practice of concentrated focus upon a sound, object, visualization, the breath, movement, or attention itself in order to increase awareness of the present moment, reduce stress, promote relaxation, and enhance personal and spiritual growth.

MEDULLARY THYROID CANCER. A slow-growing tumor associated with multiple endocrine neoplasia syndromes.

MEGACOLON. Abnormal dilation (enlargement) of the colon.

MEGALENCEPHALY. A condition in which the brain is abnormally large.

MEGALOBLAST. A large erythroblast (a red marrow cell that synthesizes hemoglobin).

MEGALOCEPHALY. An abnormally large head.

MELANIN. A pigment that creates hair, skin, and eye color. Melanin also protects the body by absorbing ultraviolet light.

MELANOMA. A tumor, usually of the skin.

MELENA. The passage of dark stools stained with blood pigments or with altered blood.

MEMBRANE OXYGENATOR. The artificial lung that adds oxygen and removes carbon dioxide.

MENARCHE. The first menstrual cycle in a girl's life.

MENINGES. The three-layer membranous covering of the brain and spinal cord, composed of the dura mater, arachnoid, and pia mater. It provides protection for the brain and spinal cord, as well as housing many blood vessels and participating in the appropriate flow of cerebrospinal fluid.

MENINGITIS. An infection or inflammation of the membranes that cover the brain and spinal cord. It is usually caused by bacteria or a virus.

MENINGOENCEPHALITIS. Inflammation of the brain and its membranes; also called cerebromeningitis or encephalomeningitis.

MENKES DISEASE. A genetic disease caused by a mutation on the X chromosome and resulting in impaired transport of copper from the digestive tract. It was first identified in 1962.

MENSTRUATION. The periodic discharge from the vagina of blood and tissues from a nonpregnant uterus.

MENTAL RETARDATION. A condition where an individual has a lower-than-normal IQ, and thus is developmentally delayed.

METABOLIC. Refers to the chemical reactions in living organisms.

METABOLISM. The sum of all chemical reactions that occur in the body resulting in growth, transformation of foodstuffs into energy, waste elimination, and other bodily functions. These include processes that break down substances to yield energy and processes that build up other substances necessary for life.

METACOGNITION. Awareness of the process of cognition.

METALINGUISTIC SKILLS. The ability to analyze language and control internal language processing; important for reading development in children.

METASTASIS. A secondary tumor resulting from the spread of cancerous cells from the primary tumor to other parts of the body.

METHEMOGLOBIN. A compound formed from hemoglobin by oxidation of its iron component. Methemoglobin cannot carry oxygen.

METHIONINE. An amino acid that, when not metabolized properly, allows homocysteine to build up in the blood. Folic acid aids methionine metabolism.

METHOTREXATE. A drug that interferes with cell growth and is used to treat rheumatoid arthritis as well as various types of cancer. Side effects may include mouth sores, digestive upsets, skin rashes, and hair loss.

METHYLATION TESTING. DNA testing that detects if a gene is active or if it is imprinted.

METHYLPREDISOLONE. A steroid drug. Methylpredisolone administered within eight hours of acute spinal cord trauma is the first drug shown to improve recovery from spinal cord injury.

METOPIC SUTURE. Suture extending from the top of the head down the middle of the forehead to the nose.

MICROCEPHALY. An abnormally small head.

MICROCYTIC. A descriptive term applied to a smaller than normal red blood cell.

MICROFLORA. The bacterial population in the intestine.

MICRONUTRIENT. An organic compound such as vitamins or minerals essential in small amounts and necessary to the growth and health of humans and animals.

MICROORGANISM. An organism that is too small to be seen with the naked eye, such as a bacterium, virus, or fungus.

MIDDLE EAR. The cavity or space between the eardrum and the inner ear. It includes the eardrum, the three little bones (hammer, anvil, and stirrup) that transmit sound to the inner ear, and the eustachian tube, which connects the inner ear to the nasopharynx (the back of the nose).

MIDGET. An individual who is short statured but has normal body proportions. The term is considered to be offensive.

MIGRAINE. A throbbing headache that usually affects only one side of the head. Nausea, vomiting, increased sensitivity to light, and other symptoms often accompany a migraine.

MIND-BODY CONNECTION. Rather than relying on an understanding of the term "psychosomatic," mind-body medicine acknowledges the influence of thinking and the cognitive process on the behavior of chemicals in the body, involving the mind in both creating the conditions for disease and helping to heal the effects of disease.

MINERALS. Inorganic chemical elements that are found in plants and animals and are essential for life. There are two types of minerals: major minerals, which the body requires in large amounts, and trace elements, which the body needs only in minute amounts.

MISBEHAVIOR. Behavior outside the norms of acceptance within the group.

MISCARRIAGE. Loss of the embryo or fetus and other products of pregnancy before the twentieth week. Often, early in a pregnancy, if the condition of the baby and/or the mother's uterus are not compatible with sustaining life, the pregnancy stops, and the contents of the uterus are expelled. For this reason, miscarriage is also referred to as spontaneous abortion.

MITE. An insect parasite belonging to the order Acarina. The organism that causes scabies is a mite.

MITOCHONDRIA. Spherical or rod-shaped structures of the cell. Mitochondria contain genetic material (DNA and RNA) and are responsible for converting food to energy.

MITOCHONDRIAL INHERITANCE. Inheritance associated with the mitochondrial genome which is inherited exclusively from the mother.

MITRAL VALVE PROLAPSE. A heart defect in which the mitral valve of the heart (which normally controls blood flow from the left atrium to the left ventricle) becomes floppy. Mitral valve prolapse may be detected as a heart murmur but there are usually no symptoms.

MITRAL VALVE STENOSIS. Narrowing of the mitral valve.

MIXED MANIA. A mental state in which symptoms of both depression and mania occur simultaneously. Also called mixed state.

MODELING. A type of teaching method used in social skills training. Therapists who use this method may offer positive and negative examples of the behaviors that make up a social skill.

MOLARS. The teeth behind the primary canines or the permanent premolars, with large crowns and broad chewing surfaces for grinding food.

MONOAMINE OXIDASE (MAO) INHIBITORS. A type of antidepressant that works by blocking the action of a chemical substance known as monoamine oxidase in the nervous system.

MONOCHORIONIC TWINS. Twins that share a single placenta.

MONONUCLEOSIS. An infection, caused by the Epstein-Barr virus, that causes swelling of lymph nodes, spleen, and liver, usually accompanied by extremely sore throat, fever, headache, and intense long-lasting fatigue. Also called infectious mononucleosis.

MONOZYGOTIC. From one zygote, as in identical twins. The zygote is the first cell formed by the union of sperm and egg.

MORBIDITY. A disease or abnormality. In statistics it also refers to the rate at which a disease or abnormality occurs.

MORO REFLEX. A startle response in a newborn, characterized by spreading the arms with the palms up and fingers flexed; the reflex usually disappears by two months of age.

MORPHINE. The principal alkaloid derived from the opium poppy for use as a pain reliever and sedative. In its purified form, it is a white, bitter-tasting crystalline powder.

MORPHOLOGY. Literally, the study of form. In medicine, morphology refers to size, shape, and structure rather than function.

MOSAIC. A term referring to a genetic situation in which an individual's cells do not have the exact same composition of chromosomes. In Down syndrome, this may mean that some of the individual's cells have a normal 46 chromosomes, while other cells have an abnormal 47 chromosomes.

MOSAICISM. A genetic condition resulting from a mutation, crossing over, or nondisjunction of chromosomes during cell division, causing a variation in the number of chromosomes in the cells.

MOTILITY. The movement or capacity for movement of an organism or body organ. Indigestion is sometimes caused by abnormal patterns in the motility of the stomach.

MOTOR COORDINATION (MC). Related to movement of parts of the body, particularly the use of the hands and coordination of eye-hand motion.

MOTOR NEURON. A nerve cell that specifically controls and stimulates voluntary muscles.

MOTOR SKILLS. Controlled movements of muscle groups. Fine motor skills involve tasks that require dexterity of small muscles, such as buttoning a shirt. Tasks such as walking or throwing a ball involve the use of gross motor skills.

MOTTLING. Fluorosis; spotting on the teeth due to excess fluoride as the tooth enamel is forming.

MOURN. To express grief or sorrow, usually for a death.

MUCIN. A protein in saliva that combines with sugars in the mouth to form plaque.

MUCOCILIARY ESCALATOR. The coordinated action of tiny projections on the surfaces of cells lining the respiratory tract, which moves mucus up and out of the lungs.

MUCOCUTANEOUS LYMPH NODE SYNDROME (MLNS). Another name for Kawasaki syndrome. The name comes from the key symptoms of the disease, which involve the mucous membranes of the mouth and throat, the skin, and the lymph nodes. MLNS is a potentially fatal inflammatory disease of unknown cause.

MUCOLYTIC. An agent that dissolves or destroys mucin, the chief component of mucus.

MUCOPOLYSACCHARIDE. A complex molecule made of smaller sugar molecules strung together to form a chain. It is found in mucous secretions and intercellular spaces.

MUCOSAL. Refers to the mucous membrane.

MUCUS. The thick fluid produced by the mucous membranes that line many body cavities and structures. It contains mucin, white blood cells, water, inorganic salts, and shed cells, and it serve to lubricate body parts and to trap particles of dirt or other contaminants.

MULTICULTURAL EDUCATION. A social or educational theory that encourages interest in many cultures within a society rather than in only a mainstream culture.

MULTIFACTORIAL. Describes a disease that is the product of the interaction of multiple genetic and environmental factors.

MULTIFOCAL. Having many focal points. When referring to a disease, it means that damage caused by the disease occurs at multiple sites. When referring to a cancer, it means that more than one tumor is present.

MULTIPLE RETINAL HEMORRHAGES. Bleeding in the back of the eye.

MULTIPLE SCLEROSIS. A progressive, autoimmune disease of the central nervous system characterized by damage to the myelin sheath that covers nerves. The disease, which causes progressive paralysis, is marked by periods of exacerbation and remission.

MULTI-TASKING. Performing multiple duties or taking on multiple responsibilities and roles simultaneously.

MUNCHAUSEN SYNDROME. A factitious disorder in which a patient intentionally acts physically ill without obvious benefit.

MUSCLE SPASM. Localized muscle contraction that occurs when the brain signals the muscle to contract.

MUSCLE TONE. Also termed tonus; the normal state of balanced tension in the tissues of the body, especially the muscles.

MUSCLE WEAKNESS. Reduction in the strength of one or more muscles.

MUSCULAR DYSTROPHY. A group of inherited diseases characterized by progressive wasting of the muscles.

MUTATION. A permanent change in the genetic material that may alter a trait or characteristic of an individual, or manifest as disease. This change can be transmitted to offspring.

MYCTOPHOBIA. Fear of darkness.

MYELIN. A fatty sheath surrounding nerves throughout the body that helps them conduct impulses more quickly.

MYELOGRAM. An x-ray image of the spinal cord, spinal canal, and nerve roots taken with the aid of a contrast dye.

MYOCARDITIS. Inflammation of the heart muscle (myocardium).

MYOCLONUS. Involuntary contractions of a muscle or an interrelated group of muscles. Also known as myoclonic seizures.

MYOPATHY. Any abnormal condition or disese of muscle tissue, characterized by muscle weakness and wasting.

MYOSITIS. Inflammation of the muscle.

MYOTONIC DYSTROPHY. A form of muscular dystrophy, also known as Steinert's disease, that affects both men and women. It is characterized by delay in the ability to relax muscles after forceful contraction (myotonia) and wasting of muscles, as well as other abnormalities.

MYRINGOTOMY. A surgical procedure in which an incision is made in the ear drum to allow fluid or pus to escape from the middle ear.

MYXEDEMA. Severe hypothyroidism, characterized by swelling of the face, hands, and feet, an enlarged tongue, horseness, and physical and mental sluggishness.

N

NAIL BED. The layer of tissue underneath the nail.

NARCOLEPSY. A life-long sleep disorder marked by four symptoms: sudden brief sleep attacks, cataplexy (a sudden loss of muscle tone usually lasting up to 30 minutes), temporary paralysis, and hallucinations. The hallucinations are associated with falling asleep or the transition from sleeping to waking.

NARCOTIC. A drug derived from opium or compounds similar to opium. Such drugs are potent pain relievers and can affect mood and behavior. Long-term use of narcotics can lead to dependence and tolerance. Also known as a narcotic analgesic.

NASAL ENDOSCOPY. A procedure that involves inserting a tiny camera into the nose in order to look at blood vessels and nasal structures.

NASAL SEPTUM. The partition that separates the nostrils.

NASOGASTRIC TUBE. A long, flexible tube inserted through the nasal passages, down the throat, and into the stomach.

NASOPHARYNX. One of the three regions of the pharynx, the nasopharynx is the region behind the nasal cavity.

NEBULIZER. A device that turns liquid forms of medication into a fine spray that can be inhaled.

NECROSIS. Localized tissue death due to disease or injury, such as a lack of oxygen supply to the tissues.

NECROTIZING. Causing the death of a specific area of tissue. Human bites frequently cause necrotizing infections.

NECROTIZING ENTEROCOLITIS. A serious bacterial infection of the intestine that occurs primarily in sick or premature newborn infants. It can cause death of intestinal tissue (necrosis) and may progress to blood poisoning (septicemia).

NEONATAL. Refers to the first 28 days of an infant's life.

NEONATE. A newborn infant, from birth until 28 days of age.

NEONATOLOGIST. A physician (pediatrician) who has special training in the care of newborn infants.

NEOPLASM. An abnormal formation of new tissue. A neoplasm may be malignant or benign.

NEPHROLOGIST. A physician who specializes in treating diseases of the kidney.

NERVE CONDITION VELOCITY (NCV). Technique for studying nerve or muscle disorders, measuring the speed at which nerves transmit signals.

NERVE GROWTH FACTOR. A protein resembling insulin that affects the growth and maintenance of nerve cells

NERVOUS SYSTEM. The system that transmits information, in the form of electrochemical impulses, throughout the body for the purpose of activation, coordination, and control of bodily functions. It is comprised of the brain, spinal cord, and nerves.

NERVOUS TIC. A repetitive, involuntary action, such as the twitching of a muscle or repeated blinking.

NEURODEGENERATIVE DISEASE. A disease in which the nervous system progressively and irreversibly deteriorates.

NEURODERMATITIS. An itchy skin disease (also called lichen simplex chronicus) found in nervous, anxious people.

NEUROFIBROMA. A soft tumor usually located on a nerve.

NEUROFIBROMATOSIS. A progressive genetic condition often including multiple café-au-lait spots, multiple raised nodules on the skin (neurofibromas), developmental delays, slightly larger head size, and freckles in the armpits, groin, and iris. Also known as von Recklinghausen's disease.

NEUROIMAGING. The use of x-ray studies and magnetic resonance imaging (MRI) to detect abnormalities or trace pathways of nerve activity in the central nervous system.

NEUROLEPTIC DRUG. Another name for the older type of antipsychotic medications, such as haloperidol and chlorpromazine, prescribed to treat psychotic conditions.

NEUROLOGICAL. Relating to the brain and central nervous system.

NEUROLOGICAL DISORDERS. Pathological conditions relating to the brain and/or nervous system.

NEUROLOGIST. A doctor who specializes in disorders of the nervous system, including the brain, spinal cord, and nerves.

NEUROLOGY. The study of nerves.

NEUROLYSIS. The destruction of nerve tissue or removal of scar tissue surrounding a nerve.

NEUROMA. Scar tissue that forms around a nerve; a tumor derived from nerve tissue.

NEURONS. Any of the conducting cells of the nervous system that transmit signals.

NEUROPATHY. A disease or abnormality of the peripheral nerves (the nerves outside the brain and spinal cord). Major symptoms include weakness, numbness, paralysis, or pain in the affected area.

NEUROPSYCHOLOGICAL. Referring to the interaction between the nervous system and cognitive function, the influence of one function on the other.

NEUROPSYCHOLOGICAL TESTING. Tests used to evaluate patients who have experienced a traumatic brain injury, brain damage, or organic neurological problems (e.g., dementia). It may also be used to evaluate the progress of a patient who has undergone treatment or rehabilitation for a neurological injury or illness.

NEUROPSYCHOLOGIST. A clinical psychologist who specializes in assessing psychological status caused by a brain disorder.

NEUROSURGEON. Physician who performs surgery on the nervous system.

NEUROTOXIN. A poison that acts directly on the central nervous system.

NEUROTRANSMITTER. A chemical messenger that transmits an impulse from one nerve cell to the next.

NEUTROPENIA. A condition in which the number of neutrophils, a type of white blood cell (leukocyte) is abnormally low.

NEUTROPHIL. The primary type of white blood cell involved in inflammation. Neutrophils are a type of granulocyte, also known as a polymorphonuclear leukocyte. They increase in response to bacterial infection and remove and kill bacteria by phagocytosis.

NEVUS (PLURAL, NEVI). The medical term for any anomaly of the skin that is present at birth, including moles and birthmarks.

NICOTINE. A colorless, oily chemical found in tobacco that makes people physically dependent on smoking. It is poisonous in large doses.

NICOTINE REPLACEMENT THERAPY. A method of weaning a smoker away from both nicotine and the oral fixation that accompanies a smoking habit by giving the smoker smaller and smaller doses of nicotine in the form of a patch or gum.

NITRATE. A food additive, commonly found in processed meats, that may be a headache trigger for some people.

NITS. The eggs produced by head or pubic lice, usually grayish white in color and visible at the base of hair shafts.

NOCICEPTOR. A nerve cell that is capable of sensing pain and transmitting a pain signal.

NOCTURNAL ENURESIS. Involuntary discharge of urine during the night.

NOCTURNAL LEG CRAMPS. Cramps that may be related to exertion and awaken a person during sleep.

NOCTURNAL MYOCLONUS. A disorder in which the patient is awakened repeatedly during the night by cramps or twitches in the calf muscles. Also sometimes called periodic limb movement disorder.

NONCOMEDOGENIC. A substance that does not contribute to the formation of blackheads or pimples on the skin.

NON-CONDUCTING MATERIALS. Also called insulators, materials through which electric current does not propagate. Examples are ceramics, rubber, wood.

NON-CUSTODIAL PARENT. A parent who does not have legal custody of a child.

NONDISJUNCTION. An event that takes place during cell division in which a chromosome pair does not separate as it should. The result is an abnormal number of chromosomes in the daughter cells produced by that cell division.

NONPHARMACOLOGICAL. Referring to therapy that does not involve drugs.

NONPRODUCTIVE. A cough in which no mucus is coughed up, also called dry cough.

NON-RAPID EYE MOVEMENT (NREM) SLEEP. A type of sleep that differs from rapid eye movement (REM) sleep. The four stages of NREM sleep account for 75–80% of total sleeping time.

NONRHYTHMIC. Having uneven sleep and eating patterns.

NONSTEROIDAL ANTI-INFLAMMATORY DRUGS (NSAIDS). A group of drugs, including aspirin, ibuprofen, and naproxen, that are taken to reduce fever and inflammation and to relieve pain. They work primarily by interfering with the formation of prostaglandins, enzymes implicated in pain and inflammation.

NOREPINEPHRINE. A hormone secreted by certain nerve endings of the sympathetic nervous system, and by the medulla (center) of the adrenal glands. Its primary function is to help maintain a constant blood pressure by stimulating certain blood vessels to constrict when the blood pressure falls below normal.

NORMOCHROMIC. A descriptive term applied to a red blood cell with a normal concentration of hemoglobin.

NORMOCYTIC. A descriptive term applied to a red blood cell of normal size.

NORM-REFERENCED TEST. A test that measures the performance of a student against the performance of a group of other individuals.

NORMS. A fixed or ideal standard; a normative or mean score for a particular age group.

NOSOCOMIAL INFECTION. An infection acquired in a hospital setting.

NUCHAL TRANSLUCENCY. A pocket of fluid at the back of an embryo's neck, visible via ultrasound. When this pocket of fluid is thickened, it may indicate that the infant will be born with a congenital cardiovascular defect.

NUCLEAR FAMILY. The basic family unit, consisting of a father, a mother, and their biological children.

NURSEMAID'S ELBOW. An injury to the ligament (strong band of tissue) that keeps the two bones of the forearm in the correct place.

NURSING UNIT. The floor or section of the hospital where patient rooms are located.

NUTRIENT. Substances in food that supply the body with the elements needed for metabolism. Examples of nutrients are vitamins, minerals, carbohydrates, fats, and proteins.

NUTRITION THERAPY. Nutrition assessment, counseling, and education, usually provided by registered dietitians.

NYSTAGMUS. An involuntary, rhythmic movement of the eyes.

O

OBESITY. An abnormal accumulation of body fat, usually 20% or more over an individual's ideal body weight.

OBSERVATION. Infants and children watch an object, although not actively engaged in it, as in watching a mobile.

OBSESSION. A persistent image, idea, or desire that dominates a person's thoughts or feelings.

OBSESSIVE-COMPULSIVE DISORDER. An anxiety disorder marked by the recurrence of intrusive or disturbing thoughts, impulses, images, or ideas (obsessions) accompanied by repeated attempts to supress these thoughts through the performance of certain irrational and ritualistic behaviors or mental acts (compulsions).

OCCLUSION. The way upper and lower teeth fit together during biting and chewing. Also refers to the blockage of some area or channel of the body.

OCCLUSIONAL. Referring to a type of injury caused by the closing of the teeth on a finger or other body part. Occlusional injuries are also called chomping injuries.

OCCULSION THERAPY. A type of treatment for amblyopia in which the good eye is patched for a period of time, thus forcing the use of the weaker eye.

OCCUPATIONAL THERAPIST. A healthcare provider who specializes in adapting the physical environment to meet a patient's needs. An occupational therapist also assists patients and caregivers with activities of daily living and provide instructions on wheelchair use or other adaptive equipment.

OCULOPHARYNGEAL MUSCULAR DYSTROPHY. A type of muscular dystrophy that affects adults of both sexes, causing weakness in the eye muscles and throat.

ODYNOPHAGIA. Pain in swallowing.

OFF-LABEL USE. Prescribing a drug for a population (e.g., pediatric) or condition for which it was not originally approved by the U.S. FDA. For example, sulfonylurea drugs are not FDA approved for use in children with type 2 diabetes due to a lack of clinical studies in pediatric populations, but a physician may prescribe them in an off-label use of the drug.

OLIGOHYDRAMNIOS. A reduced amount of amniotic fluid, whose causes include non-functioning kidneys and premature rupture of membranes. Without amniotic fluid to breathe, a baby will have underdeveloped and immature lungs.

OMPHALOCELE. A birth defect in which the bowel and sometimes the liver protrudes through an opening in the baby's abdomen near the umbilical cord.

ONCOLOGIST. A physician specializing in the diagnosis and treatment of cancer

OOCYST. A developmental stage of certain parasitic organisms, including those responsible for malaria and toxoplasmosis, in which the zygote of the organism is enclosed in a cyst.

OPEN BITE. A malocclusion in which some teeth do not meet the opposing teeth.

OPHIDIAPHOBIA. Fear of snakes.

OPHTHALMOLOGIST. A physician who specializes in the anatomy and physiology of the eyes and in the diagnosis and treatment of eye diseases and disorders.

OPIUM LATEX. The milky juice or sap of the opium poppy, used to produce morphine.

OPPORTUNISTIC INFECTION. An infection that is normally mild in a healthy individual, but which takes advantage of an ill person's weakened immune system to move into the body, grow, spread, and cause serious illness.

OPPOSITIONAL DEFIANT DISORDER. An emotional and behavioral disorder of children and adolescents characterized by hostile, deliberately argumentative, and defiant behavior towards authority figures that lasts for longer than six months.

OPTIC NERVE. A bundle of nerve fibers that carries visual messages from the retina in the form of electrical signals to the brain.

ORAL LESIONS. A single infected sore in the skin around the mouth or mucous membrane inside of the oral cavity.

ORAL REHYDRATION SOLUTION (ORS). A liquid preparation of electrolytes and glucose developed by the World Health Organization that can decrease fluid loss in persons with diarrhea. Originally developed to be prepared with materials available in the home, commercial preparations have recently come into use.

ORBIT. The eye socket which contains the eyeball, muscles, nerves, and blood vessels that serve the eye.

ORCHIOPEXY. A surgical procedure that places an undescended testicle in the scrotum and/or attaches a testicle to the scrotum.

ORCHITIS. Inflammation of one or both testes, accompanied by swelling, pain, fever, and a sensation of heaviness in the affected area.

OREXIN. Another name for hypocretin, a chemical secreted in the hypothalmus that regulates the sleep/wake cycle. Narcolepsy is sometimes described as an orexin deficiency syndrome.

ORGANELLE. A specialized structure within a cell, which is separated from the rest of the cell by a membrane composed of lipids and proteins, where chemical and metabolic functions take place.

ORGANIC CAUSES. Underlying medical or physical disorders causing failure to thrive.

ORGANISM. A single, independent unit of life, such as a bacterium, a plant, or an animal.

ORGANOGENESIS. The formation of organs during development.

ORGASM. Another word for sexual climax. In the male, orgasm is usually accompanied by ejaculation but may be experienced as distinct from ejaculation.

OROPHARYNX. One of the three regions of the pharynx, the oropharynx is the region behind the mouth.

ORTHOGNATIC SURGERY. Surgery to alter the relationships of the teeth and/or supporting bones, usually in conjunction with orthodontic treatment.

ORTHOPEDIST. A doctor specializing in treatment of the musculoskeletal system.

ORTHOSIS. An external device, such as a splint or a brace, that prevents or assists movement.

OSMOLALITY. The concentration of osmolar particles in the blood (or other solutions) that can help determine if the body is dehydrated.

OSSICLES. The three small bones of the middle ear: the malleus (hammer), the incus (anvil) and the stapes (stirrup). These bones help carry sound from the eardrum to the inner ear.

OSTEOARTHRITIS. A noninflammatory type of arthritis, usually occurring in older people, characterized by degeneration of cartilage, enlargement of the margins of the bones, and changes in the membranes in the joints. Also called degenerative arthritis.

OSTEOCLAST. A large, multinuclear cell involved in the physiological destruction and absorption of bone.

OSTEOGENESIS IMPERFECTA. An inherited disorder of the connective tissues that involves multiple symptoms, including weakened bones that break easily.

OSTEOLOGIST. A doctor who specializes in the skeletal system.

OSTEOMALACIA. A bone disease that occurs in adults due to a prolonged period of vitamin D deficiency. It is characterized by softening of the bone and is sometimes referred to as adult rickets.

OSTEOMYELITIS. An infection of the bone and bone marrow, usually caused by bacteria.

OSTEOPOROSIS. Literally meaning "porous bones," this condition occurs when bones lose an excessive amount of their protein and mineral content, particularly calcium. Over time, bone mass and strength are reduced leading to increased risk of fractures.

OSTOMY. A surgically-created opening in the abdomen for elimination of waste products (urine or stool).

OTALGIA. The medical term for pain in the ear. Impacted cerumen can sometimes cause otalgia.

OTITIS. Inflammation of the ear, which may be marked by pain, fever, abnormalities of hearing, hearing loss, noise in the ears, and dizzy spells.

OTITIS MEDIA. Inflammation or infection of the middle ear space behind the eardrum. It commonly occurs in early childhood and is characterized by ear pain, fever, and hearing problems.

OTOACOUSTIC EMISSION (OAE). Sounds or echoes created by vibrations of hair cells in the cochlea in response to sound; used to screen for hearing impairment in newborns.

OTOLARYNGOLOGIST. A doctor who is trained to treat injuries, defects, diseases, or conditions of the ear, nose, and throat. Also sometimes known as an otorhinolaryngologist.

OTOSCOPE. A hand-held instrument with a tiny light and a funnel-shaped attachment called an ear speculum, which is used to examine the ear canal and eardrum.

OUTER EAR. Outer visible portion of the ear that collects and directs sound waves toward the tympanic membrane by way of a canal which extends inward through the temporal bone.

OUTPATIENT SURGERY. Also called same-day or ambulatory surgery. The patient arrives for surgery and returns home on the same day. Outpatient surgery can take place in a hospital, surgical center, or outpatient clinic.

OVA. The plural of ovum, it is the female reproductive cell.

OVARY. One of the two almond-shaped glands in the female reproductive system responsible for producing eggs and the sex hormones estrogen and progesterone.

OVERBITE. Protrusion of the upper teeth over the lower teeth.

OVER-THE-COUNTER TREATMENTS. Medications that can be purchased without a prescription.

OVERWEIGHT. Being 25–29% over the recommended healthy body weight for a specific age and height, as established by calculating body mass index.

OVULATE. To release a mature egg for fertilization.

OVULATION. The monthly process by which an ovarian follicle ruptures releasing a mature egg cell.

OXIDATIVE STRESS. A condition where the body is producing an excess of oxygen-free radicals.

OXYGENATE. To supply with oxygen.

OXYGENATED BLOOD. Blood carrying oxygen through the body.

OXYTOCIN. A hormone that stimulates the uterus to contract during child birth and the breasts to release milk.

OZONE. A form of oxygen with three atoms in its molecule (O_3), produced by an electric spark or ultraviolet light passing through air or oxygen. A layer of ozone about 15 mi (24 km) above Earth's surface helps protect living things from the damaging effects of the sun's ultraviolet rays. Ozone is used therapeutically as a disinfectant and oxidative agent.

P

PAGET'S DISEASE. A chronic disorder of unknown cause usually affecting middle aged and elderly people and characterized by enlarged and deformed bones. Changes in the normal mechanism of bone formation occur in Paget's disease and can cause bones to weaken, resulting in bone pain, arthritis, deformities, and fractures. Also known as osteitis deformans.

PAGOPHAGIA. The compulsive eating of ice.

PALATAL LENGTHENING (PALATAL PUSHBACK). A surgical procedure in which tissue from the front part of the mouth is moved back to lengthen it.

PALATE. The roof of the mouth.

PALILALIA. A complex vocal tic in which the child repeats his or her own words, songs, or other utterances.

PALLIATIVE. Referring to a drug or a form of care that relieves pain without providing a cure. Persons in severe pain from terminal cancer are often prescribed narcotics as palliative care.

PALLOR. Extreme paleness in the color of the skin.

PALMAR. Referring to the palm of the hand.

PALMAR GRASP. A young infant's primitive ability to hold an object in the palm by wrapping fingers and thumb around it from one side.

PALPITATIONS. Rapid and forceful heartbeat.

PALSY. Uncontrolable tremors.

PANCARDITIS. Inflammation of the lining of the heart, the sac around the heart, and the muscle of the heart.

PANCREAS. A five-inch-long gland that lies behind the stomach and next to the duodenum. The pancreas releases glucagon, insulin, and some of the enzymes which aid digestion.

PANCREATIC INSUFFICIENCY. Reduction or absence of pancreatic secretions into the digestive system due to scarring and blockage of the pancreatic duct.

PANDAS DISORDERS. A group of childhood disorders associated with such streptococcal infections as scarlet fever and strep throat. The acronym stands for Pediatric Autoimmune Neuropsychiatric Disorders Associated with Streptococci.

PANDEMIC. A disease that occurs throughout a regional group, the population of a country, or the world.

PANHYPOPITUITARISM. Generalized decrease of all of the anterior pituitary hormones.

PANTOPHOBIA. Fear of everything.

PAP TEST. A screening test for precancerous and cancerous cells on the cervix. This simple test is done during a routine pelvic exam and involves scraping cells from the cervix. These cells are then stained and examined under a microscope. Also known as the Papanicolaou test.

PAPULE. A solid, raised bump on the skin.

PARALLEL PLAY. Toddlers play side by side but seldom try to interact with each other, playing separately with similar toy.

PARALYSIS. Loss of the ability to move one or more parts of the body voluntarily due to muscle or nerve damage.

PARAMYXOVIRUS. A genus of viruses that includes the causative agent of mumps.

PARASOMNIA. A type of sleep disorder characterized by abnormal changes in behavior or body functions during sleep, specific stages of sleep, or the transition from sleeping to waking.

PARASYMPATHETIC GANGLION CELL. Type of nerve cell normally found in the wall of the colon.

PARATHYROID GLAND. A pair of glands adjacent to the thyroid gland that primarily regulate blood calcium levels.

PARATHYROID HORMONE. A chemical substance produced by the parathyroid glands. This hormone plays a major role in regulating calcium concentration in the body.

PARENTERAL NUTRITION. Liquid nutrition usually provided intravenously.

PARKINSONISM. A set of symptoms originally associated with Parkinson disease that can occur as side effects of neuroleptic medications. The symptoms include trembling of the fingers or hands, a shuffling gait, and tight or rigid muscles.

PARKINSON'S DISEASE. A slowly progressive disease that destroys nerve cells in the basal ganglia and thus causes loss of dopamine, a chemical that aids in transmission of nerve signals (neurotransmitter). Parkinson's is characterized by shaking in resting muscles, a stooping posture, slurred speech, muscular stiffness, and weakness.

PAROTITIS. Inflammation and swelling of one or both of the parotid salivary glands.

PAROXYSMAL HYPERCYANOIC ATTACKS. Sudden episodes of cyanosis resulting from the circulation of deoxygenated blood to the body.

PARVOVIRUS B19. A virus that commonly infects humans; about 50% of all adults have been infected sometime during childhood or adolescence. Parvovirus B19 infects only humans. An infection in pregnancy can cause the unborn baby to have severe anemia and the woman may have a miscarriage.

PASSIVE IMMUNITY. The body reception of proteins that act as antibodies instead of making the antibodies itself. Immunoglobulins may produce this immunity. All babies have antibodies from their mothers, which give them short-term protection.

PASSIVE MOVEMENT. Movement that occurs under the power of an outside source such as a clinician. There is no voluntary muscular contraction by the individual who is being passively moved.

PASTEURELLOSIS. A bacterial wound infection caused by *Pasteurella multocida*. Pasteurellosis is characterized by inflammation around the wound site and may be accompanied by bacteria in the bloodstream and infection in tissues and organs.

PASTEURIZATION. A process during which milk is heated and maintained at a particular temperature for the purpose of killing, or retarding the development of, pathogenic bacteria.

PATCH TEST. A skin test in which different antigens (substances that cause an allergic reaction) are introduced into a patient's skin via a needle prick or scratch and then observed for evidence of an allergic reaction to one or more of them. Also known as a scratch test.

PATELLA. The kneecap.

PATENT DUCTUS ARTERIOSUS. A congenital defect in which the temporary blood vessel connecting the left pulmonary artery to the aorta in the fetus does not close after birth.

PATENT FORAMEN OVALE (PFO). A congenital heart defect characterized by an open flap that remains between the two upper chambers of the heart (the left and right atria). This opening can allow a blood clot from one part of the body to travel through the flap and up to the brain, causing a stroke.

PATHOGEN. Any disease-producing microorganism.

PATHOGENIC BACTERIA. Bacteria that produce illness.

PATHOLOGIC. Characterized by disease or by the structural and functional changes due to disease.

PATIENT EDUCATION. Instruction and information that helps patients prepare for a procedure, learn about a disease, or manage their health. Patient education may include one-on-one instruction from a health care provider, educational sessions in a group setting, or self-guided learning videos or modules. Informative and instructional handouts are usually provided to explain specific medications, tests, or procedures.

PATIENT RIGHTS AND RESPONSIBILITIES. Every hospital has an established list of patient rights and responsibilities, established by the American Hospital Association. They are usually posted throughout the hospital.

PAVOR NOCTURNUS. Another name for sleep terror disorder, or night terrors.

PEAK FLOW MEASUREMENT. Measurement of the maximum rate of airflow attained during a forced vital capacity determination.

PECTUS CARINATUM. An abnormality of the chest in which the sternum (breastbone) is pushed outward. It is sometimes called "pigeon breast."

PECTUS EXCAVATUM. An abnormality of the chest in which the sternum (breastbone) sinks inward; sometimes called "funnel chest."

PEDIATRIC ALLERGIST. A board certified physician specializing in the diagnosis and treatment of allergic conditions in children.

PEDIATRIC DENTISTRY. The dental specialty concerned with the dental treatment of children and adolescents.

PEDIATRIC INTENSIVIST. A physician who completed a three-year residency in pediatrics after medical school and an additional subspecialty fellowship training in intensive care.

PEDICULICIDE. Any substance that kills lice.

PEDICULOSIS. A lice infestation.

PEER ACCEPTANCE. The degree to which a child or adolescent is socially accepted by peers, usually of about the same age; the level of peer popularity.

PEER INFLUENCE. Peer approval or disapproval of the child's behavior or performance.

PEER PRESSURE. Social pressure exerted by a group or individual in a group on someone to adopt a particular type of behavior, dress, or attitude in order to be an accepted member of a group or clique.

PELVIC INFLAMMATORY DISEASE (PID). Any infection of the lower female reproductive tract (vagina and cervix) that spreads to the upper female reproductive tract (uterus, fallopian tubes and ovaries). Symptoms include severe abdominal pain, high fever, and vaginal discharge. PID is the most common and most serious consequence of infection with sexually transmitted diseases in women and is a leading cause of female fertility problems.

PENICILLAMINE (CUPRIMINE, DEPEN). A drug used to treat medical problems (such as excess copper in the body and rheumatoid arthritis) and to prevent kidney stones. It is also sometimes prescribed to remove excess lead from the body.

PERCUSSION. An assessment method in which the surface of the body is struck with the fingertips to obtain sounds that can be heard or vibrations that can be felt. It can determine the position, size, and consistency of an internal organ. It is performed over the chest to determine the presence of normal air content in the lungs, and over the abdomen to evaluate air in the loops of the intestine.

PERCUTANEOUS UMBILICAL BLOOD SAMPLING (PUBS). A technique used to obtain pure fetal blood from the umbilical cord while the fetus is in utero and also called cordocentesis.

PERICARDITIS. Inflammation of the pericardium, the sac that surrounds the heart and the roots of the great blood vessels.

PERICARDIUM. The thin, sac-like membrane that surrounds the heart and the roots of the great vessels. It has two layers: the inner, serous (or visceral) pericardium and the outer, fibrous (or parietal) pericardium.

PERINATAL. Referring to the period of time surrounding an infant's birth, from the last two months of pregnancy through the first 28 days of life.

PERINATAL MORTALITY. The number of late fetal deaths, 28 weeks or more gestation, and neonatal deaths that occur in the first seven days.

PERINEUM. The area between the opening of the vagina and the anus in a woman, or the area between the scrotum and the anus in a man.

PERIODIC LIMB MOVEMENT DISORDER. A disorder characterized by involuntary flexion of leg muscles, causing twitching and leg extension or kicking during sleep.

PERIODONTAL LIGAMENT. Also called the periodontal membrane, this tough fibrous tissue holds the teeth in place in the gums.

PERIODONTITIS. Inflammation of the periodontium, the tissues that support and anchor the teeth. Without treatment it can destroy the structures supporting the teeth, including bone.

PERIPHERAL NERVOUS SYSTEM (PNS). The part of the nervous system that is outside the brain and spinal cord. Sensory, motor, and autonomic nerves are included. PNS nerves link the central nervous system with sensory organs, muscles, blood vessels, and glands.

PERISTALSIS. Slow, rhythmic contractions of the muscles in a tubular organ, such as the intestines, that move the contents along.

PERITONEUM. The transparent membrane lining the abdominal and pelvic cavities (parietal peritoneum) and the membrane forming the outer layer of the stomach and interstines (visceral peritoneum). Between the visceral and parietal peritoneums is a potential space called the peritoneal cavity.

PERITONITIS. Inflammation of the peritoneum. It is most often due to bacterial infection, but can also be caused by a chemical irritant (such as spillage of acid from the stomach or bile from the gall bladder).

PERMEABLE. A condition in which fluid or certain other substances are allowed to pass through.

PERMETHRIN. A medication used to rid the scalp of head lice. Permethrin works by paralyzing the lice, so that they cannot feed within the 24 hours after hatching required for survival.

PERSONAL EXPERIENCE SCREENING QUESTIONNAIRE (PESQ). A questionnaire for alcoholism.

PERSONALITY. The organized pattern of behaviors and attitudes that makes a human being distinctive. Personality is formed by the ongoing interaction of temperament, character, and environment.

PERSPECTIVE. The way an artist shows depth or distance in a drawing or painting, usually by drawing figures and buildings larger in the front of the picture and smaller in the back.

PERTUSSIS. Whooping cough, a highly contagious disease of the respiratory system, usually affecting children, that is caused by the bacterium *Bordetella pertussis* and is characterized in its advanced stage by spasms of coughing interspersed with deep, noisy inspirations.

PERVASIVE DEVELOPMENTAL DISORDER. A category of childhood disorder that includes Asperger syndrome and Rett's disorder. The PDDs are sometimes referred to collectively as autistic spectrum disorders.

PETECHIA. Plural, petechiae. A tiny purple or red spot on the skin resulting from a hemorrhage under the skin's surface.

PETROLEUM JELLY OR OINTMENT. Petrolatum, a gelatinous substance obtained from oil that is used as a protective dressing.

PEYRONIE'S DISEASE. A disease of unknown origin which causes a hardening of the corpora cavernosa, the erectile tissue of the penis. The penis may become misshapen and/or curved as a result and erections are painful.

PFEIFFER SYNDROME. This condition includes craniosynostosis, shallow eye sockets, underdevelopment of the midface, short thumbs and big toes, and possible webbing of hands and feet.

PH. A measurement of the acidity or alkalinity of a solution. Based on a scale of 14, a pH of 7.0 is neutral. A pH below 7.0 is an acid; the lower the number, the stronger the acid. A pH above 7.0 is a base; the higher the number, the stronger the base. Blood pH is slightly alkaline (basic) with a normal range of 7.36–7.44.

PHAGOCYTOSIS. A process by which certain cells envelope and digest debris and microorganisms to remove them from the blood.

PHALANX. (plural, plananges) Any of the digital bones of the hand or foot. Humans have three phalanges to each finger and toe with the exception of the thumb and big toe which have only two each.

PHALILALIA. Involuntary echoing by an individual of the last word, phrase, sentence, or sound he/she vocalized.

PHANTOM PAIN. Pain, tingling, itching, or numbness in the place where the amputated part used to be.

PHARMACOLOGICAL. Referring to therapy that relies on drugs.

PHARYNX. The throat, a tubular structure that lies between the mouth and the esophagus.

PHASE CONTRAST MICROSCOPE. A light microscope in which light is focused on the sample at an angle to produce a clearer image.

PHENYLALANINE. An essential amino acid that must be obtained from food since the human body cannot manufacture it. It is necessary for normal growth and development and for normal protein metabolism.

PHENYLKETONURIA (PKU). A rare, inherited, metabolic disorder in which the enzyme necessary to break down and use phenylalanine, an amino acid necessary for normal growth and development, is lacking. As a result, phenylalanine builds up in the body causing mental retardation and other neurological problems.

PHENYTOIN. An anti-convulsant medication used to treat seizure disorders. Sold under the brand name Dilantin.

PHEOCHROMOCYTOMA. A tumor that originates from the adrenal gland's chromaffin cells, causing overproduction of catecholamines, powerful hormones that induce high blood pressure and other symptoms.

PHIMOSIS. A tightening of the foreskin that may close the opening of the penis.

PHLEBOTOMIST. A person who draws blood from a vein.

PHLEGM. Thick mucus produced in the air passages.

PHOBIA. An intense and irrational fear of a specific object, activity, or situation that leads to avoidance.

PHONEMES. The basic units of sound in a language.

PHONICS. A system to teach reading by teaching the speech sounds associated with single letters, letter combinations, and syllables.

PHONOLOGICAL AWARENESS. The ability to hear and manipulate the sounds that make up words.

PHONOLOGY. The science of speech sounds and sound patterns.

PHOTOCOAGULATION. A type of cancer treatment in which cancer cells are destroyed by an intense beam of laser light.

PHOTOPHOBIA. An extreme sensitivity to light.

PHOTOSENSITIZATION. Development of oversensitivity to sunlight.

PHOTOTHERAPY. Another name for light therapy in mainstream medical practice.

PHYSIATRIST. A physician who specializes in physical medicine and rehabilitation.

PHYSICAL THERAPIST. A healthcare provider who teaches patients how to perform therapeutic exercises to maintain maximum mobility and range of motion.

PHYSIOLOGIC. Refers to physiology, particularly normal, healthy, physical functioning.

PHYTOESTROGENS. Compounds found in plants that can mimic the effects of estrogen in the body.

PICA. A desire that sometimes arises in pregnancy to eat nonfood substances, such as dirt or clay.

PIMPLE. A small, red swelling of the skin.

PINCER GRIP. The ability to hold objects between thumb and index finger, which typically develops in infants between 12 and 15 months of age.

PIPERONYL BUTOXIDE. A liquid organic compound that enhances the activity of insecticides.

PITOCIN. A synthetic hormone that produces uterine contractions.

PITUITARY GLAND. The most important of the endocrine glands (glands that release hormones directly into the bloodstream), the pituitary is located at the base of the brain. Sometimes referred to as the "master gland," it regulates and controls the activities of other endocrine glands and many body processes including growth and reproductive function. Also called the hypophysis.

PLACENTA. The organ that provides oxygen and nutrition from the mother to the unborn baby during pregnancy. The placenta is attached to the wall of the uterus and leads to the unborn baby via the umbilical cord.

PLACENTA PREVIA. A condition in which the placenta totally or partially covers the cervix, preventing vaginal delivery.

PLACENTAL ABRUPTION. An abnormal separation of the placenta from the uterus before the birth of the baby, with subsequent heavy uterine bleeding. Normally, the baby is born first and then the placenta is delivered within a half hour.

PLACENTAL INFARCTION. An area of dead tissue in the placenta that is due to an obstruction of circulation in the area.

PLAGIOCEPHALY. A form of craniosynostosis that involves fusion of the right or left side of coronal suture.

PLAGUE. A serious, potentially life-threatening infectious disease caused by the bacterium *Yersinia pestis*. The disease is usually transmitted to humans by the bites of infected rodent fleas. There are three major types: bubonic, pneumonic, and septicemic.

PLANTAR. Relating to the sole of the foot.

PLAQUE. A deposit, usually of fatty material, on the inside wall of a blood vessel. Also refers to a small, round demyelinated area that develops in the brain and spinal cord of an individual with multiple sclerosis.

PLASMA. A watery fluid containing proteins, salts, and other substances that carries red blood cells, white blood cells, and platelets throughout the body. Plasma makes up 50% of human blood.

PLATELET. A cell-like particle in the blood that plays an important role in blood clotting. Platelets are activated when an injury causes a blood vessel to break. They change shape from round to spiny, "sticking" to the broken vessel wall and to each other to begin the clotting process. In addition to physically plugging breaks in blood vessel walls, platelets also release chemicals that promote clotting.

PLAY THERAPY OR THERAPEUTIC PLAY. A type of psychotherapy for young children involving the use of toys and games to build a therapeutic relationship and encourage the child's self-expression.

PLAY-BASED ASSESSMENT. A form of developmental assessment that involves observation of how a child plays alone, with peers, or with parents or other familiar caregivers, in free play or in special games.

PLEURITIS. Inflammation of the pleura, the membrane surrounding the lungs. Also called pleurisy.

PNEUMATIC OTOSCOPE. An otoscope that can also produce a small puff of air that vibrates the eardrum.

PNEUMOCYSTIS CARINII. A parasite transitional between a fungus and protozoan, frequently occurring as aggregate forms existing within rounded cystlike structures. It is the causative agent of pneumocystosis.

PNEUMONIA. An infection in which the lungs become inflamed. It can be caused by nearly any class of organism known to cause human infections, including bacteria, viruses, fungi, and parasites.

PNEUMOTHORAX. A collection of air or gas in the chest or pleural cavity that causes part or all of a lung to collapse.

POLIO. Poliomyelitis, an acute viral disease marked by inflammation of nerve cells of the brain stem and spinal cord and can cause paralysis.

POLLEN. A fine, powdery substance released by plants and trees; an allergen.

POLYCARBONATE. A very strong type of plastic often used in safety glasses, sport glasses, and children's eyeglasses. Polycarbonate lenses have approximately 50 times the impact resistance of glass lenses.

POLYHYDRAMNIOS. A condition in which there is too much fluid around the fetus in the amniotic sac.

POLYSOMNOGRAPHY. An overnight series tests designed to evaluate a patient's basic physiological processes during sleep. Polysomnography generally includes monitoring of the patient's airflow through the nose and mouth, blood pressure, electrocardiographic activity, blood oxygen level, brain wave pattern, eye movement, and the movement of respiratory muscles and limbs

POLYUNSATURATED FAT. A non-animal oil or fatty acid rich in unsaturated chemical bonds. This type of fat is not associated with the formation of cholesterol in the blood.

POLYURETHANE. A type of synthetic plastic.

PORPHYRIN. An organic compound found in living things that founds the foundation structure for hemoglobin, chlorophyll, and other respiratory pigments. In humans, porphyrins combine with iron to form hemes.

PORTFOLIO. A student-controlled collection of student work products that indicates progress over time.

POSITRON EMISSION TOMOGRAPHY (PET). A computerized diagnostic technique that uses radioactive substances to examine structures of the body. When used to assess the brain, it produces a three-dimensional image that shows anatomy and function, including such information as blood flow, oxygen consumption, glucose metabolism, and concentrations of various molecules in brain tissue.

POSTAXIAL. Situated behind or away from the axis or midline of the body.

POSTEXPOSURE PROPHYLAXIS. Any treatment given after exposure to a disease to try to prevent the disease from occurring. In the case of rabies, postexposure prophylaxis involves a series of vaccines given to an individual who has been bitten by an unknown animal or one that is potentially infected with the rabies virus.

POSTPARTUM. The six-week period following childbirth.

POST-TRAUMATIC STRESS DISORDER (PTSD). A disorder that occurs among survivors of extremely stressful or traumatic events, such as a natural disaster, an airplane crash, rape, or military combat. Symptoms include anxiety, insomnia, flashbacks, and nightmares. Patients with PTSD are unnecessarily vigilant; they may experience survivor guilt, and they sometimes cannot concentrate or experience joy.

POSTURAL. Pertaining to the position of the head, neck, trunk and lower limbs in relation to the ground and the vertical.

POSTURAL DRAINAGE. The use of positioning to drain secretions from the bronchial tubes and lungs into the trachea or windpipe where they can either be coughed up or suctioned out.

PRANAYAMA. The yoga practice of breathing correctly and deeply.

PREAXIAL. Situated in front of the axis or midline of the body.

PREDIABETES. A precursor condition to type 2 diabetes, sometimes called impaired glucose tolerance or impaired fasting glucose. Prediabetes is clinically defined as individuals who have elevated blood glucose levels that are not diagnostic of type 2 diabetes but are above normal (for the fasting plasma glucose test, this measurement would be 100 to 125 mg/dL [5.6 to 6.9 mmol/L]).

PREDNISONE. A corticosteroid medication often used to treat inflammation.

PREECLAMPSIA. A condition that develops after the twentieth week of pregnancy and results in high blood pressure, fluid retention that doesn't go away, and large amounts of protein in the urine. Without treatment, it can progress to a dangerous condition called eclampsia, in which a woman goes into convulsions.

PREGNANCY CATEGORY. A system of classifying drugs according to their established risks for use during pregnancy. Category A: Controlled human studies have demonstrated no fetal risk. Category B: Animal studies indicate no fetal risk, but no human studies, or adverse effects in animals, but not in well-controlled human studies. Category C: No adequate human or animal studies, or adverse fetal effects in animal studies, but no available human data. Category D: Evidence of fetal risk, but benefits outweigh risks. Category X: Evidence of fetal risk. Risks outweigh any benefits.

PREMATURE LABOR. Labor beginning before 36 weeks of pregnancy.

PREMAXILLA. The front central section of the upper gum, containing the four upper front teeth.

PREMOLAR. Bicuspid; the two cupped teeth between the first molars and the cuspids.

PREMUTATION. A change in a gene that precedes a mutation; this change does not alter the function of the gene.

PRENATAL DIAGNOSIS. The determination of whether a fetus possesses a disease or disorder while it is still in the womb.

PRENATAL TESTING. Testing for a disease, such as a genetic condition, in an unborn baby.

PREPUCE. A fold of skin, such as the foreskin of the penis or the skin that surrounds the clitoris.

PRESCHOOL. An early childhood program in which children combine learning with play in a program run by professionally trained adults.

PRESSURE ULCER. Also known as a decubitus ulcer or bedsore, a pressure ulcer is an open wound that forms whenever prolonged pressure is applied to skin covering bony prominences of the body. Patients who are bedridden are at risk of developing pressure ulcers.

PRIAPISM. A painful, abnormally prolonged penile erection.

PRIMARY CAREGIVER. A person who is responsible for the primary care and upbringing of a child.

PRIMARY IMMUNODEFICIENCY DISEASE. A group of approximately 70 conditions that affect the normal functioning of the immune system.

PRIMARY SLEEP DISORDER. A sleep disorder that cannot be attributed to a medical condition, another mental disorder, or prescription medications or other substances.

PROBIOTICS. Bacteria that are beneficial to a person's health, either through protecting the body against pathogenic bacteria or assisting in recovery from an illness.

PROBLEM ORIENTED SCREENING INSTRUMENT FOR TEENAGERS (POSIT). A questionnaire used specifically for teenagers to assess alcohol and drug use.

PRODROME. Early symptoms that warn of the beginning of disease. For example, the herpes prodrome consists of pain, burning, tingling, or itching at a site before blisters are visible while the migraine prodrome consists of visual disturbances.

PROGESTERONE. The hormone produced by the ovary after ovulation that prepares the uterine lining for a fertilized egg.

PROGRESSIVE. Advancing, going forward, going from bad to worse, increasing in scope or severity.

PROGRESSIVE SUPRANUCLEAR PALSY. A rare disease that gradually destroys nerve cells in the parts of the brain that control eye movements, breathing, and muscle coordination. The loss of nerve cells causes palsy, or paralysis, that slowly gets worse as the disease progresses. The palsy affects ability to move the eyes, relax the muscles, and control balance. Also called Steele-Richardson-Olszewski syndrome.

PROJECTIVE PERSONALITY TEST. A personality test in which the participant interprets ambiguous images, objects, stories.

PROJECTIVE TEST. A type of psychological test that assesses a person's thinking patterns, observational ability, feelings, and attitudes on the basis of responses to ambiguous test materials. Projective tests are often used to evaluate patients with personality disorders.

PROLACTIN. A hormone that prepares the breasts during pregnancy for milk production after childbirth.

PROMISCUOUS. Having many indiscriminate or casual sexual relationships.

PRONE. Lying on the stomach with the face downward.

PROPHYLACTIC. Preventing the spread or occurrence of disease or infection.

PROPHYLAXIS. Protection against or prevention of a disease. Antibiotic prophylaxis is the use of antibiotics to prevent a possible infection.

PROSOCIAL BEHAVIORS. Social behavior characterized by positive, cooperative, and reciprocal social exchanges.

PROSTAGLANDINS. A group of hormone-like molecules that exert local effects on a variety of processes including fluid balance, blood flow, and gastrointestinal function. They may be responsible for the production of some types of pain and inflammation.

PROSTHETIC. Referring to an artificial part of the body.

PROSTHETIST. A health care professional who is skilled in making and fitting artificial limbs and other prostheses.

PROTEIN. An important building blocks of the body, a protein is a large, complex organic molecule composed of amino acids. It is involved in the formation of body structures and in controlling the basic functions of the human body.

PROTEIN-LOSING ENTEROPATHY. Excessive loss of plasma and proteins in the gastrointestinal tract.

PROTEINURIA. Having abnormally large quantities of protein in the urine.

PROTOCOL. A plan for carrying out a scientific study or a patient's course of treatment.

PROTON PUMP. A structure in the body that produces and pumps acid into the stomach.

PROTOPORPHYRIN. A kind of porphyrin that links with iron to form the heme of hemoglobin.

PROTOPORPHYRIN IX. A protein the measurement of which is useful for the assessment of iron status. Hemoglobin consists of a complex of a protein plus heme. Heme consists of iron plus protoporphyrin IX. Normally, during the course of red blood cell formation, protoporphyrin IX acquires iron, to generate heme, and the heme becomes incorporated into hemoglobin. However, in iron deficiency, protophoryrin IX builds up.

PROXIMAL MUSCLES. The muscles closest to the center of the body.

PROXIMODISTAL DEVELOPMENT. Motor development which occurs in the first two years of life: head, trunk, and arms before hands and fingers.

PRURITUS. The symptom of itching or an uncontrollable sensation leading to the urge to scratch.

PSEUDOMONAS. A bacterium which can cause ulcers in contact lens wearers.

PSORIASIS. A chronic, noncontagious skin disease that is marked by dry, scaly, and silvery patches of skin that appear in a variety of sizes and locations on the body.

PSYCHODRAMA. A specific form of role play that focuses on acting out "scripts" of unresolved issues within the family, or helping family members adopt new approaches and understanding of one another.

PSYCHOGENIC DISORDERS. A variety of unusual, involuntary movements that occur in children with psychiatric disorders or in response to anxiety, stress, depression, anger, or grief. Psychogenic movements are thought to represent the physical expression of an intolerable mental conflict.

PSYCHOLOGICAL. Pertaining to the mind, its mental processes, and its emotional makeup.

PSYCHOLOGICAL EVALUATION. Examination of a patient by a psychologist through interviews, observation of behavior, and psychological testing with the goal of determining personality adjustment, identifying problems, and helping to diagnose and plan treatment for a mental disorder.

PSYCHOMETRICS. The development, administration, and interpretation of tests to measure mental or psychological abilities. Psychometric tests convert an individual's psychological traits and attributes into a numerical estimation or evaluation.

PSYCHOMOTOR AGITATION. Disturbed physical and mental processes (e.g., fidgeting, wringing of hands, racing thoughts); a symptom of major depressive disorder.

PSYCHOMOTOR RETARDATION. Slowed mental and physical processes characteristic of a bipolar depressive episode.

PSYCHOPATHOLOGY. The study of mental disorders or illnesses, such as schizophrenia, personality disorder, or major depressive disorder.

PSYCHOSES. Mental illness that interferes with an individual's ability to manage life's challenges and everyday activities. The impairment of cognitive ability that distorts reality.

PSYCHOTHERAPY. Psychological counseling that seeks to determine the underlying causes of a patient's depression. The form of this counseling may be cognitive/behavioral, interpersonal, or psychodynamic.

PSYCHOTROPIC DRUG. Any medication that has an effect on the mind, brain, behavior, perceptions, or emotions. Psychotropic medications are used to treat mental illnesses because they affect a patient's moods and perceptions.

PUBERTY. The point in development when the ability to reproduce begins. The gonads begin to function and secondary sexual characteristics begin to appear.

PULMONARY. Referring to the lungs and respiratory system.

PULMONARY ARTERY. An artery that carries blood from the heart to the lungs.

PULMONARY EDEMA. An accumulation of fluid in the tissue of the lungs.

PULMONARY EMBOLISM. Blockage of an artery in the lungs by foreign matter such as fat, tumor tissue, or a clot originating from a vein. A pulmonary embolism can be a very serious, and in some cases fatal, condition.

PULMONARY HYPERTENSION. A disorder in which the pressure in the blood vessels of the lungs is abnormally high.

PULMONARY HYPOPLASIA. Incomplete or defective development of the lungs.

PULP. The soft, innermost layer of a tooth that contains its blood vessels and nerves.

PULPITIS. Inflammation of the pulp of a tooth that involves the blood vessels and nerves.

PUNCTURE. An injury caused by a sharp, narrow object deeply penetrating the skin.

PUNISHMENT. The application of a negative stimulus to reduce or eliminate a behavior. The two types typically used with children are verbal reprimands and punishment involving physical pain, as in corporal punishment.

PURGING. The use of vomiting, diuretics, or laxatives to clear the stomach and intestines after a binge.

PURIFIED CHICKEN EMBRYO CELL VACCINE (PCEC). A rabies vaccine in which the virus is grown in cultures of chicken embryo cells, inactivated, and purified for IM injection.

PURPURA. A group of disorders characterized by purplish or reddish brown areas of discoloration visible through the skin. These areas of discoloration are caused by bleeding from broken capillaries.

PUS. A thick, yellowish or greenish fluid composed of the remains of dead white blood cells, pathogens, and decomposed cellular debris. It is most often associated with bacterial infection.

PYELONEPHRITIS. An inflammation of the kidney and upper urinary tract, usually caused by a bacterial infection. In its most serious form, complications can include high blood pressure (hypertension) and renal failure.

PYOGENIC. Capable of generating pus. *Streptococcus*, *Staphocococcus*, and bowel bacteria are the primary pyogenic organisms.

PYRETHRIN, PYRETHROID. A naturally occurring insecticide extracted from chrysanthemum flowers. It paralyzes lice so that they cannot feed.

PYREXIA. A medical term meaning fever.

PYRIN. A protein that regulates the body' s inflammatory response to stress or trauma. The MEFV gene involved in FMF produces an unstable form of pyrin that fails to adequately control the inflammatory response.

PYROGEN. A chemical circulating in the blood that causes a rise in body temperature.

PYROMANIA. An impulse control disorder characterized by fire setting.

Q

QUADRIPLEGIA. Paralysis of all four limbs and the trunk below the level of an associated injury to the spinal cord. Also called tetraplegia.

QUANTIFIABLE. A result or measurement that can be expressed as a number. The results of quantifiable psychological tests can be translated into numerical values, or scores.

R

RABIES IMMUNE GLOBULIN (RIG OR HRIG). A human serum preparation containing high levels of antibodies against the rabies virus; used for post-exposure prophylaxis.

RABIES VIRUS ADSORBED (RVA). A rabies vaccine in which the virus is grown in cultures of lung cells from rhesus monkeys, inactivated, and adsorbed to aluminum phosphate.

RACHITIC ROSARY. Beadlike bumps present at the junction of the ribs with their cartilages. It is often seen in children with rickets.

RADIATION THERAPY. A cancer treatment that uses high-energy rays or particles to kill or weaken cancer cells. Radiation may be delivered externally or internally via surgically implanted pellets. Also called radiotherapy.

RADIOFREQUENCY ABLATION (RFA). A procedure in which radiofrequency waves are used to destroy blood vessels and tissues.

RADIOGRAPH. The actual picture or film produced by an x-ray study.

RADIOGRAPHY. Examination of any part of the body through the use of x rays. The process produces an image of shadows and contrasts on film.

RADIOISOTOPE. One of two or more atoms with the same number of protons but a different number of neutrons with a nuclear composition. In nuclear scanning, radioactive isotopes are used as a diagnostic agent.

RADIOLOGIST. A medical doctor specially trained in radiology, the branch of medicine concerned with radioactive substances and their use for the diagnosis and treatment of disease.

RADIOPAQUE. Not penetrable by x-rays. A radiopaque object will look white or light when the x-ray film is developed. Most objects that children swallow can be detected by an x-ray study because they are radiopaque.

RADIOPAQUE DYES, RADIOCONTRAST MEDIA. Injected substances that are used to outline tissues and organs in some x-ray and other radiation procedures.

RADIUS. The bone of the forearm which joins the wrist on the same side as the thumb.

RAGAMUFFINS. A term used in nineteenth-century London to describe neglected or abandoned children who lived on the streets.

RAGGED-RED FIBERS. A microscopic accumulation of diseased mitochondria.

RANGE OF MOTION (ROM). The range of motion of a joint from full extension to full flexion (bending) measured in degrees like a circle.

RAPID EYE MOVEMENT (REM) LATENCY. The amount of time it takes for the first onset of REM sleep after a person falls asleep.

RAPID EYE MOVEMENT (REM) SLEEP. A phase of sleep during which the person's eyes move rapidly beneath the lids. It accounts for 20–25% of sleep time. Dreaming occurs during REM sleep.

RASH. A spotted, pink or red skin eruption that may be accompanied by itching and is caused by disease, contact with an allergen, food ingestion, or drug reaction.

REACTIVE HYPOGLYCEMIA. A rare condition in which blood sugars drop below normal levels approximately four hours after eating.

REACTIVITY. The level or intensity of a person's physical or emotional excitability.

READINESS TEST. A test that measures the extent of a child's acquired skills for successfully undertaking a new learning activity such as kindergarten.

RECEPTIVE APHASIA. A developmental disorder in which a child has difficulty comprehending spoken and written language.

RECEPTIVE LANGUAGE. The comprehension of language.

RECESSIVE. Refers to an inherited trait that is outwardly obvious only when two copies of the gene for that trait are present. An individual displaying a recessive trait must have inherited one copy of the defective gene from each parent.

RECESSIVE DISORDER. Disorder that requires two copies of the predisposing gene one from each parent for the child to have the disease.

RECESSIVE GENE. A type of gene that is not expressed as a trait unless inherited by both parents.

RECOMMENDED DIETARY ALLOWANCE (RDA). The Recommended Dietary Allowances (RDAs) are quantities of nutrients in the diet that are required to maintain good health in people. RDAs are established by the Food and Nutrition Board of the National Academy of Sciences, and may be revised every few years. A separate RDA value exists for each nutrient. The RDA values refer to the amount of nutrient expected to maintain good health in people. The actual amounts of each nutrient required to maintain good health in specific individuals differ from person to person.

RECURRENT. Tendency to repeat.

RED BLOOD CELL INDICES. Measurements that describe the size and hemoglobin content of red blood cells. The indices are used to help in the differential diagnosis of anemia. Also called red cell absolute values or erythrocyte indices.

RED BLOOD CELLS. Cells that carry hemoglobin (the molecule that transports oxygen) and help remove wastes from tissues throughout the body.

RED CELL DISTRIBUTION WIDTH (RDW). A measure of the variation in size of red blood cells.

REDUCIBLE HERNIA. A hernia that can be gently pushed back into place or that disappears when the person lies down.

REDUCTION. The restoration of a body part to its original position after displacement, such as the reduction of a fractured bone by bringing ends or fragments back into original alignment. The use of local or general anesthesia usually accompanies a fracture reduction.

this trait may suffer milder symptoms of sickle cell anemia or may have no symptoms. Some scientists believe that the trait actually provides an advantage in tropical environments because the slightly altered shape of the blood cells cause a person to be more resistant to malaria.

SIDESTREAM SMOKE. The smoke that is emitted from the burning end of a cigarette or cigar, or that comes from the end of a pipe. Along with exhaled smoke, it is a constituent of second-hand smoke.

SIGMOID COLON. The final portion of the large intestine that empties into the rectum.

SIGMOIDOSCOPY. A procedure in which a thin, flexible, lighted instrument, called a sigmoidoscope, is used to visually examine the lower part of the large intestine. Colonoscopy examines the entire large intestine using the same techniques.

SILENT REFLUX. An acid reflux problem that does not cause vomiting but can cause chronic, recurrent respiratory symptoms much like asthma.

SIMULTANEOUS BILINGUALISM. Acquiring two languages simultaneously before the age of three.

SINUS. A tubular channel or cavity connecting one body part with another or with the outside. Often refers to one of the air-filled cavities surrounding the eyes and nose that are lined with mucus-producing membranes. They cleanse the nose, add resonance to the voice, and partially determine the structure of the face.

SKIN GRAFTING. A surgical procedure by which skin or a skin substitute is placed over a burn or non-healing wound to permanently replace damaged or missing skin or to provide a temporary wound covering.

SKIN HEMATOMA. Blood from a broken blood vessel that has accumulated under the skin.

SLEEP APNEA. A sleep disorder characterized by periods of breathing cessation lasting for 10 seconds or more.

SLEEP DISORDER. Any condition that interferes with sleep. Sleep disorders are characterized by disturbance in the amount of sleep, in the quality or timing of sleep, or in the behaviors or physiological conditions associated with sleep.

SLEEP LATENCY. The amount of time that it takes to fall asleep. Sleep latency is measured in minutes and is important in diagnosing depression.

SLEEP PARALYSIS. An abnormal episode of sleep in which the patient cannot move for a few minutes, usually occurring on falling asleep or waking up. Often found in patients with narcolepsy.

SLOW-WAVE SLEEP (SWS). Stage of deepest sleep characterized by absence of eye movements, decreased body temperature, and involuntary body movements. Night terrors and sleepwalking occur during this stage of sleep.

SOCIAL ANXIETY DISORDER. Persistent avoidance and/or discomfort in social situations that significantly interferes with functioning.

SOCIAL PHOBIA. An anxiety disorder characterized by a strong and persistent fear of social or performance situations in which the individual might feel embarassment or humiliation.

SOCIAL PROMOTION. Passing a child on to the next grade regardless of readiness in order for the child to remain with his or her age peers.

SOCIAL SKILLS. The knowledge of and ability to use a variety of social behaviors that are appropriate to interact positively with other people.

SOCIAL WITHDRAWAL. Avoidance of social contacts.

SOCIAL WORKER. Health care professional available to help patients and families manage the changes that may occur as a result of the patient's hospitalization. Socials workers provide referrals to community resources and can help the family make arrangements for care in the home as necessary after the patient is discharged from the hospital.

SOCIALIZATION. The process by which new members of a social group are integrated in the group.

SODIUM. An element; sodium is the most common electrolyte found in animal blood serum.

SODOMY. Anal intercourse.

SOMATIC CELLS. All the cells of the body with the exception of the egg and sperm cells.

SOMNAMBULISM. Another term for sleepwalking.

SORE. A wound, lesion, or ulcer on the skin.

SPACE MAINTAINER. An orthodontic appliance that is worn to prevent adjacent teeth from moving into the space left by an unerupted or prematurely lost tooth.

SPASTIC. Refers to a condition in which the muscles are rigid, posture may be abnormal, and fine motor control is impaired.

SPASTICITY. Increased mucle tone, or stiffness, which leads to uncontrolled, awkward movements.

SPATIAL SKILLS. The ability to locate objects in a three-dimensional world using sight or touch.

SPECTROPHOTOMETRY. A testing method that measures the amount of ultraviolet light absorbed by specific substances such as bilirubin pigment. A spectrophotometer can accurately measure how much bilirubin is in a blood sample and the result can be compared to known normal values.

SPEECH PATHOLOGIST. An individual certified by the American Speech-Language-Hearing Association (ASHA) to treat speech disorders.

SPERMATIC CORD. The tissue that suspends the testis inside the scrotum.

SPERMICIDE. A substance that kills sperm. Also called a spermatocide.

SPHINCTER. A circular band of muscle that surrounds and encloses an opening to the body or to one of its hollow organs. These muscles can open or close the opening by relaxing or contracting.

SPHYGMOMANOMETER. An instrument used to measure blood pressure.

SPINA BIFIDA. A birth defect (a congenital malformation) in which part of the vertebrae fail to develop completely so that a portion of the spinal cord, which is normally protected within the vertebral column, is exposed. People with spina bifida can suffer from bladder and bowel incontinence, cognitive (learning) problems, and limited mobility.

SPINAL CANAL. The opening that runs through the center of the spinal column. The spinal cord passes through the spinal canal. Also called the vertebral canal.

SPINAL CORD. The elongated nerve bundles that lie in the spinal canal and from which the spinal nerves emerge.

SPINAL CORD INJURY. Injury to the spinal cord, via blunt or penetrating trauma.

SPIROCHETE. A type of bacterium with a long, slender, coiled shape. Syphilis and Lyme disease are caused by spirochetes.

SPIROMETRY. A test using an instrument called a spirometer that measures how much and how fast the air is moving in and out of a patient's lungs. Spirometry can help a physician diagnose a range of respiratory diseases, monitor the progress of a disease, or assess a patient's response to treatment.

SPIRULINA. A genus of blue-green algae that is sometimes added to food to increase its nutrient value.

SPLENECTOMY. Surgical removal of the spleen.

SPLINT. A thin piece of rigid or flexible material that is used to restrain, support, or immobilize a part of the body while healing takes place.

SPONDYLOSIS. A condition in which one or more to the vertebral joints in the spine become stiff and/or fixed in one position.

SPORE. A dormant form assumed by some bacteria, such as anthrax, that enable the bacterium to survive high temperatures, dryness, and lack of nourishment for long periods of time. Under proper conditions, the spore may revert to the actively multiplying form of the bacteria. Also refers to the small, thick-walled reproductive structure of a fungus.

SPUTUM. The substance that is coughed up from the lungs and spit out through the mouth. It is usually a mixture of saliva and mucus, but may contain blood or pus in patients with lung abscess or other diseases of the lungs.

STANDARD DEVIATION. A measure of the distribution of scores around the average (mean). In a normal distribution, two standard deviations above and below the mean includes about 95% of all samples.

STANDARDIZATION. The process of determining established norms and procedures for a test to act as a standard reference point for future test results.

STANDARDIZED TEST. A test that follows a regimented structure, and each individual's scores may be compared with those of groups of people. In the case of the Cognistat, test taker's scores can be compared to groups of young adults, middle-aged adults, the geriatric, and people who have undergone neurosurgery.

STANFORD-BINET INTELLIGENCE SCALES. A device designed to measure somebody's intelligence, obtained through a series of aptitude tests concentrating on different aspects of intellectual functioning. An IQ score of 100 represents "average" intelligence.

STAPHYLOCOCCAL INFECTION. Infection with one of several species of *Staphylococcus* bacteria. Staphylococcal infections can affect any part of the body and are characterized by the formation of abscesses. Also known popularly as a staph infection.

STAPHYLOCOCCUS. Any of several species of spherical bacteria that occur in groups of four or in irregular clusters. They can infect various parts of the body, especially the skin and mucous membranes.

STATIC ENCEPHALOPATHY. A disease or disorder of the brain that does not get better or worse.

STEATORRHEA. An excessive amount of fat in the feces due to poor fat absorption in the gastrointestinal tract.

STEM CELL. An undifferentiated cell that retains the ability to develop into any one of a variety of cell types.

STENOSIS. A condition in which an opening or passageway in the body is narrowed or constricted.

STENT. A slender hollow catheter or rod placed within a vessel or duct to provide support or to keep it open.

STEPFAMILY. A family formed by the marriage or long-term cohabitation of two individuals, where one or both have at least one child from a previous relationship living part-time or full-time in the household. The individual who is not the biological parent of the child or children is referred to as the stepparent.

STEREOGNOSIS. The ability to recognize objects by sense of touch.

STEREOTACTIC TECHNIQUE. A technique used by neurosurgeons to pinpoint locations within the brain. It employs computer imaging to guide the surgeon to the exact location for the surgical procedure.

STEREOTYPED. Having a persistent, repetitive, and senseless quality. Tics are stereotyped movements or sounds.

STEROID. A class of drugs resembling normal body substances that often help control inflammation in the body tissues.

STEVENS-JOHNSON SYNDROME. A severe inflammatory skin eruption that occurs as a result of an allergic reaction or respiratory infection.

STIMULUS. Anything capable of eliciting a response in an organism or a part of that organism.

STOMATITIS. Inflammation of the mucous lining of any of the structures of the mouth, including the cheeks, gums, tongue, lips, and roof or floor of the mouth.

STOOL. The solid waste that is left after food is digested. Stool forms in the intestines and passes out of the body through the anus.

STRABISMUS. A disorder in which the eyes do not point in the same direction. Also called squint.

STRANGULATED HERNIA. A hernia that is so tightly incarcerated outside the abdominal wall that the intestine is blocked and the blood supply to that part of the intestine is cut off.

STRANGULATED OBSTRUCTION. An obstruction in which a loop of the intestine has its blood supply cut off.

STRAWBERRY TONGUE. A sign of scarlet fever in which the tongue appears to have a red coating with large raised bumps.

STREET DRUG. A substance purchased from a drug dealer. It may be a legal substance, sold illicitly (without a prescription, and not for medical use), or it may be a substance which is illegal to possess.

STREP THROAT. An infection of the throat caused by *Streptococcus* bacteria. Symptoms include sore throat, chills, fever, and swollen lymph nodes in the neck.

***STREPTOCOCCUS*.** Plural, streptococci. Any of several species of spherical bacteria that form pairs or chains. They cause a wide variety of infections including scarlet fever, tonsillitis, and pneumonia.

***STREPTOCOCCUS PYOGENES*.** A common bacterium that causes strep throat and can also cause tonsillitis.

STREPTOMYCIN. An antibiotic used to treat tuberculosis.

STRESS. A physical and psychological response that results from being exposed to a demand or pressure.

STRESSOR. A stimulus, or event, that provokes a stress response in an organism. Stressors can be categorized as acute or chronic, and as external or internal to the organism.

STRICTURE. An abnormal narrowing or tightening of a body tube or passage.

STRIDOR. A term used to describe noisy breathing in general and to refer specifically to a high-pitched crowing sound associated with croup, respiratory infection, and airway obstruction.

STROKE. Interruption of blood flow to a part of the brain with consequent brain damage. A stroke may be caused by a blood clot or by hemorrhage due to a burst blood vessel. Also known as a cerebrovascular accident.

STROMAL. Pertaining to the type of tissue that is associated with the support of an organ.

STRUCTURED ENGLISH IMMERSION. Sheltered English; English-only instruction for ELLs that uses simplified language, visual aids, physical activity, and the physical environment to teach academic subjects.

STUDENTS AGAINST DRUNK DRIVING (SADD). An organization that offers a "Contract for Life" that asks teens to discuss substance use with parents, to call home for a ride if safe transportation is needed, and to wear a seat belt. Parents in turn promise to arrange for that safe transportation home "regardless of the time or circumstances," without discussion of the incident until both teens and parents are calm.

STUPOR. A trance-like state that causes a person to appear numb to their environment.

STY. An external hordeolum caused by an infection of an oil gland on the eyelid.

SUBARACHNOID. Referring to the space underneath the arachnoid membrane, the middle of the three membranes that sheath the spinal cord and brain.

SUBARACHNOID HEMORRHAGE. A collection of blood in the subarachnoid space, the space between the arachnoid and pia mater membranes that surround the brain. This space is normally filled with cerebrospinal fluid. A subarachnoid hemorrhage can lead to stroke, seizures, permanent brain damage, and other complications.

SUBCUTANEOUS. Referring to the area beneath the skin.

SUBDURAL HEMATOMA. A localized accumulation of blood, sometimes mixed with spinal fluid, in the space between the middle (arachnoid) and outer (dura mater) membranes covering the brain. It is caused by an injury to the head that tears blood vessels.

SUBPERIOSTEAL APPOSITION. The process by which bones are made thicker from the outside.

SUBSTANCE ABUSE. Maladaptive pattern of drug or alcohol use that may lead to social, occupational, psychological, or physical problems.

SUBUNGUAL HEMATOMA. Accumulation of blood under a nail.

SUCCIMER. A chelating agent that is used to remove excess lead from the body. Sold under the trade name Chemet.

SUDDEN INFANT DEATH SYNDROME (SIDS). The general term given to "crib deaths" of unknown causes.

SUGARS. Those carbohydrates having the general composition of one part carbon, two parts hydrogen, and one part oxygen.

SULFONYLUREA DRUG. A medication for type 2 diabetes that causes the pancreas to produce more insulin, and may trigger hypoglycemia in some people.

SUNSCREEN. A product that blocks the damaging rays of the sun. Good sunscreens contain either para-aminobenzoic acid (PABA) or benzophenone, or both. Sunscreen protection factors range from two to 45.

SUNSTROKE. Heatstroke caused by direct exposure to the sun in which body temperature increases to dangerously high levels.

SUPERIOR MESENTERIC ARTERY SYNDROME. A condition in which a person vomits after meals due to blockage of the blood supply to the intestine.

SUPINE. Lying on the back with the face upward.

SUPRACHIASMATIC NUCLEI (SCN). SCN is that part of the brain that functions as a person's "biological clock" to regulate many body rhythms. The SCN is located on top of the main junction of nerve fibers that connects to the eyes.

SUPRAGLOTTITIS. Another term for epiglottitis.

SUPRAVALVULAR AORTIC STENOSIS (SVAS). A narrowing of the aorta.

SURFACTANT. A protective film secreted by the alveoli in the lungs that reduces the surface tension of lung fluids, allowing gas exchange and helping maintain the elasticity of lung tissue. Surfactant is normally produced in the fetal lungs in the last months of pregnancy, which helps the air sacs to open up at the time of birth so that the newborn infant can breathe freely. Premature infants may lack surfactant and are more susceptible to respiratory problems without it.

SUTURE. A "seam" that joins two surfaces together, such as is found between the bones of the skull. Also refers to stitching together the torn or cut edges of tissue.

SWADDLING. To wrap the infant securely in clothing or blankets; to provide comfort and control.

SWIMMER'S ITCH. An allergic skin inflammation caused by a sensitivity to flatworms that die under the skin, resulting in an itchy rash.

SYMMETRIC. Occurring on both sides of the body, in a mirror-image fashion.

SYNCOPE. A loss of consciousness over a short period of time, caused by a temporary lack of oxygen in the brain; a faint.

SYNDROME. A group of signs and symptoms that collectively characterize a disease or disorder.

SYNOVIAL JOINT. A fully moveable joint in which a synovial cavity is present between two articulating bones. Also called a diarthrosis.

SYNOVIAL MEMBRANE. The membrane that lines the inside of the articular capsule of a joint, and produces a lubricating fluid called synovial fluid.

SYNOVITIS. Inflammation of the synovial membrane, the membrane that lines the inside of the articular capsule of a joint.

SYPHILIS. This disease occurs in two forms. One is a sexually transmitted disease caused by A systemic infection caused by the spirochete *Treponema pallidum*. It is most commonly transmitted by sexual contact.

SYRINGOMYELIA. Excessive fluid in the spinal cord.

SYRINX. A tubular fluid-filled cavity within the spine.

SYSTEMIC. Relating to an entire body system or the body in general.

SYSTEMIC ABSORPTION. Any substance topical, inhaled, or ingested that is absorbed into the bloodstream and distributed throughout the body.

SYSTEMIC CIRCULATION. Refers to the general blood circulation of the body, not including the lungs.

SYSTOLIC BLOOD PRESSURE. Blood pressure when the heart contracts (beats).

T

T LYMPHOCYTES. Also called T cells, a type of white blood cell that is produced in the bone marrow and matured in the thymus gland. These specialized blood cells recognize invading organisms (helper T lymphocytes) and destroy them (killer T lymphocytes).

TACHYPNEA. Rapid breathing.

TAKAYASU ARTERITIS. A disease in which the aorta and its major branches become inflamed. It is often accompanied by high blood pressure, an abnormal pulse, and visual symptoms.

TARTAR. A hardened yellow or brown mineral deposit from unremoved plaque. Also called calculus.

TASK. A goal directed activity used in assessment.

TAY-SACHS DISEASE. An inherited disease caused by a missing enzyme that is prevalent among the Ashkenazi Jewish population of the United States. Infants with the disease are unable to process a certain type of fat which accumulates in nerve and brain cells, causing mental and physical retardation, and, finally, death.

TELANGIECTASIA. Abnormal dilation of capillary blood vessels leading to the formation of telangiectases or angiomas.

TELECOMMUTING. A form of employment in which the employee works at home on a computer linked to the company's central office.

TEMPERAMENT. A person's natural disposition or inborn combination of mental and emotional traits.

TEMPORAL BONES. The compound bones that form the left and right sides of the skull and contain various cavities associated with the ear.

TEMPOROMANDIBULAR JOINT (TMJ). One of a pair of joints that attaches the mandible of the jaw to the temporal bone of the skull. It is a combination of a hinge and a gliding joint.

TEMPOROMANDIBULAR JOINT DISORDER. Inflammation, irritation, and pain of the jaw caused by improper opening and closing of the temporomandibular joint. Other symptoms include clicking of the jaw and a limited range of motion. Also called temporomandibular joint syndrome.

TENDINITIS. Inflammation of a tendon (a tough band of tissue that connects muscle to bone) that is often the result of overuse over a long period of time.

TENDON. A tough cord of dense white fibrous connective tissue that connects a muscle with some other part, especially a bone, and transmits the force which the muscle exerts.

TENOSYNOVITIS. Inflammation of a tendon and its enveloping sheath, usually resulting from overuse injury.

TENOTOMY. A surgical procedure that cuts the tendon of a contracted muscle to allow lengthening.

TERATOGEN. Any drug, chemical, maternal disease, or exposure that can cause physical or functional defects in an exposed embryo or fetus.

TESTICULAR TORSION. A condition involving the twisting of the spermatic cord inside the testicle that shuts off its blood supply and can seriously damage the testicle.

TESTOSTERONE. Male hormone produced by the testes and (in small amounts) in the ovaries. Testosterone is responsible for some masculine secondary sex characteristics such as growth of body hair and deepening voice. It also is sometimes given as part of hormone replacement therapy to women whose ovaries have been removed.

TETANUS. A potentially fatal infection caused by a toxin produced by the bacterium *Clostridium tetani*. The bacteria usually enter the body through a wound and the toxin they produce affects the central nervous system causing painful and often violent muscular contractions. Commonly called lockjaw.

TETRACYCLINE. A broad-spectrum antibiotic.

THALAMUS. A pair of oval masses of gray matter within the brain that relay sensory impulses from the spinal cord to the cerebrum.

THERMOGRAPHY. Use of a heat-sensitive device for measuring blood flow.

THIMEROSAL. A mercury-containing preservative used in some vaccines.

THRESHOLD. The minimum level of stimulation necessary to produce a response.

THROMBOCYTE. Another name for platelet.

THROMBOCYTOPENIA. A persistent decrease in the number of blood platelets usually associated with hemorrhaging.

THROMBOCYTOSIS. An abnormally high platelet count. It occurs in polycythemia vera and other disorders in which the bone marrow produces too many platelets.

THROMBOLYSIS. The process of dissolving a blood clot.

THROMBOLYTICS. Drugs that dissolve blood clots. Thrombolytics are used to treat embolisms.

THROMBOSIS. The formation of a blood clot in a vein or artery that may obstruct local blood flow or may dislodge, travel downstream, and obstruct blood flow at a remote location. The clot or thrombus may lead to infarction, or death of tissue, due to a blocked blood supply.

THROMBUS. A blood clot that forms within a blood vessel or the heart.

THRUSH. An infection of the mouth, caused by the yeast *Candida albicans* and characterized by a whitish growth and ulcers.

THYMIC APLASIA. A lack of T lymphocytes, due to failure of the thymus to develop, resulting in very reduced immunity.

THYMUS GLAND. An endocrine gland located in the upper chest just below the neck that functions as part of the lymphatic system. It coordinates the development of the immune system.

THYROIDECTOMY. Surgical removal of all or part of the thyroid gland.

THYROID-STIMULATING HORMONE (TSH). A hormone produce by the pituitary gland that stimulates the thyroid gland to produce the hormones that regulate metabolism. Also called thyrotropin.

THYROXINE (T_4). The thyroid hormone that regulates many essential body processes.

TIC. A brief and intermittent involuntary movement or sound.

TIME-OUT. A discipline strategy that entails briefly isolating a disruptive child in order to interrupt and avoid reinforcement of negative behavior.

TINNITUS. A noise, ranging from faint ringing or thumping to roaring, that originates in the ear not in the environment.

TITER. The highest dilution of a material (e.g., serum or other body fluid) that produces a reaction in an immunologic test system. Also refers to the extent to which an antibody can be diluted before it will no longer react with a specific antigen. Also spelled titre.

TOCOLYTIC DRUG. A compound given to women to stop the progression of labor.

TOLERANCE. A condition in which an addict needs higher doses of a substance to achieve the same effect previously achieved with a lower dose.

TONGUE THRUSTING. A physiological behavior that causes the tongue to flatten and thrust forward during swallowing and speaking.

TONIC-CLONIC SEIZURE. This is the most common type of seizure among all age groups and is categorized into several phases beginning with vague symptoms hours or days before an attack. These seizures are sometimes called grand mal seizures.

TONSILLECTOMY. A surgical procedure to remove the tonsils. A tonsillectomy is performed if the patient has recurrent sore throats or throat infections, or if the tonsils have become so swollen that the patient has trouble breathing or swallowing.

TONSILS. Common name for the palatine tonsils, which are lymph masses in the back of the mouth, on either side of the tongue. Tonsils act like filters to trap bacteria and viruses.

TOOTH ERUPTION. The emergence of a tooth through the gum.

TOPICAL. Not ingested; applied to the outside of the body, for example to the skin, eye, or mouth.

TOP-LEVEL REACHING. The ability of an infant to grasp an object that is within reach, looking only at the object and not at their hands. Typically develops between four and five months of age.

TOTAL PLEXUS PALSY. Erb/Klumpke palsy; a condition resulting from injury involving all of the brachial plexus nerves and affecting the entire upper extremity of the body.

TOURETTE SYNDROME. A neurological disorder characterized by multiple involuntary movements and uncontrollable vocalizations called tics that come and go over years, usually beginning in childhood and becoming chronic. Sometimes the tics include inappropriate or obscene language (coprolalia).

TOURNIQUET. Any device that is used to compress a blood vessel to stop bleeding or as part of collecting a blood sample. Phlebotomists usually use an elastic band as a tourniquet.

TOXICOLOGY. The branch of medical pharmacology dealing with the detection, effects, and antidotes of poisons.

TOXIN. A poisonous substance usually produced by a microorganism or plant.

TOXOID. A preparation made from inactivated exotoxin, used in immunization.

TOXOPLASMOSIS. A parasitic infection caused by the intracellular protozoan *Toxoplasmosis gondii*. Humans are most commonly infected by swallowing the oocyte form of the parasite in soil (or kitty litter) contaminated by feces from an infected cat; or by swallowing the cyst form of the parasite in raw or undercooked meat.

TRACE ELEMENT. An element that is required in only minute quantities for the maintenance of good health. Trace elements are also called micronutrients.

TRACHEA. The windpipe. A tube composed of cartilage and membrane that extends from below the voice box into the chest where it splits into two branches, the bronchi, that lead to each lung.

TRACHEOESOPHAGEAL FISTULA. An abnormal connection between the trachea and esophagus, frequently associated with the esophagus ending in a blind pouch.

TRACHEOSTOMY. A procedure in which a small opening is made in the neck and into the trachea or windpipe. A breathing tube is then placed through this opening.

TRACHEOTOMY. An surgical procedure in which the surgeon cuts directly through the patient's neck into the windpipe below a blockage in order to keep the airway open.

TRACHOMA. A type of chlamydia that causes blindness.

TRACTION. The process of placing a bone, limb, or group of muscles under tension by applying weights and pulleys. The goal is to realign or immobilize the part or to relieve pressure on that particular area to promote healing and restore function.

TRAIT. A distinguishing feature of an individual.

TRANQUILIZER. A medication that has a calming effect and is used to treat anxiety and mental tension.

TRANS-FATTY ACID. A type of fat created by hydrogenating polyunsaturated oils. This changes the double bond on the carbon atom from a cis configuration to a trans configuration, making the fatty acid saturated, and a greater health concern. For example, stick margarines are known to contain more trans-fatty acids than liquid oils.

TRANSGENDER. Any person who feels their assigned gender does not completely or adequately reflect their internal gender, such as a biological male who perceives himself to be female.

TRANSILLUMINATION. A technique of checking for tooth decay by shining a light behind the patient's teeth. Decayed areas show up as spots or shadows.

TRANSITIONAL BILINGUAL EDUCATION (TBE). Bilingual education that includes ESL and academic classes conducted in a child's primary language.

TRANSLOCATION. The transfer of one part of a chromosome to another chromosome during cell division. A balanced translocation occurs when pieces from two different chromosomes exchange places without loss or gain of any chromosome material. An unbalanced translocation involves the unequal loss or gain of genetic information between two chromosomes.

TRANSPLACENTAL. Passing through or occurring across the placenta.

TRANS-RACIAL ADOPTIONS. Adoption in which a family of one race adopts a child of another race.

TRANSSEXUALISM. A term used to describe a male or female that feels a strong identification with the opposite sex and experiences considerable distress because of their actual sex. Also called gender identity disorder.

TRAUMA. Serious physical injury. Also refers to a disastrous or life-threatening event that can cause severe emotional distress, including dissociative symptoms and disorders.

TRAUMATIC SHOCK. A condition of depressed body functions as a reaction to injury with loss of body fluids or lack of oxygen. Signs of traumatic shock include weak and rapid pulse, shallow and rapid breathing, and pale, cool, clammy skin.

TRAVELER'S DIARRHEA. An illness due to infection from a bacteria or parasite that occurs in persons traveling to areas where there is a high frequency of the illness. The disease is usually spread by contaminated food or water.

TREMOR. Involuntary shakiness or trembling.

TREPONEME. A term used to refer to any member of the genus *Treponema*, which is an anaerobic bacteria consisting of cells, 3–8 micrometers in length, with acute, regular, or irregular spirals and no obvious protoplasmic structure.

TRETINOIN. A drug, used in the treatment of acne, that works by increasing the turnover (death and replacement) of skin cells.

TRIANGLING. A process in which two family members lower the tension level between them by drawing in a third member.

TRICYCLIC ANTIDEPRESSANT. A class of antidepressants, named for their three-ring structure, that increase the levels of serotonin and other brain chemicals. They are used to treat depression and anxiety disorders, but have more side effects than the newer class of antidepressants called selective serotonin reuptake inhibitors (SSRIs).

TRIGGER. Any situation (people, places, times, events, etc.) that causes one to experience a negative emotional reaction, which is often accompanied by a display of symptoms or problematic behavior.

TRIGLYCERIDE. A substance formed in the body from fat in the diet. Triglycerides are the main fatty materials in the blood. Bound to protein, they make up high- and low-density lipoproteins (HDLs and LDLs). Triglyceride levels are important in the diagnosis and treatment of many diseases including high blood pressure, diabetes, and heart disease.

TRIGONOCEPHALY. An abnormal development of the skull characterized by a triangular shaped forehead.

TRIIODOTHYRONINE (T_3). A thyroid hormone similar to thyroxine but more powerful. Preparations of triiodothyronine are used in treating hypothyroidism.

TRIMESTER. The one of three periods of about 13 weeks each into which a pregnancy is divided.

TRINUCLEOTIDE REPEAT EXPANSION. A sequence of three nucleotides that is repeated too many times in a section of a gene.

TRISKAIDEKAPHOBIA. Fear of the number 13.

TRISOMY. An abnormal condition where three copies of one chromosome are present in the cells of an individual's body instead of two, the normal number.

TRUNK. That part of the body that does not include the head, arms, and legs. Also called the torso.

TRYPTOPHAN. An essential amino acid that has to consumed in the diet because it cannot be manufactured by the body. Tryptophan is converted by the body to niacin, one of the B vitamins, and serotonin, a neurotransmitter.

TUBERCULOSIS. Tuberculosis (TB) is a potentially fatal contagious disease that can affect almost any part of the body, but is mainly an infection of the lungs. It is caused by a bacterial microorganism, the tubercle bacillus or *Mycobacterium tuberculosis*. Symptoms include fever, weight loss, and coughing up blood.

TUBEROUS SCLEROSIS. A genetic condition that affects many organ systems including the brain, skin, heart, eyes, and lungs. Benign (non-cancerous) growths or tumors called hamartomas form in various parts of the body, disrupting their normal function.

TUBULE. Tissues and cells associated with the structures that connect the renal pelvis to the glomeruli.

TUMOR. A growth of tissue resulting from the uncontrolled proliferation of cells.

TUMOR-SUPPRESSOR GENE. A gene involved in controlling normal cell growth and preventing cancer.

TURNER SYNDROME. A chromosome abnormality characterized by short stature and ovarian failure caused by an absent X chromosome. It occurs only in females.

TWELVE-STEP PROGRAMS. Several programs to assist in breaking addictions, offering either support to addicted people or to friends and loved ones of addicted people. These programs are spiritual but not religious and are based on the twelve steps that are the basis of Alcoholics Anonymous (AA). Programs include AA, Narcotics Anonymous (NA), Al-Anon, Adult Children of Alcoholics (ACOA), Alateen, and Co-Dependence Anonymous (CODA).

25-HYDROXY-VITAMIN D. The form of vitamin D that is measured in order to assess vitamin D deficiency.

TWIN-TWIN TRANSFUSION SYNDROME (TTTS). A condition in identical monochorionic twins in which there is a connection between the two circulatory systems so that the donor twin pumps the blood to the recipient twin without a return of blood to the donor.

TWO-WAY BILINGUAL EDUCATION. Dual language programs in which English and a second language are both used in classes consisting of ELLs and native-English speakers.

TYMPANIC MEMBRANE. The eardrum, a thin disc of tissue that separates the outer ear from the middle ear. It can rupture if pressure in the ear is not equalized during airplane ascents and descents.

TYMPANOMETRY. A test where air pressure in the ear canal is varied to test the condition and movement of the ear drum. This test is useful in detecting disorders of the middle ear.

TYMPANOSTOMY TUBE. An ear tube. A tympanostomy tube is small tube made of metal or plastic that is inserted during myringotomy to ventilate the middle ear.

TYPE. A category used to define personality, usually based on a theory of some kind. Inhibited and uninhibited are examples of personality types.

TYPHOID FEVER. A severe infection caused by a bacterium, *Salmonella typhi*. People with this disease have a lingering fever and feel depressed and exhausted. Diarrhea and rose-colored spots on the chest and abdomen are other symptoms. The disease is spread through poor sanitation.

TYROSINASE. An enzyme in a pigment cell which helps change tyrosine to dopa during the process of making melanin.

TYROSINE. An amino acid synthesized by the body from the essential amino acid phenylalanine. It is used by the body to make melanin and several hormones, including epinephrine and thyroxin.

U

ULCER. A site of damage to the skin or mucous membrane that is characterized by the formation of pus, death of tissue, and is frequently accompanied by an inflammatory reaction.

ULCERATED. Characterized by the formation of an ulcer.

ULCERATIVE COLITIS. A form of inflammatory bowel disease characterized by inflammation of the mucous lining of the colon, ulcerated areas of tissue, and bloody diarrhea.

ULNA. One of the two bones of the forearm. Two pivot joints join it to the radius, one near the elbow, one near the wrist.

ULTRASONOGRAPHY. A medical test in which sound waves are directed against internal structures in the body. As sound waves bounce off the internal structure, they create an image on a video screen. Ultrasonography is often used to diagnose fetal abnormalities, gallstones, heart defects, and tumors. Also called ultrasound imaging.

ULTRAVIOLET (UV) RADIATION. A portion of the light spectrum with a wavelength just below that of visible light. UV radiation is damaging to DNA and can destroy microorganisms. It may be responsible for sunburms, skins cancers, and cataracts in humans. Two bands of the UV spectrum, UVA and UVB, are used to treat psoriasis and other skin diseases.

UMBILICAL. Refers to the opening in the abdominal wall where the blood vessels from the placenta enter.

UMBILICAL CORD. The blood vessels that allow the developing baby to receive nutrition and oxygen from its mother; the blood vessels also eliminate the baby's waste products. One end of the umbilical cord is attached to the placenta and the other end is attached to the baby's belly button (umbilicus).

UMBILICAL CORD PROLAPSE. A birth situation in which the umbilical cord, the structure that connects the placenta to the umbilicus of the fetus to deliver oxygen and nutrients, falls out of the uterus and becomes compressed, thus preventing the delivery of oxygen.

UNCIRCUMCISED. Not having had the foreskin of the penis removed.

UNDERLYING CONDITION. Disorder or disease that causes the appearance of another medical disorder or condition.

UNDESCENDED TESTICLE. A testicle that is still in the groin and has not made its way into the scrotum.

UNIFOCAL. Only one tumor present in one eye.

UNILATERAL. Refers to one side of the body or only one organ in a pair.

UNILATERAL CLEFT. A cleft that occurs on only the right or left side of the lip.

UNILATERAL NEGLECT. Also called one-sided neglect. A side effect of stroke in which the stroke survivor ignores or forgets the weaker side of the body caused by the stroke.

UNIPARENTAL DISOMY. Chromosome abnormality in which both chromosomes in a pair are inherited from the same parent.

URETER. The tube that carries urine from the kidney to the bladder; each kidney has one ureter.

URETEROVESICAL JUNCTION. The point where the ureter joins the bladder.

URETEROVESICAL VALVE. A sphincter (an opening controlled by a circular muscle), located where the ureter enters the bladder, that keeps urine from flowing backward toward the kidney.

URETHRA. A passageway from the bladder to the outside of the body for the discharge of urine. In the female this tube lies between the vagina and clitoris; in the male the urethra travels through the penis and opens at the tip. In males, seminal fluid and sperm also pass through the urethra.

URETHRAL MEATUS. The opening of the urethra on the body surface through which urine is discharged.

URETHRITIS. Inflammation of the urethra, the tube through which the urine moves from the bladder to the outside of the body.

UROGENITAL. Refers to both the urinary system and the sexual organs, which form together in the developing embryo.

UROLOGIST. A physician who specializes in the anatomy, physiology, diseases, and care of the urinary tract (in men and women) and male reproductive tract.

URTICARIA. An itchy rash usually associated with an allergic reaction. Also known as hives.

URUSHIOL. The oil from poison ivy, oak, and sumac that causes severe itching, blistering, and rash.

UTEROPLACENTAL INSUFFICIENCY. Designates the lack of blood flow from the uterus to the placenta, resulting in decreased nourishment and oxygen to the fetus.

UTERUS. The female reproductive organ that contains and nourishes a fetus from implantation until birth. Also called the womb.

UVEITIS. Inflammation of all or part the uvea. The uvea is a continuous layer of tissue that consists of the iris, the ciliary body, and the choroid. The uvea lies between the retina and sclera.

V

VACCINATION. Another word for immunization.

VACCINE. A substance prepared from a weakened or killed microorganism which, when injected, helps the body to form antibodies that will prevent infection by the natural microorganism.

VACCINE ADVERSE EVENT REPORTING SYSTEM (VAERS). A federal government program for reporting adverse reactions to the administration of a vaccine.

VACCINE INJURY COMPENSATION PROGRAM (VICP). A program through which victims of vaccine-induced injury or death can be awarded financial compensation.

VACCINE INJURY TABLE. The guidelines by which claims to the VICP are evaluated; includes the vaccines, injuries or other conditions, and the allowable time periods for coverage by the VICP.

VARICELLA ZOSTER. The virus that causes chickenpox (varicella).

VARICELLA-ZOSTER IMMUNE GLOBULIN. A substance that can reduce the severity of chickenpox symptoms.

VARIVAX. The brand name for varicella virus vaccine live, an immunizing agent used to prevent infection by the *Herpes (varicella) zoster* virus. The vaccine works by causing the body to produce its own protection (antibodies) against the virus.

VASCULAR. Pertaining to blood vessels.

VASCULAR MALFORMATION. Abnormally formed blood or lymph vessels.

VASCULOPATHY. Any disease or disorder that affects the blood vessels.

VECTOR. A carrier organism (such as a fly or mosquito) which serves to deliver a virus (or other agent of infection) to a host. Also refers to a retrovirus that had been modified and is used to introduce specific genes into the genome of an organism.

VEGAN. A vegetarian who does not eat eggs or dairy products.

VEIN. A blood vessel that returns blood to the heart from the body. All the veins from the body converge into two major veins that lead to the right atrium of the heart. These veins are the superior vena cava and the inferior vena cava. The pulmonary vein carries the blood from the right ventricle of the heart into the lungs.

VELAMENTOUS INSERTION OF THE UMBILICAL CORD. The attachment of the umbilical cord close to the membranes (bag of water) or in the membranes.

VENOARTERIAL (V-A) BYPASS. The type of extracorporeal membrane oxygenation that provides both heart and lung support, using two tubes (one in the jugular vein and one in the carotid artery).

VENOVENOUS (V-V) BYPASS. The type of extracorporeal membrane oxygenation that provides lung support only, using a tube inserted into the jugular vein.

VENTILATOR. A mechanical device that can take over the work of breathing for a patient whose lungs are injured or are starting to heal. Sometimes called a respirator.

VENTRICLES. The lower pumping chambers of the heart. The ventricles push blood to the lungs and the rest of the body.

VENTRICLES OF THE BRAIN. The spaces within the brain where cerebrospinal fluid is made.

VENTRICULAR FIBRILLATION. An arrhythmia characterized by a very rapid, uncoordinated, ineffective series of contractions throughout the lower chambers of the heart. Unless stopped, these chaotic impulses are fatal.

VENTRICULAR SEPTAL DEFECT. An opening between the right and left ventricles of the heart.

VENULES. The smallest veins.

VERMILION BORDER. The line between the lip and the skin.

VERTEBRAE. Singular, vertebra. The individual bones of the spinal column that are stacked on top of each other. There is a hole in the center of each bone, through which the spinal cord passes.

VERTEX. The top of the head or highest point of the skull.

VERTIGO. A feeling of dizziness together with a sensation of movement and a feeling of rotating in space.

VESICLE. A bump on the skin filled with fluid.

VESTIBULAR SYSTEM. The brain and parts of the inner ear that work together to detect movement and position.

VIBRATION. The treatment that is applied to help break up lung secretions. Vibration can be either mechanical or manual. It is performed as the patient breathes deeply. When done manually, the person performing the vibration places his or her hands against the patient's chest and creates vibrations by quickly contracting and relaxing arm and shoulder muscles while the patient exhales. The procedure is repeated several times each day for about five exhalations.

VIBROACOUSTIC STIMULATION. In the biophysical profile, use of an artificial larynx to produce a loud noise to "awaken" the fetus.

VIDEO GAME RELATED SEIZURES (VGRS). Seizures thought to be brought on by the flashing lights and complex graphics of a video game.

VILLI. Tiny, finger-like projections that enable the small intestine to absorb nutrients from food.

VIRAL MENINGITIS. Meningitis caused by a virus. Also called aseptic meningitis.

VIRILIZING SYNDROMES. Abnormalities in female hormone production that produce male characteristics.

VIRUS. A small infectious agent consisting of a core of genetic material (DNA or RNA) surrounded by a shell of protein. A virus needs a living cell to reproduce.

VISCOSITY. Thickness of a liquid.

VISUAL ACUITY. Sharpness or clearness of vision.

VISUAL PERCEPTION (VP). The ability to perceive or understand what is being seen; the integration of an image with an idea of what it represents.

VISUOSENSORY. Pertaining to the perception of visual stimuli.

VITAMIN STATUS. The state of vitamin sufficiency or deficiency of any person. For example, a test may reveal that a patient's folate status is sufficient, borderline, or severely inadequate.

VITAMINS. Small compounds required for metabolism that must be supplied by diet, microorganisms in the gut (vitamin K) or sunlight (UV light converts pre-vitamin D to vitamin D).

VITREOUS. The transparent gel that fills the back part of the eye.

VITREOUS SEEDING. Small pieces of tumor have broken off and are floating around the vitreous.

VOCATIONAL. Relating to an occupation, career, or job.

VOID. To empty the bladder.

VOIDING CYSTOGRAM. A radiographic image of the mechanics of urination.

VOLUNTARY MUSCLES. Muscles that can be moved by conscious thought.

VOLVULUS. A twisting of the intestine that causes an obstruction.

VON WILLEBRAND FACTOR (VWF). A protein found in the blood that is involved in the process of blood clotting.

VULVA. The external genital organs of a woman, including the outer and inner lips, clitoris, and opening of the vagina.

W

WARFARIN. An anticoagulant drug given to treat existing blood clots or to control the formation of new blood clots. Sold in the United States under the brand name Coumadin.

WATER-SOLUBLE VITAMINS. Vitamins that are not stored in the body and are easily excreted. They must, therefore, be consumed regularly as foods or supplements to maintain health.

WEBBING. A tissue or membrane that connects two digits at their base or for the greater part of their length.

WECHSLER INTELLIGENCE SCALES. A test that measures verbal and non-verbal intelligence.

WEPMAN'S AUDITORY DISCRIMINATION TEST (WADT). A commonly used test for evaluating auditory discrimination skills.

WHEAL. A smooth, slightly elevated area on the body surface that is redder or paler than the surrounding skin.

WHITE BLOOD CELLS. A group of several cell types that occur in the bloodstream and are essential for a properly functioning immune system; they fight infection.

WHITE MATTER. A substance, composed primarily of myelin fibers, found in the brain and nervous system that protects nerves and allows messages to be sent to and from the brain and various parts of the body. Also called white substance.

WHOLE BLOOD. Blood which contains red blood cells, white blood cells, and platelets in plasma.

WHOOPING COUGH. An infectious disease of the respiratory tract caused by a bacterium, *Bordetella pertussis*. Also known as pertussis.

WILSON'S DISEASE. A rare inherited disease in which excessive amounts of copper accumulate in the liver or brain. It is fatal unless the patient complies with lifelong treatment with penicillamine and zinc oxidase. Wilson's disease is also known as inherited copper toxicosis.

WISDOM TEETH. The third molars at that back of the mouth.

WITHDRAWAL SYMPTOMS. A group of physical and/ or mental symptoms that may occur when a person suddenly stops using a drug or other substance upon which he or she has become dependent.

WORLD HEALTH ORGANIZATION (WHO). An international organization within the United Nations system that is concerned with world health and welfare.

X

X CHROMOSOME. One of the two sex chromosomes (the other is Y) that determine a person's gender. Normal males have both an X and a Y chromosome, and normal females have two X chromosomes.

XENOPHOBIA. Fear of strangers or foreigners.

XEROSIS. The medical term for dry skin. Many children diagnosed with atopic dermatitis have a history of xerosis even as newborns.

X-LINKED. A gene carried on the X chromosome, one of the two sex chromosomes.

X RAYS. High-energy radiation used in high doses, either to diagnose or treat disease.

XYY SYNDROME. A chromosome disorder that affects males.

Y

YELLOW FEVER. An infectious disease caused by a virus. The disease, which is spread by mosquitoes, is most common in Central and South America and Central Africa. Symptoms include high fever, jaundice (yellow eyes and skin) and dark-colored vomit, a sign of internal bleeding. Yellow fever can be fatal.

YOGI (FEMALE, YOGINI). A trained yoga expert.

Z

ZOONOSIS. Any disease of animals that can be transmitted to humans. Rabies is an example of a zoonosis.

ZOOPHOBIA. Fear of animals.

ZYGOTE. The result of the sperm successfully fertilizing the ovum. The zygote is a single cell that contains the genetic material of both the mother and the father.

GROWTH CHARTS APPENDIX

The following growth charts were obtained from the United States Centers for Disease Control. These charts, updated in 2000, include norms for head circumference, weight, and length for boys and girls from birth through age three. Separate charts display percentiles for height, weight, and body mass index (BMI) for boys and girls through age 20.

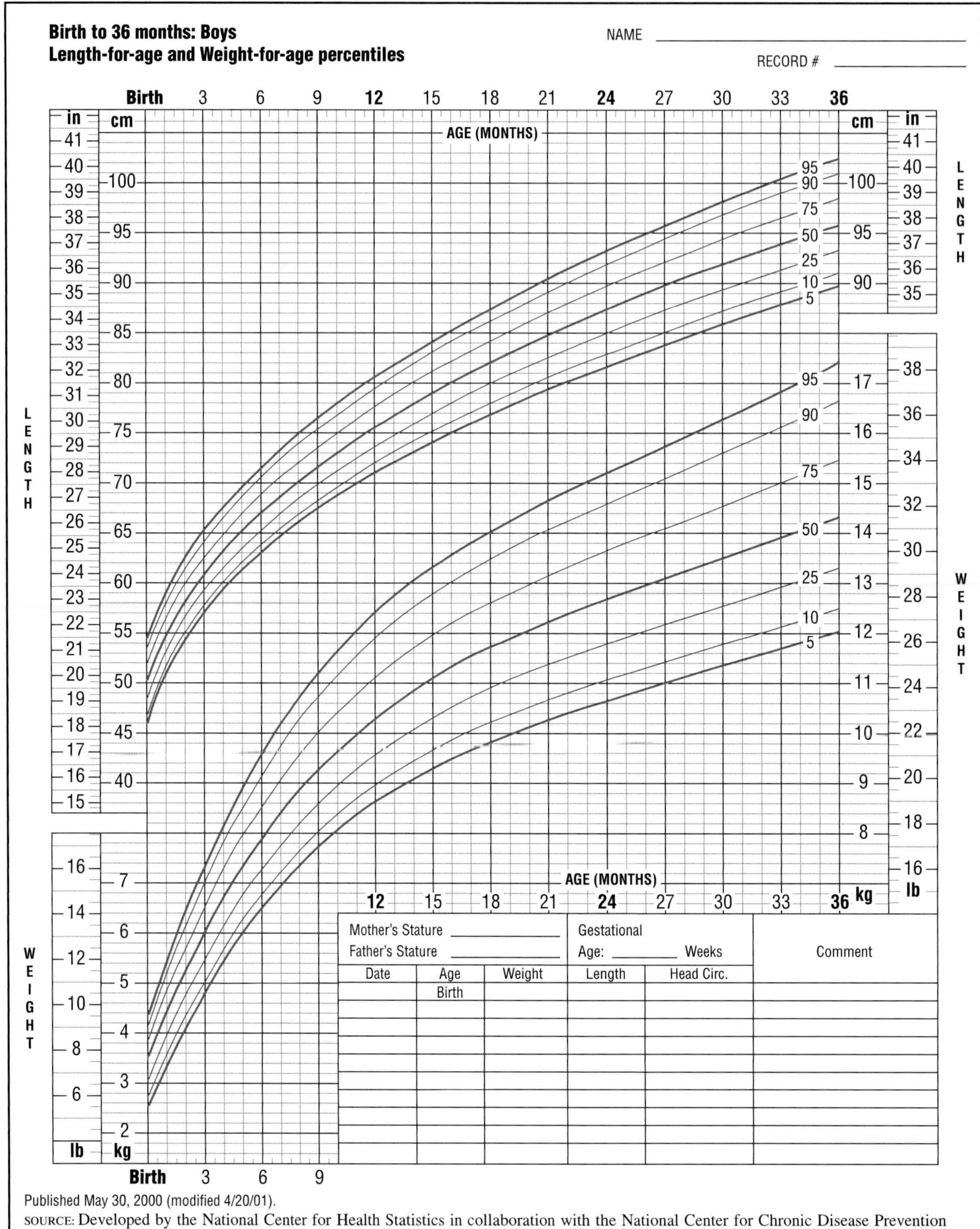

Published May 30, 2000 (modified 4/20/01).

SOURCE: Developed by the National Center for Health Statistics in collaboration with the National Center for Chronic Disease Prevention and Health Promotion (2000). http://www.cdc.gov/growthcharts

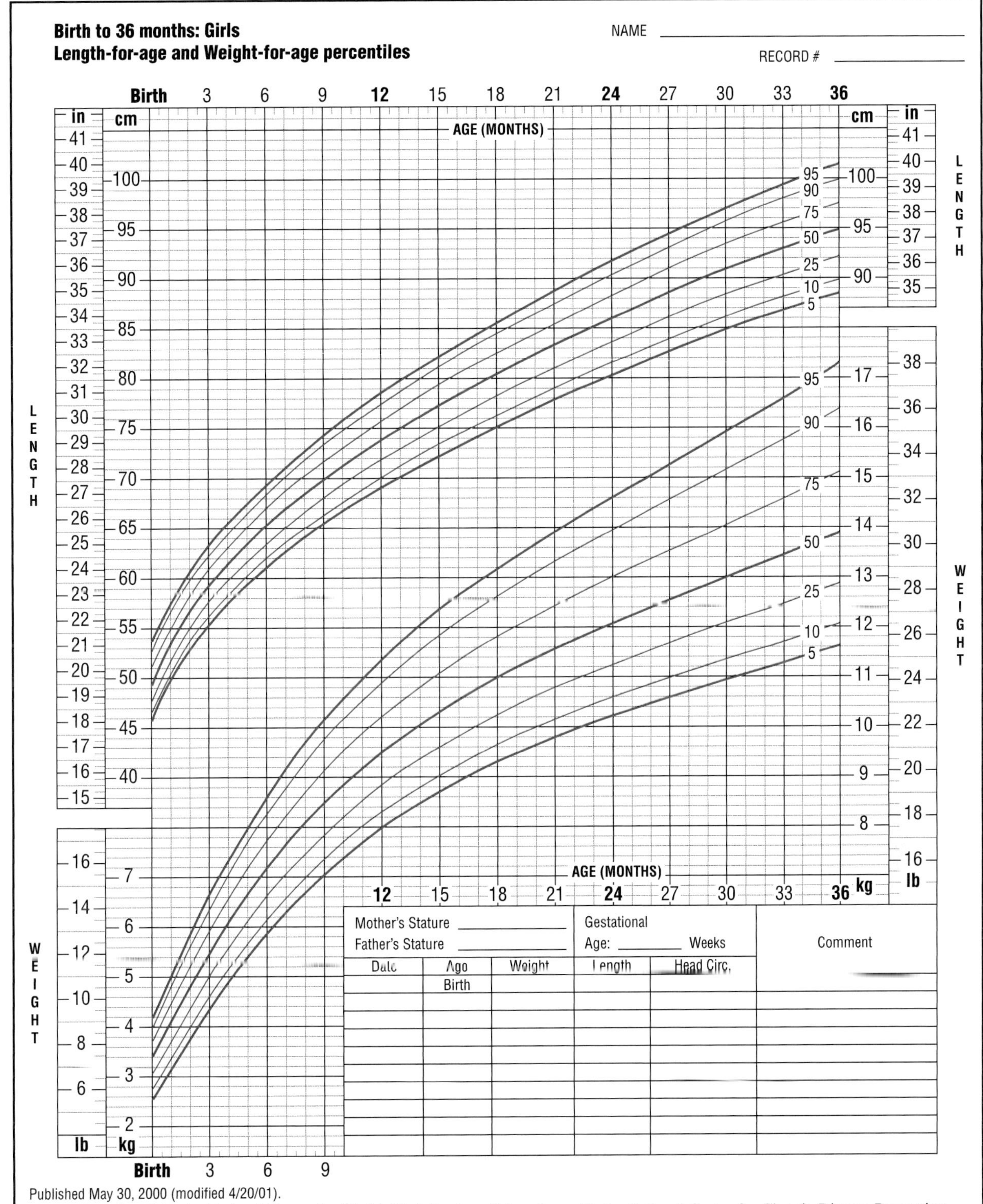

Published May 30, 2000 (modified 4/20/01).

SOURCE: Developed by the National Center for Health Statistics in collaboration with the National Center for Chronic Disease Prevention and Health Promotion (2000). http://www.cdc.gov/growthcharts

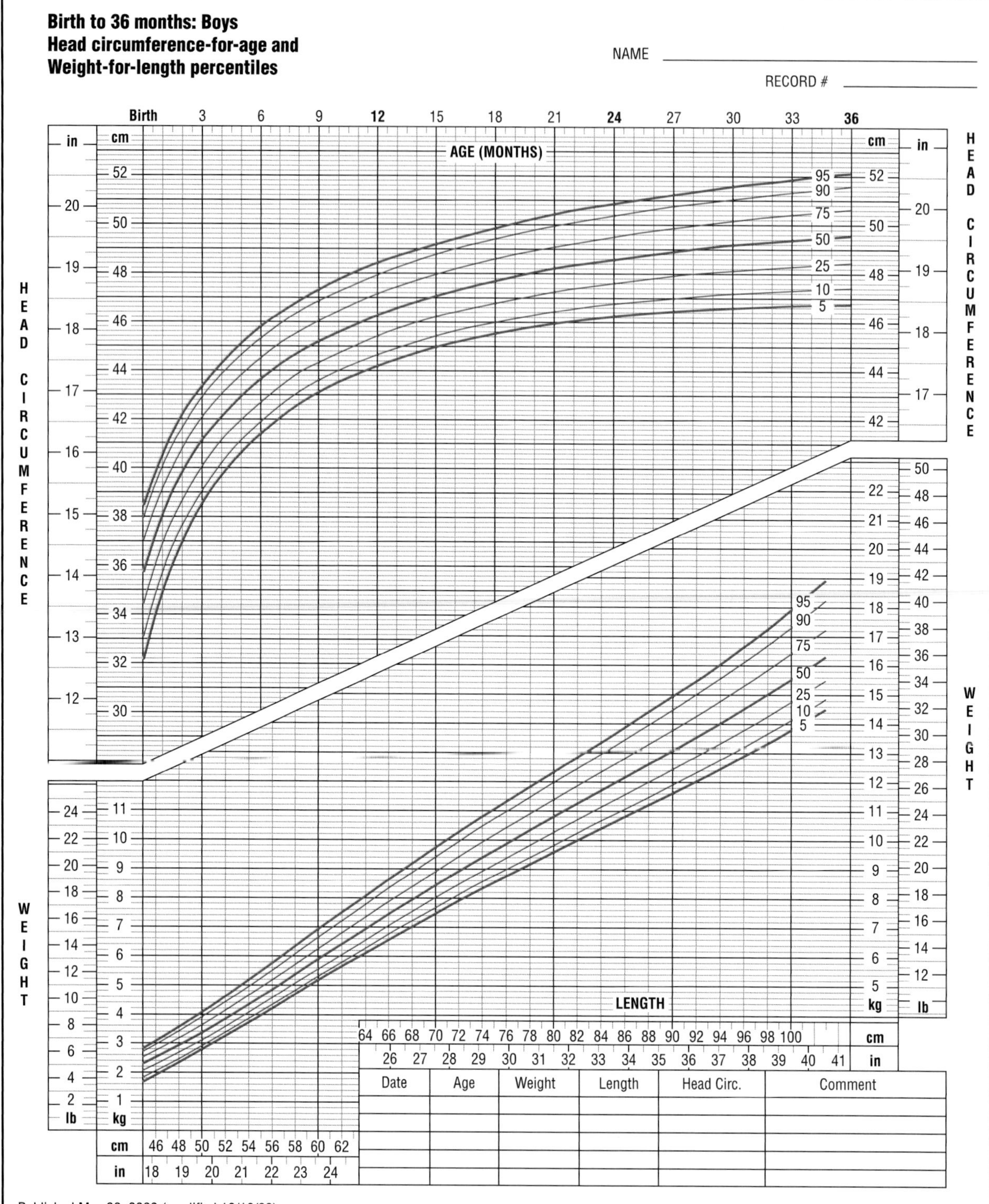

Published May 30, 2000 (modified 10/16/00).

SOURCE: Developed by the National Center for Health Statistics in collaboration with the National Center for Chronic Disease Prevention and Health Promotion (2000). http://www.cdc.gov/growthcharts

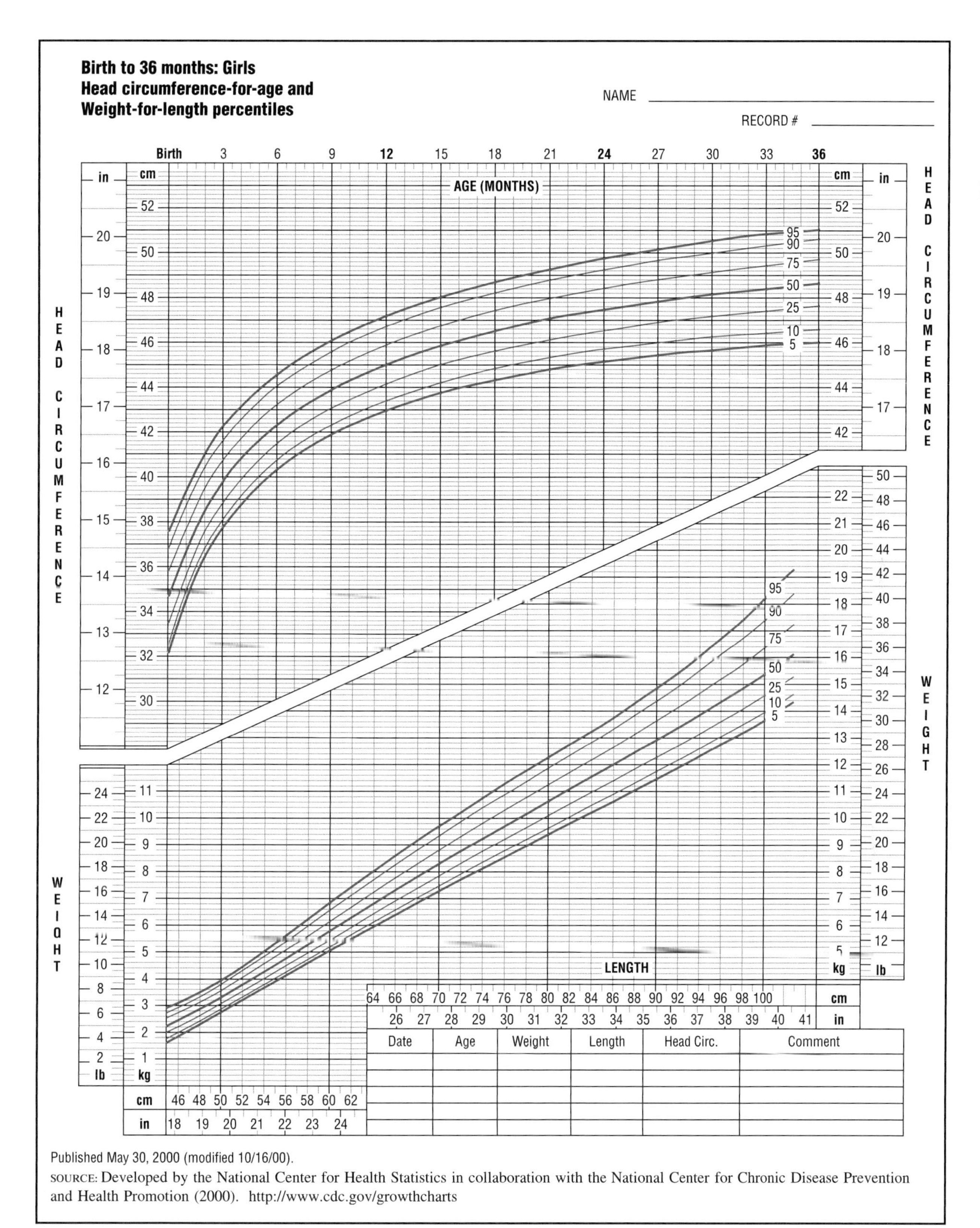

Published May 30, 2000 (modified 10/16/00).

SOURCE: Developed by the National Center for Health Statistics in collaboration with the National Center for Chronic Disease Prevention and Health Promotion (2000). http://www.cdc.gov/growthcharts

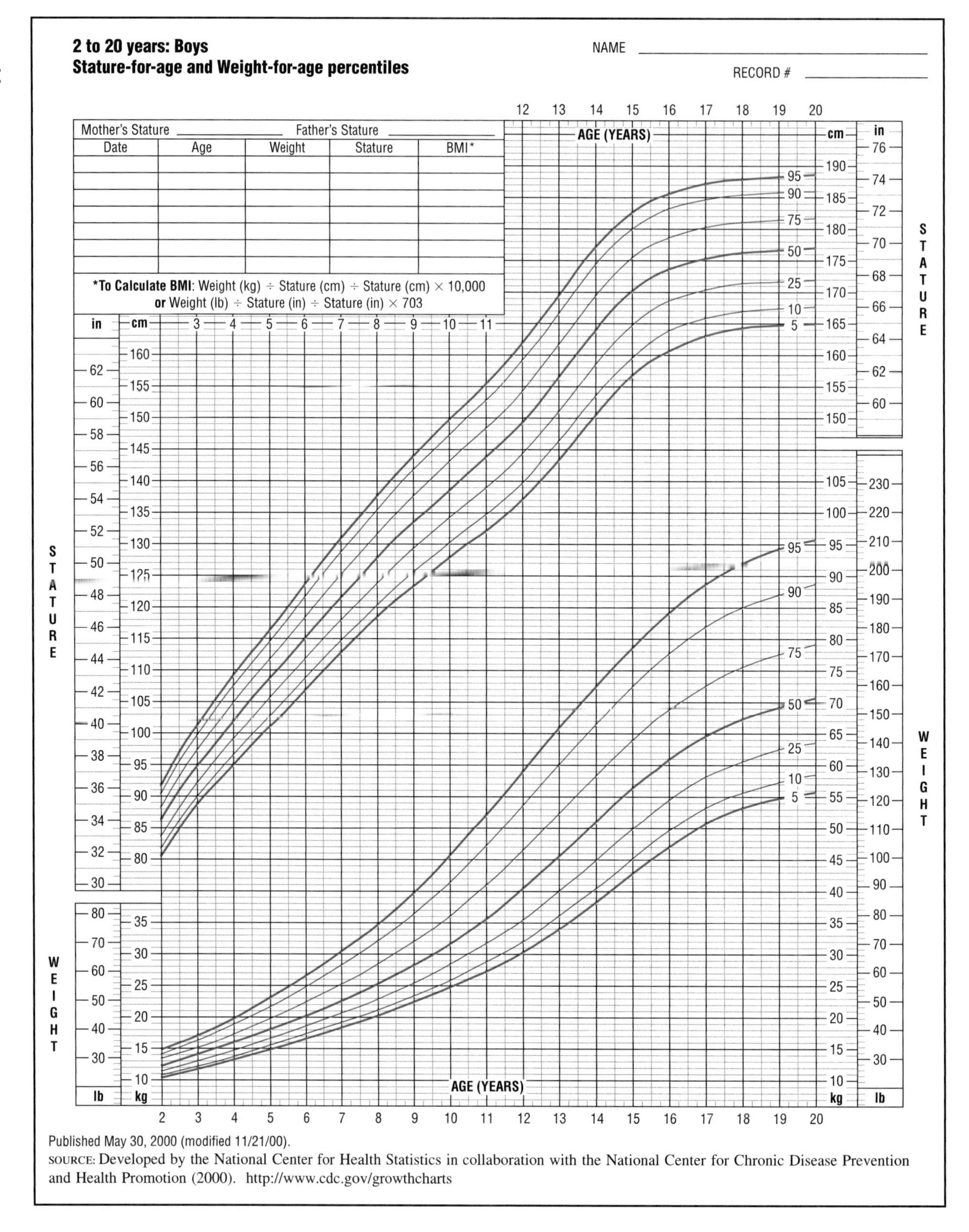

Published May 30, 2000 (modified 11/21/00).

SOURCE: Developed by the National Center for Health Statistics in collaboration with the National Center for Chronic Disease Prevention and Health Promotion (2000). http://www.cdc.gov/growthcharts

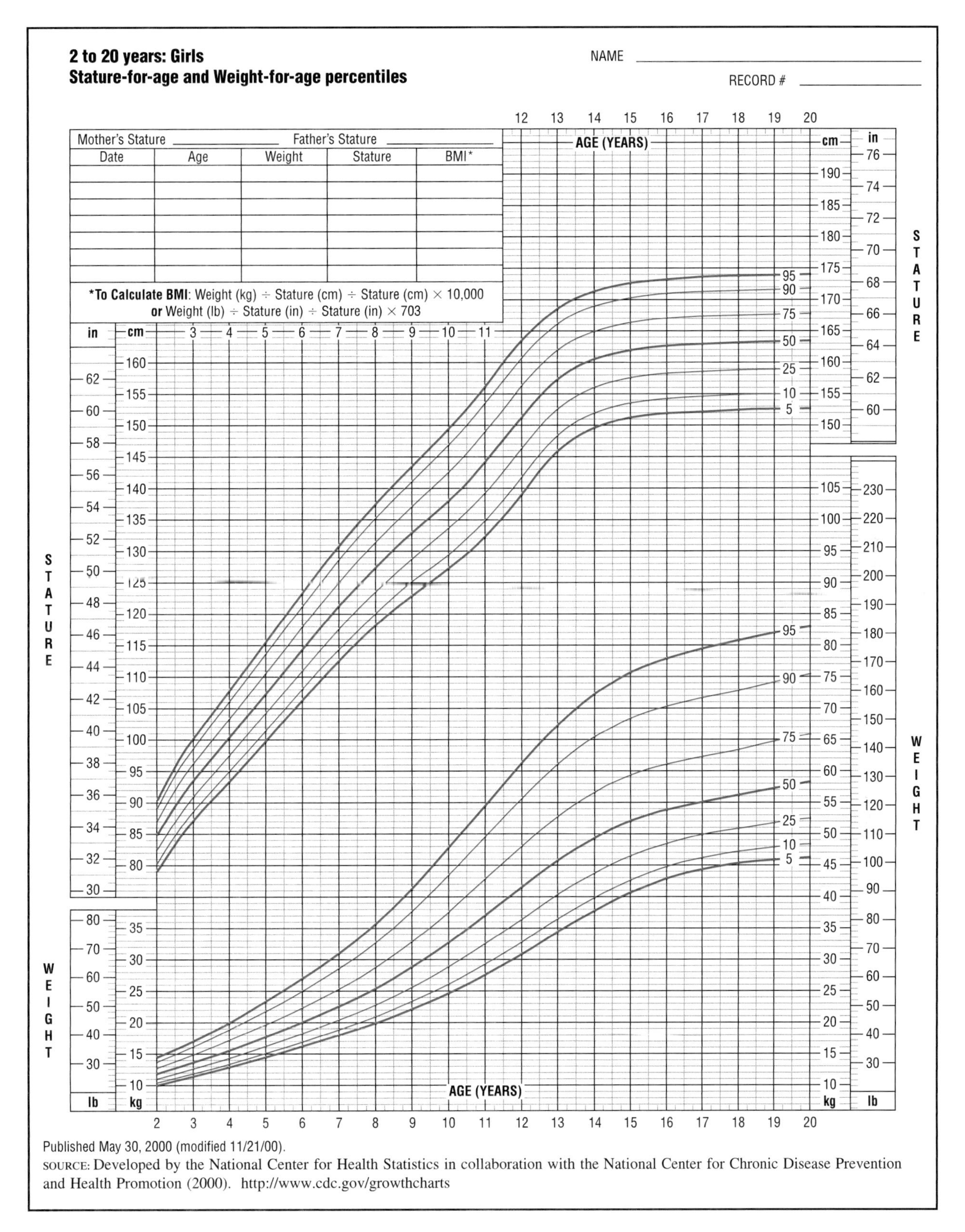

Published May 30, 2000 (modified 11/21/00).

SOURCE: Developed by the National Center for Health Statistics in collaboration with the National Center for Chronic Disease Prevention and Health Promotion (2000). http://www.cdc.gov/growthcharts

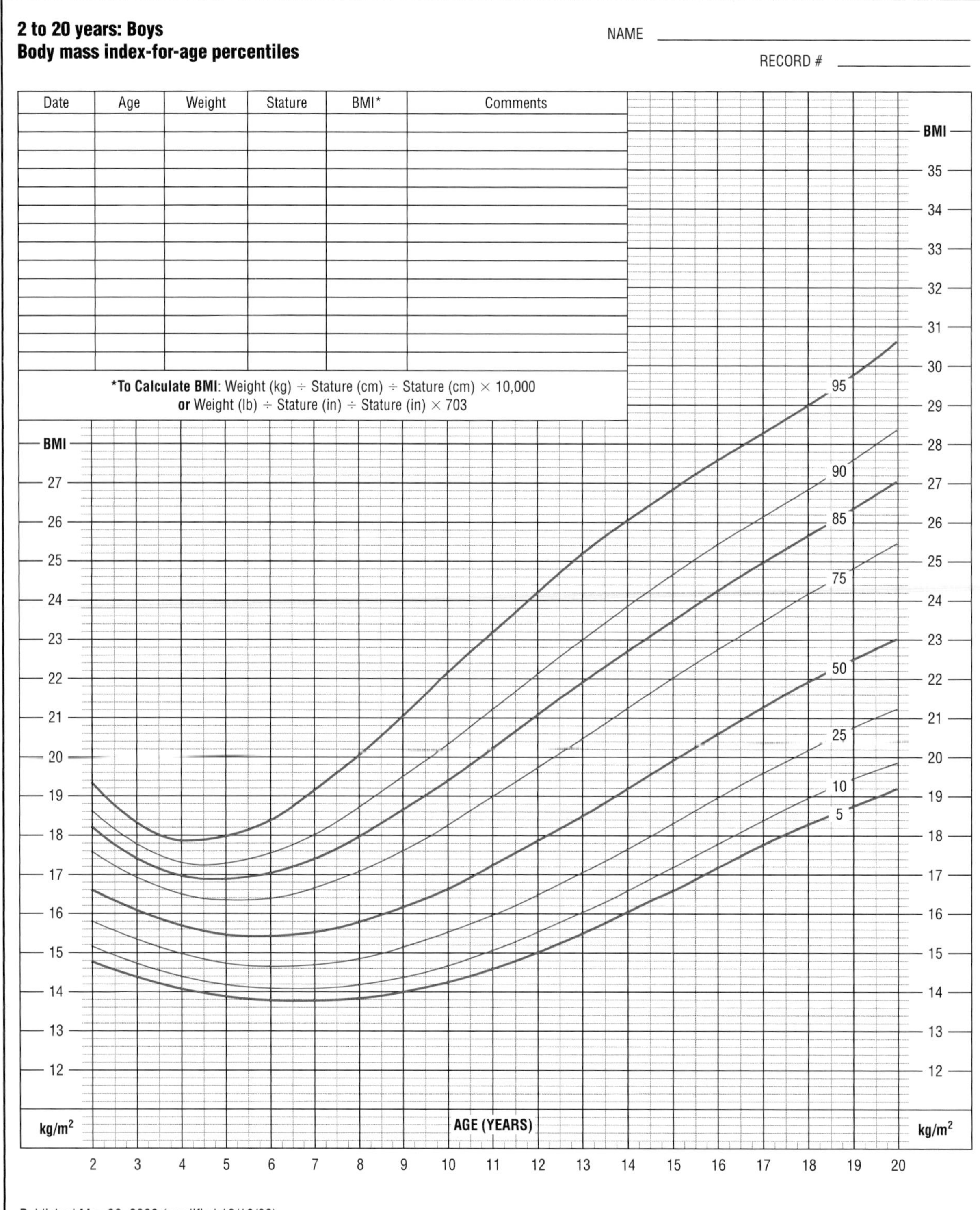

Published May 30, 2000 (modified 10/16/00).
SOURCE: Developed by the National Center for Health Statistics in collaboration with the National Center for Chronic Disease Prevention and Health Promotion (2000). http://www.cdc.gov/growthcharts

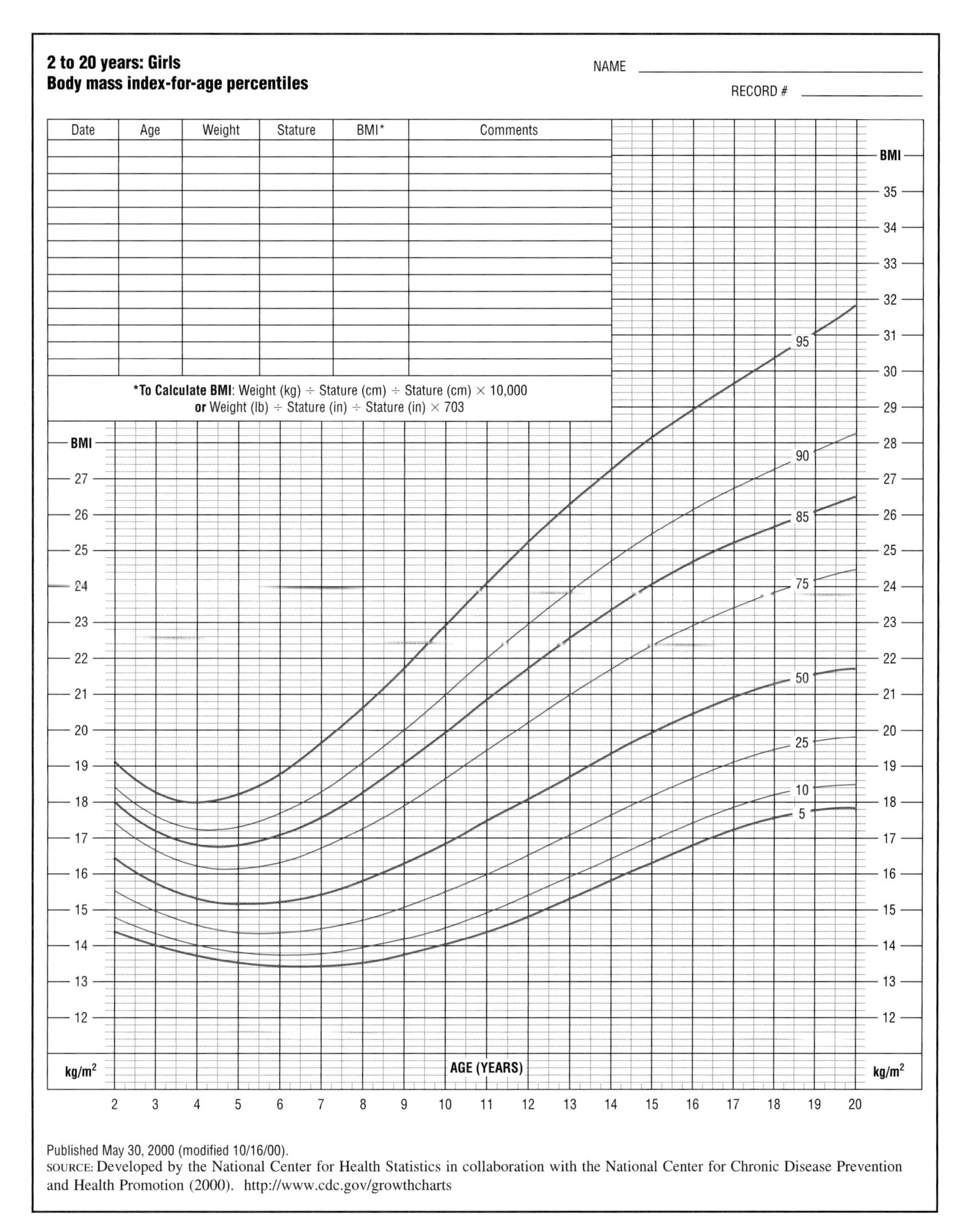

Published May 30, 2000 (modified 10/16/00).

SOURCE: Developed by the National Center for Health Statistics in collaboration with the National Center for Chronic Disease Prevention and Health Promotion (2000). http://www.cdc.gov/growthcharts

APPENDIX OF COMMON CHILDHOOD MEDICATIONS

This list of childhood medications was created from the drugs listed in the main body of the text. Short descriptions and any relevant cautionary information are included.

ABACAVIR .... Antiretroviral drug (for treatment of AIDS virus) in patients over the age of three months.

ACCUTANE .... *See* isotretinoin

ACETAMINOPHEN .... Non-narcotic analgesic and fever reducer without anti-inflammatory effects. *Use care in selecting the dosage form and measuring doses. Note that the infant drops have a higher concentration of acetaminophen than the children's formula, and should only be given in drops, never by the teaspoonful.*

ACIPHEX .... *See* rabeprazole

ACYCLOVIR .... An antiviral agent used against herpes infections. It has been used in infants, and even in newborns. Acyclovir has been reported on favorably in the treatment of chickenpox.

ADAPALENE .... A prescription drug for treatment of acne, adapalene is applied to the skin and works by keeping pores clear.

ADRENALIN .... *See* epinephrine

ADRIAMYCIN .... *See* doxorubicin

ADRUCIL .... *See* 5-fluorouracil

AFRIN .... *See* oxymetazoline

AGENERASE .... *See* amprenavir

ALEVE .... *See* naproxen

ALLEGRA .... *See* fexofenadine

ALUMINUM AND MAGNESIUM HYDROXIDES .... An antacid combination used for a number of stomach disorders.

AMANTIDINE .... Although best known for treatment of Parkinson's disease, amantidine provides protection against influenza virus in children as young as one year.

AMINOPHYLLINE .... A bronchodilator used in treatment of asthma

AMITRIPTYLINE .... A tricyclic antidepressant. *Tricyclic antidepressants are not recommended for children under the age of 12 years. Parents should discuss the safety of all antidepressants before using them in children or adolescents.*

AMLEXANOX .... The only drug approved for use in canker sores. It may work by reducing inflammation.

AMOXICILLIN .... Amoxicillin is a semi-synthetic penicillin similar to ampicillin. The semi-synthetics are effective against more bacteria than are the natural penicillins, and amoxicillin causes less diarrhea in children than does ampicillin.

AMOXICILLIN-CLAVULANATE .... A broad-spectrum antibiotic combination that is effective against bacteria which would be resistant to penicillin alone.

AMOXIL .... *See* amoxicillin

AMPHOTERICIN B .... An antifungal drug, given by vein, which may be used to treat sinus infections caused by fungi as well as other fungal infections. This drug may cause severe discomfort in patients.

AMPICILLIN .... A type of penicillin which is effective against more types of bacteria than the original drug. May cause diarrhea in children.

AMPRENAVIR .... Antiretroviral drug (for treatment of AIDS virus) in patients over the age of four years.

ANADROL .... *See* oxymetholone

ANAPROX .... *See* naproxen

ANTHRALIN .... An ingredient in creams for treatment of psoriasis or some types of hair loss.

APHTHASOL .... *See* amlexanox

ASPIRIN .... Non-narcotic pain reliever and fever reducer with anti-inflammatory effects. *Aspirin should not be given to children except on a physician's order.*

ASPIRIN-FREE ANACIN ... *See* acetaminophen

ASTALIN .... *See* azalastin

AUGMENTIN .... *See* amoxicillin-clavulanate

AVENTYL .... *See* nortriptyline

AXID .... *See* nizatidine

AZACTAM .... *See* aztreonam

AZELAIC ACID .... A prescription drug for treatment of acne. It kills bacteria and keeps pores clear.

AZELEX .... *See* azelaic acid

AZITHROMYCIHN .... An antibiotic similar to erythromycin, but with better absorption into the lungs, and greater effectiveness against some types of bacteria.

AZTREONAM .... An antibiotic which may be useful in treating infections caused by bacteria resistant to other drugs.

BABYLAX .... *See* glycerin

BAL .... Acronym for British Anti-Lewisite—*See* dimercaprol

BAYER SELECT MAXIMUM STRENGTH HEADACHE PAIN RELIEF FORMULA .... *See* acetaminophen

BENADRYL .... *See* diphenhydramine

BENZAMYCIN .... Benzoyl peroxide and erythromycin combination used in the treatment of acne.

BENZOYL PEROXIDE ..... Skin drying agent, used for treatment of acne. May be mixed with other compounds such as antibiotics.

BEXTRA .... *See* valdecoxib

BIAXIN .... *See* clarithromycin

BISACODYL .... An irritant cathartic (laxative) not recommended for children under six years old. Available as tablets and suppositories.

BLENOXANE .... *See* bleomycin

BLEOMYCIN .... An anti-cancer drug of the antibiotic type, bleomycin has been used to treat germ-cell cancers (ovaries or testis) and some other cancers in children.

BLEPH .... *See* sulfacetamide

BLISTEX .... *See* phenol

BONINE .... *See* meclizine

BOTOX .... *See* botulinum toxin

BOTULINUM TOXIN ..... Although most widely used for reduction of wrinkles, botulinum toxin may be injected as a means of reducing excessive perspiration. Its most important use in children is reduction of spasticity in children with cerebral palsy.

BRITISH ANTI-LEWISITE .. *See* dimercaprol

BROMPHENIRAMINE .... An antihistamine with only moderately sedative effects. The product is available in liquid form, and one of the branded products has a high level of taste acceptability among children.

BUPROPION .... An antidepressant which is unrelated to other types of antidepressant drugs. Bupropion has been used to treat attention deficit disorder and bipolar disorder. It is also used to help stop smoking. Although approved only for use in adults, the drug has been used to treat children. *The United States Food and Drug Administration has issued a warning that antidepressants may increase the risk of suicide when used to treat children and adolescents. The FDA warns that the risk of suicide is increased in children with bipolar disorder.*

CALAMINE LOTION ..... A preparation of zinc oxide, lime water, glycerin, and water that may relieve some insect stings and irritants like poison ivy. Preparations that contain phenol or antihistamines may be more effective than the original formula.

CALCIUM CARBONATE .. An antacid for treatment of stomach disorders. It may also be used as a diet supplement to provide extra calcium.

CALCIUM CARBONATE AND MAGNESIUM HYDROXIDE .... An antacid combination used for a number of stomach disorders.

CALCIUM DISODIUM EDETATE .... A chelating agent used as an antidote to lead poisoning.

CALCIUM DISODIUM VERSENATE .... *See* calcium disodium edetate

CARBAMAZEPINE .... An anti-epileptic drug that has been used for a wide range of neurologic conditions. It is approved for use in children above the age of six years, but has been used in younger children as well.

CASCARA SAGRADA .... An irritant cathartic (laxative) not recommended for children under six years old.

CECLOR .... *See* cefaclor

CEFACLOR .... An antibiotic given by mouth. The drug is available in a pediatric suspension that is very well accepted by children.

CEFOBID .... *See* cefotaxime

CEFOTAXIME .... A broad-spectrum antibiotic given by injection into a vein.

CEFTRIAXONE .... A broad-spectrum antibiotic given by injection into a vein. Ceftriaxone is considered to be the best treatment for late Lyme disease.

CELEBREX .... *See* celecoxib

CELECOXIB .... A COX-2 inhibitor; a type of non-steroidal anti-inflammatory drug that is often used to treat arthritis. No studies have been done on children.

CELEXA .... *See* citalopram

CELONTIN .... *See* methosuximide

CETIRIZINE .... An antihistamine with very little sedating effect. It is used to treat hay fever and other allergies.

CHLORAMPHENICOL .... A broad-spectrum antibiotic, unrelated to other antibiotics. Because this drug can cause very serious adverse reactions, it should be reserved for cases which cannot be treated with any other antibacterial agent.

CHLOROMYCETIN ...... *See* chloramphenicol

CHLORPHENIRAMINE ... An antihistamine used in the treatment of allergies that carries mild risk of drowsiness.

CHLOR-TRIMETRON ..... *See* chlorpheniramine

CHOLESTYRAMINE ...... Cholesterol reducer for children over the age of two years.

CHRONULAC .... *See* lactulose

CIMETIDINE .... A gastric acid reducer used to treat gastroesophageal reflux and diseases in which the stomach produces too much acid. An over-the-counter form is available.

CITALOPRAM .... An antidepressant of the SSRI class (serotonin specific reuptake inhibitor). These drugs are used to treat depression, and may be prescribed for bipolar disorder. *Warning: Antidepressants may increase depression or even lead to suicide when used in children and adolescents. Careful observation is essential.*

CITRUCEL .... *See* methylcellulose

CLARITHROMYCIN ...... Clarithromycin is an antibiotic similar to erythromycin, but with better absorption into the lungs, and greater effectiveness against some types of bacteria.

CLARITIN .... *See* loratidine

CLEMASTINE .... An antihistamine used to treat allergies that carries a mild risk of drowsiness.

CLEOCIN-T .... *See* clindamycin. This form is for application to the skin, commonly used for treatment of acne.

CLINDAMYCIN .... Antibiotic, used for anaerobic infections and for treatment of acne.

CLONAZEPAM .... A benzodiazepine used as a tranquilizer and anti-seizure medication. This is a controlled drug under law.

CLORAZEPATE .... A benzodiazepine used as a tranquilizer, for treatment of alcoholism, and as an anti-seizure medication. This is a controlled drug under law.

CLOTRIMAZOLE .... An antifungal drug that may be used as an oral lozenge, skin cream, lotion, or vaginal cream, depending on the location of the fungal infection.

CLOZAPINE .... Clozapine is an anti-psychotic drug which has been used in treatment of bipolar disorder. Although it is approved only for adults, it has been studied in children as young as nine years. For safe use, weekly blood counts are essential.

CLOZARIL .... *See* clozapine

COLACE .... *See* docusate

COLCHICINE .... A medicine for gout that has found uses in several other conditions, such as familial mediterranean fever. Colchicine has been used to treat children as young as three years.

CORTIZONE .... *See* hydrocotisone

COUMADIN .... *See* warfarin

CRIXAVAN .... *See* indinavir

CROMOLYN .... A mast-cell stabilizing drug used for prevention of asthmatic and allergic attacks.

CUPRIMINE .... *See* penicillamine

CYCLIZINE .... An over-the-counter antihistamine used in treatment of motion sickness in children over the age of six years.

CYCLOPHOSPHAMIDE ... An alkylating agent used in treatment of cancer. It may be used for some types of childhood leukemias.

CYTOVENE .... *See* ganciclovir

CYTOXAN .... *See* cyclophosphamide

DARVON .... *See* propoxyphene

DDAVP .... *See* desmopressin acetate

DECADRON .... *See* dexamethasone

DECADURABOLIN ...... *See* nandrolone

DELTASONE .... *See* prednisone

DEMEROL .... *See* meperidine

DEPAKENE .... *See* valproic acid

DEPAKOTE .... *See* valproic acid

DEPEN .... *See* penicillamine

DESFERAL .... *See* desferoxamine

DESFEROXAMINE .... A drug which binds iron, it is used to reduce the blood iron levels in thalassemia.. It is given only by injection.

DESIPRAMINE . . . . A tricyclic antidepressant, used to treat depression, but which may also be useful in treatment of bulimia. *Warning: Antidepressants may increase depression or even lead to suicide when used in children and adolescents. Careful observation is essential.*

DESMOPRESSIN . . . . A synthetic compound similar to antidiuretic hormone (ADH). It may be used to treat bedwetting. Because desmopressin increases the count of blood platelets, it has been used to control some types of coagulation disorders.

DEXAMETHASONE . . . . . . An anti-inflammatory steroid that is widely used. It may be given by mouth, by vein, applied to the skin, or included in eye drops or ear drops.

DEXTROMETHORPHAN . A cough suppressant that is the active ingredient in most over-the-counter cough remedies. It is usually indicated in product names as DM.

DIAZEPAM . . . . A benzodiazepine used as a tranquilizer, muscle relaxant, and anti-seizure medication. This is a controlled drug under law.

DIBASIC SODIUM PHOSPHATE . . . . A saline cathartic (laxative), it acts by drawing water into the intestine, and produces a watery stool. Children may be more sensitive than adults to toxic effects. Do not use in children under the age of six years.

DIDANOSINE . . . . Antiretroviral drug (for treatment of AIDS virus) in patients over the age of two weeks, although the drug has been used in newborn infants as well.

DIFFERIN . . . . *See* adapalene

DIGOXIN . . . . Derived from digitalis, this drug increases the strength of heart contractions.

DILANTIN . . . . *See* phenytoin

DILAUDID . . . . *See* hydromorphone

DIMENHYDRINATE . . . . . An over-the-counter antihistamine used in treatment of motion sickness in children over the age of two years.

DIMERCAPROL . . . . A chelating agent which is used as an antidote for arsenic, gold, mercury and lead poisoning.

DIMETANE . . . . *See* brompheniramine

DIPHENHYDRAMINE . . . . An antihistamine that is very effective but commonly causes drowsiness.

DOCUSATE . . . . A stool softener to relieve constipation (not a laxative). It may take as long as three days to show any benefit. Not recommended for children under six years old.

DOXORUBICIN . . . . An anti-cancer drug of the antibiotic type, doxorubicin has been used to treat Ewing's sarcoma and some types of lymphoma in children.

DTP VACCINE . . . . A vaccine that protects against diphtheria, tetanus, and pertussis. It has largely been replaced by diphtheria and tetanus toxoids and acellular pertussis (DTaP) vaccine, which has fewer unwanted side effects.

DRAMAMINE . . . . *See* dimenhydrinate

DRITHOCREME . . . . *See* anthralin

DRYSOL . . . . *See* aluminum chloride

DTAP VACCINE . . . . A vaccine that protects against diphtheria, tetanus, and pertussis. It is safer than the old DTP vaccine.

DULCOLAX . . . . *See* bisadocyl

DUPHALAC . . . . *See* lactulose

DURAGESIC . . . . *See* fentanyl

DUVOID .... *See* bethanechol

EFAVIRENZ .... Antiretroviral drug (for treatment of AIDS virus) in patients over the age of three years.

EFFEXOR .... *See* venlafaxine

ELAVIL .... *See* amitriptyline

ELIDEL .... *See* pimecrolimus

EPINEPHRINE .... A hormone that is used as a stimulant and vasoconstrictor in the treatment of anaphylaxis. It may also be used to stop bleeding during surgery.

EPIVIR .... *See* lamivudine

EPSOM SALTS .... *See* magnesium sulfate

ERTAPENEM .... A prescription antibiotic used to treat penicillin-resistant bacteria. Has not been well studied in children.

ERYTHROMYCIN .... An antibiotic which may be taken by mouth or injected to treat infections, or applied to the skin to treat acne. Erythromycin is widely used for patients who are allergic to penicillin.

ESCITALOPRAM .... An antidepressant of the SSRI class (serotonin specific reuptake inhibitor) These drugs are used to treat depression, and may be prescribed for bipolar disorder. *Warning: May increase depression or even lead to suicide when used in pediatrics. Careful observation is essential.*

ESKALITH .... *See* lithium carbonate

ESOMEPRAZOLE .... A prescription gastric acid reducer of the proton-pump inhibitor class. It has been given to children as young as three years of age.

ETHOSUXIMIDE .... A drug used in treatment of epilepsy, usually for absence seizures.

ETHOTOIN .... A drug in the same family as phenytoin, used to control epilepsy.

ETOPOSIDE .... An anti-cancer drug of the topoisomerase class. It may be used to treat some types of leukemia and other cancers in children.

FAMCICLOVIR .... An anti-viral drug which has been useful in treatment of herpes infections, including those associated with chickenpox. At present, it is not recommended that this drug be used in patients under the age of 18 years.

FAMOTIDINE .... A gastric acid reducer of the H-2 receptor blocker class used to treat gastroesophageal reflux and diseases in which there is an excess of stomach acid. An OTC form is available

FAMVIR .... *See* famciclovir

FELBAMATE .... An anti-epileptic drug approved for use in children over the age of 14 years, but which has been used in younger children as well. Should be reserved for cases not responsive to other drugs.

FELBATOL .... *See* felbamate

FENTANYL .... A narcotic pain reliever, fentanyl is often given to children to relax them before surgery. This is a controlled drug under federal law.

FEO-SOL .... *See* ferrous sulfate

FERROUS SULFATE ...... The preferred form of iron for treatment of iron deficiencies. It comes in tablet and liquid form.

FEXOFENADINE .... A non-sedating antihistamine used in the treatment of allergies. It has not been tested in children younger than six years.

FINEVIN .... *See* azelaic acid

5-FLUOROURACIL .... An antimetabolite used in the treatment of cancer. The injection has limited use in common childhood cancers, but a skin cream has been used for some types of skin cancers.

5-FU .... *See* 5-fluorouracil

FLUMADINE .... *See* rimantidine

FLUOXETINE .... An antidepressant of the SSRI class (serotonin specific reuptake inhibitor). These drugs are used to treat depression, and may be prescribed for bipolar disorder. Fluoxetine has also been used to treat bulimia. *Warning: May increase depression or even lead to suicide when used in children. Careful observation is essential.*

FLUVAX .... *See* influenza virus vaccine

FOSCARNET .... An antiviral drug used for treatment of cytomegalovirus and severe herpes virus infections. It is appropriate for adolescents, but not recommended for children.

FORTOVASE .... *See* saquinavir

FOSCAVIR .... *See* foscarnet

FULVICIN .... *See* griseofulvin

FUNGIZONE............ *See* amphotericin B

GAMIMUNE .... *See* immune serum globulin

GAMMAGARD .... *See* immune serum globulin

GANCICLOVIR.......... Antiviral agent for cytomegalovirus infections of the eye. Although not recommended for patients below the age of 12 years, the drug is has been used in children as young as three months.

GEODON............... *See* ziprasidone

GLUCAGON .... A hormone manufactured by the pancreas that triggers the release of blood glucose by the liver, often in diabetics. It is only administered by injection.

GLUCAGON EMERGENCY KIT .... See glucagon

GLYCERIN .... A hyperosmotic laxative that is used in either rectal solution or suppository form. Glycerin is used in children as young as newborns. The chemical has many uses in drug formulation since it helps products retain moisture (in lotions and creams), while in oral liquids it acts as a thickening agent and provides a slightly sweet taste.

GLYCOLIC ACID .... A chemical peel used to treat acne and for other cosmetic purposes.

GRANISETRON.......... An anti-emetic drug used to control nausea and vomiting associated with cancer therapy. The drug may be given by mouth or by vein, and is used in children over the age of two years.

GRISACTIN .... *See* griseofulvin

GRISEOFULVIN .... An antifungal agent used to treat infections of the hair and nails.

GRIS-PEG............... *See* griseofulvin

GUAIFENESIN........... Guaifenesin is commonly included in over-the-counter cough remedies as an expectorant, a drug which breaks up mucus. Although the drug has been used for a long time, there is little proof that it works.

GYNE-LOTRIMIN .... *See* clotrimazole

HALDOL .... *See* haloperidol

HALOPERIDOL .... A prescription drug commonly used for behavioral disorders such as excessive rage. It has also been useful in the treatment of Tourette's syndrome.

HEXADROL .... *See* dexamethasone

HIVID.................. *See* zalcitabine

HUMULIN.............. *See* insulin

HYDROCORTISONE ..... An anti-inflammatory steroid that may be taken by mouth, or in creams and lotions to be applied to skin and mucous membranes. Hydrocortisone creams may be used on infants and young children. Low concentrations of hydrocortisone are available in over-the-counter preparations.

HYDROMORPHONE .... Hydromorphone is a narcotic pain reliever and cough suppressant for use in children over the age of six years. It is a controlled drug under federal law.

HYDROXYCHLORO-QUINE ..... An antialarial compound that has been used to treat some autommune conditions including lupus and juvenile dermatomyositis.

HYTONE .... *See* hydrocortisone

IBUPROFEN .... Non-narcotic pain-reliever and fever reducer with anti-inflammatory effects.

IMIPRAMINE .... A tricyclic antidepressant, used primarily to treat depression, but which may also be used in treatment of bulimia. Imipramine may also be useful in control of bedwetting. *Warning: May increase depression or even lead to suicide when used in children and adolescents. Careful observation is essential.*

IMITREX .... *See* sumatriptan

IMMUNE SERUM GLOBULIN .... This is a preparation of the portion of the blood that contains antibodies. It helps the immune system prevent or fight off infections.

IMODIUM .... *See* loperamide

INDINAVIR .... Antiretroviral drug for treatment of AIDS virus. According to the manufacturer, safety in children has not been established, but the drug has been listed in standard pediatric references.

INDOCIN............... *See* indomethicin

INDOMETHACIN .... A non-steroidal anti-inflammatory drug (NSAID) available by prescription only, usually used to treat arthritis and other inflammatory conditions. Not recommended for children under the age of 14 except in special circumstances. Indomethacin has special application in some infants born with heart problems.

INFLUENZA VIRUS VACCINE ...... A vaccine used to prevent infection with the influenza virus. It may be given to infants as young as six months of age.

INSULIN .... A hormone which is essential for glucose (sugar) utilization. There are many types of modified insulins designed to give either more rapid effect or longer duration of action. Insulin must be given by injection.

INTAL .... *See* cromolyn

INVANZ................ *See* ertapenem

INVIRASE............... *See* saquinavir

ISONIAZID .... Anti-tuberculosis drug that may be used to treat tuberculosis and to protect people in close contact with tuberculosis patients. Infants and young children can tolerate higher doses of this drug than do older children and adults.

ISOTRETINOIN .... An anti-acne drug.

IVERMECTIN .... A prescription treatment for parasites which is effective against lice, although it is not FDA-approved for this purpose.

KALETRA .... *See* lopinavir/ritonavir fixed combination

KENALOG .... *See* triamcinolone

KETOCONAZOLE........ An antifungal agent that may be used as a cream for skin fungus, or in tablet form for systemic infections.

KETOPROFEN .... A non-steroidal anti-inflammatory drug (NSAID), available by prescription only. Not given to children under the age of 16 unless directed by a physician.

KETOROLAC TROMETHAMINE .... A non-teroidal anti-inflammatory drug (NSAID) given by injection. This is an effective pain reliever for short-erm use only. Its main advantage over narcotics for short-erm use is that it does not cause sedation. This drug is not normally used for treatment of children.

KLONOPIN .... *See* clonazepam

KONSIL .... *See* psyllium

KWELL .... *See* lindane

KYTRIL .... *See* granisetron

LACTULOSE.......... A hyperosmotic laxative that is also used for other conditions, including liver and brain problems. It has been used to treat children, but is not recommended for frequent use.

LAMICTAL .... *See* lamotrigene

LAMIVUDINE .... An antiretroviral drug, used to treat the AIDS virus, in children above the age of three months. Because viral resistance develops when lamivudine is used alone, the drug should be administered in combination with other antiretroviral drugs.

LAMOTRIGENE .... A anti-epileptic drug primarily for use in adults, but which has been used in children with severe epilepsy as young as two years of age. The drug has also been used to treat bipolar disorder.

LAMICTAL .... *See* lamotrigene

LANOXIN.......... *See* digoxin

LANSOPRAZOLE .... A prescription gastric acid reducer of the proton-pump inhibitor class, used to treat gastroesophageal reflux, and other disorders of excess stomach acid. A pediatric suspension is available, and the flavor had been reported to be popular with children.

LEVO-DROMORAN .... *See* levorphanol

LEVORPHANOL .... A narcotic pain reliever for severe pain. Its use in children has not been well established. It is a controlled drug under federal law.

LEXAPRO .... *See* escitalopram

LIDOCAINE.......... A local anesthetic that may be injected, or applied to skin or mucous membranes. It relieves pain from wounds and sores, including canker sores.

LINDANE.......... A prescription drug for removal of lice. Lindane may cause nerve damage even when used as directed. It should never be used on premature infants.

LINEZOLID .... A prescription antibiotic used to treat penicillin-resistant bacteria. Has not been well studied in children. Because it may cause blood problems, regular blood tests are needed while taking this drug.

LITHIUM CARBONATE ... A drug used in treatment of some psychiatric conditions including bipolar mood disorder and anorexia.

LONITEN .... *See* minoxidil (Loniten designates tablets for high blood pressure only.)

LOPERAMIDE .... An antidiarrheal drug that is available without prescription. It has been given to children as young as two years, but should not be used without first consulting a physician.

LOPINAVIR/RITONAVIR FIXED COMBINATION . A combination of antiretroviral drugs (anti-IDS drugs) that may be used in children as young as six months.

LORATIDINE .... A non-sedating antihistamine used in the treatment of asthma.

LOTRIMIN .... *See* clotrimazole

MAALOX .... *See* aluminum and magnesium hydroxides

MAGNESIUM CITRATE (CITRATE OF MAGNESIA) ... A saline cathartic (laxative), it acts by drawing water into the intestine, and produces a watery stool. Children may be more sensitive than adults to toxic effects. The oral liquid should be chilled before use. Do not use in children under the age of two years.

MAGNESIUM HYDROXIDE .... A saline cathartic (laxative), it acts by drawing water into the intestine, and produces a watery stool. Children may be more sensitive than adults to toxic effects. Do not use in children under the age of two years. May be used as an antacid.

MAGNESIUM SULFATE ... A saline cathartic (laxative), it acts by drawing water into the intestine, and produces a watery stool. Children may be more sensitive than adults to toxic effects. Do not use in children under the age of two years. May be used as a soak for bruises and sprains. Flavored forms available.

MAREZINE .... *See* cyclizine

MARIJUANA .... Abuse drug, the active component, tetrahydrocannabinol, or THC, may be used as an antinauseant to relieve some of the effects of cancer chemotherapy. Under United States law, marijuana has no legitimate medical use.

MECLIZINE .... An over-the-counter antihistamine used in treatment of motion sickness in children over the age of 12 years.

MECLOFENAMATE SODIUM ...... A non-teroidal anti-inflammatory drug (NSAID), available by prescription only. Safety and efficacy in children under 14 years of age has not been established.

MEDROL .... *See* methylprednisolone

MEFENAMIC ACID .... A non-steroidal anti-inflammatory drug (NSAID), available by prescription only. Safety and efficacy in children under 14 years of age has not been established.

MENABOL .... *See* stanzolol

MEPERIDINE .... A synthetic narcotic analgesic. This is a controlled drug under federal law.

MEPHENYTOIN .... A drug in the same family as phenytoin, used to control epilepsy.

MESANTOIN .... *See* mephenytoin

METADATE .... *See* methylphenidate

METAMUCIL .... *See* psyllium

METHSUXIMIDE .... A drug used in treatment of epilepsy, usually for absence seizures.

METHYLCELLULOSE ..... A bulk-forming laxative. Should be given in divided doses, with at least eight ounces of fluid. Not recommended for children under six years old.

METHYLPHENIDATE ..... A stimulant which is used in treatment of attention deficit/ hyperactivity disorder in children. This is a controlled drug under federal law.

METHYLPREDNISOLONE An anti-inflammatory steroid which may be administered by mouth or injection. The drug may be given to infants and children for many diseases.

METOCLOPRAMIDE ..... A prokinetic agent, metoclopramide accelerates emptying of the stomach into the intestine. It may be used for stomach disorders or in conjunction with anticancer drugs.

MICANOL .... *See* anthralin

MICROSULFON .... *See* sulfadiazine

MILK OF MAGNESIA ..... *See* magnesium hydroxide

MILONTIN.............. *See* phensuximide

MINERAL OIL .... An emollient cathartic (laxative) it acts by lubricating the intestine. Not recommended for children under six years old. Routine use may reduce absorption of essential vitamins.

MINOXIDIL............. An antihypertensive drug which has been widely used as a lotion to treat androgenetic hair loss.

MIRTAZAPINE........... An antidepressant, chemically different from most other antidepressants. *Warning: May increase depression or even lead to suicide when used in children and adolescents. Careful observation is essential.*

MODAFINIL .... A central nervous system stimulant which is chemically unrelated to other drugs such as caffeine or methylphenidate. Although officially not approved for children, the drug has been used to treat childhood narcolepsy.

MOTRIN................ *See* ibuprofen

MYCELEX .... *See* clotrimazole

MYLANTA .... *See* calcium carbonate and magnesium hydroxide

MYSOLINE.............. *See* primidone

NANDROLONE .... An anabolic steroid, used for treatment of some diseases that cause breakdown of the body, kidney disease, and anemia. May be subject to abuse. This is a controlled drug under federal law.

NAPHAZOLINE.......... A vasoconstrictor, most often used as eye drops to treat eye redness associated with colds.

NAPHCON .... *See* naphazoline

NAPROSYN............. *See* naproxen

NAPROXEN .... A non-steroidal anti-inflammatory drug (NSAID), available over-the-counter and by prescription. Safety and efficacy in children under two years of age has not been established.

NEFAZODONE .... An antidepressant which is unrelated to other types of antidepressant drugs. *Warning: May increase depression or even lead to suicide when used in children and adolescents. Careful observation is essential.*

NELFINAVIR .... Nelfinavir is an anti-retroviral drugs (anti-AIDS). The manufacturer does not recommend use of this drug for children younger than two years, but it has been studied with some success in children as young as newborns.

NEO-SYNEPHRINE....... *See* phenylephrine

NEXIUM................ *See* esomeprazole

NILSTSTAT.............. *See* nystatin

NITROSTAT............. *See* nitroglycerin

NIZATIDINE .... A gastric acid reducer of the H-2 receptor blocker class. An OTC form is available.

NIZORAL............... *See* ketoconazole

NOLVADEX............. *See* tamoxifen

NORPRAMINE .... *See* desipramine

NORTRIPTYLINE .... A tricyclic antidepressant. *Warning: May increase depression or even lead to suicide when used in children and adolescents. Careful observation is essential.*

NORVIR................ *See* ritonavir

NUMORPHAN .... *See* oxymorphone

NYSTATIN .... An antifungal drug which may be used in several forms: swallowed, used as a mouth rinse, applied to the skin, or used as a vaginal suppository, depending on the location of the fungal infection.

OLANZAPINE . . . . Olanzapine is an anti-psychotic drugs which has been used in treatment of bipolar disorder. Although it is approved only for adults, there have been reports of its use in children as young as eight years. The frequency of adverse effects is higher in children than in adults.

ONDANSETRON . . . . An anti-emetic drug used to control of nausea and vomiting that are associated with cancer therapy. The drug may be given by mouth or by vein, and is used in children over the age of four years.

ORAP . . . . *See* pimozide

ORUDIS . . . . *See* ketoprofen

ORUVAIL . . . . *See* ketoprofen

OSELTAMIVIR . . . . Antiviral drug used to treat influenza infections in patients over the age of 13 years.

OTRIVIN . . . . *See* xylometazoline

OXANDRIN . . . . *See* oxandrolone

OXANDROLONE . . . . An anabolic steroid used for treatment of some diseases that cause breakdown of the body, kidney disease, and anemia. May be subject to abuse.

OXCARBAZEPINE . . . . An anti-epileptic drug similar to carbamazepine. Approved for use in children over 16 years, but has been used in younger children as well.

OXYCODONE . . . . Oxycodone is a narcotic pain reliever which is approved for children above the age of six years. It is a controlled drug under federal law.

OXYCONTIN . . . . *See* oxycodone

OXYMETAZOLINE . . . . A vasoconstrictor which may be used as a nasal spray to relieve stuffy nose, or as an eye drop to treat eye redness associated with colds.

OXYMETHOLONE . . . . An anabolic steroid used for treatment of some diseases that cause breakdown of the body, kidney disease, and anemia. May be subject to abuse.

OXYMORPHONE . . . . A narcotic pain reliever for children over the age of two years. It is administered by injection or rectal suppository. It is a controlled drug under federal law.

PAMELOR . . . . *See* nortriptyline

PANADOL . . . . *See* acetaminophen

PANTOPRAZOLE . . . . A prescription gastric acid reducer of the proton-pump inhibitor class. It is used to treat gastroesophageal reflux and other disorders in which the stomach produces too much acid.

PARNATE . . . . *See* tranylcypromine

PAROXETINE . . . . An antidepressant of the SSRI class (serotonin specific reuptake inhibitor). These drugs are used to treat depression, and may be prescribed for bipolar disorder. *Warning: May increase depression or even lead to suicide when used in children and adolescents. Careful observation is essential.*

PAXIL . . . . *See* paroxetine

PEGANONE . . . . *See* ethotoin

PENICILLAMINE . . . . A drug used as a treatment for rheumatoid arthritis, Wilson's disease (excess copper in the blood), and as an antidote for heavy metal poisoning (iron, mercury, lead, and arsenic).

PENICILLIN . . . . An antibiotic; the parent compound of a large class of antibiotics that may be used in treatment or prevention of bacterial infections.

PEPCID . . . . *See* famotidine

PERTOFRANE . . . . *See* desipramine

PHENACEMIDE .... An anti-epileptic drug no longer in common use.

PHENOL .... A barbiturate used in treatment of epilepsy.

PHENSUXIMIDE......... A drug used in treatment of epilepsy, usually for absence seizures.

PHENYLEPHRINE........ A nasal decongestant.

PHENYTOIN .... An anti-seizure (anti-epileptic) agent used to control many different types of seizures. It is available in liquid and chewable tablets for children.

PHOSPO-SODA .... *See* dibasic sodium phosphate

PIMECROLIMUS......... Medication originally used to prevent rejection in organ transplants. An ointment of this compound is used to treat moderate to severe atopic dermatitis in adults or children two years of age and older.

PIMOZIDE .... A prescription drug for treatment of Tourrette's syndrome in children over the age of 12 years.

PLAQUENIL............. *See* hydroxychloroquine

PODOFILOX .... An agent used for wart removal, it should be used only by a physician, since it is too strong for self application. It has been used in children as young as two years old.

PODOPHYLLUM .... An agent used for wart removal, it should be used only by a physician, since it is too strong for self application.

PONSTEL .... *See* mefenamic acid

PREDNISONE .... An anti-inflammatory steroid. It is most often given by mouth and has many applications.

PREVACID .... *See* lansoprazole

PRIMIDONE .... A drug used for several different types of epilepsy. In some children it may cause agitation.

PROPOXYPHENE .... A synthetic narcotic analgesic for mild pain.

PROTONIX .... *See* pantoprazole

PROTOPIC.............. *See* tacrolimus

PROVIGIL .... *See* modafinil

PROZAC................ *See* fluoxetine

PSEUDOEPHEDRINE ..... A nasal decongestant, may be inhaled or taken by mouth.

PSYLLIUM .... A bulk-forming laxative. Should be given in divided doses, with at least eight ounces of fluid. Not recommended for children under six years old.

QUESTRAN .... *See* cholestyramine

QUETIAPINE .... An antipsychotic agent approved only for use in adults, but has been used in children both for psychosis and bipolar disorder.

RABEPRAZOLE .... A prescription gastric acid reducer of the proton-pump inhibitor class, used in the treatment of gastroesophageal reflux and other disorders in which the stomach produces too much acid.

RANITIDINE .... A gastric acid reducer of the H-2 receptor blocker class. An over-the-counter form is available. A pediatric suspension is available, but in one study, children did not like the flavor.

REBETOL .... *See* ribavirin

REGLAN................ *See* metoclopramide

RELENZA .... *See* zanamivir

RETROVIR .... *See* zidovudine

RIBAVIRIN .... Antiviral drug used to treat respiratory viruses in infants and young children.

RIMANTIDINE .... Antiviral drugs used to treat influenza virus infections in children one year old or older.

RISPERDAL .... *See* risperidone

RISPERIDONE .... An antipsychotic drug which has been used in treatment of bipolar disorder. Although it is approved only for adults, it has been studied in children as young as nine years.

RITALIN .... *See* methylphenidate

RITONAVIR .... An antiretroviral (anti-AIDS) drug for use in children over the age of two years.

ROCEFIN .... *See* ceftriaxone

ROGAIN .... *See* minoxodil (Rogain is a solution, applied to the scalp, for hair loss only. Minoxidil in tablet form is used for treatment of high blood pressure.)

SALICYLIC ACID .... Used as a skin peel, for removal or warts and treatment of acne.

SAQUINAVIR .... An anti-retroviral (anti-AIDS) drug. The manufacturer does not recommend use of this drug for children younger than 16 years, but it has been studied with some success in children as young as two years.

SEROQUEL .... *See* quetiapine

SERTRALINE .... An antidepressant of the SSRI class (serotonin specific reuptake inhibitor). *Warning: May increase depression or even lead to suicide when used in children and adolescents. Careful observation is essential.*

SERZONE .... *See* nefazodone

SOLU-MEDROL .... *See* methylprednisolone

SPIRONOLACTONE ..... Potassium-sparing diuretic used in heart disease; also has anti-androgenic effects which may be used to treat acne.

STANZOLOL .... An anabolic steroid used for treatment of some diseases that cause breakdown of the body, kidney disease, and anemia. May be subject to abuse.

STAVUDINE .... An anti-retroviral (anti-AIDS) drug that may be given to infants as young as newborns.

STERAPRED .... *See* prednisone

STROMECTOL........... *See* ivermectin

SUDAFED............... *See* pseudoephedrine

SULAMYD .... *See* sulfacetamide

SULFACETAMIDE .... A sulfa drug with antibacterial effects. It may be applied to the skin to treat acne, or used in eye drops to treat pink eye (conjunctivitis) infections.

SULFADIAZINE .... A sulfa drug that may be used to treat toxoplasmosis in infants.

SUMATRIPTAN .... A prescription drug used for treatment of migraine headaches.

SUMYCIN .... *See* teracycline

SURFAK .... *See* docusate

SURMONTIL............ *See* trimipramine

SUSTIVA................ *See* efavirenz

SYMMETREL .... *See* amantidine

TACROLIMUS .... A medication originally used to prevent rejection in organ transplants. An ointment of this compound is used to treat moderate to severe atopic dermatitis in adults or children two years of age and older.

TAGAMET .... *See* cimetidine

TAMIFLU .... *See* oseltamivir

TAMOXIFEN .... An anti-estrogen drug normally used for treatment of breast cancer in adult women. It has been reported on favorably for treatment of gynecomastic (enlarged breasts in the male) in adolescent boys.

TAVIST .... *See* clemastine

TCA..................... *See* trichloracetic acid

TEGRETOL.............. *See* carbamazepine

TETRACYCLINE .... An antibiotic which is effective against many types of bacteria and other pathogens. It is not recommended for young children because it can cause discoloration of the teeth. A solution or paste made of tetracycline may relieve the discomfort of a canker sore. It may be used for treatment of acne in adolescents.

TETRACYN.............. *See* tetracycline

TOFRANIL.............. *See* imipramine

TOLECTIN.............. *See* tolmetin sodium

TOLMETIN SODIUM..... A non-steroidal anti-inflammatory drug (NSAID), available by prescription only. Safety and efficacy in children under two years of age has not been established.

TORADOL.............. *See* ketorolac tromethamine

TRANXENE.............. *See* clorazepate

TRANYLCYPROMINE .... An antidepressant of the mono-amine oxidase inhibitor class (MAOI), has been used to treat bipolar disorder as well as depression.. Special diet restrictions are essential for safe use. *Warning: May increase depression or even lead to suicide when used in children and adolescents. Careful observation is essential.*

TRETINOIN............. A prescription drug used for treatment of acne.

TRIAMCINOLONE....... A steroid cream which is used to treat various skin conditions, including canker sores.

TRICHLORACETIC ACID . An agent used for wart removal, it should be used only by a physician, since it is too strong for self application.

TRILEPTAL.............. *See* oxcarbazepine

TRIMIPRAMINE .... A tricyclic antidepressant, not widely used. *Warning: May increase depression or even lead to suicide when used in children and adolescents. Careful observation is essential.*

TRIMOX................ *See* amoxicillin

TUMS.................. *See* calcium carbonate

TYLENOL............... *See* acetaminophen

VALACYCLOVIR .... An antiviral drug used to treat all types of herpes virus infections, it may be used in adolescents, but has not been studied in young children.

VALDECOXIB .... A COX-2 inhibitor; a type of non-steroidal anti-inflammatory drug that has a reduced risk of stomach ulcers. *Drugs in this class have been linked to an increased frequency of heart attacks and strokes. Valdecoxib has been associated with a higher frequency of severe skin reactions than other drugs in the same class.*

VALIUM................ *See* diazepam

VALPROATE SODIUM ... *See* valproic acid

VALPROIC ACID .... Anti-epileptic drug for use in a variety of seizure types. It has been used for mood disorders, bipolar disorder, and other purposes as well. Approved for use in children over the age of 10 years, but has been used in much younger children as well.

VALTREX .... *See* valacyclovir

VENLAFAXINE .... An antidepressant which is unrelated to other types of antidepressant drugs. Warning: Antidepressants may increase depression or even lead to suicide when used in children and adolescents. Careful observation is essential.

VEPESID................ *See* etoposide

VIDARABINE .... Antiviral drug used to treat severe herpes infections in newborns, but its primary value is in the form of an eye ointment to treat herpes infections of the eye.

VIDEX.................. *See* didanosine

VIR-A .... *See* vidarabi

VIRACEPT .... *See* nelfinavir

VIRAZOL .... *See* ribavirin

VISINE .... *See* oxymetazoline

WARFARIN .... A "blood thinner," a drug that helps keep blood from clotting. It is given to children who have had heart surgery until the heart has fully healed.

WELLBUTRIN .... *See* bupropion

WINSTROL .... *See* stanzolol

XYLOCAINE............. *See* lidocaine

XYLOMETAZOLINE ...... A vasoconstrictor to treat nasal congestion which may be used as a nasal spray or nose drops.

ZALCITABINE .... Zalcitabine is an anti-retroviral (anti-AIDS) drug. The manufacturer does not recommend use in patients under the age of 13 years, but it may be prescribed in younger children.

ZANAMIVIR .... Antiviral drug used to treat influenza infections caused by viruses types A and B in adults and children over the age of seven.

ZARONTIN .... *See* ethosuximide

ZERIT .... *See* stavudine

ZIAGEN .... *See* abacavir

ZIDOVUDINE .... Antiretroviral agents (anti-AIDS drug) which may be appropriate for infants and children, best used in combination with other drugs.

ZIPRASIDONE........... An antipsychotic drug. It has been approved only for use in adults, but has been used in children for treatment of schizophenia and bipolar disorder.

ZITHROMAX............ *See* azithromycin

ZOFRAN .... *See* ondansetron

ZOLOFT................ *See* sertraline

ZONEGRAN .... *See* zonisamide

ZONISAMIDE .... A drug used to treat epilepsy, particularly partial seizures. Safety in children under 16 has not been established, but this drug has a history of use in pediatrics.

ZOVIRAX............... *See* acyclovir

ZYPREXA .... *See* olanzapine

ZYRTEC .... *See* cetirizine

ZYVOX................. *See* linezolid

B

C

D

E

F

G

H

I

J

K

L

M

N

O

P

Q

S

T

U

W

X

Y

Z